Dr. Wolfgang Schuster
Carlton 'Fred' Schwan
David E. Seelye
Christian Selvais
Narendra Sengar
Joel Altman-Shafer
Ladislav Sin
Saran Singh
Evzen Sknouril
Arlie Slabaugh
Gary F. Snover
William F. Spengler
Jimmie C. Steelman
Herbert Stein
Mel Steinberg
Tim Steiner
Zeljko Stojanovic
Roger B. Stolberg
Mark Strumpf
Alim A. Sumana
Peter Symes
Imre Szatmari
Steven Tan
Reinhardt Tetting
Mike Tiitus
Eduardo R. Trujillo B.
Anthony Tumonis
Jan Vandersande
Dr. Karel Vanka
Igor Victorov-Orlov
Michael Vort-Ronald
A. Wang
James Warmus
Stewart Westdal
Michael J. Whelihan
P.L. Willems
Dr. Heinz Wirz
Yu Chien Hua
Christof Zellweger

INSTITUTIONS AND PUBLICATIONS

American Numismatic Association
American Numismatic Society
International Bank Note Society
L.A.N.S.A.
Smithsonian Institution
Note Printing Australia
National Bank of Cambodia
Ceská Národní Banka
Banco Central de la Repúublica Dominicana

Central Bank of Iceland
National Bank of Macedonia
Reserve Bank of New Zealand
Banco Central de Reserva del Peru
National Bank of Romania
Central Bank of Samoa
Bank of Slovenia
Nadrona Banka Slovenska
Banco Central del Uruguay

The Stateman's Year-Book, 2000

136th Edition

by Barry Turner, editor, The Stateman's Year-Book Office, The Macmillan Press Ltd., 4-6 Crinan Street, London N1 9SQ, England. (Statistical and Historical Annual of the States of the World).

Le Change des Monnaies Etrangers

by R. L. Martin. 12, rue Poincaré, F 55800 Revigny, France.
(Illustrated guide of current world bank notes.)

MRI Bankers' Guide to Foreign Currency

by Arnoldo Efron, Monetary Research Institute, P.O. Box 3174, Houston, Texas, U.S.A., 77253-3174.
(Quarterly illustrated guide of current world bank notes and travelers checks.)

Cover Photo Courtesy of Chester Krause

INTRODUCTION

Welcome to the Sixth Edition of the Standard Catalog of World Paper Money, Modern Issues.

For those of you already familiar with this volume, you will note numerous enhancements and additions to the text. We have expanded the "Acknowledgements" page to better introduce the reader to the contributors from around the world who assist us in making this catalog the most complete reference it can be. This incredible network of dealers, collectors, scholars, societies and central banks are providing the most comprehensive up-to-the-minute reporting of new issues as well as new varieties of previously issued notes.

In our constant endeavor to provide as much detail as possible, we have added many more illustrations, more detailed text and signature information such as the amount of signature varieties Portugal has issued by denomination and by date. We continue to update maps and introduce newly forming nations. Extensive price analysis has been performed to provide timely insight to the everchanging world paper money marketplace. Renumbering has been held to an absolute minimum by popular request.

For the ease of identification, notes are listed under their historic country name (British Honduras is no longer hidden within Belize). Notes of a particular bank are listed in release date order, and then grouped in ascending denomination order. In the cases of countries where more than one issuing authority is in effect at a single time, follow the bank headings in the listings and it will become apparent if that country's listing is by date or alphabetical by issuing authority. In the cases where a country has changed from a kingdom to a republic all the banknotes of the kingdom's era would be listed before that of the republic's.

Sending Scanned Images by Email

Over the past 2 years or so, we have been receiving an ever-increasing flow of scanned images from sources worldwide. Unfortunately, many of these scans could not be used due to the type of scan, or simple incompatibility with our systems. We appreciate the effort it takes to produce these images and accuracy they add to the catalog listings.

Here are a few simple instructions to follow when producing these scans. We encourage you to continue sending new images or upgrades to those currently illustrated and please do not hesitate to ask questions about this process.

- Scan all images within a resolution range of 200 dpi to 300 dpi
- Size setting should be at 100%
- Scan in true 4-color
- Save images as 'jpeg' or 'tiff' and name in such a way which clearly identifies the country of origin of the note
- Please email with a request to confirm receipt of the attachment
- Please send images to thernr@krause.com

A review of paper money collecting

Paper money collecting is undoubtedly as old as paper money itself. This segment of the numismatic hobby did not begin to reach a popularity approaching that of coin collecting until the latter half of the 1970's. While coins and paper money are alike in that both served as legal obligations to facilitate commerce, long-time paper money enthusiasts know the similarity ends there.

Coins were historically guaranteed by the intrinsic value of their metallic content - at least until recent years when virtually all circulating coins have become little more than legal tender tokens, containing little or no precious metal - while paper money possesses a value only when it is accepted for debts or converted into bullion or precious metals. With many note issues, this conversion privilege was limited and ultimately negated by the imposition of redemption cutoff dates.

Such conditions made dealing in bank notes a risky business, particularly with notes possessing a high face value. This is why in most instances, except where issues were withdrawn shortly after release or became virtually worthless due to hyper-inflation, early high denomination notes are extremely difficult to locate, especially in choice to uncirculated grades.

The development of widespread collector interest in paper money of most nations was inhibited by a near total absence of adequate documentation. No more than three and a half decades ago collectors could refer to only a few catalogs and dealer price lists of limited scope, most of which were difficult to acquire, or they could build their own knowledge through personal collecting pursuits and contact with fellow collectors.

This situation was somewhat corrected over the past 30 years with a number of special catalogs covering the more popular collected countries. Still, many areas remained uncataloged, and no single volume existed which contained comprehensive, detailed, illustrated listings of issues from all countries of the world.

The early catalogs authored by Albert Pick chronicled issues of Europe and the Americas and were assembled as stepping stones to the ultimate objective which became reality with publication of the first *Standard Catalog of World Paper Money* in 1975. That work provided collectors with near complete listings and up-to-date valuations of all recorded government note issues of the 20th century, incorporating Pick's previously unpublished manuscripts on Africa, Asia and Oceania, plus many earlier issues.

This completely revised and updated 6th Edition of Volume III, Modern Issues, along with the companion NINTH Edition Volume II General Issues (Scheduled Release September 2000) presents a substantial extension of the cataloging effort initiated in 1975 and revised in succeeding editions. As the most comprehensive world paper money reference ever assembled, it fully documents many and varied legal tender paper currencies issued and circulated by nearly 300 past and current governments of the world from 1300's to present.

COUNTRY INDEX

Afghanistan 42
Albania 45
Algeria 51
Angola 54
Argentina 60
Armenia 69
Aruba 70
Australia 72
Austria 76
Azerbaijan 79
Bahamas 80
Bahrain 84
Bangladesh 87
Barbados 91
Belarus 93
Belgium 96
Belize 99
Bermuda 102
Bhutan 106
Biafra 109
Bolivia 110
Bosnia - Herzegovina . . . 119
Botswana 128
Brazil 131
British Caribbean Territories 142
British Honduras 143
Brunei 144
Bulgaria 147
Burma 151
Burundi 153
Cambodia 158
Cameroon 165
Canada 168
Cape Verde 172
Cayman Islands 174
Central African Republic 176
Central African States . . . 179
Ceylon 181
Chad 183
Chile 185
China 189
Colombia 198
Comoros 204
Congo Democratic Republic 206
Congo Republic 209
Cook Islands 211
Costa Rica 213
Croatia 218
Cuba 226
Cyprus 232
Czech Republic 237
Czechoslovakia 235
Denmark 240
Djibouti 243
Dominican Republic 244
East Africa 251
East Caribbean States . . . 252
Ecuador 257
Egypt 262
El Salvador 267
Equatorial African States 273
Equatorial Guinea 275
Eritrea 277
Estonia 278
Falkland Islands 285
Faroes 284
Fiji 287
Finland 291
France 295
French Afars and Issas . . 298
French Antilles 299
Gabon 301
Gambia 303
Georgia 307
Germany - Federal Republic 311
Germany-Democratic Republic 316
Gibraltar 321
Great Britain 323
Greece 327
Guatemala 329
Guernsey 334
Guinea-Bissau 339
Guyana 341
Haiti 343
Honduras 349
Hong Kong 354
Hungary 361
Iceland 364
India 366
Indonesia 375
Iran 384
Iraq 393
Ireland - Republic 398
Ireland - Northern 401
Isle of Man 408
Israel 412
Italy 418
Jamaica 422
Japan 426
Jersey 428
Jordan 431
Katanga 434
Kazakhstan 436
Kenya 436
Kuwait 452
Kyrgystan 456
Lanka 697
Laos 458
Latvia 462
Lebanon 464
Lesotho 468
Libya 471
Lithuania 476
Luxembourg 480
Macao 482
Macedonia 486
Madagascar 488
Malasia 499
Malawi 493
Malaysia 499
Maldives 504
Mali 505
Malta 508
Mauritania 511
Mauritius 513
Mexico 516
Moldova 524
Mongolia 526
Morocco 528
Mozambique 530
Myanmar 534
Nepal 538
Netherlands 541
Netherlands Antilles 543
New Caledonia 546
New Hebrides 547
New Zealand 548
Nicaragua 553
Nigeria 562
North Korea 444
Norway 564
Oatar & Dubai 616
Oman 568
Pakistan 573
Papua New Guinea 577
Paraguay 580
Peru 583
Philippines 592
Poland 601
Portugal 608
Portuguese Guinea 612
Qatar 613
Qatar & Dubai 616
Reunion 617
Rhodesia 619
Rhodesia & Nyasaland . . 620
Romania 621
Russia 630
Rwanda 630
Rwanda-Burundi 634
Saint Helena 635
Saint Pierre & Miquelon 636
Saint Thomas & Prince . . 637
Saudi Arabia 641
Scotland 644
Seychelles 660
Sierra Leone 665
Singapore 668
Slovakia 674
Slovenia 677
Solomon Islands 680
Somalia 682
Somaliland 687
South Africa 689
South Korea 447
Spain 694
Sri Lanka 697
Sudan 702
Surinam 708
Swaziland 711
Sweden 716
Switzerland 720
Syria 725
Tahiti 727
Tajikistan 729
Tanzania 730
Tatarstan 735
Thailand 737
Tonga 746
Transnistria 749
Trindad & Tobago 754
Tunisia 755
Turkey 758
Turkmenistan 762
Uganda 763
Ukraine 769
United Arab Emirates . . . 774
United States 777
Uruguay 783
Uzbekistan 789
Vanuatu 793
Venezuela 795
Viet Nam - South 806
Viet Nam 800
West African States 811
Western Samoa 822
Yemen Arab Republic . . . 826
Yemen Democratic Republic 831
Yugoslavia 832
Zaïre 842
Zambia 851
Zimbabwe 857

ISSUER & BANK INDEX

Abkhazian Government 309
Allied Irish Banks Ltd. 401
Allied Irish Banks Public Limited Company 402
Arab Republic of Egypt 266
Armenian Republic Bank 69
Australia, Reserve Bank 73, 75
Austrian National Bank 76
Auxiliary Military Payment Certificate Coupons 450, 743
Azerbaycan Milli Banki 79
Baanka Somaliland 687
Bahamas Government 84
Bahamas Monetary Authority 81, 84
Bahrain Currency Board 84
Bahrain Monetary Agency 85
Banc Ceannais na hÉireann 398
Banca d'Italia 418
Banca Nationala a Moldovei 524
Banca Nationala a Republicii Socialiste România 621
Banca Nationala a României 622
Banca Nazionale Somala 682, 684
Banco Central de Bolivia 110, 112, 115
Banco Central de Chile 185
Banco Central de Costa Rica 213
Banco Central de Cuba 228
Banco Central de Honduras 349
Banco Central de la República Dominicana 244, 250
Banco Central de Nicaragua 553
Banco Central de Reserva de El Salvador 267
Banco Central de Reserva del Perú 583
Banco Central de S.Tomé e Príncipe 640
Banco Central de Venezuela 795
Banco Central del Ecuador 257
Banco Central del Paraguay 580, 583
Banco Central del Uruguay 783
Banco Central di Aruba 70
Banco Central do Brasil 133
Banco Central 60, 275
Banco da China 484
Banco de Angola 54
Banco De Cabo Verde 172
Banco de Credito del Perú/Banco Central de Reserva del Perú 592
Banco de España 694
Banco de Guatemala 329
Banco de Guinea Ecuatorial 276
Banco de la Nación/Banco Central de Reserva del Perú 592
Banco de la República 198
Banco de Moçambique 531
Banco de Portugal 608
Banco Nacional da Guiné-Bissau 339
Banco Nacional de Angola 56
Banco Nacional de Cuba 226, 228, 231
Banco Nacional de S. Tomé e Príncipe 638
Banco Nacional Ultramarino 172, 482, 530, 637, 745
Banco Nacional Ultramarino, Guiné 612
Banco Popular 275
Bangko Sentral ng Pilipinas 594, 600
Bangladesh Bank 88
Bank al-Maghrib 529
Bank Centrali ta' Malta 508, 510
Bank for Foreign Trade 805
Bank Indonesia 376, 382, 383
Bank Markazi Iran 384, 390
Bank Negara Malaysia 499
Bank of Afghanistan 42, 43
Bank of Biafra 109
Bank of Botswana 128, 130
Bank of China 192, 360
Bank of England 323, 327
Bank of Eritrea 277
Bank of Estonia 278, 280
Bank of Ghana 316, 320
Bank of Greece 327, 328
Bank of Guyana 341
Bank of Ireland 402, 408
Bank of Israel 412, 417
Bank of Italy 418
Bank of Jamaica 422, 426
Bank of Japan 426
Bank of Kampuchea 160
Bank of Korea 447
Bank of Libya 471
Bank of Lithuania 476
Bank of Mauritius 513, 516
Bank of Namibia 536, 537
Bank of Papua New Guinea 577
Bank of Rhodesia and Nyasaland 620
Bank of Russia 627
Bank of Scotland 644
Bank of Sierra Leone 665, 668
Bank of Sudan 702
Bank of Taiwan 193, 196
Bank of Tanzania 730
Bank of Thailand 738
Bank of the Lao PDR 461
Bank of Uganda 763
Bank of Uzbekistan 791
Bank of Western Samoa 823
Bank of Yemen 831
Bank of Zambia 851
Bank van de Nederlandse Antillen 543
Banka e Shqiperise 48
Banka e Shtetit Shqiptar 45, 46, 50
Banka Nistriana 750
Banka Slovenije 678
Banki Nasiyonali Y'u Rwanda 630
Bankiga Dhexe ee Soomaaliya 685
Bankiga Qaranka Soomaaliyeed 684
Banky Foiben'i Madagasikara 490
Banky Foiben'ny Repoblika Malagasy 490
Banque Centrale d'Algérie 51
Banque Centrale de la République de Guinée 336
Banque Centrale de la République Malgache 490
Banque Centrale de Mauritanie 511
Banque Centrale de Tunisie 754
Banque Centrale de Vanuatu 793
Banque Centrale des Comores 205
Banque Centrale des États de l'Afrique ... 273, 274
Banque Centrale des Etats de l'Afrique de l'Ouest 811
Banque Centrale du Congo 208
Banque Centrale du Mali 506
Banque Centrale 165, 183, 209, 301
Banque d'Algérie 53
Banque d'Emission du Rwanda et du Burundi 634
Banque de France 295
Banque de l'Algérie 51
Banque de l'Indochine 727
Banque de la République d'Haiti 345
Banque de la République du Burundi 154
Banque de la République du Mali 505
Banque de Madagascar et des Comores 204
Banque de Reserve de Vanuatu 794
Banque des États de l'Afrique Centrale 167, 179, 183, 209, 211, 277, 301
Banque des États del'Afrique Centrale 166, 176, 177
Banque du Canada / Bank of Canada 168
Banque du Liban 465
Banque du Maroc 529
Banque du Royaume du Burundi 153
Banque du Zaïre Branches 850
Banque du Zaïre 842
Banque Internationale a Luxembourg 480
Banque Nationale de Belgique 96, 97
Banque Nationale de la République d'Haiti 343
Banque Nationale du Cambodge 158, 159
Banque Nationale du Congo 206
Banque Nationale du Katanga 435
Banque Nationale du Laos 458
Banque Nationale du Rwanda 630
Banque Nationale 243
Belarus National Bank 94
Belarus Republic 93
Belfast Banking Company Limited 403
Benki Kuu Ya Tanzania 731
Bermuda Government 102
Bermuda Monetary Authority 103, 105
Board of Commissioners of Currency 499, 668
Bon Towarowy (Trade Voucher) 606
British Armed Forces, Special Vouchers 326
British Caribbean Territories, Eastern Group 142
British Linen Bank 648
Bulgarian National Bank 147, 148, 150
Bundeskassenschein 312
Caisse Centrale de la France d'Outre-Mer 511, 636
Cayman Islands Currency Board 174, 176
Cayman Islands Monetary Authority 176
Central Bank of Barbados 91
Central Bank of Belize 99, 101
Central Bank of Ceylon 181, 697
Central Bank of Cyprus 232
Central Bank of Egypt 262
Central Bank of Iceland 364
Central Bank of Iraq 393
Central Bank of Ireland 398
Central Bank of Jordan 431
Central Bank of Kenya 438
Central Bank of Kuwait 452, 456
Central Bank of Lesotho 468
Central Bank of Libya 472
Central Bank of Malta 508
Central Bank of Myanmar 534
Central Bank of Nigeria 562
Central Bank of Oman 569
Central Bank of Samoa 825
Central Bank of Seychelles 663
Central Bank of Solomon Islands 680
Central Bank of Somalia 685
Central Bank of Sri Lanka 699

Central Bank of Swaziland 712
Central Bank of Syria 725
Central Bank of the Bahamas 81
Central Bank of The Gambia........................... 304
Central Bank of the Islamic Republic of Iran ... 392
Central Bank of the Philippines 592
Central Bank of the Republic of Armenia 70
Central Bank of Trinidad and Tobago 752
Central Bank of Turkey.................................... 758
Central Bank of Turkmenistan......................... 762
Central Bank of Uzbekistan Republic.............. 792
Central Bank of Vanuatu/Central Bank Blong Vanuatu 793
Central Bank of Yemen 828
Central Bank.. 536
Central Committee of the National Front for the Liberation of South Vietnam 810
Central Monetary Authority.............................. 288
Centrale Bank Van Aruba................................. 71
Centrale Bank van Suriname 708, 709
Ceská Národní Banka 237
Ceskoslovenská Socialistická Republika 235
Chartered Bank 354
Clydesdale and North of Scotland Bank Ltd. 649
Clydesdale Bank Limited................................. 649
Clydesdale Bank Plc 651, 660
Collector Series... 743
Conseil Monétaire de la Répub lique du Congo 206
Corecom.. 150
Czech National Bank....................................... 237
Czechoslovak Socialist Republic..................... 235
Czechoslovak State Bank 235
Da Afghanistan Bank.................................. 43, 44
Danmarks Nationalbank 240
De Nederlandsche Bank 541
Deutsche Bundesbank 311, 312
Deutsche Notenbank....................................... 314
East African Currency Board, Nairobi 251
East Caribbean Central Bank.......................... 257
East Caribbean Currency Authority................. 252
Eastern Caribbean Central Bank..................... 254
Eesti Pank 278, 280
El Banco de México, S.A................................. 516
Équatoriale et du Cameroun 273
Équatoriale 274
Fale Tupe o Samoa I Sisifo 823
Faletupe Tutotonu O Samoa........................... 825
Federal Reserve Notes - Small Size 778
First Trust Bank 404
Føroyar.. 284
Forum-Aussenhandelsgesellschaft M.B.H. 316
Gambia Currency Board.................................. 303
Georgian Military 310
Georgian National Bank 306
Government of Antigua and Barbuda............. 257
Government of Belize.. 99
Government of British Honduras 143
Government of Brunei 144
Government of Gibraltar......................... 321, 322
Government of Hong Kong.............................. 360
Government of India....................... 370, 371, 374
Government of Pakistan 573, 574
Government of Seychelles 660
Government of St. Helena............................... 635
Government of Thailand.................................. 738
Government of the Bahamas 80
Government of the Cook Islands............ 211, 212
Government of Tonga 746, 748
Grand Duché de Luxembourg 480
Hong Kong & Shanghai Banking Corporation 355
Hong Kong & Shanghai Banking Corporation Limited... 358
Hong Kong Branch.. 355
Hungarian National Bank 361
Institut d'Emission d'Outre-Mer........ 301, 546, 728
Institut d'Emission d'Outre-Mer, Nouvelles Hébrides 547
Institut d'Émission des Comores..................... 204
Institut d'Emission des Départements d'Outre-Mer 299
Institut d'Emission des Départements d'Outre-Mer République Francaise 300, 617
Institut d'Emission Malgache 488
Institut Monetaire Luxembourgeois................. 481
International Bank in Luxembourg 480
Kazakhstan National Bank.............................. 436
Kerajaan Brunei 144
Khmer Rouge Influence 164
Kibris Merkez Bankasi 232
Kingdom of Tonga... 747
Komiti Faatino o Tupe a Samoa I Sisifo.......... 824
Korean Central Bank.............................. 444, 447
Kuwait Currency Board 452
Kyrgyzstan Bank 457
Kyrgyz Bank.. 457
Kyrgyz Republic 456
Labank Santral Sesel...................................... 663
Lesotho Monetary Authority 468
Lietuvos Bankas.. 476
Lloyds Bank Limited 408
Magyar Nemzeti Bank............................ 361, 362
Maldives Monetary Authority........................... 504
Maldivian State, Government Treasurer 504
Marynarski Bon Towarowy............................. 607
Mercantile Bank Limited.................................. 358
Military Payment Certificates 193, 781
Minister of Finance.. 524
Ministere du Tourisme du Cambodge............. 165
Mogadishu North Forces................................. 687
Monetary Authority of Belize 99
Monetary Authority of Swaziland 712, 716
Monetary Board of Western Samoa................ 824
Mongol Bank 527
Muntbiljet... 708
Narodna Banka Bosne I Hercegovine............. 119
Narodna Banka Jugoslavije 833
Narodna Banka Republike Srpske Krajine....... 222
Narodna Banka Republike Srpske.................. 127
Národná Banka Slovenska 675
Narodna Banka Srpske Republike Bosne I Hercegovine National Bank of the Serbian Republic of Bosnia-Herzegovina............... 126
Narodowy Bank Polski 601, 602, 603, 607
National Bank of Cambodia 163, 165
National Bank of Cuba 226
National Bank of Ethiopia........................ 281, 282
National Bank of Liberia.................................. 471
National Bank of Macedonia 486
National Bank of the Republic of Macedonia.. 487
National Bank of the Republic of Tajikistan 729
National Bank of the Serbian Republic - Krajina.. 222
National Bank of the Serbian Republic 127
National Bank of Viet Nam.............................. 806
National Bank of Yugoslavia 833
National Commercial Bank of Scotland Limited... 654
National Reserve Bank of Tonga 748
Nationale Bank van Belgie................................ 96
Negara Brunei Darussalam 145
Netherlands Bank 541
Ngân Hang N goai Thu'o'ng 805
Ngân-Hàng Nhà-Nu'ó'c Viêt-Nam.... 800, 801, 802
Ngân-Hàng Quô'c-Gia Viêt-Nam 806
Ngân-Hàng Viêt-Nam 809
Norges Bank.. 564
Northern Bank Limited.................................... 405
Odberní Poukaz... 237
Oesterreichische Nationalbank......................... 76
Oman Currency Board.................................... 569
Pathet Lao Government.................................. 460
Pekao Trading Co. (P.K.O.)/Bank Polska........ 606
Peoples Bank of Burma 151
Peoples Bank of China 190
Peoples National Bank of Cambodia.............. 162
Peoples Republic of Bangladesh...................... 87
Phiêu' Thay Ngoai Tê 805
Polish National Bank....................... 601, 602, 603
Provincial Bank of Ireland Limited 406, 408
Pule' Anga 'o Tonga 746
Qatar and Dubai Currency Board 616
Qatar Central Bank 615
Qatar Monetary Agency.................................. 613
Repubblica Italiana - Biglietto di Stato............ 418
Republic Indonesia 382, 383
Republic of China-Taiwan Bank 195
Republic of Croatia 219, 221
Republic of Cyprus 232
Republic of Seychelles 661
Republic of Slovakia 674
República Popular De Moçambique 532
Republik Indonesia 375
Republika Hrvatska... 219
Republika Slovenija 677
Republika Srpska Krajina 221
Reserve Bank Of Fiji....................................... 289
Reserve Bank of India 367, 370, 372, 374
Reserve Bank of Malawi 493
Reserve Bank of New Zealand 548, 552
Reserve Bank of Rhodesia 618, 619
Reserve Bank of Vanuatu/Reserve Bank Blong Vanuatu 794
Reserve Bank of Zimbabwe............................ 857
Reserve Bank 72
Royal Bank of Scotland 655
Royal Bank of Scotland Limited...................... 656
Royal Bank of Scotland plc............................. 657
Royal Government of Bhutan 106
Royal Monetary Authority of Bhutan............... 107
Royaume de Belgique - Koninkrijk Belgie.......... 96
Russian Federation... 627
Saint-Pierre-et-Miquelon................................. 636
Saudi Arabian Monetary Agency 641
Schweizerische Nationalbank.......................... 721
Seamen's Trade Vouchers 607
Sedlabanki Íslands.. 364
Seychelles Monetary Authority 662
Singapore 674
Slovak National Bank...................................... 675
Slovenska Republika 674
Solomon Islands Monetary Authority....... 680, 682
Somali National Bank 684
South African Reserve Bank........................... 689
South Arabian Currency Authority 831
Srí Lanká Maha Bänkuva 699
Staatsbank der DDR.............................. 315, 316
Standard Chartered Bank 359
State Bank Note U.S.S.R................................ 625
State Bank of Democratic Kampuchea........... 161

State Bank of Ethiopia 280
State Bank of Pakistan 573, 575, 576
State Bank of Viet Nam 800, 801, 802
State Bank 526, 538
State Treasury Note 625
States of Guernsey 334
States of Jersey, Treasury 428, 430
Státní Banka Ceskoslovenská 235
Sultanate of Muscat and Oman 568
Suomen Pankki - Finlands Bank 291
Sw(v)eriges Riksbank 716
Swiss National Bank 721
Territory of Western Samoa 822
Tesouro Nacional, Valor Legal 132
Tesouro Nacional, Valor Recebido 132
Treasury 735, 769, 771
Trésor Public, Territoire Français des Afars et des Issas 298
Türkiye Cümhuriyet Merkez Bankasi 758
Türkmenistanyñ Merkezi Döwlet Banky 762
Ukrainian National Bank 770, 771, 774
Ulster Bank Limited 407
Union Bank of Burma 152
United Arab Emirates Central Bank 775
United Arab Emirates Currency Board 774
United Arab Republic 266
United States Notes - Small Size 778
Úy Ban Trung U'O'ng 810
Westminster Bank Limited 408
Yemen Currency Board 826

ЎЗБЕКИСТОН РЕСПУБЛИКАСИ МАРКАЗИЙ БАНКИ 792
БАНК РОССИЙ 627
БАНКА НИСТРЯНЭ 750
БИЛЕТ ГОСУДАРСТВЕННОГО БАНКА С.С.С.Р. 625
БЪЛГАРСКАТА НАРОДНА БАНКА 147
БЪЛГАРСКАТА НАРОДНА БАНКА 148
БОНКИ МИЛЛИИ ЧУМХУРИИ ТОЧИКИСТОН 729
ГОСУДАРСТВЕННЫЙ КАЗНАЧЕЙСКИЙ БИЛЕТ 625
РЕПУБЛИКА СРПСКА КРАЈИНА 221
КАЗАКСТАН УЛТТЫК БАНКI 436
КУПОН РЭСПУБЛІКА БЕЛАРУСБ 93
КЫРГЫЗ РЕСПУБЛИКАСЫ 456
КЫРГЫЗСТАН БАНКЫ 457
КЫРГЫЭ БАНКЫ 457
УЗБЕКИСТОН ДАВПАТ БАНКИ 791
УЛСЫН БАНК 526
ЦЕНТРАЛНА БАНКА БОСНЕ И ХЕРЦЕГОВИНЕ Centralna Banka Bosne I Hercegovine 124
МОНГОЛ БАНК 527
KENTRIKH TRAPEZA THS KUPROU 232
KUPRIAKH DHMOKRATIA 232
НАЦІОНАЛЬНИЙ БАНК УКРАЇНИ 770
НАЦІОНАЛЬНИЙ БАНК УКРАЇНИ 771
НАЦІОНАЛЬНИЙ БАНК УКРАЇНИ 774
НАЦЫЯНАЛЬНАIА БАНКА БЕЛАРУСI 94
НАРОДНА БАНКА ЈУГОСЛАВИЈЕ 833
НАРОДНА БАНКА БОСНЕ И ХЕРЦЕГОВИНЕ 119
НАРОДНА БАНКА РЕПУБЛИКЕ СРПСКЕ КР АЈИНЕ 222
НАРОДНА БАНКА РЕПУБЛИКЕ СРПСКЕ 127
НАРОДНА БАНКА НА РЕПУБЛИКА МАКЕДОНИЈА 487
НАРОДНА БАНКА НА МАКЕДОНИЈА 486
НАРОДНА БАНКА СРПСКЕ РЕПУБЛИКЕ БОСНЕ И ХЕРЦЕГО 126
РОССИЙСКАЯ ФЕДЕРАЦИЯ 627
TRAPEZA THS ELLADOS 327
TRAPEZA THS ELLADOS 328

HOW TO USE THIS CATALOG

Catalog listings consist of all regular and provisional notes attaining wide circulation in their respective countries for the period covered. Notes have been listed under the historical country name. Thus Dahomey is not under Benin, and so on, as had been the case in past catalogs. Where catalog numbers have changed, and you will find some renumbering in this edition, the old catalog numbers appear in parentheses directly below the new number. The listings continue to be grouped by issue range rather than by denomination, and a slight change in the listing format should make the bank name, issue dates as well as catalog numbers and denominations easier to locate. These changes have been made to make the catalog as easy to use as possible for you.

The editors and publisher make no claim to absolute completeness, just as they acknowledge that some errors and pricing inequities will appear. Correspondence is invited with interested persons who have notes previously unlisted or who have information to enhance the presentation of existing listings in succeeding editions of this catalog.

Catalog Format

Listings proceed generally according to the following sequence: country, geographic or political chronology, bank name, sometimes alphabetically or by date of first note issue. Release within the bank, most often in date order, but sometimes by printer first.

Catalog number — The basic reference number at the beginning of each listing for each note. For this Modern Issues volume the regular listings require no prefix letters except when an 'A' or 'B' appear within the catalog number. (Military and Regional prefixes are explained later in this section.)

Denomination — the value as shown on the note, in western numerals. When denominations are only spelled out, consult the numerics chart.

Date — the actual issue date as printed on the note; in day-month-year order. Where more than one date appears on a note, only the latest is used. Where the note has no date, the designation ND is used, followed by a year date in parentheses when it is known. If a note is dated by the law or decree of authorization, then these dates appear with a L or D and are italicized.

Descriptions of the note are broken up into one or more items as follows:

Color — the main color(s) of the face, and the underprint are given first. If the colors of the back are different, then they follow the face design description.

Design — The identification and location of the main design elements if known. Back design elements identified if known.

If design elements and or signatures are the same for an issue group then they are printed only once at the heading of the issue, and apply for the group that follows.

Printer — often a local printer has the name shown in full. Abbreviations are used for the most prolific printers. Refer to the list of printer abbreviations elsewhere in this introduction. In these listings the use of the term "imprint" refers to the logo or the printer's name as usually appearing in the bottom frame or below in the margin of the note.

Valuations — are generally given under the grade headings of Good, Fine and Extremely Fine for early notes; and Very Good, Very Fine and Uncirculated for the later issues. Listings that do not follow these two patterns are clearly indicated. *Unc* followed by a value is used usually for specimens and proofs when lower grade headings are used for a particular series of issued notes.

Catalog prefix or suffix letters

A catalog number preceded by a capital 'A' indicated the incorporation of an earlier listing as required by type or date; a capital letter following the catalog number usually shows the addition of a later issue. Both may indicate newly discovered lower or higher denominations to a series. Listings of notes for regional circulation are distinguished from regular national issues with the prefix letter 'R'; military issues use a 'M' prefix; foreign exchange certificates are assigned a 'FX' prefix. Varieties, specific date or signature listings are shown with small letters 'a' following a number within their respective entries. Some standard variety letters include: 'p' for proof notes, 'r' for remainder notes, 's' for specimen notes and 'x' for errors.

Denominations

The denomination as indicated on many notes issued by a string of countries stretching from the eastern Orient, through western Asia and on across northern Africa often appear only in unfamiliar non-Western numeral styles. Within the listings which follow, however, denominations are always indicated in Western numerals.

A comprehensive chart keying Western numerals to their non-Western counterparts is included elsewhere in this introduction as an aid to the identification of note types. This compilation features not only the basic numeral systems such as Arabic, Japanese and Indian; but also the more restricted systems such as Burmese, Ethiopian, Siamese, Tibetan, Hebrew, Mongolian and Korean, plus other localized variations which have been applied to some paper money issues.

In consulting the numeral systems chart to determine the denomination of a note, one should remember that the actual numerals styles employed in any given area, or at a particular time, may vary significantly from these basic representations. Such variations can be deceptive to the untrained eye, just as variations from Western numeral styles can prove deceptive to individuals not acquainted with the particular style employed.

Dates and Date Listing Policy

In previous editions of this work it was the goal to provide a sampling of the many date varieties that were believed to exist. In recent times, as particular dates (and usually signature combinations) were known to be scarcer, that particular series was expanded to include listings of individual dates. At times this idea has been fully incorporated, but with some series it is not practicable, especially when just about every day in a given month could have been an issue date for the notes.

Accordingly, where it seems justifiable that date spans can be realistically filled with individual dates, this has been done. In order to accommodate the many new dates, the idea of providing small letters to break them up into narrower spans of years has been used. Within these small letter date spans, the aim has been to include no more than five or six dates. If it appears that there are too many dates for a series, with no major differences in value, then a general inclusive date span is used (beginning and ending) and individual dates within this span are not shown.

For those notes showing only a general date span, the only important dates become those that expand the range of years, months or days earlier or later. But even they would have no impact on the values shown.

Because a specific date is not listed does not necessarily mean it is rare. It may be just that it has not been reported. Those date varieties known to be scarcer are cataloged separately. Newly reported dates in a wide variety of listings are constantly being reported. This indicates that research into the whole area is very active, and a steady flow of new dates is fully expected upon publication of this edition.

Abbreviations

Certain abbreviations have been adopted for words occurring frequently in note descriptions. Following is a list of these:

#	—	number (catalog or serial)
bldg.	—	building
ctr.	—	center
dk.	—	dark
FV	—	face value
Gen.	—	General
govt.	—	government
Kg.	—	king
l.	—	left
lg.	—	large
lt.	—	light
m/c	—	multicolored
ND	—	no date
ovpt.	—	overprint
portr.	—	portrait
Qn.	—	queen
r.	—	right
sign.	—	signature or signatures
sm.	—	small
unpt.	—	underprint (background printing)
wmk.	—	watermark
w/	—	with
w/o	—	without

Valuations

Valuations are given for most notes in three grades. Earlier issues are usually priced in the grade headings of Good, Fine and Extremely Fine; later issues take the grade headings of Very Good, Very Fine and Uncirculated. While it is true that some early notes cannot be priced in Extremely Fine and some later notes have no premium value in Very Good, it is felt that this coverage provides the best uniformity of value data to the collecting community. There are exceptional cases where headings are adjusted for either single notes or a series that really needs special treatment. We have endeavored to print the grade headings often for ease of reference.

Valuations are determined generally from a consensus of individuals submitting prices for evaluation. Some notes have NO values; this does not necessarily mean they are expensive or even rare; but it shows that no pricing information was forthcoming. A number of notes have a 'Rare' designation, and no values. Such notes are generally not available on the market, and when they do appear the price is a matter between buyer and seller. No book can provide guidance in these instances except to indicate rarity.

Valuations used in this book are based on the IBNS grading standards and are stated in U.S. dollars. They serve only as aids in evaluating paper money since actual market conditions throughout the worldwide collector community are constantly changing. In addition, particularly choice examples of many issues listed may bring higher premiums than values listed.

Unless otherwise presented, values are given for types only, without regard for date or signature. In a number of instances there could be dates or signature varieties worth a substantial premium over the listed value.

FV (for Face Value) is used as a value designation on older but still redeemable legal tender notes in lower conditions. FV may appear in one or both condition columns before Uncirculated, depending on the relative age and availability of the note in question.

Collection care

The proper preservation of a collection should be of paramount importance to all in the hobby - dealers, collectors and scholars. Only a person who has housed notes in a manner giving pleasure to himself and others will keep alive the pleasure of collecting for future generations. The same applies to the way of housing as to the choice of the collecting specialty: it is chiefly a questions of what most pleases the individual collector.

Arrangement and sorting of a collection is most certainly a basic requirement. Storing the notes in safe paper envelopes and filing boxes should, perhaps, be considered only when building a new section of a collection, for accommodating varieties or for reasons of saving space when the collection has grown quickly.

The grouping of notes on large sheets and fixing them into position with photo corners had been a method practiced for many years. The collector could arrange the notes to his own taste, identify and otherwise embellish them. Difficulties arise in the accommodation of supplements and the exchanging of notes for examples in better condition, since even slight differences in the format will necessitate detaching and most likely remaking a whole page.

Most paper money collections are probably housed in some form of plastic-pocketed album which are today manufactured in many different sizes and styles to accommodate many types of world paper money.

Because of the number of bank note collectors has grown continually over the past twenty-five years, some specialty manufacturers of albums have developed a paper money selection. The notes, housed in clear plastic pockets, individually or in groups, can be viewed and exchanged without difficulty. These albums are not cheap, but the notes displayed in this manner do make a lasting impression on the viewer. A large collection will hardly be accommodated in its entirety in this manner, thus many collectors limit themselves to partial areas or especially valuable notes which are displayed thus. **A word of concern: certain types of plastic and all vinyl used for housing notes may cause notes to become brittle over time, or cause an irreversible and harmful transfer of oils from the vinyl onto the bank notes.**

The high demands which stamp collectors make on their products cannot be transferred to the paper money collecting fraternity. A postage stamp is intended for only a single use, then it is relegated to a collection. With paper money, it is nearly impossible to acquire uncirculated specimens from a number of countries due to export laws or just because of internal bank procedures. Bends from excessive counting, or even staple holes are commonplace. Once acquiring a circulated note, the collector must endeavor to maintain its state of preservation.

The fact that there is a classification and value difference between notes with greater use or even damage is a matter of course. It is part of the opinion and personal taste of the individual collector to decide what he will consider worthy of collecting and what will pay for such items.

For the purposed of strengthening and mending torn paper money, under no circumstances should one use plain cellophane tape or a similar material. These tapes warp easily, with sealing marks forming at the edges, and the tape frequently discolors. Only with the greatest of difficulty (and often not at all) can these tapes be removed, and damage to the note or the printing is almost unavoidable. The best material for mending tears is an archival tape recommended for the treatment and repair of documents.

There are collectors who, with great skill, remove unsightly spots, repair badly damaged notes, replace missing pieces and otherwise restore or clean a note. Before venturing to tackle such work, one should first experiment with cheap duplicates and not endanger a collection piece. Really difficult work of this nature should be left to the experienced restorer. There is also the question of morality of tampering with a note to improve its condition, either by repairing, starching, ironing, pressing or other methods to possibly deceive a potential future buyer. Such a question must, in the final analysis, be left to the individual collector.

IBNS GRADING STANDARDS FOR WORLD PAPER MONEY

The following introduction and Grading Guide is the result of work prepared under the guidance of the Grading Committee of the International Bank Note Society (IBNS.) It has been adopted as the official grading standards of that society.

Introduction

Grading is the most controversial component of paper money collecting today. Small differences in grade can mean significant differences in value. The process of grading is so subjective and dependent on external influences such as lighting, that even a very experienced individual may well grade the same note differently on separate occasions.

To facilitate communication between sellers and buyers, it is essential that grading terms and their meanings be as standardized and as widely used as possible. This standardization should reflect common usage as much as practicable. One difficulty with grading is that even the actual grades themselves are not used everywhere by everyone. For example, in Europe the grade 'About Uncirculated' (AU) is not in general use, yet in North America it is widespread. The European term 'Good VF' may roughly correspond to what individuals in North America call 'Extremely Fine' (EF).

The grades and definitions as set forth below cannot reconcile all the various systems and grading terminology variants. Rather, the attempt is made here to try and diminish the controversy with some common-sense grades and definitions that aim to give more precise meaning to the grading language of paper money.

How to look at a banknote

In order to ascertain the grade of a note, it is essential to examine it out of a holder and under a good light. Move the note around so that light bounces off at different angles. Try holding it up obliquely so that the not is almost even with your eye as you look up at the light. Hard-to-see folds or slight creases will show up under such examination. Some individuals also lightly feel along the surface of the note to detect creasing.

Cleaning, Washing, Pressing of Banknotes

a) Cleaning, washing or pressing paper money is generally harmful and reduces both the grade and the value of a note. At the very least, a washed or pressed note may lose its original sheen and its surface may become lifeless and dull. The defects a note had, such as folds and creases, may not necessarily be completely eliminated and their telltale marks can be detected under a good light. Carelessly washed notes may also have white streaks where the folds or creases were (or still are).

b) Processing of a note which started out as Extremely Fine will automatically reduce it at least one full grade.

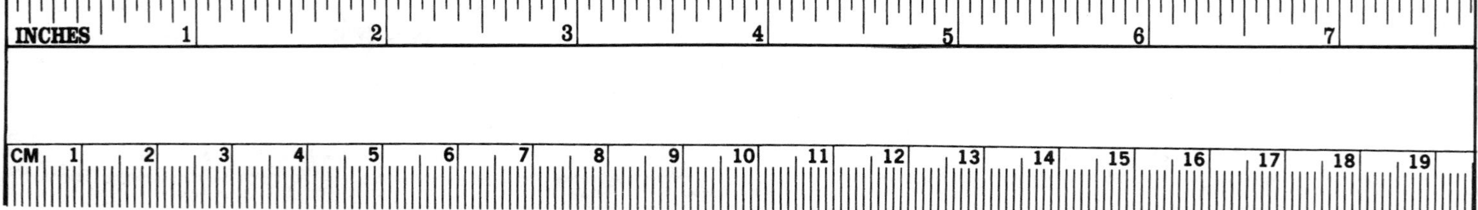

Unnatural Defects

Glue, tape or pencil marks may sometimes be successfully removed. While such removal will leave a cleaned surface, it will improve the overall appearance of the note without concealing any of its defects. Under such circumstances, the grade of that note may also be improved.

The words "pinholes", "staple holes", "trimmed", "writing on face", "tape marks" etc. should always be added to the description of a note. It is realized that certain countries routinely staple their notes together in groups before issue. In such cases, the description can include a comment such as "usual staple holes" or something similar. After all, not everyone knows that certain notes cannot be found otherwise.

The major point of this section is that one cannot lower the overall grade of a note with defects simply because of the defects. The price will reflect the lowered worth of a defective note, but the description must always include the specific defects.

The Term *Uncirculated*

The word *Uncirculated* is used in this grading guide only as a qualitive measurement of the appearance of a note. It has nothing at all to do with whether or not an issuer has actually released the note to circulation. Thus, the term About Uncirculated is justified and acceptable because so many notes that have never seen hand to hand use have been mishandled so that they are available at best in AU condition. Either a note is uncirculated in condition or it is not; there can be no degrees of uncirculated. Highlights or defects in color, centering and the like may be included in a description but the fact that a note is or is not in uncirculated condition should not be a disputable point.

GRADING GUIDE — Definitions of Terms

UNCIRCULATED: A perfectly preserved note, never mishandled by the issuing authority, a bank teller, the public or a collector.

Paper is clean and firm, without discoloration. Corners are sharp and square without any evidence of rounding. (Rounded corners are often a tell-tale sign of a cleaned or "doctored" note.)
An uncirculated note will have its original, natural sheen.

NOTE: Some note issuers are most often available with slight evidence of very light counting folds which do not "break" the paper. Also, French-printed notes usually have a slight ripple in the paper. Many collectors and dealers refer to such notes as AU-UNC.

ABOUT UNCIRCULATED: A virtually perfect note, with some minor handling. May show very slight evidence of bank counting folds at a corner or one light fold through the center, but not both. An AU note cannot be creased, a crease being a hard fold which has usually "broken" the surface of the note.

Paper is clean and bright with original sheen. Corners are not rounded.

NOTE: Europeans will refer to an About Uncirculated or AU note as "EF-Unc" or as just "EF". The Extremely Fine note described below will often be referred to as "GVF" or "Good Very Fine".

EXTREMELY FINE: A very attractive note, with light handling. May have a maximum of three light folds or one strong crease.

Paper is clean and firm, without discoloration. Corners are sharp and square without any evidence of rounding. (Rounded corners are often a tell-tale sign of a cleaned or "doctored" note.)

VERY FINE: An attractive note, but with more evidence of handling and wear. May have several folds both vertically and horizontally.

Paper may have minimal dirt, or possible color smudging. Paper itself is still relatively crisp and not floppy.

There are no tears into the border area, although the edges do show slight wear. Corners also show wear but not full rounding.

Fine: A note that shows considerable circulation, with many folds, creases and wrinkling.

Paper is not excessively dirty but may have some softness.

Edges may show much handling, with minor tears in the border area. Tears may not extend into the design. There will be no center hole because of excessive folding.

Colors are clear but not very bright. A staple hole or two would not be considered unusual wear in a Fine note. Overall appearance is still on the desirable side.

VERY GOOD: A well used note, abused but still intact.

Corners may have much wear and rounding, tiny nicks, tears may extend into the design, some discoloration may be present, staining may have occurred, and a small hole may sometimes be seen at center from excessive folding.

Staple and pinholes are usually present, and the note itself is quite limp but NO pieces of the note can be missing. A note in VG condition may still have an overall not unattractive appearance.

GOOD: A well worn and heavily used note. Normal damage from prolonged circulation will include strong multiple folds and creases, stains, pinholes and/or staple holes, dirt, discoloration, edge tears, center hole, rounded corners and an overall unattractive appearance. No large pieces of the note may be missing. Graffiti is commonly seen on notes in G condition.

FAIR: A totally limp, dirty and very well used note. Larger pieces may be half torn off or missing besides the defects mentioned under the Good category. Tears will be larger, obscured portions of the note will be bigger.

POOR: A "rag" with severe damage because of wear, staining, pieces missing, graffiti, larger holes. May have tape holding pieces of the note together. Trimming may have taken place to remove rough edges. A Poor note is desirable only as a "filler" or when such a note is the only one known of that particular issue.

STANDARD INTERNATIONAL GRADING TERMINOLOGY AND ABBREVIATIONS

U.S. and ENGLISH SPEAKING LANDS	UNCIRCULATED	EXTREMELY FINE	VERY FINE	FINE	VERY GOOD	GOOD	POOR
Abbreviation	UNC	EF or XF	VF	FF	VG	G	PR
BRAZIL	(1) DW	(3) S	(5) MBC	(7) BC	(8)	(9) R	UTGeG
DENMARK	O	O1	1+	1	1÷	2	3
FINLAND	0	01	1+	1	1?	2	3
FRANCE	NEUF	SUP	TTB or TB	TB or TB	B	TBC	BC
GERMANY	KFR	II / VZGL	III / SS	IV / S	V / S.g.E.	VI / G.e.	G.e.s.
ITALY	FdS	SPL	BB	MB	B	M	—
JAPAN	未使用	極美品	美品	並品	—	—	—
NETHERLANDS	FDC	Pr.	Z.F.	Fr.	Z.g.	G	—
NORWAY	0	01	1+	1	1÷	2	3
PORTUGAL	Novo	Soberbo	Muito bo	—	—	—	—
SPAIN	Lujo	SC, IC or EBC	MBC	BC	—	RC	MC
SWEDEN	0	01	1+	1	1?	2	—

BRAZIL

FE — Flor de Estampa
S — Soberba
MBC — Muito Bem Conservada
BC — Bem Conservada
R — Regular
UTGeG — Um Tanto Gasto e Gasto

DENMARK

O — Uncirkuleret
01 — Meget Paent Eksemplar
1+ — Paent Eksemplar
1 — Acceptabelt Eksemplar
1 —Noget Slidt Eksemplar
2 — Darlight Eksemplar
3 — Meget Darlight Eskemplar

FINLAND

00 — Kiitolyonti
0 — Lyontiveres
01 — Erittain Hyva
1+ — Hyva
1? — Keikko
3 — Huono

FRANCE

NEUF — New
SUP — Superbe
TTB — Tres Tres Beau
TB — Tres Beau
B — Beau
TBC — Tres Bien Conserve
BC — Bien Conserve

GERMANY

VZGL — Vorzüglich
SS — Sehr schön
S — Schön
S.g.E. — Sehr gut erhalten
G.e. — Gut erhalten
G.e.S. — Gering erhalten Schlect

ITALY

Fds — Fior di Stampa
SPL — Splendid
BB — Bellissimo
MB — Molto Bello
B — Bello
M — Mediocre

JAPAN

未使用 — Mishiyo
極美品 — Goku Bihin
美品 — Bihin
並品 — Futuhin

NETHERLANDS

Pr. — Prachtig
Z.F. — Zeer Fraai
Fr. — Fraai
Z.g. — Zeer Goed
G — Good

NORWAY

0 — Usirkuleret eks
01 — Meget pent eks
1+ — Pent eks
1 — Fullgodt eks
1- — Ikke Fullgodt eks
2 — Darlig eks

ROMANIA

NC — Necirculata (UNC)
FF — Foarte Frumoasa (VF)
F — Frumoasa (F)
FBC — Foarte Bine Conservata (VG)
BC — Bine Conservata (G)
M — Mediocru Conservata (POOR)
Schlecht
— Goed

SPAIN

EBC — Extraordinariamente Bien Conservada
SC — Sin Circular
IC — Incirculante
MBC — Muy Bien Conservada
BC — Bien Conservada
RC — Regular Conservada
MC — Mala Conservada

SWEDEN

0 — Ocirkulerat
01 — Mycket Vackert
1+ — Vackert
1 — Fullgott
1? — Ej Fullgott
2 — Dalight

COUNTRY / BANK IDENTIFICATION GUIDE

Afghanistan / Bank of Afghanistan

Belarus / Belarus National Bank

Algeria / Banque Centrale D'Algerie

Belarus / Belarus National Bank

Armenia / Armenia Republic Bank

Bulgaria / Bulgarian National Bank

Armenia / Armenia Republic Bank

Cambodia / National Bank of Cambodia

COUNTRY / BANK IDENTIFICATION GUIDE

Georgia / Georgian National Bank

Greece / Bank of Greece

Kazakhstan / Kazakhsta National Bank

North Korea / Korean Central Bank

Kyrgystan / Kyrgyz Bank

Laos / Bank of the Lao PDR

Libya / Bank of Libya

Macedonia / National Bank of the Republic of Macedonia

COUNTRY / BANK IDENTIFICATION GUIDE

Mongolia / Mongol Bank

Nepal / State Bank

Thailand / Bank of Thailand

Transdniestria / Banka Nistriana

Transdniestria / Banka Nistriana

Uzbekistan / Central Bank of Uzbekistan Replublic

Ukraine / Ukrainian National Bank

Dual Listings

As a general rule, the cutoff date in the Standard Catalog of World Paper Money, General Issues Volume II to Modern Issues Volume III is 1961. All notes dated 1961 and later can be found in Volume III; earlier dated issues are found in Volume II. There are numerous issues produced prior to 1961, which were reprinted with dates beyond 1961. In previous editions, such issues were split according to the beginning date of the type, without regard to the ending date, thus creating consistent treatment, but remaining somewhat confusing.

Due to popular demand and in the best interests of the collector, this edition as well as the 9th edition of General Issues Vol II will include dual-listings of such notes to present overlapping issues in their entirety, offering a more complete presentation.

Foreign Exchange Table

The latest foreign exchange fixed rates below apply to trade with banks in the country of origin. The left column shows the number of units per U.S. dollar at the official rate. The right column shows the number of units per dollar at the free market rate.

Country	Official #/$	Market #/$
Afghanistan (Afghan)	4,750	28,700
Albania (Lek)	138.85	–
Algeria (Dinar)	70.82	75.00
Andorra uses French Franc and Spanish Peseta		
Angola (Readjust Kwanza)	5.9201	–
Anguilla uses E.C.Dollar	2.70	–
Antigua uses E.C.Dollar	2.70	–
Argentina (New Peso)	.9998	–
Armenia (Dram)	540	560
Aruba (Florin)	1.79	–
Australia (Dollar)	1.5822	–
Austria (Schilling)	13.9465	–
Azerbaijan (Manat)	4,361	–
Bahamas (Dollar)	1.00	–
Bahrain Is.(Dinar)	.377	–
Bangladesh (Taka)	50.95	–
Barbados (Dollar)	2.00	–
Belarus (Ruble)	435,000	–
Belgium (Franc)	40.886	–
Belize (Dollar)	2.00	–
Benin uses CFA Franc West	664.83	–
Bermuda (Dollar)	1.00	–
Bhutan (Ngultrum)	43.61	–
Bolivia (Boliviano)	6.03	–
Bosnia-Herzegovina (Deutschmark)	1.982	–
Botswana (Pula)	4.742	–
British Virgin Islands uses U.S.Dollar	1.00	–
Brazil (Real)	1.7735	–
Brunei (Ringgit)	1.7045	–
Bulgaria (Lev)	1.9797	–
Burkina Faso uses CFA Fr.West	664.83	–
Burma (Kyat)	6.464	–
Burundi (Franc)	631.56	–
Cambodia (Riel)	3,770	–
Cameron uses CFA Franc Central	664.83	–
Canada (Dollar)	1.4497	–
Cape Verde (Escudo)	111.37	–
Cayman Is.(Dollar)	0.8333	–
Central African Rep.	664.83	–
CFA Franc Central	664.83	–
CFA Franc West	664.83	–
CFP Franc	120.88	–
Chad uses CFA Franc Central	664.83	–
Chile (Peso)	511.64	–
China, P.R. (Renminbi Yuan)	8.2772	9.30
Colombia (Peso)	1,946	2,000
Comoros (Franc)	498.62	–
Congo uses CFA Franc Central	664.83	–
Congo-Dem.Rep. (Congolese Franc)	4.50	6.50
Cook Islands (Dollar)	1.73	–
Costa Rica (Colon)	300.75	–
Croatia (Kuna)	7.8532	–
Cuba (Peso)	23.00	35.00
Cyprus (Pound)	.5823	–
Czech Republic (Koruna)	36.28	–
Denmark (Danish Krone)	7.5505	–
Djibouti (Franc)	177.72	–
Dominica uses E.C.Dollar	2.70	–
Dominican Republic (Peso)	16.039	–
East Caribbean (Dollar)	2.70	–
Ecuador (Sucre)	25,000	–
Egypt (Pound)	3.451	3.50
El Salvador (Colon)	8.755	–
Equatorial Guinea uses CFA Franc Central	664.83	–
Eritrea (Nafka)	7.25	8.00
Estonia (Kroon)	15.86	–
Ethiopia (Birr)	8.121	–
Euro	1.0149	–
Falkland Is. (Pound)	.6224	–
Faroe Islands (Krona)	7.5505	–
Fiji Islands (Dollar)	2.0239	–
Finland (Markka)	6.0262	–
France (Franc)	6.6483	–
French Polynesia uses CFP Franc	120.88	–
Gabon (CFA Franc)	664.83	–
Gambia (Dalasi)	12.023	–
Georgia (Lari)	1.86	–
Germany (D.Mark)	1.9823	–
Ghana (Cedi)	3,619	–
Gibraltar (Pound)	.6224	–
Greece (Drachma)	337.9	–
Greenland uses Danish Krone		
Grenada uses E.C.Dollar	2.70	–
Guatemala (Quetzal)	7.7824	–
Guernsey (Pound Sterling)	.6224	–
Guinea Bissau (CFA Franc)	664.83	–
Guinea Conakry (Franc)	1,600	–
Guyana (Dollar)	180.3	–
Haiti (Gourde)	17.96	–
Honduras (Lempira)	14.72	–
Hong Kong (Dollar)	7.781	–
Hungary (Forint)	257.95	–
Iceland (Krona)	72.35	–
India (Rupee)	43.61	–
Indonesia (Rupiah)	7,415	–
Iran (Rial)	3,000	8,100
Iraq (Dinar)	.311	1,800
Ireland (Punt)	.7982	–
Isle of Man (Pound Sterling)	.6224	–
Israel (New Sheqalim)	4.0478	–
Italy (Lira)	1,962.5	–
Ivory Coast uses CFA Franc West	664.83	–
Jamaica (Dollar)	41.291	–
Japan (Yen)	110.77	–
Jersey (Pound Sterling)	.6224	–
Jordan (Dinar)	.709	–
Kazakhstan (Tenge)	75.00	–
Kenya (Shilling)	73.40	–
Kiribati uses Australian Dollar		
Korea-PDR (Won)	2.20	170.0
Korea-Rep. (Won)	1,129	–
Kuwait (Dinar)	.3064	–
Kyrgyzstan (Som)	42.80	–
Laos (Kip)	7,700	–
Latvia (Lat)	.5946	–
Lebanon (Pound)	1,501	–
Lesotho (Maloti)	6.3175	–
Liberia (Dollar) "JJ"	1.00	20.00
"Liberty"	–	40.00
Libya (Dinar)	.462	3.50
Liechtenstein uses Swiss Franc		
Lithuania (Litas)	4.0009	–
Luxembourg (Franc)	40.89	–
Macao (Pataca)	8.0376	–
Macedonia (New Denar)	61.15	–
Madagascar (Franc)	6,674	–
Malawi (Kwacha)	46.77	–
Malaysia (Ringgit)	3.80	–
Maldives (Rufiya)	11.77	–
Mali uses CFA Franc West	664.83	–
Malta (Lira)	.4174	–
Marshall Islands uses U.S.Dollar		
Mauritania (Ouguiya)	225.0	–
Mauritius (Rupee)	25.54	–
Mexico (Peso)	9.36	–
Moldova (Leu)	11.05	–
Monaco uses French Franc		
Mongolia (Tugrik)	1070.0	–
Montenegro uses Yugo New Dinar		
Montserrat uses E.C.Dollar	2.70	–
Morocco (Dirham)	10.222	–
Mozambique (Metical)	13,731	–
Myanmar (Burma) (Kyat)	6.2808	350
Namibia (Rand)	6.3175	–
Nauru uses Australian Dollar		
Nepal (Rupee)	68.813	–
Netherlands (Gulden)	2.2355	–
Netherlands Antilles (Gulden)	1.79	–
New Caledonia uses CFP Franc	120.88	–
New Zealand (Dollar)	2.027	–
Nicaragua (Cordoba Oro)	12.413	–
Niger uses CFA Franc West	664.83	–
Nigeria (Naira)	102.05	105
Northern Ireland (Pound Sterling)	.6224	–
Norway (Krone)	8.2495	–
Oman (Rial)	.385	–
Pakistan (Rupee)	51.89	60.00
Palau uses U.S.Dollar		
Panama (Balboa) uses U.S.Dollar		
Papua New Guinea (Kina)	3.11	–
Paraguay (Guarani)	3,503	–
Peru (Nuevo Sol)	3.4405	–
Philippines (Peso)	40.66	–
Poland (Zloty)	4.1021	–
Portugal (Escudo)	203.19	–
Qatar (Riyal)	3.641	–
Romania (Leu)	18,763	–
Russia (New Ruble)	28.836	–
Rwanda (Franc)	342.43	–
St.Helena (Pound)	.6224	–
St.Kitts uses E.C.Dollar	2.70	–
St.Lucia uses E.C.Dollar	2.70	–
St.Vincent uses E.C.Dollar	2.70	–
San Marino uses Italian Lira		
Sao Tome e Principe (Dobra)	2,390	–
Saudi Arabia (Riyal)	3.7505	–
Scotland (Pound Sterling)	.6224	–
Senegal uses CFA Franc West	664.83	–
Seychelles (Rupee)	5.448	6.50
Sierra Leone (Leone)	1,989.3	2,500
Singapore (Dollar)	1.7045	–
Slovakia (Sk.Koruna)	42.866	–
Slovenia (Tolar)	204.04	–
Solomon Is.(Dollar)	5.0787	–
Somalia (Shilling)	2,620	–
Somaliland (Somali Shilling)	1,800	4,000
South Africa (Rand)	6.3175	–
Spain (Peseta)	168.64	–
Sri Lanka (Rupee)	73.35	–
Sudan (Dinar)	256.0	300
Surinam (Guilder)	809.5	2,000
Swaziland (Lilangeni)	6.3175	–
Sweden (Krona)	8.6473	–
Switzerland (Franc)	1.6265	–
Syria (Pound)	57.50	–
Taiwan (NTDollar)	30.715	–
Tajikistan (Ruble)	750	–
Tanzania (Shilling)	802.05	820
Thailand (Baht)	38.025	–
Togo uses CFAFranc West	664.83	–
Tonga (Paíanga)	1.6493	–
Transdniestra (New Ruble)	3,500,000	4,500,000
Trinidad & Tobago (Dollar)	6.2706	–
Tunisia (Dinar)	1.274	–
Turkey (Lira)	565,714	–
Turkmenistan (Manat)	5,200	7,500
Turks &Caicos uses U.S.Dollar		
Tuvalu uses Australian Dollar		
Uganda (Shilling)	1,506	–
Ukraine (Hryvnia)	5.42	–
United Arab Emirates (Dirham)	3.673	–
United Kingdom (Pound Sterling)	3.673	–
Uruguay (Peso Uruguayo)	11.549	–
Uzbekistan (Som)	133.0	–
Vanuatu (Vatu)	132.0	–
Vatican City uses Italian Lira		
Venezuela (Bolivar)	659.5	–
Vietnam (Dong)	14,061	–
Western Samoa (Tala)	3.126	–
Yemen (Rial)	161.05	–
Yugoslavia (Novih Dinar)	11.8868	35.00
Zambia (Kwacha)	2,870	–
Zimbabwe (Dollar)	38.035	–

ARMS AND MONETARY SYSTEMS GUIDE

EUROPE

Compliments of
Evzen Sknovril

ALBANIA

1 lek = 100 qindarka

AUSTRIA

1 Schilling = 100 Groschen

BELARUS

1 rubel = 100 kapeik

BELGIUM

1 franc = 100 centimes

BOSNIA AND HERZEGOVINA
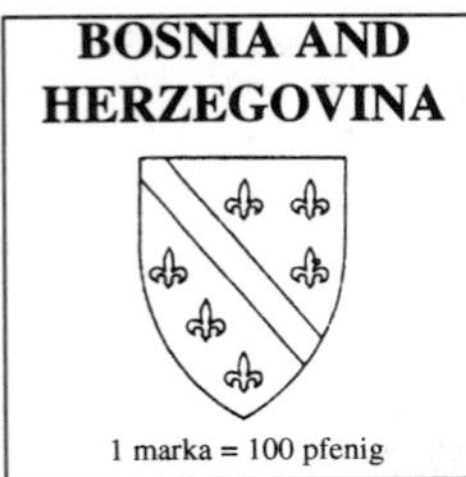
1 marka = 100 pfenig

BULGARIA

1 lev = 100 stotinki

CROATIA

1 kuna = 100 lipa

CZECH REPUBLIC

1 koruna ceska = 100 haleru

DENMARK

1 krone = 100 ore

ESTONIA

1 kroon = 100 senti

FAROE ISLANDS

1 krona = 100 ore

FINLAND

1 markka = 100 pennia

FRANCE

1 franc = 100 centimes

GERMANY

1 Deutsche Mark = 100 Pfennig

GIBRALTAR

1 pound = 100 pence

GREAT BRITAIN

1 pound = 100 pence

GREECE

1 drachme = 100 lepton

GUERNSEY
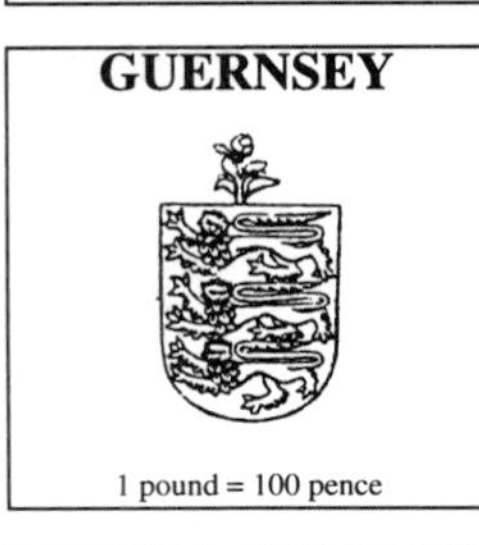
1 pound = 100 pence

HUNGARY
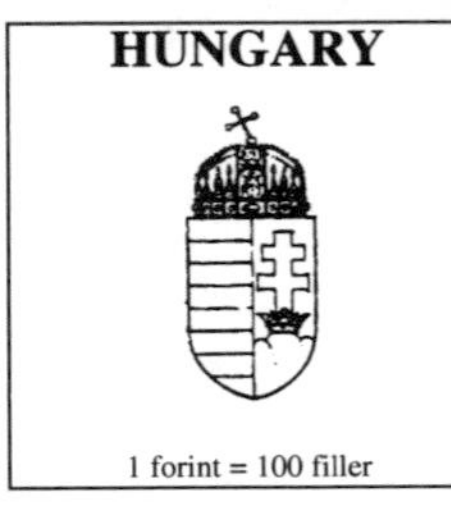
1 forint = 100 filler

ICELAND

1 krona = 100 aurar

IRELAND
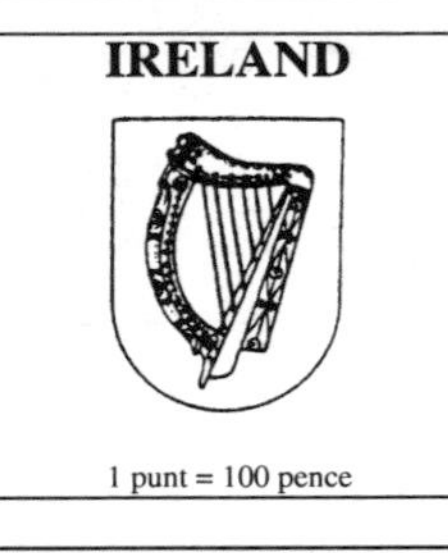
1 punt = 100 pence

IRELAND NORTHERN

1 pound = 100 pence

ISLE OF MAN

1 pound = 100 pence

ITALY

1 lira = 100 centesimi

JERSEY
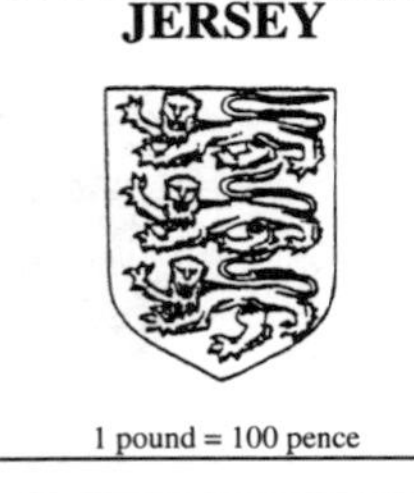
1 pound = 100 pence

LATVIA

1 lats = 100 santimu

LITHUANIA

1 litas = 100 centu

LUXEMBOURG

1 franc = 100 centimes

MACEDONIA

1 denar = 100 deni

MALTA

1 lira = 100 cents

MOLDOVA

1 leu = 100 bani

NETHERLANDS

1 gulden = 100 cent

NORWAY

1 krone = 100 ore

ARMS AND MONETARY SYSTEMS GUIDE

POLAND

1 zloty = 100 groszy

PORTUGAL
1 escudo = 100 centavos

ROMANIA

1 leu = 100 bani

RUSSIA

1 ruble = 100 kopejek

SCOTLAND

1 pound = 100 pence

SLOVAKIA

1 slovenska korun = 100 halierov

SLOVENIA

1 tolar = stotinov

SPAIN

1 peseta = 100 centimos

SWEDEN

1 krona = 100 ore

SWITZERLAND
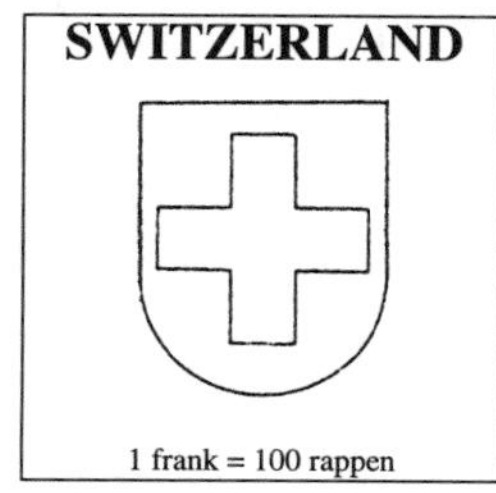
1 frank = 100 rappen

TRANSDNIESTRA

1 ruble

UKRAINE

1 hrivnja = 100 kopijok

YUGOSLAVIA

1 novi dinar = 100 para

ARGENTINA

1 peso (nuevo) = 100 centavos

ARUBA

1 florin = 100 cent

BAHAMAS

1 dollar = 100 cent

BARBADOS

1 dollar = 100 cent

BELIZE

1 dinar = 100 para

BERMUDA

1 dollar = 100 cents

BOLIVIA

1 boliviano = 100 centavos

BRAZIL

1 real = 100 centavos

CANADA

1 dollar = 100 cents

CAYMAN ISLANDS

1 dollar = 100 cents

CHILE

1 peso = 100 centavos

COLOMBIA

1 peso = 100 centavos

COSTA RICA

1 colon = 100 centimos

CUBA

1 peso = 100 centavos

DOMINICAN REPUBLIC

1 peso oro = 100 centavos

ECUADOR
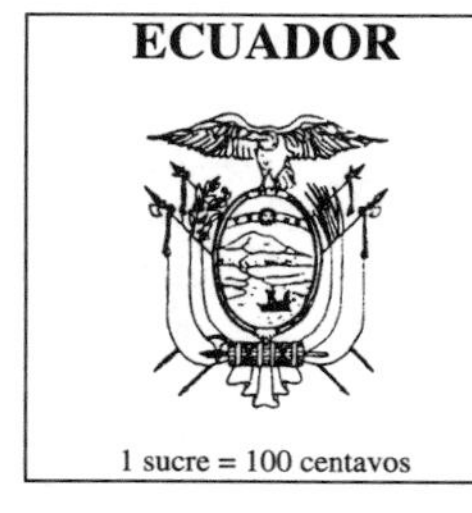
1 sucre = 100 centavos

EL SALVADOR

1 colon = 100 centavos

FALKLAND ISLANDS

1 pound = 100 pence

GUATEMALA

1 quetzal = 100 centavos

GUYANA

1 dollar = 100 cents

ARMS AND MONETARY SYSTEMS GUIDE

HAITI

1 gourde = 100 centimes

HONDURAS

1 lempira = 100 centavos

JAMAICA

1 dollar = 100 cents

MEXICO

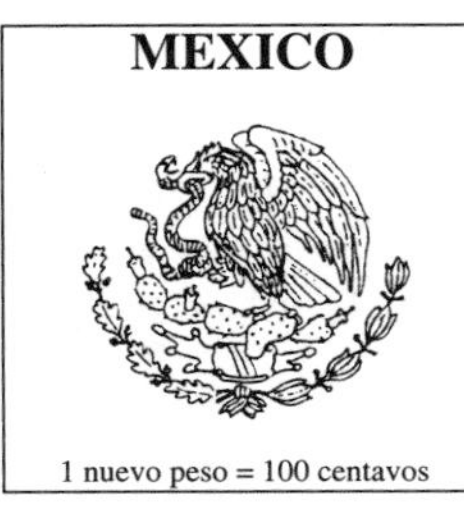

1 nuevo peso = 100 centavos

NETHERLAND ANTILLES

1 gulden = 100 cent

NICARAGUA

1 cordoba = 100 centavos

PARAGUAY

1 guarani = 100 centimos

PERU

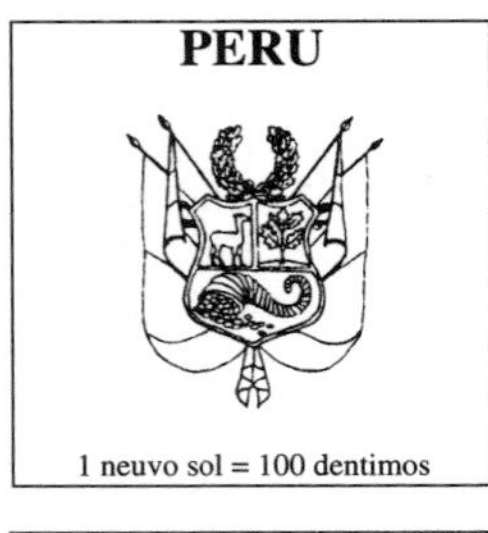

1 neuvo sol = 100 dentimos

SURINAM

1 gulden = 100 cent

TRINIDAD AND TOBAGO

1 dollar = 100 cents

UNITED STATES OF AMERICA

1 dollar = 100 cents

URUGUAY

1 Peso = 100 centesimos

VENEZUELA

1 bolivar = 100 centimos

AFGHANISTAN

1 afghani = 100 pul

ARMENIA

1 dram = 100 luma

AZERBAIJAN

1 manat = 100 qepik

BAHRAIN

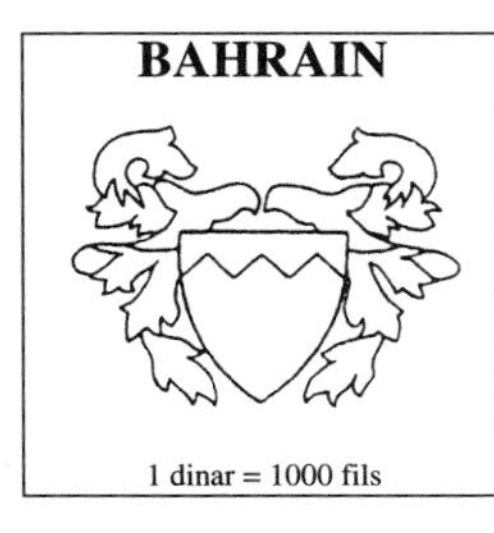

1 dinar = 1000 fils

BANGLADESH

1 taka = 100 paisa

BHUTAN

1 ngultrum = 100 chtrum

BRUNEI

1 ringgit = 100 sen

CAMBODIA

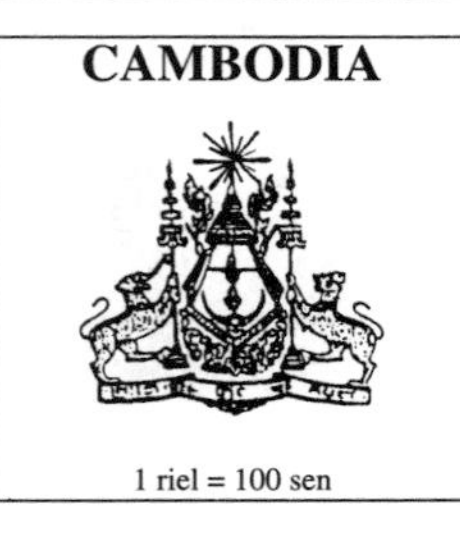

1 riel = 100 sen

CHINA

1 yuan = 10 jiao = 100 fen

CYPRUS

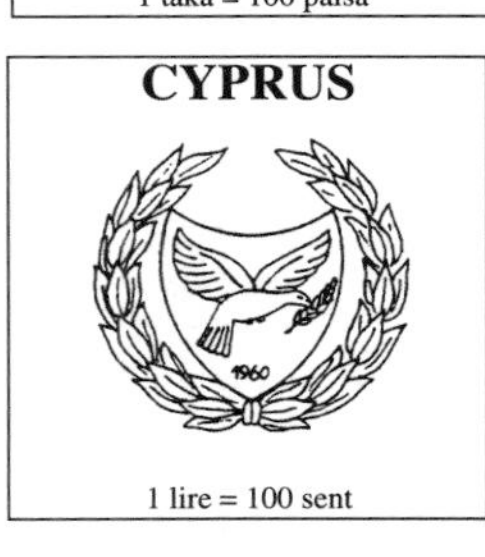

1 lire = 100 sent

GEORGIA

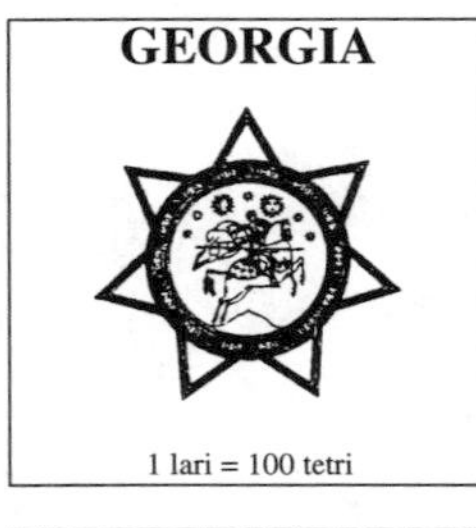

1 lari = 100 tetri

HONG KONG

1 dollar = 100 cents

INDIA

1 rupee = 100 paise

INDONESIA

1 rupiah = 100 sen

IRAN

1 rijal = 100 dinar

IRAQ

1 dinar = 1000 fils

ISRAEL

1 shekel = 100 agorot

JAPAN

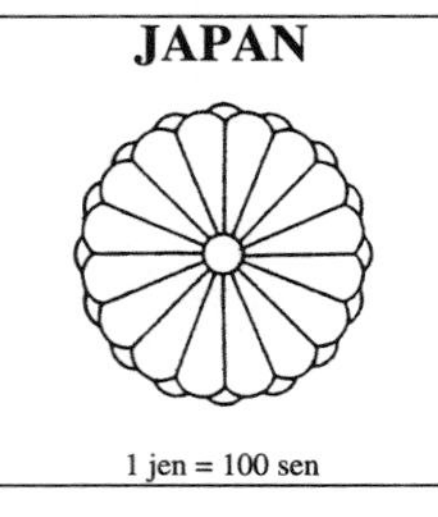

1 jen = 100 sen

JORDAN

1 dinar = 100 fils

KAZAKHSTAN

1 tenge = 100 tiyin

ARMS AND MONETARY SYSTEMS GUIDE

KOREA NORTH

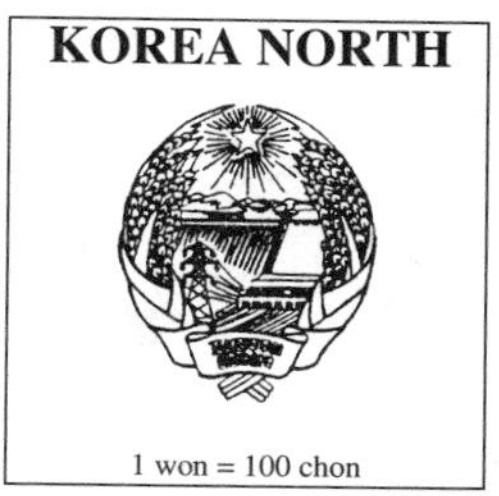

1 won = 100 chon

KOREA SOUTH

1 won = 100 chon

KUWAIT

1 dinar = 1000 fils

KYRGYZSTAN

1 som = 100 tyjin

LAOS

1 kip = 100 at

LEBANON

1 livre = 100 pisatres

MACAO

1 pataca = 100 avos

MALAYSIA

1 ringgit = 100 sen

MALDIVE ISLANDS

1 rufiyaa = 100 laari

MONGOLIA

1 togrog = 100 mongo

MYANMAR

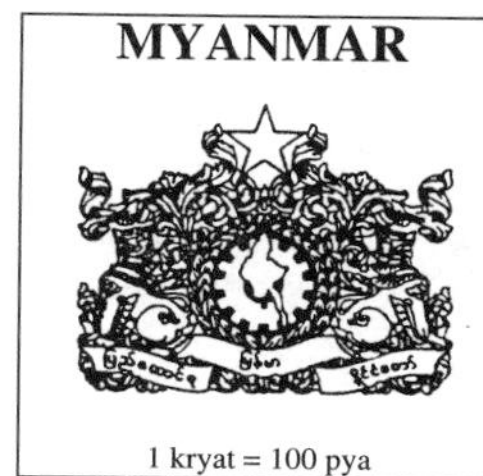

1 kryat = 100 pya

NEPAL

1 rupaja = 100 paise

OMAN

1 rial = 1000 baiza

PAKISTAN

1 rupaja = 100 pajsa

PHILIPPINES

1 pisi = 100 sentimo

QATAR

1 rijal = 100 dirham

SAUDI ARABIA

1 rijal = 100 halala

SINGAPORE

1 dollar = 100 cents

SRI LANKA

1 rupee = 100 cents

SYRIA

1 lira = 100 kirs

TAIWAN

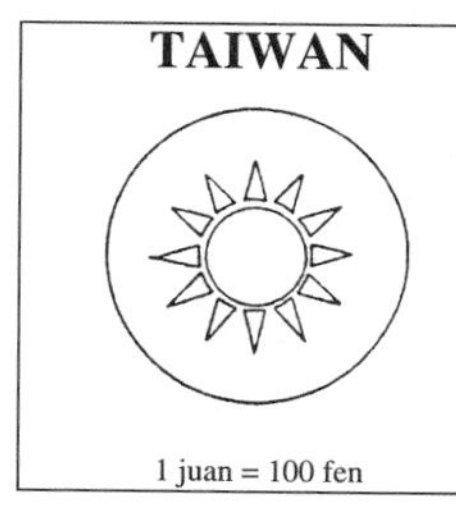

1 juan = 100 fen

TAJIKISTAN

1 tajik ruble = 100 tanga

THAILAND

1 bath = 100 satang

TURKEY

1 lira = 100 kurus

TURKMENISTAN

1 manat = 100 tenge

UNITED ARAB EMIRATES

1 dirham = 100 fils

UZBEKISTAN

1 sum = 100 tyyn

VIETNAM

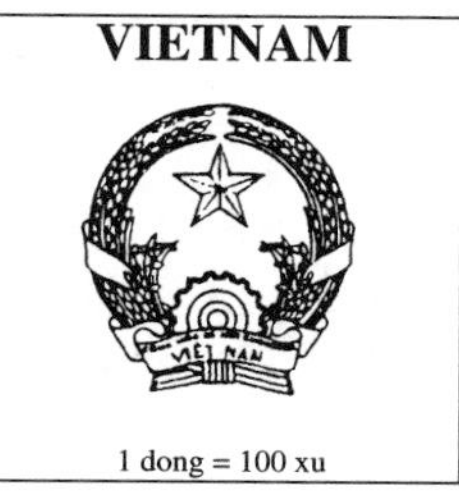

1 dong = 100 xu

YEMEN

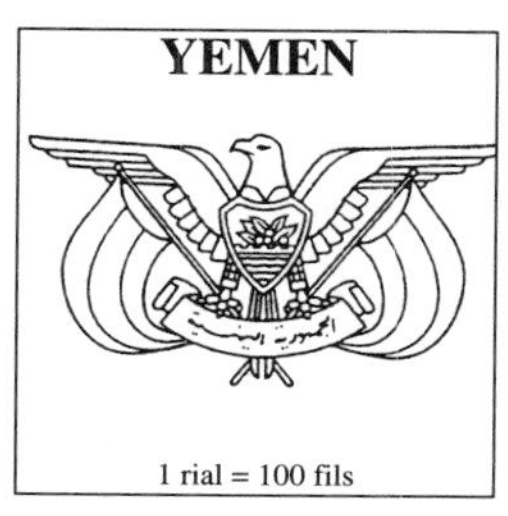

1 rial = 100 fils

AFRICA

ALGERIA

1 dinar = 100 santims

ANGOLA

1 kwanza reajustado = 100 new kwanzas

ARMS AND MONETARY SYSTEMS GUIDE

BIAFRA

1 pound = 20 shillings

BOTSWANA

1 pula = 100 thebe

BURUNDI

1 franc = 100 centimes

CAMEROON

1 CFA franc = 100 centimes

CAPE VERDE

1 escudo = 100 centavos

CENTRAL AFRICAN REPUBLIC

1 CFA franc = 100 centimes

CHAD

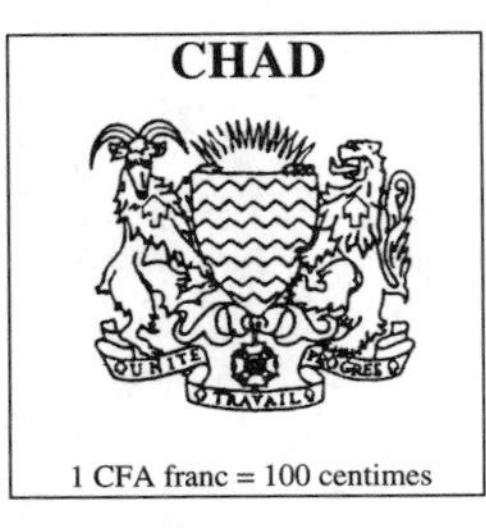

1 CFA franc = 100 centimes

COMOROS

1 franc = 100 centimos

CONGO

1 CFA franc = 100 centimes

CONGO DEMOCRATIC REPUBLIC

1 nouveau zaire = 100 nouveau makuta

DJIBOUTI

1 djibouti franc = 100 centimes

EGYPT

1 pound = 100 piastres

EQUATORIAL GUINEA

1 CFA franc = 100 centimes

ERITREA

1 nakfa = 100 cents

ETHIOPIA

1 birr = 100 santeem

GABON

1 CFA franc = centimes

GAMBIA

1 dalasi = 100 bututs

GHANA

1 cedi = 100 pesewas

GUINEA

1 franc guineen = 100 centimes

GUINEA-BISSAU

1 peso = 100 centavos

KENYA

1 shilling = 100 cents

LESOTHO

1 loti = 100 lisente

LIBERIA

1 dollar = 100 cents

LIBYA

1 dinar = 1000 dirham

MADAGASCAR

1 franc = 100 centimes

MALAWI

1 kwacha = 100 tambala

MAURITANIA

ouguiya

MAURITIUS

1 rupee = 100 cents

MOROCCO

1 dirham = 100 santimin

MOZAMBIQUE

1 metical = 100 centavos

NAMIBIA

1 dollar = 100 cents

NIGERIA

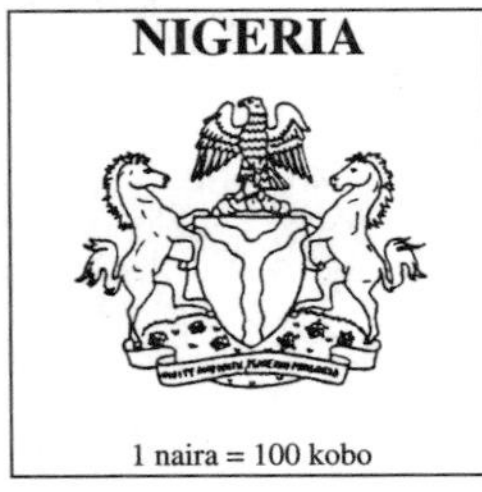

1 naira = 100 kobo

RWANDA

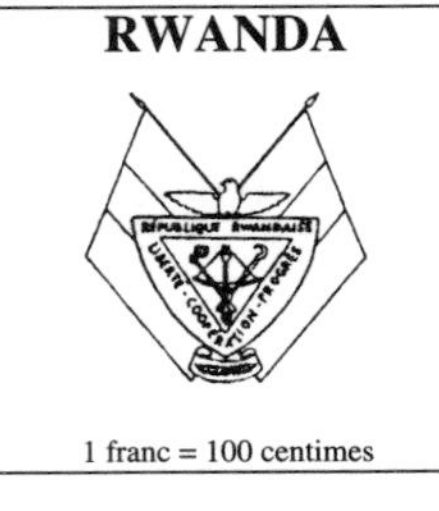

1 franc = 100 centimes

ST. HELENA

1 pound = 100 pence

ST. THOMAS & PRINCE

1 dobra = 100 centimos

ARMS AND MONETARY SYSTEMS GUIDE

SEYCHELLES
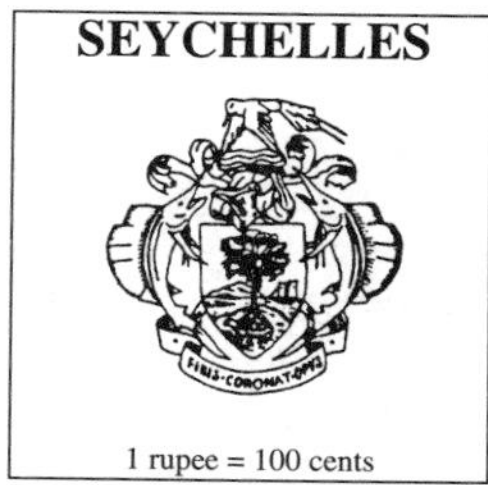
1 rupee = 100 cents

SIERRA LEONE
1 leone = 100 cents

SOMALIA

1 shilling = 100 cents

SOMALILAND

shilling

SOUTH AFRICA

1 rand = 100 cents

SUDAN

1 dinar = 100 dirham

SWAZILAND

1 lilangeni = 100 cents

TANZANIA
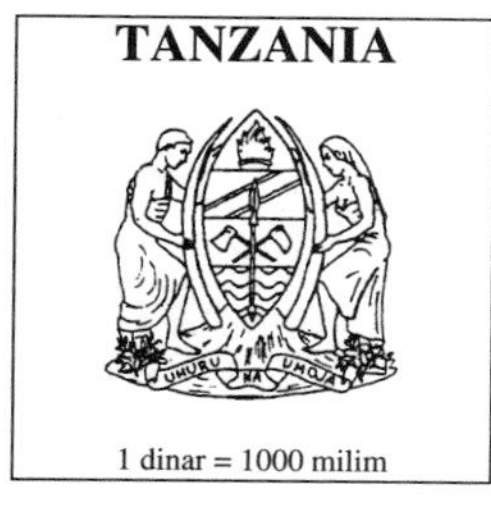
1 dinar = 1000 milim

TUNISIA
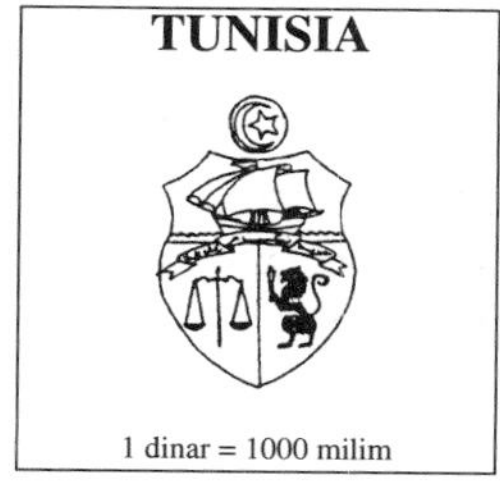
1 dinar = 1000 milim

UGANDA

1 shilling = 100 cent

ZAMBIA

1 kwacha = 100 ngwee

ZIMBABWE
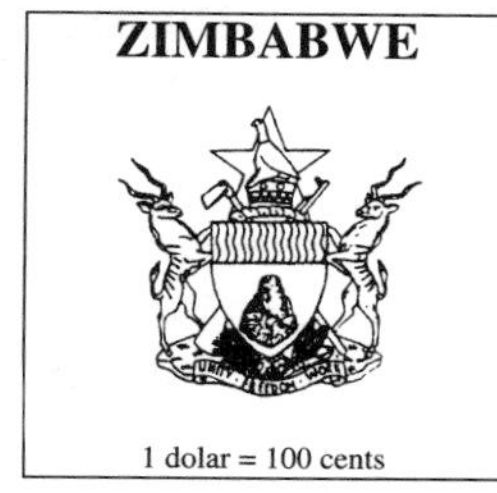
1 dolar = 100 cents

OCEANIA

ANGUILLA

1 (EC) dollar = 100 cents

ANTIGUA

1 (EC) dollar = 100 cents

AUSTRALIA

1 dolar = 100 cents

COOK ISLAND

1 dollar = 100 cents

DOMINICA

1 (EC) dollar = 100 cents

FIJI

1 dollar = 100 cents

FRENCH PACIFIC TERRITORIES
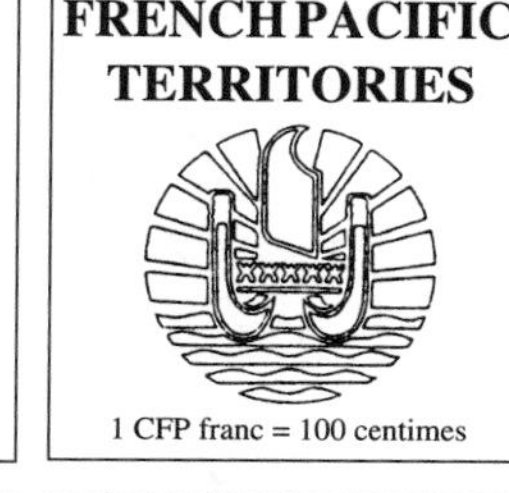
1 CFP franc = 100 centimes

GRENADA

1 (EC) dollar = 100 cents

MONTSERRAT

1 (EC) dollar = 100 cents

NEW CALEDONIA

1 CFP franc = 100 centimes

NEW ZEALAND

1 dollar = 100 cents

PAPUA NEW GUINEA

1 kina = 100 toea

St. KITTS and NEVIS

1 (EC) dollar = 100 cents

St. LUCIA

1 (EC) dollar = 100 cents

St. VINCENT

1 (EC) dollar = 100 cents

SOLOMON ISLANDS

1 dollar = 100 cents

TONGA

1 pa'anga = 100 seniti

VANUATU
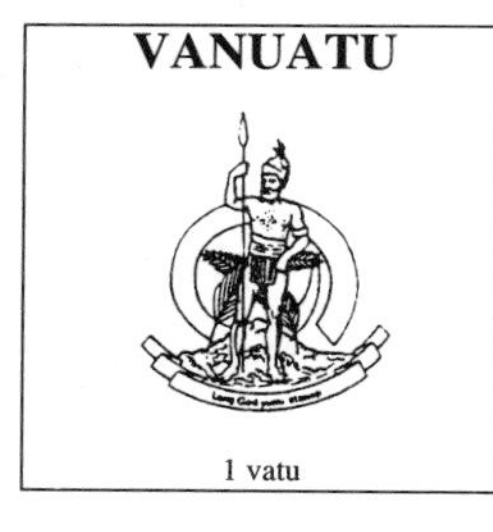
1 vatu

WESTERN SAMOA

1 tala = 100 sene

Security Devices

ASCENDING SIZE SERIAL NUMBER — A serial number with each digit slightly increasing in height and width. Both horizontal and vertical formats have been used. Czech Republic and Slovakia are among the countries where this may be found.

BAR CODE AND NUMERALS — Used mainly by banks for checks. Some countries have used these on banknotes. Scotland has a bar code, and Canada has used it with serial numbers. Sometimes magnetic.

COLORED FIBERS — Fibers usually red, blue or green, that are added either into the pulp mix to be randomly flowed onto the paper as it is made, or distributed onto the drying paper in particular areas of the page forming 'bars' of colored fibers, quite visible to the naked eye.

EMBEDDED SECURITY THREAD — A high strength thread, sometimes magnetic, embedded into the paper at the beginning of the drying stage. Looks to the eye as a solid dark strip within the paper.

FACE-BACK OPTICAL REGISTRATION DESIGN (TRANSPARENT REGISTER) — A design technique where half of an image in a framed area is printed on the face, and the other half is printed on the back, in exact register, so when held to a light, the two half images form one full image.

FOIL IMPRINTS — Shaped metal foil applied to the printed note, usually with an adhesive. Sometimes the foil is embossed with an image.

HOLOGRAM — Shiny application to the note containing an image that changes in design and color depending upon the viewing angle.

INVISIBLE PRINTING — Designs printed with inks detectable only when viewed under bright sunlight or ultraviolet light. Sometimes used to replace the more expensive watermark on low value notes.

LATENT IMPRESSIONS —Portions of the note containing sculptured engraving, making some legends or designs visible only when held to the light at certain angles.

KINEGRAM® — Similiar to a foil imprint, the design and color changes at different viewing angles.

METALLIC INK — An ink with very fine granules of metal, thus giving the ink a metallic sheen.

MICRO PRINTING — Very small letters added to an itaglio printing plate, sometimes as single lines, or in multiple repeating lines forming a larger block in the underprint design. Intaglio printing keeps the design sharp and clear, but if the note is counterfeit the microprinted area usually becomes muddy and unclear.

OPTICAL VARIABLE DEVICE (OVD) — A foil that displays a three-dimensional image when viewed under proper lighting conditions. Similar to foil imprints

OPTICALLY VARIABLE INK — An ink when printed in a special pattern changes shades when viewed and then tilted slightly.

PLANCHETTES — Tiny multicolored discs of paper embedded into the pulp mix or randomly sprinkled throughout the paper as it is drying.

RAISED MARKS — A type of braille design in notes, enabling blind people to identify note values.

SEGMENTED SECURITY THREAD —A continuous security thread, usually wide and with lettering, that is added into the paper during the drying process. Once added, a special tool is used to scrape the wet paper off only above the thread, and usually in a particular pattern, thus exposing alternate areas of the embedded thread.

UV-ULTRAVIOLET (FLOURESCENT) — When viewed in a darkened area, and exposed to a special low or high frequency UV light, a design, value, or paper fibers will glow.

WATERMARK — Extensively used as a security measure, the watermark is created by a raised design on a drying cylinder applied towards the end of the paper manufacturing process. The raised design causes a thin area in the paper which when held to the light reveals an image. This image can be words, a design, or a portrait. Recent developments have made graduations available. Thus, rather than a light/dark watermark, a gradual light to dark fade can be achieved.

DATING

Determining the date of issue of a note is a basic consideration of attribution. As the reading of dates is subject not only to the vagaries of numeric styling, but to variations in dating roots caused by the observation of differing religious eras or regal periods from country to country, making this determination can sometimes be quite difficult. Most countries outside the North Africa and Oriental spheres rely on Western date numerals and the Christian (AD) reckoning, although in a few instances note dating has been tied to the year of a reign or government.

Countries of the Arabic sphere generally date their issues to the Muslim calendar which commenced on July 16, 622 AD when the prophet Mohammed fled from Mecca to Medina. As this calendar is reckoned by the lunar year of 354 days, it is a year 3.03% shorter than the Christian year. A conversion formula requires you to subtract three percent from the AH date, and then add 621 to gain the AD date.

The Muslim calendar is not always based on the lunar year (AH), however, causing some confusion. Afghanistan and Iran (Persia) used a calendar based on a solar year (SH) introduced around 1920. These dates can be converted to AD by simply adding 621. In 1976 Iran implemented a solar calendar based on the founding of the Iranian monarchy in 559 BC. The first year observed on this new system was 2535(MS) which commenced on March 20, 1976.

Several different eras of reckoning, including the Christian (AD) and Muslim (AH), have been used to date paper money of the Indian subcontinent. The two basic systems are the Vikrama Samvat (VS) era which dates from October 18, 58 BC, and the Saka (SE) era, the origin of which is reckoned from March 3, 78 AD. Dating according to both eras appear on notes of several native states and countries of the area.

China - Republic 9th year, 1st month, 15th day (15.1.1920), read r. to l.

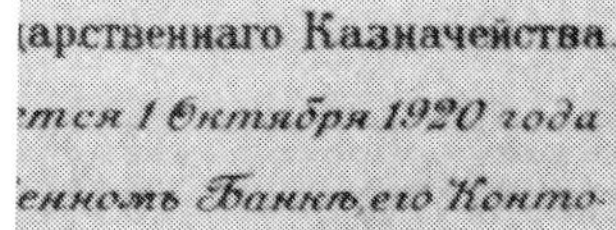

Russia - 1 October 1920

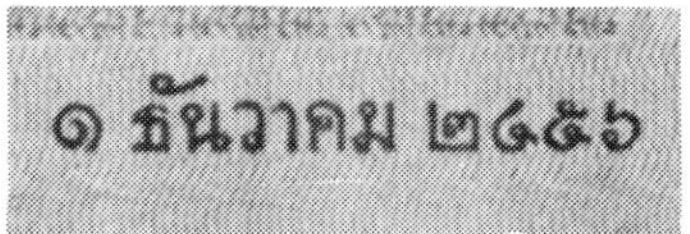

Thailand (Siam) - 1 December 2456

Korea - 4288 (1955)

Poland - 28 February 1919

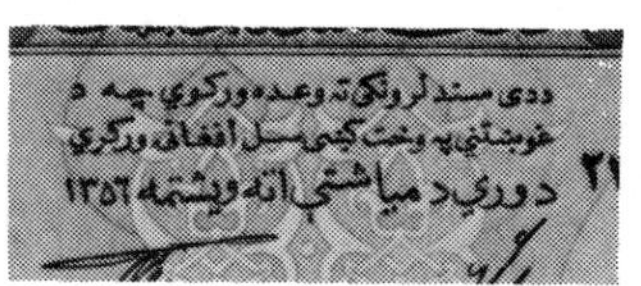

Afghanistan - Solar year 1356

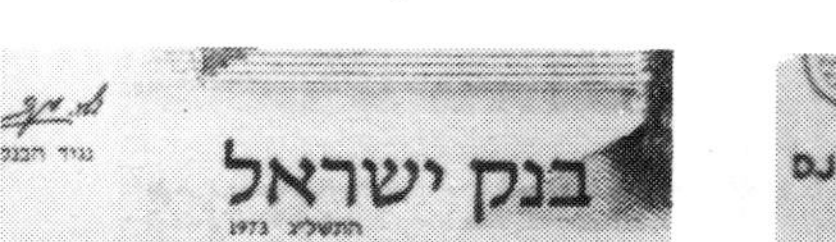
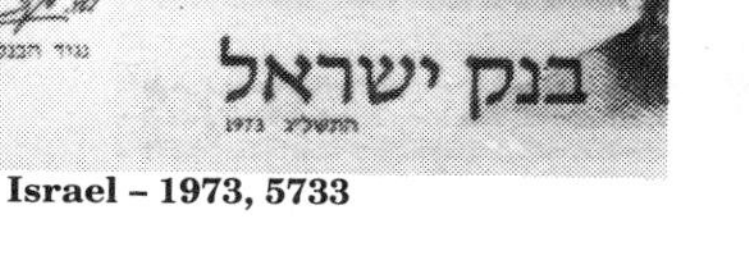

Israel - 1973, 5733

Indonesia - January 1950

Egypt - 1967 December 2

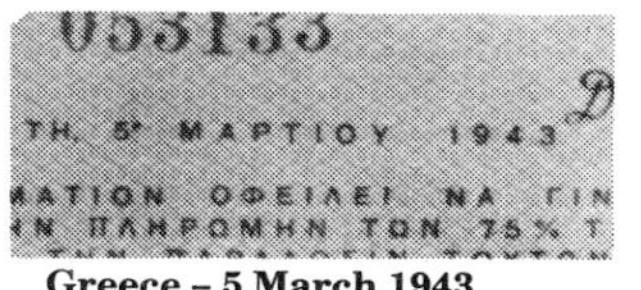

Greece - 5 March 1943

Thailand (Siam) has observed three different eras for dating. The most predominant is the Buddhist (BE) era which originated in 543 BC. Next is the Bangkok or Ratanakosind-sok (RS) era dating from 1781 AD (dates consist of only 3 numerals), followed by the Chula-Sakarat (CS) era which dates from 638 AD, with the latter also observed in Burma.

Other calendars include that of the Ethiopian (EE) era which commenced 7 years, 8 months after AD dating, and that of the Hebrew nation which commenced on October 7, 3761 BC. Korea claims a legendary dating from 2333 BC which is acknowledged on some issues.

The following table indicates the year dating for the various eras which correspond to 1999 by the Christian (AD) calendar reckoning. It must be remembered that there are overlaps between the eras in some instances:

Christian Era (AD)	—	2000
Mohammedan era (AH)	—	AH1421
Solar year (SH)	—	SH1379
Monarchic Solar era (MS)	—	MS2559
Vikrama Samvat era (VS)	—	SE2057
Saka era (SE)	—	Saka 1922
Buddhist era (BE)	—	BE2543
Bangkok era (RS)	—	RS219
Chula-Sakarat era (CS)	—	CS1362
Ethiopian era (EE)	—	EE1992
Jewish era	—	5760
Korean era	—	4333

Paper money of Oriental origin - principally Japan, Korea, China, Turkestan and Tibet generally date to the year of the government, dynastic, regnal or cyclical eras, with the dates indicated in Oriental characters which usually read from right to left. In recent years, however, some dating has been according to the Christian calendar and in western numerals reading from left to right.

More detailed guides to the application of the less prevalent dating systems than those described, and others of strictly local nature, along with the numeral designations employed are presented in conjunction with the appropriate listings.

Some notes carry dating according to both the locally observed and Christian eras. This is particularly true in the Arabic sphere, where the Muslim date may be indicated in Arabic numerals and the Christian date in western numerals.

In general the date actually carried on a given paper money issue is indicated. Notes issued by special Law or Decree will have a L or D preceding the date. Dates listed within parentheses are dates of issue which may differ from the date appearing on the note, but which is documented by other means. Undated notes are listed with ND, followed by a year when the year of actual issue is known.

Timing differentials between the 354 day Muslim and the 365 day Christian year cause situations whereby notes bearing dates of both eras have two date combinations that may overlap from one or the other calendar system.

HEJIRA DATE CONVERSION CHART

HEJIRA DATE CHART

HEJIRA (Hijra, Hegira), the name of the Mohammedan era (A.H. = Anno Hegirae) dates back to the Christian year 622 when Mohammed "fled" from Mecca, escaping to Medina to avoid persecution from the Koreish tribesmen. Based on a lunar year the Mohammedan year is 11 days shorter.

* = Leap Year (Christian Calendar)

AH Hejira	AD Christian Date
1010	1601, July 2
1011	1602, June 21
1012	1603, June 11
1013	1604, May 30
1014	1605, May 19
1015	1606, May 19
1016	1607, May 9
1017	1608, April 28
1018	1609, April 6
1019	1610, March 26
1020	1611, March 16
1021	1612, March 4
1022	1613, February 21
1023	1614, February 11
1024	1615, January 31
1025	1616, January 20
1026	1617, January 9
1027	1617, December 29
1028	1618, December 19
1029	1619, December 8
1030	1620, November 26
1031	1621, November 16
1032	1622, November 5
1033	1623, October 25
1034	1624, October 14
1035	1625, October 3
1036	1626, September 22
1037	1627, September 12
1038	1628, August 31
1039	1629, August 21
1040	1630, July 10
1041	1631, July 30
1042	1632, July 19
1043	1633, July 8
1044	1634, June 27
1045	1635, June 17
1046	1636, June 5
1047	1637, May 26
1048	1638, May 15
1049	1639, May 4
1050	1640, April 23
1051	1641, April 12
1052	1642, April 1
1053	1643, March 22
1054	1644, March 10
1055	1645, February 27
1056	1646, February 17
1057	1647, February 6
1058	1648, January 27
1059	1649, January 15
1060	1650, January 4
1061	1650, December 25
1062	1651, December 14
1063	1652, December 2
1064	1653, November 22
1065	1654, November 11
1066	1655, October 31
1067	1656, October 20
1068	1657, October 9
1069	1658, September 29
1070	1659, September 18
1071	1660, September 6
1072	1661, August 27
1073	1662, August 16
1074	1663, August 5
1075	1664, July 25
1076	1665, July 14
1077	1666, July 4
1078	1667, June 23
1079	1668, June 11
1080	1669, June 1
1081	1670, May 21
1082	1671, May 10
1083	1672, April 29
1084	1673, April 18
1085	1674, April 7
1086	1675, March 28
1087	1676, March 16*
1088	1677, March 6
1089	1678, February 23
1090	1679, February 12
1091	1680, February 2*
1092	1681, January 21
1093	1682, January 10
1094	1682, December 31
1095	1683, December 20
1096	1684, December 8*
1097	1685, November 28
1098	1686, November 17
1099	1687, November 7
1100	1688, October 26*
1101	1689, October 15
1102	1690, October 5

AH Hejira	AD Christian Date
1103	1691, September 24
1104	1692, September 12*
1105	1693, September 2
1106	1694, August 22
1107	1695, August 12
1108	1696, July 31*
1109	1697, July 20
1110	1698, July 10
1111	1699, June 29
1112	1700, June 18
1113	1701, June 8
1114	1702, May 28
1115	1703, May 17
1116	1704, May 6*
1117	1705, April 25
1118	1706, April 15
1119	1707, April 4
1120	1708, March 23*
1121	1709, March 18
1122	1710, March 2
1123	1711, February 19
1124	1712, February 9*
1125	1713, January 28
1126	1714, January 17
1127	1715, January 7
1128	1715, December 27
1129	1716, December 16*
1130	1717, December 5
1131	1718, November 24
1132	1719, November 14
1133	1720, November 2*
1134	1721, October 22
1135	1722, October 12
1136	1723, October 1
1137	1724, September 29*
1138	1725, September 9
1139	1726, August 29
1140	1727, August 19
1141	1728, August 7*
1142	1729, July 27
1143	1730, July 17
1144	1731, July 6
1145	1732, June 24*
1146	1733, June 14
1147	1734, June 3
1148	1735, May 24
1149	1736, May 12*
1150	1737, May 1
1151	1738, April 21
1152	1739, April 10
1153	1740, March 29*
1154	1741, March 19
1155	1742, March 8
1156	1743, February 25
1157	1744, February 15*
1158	1745, February 3
1159	1746, January 24
1160	1747, January 13
1161	1748, January 2
1162	1748, December 22*
1163	1749, December 11
1164	1750, November 30
1165	1751, November 20
1166	1752, November 8*
1167	1753, October 29
1168	1754, October 18
1169	1755, October 7
1170	1756, September 26*
1171	1757, September 15
1172	1758, September 4
1173	1759, August 25
1174	1760, August 13*
1175	1761, August 2
1176	1762, July 28
1177	1763, July 12
1178	1764, July 1*
1179	1765, June 20
1180	1766, June 9
1181	1767, May 30
1182	1768, May 18*
1183	1769, May 7
1184	1770, April 27
1185	1771, April 16
1186	1772, April 4*
1187	1773, March 25
1188	1774, March 14
1189	1775, March 4
1190	1776, February 21*
1191	1777, February 9
1192	1778, January 30
1193	1779, January 19
1194	1780, January 8*
1195	1780, December 28*
1196	1781, December 17
1197	1782, December 7
1198	1783, November 26
1199	1784, November 14*
1200	1785, November 4
1201	1786, October 24
1202	1787, October 13
1203	1788, October 2*
1204	1789, September 21
1205	1790, September 10
1206	1791, August 31
1207	1792, August 19*
1208	1793, August 9

AH Hejira	AD Christian Date
1209	1794, July 29
1210	1795, July 18
1211	1796, July 7*
1212	1797, June 26
1213	1798, June 15
1214	1799, June 5
1215	1800, May 25
1216	1801, May 14
1217	1802, May 4
1218	1803, April 23
1219	1804, April 12*
1220	1805, April 1
1221	1806, March 21
1222	1807, March 11
1223	1808, February 28*
1224	1809, February 16
1225	1810, February 6
1226	1811, January 26
1227	1812, January 16*
1228	1813, January 4
1229	1813, December 24
1230	1814, December 14
1231	1815, December 3
1232	1816, November 21*
1233	1817, November 11
1234	1818, October 31
1235	1819, October 20
1236	1820, October 9*
1237	1821, September 28
1238	1822, September 18
1239	1823, September 7
1240	1824, August 26*
1241	1825, August 16
1242	1826, August 5
1243	1827, July 25
1244	1828, July 14*
1245	1829, July 3
1246	1830, June 22
1247	1831, June 12
1248	1832, May 31*
1249	1833, May 21
1250	1834, May 10
1251	1835, April 29
1252	1836, April 18*
1253	1837, April 7
1254	1838, March 27
1255	1839, March 17
1256	1840, March 5*
1257	1841, February 23
1258	1842, February 12
1259	1843, February 1
1260	1844, January 22*
1261	1845, January 10
1262	1845, December 30
1263	1846, December 20
1264	1847, December 9
1265	1848, November 27*
1266	1849, November 17
1267	1850, November 6
1268	1851, October 27
1269	1852, October 15*
1270	1853, October 4
1271	1854, September 24
1272	1855, September 13
1273	1856, September 1*
1274	1857, August 22
1275	1858, August 11
1276	1859, July 31
1277	1860, July 20*
1278	1861, July 9
1279	1862, June 29
1280	1863, June 18
1281	1864, June 6*
1282	1865, May 27
1283	1866, May 16
1284	1867, May 5
1285	1868, April 24*
1286	1869, April 13
1287	1870, April 3
1288	1871, March 23
1289	1872, March 11*
1290	1873, March 1
1291	1874, February 18
1292	1875, February 7
1293	1876, January 28*
1294	1877, January 16
1295	1878, January 5
1296	1878, December 26
1297	1879, December 15
1298	1880, December 4*
1299	1881, November 23
1300	1882, November 12
1301	1883, November 2
1302	1884, October 21*
1303	1885, October 10
1304	1886, September 30
1305	1887, September 19
1306	1888, September 7*
1307	1889, August 28
1308	1890, August 17
1309	1891, August 7
1310	1892, July 26*
1311	1893, July 15
1312	1894, July 5
1313	1895, June 24
1314	1896, June 12*

AH Hejira	AD Christian Date
1315	1897, June 2
1316	1898, May 22
1317	1899, May 12
1318	1900, May 1
1319	1901, April 20
1320	1902, April 10
1321	1903, March 30
1322	1904, March 18*
1323	1905, March 8
1324	1906, February 25
1325	1907, February 14
1326	1908, February 4*
1327	1909, January 23
1328	1910, January 13
1329	1911, January 2
1330	1911, December 22
1331	1912, December 11*
1332	1913, November 30
1333	1914, November 19
1334	1915, November 9
1335	1916, October 28*
1336	1917, October 17
1337	1918, October 7
1338	1919, September 26
1339	1920, September 15*
1340	1921, September 4
1341	1922, August 24
1342	1923, August 14
1343	1924, August 2*
1344	1925, July 22
1345	1926, July 12
1346	1927, July 1
1347	1928, June 20*
1348	1929, June 9
1349	1930, May 29
1350	1931, May 19
1351	1932, May 7*
1352	1933, April 26
1353	1934, April 16
1354	1935, April 5
1355	1936, March 24*
1356	1937, March 14
1357	1938, March 3
1358	1939, February 21
1359	1940, February 10*
1360	1941, January 29
1361	1942, January 19
1362	1943, January 8
1363	1943, December 28
1364	1944, December 17*
1365	1945, December 6
1366	1946, November 25
1367	1947, November 15
1368	1948, November 3*
1369	1949, October 24
1370	1950, October 13
1371	1951, October 2
1372	1952, September 21*
1373	1953, September 10
1374	1954, August 30
1375	1955, August 20
1376	1956, August 8*
1377	1957, July 29
1378	1958, July 18
1379	1959, July 7
1380	1960, June 25*
1381	1961, June 14
1382	1962, June 4
1383	1963, May 25
1384	1964, May 13*
1385	1965, May 2
1386	1966, April 22
1387	1967, April 11
1388	1968, March 31*
1389	1969, March 20
1390	1970, March 9
1391	1971, February 27
1392	1972, February 16*
1393	1973, February 4
1394	1974, January 25
1395	1975, January 14
1396	1976, January 3*
1397	1976, December 23*
1398	1977, December 12
1399	1978, December 2
1400	1979, November 21
1401	1980, November 9*
1402	1981, October 30
1403	1982, October 19
1404	1983, October 8
1405	1984, September 27*
1406	1985, September 16
1407	1986, September 6
1408	1987, August 26
1409	1988, August 14*
1410	1989, August 3
1411	1990, July 24
1412	1991, July 13
1413	1992, July 2*
1414	1993, June 21
1415	1994, June 10
1416	1995, May 31
1417	1996, May 19*
1418	1997, May 9
1419	1998, April 28
1420	1999, April 17
1421	2000, April 6*

English	January	February	March	April	May	June	July	August	September	October	November	December
Albanian	Kallnuer	Fruer	Mars	Prill	Maj	Qershuer	Korrik	Gusht	Shtatuer	Tetuer	Nanduer	Dhetuer
Czech	Leden	Unor	Brezen	Duben	Kveten	Cerven	Cervenec	Srpen	Zari	Rijen	listopad	Prosinec
Danish	Januar	Februari	Maart	April	Maj	Juni	Juli	August	September	Oktober	November	December
Dutch	Januari	Fevruari	Maart	April	Mei	Juni	Juli	Augustus	September	Oktober	November	December
Estonian	Jaanuar	Veebruar	Marts	Aprill	Mai	Juuni	Juuli	August	September	Oktoober	November	Detsember
French	Janvier	Fevrier	Mars	Avril	Mai	Juin	Jillet	Aout	Septembre	Octobre	Novembre	Decembre
Finnish	Tammikuu	Helmikuu	Maaliskuu	Huhtikuu	Toukokuu	Kesakuu	Heinakuu	Elokuu	Syyskuu	Lokakuu	Marraskuu	Joulukuu
German	Januar	Februar	Marz	April	Mai	juni	Juli	August	September	Oktober	Novembre	Dezember
Hungarian	Januar	Februar	Marcius	Aprilis	Majus	Junius	Julius	Augusztus	Szeptember	Oktober	November	December
Indonesian	Djanuari	Februari	Maret	April	Mai	Djuni	Djuli	Augustus	September	Oktober	Nopember	Desember
Italian	Gennaio	Fabbraio	Marzo	Aprile	Maggio	Giugno	Luglio	Agosto	Settembre	Ottobre	Novembre	Dicembre
Lithuanian	Sausis	Vasaris	Kovas	Balandis	Geguzis	Birzelis	Liepos	Rugpiutis	Rugsejis	Spalis	Lapkritis	Gruodis
Norwegian	Januar	Februar	Mars	April	Mai	Juni	Juli	August	September	Oktober	November	Desember
Polish	Styczen	Luty	Marzec	Kwiecien	Maj	Cerwiec	Lipiec	Sierpien	Wrzesien	Pazdziernik	Listopad	Grudzien
Portuguese	Janerio	Fevereiro	Marco	Abril	Maio	Junho	Julho	Agosto	Setembro	Outubro	Novembro	Dezembro
Romanian	Ianuarie	Februarie	Martie	Aprilie	Mai	Iunie	Iulie	August	Septembrie	Octombrie	Noiembrie	Decembrie
Croatian	Sijecanj	Veljaca	Ozujak	Travanj	Svibanj	Lipanj	Srpanj	Kolovoz	Rujan	Listopad	Studeni	Prosinac
Spanish	Enero	Febrero	Marzo	Abril	Mayo	Junio	Julio	Agosto	Septiembre	Octubre	Noviembre	Diciembre
Swedish	Januari	Februari	Mars	April	Maj	Juni	Juli	Augusti	September	Oktober	November	December
Turkish	Ocak	Subat	Mart	Nisan	Mayis	Haziran	Temmuz	Agusto	Eylul	Ekim	Kasim	Aralik
Arabic-New (condensed)	يناير	فبراير	مارس	ابريل	مايو	يونيو	يوليو	أغسطس	سبتمبر	أكتوبر	نوفمبر	ديسمبر
(extended)	ينـايـر	فـبرايـر	مـارس	ابـريـل	مـايـو	يـونـيـه	يـولـيـه	اغسطس	سبتمبر	اكتوبر	نوفمبر	ديسمبر
Persian (Solar)	فروردين	اردیبهشت	خرداد	تیر	مرداد	شهریور	مهر	آبان	آذر	دی	بهمن	اسفند
(Lunar)	مُحَرَّم	صَفَر	رَبِيعُ ٱلْأَوَّل	رَبِيعُ ٱلْآخِر	جُمَادَى ٱلْأُولَى	جُمَادَى ٱلْآخِرَة	رَجَب	شَعْبَان	رَمَضَان	شَوَّال	ذُو ٱلْقَعْدَة	ذُو ٱلْحِجَّة
Chinese	正月	二月	三月	四月	五月	六月	七月	八月	九月	十月	十一月	十二月
Japanese	月一	月二	月三	月四	月五	月六	月七	月八	月九	月十	月一十	月十二
Greek	Ιανοναριοδ	Φεβροναριοδ	Μαρτιοδ	Απιλιοδ	Μαιοδ	Ιουνιοδ	Ιουλιοδ	Αυγουατοδ	Εεπτεμβπιοδ	Οκτωβπιοδ	Νοεμπιοσ	Δεκεμβπιοδ
Russian	ЯНВАРЬ	ФЕВРАЛЬ	МАРТ	АПРЕЛЬ	МАИ	ИЮОЬ	ИЮЛЬ	АВГУСТ	СЕИТЯБРЬ	ОКТЯБРЬ	НОЯБРЬ	ДЕКАБРЬ
Serbian	Јануар	Фебруар	Марг	Април	Мај	Јун	Јул	Август	Септембар	Октобар	Новембар	Децембар
Ukranian	Січень	Лютий	Березень	Квітень	Травень	Червень	Липень	Серпень	Вересень	Жовтень	Листопад	Грудень
Yiddish	יאַנואַר	פעברואַר	מערץ	אַפּריל	מײַ	יוני	יולי	אויגוסט	סעפּטעמבער	אָקטאָבער	נאָוועמבער	דעצעמבער
Hebrew (Israeli)	ינואר	פברואר	מרץ	אפריל	מאי	יוני	יולי	אוגוסט	ספטמבר	אוקטובר	נובמבר	דצמבר

Note: Word spellings and configurations as represented on actual notes may vary significantly from those shown on this chart.

- Free Price List on Request
- Postbank in Koln
- Quality Guaranteed
- Dependable
- Fast

MICHAEL MORRIS PAPER MONEY

BUYING AND SELLING WORLD PAPER MONEY

VISA

P.O. Box 20046
Minneapolis, MN 55420
Tel: 952-881-9403
FAX: 952-888-4874
email: morris@sihope.com
webpage: www.sihope.com/~morris

Mention this ad for a 5% Discount

WORLD PAPER MONEY

British Commonwealth, Africa, Asia, China, Latin America, etc.

New and Older Issues.

Free, Frequent Price Lists

MICHAEL E. KNABE

P.O. Box 3964
Pinedale, CA 93650
U.S.A.

NORTHWEST BANKNOTE IMPORTS

WILLIAM G. HENDERSON
P.O. Box 73037 (MPM), Puyallup, WA 98373-0037 U.S.A.
PHONE 253-848-9194 • FAX: 253-770-0880

BUYING WORLD PAPER MONEY

Older Bank Notes VF & Better
Buying Modern Bank Notes Unc Only
Chinese Paper Money Fine - Unc

BUYING WORLDWIDE NUMISMATIC BOOKS. If you are the author or distributor, please quote the best price (cost) of your books on banknotes and coins. Prices to include surface postage. Also give us the anticipated date of new editions coming out.

WORLD PAPER MONEY

5-7 Retail Lists Per Year
2-3 Wholesale Investor Lists for Bulk Buyers
15 Day Return Privilege

We are strong in - Latin American - Mexican Paper Money including specimens -Chinese Paper Money including specimens - Modern World Paper Money including specimens (some proofs).

We are also jobber/wholesale and retail dealer of many books, Worldwide, including U.S., some Foreign titles. Books are on Bank notes, coins, tokens with 2-3 lists per year on books.

Member - ANA LM 1998 **IBNS LM 17**

STANDARD INTERNATIONAL NUMERAL SYSTEMS
PREPARED ESPECIALLY FOR THE STANDARD CATALOG OF WORLD PAPER MONEY

WESTERN	0	½	1	2	3	4	5	6	7	8	9	10	50	100	500	1000
ROMAN			I	II	III	IV	V	VI	VII	VIII	IX	X	L	C	D	M
ARABIC-TURKISH	٠	١/٢	١	٢	٣	٤	٥	٦	٧	٨	٩	١٠	٥٠	١٠٠	٥٠٠	١٠٠٠
MALAY—PERSIAN	۰	۱/۲	۱	۲	۳	۴	۵	۶ or ۶	۷	۸	۹	۱۰	۵۰	۱۰۰	۵۰۰	۱۰۰۰
EASTERN ARABIC	۰	۱/۲	۱	۲	۳	۴	۵	۶	۷	۸	۹	۱۰	۵۰	۱۰۰	۵۰۰	۱۰۰۰
HYDERABAD ARABIC	۰	۱/۲	۱	۲	۳	۴	۵	۶	۷	۸	۹	۱۰	۵۰	۱۰۰	۵۰۰	۱۰۰۰
INDIAN (Sanskrit)	०	१/२	१	२	३	४	५	६	७	८	९	१०	५०	१००	५००	१०००
ASSAMESE	০	১/২	১	২	৩	৪	৫	৬	৭	৮	৯	১০	৫০	১০০	৫০০	১০০০
BENGALI	০	১/২	১	২	৩	৪	৫	৬	৭	৮	৯	১০	৫০	১০০	৫০০	১০০০
GUJARATI	૦	૧/૨	૧	૨	૩	૪	૫	૬	૭	૮	૯	૧૦	૫૦	૧૦૦	૫૦૦	૧૦૦૦
KUTCH	०	१/२	१	२	३	४	५	६	७	८	९	१०	५०	१००	५००	१०००
DEVAVNAGRI	०	१/२	१	२	३	४	५	६ or ६	७	८	९ or ९	१०	५०	१००	५००	१०००
NEPALESE	०	१/२	१ or १	२	३	४	५ or ५	६	७	८ or ८	९ or ९ or ९	१०	५०	१००	५००	१०००
TIBETAN	༠	༡/༢	༡	༢	༣	༤	༥	༦	༧	༨	༩	༡༠	༥༠	༡༠༠	༥༠༠	༡༠༠༠
MONGOLIAN	᠐	᠑/᠒	᠑	᠒	᠓	᠔	᠕	᠖	᠗	᠘	᠙	᠑᠐	᠕᠐	᠑᠐᠐	᠕᠐᠐	᠑᠐᠐᠐
BURMESE	၀	၁/၂	၁	၂	၃	၄	၅	၆	၇	၈	၉	၁၀	၅၀	၁၀၀	၅၀၀	၁၀၀၀
THAI-LAO	๐	๑/๒	๑	๒	๓	๔	๕	๖	๗	๘	๙	๑๐	๕๐	๑๐๐	๕๐๐	๑๐๐๐
JAVANESE	꧐		꧑	꧒	꧓	꧔	꧕	꧖	꧗	꧘	꧙	꧑꧐	꧕꧐	꧑꧐꧐	꧕꧐꧐	꧑꧐꧐꧐
ORDINARY CHINESE JAPANESE-KOREAN	零	半	一	二	三	四	五	六	七	八	九	十	十五	百	百五	千
OFFICIAL CHINESE			壹	貳	叁	肆	伍	陸	柒	捌	玖	拾	拾伍	佰	佰伍	仟
COMMERCIAL CHINESE			〡	〢	〣	〤	〥	〦	〧	〨	〩	十	〥十	〡百	〥百	〡千
KOREAN		반	일	이	삼	사	오	육	찰	팔	구	십	오십	백	오백	천
GEORGIAN			ა	ბ	გ	დ	ე	ვ	ზ	ჱ	თ	ი	ნ	რ	ფ	ჩ
			11 ∽	20 კ	30 ლ	40 მ	50 ნ	60 ჲ	70 ო	80 პ	90 ჟ	100 რ	200 ს 300 ტ	400 უ	600 ქ 700 ღ	800 ყ
ETHIOPIAN	◆		፩	፪	፫	፬	፭	፮	፯	፰	፱	፲	፶	፻	፭፻	፲፻
				20 ፳	30 ፴	40 ፵		60 ፷	70 ፸	80 ፹	90 ፺					
HEBREW			א	ב	ג	ד	ה	ו	ז	ח	ט	י	נ	ק	תק	
				20 כ	30 ל	40 מ		60 ס	70 ע	80 פ	90 צ		200 ר 300 ש	400 ת	600 תר 700 תש	800 תת
GREEK			Α	Β	Γ	Δ	Ε	ΣΤ	Ζ	Η	Θ	Ι	Ν	Ρ	Ο	͵Α
				20 Κ	30 Λ	40 Μ	60 Ξ	70 Ο	80 Π		200 Σ	300 Τ	400 Υ	600 Χ	700 Ψ	800 Ω

SPECIMEN NOTES

To familiarize private banks, central banks, law enforcement agencies and treasuries around the world with newly issued currency, many issuing authorities provide special 'Specimen' examples of their notes. Specimens are actual bank notes, complete with consecutive or all zero serial numbers, proper signatures and bearing an overprint or pin-hole perforation of the word SPECIMEN, sometimes in English, or in the language of the nation of issue or choice of the printing firm.

Some countries have made specimen notes available to collectors. These include Cuba, Czechoslovakia, Poland and Slovakia. Aside from these collector issues, specimen notes usually command higher prices than regular issue notes of the same type, even though there are far fewer collectors of specimens. In some cases, notably older issues in high denominations, specimens may be the only form of such notes available to collectors today. Specimen notes are not legal tender or redeemable, thus have no real 'face value' which also is indicated on some examples.

The most unusual forms of specimens were produced by the firm of Waterlow and Sons Ltd. They printed the notes with a company seal, and very often made them in several different color combinations in addition to the regularly approved colors. These were intended to be mounted in salesman's sample books. Generally these are not included in the scope of this catalog.

Some examples of how the word SPECIMEN is represented in other languages or on notes of other countries follow:

AMOSTRA: Brazil
CAMPIONE: Italy
CONTOH: Indonesia, Malaysia
EKSEMPLAAR: South Africa
ESPÉCIME: Portugal and Colonies
ESPECIMEN: Various Spanish-speaking nations
GIAY MAU: Vietnam
HAMYHA: Tajikistan
MINTA: Hungary
MODELO: Brazil
MODEL: Albania
MUSTER: Austria, Germany
MUESTRA: Various Spanish-speaking nations
NUMUNEDIR GECMEZ: Turkey
ORNEKTIR GECMEZ: Turkey
ОБРАЗЕЦ or **ОБРАЗЕЦЪ:** Bulgaria, Russia
PARAUGS: Latvia
PROFTRYK: Sweden
SPEZIMEN: Switzerland
UZORAK: Croatia
VZOREC: Slovenia
WZOR: Poland
ЗАГВАР: Mongolia

نموذج or نموذج : Arabic

نمونه : Persian

نمونه : Pakistan

דוגמא : Israel

ແບບຢ່າງ : Laos

ՆՄՈՒՇ :Armenia

Specimen of face of a Taiwan Bank year 53 (1964) dated note with perforated ancient Chinese seal script characters.

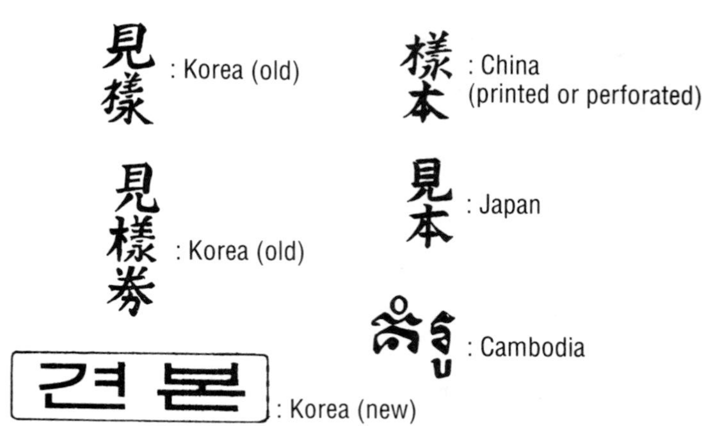

Dual Listings

As a general rule, the cutoff date in the Standard Catalog of World Paper Money, General Issues Volume II to Modern Issues Volume III is 1961. All notes dated 1961 and later can be found in Volume III; earlier dated issues are found in Volume II. There are numerous issues produced prior to 1961, which were reprinted with dates beyond 1961. In previous editions, such issues were split according to the beginning date of the type, without regard to the ending date, thus creating consistent treatment, but remaining somewhat confusing.

Due to popular demand and in the best interests of the collector, this edition as well as the 9th edition of General Issues Vol II will include dual-listings of such notes to present overlapping issues in their entirety, offering a more complete presentation.

BANKNOTE PRINTERS

Printers' names, abbreviations or monograms will usually appear as part of the frame design or below it on face and/or back. In some instances the engraver's name may also appear in a similar location on a note. The following abbreviations identify printers for many of the notes listed in this volume:

ABNC .... American Bank Note Company (USA)
ATB .... AB Tomba Bruk (Zaire)
BABN(C) .... British American Bank Note Co., Ltd. (Canada)
B&S .... Bouligny & Schmidt (Mexico)
BCdE .... Banco Central de Ecuador
BEPP .... Bureau of Engraving & Printing, Peking (China)
BF .... Banque de France (France)
BFL .... Barclay & Fry Ltd. (England)
BWC .... Bradbury, Wilkinson & Co. (England)
CABB .... Compania Americana de Billetes de Banco (ABNC)
CBC .... Columbian Banknote Co. (USA)
CBNC .... Canadian Bank Note Company (Canada)
CCBB .... Compania Columbiana de Billetes de Banco (CBC)
CdM- .... Casa da Moeda (Brazil)
CdM- .... Casa de Moneda (Argentina, Chile, etc.)
CHB .... Chung Hua Book Co. (China)
CMN .... Casa de Moneda de la Nacion (Argentina)
CMPA .... Commercial Press (China)
CNBB .... Compania Nacional de Billetes de Banco (NBNC)
CONB .... Continental Bank Note Company (USA)
CPF .... Central Printing Factory (China)
CSABB .... Compania Sud/Americana de Billetes de Banco .... (Argentina)
CS&E .... Charles Skipper & East (England)
DLR .... Thomas De La Rue (England)
DTB .... Dah Tung Book Co., and Ta Tung Printing (China)
EAW .... E. A. Wright (USA)
FCO .... Francois- Charles Oberthur
FLBN .... Franklin-Lee Bank Note Company (USA)
FNMT .... Fabrica Nacional de Moneda y Timbre (Spain)
G&D .... Giesecke & Devrient (Germany)
HBNC .... Hamilton Bank Note Company (USA)
HKB .... Hong Kong Banknote (Hong Kong)
HKP .... Hong Kong Printing Press (Hong Kong)
H&L .... Hoyer & Ludwig, Richmond, Virginia (CSA)
HLBNC .... Homer Lee Bank Note Co. (USA)
H&S .... Harrison & Sons Ltd. (England)
IBB .... Imprenta de Billetes-Bogota (Colombia)
IBSFB .... Imprenta de Billetes-Santa Fe de Bogota (Colombia)
IBNC .... International Bank Note Company (USA)
JBNC .... Jeffries Bank Note Company (USA)
JEZ .... Johann Enschede en Zonen (Netherlands)
K&B .... Keatinge & Ball (CSA)
KBNC .... Kendall Bank Note Company, New York (USA)
LN .... Litografia Nacional (Columbia)
NAL .... Nissen & Arnold (England)
NBNC .... National Bank Note Company (USA)
NBBPW .... National Bank of Belgium Printing Works
NPA .... Note Printing Australia
OCV .... Officina Carte-Valori (Italy)
ODBI .... Officina Della Banca D'Italia (Italy)
OFZ .... Orell Fussli, Zurich (Switzerland)
P&B .... Perkins & Bacon (England)
PBC .... Perkins, Bacon & Co. (England)
PB&P .... Perkins, Bacon & Petch (England)
SBNC .... Security Banknote Company (USA)
TDLR .... Thomas De La Rue (England)
UPC .... Union Printing Co. (China)
UPP .... Union Publishers & Printers Fed. Inc. (China)
USBNC .... United States Banknote Corp. (USA)
WDBN .... Western District Banknote Fed. Inc.
W&S .... Waterlow & Sons Ltd. (England)
WPCo .... Watson Printing Co. (China)
WWS .... W. W. Sprague & Co. Ltd. (England)

International Bank Note Society

The International Bank Note Society (IBNS) was formed in 1961 to promote the collecting of world paper money. A membership in excess of 2,000 in over 100 nations around the globe draw on the services of the Society in advancing their knowledge and collections.

The benefits of Society membership include the quarterly IBNS Journal, a magazine featuring learned writings on the notes of the world, their history, artistry and technical background. Additionally each member receives a directory which lists the membership by name as well as geographic location. Collector specialties are also given. A newsletter is published to announce events in a timely fashion, as well a semi-annual auctions of bank notes. Finally, an attribution service is offered by the society for persons with paper money they are unable to identify.

One of the greatest benefits of IBNS membership is the facility for correspondence with other members around the world, for purposes of exchanging notes, information and assistance with research projects.

Application for Membership in the INTERNATIONAL BANK NOTE SOCIETY

Name ______________________
Last First Initial

Street ______________________

____
City Province or State

____
Country Postal Code

Type of Membership:

Individual: ❑ $20.00 per year
Junior (Ages 11-17): ❑ $ 9.00 per year
Family (includes children under 18): ❑ $22.50 per year

Payment in US Dollars payable to IBNS.

Check ❑ Other ❑ Money Order ❑

Do you wish your name and address to appear in our Membership Directory? Yes ❑ No ❑

Collecting Interest ______________________

____

____

Mail to: Milan Alusic
P.O. Box 1642
Racine, Wisconsin
U.S.A. 53401

Northern Bank Limited
£20
£20
C0301281
Twenty
Pounds Sterling
C0301281

10
10

Reliable Numismatic Information

The #1 source for numismatic information. Includeing timely reports on market trends and news concerning collectible coins and paper money.

Weekly Publication
1 year (52 issues)
only
$32.00

A complete guide to retail values for collectible U.S. coins. A market update section (value guide) begins each issue. Includes a current coin show calendar, guide to gradin U.S. coins and a collecor Q&A.

Bi-monthly Publication
1 year (6 issues)
only
$18.98

The leading authority on world coins. Reports on new issues, market trends and other coin news from areund the world. Each issue also provides a calendar of upcomings show worldwide.

Monthly Publication
1 year (12 issues)
only
$25.98

Covers market trends, buying tips, and historical perspectives on all aspects of numistamtics. The news section wraps up the latest happenings in munismatics. Includes a calendar of upcomins show nationwide.

The finest publication for paper money collectors available. Contains news on market trends, up-to-date foreign exchange chart, price guide, world currency section, historical features and more.

Monthly Publication
1 year (12 issues)
only
$32.00

Monthly Publication
1 year (12 issues)
only
$24.98

Credit card subscriptions Call Toll Free
800-258-0929 ABAYI2
M-F, 7 am - 8 pm • Sat, 8 am - 2 pm, CST
To order by mail send your order on a 3x5 index card to:
Krause Publications • 700 E State St, Iola, WI 54990-0001
Publishers of Fine Numismatic Books & Periodicals

The Islamic Republic of Afghanistan, which occupies a mountainous region of Southwest Asia, has an area of 251,773 sq. mi. (652,090 sq. km.) and a population of 20.5 million. Presently about a fifth of the total population reside mostly in Pakistan in exile as refugees. Capital: Kabul. It is bordered by Iran, Pakistan, Russia, and Peoples Republic of China's Sinkiang Province. Agriculture and herding are the principal industries; textile mills and cement factories are recent additions to the industrial sector. Cotton, wool, fruits, nuts, sheepskin coats and hand-woven carpets are exported but foreign trade has been interrupted since 1979.

Because of its strategic position astride the ancient land route to India, Afghanistan - formerly known as Aryana and Khorasan - was conquered by Darius I, Alexander the Great, various Scythian tribes, the Arabs, the Turks, Genghis Khan, Tamerlane, the Mughals, the Persians, and in more recent times by Great Britain.

It was a powerful empire under the Kushans, Hephthalites, Ghaznavids and Ghorids. The name Afghanistan, "Land of the Afghans," came into use in the eighteenth and nineteenth centuries to describe the realm of the Afghan kings. Previously this mountainous region was the easternmost frontier of the Iranian world, with strong cultural influences from the Turks and Mongols to the north and India to the south.

The first Afghan king, Ahmad Shah Abdali, founder of the Durrani dynasty, established his rule at Qandahar in 1747. He conquered large territories in India and eastern Iran, which were lost by his grandson Zaman Shah. A new family, the Barakzays, drove the Durrani king out of Kabul, the capital, in 1819, but the Durranis were not eliminated completely until 1858. Further conflicts among the Barakzays prevented full unity until the reign of 'Abd al-Rahman in 1880. In 1929 a commoner known as Baccha-i-Saqao, "Son of the Water-Carrier," drove King Amanullah from the throne and ruled as Habibullah for less than a year before he was defeated by Muhammad Nadir Shah, a relative of the Barakzays. The last king, Muhammad Zahir Shah, became a constitutional, though still autocratic, monarch in 1964. In 1973 a coup d'etat displaced him and created the Republic of Afghanistan. A subsequent military coup established the pro-Soviet Khalq Democratic Republic of Afghanistan under Nur Muhammad Taraqi in 1978. Mounting resistance in the countryside and violence within the government led to the Soviet invasion of late 1979 and the installation of Babrak Kamal as prime minister. A brutal civil war ensued, which continues to the present, even after Soviet forces withdrew in 1989 and Kamal's government was defeated in 1992. Various militant Islamic movements have had control on and off since. Troops of President Rabbani regained possession of Kabul in March, 1995. On Sept. 26, 1996 Taliban (students of religion) forces captured Kabul and set up an interim government under Mohammed Rabbani. Afghanistan was declared a complete Islamic state under Sharia law.

RULERS:

Muhammad Zahir Shah, SH1312-1352/1933-1973AD

MONETARY SYSTEM:

1 Afghani = 100 Pul

KINGDOM

BANK OF AFGHANISTAN

1961-63 ISSUES

#37-42 Kg. Muhammad Zahir at l. and as wmk. Printer: TDLR.

		VG	VF	UNC
37	**10 AFGHANIS** SH1340 (1961). Brown on m/c unpt. Mosque of Khwajeh Mohammad Abu-Nasr Parsa in Balkh at ctr. on back.	.50	1.00	6.00

		VG	VF	UNC
38	**20 AFGHANIS** SH1340 (1961). Blue on m/c unpt. Minaret of Independence in Kabul at ctr. on back.	.50	1.00	8.00

		VG	VF	UNC
39	**50 AFGHANIS** SH1340 (1961). Green on m/c unpt. Mausoleum of Kg. Nadir Shah in Kabul at ctr. on back.	1.00	3.00	15.00
40	**100 AFGHANIS** SH1340 (1961). Red on m/c unpt.	5.00	10.00	25.00
40A (41A)	**500 AFGHANIS** SH1340 (1961). Orange on m/c unpt.	30.00	75.00	200.00

		VG	VF	UNC
41	**500 AFGHANIS** SH1342 (1963). Olive-brown on m/c unpt.	15.00	60.00	125.00

		VG	VF	UNC
42	**1000 AFGHANIS** SH1340 (1961); SH1342 (1963). Blue-gray on m/c unpt. Arch of Kalair Bost in Lashkargah at r. on back.			
	a. 8 digit serial #. SH1340.	35.00	90.00	250.00
	b. Prefix serial #. SH1342.	35.00	90.00	250.00

1967 ISSUE

#43-46 Kg. Muhammad Zahir at l. and as wmk. W/o imprint.

		VG	VF	UNC
43	**50 AFGHANIS** SH1346 (1967). Green on m/c unpt. Arge Shahi, King's palace at ctr. r. on back.	1.25	2.50	7.50

		VG	VF	UNC
44	**100 AFGHANIS** SH1346 (1967). Lilac on m/c unpt. Mausoleum of Kg. Nadir Shah in Kabul at ctr. r. on back.	2.00	4.00	12.00

		VG	VF	UNC
45	**500 AFGHANIS** SH1346 (1967). Black and dk. blue on m/c unpt.	10.00	45.00	125.00
46	**1000 AFGHANIS** SH1346 (1967). Brown on m/c unpt.	30.00	100.00	300.00

REPUBLIC

SH1352-1358/1973-1979 AD

BANK OF AFGHANISTAN

1973-78 ISSUE

#47-53 Pres. Muhammad Daud at l. and as wmk.

NOTE: It is possible that all notes #47-53 dated SH1354 are replacements. Small quantities of the above filtered into the market via Pakistan recently.

		VG	VF	UNC
47	**10 AFGHANIS** SH1352 (1973); SH1354 (1975); SH1356 (1977). Green on m/c unpt. Arch of Kalaie Bost in Lashkargah at ctr. r. on back.	.25	.75	2.25

		VG	VF	UNC
48	**20 AFGHANIS** SH1352 (1973); SH1354 (1975); SH1356 (1977). Violet on m/c unpt.	.30	1.00	3.00

		VG	VF	UNC
49	**50 AFGHANIS** SH1352 (1973); SH1354 (1975); SH1356 (1977). Green on m/c unpt. Horseman at ctr. r. on back.	.50	1.50	4.50

		VG	VF	UNC
50	**100 AFGHANIS** SH1352 (1973); SH1354 (1975); SH1356 (1977). Brown-lilac on m/c unpt. Friday Mosque in Herât at ctr. r. on back.	.65	2.00	6.00

		VG	VF	UNC
51	**500 AFGHANIS** SH1352 (1973); SH1354 (1975). Blue on m/c unpt. Fortress at ctr. r. on back.	1.00	4.00	12.50
52	**500 AFGHANIS** SH1356 (1977). Brown on m/c unpt. Like #51.	2.00	8.00	25.00

		VG	VF	UNC
53	**1000 AFGHANIS** SH1352 (1973); SH1354 (1975); SH1356 (1977). Brown on m/c unpt. Mosque of Mazâr-e Sharîf, the Noble Shrine at ctr. r. on back.	1.25	5.00	20.00

KHALQ DEMOCRATIC REPUBLIC

SH1357-1370/1978-1992 AD

DA AFGHANISTAN BANK

1978 ISSUE

#53A and 54 w/Khalq Government arms at top l. ctr.

		VG	VF	UNC
53A	**20 AFGHANIS** AH1357 (1978). Purple on m/c unpt. Fortress at ctr. on back. Specimen, punched hole cancelled.	—	—	—

		VG	VF	UNC
54	**50 AFGHANIS** SH1357 (1978). Blue-green on m/c unpt. Arms w/star at top r., and Arabic legend. Bldg. on back.	1.00	5.00	20.00

DEMOCRATIC REPUBLIC

DA AFGHANISTAN BANK

1979 ISSUE

#55-61 bank arms w/horseman at top ctr. or ctr. r. on face.

		VG	VF	UNC
55	**10 AFGHANIS** SH1358 (1979). Green and blue on m/c unpt. Mountain road scene at ctr. on back.	.15	.25	.75

		VG	VF	UNC
56	**20 AFGHANIS** SH1358 (1979). Purple on m/c unpt. Bldg. and mountains at ctr. on back. Sign. varieties.	.20	.40	1.25

		VG	VF	UNC
57	**50 AFGHANIS** SH1358-70 (1979-91). Greenish black with black text on m/c unpt. Similar to #54.			
	a. SH1358 (1979). 2 sign. varieties.	.10	.30	1.00
	b. SH1370 (1991).	.15	.20	1.50

		VG	VF	UNC
58	**100 AFGHANIS** SH1358-70 1979-91). Deep red-violet on m/c unpt. Farm worker in wheat field at r. Hydroelectric dam in mountains at ctr. on back.			
	a. SH1358 (1979). 2 sign. varieties.	.15	.40	1.25
	b. SH1369 (1990).	.35	1.00	3.50
	c. SH1370 (1991).	.35	1.00	2.50

		VG	VF	UNC
59	**500 AFGHANIS** SH1358 (1979). Violet and dk. blue on m/c unpt. Horsemen competing in Buzkashi at r. Fortress at Kabul at l. ctr. on back.	1.00	3.50	12.00
60	**500 AFGHANIS** SH1358-70 (1979-91). Reddish-brown, deep green and deep brown on m/c unpt. Like #59. Back deep green on m/c unpt.			
	a. SH1358 (1979).	.30	1.25	3.00
	b. SH1369 (1990).	.65	1.75	5.00
	c. SH1370 (1991).	.15	.50	2.00

		VG	VF	UNC
61	**1000 AFGHANIS** SH1358-70 (1979-91). Dk. brown and deep red-violet on m/c unpt. Mosque at r. Shrine w/archways at l. ctr. on back.			
	a. SH1358 (1979).	1.25	4.00	10.00
	b. SH1369 (1990).	.25	1.00	3.00
	c. SH1370 (1991).	.20	.75	3.00

1993 ISSUE

#62-64 bank arms w/horseman at top l. ctr. Wmk: Bank arms.

		VG	VF	UNC
62	**5000 AFGHANIS** SH1372 (1993). Violet and blue-black on m/c unpt. Mosque w/minaret at r. Mosque at ctr. on back.	FV	FV	2.50

63	10,000 AFGHANIS	VG	VF	UNC
	SH1372 (1993). Black, deep olive-green and deep blue-green on m/c unpt. Gateway between minarets at r. Arched gateway at ctr.			
	a. W/o small space between *Da* and *Afghanistan* on back.	FV	FV	4.00
	b. W/small space between *Da* and *Afghanistan* on back.	FV	FV	4.00

The Republic of Albania, a Balkan republic bounded by the rump Yugoslav state of Montenegro and Serbia, Macedonia, Greece and the Adriatic Sea, has an area of 11,100 sq. mi. (28,748 sq. km.) and a population of 3.5 million. Capital: Tirana. The country is mostly agricultural, although recent progress has been made in the manufacturing and mining sectors. Petroleum, chrome, iron, copper, cotton textiles, tobacco and wood products are exported.

Since it had been part of the Greek and Roman Empires, little is known of the early history of Albania. After the disintegration of the Roman Empire, Albania was overrun by Goths, Byzantines, Venetians and Turks. Skanderbeg, the national hero, resisted the Turks and established an independent Albania in 1443, but in 1468 the country again fell to the Turks and remained part of the Ottoman Empire for more than 400 years.

Independence was re-established by revolt in 1912, and the present borders established in 1913 by a conference of European powers which, in 1914, placed Prince William of Wied on the throne; popular discontent forced his abdication within months. In 1920, following World War I occupancy by several nations, a republic was set up. Ahmet Zogu seized the presidency in 1925, and in 1928 proclaimed himself king with the title of Zog I. King Zog fled when Italy occupied Albania in 1939 and enthroned King Victor Emanuel of Italy. Upon the surrender of Italy to the Allies in 1943, German troops occupied the country. They withdrew in 1944, and communist partisans seized power, naming Gen. Enver Hoxha provisional president. In 1946, following a victory by the communist front in the 1945 elections, a new constitution modeled on that of the USSR was adopted. In accordance with the constitution of Dec. 28, 1976, the official name of Albania was changed from the People's Republic of Albania to the People's Socialist Republic of Albania. A general strike by trade unions in 1991 forced the communist government to resign. A new government was elected in March 1992. In 1997 Albania had a major financial crisis which caused civil disturbances and the fall of the administration.

MONETARY SYSTEM:

1 Lek = 100 Qindarka 1948-1965
1 "heavy" Lek = 10 old Leke, 1965-1992
1 Lek Valute = 50 Leke, 1992-1993

PEOPLES REPUBLIC

BANKA E SHTETIT SHQIPTAR

1964 ISSUE

#33-39 arms at upper r. on back. Wmk: Curved *BSHSH* repeated.

33	1 LEK	VG	VF	UNC
	1964. Green and deep blue on m/c unpt. Peasant couple at ctr. Hilltop fortress at l. ctr. on back.			
	a. Issued note.	.15	.50	1.50
	s. Specimen ovpt: *MODEL*.	—	—	3.00

34	3 LEKË	VG	VF	UNC
	1964. Brown and lilac on m/c unpt. Woman w/basket of grapes at l. City view at l. ctr. on back.			
	a. Issued note.	.20	.65	2.25
	s. Specimen ovpt: *MODEL*.	—	—	4.00

35	5 LEKË	VG	VF	UNC
	1964. Purple and dk. blue on m/c unpt. Truck and steam passenger train crossing viaduct at l. ctr. Ship at l. on back.			
	a. Issued note.	.25	.90	3.00
	s. Specimen ovpt: *MODEL*.	—	—	5.00

		VG	VF	UNC
36	**10 LEKE**			
	1964. Dk. green on m/c unpt. Woman working w/cotton spinning frame. People at l. ctr., male portr. at upper r. on back.			
	a. Issued note.	.35	1.20	4.00
	s. Specimen ovpt: *MODEL.*	—	—	6.00

		VG	VF	UNC
37	**25 LEKË**			
	1964. Blue-black on m/c unpt. Peasant woman w/sheaf at l., combine and truck at ctr. Farm tractor at l. ctr. on back.			
	a. Issued note.	.60	2.00	7.00
	s. Specimen ovpt: *MODEL.*	—	—	7.50

		VG	VF	UNC
38	**50 LEKË**			
	1964. Red-brown on m/c unpt. Soldiers on parade at l. ctr., bust of Skanderbeg at upper r. Rifle and pick axe at l., modern bldg. under construction at l. ctr. on back.			
	a. Issued note.	1.00	3.50	12.00
	s. Specimen ovpt: *MODEL.*	—	—	8.50

		VG	VF	UNC
39	**100 LEKË**			
	1964. Brown-lilac. Worker and boy at coffer dam at l. ctr. Steel worker and well rigger at ctr. on back.			
	a. Issued note.	2.25	7.50	25.00
	s. Specimen ovpt: *MODEL.*	—	—	10.00

PEOPLES SOCIALIST REPUBLIC

BANKA E SHTETIT SHQIPTAR

1976 ISSUE

#40-46 like #33-39. Arms at upper r. on back. Wmk: Bank name around radiant star, repeated.

		VG	VF	UNC
40	**1 LEK**			
	1976. Green and deep blue on m/c unpt.			
	a. Issued note.	.05	.15	.50
	s1. Red ovpt: *SPECIMEN* w/all zeros serial #.	—	—	3.50
	s2. Red ovpt: *SPECIMEN* w/normal serial #.	—	—	.50
	s3. Lg. blue ovpt: *SPECIMEN* on face. Black ovpt: *E PRANUESHME* on back.	—	—	—

NOTE: #40 w/lg. blue ovpt: *SPECIMEN* on face and black rectangular ovpt. for bank 25th anniversary on back is a private issue.

		VG	VF	UNC
41	**3 LEKË**			
	1976. Brown and lilac on m/c unpt.			
	a. Issued note.	.10	.25	.75
	s1. Red ovpt: *SPECIMEN* w/all zeros serial #.	—	—	4.00
	s2. Red ovpt: *SPECIMEN* w/normal serial #.	—	—	.75

		VG	VF	UNC
42	**5 LEKË**			
	1976. Lilac and blue on m/c unpt.			
	a. Issued note.	.10	.35	1.25
	s1. Red ovpt: *SPECIMEN* w/all zeros serial #.	—	—	4.50
	s2. Red ovpt: *SPECIMEN* w/normal serial #.	—	—	1.00
	s3. Lg. blue ovpt: *SPECIMEN* on face. Black ovpt: *E PRANUESHME* on back.	—	—	—

NOTE: #42 w/lg. blue ovpt: *SPECIMEN* on face and black rectangular ovpt. for bank 25th anniversary on back is a private issue.

		VG	VF	UNC
43	**10 LEKË**			
	1976. Dk. green on m/c unpt.			
	a. Issued note.	.10	.40	1.50
	s1. Red ovpt: *SPECIMEN* w/all zeros serial #.	—	—	5.50
	s2. Red ovpt: *SPECIMEN* w/normal serial #.	—	—	1.25

44 **25 LEKË**

1976. Blue-black on m/c unpt.

	VG	VF	UNC
a. Issued note.	.15	.50	3.50
s1. Red ovpt: *SPECIMEN* w/all zeros serial #.	—	—	6.50
s2. Red ovpt: *SPECIMEN* w/normal serial #.	—	—	1.75

45 **50 LEKË**

1976. Red-brown on m/c unpt.

	VG	VF	UNC
a. Issued note.	.25	.75	5.00
s1. Red ovpt: *SPECIMEN* w/all zeros serial #.	—	—	7.50
s2. Red ovpt: *SPECIMEN* w/normal serial #.	—	—	2.50
s3. Lg. blue ovpt: *SPECIMEN* on face. Black ovpt: *E PRANUESNHME* on back.	—	—	—

NOTE: #45 w/lg. blue ovpt: *SPECIMEN* on face and black rectangular ovpt. for bank 25th anniversary on back is a private issue.

46 **100 LEKË**

1976. Brown-lilac on m/c unpt.

	VG	VF	UNC
a. Issued note.	.30	1.50	10.00
s1. Red ovpt: *SPECIMEN* w/all zeros serial #.	—	—	8.50
s2. Red ovpt: *SPECIMEN* w/normal serial #.	—	—	3.00

ND ISSUE

46A (27B) **100 LEKË**

ND. Steel workers at l., steel mill at ctr. Oil well derricks at l. ctr., arms at upper r. on back. Specimen, not issued.

	VG	VF	UNC
a. Blue and dull red on lt. green and lt. yellow unpt.	—	—	200.00
b. Brown and dull red on lt. green and lt. yellow unpt.	—	—	200.00

1991 ISSUE

#47 and 48 arms at upper r. on back. Wmk: Bank name around radiant star, repeated.

47 **100 LEKË**

1991. Deep brown and deep purple on pale orange and m/c unpt. Steel workers at l., steel mill at r. Refinery at l. ctr.

	VG	VF	UNC
a. Issued note.	.50	2.00	5.00
s. Specimen.	—	—	5.00

48 **500 LEKË**

1991; 1996. Purple, red and blue-green on lt. blue and lt. orange unpt. Peasant woman by sunflowers at l. ctr. Evergreen trees, mountains at l. ctr. on back.

	VG	VF	UNC
a. 1991.	FV	5.00	12.00
b. Enhanced UV printing. 1996.	FV	FV	10.00

1992 ND ISSUE

#48A-50 steelworker at ctr. Electrical transmission towers at l., arms at upper ctr., hydro-electric generator at r. on back. Wmk: *B.SH.SH.* below star, repeated.

48A (27B) **1 LEK VALUTË (= 50 LEKË)**

	VG	VF	UNC
ND (1992). Purple and gray-green on m/c unpt. (Not issued).	FV	FV	30.00

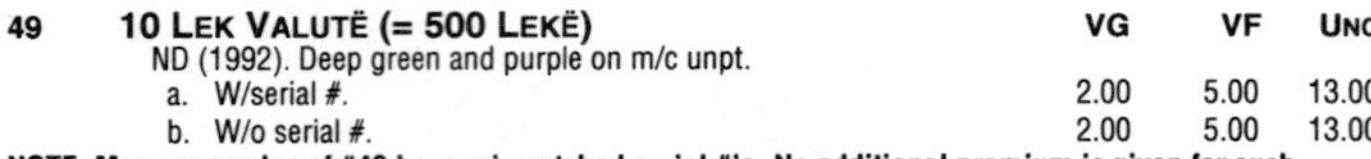

		VG	VF	UNC
49	**10 LEK VALUTË (= 500 LEKË)** ND (1992). Deep green and purple on m/c unpt.			
	a. W/serial #.	2.00	5.00	13.00
	b. W/o serial #.	2.00	5.00	13.00

NOTE: Many examples of #49 have mismatched serial #'s. No additional premium is given for such.

		VG	VF	UNC
50	**50 LEK VALUTË (= 2500 LEKË)** ND (1992). Deep brown-violet and gray-green on m/c unpt.			
	a. W/serial #.	6.00	15.00	50.00
	b. W/o serial #.	2.00	5.00	13.00
	s. Specimen.	—	—	25.00

#51 not assigned.

REPUBLIC

BANKA E SHQIPERISE

1992 ISSUE

#52-54 wmk: Repeated ring of letters *B.SH.SH.*

		VG	VF	UNC
52	**200 LEKË** 1992. Deep reddish-brown on m/c unpt. I. Qemali at l. Citizens portrayed in double-headed eagle outline on back.	FV	FV	6.00

		VG	VF	UNC
53	**500 LEKË** 1992. Deep blue on blue and m/c unpt. N. Frasheri at l. Rural mountains at l., candle at ctr. on back.	FV	FV	12.00

		VG	VF	UNC
54	**1000 LEKË** 1992. Deep green and green on m/c unpt. Skanderbeg at l. Hillside fortress tower at l., crowned arms at ctr. on back.			
	a. Issued note.	FV	FV	22.50
	s. Specimen.	—	—	12.00

1993-94 ISSUE

		VG	VF	UNC
55	**100 LEKË** 1993-96. Purple on m/c unpt. L. Kombetar at l. Mountain peaks at l. ctr., falcon at ctr. on back.			
	a. 1993.	FV	FV	3.25
	b. 1994.	FV	FV	3.00
	c. Enhanced U-V printing. 1996.	FV	FV	2.50
	s. Specimen.	—	—	2.50

		VG	VF	UNC
56	**200 LEKË** 1994. Deep reddish brown on m/c unpt. Like #52.			
	a. Issued note.	FV	FV	4.00
	s. Specimen.	—	—	4.00

The Color of Money

A Selection of Currency Printer's Art

Afghanistan #60 500 Afghanis

Albania #54 1000 Leke

Algeria #126 5 Dinars

Austria #146 100 Schilling

Austria #147 1000 Schilling

Bahamas #52 5 Dollars

Bahamas #61 50 Dollars

Bahrain #10 20 Dinars

Bahrain #15 10 Dinars

Belgium #135 500 Francs

Bhutan #8 10 Ngultrum

Brazil #200 500 Cruzieros

Brunei #21 25 Ringgit

Bulgaria #102 100 Leva

Bulgaria #109 10,000 Leva

Burundi #39 1000 Francs

Cambodia # R1 5 Riels

Cambodia #R3 20 Riels

Canada #91 100 Dollars

Peru #145 100,000 Intis

Poland #141 1000 Zlotych

Portugal #166 100 Escudos

Portugal #188 1000 Escudos

Qatar #9 10 Riyals

Romania #99 1000 Lei

St. Thomas & Prince #66 10,000 Dobras

Shri Lanka #88 100 Rupees

Slovakia #40 5000 Korun

Slovenia #17 1000 Tolarjev

South Africa #124 20 Rand

Syria #105 500 Pounds

Sudan #47 20 Pounds

Vietnam #116 50,000 Dongs

Surinam #24B $2^{1}/2$ Gulden

West African States #703T 1000 Francs

Switzerland #186 10 Francs

Switzerland #187 20 Francs

Zaire #70 10,000 Zaires

57	500 LEKË	VG	VF	UNC
	1994. Deep blue on blue and m/c unpt. Like #53.			
	a. Issued note.	FV	FV	10.00
	s. Specimen.	—	—	6.50

58	1000 LEKË	VG	VF	UNC
	1994. Deep green on green and m/c unpt. Like #54.			
	a. Issued note.	FV	FV	18.50
	s. Specimen.	—	—	13.00

1995-96 ISSUE

#59-61 like #56-58 but w/segmented foil over security thread.

59	200 LEKË	VG	VF	UNC
	1996. Deep reddish brown on m/c unpt. Like #56.	FV	FV	3.75

60	500 LEKË	VG	VF	UNC
	1996. Deep blue on blue and m/c unpt. Like #57.	FV	FV	9.00

61	1000 LEKË	VG	VF	UNC
	1995-96. Deep green and green on m/c unpt.			
	a. 1995. Olive-green sign.	FV	FV	22.50
	b. 1995. Black sign.	FV	FV	18.00
	c. 1996. Black sign.	FV	FV	17.50

1996 ISSUE

62	100 LEKË	VG	VF	UNC
	1996 (1997). Purple, dk. brown and orange on m/c unpt. F. S. Noli at l. and as wmk. Bldg. at upper r. on back.	FV	FV	2.00

63	200 LEKË	VG	VF	UNC
	1996 (1997). Brown and brown-orange on m/c unpt. N. Frasheri at l. and as wmk. Bldg. at upper r. on back.	FV	FV	3.50

NOTICE

Readers with unlisted dates, signature varieties, etc. are invited to submit photocopies of their notes to: Standard Catalog of World Paper Money, 700 East State St. Iola, WI 54990-0001, fax: 1-715-445-4087, or E-Mail: thernr@krause.com.

		VG	VF	UNC
64	**500 LEKE** 1996 (1997). Dk. blue, purple and brown on m/c unpt. I. Qemali at l. and as wmk. House at upper r. on back.	FV	FV	8.00

		VG	VF	UNC
65	**1000 LEKË** 1996 (1997). Green and dk. green on m/c unpt. P. Bogdani at l. and as wmk. Church of Vaui Dejes at upper r. on back.	FV	FV	14.00

		VG	VF	UNC
66	**5000 LEKË** 1996 (1999). Olive green and m/c. Skanderberg at l. and as wmk. Kruja castle, equestrian statue, crown on back.	FV	FV	65.00

NOTICE

Readers with unlisted dates, signature varieties, etc. are invited to submit photocopies of their notes to: Standard Catalog of World Paper Money, 700 East State St. Iola, WI 54990-0001, fax: 1-715-445-4087, or E-Mail: thernr@krause.com.

FOREIGN EXCHANGE CERTIFICATES

BANKA E SHTETIT SHQIPTAR

1965 ISSUE

#FX21-FX27 arms at r. Bank arms at ctr. on back.

		VG	VF	UNC
FX21	**.05 LEK** 1965. Deep blue-green on pink and pale yellow-orange unpt.	—	—	50.00

		VG	VF	UNC
FX22	**.10 LEK** 1965. Deep olive-brown on pink and pale blue unpt.	—	—	50.00

		VG	VF	UNC
FX23	**1/2 LEK** 1965. Deep purple on pink and lilac unpt.	—	—	50.00

		VG	VF	UNC
FX24	**1 LEK** 1965. Blackish green on pale yellow and pale yellow-orange unpt.	—	—	50.00

		VG	VF	UNC
FX25	**5 LEK** 1965. Blue-black on pale yellow-green unpt.	—	—	140.00

		VG	VF	UNC
FX26	**10 LEK** 1965. Blue-green on pale yellow and pale grayish green unpt.	—	—	140.00

		VG	VF	UNC
FX27	**50 LEK** 1965. Deep red-brown on pink and pale yellow unpt.	—	—	140.00

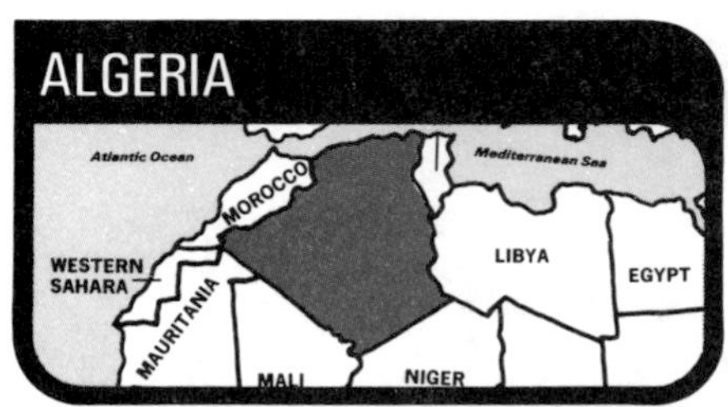

The Democratic and Popular Republic of Algeria, a North African country fronting on the Mediterranean Sea between Tunisia and Morocco, has an area of 919,595 sq. mi. (2,381,741 sq. km.) and a population of 28.6 million. Capital: Algiers (Alger). Most of the country's working population is engaged in agriculture although a recent industrial diversification, financed by oil revenues, is making steady progress. Wines, fruits, iron and zinc ores, phosphates, tobacco products, liquified natural gas, and petroleum are exported.

Algiers, the capital and chief seaport of Algeria, was the site of Phoenician and Roman settlements before the present Moslem city was founded about 950. Nominally part of the sultanate of Tlemcen, Algiers had a large measure of independence under the amirs of its own. In 1492 the Jews and Moors who had been expelled from Spain settled in Algiers and enjoyed an increasing influence until the imposition of Turkish control in 1518. For the following three centuries Algiers was the headquarters of the notorious Barbary pirates. The French took Algiers in 1830, and after a long and wearisome war completed the conquest of Algeria and annexed it to France, 1848. Following the armistice signed by France and Nazi Germany on June 22, 1940, Algeria fell under Vichy Government control until liberated by the Allied invasion forces under the command of Gen. Dwight D. Eisenhower on Nov. 8, 1942. The inability to obtain equal rights with Frenchmen led to an organized revolt which began on Nov. 1, 1954 and lasted until a ceasefire was signed on July 1, 1962. Independence was proclaimed on July 5, 1962, following a self-determination referendum.

RULERS:

French to 1962

MONETARY SYSTEM:

1 Franc = 100 Centimes to 1960
1 Nouveaux Franc = 100 Old Francs, 1960-64
1 Dinar = 100 Centimes, 1964-

FRENCH INFLUENCE

BANQUE DE L'ALGÉRIE

1959 PROVISIONAL ISSUE

#	Description	VG	VF	UNC
118	**5 NOUVEAUX FRANCS** 1959. Green and m/c. Ram at bottom ctr., Bacchus at r.			
	a. 31.7.1959; 18.12.1959.	10.00	70.00	200.00
	s. Specimen. 31.7.1959.	—	—	160.00

#	Description	VG	VF	UNC
119	**10 NOUVEAUX FRANCS** 1959-61. Brown and yellow. Isis at r.			
	a. 31.7.1959-2.6.1961.	15.00	85.00	235.00
	s. Specimen. 31.7.1959.	—	—	165.00

#	Description	VG	VF	UNC
120	**50 NOUVEAUX FRANCS** 1959. M/c. Pythian Apollo at l.			
	a. 31.7.1959; 18.12.1959.	35.00	125.00	325.00
	s. Specimen. 31.7.1959.	—	—	375.00

#	Description	VG	VF	UNC
121	**100 NOUVEAUX FRANCS** 1959-61. Blue and m/c. Seagulls w/city of Algiers in background.			
	a. 31.7.1959; 18.12.1959.	65.00	175.00	350.00
	b. 3.6.1960; 25.11.1960; 10.2.1961; 29.9.1961.	22.50	75.00	260.00
	s. Specimen. 31.7.1959.	—	—	175.00

REPUBLIC

BANQUE CENTRALE D'ALGÉRIE

1964 ISSUE

#122-125 wmk: Amir Abd el-Kader.

#	Description	VG	VF	UNC
122	**5 DINARS** 1.1.1964. Violet and lilac. Vultures perched on rocks at l. ctr. Native objects on back. 2 styles of numerals in date and serial #.	5.00	40.00	175.00

#	Description	VG	VF	UNC
123	**10 DINARS** 1.1.1964. Lilac and m/c. Pair of storks and minaret. Native craft on back. 2 styles of numerals in date and serial #.	6.00	20.00	80.00

#	Description	VG	VF	UNC
124	**50 DINARS** 1.1.1964. Lt. brown and m/c. 2 mountain sheep. Camel caravan on back.	10.00	30.00	125.00

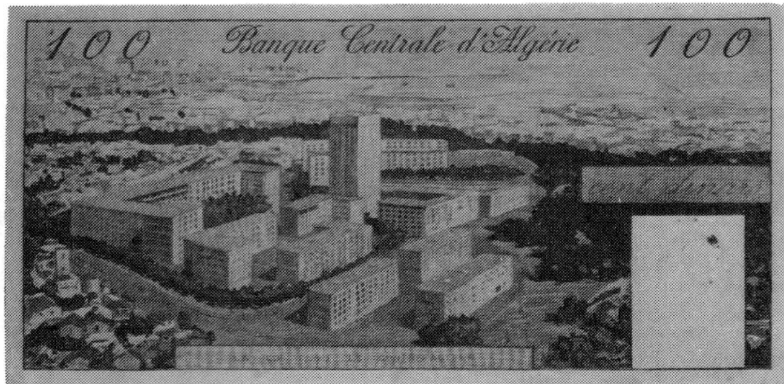

		VG	VF	UNC
125	**100 DINARS** 1.1.1964. M/c. Harbor scene. Modern bldg. complex at l. ctr. on back. 2 styles of numerals in date and serial #.	10.00	20.00	75.00

1970 ISSUE

#126 and 127 wmk: Amir Abd el-Kader.

		VG	VF	UNC
126	**5 DINARS** 1.11.1970. Blue and m/c. Warrior w/shield and sword at ctr. r. Fox head at l. ctr., village in background at ctr. r. on back. Sign. varieties.			
	a. Issued note.	.75	4.00	10.00
	s. Specimen.	—	—	30.00

		VG	VF	UNC
127	**10 DINARS** 1.11.1970. Red-brown. Sheep at l., peacock at r. Seated elderly man at l., ornate bldg. at r. on back. Minor plate varieties in legend.			
	a. Issued note.	2.00	5.00	20.00
	s. Specimen.	—	—	30.00

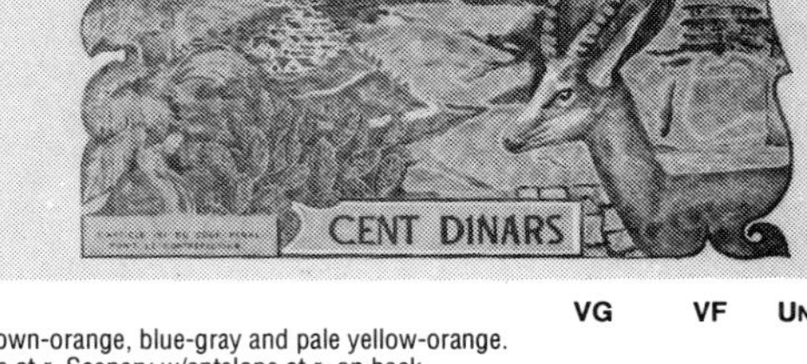

		VG	VF	UNC
128	**100 DINARS** 1.11.1970. Brown, brown-orange, blue-gray and pale yellow-orange. 2 men at l., wheat ears at r. Scenery w/antelope at r. on back.			
	a. Deep brown.	3.50	11.50	55.00
	b. Lt. brown.	3.50	10.00	45.00
	s. Specimen.	—	—	30.00

		VG	VF	UNC
129	**500 DINARS** 1.11.1970. Purple. View of city. Galleon, fortress on back.			
	a. Issued note.	7.50	30.00	65.00
	s. Specimen.	—	—	50.00

1977; 1981 ISSUE

#130 and 131 wmk: Amir Abd el-Kader.

		VG	VF	UNC
130	**50 DINARS** 1.11.1977. Dk. green on m/c unpt. Shepherd w/flock at lower l. ctr. Farm tractor on back. Sign. varieties.	1.25	2.50	7.50

		VG	VF	UNC
131	**100 DINARS** 1.11.1981. Dk. blue and blue on lt. blue unpt. Village w/minarets at l. Man working w/plants at ctr. on back.	2.00	4.50	13.50

1982-83 ISSUE

#132-135 wmk: Amir Abd el-Kader.

		VG	VF	UNC
132	**10 DINARS** 2.12.1983. Black on brown and blue-green unpt. Diesel passenger train at ctr. Back blue, blue-green and brown; mountain village at ctr.	FV	.40	2.00

		VG	VF	UNC
133	**20 DINARS** 2.1.1983. Red-brown on ochre unpt. Vase at l. ctr., handcrafts at r. Tower at ctr. on back.	FV	.50	2.50

		VG	VF	UNC
134	**100 DINARS** 8.6.1982. Pale blue and gray. Similar to #131 but w/o bird at upper r. on face.	FV	20.00	50.00

		VG	VF	UNC
135	**200 DINARS** 23.3.1983. Brown, dk. green on m/c unpt. Monument to the Algerian martyrs at l. Canyon at ctr., amphora at r. on back.	FV	8.00	20.00

#136 not assigned.

BANQUE D'ALGÉRIE

1992 DATED (1995; 1996) ISSUE

		VG	VF	UNC
137	**100 DINARS** 21.5.1992 (1996). Dk. blue w/black text on pale blue and m/c unpt. Army charging at r. Seal w/horsemen charging at l., ancient galley at ctr. on back. Wmk: Horse's head.	FV	FV	7.50
138	**200 DINARS** 21.5.1992 (1996). Dk. brown and red-brown on m/c unpt. Koranic school at ctr. r., bldg. at ctr. on back. Wmk: Horse's head.	FV	FV	11.50

		VG	VF	UNC
139	**500 DINARS** 21.5.1992 (1996). Deep purple, violet and red-violet on m/c unpt. Hannibal's troops and elephants engaging the Romans at ctr. r. Waterfalls at l., tomb ruins of Numid Kg. Massinissa at l. ctr., elephant mounted troops at ctr. r. on back. Wmk: Elephant heads.	FV	FV	25.00

		VG	VF	UNC
140	**1000 DINARS** 21.5.1992 (1995). Red-brown and orange on m/c unpt. Tassili cave carvings of animals at lower ctr., water buffalo's head at r. and as wmk. Hoggar cave painting of antelope at l., ruins at ctr. on back.	FV	FV	37.50

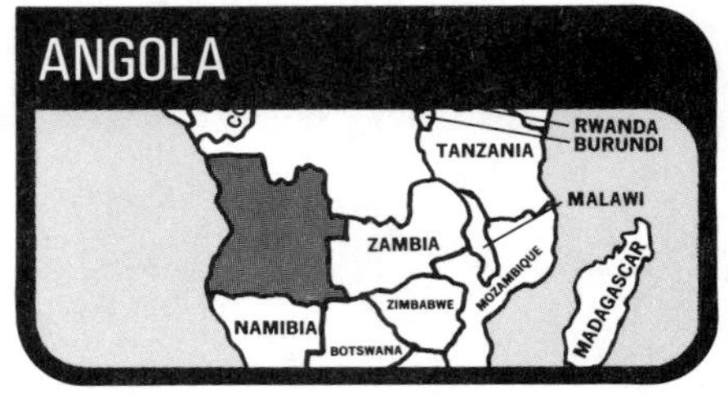

The Peoples Republic of Angola, a country on the west coast of southern Africa bounded by Zaïre, Zambia and Namibia (South-West Africa), has an area of 481,354 sq. mi. (1,246,700 sq. km.) and a population of 11.5 million, predominantly Bantu in origin. Capital: Luanda. Most of the people are engaged in subsistence agriculture. However, important oil and mineral deposits make Angola potentially one of the richest countries in Africa. Iron and diamonds are exported.

Angola was discovered by Portuguese navigator Diogo Cao in 1482. Portuguese settlers arrived in 1491, and established Angola as a major slaving center which sent about 3 million slaves to the New World.

A revolt against Portuguese rule, characterized by guerrilla warfare, began in 1961 and continued until 1974, when a new regime in Portugal offered independence. The independence movement was actively supported by three groups, the National Front, based in Zaïre, the Soviet-backed Popular Movement, and the moderate National Union. Independence was proclaimed on Nov. 11, 1975.

RULERS:

Portuguese to 1975

MONETARY SYSTEM:

1 Escudo = 100 Centavos, 1954-77
1 Kwanza = 100 Lwei, 1977-95
1 Kwanza Reajustado = 1,000 "old" Kwanzas, 1995-

SIGNATURE VARIETIES

1	Governor	Administrator
2	Governor	Administrator
3	Governor	Administrator
4	Governor	Vice-Governor
5	Governor	Vice-Governor
6	Governor	Vice-Governor
7	Governor	Administrator
8	Governor	Administrator
9	Governor	Administrator
10	Governor	Administrator
11	Governor	Vice-Governor
12	Governor	Administrator
13	Governor	Administrator
14	Governor	Vice-Governor
15	Vice-Governor	Vice-Governor
16	Governor	Vice-Governorr
17	Governor	Vice-Governor
18	Governor	Vice-Governorr
19	Governor	Vice-Governorr
20	Governor	Administrator

PORTUGUESE INFLUENCE

BANCO DE ANGOLA

1962 ISSUE

Escudo System

#92-96 portr. Americo Tomas. at l. or r. Printer: TDLR.

		VG	VF	UNC
92	**20 ESCUDOS** 10.6.1962. Black on m/c unpt. Dock at l. Gazelles running on back. Sign. 1.	1.50	5.00	20.00

		VG	VF	UNC
93	**50 ESCUDOS** 10.6.1962. Lt. blue on m/c unpt. Airport at l. Various animals at water hole on back. Sign. 2.	2.50	9.00	35.00

		VG	VF	UNC
94	**100 ESCUDOS** 10.6.1962. Lilac on m/c unpt. Salazar bridge at l. Elephants at watering hole on back. Sign. 3.	4.00	22.00	75.00
95	**500 ESCUDOS** 10.6.1962. Red on m/c unpt. Port of Luanda at ctr. 2 rhinoceros on back. Sign. 4.	10.00	50.00	250.00
96	**1000 ESCUDOS** 10.6.1962. Blue on m/c unpt. Dam at ctr. Herd on back. Sign. 4.	17.50	65.00	350.00

1970 ISSUE

#97-98 portr. Americo Tomas at l. or r. Printer: TDLR.

		VG	VF	UNC
97	**500 ESCUDOS** 10.6.1970. Red on m/c unpt. Like #95. Sign. 5.	13.00	45.00	160.00
98	**1000 ESCUDOS** 10.6.1970. Blue on m/c unpt. Like #96. Sign. 5.	15.00	55.00	180.00

1972 ISSUE

#99-103 M. Carmona at ctr. r. Printer: TDLR.

		VG	VF	UNC
99	**20 ESCUDOS** 24.11.1972. Red and brown on m/c unpt. Flowers on back. Sign. 7.	.50	1.25	6.00

		VG	VF	UNC
100	**50 ESCUDOS** 24.11.1972. Green and brown on m/c unpt. Plants on back. Sign. 8.	.50	2.00	7.50

		VG	VF	UNC
101	**100 ESCUDOS** 24.11.1972. Lt. and dk. brown on m/c unpt. Tree and plants on back. Sign. 7.	.75	1.75	8.00

		VG	VF	UNC
102	**500 ESCUDOS** 24.11.1972. Blue on m/c unpt. Rock formation at Pungo Andongo at ctr. r. on back. Sign. 8.	1.50	4.50	20.00
103	**1000 ESCUDOS** 24.11.1972. Purple on m/c unpt. Waterfalls on back. Sign. 6.	2.00	7.00	30.00

1973 ISSUE

#104-108 Luiz de Camoes at r. and as wmk.

		VG	VF	UNC
104	**20 ESCUDOS** 10.6.1973. Blue, purple and green on m/c unpt. Cotton plant on back. Sign. 10.	2.00	8.00	25.00

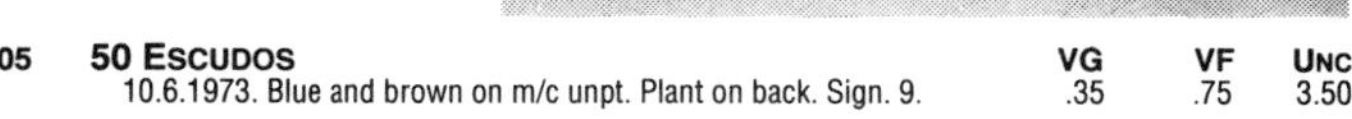

		VG	VF	UNC
105	**50 ESCUDOS** 10.6.1973. Blue and brown on m/c unpt. Plant on back. Sign. 9.	.35	.75	3.50

106 **100 ESCUDOS** | VG | VF | UNC
10.6.1973. Brown, black and maroon on m/c unpt. Back dk. green and maroon on m/c unpt. Tree at l. Sign. 10. | .50 | 1.25 | 4.00

107 **500 ESCUDOS** | VG | VF | UNC
10.6.1973. Dk. brown, violet and purple on m/c unpt. High rock formation on back. Sign. 11. | 1.50 | 3.50 | 12.50

108 **1000 ESCUDOS** | VG | VF | UNC
10.6.1973. Olive and blue on m/c unpt. Waterfalls on back. Sign. 11. | 2.00 | 7.50 | 22.50

PEOPLES REPUBLIC

BANCO NACIONAL DE ANGOLA

1976 ISSUE

Kwanza System

#109-113 Antonio Agostinho Neto at r. Arms at lower l. on back.

109 **20 KWANZAS** | VG | VF | UNC
11.11.1976. Brown, green and orange. Soldiers in field on back. Sign. 12. | 1.00 | 3.50 | 10.00

110 **50 KWANZAS** | VG | VF | UNC
11.11.1976. Purple, brown and black. Field workers on back. Sign. 12. | .75 | 1.75 | 6.00

111 **100 KWANZAS** | VG | VF | UNC
11.11.1976. Green on m/c unpt. Textile factory workers on back. Sign. 12. | .75 | 1.50 | 7.50

112 **500 KWANZAS** | VG | VF | UNC
11.11.1976. Blue on m/c unpt. Cargo ships dockside on back. Sign. 12. | 2.00 | 7.00 | 17.50

113 **1000 KWANZAS** | VG | VF | UNC
11.11.1976. Red on m/c unpt. School class on back. Sign. 12. | 2.50 | 9.00 | 27.50

1979 ISSUE

#114-117 w/2 serial #. Sign. titles, date of independence added under bank name on face. Arms at lower l. on back.

114 **50 KWANZAS** | VG | VF | UNC
14.8.1979. Purple, brown and black. Like #110. Sign. 13. | 1.00 | 2.50 | 12.00

		VG	VF	UNC
115	**100 KWANZAS** 14.8.1979. Green on m/c unpt. Like #111. Sign. 13.	1.25	3.00	15.00
116	**500 KWANZAS** 14.8.1979. Blue on m/c unpt. Like #112. Sign. 13.	3.00	16.00	55.00

		VG	VF	UNC
117	**1000 KWANZAS** 14.8.1979. Red on m/c unpt. Like #113. Sign. 13.	3.00	12.00	33.00

1984-87 ISSUE

#118-125 conjoined busts of Jose Eduardo Dos Santos and Antonio Agostinho Neto at r. Arms at lower l. on back. Wmk: bird (weak).

Replacement notes: Serial # prefixes *ZA, ZB, ZC*, etc.

		VG	VF	UNC
118	**50 KWANZAS** 7.1.1984. Deep brown and green on lt. green and tan unpt. Classroom and teacher on back. Sign. 14.	.40	1.00	3.50

NOTE: #118 dated 11.11.1987 may exist. (see #122).

		VG	VF	UNC
119	**100 KWANZAS** 7.1.1984; 11.11.1987. Deep blue, violet and brown on lt. blue and m/c unpt. Picking cotton on back. Sign. 14.	3.50	10.00	12.50

NOTE: #119 dated 1987 was only issued w/ovpt. (see #125).

		VG	VF	UNC
120	**500 KWANZAS** 1984; 1987. Black, red-brown and red on lilac and m/c unpt. Offshore oil platform at l., worker at r. on back. Wmk: Sculpture.			
	a. Sign. 14. 7.1.1984.	3.00	10.00	35.00
	b. Sign. 15. 11.11.1987.	3.00	10.00	32.00

		VG	VF	UNC
121	**1000 KWANZAS** 1984; 1987. Purple, blue-black and blue on lt. blue and m/c unpt. Soldiers embarking dockside at l. ctr. and soldier at r. on back. Wmk: Sculpture.			
	a. Sign. 14. 7.1.1984.	4.50	15.00	45.00
	b. Sign. 15. 11.11.1987.	4.00	14.00	40.00

1991 PROVISIONAL ISSUE

#121-125 portr. conjoined bust of Jose Eduardo dos Santos and Antonio Agostinho Neto at r. and as wmk. Arms at lower l. on back.

		VG	VF	UNC
122	**50 NOVO KWANZA ON 50 KWANZAS** ND (-old date 11.11.1987). Ovpt: *NOVO KWANZA* on unissued date of #118. Sign. 15.	Reported Not Confirmed		

		VG	VF	UNC
123	**500 NOVO KWANZA ON 500 KWANZAS** ND (-old date 11.11.1987). Ovpt: *NOVO KWANZA* in lt. green on #120. Sign. 15.	8.00	20.00	75.00

		VG	VF	UNC
124	**1000 NOVO KWANZA ON 1000 KWANZAS** ND (-old date 11.11.1987). Ovpt: *NOVO KWANZA* in red on #121. Sign. 15.	6.00	15.00	70.00

125	5000 NOVO KWANZA ON 100 KWANZAS	VG	VF	UNC
	ND (-old date 11.11.1987). Ovpt: *NOVO KWANZA 5000* in brown on unissued date of #119. Sign. 15.	35.00	100.00	200.00

1991 ISSUE

#126-134 portr. conjoined busts of Jose Eduardo dos Santos and Antonio Agostinho Neto at r. and as wmk. Arms at lower l. on back.

#126-131 replacement notes: Serial # prefixes *AZ, BZ, CZ, DZ, EZ.*

126	100 KWANZAS	VG	VF	UNC
	4.2.1991. Purple, green and brown. Rock formation at Pungo Andongo at l. ctr. Tribal mask at r. on back. Sign. 16.	.25	1.00	4.00
127	500 KWANZAS			
	4.2.1991. Blue and violet. Back blue, violet, green and brown. Like #126. Specimen.	—	—	—

128	500 KWANZAS	VG	VF	UNC
	4.2.1991. Purple and deep blue-green on m/c unpt. Serra da Leba at l. ctr; native pot at r. on back.			
	a. Sign. 16.	1.00	4.00	15.00
	b. Sign. 17.	.50	2.00	8.50
	c. Sign. 18.	1.00	4.00	15.00

129	1000 KWANZAS	VG	VF	UNC
	4.2.1991. Brown, orange, purple and red-violet on m/c unpt. Banco Nacional at l. ctr, native doll at r. on back.			
	a. Sign. 16.	1.50	6.00	24.00
	b. Sign. 17.	.75	2.25	12.00
	c. Sign. 18.	1.25	5.00	18.00

130	5000 KWANZAS	VG	VF	UNC
	4.2.1991. Dk. green, blue-green and dk. brown on m/c unpt. Waterfalls and stylized statue of "The Thinker" on back.			
	a. Sign. 16.	3.00	13.00	45.00
	b. Sign. 17.	2.00	7.00	25.00
	c. Sign. 18.	2.50	10.00	30.00

131	10,000 KWANZAS	VG	VF	UNC
	4.2.1991. Red, olive-green and purple on m/c unpt. Palanca Negra, antelope herd and shell on back.			
	a. Sign. 17.	2.50	12.00	55.00
	b. Sign. 18.	.50	2.00	15.00

132	50,000 KWANZAS	VG	VF	UNC
	4.2.1991. Bright green, yellow-green and dk. brown on m/c unpt. Like #130. Sign. 18.	.60	2.25	12.00

133	100,000 KWANZAS	VG	VF	UNC
	4.2.1991 (1993). Orange and aqua on emerald green and m/c unpt. Like #129 except for value. Sign. 18.			
	a. Microprint around wmk area reads: *100000 BNA*, latent print: *100000 CEM MIL*. Wmk: *100000*.	1.00	4.00	15.00
	x. Microprint around wmk. area reads: *10000 BNA*, latent print: *10000 DEZ MIL*. Wmk: *10,000*. (error).	3.50	15.00	45.00

		VG	VF	UNC
134	**500,000 KWANZAS** 4.2.1991 (1994). Red, brown and violet on m/c unpt. Rhinoceros at l. on back. Sign. 19.	.50	2.50	12.00
134A	**1,000,000 KWANZAS** 4.2.1991.	Reported Not Confirmed		

1995 ISSUE

Kwanza Reajustado System

#135-142 portr. conjoined busts of Jose Eduardo Dos Santos and Antonio Agostinho Neto at r. Arms at lower l., mask at upper r. on back. Wmk: Sculpture.

		VG	VF	UNC
135	**1000 KWANZAS REAJUSTADOS** 1.5.1995. Black and blue on m/c unpt. Palanca Negra Real, antelope at l. on back. Sign. 20.	.50	.75	2.00

		VG	VF	UNC
136	**5000 KWANZAS REAJUSTADOS** 1.5.1995. Green and brown on m/c unpt. Banco Nacional at l. on back. Sign. 20.	.50	.75	6.00

		VG	VF	UNC
137	**10,000 KWANZAS REAJUSTADOS** 1.5.1995. Red and purple on m/c unpt. Off shore oil platform at l. on back. Sign. 20.	.50	.75	5.00

		VG	VF	UNC
138	**50,000 KWANZAS REAJUSTADOS** 1.5.1995. Orange and green on m/c unpt. Telecommunications station in Luanda at l. ctr. on back. Sign. 20.	.50	.75	6.00
139	**100,000 KWANZAS REAJUSTADOS** 1.5.1995. Dk. blue and brown-violet on m/c unpt. Mask and pottery at l. ctr. on back. Sign. 20.	.50	.75	7.00
140	**500,000 KWANZAS REAJUSTADOS** 1.5.1995. Dk. brown and red-brown on m/c unpt. Matala dam at l. ctr. on back. Sign. 20.	FV	FV	10.00
141	**1,000,000 KWANZAS REAJUSTADOS** 1.5.1995. Bright blue and red-brown on m/c unpt. School girl at l. ctr. on back. Sign. 20.	FV	FV	15.00

		VG	VF	UNC
142	**5,000,000 KWANZAS REAJUSTADOS** 1.5.1995. Violet and red-brown on m/c unpt. Serra da Leba at l. ctr. on back. Sign. 20.	FV	FV	45.00

The Argentine Republic, located in South America, has an area of 1,068,301 sq. mi. (2,766,889 sq. km.) and a population of 34.6 million. Capital: Buenos Aires. Its varied topography ranges from the subtropical lowlands of the north to the towering Andean Mountains in the west and the windswept Patagonian steppe in the south. The rolling, fertile pampas of central Argentina are ideal for agriculture and grazing, and support most of the republic's population. Meat packing, flour milling, textiles, sugar refining and dairy products are the principal industries. Oil is found in Patagonia, but most of the mineral requirements must be imported.

Argentina was discovered in 1516 by the Spanish navigator Juan de Solis. A permanent Spanish colony was established at Buenos Aires in 1580, but the colony developed slowly. When Napoleon conquered Spain, the Argentines set up their own government in the name of the Spanish king on May 25, 1810. Independence was formally declared on July 9, 1816.

MONETARY SYSTEM:

- 1 Peso (m/n) = 100 Centavos to 1970
- 1 'New' Peso (Ley 18.188) = 100 'Old' Pesos (m/n), 1970-83
- 1 Peso Argentino = 10,000 Pesos, (Ley 18.188) 1983-85
- 1 Austral = 100 Centavos = 1000 Pesos Argentinos, 1985-92
- 1 Peso = 10,000 Australes, 1992-

REPUBLIC

BANCO CENTRAL

Signature Titles:

- A - ***GERENTE GENERAL***
- B - ***SUBGERENTE GENERAL***
- C - ***GERENTE GENERAL* and *PRESIDENTE***
- D - ***SUBGERENTE GENERAL* and *VICE-PRESIDENTE***
- E - ***SUBGERENTE GENERAL* and *PRESIDENTE***
- F - ***VICE PRESIDENTE* and *PRESIDENTE***
- G - ***PRESIDENTE B.C.R.A.* and *PRESIDENTE H.C. SENADORES***
- H - ***PRESIDENTE B.C.R.A.* and *PRESIDENTE H.C. DIPUTADOS***

1960-67 ND ISSUE

W/o Ley

#275-281 replacement notes: Serial # prefix *R*.

#275-277, 279-280 Portr. Gen. José de San Martín in uniform at r. Sign. varieties.

275	**5 PESOS**	VG	VF	UNC
	ND (1960). Brown on yellow unpt. People gathering before bldg. on back. Printer: CMN.			
	a. Sign. titles: D.	.30	1.35	5.00
	b. Sign. titles: C.	.75	3.25	10.00
	c. Sign. titles: E.	.40	1.50	4.50

276	**50 PESOS**	VG	VF	UNC
	ND (1969). Green on m/c unpt.	.35	1.25	3.75

277	**100 PESOS**	VG	VF	UNC
	ND (1967). Brown on m/c unpt. 2 sign. varieties.	.25	1.00	3.00

278	**500 PESOS**	VG	VF	UNC
	ND (1964). Blue on m/c unpt. Portr. elderly Gen J. de San Martín not in uniform at r. Grand Bourg House in France on back. 4 sign. varieties.			
	a. Sign. titles: E.	1.00	4.00	12.00
	b. Sign. titles: C.	.75	3.00	8.50

279	**1000 PESOS**	VG	VF	UNC
	ND (1966). Violet on m/c unpt. Portr. young Gen. J. de San Martín in uniform at r. Sailing ship on back. 3 sign. varieties.			
	a. Sign. titles: E.	1.00	3.50	12.00
	b. Sign. titles: C.	.75	3.00	8.50

280	**5000 PESOS**	VG	VF	UNC
	ND (1962). Brown on yellow-green unpt. Portr. young Gen. J. de San Martín in uniform. Capitol on back. 6 sign. varieties.			
	a. Sign. titles: E.	4.50	13.50	40.00
	b. Sign. titles: C.	4.00	12.00	36.00

281	**10,000 PESOS**	VG	VF	UNC
	ND (1961). Red-brown on m/c unpt. Portr. elderly Gen J. de San Martín not in uniform at r. Armies in the field on back. 5 sign. varieties.			
	a. Sign. titles: E.	4.50	13.50	40.00
	b. Sign. titles: C.	2.50	10.00	30.00

1969 ND PROVISIONAL ISSUE

Ley 18.188

		VG	VF	UNC
282	**1 PESO ON 100 PESOS** ND (1969). Brown on m/c unpt. Ovpt: New denomination on #277.	.20	2.00	5.00

		VG	VF	UNC
283	**5 PESOS ON 500 PESOS** ND (1969). Blue on m/c unpt. Ovpt: New denomination on #278. 2 sign. varieties.	1.00	4.00	12.00

		VG	VF	UNC
284	**10 PESOS ON 1000 PESOS** ND (1969). Violet on m/c unpt. Ovpt: New denomination on #279.	.75	3.00	9.00

		VG	VF	UNC
285	**50 PESOS ON 5000 PESOS** ND (1969). Brown on yellow green unpt. Ovpt: New denomination on #280.	1.50	6.50	20.00

		VG	VF	UNC
286	**100 PESOS ON 10,000 PESOS** ND (1969). Red brown on m/c unpt. Ovpt: New denomination on #281. 2 sign. varieties.	6.00	15.00	45.00

LEY 18.188; 1970-72 ND ISSUE

#287-292 replacement notes: Serial # prefix *R*.

#287-289 Gen. Manuel Belgrano at r. Printer: CMN. Many sign. varieties. W/o colored threads in white or grayish tint paper.

		VG	VF	UNC
287	**1 PESO** ND (1970-73). Orange on m/c unpt. Scene of Bariloche-Llao-Llao at ctr. on back. 5 sign. varieties.	.15	.40	1.50

		VG	VF	UNC
288	**5 PESOS** ND (1971-73). Blue on m/c unpt. Monument to the Flag at Rosario at ctr. on back. 2 sign. varieties.	.25	1.00	4.00

		VG	VF	UNC
289	**10 PESOS** ND (1970-73). Violet on m/c unpt. Waterfalls at Iguazu at ctr. on back. 6 sign. varieties.	.10	.30	1.00

#290-292 Gen. José de San Martín at r. Colored threads in paper.

		VG	VF	UNC
290	**50 PESOS** ND (1972-73). Black and brown on m/c unpt. Hot springs at Jujuy at ctr. on back. 3 sign. varieties.	1.00	3.00	10.00
291	**100 PESOS** ND (1971-73). Red on m/c unpt. Coastline at Ushuaia at ctr. on back. 4 sign. varieties.	1.50	5.00	15.00
292	**500 PESOS** ND (1972-73). Green on m/c unpt. Army monument at Mendoza at ctr. on back. 2 sign. varieties.	2.00	6.50	20.00

DECRETO-LEY 18.188/69; 1973-74 ND ISSUE

#293-299 replacement notes: Serial # prefix *R*.

#293-295 Gen. Manuel Belgrano at r. Sign. varieties. W/o colored threads in paper (varieties). Wmk. varieties.

		VG	VF	UNC
293	**1 PESO** ND (1974). Orange on m/c unpt. Scene of Bariloche-Llao-Llao at ctr. on back.	.15	.65	2.00
294	**5 PESOS** ND (1974-76). Blue on m/c unpt. Monument to the Flag at Rosario at ctr. on back. 2 sign. varieties.	.10	.40	1.25
295	**10 PESOS** ND (1973-76). Violet on m/c unpt. Waterfalls at Iguazu at ctr. on back. 4 sign. varieties.	.15	.65	2.00

#296-299 Gen. José de San Martín at r. Sign. varieties. Colored threads in paper.

		VG	VF	UNC
296	**50 PESOS** ND (1974-76). Black and brown on m/c unpt. Hot springs at Jujuy at ctr. on back. 3 sign. varieties.	.15	.50	1.50

		VG	VF	UNC
297	**100 PESOS** ND (1973-76). Red on m/c unpt. Usukaja Harbor scene at ctr. on back. 3 sign. varieties.	.25	1.00	3.00
298	**500 PESOS** ND (1974-75). Green on m/c unpt. Army monument at Mendoza at ctr.	1.00	3.00	7.00

		VG	VF	UNC
299	**1000 PESOS** ND (1973-76). Brown on m/c unpt. *Plaza de Mayo* in Buenos Aires at ctr. on back. 3 sign. varieties.	1.25	5.00	15.00

1976-81 ND ISSUE

W/o Decreto or Ley

#301-310 Gen. José de San Martín at r. Sign. and wmk. varieties. Replacement notes: Serial # prefix *R*.

#300-302 wmk: Arms.

		VG	VF	UNC
300	**10 PESOS** ND (1976). Violet on m/c unpt. Gen. M. Belgrano at r. Waterfalls at Iguazu at ctr. on back.	.10	.20	.85

		VG	VF	UNC
301	**50 PESOS** ND (1976-78). Black on m/c unpt. Hot springs at Jujuy at ctr. on back. 2 sign. varieties.			
	a. W/o colored threads in paper.	1.25	5.00	15.00
	b. Colored threads in paper.	.10	.20	.85

		VG	VF	UNC
302	**100 PESOS**			
	ND (1976-78). Red on m/c unpt. Coastline at Ushuaia at ctr. on back.			
	a. W/o colored threads in paper. 2 sign. varieties.	.15	.65	2.00
	b. Colored threads in paper. 2 sign. varieties.	.10	.30	1.00

		VG	VF	UNC
303	**500 PESOS**			
	ND (1977-82). Green on m/c unpt. Army monument at Mendoza at ctr. on back. 4 sign. varieties.			
	a. Wmk: Arms. W/o colored threads in paper.	.10	.20	1.00
	b. Wmk: Arms. Colored threads in paper.	.15	.65	2.00
	c. Wmk: Multiple sunbursts. Colored threads. Back lithographed.	.05	.20	.60

		VG	VF	UNC
304	**1000 PESOS**			
	ND (1976-82). Brown on m/c unpt. *Plaza de Mayo* in Buenos Aires at ctr. on back. 5 sign. varieties.			
	a. Wmk: Arms. W/o colored threads in paper.	.10	.30	1.50
	b. Wmk: Arms. Colored threads in paper. 2 sign. varieties.	.05	.20	1.00
	c. Wmk: Multiple sunbursts. Back engraved.	.05	.20	1.00
	d. Wmk: Multiple sunbursts. Back lithographed.	.05	.15	.75

#305-310 w/colored threads.

		VG	VF	UNC
305	**5000 PESOS**			
	ND (1977-83). Blue and green on m/c unpt. Coastline of Mar del Plata on back.			
	a. Wmk: Arms. 2 sign. varieties.	.20	.50	3.50
	b. Wmk: Multiple sunbursts. 2 sign. varieties.	.10	.20	.85

		VG	VF	UNC
306	**10,000 PESOS**			
	ND (1976-83). Orange on m/c unpt. National park on back. 4 sign. varieties.			
	a. Wmk: Arms. 3 sign. varieties.	.25	.75	3.00
	b. Wmk: Multiple sunbursts.	.20	.50	1.35

		VG	VF	UNC
307	**50,000 PESOS**			
	ND (1979-83). Brown on m/c unpt. Banco Central bldg. at l. ctr. on back. Wmk: Arms. 2 sign. varieties.	.30	1.00	3.00

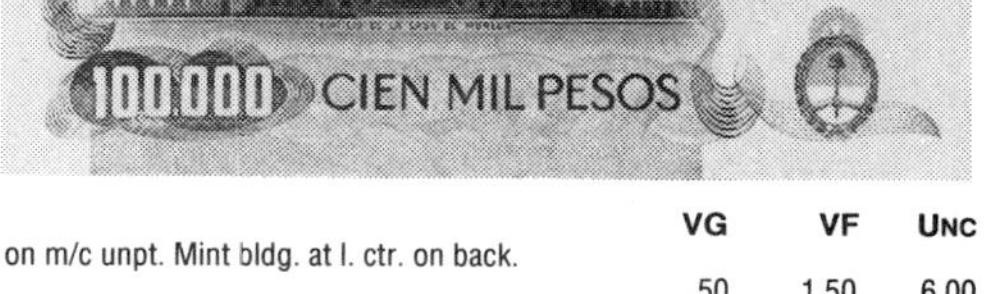

		VG	VF	UNC
308	**100,000 PESOS**			
	ND (1979-83). Gray on m/c unpt. Mint bldg. at l. ctr. on back.			
	a. Wmk: Arms.	.50	1.50	6.00
	b. Wmk: Multiple sunbursts.	.30	1.00	3.00

		VG	VF	UNC
309	**500,000 PESOS**			
	ND (1980-83). Green and brown on m/c unpt. Founding of Buenos Aires at l. ctr. on back. Wmk: Multiple sunbursts. 2 sign. varieties.	.30	1.00	5.00

		VG	VF	UNC
310	**1,000,000 PESOS** ND (1981). Pink and blue on m/c unpt. Independence Declaration w/*25 de Mayo* at l. ctr. on back. Wmk: Multiple sunbursts. 2 sign. varieties.	1.00	3.00	16.50

1983-85 ND ISSUE

Peso Argentino System

#311-319 w/colored threads. Replacement notes: Serial # prefix *R*.

#311-317 face design w/San Martín at r.

#311-316 wmk: Multiple sunbursts. Printer: CdM.

		VG	VF	UNC
311	**1 PESO ARGENTINO** ND (1983-84). Red-orange and purple on m/c unpt. Scene of Bariloche-Llao-Llao at ctr. on back. 2 sign. varieties.	.05	.15	.50

		VG	VF	UNC
312	**5 PESOS ARGENTINOS** ND (1983-84). Brown-violet and black on m/c unpt. Monument to the Flag at Rosario at ctr. on back. 2 sign. varieties.	.05	.15	.50

		VG	VF	UNC
313	**10 PESOS ARGENTINOS** ND (1983-84). Black and red-brown on green and m/c unpt. Waterfalls at Iguazu at ctr. on back. 2 sign. varieties. White or grayish tint paper.	.05	.15	.50
314	**50 PESOS ARGENTINOS** ND (1983-85). Brown on m/c unpt. Hot springs at Jujuy at ctr. on back. 2 sign. varieties.	.05	.15	.50

		SVG	VF	UN
315	**100 PESOS ARGENTINO** ND (1983-85). Blue on m/c unpt. Coastline at Ushuaia at ctr. on back. 2 sign. varieties.	.15	.35	1.25

		VG	VF	UNC
316	**500 PESOS ARGENTINOS** ND (1984). Violet on m/c unpt. Town meeting of May 22, 1810 on back.	.15	.50	1.75

		VG	VF	UNC
317	**1000 PESOS ARGENTINOS** ND (1983-84). ND. Blue-green and brown on m/c unpt. *El Paso de los Andes* battle scene on back.			
	a. Wmk: San Martín. (1983). 2 sign. varieties.	.40	1.25	5.00
	b. Wmk: Multiple sunbursts (1984).	.15	.50	1.50
	s1. As a. Specimen. Ovpt: *MUESTRA*	—	—	75.00
	s2. As b. Specimen. Ovpt.: *MUESTRA*	—	—	75.00
318	**5000 PESOS ARGENTINOS** ND (1984-85). Red-brown on m/c unpt. J. B. Alberdi at r. Constitutional meeting of 1853 on back. Wmk: Young San Martín.	.35	1.00	3.00
319	**10,000 PESOS ARGENTINOS** ND (1985). Blue-violet on m/c unpt. M. Belgrano at r. Creation of Argentine flag on back. Wmk: Young San Martín.	1.25	3.50	12.50

1985 ND PROVISIONAL ISSUE

Austral System

#320-322 ovpt. on Peso Argentino notes.

		VG	VF	UNC
320	**1 AUSTRAL** ND (1985). New denomination ovpt. in numeral and wording in box, green on face and blue on back of #317b. Series D.	.15	.65	2.00

		VG	VF	UNC
321	**5 AUSTRALES** ND (1985). New denomination ovpt. as #320, purple on face and brown on back of #318, Series B.	.20	.90	2.75

		VG	VF	UNC
322	**10 AUSTRALES** ND (1985). New denomination ovpt. as #320 on #319.			
	a. Blue ovpt. on face and back. Wmk: San Martín. Series A.	1.00	4.00	8.00
	b. Like a. but wmk: Multiple sunbursts. Series B; C.	.40	1.75	4.00
	c. Blue ovpt on face, lt. olive-green ovpt. on back. Series B; C.	.40	1.75	4.00

1985-89 ND ISSUE

#323-330 latent image "BCRA" on face. Liberty (Progreso) w/torch and shield seated at l. ctr. on back. Printer: CdM. Sign. varieties.

Replacement notes: Serial # prefix *R*.

		VG	VF	UNC
323	**1 AUSTRAL** ND (1985). Blue-green and purple on m/c unpt. B. Rivadavia at ctr. Wmk: Multiple sunbursts.			
	a. Sign. titles E. Series A.	.10	.50	2.00
	b. Sign. titles C. Series B; C.	.05	.15	.40

		VG	VF	UNC
324	**5 AUSTRALES** ND (1986). Brown and deep olive-green on m/c unpt. J. J. de Urquiza at ctr. Wmk: Multiple sunbursts.			
	a. Sign. titles E. Series A.	.10	.25	2.00
	b. Sign. titles C. Series A.	.05	.15	.40

		VG	VF	UNC
325	**10 AUSTRALES** ND (1986). Dk. blue and purple on m/c unpt. S. Derqui at ctr. Wmk: Multiple sunbursts.			
	a. Coarse portrait in heavy horizontal wavy lines. Sign. titles E. Series A.	.25	1.00	4.00
	b. Modified portrait in finer horizontal wavy lines. Sign. titles C. Series A; B; C.	.05	.15	.40

		VG	VF	UNC
326	**50 AUSTRALES** ND (1986). Violet and deep brown on m/c unpt. B. Mitre at ctr. Wmk: Multiple sunbursts.			
	a. Sign. titles E. Series A.	.75	6.00	20.00
	b. Sign. titles C. Series A.	.10	.15	.40

		VG	VF	UNC
327	**100 AUSTRALES** ND (1985). Dk. red and purple on m/c unpt. D. F. Sarmiento at ctr. Wmk: Multiple sunbursts.			
	a. Sign. titles E. Series A.	.50	4.00	12.00
	b. Sign. titles C. Engraved back. Series A; B.	.10	.20	.75
	c. Sign. titles C. Back pink and lithographed; w/o purple and blue. Series C; D.	.05	.15	.50

NOTICE

Readers with unlisted dates, signature varieties, etc. are invited to submit photocopies of their notes to: Standard Catalog of World Paper Money, 700 East State St. Iola, WI 54990-0001, fax: 1-715-445-4087, or E-Mail: thernr@krause.com.

		VG	VF	UNC
328	**500 AUSTRALES** ND (1988). Pale olive-green on m/c unpt. N. Avellaneda at ctr. Sign. titles: C.			
	a. Metallic green guilloche by *500*. Back olive-green, black and m/c. Wmk: Liberty. Series A. (1988).	.10	.50	2.00
	b. Dk. olive-green guilloche by *500*. Back pale olive-green and m/c; lithographed (w/o black). Wmk: Multiple sunbursts. Series A. (1990).	.05	.20	.75

		VG	VF	UNC
329	**1000 AUSTRALES** ND (1989). Violet-brown and purple on m/c unpt. J. A. Roca at ctr. Sign. titles: *GERENTE GENERAL* and *PRESIDENTE*.			
	a. Vertical green guilloche near *1000*. Wmk: Liberty. Series A.	.05	.20	.75
	b. Vertical brown-violet guilloche near *1000*. Wmk: Multiple sunbursts. Series B.	.05	.20	.75
	c. Like b. but sign. titles: F. Series C.	.10	.50	1.50

		VG	VF	UNC
330	**5000 AUSTRALES** ND (1989). Dk. brown and red-brown on m/c unpt. M. Juarez at ctr.			
	a. Green shield design at upper ctr. r. Sign titles: E. Wmk: Liberty. Series A.	.75	3.00	10.00
	b. Green shield design at upper ctr. r. Sign titles: C. Wmk: Liberty. Series A.	1.25	5.00	15.00
	c. Dk. brown shield design at upper ctr. r. Sign. titles: E. Wmk: Liberty. Series B.	.60	2.50	8.00
	d. Dk. brown shield design. Sign. titles: C. Wmk: Liberty. Series B.	.50	2.00	6.00
	e. Dk. brown shield design. Sign. titles: F. Lithographed back. Wmk: Multiple sunbursts. Series C.	.20	1.00	3.00

1989; 1991 ND PROVISIONAL ISSUE

#331-333 use modified face plates from earlier issue. Wmk: Multiple sunbursts. Series M. Printer: CdM-A. Replacement notes: Serial # prefix *R*.

		VG	VF	UNC
331	**10,000 AUSTRALES** ND (1989). Black-blue, deep blue-green and brown on m/c unpt. Face similar to #306. Ovpt. value in olive-green in box at l. Word "PESOS" at ctr. blocked out. Denomination repeated in lines of text and ovpt. value at r. on back. Sign. titles: C.	2.00	7.50	20.00

		VG	VF	UNC
332	**50,000 AUSTRALES** ND (1989). Deep olive-green and blue on m/c unpt. Face similar to #307. Ovpt. value in violet in box at l. Word "PESOS" at ctr. blocked out. Back similar to #331. Value in lt. brown at r. Sign. titles: E.	2.00	8.00	25.00
333	**500,000 AUSTRALES** ND (1991). Black, purple and red on m/c unpt. Face similar to #309. Ovpt. value in box at l. Word "PESOS" at bottom r. blocked out. Back similar to #331. Value at r. Sign. titles: F.	10.00	30.00	75.00

1989-91 ND ISSUE

#334-338 Liberty (Progreso) w/torch and shield seated at l. ctr. on back. Wmk: Liberty head. Printer: CdM-A. Replacement notes: Serial # prefix *R*.

		VG	VF	UNC
334	**10,000 AUSTRALES** ND (1989). Black on deep blue, brown and m/c unpt. w/brown diamond design at upper ctr. R. C. Pellegrini at ctr.			
	a. Sign. titles: C. Series A; B.	.40	1.25	3.50
	b. Sign. titles: F. Series C.	.50	1.50	4.50

		VG	VF	UNC
335	**50,000 AUSTRALES** ND (1989). Black on ochre, olive-green and m/c unpt. w/black flower design at upper ctr. r. L. Saenz Peña at ctr. Sign. titles: C. Series A; B.	1.50	6.00	20.00

336 100,000 AUSTRALES

	VG	VF	UNC
ND (1990-91). Dk. brown and reddish brown on pale brown and m/c unpt. Coarsely engraved portr. of J. Evaristo Uriburu at ctr. Black sign. titles: F. Series A; B.	2.50	10.00	35.00

337 100,000 AUSTRALES

	VG	VF	UNC
ND (1991). Dk. brown and reddish brown on brown and m/c unpt. Finely engraved portr. of J. Evaristo Uriburu at ctr. Brown sign. titles. Series B.	2.00	8.00	40.00

338 500,000 AUSTRALES

	VG	VF	UNC
ND (1990). Black-violet, red and blue on m/c unpt. M. Quintana at ctr. Series A.	5.00	25.00	75.00

1992 ND ISSUE

Peso System

#339-345 replacement notes: Serial # prefix *R*.

#339-341 wmk: Multiple sunbursts. Printer: CdM-A.

339 1 PESO

	VG	VF	UNC
ND (1992-94). Black and violet-brown on m/c unpt. C. Pelligrini at r. Back gray on m/c unpt; National Congress bldg. at l. ctr.			
a. Sign. titles: F. (1992).	FV	1.50	3.00
b. Sign. titles: G. (1993).	FV	1.25	2.75
c. Sign. titles as a. Serial # prefix L. (1994).	FV	2.00	6.00

340 2 PESOS

	VG	VF	UNC
ND (1992-96). Deep blue and red-violet on m/c unpt. B. Mitre at r. Back lt. blue on m/c unpt; Mitre Museum at l. ctr.			
a. Sign. titles: F. (1992).	FV	FV	5.00
b. Sign. titles: H. (1993).	FV	FV	4.50

341 5 PESOS

	VG	VF	UNC
ND (1992-96). Deep olive-green and red-orange on m/c unpt. Gen. J. de San Martín at r. Back lt. olive-gray on m/c unpt; monument to the Glory of Mendoza at l. ctr.			
a. Sign. titles: F. (1992).	FV	FV	11.00
b. Sign. titles: G. (1993).	FV	FV	10.00
c. Sign. titles as a. Serial # prefix L. (1994).	FV	4.00	12.50

#342-343 wmk: Liberty head. Printer: CdM-A.

342 10 PESOS

	VG	VF	UNC
ND (1992-96). Deep brown and dk. green on m/c unpt. M. Belgrano at r. Monument to the Flag at Rosario w/city in background at l. ctr. on back.			
a. Sign. titles: F. (1992).	FV	FV	20.00
b. Sign. titles: H. (1993).	FV	FV	18.50

343 20 PESOS

	VG	VF	UNC
ND (1992-). Carmine and deep blue on m/c unpt. J. Manuel de Rosas at r. *Vuelta de Obligado* battle scene at l. ctr. on back.			
a. Sign. titles: F. (1992).	FV	FV	37.50
b. Sign. titles: G. (1993).	FV	FV	35.00

		VG	VF	UNC
344	**50 PESOS** ND (1992-). Black and red on m/c unpt. D. Faustino Sarmiento at r. and as wmk. Plaza de Mayo in Buenos Aires at l. ctr. on back.			
	a. Sign. titles: F. (1992).	FV	FV	80.00
	b. Sign. titles: H. (1993).	FV	FV	75.00

		VG	VF	UNC
345	**100 PESOS** ND (1992-). Violet, lilac and green on m/c unpt. J. A. Roca at r. and as wmk. Back violet and m/c; *La Conquista del Desierto* scene at l. ctr.			
	a. Sign. titles: F. (1992).	FV	FV	150.00
	b. Sign. titles: G. (1993).	FV	FV	140.00

1997 ND ISSUE

#346-351 ascending serial # at upper r. Printer: CdM-A. Replacement notes: Serial # prefix *R*.

		VG	VF	UNC
346	**2 PESOS** ND (1997). Deep blue and brown-violet on m/c unpt. B. Mitre at r. and as wmk., ornate gate at ctr. Mitre Museum at l. ctr. on back. Sign. titles: H.	FV	FV	4.00

		VG	VF	UNC
347	**5 PESOS** ND (1997). Deep olive-green and purple on m/c unpt. Gen. J. de. San Martín at r. and as wmk., Gen. San Martín on horseback w/troops at ctr. Monument to the Glory at Mendoza at l. ctr. on back. Sign. titles: G.	FV	FV	8.50

		VG	VF	UNC
348	**10 PESOS** ND (1998). Deep brown and dk. green on m/c unpt. M. Belgrano at r. and as wmk., Liberty w/flag at ctr. Monument to the Flag at Rosario w/city in background at l. ctr. on back. Sign. titles: H.	FV	FV	16.50
349	**20 PESOS** ND (2000). M/c. J. Manuel de Rosas at r. and as wmk. *Vuelta de Obligado* battle scene at l. ctr. on back.	Expected New Issue		
350	**50 PESOS** ND (1999). M/c. D. Faustino Sarmiento at r. and as wmk. Government office w/monuments, palm trees in foreground at l. ctr. on back.	Expected New Issue		
351	**100 PESOS** ND (2000). M/c. J. A. Roca at r. and as wmk. *La Conquista del Desierto* scene at l. ctr. on back.	Expected New Issue		

NOTICE

Readers with unlisted dates, signature varieties, etc. are invited to submit photocopies of their notes to: Standard Catalog of World Paper Money, 700 East State St. Iola, WI 54990-0001, fax: 1-715-445-4087, or E-Mail: thernr@krause.com.

The Republic of Armenia (formerly Armenian S.S.R.) is bounded in the north by Georgia, to the east by Azerbaijan and to the south and west by Turkey and Iran. It has an area of 11,490 sq. mi. (29,800 sq. km) and a population of 3.7 million. Capital: Yerevan. Agriculture including cotton, vineyards and orchards, hydroelectricity, chemicals - primarily synthetic rubber and fertilizers, and vast mineral deposits of copper, zinc and aluminum and production of steel and paper are major industries.

The earliest history of Armenia records continuous struggles with expanding Babylonia and later Assyria. In the sixth century B.C. it was called Armina. Later under the Persian empire it enjoyed the position of a vassal state. Conquered by Macedonia, it later defeated the Seleucids and Greater Armenia was founded under the Artaxis dynasty. Christianity was established in 303 A.D. which led to religious wars with the Persians and Romans who divided it into two zones of influence. The Arabs succeeded the Persian Empire of the Sassanids which later allowed the Armenian princes to conclude a treaty in 653 A.D. In 862 A.D. Ashot V was recognized as the "prince of princes" and established a throne recognized by Baghdad and Constantinople in 886 A.D. The Seljuks overran the whole country and united with Kurdistan which eventually ran the new government. In 1240 A.D. onward the Mongols occupied almost all of western Asia until their downfall in 1375 A.D. when various Kurdish, Armenian and Turkoman independent principalities arose. After the defeat of the Persians in 1516 A.D. the Ottoman Turks gradually took control over a period of some 40 years, with Kurdish tribes settling within Armenian lands. In 1605 A.D. the Persians moved thousands of Armenians as far as India developing prosperous colonies. Persia and the Ottoman Turks were again at war, with the Ottomans once again prevailing. The Ottomans later gave absolute civil authority to a Christian bishop allowing them free enjoyment of their religion and traditions.

Russia occupied Armenia in 1801 until the Russo-Turkish war of 1878. British intervention excluded either side from remaining although the Armenians remained more loyal to the Ottoman Turks, but in 1894 the Ottoman Turks sent in an expeditionary force of Kurds fearing a revolutionary movement. Large massacres were followed by retaliations, then amnesty was proclaimed which led right into WW I and once again occupation by Russian forces in 1916. After the Russian revolution the Georgians, Armenians and Azerbaijanis formed the short lived Transcaucasian Federal Republic on Sept. 20, 1917 which broke up into three independent republics on May 26, 1918. Communism developed and in Sept. 1920 the Turks attacked the Armenian Republic; the Russians soon followed suit from Azerbaijan routing the Turks. On Nov. 29, 1920 Armenia was proclaimed a Soviet Socialist Republic. On March 12, 1922, Armenia, Georgia and Azerbaijan were combined to form the Transcaucasian Soviet Federated Socialist republic, which on Dec. 30, 1922, became a part of U.S.S.R. On Dec. 5, 1936, the Transcaucasian federation was dissolved and Armenia became a constituent republic of the U.S.S.R. A new constitution was adopted in April 1978. Elections took place on May 20, 1990. The Supreme Soviet adopted a declaration of sovereignty in Aug. 1991, voting to unite Armenia with Nagorno-Karabakh. This newly constituted "Republic of Armenia" became fully independent by popular vote in Sept. 1991. It became a member of the CIS in Dec.1991.

Fighting between Christians in Armenia and Muslim forces of Azerbaijan escalated in 1992 and continued through early 1994. Each country claimed the Nagorno-Karabakh, an Armenian ethnic enclave in Azerbaijan. A temporary cease-fire was announced in May 1994.

MONETARY SYSTEM:

1 Dram = 100 Lumma

REPUBLIC

ARMENIAN REPUBLIC BANK

1993-95 ISSUE

#33-38 wmk: Decorative design.

		VG	VF	UNC
33	**10 DRAM** 1993. Dk. brown, lt. blue and pale orange on m/c unpt. Statue of David from Sasoun at upper ctr. r., main railway station in Yerevan at upper l. ctr. Mt. Ararat at upper ctr. r. on back.	FV	FV	.45

		VG	VF	UNC
34	**25 DRAM** 1993. Brown, yellow and blue. Frieze w/lion from Erebuni Castle at ctr. r., cuneiform tablet at upper l. ctr. Arched ornament at upper ctr. r. on back.	FV	FV	.90

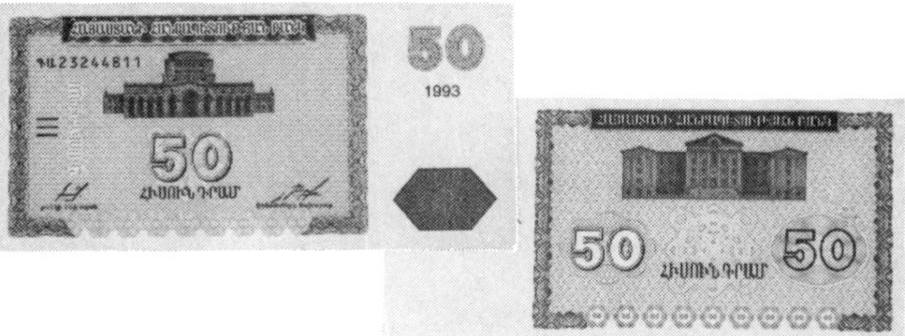

		VG	VF	UNC
35	**50 DRAM** 1993. Blue, red and violet. State Museum of History and National Gallery at upper l. ctr. Parliament bldg. at upper ctr. r. on back.	FV	FV	1.35

		VG	VF	UNC
36	**100 DRAM** 1993. Violet, red and blue. Mt. Ararat at upper l. ctr., Zvarnots Temple at ctr. r. Opera and ballet theater in Yerevan at upper ctr. r. on back.	FV	FV	2.25

		VG	VF	UNC
37	**200 DRAM** 1993. Brown, green and red. St. Hegine Temple in Echmiadzin at ctr. r. Circular design at upper ctr. r. on back.	FV	FV	4.00

		VG	VF	UNC
38	**500 DRAM** 1993. Dk. green and red-brown on m/c unpt. Tetradrachm of Kg. Tigran II the Great at ctr. r., Mt. Ararat at upper l. ctr. Open book and quill pen at upper ctr. r. on back.	FV	FV	7.50

		VG	VF	UNC
39	**1000 DRAM** 1994. Dk. brown and brown on m/c unpt. Ancient statue at l. Ancient ruins at r. on back. Wmk: Arms.	FV	FV	13.50

		VG	VF	UNC
40	**5000 DRAM** 1995. Brown-violet on m/c unpt. Temple of Garni at ctr. Goddess Anahid on back.	FV	FV	35.00

CENTRAL BANK OF THE REPUBLIC OF ARMENIA

1998-99 ISSUE

#41-48 printer: (T)DLR. Wmk. is portr.

		VG	VF	UNC
41	**50 DRAM** 1998. Brownish pink and slate blue. A. Khachaturyan at l., opera house at r. Scene from *Gayane* Ballet and Mt. Ararat on back.	FV	FV	1.75

		VG	VF	UNC
42	**100 DRAM** 1998. Lt. and dk. blue, pink. V. Hambardzumyan at l., solar system map at r. Buragan Observatory on Mt. Arakadz on back.	FV	FV	2.50
43	**200 DRAM** 1999.	Expected New Issue		
44	**500 DRAM** 1999.	Expected New Issue		
45	**1000 DRAM** 1999. Teal and green. E. Charents at l., lines of poetry at r. *Fiacre* scene on back.	FV	FV	17.50
46	**5000 DRAM** 1999.	Expected New Issue		
47	**10,000 DRAM** 1999.	Expected New Issue		
48	**20,000 DRAM** 1999. Brown and yellow on m/c unpt. Martiros Saryan, painter at l., abstract painting in ctr. Wmk: portr. Hologram. Mt. Ararat and Sarjan painting, yellow and lt. brown on m/c unpt. on back.	FV	FV	85.00

ARUBA

Caribbean Sea
COLOMBIA
VENEZUELA

Aruba, formerly a part of the Netherlands Antilles, achieved on Jan. 1, 1986 a special status "status aparte" as the third state under the Dutch crown, together with the Netherlands and the remaining five islands of the Netherlands Antilles. On Dec. 15, 1954 the Netherlands Antilles were given complete domestic autonomy and granted equality within the Kingdom of the Netherlands.

Aruba was the second-largest island of the Netherlands Antilles and is situated near the Venezuelan coast. The island has an area of 74 1/2 sq. mi. (193 sq. km.) and a population of 68,000. Capital: Oranjestad, named after the Dutch royal family. Chief industry is tourism. For earlier issues see Curaçao and the Netherlands Antilles. During Jan. 1986 the banknotes of the Netherlands Antilles were redeemed at a ratio of 1 to 1.

MONETARY SYSTEM:

1 Florin = 100 Cents

DUTCH INFLUENCE

BANCO CENTRAL DI ARUBA

1986 ISSUE

#1-5 flag at l., coastal hotels at ctr. Arms of Aruba at ctr. on back. Printer: JEZ.

		VG	VF	UNC
1	**5 FLORIN** 1.1.1986. Green.	FV	FV	6.50

		VG	VF	UNC
2	**10 FLORIN** 1.1.1986. Green.	FV	FV	17.00

		VG	VF	UNC
3	**25 FLORIN** 1.1.1986. Green.	FV	FV	35.00

		VG	VF	UNC
4	**50 FLORIN** 1.1.1986. Green.	FV	FV	65.00

		VG	VF	UNC
5	**100 FLORIN** 1.1.1986. Green.	FV	FV	125.00

CENTRALE BANK VAN ARUBA

1990 ISSUE

#6-10 geometric forms with pre-Columbian Aruban art on back. Wmk: Stylized tree. Printer: JEZ.

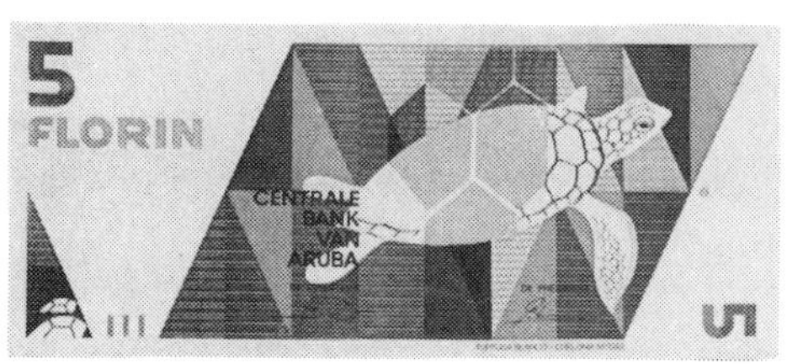

		VG	VF	UNC
6	**5 FLORIN** 1.1.1990. Purple and m/c. Tortuga Blanco (sea turtle) at ctr. r.	FV	FV	6.50

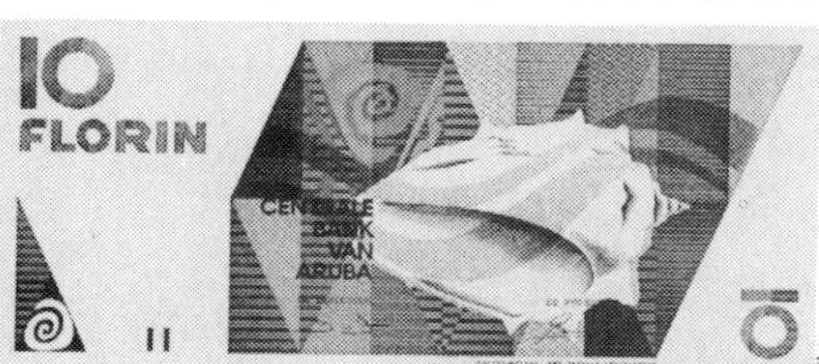

		VG	VF	UNC
7	**10 FLORIN** 1.1.1990. Blue and m/c. Calco Indian conch at ctr. r.	FV	FV	11.50

		VG	VF	UNC
8	**25 FLORIN** 1.1.1990. Brown and m/c. Cascabel snake at r.	FV	FV	28.50

		VG	VF	UNC
9	**50 FLORIN** 1.1.1990. Red-brown and m/c. Shoco owl at ctr. r.	FV	FV	55.00

		VG	VF	UNC
10	**100 FLORIN** 1.1.1990. Olive-green and m/c. Frog at ctr. r.	FV	FV	100.00

1993 (1996) ISSUE

#11-15 like #7-10 but w/text: *Wettig Betaaimiddel* (legal tender). Wmk: Stylized tree. Printer: JEZ.

		VG	VF	UNC
11	**10 FLORIN** 16.7.1993 (1996). Blue and m/c. Like #7.	FV	FV	11.00
12	**25 FLORIN** 16.7.1993 (1996). Brown and m/c. Like #8.	FV	FV	25.00
13	**50 FLORIN** 16.7.1993 (1996). Red-brown and m/c. Like #9.	FV	FV	48.50
14	**100 FLORIN** 16.7.1993 (1996). Olive-green and m/c. Like #10.	FV	FV	95.00
15 (11)	**500 FLORIN** 16.7.1993. Blue and m/c. Mero fish at ctr r.	FV	FV	375.00

COLLECTOR SERIES

CENTRALE BANK VAN ARUBA

1995 ISSUE

		ISSUE PRICE	MKT. VALUE
CS1	**1990 (1995) 5-100 FLORIN** #6-10 w/matched serial # in special presentation folder.	—	200.00

The Commonwealth of Australia, the smallest continent and largest island in the world, is located south of Indonesia between the Indian and Pacific oceans. It has an area of 2,967,909 sq. mi. (7,686,849 sq. km.) and a population of 17.9 million. Capital: Canberra. Due to its early and sustained isolation, Australia is the habitat of such curious and unique fauna as the kangaroo, koala, platypus, wombat and barking lizard. The continent possesses extensive mineral deposits, the most important of which are gold, coal, silver, nickel, uranium, lead and zinc. Livestock raising, mining and manufacturing are the principal industries. Chief exports are wool, meat, wheat, iron ore, coal and nonferrous metals.

The first caucasians to see Australia probably were Portuguese and Spanish navigators of the late 16th century. In 1770, Captain James Cook explored the east coast and annexed it for Great Britain. The Colony of New South Wales was founded by Captain Arthur Phillip on Jan. 26, 1788, a date now celebrated as Australia Day. Dates of creation of six colonies that now comprise the states of the Australian Commonwealth are: New South Wales, 1823; Tasmania, 1825; Western Australia, 1838; South Australia, 1842; Victoria, 1851; Queensland, 1859. A constitution providing for federation of the colonies was approved by the British Parliament in 1900; the Commonwealth of Australia came into being in 1901. Australia passed the Statute of Westminster Adoption Act on Oct. 9, 1942, which officially established Australia's complete autonomy in external and internal affairs, thereby formalizing a situation that had existed for years.

During WWII Australia was the primary supply and staging area for Allied forces in the South Pacific Theatre.

Australia is a member of the Commonwealth of Nations. Elizabeth II is Head of State as Queen of Australia.

RULERS:

British

MONETARY SYSTEM:

1 Shilling = 12 Pence
1 Pound = 20 Shillings; to 1966
1 Dollar = 100 Cents, 1966-

COMMONWEALTH OF AUSTRALIA

RESERVE BANK

1960-61 ND ISSUE

#33-36 sign. H. C. Coombs w/title: *GOVERNOR/RESERVE BANK of AUSTRALIA* below lower l. sign. R. Wilson. Wmk: Capt. James Cook. Replacement notes: Serial # suffix *.

		VG	VF	UNC
33	**10 SHILLINGS** ND (1961-65). Brown on m/c unpt. Portr. M. Flinders at r. Parliament in Canberra on back.	3.00	9.00	45.00

		VG	VF	UNC
34	**1 POUND** ND (1961-65). Green on m/c unpt. Cameo portr. Qn. Elizabeth II at r. Facing portr. C. Sturt and H. Hume on back.	2.00	6.00	30.00

		VG	VF	UNC
35	**5 POUNDS** ND (1960-65). Blue on m/c unpt. Portr. Sir J. Franklin at r. Cattle, sheep and agricultural products on back.	7.00	15.00	110.00

		VG	VF	UNC
36	**10 POUNDS** ND (1960-65). Red on m/c. Portr. Gov. Philip at l. Symbols of science and industry on back.	15.00	30.00	210.00

1966-67 ND ISSUE

#37-41 w/text: *COMMONWEALTH OF* in heading. Wmk: Capt. James Cook. Replacement notes: Serial # prefixes *ZAA-ZXA* w/suffix *.

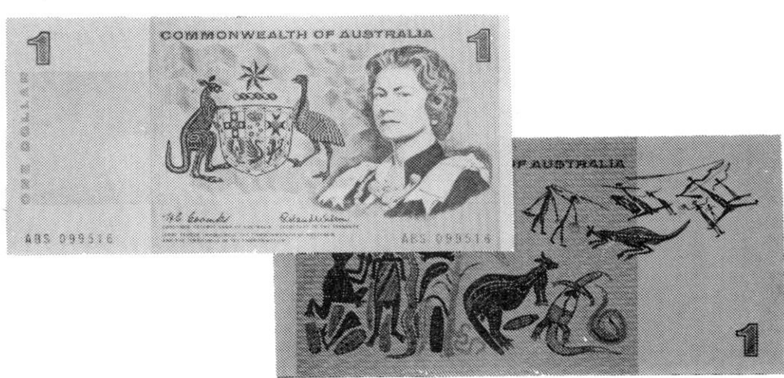

		VG	VF	UNC
37	**1 DOLLAR** ND (1966-72). Dk. brown on orange and m/c unpt. Arms at ctr., Qn. Elizabeth II at r. Stylized Aboriginal figures and animals on back.			
	a. Sign. H. C. Coombs and R. Wilson. (1966).	1.50	6.00	25.00
	b. Sign. H. C. Coombs and R. J. Randall. (1968).	30.00	60.00	210.00
	c. Sign. J. G. Phillips and R. J. Randall. (1969).	.75	3.00	20.00
	d. Sign. J. G. Phillips and F. H. Wheeler. (1972).	.85	4.00	15.00

		VG	VF	UNC
38	**2 DOLLARS** ND (1966-72). Black on green, blue and yellow m/c unpt. J. MacArthur at r., sheep at ctr. W. Farrer at l., wheat at ctr. on back.			
	a. Sign. H. C. Coombs and R. Wilson. (1966).	FV	4.00	12.00
	b. Sign. H. C. Coombs and R. J. Randall. (1967).	5.00	12.00	45.00
	c. Sign. J. G. Phillips and R. J. Randall. (1968).	1.50	4.00	12.00
	d. Sign. J. G. Phillips and F. H. Wheeler. (1972).	1.50	4.00	12.00
39	**5 DOLLARS** ND (1967-72). Deep purple on m/c unpt. Sir J. Banks at r., plants at ctr. C. Chisholm, ship, bldgs., and women on back.			
	a. Sign. H. C. Coombs and R. J. Randall. (1967).	3.50	7.00	50.00
	b. Sign. J. G. Phillips and R. J. Randall. (1969).	3.50	10.00	45.00
	c. Sign. J. G. Phillips and F. H. Wheeler. (1972).	3.50	8.00	30.00

40	10 DOLLARS	VG	VF	UNC
	ND (1966-72). Black on blue, orange and m/c unpt. F. Greenway at r., village scene at ctr. H. Lawson and bldgs. on back.			
	a. Sign. H. C. Coombs and R. Wilson. (1966).	6.50	7.50	22.50
	b. Sign. H. G. Coombs and R. J. Randall. (1967).	7.50	30.00	110.00
	c. Sign. J. G. Phillips and R. J. Randall. (1968).	6.50	8.00	25.00
	d. Sign. J. G. Phillips and F. H. Wheeler. (1972).	6.50	8.00	25.00

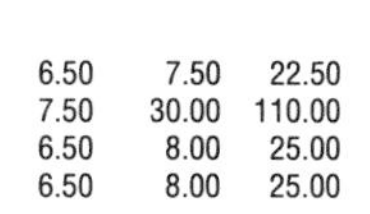

41	20 DOLLARS	VG	VF	UNC
	ND (1966-72). Black on red, yellow and m/c unpt. Sir C. Kingsford-Smith at r. L. Hargrave at l., aeronautical devices on back.			
	a. Sign. H. C. Coombs and R. Wilson. (1966).	13.50	15.00	30.00
	b. Sign. H. G. Coombs and R. J. Randall. (1968).	60.00	240.00	2150.
	c. Sign. J. G. Phillips and R. J. Randall. (1968).	13.50	15.00	50.00
	d. Sign. J. G. Phillips and F. H. Wheeler. (1972).	13.50	16.50	70.00

AUSTRALIA, RESERVE BANK

1973; 1984 ND ISSUE

#42-48 w/o text: *COMMONWEALTH OF* in heading.

#42-46 like #37-41. Wmk: Capt. James Cook.

42	1 DOLLAR	VG	VF	UNC
	ND (1974-83). Dk. brown on orange and m/c unpt.			
	a. Sign. J. G. Phillips and F. H. Wheeler. (1974).	FV	3.00	15.00
	b. Sign. H. M. Knight and F. H. Wheeler. (1976).	FV	2.00	7.00
	c. Sign. H. M. Knight and J. Stone. (1979).	FV	1.00	3.00
	d. Sign. R. A. Johnston and J. Stone. (1983).	FV	FV	2.00

43	2 DOLLARS	VG	VF	UNC
	ND (1974-85). Black on green, blue and yellow unpt.			
	a. Sign. J. G. Phillips and F. H. Wheeler. (1974).	FV	4.00	15.00
	b. Sign. H. M. Knight and F. H. Wheeler. (1976). 2 serial # varieties.	FV	2.00	8.00
	c. Sign. H. M. Knight and J. Stone. (1979).	FV	FV	5.00
	d. Sign. R. A. Johnston and J. Stone. (1983).	FV	FV	4.00
	e. Sign. R. A. Johnston and B. W. Fraser. (1985).	FV	FV	4.00

44	5 DOLLARS	VG	VF	UNC
	ND (1974-91). Deep purple on m/c unpt.			
	a. Sign. J. G. Phillips and F. H. Wheeler. (1974).	FV	15.00	55.00
	b. Sign. H. M. Knight and F. H. Wheeler. (1976).	FV	7.50	25.00
	c. Sign. H. M. Knight and J. Stone. (1979). 2 serial # varieties.	FV	FV	10.00
	d. Sign. R. A. Johnston and J. Stone. (1983).	FV	FV	9.00
	e. Sign. R. A. Johnston and B. W. Fraser. (1985). 2 serial # varieties.	FV	FV	8.00
	f. Sign. B. W. Fraser and C. I. Higgins. (1990).	FV	FV	7.00
	g. Sign. B. W. Fraser and A. S. Cole. (1991).	FV	FV	7.00

45	10 DOLLARS	VG	VF	UNC
	ND (1974-91). Black on blue and orange unpt.			
	a. Sign. J. G. Phillips and F. H. Wheeler. (1974).	10.00	20.00	100.00
	b. Sign. H. M. Knight and F. H. Wheeler. (1976).	FV	12.00	25.00
	c. Sign. H. M. Knight and J. Stone. (1979). 2 serial # varieties.	FV	FV	35.00
	d. Sign. R. A. Johnston and J. Stone. (1983).	FV	FV	35.00
	e. Sign. R. A. Johnston and B. W. Fraser. (1985).	FV	FV	13.50
	f. Sign. B. W. Fraser and C. I. Higgins. (1990).	FV	FV	13.50
	g. Sign. B. W. Fraser and A. S. Cole. (1991).	FV	FV	13.50

46	20 DOLLARS	VG	VF	UNC
	ND (1974-94). Black on red, yellow and m/c unpt.			
	a. Sign. J. G. Phillips and F. H. Wheeler. (1974).	FV	20.00	80.00
	b. Sign. H. M. Knight and F. H. Wheeler. (1975).	FV	FV	65.00
	c. Sign. H. M. Knight and J. Stone. (1979). 2 serial # varieties.	FV	FV	35.00
	d. Sign. R. A. Johnston and J. Stone. (1983).	FV	FV	55.00
	e. Sign. R. A. Johnston and B. W. Fraser. (1985) 2 serial # varieties.	FV	FV	27.50
	f. Sign. M. J. Phillips and B. W. Fraser. (1989).	FV	FV	25.00
	g. Sign. B. W. Fraser and C. I. Higgins. (1989).	FV	FV	45.00
	h. Sign. B. W. Fraser and A. S. Cole. (1991).	FV	FV	30.00
	i. Sign. B. W. Fraser and E. A. Evans. (1994).	FV	FV	32.50

		VG	VF	UNC
47	**50 DOLLARS** ND. (1973-94). Dk. brown on m/c unpt. Teaching implements at ctr., Lord H. W. Florey at r., I. Clunies-Ross at l., space research at ctr. on back.			
	a. Sign. J. G. Phillips and F. H. Wheeler. (1973).	FV	40.00	85.00
	b. Sign. H. M. Knight and F. H. Wheeler. (1975).	FV	37.50	110.00
	c. Sign. H. M. Knight and J. Stone. (1979).	FV	FV	80.00
	d. Sign. R. A. Johnston and J. Stone. (1983).	FV	FV	85.00
	e. Sign. R. A. Johnston and B. W. Fraser. (1985). 2 serial # varieties.	FV	FV	70.00
	f. Sign. M. J. Phillips and B. W. Fraser. (1989).	FV	FV	55.00
	g. Sign. B. W. Fraser and C. I. Higgins. (1989).	FV	FV	90.00
	h. Sign. B. W. Fraser and A. S. Cole. (1991).	FV	FV	50.00
	i. Sign. B. W. Fraser and E. A. Evans. (1994).	FV	FV	48.50

		VG	VF	UNC
48	**100 DOLLARS** ND (1984-92). Blue and gray on m/c unpt. Sir Douglas Mawson at ctr. J. Tebbutt at l. ctr. on back.			
	a. Sign. R. A. Johnston and J. Stone. (1984).	FV	FV	100.00
	b. Sign. R. A. Johnston and B. W. Fraser. (1985).	FV	FV	100.00
	c. Sign. B. W. Fraser and C. I. Higgins. (1990).	FV	FV	97.50
	d. Sign. B. W. Fraser and A. S. Cole. (1992).	FV	FV	110.00

NOTE: See also "Collector Series" following note listings.

NOTICE

Readers with unlisted dates, signature varieties, etc. are invited to submit photocopies of their notes to: Standard Catalog of World Paper Money, 700 East State St. Iola, WI 54990-0001, fax: 1-715-445-4087, or E-Mail: thernr@krause.com.

1988 ND COMMEMORATIVE ISSUE

#49 Bicentennial of British Settlement.

Polymer plastic. Printer: NPA.

		VG	VF	UNC
49	**10 DOLLARS** ND (1988). Brown and green on m/c unpt. Capt. Cook OVD at upper l., colonists across background; Cook's ship *Supply* at lower r. shoreline. Aboriginal youth, rock painting and ceremonial "Morning Star" pole at ctr. on back. Sign. R. A. Johnston and B. W. Fraser. Polymer plastic. Serial # prefix *AA* and *AB*	FV	FV	15.00

1992-96 ND ISSUES

#50-55 printed on polymer plastic. Printer: NPA.

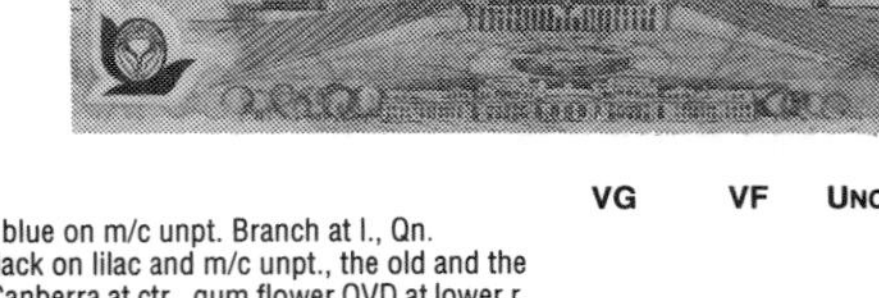

		VG	VF	UNC
50	**5 DOLLARS** ND (1992-). Black, red and blue on m/c unpt. Branch at l., Qn. Elizabeth II at ctr. r. Back black on lilac and m/c unpt., the old and the new Parliament Houses in Canberra at ctr., gum flower OVD at lower r.			
	a. Sign. B. W. Fraser and A. S. Cole.	FV	FV	6.00
	b. Sign. B. W. Fraser and E. A. Evans.	FV	FV	6.00

		VG	VF	UNC
51	**5 DOLLARS** ND (1995-). Black, red and bright purple. Like #50 but w/orientation bands in upper and lower margins, gum flower OVD at lower r. Back w/darker unpt. colors.			
	a. W/4 diagonal white lines. Sign. B. W. Fraser and E. A. Evans.	FV	FV	7.00
	b. As a. but w/11 diagonal white lines.	FV	FV	20.00
	c. Sign. I. Macfarlane and E. A. Evans.	FV	FV	6.00

		VG	VF	UNC
52	**10 DOLLARS** ND (1993-). Purple on dk. blue and m/c unpt. Man on horseback at l., "Banjo" Paterson at ctr., windmill OVD in transparent window at lower r. Dame M. Gilmore at ctr. r. on back.			
	a. Sign. B. W. Fraser and E. A. Evans.	FV	FV	9.00
	b. Sign. I. Macfarlane and E. A. Evans.	FV	FV	9.00

		VG	VF	UNC
53	**20 DOLLARS** ND (1994-). Black and red on orange and pale green unpt. Biplane at l., Rev. J. Flynn at ctr. r., camel back at r. Sailing ship at l., M. Reiby at ctr. on back. Compass OVD in transparent window at lower r.			
	a. Sign. B. W. Fraser and E. A. Evans.	FV	FV	20.00
	b. Sign. I. Macfarlane and E. A. Evans.	FV	FV	18.50

		VG	VF	UNC
54	**50 DOLLARS** ND (1995-). Black and deep purple on yellow-brown, green and m/c unpt. D. Unaipon at l. ctr., Mission Church at Point McLeay at lower l., patent drawings at upper ctr. r., Southern Cross constellation OVD in transparent window at lower r. Portr. E. Cowan, foster mother w/children at ctr., W. Australia's Parliament House at upper l., Cowan at lectern at r.			
	a. Sign. B. W. Fraser and E. A. Evans.	FV	FV	47.50
	b. Sign. I. Macfarlane and E. A. Evans.	FV	FV	45.00
55	**100 DOLLARS** ND (1996-). Black and green on orange and m/c unpt. Opera stage at l. Dame N. Melba at ctr., stylized peacock OVD in transparent window at lower r. Sir J. Monash and WWI battle scenes and insignia on back.			
	a. Sign. B. W. Fraser and E. A. Evans.	FV	FV	90.00
	b. Sign. I. Macfarlane and E. A. Evans.	FV	FV	87.50

COLLECTOR SERIES

AUSTRALIA, RESERVE BANK

Many varieties of products have been produced for collectors in the form of uncut sheets, special serial # prefixes, various coin fair ovpts., souvenir folders including coin and bank note sets too numerous to list. These are documented occasionally in *Australian Coin Review* by Michael Vort-Ronald.

1994 DATED ISSUE

		ISSUE PRICE	MKT. VALUE
CS50	**5 DOLLARS** ISSUE PRI 1992; 1994. Ovpt. on #50.		
	a. 7.7.1992.	—	8.50
	b. Sign. B. W. Fraser and E. A. Evans. Red serial #. (900). 1994.	32.00	75.00
	c. As. a. Black serial #. (9,000). 1994.	10.50	15.00

1994-97 DATED ISSUES

		ISSUE PRICE	MKT. VALUE
CS51	**5 DOLLARS** ISSUE PRI 1995-97. Ovpt. on #51.		
	a. Sign. B. W. Fraser and E. A. Evans. Red serial #. (900). 1995.	35.00	55.00
	b. Sign. as a. Black serial #. (9,000). 1995.	10.50	15.00
	c. As a. (900). 1996.	35.00	50.00
	d. As b. (8,000). 1996.	10.50	25.00
	e. Sign. I. Macfarlane and E. A. Evans. Red serial #. (900). 1997.	35.00	40.00
	f. Sign. as e. Black serial #. (7,000). 1997.	10.50	14.00
	g. As f. (900) 1998.	360.00	400.00
	h. As g. (2,000) 1998.	215.00	250.00
	i. As h. (900) 1999.	360.00	400.00
	j. As i. (1,200) 1999.	245.00	275.00
CS52	**10 DOLLARS** 1993-97. Ovpt. on #52.		
	a. Red serial #. 1993.	—	150.00
	b. Sign. B. W. Fraser and E. A. Evans. Red serial #. (900). 1994.	35.00	85.00
	c. Sign. as b. Blue serial #. (9,000). 1994.	14.00	20.00
	d. As b. (900). 1995.	45.00	70.00
	e. As c. (9,000). 1995.	14.00	20.00
	f. As b. (900). 1996.	45.00	55.00
	g. As c. (8,000). 1996.	14.00	20.00
	h. Sign. I. Macfarlane and E. A. Evans. Red serial #. (900). 1997.	45.00	45.00
	i. Sign. as h. Blue serial #. (7,000). 1997.	14.00	20.00
CS53	**20 DOLLARS** 1994-97. Ovpt. on #53.		
	a. Red serial #. 1994.	—	165.00
	b. Sign. B. W. Fraser and E. A. Evans. Red serial #. (900). 1995.	60.00	90.00
	c. Sign. as b. Black serial #. (6,000). 1995.	21.00	25.00
	d. As b. (900). 1996.	60.00	60.00
	e. As c. (6,000). 1996.	21.00	25.00
	f. Sign. I. Macfarlane and E. A. Evans. Red serial #. (900). 1997.	60.00	55.00
	g. Sign. as f. Black serial #. (6,000). 1997.	21.00	25.00
CS54	**50 DOLLARS** 1995-97. Ovpt. on #54.		
	a. 1995.	—	180.00
	b. Sign. B. W. Fraser and E. A. Evans. Red serial #. (900). 1996.	80.00	90.00
	c. Sign. as b. Black serial #. (4,000). 1996.	48.50	52.50
	d. Sign. I. Macfarlane and E. A. Evans. Red serial #. (900). 1997.	80.00	70.00
	e. Sign. as d. Black serial #. (4,000). 1997.	48.50	52.50
CS55	**100 DOLLARS** 1996; 1997. Ovpt. on #55.		
	a. Red serial #. 1996. (3,000).	—	200.00
	b. Sign. I. Macfarlane and E. A. Evans. Red serial #. (900). 1997.	115.00	120.00
	c. Sign. as b. Black serial #. (4,000). 1997.	90.00	75.00

The Republic of Austria (Oesterreich), a parliamentary democracy located in mountainous central Europe, has an area of 32,374 sq. mi. (83,849 sq. km.) and a population of 8 million. Capital: Vienna. Austria is primarily an industrial country. Machinery, iron and steel, textiles, yarns and timber are exported.

The territories later to be known as Austria were overrun in pre-Roman times by various tribes, including the Celts. Upon the fall of the Roman Empire, the country became a margravate of Charlemagne's Empire. Ottokar, King of Bohemia, gained possession in 1252, only to lose the territory to Rudolf of Habsburg in 1276. Thereafter, until World War I, the story of Austria was that of the ruling Habsburgs, German emperors from 1438-1806. From 1815-1867 it was a member of the "Deutsche Bund" (German Union).

During World War I, the Austro-Hungarian Empire was one of the Central Powers with Germany, Bulgaria and Turkey. At the end of the war, the Empire was dissolved and Austria established as an independent republic. In March 1938, Austria was incorporated into Hitler's short-lived German Third Reich. Allied forces of both East and West liberated Austria in April 1945, and subsequently divided it into four zones of military occupation. On May 15, 1955, the four powers formally recognized Austria as a "sovereign," independent democratic state.

MONETARY SYSTEM:

1 Schilling = 100 Groschen, 1945-

Republic

Oesterreichische Nationalbank

Austrian National Bank

1956-65 Issues

		VG	VF	Unc
136	**20 Schilling** 2.7.1956. Brown on red-brown and olive unpt. A. von Welsbach at r., arms at l. Village Maria Rain, Church and Karawanken mountains on back.	1.50	7.50	15.00

		VG	VF	Unc
137	**50 Schilling** 2.7.1962 (1963). Purple on m/c unpt. R. Wettstein at r., arms at bottom ctr. Mauterndorf castle in Salzburg on back.	3.00	9.00	20.00

		VG	VF	Unc
138	**100 Schilling** 1.7.1960 (1961). Dk. green on violet and m/c unpt. Violin and music at lower l., J. Strauss at r., arms at l. Schönbrunn Castle on back.	6.00	15.00	32.50

		VG	VF	Unc
139	**500 Schilling** 1.7.1965 (1966). Red-brown on m/c unpt. J. Ressel at r. Steam powered screw propeller ship *Civetta* at l., arms at lower r. on back.	45.00	60.00	90.00
140	**1000 Schilling** 2.1.1961 (1962). Dk. blue on m/c unpt. V. Kaplan at r. Dam and Persenburg Castle, arms at r. on back. 148 x 75mm.	350.00	800.00	1300.

NOTE: #140 was in use for only 11 weeks.

		VG	VF	Unc
141	**1000 Schilling** 2.1.1961 (1962). Dk. blue on m/c unpt. Like #140 but w/blue lined unpt. up to margin. 158 x 85mm.			
	a. Issued note.	35.00	90.00	185.00
	s. Specimen. Ovpt. and perforated: *Muster.*	—	—	1500.

1966-70 Issues

		VG	VF	Unc
142	**20 Schilling** 2.7.1967 (1968). Brown on olive and lilac unpt. C. Ritter von Ghega at r., arms at lower ctr. Semmering Railway bridge over the Semmering Pass (986 meters) on back.	2.00	2.75	4.50

		VG	VF	UNC
143	**50 SCHILLING** 2.1.1970 (1972). Purple on m/c unpt. F. Raimund at r., arms at l. Burg Theater in Vienna at l. ctr. on back.			
	a. Issued note.	4.50	6.00	12.00
	s. Specimen. Ovpt: *Muster.*	—	—	500.00

		VG	VF	UNC
144	**50 SCHILLING** 2.1.1970 (1983). Like #143 but w/ovpt. *2. AUFLAGE* (2nd issue) at lower l. ctr.	4.50	6.00	12.00

		VG	VF	UNC
145	**100 SCHILLING** 2.1.1969 (1970). Dk. green on m/c unpt. A. Kauffmann at r. Large house on back.			
	a. Issued note.	FV	11.00	22.50
	s. Specimen. Ovpt: *Muster.*	—	—	750.00

		VG	VF	UNC
146	**100 SCHILLING** 2.1.1969 (1981). Like #145 but w/ovpt: *2 AUFLAGE* (2nd issue) at upper l.	8.00	12.00	22.50

		VG	VF	UNC
147	**1000 SCHILLING** 1.7.1966 (1970). Blue-violet on m/c unpt. B. von Suttner at ctr. r., arms at r. Leopoldskron Castle and Hohensalzburg Fortress on back.			
	a. Issued note.	FV	90.00	150.00
	s. Specimen. Ovpt: *Muster.*	—	—	1250.

1983-88 ISSUE

#148-153 Federal arms at upper l. Wmk: Federal arms and parallel vertical lines.

		VG	VF	UNC
148	**20 SCHILLING** 1.10.1986 (1988). Dk. brown and brown on m/c unpt. M. Daffinger at r. Vienna's Albertina Museum at l. ctr. on back.	FV	FV	3.25

		VG	VF	UNC
149	**50 SCHILLING** 2.1.1986 (1987). Purple and violet on m/c unpt. S. Freud at r. Vienna's *Josephinum* Medical School at l. ctr. on back.	FV	FV	7.00

		VG	VF	UNC
150	**100 SCHILLING** 2.1.1984 (1985). Dk. green, gray and dk. brown on m/c unpt. E. Böhm v. Bawerk at r. Wissenschafften Academy in Vienna at l. ctr. on back. 3 serial # varieties.	FV	FV	13.50

		VG	VF	UNC
151	**500 SCHILLING** 1.7.1985 (1986). Dk. brown, deep violet and orange-brown on m/c unpt. Architect O. Wagner at r. Post Office Savings Bank in Vienna at l. ctr. on back.	FV	FV	65.00

		VG	VF	UNC
152	**1000 SCHILLING** 3.1.1983. Dk. blue and purple on m/c unpt. E. Schrödinger at r. Vienna University at l. ctr. on back.	FV	FV	110.00

		VG	VF	UNC
153	**5000 SCHILLING** 4.1.1988 (1989). Lt. brown and purple on m/c unpt. W. A. Mozart at r., kinegram of Mozart's head at lower l. Vienna Opera House at ctr. on back.	FV	FV	475.00

1997 ISSUE

		VG	VF	UNC
154	**500 SCHILLING** 1.1.1997. Brown on m/c unpt. Rosa Mayreder at l. Rosa and Karl Mayreder w/group at r. on back.	FV	FV	57.50

		VG	VF	UNC
155	**1000 SCHILLING** 1.1.1997. Blue on m/c unpt. K. Landsteiner at l. Landsteiner working in his laboratory in Licenter at r. on back.	FV	FV	110.00

The Republic of Azerbaijan includes the Nakhichevan Autonomous Republic and Nagorno-Karabakh Autonomous Region (which was abolished in 1991). Situated in the eastern area of Transcaucasia, it is bordered in the west by Armenia, in the north by Georgia and the Russian Federation of Dagestan, to the east by the Caspian Sea and to the south by Iran. It has an area of 33,430 sq. mi. (86,600 sq. km.) and a population of 7.43 million. Capital: Baku. The area is rich in mineral deposits of aluminum, copper, iron, lead, salt and zinc, with oil as its leading industry. Agriculture and livestock follow in importance.

In ancient times home of Scythian tribes and known under the Romans as Albania and to the Arabs as Arran, the country of Azerbaijan formed at the time of its invasion by Seljuk Turks a prosperous state under Persian suzerainty. From the 16th century the country was a theatre of fighting and political rivalry between Turkey, Persia and later Russia. Baku was first annexed to Russia by Czar Peter I in 1723. After the Russian retreat in 1735, the whole of Azerbaijan north of the Aras River became a khanate under Persian control until 1813 when annexed by Czar Alexander I into the Russian empire.

Until the Russian Revolution of 1905 there was no political life in Azerbaijan. A Mussavat (Equality) party was formed in 1911. After the Russian Revolution of March 1917, the party started a campaign for independence, but Baku, the capital, with its mixed population, constituted an alien enclave in the country. While a national Azerbaijani government was established at Gandzha (Elizavetpol), a Communist-controlled council assumed power at Baku. The Gandzha government joined first, on Sept. 20, 1917, a Transcaucasian federal republic, but on May 28, 1918, proclaimed the independence of Azerbaijan. On June 4, 1918, at Batum, a peace treaty was signed with Turkey and a Turko-Azerbaijani force started an offensive against Baku, but it was occupied on Aug. 17, 1918 by 1,400 British troops coming by sea from Anzali, Persia. On Sept. 14 the British evacuated Baku, returning to Anzali, and three days later the Azerbaijan government, headed by Fath Ali Khan Khoysky, established itself at Baku.

After the collapse of the Ottoman empire the British returned to Baku, at first ignoring the Azerbaijan government. A general election with universal suffrage for the Azerbaijan constituent assembly took place on Dec. 7, 1918 and out of 120 members there were 84 Mussavat supporters; Ali Marden Topchibashev was elected speaker, and Nasib Usubekov formed a new government. On Jan. 15, 1920, the Allied powers recognized Azerbaijan de facto but on April 27 of the same year the Red army invaded the country and a Soviet Republic of Azerbaijan was proclaimed the next day.

The Azerbaijan Communist party held its first congress at Baku in Feb. 1920. From 1921 to 1925 its first secretary was a Russian, S.M. Kirov, who directed a mass deportation to Siberia of about 120,000 Azerbaijani "nationalist deviationists," among them the country's first two premiers. Later it became a member of the Transcaucasian Federation joining the U.S.S.R. on Dec. 30, 1922. It became a self-constituent republic in 1936.

In 1990 it adopted a declaration of republican sovereignty, and in Aug. 1991 declared itself formally independent; this was approved by a vote of referendum in Jan. 1992.

The Armed forces of Azerbaijan and the Armenian separatists of the Armenian ethnic enclave of Nagurno-Karabakh supported in all spheres by Armenia fought over the control of the enclave in 1992-94. A cease-fire was declared in May 1994 with Azerbaijan actually losing control over the territory. A Treaty of Friendship and Cooperation w/Russia was signed on 3 July 1997.

REPUBLIC

AZERBAYCAN MILLI BANKI

1992 ND ISSUE

#11-13 Maiden Tower at ctr. Wmk: 3 flames.

		VG	VF	UNC
11	**1 MANAT** ND (1992). Deep olive-green on m/c unpt.	.10	.50	1.50
12	**10 MANAT** ND (1992). Deep brown-violet on m/c unpt.	.20	1.00	3.50

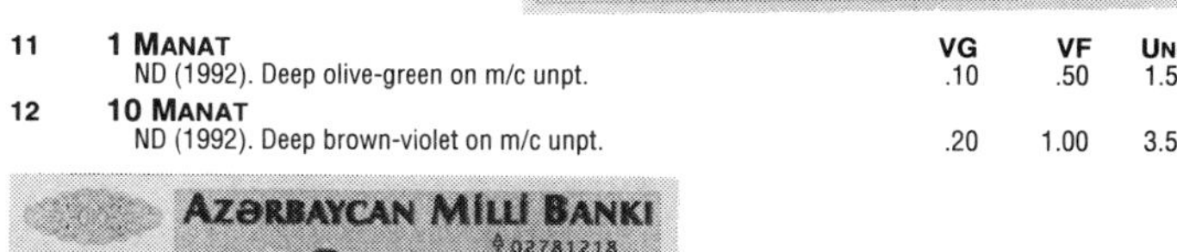

		VG	VF	UNC
13	**250 MANAT** ND (1992). Deep blue-gray on m/c unpt.	1.50	10.00	40.00

1993 ND; 1994-95 ISSUE

#14-20 ornate "value" backs. Wmk: 3 flames.

#14-18 different view Maiden Tower ruins at ctr.

		VG	VF	UNC
14	**1 MANAT** ND (1993). Deep blue and tan on dull orange and green unpt.	FV	FV	1.00

		VG	VF	UNC
15	**5 MANAT** ND (1993). Deep brown and pale purple on lilac and m/c unpt.	FV	FV	1.50

		VG	VF	UNC
16	**10 MANAT** ND (1993). Deep grayish blue-green on pale blue and m/c unpt.	FV	FV	1.65

		VG	VF	UNC
17	**50 MANAT** ND (1993). Brownish red and tan on ochre and m/c unpt.	FV	FV	3.00

		VG	VF	UNC
18	**100 MANAT** ND (1993). Red-violet and pale blue on m/c unpt.	FV	FV	4.50

		VG	VF	UNC
19	**500 MANAT** ND (1993). Deep brown on pale blue, pink and m/c unpt. Portr. N. Gencevi at r.	FV	FV	8.50

		VG	VF	UNC
20	**1000 MANAT** ND (1993). Dk. brown and blue on pink and m/c unpt. M. E. Resulzado at r.	FV	FV	6.00

		VG	VF	UNC
21	**10,000 MANAT** 1994. Dull dk. brown and pale violet on m/c unpt. Shirvansha's Palace at ctr. r. Wmk: AMB repeated.			
	a. Security thread.	FV	FV	30.00
	b. Segmented foil over security thread.	FV	FV	10.00

		VG	VF	UNC
22	**50,000 MANAT** 1995. Blue-green on m/c unpt. Mausoleum in Nachziban at ctr. r. Carpet design at l. on back. Segmented foil over security thread.	FV	FV	25.00

BAHAMAS

The Commonwealth of The Bahamas is an archipelago of about 3,000 islands, cays and rocks located in the Atlantic Ocean east of Florida and north of Cuba. The total land area of the 800-mile (1.287 km.) long chain of islands is 5,380 sq. mi. (13,935 sq. km.). They have a population of 284,000. Capital: Nassau. The Bahamas imports most of their food and manufactured products and exports cement, refined oil, pulpwood and lobsters. Tourism is the principal industry.

The Bahamas were discovered by Columbus in October, 1492, but Spain made no attempt to settle them. British influence began in 1626 when Charles I granted them to the lord proprietors of Carolina. They continued under British proprietors until 1717, when the civil and military governments were surrendered to the King and the islands designated a British Crown Colony. The Bahamas obtained complete internal self-government under the constitution of Jan. 7, 1964. Full independence was achieved on July 10, 1973. The Bahamas is a member of the Commonwealth of Nations. Elizabeth II is Head of State, as Queen of the Bahamas.

RULERS:

British

MONETARY SYSTEM:

1 Shilling = 12 Pence
1 Pound = 20 Shillings to 1966
1 Dollar = 100 Cents 1966-

COMMONWEALTH

GOVERNMENT OF THE BAHAMAS

1965 CURRENCY NOTE ACT

#17-25 Qn. Elizabeth II at l. Sign. varieties. Arms at r. on back. Wmk: Shellfish. Printer: TDLR. Replacement notes: Serial # prefix *Z*.

		VG	VF	UNC
17	**1/2 DOLLAR** *L.1965.* Purple on m/c unpt. Straw market on back.	.75	1.35	7.00

		VG	VF	UNC
18	**1 DOLLAR** *L.1965.* Green on m/c unpt. Sea garden on back.			
	a. 2 sign.	1.35	3.00	32.50
	b. 3 sign.	1.50	5.00	40.00

		VG	VF	UNC
19	**3 DOLLARS** *L.1965.* Red on m/c unpt. Paradise Beach on back.			
	a. Sign. Sands and Higgs.	4.00	7.50	25.00
	b. Sign. Francis and Higgs. Specimen.	—	—	225.00

		VG	VF	UNC
20	**5 DOLLARS** *L.1965.* Green on m/c unpt. Government House on back.	8.00	17.50	100.00
21	**5 DOLLARS** *L.1965.* Orange on m/c unpt. Like #20.			
	a. 2 sign.	10.00	30.00	250.00
	b. 3 sign.	15.00	65.00	450.00

		VG	VF	UNC
22	**10 DOLLARS** *L.1965.* Dk. blue on m/c unpt. Flamingos on back.			
	a. 2 sign.	15.00	55.00	450.00
	b. 3 sign.	25.00	150.00	850.00
23	**20 DOLLARS** *L.1965.* Dk. brown on m/c unpt. Surrey on back.			
	a. Issued note.	50.00	200.00	625.00
	s. Specimen. 3 sign.	—	—	—
24	**50 DOLLARS** *L.1965.* Brown on m/c unpt. Produce market on back.			
	a. Issued note.	100.00	300.00	1500.
	s. Specimen. 3 sign.	—	—	—
25	**100 DOLLARS** *L.1965.* Blue on m/c unpt. Deep sea fishing on back.			
	a. Issued note.	200.00	600.00	2500.
	s. Specimen. 3 sign.	—	—	—

BAHAMAS MONETARY AUTHORITY

1968 MONETARY AUTHORITY ACT

#26-33 Qn. Elizabeth II at l. Arms at r. on back. Wmk: Shellfish. Printer: TDLR. Replacement notes: Serial # prefix *Z*.

		VG	VF	UNC
26	**1/2 DOLLAR** *L.1968.* Purple on m/c unpt. Back similar to #17.	.65	1.25	4.50

		VG	VF	UNC
27	**1 DOLLAR** *L.1968.* Green on m/c unpt. Back similar to #18.	1.25	2.25	15.00

		VG	VF	UNC
28	**3 DOLLARS** *L.1968.* Red on m/c unpt. Back similar to #19.	3.50	5.50	20.00

		VG	VF	UNC
29	**5 DOLLARS** *L.1968.* Orange on m/c unpt. Back similar to #20.	7.00	50.00	175.00
30	**10 DOLLARS** *L.1968.* Dk. blue on m/c unpt. Back similar to #22.	22.50	100.00	585.00

		VG	VF	UNC
31	**20 DOLLARS** *L.1968.* Dk. brown on m/c unpt. Back similar to #23.	60.00	300.00	1000.
32	**50 DOLLARS** *L.1968.* Brown on m/c unpt. Back similar to #24.	150.00	450.00	1800.
33	**100 DOLLARS** *L.1968.* Blue on m/c unpt. Back similar to #25.	300.00	700.00	2850.

#34 not assigned.

CENTRAL BANK OF THE BAHAMAS

1974 CENTRAL BANK ACT

#35-41 Qn. Elizabeth II at l. Arms at r. on back. Wmk: Shellfish. Printer: TDLR. Replacement notes: Serial # prefix *Z*.

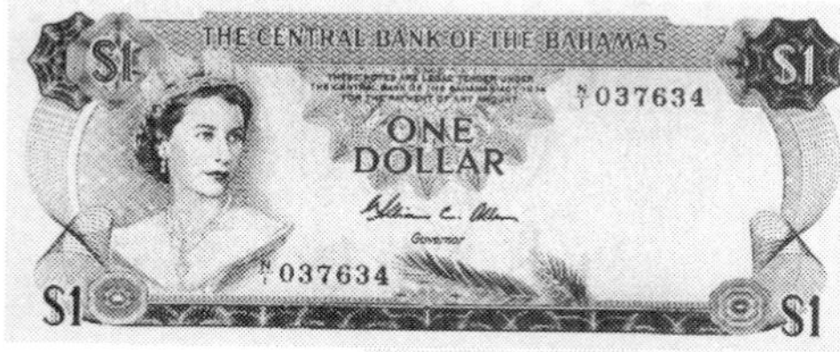

		VG	VF	UNC
35	**1 DOLLAR** *L.1974.* Dk. blue-green on m/c unpt. Back similar to #27.			
	a. Sign. T. B. Donaldson.	1.25	2.00	15.00
	b. Sign. W. C. Allen.	1.50	7.50	25.00

		VG	VF	UNC
37	**5 DOLLARS** *L.1974.* Orange on m/c unpt. Back similar to #29.			
	a. Sign. T. B. Donaldson.	6.50	18.50	65.00
	b. Sign. W. C. Allen.	10.00	65.00	285.00

		VG	VF	UNC
38	**10 DOLLARS** *L.1974.* Dk. blue on m/c unpt. Back similar to #30.			
	a. Sign. T. B. Donaldson.	11.00	35.00	225.00
	b. Sign. W. C. Allen.	20.00	125.00	500.00

		VG	VF	UNC
39	**20 DOLLARS** *L.1974.* Dk. brown on m/c unpt. Back similar to #31.			
	a. Sign. T. B. Donaldson.	27.50	85.00	335.00
	b. Sign. W. C. Allen.	42.50	185.00	700.00
40	**50 DOLLARS** *L.1974.* Brown on m/c unpt. Back similar to #32.			
	a. Sign. T. B. Donaldson.	75.00	150.00	685.00
	b. Sign. W. C. Allen.	85.00	275.00	1250.
41	**100 DOLLARS** *L.1974.* Blue on m/c unpt. Back similar to #33.			
	a. Sign. T. B. Donaldson.	135.00	300.00	1600.
	b. Sign. W. C. Allen.	165.00	425.00	1850.

1974 CENTRAL BANK ACT; 1984 ND ISSUE

#42-49 map at l., mature portr. Qn. Elizabeth II at ctr. r. Arms at r. on back. Wmk: Sailing ship. Printer: TDLR. Replacement notes: Serial # prefix *Z*.

		VG	VF	UNC
42	**1/2 DOLLAR** *L.1974* (1984). Green on m/c unpt. Baskets at l. Sister Sarah in Nassau market on back. Sign. W. C. Allen.	FV	FV	1.50

		VG	VF	UNC
43	**1 DOLLAR** *L.1974* (1984). Deep green on m/c unpt. Fish at l. Royal Bahamas Police band at ctr. on back.			
	a. Sign. W. C. Allen.	FV	FV	4.00
	b. Sign. F. H. Smith.	FV	FV	3.50

		VG	VF	UNC
44	**3 DOLLARS** *L.1974* (1984). Red-violet on m/c unpt. Paradise Beach at l. Family Island sailing regatta on back. Sign. W. C. Allen.	FV	FV	6.00

		VG	VF	UNC
45	**5 DOLLARS** *L.1974* (1984). Orange on m/c unpt. Statue at l. Local dancers *Junkanoo* at ctr.			
	a. Sign. W. C. Allen.	FV	7.50	30.00
	b. Sign. F. H. Smith. 2 horizontal serial #.	FV	6.00	22.50
46	**10 DOLLARS** *L.1974* (1984). Pale blue on m/c unpt. 2 flamingos at l. Lighthouse and Abaco Settlement on back.			
	a. Sign. W. C. Allen.	FV	12.00	35.00
	b. Sign. F. H. Smith. 2 horizontal serial #.	FV	20.00	65.00

		VG	VF	UNC
47	**20 DOLLARS** *L.1974* (1984). Red and black on m/c unpt. Horse and carriage at l. Nassau harbor on back.			
	a. Sign. W. C. Allen.	FV	25.00	110.00
	b. Sign. F. H. Smith. 2 horizontal serial #.	FV	22.50	55.00

		VG	VF	UNC
48	**50 DOLLARS** *L.1974* (1984). Purple, orange and green on m/c unpt. Lighthouse at l. Central Bank on back.			
	a. Sign. W. C. Allen.	FV	65.00	185.00
	b. Sign. F. H. Smith. 2 horizontal serial #.	60.00	100.00	450.00
49	**100 DOLLARS** *L.1974* (1984). Purple, deep blue and red-violet on m/c unpt. Sailboat at l. Blue marlin on back. Sign. W. C. Allen.	FV	125.00	425.00

1992 COMMEMORATIVE ISSUE

#50, Quincentennial of First Landfall by Christopher Columbus

		VG	VF	UNC
50	**1 DOLLAR** ND (1992). Dk. blue and deep violet on m/c unpt. Commercial seal at l., bust of C. Columbus r. w/compass face behind. Birds, lizard, islands outlined, ships across back w/arms at lower r. Printer: CBNC.	FV	FV	2.75

1974 CENTRAL BANK ACT; 1992-95 ND ISSUE

#51-56 arms at r. on back. Wmk: Caravel sailing ship. Sign. F.H. Smith.

		VG	VF	UNC
51	**1 DOLLAR** *L.1974* (1992). Deep green on m/c unpt. Like #43b but w/serial # vertical and horizontal. Printer: BABN.	FV	FV	3.00
52	**5 DOLLARS** *L.1974* (1995). Dk. brown, brown and orange on m/c unpt. Statue of Columbus at l., Wallace-Whitfield at r. Back like #45. Printer: TDLR.	FV	FV	15.00

		VG	VF	UNC
53	**10 DOLLARS** *L.1974* (1992). Pale blue on m/c unpt. Like #46b but w/serial # vertical and horizontal. Printer: CBNC.	FV	12.50	30.00

#54-56 printer: TDLR.

54	**20 DOLLARS** *L.1974* (1993). Black and red on m/c unpt. Sir M. B. Butler at r., horse drawn surrey at l. Aerial view of ships in Nassau's harbor at ctr.	FV	FV	42.50

		VG	VF	UNC
55	**50 DOLLARS** *L.1974* (1992). Brown, blue-green and orange on m/c unpt. Like #48b but w/serial # vertical and horizontal.	FV	FV	115.00

		VG	VF	UNC
56	**100 DOLLARS** *L.1974* (1992). Purple, deep blue and red-violet on m/c unpt. Like #49 but w/serial # vertical and horizontal.	FV	FV	225.00

1974 CENTRAL BANK ACT; 1996 ISSUE

#57, 59, 61, and 62 mature bust of Qn. Elizabeth II. Ascending size serial # at lower l. Arms at r. on back. Sign. F. H. Smith.

		VG	VF	UNC
57	**1 DOLLAR** 1996. Deep green on m/c unpt. Like #51. Printer: BABN.	FV	FV	2.75

#58 *Deleted.* See #63.

		VG	VF	UNC
59	**10 DOLLARS** 1996. Deep blue-green, green and violet on m/c unpt. Like #53. Printer: TDLR.	FV	FV	18.50

#60 not assigned.

		VG	VF	UNC
61	**50 DOLLARS** 1996. Red-brown and deep green on m/c unpt. Like #55. Printer: TDLR.	FV	FV	75.00

NOTE: The following notes were stolen and are not redeemable. Serial # G101,001-103,000; G104,001-G105,000; G108,001-G109,000.

		VG	VF	UNC
62	**100 DOLLARS** 1996. Purple, deep blue and violet on m/c unpt. Like #56. Printer: BABN.	FV	FV	150.00

NOTE: The following notes were stolen and are not redeemable. Serial # G541,001-G548,000.

1974 CENTRAL BANK ACT; 1997 ISSUE

Series #'s vertical and horizontal (Ascending horizontal).

		VG	VF	UNC
63	**5 DOLLARS** 1997. Dk. brown, brown and orange on m/c unpt. Like #52. Printer: TDLR. 2 sign. varieties.	FV	FV	10.00
64	**20 DOLLARS** 1997. M/c. 2 sign. varieties.	FV	FV	35.00

COLLECTOR SERIES

BAHAMAS GOVERNMENT

1965 ISSUE

		ISSUE PRICE	MKT. VALUE
CS1	**1/2-100 DOLLARS** *L.1965.* #17-25 ovpt: *SPECIMEN.* (100 sets).	—	2100.

BAHAMAS MONETARY AUTHORITY

1968 ISSUES

		ISSUE PRICE	MKT. VALUE
CS2	**1/2-100 DOLLARS** *L.1968.* #26-33 ovpt: *SPECIMEN.*	—	325.00
CS3	**1/2-100 DOLLARS** *L.1968.* #26-33 ovpt: *SPECIMEN*, punched hole cancelled.	60.00	90.00

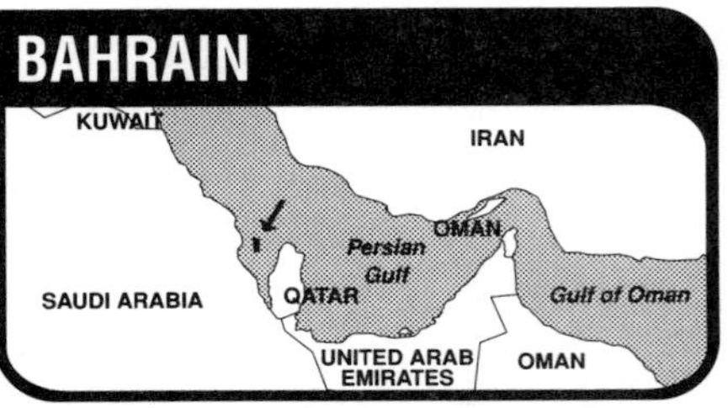

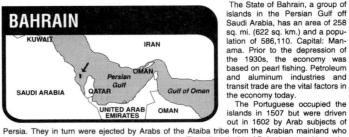

The State of Bahrain, a group of islands in the Persian Gulf off Saudi Arabia, has an area of 258 sq. mi. (622 sq. km.) and a population of 586,110. Capital: Manama. Prior to the depression of the 1930s, the economy was based on pearl fishing. Petroleum and aluminum industries and transit trade are the vital factors in the economy today.

The Portuguese occupied the islands in 1507 but were driven out in 1602 by Arab subjects of Persia. They in turn were ejected by Arabs of the Ataiba tribe from the Arabian mainland who have maintained possession up to the present time. The ruling sheikh of Bahrain entered into relations with Great Britain in 1805 and concluded a binding treaty of protection in 1861. In 1968 Great Britain decided to terminate treaty relations with the Persian Gulf sheikhdoms. Unable to agree on terms of union with the other sheikhdoms, Bahrain decided to seek independence as a separate entity and became fully independent on August 15, 1971.

RULERS:

Isa Bin Sulman al-Khalifa, 1961-

MONETARY SYSTEM:

1 Dinar = 1000 Fils

STATE

BAHRAIN CURRENCY BOARD

AUTHORIZATION 6/1964

#1-6 dhow at l., arms at r. Wmk: Falcon's head.

		VG	VF	UNC
1	**100 FILS** *L.1964.* Ochre on m/c unpt. Palm trees on back.	.25	1.00	6.00

		VG	VF	UNC
2	**1/4 DINAR** *L.1964.* Brown on m/c unpt. Oil derricks on back.	.50	1.50	9.00

		VG	VF	UNC
3	**1/2 DINAR** *L.1964.* Purple on m/c unpt. Ships on back.	.75	2.00	8.00

		VG	VF	UNC
4	**1 DINAR** *L.1964.* Reddish brown on m/c unpt. Minarets on back.	1.50	4.50	13.00

		VG	VF	UNC
5	**5 DINARS** *L.1964.* Blue black on m/c unpt. Dhows on back.	15.00	60.00	150.00

		VG	VF	UNC
6	**10 DINARS** *L.1964.* Green on m/c unpt. Aerial view of Manama at ctr. on back.	20.00	37.50	100.00

BAHRAIN MONETARY AGENCY

AUTHORIZATION 23/1973

#7-11 map at l., dhow at ctr., arms at r. Wmk: Falcon's head.

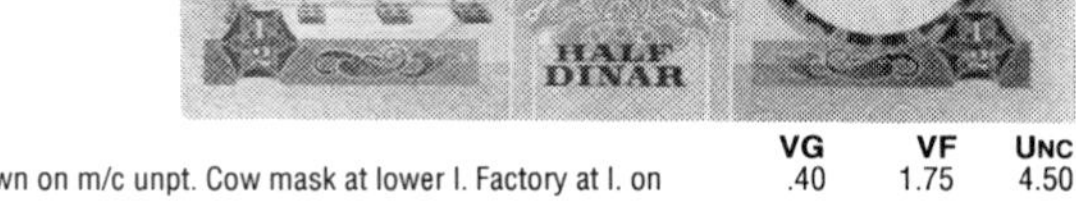

		VG	VF	UNC
7	**1/2 DINAR** *L.1973.* Brown on m/c unpt. Cow mask at lower l. Factory at l. on back.	.40	1.75	4.50

		VG	VF	UNC
8	**1 DINAR** *L.1973.* Red on m/c unpt. Tower at l. Bahrain Monetary Agency bldg. at l. on back.	.80	3.25	7.00

		VG	VF	UNC
8A	**5 DINARS** *L.1973.* Blue black on m/c unpt. Mosque at l. Pearl fishing scene at l. on back.	1.50	6.00	30.00

		VG	VF	UNC
9	**10 DINARS** *L.1973.* Green on m/c unpt. Wind tower at l. Dry dock at l. on back.			
	a. 2 horizontal serial #.	7.50	30.00	50.00
	b. Serial # vertical and horizontal.	8.50	35.00	60.00

		VG	VF	UNC
10	**20 DINARS** *L.1973.* Reddish-brown on m/c unpt. Tower at l. Modern bldg. at l. on back.	21.50	85.00	185.00

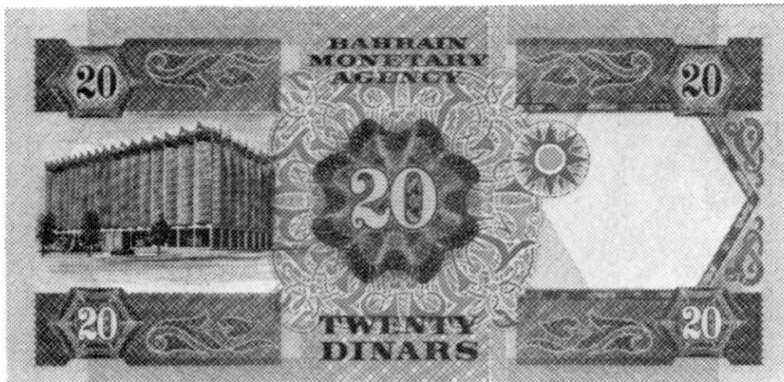

11	20 DINARS	VG	VF	UNC
	L.1973. Face like #10, but w/symbol changed at r. of map. Silvering added at lower l. denomination. Back has open frame and symbol around wmk. area. Also various color differences.			
	a. 2 horizontal serial #.	20.00	60.00	90.00
	b. Serial # vertical and horizontal.	20.00	65.00	100.00

AUTHORIZATION 23/1973; 1993 ND ISSUE

#12-16 arms at ctr., outline map at l. Wmk: Antelope's head.

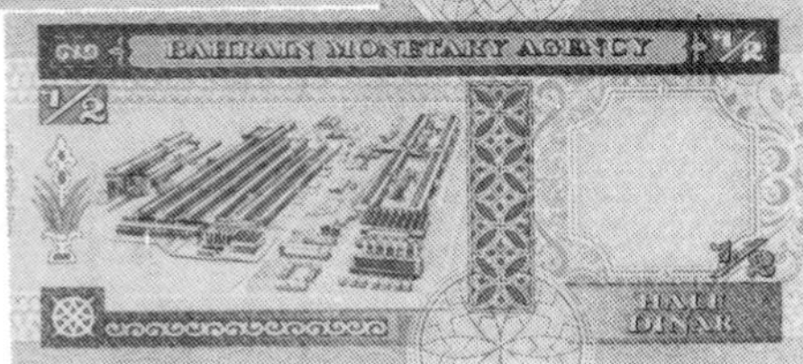

12	1/2 DINAR	VG	VF	UNC
	L.1973 (1993). Deep brown, violet and brown orange w/red shield at ctr. on m/c unpt. Man weaving at r. "Aluminum Bahrain" facility at l. ctr. on back.	FV	1.50	3.75

13	1 DINAR	VG	VF	UNC
	L.1973 (1993). Violet and red-orange on m/c unpt. Ancient Dilmun seal at r. Bahrain Monetary Agency bldg. at l. ctr. on back.	FV	FV	6.50

14	5 DINARS	VG	VF	UNC
	L.1973 (1993). Blue-black and deep blue-green on m/c unpt. Riffa Fortress at r. Bahrain International Airport at l. ctr. on back.	FV	FV	26.50

15	10 DINARS	VG	VF	UNC
	L.1973 (1993). Deep olive-green and green on m/c unpt. Dhow at r. Aerial view of Kg. Fahad Causeway at l. ctr. on back.	FV	FV	48.50

16	20 DINARS	VG	VF	UNC
	L.1973 (1993). Purple and violet m/c unpt. Bab al-Bahrain gate at r. Ahmed al-Fateh Islamic Center at l. ctr. on back.	—	—	100.00

NOTE: A second printing was ordered w/o authorization. They are easily distinguished by a space between the 2 Arabic letters in the serial # prefix and are not redeemable. Value approximately $85.00.

AUTHORIZATION 23/1973; 1996 ND ISSUE

17	1/2 DINAR	VG	VF	UNC
	L.1973 (1996). Deep brown, violet and brown w/deep brown shield at ctr. Like #12.	FV	FV	3.50

AUTHORIZATION 23/1973; 1998 ND ISSUE

#18-20 arms at lower ctr., hologram at lower l.

		VG	VF	UNC
18	5 DINARS *L.1973* (1998). Blue on m/c unpt. Like #14.	FV	FV	25.00
19	10 DINARS *L.1973* (1998). Green on m/c unpt. Like #15.	FV	FV	45.00
20	20 DINARS *L.1973* (1998). Orange on m/c unpt. Like #16.	FV	FV	85.00

COLLECTOR SERIES

CS1	100 FILS - 20 DINARS	ISSUE PRICE	MKT. VALUE
	ND (1978). #1-6 and 10 w/ovpt: *SPECIMEN* and Maltese cross serial # prefix.	14.00	50.00

BANGLADESH

NEPAL CHINA BHUTAN CHINA INDIA MYANMAR Bay of Bengal LAOS

The Peoples Republic of Bangladesh (formerly East Pakistan), a parliamentary democracy located on the Bay of Bengal bordered by India and Burma, has an area of 55,598 sq. mi. (143,998 sq. km.) and a population of 124.34 million. Capital: Dacca. The economy is predominantly agricultural. Jute products and tea are exported.

British rule over the vast Indian sub-continent ended in 1947 when British India attained independence and was partitioned into the two successor states of India and Pakistan. Pakistan consisted of East and West Pakistan, two areas united by the Moslem religion but separated by culture and 1,000 miles of Indian territory. Restive under the de facto rule of the militant but fewer West Pakistanis, the East Pakistanis unsuccessfully demanded greater economic benefits and political reforms. The inability of the leaders of East and West Pakistan to resolve a political breakdown occasioned by the East Pakistan success in the general elections of 1970 precipitated massive civil disobedience n East Pakistan which West Pakistan sought to suppress militarily. East Pakistan seceded from Pakistan, March 26, 1971, and with the support of India declared an independent Peoples Republic of Bangladesh led by Mujibur Rahman who was later assassinated on Aug. 15, 1975. Bangladesh is a member of the Commonwealth of Nations. The president is the Head of State and of Government.

MONETARY SYSTEM:

1 Rupee = 100 Paise to 1972
1 Taka = 100 Paisas 1972-

REPUBLIC

PEOPLES REPUBLIC OF BANGLADESH

1971 ND PROVISIONAL ISSUE

#1-3 w/*BANGLADESH* ovpt. in English or Bengali on Pakistan notes. The Bangladesh Bank never officially issued any Pakistan notes w/ovpt. These are considered locally issued by some authorities.

		VG	VF	UNC
1	**1 RUPEE** ND (1971). Blue. Purple ovpt. *BANGLADESH* on Pakistan #9.	10.00	30.00	90.00

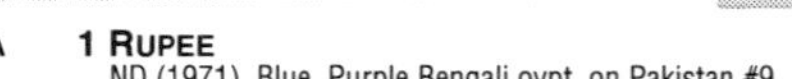

		VG	VF	UNC
1A	**1 RUPEE** ND (1971). Blue. Purple Bengali ovpt. on Pakistan #9.	10.00	30.00	90.00

		VG	VF	UNC
2	**5 RUPEES** ND (1971). Brown-violet. Purple Bengali ovpt. on Pakistan #15.	10.00	32.50	100.00

		VG	VF	UNC
3	**10 RUPEES** ND (1971). Brown. Purple Bengali ovpt. on Pakistan #13.	10.00	35.00	120.00

1972-89 ND ISSUES

		VG	VF	UNC
4	**1 TAKA** ND (1972). Brown. Map of Bangladesh at l.	.35	1.00	3.75

		VG	VF	UNC
5	**1 TAKA** ND (1973). Violet and ochre. Hand holding rice plants at l. Arms at r. on back.			
	a. W/wmk.	.25	.75	2.75
	b. W/o wmk. (different sign.).	.25	.75	2.50

		VG	VF	UNC
6	**1 TAKA** ND (1974). Violet. Woman preparing grain at l. Hand holding rice plants at ctr., arms at r. on back.	.20	.50	1.75

		VG	VF	UNC
6A	**1 TAKA** ND (1980). Purple on m/c. unpt. Arms at r. Deer at l. ctr. on back.	.10	.35	1.50

		VG	VF	UNC
6B	**1 TAKA** ND (1984). Purple on m/c unpt. Similar to #6A but no printing on wmk. area at l. Modified tiger wmk.	.05	.10	.50

		VG	VF	UNC
6C	**2 TAKA** ND (1989). Gray-green on orange and green unpt. Monument at r. Bird on branch at l. on back. 2 sign. varieties.	FV	FV	.50

BANGLADESH BANK

1972 ND ISSUE

#7-9 map of Bangladesh at l., portr. Mujibur Rahman at r.

		VG	VF	UNC
7	**5 TAKA** ND (1972). Purple on m/c unpt.	.50	1.50	7.50

		VG	VF	UNC
8	**10 TAKA** ND (1972). Blue on m/c unpt.	1.00	3.00	10.00

		VG	VF	UNC
9	**100 TAKA** ND (1972). Green on m/c unpt.	2.00	7.50	22.50

1973 ND ISSUE

#10-12 Mujibur Rahman at l. Wmk: Tiger's head.

		VG	VF	UNC
10	**5 TAKA** ND (1973). Red on m/c unpt. Lotus plants at ctr. r. on back.	.35	1.50	5.00

NOTICE

Readers with unlisted dates, signature varieties, etc. are invited to submit photocopies of their notes to: Standard Catalog of World Paper Money, 700 East State St. Iola, WI 54990-0001, fax: 1-715-445-4087, or E-Mail: thernr@krause.com.

		VG	VF	UNC
11	**10 TAKA** ND (1973). Green on m/c unpt. River scene on back.			
	a. Serial # in Western numerals.	.50	2.50	10.00

		VG	VF	UNC
	b. Serial # in Bengali numerals.	.50	1.75	7.00

		VG	VF	UNC
12	**100 TAKA** ND (1973). Brown on m/c unpt. River scene on back.	.75	3.00	10.00

1974 ND ISSUE

#13-14 Mujibur Rahman at r. Wmk: Tiger's head.

		VG	VF	UNC
13	**5 TAKA** ND (1974). Red on m/c unpt. Aerial view of factory on back.	.25	.75	4.00

		VG	VF	UNC
14	**10 TAKA** ND (1974). Green on m/c unpt. *Atiya Jam-e* mosque in Tangali at r. Rice harvesting scene at l. ctr. on back.	.50	1.50	7.50

1976; 1977 ND ISSUE

#15-17, 19 Star mosque in Dhaka at r. Wmk: Tiger's head.

		VG	VF	UNC
15	**5 TAKA** ND (1977). Lt. brown on m/c unpt. Back like #13.	.15	.35	3.00

		VG	VF	UNC
16	**10 TAKA** ND (1977). Purple on m/c unpt. Back like #14.	.25	.75	5.00

		VG	VF	UNC
17	**50 TAKA** ND (1976). Orange. Harvesting scene on back.	1.00	3.00	7.50

		VG	VF	UNC
18	**100 TAKA** ND (1976). Blue-violet on m/c unpt. Star mosque in Dhaka at l. Back like #12. Wmk: Tiger's head.	3.00	7.50	17.50

		VG	VF	UNC
19	**500 TAKA** ND (1977). Blue and lilac on m/c unpt. High Court in Dhaka on back.	12.50	30.00	135.00

1978-82 ND ISSUE

#20-24 wmk: Tiger's head.

		VG	VF	UNC
20	**5 TAKA** ND (1978). Lt. brown on m/c unpt. Doorway of *Kushumba* mosque at r. Back like #14.	.20	.50	2.00

		VG	VF	UNC
21	**10 TAKA** ND (1978). Purple on m/c unpt. *Atiya Jam-e* mosque in Tangali at r. Back like #14.	.25	.75	3.50

		VG	VF	UNC
22	**20 TAKA** ND (1980). Blue-green on m/c unpt. *Chote Sona* mosque at r. Harvesting scene on back.	.50	1.50	5.00

		VG	VF	UNC
23	**50 TAKA** ND (1980). Orange on m/c unpt. Bldg. at r. Women harvesting on back.	.75	2.00	8.00

		VG	VF	UNC
24	**100 TAKA** ND (1982). Blue-violet, deep brown and orange on m/c unpt. Star mosque in Dhaka at r. Unpt. throughout wmk. area at l. Ruins of Lalbagh Fort at l. ctr. on back.	1.25	5.00	14.00

1982-88 ND ISSUE

#25-32 wmk: Modified tiger's head. Sign. varieties.

		VG	VF	UNC
25	**5 TAKA** ND (1983). Similar to #20 but w/o printing on wmk. area at l. on face.			
	a. Black sign. Lg. serial #.	.15	.30	1.35
	b. Black sign. Sm. serial #.	FV	.15	1.10
	c. Brown sign. Sm. serial #.	FV	FV	.60

		VG	VF	UNC
26	**10 TAKA** ND (1982). Violet and red-violet on m/c unpt. Atiya Jam-e mosque in Tangali at r. Hydroelectric dam at l. ctr. on back. 3 sign. varieties.			
	a. W/curved line of text above and below mosque.	.30	.50	2.50

		VG	VF	UNC
	b. W/o curved line of text above mosque.	FV	.40	1.25

		VG	VF	UNC
27	**20 TAKA** ND (1988). Blue-green on m/c unpt. W/o printing on wmk. area.			
	a. Black sign. Lg. serial #.	FV	FV	2.75
	b. Green sign. Sm. serial #.	FV	FV	2.25

		VG	VF	UNC
28	**50 TAKA** ND (1986). Black, red and deep green on m/c unpt. National Monument at Savar at ctr. National Assembly bldg. at ctr. on back.	FV	FV	5.00

		VG	VF	UNC
29	**100 TAKA** ND (1984). Blue-violet, deep brown and orange on m/c unpt. W/o printing on wmk. area at l. on face.	FV	FV	8.50

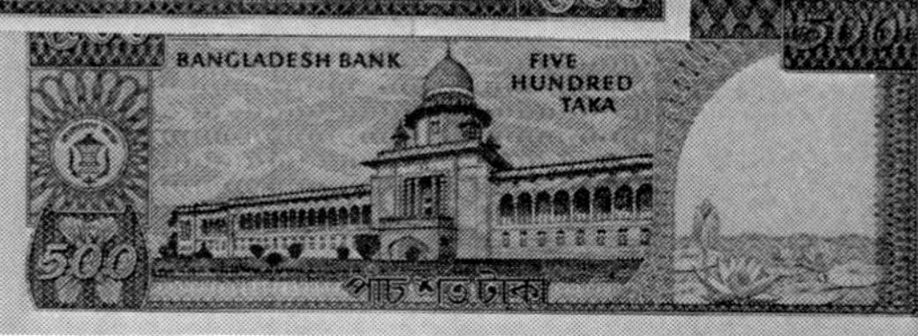

		VG	VF	UNC
30	**500 TAKA** ND (1984). Gray, blue and violet on m/c unpt. Similar to #19 but w/o printing on wmk. area at l. on face.			
	a. W/o segmented foil.	FV	FV	42.50
	b. W/segmented foil over security thread.	FV	FV	25.00

1992-93 ND ISSUE

		VG	VF	UNC
31 (32)	**100 TAKA** ND (1992). Like #29 but w/circular toothed border added around wmk. area on face and back.			
	a. W/o segmented foil.	FV	FV	6.50
	b. W/segmented foil over security thread.	FV	FV	6.00

1997 ND ISSUE

		VG	VF	UNC
32 (34)	**10 TAKA** ND (1997). Dk. brown and deep blue-green on m/c unpt. M. Rahman at r. and as wmk. Arms at l., mosque in Tangali at l. ctr. on back.	FV	FV	2.00

1998 ND COMMEMORATIVE ISSUE

#35, Victory Day

		VG	VF	UNC
33 (35)	**10 TAKA** ND (1998). Violet on m/c unpt. Commemorative ovpt. at lower l. in wmk. area.	FV	FV	12.50

1999 ND ISSUE

		VG	VF	UNC
34	**500 TAKA** ND(1999). National Monument in Savan. High Court building in Dhaka.	Expected New Issue		

BARBADOS

DOMINICA
MARTINIQUE
ST. LUCIA
ST. VINCENT AND THE GRENADINES
GRENADA

Barbados, an independent state within the British Commonwealth, is located in the Windward Islands of the West Indies east of St. Vincent. The coral island has an area of 166 sq. mi. (431 sq. km) and a population of 300,000. Capital: Bridgetown. The economy is based on sugar and tourism. Sugar, petroleum products, molasses and rum are exported.

Barbados was named by the Portuguese who achieved the first landing on the island in 1563. British sailors landed at the site of present-day Holetown in 1624. Barbados was under uninterrupted British control from the time of the first British settlement in 1627 until it obtained independence on Nov. 30, 1966. It is a member of the Commonwealth of Nations. Elizabeth II is Head of State, as Queen of Barbados.

Barbados was included in the issues of the British Caribbean Territories - Eastern Group and later the East Caribbean Currency Authority until 1973.

RULERS:
British to 1966

MONETARY SYSTEM:
1 Dollar = 100 Cents, 1950-

STATE

CENTRAL BANK OF BARBADOS

1973 ND ISSUE

#29-33 arms at l. ctr. Trafalgar Square in Bridgetown on back. Wmk: Map of Barbados. Printer: (T)DLR. Replacement notes: Serial # prefix *Z1*.

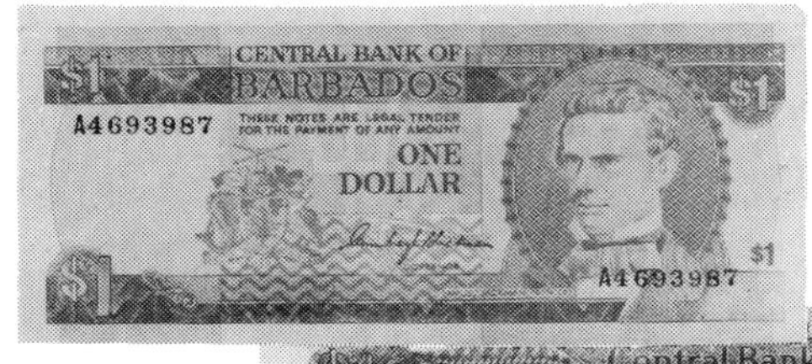

		VG	VF	UNC
29	**1 DOLLAR** ND (1973). Red on m/c unpt. Portr. S. J. Prescod at r.	FV	.75	2.25

		VG	VF	UNC
30	**5 DOLLARS** ND (1973). Green on m/c unpt. Portr. S. J. Prescod at r.	FV	4.00	13.50

		VG	VF	UNC
31	**10 DOLLARS** ND (1973). Dk. brown on m/c unpt. Portr. C. D. O'Neal at r.			

		VG	VF	UNC
	a. Sign. C. Blackman.	FV	7.00	15.00
	b. Sign K. King.	FV	6.00	11.50
32	**20 DOLLARS** ND (1973). Purple on m/c unpt. Portr. S. J. Prescod at r.	FV	12.00	27.50
33	**100 DOLLARS** ND (1973). Gray, blue on m/c unpt. Portr. Sir G. H. Adams at r. Treetops are grayish blue on back. Serial # to E3,200,000.	FV	70.00	125.00

1975; 1980 ND ISSUE

#34 *Deleted.* See #36.

#35-40 arms at l. ctr. Trafalgar Square in Bridgetown on back. Wmk: Map of Barbados. Printer: (T)DLR. Replacement notes: Serial # prefix *Z1*.

		VG	VF	UNC
35	**2 DOLLARS** ND (1980). Blue on m/c unpt. Portr. J. R. Bovell at r.			
	a. Sign. C. Blackman.	FV	1.50	3.50
	b. Sign. K. King.	FV	1.25	3.00
	c. Sign. C. M. Springer.	FV	FV	2.75

		VG	VF	UNC
36	**5 DOLLARS** ND (1975).Dk. green on m/c unpt. Portr. Sir F. Worrell at r.			
	a. Sign C. Blackman.	FV	3.50	7.50
	b. Sign. K. King.	FV	5.50	7.00

1986-94 ND ISSUE

#37-40 printer: (T)DLR.

		VG	VF	UNC
37	**10 DOLLARS** ND (1994). Dk. brown and green on m/c unpt. Like #31 but seahorse in rectange at l. on face, at r. on back.	FV	6.00	12.50
38	**20 DOLLARS** ND (1988). Purple on m/c unpt. Like #32, but bird emblem in rectangle at l. on face, at r. on back. Sign. K. King.	FV	11.50	22.50

		VG	VF	UNC
39	**50 DOLLARS** ND (1989). Orange, blue and gray on m/c unpt. Portr. Prime Minister E. W. Barrow at r.	FV	FV	50.00

		VG	VF	UNC
40	**100 DOLLARS** ND (1986). Brown, purple and gray-blue on m/c unpt. Like #33, but seahorse emblem in rectangle at l. on face. Treetops are green, seahorse emblem at r. on back. Serial # above E3,200,000.			
	a. Sign. C. Blackman.	FV	55.00	100.00
	b. Sign. K. King.	FV	55.00	85.00
	c. Sign. C. H. Springer.	FV	FV	82.50

1995-96 ND ISSUE

#41-44 like #35-38 but w/enhanced security features. Descending and ascending serial # at upper l. Sign. C. M. Springer or W. Cox. Printer: (T)DLR. Replacement notes: Serial # prefix *Z1*.

		VG	VF	UNC
41	**2 DOLLARS** ND (1995-). Blue on m/c unpt.	FV	FV	3.50
42	**5 DOLLARS** ND (1995-). Dk. green on m/c unpt.	FV	FV	6.50
43	**10 DOLLARS** ND (1995-). Dk. brown and green on m/c unpt.	FV	FV	12.50
44	**20 DOLLARS** ND (1996-). Red-violet and purple on m/c unpt.	FV	FV	20.00
45	**50 DOLLARS** ND (1997-). Orange, blue and gray on m/c unpt.	FV	FV	43.50
46	**100 DOLLARS** ND (1996-). Brown, purple and blue-gray on m/c unpt.			
	a. Sign. C. M. Springer (1996).	FV	FV	85.00
	b. Sign. W. Cox (1998).	FV	FV	80.00

1997 COMMEMORATIVE ISSUE

#47, 25th Anniversary Central Bank

		VG	VF	UNC
47	**100 DOLLARS** 1997. Brown, purple and blue-gray on m/c unpt. Commemorative ovpt. on #46 at l. Sign. C. M. Springer.	FV	FV	90.00

1999 ISSUE

#48-53 like #41-46. Enhanced security features. Sign: W. Cox.

		VG VF UNC
48	**2 DOLLARS** 1999.	Expected New Issue
49	**5 DOLLARS** 1999.	Expected New Issue
50	**10 DOLLARS** 1999.	Expected New Issue
51	**20 DOLLARS** 1999.	Expected New Issue
52	**50 DOLLARS** 1999.	Expected New Issue
53	**100 DOLLARS** 1999.	Expected New Issue

Belarus (Byelorussia, Belorussia, or White Russia) is situated along the Western Dvina and Dnieper, bounded in the west by Poland, to the north by Latvia and Lithuania, to the east by Russia and the south by the Ukraine. It has an area of 80,134 sq. mi. (207,600 sq. km.) and a population of 10.3 million. Capital: Minsk. Peat, salt, agriculture including flax, fodder and grasses for cattle breeding and dairy products, along with general manufacturing industries comprise the economy.

There never existed an independent state of Byelorussia. When Kiev was the center of Rus, there were a few feudal principalities in the Byelorussian lands, those of Polotsk, Smolensk and Turov being the most important. The principalities, protected by the Pripet marshes, escaped invasion when, in the first half of the 13th century, the Tatars destroyed the Kievan Rus, but soon they were all incorporated into the Grand Duchy of Lithuania. The Lithuanian conquerors were pagan and illiterate but politically wise. They respected the Christianity of the conquered and gradually Byelorussian became the official language of the grand duchy. When this greater Lithuania was absorbed by Poland in the 16th century, Polish replaced Byelorussian as the official language of the country. Until the partitions of Poland at the end of the 18th century, the history of Byelorussia is identical with that of greater Lithuania.

When Russia incorporated the whole of Byelorussia into its territories in 1795, it claimed to be recovering old Russian lands and denied that the Byelorussians were a separate nation. The country was named Northwestern territory and in 1839 Byelorussian Roman Catholics of the Uniate rite were forced to accept Orthodoxy. A minority remained faithful to the Latin rite. The German occupation of western Byelorussia in 1915 created an opportunity for Byelorussian leaders to formulate in Dec. 1917 their desire for an independent Byelorussia. On Feb. 25, 1918, Minsk was occupied by the Germans, and in the Brest- Litovsk peace treaty of March 3 between the Central Powers and Soviet Russia the existence of Byelorussia was ignored. Nevertheless, on March 25, the National council headed by Lutskievich, Vatslav Lastovski and others proclaimed an independent republic. After the collapse of Germany the Soviet government repudiated the Brest treaties and on Jan. 1, 1919, proclaimed a Byelorussian S.S.R. The Red army occupied the lands evacuated by the Germans, and by February all Byelorussia was in Communist hands. The Polish army started an eastward offensive, however, and on Aug. 8 entered Minsk. In Dec. 1919 the Byelorussian National council gathered there but a split occurred in its ranks: Lastovski formed a pro-Soviet government, while Lutskievich formed an anti-Communist council. The Lastovski "government" soon took refuge in Lithuania, and later in Czechoslovakia. The peace treaty between Poland and the U.S.S.R. in March 1921 partitioned Byelorussia. In its eastern and larger part a Soviet republic was formed, which in 1922 became a founder member of the U.S.S.R. The eastern frontier was identical with the corresponding section of the Polish-Russian frontier before 1772. The first premier of the Byelorussian S.S.R., Dmitro Zhylunovich, persuaded Lastovski to return. Both perished in the purges of the 1930s. On Sept. 17, 1939, in accordance with the secret treaty partitioning Poland signed on Aug. 23 between Germany and the U.S.S.R., the Soviet army occupied eastern Poland, where a western Byelorussian people's assembly was elected on Oct. 22. The assembly "unanimously" demanded the incorporation of western Byelorussia into the U.S.S.R. On Nov. 2 the supreme soviet of the union proclaimed the unification of all Byelorussia. However, when the Moscow treaty of Aug. 16, 1945, fixed the Polish-Soviet frontier, it left Bialystok to Poland. From Jan. 1, 1955, the republic was divided into 7 oblasti or provinces; Minsk, Brest, Grodno, Molodechno, Mohylev (Mogilev), Homel (Gomel) and Vitebsk. On Aug. 25, 1991, following an unsuccessful coup, the Supreme Soviet adopted a declaration of independence, and the "Republic of Belarus" was proclaimed in Sept. Later in Dec. it became a founding member of the CIS.

MONETARY SYSTEM:

1 Rubel = 100 Kapeek

REPUBLIC

КУПОН РЭСПУБЛІКА БЕЛАРУСЬ

BELARUS REPUBLIC

1991 FIRST RUBEL CONTROL COUPON ISSUE

		VG	VF	UNC
AA1	**20 RUBLEI** ND (1991).	—	—	3.00

NOTE: The 20 Rublei denomination was issued on a sheet of 14 coupons. Uniface.

		VG	VF	UNC
A1	**RUBLEI - VARIOUS AMOUNTS** ND (1991).	—	—	4.00

NOTE: The 50, 75, and 100 Rublei denominations were issued in various colors on a sheet of 28 coupons. Uniface.

1991 SECOND RUBEL CONTROL COUPON ISSUE

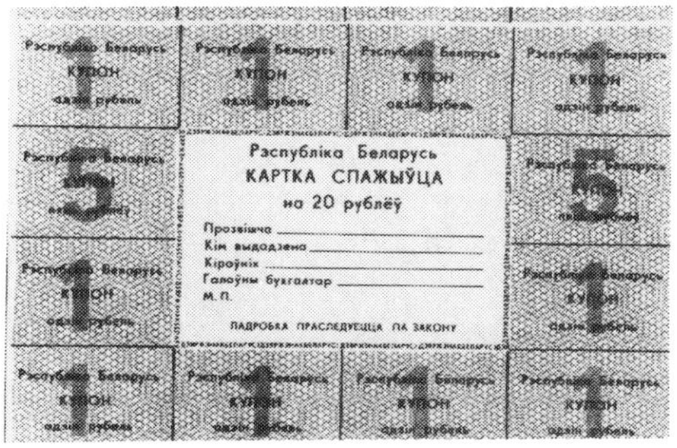

		VG	VF	UNC
A3	**20 RUBLEI** ND (1991).	—	—	3.00

NOTE: The 20 Rublei denomination was issued on a sheet of 14 coupons. Uniface.

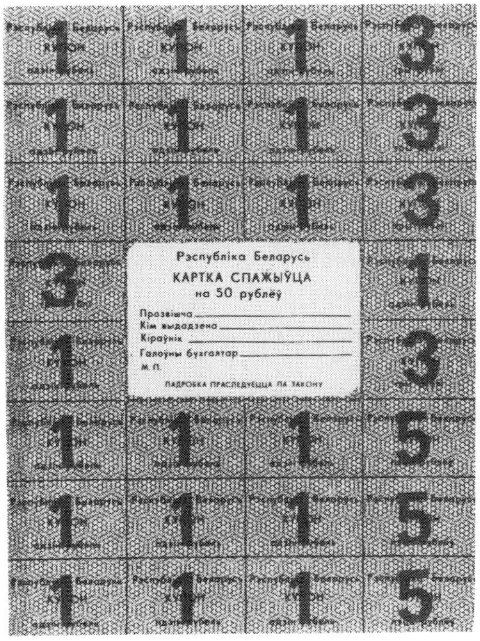

		VG	VF	UNC
A4	**RUBLEI - VARIOUS AMOUNTS** ND (1991).	—	—	3.00

NOTE: The 50, 75, 100, 200, 300, and 500 Rublei denominations were issued in various colors on a sheet of 28 coupons. Uniface.

НАЦЫЯНАЛЬНАIА БАНКА БЕЛАРУСI
BELARUS NATIONAL BANK

1992-96 РАЗЛIКОВЫ БIЛЕТ - EXCHANGE NOTE ISSUE

#1-10 "Pagonya," a defending warrior wielding sword on horseback at ctr. Wmk. paper.

		VG	VF	UNC
1	**50 KAPEEK** 1992. Red and brown-orange on pink unpt. Squirrel at ctr. r. on back.	—	.05	.30

		VG	VF	UNC
2	**1 RUBEL** 1992. Yellow on green, purple and blue unpt. Rabbit at ctr. r. on back.	.05	.10	.60

		VG	VF	UNC
3	**3 RUBLEI** 1992. Green, red-orange and pale olive-green on m/c unpt. 2 beavers at ctr. r. on back.	.10	.50	1.00

		VG	VF	UNC
4	**5 RUBLEI** 1992. Deep blue on lt. blue, lilac, violet and m/c unpt. 2 wolves at ctr. r. on back.	.05	.10	.40

		VG	VF	UNC
5	**10 RUBLEI** 1992. Deep green on lt. green, orange and m/c unpt. Lynx w/kitten at ctr. r. on back.	.05	.10	.40

		VG	VF	UNC
6	**25 RUBLEI** 1992. Violet on red, green and m/c unpt. Moose at ctr. r. on back.	.05	.10	.40

		VG	VF	UNC
7	**50 RUBLEI** 1992. Deep purple on red and green unpt. Bear at ctr. r. on back.	.05	.10	.40

		VG	VF	UNC
8	**100 RUBLEI** 1992. Brown, gray and tan on m/c unpt. Wisent (European Bison) at ctr. on back.	.05	.10	.40

		VG	VF	UNC
9	**200 RUBLEI** 1992. Deep brown-violet, orange, green and ochre on m/c unpt. City view at ctr. r. on back.	.10	.25	1.25

		VG	VF	UNC
10	**500 RUBLEI** 1992. Violet, tan, lt. blue and orange on m/c unpt. Victory Plaza in Minsk at ctr. r. on back.	.10	.50	2.00

		VG	VF	UNC
11	**1000 RUBLEI** 1992 (1993). Lt. blue, pale olive-green and pink. Back black, dk. blue and dk. green on m/c unpt.; Academy of Sciences bldg. at ctr. r. on back.	.05	.25	1.35

		VG	VF	UNC
12	**5000 RUBLEI** 1992 (1993). Purple and red-violet on m/c unpt. Back brown-violet and olive-green on m/c unpt. Bldgs. in Minsk lower city at ctr. r.	.10	.50	2.65

1994-96 ISSUE

		VG	VF	UNC
13	**20,000 RUBLEI** 1994. Dk. brown on m/c unpt. National Bank bldg. at l. ctr., *Pagonya* (National emblem) on back. Wmk: Tower and tree.	FV	FV	6.00

		VG	VF	UNC
14	**50,000 RUBLEI** 1995. Dk. brown on m/c unpt. Brest's tower, Holmsky gate at l., tapestry at ctr. r. Star shaped war memorial gateway at ctr. r. on back.	FV	FV	8.00
15	**100,000 RUBLEI** 1996. Deep blue and violet on m/c unpt. Bolshoi Opera and Ballet Theatre at ctr., tapestry at l. Scene from Glebov's ballet *Izbrannitsa* at ctr. on back.	FV	FV	15.00

1998 ISSUE

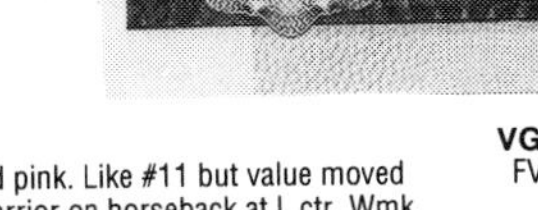

		VG	VF	UNC
16	**1000 RUBLEI** 1998. Lt. blue, pale olive-green and pink. Like #11 but value moved within oval replacing "Pagonya", warrior on horseback at l. ctr. Wmk. paper.	FV	FV	1.25

		VG	VF	UNC
17	**5000 RUBLEI** 1998. M/c.	FV	FV	2.50

1998-99 ISSUE

		VG	VF	UNC
18	**500,000 RUBLEI** 1998. Lt. red on yellow unpt. Palace of Culture bldg. at ctr. Façade fragment on back.	FV	FV	15.00

		VG	VF	UNC
19	**1,000,000 RUBLEI** 1999. Green on m/c unpt. National Museum of Art at ctr. Artwork: *Wife's Portrait w/Flowers and Fruits* on back.	FV	FV	20.00
20	**5,000,000 RUBLEI** 1999.	FV	FV	30.00

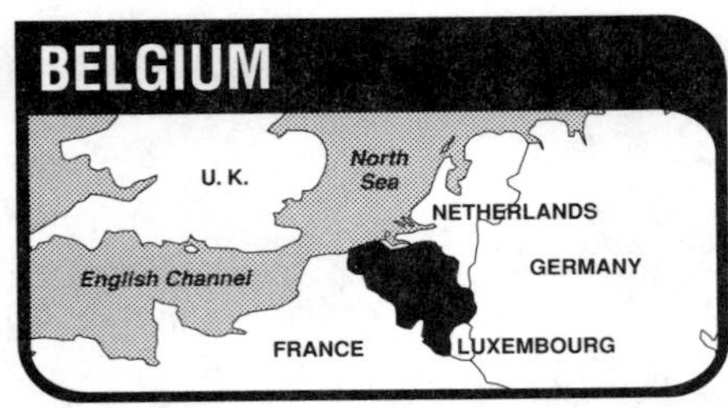

The Kingdom of Belgium, a constitutional monarchy in northwest Europe, has an area of 11,779 sq. mi. (30,513 sq. km.) and a population of 10.1 million, chiefly Dutch-speaking Flemish and French-speaking Walloons. Capital: Brussels. Agriculture, dairy farming, and the processing of raw materials for re-export are the principal industries. "Beurs voor Diamant" in Antwerp is the world's largest diamond trading center. Iron and steel, machinery, motor vehicles, chemicals, textile yarns and fabrics comprise the principal exports.

The Celtic tribe called "Belgae," from which Belgium derived its name, was described by Caesar as the most courageous of all the tribes of Gaul. The Belgae eventually capitulated to Rome and the area remained for centuries as a part of the Roman Empire known as Belgica.

As Rome began its decline, Frankish tribes migrated westward and established the Merovingian, and subsequently, the Carolingian empires. At the death of Charlemagne, Europe was divided among his three sons Karl, Lothar and Ludwig. The eastern part of today's Belgium lay in the Duchy of Lower Lorraine while much of the western parts eventually became the County of Flanders. After further divisions, the area was absorbed into the Duchy of Burgundy from whence it passed into Hapsburg control when Marie of Burgundy married Maximilian of Austria. Phillip I (the Fair), son of Maximilian and Marie, then added Spain to the Hapsburg empire by marrying Johanna, daughter of Ferdinand and Isabella. Charles and Ferdinand, sons of Phillip and Johanna, began the separate Spanish and Austrian lines of the Hapsburg family. The Burgundian lands, along with the northern provinces which make up present day Netherlands, became the Spanish Netherlands. The northern provinces successfully rebelled and broke away from Hapsburg rule in the late 16th century and early 17th century. The southern provinces along with the Duchy of Luxembourg remained under the influence of Spain until the year 1700 when Charles II, last of the Spanish Hapsburg line, died without leaving an heir and the Spanish crown went to the Bourbon family of France. The Spanish Netherlands then reverted to the control of the Austrian line of Hapsburgs and became the Austrian Netherlands. The Austrian Netherlands along with the Bishopric of Liege fell to the French Republic in 1794.

At the Congress of Vienna in 1815 the area was united with the Netherlands but in 1830 independence was gained and the constitutional monarchy of Belgium was established. A large part of the Duchy of Luxembourg was incorporated into Belgium and the first king was Leopold I of Saxe-Coburg-Gotha. It was invaded by the German army in Aug. 1914 and the German forces carried on a devastating occupation of most of the territory until the Armistice. Belgium joined the League of Nations. On May 10, 1940 it was invaded again by Nazi German armies. The Belgian and Allied forces were quickly overwhelmed and were evacuated through Dunkirk. Allied troops reached Belgium again in Sept. 1944. Prince Charles, Count of Flanders assumed King Leopold's responsibilities until his liberation by the U.S. army in Austria on May 8, 1945. From 1920-1940 and since 1944 Eupen-Malmedy went from Germany to Belgium.

RULERS:

Baudouin I, 1951-93
Albert II, 1993-

MONETARY SYSTEM:

1 Franc = 100 Centimes

KINGDOM

BANQUE NATIONALE DE BELGIQUE

NATIONALE BANK VAN BELGIE

1961-71 ISSUE

#134-137 wmk: Kg. Baudouin I.

		VG	VF	UNC
134	**100 FRANCS** 1.2.1962-2.6.1977. Violet on m/c unpt. Lombard at l. Allegorical figure at ctr. on back. 4 sign. varieties.	2.00	3.00	5.00

NOTICE

Readers with unlisted dates, signature varieties, etc. are invited to submit photocopies of their notes to: Standard Catalog of World Paper Money, 700 East State St. Iola, WI 54990-0001, fax: 1-715-445-4087, or E-Mail: thernr@krause.com.

#135-137 replacement notes: Serial # prefix *Z/1*.

		VG	VF	UNC
135	**500 FRANCS** 2.5.1961-28.4.1975. Blue-gray and m/c. B. Van Orley at ctr. Margaret of Austria on back. 4 sign. varieties.	12.50	15.00	25.00

		VG	VF	UNC
136	**1000 FRANCS** 2.1.1961-8.12.1975. Brown and blue. Kremer (called Mercator) at l. Atlas holding globe on back. 4 sign. varieties.	25.00	35.00	45.00

		VG	VF	UNC
137	**5000 FRANCS** 6.1.1971-15.9.1977. Green. A. Vesalius at ctr. r. Statue and temple on back. 4 sign. varieties.	125.00	150.00	200.00

KINGDOM

ROYAUME DE BELGIQUE - KONINKRIJK BELGIE

TRÉSORERIE - THESAURIE (TREASURY NOTES)

1964-66 ISSUE

#138 and 139 replacement notes: Serial # prefix *Z/1*.

		VG	VF	UNC
138	**20 FRANCS** 15.6.1964. Black on blue, orange and m/c unpt. Kg. Baudouin I at l. and as wmk., arms at lower r. Atomium complex in Brussels at r. on back. Wmk: Baudouin I. 3 sign. varieties.	.25	.50	1.50

		VG	VF	UNC
139	**50 FRANCS** 16.5.1966. Brown-violet and orange-brown on m/c unpt. Arms at lower l. ctr., Kg. Baudouin I and Qn. Fabiola at r. Parliament bldg. in Brussels on back. Wmk: Baudouin I. 4 sign. varieties.	.50	.75	2.00

BANQUE NATIONALE DE BELGIQUE

1978; 1980 ND ISSUE

#140-145 wmk: Kg. Baudouin I.

		VG	VF	UNC
140	**100 FRANCS** ND (1978-81). Maroon, blue and olive-green on m/c unpt. H. Beyaert at ctr. r. Architectural view and plan at l. Geometric design on back. 2 sign. varieties.	FV	4.00	6.50

		VG	VF	UNC
141	**500 FRANCS** ND (1980-81). Deep blue-violet and deep green on blue and m/c unpt. C. Meunier at l. ctr. Unpt. of 2 coal miners and mine conveyor tower at ctr. r. 5 circular designs on back.	FV	20.00	30.00

1981-82 ND ISSUE

		VG	VF	UNC
142	**100 FRANCS** ND (1982-94). Like #140 but w/sign. on face and back. 7 sign. varieties.	FV	3.00	4.00

		VG	VF	UNC
143	**500 FRANCS** ND (1982-98). Like #141 but w/sign. on face and back. 7 sign. varieties.	12.50	15.00	20.00

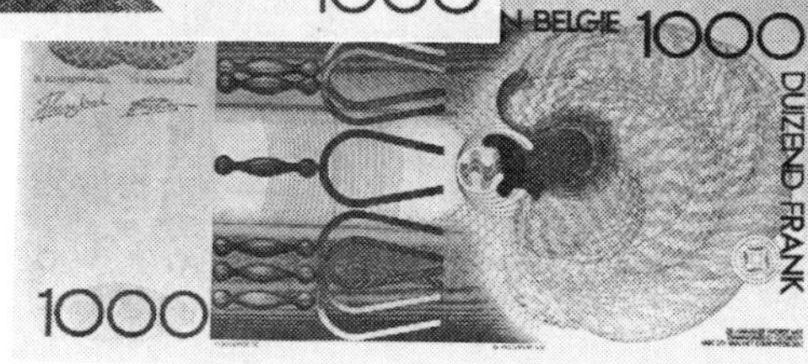

		VG	VF	UNC
144	**1000 FRANCS** ND (1980-96). Brown and m/c. A. Gretry at l. ctr., violin ctr. r. in background. Tuning forks and sound wave designs on back. 7 sign. varieties.			
	a. Name as: *ANDRÉ ERNEST MODESTE GRETRY. 1741-1813.*	25.00	30.00	35.00
	x1. Name as: *• ERNEST • MODESTE.*	50.00	100.00	200.00
	x2. Name as: *ANDRÉ ERNEST MODESTE GRETRY.*	30.00	40.00	80.00

		VG	VF	UNC
145	**5000 FRANCS** ND (1982-92). Green. G. Gezelle at l. ctr. Tree and stained glass window behind. Back green, red and brown; dragonfly and leaf at ctr. 5 sign. varieties.	125.00	140.00	175.00

1992 ND ISSUE

		VG	VF	UNC
146	**10,000 FRANCS** ND (1992-97). Grayish purple on m/c unpt. Kg. Baudouin I and Qn. Fabiola at l. and as wmk., aerial map as unpt. Flora and greenhouses at Lacken (royal residence) at ctr. on back.	250.00	275.00	300.00

NOTICE

Readers with unlisted dates, signature varieties, etc. are invited to submit photocopies of their notes to: Standard Catalog of World Paper Money, 700 East State St. Iola, WI 54990-0001, fax: 1-715-445-4087, or E-Mail: thernr@krause.com.

1994-97 ND ISSUE

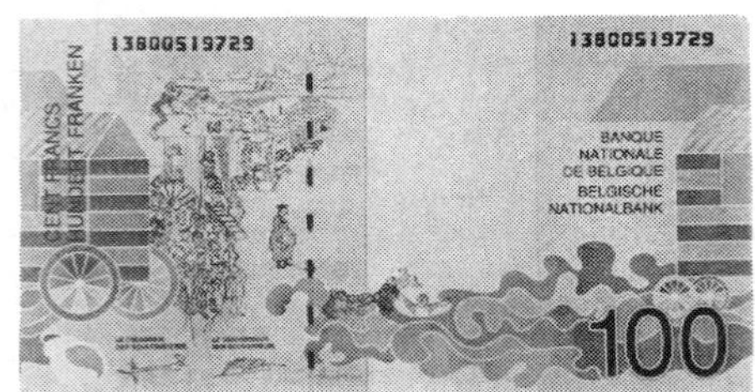

147 **100 FRANCS** — VG FV | VF FV | UNC 4.50
ND (1995-). Red-violet and black on m/c unpt. James Ensor at l. and as wmk., masks at lower ctr. and at r. Beach scene at l. on back.

148 **200 FRANCS** — VG FV | VF FV | UNC 8.00
ND (1995). Black and brown on yellow and orange unpt. Adolphe Sax at l. and as wmk., saxophone at r. Saxophone players outlined at l., church, houses in Dinant outlined at lower r. on back.

149 **500 FRANCS** — VG FV | VF FV | UNC 20.00
ND (1998). Blue-black, purple and blue-green on m/c unpt. René Magritte at l. and as wmk., birds in plants at lower ctr., tree at r. 6 men, chair at l., men at ctr. r. on back.

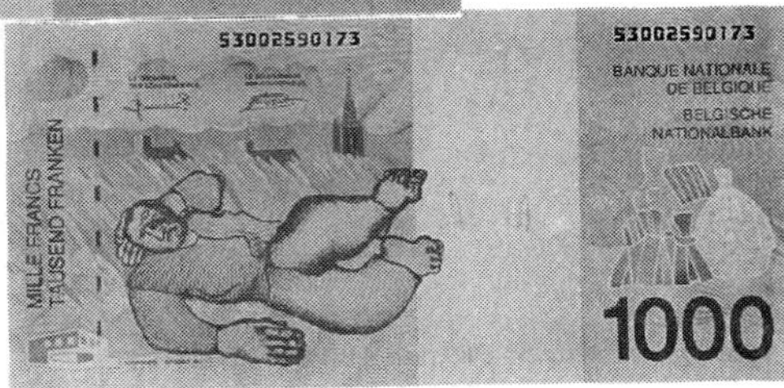

150 **1000 FRANCS** — VG FV | VF FV | UNC 30.00
ND (1997). Brown-violet on m/c unpt. Constant Permeke at l. and as wmk., sailboat at ctr. "Sleeping Farmer" painting at l. on back.

151 **2000 FRANCS** — VG FV | VF FV | UNC 65.00
ND (1994-). Purple and blue-green on m/c unpt. Baron Victor Horta at l. and as wmk. Flora and *Art Nouveau* design at l. on back.

152 **10,000 FRANCS** — VG FV | VF FV | UNC 275.00
ND (1997). Deep purple on m/c unpt. Kg. Albert II and Queen Paola at l., aerial view of Parliamentary chamber at r. Greenhouses at Lacken royal residence on back. Wmk: Kg. Albert II.

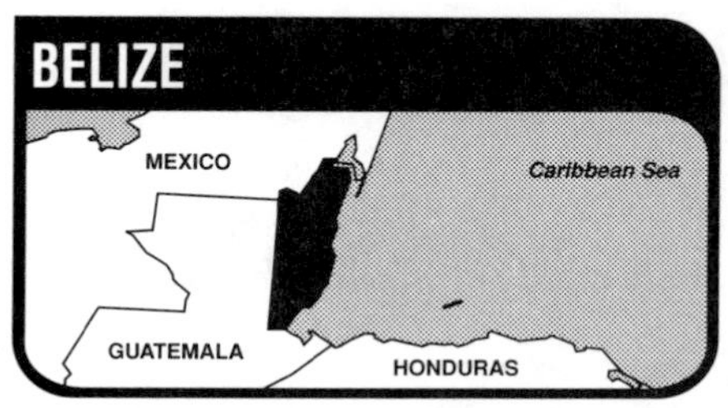

Belize (formerly British Honduras) is situated in Central America south of Mexico and east and north of Guatemala. It has an area of 8,867 sq. mi. (22,965 sq. km.) and a population of 219,300. Capital: Belmopan. Sugar, citrus fruits, chicle and hard woods are exported.

The area, site of the ancient Mayan civilization, was sighted by Columbus in 1502, and settled by shipwrecked English seamen in 1638. British buccaneers settled the former capital of Belize in the 17th Century. Britian claimed administrative right over the area after the emancipation of Central America from Spain, and declared it a dependency of the Colony of Jamaica in 1862. It was established as the separate Crown Colony of British Honduras in 1884. The anti-British People's United Party, which attained power in 1954, won a constitution, effective in 1964 which established self-government under a British appointed Governor. British Honduras became Belize on June 1, 1973, following the passage of a surprise bill by the People's United Party, but the consititutional relationship with Britain remained unchanged.

In Dec. 1975, the U.N. General Assembly adopted a resolution supporting the right of the people of Belize to self-determination, and asked Britian and Guatemala to renew their negotiations on the future of Belize. They obtained independence on Sept. 21, 1981. Elizabeth II is Head of State, as Queen of Belize.

For earlier bank notes, see British Honduras.

MONETARY SYSTEM:

1 Dollar = 100 Cents

BELIZE

GOVERNMENT OF BELIZE

1974-75 ISSUE

#33-37 arms at l., portr. Qn. Elizabeth II at r.

		VG	VF	UNC
33	**1 DOLLAR**			
	1974-76. Green on m/c unpt.			
	a. 1.1.1974.	.75	3.50	30.00
	b. 1.6.1975.	.75	2.25	25.00
	c. 1.1.1976.	.75	2.00	22.50
34	**2 DOLLARS**			
	1974-76. Violet on lilac and m/c unpt.			
	a. 1.1.1974.	3.00	9.00	50.00
	b. 1.6.1975.	2.50	7.00	40.00
	c. 1.1.1976.	2.00	5.00	35.00

		VG	VF	UNC
35	**5 DOLLARS**			
	1975; 1976. Red on m/c unpt.			
	a. 1.6.1975.	5.00	12.50	85.00
	b. 1.1.1976.	3.00	8.50	65.00

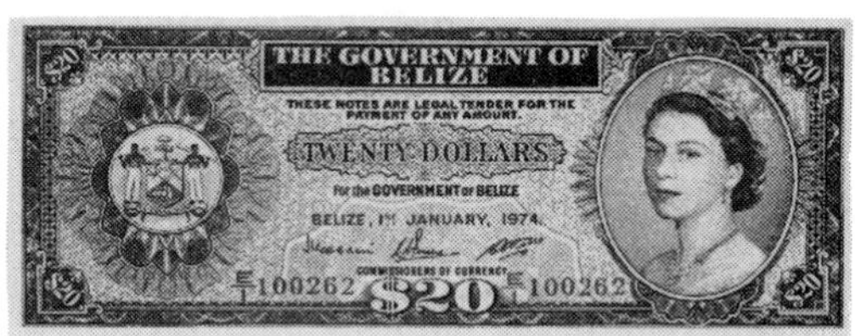

		VG	VF	UNC
36	**10 DOLLARS**			
	1974-76. Black on m/c unpt.			
	a. 1.1.1974.	10.00	50.00	350.00
	b. 1.6.1975.	8.00	35.00	250.00
	c. 1.1.1976.	7.50	30.00	225.00

		VG	VF	UNC
	1974-76. Brown on m/c unpt.			
	a. 1.1.1974.	14.00	75.00	550.00
	b. 1.6.1975.	13.00	60.00	400.00
	c. 1.1.1976.	12.00	55.00	385.00

MONETARY AUTHORITY OF BELIZE

ORDINANCE NO. 9 OF 1976; 1980 ISSUE

#38-42 linear border on arms in upper l. corner, Qn. Elizabeth II at ctr. r. 3/4 looking l., underwater scene w/reef and fish in ctr. background. House of Representatives in Belize on back. Wmk: Carved head of the "sleeping giant." Replacement notes: Serial # prefix *Z/1; Z/2; Z/3; Z/4; Z/5*.

		VG	VF	UNC
38	**1 DOLLAR**			
	1.6.1980. Green on m/c unpt.	1.25	1.50	7.50

		VG	VF	UNC
39	**5 DOLLARS**			
	1.6.1980. Red on m/c unpt.	3.00	4.50	20.00
40	**10 DOLLARS**			
	1.6.1980. Violet on m/c unpt.	6.00	9.00	70.00

		VG	VF	UNC
41	**20 DOLLARS**			
	1.6.1980. Brown on m/c unpt.	11.50	20.00	175.00

		VG	VF	UNC
42	**100 DOLLARS**			
	1.6.1980. Blue on m/c unpt.	60.00	120.00	850.00

CENTRAL BANK OF BELIZE

ACT 1981; 1983 ISSUE

#43-45 similar to #38, 40 and 41. Wreath border on arms at upper l. Replacement notes: Serial # prefix *Z/1; Z/3; Z/4*.

		VG	VF	UNC
43	**1 DOLLAR** 1.7.1983. Green on m/c unpt.	1.25	1.50	10.00

		VG	VF	UNC
44	**10 DOLLARS** 1.7.1983. Gray on m/c unpt.	6.00	8.00	47.50

		VG	VF	UNC
45	**20 DOLLARS** 1.7.1983. Brown on m/c unpt.	11.00	20.00	250.00

ACT 1982; 1983-87 ISSUE

#46-50 like #38-42. Lg. tree behind arms at upper l. Sign. varieties. Replacement notes: Serial # prefix Z/1; Z/2; Z/3; Z/4; Z/5.

		VG	VF	UNC
46	**1 DOLLAR** 1983-87. Green on m/c unpt.			
	a. 1.11.1983.	FV	1.00	7.00
	b. 1.1.1986.	FV	.75	5.00
	c. 1.1.1987.	FV	FV	4.00

		VG	VF	UNC
47	**5 DOLLARS** 1987; 1989. Red on m/c unpt.			
	a. 1.1.1987.	3.50	20.00	150.00
	b. 1.1.1989.	FV	4.00	15.00

		VG	VF	UNC
48	**10 DOLLARS** 1987; 1989. Violet on m/c unpt.			
	a. 1.1.1987.	FV	6.00	35.00
	b. 1.1.1989.	6.00	30.00	150.00

		VG	VF	UNC
49	**20 DOLLARS** 1986; 1987. Brown on m/c unpt.			
	a. 1.1.1986.	FV	15.00	85.00
	b. 1.1.1987.	FV	12.50	50.00

		VG	VF	UNC
50	**100 DOLLARS** 1983; 1989. Blue on m/c unpt.			
	a. 1.11.1983.	FV	95.00	425.00
	b. 1.1.1989.	FV	95.00	425.00

ACT 1982; 1990 ISSUE

#51-57 older facing portr. of Qn. Elizabeth II at r. Wmk: Carved head of the "sleeping giant." Printer: TDLR.

		VG	VF	UNC
51	**1 DOLLAR** 1.5.1990. Green on lt. brown, blue and m/c unpt. Crustacean at l. Back green and red; marine life of Belize across ctr.	FV	.75	3.50

		VG	VF	UNC
52	**2 DOLLARS** 1990; 1991. Purple on lt. green, blue and m/c unpt. Carved stone pillar at l. Mayan ruins of Belize on back.			
	a. 1.5.1990.	FV	1.25	5.00
	b. 1.6.1991.	FV	1.25	5.00

		VG	VF	UNC
53	**5 DOLLARS** 1990; 1991. Red-orange, orange and violet on m/c unpt. C. Columbus medallion at l, silver trigger fish below. St. George's Caye, coffin, outline map and bldg. on back.			
	a. 1.5.1990.	FV	3.00	10.00
	b. 1.6.1991.	FV	3.00	8.50

		VG	VF	UNC
54	**10 DOLLARS** 1990; 1991. Black, olive-brown and deep blue-green on m/c unpt. Court House clock tower at l. Government House, Court House and St. John's Cathedral on back.			
	a. 1.5.1990.	FV	6.00	20.00
	b. 1.6.1991.	FV	6.00	15.00

		VG	VF	UNC
55	**20 DOLLARS** 1.5.1990. Dk. brown on m/c unpt. Jaguar at l. Fauna of Belize on back.	FV	12.00	25.00

		VG	VF	UNC
56	**50 DOLLARS** 1990; 1991. Purple, brown and red on m/c unpt. Boats at l. Bridges of Belize on back.			
	a. 1.5.1990.	FV	FV	50.00
	b. 1.6.1991.	FV	FV	55.00

		VG	VF	UNC
57	**100 DOLLARS** 1990-94. Blue-violet, orange and red on m/c unpt. Toucan at l. Birds of Belize on back.			
	a. 1.5.1990.	FV	65.00	175.00
	b. 1.6.1991.	FV	60.00	150.00
	c. 1.5.1994.	FV	FV	100.00

ACT 1982; 1996 ISSUE

#58, 59, 60-63 like #53-57 but w/segmented foil over security strip and ascending serial # at upper r. Printer: TDLR.

		VG	VF	UNC
58	**5 DOLLARS** 1.3.1996. Red-orange, orange and violet on m/c unpt. Like #53.	FV	FV	5.50
59	**10 DOLLARS** 1.3.1996. Black, olive brown and deep blue-green on m/c unpt. Like #54.	FV	FV	10.00

1997 ISSUE

#60-63 reduced size.

		VG	VF	UNC
60	**10 DOLLARS** 1.6.1997. Black, olive-brown and deep blue-green on m/c unpt. Like #59.	FV	FV	8.50
61	**20 DOLLARS** 1.6.1997. Dk. brown on m/c unpt. Like #55.	FV	FV	18.50
62	**50 DOLLARS** 1.6.1997. Purple, brown and red on m/c unpt. Like #56.	FV	FV	43.50
63	**100 DOLLARS** 1.6.1997. Blue-violet, orange and red on m/c unpt. Like #57.	FV	FV	85.00

1999 ISSUE

#64 and 65 reduced size.

		VG	VF	UNC
64	**2 DOLLARS** 1.1.1999. Purple on lt. green, blue and m/c unpt. Like #52.	FV	FV	2.00
65	**5 DOLLARS** 1.1.1999. Red-orange, orange and violet on m/c unpt. Like #53.	FV	FV	4.50

COLLECTOR SERIES

CENTRAL BANK OF BELIZE

1984 ISSUE

NOTE: The Central Bank of Belize will no longer exchange these notes for regular currency. (It is illegal to export the currency afterwards). Value is thus speculative.

		ISSUE PRICE	MKT. VALUE
CS1	**ND (1984) COLLECTION** Stamped from paper bonded within gold foil. Denominations: $1 (1 pc.), $2 (2 pcs.) $5 (3 pcs.), $10 (4 pcs.), $20 (2 pcs.), $25 (6 pcs.), $50 (7 pcs.), $75 (5 pcs.), $100 (6 pcs.). Total 36 pcs. All have QE II and bldg. on face, different animals, ships, fish, birds etc. on backs.	—	350.00

The Parliamentary British Colony of Bermuda, situated in the western Atlantic Ocean 660 miles (1,062 km.) east of North Carolina, has an area of 20.6 sq. mi. (53 sq. km.) and a population of 60,470. Capital: Hamilton. Concentrated essences, beauty preparations, and cut flowers are exported. Most Bermudians derive their livelihood from tourism.

Bermuda was discovered by Juan de Bermudez, a Spanish navigator, in 1503. British influence dates from 1609 when a group of Virginia-bound British colonists under the command of Sir George Somers was shipwrecked on the islands for 10 months. The islands were settled in 1612 by 60 British colonists from the Virginia Colony and became a crown colony in 1684. Internal autonomy was obtained by the constitution of June 8, 1968.

In February, 1970, Bermuda converted from its former currency, the British pound, to a decimal currency, termed a dollar, On July 31, 1972, Bermuda severed its monetary link with the British pound and pegged its dollar to be the same value as the U.S. dollar.

RULERS:
British

MONETARY SYSTEM:
1 Shilling = 12 Pence
1 Pound = 20 Shillings, to 1970
1 Dollar = 100 Cents, 1970-

BRITISH INFLUENCE

BERMUDA GOVERNMENT

1952-66 ISSUE

#19-22 printer: BWC.

		VG	VF	UNC
19	**10 SHILLINGS** 1952-66. Red on m/c unpt. Portr. Qn. Elizabeth at upper ctr. Gate's Fort in St. George in frame at bottom ctr.			
	a. 20.10.1952.	5.00	35.00	225.00
	b. 1.5.1957.	3.00	15.00	100.00
	c. 1.10.1966.	4.00	20.00	225.00

		VG	VF	UNC
20	**1 POUND** 1952-66. Blue on m/c unpt. Portr. Qn. Elizabeth at r. Bridge at l.			
	a. 20.10.1952.	7.50	30.00	225.00
	b. 1.5.1957. W/o security strip.	5.00	20.00	225.00
	c. 1.5.1957. W/security strip.	3.50	15.00	185.00
	d. 1.10.1966.	3.00	13.00	140.00
21	**5 POUNDS** 1952-66. Orange on m/c unpt. Portr. Qn. Elizabeth II at r., ship entering Hamilton Harbor at l.			
	a. 20.10.1952.	25.00	120.00	600.00
	b. 1.5.1957. W/o security strip.	17.50	75.00	450.00
	c. 1.5.1957. W/security strip.	15.00	70.00	425.00
	d. 1.10.1966.	15.00	55.00	375.00
22	**10 POUNDS** 28.7.1964. Purple on m/c unpt. Portr. Qn. Elizabeth II at r.	100.00	400.00	1500.

1970 ISSUE

#23-27 Qn. Elizabeth II at r. looking 3/4 to l., arms at l. ctr. Wmk: Tuna fish.

		VG	VF	UNC
23	**1 DOLLAR** 6.2.1970. Dk. blue on tan and aqua unpt. Sailboats at l. ctr., bldgs. at upper r. on back.	1.50	3.00	22.50

		VG	VF	UNC
24	**5 DOLLARS** 6.2.1970. Red-violet on aqua and m/c unpt. Lighthouse at l., bldgs. at ctr. r. on back.	6.50	8.50	30.00

		VG	VF	UNC
25	**10 DOLLARS** 6.2.1970. Purple on brown and m/c unpt. Bird and seashell at ctr., beach at l. on back.	FV	12.50	60.00
26	**20 DOLLARS** 6.2.1970. Green on m/c unpt. Bldg., sailboat and bridge at l. ctr. on back.	FV	25.00	100.00
27	**50 DOLLARS** 6.2.1970. Brown on m/c unpt. Lighthouse at l., map at upper r. on back.	FV	70.00	225.00

NOTICE

Readers with unlisted dates, signature varieties, etc. are invited to submit photocopies of their notes to: Standard Catalog of World Paper Money, 700 East State St. Iola, WI 54990-0001, fax: 1-715-445-4087, or E-Mail: thernr@krause.com.

BERMUDA MONETARY AUTHORITY

1974-82 ISSUE

#28-33 Qn. Elizabeth II at r. looking 3/4 to l. Wmk: Tuna fish. Replacement notes: Serial # prefix *Z/1*.

#28-32 like #23-27.

		VG	VF	UNC
28	**1 DOLLAR** 1975-88. Dk. blue on tan and aqua unpt.			
	a. Sign. titles: *CHAIRMAN* and *MANAGING DIRECTOR*. 1.7.1975; 1.12.1976.	FV	2.50	22.50
	b. 1.4.1978; 1.9.1979; 2.1.1982; 1.5.1984.	FV	1.50	10.00
	c. Sign. titles: *CHAIRMAN* and *GENERAL MANAGER*. 1.1.1986.	FV	1.50	11.00
	d. Sign. titles: *CHAIRMAN* and *DIRECTOR*. 1.1.1988.	FV	1.50	9.50

		VG	VF	UNC
29	**5 DOLLARS** 1978-88. Red-violet on aqua and m/c unpt.			
	a. Sign. titles: *CHAIRMAN* and *MANAGING DIRECTOR*. 1.4.1978.	FV	6.50	22.50
	b. 2.1.1981.	FV	6.00	22.50
	c. Sign. titles: *CHAIRMAN* and *GENERAL MANAGER*. 1.1.1986.	FV	6.00	18.50
	d. Sign. titles: *CHAIRMAN* and *DIRECTOR*. 1.1.1988.	FV	6.00	17.50

		VG	VF	UNC
30	**10 DOLLARS** 1978; 1982. Purple on brown and m/c unpt.			
	a. 1.4.1978.	FV	17.50	90.00
	b. 2.1.1982.	FV	15.00	75.00

		VG	VF	UNC
31	**20 DOLLARS** 1974-86. Green on m/c unpt.			
	a. 1.4.1974.	25.00	45.00	275.00
	b. 1.3.1976.	FV	25.00	175.00
	c. 2.1.1981; 1.5.1984.	FV	FV	65.00
	d. Sign. title: *GENERAL MANAGER* at r. 1.1.1986.	FV	FV	60.00

		VG	VF	UNC
32	**50 DOLLARS** 1974-82. Brown on m/c unpt.			
	a. 1.5.1974.	60.00	150.00	750.00
	b. 1.4.1978; 2.1.1982.	FV	85.00	400.00

		VG	VF	UNC
33	**100 DOLLARS** 1982-86. Orange and brown on m/c unpt. House of Assembly at l., Camden bldg. at upper ctr. r. on back.			
	a. 2.1.1982.	FV	FV	290.00
	b. Sign. title: *GENERAL MANAGER* ovpt. at r. 14.11.1984.	FV	FV	250.00
	c. Sign. title: *GENERAL MANAGER* at r. 1.1.1986.	FV	FV	200.00

1988-89 ISSUE

#34-39 mature bust of Qn. Elizabeth II at r. Back similar to #29-33 but w/stylistic changes; arms added at upper l. Sign. titles: *CHAIRMAN* and *DIRECTOR*. Wmk.: Tuna fish. Replacement notes: Serial # prefix *Z/1*.

		VG	VF	UNC
34	**2 DOLLARS** 1988; 1989. Blue-green on green and m/c unpt. Dockyards clock tower bldg. at upper l., map at ctr., arms at ctr. r. on back.			
	a. Serial # prefix: *B/1*. 1.10.1988.	FV	FV	5.00
	b. Serial # prefix: *B/2*. 1.8.1989.	FV	FV	6.50

		VG	VF	UNC
35	**5 DOLLARS** 20.2.1989. Red-violet and purple on m/c unpt.			
	a. Sign. title: *DIRECTOR* on silver background at bottom ctr. Serial # prefix: *B/1*.	FV	7.00	25.00
	b. Sign. title: *DIRECTOR* w/o silver background. Serial # prefix: *B/1, B/2*.	FV	FV	11.50

		VG	VF	UNC
36	**10 DOLLARS** 20.2.1989. Purple, blue and ochre on m/c unpt.	FV	FV	25.00

		VG	VF	UNC
37	**20 DOLLARS** 20.2.1989. Green and red on m/c unpt.			
	a. Serial # prefix: *B/1*.	FV	FV	42.50
	b. Serial # prefix: *B/2*.	FV	FV	40.00

		VG	VF	UNC
38	**50 DOLLARS** 20.2.1989. Brown and olive on m/c unpt.	FV	FV	100.00

		VG	VF	UNC
39	**100 DOLLARS** 20.2.1989. Orange, brown and violet on m/c unpt.	FV	FV	165.00

1992 COMMEMORATIVE ISSUE

#40, Quincentenary of Christopher Columbus

		VG	VF	UNC
40	**50 DOLLARS** 12.10.1992. Dk. blue, brown and red on m/c unpt. Like #44 but w/commemorative details. Maltese cross as serial # prefix at upper l., c/c fractional prefix at r., and ovpt: *Christopher Columbus/Quincentenary/ 1492-1992* at l.	FV	FV	120.00

ACT 1969; 1992-96 ISSUE

#40A-45 issued under Bermuda Monetary Authority Act 1969. Like #34-39 but w/Authorization text in 3 lines at ctr. Wmk: Tuna fish.

		VG	VF	UNC
40A	**2 DOLLARS** 29.2.1996; 6.6.1997. Blue and green on m/c unpt.			
	a. 29.2.1996.	FV	FV	6.50
	b. 6.6.1997.	FV	FV	4.50

		VG	VF	UNC
41	**5 DOLLARS** 1992-97. Red-violet and purple on m/c unpt. Like #35 but new 3-line text under value at ctr.			
	a. 12.11.1992.	FV	FV	10.00
	b. 25.3.1995.	FV	FV	9.00
	c. 20.2.1996.	FV	FV	8.50
	d. 10.6.1997.	FV	FV	8.00

		VG	VF	UNC
42	**10 DOLLARS** 1993-97. Purple, deep blue and orange on m/c unpt. Like #36 but w/new text at #41.			
	a. 4.1.1993.	FV	FV	18.50
	b. 15.3.1996.	FV	FV	17.50
	c. 17.6.1997.	FV	FV	17.00
43	**20 DOLLARS** 27.2.1996. Green and red on m/c unpt.	FV	FV	37.50

		VG	VF	UNC
44	**50 DOLLARS** 1992-96. Dk. blue, brown and red on m/c unpt. Face similar to #38 but w/new text similar to #41. Scuba divers, shipwreck at l., island outline at upper r. above arms.			
	a. 12.10.1992.	FV	FV	95.00
	b. 25.3.1995.	FV	FV	90.00
	c. 23.2.1996.	FV	FV	85.00

		VG	VF	UNC
45	**100 DOLLARS** 14.2.1996. Orange, brown and violet on m/c unpt. Arms at upper l., House of Assembly at l., Camden bldg. at upper ctr. r. on back.	FV	FV	165.00

1994 COMMEMORATIVE ISSUE

#46, 25th Anniversary Bermuda Monetary Authority

		VG	VF	UNC
46	**100 DOLLARS** 20.2.1994. Orange, brown and violet on m/c unpt. Similar to #39 but new 3-line text under value. Ovpt: *25th Anniversary....*	FV	FV	170.00

NOTICE

Readers with unlisted dates, signature varieties, etc. are invited to submit photocopies of their notes to: Standard Catalog of World Paper Money, 700 East State St. Iola, WI 54990-0001, fax: 1-715-445-4087, or E-Mail: thernr@krause.com.

1997 COMMEMORATIVE ISSUE

#47, Opening of Burnaby House

		VG	VF	UNC
47	**20 DOLLARS** 17.1.1997. Green and red on m/c unpt. Ovpt. on #43.	FV	FV	35.00

1997 REGULAR ISSUE

		VG	VF	UNC
48	**50 DOLLARS** 6.6.1997. Dk. blue, brown and red on m/c ovpt. Like #44 but w/segmented foil over security thread.	FV	FV	87.50

		VG	VF	UNC
49	**100 DOLLARS** 30.6.1997. Orange and brown on m/c unpt. Like #45 but w/segmented foil over security thread.	FV	FV	165.00

COLLECTOR SERIES

BERMUDA MONETARY AUTHORITY

		ISSUE PRICE	MKT. VALUE
CS1	**1978-84 1-100 DOLLARS** #22-33 w/normal serial #, punched hole cancelled, ovpt: *SPECIMEN* (1985).	—	30.00

1981-82 ISSUE (1985)

		ISSUE PRICE	MKT. VALUE
CS2	**1981-82 1-100 DOLLARS** #28-33 w/all zero serial #, punched hole cancelled in all 4 corners, ovpt: *SPECIMEN* (1985).	—	30.00

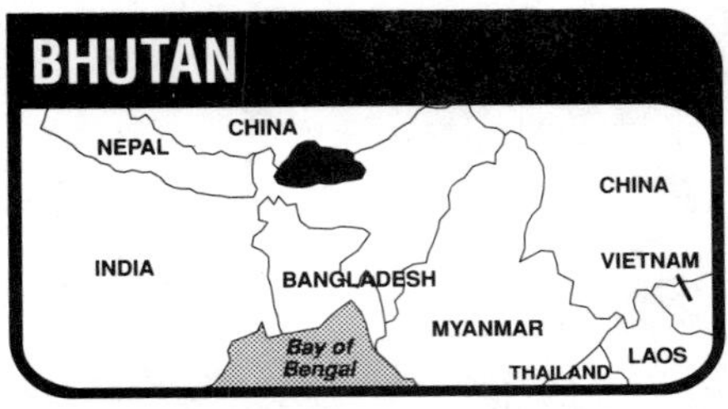

The Kingdom of Bhutan, a landlocked Himalayan country bordered by Tibet, India, and Sikkim, has an area of 18,147 sq. mi. (47,000 sq. km.) and a population of 600,000. Capital: Thimphu; Paro is the administrative capital. Virtually the entire population is engaged in agricultural and pastoral activities. Rice, wheat, barley, and yak butter are produced in sufficient quantity to make the country self-sufficient in food. The economy of Bhutan is primitive and many transactions are conducted on a barter basis.

Bhutan's early history is obscure, but is thought to have resembled that of rural medieval Europe. The country was conquered by Tibet, which still claims sovereignty over Bhutan, in the 9th century, and subjected to a dual temporal and spiritual rule until the mid-19th century, when the southern part of the country was occupied by the British and annexed to British India. Bhutan was established as a hereditary monarchy in 1907, and in 1910 agreed to British control of its external affairs. In 1949, India and Bhutan concluded a treaty whereby India assumed Britain's role in subsidizing Bhutan and conducting its foreign affairs.

RULERS:

Jigme Singye Wangchuk, 1972-

MONETARY SYSTEM:

1 Ngultrum (= 1 Indian Rupee) = 100 Chetrums, 1974-

Signature Chart:

Chairman	Ashi Sonam Wangchuck
Bank of Bhutan	Yeshe Dorji
Chairman	Dorji Tsering

Kingdom

Royal Government of Bhutan

1974-78 ND Issue

1 **1 Ngultrum** VG 1.00 VF 2.75 Unc 7.50
ND (1974). Blue on m/c unpt.

2 **5 Ngultrums** VG 3.00 VF 15.00 Unc 45.00
ND (1974). Brown on m/c unpt. Portr. J. Singye Wangchuk at ctr. Simtokha Dzong palace ctr. r. on back.

3 **10 Ngultrums** VG 10.00 VF 30.00 Unc 150.00
ND (1974). Blue-violet on m/c unpt. Portr. J. Dorji Wangchuk at top ctr. Paro Dzong palace ctr. r. on back.

4 **100 Ngultrums** VG 350.00 VF 1200. Unc —
ND (1978). Green and brown on m/c unpt. Portr. J. Singye Wangchuk at ctr., circle w/8 good luck symbols at r. Tashichho Dzong palace at l. ctr. on back.

1981 ND Issue

#5-11 serial # at upper l. and r.

5 **1 Ngultrum** VG .10 VF .20 Unc 2.50
ND (1981). Blue on m/c unpt. Royal emblem between facing dragons at ctr. Simtokha Dzong palace at ctr. on back.

6 **2 Ngultrums** VG .15 VF .50 Unc 3.50
ND (1981). Brown and green on m/c unpt. Royal emblem between facing dragons at ctr. Simtokha Dzong palace at ctr. on back.

7 **5 NGULTRUMS**
ND (1981). Brown on m/c unpt. Royal emblem between facing birds at ctr. Paro Dzong palace at ctr. on back.

VG	VF	UNC
.85	2.50	8.50

#8-11 royal emblem at l.

8 **10 NGULTRUMS**
ND (1981). Blue-violet on m/c unpt. Portr. J. Singye Wangchuk at r. Paro Dzong palace at ctr. on back.

VG	VF	UNC
1.25	4.00	13.50

9 **20 NGULTRUMS**
ND (1981). Olive on m/c unpt. Portr. Jigme Dorji Wangchuk at r. Punakha Dzong palace at ctr. on back.

VG	VF	UNC
2.00	6.00	22.50

10 **50 NGULTRUMS**
ND (1981). Purple, violet and brown on m/c unpt. Portr. J. Dorji Wangchuk at r. Tongsa Dzong palace at ctr. on back.

VG	VF	UNC
4.50	15.00	60.00

11 **100 NGULTRUMS**
ND (1981). Dk. green, olive-green and brown-violet on m/c unpt. Bird at ctr., Portr. J. Singye Wangchuk at r. Tashichho Dzong palace at ctr. on back.

VG	VF	UNC
6.50	26.50	135.00

ROYAL MONETARY AUTHORITY OF BHUTAN

1985-92 ND ISSUE

#12-18 similar to #5-11 but reduced size w/serial # at lower l. and upper r.

12 **1 NGULTRUM**
ND (1986). Blue on m/c unpt.

VG	VF	UNC
FV	FV	.40

13 **2 NGULTRUMS**
ND (1986). Brown and green on m/c unpt.

VG	VF	UNC
FV	FV	.75

14 **5 NGULTRUMS**
ND (1985). Brown on m/c unpt.

VG	VF	UNC
FV	FV	1.50

15 **10 NGULTRUMS**
ND (1986; 1992). Blue-violet on m/c unpt. Portr. King Jigme Singye Wangchuk at l. Paro Dzong palace at ctr. on back.

	VG	VF	UNC
a. Serial # prefix fractional style. (1986).	FV	FV	1.75
b. Serial # prefix 2 lg. letters (printed in China.) (1992).	FV	FV	2.00

		VG	VF	UNC
16	**20 NGULTRUMS**			
	ND (1986; 1992). Olive on m/c unpt.			
	a. Serial # prefix fractional style. (1986).	FV	FV	4.00
	b. Serial # prefix 2 lg. letters (printed in China.) (1992).	FV	FV	3.50

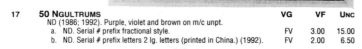

		VG	VF	UNC
17	**50 NGULTRUMS**			
	ND (1986; 1992). Purple, violet and brown on m/c unpt.			
	a. ND. Serial # prefix fractional style.	FV	3.00	15.00
	b. ND. Serial # prefix letters 2 lg. letters (printed in China.) (1992).	FV	2.00	6.50

		VG	VF	UNC
18	**100 NGULTRUMS**			
	ND (1986; 1992). Green and brown on m/c unpt.			
	a. Serial # prefix fractional style. (1986).	FV	5.00	25.00
	b. Serial # prefix 2 lg. letters (printed in China.) (1992).	FV	4.00	17.50

1994 ND ISSUE

#19 and 20 similar to #17 and 18 but with modified unpt. including floral diamond shaped registry design at upper ctr. Wmk: Wavy *ROYAL MONETARY AUTHORITY* repeated.

		VG	VF	UNC
19	**50 NGULTRUMS**			
	ND (1994). Purple, violet and brown on m/c unpt.	FV	FV	6.00

		VG	VF	UNC
20	**100 NGULTRUMS**			
	ND (1994). Green and brown on m/c unpt.	FV	FV	9.00

1994 ND COMMEMORATIVE ISSUE

#21, National Day

		VG	VF	UNC
21	**500 NGULTRUMS**			
	ND (1994). Orange on m/c unpt.	FV	FV	40.00

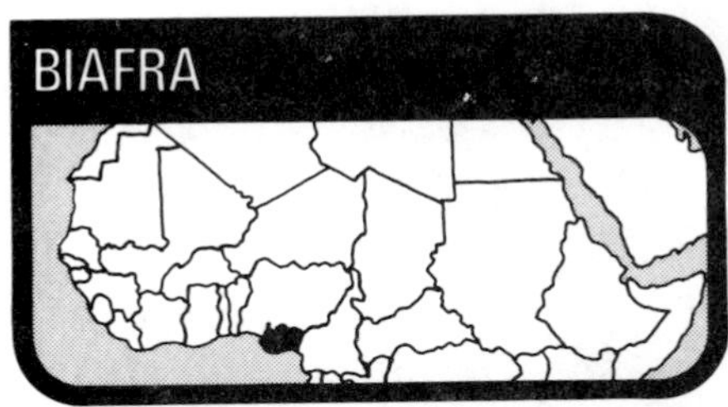

On May 27, 1967, Gen. Yakubu Gowon, head of the Federal Military Government of Nigeria, created three states from the Eastern Region of the country. Separation of the region, undertaken to achieve better regional and ethnic balance, caused Lt. Col. E. O. Ojukwu, Military Governor of the Eastern Region, to proclaim on May 30, 1967, the independence of the Eastern Region as the "Republic of Biafra." Fighting broke out between the Federal Military Government and the forces of Lt. Col. Ojukwu and continued until Biafra surrendered on Jan. 15, 1970. Biafra was then reintegrated into the Republic of Nigeria as three states: East-Central, Rivers, and South-Eastern.

For additional history, see Nigeria.

MONETARY SYSTEM:

1 Shilling = 12 Pence
1 Pound = 20 Shillings

Republic

Bank of Biafra

1967 ND Issue

#1-2 palm tree, lg. rising sun at l.

		VG	VF	Unc
1	**5 Shillings** ND (1967). Blue on lilac unpt. (Color varies from orange to yellow for rising sun.) 4 girls at r. on back.			
	a. Issued note.	.75	3.00	11.00
	b. W/o serial #.	Reported Not Confirmed		

		VG	VF	Unc
2	**1 Pound** ND (1967). Blue and orange. Back brown; arms at r.	1.75	15.00	90.00

1968 ND Issue

#3-7 palm tree and small rising sun at l. to ctr.

		VG	VF	Unc
3	**5 Shillings** ND (1968-69). Blue on green and orange unpt. Back similar to #1.			
	a. Issued note.	1.00	3.00	12.50
	b. W/o serial #.	2.00	6.00	20.00

		VG	VF	Unc
4	**10 Shillings** ND (1968-69). Green on blue and orange unpt. Bldgs. at r. on back.			
	a. Issued note.	.35	1.40	4.25
	b. W/o serial #.	Reported Not Confirmed		

		VG	VF	Unc
5	**1 Pound** ND (1968-69). Dk. brown on green and brown unpt. Back similar to #2.			
	a. Issued note.	.10	.25	1.00
	b. W/o serial #.	.75	3.00	13.50

		VG	VF	Unc
6	**5 Pounds** ND (1968-69). Violet on m/c unpt. Arms at l., weaving at l. ctr. on back.			
	a. Issued note.	4.00	15.00	50.00
	b. W/o serial #.	2.00	6.00	27.50

		VG	VF	Unc
7	**10 Pounds** ND (1968-69). Blue and brown on m/c unpt. Arms at l., carver at l. ctr. on back.			
	a. Issued note.	4.00	15.00	50.00
	b. W/o serial #.	2.50	7.50	30.00

The Republic of Bolivia, a landlocked country in west central South America, has an area of 424,165 sq. mi. (1,098,581 sq. km.) and a population of 7.6 million. Capitals: La Paz (administrative); Sucre (constitutional). Mining is the principal industry and tin the most important metal. Minerals, petroleum, natural gas, cotton and coffee are exported.

The Incas, who ruled one of the world's greatest dynasties, incorporated the area that is now western Bolivia into their empire about 1200AD. Their control was maintained until the Spaniards arrived in 1535 and reduced the predominantly Indian population to slavery. When Napoleon occupied Madrid in 1808 and placed his brother Joseph on the Spanish throne, a fervor of revolutionary activity quickened in Bolivia, culminating with the 1809 proclamation of independence. Sixteen years of struggle ensued before the republic, named for the famed liberator General Simón Bolívar, was established on August 6, 1825. Since then, Bolivia has had more than 60 revolutions, 70 presidents and 11 constitutions.

RULERS:

Spanish to 1825

MONETARY SYSTEM:

1 Bolivar = 100 Centavos, 1945-1962
1 Peso Boliviano = 100 Centavos, 1962-1987
1 Boliviano = 100 Centavos, 1987-

SPECIMEN NOTES:

All specimen, *muestra, muestra sin valor* and *especimen* notes always have serial #'s of zero.

REPUBLIC

BANCO CENTRAL DE BOLIVIA

LEY DE 13 DE JULIO DE 1962 - FIRST ISSUE

Peso Boliviano System

#152-157 old and new denomination on back at bottom. Arms at l. Sign. varieties. Printer: TDLR.

152	1 PESO BOLIVIANO	VG	VF	UNC
	L.1962. Black on m/c unpt. Portr. Campesino at r. Agricultural scene at ctr. r. on back. Series A-E.			
	a. Issued note.	2.00	5.00	10.00
	s. Specimen w/red ovpt: *SPECIMEN.* Series A.	—	—	—

153	5 PESOS BOLIVIANOS	VG	VF	UNC
	L.1962. Blue on m/c unpt. Portr. G. Villarroel at r. Petroleum refinery on back. Series A-B1.			
	a. Issued note.	1.00	3.00	12.00
	b. Uncut sheet of 4 signed notes.	—	—	100.00
	s. Specimen w/red ovpt: *SPECIMEN.* Series A; T; Z.	—	—	—

154	10 PESOS BOLIVIANOS	VG	VF	UNC
	L.1962. Olive-green on m/c unpt. Portr. Busch at r. Mountain of Potosí on back. Series A-U3.			
	a. Issued note.	.05	.20	.65
	b. Uncut sheet of 4 signed notes. Series U2.	—	—	30.00
	s2. Specimen w/red ovpt: *SPECIMEN.* Series A.	—	—	—
	s3. As s1 but w/punched hole cancellation and TDLR oval stamp. Series A.	—	—	—
	s4. Specimen ovpt: *SPECIMEN.*	—	—	7.00
	s4. Uncut sheet of 4 specimen notes. Series U2.	—	—	25.00

155	20 PESOS BOLIVIANOS	VG	VF	UNC
	L.1962. Purple on m/c unpt. Portr. Murillo at r. La Paz mountain on back. Series A.			
	a. Issued note.	.75	4.00	25.00
	s. Specimen w/red ovpt: *SPECIMEN.* Series A.	—	—	—

156	50 PESOS BOLIVIANOS	VG	VF	UNC
	L.1962. Orange on m/c unpt. Portr. A. J. de Sucre at r. Puerta del Sol on back. Series A.			
	a. Issued note.	30.00	70.00	150.00
	s. Specimen w/red ovpt: *SPECIMEN.* Series A.	—	—	—

		VG	VF	UNC
157	**100 PESOS BOLIVIANOS** *L.1962.* Red on m/c unpt. Unpt. w/green at l., blue at r. Portr. S. Bolívar at r. Red serial #, and security thread at l. ctr. Back darker red; engraved, scene of the declaration of the Bolivian Republic. Series A.			
	a. Issued note. Large, wide, dark signatures.	20.00	55.00	100.00
	b. Issued note. Small, thin, light signatures.	20.00	55.00	100.00
	s. Specimen w/red ovpt: *SPECIMEN.* Series A.	—	—	—

LEY DE 13 DE JULIO DE 1962 - SECOND ISSUE

#158, 161-164A only new denomination on back. Sign. varieties. Printer: TDLR.

		VG	VF	UNC
158	**1 PESO BOLIVIANO** *L.1962.* Like #152. Series F-F1.			
	a. Issued note.	1.00	2.00	7.00
	s. Specimen w/red ovpt: *SPECIMEN.* Series Y.	—	—	—

#159, 160 Not assigned.

		VG	VF	UNC
161	**20 PESOS BOLIVIANOS** *L.1962.* Like #155. Series B-H.			
	a. Issued note.	.30	1.00	7.50
	s. Specimen w/red ovpt: *SPECIMEN.* Series E.	—	—	—

#162-164 replacement notes: Serial # prefixes: *ZX; ZY; ZZ.*

		VG	VF	UNC
162	**50 PESOS BOLIVIANOS** *L.1962.* Like #156. Series B-D9; ZY; ZZ.			
	a. Issued note.	.10	.25	.75
	b. Uncut sheet of 4 signed notes. Series L2, Y2.	—	—	10.00
	bx. Uncut sheet of 4 notes w/sign. at top of notes. Series L2; Y2. (error).	—	—	10.00
	r. Uncut sheet of 4 unsigned notes. Series AZ.	—	—	12.50
	s. Specimen w/red ovpt: *SPECIMEN.* Series F; X.	—	—	—

> **NOTICE**
>
> Readers with unlisted dates, signature varieties, etc. are invited to submit photocopies of their notes to: Standard Catalog of World Paper Money, 700 East State St. Iola, WI 54990-0001, fax: 1-715-445-4087, or E-Mail: thernr@krause.com.

	VG	VF	UNC
L.1962. Red w/green unpt. at l. and r. on face. Like #157. Brighter red back, engraved. Lower # prefixes (from B to 10D; ZX; ZY).			
a. Issued note.	.10	.25	.85
b. Uncut sheet of 4 signed notes. Series X4; D5; U5.	—	—	—
r. Uncut sheet of 4 unsigned notes. Series AZ.			
s. Specimen w/red ovpt: *SPECIMEN.* Series G.	—	—	—

		VG	VF	UNC
164	**100 PESOS BOLIVIANOS** *L.1962* (1983). Red on m/c unpt. Like #163.			
	a. Back dull red, lithographed w/poor detail. Black serial #. W/o security thread. Prefixes #10E-13D; ZZ.	.25	.75	3.50
	b. As a. but w/solid black security thread.	.25	.75	4.00
	c. As a. but w/segmented security thread.	.75	2.00	7.00
	r. Unsigned remainder. Prefix #12H.	—	—	15.00
	s. Specimen w/red ovpt: *SPECIMEN.* Prefix #10E.	—	—	—
164A	**100 PESOS BOLIVIANOS** *L.1962.* Red on m/c unpt. Like #163 including engraved back, security thread and red serial #. Higher # prefixes 13E-19T; ZX; ZY than for 164a.	.10	.25	1.00

1981-84 VARIOUS DECREES ND ISSUE

#165-171 replacement notes: Serial # prefixes: *Z; ZY; ZZ.*

		VG	VF	UNC
165	**500 PESOS BOLIVIANOS** *D. 1.6.1981.* Deep blue, blue-green and black on m/c unpt. Arms at ctr., portr. Avaroa at r. and as wmk at l. Back blue on m/c unpt. View of Puerto de Antofagasta, ca. 1879 at ctr. Series A; Z. Printer: ABNC.			
	a. Issued note. 2 sign. varieties.	.10	.25	1.00
	r. Remainder w/o series, decreto or sign. printing.	25.00	45.00	75.00
	s. Specimen w/red ovpt: *MUESTRA.*	—	—	—
166	**500 PESOS BOLIVIANOS** *D. 1.6.1981.* Like #165 but Series B; C; Z. Printer: TDLR.			
	a. Issued note.	.10	.30	1.25
	b. Specimen w/red ovpt: *SPECIMEN.* Series B.	—	—	—

167 **1000 Pesos Bolivianos**
D. 25.6.1982. Black on m/c unpt. Arms at ctr., portr. Juana Z. de Padilla at r. and as wmk. at l. House of Liberty on back. Sign. varieties. Series A1-Z9; ZY; ZZ; (6 digits) A-L; (8 digits) each only to 49,999,999); Z (8 digits). Printer: TDLR.

	VG	VF	UNC
a. Issued note.	.10	.30	1.25
s. Specimen w/red ovpt: *SPECIMEN*. Series A1.	—	—	—

168 **5000 Pesos Bolivianos**
D. 10.2.1984. Deep brown on m/c unpt. Arms at ctr., Marshall J. Ballivian y Segurola at r. and as wmk. at l. Stylized condor and leopard on back. Printer: BDDK. Series A; Z.

	VG	VF	UNC
a. Issued note. 2 sign. varieties.	.50	1.00	2.50
s1. Specimen w/red ovpt: *MUESTRA SIN VALOR*. Series A.	—	—	—
s2. Specimen pin-holed cancelled: *SPECIMEN*.	—	—	—

169 **10,000 Pesos Bolivianos**
D. 10.2.1984. Blackish purple and purple w/dk. green arms on m/c unpt. Arms at ctr. Portr. Marshall A. de Santa Cruz at r. and as wmk. at l. Back brown, bluish purple and green; Legislative palace at ctr. Printer: BDDK. Series A; Z.

	VG	VF	UNC
a. Issued note.	.05	.20	.65
s. Specimen w/red ovpt: *MUESTRA SIN VALOR*. Series A.	—	—	—

170 **50,000 Pesos Bolivianos**
D. 5.6.1984. Deep green on m/c unpt. Arms at l., portr. Villaroel at r. Petroleum refinery on back. Printer: TDLR. Series A; B; Z.

	VG	VF	UNC
a. Issued note. 2 sign. varieties.	.05	.20	.65
s. Specimen w/red ovpt: *MUESTRA SIN VALOR*. Series A.	—	—	—

171 **100,000 Pesos Bolivianos**
D. 5.6.1984. Brown-violet on m/c unpt. Arms at l., Portr. Campesino at r. Agricultural scene at ctr. r. on back. Printer: TDLR. Series A; B; Z.

	VG	VF	UNC
a. Issued note. 2 sign. varieties.	.15	.50	2.00
s. Specimen w/red ovpt: *MUESTRA SIN VALOR*. Series A.	—	—	—

1982-86 Monetary Emergency

Banco Central de Bolivia

W/o Branch

Decreto Supremo No. 19078, 28 Julio 1982

Cheque de Gerencia Issue

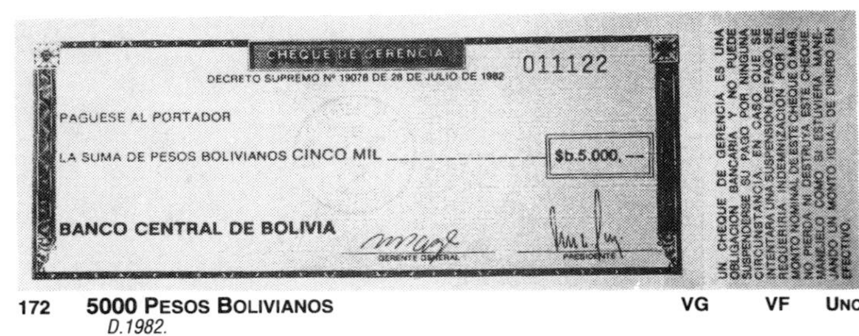

CHEQUE DE GERENCIA
DECRETO SUPREMO Nº 19078 DE 28 DE JULIO DE 1982
011122
PAGUESE AL PORTADOR
LA SUMA DE PESOS BOLIVIANOS CINCO MIL
$b.5.000,--
BANCO CENTRAL DE BOLIVIA
GERENTE GENERAL
PRESIDENTE

172 **5000 Pesos Bolivianos**
D.1982.

	VG	VF	UNC
a. Stub w/text attached at r.	—	—	6.50
b. W/o stub at r.	—	—	5.50

CHEQUE DE GERENCIA
DECRETO SUPREMO Nº 19078 DE 28 DE JULIO DE 1982
002015
PAGUESE AL PORTADOR
LA SUMA DE PESOS BOLIVIANOS DIEZ MIL
$b.10.000,--
BANCO CENTRAL DE BOLIVIA
GERENTE GENERAL
PRESIDENTE

173 **10,000 Pesos Bolivianos**
D.1982.

	VG	VF	UNC
a. Stub w/text attached at r.	—	—	10.00
b. W/o stub at r.	—	—	7.00

#174 and 175 not assigned.

Santa Cruz Branch

1984 Cheque de Gerencia Issue

#176; 178 black, Mercury in green circular unpt. at ctr.

BANCO CENTRAL DE BOLIVIA
CHEQUE DE GERENCIA
LA SUMA DE $b 50=000=00
Nº 080219
Santa Cruz, Junio 4 de 1984
$b 50.000,-
Portador
CINCUENTA MIL 00/100
ANULADO
BANCO CENTRAL DE BOLIVIA Nº 080219

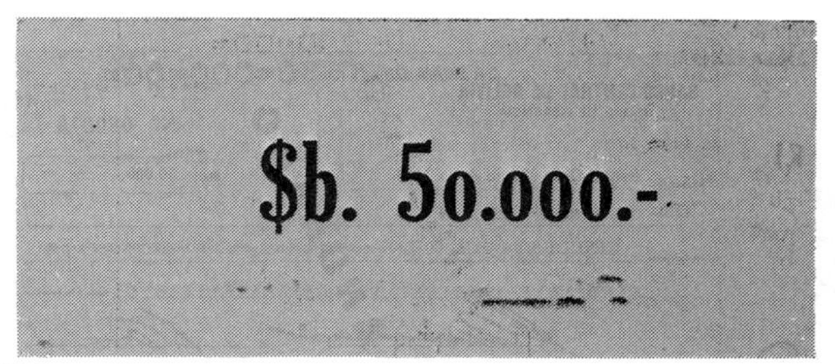

		Good	Fine	XF
176	**50,000 Pesos Bolivianos**			
	4.6.1984; 7.6.1984.			
	a. Issued note.	—	—	—
	b. Ovpt: *ANULADO* (cancelled) across face.	40.00	90.00	200.00

#177 not assigned.

		Good	Fine	XF
178	**1,000,000 Pesos Bolivianos**			
	4.6.1984; 7.6.1984.			
	a. Issued note.	—	—	—
	b. Ovpt: *ANULADO* across face.	60.00	100.00	250.00

#179 not assigned.

La Paz Branch

1984 Cheque de Gerencia Issue

#180-182 like #176-178.

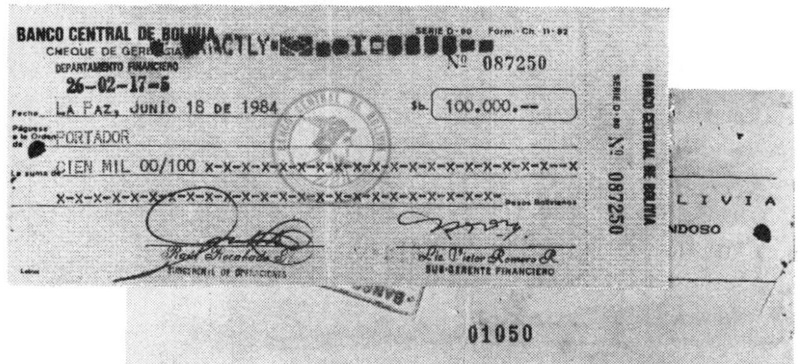

		Good	Fine	XF
180	**100,000 Pesos Bolivianos**			
	18.6.1984. Olive-green text on pale green unpt. Black text on back.			
	a. Issued note.	—	—	—
	b. Ovpt: *ANULADO* across face.	50.00	100.00	210.00
	c. Paid. Punched hole cancelled.	70.00	150.00	275.00

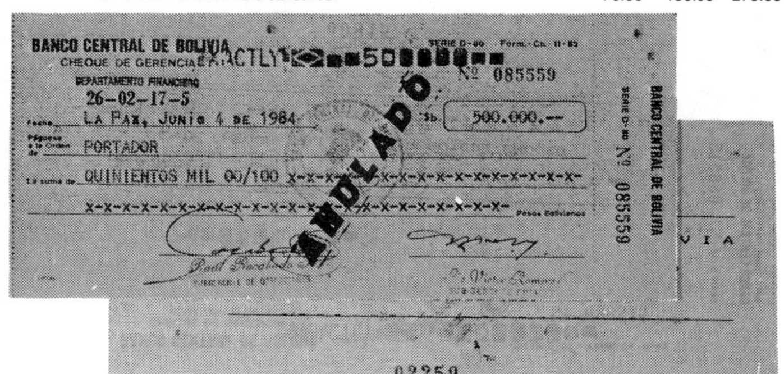

		Good	Fine	XF
181	**500,000 Pesos Bolivianos**			
	4.6.1984; 18.6.1984.			
	a. Issued note.	—	—	—
	b. Ovpt: *ANULADO* across face.	60.00	110.00	225.00
	c. Paid. Punched hole cancelled.	60.00	175.00	300.00

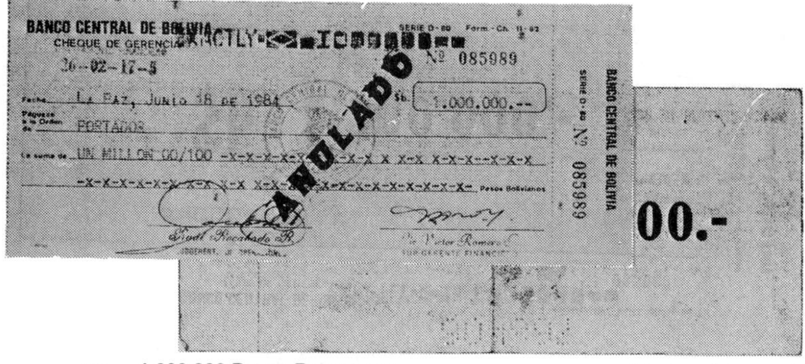

		Good	Fine	XF
182	**1,000,000 Pesos Bolivianos**			
	18.6.1984.			
	a. Issued note.	—	—	—
	b. Ovpt: *ANULADO* across face.	70.00	120.00	240.00
	c. Paid. Punched hole cancelled.	100.00	210.00	420.00

Decreto Supremo No. 20272, 5 Junio 1984, First Issue

#183-185 brown on pink unpt. Mercury at upper l. Series A. Printer: JBNC. Usable for 90 days after date of issue (Spanish text at lower r. on back).

NOTE: Unpt. of "B.C.B." and denom. boxes easily fade from pink to lt. tan to pale yellow.

		VG	VF	Unc
183	**10,000 Pesos Bolivianos**			
	D.1984.	3.00	7.00	15.00

		VG	VF	Unc
184	**20,000 Pesos Bolivianos**			
	D.1984.	15.00	40.00	100.00

		VG	VF	Unc
185	**50,000 Pesos Bolivianos**			
	D.1984.	1.25	5.00	12.50

Decreto Supremo No. 20272, 5 Junio 1984, Second Issue

#186-187 like #183-184 but w/o 90 day use restriction text on back.

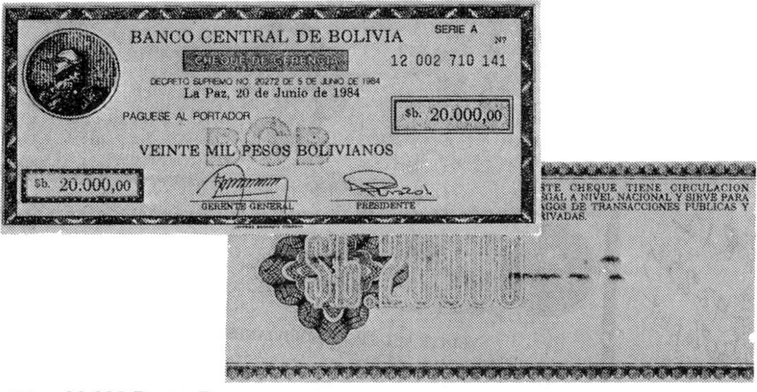

		VG	VF	Unc
186	**10,000 Pesos Bolivianos**			
	D.1984. Lt. blue on pink unpt. Series A.	1.00	2.50	7.50

		VG	VF	Unc
187	**20,000 Pesos Bolivianos**			
	D.1984. Green on pink unpt. Series A.	1.00	2.50	7.50

#188 has 90-day use restriction clause similar to #183-185.

		VG	VF	UNC
188	**100,000 Pesos Bolivianos** 21.12.1984. Reddish brown on lt. blue and lt. reddish brown unpt. 90 day usage clause at lower r. on back. Series A. Imprint and wmk: CdMB.	.20	.85	3.25

W/o Branch

Decreto Supremo No. 20272, de 5 de Junio de 1984

		VG	VF	UNC
189	**500,000 Pesos Bolivianos** *D.1984.* Deep green on green and peach unpt. No 90-day clause on back. Wmk: CdMB. W/o imprint.	.20	.85	3.25

Decreto Supremo No. 20732, 8 Marzo 1985; First Issue

		VG	VF	UNC
190	**1 Million Pesos Bolivianos** *D.1985.* Blue on yellow and pale blue unpt. Similar to previous issue. No 90-day restriction clause at lower r. on back. Series A. Wmk: CdMB. W/o imprint.			
	a. Issued note.	.25	1.00	4.50
	s. Specimen perforated: *SPECIMEN.*	—	—	—

#191 and 192 Series A. Printer: G&D.

		VG	VF	UNC
191	**5 Million Pesos Bolivianos** *D.1985.* Brown-orange and red-brown on m/c unpt. Similar to previous issues but higher quality printing and appearance. M/c back; bank initials in ornate guilloche at ctr. No 90-day restriction clause. Series A.			
	a. Issued note.	.30	1.25	5.50
	s. Specimen ovpt: *SPECIMEN.*	—	—	—

		VG	VF	UNC
192	**10 Million Pesos Bolivianos** *D.1985.* Rose and blue on tan unpt. Similar to #191. Series A.			
	a. Issued note.	2.00	8.00	18.50
	s. Specimen ovpt: *SPECIMEN.*	—	—	—

Decreto Supremo No. 20732, 8 Marzo 1985; Second Issue

#192A and 192B similar to #191 and 192. Printer: CdM-Brazil.

		VG	VF	UNC
192A (191A)	**5 Million Pesos Bolivianos** *D.1985.* Similar to #191. Series B.	.50	2.00	6.50

		VG	VF	UNC
192B (192A)	**10 Million Pesos Bolivianos** *D.1985.* Rose, violet and purple on m/c unpt. Similar to #192. Series B.	.75	3.25	8.50

DECRETO SUPREMO NO. 20732, 8 MARZO 1985; THIRD ISSUE

#192C-194 printer: CdM-Argentina.

		VG	VF	UNC
192C (A193)	**1 MILLION PESOS BOLIVIANOS** *D.1985.* Blue and m/c. Lg. guilloche at l., Mercury head in unpt. at r. Series L.			
	a. Issued note.	.20	.75	3.25
	s. Specimen w/black ovpt: *MUESTRA.*	—	—	—

		VG	VF	UNC
193	**5 MILLION PESOS BOLIVIANOS** *D.1985.* Brown w/reddish brown text on m/c unpt. Similar to #192C. Series N.			
	a. Issued note.	.75	3.25	6.50
	s. Specimen w/black ovpt: *MUESTRA.*	—	—	—

		VG	VF	UNC
194	**10 MILLION PESOS BOLIVIANOS** *D.1985.* Violet w/lilac text on m/c unpt. Similar to #192C. Series M.			
	a. Issued note.	1.00	4.00	12.00
	s. Specimen w/black ovpt: *MUESTRA.*	—	—	—

NOTICE

Readers with unlisted dates, signature varieties, etc. are invited to submit photocopies of their notes to: Standard Catalog of World Paper Money, 700 East State St. Iola, WI 54990-0001, fax: 1-715-445-4087, or E-Mail: thernr@krause.com.

REPUBLIC, 1986-

BANCO CENTRAL DE BOLIVIA

1987 ND PROVISIONAL ISSUE

		VG	VF	UNC
195	**1 CENTAVO ON 10,000 PESOS BOLIVIANOS** ND (1987). Ovpt. at r. on back of #169.	.10	.25	1.00

		VG	VF	UNC
196	**5 CENTAVOS ON 50,000 PESOS BOLIVIANOS** ND (1987). Ovpt. at r. on back of #170.	.15	.50	2.25
196A	**10 CENTAVOS ON 100,000 PESOS BOLIVIANOS** ND (1987). Ovpt. at r. on back of #171.	.50	1.50	5.00

		VG	VF	UNC
197	**10 CENTAVOS ON 100,000 PESOS BOLIVIANOS** ND (1987). Ovpt. at r. on back of #188.	.15	.50	2.25

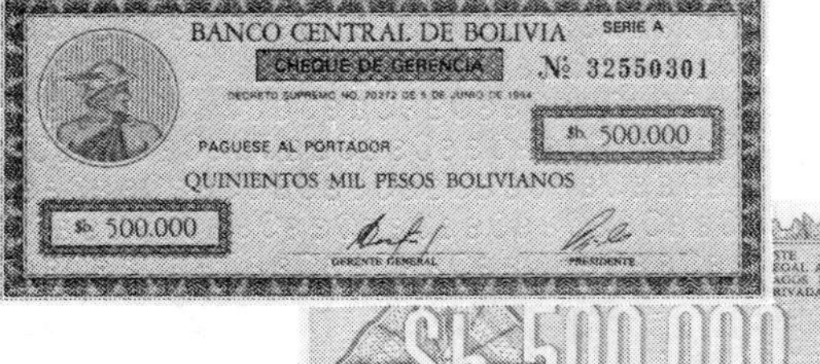

		VG	VF	UNC
198	**50 CENTAVOS ON 500,000 PESOS BOLIVIANOS** ND (1987). Ovpt. at r. on back of #189.	.20	.85	3.25

		VG	VF	UNC
199	**1 BOLIVIANO ON 1,000,000 PESOS BOLIVIANOS** ND (1987). Ovpt. at r. on back of #192C.	.25	.60	2.50

		VG	VF	UNC
200	**5 BOLIVIANOS ON 5,000,000 PESOS BOLIVIANOS** ND (1987). Ovpt. at l. on back of #192A.			
	a. Issued note.	.30	1.25	5.00
	x1. Error. Inverted ovpt. on left end.	1.00	5.50	15.00
	x2. Error. Ovpt. on r. end.	—	—	—

		VG	VF	UNC
201	**10 BOLIVIANOS ON 10,000,000 PESOS BOLIVIANOS** ND (1987). Ovpt. at l. on back of #192B.	1.00	4.00	12.00

LEY 901 DE 28.11.1986; 1987-97 ND ISSUES

#202-208 arms at lower l., ctr. or r. Wmk: S. Bolívar. Printer: F-CO

Series A sign. titles: *PRESIDENTE BCB* and *MINISTRO DE FINANZAS*. Serial # suffix *A*.

Series B sign. titles: *PRESIDENTE DEL B.C.B.* and *GERENTE GENERAL B.C.B.* Serial # suffix *B*.

Series E sign. titles: *PRESIDENTE BCB* and *GERENTE GENERAL BCB*. Serial # suffix *E*.

		VG	VF	UNC
202	**2 BOLIVIANOS** *L.1986.* (1987; 1990). Black on m/c unpt. A. Vaca Diez at r., arms at lower ctr. Trees and bldgs. at ctr. on back.			
	a. Series A (1987). W/control #'s.	FV	FV	3.25
	b. Series B. (1990). W/control #'s.	FV	FV	4.00
	s. As a. Specimen w/red ovpt: *ESPECIMEN.*	—	—	—

		VG	VF	UNC
203	**5 BOLIVIANOS** *L.1986.* (1987; 1990). Olive-green on m/c unpt. Adela Zamudio at r., arms at lower l. Religious shrine at l. ctr. on back.			
	a. Series A (1987). W/control #.	FV	FV	5.00
	b. Series B (1990). W/control #.	FV	FV	6.50
	c. Series E (1998). W/o control #.	FV	FV	3.00
	s. As a. Specimen w/red ovpt: *ESPECIMEN.*	—	—	—

		VG	VF	UNC
204	**10 BOLIVIANOS** *L.1986.* (1987-97). Blue-black on m/c unpt. C. Guzman R. at r., arms at lower l. Figures overlooking city view on back.			
	a. Series A (1987). W/control #.	FV	FV	9.50
	b. Series B (1990). W/control #.	FV	FV	12.50
	c. Series E (1997). W/o control #.	FV	FV	5.00
	s. As a. Specimen w/red ovpt: *ESPECIMEN.*	—	—	—

		VG	VF	UNC
205	**20 BOLIVIANOS** *L.1986.* (1987; 1990). Orange and brown-orange on m/c unpt. P. Dalence at r., arms at lower ctr. Bldg. at ctr. on back.			
	a. Series A (1987). W/control #.	FV	FV	20.00
	b. Series B (1990). W/control #.	FV	FV	25.00

		VG	VF	UNC
	c. Series E (1997). W/o control #.	FV	FV	8.50
	s. As a. Specimen w/red ovpt: *ESPECIMEN.*	—	—	—

		VG	VF	UNC
206	**50 BOLIVIANOS** *L.1986* (1987; 1997). Purple on m/c unpt. M. Perez de Holguin at r., arms at lower ctr. Tall bldg. at ctr. on back.			
	a. Series A (1987). W/control #.	FV	FV	50.00
	b. Series E (1997). W/o control #.	FV	FV	16.50
	s. As a. Specimen w/red ovpt: *ESPECIMEN.*	—	—	—

		VG	VF	UNC
207	**100 BOLIVIANOS** *L.1986* (1987; 1997). Red-violet and orange on m/c unpt. G. Rene Moreno at r., arms at lower r. University bldg. at ctr. on back.			
	a. Series A (1987). W/control #.	FV	FV	110.00
	b. Series E (1997). W/o control #.	FV	FV	32.50
	s. As a. Specimen w/red ovpt: *ESPECIMEN.*	—	—	—

		VG	VF	UNC
208	**200 BOLIVIANOS** *L.1986* (1987; 1997). Brown and dk. brown on m/c unpt. F. Tamayo at r., arms at lower ctr. Ancient statuary on back.			
	a. Series A (1987). W/control #.	FV	FV	225.00
	b. Series E (1997). W/o control #.	FV	FV	60.00
	s. As a. Specimen w/red ovpt: *ESPECIMEN.*	—	—	—

LEY 901 DE 28.11.1986; 1993 ND ISSUE

#209-214 similar to #203-208 but many stylistic differences. Sign. titles: *PRESIDENTE BCB* and *GERENTE GENERAL BCB*. Serial # suffix *C*. Printer: FNMT.

#209-212 wmk: S. Bolívar.

		VG	VF	UNC
209	**5 BOLIVIANOS** *L.1986* (1993). Olive-green on m/c unpt. Series C.	FV	FV	4.00

		VG	VF	UNC
210	**10 BOLIVIANOS** *L.1986* (1993). Blue-black on m/c unpt. Series C.	FV	FV	6.50

		VG	VF	UNC
211	**20 BOLIVIANOS** *L.1986* (1993). Orange and brown-orange on m/c unpt. Series C.	FV	FV	11.00

		VG	VF	UNC
212	**50 BOLIVIANOS** *L.1986* (1993). Purple on m/c unpt. Series C.	FV	FV	22.50

NOTICE

Readers with unlisted dates, signature varieties, etc. are invited to submit photocopies of their notes to: Standard Catalog of World Paper Money, 700 East State St. Iola, WI 54990-0001, fax: 1-715-445-4087, or E-Mail: thernr@krause.com.

		VG	VF	UNC
213	**100 BOLIVIANOS** *L.1986* (1993). Red and orange on m/c unpt. Series C.	FV	FV	45.00

		VG	VF	UNC
214	**200 BOLIVIANOS** *L.1986* (1993). Brown and dk. brown on m/c unpt. Series C.	FV	FV	90.00

LEY 901 DE 28.11.1986; 1995 ND INTERIM ISSUE

#215 and 216 like #209 and 210 but w/many stylistic differences including sign. titles. Wmk: S. Bolívar. Printer: TDLR.

		VG	VF	UNC
215	**5 BOLIVIANOS** *L.1986* (1995). Olive-green on m/c unpt. Series C.			
	a. Issued note.	FV	FV	6.00
	s. Specimen w/red ovpt: *MUESTRA SIN VALOR.*	—	—	—
216	**10 BOLIVIANOS**			

		VG	VF	UNC
	L.1986 (1995). Blue-black on m/c unpt. Series C.			
	a. Issued note.	FV	FV	12.00
	s. Specimen w/red ovpt: *MUESTRA SIN VALOR.*	—	—	—

LEY 901 DE 28.11.1986; 1995-96 ND ISSUE

#217-222 like #209-214 but w/many stylistic differences and sign. titles: *PRESIDENTE BCB* and *GERENTE GENERAL BCB*. W/o 4 control #'s. Printer: TDLR.

#217-220 wmk: S. Bolívar.

		VG	VF	UNC
217	**5 BOLIVIANOS** *L.1986* (1995). Olive-green on m/c unpt. Series D.	FV	FV	3.25

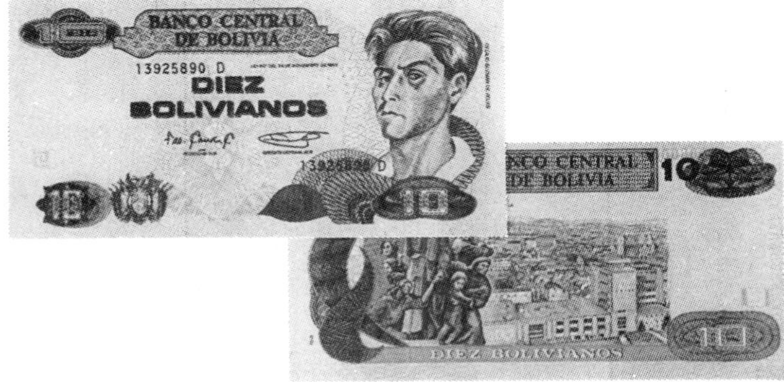

		VG	VF	UNC
218	**10 BOLIVIANOS** *L.1986* (1995). Blue-black on m/c unpt. Series D.	FV	FV	5.00

		VG	VF	UNC
219	**20 BOLIVIANOS** *L.1986* (1995). Orange and brown-orange on m/c unpt. Series D.	FV	FV	8.00

		VG	VF	UNC
220	**50 BOLIVIANOS** *L.1986* (1995). Purple on m/c unpt. Series D. Wmk: M. P. de Holguín.			
	a. Issued note.	FV	FV	18.50
	s. Specimen w/red ovpt: *MUESTRA SIN VALOR.*	—	—	—
221	**100 BOLIVIANOS** *L.1986* (1996). Red and orange on m/c unpt. Wmk: G. Rene Moreno. Series D.	FV	FV	35.00
222	**200 BOLIVIANOS** *L.1986* (1996). Brown and dk. brown on m/c unpt. Wmk: F. Tamayo. Series D.	FV	FV	65.00

The Republic of Bosnia-Herzegovina borders Croatia to the north and west, Serbia to the east and Montenegro in the southeast with only 12.4 miles of coastline. The total land area is 19,735 sq. mi. (51,129 sq. km.). It has a population of 4.37 million. Capital: Sarajevo. Electricity, mining and agriculture are leading industries.

Bosnia's first ruler of importance was the Ban Kulin, 1180-1204. Stephen Kotromanió was invested with Bosnia, held loyalty to Hungary and extended his rule to the principality of Hum or Zahumlje, the future Herzegovina. His daughter Elisabeth married Louis the Great and he died in the same year. His nephew Tvrtko succeeded and during the weakening of Serbian power he assumed the title "Stephen Tvrtko, in Christ God King of the Serbs and Bosnia and the Coastland." Later he assumed the title of "King of Dalmatia and Croatia," but died before he could consolidate power. Successors also asserted their right to the Serbian throne.

In 1459 the Turks invaded Serbia. Bosnia was invaded in 1463 and Herzegovina in 1483. During Turkish rule Islam was accepted rather than Catholicism. During the 16th and 17th centuries Bosnia was an important Turkish outpost in continuing warfare with the Habsburgs and Venice. When Hungary was freed of the Turkish yoke, the imperialists penetrated Bosnia, and in 1697 Prince Eugene captured Sarajevo. Later, by the Treaty of Karlowitz in 1699, the northern boundary of Bosnia became the northernmost limit of the Turkish empire while the eastern area was ceded to Austria, but later restored to Turkey in 1739 lasting until 1878 following revolts of 1821, 1828, 1831 and 1862. On June 30, 1871 Serbia and Montenegro declared war on Turkey and were quickly defeated. The Turkish war with Russia led to the occupation by Austria-Hungary. Insurgents attempted armed resistance and Austria-Hungary invaded, quelling the uprising in 1878. The Austrian occupation provided a period of prosperity while at the same time prevented relations with Serbia and Croatia. Strengthening political and religious movements from within forced the annexation by Austria on Oct. 7, 1908. Hungary's establishment of a dictatorship in Croatia following the victories of Serbian forces in the Balkan War roused the whole Yugoslav population of Austria-Hungary to feverish excitement. The Bosnian group, mainly students, devoted its efforts to revolutionary ideas. After Austria's Balkan front collapsed in Oct. 1918 the union with Yugoslavia developed and on Dec. 1, 1918 the former Kingdom of the Serbs, Croats and Slovenes was proclaimed (later to become the Kingdom of Yugoslavia on Oct. 3, 1929).

After the defeat of Germany in WWII during which Bosnia was under the control of Pavelic of Croatia, a new Socialist Republic was formed under Marshal Tito having six constituent republics all subservient, quite similar to the constitution of the U.S.S.R. Military and civil loyalty was with Tito. In Jan. 1990 the Yugoslav government announced a rewriting of the constitution, abolishing the Communist Party's monopoly of power. Opposition parties were legalized in July 1990. On Oct. 15, 1991 the National Assembly adopted a Memorandum on Sovereignty that envisaged Bosnian autonomy within a Yugoslav Federation. In March 1992 an agreement was reached under EC auspices by Moslems, Serbs and Croats to set up 3 autonomous ethnic communities under a central Bosnian authority. Independence was declared on April 5, 1992. The 2 Serbian members of government resigned and fighting broke out between all 3 ethnic communities. The Dayton (Ohio, USA) Peace Accord was signed in 1995 which recognized the Federation of Bosnia-Herzegovina and the Srpska (Serbian) Republic. Both governments maintain separate military forces, schools, etc., providing humanitarian aid while a treaty allowed NATO "Peace Keeping" forces be deployed in Dec. 1995 replacing the United Nations troops previously acting in a similar role.

RULERS:

Ottoman, until 1878
Austrian, 1878-1918
Yugoslavian, 1918-1941

MONETARY SYSTEM:

1 Dinar = 100 Para 1992-1998
1 Convertible Marka = 1 Deutschemark
1 Convertible Marka = 100 Convertible Pfeniga, 1998-

REPUBLIKA BOSNA I HERCEGOVINA

MOSLEM REPUBLIC

НАРОДНА БАНКА БОСНЕ И ХЕРЦЕГОВИНЕ

NARODNA BANKA BOSNE I HERCEGOVINE

Ceased operations in August 1997.

W/O BRANCH

1992 FIRST PROVISIONAL ISSUE

#1-2 violet handstamp: *NARODNA BANKA BOSNE I HERCEGOVINE,* also in Cyrillic around Yugoslav arms, on Yugoslav regular issues. Handstamp varieties exist.

1	500 DINARA	GOOD	FINE	XF
	ND (1992). 31mm handstamp on Yugoslavia #109.			
	a. Handstamp w/o numeral.	10.00	30.00	100.00
	b. Handstamp w/numeral: *1.*	10.00	30.00	100.00
	c. Handstamp w/numeral: *2.*	10.00	30.00	100.00

2	1000 DINARA	GOOD	FINE	XF
	ND (1992). 48mm handstamp on Yugoslavia #110.			
	a. Handstamp w/o numeral.	8.00	25.00	125.00
	b. Handstamp w/numeral 1.	8.00	25.00	125.00
	c. Handstamp w/numeral 2.	8.00	25.00	125.00

#3 and 4 not assigned.

1992 SECOND PROVISIONAL NOVCANI BON ISSUE

#5-9 issued in various Moslem cities. Peace dove at upper l. ctr. Example w/o indication of city of issue are remainders.

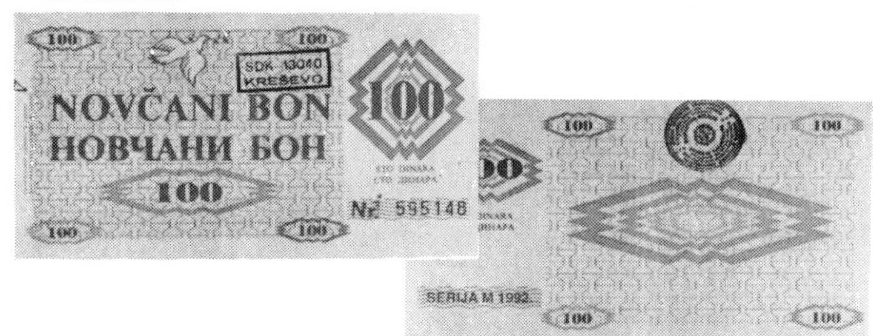

6	100 DINARA	GOOD	FINE	XF
	1992. Deep pink on gray and yellow unpt.			
	a. Handstamped: *BREZA* on back.	3.00	9.00	25.00
	b. Circular red handstamp: *FOJNICA* on back.	2.50	7.50	22.50
	c. Rectangular purple handstamp on face, circular purple handstamp: *KRESEVO* on back.	6.50	20.00	60.00
	d. Handstamped: *TESANJ* on back.	6.50	20.00	60.00
	e. Handstamped: *VARES* on back.	2.50	7.50	22.50
	f. Handstamped: *VISOKO* on back (2 varieties).	2.00	6.00	18.00
	g. Circular red ovpt: *ZENICA,* 11.5.1992. on back r. W/printed sign. at either side.	1.00	3.00	9.00
	r. Remainder, w/o handstamp or ovpt.	—	2.00	7.00

7	500 DINARA	GOOD	FINE	XF
	1992. Pale greenish-gray on gray and yellow unpt.			
	a. Handstamped: *BREZA* on back.	2.50	8.00	24.00
	b. Circular red handstamp: *FOJNICA* on back.	2.50	7.50	22.50
	c. Handstamped: *KRESEVO* on back.	6.50	20.00	60.00
	d. Handstamped: *TESANJ* on back.	2.50	7.50	22.50
	e. Handstamped: *VARES* on back.	6.50	20.00	60.00
	f. Circular red handstamp: *VISOKO* on back.	4.50	14.00	42.00
	g. Circular red handstamp on back, details as #6g: *ZENICA* (small or large), 11.5.1992.	.50	2.00	7.00

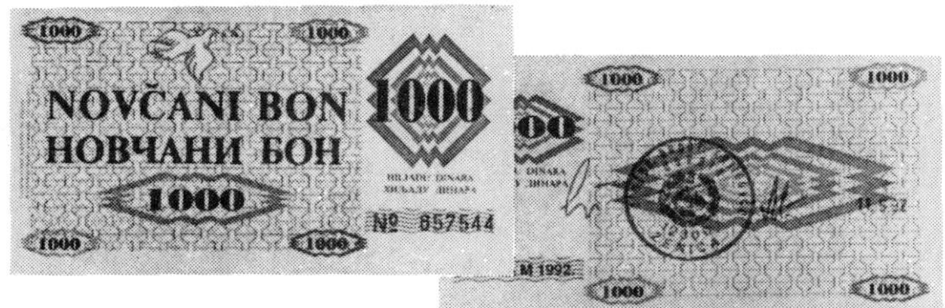

8	1000 DINARA	GOOD	FINE	XF
	1992. Blue on gray unpt.			
	a. Handstamped: *BREZA* on back.	5.00	16.00	48.00
	b. Handstamped: *FOJNICA* on back.	5.00	16.00	48.00
	c. Handstamped: *KHESEVO* on back.	8.00	25.00	75.00
	d. Handstamped: *TESANJ* on back.	6.50	20.00	60.00
	e. Handstamped: *VARES* on back.	6.50	20.00	60.00
	f. Handstamped: *VISOKO* on back (small or large).	2.00	6.00	18.00
	g. Handstamped: *ZENICA* on face, no date on stamping.	8.00	25.00	75.00
	h. Circular red ovpt. on back, details as 6g: *ZENICA,* 11.5.1992.	.25	1.00	18.50

#		Good	Fine	XF
9	**5000 Dinara**			
	1992. Dull brown on gray and yellow unpt.			
	a. Handstamped: *BREZA* on back.	4.00	12.00	36.00
	b. Circular red handstamp: *FOJNICA* on back.	3.25	10.00	30.00
	c. Handstamped: *KRESEVO* on back.	6.50	20.00	60.00
	d. Handstamped: *TESANJ* on back.	10.00	30.00	—
	e. Handstamped: *VARES* on back.	3.25	10.00	30.00
	f. Handstamped: *VISOKO* on back (3 varieties).	2.00	6.00	18.00
	g. Handstamped: *ZENICA* on face, w/o date in stamping.	6.50	20.00	60.00
	h. Circular violet ovpt. on back, details as 6g: *ZENICA*, 11.5.1992.	.25	1.00	3.00
	r. Remainder, w/o handstamp or ovpt.	5.00	16.00	48.00

1992-93 Issues

#10-15 guilloche at l. ctr. 145x73mm. Wmk: Repeated diamonds. Printer: Cetis (Celje, Slovenia).

#10-18 serial # varieties.

#		VG	VF	Unc
10	**10 Dinara**			
	1.7.1992. Purple on pink unpt. Mostar stone arch bridge at r. on back.			
	a. Issued note.	.10	.25	1.00
	s. Specimen.	—	—	30.00

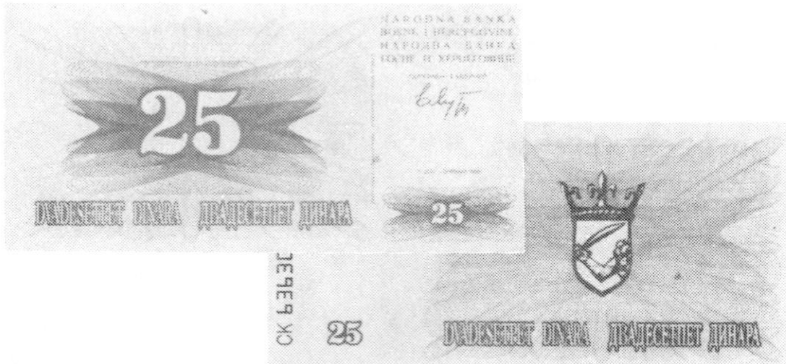

#		VG	VF	Unc
11	**25 Dinara**			
	1.7.1992. Blue-black on lt. blue unpt. Crowned arms at ctr. r. on back.			
	a. Issued note.	.10	.20	1.25
	s. Specimen.	—	—	30.00

#		VG	VF	Unc
12	**50 Dinara**			
	1.7.1992. Blue-black on red-violet unpt. Mostar stone arch bridge at r. on back.			
	a. Issued note.	10	.35	1.50
	s. Specimen.	—	—	30.00

#		VG	VF	Unc
13	**100 Dinara**			
	1.7.1992. Dull black on olive-green unpt. Crowned arms at ctr. r. on back.			
	a. Issued note.	.10	.45	1.75
	s. Specimen.	—	—	30.00

#		VG	VF	Unc
14	**500 Dinara**			
	1.7.1992. Dull violet-brown on pink and ochre unpt. Crowned arms at ctr. r. on back.			
	a. Issued note.	.20	.85	3.50
	s. Specimen.	—	—	30.00

#		VG	VF	Unc
15	**1000 Dinara**			
	1.7.1992. Deep purple on lt. green and lilac unpt. Mostar stone arch bridge at r. on back.			
	a. Issued note.	.25	1.00	4.50
	s. Specimen.	—	—	30.00

#16 and 17 grayish blue shield w/fleur-de-lis replaces crowned shield w/raised scimitar on back. Reduced size notes. Printed in Zenica.

#		VG	VF	Unc
16	**5000 Dinara**			
	25.1.1993. Pale olive-green on yellow-orange unpt. Arms at r. on back.			
	a. Issued note.	1.00	3.00	7.50
	b. W/ovpt: *SDK*.	1.75	5.00	15.00

17	10,000 DINARA	VG	VF	UNC
	25.1.1993. Brown on pink unpt. Arms at r. on back.			
	a. Issued note.	1.25	3.50	8.50
	b. W/ovpt: *SDK*.	1.75	5.00	15.00

1992; 1993 BON ISSUE

#21-27 shield at l. on back. Issued for the Sarajevo area. Grayish green or yellow unpt. on back.

21	10 DINARA	VG	VF	UNC
	1.8.1992. Violet.			
	a. Issued note.	3.25	10.00	25.00
	s. Specimen.	—	—	30.00

22	20 DINARA	VG	VF	UNC
	1.8.1992. Blue-violet.			
	a. Issued note.	2.00	6.00	15.00
	s. Specimen.	—	—	30.00

23	50 DINARA	VG	VF	UNC
	1.8.1992. Pink.			
	a. Issued note.	2.00	6.00	15.00
	s. Specimen.	—	—	30.00

24	100 DINARA	VG	VF	UNC
	1.8.1992. Green.			
	a. Issued note.	3.25	10.00	25.00
	s. Specimen.	—	—	30.00

25	500 DINARA	VG	VF	UNC
	1.8.1992. Orange. Back red-orange on pale purple and grayish green unpt.			
	a. Issued note.	3.25	10.00	25.00
	s. Specimen.	—	—	30.00

26	1000 DINARA	VG	VF	UNC
	1.8.1992. Brown.			
	a. Issued note.	2.00	6.00	15.00
	s. Specimen.	—	—	30.00

27	5000 DINARA	VG	VF	UNC
	1.8.1992. Violet.			
	a. Issued note.	2.25	7.50	18.00
	s. Specimen.	—	—	30.00

NOTICE

Readers with unlisted dates, signature varieties, etc. are invited to submit photocopies of their notes to: Standard Catalog of World Paper Money, 700 East State St. Iola, WI 54990-0001, fax: 1-715-445-4087, or E-Mail: thernr@krause.com.

		VG	VF	UNC
28	**10,000 DINARA** 6.4.1993. Lt. Blue.	2.25	7.50	18.00

		VG	VF	UNC
29	**50,000 DINARA** 1.5.1993. Pink.	5.00	15.00	25.00

		VG	VF	UNC
30	**100,000 DINARA** 1.8.1993. Green on m/c unpt. Back green on gray unpt.	1.65	5.00	12.00

		VG	VF	UNC
31	**100,000 DINARA** 1.8.1993. Green. Back green on yellow unpt.	2.50	7.50	18.50

1993 NOVCANI BON EMERGENCY ISSUE

		VG	VF	UNC
32	**100,000 DINARA** 1993 (-old date 1.7.1992). Rectangular crenalated framed ovpt: *NOVCANI BON 100,000...*on face and back of #10.			

	VG	VF	UNC
a. Purple ovpt. 1.9.1993.	.50	7.00	18.00

	VG	VF	UNC
b. Blue ovpt. and lt. blue sign. ovpt. 10.11.1993.	.50	3.50	9.00

		VG	VF	UNC
33	**1,000,000 DINARA** 10.11.1993 (old date-1.7.1992). Blue-violet ovpt. on #11. (Not issued)	—	6.00	15.00

		VG	VF	UNC
34	**10,000,000 DINARA** 10.11.1993 (old date-1.7.1992). Blue-violet ovpt. on #12. (Not issued)	—	4.00	12.50

		VG	VF	UNC
35	**100,000,000 DINARA** 10.11.1993 (old date-1.7.1992). Blue-violet ovpt. on #12. (Not issued)	—	4.00	12.50

1994 FIRST ISSUE

#36 Not assigned.

		VG	VF	UNC
37	**500,000 DINARA** 1.1.1994. Brown. Back brown on pale yellow-green unpt.	2.50	7.50	18.50
38	**1,000,000 DINARA** 1.1.1994. Red.	2.00	5.00	15.00

1994 SECOND ISSUE

Currency Reform, 1994

1 New' Dinar = 10,000 "Old" Dinara

#39-46 alternate with shield or Mostar stone bridge at ctr. r. on back. Wmk: block design. Printer: DD "Dom Stampe" Zenica.

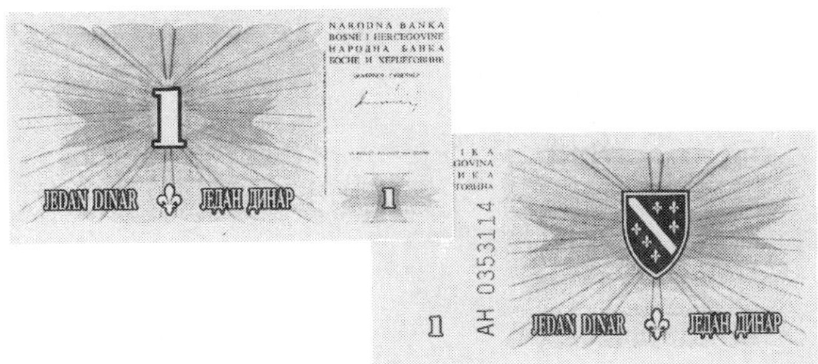

		VG	VF	UNC
39	**1 DINAR** 15.8.1994. Purplish gray on red-violet and pale green unpt.	.05	.15	.75

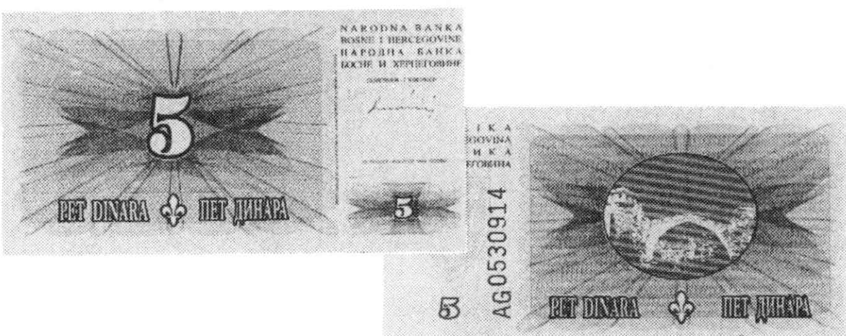

		VG	VF	UNC
40	**5 DINARA** 15.8.1994. Purplish gray on lilac, red and orange unpt.	.05	.15	.75

		VG	VF	UNC
41	**10 DINARA** 15.8.1994. Purple on red, orange and red-violet unpt.	.10	.25	1.00

		VG	VF	UNC
42	**20 DINARA** 15.8.1994. Brown on violet, red and yellow unpt.	.15	.35	1.50

		VG	VF	UNC
43	**50 DINARA** 15.8.1994. Purplish gray on red-violet and pale purple unpt.	.15	.50	2.00

NOTICE

Readers with unlisted dates, signature varieties, etc. are invited to submit photocopies of their notes to: Standard Catalog of World Paper Money, 700 East State St. Iola, WI 54990-0001, fax: 1-715-445-4087, or E-Mail: thernr@krause.com.

		VG	VF	UNC
44	**100 DINARA** 15.8.1994. Dull black on aqua, yellow and olive-green unpt.	.15	.50	2.25

		VG	VF	UNC
45	**500 DINARA** 15.8.1994. Dull brown on lilac and yellow unpt.			
	a. Large #'s.	.35	1.50	6.00
	b. Small #'s.	.35	1.50	6.00

		VG	VF	UNC
46	**1000 DINARA** 15.8.1994. Blue-gray on gray-green, red-violet and lt. green unpt.			
	a. Large #'s.	1.00	4.50	12.50
	b. Small #'s.	1.00	4.50	12.50

1995 ND ISSUE

		VG	VF	UNC
47	**50 DINARA** ND (1995). Purple on pink and ochre unpt. Bridge at r. Wmk: Lis.	—	4.00	12.50

TRAVNIK BRANCH

1992 ND NOVCANI BON ISSUE

#48-52 plain design w/value at ctr. w/Travnik Branch handstamp.

		VG	VF	UNC
48	**200 DINARA** ND(1992). Orange.	10.00	30.00	60.00
49	**500 DINARA** ND(1992). Brown.	10.00	30.00	60.00

		VG	VF	UNC
50	**1000 DINARA** ND(1992). Lilac.	7.50	20.00	40.00

51 **5000 Dinara**
ND(1992). Lt. blue. 15.00 40.00 80.00

		VG	VF	UNC
52	**10,000 Dinara** ND(1992). Red on blue unpt.	15.00	40.00	80.00

1993 Emergency Issue

#53-56 like #10-13 w/additional 3 solid zeroes printed after large value on face w/Travnik Branch dated handstamp.

		VG	VF	UNC
53	**10,000 Dinara** 15.10.1993. Red on yellow unpt.	7.00	17.50	35.00

		VG	VF	UNC
54	**25,000 Dinara** 15.10.1993. Green on blue unpt.	7.00	17.50	35.00

		VG	VF	UNC
		7.00	17.50	35.00

...tc. are invited to submit pho-

		VG	VF	UNC
56	**100,000 Dinara** 15.10.1993. Green.	7.00	17.50	35.00

ЦЕНТРАЛНА БАНКА БОСНЕ И ХЕРЦЕГОВИНЕ
Centralna Banka Bosne I Hercegovine

Established in Sarajevo on Aug. 11, 1997.

1998 ND Issue

#57-70 w/alternating texts of bank name and denominations. Wmk: Central bank monogram repeated vertically. Printer: FC-O.

		VG	VF	UNC
57	**50 Convertible Pfeniga** ND (1998). Dk. blue on blue and lilac unpt. Portr. S. Kulenovic at r. *Stecak Zgosca* fragment at l. ctr. on back.	FV	FV	.75

		VG	VF	UNC
58	**50 Convertible Pfeniga** ND (1998). Dk. blue on blue and lilac unpt. Portr. B. Copic at r. Open book, cabin at l. ctr. on back.	FV	FV	.75

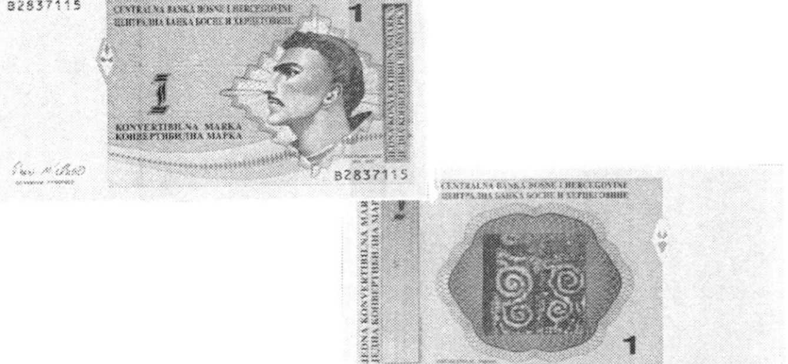

		VG	VF	UNC
59	**1 Convertible Marka** ND (1998). Dk. green on green and yellow-green unpt. I. F. Jukic at r. "Stecak Stolac" fragment at l. ctr. on back.	FV	FV	1.35

		VG	VF	UNC
60	**1 CONVERTIBLE MARKA** ND (1998). Dk. green on green and yellow-green unpt. I. Andric at r. Bridge at l. ctr. on back.	FV	FV	1.35

		VG	VF	UNC
61	**5 CONVERTIBLE MARAKA** ND (1998). Violet on m/c unpt. M. Selimovic at r. Trees at l. ctr. on back.	FV	FV	5.50

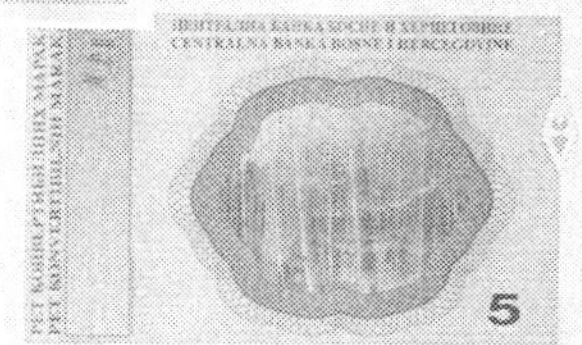

		VG	VF	UNC
62	**5 CONVERTIBLE MARAKA** ND (1998). Violet on m/c unpt. Like #61 but cyrillic bank name and denomination first.	FV	FV	5.50

		VG	VF	UNC
63	**10 CONVERTIBLE MARAKA** ND (1998). Orange-brown on dull purple and orange-brown unpt. M. M. Dizdar at r. "Stecak Radimlja" fragment at l. ctr. on back.	FV	FV	10.00
64	**10 CONVERTIBLE MARAKA** ND (1998). Orange-brown on dull purple and orange-brown unpt. A. Santic at r. Loaf of bread at l. ctr. on back.	FV	FV	10.00

#65-70 variable optical device at upper l. ctr.

		VG	VF	UNC
65	**20 CONVERTIBLE MARAKA** ND (1998). Dk. brown on m/c unpt. A. B. Simic at r. "Stecak Radimilja" fragment at l. ctr. on back.	FV	FV	18.50

		VG	VF	UNC
66	**20 CONVERTIBLE MARAKA** ND (1998). Dk. brown on m/c unpt. F. Visjic at r. "Gusle" musical instrument at l. ctr. on back.	FV	FV	18.50

		VG	VF	UNC
67	**50 CONVERTIBLE MARAKA** ND (1998). Purple on lilac and m/c unpt. M. C. Catic at r. Stone relief at l. ctr. on back.	FV	FV	45.00

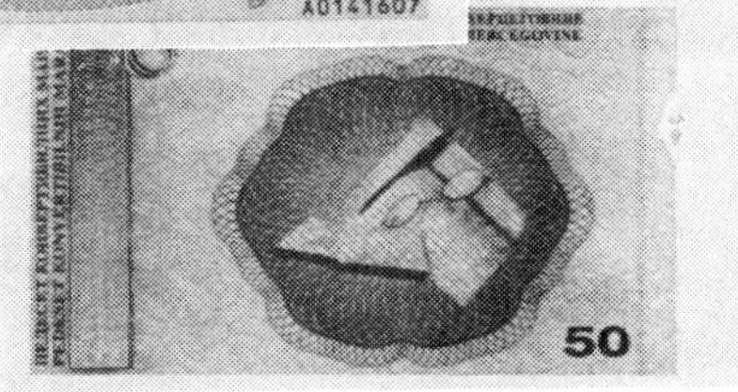

		VG	VF	UNC
68	**50 CONVERTIBLE MARAKA** ND (1998). Purple on lilac and m/c unpt. I. Ducic at r. Pen, glasses and book at l. ctr. on back.	FV	FV	45.00

		VG	VF	UNC
69	**100 CONVERTIBLE MARAKA** ND (1998). Dk. brown on yellow and m/c unpt. N. Sop at r. "Stecak Sgosca" fragment at l. ctr. on back.	FV	FV	85.00

		VG	VF	Unc
70	**100 Convertible Maraka** ND (1998). Dk. brown on yellow and m/c unpt. P. Kocic at r. Pen, glasses and book at l. ctr. on back.	FV	FV	85.00

Srpska (Serbian) Republic

НАРОДНА БАНКА СРПСКЕ РЕПУБЛИКЕ БОСНЕ И ХЕРЦЕГО

Narodna Banka Srpske Republike Bosne I Hercegovine National Bank of the Serbian Republic of Bosnia-Herzegovina

Ceased operations in August 1997.

1992-93 Banja Luka Issue

#133-139 arms at l., numerals in heart-shaped design below guilloche at ctr. r. Curved artistic design at l. ctr., arms at r. on back.

#133-135 wmk: Portr. of a young girl.

		VG	VF	Unc
133	**10 Dinara** 1992. Deep brown or orange and silver unpt. Back with ochre unpt.			
	a. Issued note.	.10	.35	1.50
	s. Specimen.	—	—	5.00

		VG	VF	Unc
134	**50 Dinara** 1992. Deep olive-gray on ochre and m/c unpt.			
	a. Issued note.	.15	.40	1.50
	s. Specimen.	—	—	5.00

		VG	VF	Unc
135	**100 Dinara** 1992. Dk. blue on lilac and silver unpt.			
	a. Issued note.	.35	1.00	3.00
	s. Specimen.	—	—	5.00

#136-140 wmk: Portr. of a young boy.

		VG	VF	Unc
136	**500 Dinara** 1992. Dk. blue on pink and m/c unpt.			
	a. Issued note.	.50	1.50	4.50
	s. Specimen.	—	—	5.00

		VG	VF	Unc
137	**1000 Dinara** 1992. Slate gray on pink and tan unpt. Back with orange unpt.			
	a. Issued note.	.40	1.20	3.75
	s. Specimen.	—	—	5.00
138	**5000 Dinara** 1992. Violet on lilac and lt. blue unpt.			
	a. Issued note.	.60	2.50	10.00
	s. Specimen.	—	—	5.00
139	**10,000 Dinara** 1992. Gray on tan and lt. blue unpt.			
	a. Issued note.	.60	2.50	10.00
	s. Specimen.	—	—	5.00
140	**50,000 Dinara** 1993. Brown on olive-green and m/c unpt.			
	a. Issued note.	2.00	8.00	30.00
	s. Specimen.	—	—	7.50

NOTE: For similar notes to #136-140 but differing only in text at top, sign., and Knin as place of issue, see Croatia-Regional.

		VG	VF	Unc
141	**100,000 Dinara** 1993. Purple on brown and m/c unpt. Wmk: Portr. of young woman w/head covering.			
	a. Issued note.	.40	1.35	4.00
	s. Specimen.	—	—	7.50

#142-144 wmk: Portr. of a young girl.

		VG	VF	UNC
142	**1 Million Dinara** 1993. Dp. purple on pink, yellow and m/c unpt.			
	a. Issued note.	2.00	8.00	40.00
	s. Specimen.	—	—	7.50
143	**5 Million Dinara** 1993. Dk. brown on lt. blue and yellow-orange unpt.			
	a. Issued note.	.35	1.00	3.00
	s. Specimen.	—	—	7.50

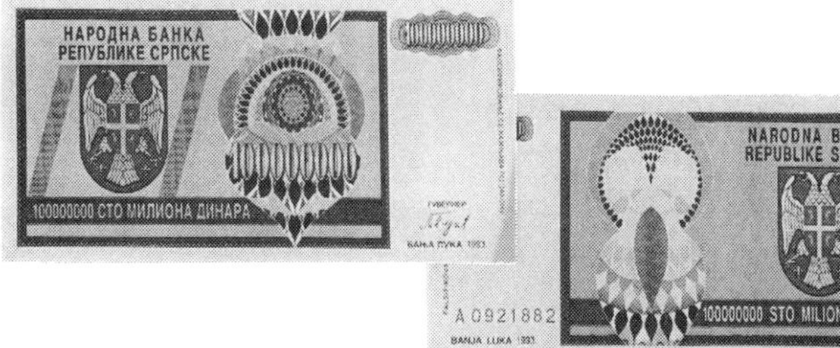

		VG	VF	UNC
144	**10 Million Dinara** 1993. Dk. blue-violet on olive-green and yellow-orange unpt.			
	a. Issued note.	.50	1.50	4.50
	s. Specimen.	—	—	7.50

НАРОДНА БАНКА РЕПУБЛИКЕ СРПСКЕ
Narodna Banka Republike Srpske
National Bank of the Serbian Republic

1993 Banja Luka First Issue

		VG	VF	UNC
145	**50 Million Dinara** 1993. Dk. brown on pink and gray unpt.			
	a. Issued note.	.85	2.50	7.50
	s. Specimen.	—	—	5.00

		VG	VF	UNC
146	**100 Million Dinara** 1993. Pale blue-gray on lt. blue and gray unpt.			
	a. Issued note.	.40	1.25	4.00
	s. Specimen.	—	—	5.00

		VG	VF	UNC
147	**1 Milliard Dinara** 1993. Orange on pale blue and lt. orange unpt.			
	a. Issued note.	.50	1.50	5.00
	s. Specimen.	—	—	5.00

		VG	VF	UNC
148	**10 Milliard Dinara** 1993. Black on pink and pale orange unpt.			
	a. Issued note.	.50	1.50	5.00
	s. Specimen.	—	—	5.00

1993 Banja Luka Second Issue

#149-155 P. Kocic at l. Serbian arms at ctr. r. on back. Wmk: Greek design repeated.

		VG	VF	UNC
149	**5000 Dinara** 1993. Red-violet and purple on pale blue-gray unpt.			
	a. Issued note.	.35	1.00	3.00
	s. Specimen.	—	—	7.50

		VG	VF	UNC
150	**50,000 Dinara** 1993. Brown and dull red on ochre unpt.			
	a. Issued note.	.35	1.00	3.00
	s. Specimen.	—	—	7.50

		VG	VF	UNC
151	**100,000 Dinara** 1993. Violet and blue-gray on pink unpt.			
	a. Issued note.	.35	1.00	3.00
	s. Specimen.	—	—	7.50

		VG	VF	UNC
152	**1,000,000 DINARA**			
	1993. Black and blue-gray on pale purple unpt.			
	a. Issued note.	.50	1.50	5.00
	s. Specimen.	—	—	7.50

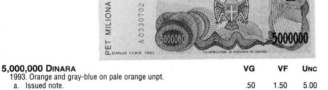

		VG	VF	UNC
153	**5,000,000 DINARA**			
	1993. Orange and gray-blue on pale orange unpt.			
	a. Issued note.	.50	1.50	5.00
	s. Specimen.	—	—	7.50

		VG	VF	UNC
154	**100,000,000 DINARA**			
	1993. Dull grayish green and pale olive-brown on lt. blue unpt.			
	a. Issued note.	.50	1.50	5.00
	s. Specimen.	—	—	7.50

		VG	VF	UNC
155	**500,000,000 DINARA**			
	1993. Brown-violet and grayish green on pale olive-brown unpt.			
	a. Issued note.	.50	1.50	5.00
	s. Specimen.	—	—	7.50

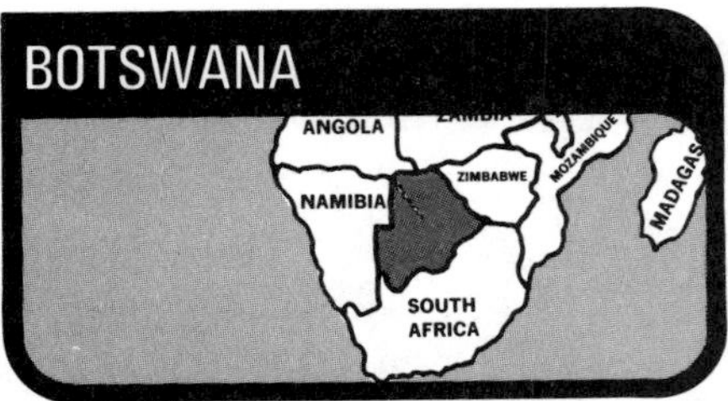

The Republic of Botswana (formerly Bechuanaland), located in south central Africa between Southwest Africa, (Namibia) and Zimbabwe has an area of 231,805 sq. km.) and a population of 1.48 million. Capital: Gaborone. Botswana is a member of a Customs Union with South Africa, Lesotho, and Swaziland. The economy is primarily pastoral with a rapidly developing mining industry, of which diamonds, copper and nickel are the chief elements. Meat products and diamonds comprise 85 percent of the exports.

Little is known of the origin of the peoples of Botswana. The early inhabitants, the Bushmen, did not develop a recorded history and are now dying out. The ancesters of the present Botswana probably arrived about 1600 AD in Bantu migrations from the north and east. Bechuanaland was first united early in the 19th century under Chief Khama III to more effectively resist incursions by the Boer trekkers from Transvaal and by the neighboring Matabeles. As the Boer threat intensified, appeals for protection were made to the British Government, which proclaimed the whole of Bechuanaland a British protectorate in 1885. In 1895, the southern part of the protectorate was annexed to Cape Province. The northern part, known as the Bechuanaland Protectorate, remained under British administration until it became the independent Republic of Botswana on Sept. 30, 1966. Botswana is a member of the Commonwealth of Nations. The president is Chief of State and Head of Government.

MONETARY SYSTEM:

1 Pula (Rand) = 100 Thebe (Cents)

Signature Chart

	Minister of Finance	Governor
1.	Sir Q.K.J. Masire	Q. Hermans
2.	Sir Q.K.J. Masire	B.C. Leavitt
3.	P.S. Mmusi	F.G. Mogae
4.	P.S. Mmusi	C. Kikonyogo
5.	P.S. Mmusi	Q. Hermans
6.	F.G. Mogae	Q. Hermans
7.	P.H.K. Kedikilwe	B. Gaolthe

REPUBLIC

BANK OF BOTSWANA

1976-79 ND ISSUE

#1-5 Pres. Sir Seretse Khama at l., arms at upper r. Wmk: Rearing zebra. Printer: TDLR. Replacement notes: Serial # prefixes *Z/1*, *X/1*, *Y/1* for 1, 10, and 20 respectively.

		VG	VF	UNC
1	**1 PULA**			
	ND (1976). Brown on m/c unpt. Bird at ctr. Farmer milking cow at ctr. r. on back.			
	a. Issued note.	.60	1.75	5.00
	s. Specimen. Serial # prefix: *A/1*.	—	—	80.00

		VG	VF	UNC
2	**2 PULA** ND (1976). Blue on m/c unpt. Bird at ctr. Various workers at ctr. r. on back.			
	a. Issued note.	1.25	4.00	16.00
	s. Specimen. Serial # prefix: *C/1.*	—	—	80.00

		VG	VF	UNC
3	**5 PULA** ND (1976). Purple on m/c unpt. Bird at ctr. Gemsbok antelope at ctr. r. on back.			
	a. Issued note.	2.75	10.00	45.00
	s. Specimen. Serial # prefix: *C/1.*	—	—	80.00

		VG	VF	UNC
4	**10 PULA** ND (1976). Green on m/c unpt. Bird at ctr. Lg. bldg. at ctr. r. on back.			
	a. Sign. 1.	7.00	25.00	95.00
	b. Sign. 2.	15.00	80.00	250.00
	s1. As a. Specimen. Serial # prefix: *D/1.*	—	—	13.50
	s2. As b. Specimen. Serial # prefix: *D/4.*	—	—	80.00
5	**20 PULA** ND (1979). Red, purple and brown on m/c unpt. Bird at ctr. Mining conveyors at ctr. r. on back.			
	a. Sign. 1.	20.00	85.00	250.00
	b. Sign. 2.	25.00	110.00	375.00
	s1. As a. Specimen. Serial # prefix: *E/1.*	—	—	175.00
	s2. As b. Specimen. Serial # prefix: *E/2.*	—	—	80.00

1982-83 ND ISSUE

#6-10 Pres. Q.K.J. Masire at l. Printer: TDLR. Replacement notes: Serial # prefix *Z/1, X/1, Y/1* for 1, 10 and 20 respectively.

		VG	VF	UNC
6	**1 PULA** ND (1983). Dk. brown. Pres. O. Masire at l. Cattle, arms and plants on back.			
	a. Issued note.	.20	1.25	4.50
	s. Specimen. Serial # prefix: *A/1.*	—	—	60.00

#7-10 Pres. Q.K.C. Masire at l., arms at upper r. Wmk: Rearing zebra.

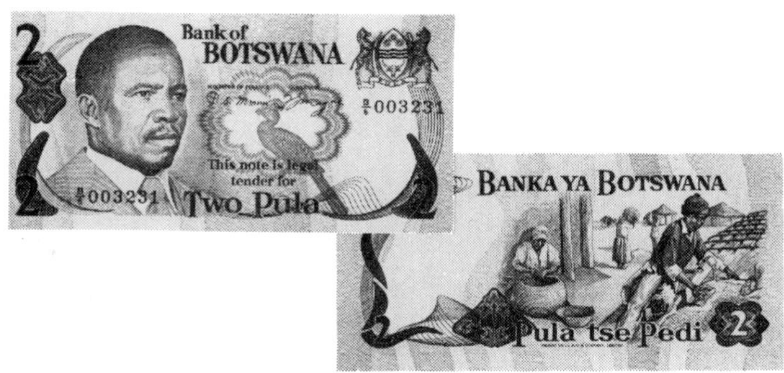

		VG	VF	UNC
7	**2 PULA** ND (1982). Blue on m/c unpt. Bird at ctr. Various workers at ctr. r. on back.			
	a. Sign. 3.	.75	4.00	20.00
	b. Sign. 4.	.75	1.85	5.50
	c. Sign. 5.	.65	2.00	7.50
	d. Sign. 6.	.65	1.75	4.00
	s. As a. Specimen.	—	—	60.00

		VG	VF	UNC
8	**5 PULA** ND (1982). Deep violet on m/c unpt. Bird at ctr. Gemsbok antelope at ctr. r. on back.			
	a. Sign. 3.	2.00	10.00	50.00
	b. Sign. 4.	1.75	5.00	18.00
	c. Sign. 5.	1.65	4.50	12.00

		VG	VF	UNC
9	**10 PULA** ND (1982). Green on m/c unpt. Bird at ctr. Lg. bldg. at ctr. r. on back.			
	a. Sign. 3.	4.00	12.00	65.00
	b. Sign. 4.	3.75	7.50	20.00
	c. Sign. 5.	3.50	8.00	25.00
	d. Sign. 6.	3.25	6.00	20.00
	s1. As a. Specimen. Serial # prefix: *D/7.*	—	—	60.00
	s2. As b. Specimen. Serial # prefix: *D/12.*	—	—	60.00
	s3. As c. Specimen. Serial # prefix: *D/21.*	—	—	60.00
	s4. As d. Specimen. Serial # prefix: *D/26.*	—	—	60.00

		VG	VF	UNC
10	**20 PULA** ND (1982). Red, purple and brown on m/c unpt. Ostrich at ctr. Mining conveyors at ctr. r. on back.			
	a. Sign. 3.	5.00	25.00	95.00
	b. Sign. 4.	FV	14.00	45.00
	c. Sign. 5.	FV	14.50	50.00
	d. Sign. 6.	FV	12.50	30.00
	s1. As a. Specimen. Serial # prefix: *E/2.*	—	—	60.00
	s2. As b. Specimen. Serial # prefix: *E/5.*	—	—	60.00
	s3. As c. Specimen. Serial # prefix: *E/9.*	—	—	60.00
	s4. As d. Specimen. Serial # prefix: *E/13.*	—	—	60.00

1992-95 ND ISSUE

#11-15 Pres. Q.K.J. Masire at l., arms at upper r. Wmk: Rearing zebra.

#11-13 printer: Harrison.

		VG	VF	UNC
11	**5 PULA** ND (1992). Deep violet on m/c unpt. Similar to #8; sm. stylistic differences. Sign. 6.			
	a. Issued note.	FV	FV	4.50
	s. Specimen.	—	—	50.00
12	**10 PULA** ND (1992). Green on m/c unpt. Similar to #9; sm. stylistic differences. Sign. 6.			
	a. Issued note.	FV	FV	8.00
	s. Specimen. Serial # prefix: *D/46.*	—	—	50.00
13	**20 PULA** ND (1993). Red, purple and brown on m/c unpt. Similar to #10; sm. stylistic differences. Sign. 6.			
	a. Issued note.	FV	FV	14.00
	s. Specimen. Serial # prefix: *E/29.*	—	—	50.00

		VG	VF	UNC
14	**50 PULA** ND (1990). Dk. brown and dk. green on m/c unpt. Bird at ctr. Man in canoe and bird w/fish at ctr. r. on back. W/o imprint. Sign. 6. Printer: Fidelity Printers. (Zimbabwe - Harare)			
	a. Issued note.	FV	FV	40.00
	s. Specimen. Serial # prefix: *F*, suffix: *B.*	—	—	50.00
16	**50 PULA** ND(1995). Similar to #14. Printer: ABNC.			
	a. Issued note.	FV	FV	35.00
	s. Specimen. Serial # prefix: *F.....C.* (suffix)	—	—	50.00

		VG	VF	UNC
15	**100 PULA** ND (1993). Blue-violet and ochre on m/c unpt. Diamond and eagle at ctr. Worker sorting rough diamonds at ctr. r. on back. Sign. 6. Printer: TDLR.			
	a. Issued note.	FV	FV	60.00
	b. Specimen. Serial # prefix: *G/1, G/6.*	—	—	50.00

1997 ND ISSUE

#17-19 President Q.K.J. Masire at l., arms at upper r. Wmk: Rearing zebra. Printer: TDLR. Sign. 6.

		VG	VF	UNC
17	**10 PULA** ND(1997). Similar to #12.			
	a. Issued note.	FV	FV	4.50
	s. Specimen. Serial # prefix: *D/54.*	—	—	50.00
18	**20 PULA** ND(1997). Similar to #13.			
	a. Issued note.	FV	FV	8.00
	s. Specimen. Serial # prefix: *E/33.*	—	—	50.00
19	**50 PULA** ND(1997). Similar to #14.			
	a. Issued note.	FV	FV	23.00
	s. Specimen. Serial # prefix: *F/13.*	—	—	50.00

1999 ND ISSUE

#20-23 Wmk: Rearing zebra. Sign. 7.

		VG	VF	UNC
20	**10 PULA** ND(1999). Green on m/c unpt. Pres. F. Mogae at l., arms at upper r. Parliament on back. Printer: FCOF.			
	a. Issued note.	FV	FV	8.00
	s. Specimen. Serial # prefix: *D/62.*	—	—	—
21	**20 PULA**	Expected New Issue		
22	**50 PULA**	Expected New Issue		
23	**100 PULA**	Expected New Issue		

COLLECTOR SERIES

BANK OF BOTSWANA

1979 ND ISSUE

		ISSUE PRICE	MKT. VALUE
CS1	**ND (1979) 1-20 PULA** #1-3, 4a, 5a. Ovpt: *SPECIMEN* and Maltese cross serial # prefix.	14.00	30.00

1982 ND ISSUE

#CS2 and CS3 were released in quantity by the Bank of Botswana.

		ISSUE PRICE	MKT. VALUE
CS2	**ND (1982) 1-20 PULA** #1-5 ovpt: *SPECIMEN* w/4 punched hole cancellation.	—	40.00
CS3	**ND (1982) 1-20 PULA** #6-10 ovpt: *SPECIMEN* w/4 punched hole cancellation.	—	30.00

The Federative Republic of Brazil, which comprises half the continent of South America, is the only Latin American country deriving its culture and language from Portugal. It has an area of 3,286,470 sq. mi. (8,511,965 sq. km.) and a population of 157.1 million. Capital: Brasília. The economy of Brazil is as varied and complex as any in the developing world. Agriculture is a mainstay of the economy, although but 4 percent of the area is under cultivation. Known mineral resources are almost unlimited in variety and size of reserves. A large, relatively sophisticated industry ranges from basic steel and chemical production to finished consumer goods. Coffee, cotton, iron ore and cocoa are the chief exports.

Brazil was discovered and claimed for Portugal by Admiral Pedro Alvares Cabral in 1500. Portugal established a settlement in 1532 and proclaimed the area a royal colony in 1549. During the Napoleonic Wars, Dom João VI established the seat of Portuguese government in Rio de Janeiro. When he returned to Portugal, his son Dom Pedro I declared Brazil's independence on Sept. 7, 1822, and became emperor of Brazil. The Empire of Brazil was maintained until 1889 when a republic was established. The Federative Republic was established in 1946 by terms of a constitution drawn up by a constituent assembly. Following a coup in 1964, the armed forces retained overall control under dictatorship until a civilian government was restored on March 15, 1985. The current constitution was adopted in 1988.

MONETARY SYSTEM:

1 Cruzeiro = 100 Centavos, 1942-1967
1 Cruzeiro Novo = 1000 Old Cruzeiros, 1966-1985
1 Cruzado = 1000 Cruzeiros Novos, 1986-1989
1 Cruzado Novo = 1000 Cruzados, 1989-1990
1 Cruzeiro = 1 Cruzado Novo, 1990-1993
1 Cruzeiro Real (pl. Reais) = 1000 Cruzeiros, 1993
1 Real (pl. Reais) = 100 Centavos, 1994-

SIGNATURE VARIETIES

8	SEBASTIÃO P. ALMEIDA	CARLOS A. CARRÍLHO
9	CLEMENTE MARIANI	CARLOS A. CARRÍLHO
10	WALTER M. SALLES	REGINALDO F. NUNES
11	REGINALDO F. NUNES, 1962	WALTER M. SALLES
12	REGINALDO F. NUNES, 1963	MIGUEL CALMON
13	REGINALDO F. NUNES, 1964	OTÁVIO GOUVEX BULHÕES
14	SÉRGIO A. RIBEIRO, 1964-66	OTÁVIO GOUVEX BULHÕES
15	DÉNIO NOGUEIRA, 1966-67	OTÁVIO GOUVEX BULHÕES
16	RUY LEME, 1967	ANTÔNIO DELFIM NETTO
17	ERNANE GALVÊAS, 1967-72	ANTÔNIO DELFIM NETTO
18	MÁRIO HENRIQUE SIMONSEN, 1974-79	PAULO H.P. LIRA

SIGNATURE VARIETIES

19	KARLOS RISCHBIETER, 1979-80	ERNANE GALVÊAS
20	ERNANE GALVÊAS, 1980-81	CARLOS P. LANGONI
21	ERNANE GALVÊAS, 1983-85	ALFONSO C. PASTORE
22	FRANCISCO DORNÉLLES, 1985	ANTONIO LENGRUBER
23	DILSON FUNARO, 1985-86	FERNÃO C.B. BRACHER
24	DILSON FUNARO, 1987	FRANCISCO GROSS
25	LUIZ CARLOS BRESSER PEREIRA, 1987	FERNANDO M. OLIVEIRA
26	MAÍLSON FERREIRA DA NÓBREGA, 1988-89	ELMO CAMÕES
27	MAÍLSON FERREIRA DA NÓBREGA, 1989-90	WADICO BUCCHI
28	ZÉLIA CARDOSO DE MELLO, 1990	IBRAHIM ÉRIS
29	MARCÍLIO M. MOREIRA, 1991-92	FRANCISCO GROSS
30	PAULO R. HADDAD, 1993	GUSTAVO LOYOLA
31	ELIZEU RESENDE, 1993	PAULO XIMENES
32	FERNANDO H. CARDOSO, 1993	PAULO XIMENES
33	FERNANDO H. CARDOSO, 1993-94	PEDRO MALAN
34	RUBENS RICUPERO, 1994	PEDRO MALAN
35	CIRO GOMES, 1994	PEDRO MALAN
36	PEDRO MALAN, 1995	PÉRSIO ARIDA
37	PEDRO MALAN, 1995-96	GUSTAVO LOYOLA

REPUBLIC

NO LOCALE

TESOURO NACIONAL, VALOR RECEBIDO

ESTAMPA 3; 1961 ND ISSUE

		VG	VF	UNC
166	**5 CRUZEIROS** ND (1961-62). Dk. brown and brown. Raft w/sail at l., male male Indian at r. Flower on back. Printer: CdM-B.			
	a. Sign. 8. Series #1-75.	.10	.35	2.00
	b. Sign. 10. Series #76-111.	.10	.30	1.25

TESOURO NACIONAL, VALOR LEGAL

ESTAMPA 1A; 1961 ND ISSUE

#167-173 dk. blue on m/c unpt. 2 printed sign. Printer: ABNC.

		VG	VF	UNC
167	**10 CRUZEIROS** ND (1961-63). Portr. G. Vargas at ctr. Back green; allegory of "Industry" at ctr.			
	a. Sign. 9. Series #331-630. (1961).	.15	.50	1.85
	b. Sign. 12. Series #631-930. (1963).	.15	.50	1.65

		VG	VF	UNC
168	**20 CRUZEIROS** ND (1961-63). Portr. D. da Fonseca at ctr. Back red; allegory of "the Republic" at ctr.			
	a. Sign. 9. Series #461-960. (1961).	.15	.50	2.25
	b. Sign. 12. Series #961-1260. (1963).	.15	.50	2.00

		VG	VF	UNC
169	**50 CRUZEIROS** ND (1961). Portr. Princess Isabel at ctr. Back purple; allegory of "Law" at ctr. Sign. 9. Series #721-1220.	.15	1.50	7.50

		VG	VF	UNC
170	**100 CRUZEIROS** ND (1961-64). Portr. D. Pedro at ctr. Back red-brown; allegory of "National Culture" at ctr.			
	a. Sign. 9. Series #761-1160. (1961).	.30	2.25	9.00
	b. Sign. 13. Series #1161-1360. (1964).	.30	1.00	4.50
	c. Sign. 14. Series #1361-1560. (1964).	.30	2.00	8.00

		VG	VF	UNC
171	**200 CRUZEIROS** ND (1961-64). Portr. D. Pedro at ctr. Back olive-green; battle scene at ctr.			
	a. Sign. 9. Series #671-1070. (1961).	.50	3.50	15.00
	b. Sign. 13. Series #1071-1370. (1964).	.50	3.00	12.00
	c. Sign. 14. Series #1371-1570. (1964).	.50	3.00	12.00

		VG	VF	UNC
172	**500 CRUZEIROS** ND (1961-62). Portr. D. Joao VI at ctr. Back blue-black; allegory of "Maritime Industry" at ctr.			
	a. Sign. 9. Series #261-660. (1961).	1.00	5.00	25.00
	b. Sign. 11. Series #661-1460. (1962).	.75	4.00	20.00
173	**1000 CRUZEIROS** ND (1961-63). Portr. P. Alvares Cabral at ctr. Back orange; scene of the "First Mass" at ctr.			
	a. Sign. 9. Series #1331-1730. (1961).	.75	8.00	50.00
	b. Sign. 11. Series #1731-3030. (1962).	.75	6.00	40.00
	c. Sign. 12. Series #3031-3830. (1963).	1.00	7.00	45.00

		VG	VF	UNC
174	**5000 CRUZEIROS** ND (1963-64). Blue-gray on m/c unpt. Portr. Tiradentes at r. Back red; Tiradentes in historical scene at ctr. Printer: ABNC.			
	a. Sign. 12. Series #1-400. (1963).	1.00	5.00	35.00
	b. Sign. 13. Series #401-1400. (1964).	1.00	4.50	30.00
	c. Sign. 14. Series #1401-1650. (1965).	1.75	8.00	50.00

ESTAMPA 2A; 1962-63 ND ISSUE

#175 *Deleted*, see #182B.

#176-182 2 printed sign. Printer: TDLR.

		VG	VF	UNC
176	**5 CRUZEIROS** ND (1962-64). Brown on m/c unpt. Portr. Baron de Rio Branco at ctr.			
	a. Sign. 11. Series #2301-3500. (1962).	.10	.25	1.00
	b. Sign. 12. Series #3501-3700. (1963).	.10	.25	2.50
	c. Sign. 13. Series #3701-3748; 4149-4180; 4201-4232. (1964).	.10	.25	5.00
	d. Sign. 14. Series #3749-4148; 4181-4200; 4233-4700. (1964).	.10	.25	.75
177	**10 CRUZEIROS** ND (1962). Green on m/c unpt. Like #167.			
	a. Sign. 10. Series #2365-3055.	.10	.25	1.50
	b. Sign. 11. Series 2394A.	.10	.25	1.50

		VG	VF	UNC
178	**20 CRUZEIROS** ND (1962). Red-brown on m/c unpt. Like #168. Sign. 11. Series #1576-2275.	.15	.50	2.25
179	**50 CRUZEIROS** ND (1963.) Purple on m/c unpt. Like #169. Sign. 12. Series #586-785.	.25	1.00	4.00
180	**100 CRUZEIROS** ND (1963). Red on m/c unpt. Like #170. Sign. 12. Series #216-415.	.35	2.00	9.00

		VG	VF	UNC
181	**1000 CRUZEIROS** ND (1963). Orange on m/c unpt. Like #173. Sign. 12. Series #791-1590.	.50	3.00	15.00

		VG	VF	UNC
182	**5000 CRUZEIROS** ND (1963-64). Red on m/c unpt. Like #174. Sign. at l. w/*Director Caixa de Amortizacao.*			
	a. Sign. 12. Series #1-400. (1963).	1.00	4.50	30.00
	b. Sign. 13. Series #401-1400. (1964).	.85	4.00	25.00
	c. Sign. 14. Series #1401-1700. (1964).	1.50	6.00	40.00

BANCO CENTRAL DO BRASIL

1965; 1966 ND ISSUE

		VG	VF	UNC
182A (A182)	**5000 CRUZEIROS** ND (1965). Red on m/c unpt. Like #174. Sign. D. Nogueira w/title: *Presidente do Banco Central* and O. Gouvea de Bulhões. Sign 15. Series #1701-2200.	1.00	5.00	35.00

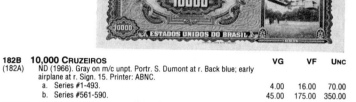

		VG	VF	UNC
182B (182A)	**10,000 CRUZEIROS** ND (1966). Gray on m/c unpt. Portr. S. Dumont at r. Back blue; early airplane at r. Sign. 15. Printer: ABNC.			
	a. Series #1-493.	4.00	16.00	70.00
	b. Series #561-590.	45.00	175.00	350.00

1966; 1967 ND PROVISIONAL ISSUE

Feb. 1967 Monetary Reform: 1 Cruzeiro Novo = 1,000 Cruzeiros

#183-190 black circular ovpt: *BANCO CENTRAL* and new currency unit in black circle on Tesouro Nacional notes.

		VG	VF	UNC
183	**1 CENTAVO ON 10 CRUZEIROS** ND (1966-67). Green on m/c unpt. Ovpt. on #177. Sign. 15.			
	a. Error: *Minstro* below r. sign. (2 types of 1 in ovpt.) (1966). Series #3056-3151.	.10	.20	1.00
	b. *Ministro* below r. sign. (1967). Series # 3152-4055.	.10	.20	1.00
	s. As b. Specimen ovpt: *MODELO.*	—	—	—

		VG	VF	UNC
184	**5 CENTAVOS ON 50 CRUZEIROS** ND (1966-67). Purple on m/c unpt. Ovpt. on #179. Sign. 15.			
	a. Type of #183a. Series #786-1313.	.10	.30	1.50
	b. Type of #183b. Series #1314-1885.	.10	.30	1.50

		VG	VF	UNC
185	**10 CENTAVOS ON 100 CRUZEIROS** ND (1966-67). Red on m/c unpt. Ovpt. on #180. Sign. 15.			
	a. Type of #183a. Series #416-911.	.10	.30	2.00
	b. Type of #183b. Series #912-1515.	.10	.30	1.75

		VG	VF	UNC
186	**50 CENTAVOS ON 500 CRUZEIROS** ND (1967). Blue on m/c unpt. Ovpt. on #172. Sign. 15. Series #1461-2360.	.75	2.00	4.50

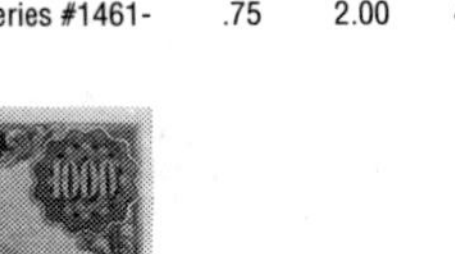

		VG	VF	UNC
187	**1 CRUZEIRO NOVO ON 1000 CRUZEIROS** ND (1966-67). Blue on m/c unpt. Ovpt. on #173.			
	a. Sign. 14. Series #3831-3930.	2.00	7.50	22.50
	b. Sign. 15. Series #3931-4830.	1.50	2.50	7.50

		VG	VF	UNC
188	**5 CRUZEIROS NOVOS ON 5000 CRUZEIROS** ND (1966-67). Blue-green on m/c unpt. Ovpt. on #174.			
	a. Sign. 14. Series #1651-1700.	10.00	30.00	60.00
	b. Sign. 15. Series #1701-2900.	2.00	8.00	22.50

		VG	VF	UNC
189	**10 CRUZEIROS NOVOS ON 10,000 CRUZEIROS** ND (1966-67). Gray on m/c unpt. Bold or semi-bold ovpt. on #182B. Printer: ABNC.			
	a. Sign. 15. Series #494-560 and 591-700. (1966).	2.50	25.00	85.00
	b. Sign. 16. Series #701-1700. (1967).	1.00	6.00	25.00
	c. Sign. 17. Series #1701-2700. (1967).	1.00	5.00	20.00
190	**10 CRUZEIROS NOVOS ON 10,000 CRUZEIROS** ND (1967). Brown on pink and m/c unpt. Like #182B. Printer: TDLR.			
	a. Sign. 16. Series #1-1000.	1.00	3.50	15.00
	b. Sign. 17. Series #1001-2100.	.75	2.25	10.00

1970 ND ISSUES

#191-195 portr. as wmk. Sign. varieties. 5 digit series # above serial #.

#191-194, 195A printer: CdM-B.

		VG	VF	UNC
191	**1 CRUZEIRO** ND (1970-72). Dk. green and blue on ochre and green unpt. w/medallic Liberty head at r. in brown. Banco Central bldg. at l. on back. Series # prefix A. Sign. 17.			
	a. Series #1-3000.	.20	.50	1.50
	s. Specimen ovpt: *MODELO.*	—	—	—

		VG	VF	UNC
191A	**1 CRUZEIRO** ND (1972-80). Dk. green w/medallic Liberty head in green. Series # prefix B.			
	a. Sign. 17. Series #1-3781 (1972).	.10	.25	.90
	b. Sign. 18. Series #3782-13194 (1975).	.05	.15	.75
	c. Sign. 20. Series #13195-18094 (1980).	.05	.10	.40
	s. As a. Specimen ovpt. and perforated: *MODELO.*	—	—	—

		VG	VF	UNC
192	**5 CRUZEIROS** ND (1970-80). Blue on orange and green unpt. Portr. D. Pedro I at r. Back maroon; parade square at l.			
	a. Back darkly printed. Sign. 17. Series # prefix A. Series #1-107 (1970-71).	.10	4.00	15.00
	b. Back lightly printed. Sign. 17. Series # prefix B. Series #1-2467 (1973).	.10	.25	1.25
	c. Sign. 18. Series #2468-6050 (1974).	.10	.25	1.50
	d. Sign. 19. Series #6051-6841 (1979).	.10	.25	2.00
	s. As a. Specimen ovpt: *SEM VALOR,* perforated: *MODELO.*	—	—	—

		VG	VF	UNC
193	**10 CRUZEIROS** ND (1970-80). Grayish purple and dk. brown on orange-brown blue-green and m/c unpt. Portr. D. Pedro II at r. Back green, violet and brown; statue of the Prophet Daniel.			
	a. Back darkly printed. Sign. 17. Series # prefix A. Series #1-1429 (1970).	.50	2.50	15.00
	b. As a. Sign. 18. Series #1430-7745 (1974).	.15	.50	1.75
	c. Back lightly printed. Sign. 18. Series # prefix B. Series #1-2394 (1979).	.25	1.00	5.00
	d. As c. Sign. 19. Series #2395-2870 (1980).	.15	.50	2.50
	e. As d. Sign. 20. Series #2871-5131 (1980).	.10	.40	2.00

		VG	VF	UNC
194	**50 CRUZEIROS**			
	ND (1970-81). Black, purple, blue-black and violet on lilac and m/c unpt. Portr. D. da Fonseca at r. Back brown, lilac and blue; coffee loading at l.			
	a. Sign. 17. Series #1-1250 (1970).	1.00	3.00	20.00
	b. Sign. 18. Series #1251-3841 (1974).	.20	.60	3.00
	c. Sign. 20. Series #3842-5233 (1980).	.15	.50	2.50
195	**100 CRUZEIROS**			
	ND (1970-81). Purple and violet on pink and m/c unpt. Portr. Marshal F. Peixoto at r. Back blue, brown and violet; National Congress at l. Printer: TDLR. Sign. 17 (w/imprint CdM-B). Series #1-01358.	1.50	6.00	35.00

		VG	VF	UNC
195A	**100 CRUZEIROS**			
	ND (1974-81). Purple and violet on pink and m/c unpt. Like #195. Printer CdM-B.			
	a. Sign. 18. Series #01359-10455 (1974).	.25	.75	6.00
	b. Sign. 20. Series #10456-12681 (1981).	.25	.75	6.00

NOTE: The difference between #195 and 195A is in the wmk.

1972 COMMEMORATIVE ISSUE

#196, 150th Anniversary of Brazilian Independence

		VG	VF	UNC
196	**500 CRUZEIROS**			
	1972 (1972-74). Dk. olive-green and brown on violet and m/c unpt. Portr. of 5 men of differing racial groups. Wmk: Dates *1822 1972* in clear area at l. 5 different historical maps of Brazil on back. Printer: CdM-B.			
	a. Sign. 17. Series # prefix A. #1-90 (1972).	10.00	50.00	225.00
	b. As a. Sign. 18. Series #91-2636 (1974).	1.00	5.00	32.50
	s. Specimen. Ovpt: *MODELO*.	—	—	50.00
196A	**500 CRUZEIROS**			
	1972 (1979-80). Like #196 but wmk. area has vertical lines printed on face and back.			
	a. Sign. 18. Series # prefix B. #1-1401 (1979).	.65	3.50	20.00
	b. As a. Sign. 19. Series #1402-1959 (1979).	.50	2.75	16.50
	c. As a. Sign. 20. Series #1960-2763 (1980).	.65	3.50	20.00
	s. Specimen.	—	—	50.00

1978 ND ISSUE

#197, the first 4 digits of the serial # represent the series #.

		VG	VF	UNC
197	**1000 CRUZEIROS**			
	ND (1978-80). Green and brown. Double portr. B. do Rio Branco and as wmk. *BANCO CENTRAL DO BRASIL* in 2 lines. Double view of machinery on back. Also, small plate modification on back.			
	a. Sign. 18. Series #1-665 (1978).	1.50	8.00	50.00
	b. Sign. 19. Series #666-2072 (1979).	1.75	6.00	32.50
	c. Sign. 20. Series #2073-3297 (1980).	.80	6.00	35.00

1981-85 ND ISSUE

#198-205 portr. as wmk. Sign. varieties. Printer: CdM-B. The first 4 digits of the serial # represent the series #.

#198-202 double portr. and vignettes.

		VG	VF	UNC
198	**100 CRUZEIROS**			
	ND (1981-84). Red and purple on m/c unpt. D. de Caxias at ctr. Back gray-blue and red; battle scene and sword at ctr.			
	a. Sign. 20. Series #1-4081 (1981).	.05	.15	.60
	b. Sign. 21. Series #4082-8176 (1984).	.05	.15	.60

		VG	VF	UNC
199	**200 CRUZEIROS**			
	ND (1981-84). Green and violet on m/c unpt. Princess Isabel at ctr. Back brown and green; 2 women cooking outdoors.			
	a. Sign. 20. Series #1-2996 (1981).	.05	.15	.60
	b. Sign. 21. Series #2997-4960 (1984).	.05	.15	.60

		VG	VF	UNC
200	**500 CRUZEIROS**			
	ND (1981-85). Blue and brown on m/c unpt. D. da Fonseca at ctr. Back pink, brown and purple; group of legislators.			
	a. Sign. 20. Series #1-3510 (1981).	.05	.20	.85
	b. Sign. 21. Series #3511-4238 (1985).	.05	.15	.75

201	1000 CRUZEIROS	VG	VF	UNC
	ND (1981-86). Brown and dk. olive on m/c unpt. Similar to #197, but bank name in 1 line. Back tan and blue.			
	a. Sign. 20. Series # prefix A, #1-5733 (1981).	.10	.35	2.50
	b. As a. Sign. 21. Series #5734-7019 (1984).	.05	.15	.75
	c. As b. Sign. 22. Series #7020-9999 (1985).	.05	.15	.75
	d. Sign. 22. Series # prefix B, #1-788 (1986).	.05	.15	.75

202	5000 CRUZEIROS	VG	VF	UNC
	ND (1981-85). Purple and brown on m/c unpt. C. Branco at ctr. Back brown, purple and blue; antennas.			
	a. Sign. 20. Series # prefix A, #1-9205 (1981).	.15	.85	6.50
	b. As a. Sign. 21. Series #9206-9999 (1983).	.10	.35	1.50
	c. Sign. 21. Series # prefix B, #1-2118 (1984).	.10	.30	1.00
	d. As c. Sign. 22. Series #2119-2342 (1985).	.20	.60	2.00

203	10,000 CRUZEIROS	VG	VF	UNC
	ND (1984-85). Brown on m/c unpt. Desk top at ctr., Rui Barbosa at ctr. r. Conference scene on back.			
	a. Sign. 21. Series #1-3619 (1984).	.25	1.25	4.50
	b. Sign. 22. Series #3620-3696 (1985).	.75	4.00	22.50

204	50,000 CRUZEIROS	VG	VF	UNC
	ND (1984-86). Violet on m/c unpt. Microscope at ctr., O. Cruz at r. Cruz Institute at ctr. on back.			
	a. Sign. 21. Series #1-1673 (1984).	.60	3.75	20.00
	b. Sign. 22 (reversed). Series #1674-2170 (1985).	1.00	5.00	15.00
	c. Sign. 22 (corrected). Series #2171-3248 (1985).	.30	1.75	7.00
	d. Sign. 23. Series #3249-3290 (1986).	.35	2.00	11.50

205	100,000 CRUZEIROS	VG	VF	UNC
	ND (1985). Black on blue, gold and m/c unpt. Electric power station at ctr., Pres. J. Kubitschek at r. Old and modern bldgs. at ctr. on back. Sign. 23. Series #1-4347.	.50	2.50	5.50

1986 ND PROVISIONAL ISSUE

Feb. 1986 Monetary Reform: 1 Cruzado = 1,000 Cruzeiros

#206-208 black circular ovpt: *Banco Central Do Brazil* and new currency unit on #203-205.

206	10 CRUZADOS ON 10,000 CRUZEIROS	VG	VF	UNC
	ND (1986). Ovpt. on #203. Sign. 23. Series #3697-5124.	.10	.20	1.35

207	50 CRUZADOS ON 50,000 CRUZEIROS	VG	VF	UNC
	ND (1986). Ovpt. on #204. Sign. 23. Series #3291-4592.	.20	.75	2.50

208	100 CRUZADOS ON 100,000 CRUZEIROS	VG	VF	UNC
	ND (1986). Ovpt. on #205. Sign. 23. Series #4348-6209.	.20	.75	5.00

1986 ND ISSUE

#209-211 printer: CdM-B.

		VG	VF	UNC
209	**10 CRUZADOS** ND (1986-87). Similar to #203 except for denomination.			
	a. Sign. 23. Series #1-1155 (1986).	.05	.20	1.00
	b. Sign. 25. Series #1156-1505 (1987).	.05	.15	.50

		VG	VF	UNC
210	**50 CRUZADOS** ND (1986-88). Similar to #204 except for denomination.			
	a. Sign. 23. Series #1-1617 (1986).	.05	.20	.60
	b. Sign. 25. Series #1618-2044 (1987).	.05	.20	.60
	c. Sign. 26. Series #2045-2051 (1988).	2.50	15.00	100.00

		VG	VF	UNC
211	**100 CRUZADOS** ND (1986-88). Similar to #205 except for denomination.			
	a. Sign. 23. Series #1-1176 (1986).	.10	.40	2.00
	b. Sign. 24. Series #1177-1582 (1987).	.10	.40	2.00
	c. Sign. 25. Series #1583-3045 (1987).	.05	.15	.50
	d. Sign. 26. Series #3046-3059 (1988).	.60	3.00	17.50

1986 ND COMMEMORATIVE ISSUE

#212, Centennial - Birth of H. Villa-Lobos

		VG	VF	UNC
212	**500 CRUZADOS** ND (1986). Blue-green on m/c unpt. H. Villa-Lobos at ctr. r. and as wmk. Villa-Lobos at l. ctr. on back. Printer: CdM-B.			
	a. Sign. 23. Series #1-2352 (1986).	.10	.50	3.00
	b. Sign. 24. Series #2353-2842 (1987).	.10	.40	2.50
	c. Sign. 25. Series #2843-7504 (1987).	.05	.15	.50
	d. Sign. 26. Series #7505-8309 (1988).	.05	.20	1.00

1987 ND REGULAR ISSUE

#213-215 portr. as wmk. Printer: CdM-B. Series # are first 4 digits of serial #.

		VG	VF	UNC
213	**1000 CRUZADOS** ND (1987-88). Purple and brown-violet on m/c unpt. J. Machado at r. Street scene from old Rio de Janeiro on back.			
	a. Sign. 25. Series #1-2744 (1987).	.20	1.00	6.00
	b. Sign. 26. Series #2745-9919 (1988)	.05	.15	.65

		VG	VF	UNC
214	**5000 CRUZADOS** ND (1988). Blue on m/c unpt. Portion of mural at l. ctr., C. Portinari at r. C. Portinari painting at ctr. on back. Sign. 26. Series #1-1757.	.25	1.00	4.00

		VG	VF	UNC
215	**10,000 CRUZADOS** ND (1989). Red and brown on m/c unpt. C. Chagas at r. Chagas w/lab instruments on back. Sign. 26. Series #1-1841.	.25	1.00	7.00

1989 ND PROVISIONAL ISSUE

Jan. 1989 Monetary Reform: 1 Cruzado Novo = 1,000 Cruzados

#216-218 black triangular ovpt. of new currency unit on #213-215.

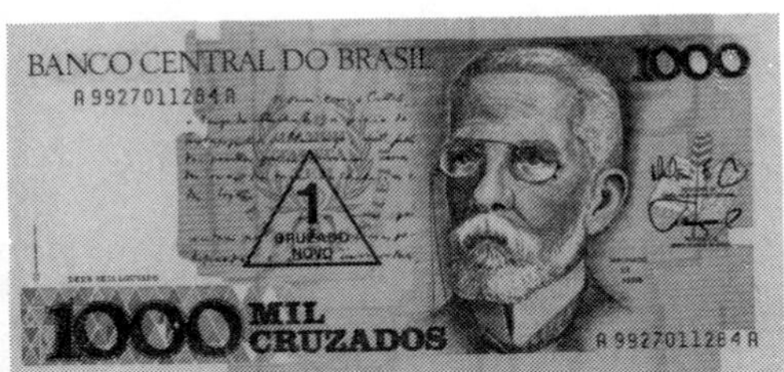

216	**1 CRUZADO NOVO ON 1000 CRUZADOS**	VG	VF	UNC
	ND (1989). Purple and brown-violet on m/c unpt. Ovpt. on #213.			
	a. Sign. 26. Series # prefix A, #9920-9999 (1989).	.10	.50	2.00
	b. Sign. 26. Series # prefix B, #1-1617 (1989).	.10	.15	.50
	c. As b. Sign. 27. Series #1618-1792 (1989).	.10	.30	1.25

217	**5 CRUZADOS NOVOS ON 5000 CRUZADOS**	VG	VF	UNC
	ND (1989). Blue on m/c unpt. Ovpt. on #214.			
	a. Sign. 26. Series #1758-3531 (1989).	.15	.40	1.75
	b. Sign. 27. Series #3532-3818 (1989).	.15	.40	1.75

218	**10 CRUZADOS NOVOS ON 10,000 CRUZADOS**	VG	VF	UNC
	ND (1989-90). Red and brown on m/c unpt. Ovpt. on #215.			
	a. Sign. 26. Series #1842-4171 (1989).	.10	.35	1.50
	b. Sign. 27. Series #4172-4502 (1990).	.10	.40	2.50

1989 ND ISSUE

#219 and 220 printer: CdM-B. Wmk: Liberty head.

219	**50 CRUZADOS NOVOS**	VG	VF	UNC
	ND (1989-90). Brown and black on m/c unpt. C. Drummond de Andrade at r. Back black, red-brown and blue; de Andrade writing poetry.			
	a. Sign. 26. Series #1-3340 (1989).	.10	.35	1.50
	b. Sign. 27. Series #3341-3358 (1990).	.25	2.00	15.00

220	**100 CRUZADOS NOVOS**	VG	VF	UNC
	ND (1989). Orange, purple and green on m/c unpt. C. Meireles at r. Back brown, black and m/c; child reading and people dancing.			
	a. Sign. 26. Series #1-6772.	.15	.65	1.50
	b. Sign. 27. Series #6773-8794.	.20	.90	5.00

1989 ND COMMEMORATIVE ISSUE

#221, Centenary of the Republic

221	**200 CRUZADOS NOVOS**	VG	VF	UNC
	ND (1989). Blue and black on m/c unpt. Political leaders at ctr., sculpture of the Republic at ctr. r., arms at r. Oil painting "Patria" by P. Bruno w/flag being embroidered by a family on back. Wmk: Liberty head. Printer: CdM-B. Sign. 27. Series #1-1964.	.20	1.00	5.00

1990 ND ISSUE

222	**500 CRUZADOS NOVOS**	VG	VF	UNC
	ND (1990). Green and purple on m/c unpt. Orchids at ctr., A. Ruschi at r. Back lt. orange, purple and blue; hummingbird, orchids and A. Ruschi at ctr. Wmk: Liberty head. Sign. 27. Series #1-3700.	.75	2.00	7.50

1990 ND PROVISIONAL ISSUE

March 1990 Monetary Reform: 1 Cruzeiro = 1 Cruzado Novo

#223-226 black rectangular ovpt. of new currency unit on #219-222. Sign. 27.

223	**50 CRUZEIROS ON 50 CRUZADOS NOVOS**	VG	VF	UNC
	ND (1990). Brown and black on m/c unpt. Ovpt. on #219. Series #3359-5338.	.10	.15	.60

224	**100 CRUZEIROS ON 100 CRUZADOS NOVOS**	VG	VF	UNC
	ND (1990). Orange, purple and green on m/c unpt. Ovpt. on #220.			
	a. Series #8601.	10.00	50.00	140.00
	b. Series #8795-9447.	.10	.40	1.50

225	**200 CRUZEIROS ON 200 CRUZADOS NOVOS**	VG	VF	UNC
	ND (1990). Blue and black on m/c unpt. Ovpt. on #221.			
	a. Series #1725.	20.00	75.00	175.00
	b. Series #1965-2668.	.10	.40	1.00

226 **500 CRUZEIROS ON 500 CRUZADOS NOVOS**
ND (1990). Green and purple on m/c unpt. Ovpt. on #222.

	VG	VF	UNC
a. Series #3111.	10.00	35.00	100.00
b. Series #3701-7700.	.10	.25	.75

1992 ND EMERGENCY ISSUE

227 **5000 CRUZEIROS**
ND (1990). Deep olive-green and deep brown on m/c unpt. Liberty head at r. and as wmk. Arms at l. on back. Printer: CdM-B. Provisional type. Sign. 28. Series #1-1520.

VG	VF	UNC
.20	.75	2.00

1990-93 ND REGULAR ISSUE

#228-236 printer: CdM-B.

#228-231 similar to #220-223 but w/new currency unit and new sign. titles.

228 **100 CRUZEIROS**
ND (1990). Like #220. Sign. 28. Series #1-1045.

VG	VF	UNC
.10	.20	.50

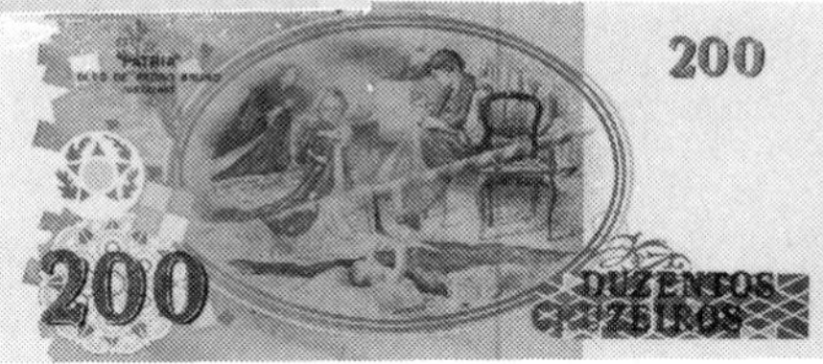

229 **200 CRUZEIROS**
ND (1990). Like #221. Sign. 28. Series #1-1646.

VG	VF	UNC
.05	.15	.35

230 **500 CRUZEIROS**
ND (1990). Like #222. Sign. 28. Series #1-0210.

VG	VF	UNC
.30	.75	3.00

231 **1000 CRUZEIROS**
ND (1990-91). Dk. brown, brown, violet and black on m/c unpt. C. Rondon at r., native hut at ctr., map of Brazil in background. 2 Indian children and local food from Amazonia on back. Wmk: Liberty head.

	VG	VF	UNC
a. Sign. 28. Upper sign. title: *MINISTRO DA ECONOMIA,...* Series #1-4268 (1990).	.10	.40	2.50
b. Upper sign. title: *MINISTRA DA ECONOMIA,...* Series #4269-6796 (1990).	.10	.30	2.00
c. Sign. 29. Series #6797-8453 (1991).	.05	.15	.50

232 **5000 CRUZEIROS**
ND (1990-93). Blue-black, black, and deep brown on lt. blue and m/c unpt. C. Gomes at ctr. r., Brazilian youths at ctr. Statue of Gomes seated, grand piano in background at ctr. on back.

	VG	VF	UNC
a. Sign. 28. Series #1-4489 (1990).	.10	.50	2.00
b. Sign. 29. Series #4490-5501 (1992).	.10	.25	1.50
c. Sign. 30. Series #5502-6041 (1993).	.10	.20	1.00

233 **10,000 CRUZEIROS**
ND (1991-93). Black and brown-violet on m/c unpt. V. Brazil at r. and as wmk. Extracting poisonous venom at ctr. One snake swallowing another at ctr. on back.

	VG	VF	UNC
a. Sign. 28. Series #1-3136 (1991).	.10	.30	3.00
b. Sign. 29. Series #3137-6937 (1992).	.10	.30	1.25
c. Sign. 30. Series #6938-7365 (1993).	.05	.15	1.00

		VG	VF	UNC
234	**50,000 CRUZEIROS** ND (1992). Dk. brown and red-orange on m/c unpt. C. Cascudo at ctr. r. and as wmk. 2 men on raft in background at l. ctr. Folklore dancers at l. ctr. on back. Sign. 29. Series #1-6289.	.10	.35	1.25

#235 and 236 wmk: Sculptured head of *Brasilia*.

		VG	VF	UNC
235	**100,000 CRUZEIROS** ND (1992-93). Brown, green and purple on m/c unpt. Hummingbird feeding nestlings at ctr., butterfly at r. Butterfly at l., Iguacú cataract at ctr. on back.			
	a. Sign. 29. Series #1-6052 (1992).	.15	.50	6.00
	b. Sign. 30. Series #6053-6226 (1993).	.15	.45	5.00
	c. Sign. 31. Series #6227-6290 (1993).	.15	.45	5.00
	d. Sign. 32. Series #6291-6733 (1993).	.10	.25	1.25

		VG	VF	UNC
236	**500,000 CRUZEIROS** ND (1993). Red-violet, brown and deep purple on m/c unpt. M. de Andrade at r., native indian art in unpt. Bldg., de Andrade teaching children at ctr. on back.			
	a. Sign. 30. Series #1-3410 (1993).	.50	2.50	12.00
	b. Sign. 31. Series #3411-4404 (1993).	.50	2.00	10.00
	c. Sign. 32. Series #4405-8291 (1993).	.20	.50	4.00

1993 ND PROVISIONAL ISSUE

August 1993 Monetary Reform: 1 Cruzeiro Real = 1,000 Cruzeiros

#237-239 black circular ovpt. of new value on #234-236. Sign. 32.

		VG	VF	UNC
237	**50 CRUZEIROS REAIS ON 50,000 CRUZEIROS** ND (1993). Dk. brown and red-orange on m/c unpt. Ovpt. on #234. Series #6290-6591.	.05	.20	1.00

		VG	VF	UNC
238	**100 CRUZEIROS REAIS ON 100,000 CRUZEIROS** ND (1993). Brown, green and purple on m/c unpt. Ovpt. on #235d. Series #6734-7144.	.10	.20	1.00

		VG	VF	UNC
239	**500 CRUZEIROS REAIS ON 500,000 CRUZEIROS** ND (1993). Red-violet, brown and deep purple on m/c unpt. Ovpt. on #236c.			
	a. Series prefix A, #8292-9999.	.10	.40	3.00
	b. Series prefix B, #1-607.	.10	.30	2.25

1993-94 ND ISSUE

#240-242 wmk: Sculptured head of *"Brasilia."* Printer: CdM-B. Sign. 33.

		VG	VF	UNC
240	**1000 CRUZEIROS REAIS** ND (1993). Black, dk. blue and brown on m/c unpt. A. Teixeira at ctr. r. "Parque" school at l. ctr. Children and workers on back. Series #1-2515.	.10	.50	2.00

		VG	VF	UNC
241	**5000 CRUZEIROS REAIS** ND (1993). Black, red-brown and dk. olive-green on m/c unpt. Gaucho at ctr. r., ruins of São Miguel das Missões at l. ctr. Back vertical format; gaucho on horseback roping steer at ctr. Series #1-9999.	.50	2.50	12.50

		VG	VF	UNC
242	**50,000 CRUZEIROS REAIS** ND (1994). Deep purple and brown-violet on m/c unpt. Dancer at l. ctr., Baiana at ctr. r. Back vertical format; Baiana Acarajé preparing food at ctr. Series #1-1200.	5.00	25.00	50.00

1994 ND ISSUE

July 1994 Monetary Reform: 1 Real = 2750 Cruzeiros Reals

#243-247 sculpture of the Republic at ctr. r. Back vertical format. Printer: CdM-B or w/additional imprint of secondary printer. Series # is first 4 digits of serial #.

		VG	VF	UNC
243	**1 REAL** ND (1994-). Black, olive-green and blue-green on aqua and pale green unpt. Hummingbirds at ctr. on back. Sign. 33-.			
	a. Wmk: Republic. W/o text. Sign. 33. Series #1-2409 (1994).	FV	FV	4.00
	b. Sign. 34. Series #2410-3833 (1994).	FV	FV	4.00
	c. Sign. 34. W/text: *DEUS SEJA LOUVADO* at lower l. Series #3834- . FVFV2.50	FV	FV	3.00
	d. Wmk: Flag. W/o security thread.			

		VG	VF	UNC
244	**5 REAIS** ND (1994-). Violet, dk. brown and blue on lilac unpt. Crane at ctr. on back. Sign. 33-37.			
	a. Wmk: Republic. Sign. 33. W/o text or G & D imprint. Series A-A: #0001-1411.	FV	FV	11.00
	b. W/o text. Printer: G & D. Series A-B:#1-1000.	FV	FV	10.00
	c. W/text: *DEUS SEJA LOUVADO* at lower left. Series A-A: #1412-.	FV	FV	9.00
	d. Wmk: Flag. W/o security thread.	FV	FV	8.00
	e. Wmk: Republic. Sign. 34. Printer: CdM. Series A-A: #1540.	FV	FV	8.00

		VG	VF	UNC
245	**10 REAIS** ND (1994). Dk. brown, brown-violet and brown-orange on lilac and pale orange unpt. Arara bird at ctr. on back. Sign. 33-37.			
	a. Wmk: Republic. Sign. 33. W/o text or TDLR imprint. Series A-A: #1-1817.	FV	FV	20.00
	b. W/o text. Printer: TDLR. Series #A-B: #1-1200.	FV	FV	18.50
	c. W/text: *DEUS SEJA LOUVADO* at lower l. Series #1818-.	FV	FV	16.50
	d. Wmk: Flag.	FV	FV	15.00
246	**50 REAIS** ND (1994-). Dk. brown and red-brown on m/c unpt. Onça pintada leopard on back. Sign. 33; 34; 36; 37.			
	a. W/o text or F-CO imprint. Sign. 33. Series A-A: #1-1338.	FV	FV	80.00
	b. W/o text. Printer: F-CO. Series A-B: #1-0400.	FV	FV	75.00
	c. W/text: *DEUS SEJA LOUVADO* at lower l. Series #1339-.	FV	FV	90.00
247	**100 REAIS** ND (1994-). Blue-green and purple on m/c unpt. Garoupa fish on back.			
	a. W/o text. Sign. 33. Series #1-1201.	FV	FV	140.00
	b. W/o text. Sign. 34. Series #1199-1201.	FV	FV	200.00
	c. W/text: *DEUS SEJA LOUVADO* at lower l. Sign. 34. Series #1202-1301.	FV	FV	175.00

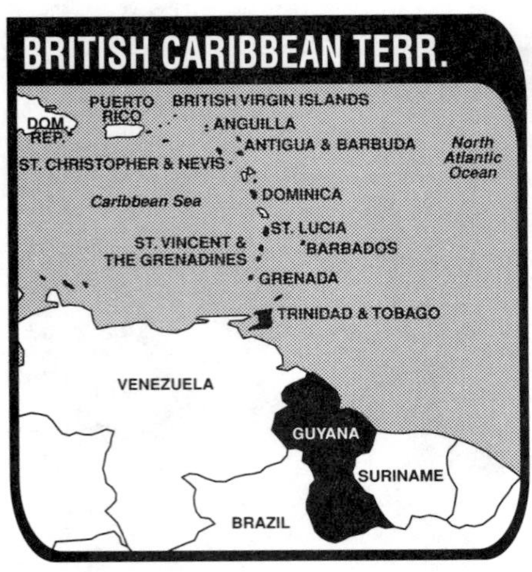

The British Caribbean Territories (Eastern Group), a currency board formed in 1950, comprised the British West Indies territories of Trinidad and Tobago; Barbados; the Leeward Islands of Anguilla, Saba, St. Christopher, Nevis and Antigua; the Windward Islands of St. Lucia, Dominica, St. Vincent and Grenada; British Guiana and the British Virgin Islands. As time progressed, the members of this Eastern Group varied.

For later issues see the East Caribbean States.

RULERS:
British

MONETARY SYSTEM:
1 Dollar = 100 Cents

BRITISH INFLUENCE

BRITISH CARIBBEAN TERRITORIES, EASTERN GROUP

1953 ISSUE

#7-12 map at lower l., portr. Qn. Elizabeth II at r. Arms in all 4 corners on back. Printer: BWC.

		VG	VF	UNC
7	**1 DOLLAR** 1953-64. Red on m/c unpt.			
	a. Wmk: Sailing ship. 5.1.1953.	6.00	35.00	150.00
	b. Wmk: Qn. Elizabeth II. 1.3.1954-2.1.1957.	3.00	15.00	75.00
	c. 2.1.1958-2.1.1964.	1.50	12.00	60.00

		VG	VF	UNC
8	**2 DOLLARS** 1953-64. Blue on m/c unpt.			
	a. Wmk: Sailing ship. 5.1.1953.	20.00	175.00	450.00
	b. Wmk: Qn. Elizabeth II. 1.3.1954-1.7.1960.	7.50	55.00	325.00
	c. 2.1.1961-2.1.1964.	3.00	35.00	250.00

NOTICE

Readers with unlisted dates, signature varieties, etc. are invited to submit photocopies of their notes to: Standard Catalog of World Paper Money, 700 East State St. Iola, WI 54990-0001, fax: 1-715-445-4087, or E-Mail: thernr@krause.com.

		VG	VF	UNC
9	**5 DOLLARS** 1953-64. Green on m/c unpt.			
	a. Wmk: Sailing ship. 5.1.1953.	22.50	185.00	450.00
	b. Wmk: Qn. Elizabeth II. 3.1.1955-2.1.1959.	10.00	65.00	375.00
	c. 2.1.1961-2.1.1964.	7.50	50.00	350.00

		VG	VF	UNC
10	**10 DOLLARS** 1953-64. Brown on m/c unpt.			
	a. Wmk: Sailing ship. 5.1.1953.	37.50	300.00	1500.
	b. Wmk: Qn. Elizabeth II. 3.1.1955-2.1.1959.	20.00	150.00	950.00
	c. 2.1.1961; 2.1.1962; 2.1.1964.	15.00	110.00	525.00

		VG	VF	UNC
11	**20 DOLLARS** 1953-64. Purple on m/c unpt.			
	a. Wmk: Sailing ship. 5.1.1953.	50.00	400.00	2000.
	b. Wmk: Qn. Elizabeth II. 2.1.1957-2.1.1964.	25.00	200.00	1000.
12	**100 DOLLARS** 1953-63. Black on m/c unpt.			
	a. Wmk: Sailing ship. 5.1.1953.	375.00	1250.	—
	b. Wmk: Queen Elizabeth II. 1.3.1954; 2.1.1957; 2.1.1963.	225.00	750.00	—

The British colony of Belize, formerly British Honduras, a self-governing dependency of the United Kingdom situated in Central America south of Mexico and east and north of Guatemala, has an area of 8,867 sq. mi. (22,965 sq. km.) and a population of 209,000. Capital: Belmopan. Sugar, citrus fruits, chicle and hard woods are exported.

The area, site of the ancient Mayan civilization, was sighted by Columbus in 1502, and settled by shipwrecked English seamen in 1638. British buccaneers settled the former capital of Belize in the 17th century. Britain claimed administrative right over the area after the emancipation of Central America from Spain, and declared it a colony subordinate to Jamaica in 1862. It established as the separate Crown Colony of British Honduras in 1884. The anti-British People's United Party, which attained power in 1954, won a constitution, effective in 1964 which established self-government under a British appointed governor. British Honduras became Belize on June 1, 1973, following the passage of a surprise bill by the Peoples United Party, but the constitutional relationship with Britain remained unchanged.

In Dec. 1975, the U.N. General Assembly adopted a resolution supporting the right of the people of Belize to self-determination, and asking Britain and Guatemala to renew their negotiations on the future of Belize. Belize obtained independence on Sept. 21, 1981.

See listings of Belize for later issues.

RULERS:
British

MONETARY SYSTEM:
1 Dollar = 100 Cents

BRITISH HONDURAS

GOVERNMENT OF BRITISH HONDURAS

1952-53 ISSUE

#28-32 arms at l., portr. Qn. Elizabeth II at r.

		VG	VF	UNC
28	**1 DOLLAR** 1952-73. Green on m/c unpt.			
	a. 15.4.1953-1.10.1958.	4.00	25.00	125.00
	b. 1.1.1961-1.5.1969.	2.00	10.00	50.00
	c. 1.1.1970-1.1.1973.	1.50	7.00	35.00

		VG	VF	UNC
29	**2 DOLLARS** 1953-73. Purple on m/c unpt.			
	a. 15.4.1953-1.10.1958.	7.50	40.00	350.00
	b. 1.10.1960-1.5.1965.	3.00	20.00	125.00
	c. 1.1.1971-1.1.1973.	2.00	15.00	55.00

		VG	VF	UNC
30	**5 DOLLARS** 1953-73. Red on m/c unpt.			
	a. 15.4.1953-1.1.1958.	10.00	50.00	350.00
	b. 1.3.1960-1.5.1969.	5.00	30.00	225.00
	c. 1.1.1970-1.1.1973.	4.50	20.00	150.00

		VG	VF	UNC
31	**10 DOLLARS** 1953-73. Black on m/c unpt.			
	a. 15.4.1953-1.10.1958.	15.00	100.00	700.00
	b. 1.4.1964-1.5.1969.	10.00	50.00	500.00
	c. 1.1.1971-1.1.1973.	7.50	35.00	375.00
32	**20 DOLLARS** 1952-73. Brown on m/c unpt.			
	a. 1.12.1952-1.10.1958.	30.00	150.00	1000.
	b. 1.3.1960-1.5.1969.	20.00	120.00	750.00
	c. 1.1.1970-1.1.1973.	15.00	100.00	675.00

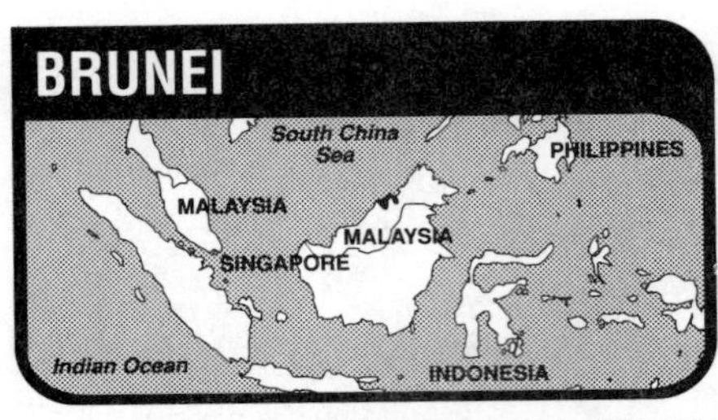

Negara Brunei Darussalam (The State of Brunei), a member of the British Commonwealth is located on the northwest coast of the island of Borneo, has an area of 2,226 sq. mi. (5,765 sq. km.) and a population of 299,940. Capital: Bandar Seri Begawan. Crude oil and rubber are exported.

Magellan was the first European to visit Brunei in 1521. It was a powerful state, ruling over Northern Borneo and adjacent islands from the 16th to the 19th century. Brunei became a British protectorate in 1888 and a British dependency in 1905. The Constitution of 1959 restored control over internal affairs to the sultan, while delegating responsibility for defense and foreign affairs to Britain.

On Jan. 1, 1984, Brunei became a fully independent member of the Commonwealth.

RULERS:

Sultan Sir Omar Ali Saifuddin III, 1950-1967
Sultan Hassanal Bolkiah I, 1967-

MONETARY SYSTEM:

1 Dollar = 100 Sen to 1967
1 Ringgit (Dollar) = 100 Sen, 1967-

STATE

KERAJAAN BRUNEI

GOVERNMENT OF BRUNEI

1967 ISSUE

#1-5 Sultan Omar Ali Saifuddin III w/military cap at r. and as wmk. Mosque on back. Printer: BWC.

		VG	VF	UNC
1	**1 RINGGIT** 1967. Dk. blue on m/c unpt. Back gray, lavender and pink.	2.00	10.00	35.00

		VG	VF	UNC
2	**5 RINGGIT** 1967. Dk. green on m/c unpt. Back green and pink.	7.00	17.50	62.50
3	**10 RINGGIT** 1967. Red on m/c unpt. Back red.	10.00	20.00	75.00
4	**50 RINGGIT** 1967. Dk. brown on m/c unpt. Back olive.	45.00	80.00	250.00

		VG	VF	UNC
5	**100 RINGGIT** 1967. Blue on m/c unpt. Back purple.	55.00	150.00	375.00

1972-79 ISSUE

#6-10 Sultan Hassanal Bolkiah I in military uniform at r. and as wmk. Mosque on back. Printer: BWC.

		VG	VF	UNC
6	**1 RINGGIT** 1972-88. Blue on m/c unpt.			
	a. 1972; 1976; 1978.	FV	2.00	7.00
	b. 1980; 1982.	FV	1.50	5.00
	c. 1983-1986.	FV	1.25	8.00
	d. 1988.	FV	FV	5.00

		VG	VF	UNC
7	**5 RINGGIT** 1979-86. Green on m/c unpt.			
	a. 1979; 1981.	1.50	6.00	15.00
	b. 1983; 1984; 1986.	1.00	4.00	15.00
8	**10 RINGGIT** 1976-86. Red on m/c unpt.	VG	VF	UNC
	a. 1976; 1981.	2.00	10.00	25.00
	b. 1983; 1986.	1.50	6.50	25.00

		VG	VF	UNC
9	**50 RINGGIT** 1973-86. Dk. brown on m/c unpt.			
	a. 1973.	FV	45.00	100.00
	b. 1977; 1982.	FV	40.00	90.00
	c. 1986.	FV	35.00	60.00

		VG	VF	UNC
10	**100 RINGGIT** 1972-88. Blue on m/c unpt.			
	a. 1972; 1976.	FV	95.00	225.00
	b. 1978; 1980.	FV	80.00	165.00
	c. 1982; 1983; 1988.	FV	75.00	140.00

1979; 1987 ISSUE

#11 and 12 Sultan Hassanal Bolkiah I in royal uniform at r. and as wmk. Printer: BWC.

		VG	VF	UNC
11	**500 RINGGIT** 1979; 1987. Orange on m/c unpt. Mosque at ctr. on back.			
	a. 1979.	FV	425.00	700.00
	b. 1987.	FV	400.00	650.00

		VG	VF	UNC
12	**1000 RINGGIT** 1979; 1986; 1987. Gray, brown and greenish blue. Brunei Museum on back.			
	a. 1979.	FV	850.00	1350.
	b. 1986-87.	FV	800.00	1250.

NEGARA BRUNEI DARUSSALAM

1989 ISSUE

#13-20 Sultan Hassanal Bolkiah I at r. and as wmk.

		VG	VF	UNC
13	**1 RINGGIT** 1989-95. Purple on m/c unpt. Aerial view on back.			
	a. 1989; 1991.	FV	.50	3.00
	b. 1994-95.	FV	FV	2.50

		VG	VF	UNC
14	**5 RINGGIT** 1989-91; 1993; 1995. Blue-gray and deep green on m/c unpt. Houses and boats on back.	FV	1.00	10.00

		VG	VF	UNC
15	**10 RINGGIT** 1989-92; 1995. Purple and red-orange on m/c unpt. Waterfront village w/mosque on back.	FV	FV	14.00

		VG	VF	UNC
16	**50 RINGGIT** 1989-91; 1995. Brown, olive-green, and orange on m/c unpt. People in power launch on back.	FV	FV	57.50

		VG	VF	UNC
17	**100 RINGGIT** 1989-92; 1994. Blue and violet on m/c unpt. River scene on back.	FV	FV	110.00

		VG	VF	UNC
18	**500 RINGGIT** 1989-92. Red-orange, purple, olive and black on m/c unpt. Woman in boat on back.	FV	FV	475.00
19	**1000 RINGGIT** 1989-91. Red-violet, purple, olive and blue-green on m/c unpt. Waterfront village w/mosque on back.	FV	FV	800.00

NOTICE

Readers with unlisted dates, signature varieties, etc. are invited to submit photocopies of their notes to: Standard Catalog of World Paper Money, 700 East State St. Iola, WI 54990-0001, fax: 1-715-445-4087, or E-Mail: thernr@krause.com.

20 **10,000 RINGGIT**
1989. Dk. brown and dk. green on m/c unpt. Aerial view of Bandar Seri Begawan harbor on back.

	VG	VF	UNC
a. Issued note.	FV	FV	7650.
s. Specimen.	—	—	5000.

1992 COMMEMORATIVE ISSUE

#21, 25th Anniversary of Accession

	VG	VF	UNC
21 **25 RINGGIT** 1992. Brown, lilac, green and m/c. Royal procession at ctr., Sultan at r. and as wmk. at l. Crown at l., coronation at ctr. on back. Dates *1967* and *1992* w/text at top.	FV	FV	35.00

1996 ISSUE

#22-26 Sultan Hassanal Bolkiah I at r.

#22-24 arms at upper l. Polymer plastic. Printer: NPA (w/o imprint).

	VG	VF	UNC
22 **1 RINGGIT** 1996. Blue-black and deep green on m/c unpt. Riverside simpur plant at l. ctr. Back blue and m/c; rain forest waterfall at l. ctr.	FV	FV	2.00

	VG	VF	UNC
23 **5 RINGGIT** 1996. Black on green and m/c unpt. Pitcher plant at l. ctr. Rain forest floor on back.	FV	FV	6.00

	VG	VF	UNC
24 **10 RINGGIT** 1996. Dk. brown and brown on red and m/c unpt. Purple-leafed forest yam at l. ctr. Rain forest canopy on back.	FV	FV	11.50
25 **50 RINGGIT** 1996. Brown, blue and purple on m/c unpt. Marine installation on back.	FV	FV	52.50
26 **100 RINGGIT** 1996. Brown and orange on m/c unpt. Airport on back.	FV	FV	90.00
27 **500 RINGGIT** 199x.	Expected New Issue		
28 **1000 RINGGIT** 199x.	Expected New Issue		
29 **10,000 RINGGIT** 199x.	Expected New Issue		

The Republic of Bulgaria (formerly the Peoples Republic of Bulgaria), a Balkan country on the Black Sea in southeastern Europe, has an area of 44,365 sq. mi. (110,912 sq. km.) and a population of 8.47 million. Capital: Sofia. Agriculture remains a key component of the economy but industrialization, particularly he- avy industry, has been emphasized since the late 1940's. Machinery, tobacco and cigarettes, wines and spirits, clothing and metals are the chief exports.

The area now occupied by Bulgaria was conquered by the Bulgars, an Asiatic tribe, in the 7th century. Bulgarian kingdoms continued to exist on the peninsula until it came under Turkish rule in 1395. In 1878, after nearly 500 years of Turkish rule, Bulgaria was made a principality under Turkish suzerainty. Union seven years later with Eastern Rumelia created a Balkan state with borders approximating those of present-day Bulgaria. A Bulgarian kingdom fully independent of Turkey was proclaimed Sept. 22, 1908.

During WWI Bulgaria had been aligned with Germany. After the Armistice certain land concessions were granted to Greece and Romania. In 1934 King Boris III suspended all political parties and established a dictatorial monarchy. In 1938 the military began rearming through the aid of the Anglo-French loan. As WWII developed Bulgaria again supported the Germans but Boris protected its Jewish community. Boris died mysteriously in 1943 and Simeon II became king at the age of six. The country was then ruled by a pro-Nazi regency until it was invaded by Soviet forces in 1944. The monarchy was abolished and Simeon was ousted by plebiscite in 1946, and Bulgaria became a People's Republic in the Soviet pattern. Following demonstrations and a general strike, the communist government resigned in Nov. 1990. A new government was elected in Oct. 1991.

TITLES:

Bulgarian People's Republic: НАРОДНАРЕПУБЛИКАБЪЛГАРИЯ
Bulgarian National Bank: БЪЛГАРСКАТАНАРОДНАБАНКА

MONETARY SYSTEM:

1 Lev ЛЕВ = 100 Stotinki СТОТИНКИ, until 1999
1 Lev = 1,000 "Old" Lev, 1999

PEOPLES REPUBLIC

БЪЛГАРСКАТА НАРОДНА БАНКА

BULGARIAN NATIONAL BANK

1962 ISSUE

#88-92 arms at l.

		VG	VF	UNC
88	**1 LEV** 1962. Brown-lilac. Monument for the Battle of Shipka Pass (1877) at l. ctr. on back.			
	a. Issued note.	.10	.25	2.00
	s. Specimen.	—	—	17.50

		VG	VF	UNC
89	**2 LEVA** 1962. Green. Woman picking grapes in vineyard on back.			
	a. Issued note.	.20	.40	3.00
	s. Specimen.	—	—	18.50
90	**5 LEVA** 1962. Red-brown. Coastline village.			
	a. Issued note.	.25	.50	5.00
	s. Specimen.	—	—	20.00
91	**10 LEVA** 1962. Blue. Factory. Dimitrov on back.			
	a. Issued note.	.35	.70	8.50
	s. Specimen.	—	—	22.50
92	**20 LEVA** 1962. Brown-lilac. Factory. Dimitrov on back.			
	a. Issued note.	.50	1.00	15.00
	s. Specimen.	—	—	25.00

1974 ISSUE

#93-97 modified arms w/dates *681-1944* at l.

#93-95 wmk: Decorative design.

		VG	VF	UNC
93	**1 LEV** 1974. Brown. Like #88.			
	a. Issued note.	.10	.20	1.00
	s. Specimen.	—	—	17.50

		VG	VF	UNC
94	**2 LEVA** 1974. Green. Like #89.			
	a. Issued note.	.10	.25	2.50
	s. Specimen.	—	—	18.50

		VG	VF	UNC
95	**5 LEVA** 1974. Red-brown. Like #90.			
	a. Issued note.	.15	.30	1.10
	s. Specimen.	—	—	20.00

#96 and 97 wmk: Hands holding hammer and sickle.

		VG	VF	UNC
96	**10 LEVA** 1974. Blue. Like #91.			
	a. Issued note.	.25	.75	2.50
	s. Specimen.	—	—	22.50

		VG	VF	UNC
97	**20 LEVA** 1974. Brown-lilac. Like #92.			
	a. Issued note.	.50	1.00	10.00
	s. Specimen.	—	—	25.00

1989; 1990 ISSUES

98 **50 LEVA**

1990. Brown and dk. blue on m/c unpt. Arms at l. ctr. Back brown and dk. green; castle ruins at ctr. r. on back. Wmk: Hands holding hammer and sickle.

	VG	VF	UNC
a. Issued note.	1.25	2.50	12.50
s. Specimen.	—	—	150.00

#98 was withdrawn from circulation shortly after its release.

99 **100 LEVA**

	VG	VF	UNC
1989. Purple on lilac unpt. Arms at l. ctr. Horseman w/2 dogs at ctr. r. on back. Wmk: Rampant lion. (Not issued).	—	—	150.00

#99 carries the name of the Bulgarian Peoples Republic, probably the reason it was not released. An estimated 500-600 pieces were "liberated" from the recycling process.

REPUBLIC

БЪЛГАРСКАТА НАРОДНА БАНКА

BULGARIAN NATIONAL BANK

1991-96 ND ISSUE

#100-103 wmk: Arms (lion).

100 **20 LEVA**

	VG	VF	UNC
1991. Blue-black and blue-green on m/c unpt. Dutchess Sevastokrat Oritza Desislava at l. ctr. Boyana Church at r. on back.	FV	FV	.35

101 **50 LEVA**

	VG	VF	UNC
1992. Purple and violet on m/c unpt. Khristo G. Danov at l. Platen printing press at r. on back.	FV	FV	.40

102 **100 LEVA**

1991; 1993. Dk. brown and maroon on m/c unpt. Zhary Zograf (artist) at l. ctr. Wheel of Life at r. on back.

	VG	VF	UNC
a. 1991.	FV	FV	1.50
b. 1993.	FV	FV	.65

103 **200 LEVA**

	VG	VF	UNC
1992. Deep violet and brown-orange on m/c unpt. Ivan Vazov at l., village in unpt. Lyre w/laurel wreath at r. on back.	FV	FV	.75

104 **500 LEVA**

	VG	VF	UNC
1993. Dk. green and black on m/c unpt. D. Hristov at l. and as wmk. Opera house in Varna at ctr. r., sea gulls at lower r. on back.	FV	FV	1.25

105 **1000 LEVA**

	VG	VF	UNC
1994; 1996. Dk. green and olive-brown on m/c unpt. V. Levski at l. and as wmk., Liberty w/flag, sword and lion at upper ctr. r. Monument and writings of Levski at ctr. r. on back.	FV	FV	1.50

106 (107) **1000 LEVA**

	VG	VF	UNC
1996. Dk. green and olive-brown on m/c unpt. Like #105 but w/wide hologram foil strip at l.	FV	FV	1.00

107 (106) **2000 LEVA**

	VG	VF	UNC
1994; 1996. Black and dk. blue on m/c unpt. N. Ficev at l. and as wmk., bldg. outlines at ctr., wide hologram foil strip at l. Steeple, bldg. plans at ctr. r. on back.	FV	FV	2.00

1996 ISSUE

#108-109 w/wide hologram foil strip at l.

		VG	VF	UNC
108	**5000 LEVA** 1996. Violet on m/c unpt. Z. Stoyanov at l. and as wmk. quill pen at ctr. r. Monument (2 views) at ctr., and *1885 Proclamation to the Bulgarian People* at r. on back.	FV	FV	5.00

		VG	VF	UNC
109	**10,000 LEVA** 1996. Brown and purple on m/c unpt. V. Dimitrov at l. and as wmk., palette, brushes, Academy of the Arts at ctr. Sketches at ctr., "Bulgarian Madonna" at r. on back.	FV	FV	10.00

1997 ISSUE

#110-111 like #106-108 but w/o wide hologram foil strip at l.

		VG	VF	UNC
110	**1000 LEVA** 1997. Dk. green and olive-brown on m/c unpt.	FV	FV	2.00
111 (112)	**5000 LEVA** 1997. Violet on m/c unpt.	FV	FV	5.00

#112 and 113 w/wide hologram foil strip at l. Reduced size.

		VG	VF	UNC
112 (113)	**10,000 LEVA** 1997. M/c. Dr. P. Beron at l. Telescope at r. on back.	FV	FV	10.00
113 (114)	**50,000 LEVA** 1997. Purple on m/c unpt. St. Cyril at l., St. Methodius at ctr. r. Architectural monuments of the ancient Bulgarian capitals of Pliska and Preslav on back.	FV	FV	45.00

1999 ISSUE

Monetary reform: 1 "New" Lev = 1000 "Old" Lev

		VG	VF	UNC
114	**1 LEV** 1999. Red and blue on yellow unpt. Icon of St. John of Rila at l. Rila Monastery on back.	FV	FV	1.00

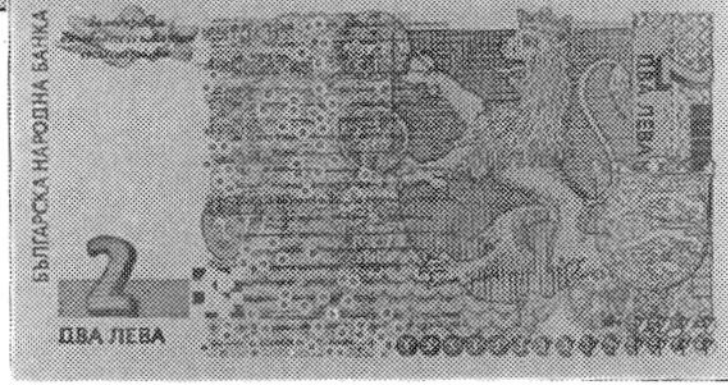

		VG	VF	UNC
115	**2 LEVA** 1999. Violet and pink on lt. blue unpt. Paisii Hilendarski at l. Heraldic lion on back.	FV	FV	2.00

		VG	VF	UNC
116	**5 LEVA** 1999. Red, brown and green on m/c unpt. Ivan Milev at l. Parts of paintings on back.	FV	FV	5.00

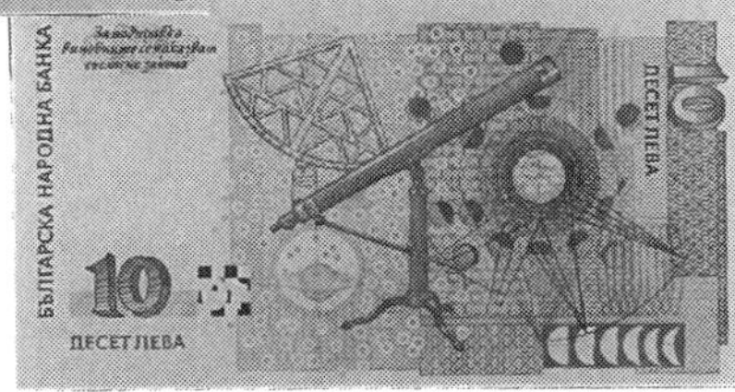

		VG	VF	UNC
117	**10 LEVA** 1999. Dk. green on ochre unpt. Dr. Peter Beron at l. Astronomy sketches and telescope on back.	FV	FV	10.00
118	**20 LEVA** 1999. Blue on m/c unpt. Stambolov at l. National Assembly bldg. and Eagles' and Lions' Bridges in Sofia on back.	FV	FV	20.00
119	**50 LEVA** 1999. Brown and yellow on m/c unpt. Pencho Slaveykov at l. Illustrations from his poetry works on back.	FV	FV	50.00

Foreign Exchange Certificates

Corecom

1966 ND Issue

		VG	VF	UNC
FX1	**1 Lev** ND (1966). Lt. brown on yellow unpt.	—	—	5.00
FX2	**2 Leva** ND (1966). Lt. brown on yellow unpt.	—	—	7.50
FX3	**5 Leva** ND (1966). Lt. brown on yellow unpt.	—	—	10.00
FX4	**10 Leva** ND (1966). Lt. brown on yellow unpt.	—	—	20.00
FX5	**20 Leva** ND (1966). Lt. brown on yellow unpt.	—	—	30.00
FX6	**50 Leva** ND (1966). Lt. brown on yellow unpt.	—	—	40.00
FX7	**100 Leva** ND (1966). Lt. brown on yellow unpt.	—	—	50.00

1968 ND Issue

		VG	VF	UNC
FX8	**1 Lev** ND (1968). Brown on lt. green unpt.	—	—	5.00
FX9	**2 Leva** ND (1968). Brown on lt. green unpt.	—	—	6.50
FX10	**5 Leva** ND (1968). Brown on lt. green unpt.	—	—	8.50
FX11	**10 Leva** ND (1968). Brown on lt. green unpt.	—	—	10.00
FX12	**20 Leva** ND (1968). Brown on lt. green unpt.	—	—	15.00
FX13	**50 Leva** ND (1968). Brown on lt. green unpt.	—	—	25.00
FX14	**100 Leva** ND (1968). Brown on lt. green unpt.	—	—	50.00

1975 ND Issue

		VG	VF	UNC
FX15	**1 Lev** ND (1975). Brown on lt. pink unpt.	—	—	5.00

		VG	VF	UNC
FX16	**2 Leva** ND (1975).	—	—	7.50
FX17	**5 Lev** ND (1975).	—	—	10.00
FX18	**10 Leva** ND (1975).	—	—	15.00
FX19	**20 Leva** ND (1975).	—	—	20.00
FX20	**50 Leva** ND (1975).	—	—	30.00
FX21	**100 Leva** ND (1975).	—	—	50.00

1978 ND Issue

#FX22-28 Wmk: Wavy lines.

		VG	VF	UNC
FX22	**1 Lev** ND (1978). Red on lt. blue unpt.	—	—	5.00
FX23	**2 Leva** ND (1978).	—	—	7.50
FX24	**5 Leva** ND (1978).	—	—	10.00
FX25	**10 Leva** ND (1978).	—	—	15.00
FX26	**20 Leva** ND (1978).	—	—	20.00
FX27	**50 Leva** ND (1978).	—	—	30.00
FX28	**100 Leva** ND (1978).	—	—	50.00

Bulgarian National Bank

1981 Issue

#FX29-35 Wmk: BHB in oval, repeated.

		VG	VF	UNC
FX29	**1 Lev** 1981. Lt. brown on pale red unpt.	—	—	5.00
FX30	**2 Leva** 1981.	—	—	7.50

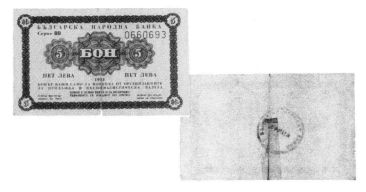

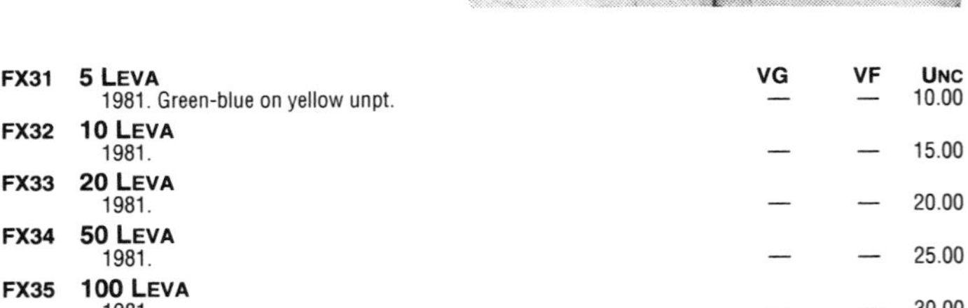

		VG	VF	UNC
FX31	**5 Leva** 1981. Green-blue on yellow unpt.	—	—	10.00
FX32	**10 Leva** 1981.	—	—	15.00
FX33	**20 Leva** 1981.	—	—	20.00
FX34	**50 Leva** 1981.	—	—	25.00
FX35	**100 Leva** 1981.	—	—	30.00

Sending Scanned Images by Email

Over the past 2 years or so, we have been receiving an ever-increasing flow of scanned images from sources worldwide. Unfortunately, many of these scans could not be used due to the type of scan, or simple incompatibility with our systems. We appreciate the effort it takes to produce these images and accuracy they add to the catalog listings.

Here are a few simple instructions to follow when producing these scans. We encourage you to continue sending new images or upgrades to those currently illustrated and please do not hesitate to ask questions about this process.

- Scan all images within a resolution range of 200 dpi to 300 dpi
- Size setting should be at 100%
- Scan in true 4-color
- Save images as 'jpeg' or 'tiff' and name in such a way which clearly identifies the country of origin of the note
- Please email with a request to confirm receipt of the attachment
- Please send images to thernr@krause.com

1986 ISSUE

		VG	VF	UNC
FX36	**1 LEV** (19)86. Red on ochre unpt.	—	—	5.00
FX37	**2 LEVA** (19)86. Blue on grey unpt.	—	—	7.50
FX38	**5 LEVA** (19)86.	—	—	10.00
FX39	**10 LEVA** (19)86.	—	—	15.00
FX40	**20 LEVA** (19)86.	—	—	20.00
FX41	**50 LEVA** (19)86.	—	—	25.00
FX42	**100 LEVA** (19)86. Olive on lt. brown unpt.	—	—	30.00

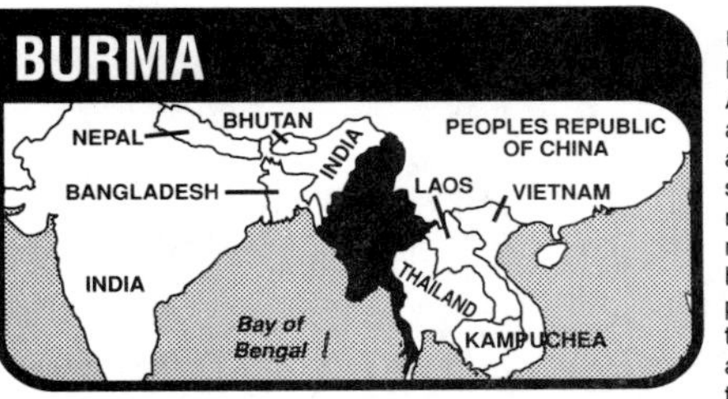

The Socialist Republic of the Union of Burma (now called Myanmar), a country of Southeast Asia fronting on the Bay of Bengal and the Andaman Sea, has an area of 261,789 sq. mi. (676,522 sq. km.) and a population of 41.5 million. Capital: Rangoon. Myanmar is an agricultural country heavily dependent on its leading product (rice) which embodies two-thirds of the cultivated area and accounts for 40 percent of the value of exports. Petroleum, lead, tin, silver, zinc, nickel, cobalt and precious stones are exported.

The first European to reach Burma, about 1435, was Nicolo Di Conti, a merchant of Venice. During the beginning of the reign of Bodawpaya (1782-1819AD) the kingdom comprised most of the same area as it does today including Arakan which was taken over in 1784-85. The British East India Company, while unsuccessful in its 1612 effort to establish posts along the Bay of Bengal, was enabled by the Anglo-Burmese Wars of 1824-86 to expand to the whole of Burma and to secure its annexation to British India. In 1937, Burma was separated from India, becoming a separate British colony with limited self-government. The Japanese occupied Burma in 1942, and on Aug. 1, 1943 Burma became an "independent and sovereign state" under Dr. Ba Maw who was appointed the Adipadi (head of state) which later collapsed with the surrender of Japanese forces. Burma became an independent nation outside the British Commonwealth on Jan. 4, 1948, the constitution of 1948 providing for a parliamentary democracy and the nationalization of certain industries. However, political and economic problems persisted, and on March 2, 1962, Gen. Ne Win took over the government, suspended the constitution, installed himself as chief of state, and pursued a socialistic program with nationalization of nearly all industry and trade. On Jan. 4, 1974, a new constitution adopted by referendum established Burma as a "socialist republic" under one-party rule. The country name was changed formally to the Union of Myanmar in 1989.

For later issues refer to Myanmar.

MONETARY SYSTEM:

1 Kyat = 100 Pya, 1943-45, 1952-

REPUBLIC

PEOPLES BANK OF BURMA

1965 ND ISSUE

#52-55 portr. Gen. Aung San at ctr. Wmk. pattern throughout paper. Printed in East Berlin. Replacement notes have special Burmese characters w/serial #.

		VG	VF	UNC
52	**1 KYAT** ND (1965). Violet and blue. Back violet; fisherman at ctr. Serial # varieties.	.15	.30	1.00

		VG	VF	UNC
53	**5 KYATS** ND (1965). Green and lt. blue. Back green; man w/ox at ctr.	.50	1.00	2.50

		VG	VF	UNC
54	**10 KYATS** ND (1965). Red-brown and violet. Back red-brown, woman picking cotton at r.	.75	1.50	5.00

		VG	VF	UNC
55	**20 KYATS** ND (1965). Brown and tan. Back brown; farmer on tractor at ctr. r.	1.00	2.50	8.00

UNION BANK OF BURMA

1972-79 ND ISSUE

#56-61 various military portrs. of Gen. Aung at l. and as wmk.

		VG	VF	UNC
56	**1 KYAT** ND (1972). Green and blue on m/c unpt. Ornate native wheel assembly at r. on back.	.10	.15	.40

		VG	VF	UNC
57	**5 KYATS** ND (1973). Blue and purple on m/c unpt. Palm tree at l. ctr. on back.	.15	.35	.90

		VG	VF	UNC
58	**10 KYATS** ND (1973). Red and violet on m/c unpt. Native ornaments at ctr. on back.	.15	.40	1.00

		VG	VF	UNC
59	**25 KYATS** ND (1972). Brown and tan on m/c unpt. Mythical winged creature at ctr. on back.	.25	.60	1.50

		VG	VF	UNC
60	**50 KYATS** ND (1979). Brown and violet on m/c unpt. Mythical dancer at l. ctr. on back.	2.00	5.00	17.50

		VG	VF	UNC
61	**100 KYATS** ND (1976). Blue and green on m/c unpt. Native wheel and musical string instrument at l. ctr. on back.	1.50	4.00	15.00

1985-87 ND ISSUE

#62-66 reduced size notes. Various portrs. Gen. Aung San as wmk.

		VG	VF	UNC
62	**15 KYATS** ND (1986). Blue-gray and green on m/c unpt. Gen. Aung San at l. ctr. Mythical dancer at l. on back.	FV	FV	2.00

63 **35 KYATS**

	VG	VF	UNC
ND (1986). Brown-violet and purple on m/c unpt. Gen. Aung San in military hat at l. ctr. Mythical dancer at l. on back.	.20	.50	1.50

64 **45 KYATS**

	VG	VF	UNC
ND (1987). Blue-gray and blue on m/c unpt. Po Hla Gyi at r. 2 workers w/rope and bucket at l. ctr., oil field at ctr. r. on back.	FV	FV	4.00

65 **75 KYATS**

	VG	VF	UNC
ND (1985). Brown on m/c unpt. Gen. Aung San at l. ctr. Dancer at l. on back.	.20	.75	2.75

66 **90 KYATS**

	VG	VF	UNC
ND (1987). Brown and green on m/c unpt. Seya San at r. Farmer plowing w/oxen at l. ctr., rice planting at upper r. on back.	FV	FV	6.00

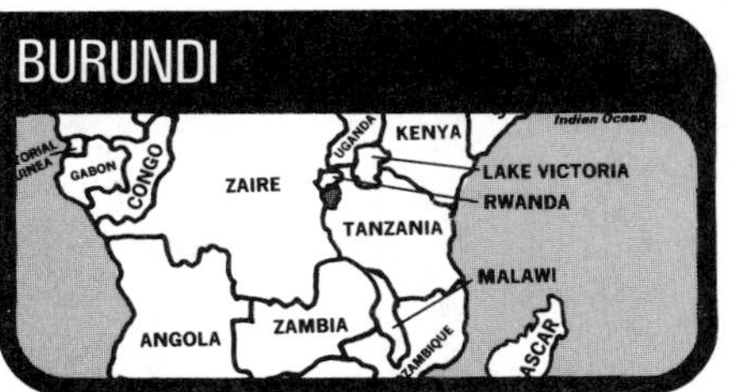

The Republic of Burundi, a landlocked country in central Africa, east of Lake Taganyila has an area of 10,759 sq. mi. (27.834 sq. km.) and a population of 5.36 million. Capital: Bujumbura. Burundi has a predominantly agricultural economy. Coffee, tea and cotton are exported.

. The original inhabitants of Burundi are believed to be the Twa (pygmy); they were there when the Hutu (Bantu) arrived in the 14th century, imposing their language and customs. The development of the state structure began in the 15th centruy when migrating Tutsi, imposed themselves as feudal rulers over the Hutu. Burundi had a caste system and was ruled by a monarch, so-called the *Mwami;* however, the political and social structures were not rigid, the marriages between the two communites were common, and the Hutu enjoyed greater economic independence.

Since 1820, the caravans of Zanzibar traversed the country, but the Islamic infulence was minimal. In 1858 the first British travelers arrived in the country, and in 1871 the explorer Livingstone and journalist Stanley. As a result of Bismark's continuing interest in Africa, Burundi (then called Urundi) was occupied in the 1880s and the German Protectorate established in 1890. The country was incorporated with Rwanda (called Ruanda), into German East Africa.

During World War I, Belgium occupied Ruanda-Urundi and later the League of Nations gave the mandate area as part of Belgian Congo. After World War II, it was made a UN trust territory administrated by Belgium. The indigenous social structures were maintained in Urundi, including the presence of a local monarch, King Mwambutsa IV Bangiricenge The UN supervised election of 1961 established limited self-governoment. Burundi became a constitutional monarchy on July 1, 1962 and was admitted to the UN. Political rivalry between the Hutu and Tutsi intensified. The monarchy was overthrown in a military *coup* in 1966, A 1972 Hutu uprising lead to widespread massacres. Additional *coups* occured in 1976, 1987 and 1992. Since elections of 1993, there has been continual civil unrest.

RULERS:

Mwambutsa IV, 1962-1966
Ntare V, 1966

MONETARY SYSTEM:

1 Franc = 100 Centimes

KINGDOM

BANQUE DU ROYAUME DU BURUNDI

1964 ND PROVISIONAL ISSUE

#1-7 lg. *BURUNDI* ovpt. on face only of Banque d'Emission du Rwanda et du Burundi notes.

1 **5 FRANCS**

	GOOD	FINE	XF
ND (1964 - old dates 15.5.1961; 15.4.1963). Lt. brown. Black ovpt. on Rwanda-Burundi #1.	10.00	45.00	185.00

2 **10 FRANCS**

	GOOD	FINE	XF
ND (1964 - old date 5.10.1960). Gray. Red ovpt. on Rwanda-Burundi #2.	15.00	50.00	190.00

3 **20 FRANCS**

	GOOD	FINE	XF
ND (1964 - old date 5.10.1960). Green. Black ovpt. on Rwanda-Burundi #3.	20.00	60.00	200.00

4 **50 FRANCS**

	GOOD	FINE	XF
ND (1964 - old dates 15.9.1960-1.10.1960). Red. Black ovpt. on Rwanda-Burundi #4.	20.00	65.00	225.00

5 **100 Francs** | Good | Fine | XF
ND (1964 - old dates 1.10.1960; 31.7.1962). Blue. Red ovpt. on Rwanda-Burundi #5. | 15.00 | 55.00 | 200.00

6 **500 Francs**
ND (1964 - old dates 15.9.1960-15.5.1961). Lilac brown. Black ovpt. on Rwanda-Burundi #6. | 150.00 | 650.00 | 1100.

7 **1000 Francs** | Good | Fine | XF
ND (1964 - old date 31.7.1962). Green. Black ovpt. on Rwanda-Burundi #7. | 100.00 | 400.00 | 900.00

1964; 1965 Regular Issue

#8-14 arms at ctr. on back.

8 **5 Francs** | VG | VF | Unc
1.10.1964; 1.12.1964; 1.5.1965. Lt. brown on gray-green unpt. 2 young men picking coffee beans at l. | 2.00 | 7.50 | 25.00

9 **10 Francs** | VG | VF | Unc
20.11.1964; 25.2.1965; 20.3.1965; 31.12.1965. Dk. brown on lilac-brown unpt. Cattle at ctr. | 2.00 | 7.50 | 30.00

10 **20 Francs** | VG | VF | Unc
20.11.1964; 25.2.1965; 20.3.1965. Blue-green. Dancer at ctr. | 7.50 | 30.00 | 100.00

11 **50 Francs** | VG | VF | Unc
1964-66. Red-orange. View of Bujumbura.
a. Sign. titles: *LE VICE PRESIDENT* and *LE PRESIDENT*. 1.10.1964-31.12.1965. | 15.00 | 50.00 | 175.00
b. Sign. titles: *L'ADMINISTRATEUR* and *LE PRESIDENT*. 1.7.1966. | — | — | —

NOTE: #11b was prepared but apparently not released w/o ovpt. See #16b.

12 **100 Francs** | VG | VF | Unc
1964-66. Bluish purple. Prince Rwagasore at ctr.
a. Sign. titles: *LE VICE PRESIDENT* and *LE PRESIDENT*. 1.10.1964; 1.12.1964; 1.5.1965. | 6.00 | 32.50 | 175.00
b. Sign. titles: *L'ADMINISTRATEUR* and *LE PRESIDENT*. 1.7.1966. | — | — | —

13 **500 Francs** | VG | VF | Unc
5.12.1964; 1.8.1966. Brown on yellow unpt. Bank at r. | 45.00 | 175.00 | —

14 **1000 Francs** | VG | VF | Unc
1.2.1965. Green on m/c unpt. Kg. Mwami Mwambutsa IV at r. | 150.00 | 550.00 | —

Republic

Banque de la République du Burundi

1966 Provisional Issue

#15-19 black ovpt: *DE LA REPUBLIQUE* and *YA REPUBLIKA* on face only of Banque du Royaume du Burundi notes.

NOTE: Ovpt. on #17 has letters either 3, 2 or 2.6mm high.

15 **20 Francs** | VG | VF | Unc
ND (1966 - old date 20.3.1965). Ovpt. on #10. | 15.00 | 45.00 | 150.00

16 **50 Francs**
ND (1966 - old dates 1.5.1965; 31.12.1965; 1.7.1966).
a. Ovpt. on #11a. | 17.50 | 60.00 | 200.00
b. Ovpt. on #11b. | 22.50 | 85.00 | 260.00

17	100 FRANCS	VG	VF	UNC
	ND (1966).			
	a. Ovpt. on #12a. (- old date 1.5.1965).	10.00	45.00	150.00
	b. Ovpt. on #12b. (- old date 1.7.1966).	10.00	45.00	150.00

NOTE: Ovpt. on #17 has letters either 3.2 or 2.6mm high.

18	500 FRANCS	VG	VF	UNC
	ND (1966 - old dates 5.12.1964; 1.8.1966). Ovpt. on #13.	85.00	250.00	—

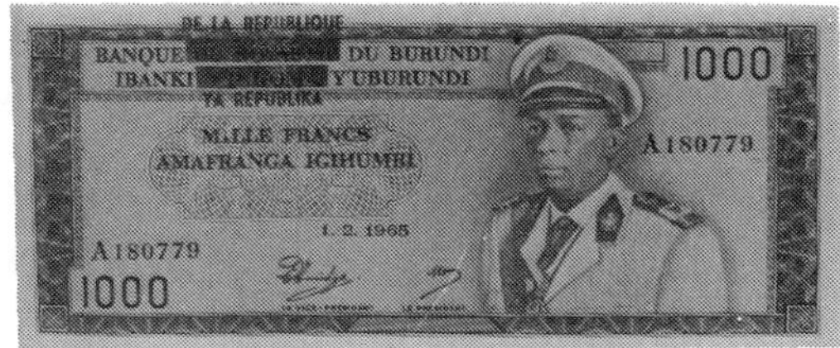

19	1000 FRANCS	VG	VF	UNC
	ND (1966 - old date 1.2.1965). Ovpt. on #14.	200.00	650.00	—

1968-75 ISSUES

Sign. varieties.

20	10 FRANCS	VG	VF	UNC
	1968; 1970. Red on green and blue unpt. "Place De La Revolution" monument at r. Sign. titles: *L'ADMINISTRATEUR* and *LE PRESIDENT*.			
	a. 1.11.1968.	1.25	3.00	10.00
	b. 1.4.1970.	.75	1.25	4.00

21	20 FRANCS	VG	VF	UNC
	1968-73. Blue on green and violet unpt. Dancer at ctr. Text on back.			
	a. Sign. titles: *LE PRESIDENT* and *LE VICE-PRESIDENT*. 1.11.1968.	3.00	8.00	35.00
	b. Sign. titles: *LE PRESIDENT* and *L'ADMINISTRATEUR*. 1.4.1970; 1.11.1971; 1.7.1973.	3.00	7.00	30.00
22	**50 FRANCS**			
	1968-73. Pale red on m/c unpt. Drummer at l. ctr.			
	a. Sign. titles: *L'ADMINISTRATEUR* and *LE PRESIDENT*. 15.5.1968; 1.10.1968.	3.50	15.00	65.00
	b. Sign. titles: *ADMINISTRATEUR* and *PRESIDENT*. 1.2.1970; 1.8.1971; 1.7.1973.	2.50	10.00	35.00

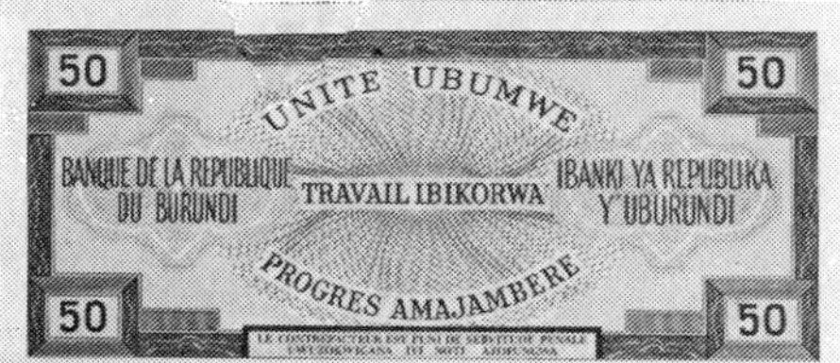

22A	50 FRANCS	VG	VF	UNC
	1.6.1975. Brown. Like #22b.	5.00	20.00	70.00

23	100 FRANCS	VG	VF	UNC
	1968-75. Brown on pale orange, lilac and blue unpt. Prince Rwagasore at r.			
	a. Sign. titles: *LE VICE-PRESIDENT* and *LE PRESIDENT*. 15.5.1968; 1.10.1968.	5.00	20.00	75.00
	b. Sign. titles: *ADMINISTRATEUR* and *LE PRESIDENT*. 1.2.1970; 1.8.1971; 1.7.1973; 1.6. 1975.	4.00	15.00	60.00

24	500 FRANCS	VG	VF	UNC
	1968-75. Brown. Bank bldg. at r.			
	a. Sign. titles: *LE PRESIDENT* and *LE VICE-PRESIDENT*.1.8.1968.	50.00	135.00	400.00
	b. Sign. titles: *LE PRESIDENT* and *L'ADMINISTRATEUR*. 1.4.1970; 1.8.1971.	50.00	135.00	400.00
	c. Sign. titles: *LE PRESIDENT* and *LE VICE-PRESIDENT*. 1.7.1973; 1.6.1975.	50.00	135.00	400.00

25	1000 FRANCS	VG	VF	UNC
	1968-75. Blue and m/c. Bird and flowers. Back blue and lt. brown; cattle at ctr.			
	a. Sign. titles: *L'ADMINISTRATEUR* and *LE PRESIDENT*. 1.4.1968; 1.5.1971; 1.2.1973.	45.00	150.00	425.00
	b. Sign. title: *LE VICE-PRESIDENT* 1.6.1975; 1.9.1976.	35.00	120.00	325.00

26	5000 FRANCS	VG	VF	UNC
	1968; 1971; 1973. Blue. Pres. Micombero in military uniform at r. Loading at dockside on back.			
	a. Sign. titles: *LE VICE-PRESIDENT* and *LE PRESIDENT*. 1.4.1968; 1.7.1973.	200.00	500.00	1000.
	b. Sign. title: *L'ADMINISTRATEUR*. 1.5.1971.	200.00	500.00	1000.

1975-78 ISSUE

#27-31 face like #20-26. Arms at ctr. on back.

27	20 FRANCS	VG	VF	UNC
	1977-95. Red on m/c unpt. Face design like #21. Sign. titles: *LE GOUVERNEUR* and *L'ADMINISTRATEUR*.			
	a. 1.7.1977; 1.6.1979; 1.12.1981.	FV	.50	2.00
	b. 1.12.1983; 1.12.1986; 1.5.1988; 1.10.1989.	FV	.40	1.25
	c. 1.10.1991; 25.5.1995.	FV	FV	.75
	d. 5.2.1997.	FV	FV	.75

28	50 FRANCS	VG	VF	UNC
	1977-93. Brown on m/c unpt. Face like #22.			
	a. 1.7.1977; 1.5.1979.	.15	.75	3.00
	b. 1.12.1981; 1.12.1983.	FV	.50	2.00
	c. 1.5.1988; 1.10.1989; 1.10.1991; 1.5.1993.	FV	FV	1.25

29	100 FRANCS	VG	VF	UNC
	1977-93. Purple. Face design like #23. Sign. titles: *L'ADMINISTRATEUR* and *LE GOUVERNEUR*.			
	a. 1.7.1977; 1.5.1979.	FV	1.00	3.50
	b. 1.1.1981; 1.7.1982; 1.11.1984; 1.11.1986.	FV	.85	3.00
	c. 1.5.1988; 1.7.1990; 1.5.1993.	FV	FV	2.00

30	500 FRANCS	VG	VF	UNC
	1977-88. Dk. blue on m/c unpt. Face design like #24. Numeral and date style varieties. Sign. titles: *LE GOUVERNEUR* and *LE VICE-GOUVERNEUR*.			
	a. 1.7.1977; 1.9.1981.	FV	6.00	22.50
	b. 1.7.1985; 1.9.1986; 1.5.1988.	FV	5.00	12.50

31	1000 FRANCS	VG	VF	UNC
	1977-91. Dk. green on m/c unpt. Like #25.			
	a. Sign. titles: *LE VICE-GOUVERNEUR* and *LE GOUVERNEUR*. 1.7.1977; 1.1.1978; 1.5.1979; 1.1.1980.	FV	12.50	35.00
	b. 1.1.1981; 1.5.1982; 1.1.1984; 1.12.1986.	FV	10.00	30.00
	c. Sign. titles: *L'ADMINISTRATEUR* and *LE VICE-GOUVERNEUR*. 1.6.1987.	FV	15.00	50.00
	d. Sign. titles: *LE VICE-GOUVERNEUR* and *LE GOUVERNEUR*. 1.5.1988; 1.10.1989; 1.10.1991.	FV	7.50	11.50

32	5000 FRANCS	VG	VF	UNC
	1978-95. Dk. brown and grayish purple on m/c unpt. Arms at upper ctr.; bldg. at lower r. Ship dockside on back.			
	a. 1.7.1978; 1.10.1981.	30.00	60.00	175.00
	b. 1.1.1984; 1.9.1986.	FV	28.00	85.00
	c. 1.10.1989; 1.10.1991.	FV	FV	70.00
	d. Sign titles: *LE 1ER VICE-GOUVERNEUR* and *LE GOUVERNEUR*. 10.5.1994; 25.5.1995.	FV	FV	62.50

1979-81 ISSUES

#33 and 34 replacement notes: Serial # prefix *Z*.

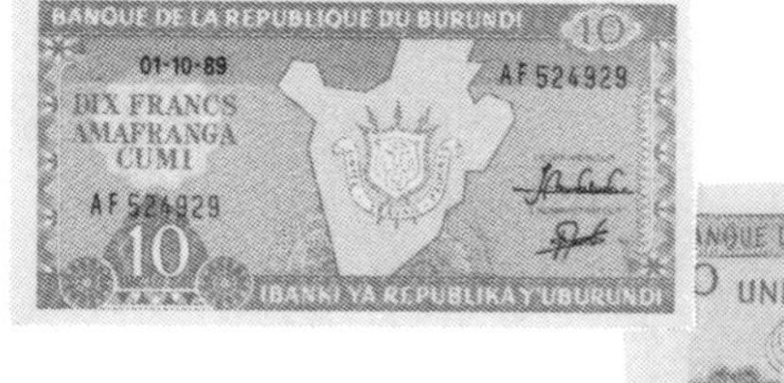

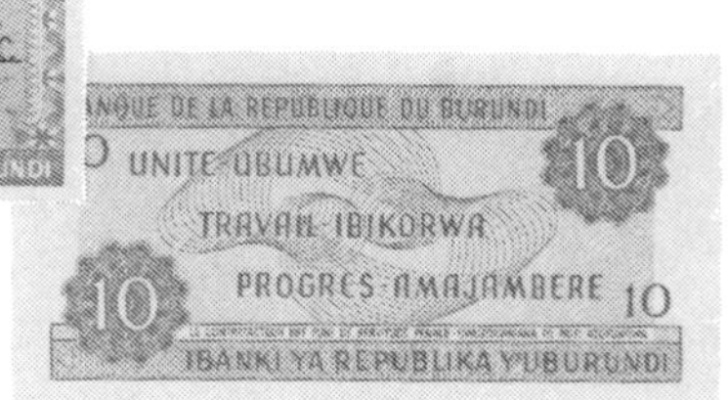

33	10 FRANCS	VG	VF	UNC
	1981-95. Blue-green on tan unpt. Map of Burundi w/arms superimposed at ctr. Text on back.			
	a. Sign. titles: *LE GOUVERNEUR* and *ADMINISTRATEUR*. 1.6.1981; 1.12.1983.	FV	FV	1.00
	b. 1.12.1986; 1.5.1988; 1.10.1989; 1.10.1991.	FV	FV	.75
	c. 25.5.1995.	FV	FV	.50
	d. Sign. titles: *LE GOUVERNEUR* and *LE 2E GOUVERNEUR*. 5.2.1997.	FV	FV	.50

		VG	VF	UNC
34	**500 FRANCS** 1.6.1979; 1.1.1980. Tan, blue-black, purple and green on m/c unpt. Back purple on m/c unpt. Similar to #30. Sign. titles: *LE GOUVERNEUR* and *LE VICE-GOUVERNEUR*.	5.00	12.50	50.00

1993-97 ISSUE

		VG	VF	UNC
35	**20 FRANCS** 1995. M/c.	FV	FV	1.00

		VG	VF	UNC
36	**50 FRANCS** 19.5.1994. Dull brown-violet on m/c unpt. Man in canoe at l., arms at lower ctr. Natives w/boat at ctr., hippopotamus at lower r.	FV	FV	1.85

		VG	VF	UNC
37 (35)	**100 FRANCS** 1.10.1993; 1.12.1997. Dull purple on m/c unpt. Similar to #29. Arms at lower l., brick home construction at ctr. on back. Sign. titles: *LE 1ER VICE-GOUVERNEUR* and *LE GOUVERNEUR*.	FV	FV	3.00

		VG	VF	UNC
38	**500 FRANCS** 1.5.1997. Gray and violet on m/c unpt. Native painting at l. Back blue on m/c unpt.; bank bldg. at ctr., arms at r. Wmk: Ox.	FV	FV	7.50

		VG	VF	UNC
39 (36)	**1000 FRANCS** 19.5.1994. Greenish black and brown-violet on m/c unpt. Steers at l., arms at lower ctr. Monument at ctr. on back. Sign. titles: *LE GOUVERNEUR* and *LE 1ER VICE-GOUVERNEUR*. Wmk: Pres. Micombero.	FV	FV	17.50

		VG	VF	UNC
40	**5000 FRANCS** 5.2.1997. Olive-green and dk. green on m/c unpt. Like #32 but w/date moved to l. and segmented foil over security thread.	FV	FV	55.00

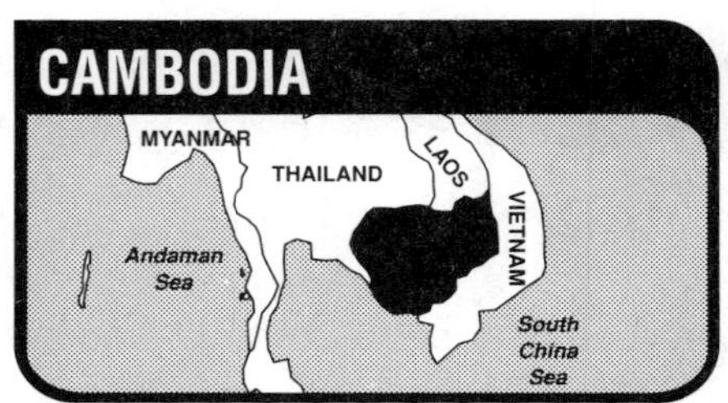

Cambodia, formerly known as Democratic Kampuchea and the Khmer Republic, a land of paddy fields and forest-clad hills located on the Indo-Chinese peninsula fronting on the Gulf of Thailand, has an area of 69,898 sq. mi. (181,035 sq. km.) and a population of 9.86 million. Capital: Phnom Penh. Agriculture is the basis of the economy, with rice the chief crop. Native industries include cattle breeding, weaving and rice milling. Rubber, cattle, corn, and timber are exported.

The region was the nucleus of the Khmer empire which flourished from the 5th to the 12th century and attained an excellence in art and architecture still evident in the magnificent ruins at Angkor. The Khmer empire once ruled over much of Southeast Asia, but began to decline in the 13th century as the Thai and Vietnamese invaded the region and attached its territories. At the request of the Cambodian king, a French protectorate attached to Cochin-China was established over the country in 1863, saving it from dissolution, and in 1885, Cambodia was included in the French Union of Indo-China. France established a constitutional monarchy for Cambodia within the French Union in 1949. The 1954 Geneva Convention resulted in full independence for the Kingdom of Cambodia. King Sihanouk abdicated to his father and won the office of Prime Minister.

Prince Sihanouk was toppled by a bloodless coup led by Lon Nol in March of 1970. Sihanouk moved to Peking to head a government-in-exile. On Oct. 9, 1970, Cambodia became the Khmer Republic, and Lon Nol its President. The government of Lon Nol was in turn toppled, April 17, 1975, by the Khmer Rouge insurgents who took control of the government and renamed the country Democratic Kampuchea.

The Khmer Rouge completely eliminated the economy and created a state without money, exchange or barter. Everyone worked for the state and was taken care of by the state. The Vietnamese supported People's Republic of Kampuchea was installed in accordance with the constitution of January 5, 1976. The name of the country was changed from Democratic Cambodia to Democratic Kampuchea, afterwards reverting to Cambodia.

In the early 1990's the UN supervised a ceasefire and in 1992 Norodom Sihanouk returned as Chief of State.

RULERS:

Norodom Sihanouk, (as Chief of State), 1960-1970
Lon Nol, 1970-1975
Pol Pot, 1975-1979, 1985
Heng Samrin, 1979-1985
Hun Sen, 1985-1991
Norodom Sihanouk (Chairman, Supreme National Council), 1991-1993
Norodom Sihanouk (as King), 1993-

MONETARY SYSTEM:

1 Riel = 100 Sen

Signature Chart:

	Governor [illegible]	chief inspector [អគ្គាធិការ]	Advisor [ទីប្រឹក្សាមួយនាក់]	DATE
1				28.10.1955
2				1956
3				1956
4				Late 1961
5				Mid 1962
6				1963
7				1965
8				1968
9				1968
10				1969
11				1970
12				1972
13				1972
14				1974
15				march, 1975 (printed1974)
16	Le Gouverneur Thor Peng Leath (08-07-93 / 23-03-98)		Le Caissier General Tieng Seng, 1995-	
17	Le Gouverneur Chea Chanto 23-03-98-		Le Caissier General Tieng Seng, 1995-	

CAMBODIA - KINGDOM

BANQUE NATIONALE DU CAMBODGE

1956 ND FIRST ISSUE

#6 Deleted. See #3a in Volume II, General Issues.

		VG	VF	UNC
4	**1 RIEL** ND (1956-75). Grayish green on m/c unpt. Boats dockside in port of Phnom-Penh. Royal palace throne room on back. Printer: BW (w/o imprint).			
	a. Sign. 1; 2.	1.00	3.00	15.00
	b. Sign. 6; 7; 8; 10; 11.	.15	.25	1.25
	c. Sign. 12.	.10	.15	.25
5	**20 RIELS** ND (1956-75). Brown. Combine harvester at r. Phnom Penh pagoda on back. Wmk: Buddha. Printer: BWC (w/o imprint).			
	a. Sign. 3.	.25	1.00	5.00
	b. Sign. 6; 7; 8; 10.	.20	.50	2.00
	c. Sign. 12.	.10	.25	.65

#6 not assigned.

7 **50 RIELS**
ND (1956-75). Blue and orange. Fishermen fishing from boats w/lg. nets in Lake Tonle Sap at l. and r. Back blue and brown; Angkor Wat. Wmk: Buddha. Printer: TDLR (w/o imprint).

	VG	VF	UNC
a. Western numeral in plate block designator. Sign. 3.	1.00	3.00	20.00
b. Cambodian numeral in plate block designator. 5-digit serial #. Sign. 7; 10.	.50	1.00	3.00
c. As b. Sign. 12.	.25	.50	1.00
d. Cambodian serial # 6-digits. Sign. 12.	.10	.20	.35

8 **100 RIELS**
ND (1957-75). Brown and green on m/c unpt. Statue of Lokecvara at l. Long boat on back. Wmk: Buddha.

	VG	VF	UNC
a. Imprint: *Giesecke & Devrient Munchen, AG MUNCHEN.* Sign. 3; 7; 8; 11.	1.00	3.00	20.00
b. As a. Sign. 7; 8; 11.	.50	1.00	3.00
c. Imprint: *Giesecke & Devrient Munchen.* Sign. 12; 13.	.50	1.00	3.00

9 **500 RIELS**
ND (1958-70). Green and brown on m/c unpt. Sculpture of 2 royal women dancers "Devatas" at l. 2 royal dancers in ceremonial costumes on back. Wmk: Buddha. Printer: G&D.

	VG	VF	UNC
a. Sign. 3.	3.00	20.00	75.00
b. Sign. 6; 9.	1.00	3.00	10.00

1956; 1958 ND SECOND ISSUE

10 **5 RIELS**
(12)
ND (1962-75). Red on m/c unpt. Bayon stone 4 faces of Avalokitesvara at l. Royal Palace Entrance - Chanchhaya on back. Wmk: Buddha. Printer: BWC (w/o imprint).

	VG	VF	UNC
a. Sign. 4; 6.	1.00	3.00	20.00
b. Sign. 7; 8; 11.	.20	.50	2.00
c. Sign. 12.	.10	.25	.65

11 **10 RIELS**
(13)
ND (1962-75). Brown on m/c unpt. Temple of Banteay Srei. Central Market bldg. at Phnom-Penh at l. on back. Wmk: Buddha. Printer: TDLR (w/o imprint).

	VG	VF	UNC
a. Sign. 5; 6.	1.00	3.00	20.00
b. Sign. 7; 8; 11.	.20	.50	2.00
c. Sign. 12. 5 digit serial #.	.10	.25	.65
d. As c. 6 digit serial #.	.20	.50	2.00

12 **100 RIELS**
(14)
ND (1963-72). Blue-black, dk. green and dk. brown on m/c unpt. Sun rising behind Temple of Preah Vihear at l. Back blue, green and brown; aerial view of the Temple of Preah Vihear. Wmk: Buddha. Printer: G&D.

	VG	VF	UNC
a. Sign. 6.	1.00	3.00	20.00
b. Sign. 13. (Not issued).	.10	.20	.60

KHMER REPUBLIC

BANQUE NATIONALE DU CAMBODGE

1970 ND ISSUE

13 **100 RIELS**
ND (1970). Blue on m/c unpt. 2 oxen at r. 3 ceremonial women on back.

	VG	VF	UNC
a. Printer: ABNC w/ imprint on lower margins, face and back. Sign. 3.	3.00	20.00	75.00
b. W/o imprint on either side. Sign. 12.	.10	.25	1.00

14 **500 RIELS**
ND (1970). M/c. Farmer plowing w/2 water buffalo. Pagoda at r., doorway of Preah Vihear at l. on back. Wmk: Buddha. Printer: BdF (w/o imprint).

	VG	VF	UNC
a. Sign. 3.	.50	3.00	20.00
b. Sign. 5; 7.	.50	2.00	8.00
c. Sign. 9.	.50	1.50	6.00
d. Sign. 12.	.15	.50	1.00
x. Lithograph counterfeit; wmk. barely visible. Sign. 3; 5.	20.00	65.00	110.00
y. As x. Sign 7; 9.	15.00	55.00	90.00

1973 ND Issue

#15 and 16 replacement notes: Series #90.

		VG	VF	UNC
15	**100 Riels** ND. Purple on m/c unpt. Carpet weaving. Angkor Wat on back. Wmk: Man's head. Printer: TDLR (w/o imprint). (Not issued).			
	a. Sign. 13.	.10	.20	.75
	b. Sign. 14.	1.00	2.00	10.00

		VG	VF	UNC
16	**500 Riels** ND(1973-75). Green on m/c unpt. Girl w/vessel on head at l. Rice paddy scene on back. Wmk: Man's head. Printer: TDLR (w/o imprint).			
	a. Sign. 13; 14.	.15	.25	3.00
	b. Sign. 15.	.10	.20	.75

		VG	VF	UNC
17	**1000 Riels** ND. Green on m/c unpt. School children. Head of Lokecvara at Ta Som on back. Wmk: School girl. Sign. 13. Printer: BWC. (Not issued).	.10	.20	.75

NOTICE

Readers with unlisted dates, signature varieties, etc. are invited to submit photocopies of their notes to: Standard Catalog of World Paper Money, 700 East State St. Iola, WI 54990-0001, fax: 1-715-445-4087, or E-Mail: thernr@krause.com.

Kampuchea

Bank of Kampuchea

1975 Issue

#18-24 prepared by the Khmer Rouge but not issued. New regime under Pol Pot instituted an "agrarian moneyless society." All notes dated 1975.

#20-24 wmk: Angkor Wat.

		VG	VF	UNC
18	**0.1 Riel (1 Kak)** 1975. Purple, green, and orange on m/c unpt. Mortar crew l. Threshing rice on back.	.20	.50	3.00

		VG	VF	UNC
19	**0.5 Riel (5 Kak)** 1975. Red on lt. green and m/c unpt. Troops marching at l. ctr. Bayon sculpture at l., machine and worker at r. on back.	.20	.50	3.00

		VG	VF	UNC
20	**1 Riel** 1975. Red-violet and red on m/c unpt. Farm workers. at l. ctr. Woman operating machine on back.	.20	.50	3.00

		VG	VF	UNC
21	**5 Riels** 1975. Deep green on m/c unpt. Ancient temples of Angkor Wat at ctr. r. Landscaping crew on back.	.20	.40	2.50

		VG	VF	UNC
22	**10 Riels** 1975. Brown and red on m/c unpt. Machine gun crew at ctr. r. Harvesting rice on back.	.20	.50	3.00

		VG	VF	UNC
23	**50 RIELS** 1975. Purple on m/c unpt. Planting rice at l., Bayon sculpture at r. Woman's militia at ctr. r. on back.	.50	2.00	15.00

		VG	VF	UNC
24	**100 RIELS** 1975. Deep green on m/c unpt. Factory workers at l. ctr. Back black; harvesting rice.	.50	2.25	15.00

STATE BANK OF DEMOCRATIC KAMPUCHEA

1979 ISSUE

#25-32 issued 20.3.1980 by the Vietnamese-backed regime of Heng Samrin which overthrew Pol Pot in 1979.

		VG	VF	UNC
25	**0.1 RIEL (1 KAK)** 1979. Olive-green on lt. blue unpt. Arms at ctr. Water buffalos on back.			
	a. Issued note.	.05	.15	.25
	s. Specimen.	—	—	50.00

		VG	VF	UNC
26	**0.2 RIEL (2 KAK)** 1979. Grayish green on tan unpt. Arms at ctr. Rice workers on back.			
	a. Issued note.	.10	.20	.50
	s. Specimen.	—	—	50.00

		VG	VF	UNC
27	**0.5 RIEL (5 KAK)** 1979. Red-orange on tan and gray unpt. Arms at l., modern passenger train at r. Men fishing from boats w/nets on back.			
	a. Issued note.	.10	.20	.50
	s. Specimen.	—	—	50.00

		VG	VF	UNC
28	**1 RIEL** 1979. Brown on yellow and m/c unpt. Arms at ctr. Women harvesting rice on back.			
	a. Issued note.	.10	.20	.50
	s. Specimen.	—	—	50.00

		VG	VF	UNC
29	**5 RIELS** 1979. Dk. brown on lt. green and m/c unpt. 4 people at l., arms at r. Independence from France (now Victory) monument on back.			
	a. Issued note.	.10	.30	1.00
	s. Specimen.	—	—	50.00

		VG	VF	UNC
30	**10 RIELS** 1979. Dk. gray on lilac and m/c unpt. Arms at l., harvesting fruit trees at r. School on back.			
	a. Issued note.	.20	.50	2.00
	s. Specimen.	—	—	50.00

#31 and 32 wmk: Arms.

		VG	VF	UNC
31	**20 RIELS** 1979. Purple on pink and m/c unpt. Arms at l. Water buffalos hauling logs on back. Wmk: Arms.			
	a. Issued note.	.10	.35	1.50
	s. Specimen.	—	—	50.00

		VG	VF	UNC
32	**50 RIELS** 1979. Deep red and red, yellow-green and m/c unpt. Arms at l., Bayon stone head at ctr. Angkor Wat on back. Wmk: Arms.			
	a. Issued note.	.10	.35	3.00
	s. Specimen.	—	—	50.00

1987 ISSUE

		VG	VF	UNC
33	**5 RIELS** 1987. Like #29 but red and brown on lt. yellow and lt. green unpt. Back red on pale yellow unpt.	.10	.35	1.25

		VG	VF	UNC
34	**10 RIELS** 1987. Like #30 but green on lt. blue and m/c unpt. Back deep green and lilac on lt. blue unpt.	.10	.35	1.50

CAMBODIA

PEOPLES NATIONAL BANK OF CAMBODIA

1990-92 ISSUE

#35-37 wmk: Stylized lotus flowers.

		VG	VF	UNC
35	**50 RIELS** 1992. Dull brown on m/c. Arms at ctr., male portrait at r. Ships dockside on back. Wmk: Lotus flowers. Printer: NBC.			
	a. Issued note.	FV	FV	.50
	s. Specimen.	—	—	75.00
36	**100 RIELS** 1990. Dk. green and brown on lt. blue and lilac unpt. Independence from France (Now Victory) monument at l. ctr., Achar Mean at r. Rubber trees on back. Wmk: Crowned monogram C-C. Issuer: State Bank.	FV	FV	2.50

		VG	VF	UNC
37	**200 RIELS** 1992. Dull olive-green and tan on m/c unpt. Floodgates at r. Bayon sculpture in Angkor Wat ctr. on back. Printer: NBC.			
	a. Issued note.	FV	FV	1.50
	s. Specimen. 1993.	—	—	75.00

		VG	VF	UNC
38	**500 RIELS** 1991. Red, purple and brown-violet on m/c unpt. Arms above Angkor Wat at ctr. Animal statue at l., cultivating with tractors at ctr. on back. Wmk: Sculptured heads.			
	a. Issued note.	FV	FV	3.00
	s. Specimen.	—	—	75.00

		VG	VF	UNC
39	**1000 RIELS** 1992. Dk. green, brown and black on m/c unpt. Bayon Temple ruins in Angkor Wat. Fishermen fishing in boats w/lg. nets in Lake Tonle Sap on back. Wmk: Chinze. (Not released).	—	—	2.00

		VG	VF	UNC
40	**2000 RIELS** 1992. Black on dp. blue and violet-brown and m/c unpt. Prince N. Sihanouk at l. and as wmk., Temple portal at Preah Vihear at r. (Not released).	—	—	2.50

NATIONAL BANK OF CAMBODIA

1995 ISSUE

SIGNATURE VARIETIES		
	Le Gouverneur	Le Caissier Général
16	Thor Peng Leath 1995-98	Tieng Seng, 1995-
17	Chea Chanto, 1999-	

#41-43 arms at upper l. Wmk: Stylized lotus flowers. Printer: NBC. Sign. 16.

		VG	VF	UNC
41	**100 RIELS** 1995; 1998. Grayish green and brown on m/c unpt. Chinze, Independence from France (Now Victory) monument at r. Tapping rubber trees on back.			
	a. 1995.	FV	FV	1.00
	b. 1998.	FV	FV	.50
	s. Specimen.	—	—	50.00

		VG	VF	UNC
42	**200 RIELS** 1995; 1998. Dk. olive-green and brown on m/c unpt. Similar to #37.			
	a. 1995.	FV	FV	.50
	b. 1998.	FV	FV	.35
	s. Specimen. 1995.	—	—	50.00

		VG	VF	UNC
43	**500 RIELS** 1996. Red-violet and purple on m/c unpt. Angkor Wot at r. Mythical animal at l., rice fields at ctr. on back.			
	a. Issued note.	FV	FV	1.10
	s. Specimen.	—	—	50.00

#44-50 printer: F-CO.

#44 and 45 wmk: Cube design.

		VG	VF	UNC
44	**1000 RIELS** ND. (1995). Blue-green on m/c unpt. Bayon stone 4 faces of Avalokitesvara at l. Back green on m/c unpt.; Prasat Chan Chaya at r.			
	a. Issued note.	FV	FV	2.00
	s. Specimen.	—	—	50.00

		VG	VF	UNC
45	**2000 RIELS** ND (1995). Reddish brown on m/c unpt. Fishermen fishing from boats w/nets in Lake Tonie Sap at l. and r. Temple ruins at Angkor Wat on back.			
	a. Issued note.	FV	FV	3.50
	s. Specimen.	—	—	50.00

#46-49 N. Sihanouk at r. and as wmk.

		VG	VF	UNC
46	**5000 RIELS** ND (1995); 1998. Deep purple and blue-black w/black text on m/c unpt. Temple of Banteai Srei at lower l. ctr. Central market in Phnom-Penh on back.			
	a. ND (1995).	FV	FV	7.00
	b. 1998.	FV	FV	6.50
	s. Specimen. ND (1995); 1998.	—	—	50.00

		VG	VF	UNC
47	**10,000 RIELS** ND (1995); 1998. Blue-black, black and dk. green on m/c unpt. Statue of Lokecvara at lower l. ctr. People rowing long boat during the water festival at lower ctr. on back.			
	a. ND (1995).	FV	FV	13.00
	b. 1998.	FV	FV	12.00
	s. Specimen. ND(1995); 1998.	—	—	50.00

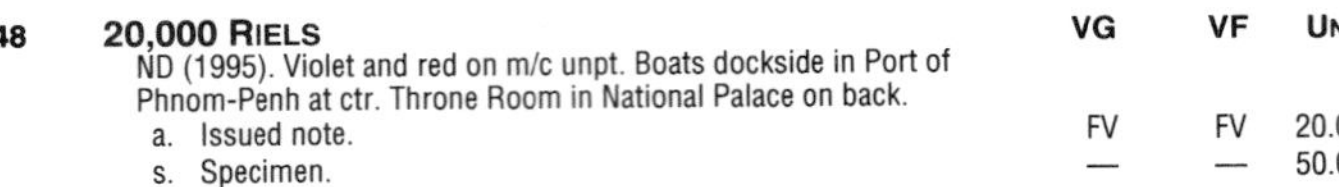

		VG	VF	UNC
48	**20,000 RIELS** ND (1995). Violet and red on m/c unpt. Boats dockside in Port of Phnom-Penh at ctr. Throne Room in National Palace on back.			
	a. Issued note.	FV	FV	20.00
	s. Specimen.	—	—	50.00

		VG	VF	UNC
49	**50,000 RIELS** ND (1995); 1998. Dk. brown, brown and deep olive-green on m/c unpt. Preah Vihear Temple at ctr. Road to Preah Vihear Temple on back.			
	a. ND (1995).	FV	FV	52.50
	b. 1998.	FV	FV	50.00
	s. Specimen. ND(1995); 1998.	—	—	50.00

		VG	VF	UNC
50	**100,000 RIELS** ND (1995). Green, blue-green and black on m/c unpt. Chief and First Lady at r. and as wmk. Chief and First Lady receiving homage of people at ctr. r. on back.			
	a. Issued note.	FV	FV	95.00
	s. Specimen. Perforated *SPECIMEN.*	—	—	50.00

REGIONAL

KHMER ROUGE INFLUENCE

Issued for circulation in Khmer Rouge occupied areas in exchange for Thailand Bahts. Printed in Thailand. Issue was ordered destroyed.

1993-94 ND ISSUE

#R1-R5 w/sign. of Pres. Khieu Samphan.

		GOOD	FINE	XF
R1	**5 RIELS** ND (1993-94). M/c. Children harvesting vegetables at ctr., temple carvings at l. and r. Caravan of ox carts at ctr., temple carvings at l. on back.	50.00	100.00	250.00

		GOOD	FINE	XF
R2	**10 RIELS** ND (1993-94). M/c. Village at ctr. r., temple carvings at l. and r. Fishing village, boats at ctr., temple carvings at l. and r. on back.	50.00	100.00	250.00

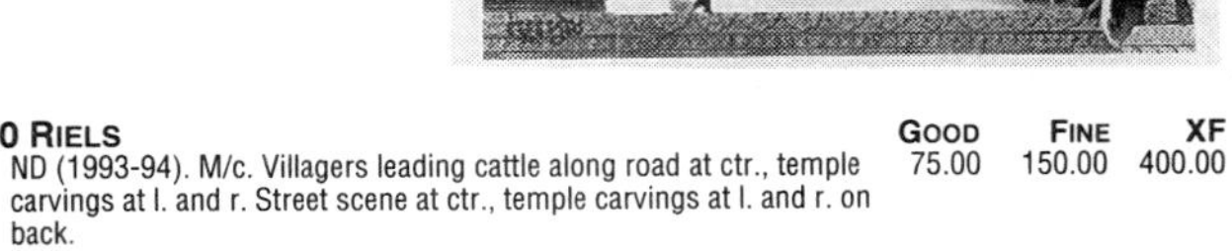

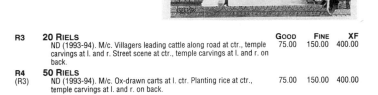

		GOOD	FINE	XF
R3	**20 RIELS** ND (1993-94). M/c. Villagers leading cattle along road at ctr., temple carvings at l. and r. Street scene at ctr., temple carvings at l. and r. on back.	75.00	150.00	400.00
R4 (R3)	**50 RIELS** ND (1993-94). M/c. Ox-drawn carts at l. ctr. Planting rice at ctr., temple carvings at l. and r. on back.	75.00	150.00	400.00

		GOOD	FINE	XF
R5 (R4)	**100 RIELS** ND (1993-94). M/c. Field workers at ctr., temple carvings at l. Temples of Angkor Wat at ctr., temple carvings at l. and r. on back.	100.00	300.00	600.00

FOREIGN EXCHANGE CERTIFICATES

MINISTERE DU TOURISME DU CAMBODGE

1960'S BON TOURISTIQUE ISSUE

#FX1-FX5 black text. Shoreline at l. ctr., royal dancer at r. Black text on back. Perforated along l. edge.

		VG	VF	UNC
FX1	**1 RIEL** ca. 1960's. Pink and tan.	7.00	30.00	75.00

		VG	VF	UNC
FX2	**2 RIELS** 1961. Lt. green and violet.	7.00	30.00	75.00

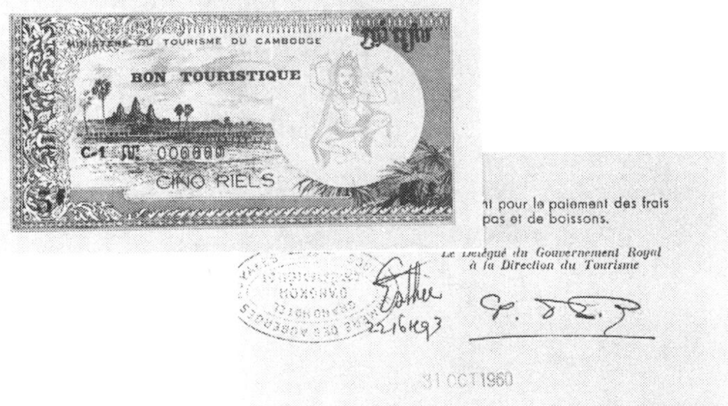

		VG	VF	UNC
FX3 (FX2)	**5 RIELS** ca. 1960's. Blue-violet and orange.	7.00	30.00	75.00
FX4 (FX3)	**10 RIELS** ca. 1960's.	7.00	30.00	75.00
FX5	**20 RIELS** ca. 1960's. Brown.	7.00	30.00	75.00

COLLECTOR SERIES

NATIONAL BANK OF CAMBODIA

1995 ND ISSUE

		ISSUE PRICE	MKT. VALUE
CS1	**1000 - 100,000 RIELS** ND (1995). #44-50. Specimen.	—	400.00

NOTE: Issued in a special folder w/notes laminated in plastic including 50, 100, 200 and 500 Riels coins dated BE2538 (1994).

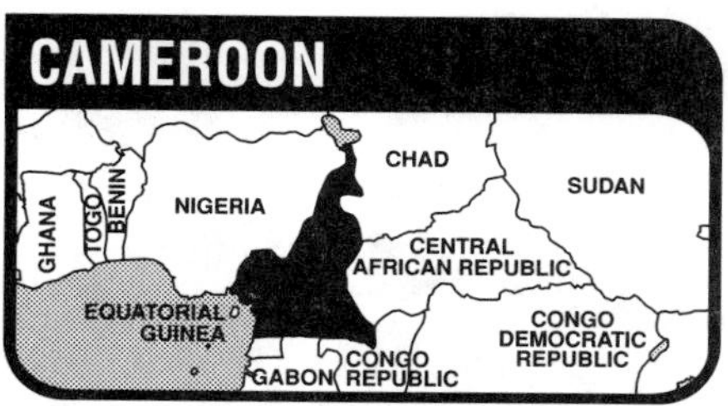

The United Republic of Cameroon, located in west-central Africa on the Gulf of Guinea, has an area of 185,568 sq. mi. (475,442 sq. km.) and a population of 14.3 million. Capital: Yaounde. About 90 percent of the labor force is employed on the land; cash crops account for 80 percent of the country's export revenue. Cocoa, coffee, aluminum, cotton, rubber and timber are exported.

European contact with what is now the United Republic of Cameroon began in the 16th century with the voyage of Portuguese navigator Fernando Po. The following three centuries saw continuous activity by Spanish, Dutch and British traders and missionaries. The land was spared colonial rule until 1884, when treaties with tribal chiefs brought German domination. After Germany's defeat in WWI, the League of Nations in 1919, divided the Cameroons between Great Britain and France, with larger eastern area going to France. The French and British mandates were converted into United Nations trusteeships in 1946. French Cameroon became the independent Cameroon Republic on Jan. 1, 1960. The federation of East (French) and West (British) Cameroon was established in 1961 when the southern part of British Cameroon voted for reunification with the Cameroon Republic, and the northern part for union with Nigeria. On Nov. 1, 1995 the Republic of Cameroon joined the Commonwealth. Issues continue under Central African States.

MONETARY SYSTEM:

1 Franc = 100 Centimes

SIGNATURE VARIETIES:

Refer to introduction to Central African States.

RÉPUBLIQUE DU CAMEROUN

BANQUE CENTRALE

1961 ND ISSUE

#7-9 denominations in French only, or French and English.

		GOOD	FINE	XF
7	**1000 FRANCS** ND (1961). M/c. Man w/basket harvesting cocoa. Sign. 1A.	150.00	500.00	1200.
8	**5000 FRANCS** ND (1961). M/c. Pres. A. Ahidjo at r. Sign. 1A.	75.00	250.00	900.00

		GOOD	FINE	XF
9	**5000 FRANCS** ND. Like #8 but denomination also in English words at lower l. ctr. Sign. 1A.	150.00	500.00	1200.

RÉPUBLIQUE FÉDÉRALE DU CAMEROUN

BANQUE CENTRALE

1962 ND ISSUE

#10-13 denominations in French and English.

		VG	VF	UNC
10	**100 FRANCS** ND (1962). M/c. Pres. of the Republic at l. Ships on back. Sign. 1A.	5.00	25.00	85.00

		VG	VF	UNC
11	**500 FRANCS** ND (1962). M/c. Man w/2 oxen. Man w/bananas at l., truck on road at ctr. r., 2 ships in background at upper r. on back. Sign. 1A.	12.00	40.00	225.00

NOTE: Engraved (intaglio) and lithographic varieties

		VG	VF	UNC
12	**1000 FRANCS** ND (1962). M/c. Like #7 but w/title: *RÉPUBLIQUE FÉDÉRALE . . .* on back. Sign. 1A.	15.00	60.00	285.00

NOTE: Engraved (intaglio) and lithographic varieties.

		VG	VF	UNC
13	**5000 FRANCS** ND (1962). M/c. Like #9 but w/title: *RÉPUBLIQUE FÉDÉRALE . . .* on back. Sign. 1A.	50.00	200.00	600.00

1972 ND ISSUE

		VG	VF	UNC
14	**10,000 FRANCS** ND (1972). M/c. Pres. A. Ahidjo at l., fruit at ctr., wood carving at r. Statue at l. and r., tractor plowing at ctr. on back. Sign. 2.	35.00	75.00	225.00

RÉPUBLIQUE UNIE DU CAMEROUN

BANQUE DES ÉTATS DEL'AFRIQUE CENTRALE

1974 ND ISSUE

		VG	VF	UNC
15	**500 FRANCS** ND (1974; 1984); 1978-83. Red-brown and m/c. Woman wearing hat at l., aerial view of modern bldgs. at ctr. Mask at l., students and chemical testing at ctr., statue at r. on back.			
	a. Sign. titles: *LE DIRECTEUR GÉNÉRAL* and *UN CENSEUR.* Engraved. Wmk: Antelope in half profile. Sign. 3. ND (1974).	15.00	60.00	150.00
	b. As a. Sign. 5.	FV	6.00	15.00
	c. Sign. titles: *LE GOUVERNEUR* and *UN CENSEUR.* Wmk: Antelope in profile. Sign. 10. 1.4.1978.	FV	4.00	10.00
	d. Sign. 12. 1.6.1981; 1.1.1983.	FV	3.00	8.50
	e. Sign. 12. 1.1.1982.	5.00	25.00	75.00
	f. Sign. 15.	FV	3.00	7.50

		VG	VF	UNC
16	**1000 FRANCS** ND (1974); 1978-82. Blue and m/c. Hut at ctr., girl w/plaits at r. Mask at l., trains, planes and bridge at ctr., statue at r. on back.			
	a. Sign. titles: *LE DIRECTEUR GÉNÉRAL* and *UN CENSEUR.* Engraved. Wmk: Antelope in half profile. Sign. 5. ND (1974).	FV	8.00	25.00
	b. Sign. titles like a. Lithographed. Wmk. like c. Sign. 8. ND (1978).	20.00	55.00	135.00
	c. Sign. titles: *LE GOUVERNEUR* and *UN CENSEUR.* Lithographed. Wmk: Antelope in profile. Sign. 10. 1.4.1978, 1.7.1980.	FV	5.00	18.00
	d. Sign. 12. 1.6.1981; 1.1.1982; 2; 1.1.1983.	FV	4.50	15.00

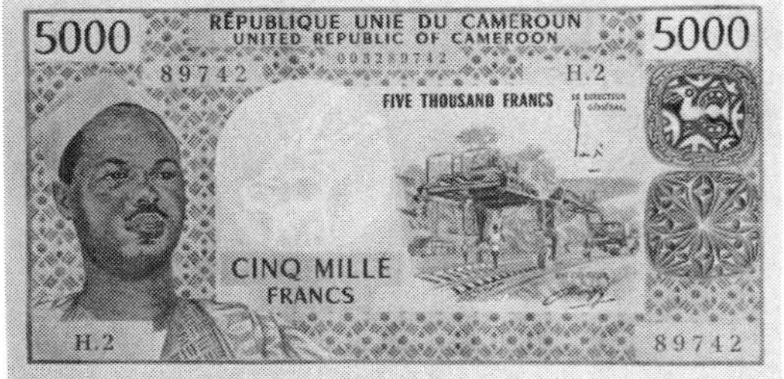

		VG	VF	UNC
17	**5000 FRANCS** ND (1974). Brown and m/c. Pres. A. Ahidjo at l., railway loading equipment at r. Mask at l., industrial college at ctr., statue at r. on back.			
	a. Sign. titles: *LE DIRECTEUR GÉNÉRAL* and *UN CENSEUR.* Engraved. Sign. 3. ND (1974).	50.00	175.00	375.00
	b. Like a. Sign. 5.	30.00	60.00	200.00
	c. Sign. titles: *LE GOUVERNEUR* and *UN CENSEUR.* Sign. 11; 12.	7.50	35.00	60.00
18	**10,000 FRANCS** ND (1974; 1978; 1981). M/c. Pres. A. Ahidjo at l. Similar to #14 except for new bank name on back.			
	a. Sign. titles: *LE DIRECTEUR GÉNÉRAL* and *UN CENSEUR.* Sign. 5. ND (1974).	15.00	50.00	130.00
	b. Sign. titles: *LE GOUVERNEUR* and *UN CENSEUR.* Sign. 11; 12. ND (1978; 1981).	10.00	45.00	100.00

1981 ND ISSUE

		VG	VF	UNC
19	**5000 FRANCS** ND (1981). Brown and m/c. Mask at l., woman carrying bundle of fronds at r. Plowing and mine ore conveyor on back. Sign. 12.	FV	15.00	50.00

		VG	VF	UNC
20	**10,000 FRANCS** ND (1981). Brown, green and m/c. Stylized antelope heads at l., woman at r. Loading of fruit onto truck at l. on back. Sign. 12.	FV	30.00	80.00

RÉPUBLIQUE DU CAMEROON

BANQUE DES ÉTATS DE L'AFRIQUE CENTRALE

1984 ND ISSUE

		VG	VF	UNC
21	**1000 FRANCS** 1.6.1984. Blue and m/c. Like #16 except for new country name. Sign. 12.	2.50	7.00	20.00
22	**5000 FRANCS** ND (1984; 1990; 1992). Brown and m/c. Like #19 except for new country name. Sign. 12; 13; 15.	Fv	12.50	35.00
23	**10,000 FRANCS** ND (1984; 1990). Brown, green and m/c. Like #20 except for new country name. Sign. 12; 13.	FV	25.00	60.00

1985-86 ISSUE

#24-26 wmk: Carving (as on notes).

		VG	VF	UNC
24	**500 FRANCS** 1985-90. Brown on m/c unpt. Carving and jug at ctr. Man carving mask at l. ctr. on back.			
	a. Sign. 12. 1.1.1985-1.1.1988.	FV	2.50	5.00
	b. Sign. 13. 1.1.1990.	FV	FV	4.00

		VG	VF	UNC
25	**1000 FRANCS** 1.1.1985. Dk. blue on m/c unpt. Carving at l., small figurines at ctr., man at r. Incomplete map of Chad at top. Elephant at l., carving at r. on back.	FV	5.00	18.50

		VG	VF	UNC
26	**1000 FRANCS** 1986-92. Like #25 but w/completed outline map of Chad at top ctr.			
	a. Sign. 12. 1.1.1986-1.1.1989.	FV	4.00	10.00
	b. Sign. 13. 1.1.1990.	FV	4.50	11.00
	c. Sign. 15.1.1.1992.	FV	3.75	8.00

CANADA

Canada is located to the north of the United States, and spans the full breadth of the northern portion of North America from Atlantic to Pacific oceans, except for the State of Alaska. It has a total area of 3,850,000 sq. mi. (9,971,550 sq. km.) and a population of 30.29 million. Capital: Ottawa.

Jacques Cartier, a French explorer, took possession of Canada for France in 1534, and for more than a century the history of Canada was that of a French colony. Samuel de Champlain helped to establish the first permanent colony in North America, in 1604 at Port Royal, Acadia - now Annapolis Royal, Nova Scotia. Four years later he founded the settlement in Quebec.

The British settled along the coast to the south while the French, motivated by a grand design, pushed into the interior. France's plan for a great American empire was to occupy the Mississippi heartland of the country, and from there to press in upon the narrow strip of English coastal settlements from the rear. Inevitably, armed conflict erupted between the French and the British; consequently, Britain acquired Hudson Bay, Newfoundland and Nova Scotia from the French in 1713. British control of the rest of New France was secured in 1763, largely because of James Wolfe's great victory over Montcalm near Quebec in 1759.

During the American Revolution, Canada became a refuge for great numbers of American Royalists, most of whom settled in Ontario, thereby creating an English majority west of the Ottawa River. The ethnic imbalance contravened the effectiveness of the prevailing French type of government, and in 1791 the Constitutional act was passed by the British parliament, dividing Canada at the Ottawa River into two parts, each with its own government: Upper Canada, chiefly English and consisting of the southern section of what is now Ontario; and Lower Canada, chiefly French and consisting principally of the southern section of Quebec. Subsequent revolt by dissidents in both sections caused the British government to pass the Union act, July 23, 1840, which united Lower and Upper Canada (as Canada East and Canada West) to form the Province of Canada, with one council and one assembly in which the two sections had equal numbers.

The union of the two provinces did not encourage political stability; the equal strength of the French and British made the task of government all but impossible. A further change was made with the passage of the British North American act, which took effect on July 1, 1867, and established Canada as the first federal union in the British Empire. Four provinces entered the union at first: Upper Canada as Ontario, Lower Canada as Quebec, Nova Scotia and New Brunswick. The Hudson's Bay Company's territories were acquired in 1869 out of which were formed the provinces of Manitoba, Saskatchewan and Alberta. British Columbia joined in 1871 and Prince Edward Island in 1873. Canada took over the Arctic Archipelago in 1895. In 1949 Newfoundland came into the confederation. Canada is a member of the Commonwealth. Elizabeth II is Head of State as Queen of Canada.

RULERS:

British 1763-

MONETARY SYSTEM:

1 Dollar = 100 Cents

BANQUE DU CANADA / BANK OF CANADA

1954 MODIFIED HAIR STYLE ISSUE

#		VG	VF	UNC
74	**1 DOLLAR** 1954 (1955-72). Black on green unpt. Qn.'s hair in modified style. Back green. Western prairie scene. Printer: CBNC.			
	a. Sign. Beattie-Coyne. (1955-61).	1.00	2.00	12.00
	b. Sign. Beattie-Rasminsky. (1961-72).	1.00	2.50	15.00
75	**1 DOLLAR** 1954. (1955-74). Like #74. Printer: BABNC.			
	a. Sign. Beattie-Coyne. (1955-61).	1.00	2.00	15.00
	b. Sign. Beattie-Rasminsky. (1961-72).	1.00	1.50	7.50
	c. Sign. Bouey-Rasminsky. (1972-73).	1.00	1.50	8.50
	d. Sign. Lawson-Bouey. (1973-74).	1.00	1.50	7.50

#		VG	VF	UNC
76	**2 DOLLARS** 1954. (1955-75). Black on red-brown unpt. Qn's hair in modified style. Back red-brown. Quebec scenery. Printer: BABNC.			
	a. Sign. Beattie-Coyne. (1955-61).	2.00	5.50	35.00
	b. Sign. Beattie-Rasminsky. (1961-72).	2.00	3.50	25.00
	c. Sign. Bouey-Rasminsky. (1972-73).	2.00	3.50	15.00
	d. Sign. Lawson-Bouey. (1973-75).	2.00	3.00	13.50

#		VG	VF	UNC
77	**5 DOLLARS** 1954 (1955-72). Black on blue unpt. Qn.'s hair in modified style. Back blue; river in the north country. Printer: CBNC.			
	a. Sign. Beattie-Coyne. (1955-61).	7.50	15.00	65.00
	b. Sign. Beattie-Rasminsky. (1961-72).	5.00	7.50	35.00
	c. Sign. Bouey-Rasminsky. (1972).	5.00	7.50	30.00
78	**5 DOLLARS** 1954 (1955-61). Like #77. Sign. Beattie-Coyne. Printer: BABNC.	7.50	15.00	65.00

#		VG	VF	UNC
79	**10 DOLLARS** 1954 (1955-71). Black on purple unpt. Qn.'s hair in modified style. Back purple; Rocky Mountain scene. Printer: BABNC.			
	a. Sign. Beattie-Coyne. (1955-61).	10.00	12.50	65.00
	b. Sign. Beattie-Rasminsky. (1961-71).	10.00	12.50	50.00

#		VG	VF	UNC
80	**20 DOLLARS** 1954 (1955-70) Black on olive green unpt. Qn's hair in modified style. Back olive green. Laurentian hills in winter. Printer: CBNC.			
	a. Sign. Beattie-Coyne. (1955-61).	22.50	27.50	100.00
	b. Sign. Beattie-Rasminsky. (1961-70).	20.00	25.00	75.00

81	50 DOLLARS	VG	VF	UNC
	1954 (1955-75). Black on orange unpt. Qn's hair in modified style. Back orange; Atlantic coastline. Printer: CBNC.			
	a. Sign. Beattie-Coyne. (1955-61).	50.00	65.00	165.00
	b. Sign. Beattie-Rasminsky. (1961-72).	50.00	65.00	150.00
	c. Sign. Lawson-Bouey. (1973-75).	50.00	85.00	275.00

82	100 DOLLARS	VG	VF	UNC
	1954 (1955-76). Black on brown unpt. Qn.'s hair in modified style. Back brown; mountain lake. Printer: CBNC.			
	a. Sign. Beattie-Coyne. (1955-61).	100.00	135.00	300.00
	b. Sign. Beattie-Rasminsky. (1961-72).	100.00	125.00	235.00
	c. Sign. Lawson-Bouey. (1973-76).	100.00	135.00	250.00
83	1000 DOLLARS			
	1954 (1955-87). Black on rose unpt. Qn's hair in modified style. Back rose; central Canadian landscape.			
	a. Sign. Beattie-Coyne. (1955-61).	1000.	1200.	1750.
	b. Sign. Beattie-Rasminsky. (1961-72).	950.00	1100.	1750.
	c. Sign. Bouey-Rasminsky. (1972).	950.00	1100.	1500.
	d. Sign. Lawson-Bouey. (1973-84).	900.00	1050.	1250.
	e. Sign. Thiessen-Crow. (1987).	950.00	1100.	1500.

1967 COMMEMORATIVE ISSUE

#84, Centennial of Canadian Confederation

84	1 DOLLAR	VG	VF	UNC
	1967. Black on green unpt. Qn. Elizabeth II at r. Back green; First Parliament Building. Sign. Beattie-Rasminsky.			
	a. *1867-1967* replacing serial #.	1.00	1.50	3.50

	VG	VF	UNC
b. Regular serial #'s.	1.00	1.50	5.00

1969-75 ISSUE

#85-91 arms at l.

85	1 DOLLAR	VG	VF	UNC
	1973. Black, lt. green on m/c unpt. Qn. Elizabeth II at r. Parliament Building as seen from across the Ottawa River on back.			
	a. Engraaved back. Sign. Lawson-Bouey.	FV	1.00	5.00
	b. Lithographed back. Sign. as a. Serial # prefix: *AFF-*.			
	c. Sign. Crow-Bouey.	FV	1.00	5.00

NOTE: Two formats of uncut 40-note sheets of #85b were sold to collectors in 1988 (BABN) and again in 1989 (CBNC). BABN format: 5x8 notes regular serial # prefixes *BFD, BFK, BFL* and replacement prefix *BAX*. CBNC format: 4x10 notes regular serial # prefixes *ECP, ECR, ECV, ECW* and replacement prefix *EAX*.

86	2 DOLLARS	VG	VF	UNC
	1974. Red-brown on m/c unpt. Qn. Elizabeth II at r. Inuits preparing for hunt on back.			
	a. Sign. Lawson-Bouey.	FV	2.00	9.50
	b. Sign. Crow-Bouey.	FV	2.00	10.00

NOTE: Two formats of uncut 40-note sheets of #86b were sold to collectors in 1995-96. BABN format: 5x8 notes. CBNC format: 4x10 notes.

87	5 DOLLARS	VG	VF	UNC
	1972. Blue on m/c unpt. Sir Wilfred Laurier at r. Serial # on face. Salmon fishing boat at Vancouver Island on back.			
	a. Sign. Bouey-Rasminsky.	FV	6.00	35.00
	b. Sign. Lawson-Bouey.	FV	6.00	30.00

88 **10 Dollars**

1971. Purple on m/c unpt. Sir John A. MacDonald at r. Oil refinery at Sarnia, Ontario, on back.

	VG	VF	Unc
a. Sign. Beattie-Rasminsky.	FV	12.50	60.00
b. Sign. Bouey-Rasminsky.	FV	13.50	65.00
c. Sign. Lawson-Bouey.	FV	FV	32.50
d. Sign. Crow-Bouey.	FV	FV	27.50
e. Sign. Thiessen-Crow.	FV	FV	25.00

89 **20 Dollars**

1969. Green on m/c unpt. Arms at l. Qn. Elizabeth II at r. Serial # on face. Alberta's Lake Moraine and Rocky Mountains on back.

	VG	VF	Unc
a. Sign. Beattie-Rasminsky.	FV	22.50	75.00
b. Sign. Lawson-Bouey.	FV	21.50	70.00

90 **50 Dollars**

1975. Red on m/c unpt. W. L. MacKenzie King at r. Mounted Police in *Dome* formation (from their Musical Ride program) on back.

	VG	VF	Unc
a. Sign. Lawson-Bouey.	FV	55.00	135.00
b. Sign. Crow-Bouey.	FV	50.00	130.00

91 **100 Dollars**

1975. Brown on m/c unpt. Sir Robert Borden at r. Lunenburg, Nova Scotia harbor scene on back.

	VG	VF	Unc
a. Sign. Lawson-Bouey.	FV	105.00	225.00
b. Sign. Crow-Bouey.	FV	100.00	165.00

1979 Issue

#92 and 93 arms at l.

92 **5 Dollars**

1979. Blue on m/c unpt. Similar to #87, but different guilloches on face. Serial # on back.

	VG	VF	Unc
a. Sign. Lawson-Bouey.	FV	FV	30.00
b. Sign. Crow-Bouey.	FV	FV	25.00

93 **20 Dollars**

1979. Deep olive-green on m/c unpt. Similar to #89, but different guilloches on face. Serial # on back.

	VG	VF	Unc
a. Sign. Lawson-Bouey.	FV	FV	65.00
b. Sign. Crow-Bouey.	FV	FV	50.00
c. Sign. Thiessen-Crow.	FV	FV	40.00

1986-91 Issue

#94-100 arms at upper l. ctr. Replacement notes: Third letter of serial # prefix is *X*.

94 **2 Dollars**

1986. Brown on m/c unpt. Qn. Elizabeth II, Parliament Bldg. at r. Pair of robins on back.

	VG	VF	Unc
a. Sign. Crow-Bouey.	FV	FV	8.50
b. Sign. Thiessen-Crow.	FV	FV	3.50
c. Sign. Bonin-Thiessen.	FV	FV	3.00

95	**5 Dollars**	VG	VF	Unc
	1986. Blue-gray on m/c unpt. Sir Wilfred Laurier, Parliament bldgs. at r. Kingfisher on back.			
	a1. Sign. Crow-Bouey. W/yellow plate # on back.	FV	FV	17.50
	a2. Sign. Crow-Bouey. W/blue plate # on back.	FV	FV	13.50
	b. Sign. Thiessen-Crow.	FV	FV	8.00
	c. Sign. Bonin-Thiessen.	FV	FV	6.50

96	**10 Dollars**	VG	VF	Unc
	1989. Purple on m/c unpt. Sir John A. Macdonald. Parliament bldgs. at r. Osprey in flight on back.			
	a. Sign. Thiessen-Crow.	FV	FV	14.00
	b. Sign. Bonin-Thiessen.	FV	FV	12.00

97	**20 Dollars**	VG	VF	Unc
	1991. Deep olive-green and olive-green on m/c unpt. Green foil optical device w/denom. at upper l. Qn. Elizabeth II, Parliament library at r. Loon on back.			
	a. Sign. Thiessen-Crow.	FV	FV	25.00
	b. Sign. Bonin-Thiessen.	FV	FV	22.50

NOTE: The letter "I" in prefix exists serif and sans-serif.

98	**50 Dollars**	VG	VF	Unc
	1988. Red on m/c unpt. W. L. MacKenzie King, Parliament bldg. at r., gold optical device w/denomination at upper l. Snowy owl on back.			
	a. Sign. Thiessen-Crow.	FV	FV	52.50
	b. Sign. Bonin-Thiessen.	FV	FV	47.50

99	**100 Dollars**	VG	VF	Unc
	1988. Dk. brown on m/c unpt. Sir R. Bordon, Parliament bldg. at r., green optical device w/denomination at upper l. Canadian geese on back.			
	a. Sign. Thiessen-Crow.	FV	FV	100.00
	b. Sign. Bonin-Thiessen.	FV	FV	95.00

100	**1000 Dollars**	VG	VF	Unc
	1988. Pink on m/c unpt. Qn. Elizabeth II, Parliament library at r. Optical device w/denomination at upper l. Pine grosbeak pair on branch at r. on back.			
	a. Sign. Thiessen-Crow.	FV	FV	900.00
	b. Sign. Bonin-Thiessen	FV	FV	875.00

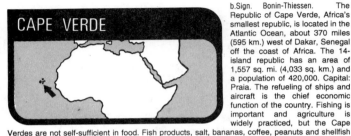

b.Sign. Bonin-Thiessen. The Republic of Cape Verde, Africa's smallest republic, is located in the Atlantic Ocean, about 370 miles (595 km.) west of Dakar, Senegal off the coast of Africa. The 14-island republic has an area of 1,557 sq. mi. (4,033 sq. km.) and a population of 420,000. Capital: Praia. The refueling of ships and aircraft is the chief economic function of the country. Fishing is important and agriculture is widely practiced, but the Cape Verdes are not self-sufficient in food. Fish products, salt, bananas, coffee, peanuts and shellfish are exported.

The date of discovery of the islands is uncertain. Possibly they were visited by Venetian Captain Alvise Cadamosto in 1456. Portuguese navigator Diogo Gomes claimed them for Portugal in May of 1460. Settlement began two years later. The early importance and wealth of the islands, which caused them to be attacked by Sir Francis Drake and the Dutch, resulted from the monopoly of the Guinea slave trade granted the inhabitants in 1466. Poverty and famine occasioned by frequent periods of severe drought have marked the history of the country since abolition of the slave trade in 1876.

After 500 years of Portuguese rule, the Cape Verdes became independent on July 5, 1975. At the first general election, all seats of the new national assembly were won by the Party for the Independence of Guinea-Bissau and Cape Verde (PAIGC). The PAIGC once had plans to possibly link the two former Portuguese colonies into a common state.

RULERS:

Portuguese to 1975

MONETARY SYSTEM:

1 Escudo = 100 Centavos, 1911-

PORTUGUESE INFLUENCE

BANCO NACIONAL ULTRAMARINO

CABO VERDE BRANCH

1971; 1972 ISSUE

Decreto Lei 39221 and 44891

#52 and 53 portr. S. Pinto at r., bank seal at l., arms at lower ctr. W/security thread. Sign. titles: *ADMINISTRADOR* and *VICE-GOVERNADOR*.

		VG	VF	UNC
52	**20 ESCUDOS** 4.4.1972. Green on m/c unpt. 2 sign. varieties.	3.00	12.00	30.00

		VG	VF	UNC
53	**50 ESCUDOS** 4.4.1972. Blue on m/c unpt.	4.00	16.00	40.00
53A	**500 ESCUDOS** 16.6.1971; 29.6.1971. Olive-green on m/c unpt. Infante D. Henrique at r.	15.00	50.00	150.00

REPUBLIC

BANCO DE CABO VERDE

1977 ISSUE

#54-56 A. Cabral w/native hat at r. and as wmk. Printer: BWC.

		VG	VF	UNC
54	**100 ESCUDOS** 20.1.1977. Red and m/c. Bow and musical instruments at l. Mountain at l. ctr. on back.	1.25	2.50	10.00

		VG	VF	UNC
55	**500 ESCUDOS** 20.1.1977. Blue and m/c. Shark at l. Harbor at Praia on back.			
	a. Issued note.	6.00	12.50	22.50
	s. Specimen.	—	—	22.50

		VG	VF	UNC
56	**1000 ESCUDOS** 20.1.1977. Brown and m/c. Electrical appliance at l. Workers at quarry at l. ctr., banana stalk at r. on back.	11.00	23.50	42.50

1989 ISSUE

#57-61 A. Cabral at r. and as wmk. Serial # black at l., red at r. Printer: TDLR.

		VG	VF	UNC
57	**100 ESCUDOS** 20.1.1989. Red and brown on m/c unpt. Festival at l. ctr. on back.	FV	FV	5.00

		VG	VF	UNC
58	**200 ESCUDOS** 20.1.1989. Green and black on m/c unpt. Modern airport collage in vertical format on back.	FV	FV	8.00
59	**500 ESCUDOS** 20.1.1989. Blue on m/c unpt. Shipyard on back.	FV	FV	17.50

		VG	VF	UNC
60	**1000 ESCUDOS** 20.1.1989. Brown and red-brown on m/c unpt. Insects at l. ctr. on back.	FV	FV	35.00
61	**2500 ESCUDOS** 20.1.1989. Violet on m/c unpt. Palace of National Assembly on back.	FV	FV	67.50

1992 ISSUE

#63-64 wmk: A. Cabral. Printer: TDLR.

		VG	VF	UNC
63	**200 ESCUDOS** 8.8.1992. Black and blue-green on m/c unpt. Sailing ship *Ernestina* at ctr. r. Back like #58.	FV	FV	6.00

		VG	VF	UNC
64	**500 ESCUDOS** 23.4.1992. Purple, blue and dk. brown on m/c unpt. Dr. B. Lopes da Silva at ctr. r. Back like #59.	FV	FV	12.50

		VG	VF	UNC
65	**1000 ESCUDOS** 5.6.1992.Dk brown, red-orange and purple on m/c unpt. Bird at ctr.r. Insects at l. ctr. on back	FV	FV	23.50

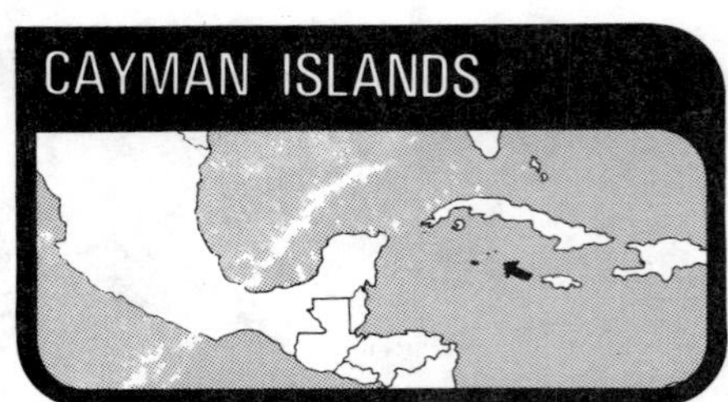

The Cayman Islands, a British Crown Colony situated about 180 miles (290 km.) northwest of Jamaica, consists of three islands: Grand Cayman, Little Cayman and Cayman Brac. The islands have an area of 102 sq. mi. (259 sq. km.) and a population of 26,950. Capital: Georgetown. Seafaring, commerce, banking and tourism are the principal industries. Rope, turtle shells and shark skins are exported.

he islands were discovered by Columbus in 1503, and were named by him, Tortugas (Spanish for "turtles") because of the great number of turtles in the nearby waters. The Cayman Islands were colonized from Jamaica by the British and remained dependencies of Jamaica until 1959, when they became a unit territory within the West Indies Federation. They became a separate colony when the Federation was dissolved in 1962.

RULERS:

British

MONETARY SYSTEM:

1 Dollar = 100 Cents

BRITISH INFLUENCE

CAYMAN ISLANDS CURRENCY BOARD

1971 CURRENCY LAW

#1-4 arms at upper ctr., Qn. Elizabeth II at r. Wmk: Tortoise. Printer: TDLR. Replacement notes: Serial # prefix *Z/1*.

		VG	VF	UNC
1	**1 DOLLAR** *L.1971* (1972). Blue on m/c unpt. Fish, coral at ctr. on back.	1.75	2.00	9.00

		VG	VF	UNC
2	**5 DOLLARS** *L.1971* (1972). Green on m/c unpt. Sailboat at ctr. on back.	8.00	10.00	35.00

		VG	VF	UNC
3	**10 DOLLARS** *L.1971* (1972). Red on m/c unpt. Beach scene at ctr. on back.	15.00	18.00	120.00

		VG	VF	UNC
4	**25 DOLLARS** *L.1971* (1972). Brown on m/c unpt. Compass and map at ctr. on back.	33.50	70.00	450.00

1974 CURRENCY LAW

#5-11 arms at upper ctr., Qn. Elizabeth II at r. Wmk: Tortoise. Printer: TDLR. Replacement notes: Serial # prefix *Z/1*.

		VG	VF	UNC
5	**1 DOLLAR** *L.1974* (1985). Blue on m/c unpt. Like #1.			
	a. Sign. as #1 illustration.	1.50	2.25	13.00
	b. Sign. Jefferson.	1.50	2.00	3.50

		VG	VF	UNC
6	**5 DOLLARS** *L.1974*. Green on m/c unpt. Like #2.	7.00	8.50	25.00

		VG	VF	UNC
7	**10 DOLLARS** *L.1974*. Red on m/c unpt. Like #3.	13.50	30.00	85.00

		VG	VF	UNC
8	**25 DOLLARS** *L.1974*. Brown on m/c unpt. Like #4.	32.50	36.50	60.00

		VG	VF	UNC
9	**40 DOLLARS** *L.1974* (1981). Purple on m/c unpt. Pirates Week Festival (crowd on beach) at ctr. on back.	50.00	65.00	87.50

		VG	VF	UNC
10	**50 DOLLARS** *L.1974* (1987). Blue on m/c unpt. Govt. house at ctr. on back.	65.00	72.50	100.00

		VG	VF	UNC
11	**100 DOLLARS** *L.1974* (1982). Deep orange on m/c unpt. Seacoast view of George Town at ctr. on back.	125.00	135.00	200.00

1991 ISSUE

#12-15 arms at upper ctr., Qn. Elizabeth II at r., treasure chest at lower l. ctr. Red coral at l. on back. Wmk: Tortoise. Printer: TDLR. Replacement notes: Serial # prefix *Z/1*.

		VG	VF	UNC
12	**5 DOLLARS** 1991. Dk. green, blue-green and olive-brown on m/c unpt. Sailboat in harbor waters at ctr. on back.	FV	FV	15.00

		VG	VF	UNC
13	**10 DOLLARS** 1991. Red, gray-green and purple on m/c unpt. Open chest, palm tree along coastline at ctr. on back. (2 varieties in color of conch shell at upper ctr. on back.)	FV	FV	30.00

		VG	VF	UNC
14	**25 DOLLARS** 1991. Deep brown, tan and orange on m/c unpt. Island outlines and compass at ctr. on back.	FV	FV	55.00

		VG	VF	UNC
15	**100 DOLLARS** 1991. Orange and dk. brown on m/c unpt. Harbor view at ctr. on back.	FV	FV	190.00

1996 ISSUE

#16-20 Qn. Elizabeth at r. Wmk: Tortoise. Printer: TDLR.

		VG	VF	UNC
16	**1 DOLLAR** 1996. Purple, orange and deep blue on m/c unpt. Back similar to #1.	FV	FV	3.50

		VG	VF	UNC
17	**5 DOLLARS** 1996. Dk. green, blue-green and olive-brown on m/c unpt. Back similar to #12.	FV	FV	12.50

		VG	VF	UNC
18	**10 DOLLARS** 1996. Red, gray-green and purple on m/c unpt. Back similar to #13.	FV	FV	20.00

		VG	VF	UNC
19	**25 DOLLARS** 1996. Deep brown, tan and orange on m/c unpt. Back similar to #14.	FV	FV	47.50

		VG	VF	UNC
20	**100 DOLLARS** 1996. Orange and brown on m/c unpt. Back similar to #15.	FV	FV	185.00

CAYMAN ISLANDS MONETARY AUTHORITY

LAW 1996; 1998 ISSUE

#21-23 Qn. Elizabeth at r. Segmented foil over security thread. Wmk: Tortoise. Printer: DLR.

		VG	VF	UNC
21	**1 DOLLAR** 1998. Purple, orange and deep blue on m/c unpt. Like #16.	FV	FV	3.00
22	**5 DOLLARS** 1998. Olive-green and blue-green on m/c unpt. Like #17.	FV	FV	11.50
23	**10 DOLLARS** 1998. Red and purple on m/c unpt. Like #18.	FV	FV	20.00
24	**25 DOLLARS** 1998. M/c.	FV	FV	47.50
25	**100 DOLLARS** 1998. M/c.	FV	FV	185.00

COLLECTOR SERIES

CAYMAN ISLANDS CURRENCY BOARD

1974 CURRENCY LAW ISSUE

		ISSUE PRICE	MKT. VALUE
CS1	*L.1974.* **1-100 DOLLARS** #5-11 ovpt: *SPECIMEN.* (300 sets.)	61.35	150.00

1991 ISSUE

		ISSUE PRICE	MKT. VALUE
CS2	**1991 5-100 DOLLARS** #12-15 ovpt: *SPECIMEN.* (300 sets.)	61.35	110.00

1996 ISSUE

		ISSUE PRICE	MKT. VALUE
CS3	**1996 1-100 DOLLARS** #16-20 ovpt: *SPECIMEN.* (300 sets.)	61.35	90.00

1998 ISSUE

		ISSUE PRICE	MKT. VALUE
CS4	**1998 1-100 DOLLARS** #21-25 ovpt: *SPECIMEN.* (300 sets.)	61.35	90.00

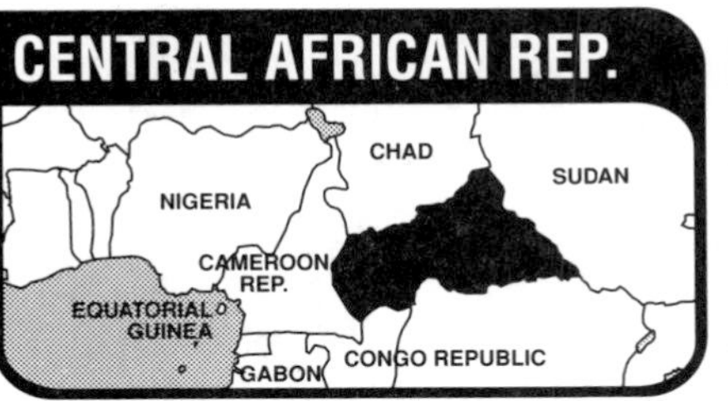

The Central African Republic, a landlocked country in Central Africa, bounded by Chad on the north, Cameroon on the west, Congo (Brazzaville) and Zaire on the south, and The Sudan on the east, has an area of 240,535 sq. mi. (622,984 sq. km.) and a population of 3.27 million. Capital: Bangui. Deposits of uranium, iron ore, manganese and copper remain to be developed. Diamonds, cotton, timber and coffee are exported.

The area that is now the Central African Republic was constituted as the French territory of Ubangi-Shari in 1894. It was united with Chad in 1905 and joined with Middle Congo and Gabon in 1910, becoming one of the four territories of French Equatorial Africa. Upon dissolution of the federation on Dec. 1, 1958, the constituent territories became full autonomous members of the French Community. Ubangi-Shari proclaimed its complete independence as the Central African Republic on Aug. 13, 1960.

On Jan. 1, 1966, Col. Jean-Bedel Bokassa, Chief of Staff of the Armed Forces, overthrew the government of President David Dacko and assumed power as president of the republic. President Bokassa abolished the constitution of 1959 and dissolved the National Assembly. In 1972 the Congress of the sole political party appointed Bokassa president for life. The republic became a constitutional monarchy on Dec. 4, 1976; President Bokassa was named Emperor Bokassa I. Bokassa was ousted as Central African emperor in a bloodless takeover of the government led by former president David Dacko on Sept. 20, 1979, and the African nation was proclaimed once again a republic. In 1996-97 a mutiny of army personnel created great tensions. It is a member of the "Union Monetaire des Etats de l'Afrique Centrale."

See also Central African States, Equatorial African States, and French African States.

RULERS:

Emperor J. B. Bokassa I, 1976-79

MONETARY SYSTEM:

1 Franc = 100 Centimes

SIGNATURE VARIETIES:

Refer to introduction to Central African States.

RÉPUBLIQUE CENTRAFRICAINE

BANQUE DES ÉTATS DEL'AFRIQUE CENTRALE

1974-76 ND ISSUE

#1-4 Pres. J. B. Bokassa at r. Wmk: Antelope's head.

		VG	VF	UNC
1	**500 FRANCS** ND (1974). Lilac-brown and m/c. Landscape at ctr. Mask at l., students and chemical testing at ctr., statue at r. on back. Sign. 6.	6.00	25.00	85.00

		VG	VF	UNC
2	**1000 FRANCS** ND (1974). Blue and m/c. Rhinoceros at l., water buffalo at ctr. Mask at l., trains, planes and bridge at ctr., statue at r. on back. Sign. 6.	10.00	35.00	150.00

		VG	VF	UNC
3	**5000 FRANCS** ND (1974). Brown and m/c. Field workers hoeing at l., combine at ctr. Mask at l., bldgs. at ctr., statue at r. on back.			
	a. Sign. 4.	30.00	110.00	300.00
	b. Sign. 6.	25.00	95.00	250.00

		VG	VF	UNC
4	**10,000 FRANCS** ND (1976). M/c. Sword hilts at l. and ctr. Mask at l., tractor cultivating at ctr., statue at r. on back. Sign. 6.	75.00	200.00	525.00

EMPIRE CENTRAFRICAIN
BANQUE DES ÉTATS DEL'AFRIQUE CENTRALE

1978-79 ISSUE

#5-8 Emp. J. B. Bokassa I at r. Wmk: Antelope's head.

		VG	VF	UNC
5	**500 FRANCS** 1.4.1978. Similar to #1. Specimen.	—	—	1500.

		VG	VF	UNC
6	**1000 FRANCS** 1.4.1978. Similar to #2. Sign. 9.	50.00	150.00	500.00

		VG	VF	UNC
7	**5000 FRANCS** ND (1979). Similar to #3. Sign. 9.	50.00	150.00	450.00

		VG	VF	UNC
8	**10,000 FRANCS** ND (1978). Similar to #4. Sign. 6.	50.00	150.00	350.00

RÉPUBLIQUE CENTRAFRICAINE
BANQUE DES ÉTATS DEL'AFRIQUE CENTRALE

NOTE: For notes with similar back designs see Cameroon Republic, Chad, Congo (Brazzaville) and Gabon.
#9-10 wmk: Antelope's head.

1980 ISSUE

		VG	VF	UNC
9	**500 FRANCS** 1.1.1980; 1.7.1980; 1.6.1981. Red and m/c. Woman weaving basket at r. Back like #1. Lithographed. Sign. 9.	1.50	3.00	8.00

		VG	VF	UNC
10	**1000 FRANCS** 1.1.1980; 1.7.1980; 1.6.1981; 1.1.1982; 1.6.1984. Blue and m/c. Butterfly at l., waterfalls at ctr., water buffalo at r. Back like #2. Lithographed. Sign. 9.	4.50	8.00	22.50

		VG	VF	UNC
11	**5000 FRANCS** 1.1.1980. Brown and m/c. Girl at l., village scene at ctr. Carving at l., airplane, train crossing bridge and tractor hauling logs at ctr., man smoking a pipe at r. Similar to Equatorial African States #6. Sign. 9.	12.50	30.00	80.00

1983-84 ND ISSUE

		VG	VF	UNC
12	**5000 FRANCS** ND (1984). Brown and m/c. Mask at l., woman w/bundle of fronds at r. Plowing and mine ore conveyor on back.			
	a. Sign. 9.	12.50	20.00	40.00
	b. Sign. 14.	11.50	18.50	35.00

		VG	VF	UNC
13	**10,000 FRANCS** ND (1983). Brown, green and m/c. Stylized antelope heads at l., woman at r. Loading fruit onto truck at l. on back. Sign. 9.	22.50	35.00	70.00

1985 ISSUE

#14-16 wmk: Carving (as printed on notes). Sign. 9.

		VG	VF	UNC
14	**500 FRANCS** 1985-91. Brown on orange and m/c unpt. Carving and jug at ctr. Man carving mask at l. ctr. on back.			
	a. 1.1.1985.	2.00	4.00	9.00
	b. 1.1.1986.	1.75	3.50	8.00
	c. 1.1.1987.	1.75	3.25	7.00
	d. 1.1.1989; 1.1.1991.	1.75	3.00	6.00

		VG	VF	UNC
15	**1000 FRANCS** 1.1.1985. Dull blue-violet on m/c unpt. Carving at l., map at ctr., Gen. Kolingba at r. Incomplete map of Chad at top ctr. Elephant at l., animals at ctr., carving at r. on back.	3.50	7.50	20.00

1986 ISSUE

		VG	VF	UNC
16	**1000 FRANCS** 1.1.1986-1.1.1990. Dull blue-violet on m/c umpt. Like # 15 but complete outline map of Chad at top ctr. Wmk:: Carving. sign. 9.	2.75	500	12.50

The Bank of the Central African States (BEAC) is a regional central bank for the monetary and customs union formed by Cameroon, Central African Republic, Chad, Congo (Brazzaville), Gabon, and (since 1985) Equatorial Guinea. It succeeded the Equatorial African States Bank in 1972-73 when the latter was reorganized and renamed to provide greater African control over its operations. The seat of the BEAC was transferred from Paris to Yaounde in 1977 and an African governor assumed responsibility for direction of the bank in 1978. The BEAC is a member of the franc zone with its currency denominated in CFA francs and pegged to the French franc at a rate of 50-1.

BEAC notes carry country names on the face and the central bank name on the back. The 1974-84 series had common back designs but were face-different. A new series begun in 1983-85 uses common designs also on the face except for some 1000 franc notes. The notes carry the signatures of *LE GOUVERNEUR (LE DIRECTEUR GENERAL* prior to 1-4-78) and *UN CENSEUR* (since 1972). Cameroon, Gabon, and France each appoint one censeur and one alternate. Cameroon and Congo notes carry the Cameroon censeur signature. Central African Republic, Equatorial Guinea, and Gabon notes carry the Gabon censeur signature. Chad notes have been divided between the two.

Prior to 1978, all BEAC notes were printed by the Bank of France. Since 1978, the 500 and 1000 franc notes have been printed by the private French firm F. C. Oberthur. The Bank of France notes are engraved and usually undated. The F. C. Oberthur notes are lithographed and most carry dates.

See individual member countries for additional note listings. Also see Equatorial African States and French Equatorial Africa.

CONTROL LETTER or CODE

Country	1993 onward
Cameroun	E
Central African Republic	F
Chad	P
Congo	C
Equatorial Guinea	N
Gabon	L

SIGNATURE COMBINATIONS

No.			Date
1	Panouillot Le Directeur-General	Gautier Le President	1955–72
1A	Panouillot Le Directeur-General	Duouedi Un Censeur	1961–72
2.	Panouillot Le Directeur-General	Koulla Un Censeur	1972–73
3	Joudiou Le Directeur-General	Koulla Un Censeur	1974
4	Joudiou Le Directeur-General	Renombo Un Censeur	1974
5	Joudiou Le Directeur-General	Ntang Un Censeur	1974–77
6	Joudiou Le Directeur-General	Ntoutoume Un Censeur	1974–78
7	Joudiou Le Directeur-General	Beke Bihege Un Censeur	1977
8	Joudiou Le Directeur-General	Kamgueu Un Censeur	1978
9	Oye Mba Le Gouverneur	Ntoutoume Un Censeur	1978–90
10	Oye Mba Le Gouverneur	Kamgueu Un Censeur	1978–86
11	Oye Mba Le Gouverneur	Kamgueu Un Censeur	1978–80
12	Oye Mba Le Gouverneur	Tchepannou Un Censeur	1981–89
13	Oye Mba Le Gouverneur	Dang Un Censeur	1990
14	Mamalepot Le Gouverneur	Ntoutoume Un Censeur	1991
15	Mamalepot Le Gouverneur	Mebara Un Censeur	1991–93
16	Mamalepot Le Gouverneur	Ognagna Un Censeur	1994
17	Mamalepot Le Gouverneur	Kaltjob Un Censeur	1994–

CENTRAL AFRICAN STATES

BANQUE DES ÉTATS DE L'AFRIQUE CENTRALE

C FOR CONGO

1993; 1994 ISSUE

#101C-103C map of Central African States at lower l. ctr. First 2 digits of serial # are year of issue.

		VG	VF	UNC
101C	**500 FRANCS** (19)93-. Dk. brown and gray on m/c unpt. Shepherd at r. and as wmk., zebus at ctr. Baobab, antelopes and Kota mask on back.			
	a. Sign. 15. (19)93.	FV	FV	5.00
	b. Sign. 16. (19)94.	FV	FV	4.50
	c. Sign. 16. (19)95.	FV	FV	4.50
	d. Sign. 16. (19)97.	FV	FV	4.00
102C	**1000 FRANCS** (19)93-. Dk. brown and red w/black text on m/c unpt. Young man at r. and as wmk., harvesting coffee beans at ctr. Forest harvesting, Okoume raft and Bakele wood mask on back.			
	a. Sign. 15. (19)93.	FV	FV	9.00
	b. Sign. 16. (19)94.	FV	FV	8.00
	c. Sign. 16. (19)95.	FV	FV	8.00
	d. Sign. 16. (19)97.	FV	FV	7.50
103C	**2000 FRANCS** (19)93-. Dk. brown and green w/black text on m/c unpt. Woman's head at r. and as wmk. surrounded by tropical fruit. Exchange of passengers and produce w/ship at l. ctr. on back.			
	a. Sign. 15. (19)93.	FV	FV	14.00
	b. Sign. 16. (19)94.	FV	FV	12.50
	c. Sign. 16. (19)97.	FV	FV	12.00
104C	**5000 FRANCS** (19)94-. Dk. brown, brown and blue w/violet text on m/c unpt. Laborer wearing hard hat at ctr. r., riggers w/well drill at r. Woman w/head basket at lower l., gathering cotton at ctr. on back.			
	a. Sign. 16. (19)94.	FV	FV	27.50
	b. Sign. 16. (19)97.	FV	FV	27.50
105C	**10,000 FRANCS** (19)94-. Dk. brown and blue w/blue-black text on m/c unpt. Modern bldg. at ctr., young woman at r. Fisherman, boats and villagers along shoreline at l. ctr. on back.			
	a. Sign. 16. (19)94.	FV	FV	47.50
	b. Sign. 16. (19)95.	FV	FV	45.00
	c. Sign. 16. (19)97.	FV	FV	42.50

E FOR CAMEROON

1993; 1994 ISSUE

		VG	VF	UNC
201E	**500 FRANCS** (19)93-. Dk. brown and gray on m/c unpt. Like #101C.			
	a. Sign. 15. (19)93.	FV	FV	5.00
	b. Sign. 17. (19)94.	FV	FV	4.50
	c. Sign. 17. (19)95.	FV	FV	4.50
	d. Sign. 17. (19)97.	FV	FV	4.50

		VG	VF	UNC
202E	**1000 FRANCS** (19)93-. Dk. brown and red w/black text on m/c unpt. Like #102C.			
	a. Sign. 15. (19)93.	FV	FV	9.00
	b. Sign. 17. (19)94.	FV	FV	8.00
	c. Sign. 17. (19)95.	FV	FV	8.00
	d. Sign. 17. (19)95.	FV	FV	8.00

		VG	VF	UNC
203E	**2000 FRANCS** (19)93-. Dk. brown and green w/black text on m/c unpt. Like #103C.			
	a. Sign. 15. (19)93.	FV	FV	13.50
	b. Sign. 17. (19)94.	FV	FV	12.50
	c. Sign. 17. (19)95.	FV	FV	12.50
204E	**5000 FRANCS** (19)94-. Dk. brown, brown and blue w/violet text on m/c unpt. Like #104C.			
	a. Sign. 17. (19)94.	FV	FV	27.50
	b. Sign. 17. (19)95.	FV	FV	27.50
205E	**10,000 FRANCS** (19)94-. Dk. brown and blue w/blue-black text on m/c unpt. Like #105C.			
	a. Sign. 17. (19)94.	FV	FV	45.00
	b. Sign. 17. (19)95.	FV	FV	45.00
	c. Sign. 17. (19)97.	FV	FV	45.00

F FOR CENTRAL AFRICAN REPUBLIC

1993; 1994 ISSUE

		VG	VF	UNC
301F	**500 FRANCS** (19)93-. Dk. brown and gray on m/c unpt. Like #101C.			
	a. Sign. 15. (19)93.	FV	FV	6.00
	b. Sign. 16. (19)94.	FV	FV	5.00
	c. Sign. 16. (19)95.	FV	FV	5.00
302F	**1000 FRANCS** (19)93-. Dk. brown and red w/black text on m/c unpt. Like #102C.			
	a. Sign. 15. (19)93.	FV	FV	9.00
	b. Sign. 16. (19)94.	FV	FV	8.50
	c. Sign. 16. (19)95.	FV	FV	8.00
303F	**2000 FRANCS** (19)93-. Dk. brown and green w/black text on m/c unpt. Like #103C.			
	a. Sign. 15. (19)93.	FV	FV	16.00
	b. Sign. 16. (19)94.	FV	FV	15.00
304F	**5000 FRANCS** (19)4-. Dk. brown, brown and blue w/violet text on m/c unpt. Like #104C.			
	a. Sign. 16. (19)94.	FV	FV	32.50
	b. Sign. 16. (19)95.	FV	FV	30.00
305F	**10,000 FRANCS** (19)94-. Dk. brown and blue w/blue-black text on m/c unpt. Like #105C.			
	a. Sign. 16. (19)94.	FV	FV	55.00
	b. Sign. 16. (19)95.	FV	FV	50.00
	c. Sign. 16. (19)95.	FV	FV	50.00

L FOR GABON

1993; 1994 ISSUE

		VG	VF	UNC
401L	**500 FRANCS** (19)93-. Dk. brown and gray on m/c unpt. Like #101C.			
	a. Sign. 15. (19)93.	FV	FV	5.00
	b. Sign. 16. (19)94.	FV	FV	4.50

		VG	VF	UNC
402L	**1000 FRANCS** (19)93-. Dk. brown and red w/black text on m/c unpt. Like #102C.			
	a. Sign. 15. (19)93.	FV	FV	8.50
	b. Sign. 16. (19)94.	FV	FV	8.00
	c. Sign. 16. (19)95.	FV	FV	7.50
	d. Sign. 16. (19)97.	FV	FV	7.50

		VG	VF	UNC
403L	**2000 FRANCS** (19)93-. Dk. brown and green w/black text on m/c unpt. Like #103C.			
	a. Sign. 15. (19)93.	FV	FV	13.50
	b. Sign. 16. (19)94.	FV	FV	13.50
	c. Sign. 16. (19)97.	FV	FV	12.50
404L	**5000 FRANCS** (19)94-. Dk. brown, brown and blue w/violet text on m/c unpt. Like #104C.			
	a. Sign. 16. (19)94.	FV	FV	25.00
	b. Sign. 16. (19)95.	FV	FV	25.00
	c. Sign. 16. (19)97.	FV	FV	25.00
405L	**10,000 FRANCS** (19)94-. Dk. brown and blue w/blue-black text on m/c unpt. Like #105C.			
	a. Sign. 16. (19)94.	FV	FV	52.50
	b. Sign. 16. (19)95.	FV	FV	47.50
	c. (19)97.	FV	FV	45.00

N FOR EQUATORIAL GUINEA

1993; 1994 ISSUE

		VG	VF	UNC
501N	**500 FRANCS** (19)93-. Dk. brown and gray on m/c unpt. Like #101C.			
	a. Sign. 15. (19)93.	FV	FV	6.00
	b. Sign. 16. (19)94.	FV	FV	6.00
	c. Sign. 16. (19)97.	FV	FV	6.00
502N	**1000 FRANCS** (19)93-. Dk. brown and red w/black text on m/c unpt. Like #102C.			
	a. Sign. 15. (19)93.	FV	FV	9.00
	b. Sign. 16. (19)94.	FV	FV	8.00
	c. Sign. 16. (19)95.	FV	FV	7.50

		VG	VF	UNC
503N	**2000 FRANCS** (19)93-. Dk. brown and green w/black text on m/c unpt. Like #103C.			
	a. Sign. 15. (19)93.	FV	FV	13.50
	b. Sign. 16. (19)94.	FV	FV	13.50
	c. Sign. 16. (19)95.	FV	FV	13.50
504N	**5000 FRANCS** (19)94-. Dk. brown, brown and blue w/violet text on m/c unpt. Like 104C.			
	a. Sign. 16. (19)94.	FV	FV	25.00
	b. Sign. 16. (19)95.	FV	FV	25.00
505N	**10,000 FRANCS** (19)94-. Dk. brown and blue w/blue-black text on m/c unpt. Like #105C.			
	a. Sign. 16. (19)94.	FV	FV	47.50
	b. Sign. 16. (19)95.	FV	FV	47.50

P FOR CHAD

1993; 1994 ISSUE

		VG	VF	UNC
601P	**500 FRANCS** (19)93-. Dk. brown and gray on m/c unpt. Like #101C.			
	a. Sign. 15. (19)93.	FV	FV	6.00
	b. Sign. 16. (19)94.	FV	FV	5.00
	c. Sign. 16. (19)95.	FV	FV	5.00
	d. Sign. 16. (19)97.	FV	FV	5.00

		VG	VF	UNC
602P	**1000 FRANCS** (19)93-. Dk. brown and red w/black text on m/c unpt. Like #102C.			
	a. Sign. 15. (19)93.	FV	FV	8.50
	b. Sign. 16. (19)94.	FV	FV	7.50
	c. Sign. 16. (19)95.	FV	FV	7.00
	d. Sign. 16. (19)97.	FV	FV	7.00
603P	**2000 FRANCS** (19)93-. Dk. brown and green w/black text on m/c unpt. Like #103C.			
	a. Sign. 15. (19)93.	FV	FV	15.00
	b. Sign. 16. (19)94.	FV	FV	15.00
	c. Sign. 16. (19)95.	FV	FV	13.50
	d. Sign. 16. (19)97.	FV	FV	12.50

		VG	VF	UNC
604P	**5000 FRANCS** (19)94-. Dk. brown, brown and blue w/violet text on m/c unpt. Like #104C.			
	a. Sign. 16. (19)94.	FV	FV	30.00
	b. Sign. 16. (19)95.	FV	FV	27.50
	c. Sign. 16. (19)97.	FV	FV	26.50

		VG	VF	UNC
605P	**10,000 FRANCS** (19)94-. Dk. brown and blue w/blue-black text on m/c unpt. Like #105C.			
	a. Sign. 16. (19)94.	FV	FV	50.00
	b. Sign. 16. (19)95.	FV	FV	50.00
	c. Sign. 16. (19)97.	FV	FV	47.50

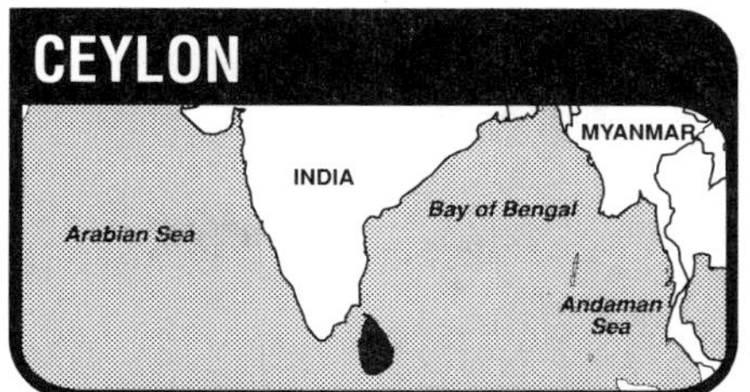

Ceylon (later to become the Democratic Socialist Republic of Sri Lanka), situated in the Indian Ocean 18 miles (29 km.) southeast of India, has an area of 25,332 sq. mi. (65,610 sq. km.) and population of 17.25 million. Capital: Colombo. The economy is chiefly agricultural. Tea, coconut products and rubber are exported.

The earliest known inhabitants of Ceylon, the Veddahs, were subjugated by the Sinhalese from northern India in the 6th century BC. Sinhalese rule was maintained until 1498, after which the island was controlled by China for 30 years. The Portuguese came to Ceylon in 1505 and maintained control of the coastal area for 150 years. They were supplanted by the Dutch in 1658, who were in turn supplanted by the British who seized the Dutch colonies in 1796, and made them a Crown Colony in 1802. In 1815, the British conquered the independent Kingdom of Kandy in the central part of the island. Constitutional changes in 1931 and 1946 granted the Ceylonese a measure of autonomy and a parliamentary form of government. Ceylon became a self-governing dominion of the British Commonwealth on February 4, 1948. On May 22, 1972, the Ceylonese adopted a new constitution which declared Ceylon to be the Republic of Sri Lanka - "Resplendent Island." Sri Lanka is a member of the Commonwealth of Nations. The president is Chief of State. The prime minister is Head of Government. For later issues, see Sri Lanka.

RULERS:

Dutch to 1796
British, 1796-1972

MONETARY SYSTEM:

1 Rupee = 100 Cents

STATE

CENTRAL BANK OF CEYLON

1962-64 ISSUE

#62-66 S. Bandaranaike at r. Wmk: Chinze. Printer: BWC.

		VG	VF	UNC
62	**2 RUPEES** 1962-65. Brown on lilac, green and blue unpt. Pavilion at ctr. r. on back.			
	a. Sign. P. B. G. Kaluga and D. W. Rajapatirana. 8.11.1962.	.75	3.00	12.00
	b. Sign. T. B. Illangaratue and D. W. Rajapatirana. 11.4.1964; 12.6.1964.	.65	2.50	10.00
	c. Sign. U. B. Wanninayake and D. W. Rajapatirana. 6.4.1965.	.50	2.00	8.00

		VG	VF	UNC
63	**5 RUPEES** 1962; 1964. Orange on brown and green unpt. Standing figure at ctr. on back.			
	a. Sign. P. B. G. Kalugalla and D. W. Rajapatirana. 8.11.1962.	.90	3.75	15.00
	b. Sign. N. M. Perera and D. W. Rajapatirana. 12.6.1964.	.75	3.00	12.00

		VG	VF	UNC
64	**10 RUPEES** 12.6.1964; 28.8.1964; 19.9.1964. Green on purple, orange and blue unpt. Ceremonial figures on back.	2.00	6.00	20.00

		VG	VF	UNC
65	**50 RUPEES** 1961-65. Blue and violet on m/c unpt. Ornate stairway on back.			
	a. Sign. F. R. D. Bandaranaike and D. W. Rajapatirana. 2.11.1961.	5.00	20.00	80.00
	b. Sign. T. B. Illangaratne and D. W. Rajapatirana. 5.6.1963.	4.50	17.50	70.00
	c. Sign. U. B. Wanninayake and D. W. Rajapatirana. 6.4.1965.	3.75	15.00	60.00

NOTE: An issue was prepared dated 12.6.1964 which was later destroyed.

		VG	VF	UNC
66	**100 RUPEES** 5.6.1963. Brown on m/c unpt. 2 women in national costumes on back.	12.50	30.00	100.00

1965-68 ISSUE

#67-71 statue of Kg. Parakkrama at r. Back designs like #56-61. Various date and sign. varieties. Wmk.: Chinze. Printer: BWC.

		VG	VF	UNC
67	**2 RUPEES** 1965-68. Brown on lilac, lt. green and blue unpt.			
	a. Sign. U. B. Wanninayake and D. W. Rajapatirana. 9.9.1965; 15.7.1967.	.50	1.75	7.00
	b. Sign. U. B. Wanninayake and W. Tennekoon. 10.1.1968.	.40	1.50	6.00
68	**5 RUPEES** 1965-68. Orange on brown and green unpt.			
	a. Sign. U. B. Wanninayake and D. W. Rajapatirana. 9.9.1965; 15.7.1967.	.65	2.50	10.00
	b. Sign. U. B. Wanninayake and W. Tennekoon. 1.9.1967; 10.1.1968.	.50	2.00	8.00
69	**10 RUPEES** 10.1.1968. Green on purple, orange and blue unpt.	1.50	4.00	12.50
70	**50 RUPEES** 1967; 1968. Blue on m/c unpt.			
	a. Sign. U. W. Wanninayake and D. W. Rajapatirana. 7.3.1967.	3.25	12.50	50.00
	b. Sign. U. B. Wanninayake and W. Tennekoon. 10.1.1968.	3.00	11.50	45.00
71	**100 RUPEES** 1966-68. Brown on m/c unpt.			
	a. Sign. U. W. Wanninayake and D. W. Rajapatirana. 28.5.1966; 22.11.1966.	4.50	17.50	70.00
	b. Sign. U. B. Wanninayake and W. Tennekoon. 10.1.1968.	4.00	16.00	65.00

1968-69 ISSUE

#72-76 w/bank name in English on both sides. Various date and sign. varieties. Wmk.: Chinze. Printer: BWC.

		VG	VF	UNC
72	**2 RUPEES** 1969-77. Brown on lilac, lt. green and blue unpt. Like #67.			
	a. Sign. U. B. Wanninayake and W. Tennekoon. 10.5.1969.	.35	1.50	6.00
	b. Sign. N. M. Perera and W. Tennekoon. 1.6.1970; 1.2.1971; 7.6.1971; 12.5.1972; 21.8.1973; 27.8.1974.	.30	1.25	5.00
	c. Sign. R. J. G. de Mel and H. E. Tennekoon. 26.8.1977.	.25	1.00	4.00

		VG	VF	UNC
73	**5 RUPEES** 1969-77. Orange on brown and green unpt. Like #68.			
	a. Sign. U. B. Wanninayake and W. Tennekoon. 10.5.1969.	.50	2.00	8.00
	b. Sign. N. M. Perera and W. Tennekoon. 1.6.1970; 1.2.1971; 21.8.1973; 16.7.1974; 27.8.1974.	.90	3.50	7.00
	c. Sign. F. R. D. Bandaranaike and H. E. Tennekoon. 26.8.1977.	.40	1.50	6.00

		VG	VF	UNC
74	**10 RUPEES** 1969-77. Green on purple, orange and blue unpt. Like #69.			
	a. Sign. U. B. Wanninayake and W. Tennekoon. 20.10.1969.	.75	3.00	12.00
	b. Sign. N. M. Perera and W. Tennekoon. 1.6.1970; 1.2.1971; 7.6.1971; 21.8.1973; 16.7.1974.	.65	2.50	10.00
	c. Sign. F. R. D. Bandaranaike and H. E. Tennekoon. 6.10.1975.	.60	2.25	9.00
	d. Sign. R. J. G. de Mel and H. E. Tennekoon. 26.8.1977.	.50	2.00	8.00
75	**50 RUPEES** 20.10.1969. Blue on m/c unpt. Like #70.	3.50	7.50	37.50

		VG	VF	UNC
76	**100 RUPEES** 10.5.1969. Brown on m/c unpt. Like #71.	4.00	12.50	50.00

NOTICE

Readers with unlisted dates, signature varieties, etc. are invited to submit photocopies of their notes to: Standard Catalog of World Paper Money, 700 East State St. Iola, WI 54990-0001, fax: 1-715-445-4087, or E-Mail: thernr@krause.com.

1970 ISSUE

#58 and 59 Smiling Pres. Bandaranaike w/raised hand. Wmk.: Chinze. Printer: TDLR. Replacement notes serial # prefix *W/1* and *V/1*.

		VG	VF	UNC
77	**50 RUPEES** 26.10.1970; 29.12.1970. Blue on lilac, yellow and brown unpt. Monument on back.	3.00	12.50	45.00
78	**100 RUPEES** 26.10.1970; 29.12.1970. Purple on m/c unpt. Female dancers on back.	5.50	20.00	65.00

1971-72 ISSUE

#79 and 80 smiling Pres. Bandaranaike w/o hand raised. Wmk.: Chinze. Printer: BWC.

		VG	VF	UNC
79	**50 RUPEES** 28.12.1972; 27.8.1974. Purple and m/c. Landscape on back.	3.00	12.00	40.00

		VG	VF	UNC
80	**100 RUPEES** 1971-75. Purple on m/c unpt. Ornate stairway on back.			
	a. Sign. N. M. Perera and H. E. Tennekoon. 18.12.1971; 16.7.1974; 27.8.1974.	4.00	16.50	65.00
	b. Sign. F. R. D. Bandaranaike and H. E. Tennekoon. 6.10.1975.	3.75	15.00	60.00

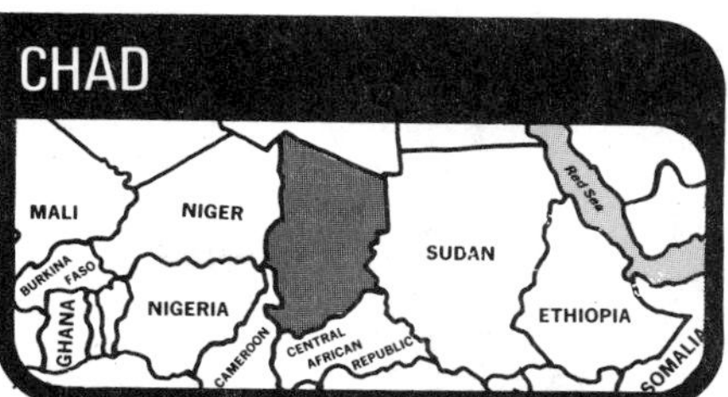

The Republic of Chad, a landlocked country of central Africa, is the largest country of former French Equatorial Africa. It has an area of 495,755 sq. mi. (1,284,000 sq. km.) and a population of 6.98 million. Capital. N'Djamâna. An expanding livestock industry produces camels, cattle and sheep. Cotton (the chief product), ivory and palm oil are important exports.

Although supposedly known to Ptolemy, the Chad area was first visited by white men in 1823. Exaggerated estimates of its economic importance led to a race for its possession (1890-93) which resulted in territory being divided by treaty between Great Britain, France and Germany. As a consequence of World War I, the German area was mandated to France in 1919. Chad was absorbed into the colony of French Equatorial Africa, as a part of Ubangi-Shari, in 1910 and became a separate colony in 1920. Upon dissolution of French Equatorial Africa in 1959, the component states became autonomous members of the French Union. Chad became an independent republic on Aug. 11, 1960.

Conflicts between the government and secessionists began in 1965 and developed into civil war. A ceasefire in 1987 was followed by an attempted coup. In 1990, Idress Déby declared himself president.

For later issues, see Central African States.

MONETARY SYSTEM:

1 Franc = 100 Centimes

SIGNATURE VARIETIES:

Refer to introduction to Central African States.

RÉPUBLIQUE DU TCHAD

BANQUE CENTRALE

1971 ISSUE

		VG	VF	UNC
1	**10,000 FRANCS** ND (1971). M/c. Pres. Tombalbaye at l., cattle watering at ctr. r. Mask at l., tractor plowing at ctr., statue at r. on back. Sign. 1.	125.00	350.00	900.00

BANQUE DES ÉTATS DE L'AFRIQUE CENTRALE

1974-78; ND ISSUE

		VG	VF	UNC
2	**500 FRANCS** ND (1974); 1978. Brown on m/c unpt. Woman at l., birds at ctr. and at r. Mask at l., students and chemical testing at ctr., statue at r. on back.			
	a. Sign. titles and wmk. like #3a. Sign. 6. (1974).	2.50	7.50	20.00
	b. Sign. titles, wmk. and date like #3c. Sign. 10. 1.4.1978.	20.00	75.00	150.00

		VG	VF	UNC
3	**1000 FRANCS** ND; 1.4.1978. Blue on m/c unpt. Woman at r. Mask at l., trains, planes and bridge at ctr., statue at r. on back.			
	a. Sign. titles: *LE DIRECTEUR GÉNÉRAL* and *UN CENSEUR*. Engraved. Wmk: Antelope. in half profile. Sign. 5; 7.	4.00	15.00	50.00
	b. Sign. titles: *LE DIRECTEUR GÉNÉRAL* and *UN CENSEUR*. Lithographed. Wmk: Antelope in profile. Sign. 8.	3.00	11.50	30.00
	c. Sign. titles: *LE GOUVERNEUR* and *UN CENSEUR*. Sign. 10. 1.4.1978.	FV	8.00	22.50
4	**5000 FRANCS** ND (1974). Brown-orange on m/c unpt. Pres. Tombalbaye at l. Mask at l., industrial college at ctr., statue at r. on back. Sign. 4.	100.00	250.00	650.00
5	**5000 FRANCS** ND. Brown on m/c unpt. Woman at l. Like #4 on back.			
	a. Sign. 6. (1976).	22.50	40.00	120.00
	b. Sign. 9. (1978).	20.00	35.00	80.00

1980 ISSUE

		VG	VF	UNC
6	**500 FRANCS** 1.6.1980; 1.6.1984. Red on m/c unpt. Woman weaving basket at r. Sign. 10.	1.50	3.00	15.00

		VG	VF	UNC
7	**1000 FRANCS** 1.6.1980; 1.6.1984. Blue on m/c unpt. Water buffalo at r. Back like #3. Sign. 9; 10.	3.00	8.50	25.00

		VG	VF	UNC
8	**5000 FRANCS** 1.1.1980. Brown and m/c. Girl at lower l., village scene at ctr. Back w/carving, airplane, train, tractor and man smoking pipe. Similar to Central African Republic #11 and others. Sign. 9.	13.50	35.00	85.00

1984-85; ND ISSUE

		VG	VF	UNC
9	**500 FRANCS** 1985-92. Brown on m/c unpt. Carved statue and jug at ctr. Man carving mask at l. ctr. on back. Wmk: Carving.			
	a. Sign. 10. 1.1.1985; 1.1.1986.	FV	FV	8.00
	b. Sign. 12. 1.1.1987.	FV	FV	7.00
	c. Sign. 13. 1.1.1990.	FV	FV	7.00
	d. Sign. 15. 1.1.1991.	FV	FV	6.50
	e. Sign. 15. 1.1.1992.	FV	FV	6.00

		VG	VF	UNC
10	**1000 FRANCS** 1.1.1985. Dull blue-violet on m/c unpt. Animal carving at lower l., map at ctr., starburst at lower r. Incomplete outline map of Chad at top ctr. Elephants at l., statue at r. on back. Wmk: Animal carving. Sign. 9.	13.50	35.00	75.00

#10 was withdrawn shortly after issue because of the incompleteness of the map at top.

10A **1000 FRANCS**
1985-91. Like #10 but complete outline map of Chad at top ctr.

		VG	VF	UNC
a.	Sign. 9. 1.1.1985; 1.1.1988; 1.1.1989; 1.1.1990.	FV	FV	12.50
b.	Sign. 15. 1.1.1991.	3.50	15.00	35.00
c.	Sign. 15. 1.1.1992.	FV	FV	11.50

11 **5000 FRANCS**
ND (1984-91). Brown on m/c unpt. Mask at l., woman w/bundle of fronds at r. Plowing and mine ore conveyor on back. Sign. 9; 15.

VG	VF	UNC
FV	FV	40.00

12 **10,000 FRANCS**
ND (1984-91). Black, brown and dk. green on m/c unpt. Stylized antelope heads at l., woman at r. and as wmk. Loading fruit onto truck at l. on back.

		VG	VF	UNC
a.	Sign. 9.	FV	FV	65.00
b.	Sign. 15.	FV	FV	55.00

NOTE: For notes with similar back designs see Cameroon Republic, Central African Republic, Congo (Brazzaville) and Gabon.

The Republic of Chile, a ribbon-like country on the Pacific coast of southern South America, has an area of 292,258 sq. mi. (756,945 sq. km.) and a population of 14.66 million. Capital: Santiago. Historically, the economic base of Chile has been the rich mineral deposits of its northern provinces. Copper, of which Chile has 25 percent of the free world's reserves, has accounted for more than 75 per cent of Chile's export earnings in recent years. Other important exports are iron ore, iodine, fruit and nitrate of soda.

Diego de Almargo was the first Spaniard to attempt to wrest Chile from the Incas and Araucanian tribes, 1536. He failed, and was followed by Pedro de Valdivia, a favorite of Pizarro, who founded Santiago in 1541. When the Napoleonic Wars involved Spain, leaving the constituent parts of the Spanish Empire to their own devices, Chilean patriots formed a national government and proclaimed the country's independence, Sept. 18, 1810. Independence, however, was not secured until Feb. 12, 1818, after a bitter struggle led by Generals Bernardo O'Higgins and José de San Martín.

In 1925, the constitution was ratified to strengthen the Executive branch at the expense of the Legislature.

MONETARY SYSTEM:

1 Escudo = 100 Centesimos, 1960-75
1 Peso = 100 Escudos, 1975-

REPUBLIC

BANCO CENTRAL DE CHILE

1960 ND PROVISIONAL ISSUE

#124-133 Escudo denominations in red as part of new plates (not ovpt., except #124). on back. Wmk: D. Diego Portales P. Sign. varieties. Printer: CdM- Chile.

124 **1/2 CENTESIMO ON 5 PESOS**
ND (1960-61). Blue. Ovpt. on #119.

VG	VF	UNC
—	—	—

125 **1 CENTESIMO ON 10 PESOS**
ND (1960-61). Red-brown. Ovpt. on #120.

VG	VF	UNC
1.00	2.50	10.00

126 **5 CENTESIMOS ON 50 PESOS**
ND (1960-61). Green ovpt. on #121. Wmk: *L*, *V* or *X* below portr.

		VG	VF	UNC
a.	Imprint 25mm wide. 2 sign. varieties.	.50	2.00	5.00
b.	Imprint 22mm wide. 3 sign. varieties.	.10	.20	.50
s.	Specimen.	—	—	10.00

127 **10 CENTESIMOS ON 100 PESOS**
ND (1960-61). Red on yellow-green unpt. Ovpt. on #122. Wmk: *C*, *L*, *V* or *X* below portr. 2 sign. varieties.

		VG	VF	UNC
a.	Issued note.	.10	.25	.75
s.	Specimen.	—	—	10.00

		VG	VF	UNC
128	**50 CENTESIMOS ON 500 PESOS** ND (1960-61). Blue. Ovpt. on #115.	.50	2.50	10.00

		VG	VF	UNC
129	**1 ESCUDO ON 1000 PESOS** ND (1960-61). Brown. Ovpt. on #116.	.50	1.50	7.50

		VG	VF	UNC
130	**5 ESCUDOS ON 5000 PESOS** ND (1960-61). Brown-violet. Ovpt. on #117. 2 sign. varieties.	1.00	3.00	15.00

		VG	VF	UNC
131	**10 ESCUDOS ON 10,000 PESOS** ND (1960-61). Purple on lt. blue unpt. Ovpt. on #118. Dual wmk: Head at l., words *DIEZ MIL* at r.	2.00	10.00	35.00
132	**10 ESCUDOS ON 10,000 PESOS** ND (1960-61). Red-brown. Similar to #131 but w/o wmk. at r.	2.50	15.00	45.00
133	**50 ESCUDOS ON 50,000 PESOS** ND (1960-61). Blue-green and brown on m/c unpt. Ovpt. on #123.	4.50	17.50	60.00

1962-70 ND ISSUE

#134-140 sign. varieties. Wmk: D. Diego Portales P. at l. Printer: CdM-Chile.

		VG	VF	UNC
134	**1/2 ESCUDO** ND. Dk. blue on pale orange and lt. blue unpt. Portr. Gen. B. O'Higgins at ctr. Explorer on horseback at l. ctr. on back. Red serial #.			
	a. Paper of #122. Series A.	.15	.50	2.50
	b. Paper of #121. Series B.	.15	.50	2.50
	s. Specimen.	—	—	10.00

		GOOD	VF	UNC
134A	**1/2 ESCUDO** ND. Like #134, but tan unpt. Black serial #.			
	a. Paper of #121. Series B-G.	.10	.25	1.00
	s. Specimen.	—	—	15.00

		VG	VF	UNC
135	**1 ESCUDO** ND. Brown-violet w/lilac guilloche on tan unpt. Portr. A. Prat at ctr. Red-brown arms w/founding of Santiago on back. Engraved. 3 sign. varieties.			
	a. Lg. brown serial #. Wmk: *1000* at r. Series A.	.50	2.00	7.50
	b. Sm. black serial #. Wmk: *1000* at r. Series A.	1.00	4.00	15.00
	c. Wmk: *500* at r. Series A; B.	.50	1.50	4.00
	d. Sm. black serial #. W/o wmk. at r. Arms in red-brown at l. on back.	.20	.50	1.00
	s. As c. Specimen.	—	—	15.00
135A	**1 ESCUDO** ND. Like #135c but w/arms in olive at l. on back.			
	a. Series G-I. W/o wmk. at r.	.10	.20	.75
	b. W/*V* under portr. Paper of #121. Series J-N.	.10	.20	.75

		VG	VF	UNC
136	**1 ESCUDO** ND (1964). Dull violet on tan unpt. Like #135 but arms on back in lt. olive. Lithographed. 2 sign. varieties w/1 sub-variety. Series N; P; Q.	.10	.30	.50

		VG	VF	UNC
137	**5 ESCUDOS** ND. Brown on m/c unpt. Portr. Bulnes at ctr. Battle of Rancagua at ctr., yellow-orange arms at l. on back.			
	a. Series A.	.75	2.00	10.00
	s. Specimen.	—	—	15.00

138 5 ESCUDOS
ND (1964). Red and brown-violet on m/c unpt. Like #137. Red-brown arms at l. on back. 4 sign. varieties. Series A-E. .10 .25 1.00

		VG	VF	UNC
139	**10 ESCUDOS**			
	ND. Violet, blue-gray and dull purple on m/c unpt. Portr. J. M. Balmaceda at ctr. Dk. or lt. brown arms at l.,soldiers meeting at ctr. on back. 3 sign. varieties.			
	a. Series A-G.	.25	.75	4.00
	s. Specimen.	—	—	20.00

		VG	VF	UNC
140	**50 ESCUDOS**			
	ND. Dk. green and olive-brown on m/c unpt. Portr. Alessandri at ctr. Back brown and green; Banco Central bldg. 5 sign. varieties.			
	a. Series A-D.	1.00	1.75	7.00
	b. Series E-F.	.10	.25	1.00
	s. Specimen.	—	—	20.00

		VG	VF	UNC
141	**100 ESCUDOS**			
	ND. Blue-gray and violet-brown on tan unpt. Rengifo at r. Sailing ships at ctr. arms at l. on back.			
	a. Series A-G.	.25	.75	3.00
	s. Specimen.	—	—	20.00

1967-76 ND ISSUES

#142-148 sign. varieties. Wmk: D. Diego Portales P. Printer: CdM-Chile. Replacement notes: Serial # suffix *R* or *R* in area of sheet position #.

		VG	VF	UNC
142	**10 ESCUDOS**			
	ND (1970). Gray-green, violet-brown and blue-gray on m/c unpt. J. M. Balmaceda at r. Red-brown lower margin on back. Engraved. Series A.	.20	.50	2.00
142A (142b)	**10 ESCUDOS**			
	ND. Like #142a but w/green lower margin on back. Lithographed.			
	a. Series B.	.20	.50	2.00
	s. Specimen.	—	—	17.50
143	**10 ESCUDOS**			
	ND. Grayish brown on tan unpt. Like #142. Lithographed. 3 sign. varieties. Series A.	.10	.25	.75
144	**500 ESCUDOS**			
	ND. Red-brown on m/c unpt. Steel worker at l. Strip mining at ctr. r. on back. W/o 3-line text: *NO DEBEMOS CONSENTIRE* at bottom.	65.00	200.00	—

		VG	VF	UNC
145	**500 ESCUDOS**			
	ND. Like #144 but w/3-line text: *NO DEBEMOS CONSENTIRE* at bottom on back. 2 sign. varieties. Series A; B.	.15	.50	2.50

		VG	VF	UNC
146	**1000 ESCUDOS**			
	ND. Purple on m/c unpt. I. Carrera Pinto at l. Back like #147. 2 sign. varieties. Series A; B.	.15	.50	3.00

		VG	VF	UNC
147	**5000 ESCUDOS**			
	ND. Dk. green and brown on m/c unpt. I. Carrera Pinto at l. Carrera House at ctr. r. on back.			
	a. Back w/deep green vignette. Lithographed. Series A.	.50	1.50	5.00
	b. Back w/dk. olive-green vignette. Partially engraved. Series B. 2 sign. varieties.	.30	.75	3.00

		VG	VF	UNC
148	**10,000 ESCUDOS**			
	ND. Red-brown on m/c unpt. Gen. B. O'Higgins at l. Blue serial #. Battle of Rancagua on back. Series A. 2 sign. varieties.	.50	2.00	6.00

1975-89 ISSUES

#149-152 wmk: D. Diego Portales P. Sign. varieties.

#152-156 printer: CdM-Chile.

149 5 PESOS
1975-76. Green on olive unpt. I. Carrera Pinto at r. Back similar to #147.

	VG	VF	UNC
a. 1975.	.50	1.50	5.00
b. 1976.	5.00	20.00	50.00
s. As a. Specimen.	—	—	22.50

150 10 PESOS
1975-76. Red on m/c unpt. Gen. B. O'Higgins at r. and as wmk. Back similar to #148.

	VG	VF	UNC
a. *B. O'HIGGINS* under portr. 1975.	.75	.75	6.50
b. *LIBERTADOR B. O'HIGGINS* under portr. 1975; 1976.	.50	1.00	4.00
s. As a. Specimen.	—	—	22.50

151 50 PESOS
1975-81. Purple and green on aqua and m/c unpt. Portr. Capt. A. Prat at r. Sailing ships at ctr. on back. 4 sign. varieties.

	VG	VF	UNC
a. 1975-78.	.20	.50	2.00
b. 1980; 1981.	.15	.25	1.00
s. Specimen. 1975.	—	—	15.00

152 100 PESOS
1976-84. Purple and m/c unpt. Portales at r. 1837 meeting at l. ctr. on back. 6 sign. varieties.

	VG	VF	UNC
a. Normal serial #. 1976.	.35	1.50	7.50
b. Electronic sorting serial #. 1976-84.	.30	.50	2.50
s. Specimen. 1976.	—	—	25.00

153 500 PESOS
1977-. Dk. brown and brown-violet w/black text on m/c unpt. P. de Valdivia at r. Wmk: Carrera. Founding of Santiago at ctr. on back.

	VG	VF	UNC
a. 1977; 1978.	FV	1.50	6.00
b. 1980-82; 1985-90.	FV	FV	3.50
c. Sign. titles: *PRESIDENTE* and *GERENTE GENERAL INTERINO.* 1991.	FV	2.00	6.00
d. 1991-93.	FV	FV	3.00
e. 1994-98.	FV	FV	2.75
s. Specimen. 1977.	—	—	25.00

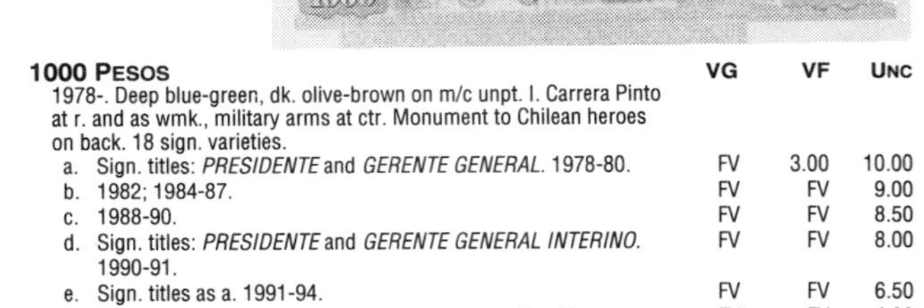

154 1000 PESOS
1978-. Deep blue-green, dk. olive-brown on m/c unpt. I. Carrera Pinto at r. and as wmk., military arms at ctr. Monument to Chilean heroes on back. 18 sign. varieties.

	VG	VF	UNC
a. Sign. titles: *PRESIDENTE* and *GERENTE GENERAL.* 1978-80.	FV	3.00	10.00
b. 1982; 1984-87.	FV	FV	9.00
c. 1988-90.	FV	FV	8.50
d. Sign. titles: *PRESIDENTE* and *GERENTE GENERAL INTERINO.* 1990-91.	FV	FV	8.00
e. Sign. titles as a. 1991-94.	FV	FV	6.50
f. Designers names omitted from lower l. and r. 1995-98.	FV	FV	4.00
s. Specimen.	—	—	50.00

155 5000 PESOS
1981-. Brown and red-violet on m/c unpt. Allegorical woman w/musical instrument, seated male at ctr. Statue of woman w/children at l. ctr., G. Mistral at r. on back and as wmk.

	VG	VF	UNC
a. Sign. titles: *PRESIDENTE* and *GERENTE GENERAL.* 1981. Plain security thread.	FV	FV	55.00
b. 1986-90.	FV	FV	45.00
c. Sign. titles: *PRESIDENTE* and *GERENTE GENERAL INTERINO.* 1991.	FV	FV	30.00
d. Sign. titles: *PRESIDENTE* and *GERENTE GENERAL.* 1992-93.	FV	FV	22.50
e. As d but w/segmented foil security thread. 1994-98.	FV	FV	18.50
s. Specimen. 1981.	—	—	100.00

		VG	VF	UNC
156	**10,000 PESOS** 1989-94. Dk. blue and dk. olive-green on m/c unpt. Capt. A. Prat at r. and as wmk. Statue of Liberty at l., Hacienda San Agustin de Punual Cuna at l. ctr. on back. 5 sign. varieties.			
	a. Plain security thread. 1989-91.	FV	FV	55.00
	b. As a. 1992-94.	FV	FV	45.00
	c. Segmented foil over security thread. 1994.	FV	FV	42.50
	s. Specimen.	—	—	100.00

1994 ISSUE

		VG	VF	UNC
157 (156)	**10,000 PESOS** 1994; 1995; 1997. Dk. blue and deep olive-green on m/c unpt. Like #156b. Printer: TDLR (w/o imprint).	FV	FV	40.00

1997 ISSUE

		VG	VF	UNC
158	**2000 PESOS** 1997. Violet, purple and dk. brown on m/c unpt. M. Rodríguez E. at r. and as wmk., statue of M. Rodríguez on horseback at ctr. Iglesia de los Dominicos at ctr. on back. Printer: CdM-C.	FV	FV	11.00

1998 ISSUE

		VG	VF	UNC
159	**20,000 PESOS** 1998. Don A. Bello at l. University bldg. on back.	FV	FV	11.00

CHINA

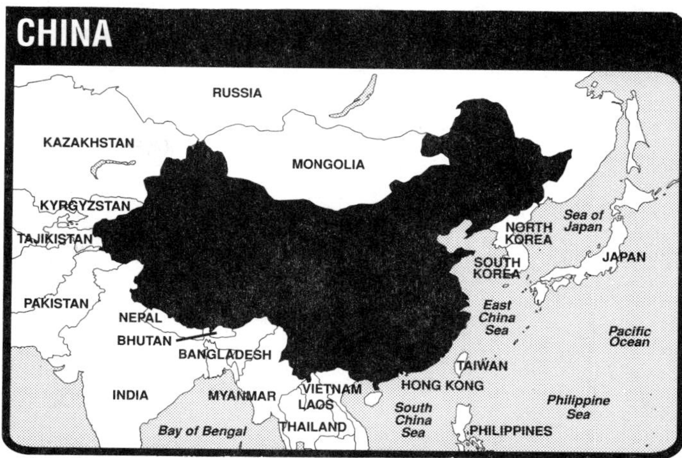

The Peoples Republic of China, located in eastern Asia, has an area of 3,696,100 sq. mi. (9,572,900 sq. km.), including Manchuria and Tibet, and a population of 1.224 billion. Capital: Beijing (Peking). The economy is based on agriculture, mining and manufacturing. Textiles, clothing, metal ores, tea and rice are exported.

In the fall of 1911, the middle business class of China and Chinese students educated in Western universities started a general uprising against the Manchu dynasty which forced the abdication on Feb. 12, 1912, of the boy emperor Hsuan T'ung (Pu-yi), thus bringing to an end the dynasty that had ruled China since 1644. Five days later, China formally became a republic with physician and revolutionist Sun Yat-sen as first provisional president.

Dr. Sun and his supporters founded a new party called the Kuomintang, and planned a Chinese republic based upon the Three Principles of Nationalism, Democracy and People's Livelihood. They failed, however, to win control over all of China, and Dr. Sun resigned the presidency in favor of Yuan Shih Kai, the most powerful of the Chinese Army generals. Yuan ignored the constitution of the new republic and tried to make himself emperor.

After the death of Yuan in 1917, Sun Yat-sen and the Kuomintang established a republic in Canton. It failed to achieve the unification of China, and in 1923 Dr. Sun entered into an agreement with the Soviet Union known as the Canton-Moscow Entente. The Kuomintang agreed to admit Chinese communists to the party. The Soviet Union agreed to furnish military advisers to train the army of the Canton Republic. Dr. Sun died in 1925 and was succeeded by one of his supporters, General Chiang Kai-shek.

Chiang Kai-shek launched a vigorous campaign to educate the Chinese and modernize their industries and agriculture. Under his command, the armies of the Kuomintang captured Nanking (1927) and Peking (1928). In 1928, Chiang was made president of the Chinese Republic. His government was recognized by most of the great powers, but he soon began to exercise dictatorial powers. Prodded by the conservative members of the Kuomintang, he initiated a break between these members and the Chinese Communists which, once again, prevented the unification of China.

Persuaded that China would fare better under the leadership of its businessmen in alliance with the capitalist countries than under the guidance of the Chinese Communists in alliance with the Soviet Union, Chiang expelled all Communists from the Kuomintang, sent the Russian advisers home, and hired German generals to train his army.

The Communists responded by setting up a government and raising an army that during the period of 1930-34 acquired control over large parts of Kiangsi, Fukien, Hunan, Hupeh and other provinces.

When his army was sufficiently trained and equipped, Chiang Kai-shek led several military expeditions against the Communist Chinese which, while unable to subdue them, dislodged them south of the Yangtze, forcing them to undertake in 1935 a celebrated "Long March" of 6,000 miles (9,654 km.) from Hunan northwest to a refuge in Shensi province just south of Inner Mongolia from which Chiang was unable to displace them.

The Japanese had now assumed warlike proportions. Chiang rejected a Japanese offer of cooperation against the Communists, but agreed to suppress the movement himself. His generals, however, persuaded him to negotiate a truce with the Communists to permit united action against the greater of Japanese aggression. Under the terms of the truce, Communists were again admitted to the Kuomintang. They, in turn, promised to dissolve the Soviet Republic of China and to cease issuing their own currency.

The war with Japan all but extinguished the appeal of the Kuomintang, appreciably increased the power of the Communists, and divided China into three parts. The east coast and its principal cities - Peking, Tientsin, Nanking, Shanghai and Canton - were in Japanese-controlled, puppet-ruled states. The Communists controlled the countryside in the north where they were the de facto rulers of 100 million peasants. Chiang and the Kuomintang were driven toward the west, from where they returned with their prestige seriously damaged by their wartime performance.

At the end of World War II, the United States tried to bring the Chinese factions together in a coalition government. American mediation failed, and within weeks the civil war resumed.

By the fall of 1947, most of northeast China was under Communist control. During the following year, the war turned wholly in favor of the Communists. The Kuomintang armies in the northeast surrendered, two provincial capitals in the north were captured, a large Kuomintang army in the Huai river basin surrendered. Four Communist armies converged upon the demoralized Kuomintang forces. The Communists crossed the Yangtse in April 1949. Nanking, the Nationalist capital, fell. The civil war on the mainland was virtually over.

Chiang Kai-shek relinquished the presidency to Li Tsung-jen, his deputy, and after moving to Canton, to Chungking and Chengtu, retreated from the mainland to Taiwan (Formosa) where he resumed the presidency.

The Communist Peoples Republic of China was proclaimed on September 21, 1949. Thereafter relations between the Peoples Republic and the Soviet Union steadily deteriorated. China emerged as an independent center of Communist power in 1958.

MONETARY SYSTEM:

1 Yüan = 10 Chiao
1 Chiao = 10 Fen

MONETARY UNITS	
Yuan	圓 *or* 圜
Pan Yuan	圓 半
5 Jiao	角伍
1 Jiao	角壹
1 Fen	分壹

NUMERICAL CHARACTERS

No.	CONVENTIONAL			FORMAL	
1	一	正	元	壹	弌
2	二			弍	貳
3	三			弎	叁
4	四			肆	
5	五			伍	
6	六			陸	
7	七			柒	
8	八			捌	
9	九			玖	
10	十			拾	什
20	十 二	廿		拾貳	念
25	五 十 二	五廿		伍拾貳	
30	十 三	卅		拾叁	
100	百 一			佰壹	
1,000	千 一			仟壹	
10,000	萬 一			萬壹	
100,000	萬 十	億 一		萬拾	億壹
1,000,000	萬百一			萬佰壹	

PEOPLES BANK OF CHINA

行銀民人國中
Chung Kuo Jen Min Yin Hang
中國人民銀行
Zhong Guo Ren Min Yin Hang

1962; 1965 ISSUE

#877-879 arms at r. on back.

		VG	VF	UNC
877	**1 JIAO** 1962. Brown on m/c unpt. Workers at l.			
	a. Back brown on green and lt. orange unpt. W/o wmk.	4.00	17.50	50.00
	b. Serial # prefix: 3 blue Roman numerals. Back: Brown w/o wmk.	.05	.20	.50
	c. As b, serial # prefix: 3 blue Roman numerals. Wmk: Stars.	.05	.15	.40
	d. Like c, serial # prefix: 2 blue Roman numerals.	.10	.30	1.00
	e. Like b, partially engraved. Serial # prefix: 3 red Roman numerals. Wmk: Stars.	.05	.15	.40
	f. Lithographed, serial # prefix: 2 red Roman numerals. W/o wmk.	.05	.15	.40
	g. Like c. Serial # prefix: 2 red Roman numerals. W/o wmk.	.05	.10	.30

		VG	VF	UNC
878	**2 JIAO** 1962. Green. Bridge over Yangtze River at l.			
	a. Engraved face. Serial # prefix: 3 Roman numerals.	.20	1.00	3.00
	b. Lithographed face. Serial # prefix: 3 Roman numerals.	.05	.20	.50
	c. As b. Serial # prefix: 2 Roman numerals.	.05	.10	.30
	x. As b. Red back.	.20	1.00	3.00

		VG	VF	UNC
879	**10 YÜAN** 1965. Black on m/c unpt. Representatives of the National Assembly at ctr. Wmk: Great Hall w/rays.			
	a. Serial # prefix: 3 Roman numerals.	FV	2.00	5.50
	b. Serial # prefix: 2 Roman numerals.	FV	1.75	3.50

1972 ISSUE

		VG	VF	UNC
880	**5 JIAO** 1972. Purple and m/c. Women working in textile factory. Arms at r. on back.			
	a. Engraved bank title and denomination. Serial # prefix: 3 Roman numerals. Wmk: Stars.	FV	.75	2.00
	b. As a. but lithographed face. W/wmk.	FV	.80	1.50
	c. Lithographed face. W/o wmk.	FV	.20	.50

1980 ISSUE

#881-888 illustrate 14 persons of various minorities.

#881-883 arms at ctr. on back.

		VG	VF	UNC
881	**1 JIAO** 1980. Brown and dk. brown on m/c unpt. 2 Taiwanese men at l.	FV	FV	.15

		VG	VF	UNC
882	**2 JIAO** 1980. Grayish olive-green on m/c unpt. Native *Pu Yi* and Korean youth at l.	FV	FV	.15

		VG	VF	UNC
883	**5 JIAO** 1980. Purple and red-violet on m/c unpt. *Miao* and *Zhuang* children at l. Back: brown-violet on m/c unpt.	FV	FV	.25

#884-889 arms at upper l., stylized birds in unpt. at ctr., dot patterns for poor of sight at lower l. or r.

		VG	VF	UNC
884	**1 YÜAN** 1980. Brown-violet on m/c unpt. *Dong* and *Yao* youths at r. Great Wall at ctr. on back.			
	a. Engraved. Dk. blue serial #. Wmk: Ancient *Pu* (pants) coin repeated. 1980.	FV	FV	.50
	b. Partially engraved. Wmk. as a. Black serial #. 1990.	FV	FV	.30
	c. Litho. Wmk: Stars. Black serial #. 1996.	FV	FV	.20

		VG	VF	UNC
885	**2 YÜAN** 1980; 1990. Dk. olive-green on m/c unpt. *Hyger* and *Ye Yien* youths at r. Rocky shoreline of South Sea on back. Wmk: Ancient *Pu* (pants) coin repeated.			
	a. Engraved back. 1980.	FV	FV	.70
	b. Litho. back. 1990.	FV	FV	.35

		VG	VF	UNC
886	**5 YÜAN** 1980. Dk. brown on m/c unpt. Old Tibetan man and young Islamic woman at r. Yangtze Gorges on back. Wmk: Ancient *Pu* (pants) coin repeated.	FV	FV	1.50

		VG	VF	UNC
887	**10 YÜAN** 1980. Black on blue and m/c unpt. Elder Han and youthful Mongolian man at r. Mountains on back. Wmk: Young Mongolian man.	FV	FV	2.50

		VG	VF	UNC
888	**50 YÜAN** 1980; 1990. Black on lt. green and m/c unpt. Intellectual, farm girl and industrial male worker at ctr. Waterfalls of Yellow River on back. Wmk: Industrial male worker.			
	a. 1980.	FV	FV	12.50
	b. Security thread at r. 1990.	FV	FV	9.00

		VG	VF	UNC
889	**100 YÜAN** 1980; 1990. Black on m/c unpt. 4 great leaders at ctr. Mountains at Ding Gang Sha (starting point of the "Long March") on back. Wmk: Bust of Mao Tse-tung.			
	a. 1980.	FV	FV	23.00
	b. Security thread at r. 1990.	FV	FV	15.00
890	**500 YÜAN** 1990. *(S/M #C284-51).*	—	—	—

NOTE: #890 used in inter-bank transfers only.

1999 COMMEMORATIVE ISSUE

50th Anniversary of Revolution

		VG	VF	UNC
891	**50 YÜAN** 1999. Red on m/c unpt. Mao Tse-tung delivering speech. 5 birds in flight, carvings to l. and r. on back.	FV	FV	10.00

1999 REGULAR ISSUE

		VG	VF	UNC
892	**1 JIAO** 1999.	Expected New Issue		
893	**2 JIAO** 1999.	Expected New Issue		
894	**5 JIAO** 1999.	Expected New Issue		
895	**1 YÜAN** 1999.	Expected New Issue		
896	**2 YÜAN** 1999.	Expected New Issue		
897	**5 YÜAN** 1999.	Expected New Issue		
898	**10 YÜAN** 1999.	Expected New Issue		
899 (892)	**50 YÜAN** 1999.	Expected New Issue		

		VG	VF	UNC
900 (893)	**100 YÜAN** 1999. Mao Tse-tung at r. Hall of the People on back.	FV	FV	20.00

FOREIGN EXCHANGE CERTIFICATES

BANK OF CHINA

This series has been discontinued.

中國銀行
Chung Kuo Yin Hang

1979 ISSUE

FX1 **10 FEN** — VG VF UNC

1979. Brown on m/c unpt. waterfalls at ctr. *(S/M #C294-301).*

	VG	VF	UNC
a. Wmk: 1 lg. and 4 sm. stars.	.05	.30	.75
b. Wmk: Star and torch.	.20	1.25	3.50

#FX2-FX4 wmk: Star and Torch.

		VG	VF	UNC
FX2	**50 FEN** 1979. Purple on m/c unpt. Temple of Heaven at l. ctr. *(S/M #C294-302).*	.10	.65	1.75
FX3	**1 YÜAN** 1979. Deep green on m/c unpt. Pleasure boats in lake w/mountains behind at ctr. *(S/M #C294-303).*	.20	1.00	2.50
FX4	**5 YÜAN** 1979. Deep brown on m/c unpt. Mountain scenery at ctr. *(S/M #C294-304).*	.50	2.50	8.00

		VG	VF	UNC
FX5	**10 YÜAN** 1979. Deep blue on m/c/ unpt. Yangtze Gorges at ctr. *(S/M #C294-305).*	.75	4.00	10.00

#FX6-FX9 wmk: National badge.

		VG	VF	UNC
FX6	**50 YÜAN** 1979. Purple and red on m/c unpt. Mountain lake at Kweilin at ctr. *(S/M #C294-306).*	7.50	32.50	100.00

		VG	VF	UNC
FX7	**100 YÜAN** 1979. Black and blue on m/c unpt. Great Wall at ctr. *(S/M #C294-307).*	7.50	40.00	130.00

1988 ISSUE

		VG	VF	UNC
FX8	**50 YÜAN** 1988. Black, orange-brown and green on m/c unpt. Shoreline rock formations at ctr. *(S/M #C294-308).*	3.00	12.50	50.00
FX9	**100 YÜAN** 1988. Olive-green on m/c unpt. Great Wall at ctr. *(S/M #C294-309).*	4.00	15.00	65.00

MILITARY

MILITARY PAYMENT CERTIFICATES

軍用代金券

Chün Yung Tai Chin Ch'üan

1965 ISSUE

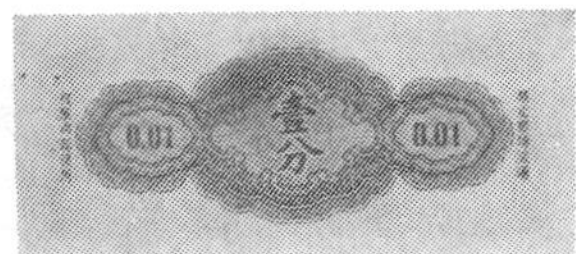

		VG	VF	UNC
M41	**1 FEN** 1965. Greenish brown. Airplane at l. ctr.	1.00	5.00	30.00

		VG	VF	UNC
M42	**5 FEN** 1965. Red. Airplane at ctr.	2.00	15.00	50.00

		VG	VF	UNC
M43	**1 CHIAO** 1965. Purple. Steam passenger train at ctr. r.	3.00	20.00	100.00

#M44 NOT ASSIGNED.

		VG	VF	UNC
M45	**1 YÜAN** 1965. Green. Truck convoy at l.	8.00	40.00	175.00
M46	**5 YÜAN** 1965. Truck convoy at l.	17.50	85.00	300.00

CHINESE ADMINISTRATION OF TAIWAN

The Republic of China, comprising Taiwan (an island located 90 miles off the southeastern coast of mainland China), the islands of Quemoy and Matsu and nearby islets of the Pescadores chain, has an area of 14,000 sq. mi. (35,981 sq. km.). and a population of 20.2 million. Capital: Taipei. In recent years, manufacturing has replaced agriculture in importance. Fruits, vegetables, plywood, textile yarns, fabrics and clothing are exported.

Chinese migration to Taiwan began as early as the sixth century. The Dutch established a base on the island in 1624 and held it until 1661, when they were driven out by supporters of the Ming dynasty who used it as a stage for their unsuccessful attempt to displace the ruling Manchu dynasty on the mainland. Manchu forces occupied the island in 1683 and remained under the suzerainty of China until its cession to Japan in 1895. Following World War II Taiwan was returned to China, and on December 8, 1949 it became the last remnant of Dr. Sun Yat-sen's Republic of China when Chiang Kai-shek moved his army and government from the mainland to the islands following his defeat by the Communist forces of Mao Tse-tung.

BANK OF TAIWAN

行銀灣臺

T'ai Wan Yin Hang

PORTRAIT ABBREVIATIONS

SYS = Dr. Sun Yat-sen, 1867-1925 President of Canton Government, 1917-25

CKS = Chiang Kai-shek, 1886-1975 President in Nanking, 1927-31 Head of Formosa Government, Taiwan, 1949-1975

NOTE: Because of the frequency of the above appearing in the following listings, their initials are used only in reference to their portraits.

NOTE: S/M # reference to *CHINESE BANKNOTES* by Ward D. Smith and Brian Matravers.

PRINTERS 1946-

CPF: (Central Printing Factory) 廠製印央中

CPFT: (Central Printing Factory, Taipei) 廠北台廠製印央中

FPFT: (First Printing Factory) 廠刷印一第

PFBT: (Printing Factory of Taiwan Bank) 所刷印行銀灣臺

1961 ISSUE

#971-975 portr. SYS at l. Printer: CPF.

		VG	VF	UNC
1971 (971)	**1 YÜAN** 1961. Dk. blue-green and purple on m/c unpt. Steep coastline at r. Printer: PFBT.			
	a. Engraved. *(S/M #T73-60).*	.20	.75	3.50
	b. Lithographed. (1972). *(S/M #T73-60).*	.10	1.50	2.50

		VG	VF	UNC
1972	**5 YÜAN** 1961. Red on m/c unpt. House w/tower at r. *(S/M #T73-61).*	.20	.75	3.00

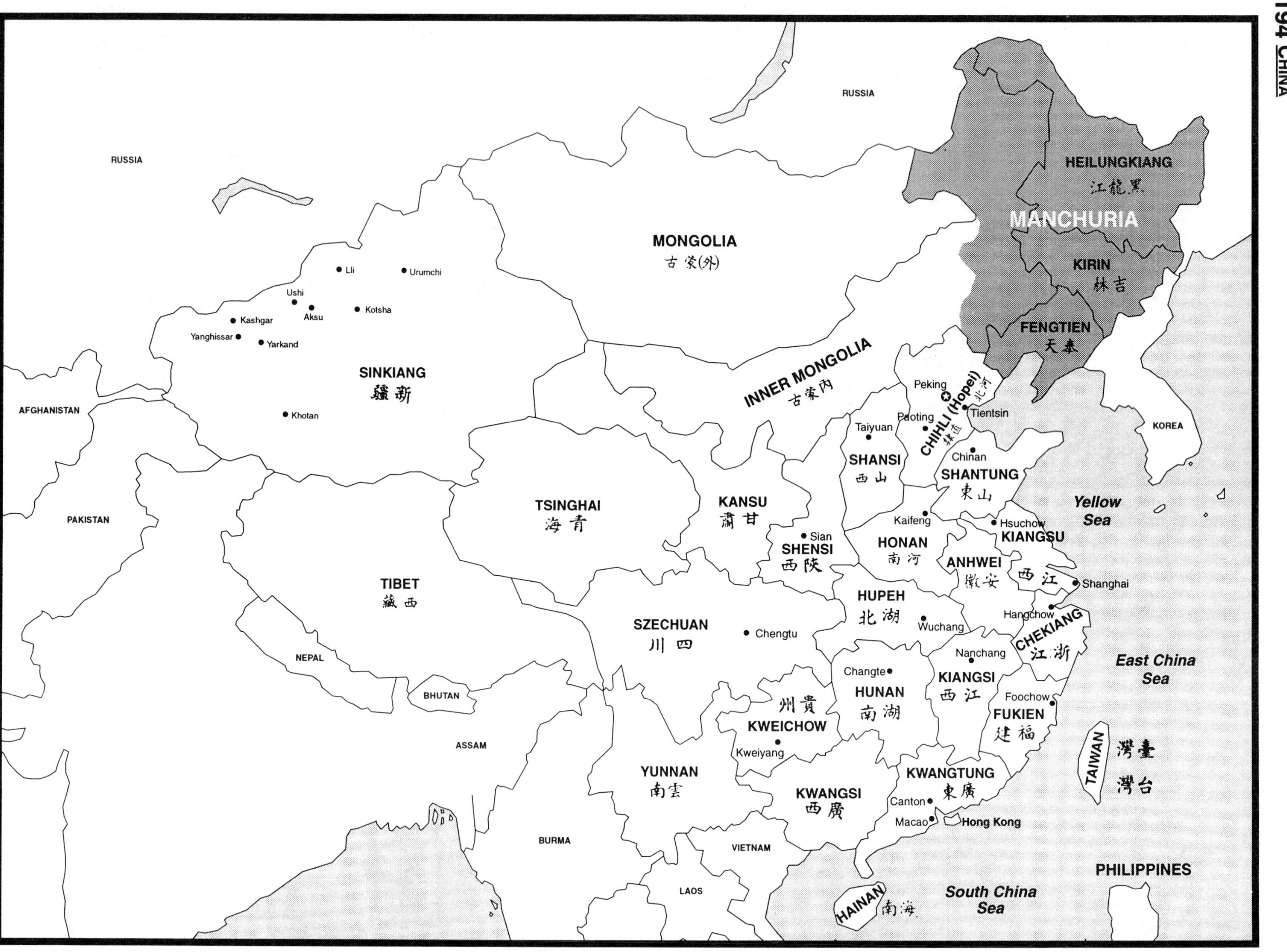
RUSSIA
RUSSIA
MONGOLIA
HEILUNGKIANG
MANCHURIA
KIRIN
FENGTIEN
Lli
Urumchi
Ushi
Kashgar
Aksu
Kotsha
Yanghissar
Yarkand
SINKIANG
Khotan
AFGHANISTAN
INNER MONGOLIA
Peking
CHIHLI (Hopei)
Tientsin
Paoting
Taiyuan
KOREA
Chinan
SHANSI
SHANTUNG
PAKISTAN
TSINGHAI
KANSU
Yellow Sea
Kaifeng
Hsuchow
Sian
KIANGSU
SHENSI
HONAN
ANHWEI
TIBET
Shanghai
HUPEH
Hangchow
SZECHUAN
Chengtu
Wuchang
CHEKIANG
NEPAL
Nanchang
East China Sea
Changte
KIANGSI
BHUTAN
HUNAN
Foochow
FUKIEN
KWEICHOW
ASSAM
Kweiyang
TAIWAN
YUNNAN
KWANGTUNG
KWANGSI
Canton
Macao
Hong Kong
BURMA
VIETNAM
PHILIPPINES
LAOS
South China Sea
HAINAN

		VG	VF	UNC
1973 (973)	**5 YÜAN** 1961. Brown on m/c unpt. Similar to #972. *S/M #T73-62).*	.25	1.00	5.50
1974 (974)	**50 YÜAN** 1961. Violet on m/c unpt. *(S/M #T73-63).*	FV	2.50	12.00
1975 (975)	**100 YÜAN** 1961. Green on m/c unpt. SYS at l. *(S/M #T73-64).*	FV	3.00	15.00

1964 ISSUE

#976 and 977 portr. SYS at l. Printer: CPF.

		VG	VF	UNC
1976 (976)	**50 YÜAN** 1964. Violet on m/c unpt. Similar to #974. *(S/M #T73-70).*	FV	2.00	10.00

		VG	VF	UNC
1977 (977)	**100 YÜAN** 1964. Green on m/c unpt. Similar to #975. *(S/M #T73-71).*	FV	3.00	12.00

REPUBLIC OF CHINA-TAIWAN BANK

中華民國臺灣銀行

Chung Hua Min Kuo-T'ai Wan Yin Hang

1969 ISSUE

		VG	VF	UNC
1978 (978)	**5 YÜAN** 1969. Blue on m/c unpt. *(S/M #T73-72).*	.15	.35	1.50

		VG	VF	UNC
1979 (979)	**10 YÜAN** 1969. Red on m/c unpt. Similar to #978. *(S/M #T73-73).*			
	a. W/o plate letter.	.20	.50	2.00
	b. Plate letter A at lower r. on face.	.15	.35	1.50

1970 ISSUE

#980-983 SYS at l. Printer: CPF.

		VG	VF	UNC
1980 (980)	**50 YÜAN** 1970. Violet on m/c unpt. *(S/M #T73-75).*	FV	2.25	6.00
1981 (981)	**100 YÜAN** 1970. Green on m/c unpt. *(S/M #T73-).*	FV	4.50	10.00

1972 ISSUE

		VG	VF	UNC
1982 (982)	**50 YÜAN** 1972. Violet, purple and lt. blue on m/c unpt. Chungshan bldg. on back. Wide margin w/guilloche at r. *(S/M #T73-76).*	FV	2.00	5.50

		VG	VF	UNC
1983 (983)	**100 YÜAN** 1972. Dk. green, lt. green and orange on m/c unpt. Palace on back. *(S/M #T73-77).*	FV	4.00	9.00

1976 ISSUE

#984-986 printer: CPF.

		VG	VF	UNC
1984 (984)	**10 YÜAN** 1976. Red on m/c unpt. SYS at l. Bank on back. *(S/M #T73-78).*	FV	.50	1.50

		VG	VF	UNC
1985 (985)	**500 YÜAN** 1976. Olive, purple and m/c. CKS at l. Chungshan bldg. on back. W/o wmk. at r. *(S/M #T73-79).*	FV	20.00	40.00

		VG	VF	UNC
1986 (986)	**1000 YÜAN** 1976. Blue-black, olive-brown and violet on m/c. unpt. CKS at l. Presidential Office bldg. on back. W/o wmk. at r. *(S/M #T73-80).*	FV	40.00	70.00

1981 ISSUE

#987 and 988 CKS at l. Printer: CPF.

		VG	VF	UNC
1987 (987)	**500 YÜAN** 1981. Brown and red-brown on m/c unpt. Similar to #985 but wmk. of CKS at r. *(S/M #T73-81).*	FV	FV	35.00

		VG	VF	UNC
1988 (988)	**1000 YÜAN** 1981. Blue-black on m/c unpt. Similar to #986 but wmk: CKS at r. *(S/M #T73-82).*	FV	FV	60.00

1987 ISSUE

		VG	VF	UNC
1989 (989)	**100 YÜAN** 1987 (1988). Red, red-brown and brown-violet on m/c unpt. SYS at l. and as wmk. Chungshan bldg. on back. *(S/M #T73-83).*	FV	FV	8.00

1999 COMMEMORATIVE ISSUE

#1990 50th Anniversary of Taiwan. Polymer plastic.

		VG	VF	UNC
1990 (990)	**50 YÜAN** 1999 Red on m/c unpt. Currency and high-speed train at l. Bank bldg. on back.	FV	FV	3.50

1999 ISSUE

		VG	VF	UNC
1991 (991)	**100 YÜAN** 1999.	Expected New Issue		
1992 (992)	**500 YÜAN** 1999.	Expected New Issue		
1993 (993)	**1000 YÜAN** 1999.	Expected New Issue		
1994 (994)	**2000 YÜAN** 1999.	Expected New Issue		

OFF-SHORE ISLAND CURRENCY

BANK OF TAIWAN

行銀灣臺

T'ai Wan Yin Hang

KINMEN (QUEMOY) BRANCH

Notes of the Bank of Taiwan and later notes of the Republic of China/Bank of Taiwan w/ovpt: 門金

用通門金限

Hsien Chin Men T'ung Yung

1949-51 (1963; 1967) ISSUE

#R101-R109 portr. SYS at upper ctr. Vertical format.

		VG	VF	UNC
R101 (R1001)	**1 YÜAN** 1949 (1963). Green on m/c unpt. Printer: CPF. *(S/M #T74-1).*	.25	1.25	6.00

1950-51 ISSUES

		VG	VF	UNC
R106 (R1006)	**10 YÜAN** 1950 (1963). Blue. Printer: CPF. *(S/M #T74-20).*	.50	1.50	7.50

		VG	VF	UNC
R107 (R1007)	**50 YÜAN** 1951 (1967). Green. Printer: FPFT. *(S/M #T74-30).*	3.00	10.00	55.00

1966-72 ISSUE

	VG	VF	UNC
R109 5 YÜAN (R1009) 1966. Violet-brown. Printer: CPF. *(S/M #T74-50).*	.75	3.00	15.00

	VG	VF	UNC
R110 10 YÜAN (R1010) 1969 (1975). Red on m/c unpt. Red ovpt. on #979a. *(S/M #T74-60).*	1.35	2.00	6.00

	VG	VF	UNC
R111 50 YÜAN (R1011) 1969 (1970). Dk. blue on m/c m/c unpt. SYS at r. *(S/M #T74-61).*	2.00	3.50	15.00

	VG	VF	UNC
R112 100 YÜAN (R1012) 1972 (1975). Green ovpt. on #983. *(S/M #T74-70).*	4.00	7.50	25.00

1976; 1981 ISSUE

	VG	VF	UNC
R112A 10 YÜAN (R1012A) 1976. Ovpt. on #984. *(S/M #T74-).*	.40	.75	5.00
R112B 100 YÜAN (R1012B) 1981. Ovpt. on #988. *(S/M #T74-).*	5.00	8.00	25.00
R112C 1000 YÜAN (R1012C) 1981. Ovpt. on #988. *(S/M #T74-).*	35.00	50.00	100.00

MATSU BRANCH

Notes of the Bank of Taiwan and later notes of the Republic of China/Bank of Taiwan w/ovpt:

1950-51 DATED (1964; 1967) ISSUE

#R117 and 118 portr. SYS at upper ctr. Vertical format.

	VG	VF	UNC
R117 10 YÜAN (R1017) 1950 (1964). Blue on m/c unpt. Printer: CPF. *(S/M #T75-2).*	1.00	3.00	17.50

	VG	VF	UNC
R118 50 YÜAN (R1018) 1951 (1967). Green on m/c unpt. Printer: FPFT. *(S/M #T75-10).*	3.00	8.00	35.00

1969; 1972 ISSUE

	VG	VF	UNC
R122 10 YÜAN (R1022) 1969 (1975). Red on m/c unpt. Ovpt. on #979a. Printer: CPF. *(S/M #T75-40).*	.50	1.00	6.00

	VG	VF	UNC
R123 50 YÜAN (R1023) 1969 (1970). Violet on m/c unpt. Printer: CPF. *(S/M #T75-45).*	2.00	4.00	22.50
R124 100 YÜAN (R1024) 1972 (1975). Dk. green, lt. green and orange on m/c unpt. Green ovpt. on #983. Printer: CPF. *(S/M #T75-50).*	4.00	10.00	40.00

1976; 1981 ISSUE

	VG	VF	UNC
R125 10 YÜAN (R1025) 1976. Red on m/c unpt. Ovpt. on #984. *(S/M #T75-55).*	.40	1.00	5.00
R126 500 YÜAN (R1026) 1981. Brown and red-brown on m/c unpt. Ovpt. on #987. *(S/M #T75-60).*	FV	20.00	50.00
R127 1000 YÜAN (R1027) 1981. Blue-black on m/c unpt. Ovpt. on #988. *(S/M #T75-61).*	FV	37.50	100.00

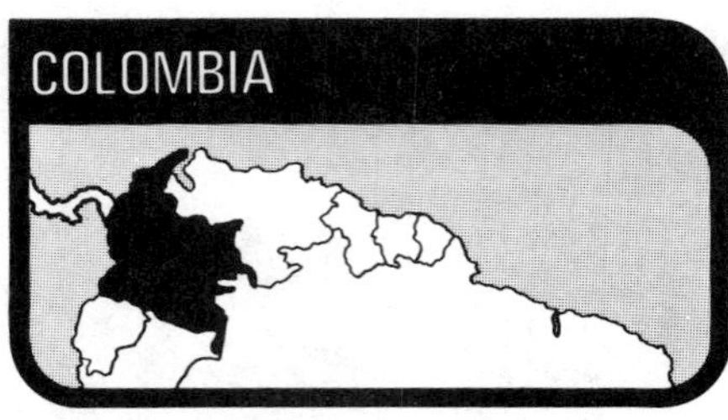

The Republic of Colombia, located in the northwestern corner of South America, has an area of 439,737 sq. mi. (1,138,914 sq. km.) and a population of 33.4 million. Capital: Bogotá. The economy is primarily agricultural with a mild, rich coffee the chief crop. Colombia has the world's largest platinum deposits and important reserves of coal, iron ore, petroleum and limestone; precious metals and emeralds are also mined. Coffee, crude oil, bananas, sugar, coal and flowers are exported.

The northern coast of present Colombia was one of the first parts of the American continent to be visited by Spanish navigators, and the site, at Darien in Panama, of the first permanent European settlement on the American mainland in 1510. New Granada, as Colombia was known until 1861, stemmed from the settlement of Santa Maria in 1525. New Granada was established as a Spanish Colony in 1549. Independence was declared in 1810, and secured in 1824. In 1819, Simón Bolívar united Colombia, Venezuela, Panama and Ecuador as the Republic of Greater Colombia. Venezuela withdrew from the Republic in 1829; Ecuador in 1830; and Panama in 1903.

MONETARY SYSTEM:

1 Peso = 100 Centavos

REPLACEMENT NOTES:

Earlier issues, small *R* just below and between signatures. Larger *R* used later. Some TDLR printings have *R* preceding serial number. Later Colombian-printed notes use circled asterisk usually close to sign. or a star at r. of upper serial #. Known replacements: #389-407, 409, 413-15, 417-19, 421-22, 425-29, 431-433, 436-41, 443, 445-48.

REPUBLIC

BANCO DE LA REPÚBLICA

1940 *CERTIFICADOS DE ORO* (GOLD CERTIFICATES) ISSUE

		VG	VF	UNC
389	**10 PESOS ORO** 1940-54. Portr. Gen. A. Nariño at lower r. w/o title: *CAJERO* and sign. on back.			
	a. Series R in red. 20.7.1940.	4.00	20.00	100.00
	b. As a. 20.7.1942; 20.7.1943.	1.00	5.00	30.00
	c. Series *R* in blue. 20.7.1944; 20.7.1946; 7.8.1947.	1.50	8.00	40.00
	d. As c. 1.1.1945.	3.00	16.00	80.00
	e. 12.10.1949.	.25	2.00	25.00
	f. Series HH. 1.1.1950.	.25	2.00	22.50
	g. 1.1.1954.	.20	1.50	20.00
	p1. Faceproof. As a. W/o series. 20.7.1943.	—	—	100.00
	p2. Faceproof. As e. Punched hole cancelled.	—	—	100.00
	p3. Faceproof. As f. Punched hole cancelled.	—	—	100.00
	s. As b. 7.8.1947. Specimen. Ovpt. *SPECIMEN* and punched hole cancelled.	—	—	150.00

1943 ISSUE

#392 printer: ABNC.

		VG	VF	UNC
392 (395)	**20 PESOS ORO** 1943-63. Purple and m/c. Bust of Caldas at l., bust of S. Bolívar at r. Liberty at ctr. on back.			
	a. Series U in red. 20.7.1943.	20.00	200.00	500.00
	b. Series U in purple. 20.7.1944; 1.1.1945.	10.00	40.00	200.00
	c. Series U. Prefix A. 7.8.1947.	1.00	4.00	40.00
	d. Series DD. 1.1.1950; 1.1.1951.	50.00	2.00	20.00
	e. Series DD. 2.1.1963.	.50	2.00	20.00

1953 ISSUE

#399-401 printer: TDLR.

		VG	VF	UNC
400	**10 PESOS ORO** 1953-61. Blue on m/c unpt. Portr. Gen. A. Nariño w/Mercury alongside at l., trees at r. Bank bldg. at Cali on back. Series N.			
	a. 1.1.1953.	.25	2.00	25.00
	b. 1.1.1958; 1.1.1960.	.25	1.25	20.00
	c. 2.1.1961.	.25	1.00	17.50
	s. As b. 1.1.1960. Specimen. W/red TDLR and *SPECIMEN* ovpt. Punched hole cancelled.	—	—	200.00

		VG	VF	UNC
401	**20 PESOS ORO** 1953-65. Red-brown on m/c unpt. Portr. Caldas and allegory at l. Liberty in frame at r. Newer bank at Barranquilla on back. Series O.			
	a. 1.1.1953.	.25	3.00	20.00
	b. 1.1.1960.	.25	3.50	25.00
	c. 2.1.1961; 2.1.1965.	.20	1.00	15.00
	s. As b. 1.1.1960. Specimen. W/ red TDLR ovpt. and *SPECIMEN*. Punched hole cancelled.	—	—	200.00

1958 ISSUE

#402-403 printer: ABNC.

		VG	VF	UNC
402	**50 PESOS ORO** 1958-67. Lt. brown on m/c unpt. Portr. A. J. de Sucre at lower l. Back olive-green; Liberty at ctr. Series Z.			
	a. 20.7.1958; 7.8.1960.	.50	3.50	22.50
	b. 1.1.1964; 12.10.1967.	.25	2.50	20.00

		VG	VF	UNC
403	**100 PESOS ORO** 1958-67. Gray on m/c unpt. Portr. Gen. F. de Paula Santander at r. Back green; like #402. Series Y.			
	a. 7.8.1958.	.75	3.75	30.00
	b. 1.1.1960; 1.1.1964; 20.7.1965; 20.7.1967.	.50	1.25	10.00
	p1. Face proof. W/o date, signatures, series or serial #. Punched hole cancelled.	—	—	150.00

1959-64 ISSUES

		VG	VF	UNC
404	**1 PESO ORO** 1959-77. Blue on m/c unpt. Portr. S. Bolívar at l., portr. Gen. F. de Paula Santander at r. Liberty head and condor w/waterfall and mountain at ctr. on back.			
	a. Security thread. 12.10.1959.	.25	2.00	6.50
	b. Security thread. 2.1.1961; 7.8.1962; 2.1.1963; 12.10.1963; 2.1.1964; 12.10.1964.	.20	1.50	4.00
	c. As b. 20.7.1966.	.75	2.75	20.00
	d. W/o security thread. 20.7.1966; 20.7.1967; 1.2.1968; 2.1.1969.	.15	1.00	3.00
	e. W/o security thread. 1.5.1970; 12.10.1970; 7.8.1971; 20.7.1972; 7.8.1973; 7.8.1974.	.10	.35	1.25
	f. As e. 1.1.1977.	.75	2.75	17.50

1961-64 ISSUE

Pesos Oro System

#406-407 replacement notes: Serial # prefix *R* or *.

		VG	VF	UNC
406	**5 PESOS ORO** 1961-81. Deep greenish black and deep brown on m/c unpt. Condor at l., Córdoba at r. Fortress at Cartagena at ctr. on back.			
	a. Security thread. 2.1.1961; 1.5.1963; 11.11.1963; 2.1.1964.	1.00	4.00	18.50
	b. Security thread. 11.11.1965; 12.10.1967; 20.7.1968.	.40	2.00	6.50
	c. Security thread. 20.7.1971.	.25	1.00	5.00
	d. As c. 1.1.1973.	7.50	37.50	150.00
	e. W/o security thread. 1.1.1973; 20.7.1974; 20.7.1975; 20.7.1976; 20.7.1977.	.15	.75	1.25
	f. W/o security thread. 1.10.1978; 1.4.1979; 1.1.1980; 1.1.1981.	.10	.50	1.00
	s. Specimen. 1.4.1979.	—	—	—

		VG	VF	UNC
407	**10 PESOS ORO** 1963-80. Lilac and slate blue on green and m/c unpt. Gen. A. Nariño at l., condor at r. Back red-brown and slate blue; archaeological site w/monoliths.			
	a. Security thread. 20.7.1963.	1.00	5.00	25.00
	b. As a. 20.7.1964.	.75	3.75	15.00
	c. 20.7.1965; 20.7.1967; 2.1.1969.	.50	2.50	8.00
	d. W/segmented security thread. As c. 12.10.1970; 1.1.1973.	.30	1.50	6.00
	e. As d. 20.7.1974.	15.00	75.00	300.00
	f. W/o security thread. 20.7.1974; 1.1.1975; 20.7.1976; 1.1.1978.	.10	.50	1.50
	g. As f. 7.8.1979; 7.8.1980.	.05	.35	1.00
	h. Like f., but *SERIE AZ* at l. ctr. and upper r. on face. 7.8.1980.	.10	.50	3.00
	s. As d. Specimen.	—	—	35.00

		VG	VF	UNC
408	**500 PESOS ORO** 20.7.1964. Olive-green on m/c unpt. Portr. S. Bolívar at r. Back has no open space under Liberty head. Printer: ABNC. Series *AA*.			
	a. Issued note.	5.00	17.50	75.00
	s. Specimen. Ovpt. *MUESTRA* and punched hole cancelled.	—	—	200.00

1966-68 ISSUE

#409 replacement note: Serial # prefix *R* or *.

		VG	VF	UNC
409	**20 PESOS ORO** 1966-83. Brown, gray and green on m/c unpt. Caldas w/globe at r. Back brown and green on m/c unpt.; artifacts from the Gold Museum.			
	a. Security thread. 12.10.1966; 2.1.1969; 1.5.1972; 1.5.1973.	.75	3.00	12.50
	b. As a. 20.7.1974.	20.00	100.00	400.00
	c. W/o security thread. 20.7.1974; 20.7.1975; 20.7.1977.	.35	1.00	5.00
	d. As c. 1.4.1979; 1.1.1981; 1.1.1982; 1.1.1983.	.20	.40	1.75
	s. As a.	—	—	35.00

		VG	VF	UNC
410	**100 PESOS ORO** 1968-71. Blue on m/c unpt. Gen F. de Paula Santander at r. Capitol at Bogotá on back. Wmk: Bolívar. Series Y. Printer: TDLR.			
	a. 1.1.1968.	1.25	5.00	20.00
	b. 2.1.1969.	1.00	3.00	15.00
	c. 1.5.1970; 20.7.1971.	.60	1.75	8.50
	s. As a. Specimen. 2.1.1969.	—	—	25.00

		VG	VF	UNC
411	**500 PESOS ORO** 1968-71. Green on m/c unpt. S. Bolívar at r. Subterranean church on back. Wmk: Liberty head. Series A. Printer: ABNC.			
	a. 1.1.1968.	5.00	15.00	40.00
	b. 12.10.1971.	6.00	20.00	50.00
	s. As a. Specimen.	—	—	50.00

1969 ISSUE

		VG	VF	UNC
412	**50 PESOS ORO** 1969-70. Purple on pale blue, lilac and pink unpt. Blue design w/o border at l., Torres at r. and as wmk. Arms and flowers on back. Printer: TDLR.			
	a. 2.1.1969.	.75	3.00	15.00
	b. 12.10.1970.	.25	1.00	5.00
	s. As a. Specimen. Punched hole cancelled.	—	—	75.00

1972-73 ISSUE

#413-415 replacement notes: Serial # prefix *R* or *.

		VG	VF	UNC
413	**2 PESOS ORO** 1972-77. Purple on m/c unpt. P. Salavarietta at l. Back brown; *El Dorado* replica from the Gold Museum.			
	a. Lg. size serial #, and # at r. near upper border. 1.1.1972; 20.7.1972; 1.1.1973.	.15	.75	3.50
	b. Sm. size serial #, and # at r. far from upper border. 20.7.1976; 1.1.1977; 20.7.1977.	.10	.50	2.75
	s. Specimen. 20.7.1976.	—	—	30.00

		VG	VF	UNC
414	**50 PESOS ORO** 20.7.1973; 20.7.1974. Purple on pale blue, lilac and pink unpt. Curved dk. border added at l. and r., also at r. on back. Printer: TDLR.	.50	1.35	7.50

		VG	VF	UNC
415	**100 PESOS ORO** 20.7.1973; 20.7.1974. Similar to #410 but curved dk. border added at l. and r., also at r. on back. Series Y. Printer: TDLR.	.65	2.00	12.50

		VG	VF	UNC
416	**500 PESOS ORO** 7.8.1973. Red on m/c unpt. Like #411. Series A. Printer: ABNC.			
	a. Issued note.	2.00		30.00
	s. Specimen.	—	—	50.00

1974 ISSUE

#417 replacement note: Serial # prefix *R*.

		VG	VF	UNC
417	**200 PESOS ORO** 1974; 1975. Green on m/c unpt. S. Bolívar at ctr. r. and as wmk., church at r. *BOGOTÁ COLOMBIA* at lower l. ctr. Man picking coffee beans on back. Printer: TDLR.			
	a. 20.7.1974.	1.00	5.00	25.00
	b. 7.8.1975.	.50	1.35	7.50

1977-79 ISSUE

#418-420 replacement notes: Serial # prefix *R* or *.

		VG	VF	UNC
418	**100 PESOS ORO** 1977-80. Violet on m/c unpt. Gen F. de Paula Santander at ctr. r. Capitol at Bogotá on back. Wmk: Liberty head. Printer: TDLR.			
	a. 1.1.1977.	.25	1.00	4.00
	b. 1.1.1980.	.20	.75	3.50
	c. Serial # prefix *A-C*. 1.1.1980.	.20	.75	3.25
	s. As a. Specimen.	—	—	—

NOTE: Numerals at upper ctr. and upper r. are darker on 1980 dated notes, also the word *CIEN*.

		VG	VF	UNC
419 (420)	**200 PESOS ORO** 20.7.1978; 1.1.1979; 1.1.1980. Like #417 but w/only *COLOMBIA* at lower l. ctr. Printer: TDLR.	.30	1.25	5.00

		VG	VF	UNC
420 (419)	**500 PESOS ORO** 1977-79. Olive and m/c. Gen. F. de Paula Santander at l. and in profile as wmk. Back gray; subterranean church and Liberty head. Printer: ABNC.			
	a. 20.7.1977.	.65	1.50	12.50
	b. 1.4.1979.	.60	1.25	7.50

		VG	VF	UNC
421	**1000 PESOS ORO** 1.4.1979. Black and m/c. J. A. Galan at r. and as wmk. Nariño Palace on back. Printer: ABNC.			
	a. Issued note.	1.00	3.00	25.00
	s. Specimen.	—	—	40.00

1980-82 ISSUES

#422 replacement note: Serial # prefix *.

		VG	VF	UNC
422	**50 PESOS ORO** 1980-83. Purple on pale blue, lilac and pink unpt. *COLOMBIA* added near border at upper l. ctr. Printer: TDLR (w/o imprint).			
	a. 1.1.1980; 7.8.1981.	FV	.75	2.00
	b. 1.1.1983.	FV	.50	1.50
	s. Specimen. 1.1.1980.	—	—	—

		VG	VF	UNC
423	**500 PESOS ORO** 1981-86. Brown, dk. green and red-brown on m/c unpt. Gen. F. de Paula Santander at l. and in profile as wmk., Bogotá on back; screw coinage press at lower r. Printer: TDLR.			
	a. 20.7.1981.	FV	2.00	15.00
	b. 20.7.1984; 20.7.1985.	FV	1.00	4.50
	c. 12.10.1985; 20.7.1986.	FV	.75	4.00
	s1. Specimen. 20.7.1981.	—	—	30.00
	s2. Specimen. 20.7.1984.	—	—	30.00

		VG	VF	UNC
424	**1000 PESOS ORO** 1982-87. Black, blue-green and deep olive-brown on m/c unpt. S. Bolívar at l. and as wmk. Scene honoring 1819 battle heroes on back. Printer: TDLR.			
	a. 1.1.1982.	FV	3.00	15.00
	b. 7.8.1984.	FV	2.25	8.00
	c. 1.1.1986; 1.1.1987.	FV	FV	5.00
	s. Specimen.	—	—	30.00

1982-84 ISSUES

#425-430 replacement notes: Serial # prefix *.

		VG	VF	UNC
425 (422a)	**50 PESOS ORO** 1984-86. Purple on pale blue, lilac and pink unpt. W/o wmk. Printer: IBB.			
	a. 12.10.1984; 1.1.1985.	FV	.20	1.25
	b. 1.1.1986.	FV	FV	1.00

		VG	VF	UNC
426 (425)	**100 PESOS ORO** 1983-91. Violet, brown, orange and dk. red on m/c unpt. Gen A. Nariño at l. and as wmk. Villa de Leyva on back; flat bed printing press at lower r.			
	a. Printer: IBB. 1.1.1983; 12.10.1984.	FV	FV	2.00
	b. 12.10.1985; 1.1.1986; 12.10.1986.	FV	FV	1.50
	c. Larger stylized serial #. 1.1.1987; 12.10.1988.	FV	FV	1.50
	d. Back colors slightly off shade from earlier issues. 7.8.1989.	FV	FV	1.25
	e. Sign. titles: *GERENTE* and *SECRETARIO.* 1.1.1990; 1.1.1991.	FV	FV	1.00
	f. Printer: IBSFB. 7.8.1991.	FV	FV	1.00
	s. Specimen. 1.1.1983; 12.10.1984.	—	—	30.00
427 (426)	**200 PESOS ORO** 1.1.1982. Like #419 but printer: IBB.	FV	FV	4.00

		VG	VF	UNC
428 (426a)	**200 PESOS ORO** 1.4.1983. Deep green and black on m/c unpt. Church and Fr. Mutis at l. and as wmk., arms at upper r. Cloister in Bogotá at r. on back. Printer: TDLR.	FV	1.50	6.00

		VG	VF	UNC
429 (426b)	**200 Pesos Oro** 1983-92. Deep green and black on m/c unpt. Like #428.			
	a. Printer: IBB. 1.4.1983.	FV	FV	3.00
	b. 20.7.1984; 1.11.1984; 1.4.1985.	FV	3.00	15.00
	c. 1.11.1985.	FV	FV	3.00
	d. Larger stylized and bold serial #. 1.4.1987; 1.4.1988; 1.11.1988; 1.4.1989; 1.11.1989; 1.4.1991.	FV	FV	2.00
	e. Printer: IBSFB. 10.8.1992.	FV	FV	1.25

		VG	VF	UNC
430 (427)	**2000 Pesos Oro** 1983-86. Dk. brown and brown-orange on m/c unpt. S. Bolívar at l. and as wmk. Scene at *Paso del Paramo de Pisba* at ctr. r. on back. Printer: TDLR.			
	a. 24.7.1983.	FV	3.00	25.00
	b. 24.7.1984.	FV	2.75	12.00
	c. 17.12.1985.	FV	2.50	10.00
	d. 17.12.1986.	FV	2.25	9.00
	s1. As a. Specimen. Punched hole cancelled.	—	—	35.00
	s2. As b. Specimen.	—	—	—
	s3. As c. Specimen. Punched hole cancelled.	—	—	35.00

1986-87 Issue

#431-433 replacement notes: Serial # prefix *.

		VG	VF	UNC
431 (429)	**500 Pesos Oro** 1986-93. Like #423.			
	a. Printer: IBB. 20.7.1986; 12.10.1987; 20.7.1989; 12.10.1990.	FV	FV	3.00
	b. Green omited from back. Printer: IBSFB. 2.3.1992.	FV	FV	2.50
	c. 4.1.1993.	FV	FV	2.00
432 (430)	**1000 Pesos Oro** 1987-94. Black, blue-green and deep olive-brown on m/c unpt. Like #424.			
	a. Printer: IBB. 1.1.1987; 1.1.1990; 1.1.1991.	FV	FV	7.50
	b. Printer: IBSFB. 31.1.1992; 1.4.1992; 4.1.1993.	FV	FV	4.50
433 (431)	**2000 Pesos Oro** 1986-92. Dk. brown and brown-orange on m/c unpt. Like #430 but w/redesigned *2's* in denomination.			
	a. Printer: IBB. 17.12.1986; 17.12.1988; 17.12.1990.	FV	FV	5.00
	b. Printer: IBSFB. 2.3.1992; 1.4.1992.	FV	FV	5.00
	c. As b. 3.8.1992.	5.00	10.00	30.00

1986 Commemorative Issue

#434, Centennial of the Constitution

		VG	VF	UNC
434 (432)	**5000 Pesos Oro** 5.8.1986. Deep violet and red-violet on m/c unpt. R. Nuñez at l. and as wmk. Statue at ctr. r. on back. Printer: BDDK.			
	a. Issued note.	FV	FV	25.00
	s. Specimen w/red serial # at upper r.	—	—	30.00

1987 Issue

		VG	VF	UNC
435 (433)	**5000 Pesos Oro** 5.8.1987; 5.8.1988. Deep violet and red-violet on m/c unpt. Similar to #434 but printer: IPS-Roma.	FV	FV	15.00

1990 Issue

#436 replacement note: Serial # prefix *.

		VG	VF	UNC
436 (434)	**5000 Pesos Oro** 1990-93. Deep violet and red-violet on m/c unpt. Like #435.			
	a. Printer: IBB. 1.1.1990.	FV	FV	12.50
	b. Printer: IBSFB. 31.1.1992; 4.1.1993.	FV	FV	12.50

1992 Commemorative Issue

#437 Quincentennial of Columbus' Voyage, 12.10.1492

		VG	VF	UNC
437 (435)	**10,000 Pesos Oro** 1992. Deep brown and black on m/c unpt. Early sailing ships at ctr., youthful woman *Mujer Embera* at ctr. r. and as wmk, native gold statue at r. Native birds around antique world map at l. ctr., Santa Maria sailing ship at lower r. on back. Printer: BDM.			
	a. Issued note.	FV	FV	30.00
	s. Specimen.	—	—	50.00

1993 Issue

		VG	VF	UNC
437A	**10,000 Pesos Oro** 1993; 1994. Deep brown and black on m/c unpt. Like #437. Printer: IBSFB.	FV	FV	20.00

NOTE: 1,000,000 pieces of #437A dated 1993 were stolen in 1994.

1993-95 Issues

Pesos System

#437A-441 printer: IBSFB.

		VG	VF	UNC
438	**1000 Pesos** 3.1.1994; 1.11.1994; 1.7.1995; 2.8.1995; 2.10.1995. Like #432 but *EL* omitted from title and *ORO* omitted from value. Black omitted on back.	FV	FV	2.75

#439-443 portr. as wmk.

		VG	VF	UNC
439 (436)	**2000 Pesos** 1993-94. Dk. brown and brown-orange on m/c unpt. Like #433 but *EL* deleted from title, *ORO* deleted from value.			
	a. 1.7.1993.	FV	FV	4.00
	b. Orange omitted from back. 1.7.1994; 1.11.1994; 17.12.1994.	FV	FV	4.00

NOTE: 1,700,000 pieces of #439a were stolen.

440 (437) **5000 PESOS** | VG | VF | UNC
3.1.1994; 4.7.1994; 2.1.1995. Deep violet and red-violet on m/c unpt. Like #434-436 but *EL* deleted from the title, *ORO* deleted from the value. | FV | FV | 15.00

NOTE: 2,200,000 pieces of #440 dated 3.1.1994 were stolen in 1994.

441 (438) **5000 PESOS** | VG | VF | UNC
1.3.1995; 1.3.1996. Dk. brown, brown and deep blue-green on m/c unpt. J. Asunción Silva and bug at upper r., trees at l. and ctr. Wmk: Asunción Silva. Woman, trees and monument at ctr. on back. | FV | FV | 15.00

442 (439) **5000 PESOS**
1.7.1995. Dk. brown, brown and deep blue-green on m/c unpt. Like #441. Printer: TDLR. | FV | FV | 9.00

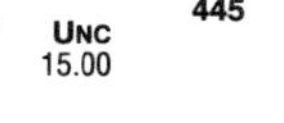

443 (440) **10,000 PESOS** | VG | VF | UNC
1.3.1995; 1.8.1996. Deep brown and black on m/c unpt. Like #437, but *EL* omitted from title, *ORO* omitted from value, diff. sign. and titles. Printer: IBSFB. | FV | FV | 22.50

1995 COMMEMORATIVE ISSUE

#444, 200th Anniversary of P. Salavarrieta *"La Pola"*

Replacement note: Serial # prefix *.

444 **10,000 PESOS** | VG | VF | UNC
1.7.1995; 1.8.1995; 23.7.1997. Red-brown and black on m/c unpt. P. Salavarrieta at r., village of Guaduas (ca. 1846) at l. ctr. on back. Printer: TDLR. | FV | FV | 22.50

1996; 1997 ISSUES

#445-448 printer: IBSFB.

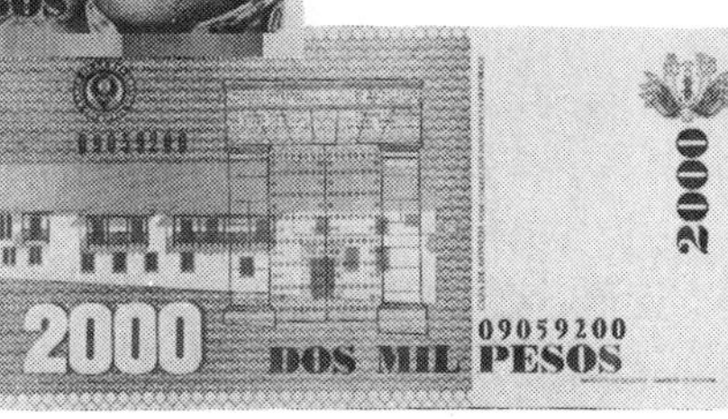

445 **2000 PESOS** | VG | VF | UNC
2.4.1996; 6.5.1997; 6.1.1998; 7.8.1998. Black, olive-green, red-brown and dk. brown on m/c unpt. Gen. F. de Paula Santander at r. Casa de Moneda bldg., entrance at l. ctr. on back. | FV | FV | 5.00

446 **5000 PESOS** | VG | VF | UNC
2.1.1997; 7.8.1998. Dk. brown and deep blue-green on m/c unpt. Like #442. | FV | FV | 9.50

447 **5000 PESOS**
12.10.1997; 2.4.1998. Deep violet and red-violet on m/c unpt. Like #446 but w/bank seal at ctr. | FV | FV | 9.50

448 **20,000 PESOS**
23.7.1996; 6.1.1998. Black, deep green ad dk. blue on m/c unpt. J. Garauito A. at r. and as wmk. view of the moon at ctr. Satellite view of earth at ctr.r., moon's surface along bottom, geometric forms in unpt. on back. | FV | FV | 27.50

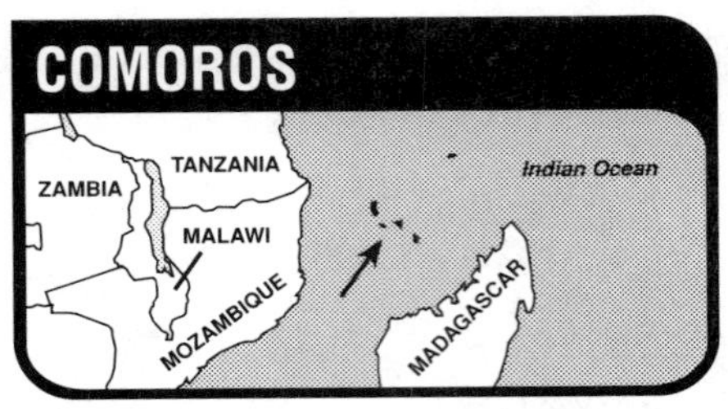

The Federal Islamic Republic of the Comoros, a volcanic archipelago located in the Mozambique Channel of the Indian Ocean 300 miles (483 km.) northwest of Madagascar, has an area of 838 sq. mi. (1,797 sq. km.) and a population of 569,240. Capital: Moroni. The economy of the islands is based on agriculture. There are practically no mineral resources. Vanilla, essence for perfumes, copra and sisal are exported.

Ancient Phoenician traders were probably the first visitors to the Comoros Islands, but the first detailed knowledge of the area was gathered by Arab sailors. Arab dominion and culture were firmly established when the Portuguese, Dutch and French arrived in the 16th century. In 1843 a Malagasy ruler ceded the island of Mayotte to France; the other three principal islands of the archipelago - Anjouan, Moheli and Grand Comore - came under French protection in 1886. The islands were joined administratively with Madagascar in 1912. The Comoros became partially autonomous, with the status of a French overseas territory in 1946 and achieved complete internal autonomy in 1961. On Dec. 31, 1975, after 133 years of French association, the Comoros Islands became the independent Republic of the Comoros.

Mayotte retained the option of determining its future ties and in 1976 voted to remain French. Its present status is that of a French Territorial Collectivity. French coinage and currency circulates there.

RULERS:

French to 1975

MONETARY SYSTEM:

1 Franc = 100 Centimes

REPUBLIC

BANQUE DE MADAGASCAR ET DES COMORES

1960 ND PROVISIONAL ISSUE

#2-6 additional red ovpt: *COMORES*.

#4-6 dated through 1952 have titles "A", those dated 1955 or ND have titles "B".

		VG	VF	UNC
2	**50 FRANCS** ND (1960-63). Brown and m/c. Woman w/hat at r. Man on back. Ovpt. on Madagascar #45.			
	a. Sign. titles: *LE CONTROLEUR GAL.* and *LE DIRECTEUR GAL.* ND (1960).	Reported Not Confirmed		
	b. Sign. titles: *LE DIRECTEUR GAL. ADJOINT* and *LE PRESIDENT DIRECTEUR GAL.* ND (1963). 2 sign varieties.	2.00	5.00	20.00

		VG	VF	UNC
3	**100 FRANCS** ND (1960-63). M/c. Woman at r., palace of the Qn. of Tananariva in background. Woman, boats and animals on back. Ovpt. on Madagascar #46.			
	a. Sign. titles: *LE CONTROLEUR GAL.* and *LE DIRECTEUR GAL.* ND (1960).	6.00	25.00	80.00
	b. Sign. titles: *LE DIRECTEUR GAL. ADJOINT* and *LE PRESIDENT DIRECTEUR GAL.* ND (1963).	1.00	5.00	18.50

		VG	VF	UNC
4	**500 FRANCS** ND (1960-63). M/c. Man w/fruit at ctr. Ovpt. on Madagascar #47.			
	a. Sign. titles: *LE CONTROLEUR GAL* and *LE DIRECTEUR GAL.* - old date 30.6.1950; 9.10.1952 (1960).	30.00	100.00	325.00
	b. Sign. titles: *LE DIRECTEUR GAL. ADJOINT* and *LE PRESIDENT DIRECTEUR GAL.* ND (1963).	15.00	75.00	250.00
5	**1000 FRANCS** ND (1960-63). M/c. Woman and man at l. ctr. Ox cart on back. Ovpt. on Madagascar #48.			
	a. Sign. titles: *LE CONTROLEUR GAL.* and *LE DIRECTEUR GAL.* - old date 1950-52; 9.10.1952 (1960).	45.00	125.00	425.00
	b. Sign. titles: *LE DIRECTEUR GAL. ADJOINT* and *LE PRESIDENT DIRECTEUR GAL.* ND (1963).	25.00	90.00	350.00

		VG	VF	UNC
6	**5000 FRANCS** ND (1960-63). M/c. Portr. Gallieni at upper l., young woman at r. Huts at l., woman w/baby at r. on back. Ovpt. on Madagascar #49.			
	a. Sign. titles: *LE CONTROLEUR GAL.* and *LE DIRECTEUR GAL.* - old date 30.6.1950 (1960).	175.00	425.00	875.00
	b. Sign. titles: *LE DIRECTEUR GAL. ADJOINT* and *LE PRESIDENT DIRECTEUR GAL.* ND (1963).	125.00	325.00	750.00
	c. Sign. titles: *LE DIRECTEUR GÉNÉRAL* and *LE PRÉSIDENT DIRECTEUR GAL.*	150.00	350.00	600.00

INSTITUT D'ÉMISSION DES COMORES

1976 ND ISSUE

#7-9 wmk: Crescent on Maltese cross.

		VG	VF	UNC
7	**500 FRANCS** ND (1976). Blue-gray, brown and red on m/c unpt. Bldg. at ctr., young woman wearing a hood at r. 2 women at l., boat at r. on back. 2 sign. varieties.	FV	3.00	9.00

		VG	VF	UNC
8	**1000 FRANCS** ND (1976). Blue-gray, brown and red on m/c unpt. Woman at r., palm trees at water's edge in background. Women on back.	FV	6.00	17.50
9	**5000 FRANCS** ND (1976). Green on m/c unpt. Man and woman at ctr., boats and bldg. in l. background. Man at ctr. on back.	FV	35.00	90.00

BANQUE CENTRALE DES COMORES

1984-86 ND ISSUE

#10-12 like to #7-9 but w/new bank name. Wmk: Maltese cross w/crescent.

		VG	VF	UNC
10	**500 FRANCS** ND (1986-). Blue-gray, brown and red on m/c unpt. Like #7.			
	a. Partially engraved. Sign. titles: *LE DIRECTEUR GÉNÉRAL* and *LE PRÉSIDENT DU CONSEIL D'ADMINISTRATION* (1986). Wmk. is inverted - crescent facing down above Maltese cross.	FV	2.25	7.50
	b. Offset. Sign. titles: *LE GOUVERNEUR* and *PRÉSIDENT DU...* (1994). Corrected wmk. crescent facing up under Maltese cross.	FV	FV	5.00

		VG	VF	UNC
11	**1000 FRANCS** ND (1984-). Blue-gray, brown and red on m/c unpt. Like #8.			
	a. Partially engraved. Sign. titles: *LE DIRECTEUR GÉNÉRAL* and *LE PRÉSIDENT DU CONSEIL D'ADMINISTRATION.* (1986).	FV	4.00	11.50
	b. Offset. Sign. titles: *LE GOUVERNEUR* and *PRÉSIDENT DU....* (1994).	FV	3.25	8.50

		VG	VF	UNC
12	**5000 FRANCS** ND (1984-). Green on m/c unpt. Like #9. Engraved sign titles: *LE DIRECTEUR GÉNÉRAL* and *LE PRÉSIDENT DU CONSEIL D'ADMINISTRATION.*	FV	16.50	40.00

1997 ND ISSUE

#13 and 14 wmk: 4 stars below crescent (arms).

		VG	VF	UNC
13	**2500 FRANCS** ND (1997). Purple and blue on m/c unpt. Woman wearing colorful scarf at l. Sea turtle at lower l. ctr. on back.	FV	FV	21.50

		VG	VF	UNC
14	**10,000 FRANCS** ND (1997). Brown on m/c unpt. 2 seated women weaving baskets at ctr. Al-Habib Seyyid O. Bin Sumeit at l., mosque at ctr. on back.	FV	FV	70.00

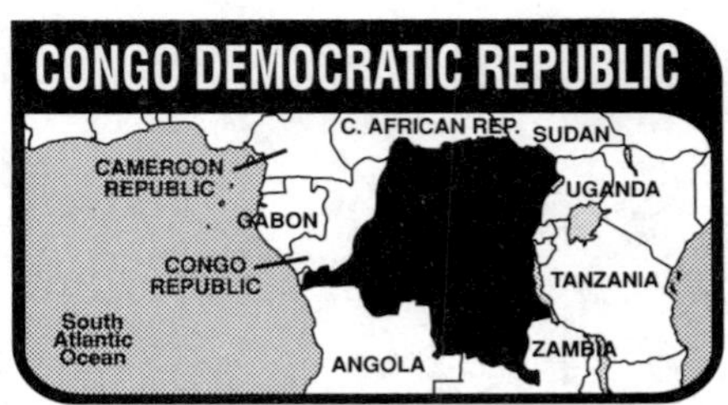

The Congo Democratic Republic (formerly Zaïre), located in the south-central part of Africa, has an area of 905,568 sq. mi. (2,345,409 sq. km.) and a population of 47.44 million. Capital: Kinshasa. The mineral-rich country produces copper, tin, diamonds, gold, zinc, cobalt and uranium.

In ancient times the territory comprising Zaïre was occupied by Negrito peoples (Pygmies) pushed into the mountains by Bantu and Nilotic invaders. The interior was first explored by the American correspondent Henry Stanley, who was subsequently commissioned by King Leopold II of Belgium to conclude development treaties with the local chiefs. The Berlin conference of 1885 awarded the area to Leopold, who administered and exploited it as his private property until it was annexed to Belgium in 1908. Following the eruption of bloody independence riots in 1959, Belgium granted the Belgian Congo independence as the Republic of the Congo on June 30, 1960. The Belgian Congo attained independence with the distinction of being the most ill-prepared country to ever undertake self-government. Without a single doctor, lawyer or engineer, with no organized unit capable of maintaining law and order, independence disintegrated into an orgy of anarchy. Provinces seceded. Intertribal warfare erupted. Belgian troops intervened to protect Belgian citizens from retributive massacre. By 1961, four groups were fighting for political dominance. The most serious threat to the viability of the country was posed by the secession of mineral-rich Katanga province on July 11, 1960.

After two and one-half years of sporadic warfare with a U.N. military force, Katanga's leaders capitulated, Jan. 14, 1963 and the rebellious province was partitioned into three provinces. The nation officially changed its name to Zaïre on Oct. 27, 1971. In May 1997, the dictator was overthrown after a three year rebellion. The country changed its name to the Democratic Republic of the Congo. A change to a Francs-Congolese currency has been considered, but meanwhile "hard" currency such as U.S.A. dollars circulate freely.

See also Rwanda, Rwanda-Burundi, and Zaïre.

MONETARY SYSTEM:

1 Franc = 100 Centimes to 1967
1 Zaïre = 100 Makuta, 1967-71
1 Franc = 100 Centimes, 1997-

Banque Nationale du Congo

Governor	Governor
1. A. Ndélé	2.J. Sambwa Mbagui

CONGO (KINSHASA)

CONSEIL MONÉTAIRE DE LA RÉPUB LIQUE DU CONGO

1962-63 ISSUE

#1-3 various date and sign varieties.

		VG	VF	UNC
1	**100 FRANCS**			
	1.6.1963-8.7.1963. Green and m/c. Dam at l. Dredging at r. on back.			
	a. Issued note.	5.00	25.00	100.00
	s. Specimen.	—	85.00	125.00

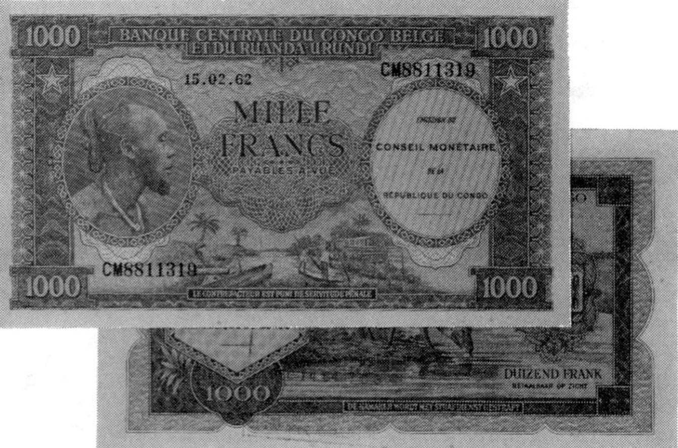

		VG	VF	UNC
2	**1000 FRANCS**			
	15.2.1962. Purple on m/c unpt. Portr. African man at l. Text: *EMISSION DU CONSEIL MONÉTAIRE DE LA REPUBLIQUE DU CONGO* in place of wmk. Back deep violet on pink unpt; longhorn animal drinking in stream.			
	a. Issued note.	15.00	55.00	300.00
	s. Specimen.	—	—	325.00

		VG	VF	UNC
3	**5000 FRANCS**			
	1.12.1963. Gray-green. Portr. African woman at l. Oarsmen on back.			
	a. Issued note.	400.00	1350.	—
	s. Specimen.	—	2250.	3450.

BANQUE NATIONALE DU CONGO

1961 ISSUE

#4-8 sign. 1.

		VG	VF	UNC
4	**20 FRANCS**			
	15.11.1961-15.9.1962. Green, blue and brown. Girl seated at r. and as wmk. Stylized tree at ctr. on back. Printer: JEZ.			
	a. Issued note.	2.00	8.00	30.00
	s. Specimen.	—	45.00	75.00

#5-8 long bldg. at bottom on back.

		VG	VF	UNC
5	**50 FRANCS**			
	1.9.1961-1.7.1962. Green. Lion at l., bridge and lake at ctr. r. in background.			
	a. Issued note.	2.50	12.50	40.00
	s. Specimen.	—	60.00	85.00

		VG	VF	UNC
6	**100 FRANCS**			
	1.9.1961-1.8.1964. Dk. brown on m/c unpt. J. Kasavubu at l., 2 birds at r. Printer: TDLR.			
	a. Issued note.	4.00	17.50	65.00
	s. Specimen.	—	70.00	95.00

		VG	VF	UNC
7	**500 FRANCS** 15.10.1961; 1.12.1961; 1.1.1962; 1.8.1964. Lilac. Mask at l. Wmk: Bird.			
	a. Issued note.	10.00	35.00	135.00
	s. Specimen.	—	120.00	145.00

		VG	VF	UNC
8	**1000 FRANCS** 15.10.1961; 15.12.1961; 1.8.1964. Dk. blue on m/c unpt. J. Kasavubu at l., carving at r. Wmk: Antelope's head. Printer: TDLR.			
	a. Issued note.	8.00	25.00	120.00
	s. Specimen.	—	100.00	120.00

1967 ISSUE

#9-13 various date and sign. varieties. Printer: TDLR. Replacement notes: Serial # prefix ZZ.

		VG	VF	UNC
9	**10 MAKUTA** 2.1.1967; 1.9.1968; 14.1.1970; 21.1.1970. Blue on olive-green and m/c unpt. Stadium at l., Mobutu at r. Long bldg. on back. Sign. 1.			
	a. Issued note.	2.00	6.00	35.00
	s. Specimen.	—	30.00	35.00

		VG	VF	UNC
10	**20 MAKUTA** 1967-70. Black on green, blue and m/c unpt. Man w/flag at ctr., P. Lumumba at r. People in long boat at l. ctr. on back. Wmk: Antelope's head.			
	a. Sign. 1. 24.11.1967; 21.1.1970.	4.00	25.00	80.00
	b. Sign. 2. 1.10.1970.	4.00	25.00	80.00
	s. Specimen. 21.1.1970.	—	75.00	100.00

		VG	VF	UNC
11	**50 MAKUTA** 1967-70. Red on olive-green and m/c unpt. Stadium at ctr. l., Mobutu at r. Gathering coconuts on back.			
	a. Sign. 1. 2.1.1967; 1.9.1968; 21.1.1970.	3.50	20.00	90.00
	b. Sign. 2. 1.10.1970.	3.50	20.00	90.00
	s. Specimen. 1.9.1968.	—	90.00	125.00

		VG	VF	UNC
12	**1 ZAÏRE = 100 MAKUTA** 1967-70. Brown and green on m/c unpt. Stadium at l., Mobutu at r. Mobutu's "time to work" to gathering of people at l. ctr. on back. Wmk: Antelope's head.			
	a. Sign. 1. 2.1.1967; 24.11.1967; 1.9.1968.	4.00	15.00	100.00
	b. Sign. 2. 1.10.1970.	4.00	15.00	100.00
	s1. Specimen. 24.11.1967.	—	80.00	125.00
	s2. Specimen. 1.10.1970.	—	80.00	125.00

		VG	VF	UNC
13	**5 ZAÏRES = 500 MAKUTA** 1967-70. Green and m/c. Mobutu at r. Long bldg. at l. ctr. on back. Wmk: Antelope's head.			
	a. Sign. 1 above title: *LE GOUVERNEUR*. Green date. 2.1.1967; 24.6.1967.	13.50	60.00	275.00
	b. Sign. 2 below title: *LE GOUVERNEUR*. Black date. 2.1.1967; 24.11.1967; 1.9.1968; 21.1.1970.	12.50	55.00	200.00
	s1. Specimen. 2.1.1967.	—	225.00	275.00
	s2. Specimen. 21.1.1970.	—	225.00	275.00

1971 ISSUE

#14 and 15 portr. Mobutu at l. and as wmk., leopard at lower r. facing r. Sign. 2. Printer: G&D. Replacement notes: Serial # suffix Z.

		VG	VF	UNC
14	**5 ZAÏRES** 24.11.1971. Green, black and m/c. Carving at l. ctr., hydroelectric dam at ctr. r. on back.			
	a. Issued note.	17.50	70.00	225.00
	s. Specimen.	—	180.00	225.00

		VG	VF	UNC
15	**10 ZAÏRES** 30.6.1971. Blue, brown and m/c. Arms on back w/yellow star.			
	a. Issued note.	20.00	75.00	200.00
	s. Specimen.	—	175.00	225.00

DEMOCRATIC REPUBLIC

BANQUE CENTRALE DU CONGO

#80-88 bank monogram at ctr. Wmk: Single Okapi head or multiple heads repeated vertically.

1997 ISSUE

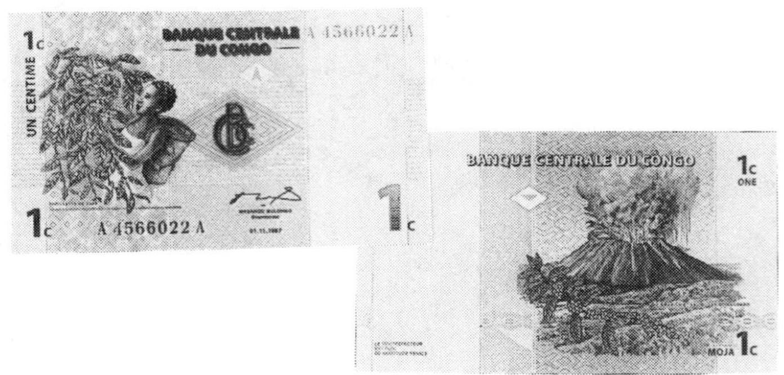

		VG	VF	UNC
80	**1 CENTIME** 1.11.1997. Deep olive-green, violet and dk. brown on m/c unpt. Woman harvesting coffee beans at l. Nyiragongo volcano at r. on back. Printer: ATB.			
	a. Issued note.	FV	FV	2.00
	s. Specimen.	—	—	5.00

		VG	VF	UNC
81	**5 CENTIMES** 1.11.1997. Purple on m/c unpt. Suku mask at l. Zande Harp at ctr. r. on back. Printer: G & D.			
	a. Issued note.	FV	FV	3.00
	s. Specimen.	—	—	30.00

		VG	VF	UNC
82	**10 CENTIMES** 1.11.1997. Red-violet and dk. brown on m/c unpt. Pende mask at l. Pende dancers at ctr. r. on back. Printer: ATB.			
	a. Issued note.	FV	FV	4.00
	s. Specimen.	—	—	5.00

		VG	VF	UNC
83	**20 CENTIMES** 1.11.1997. Blue-green and black on m/c unpt. Antelope at l. Antelope herd by lg. tree at ctr. r. on back. Printer: ATB.			
	a. Issued note.	FV	FV	5.00
	s. Specimen.	—	—	6.00

		VG	VF	UNC
84	**50 CENTIMES** 1.11.1997. Dk. brown and brown on m/c unpt. Okapi's head at l. Family of Okapi's at l. ctr. on back. Printer: G & D.			
	a. Issued note.	FV	FV	7.50
	s. Specimen.	—	—	8.00
84A	**50 CENTIMES** 1.11.1997. As #84. Printer: ATB. Serial # prefix: E; suffix: D.	FV	FV	7.50

		VG	VF	UNC
85	**1 FRANC** 1.11.1997 (1998). Deep purple and blue-violet on m/c unpt. Lg. mining complex at l. Prisoners Lumumba and 2 companions at ctr. r. on back. Printer: G & D.			
	a. Issued note.	FV	FV	15.00
	s. Specimen.	—	—	10.00

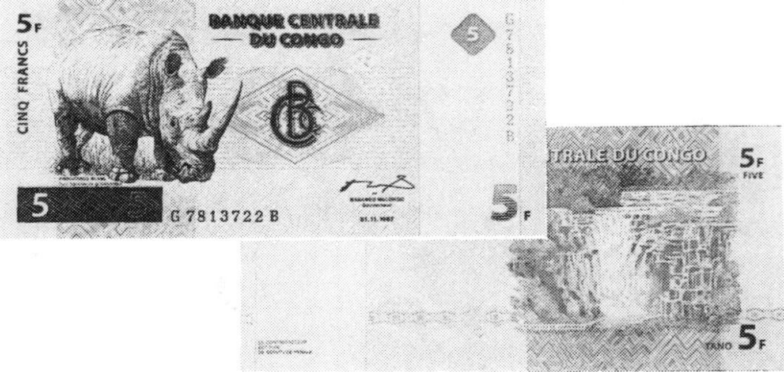

		VG	VF	UNC
86	**5 FRANCS** 1.11.1997 (1998). Purple and black on m/c unpt. White rhinocerus at l. Kamwanga Falls at ctr. r. on back. Printer: NBBPW.			
	a. Issued note.	FV	FV	25.00
	s. Specimen.	—	—	20.00

		VG	VF	UNC
87	**10 FRANCS** 1.11.1997 (1998). Olive-brown, olive-green and deep blue-green on m/c unpt. "Apui-tete Chef Luba" carving of a couple at l. "Coupe en Bois Luba" carving at r. on back. Printer: NBBPW. Serial # prefix: *H*; suffix: *A*.			
	a. Issued note.	FV	FV	35.00
	s. Specimen.	—	—	30.00

		VG	VF	UNC
87A	**10 FRANCS** 1.11.1997. As #87 but printer G & D. Serial # prefix: B; suffix: C.	FV	FV	35.00

		VG	VF	UNC
88	**20 FRANCS** 1.11.1997 (1998). Brown-orange and red-orange on m/c unpt. Male lion's head at l. Female lion lying w/2 cubs at ctr. r. on back. Printer: NBBPW.			
	a. Issued note.	FV	FV	50.00
	s. Specimen.	—	—	40.00
89	**50 FRANCS** 1.11.1997 (1998). Head at l. Village scene on back. Printer: NBBPW.			
	a. Issued note.	FV	FV	90.00
	s. Specimen.	—	—	65.00
90	**100 FRANCS** 1.11.1997 (1998). Elephant at l. Dam on back. Printer: NBBPW.			
	a. Issued note.	FV	FV	150.00
	s. Specimen.	—	—	120.00

The Republic of the Congo (formerly the Peoples Republic of the Congo), located on the equator in west-central Africa, has an area of 132,047 sq. mi. (342,000 sq. km.) and a population of 2.58 million. Capital: Brazzaville. Agriculture forestry, mining, and food processing are the principal industries. Timber, industrial diamonds, potash, peanuts, and cocoa beans are exported.

The Portuguese were the first Europeans to explore the Congo (Brazzaville) area, 14th century. They conducted a slave trade with the tribal kingdoms of Teke, Loango, and Kongo without attempting developmental colonization. French influence was established in 1883 when the King of Teke signed a treaty with Savorgnan dè Brazza, thereby placing his kingdom under the protection of France. While a French protectorate, the area was known as Middle Congo. In 1910 Middle Congo became a part of French Equatorial Africa, which also included Gabon, Ubangi-Shari (now the Central African Republic), and Chad. Following World War II, during which it was an important center of Free French activities, the Middle Congo was given a large measure of internal autonomy, and its inhabitants were made French citizens. Upon approval of the constitution of the Fifth French Republic, 1958, it became a member of the new French Community. On Aug. 15, 1960, Middle Congo became the independent Republic of the Congo-Brazzaville. In Jan. 1970 the country's name was changed to Peoples Republic of the Congo. A new constitution which asserts the government's advocacy of socialism was adopted in 1973. In June and July of 1992, a new 125-member National Assembly was elected. Later that year a new president, Pascal Lissouba, was elected. In November, President Lissouba dismissed the previous government and dissolved the National Assembly. A new 23-member government, including members of the opposition, was formed in December 1992 and the name was changed to République du Congo.

Violence erupted in 1997 nearly emptying the capitol.

NOTE: For later issues and signature chart, see Central African States.

RULERS:

French to 1960

MONETARY SYSTEM:

1 Franc = 100 Centimes

RÉPUBLIQUE POPULAIRE DU CONGO

BANQUE CENTRALE

1971 ISSUE

		VG	VF	UNC
1	**10,000 FRANCS** ND (1971). M/c. Young Congolese woman at l., people marching w/sign at ctr. Statue at l. and r., tractor plowing at ctr. on back. Sign. 1.	125.00	400.00	1000.

BANQUE DES ÉTATS DE L'AFRIQUE CENTRALE

1974 ND ISSUE

		VG	VF	UNC
2	**500 FRANCS** ND (1974)-1983. Lilac-brown and m/c. Woman at l., river scene at ctr. Mask at l., students and chemical testing at ctr., statue at r. on back.			
	a. Sign. titles: *LE DIRECTEUR GENERAL* and *UN CENSEUR*. Engraved. Sign. 5. ND (1974).	2.00	6.00	15.00
	b. Sign. titles: *LE GOUVERNEUR* and *UN CENSEUR*. Lithographed. Sign. 10. 1.4.1978.	4.00	15.00	45.00
	c. Titles as b. Sign. 10; 1.7.1980.	1.50	6.00	15.00
	d. Titles as b. Sign. 12. 1.6.1981; 1.1.1982; 1.1.1983; 1.6.1984.	1.25	3.00	10.00

		VG	VF	UNC
3	**1000 FRANCS** ND (1974)-1984. Blue and m/c. Industrial plant at ctr., man at r. Mask at l., trains, planes and bridge at ctr., statue at r. on back.			
	a. Sign. titles: *LE DIRECTEUR GENERAL* and *UN CENSEUR*. Engraved. Wmk: Antelope head in half profile. Sign. 3. ND (1974).	10.00	25.00	75.00
	b. Like a. Sign. 5.	4.00	10.00	30.00
	c. Sign. titles: *LE DIRECTEUR GENERAL* and *UN CENSEUR*. Lithographed. Wmk: Antelope head in profile. Sign. 8. ND (1978).	3.00	8.50	27.50
	d. Sign. titles: *LE GOUVERNEUR* and *UN CENSEUR*. Lithographed. Wmk: like b. Sign. 10. 1.4.1978.	2.75	7.50	23.50
	e. Titles as c. Sign. 12; 1.6.1981; 1.1.1982; 1.1.1983; 1.6.1984.	2.25	6.50	20.00

		VG	VF	UNC
4	**5000 FRANCS** ND (1974; 1978). Brown. Woman at l. Mask at l., bldgs. at ctr., statue at r. on back.			
	a. Sign. titles: *LE DIRECTEUR GENERAL* and *UN CENSEUR*. Sign. 3. ND (1974).	30.00	75.00	225.00
	b. Like a. Sign. 5.	15.00	40.00	100.00
	c. Sign. titles: *LE GOUVERNEUR* and *UN CENSEUR*. Sign. 11; 12. ND (1978).	13.50	20.00	50.00

		VG	VF	UNC
5	**10,000 FRANCS** ND (1974-81). M/c. Like #1 except for new bank name on back.			
	a. Sign. titles: *LE DIRECTEUR GENERAL* and *UN CENSEUR*. Sign. 5; 7. ND (1974; 1977).	30.00	60.00	150.00
	b. Sign. titles: *LE GOUVERNEUR* and *UN CENSEUR*. Sign. 11; 12. ND (1978; 1981).	22.50	45.00	125.00

1983-84 ND ISSUE

		VG	VF	UNC
6	**5000 FRANCS** ND (1984; 1991). Brown and m/c. Mask at l., woman w/bundle of fronds at r. Plowing and mine ore conveyor on back. Sign. 12; 15.			
	a. Sign. 12. (1984).	13.50	25.00	40.00
	b. Sign. 15. (1991).	12.50	22.50	37.50
7	**10,000 FRANCS** ND (1983). Brown, green and m/c. Stylized antelope heads at l., woman at r. Loading fruit onto truck at l. on back. Sign. 12.	22.50	35.00	75.00

1985-87 ISSUES

NOTE: For issues w/similar back designs see Cameroon Republic, Central African Republic, Chad and Gabon.

#8-10 sign. titles: *LE GOUVERNEUR* and *UN CENSEUR*.

		VG	VF	UNC
8	**500 FRANCS** 1985-91. Brown on m/c unpt. Statue at l. ctr. and as wmk., jug at ctr. Man carving mask at l. ctr. on back.			
	a. Sign. 12. 1.1.1985; 1.1.1987; 1.1.1988; 1.1.1989.	.50	2.50	7.50
	b. Sign. 13. 1.1.1990.	.40	2.00	6.00
	c. Sign. 15. 1.1.1991.	.35	1.65	5.00

		VG	VF	UNC
9	**1000 FRANCS** 1.1.1985. Dull blue-violet on m/c unpt. Animal carving at lower l., map of 6 member states at ctr. Unfinished map of Chad at upper ctr. Elephant at l., animals at ctr., carving at r. on back. Wmk: Animal carving. Sign. 12.	1.25	6.50	20.00

		VG	VF	UNC
10	**1000 FRANCS** 1987-91. Dull blue-violet on m/c unpt. Like #9 but completed map of Chad at top on face.			
	a. Sign. 12. 1.1.1987; 1.1.1988; 1.1.1989.	.90	4.50	13.50
	b. Sign. 13. 1.1.1990.	.80	4.00	12.00
	c. Sign. 15. 1.1.1991.	.70	3.50	10.00

RÉPUBLIQUE DU CONGO

BANQUE DES ÉTATS DE L'AFRIQUE CENTRALE

1992 ISSUE

		VG	VF	UNC
11	**1000 FRANCS** 1.1.1992. Dull blue-violet on m/c unpt. Like #10, but w/new country name. Sign. 15.	FV	FV	9.00

1992 ND ISSUE

		VG	VF	UNC
12 (11)	**5000 FRANCS** ND (1992). Black text and brown on pale yellow and m/c unpt. African mask at l. and as wmk., woman carrying bundle of cane at r. African string instrument at far l., farm tractor plowing at l. ctr., mineshaft cable ore bucket lift at r. on back. Sign. 15.	FV	FV	35.00

		VG	VF	UNC
13	**10,000 FRANCS** ND (1992). Greenish-black text, brown on pale green and m/c unpt. Artistic antelope masks at 1., Woman's head at r. and as wmk. Loading produce truck w/bananas at l. on back. Sign. 15.	FV	FV	65.00

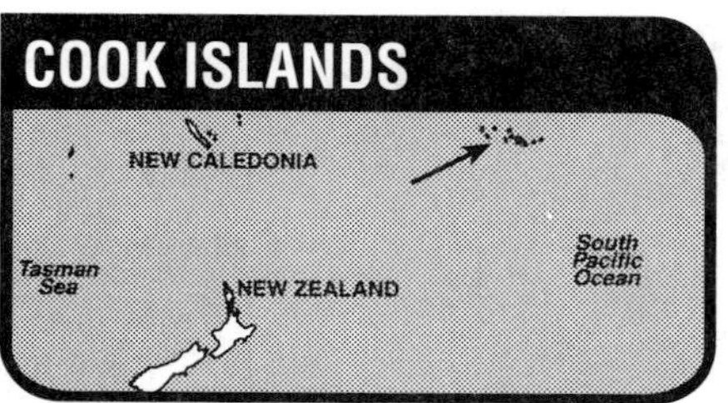

Cook Islands, a political dependency of New Zealand consisting of 15 islands located in the South Pacific Ocean about 2,000 miles (3,218 km.) northeast of New Zealand, has an area of 93 sq. mi. (234 sq. km.) and a population of 16,900. Capital: Avarua. The United States claims the islands of Danger, Manahiki, Penrhyn and Rakahanga atolls. Citrus and canned fruits and juices, copra, clothing, jewelry and mother-of-pearl shell are exported.

The islands were first sighted by Spanish navigator Alvaro de Mendada in 1595. Portuguese navigator Pedro Fernandes de Quieros landed on Rakahanga in 1606. English navigator Capt. James Cook sailed to the islands on three occasions: 1773, 1774 and 1777. He named them Hervey Islands, in honor of Augustus John Hervey, a lord of the Admiralty. The islands were declared a British protectorate in 1888, and were annexed to New Zealand in 1901. They were granted internal self-government in 1965. New Zealand provides an annual subsidy and retains responsibility for defense and foreign affairs.

As a territory of New Zealand, the Cook Islands are considered to be within the Commonwealth of Nations.

NOTE: In June 1995 the Government of the Cook Islands began redeeming all 10, 20 and 50 dollar notes in exchange for New Zealand currency while most coins originally intended for circulation along with their 3 dollar notes will remain in use.

RULERS:

New Zealand, 1901-

MONETARY SYSTEM:

1 Shilling = 12 Pence
1 Pound = 20 Shillings, to 1967
1 Dollar = 100 Cents, 1967-

NEW ZEALAND INFLUENCE

GOVERNMENT OF THE COOK ISLANDS

1987 ND ISSUE

#3-5 Ina and the shark at l.

		VG	VF	UNC
3	**3 DOLLARS** ND (1987). Deep green, blue-black and black on m/c unpt. Fishing canoe and statue of the god of Te-Rongo on back.	FV	2.75	4.50

		VG	VF	UNC
4	**10 DOLLARS** ND (1987). Violet-brown, blue-black and black on m/c unpt. Pantheon of gods on back.			
	a. Issued note.	FV	8.50	16.50
	s. Specimen.	—	—	17.50

		VG	VF	UNC
5	**20 DOLLARS** ND (1987). Purple, blue-black and black on m/c unpt. Conch shell, turtle shell and drum on back.			
	a. Sign. T. Davis.	FV	16.50	32.50
	b. Sign. M. J. Fleming.	FV	16.00	30.00
	s. Specimen.	—	—	20.00

1992 COMMEMORATIVE ISSUE

#6, 6th Festival of Pacific Arts, Rarotonga, Oct. 10-27, 1992.

		VG	VF	UNC
6	**3 DOLLARS** Oct. 1992. Black commemorative text ovpt. at l. on back of #3.	FV	3.00	5.00

1992 ND ISSUE

#7-10 worshippers at church w/cemetery at ctr. Wmk: Sea turtle.

		VG	VF	UNC
7	**3 DOLLARS** ND (1992). Lilac and green on m/c unpt. Back purple, orange and m/c. *AITUTAKI* at upper ctr., local drummers at l., dancers at ctr., fish at r.			
	a. Issued note.	FV	FV	4.50
	s. Specimen. ND.	—	—	50.00

		VG	VF	UNC
8	**10 DOLLARS** ND (1992). Green and olive on m/c unpt. *RAROTONGA* above hillside gathering on back.	FV	FV	12.50

		VG	VF	UNC
9	**20 DOLLARS** ND (1992). Brown-orange and olive on m/c unpt. *NGAPUTORU & MANGAIA* above 2 islanders w/canoe at ctr. on back.			
	a. Issued note.	FV	FV	22.50
	s. Specimen.	—	—	20.00

		VG	VF	UNC
10	**50 DOLLARS** ND (1992). Blue and green on m/c unpt. 3 islanders in canoe at l., *NORTHERN GROUP* above 2 seated women weaving at ctr. on back.			
	a. Issued note.	FV	FV	55.00
	s. Specimen.	—	—	25.00

COLLECTOR SERIES

GOVERNMENT OF THE COOK ISLANDS

1987 ND ISSUE

		ISSUE PRICE	MKT. VALUE
CS1	**ND (1987) 3-20 DOLLARS** #3-5 w/matched serial # in special pack.	55.00	60.00

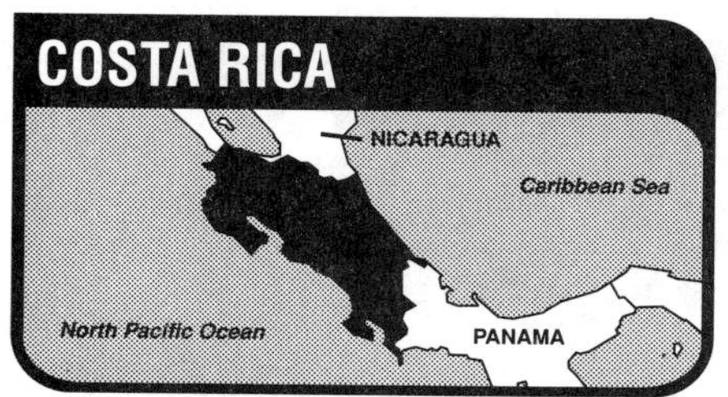

The Republic of Costa Rica, located in southern Central America between Nicaragua and Panama, has an area of 19,575 sq. mi. (50,700 sq. km.) and a population of 3.37 million. Capital: San Jose. Agriculture predominates; coffee, bananas, beef and sugar contribute heavily to the country's export earnings.

Costa Rica was discovered by Christopher Columbus in 1502, during his last voyage to the new world, and was a colony of Spain from 1522 until independence in 1821. Columbus named the territory Nueva Cartago; the name Costa Rica wasn't generally employed until 1540. Bartholomew Columbus attempted to found the first settlement but was driven off by Indian attacks and the country wasn't pacified until 1530. Costa Rica was absorbed for two years (1821-23) into the Mexican Empire of Agustin de Iturbide. From 1823 to 1848 it was a constituent state of the Central American Republic (q.v.). It was established as a republic in 1848.

Constitution revisions followed in 1871 and 1948. In the early 1990's, Costa Rica was beset with economic problems.

MONETARY SYSTEM:

1 Colon = 100 Centavos

REPUBLIC

BANCO CENTRAL DE COSTA RICA

1951; 1952 ISSUE

#221-224 printer: W&S.

		VG	VF	UNC
221	**10 COLONES** 1951-62. Blue on m/c unpt. Portr. A. Echeverria at ctr. Back blue; ox-cart at ctr.			
	a. W/*POR* added to sign. title at l. 24.10.1951; 8.11.1951; 19.11.1951; 5.12.1951; 29.10.1952.	5.00	20.00	80.00
	b. W/*POR* added to both sign. titles. 28.11.1951.	5.00	20.00	80.00
	c. W/o *POR* title changes. 2.7.1952; 28.10.1953-27.6.1962.	5.00	20.00	80.00
	d. W/*POR* added to sign. title at r. 20.11.1952.	5.00	20.00	80.00

		VG	VF	UNC
222	**20 COLONES** 1952-64. Red on m/c unpt. Portr. C. Picado at ctr. Back red; University bldg. at ctr.			
	a. Date at l. ctr., w/o sign. title changes. 20.2.1952; 13.2.1957.	8.50	37.50	140.00
	b. Sign. title: *SUB-GERENTE* ovpt. at r. 20.4.1955.	8.50	37.50	140.00
	c. Date at lower l. 7.11.1957-9.9.1964.	9.00	40.00	140.00
	d. *POR* added at l. of sign. title at l. 25.3.1953; 25.2.1954.	8.50	37.50	140.00

		VG	VF	UNC
223	**50 COLONES** 1952-64. Olive on m/c unpt. Portr. R. F. Guardia at ctr. Back olive; National Library at ctr.			
	a. 10.6.1952-25.11.1959.	11.50	45.00	190.00
	b. 14.9.1960-9.9.1964.	9.00	40.00	175.00

		VG	VF	UNC
225	**500 COLONES** 1951-77. Purple on m/c unpt. Portr. M. M. Gutiérrez at r. Back purple; National Theater at ctr. Printer: ABNC.			
	a. 10.10.1951-6.5.1969.	60.00	250.00	700.00
	b. 7.4.1970-26.4.1977.	50.00	225.00	500.00

		VG	VF	UNC
226	**1000 COLONES** 1952-74. Red on m/c unpt. Portr. J. Pena at l. Back red; Central and National Bank at ctr.			
	a. 11.6.1952-6.10.1959.	100.00	350.00	650.00
	b. 25.4.1962-6.5.1969.	100.00	300.00	750.00
	c. 7.4.1970-12.6.1974.	50.00	125.00	350.00

1959 ISSUE

		VG	VF	UNC
227	**5 COLONES** 20.5.1959-3.11.1962. Green on m/c unpt. Portr. B. Carrillo at ctr. Back: green; coffee worker at ctr. Series B. Printer: W&S.	3.50	15.00	45.00

1963-70 ISSUES

#228 and 229 printer: TDLR.

		VG	VF	UNC
228	**5 COLONES** 3.10.1963-29.5.1967. Green on m/c unpt. Portr. B. Carrillo at ctr. Back green; coffee worker at ctr. Series C.	2.50	10.00	40.00

		VG	VF	UNC
229	**10 COLONES** 19.9.1962-9.10.1967. Blue on m/c unpt. Portr. Echeverría at ctr. Back blue; ox-cart at ctr. Series B.	5.00	20.00	80.00

		VG	VF	UNC
230	**10 COLONES** 1969-70; ND. Blue on m/c unpt. Portr. R. Facio Brenes at r. Back blue; Banco Central bldg. at ctr. Series C. Printer: ABNC.			
	a. 4.3.1969; 17.6.1969.	1.50	7.50	25.00
	b. 30.6.1970.	1.00	3.50	17.50
	x. W/o date or sign.	—	—	—

NOTE: It is reported that 10,000 pieces of #230x mistakenly reached circulation.

#231-234 printer: TDLR.

		VG	VF	UNC
231	**20 COLONES** 11.11.1964-30.6.1970. Brown on m/c unpt. Portr. Picado at ctr. Back brown; University bldg. at ctr. Series B.	4.00	15.00	60.00

		VG	VF	UNC
232	**50 COLONES** 9.6.1965-30.6.1970. Greenish-brown on m/c unpt. Portr. Guardia at ctr. Back greenish brown; National Library at ctr. Series B.	7.50	30.00	120.00

		VG	VF	UNC
233	**100 COLONES** 1961-66. Black on m/c unpt. Portr. J. R. Mora at ctr. Statue of J. Santamaría at ctr. on back. Series B.			
	a. Brown unpt. 18.10.1961-3.12.1964.	10.00	40.00	150.00
	b. Olive unpt. and w/security thread. 9.6.1965; 14.12.1965; 27.4.1966.	7.50	30.00	135.00

		VG	VF	UNC
234	**100 COLONES** 29.8.1966-27.8.1968. Black on m/c unpt. Portr. Mora at ctr., w/o *C* in corners or at r. Back black; statue of J. Santamaría at ctr. Series C.			
	a. Issued note.	7.50	30.00	120.00
	s. Specimen. Ovpt: *MUESTRA*.	—	—	500.00

1967 PROVISIONAL ISSUE

#235 ovpt: *BANCO CENTRAL DE COSTA RICA/SERIE PROVISIONAL* on Banco Nacional notes.

		VG	VF	UNC
235	**2 COLONES** 5.12.1967. Black ovpt. on #203 (Vol. 2). Series F.	3.00	10.00	40.00

NOTICE

Readers with unlisted dates, signature varieties, etc. are invited to submit photocopies of their notes to: Standard Catalog of World Paper Money, 700 East State St. Iola, WI 54990-0001, fax: 1-715-445-4087, or E-Mail: thernr@krause.com.

1968-72 ISSUES

236	5 COLONES	VG	VF	UNC
	1968-92. Deep green and lilac on m/c unpt. R. Y. Castro at l., flowers at r. Back green on m/c unpt; National Theater scene. Series D. Printer: TDLR.			
	a. Date at ctr. Wmk: *BCCR CINCO.* Security thread. Error name *T. VILLA* on back. 20.8.1968; 11.12.1968.	1.50	5.00	15.00
	b. Date at ctr. r. w/wmk. and security thread. Error name *T. VILLA* on back. 1.4.1969; 30.6.1970; 24.5.1971; 8.5.1972.	.50	1.00	4.00
	c. Date at ctr. r. wmk. and security thread. Corrected name *J. VILLA* on back. 4.5.1973-4.5.1976.	FV	.75	3.00
	d. W/o wmk. or security thread. Changed sign. titles. 28.6.1977-4.10.1989.	FV	FV	1.50
	e. As d. 24.1.1990-15.1.1992.	FV	FV	1.00
	s. As d. Specimen. Ovpt: *MUESTRA.*	—	—	50.00
	x. As d. but w/error date: 7.4.1933 (instead of 1983).	5.00	10.00	25.00

237	10 COLONES	VG	VF	UNC
	1972-87. Dk. blue on m/c unpt. University bldg. at l., R. Facio Brenes at r. Central Bank on back. Wmk: *BCCR 10.* Printer: ABNC (w/o imprint). Series D.			
	a. Security thread. 6.9.1972-26.4.1977.	.75	3.00	9.00
	b. W/o security thread. 13.3.1978-18.2.1987.	.50	1.00	3.00
	s. As a. Specimen. Ovpt: *MUESTRA.*	—	—	60.00

238	20 COLONES	VG	VF	UNC
	1972-83. Dk. brown on m/c unpt. C. G. Viquez at l., bldgs. and trees at r. Allegorical scene on back. Printer: ABNC (w/o imprint). Series C.			
	a. Wmk: *BCCR 20.* (error). *BARBA* - etc. text under bldgs. at ctr. Sign. titles: *EL PRESIDENTE DE LA JUNTA DIRECTIVA* and *EL GERENTE DEL BANCO.* Date at upper r., w/security strip. 10.7.1972; 6.9.1972.	1.50	5.00	20.00
	b. Wmk. as a. Text and sign. as a., date position at upper ctr., w/security strip. 13.11.1972-26.4.1977.	1.00	3.00	15.00
	c. W/o wmk. Lt. brown. Sign. titles: *PRESIDENTE EJECUTIVO* and *GERENTE.* W/o security thread. (corrected). *BARVA...* etc. text under bldgs. at ctr. Date at upper ctr. r. or upper ctr. 1.6.1978-7.4.1983.	—	1.00	4.00
	s1. Specimen. Ovpt: *MUESTRA.* 1.6.1978.	—	—	80.00
	s2. Specimen. ND.	—	—	80.00

239	50 COLONES	VG	VF	UNC
	6.9.1972-26.4.1977. Olive on m/c unpt. Meeting scene at at l., M. M. de Peralta y Alfaro at r. Casa *Amarilla* (Yellow House) on back. Printer: TDLR (w/o imprint). Series C.	1.50	—	30.00

240	100 COLONES	VG	VF	UNC
	26.8.1969-26.4.1977. Black on m/c unpt. R. Jimenez O. at l., cows and mountains at ctr. Supreme Court at l. ctr., figures at r. on back. Printer: TDLR. Series D.	3.50	12.00	40.00

1971 COMMEMORATIVE ISSUE

#241-246 circular ovpt: 150 *AÑOS DE INDEPENDENCIA* 1821-1971

241	5 COLONES	VG	VF	UNC
	24.5.1971. Ovpt. on #236b. Series D.	2.00	7.50	25.00

242	10 COLONES	VG	VF	UNC
	24.5.1971. Ovpt. on #230. Series C.	5.00	25.00	75.00

		VG	VF	Unc
243	**50 Colones** 24.5.1971. Ovpt. on #232. Series B.	20.00	75.00	250.00

		VG	VF	Unc
244	**100 Colones** 24.5.1971; 13.12.1971. Ovpt. on #240. Series D.	30.00	100.00	450.00

		VG	VF	Unc
245	**500 Colones** 24.5.1971. Ovpt. on #225 (Vol. 2). Series A.	125.00	500.00	1000.

		VG	VF	Unc
246	**1000 Colones** 24.5.1971. Ovpt. on #226 (Vol. 2). Series A.	200.00	650.00	1500.

1975 Commemorative Issue

#247 circular ovpt: *XXV ANIVERSARIO BANCO CENTRAL DE COSTA RICA.*

		VG	VF	Unc
247	**5 Colones** 20.3.1975. Ovpt. on #236. Series D.	1.50	10.00	30.00

1975-79 Issue

		VG	VF	Unc
248	**100 Colones** 1977-88. M/c. R. Jimenez O. at l. Similar to #240. Series E. Printer: TDLR.			
	a. 26.4.1977-24.12.1981.	1.00	4.00	15.00
	b. 18.5.1982-9.11.1988.	.75	3.00	12.00

		VG	VF	Unc
249	**500 Colones** 1979-85. Purple on m/c unpt. M. M. Gutiérrez at r. National Theatre at ctr. r. on back. Series B. Printer: TDLR.			
	a. Red serial #. 4.6.1979-12.3.1981.	3.50	15.00	60.00
	b. Black serial #. 17.9.1981; 24.12.1981; 18.5.1982; 7.8.1984; 20.3.1985.	2.50	10.00	40.00

		VG	VF	Unc
250	**1000 Colones** 9.6.1975; 24.12.1981; 8.7.1982; 4.11.1982; 7.4.1983; 2.10.1984; 20.3.1985. Red on m/c unpt. T. Soley Guell at l. National Insurance Institute at ctr. r. on back. Series B. Printer: ABNC.	FV	10.00	40.00

1978 Commemorative Issue

#251, Centennial - Bank of Costa Rica 1877-1977

		VG	VF	Unc
251	**50 Colones** 1978-86. Olive-green and m/c. Obverse of 1866-dated 50 Centimos coin at l., G. Ortuno y Ors at r. Bank, reverse of 50 Centimos coin and commemorative text: *1877-CENTENARIO...* on back. Series D. Printer: TDLR.			
	a. 30.10.1978; 30.4.1979; 18.3.1980; 2.4.1981.	1.50	6.00	20.00
	b. 18.5.1982; 28.8.1984; 22.11.1984; 20.3.1985; 2.4.1986.	1.00	4.00	15.00

1983-88 ISSUE

		VG	VF	UNC
252	**20 COLONES** 28.6.1983. Design like #238d, but Series Z. Printed on Tyvek (plastic).	1.00	5.00	20.00

		VG	VF	UNC
253	**50 COLONES** 15.7.1987; 26.4.1988. Olive-green on m/c unpt. Similar to 251 but text: *ANTIGUO EDIFICIO...* on back. Wmk: *BCCR 50* w/security thread. Series E. Printer: CdM-Brazil.	FV	1.50	5.00

1986; 1987 ISSUE

		VG	VF	UNC
254	**100 COLONES** 30.11.1988; 4.10.1989; 5.10.1990. Black on m/c unpt. Similar to #240 and 248. Series F. Printer: ABNC.	.50	2.00	8.00

		VG	VF	UNC
255	**500 COLONES** 21.1.1987; 14.6.1989. Brown-orange, brown and olive-brown on m/c unpt. Similar to #249, but clear wmk. area at l. Series C. Printer: TDLR.	FV	3.50	15.00

		VG	VF	UNC
256	**1000 COLONES** 19.11.1986; 17.6.1987; 6.1.1988; 17.1.1989. Red on m/c unpt. Similar to #250. Series C. Printer: ABNC.	FV	7.50	30.00

1990-92 ISSUE

		VG	VF	UNC
257	**50 COLONES** 19.6.1991; 28.8.1991; 29.7.1992; 2.6.1993; 7.7.1993. Olive-green on m/c unpt. Similar to #253. Series E. W/o security thread. Printer: TDLR.			
	a. Issued note.	FV	.50	2.50
	s. Specimen. Ovpt: *MUESTRA*.	—	—	120.00

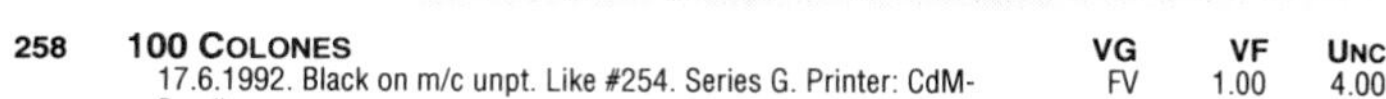

		VG	VF	UNC
258	**100 COLONES** 17.6.1992. Black on m/c unpt. Like #254. Series G. Printer: CdM-Brazil.	FV	1.00	4.00

		VG	VF	UNC
259	**1000 COLONES** 1990-94. Red on m/c unpt. Similar to #250 and #256. Series C. Printer: USBN.			
	a. 24.4.1990; 3.10.1990; 23.10.1991.	FV	4.00	15.00
	b. 2.2.1994; 20.4.1994; 15.6.1994; 10.10.1994.	FV	FV	12.50

		VG	VF	UNC
260	**5000 COLONES** 1991-95. Dk. blue, blue and dk. brown on m/c unpt. Local sculpture at l. ctr. Bird, leopard, local carving, foliage and sphere on back. Series A. Printer: TDLR.			
	a. 28.8.1991;11.3.1992; 29.7.1992.	FV	20.00	65.00
	b. 4.5.1994; 18.1.1995.	FV	FV	50.00

1993-97 ISSUE

		VG	VF	UNC
261	**100 COLONES** 28.9.1993. Black on m/c unpt. Like #258. Wmk: *BCCR-100* (repeated). Series H. Printer: ABNC.			
	a. Issued note.	FV	.75	3.50
	s. Specimen. Ovpt: *MUESTRA.* 28.9.1993.	—	—	175.00

		VG	VF	UNC
262	**500 COLONES** 6.7.1994. Brown-orange, brown and olive-brown on m/c unpt. Similar to #255 but w/printing in wmk. area at l. Ascending size serial # at lower l. Series D. Printer: TDLR.			
	a. Issued note.	FV	FV	7.50
	s. Specimen. Ovpt: *MUESTRA.* 6.7.1994.	—	—	200.00

#263 *Deleted.* See #259.

#264-267 printer: F-CO.

		VG	VF	UNC
264	**1000 COLONES** 23.7.1997. Red on m/c unpt. Like #263 but w/ascending size serial # at upper r. Series D.			
	a. Issued note.	FV	FV	10.00
	s. Specimen. Ovpt: *MUESTRA.* 23.7.1997.	—	—	300.00

		VG	VF	UNC
265	**2000 COLONES** 30.7.1997 (1998). Brown-orange and dk. brown on m/c unpt. C. Picado T. at ctr. r. and as wmk., Coco Island in unpt. at ctr. Hammerhead shark at l., dolphin at lower ctr. on back. Series A.			
	a. Issued note.	FV	FV	20.00
	s. Specimen. Ovpt: *MUESTRA.* 30.7.1997.	—	—	500.00

		VG	VF	UNC
266	**5000 COLONES** 27.3.1996 (1997). Dk. blue and dk. brown on m/c unpt. Like #261 but w/ascending size serial #. Series B. Printer: TDLR.			
	a. Issued note.	FV	FV	40.00
	s. Specimen. Ovpt: *MUESTRA.* 27.3.1996.	—	—	500.00

		VG	VF	UNC
267	**10,000 COLONES** 30.7.1997 (1998). Dk. blue and deep blue-green on m/c unpt. E. Gamboa A. at ctr. r. and as wmk., volcanoes in unpt. at ctr. Puma at upper ctr. on back. Series A.			
	a. Issued note.	FV	FV	95.00
	s. Specimen. Ovpt: *MUESTRA.* 30.7.1997.	—	—	900.00

The Republic of Croatia (Hrvatska), formerly a federal republic of the Socialist Federal Republic of Yugoslavia, has an area of 21,829 sq. mi. (56,538 sq. km.) and a population of 4.66 million. Capital: Zagreb.

Countless archeological sites witness the rich history of the area dating from Greek and Roman times, continuing uninterruptedly through the Middle Ages until today. An Independent state under the first Count Borna (about 800 AD) Croatia was proclaimed a kingdom under Tomislav in 925. In 1102 the country joined the personal union with Hungary, and by 1527 all Croatian lands were included in the Habsburg kingdom, staying in the union until 1918, when Croatia became part of the Yugoslav kingdom together with Slovenia and Serbia. In the past, Croats played a leading role in the wars against the Turks, the Antemuralis Christianitatis, and were renown soldiers in the Napoleonic army. From 1941 to 1945 Croatia was an independent puppet state; from 1945 to 1991 it was part of the Socialist state of Yugoslavia. Croatia proclaimed its independence from Yugoslavia on Oct. 8, 1991.

Local Serbian forces supported by the Yugoslav Federal Army had developed a military stronghold and proclaimed an independent "SRPSKE KRAJINA" state in the area around Knin, located in southern Croatia. In August 1995 Croat forces overran this political-military enclave.

MONETARY SYSTEM:

1 Dinar = 100 Para

REPUBLIC

REPUBLIKA HRVATSKA

REPUBLIC OF CROATIA

1991-93 ISSUE

#16-27 R. Boskovic at ctr., geometric calculations at upper r. (Printed in Sweden).

#16-22 vertical back with Zagreb cathedral and artistic rendition of city buildings behind.

		VG	VF	UNC
16	**1 DINAR** 8.10.1991. Dull orange-brown on m/c unpt. 4.5mm serial #. Wmk: Lozenges.			
	a. Issued note.	—	.05	.10
	s. Specimen.	—	—	20.00

		VG	VF	UNC
17	**5 DINARA** 8.10.1991. Pale violet on m/c unpt. 4mm serial #. Wmk: Lozenges.			
	a. Issued note.	—	.05	.15
	s. Specimen.	—	—	20.00

		VG	VF	UNC
18	**10 DINARA** 8.10.1991. Pale red-brown on m/c unpt. 4.5mm serial #. Wmk: Lozenges.			
	a. Issued note.	.05	.15	.30
	s. Specimen.	—	—	20.00

		VG	VF	UNC
19	**25 DINARA** 8.10.1991. Dull violet on m/c unpt. Buff paper w/2.8mm serial #. Wmk: 5's in crossed wavy lines.			
	a. Issued note.	.10	.25	.50
	b. Inverted wmk.	6.50	16.00	32.50
	s. Specimen.	—	—	30.00

NOTE: The wmk. paper actually used in the production for #19 was originally prepared for printing Sweden 5 Kroner, #51.

		VG	VF	UNC
20	**100 DINARA** 8.10.1991. Pale green on m/c unpt. W/o wmk.			
	a. Issued note.	.10	.40	1.00
	s. Specimen.	—	—	40.00

#21-26 wmk: Baptismal font.

		VG	VF	UNC
21	**500 DINARA** 8.10.1991. Lilac on m/c unpt.			
	a. Issued note.	.50	2.00	9.00
	s. Specimen.	—	—	30.00

		VG	VF	UNC
22	**1000 DINARA** 8.10.1991. Pale blue-violet on m/c unpt.			
	a. Issued note.	.60	2.40	10.00
	s. Specimen.	—	—	30.00

#23-26 statue of seated Glagolica *Mother Croatia* at ctr. on back.

		VG	VF	UNC
23	**2000 DINARA** 15.1.1992. Deep brown on m/c unpt.			
	a. Issued note.	.35	1.50	6.50
	s. Specimen.	—	—	30.00

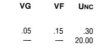

		VG	VF	UNC
24	**5000 DINARA** 15.1.1992. Dark gray on m/c unpt.			
	a. Issued note.	.40	1.60	6.50
	s. Specimen.	—	—	30.00

		VG	VF	UNC
25	**10,000 DINARA** 15.1.1992. Olive-green on m/c unpt.			
	a. Issued note.	.20	1.00	5.00
	s. Specimen.	—	—	30.00

		VG	VF	UNC
26	**50,000 DINARA** 30.5.1993. Deep red on m/c unpt.			
	a. Issued note.	.05	.15	.50
	s. Specimen.	—	—	30.00

		VG	VF	UNC
27	**100,000 DINARA** 30.5.1993. Dk. blue-green on m/c unpt.			
	a. Issued note.	.10	.25	.75
	s. Specimen.	—	—	30.00

1994 ISSUE

#28-35 shield at upper l. ctr. Printer: G & D.

		VG	VF	UNC
28	**5 KUNA** 31.10.1993 (1994). Dk. green and green on m/c unpt. F. K. Frankopan and P. Zrinski at r. and as wmk. Fortress in Varazdin at l. ctr. on back.			
	a. Issued note.	FV	FV	3.00
	x. Error w/o date or sign.	12.00	30.00	60.00
	s. Specimen.	—	—	40.00

		VG	VF	UNC
29	**10 KUNA** 31.10.1993 (1994). Purple and violet on m/c unpt. J. Dobrila at r. and as wmk. Pula arena at l. ctr. on back.			
	a. Issued note.	FV	FV	7.00
	s. Specimen.	—	—	40.00

		VG	VF	UNC
30	**20 KUNA** 31.10.1993 (1994). Brown, red and violet on m/c unpt. J. Jelacic at r. and as wmk. Pottery dove and castle of Count Eltz in Vukovar at l. ctr. on back.			
	a. Issued note.	FV	FV	10.00
	s. Specimen.	—	—	40.00

		VG	VF	UNC
31	**50 KUNA** 31.10.1993 (1994). Dk. blue and blue-green on m/c unpt. I. Gundulic at r. and as wmk. Aerial view of old Dubrovnik at l. ctr. on back.			
	a. Issued note.	FV	FV	20.00
	s. Specimen.	—	—	40.00

		VG	VF	UNC
32	**100 KUNA** 31.10.1993 (1994). Red-brown and brown-orange on m/c unpt. I. Mazuranic at r. and as wmk. Plan of and church of St. Vitus in Rijeka at l. ctr. on back.			
	a. Issued note.	FV	FV	35.00
	x. Error w/o serial #.	13.50	32.50	65.00
	s. Specimen.	—	—	40.00

		VG	VF	UNC
33	**200 KUNA** 31.10.1993 (1994). Dk. brown and brown on m/c unpt. S. Radic at r. and as wmk. Town command in Osijek at l. ctr. on back.			
	a. Issued note.	FV	FV	55.00
	s. Specimen.	—	—	40.00
34	**500 KUNA** 31.10.1993 (1994). Dk. brown and olive-brown on m/c unpt. M. Marulic at r. and as wmk. Palace of Diocletian in Spit at l. ctr. on back.			
	a. Issued note.	FV	FV	130.00
	s. Specimen.	—	—	40.00
35	**1000 KUNA** 31.10.1993 (1994). Dk. brown and purple on m/c unpt. A. Star cevic at r. and as wmk. Equestrian statue of Kg. Tomislav at l. ctr., Zagreb Cathedral at ctr. r. on back.			
	a. Issued note.	FV	FV	240.00
	s. Specimen.	—	—	40.00

1995 ISSUE

		VG	VF	UNC
36	**10 KUNA** 15.1.1995. Black and brown on m/c unpt. Like #29. Printer: G&D.			
	a. Issued note.	FV	FV	4.00
	s. Specimen.	—	—	40.00

COLLECTOR SERIES

REPUBLIC OF CROATIA

1998 ISSUE

		ISSUE PRICE	MKT. VALUE
CS1	**1991-93 1-100,000 DINARA** #16-27 w/matched serial #. (50,000).	38.50	—
CS2	**1993 5-1000 KUNA** #28-36 w/matched serial #. (50,000).	385.00	—

NOTE: #CS1 and CS2 are sold by the Croatian National Bank.

REGIONAL

KNIN

РЕПУБЛИКА СРПСКА КРАЈИНА

REPUBLIKA SRPSKA KRAJINA

1991 ВРИЈЕДНОСНИ БОН ISSUE

#RA1-RA3 Serbian arms at upper l. Uniface.

		VG	VF	UNC
RA1	**10,000 DINARA** 1991.	—	120.00	450.00

		VG	VF	UNC
RA2	**20,000 DINARA** 1991.	—	60.00	350.00

		VG	VF	UNC
RA3	**50,000 DINARA** 1991.	—	80.00	450.00

1992 ISSUE

#R1-R6 arms at l., numerals in heartshaped design below guilloche at ctr. r. Curved artistic design at l. ctr., arms at r. on back. Headings in Serbo-Croatian and Cyrillic.

#R1-R3 wmk: Young girl.

Replacement notes: #R1-R34, ZA prefix letters.

NOTE: For notes identical in color and design to #R1-R19 but differing only in text at top, sign. and place of issue Banja Luka, see Bosnia & Hercegovina #133-147.

		VG	VF	UNC
R1	**10 DINARA** 1992. Deep brown on orange and silver unpt. Back with ochre unpt.			
	a. Issued note.	.25	1.00	4.00
	b. Specimen.	—	—	13.50

		VG	VF	UNC
R2	**50 DINARA** 1992. Gray on tan and yellow unpt.			
	a. Issued note.	.30	1.25	5.00
	s. Specimen.	—	—	13.50

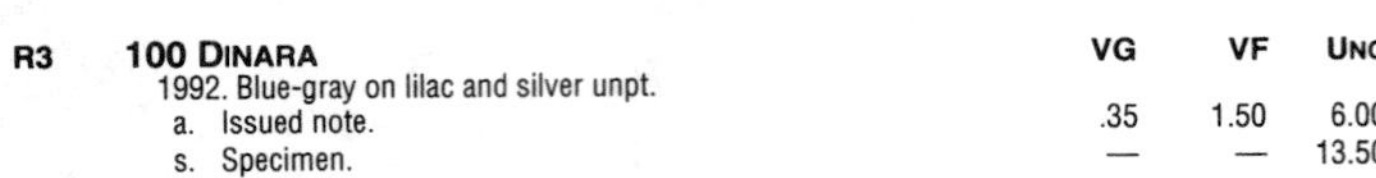

		VG	VF	UNC
R3	**100 DINARA**			
	1992. Blue-gray on lilac and silver unpt.			
	a. Issued note.	.35	1.50	6.00
	s. Specimen.	—	—	13.50

		VG	VF	UNC
R4	**500 DINARA**			
	1992. Blue-gray on pink and m/c unpt. Wmk: Young boy.			
	a. Issued note.	1.00	5.00	20.00
	s. Specimen.	—	—	13.50

		VG	VF	UNC
R5	**1000 DINARA**			
	1992. Deep gray on pink and tan unpt.			
	a. Issued note.	1.00	5.00	20.00
	s. Specimen.	—	—	13.50
R6	**5000 DINARA**			
	1992. Violet on lt. blue, pink and lilac unpt.			
	a. Issued note.	.85	3.75	15.00
	s. Specimen.	—	—	13.50

НАРОДНА БАНКА РЕПУБЛИКЕ СРПСКЕ КРАЈИНЕ

NARODNA BANKA REPUBLIKE SRPSKE KRAJINE

NATIONAL BANK OF THE SERBIAN REPUBLIC - KRAJINA

1992-93 ISSUE

#R7-R12 replacement notes: Serial # prefix *ZA*.

#R7-R16 like #R1-R6.

		VG	VF	UNC
R7	**10,000 DINARA**			
	1992. Deep gray-green on lt. blue and tan unpt.			
	a. Issued note.	.60	2.50	20.00
	s. Specimen.	—	—	13.50

		VG	VF	UNC
R8	**50,000 DINARA**			
	1992. Brown on pale orange and pale olive-green unpt. Wmk: Young boy.			
	a. Issued note.	.60	4.00	35.00
	s. Specimen.	—	—	13.50

		VG	VF	UNC
R9	**100,000 DINARA**			
	1993. Dull purple and brown on m/c unpt. Wmk: Young women.			
	a. Issued note.	.60	2.75	22.50
	s. Specimen.	—	—	13.50

#R10-R12 wmk: Young girl.

		VG	VF	UNC
R10	**1 MILLION DINARA**			
	1993. Deep purple on m/c unpt.			
	a. Issued note.	1.25	4.00	37.00
	s. Specimen.	—	—	13.50

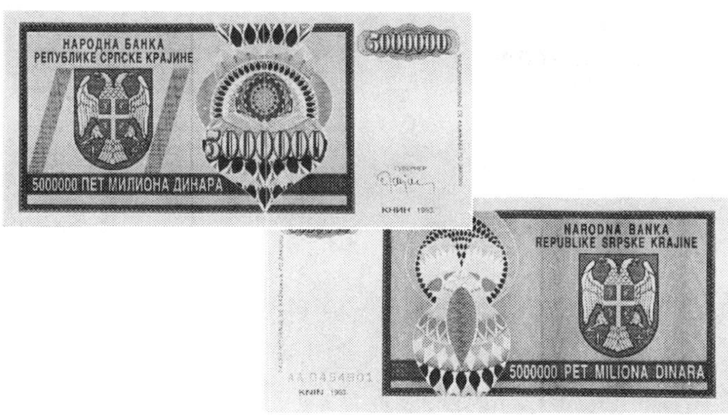

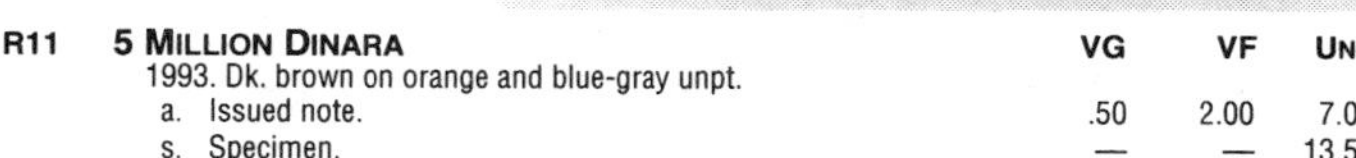

		VG	VF	UNC
R11	**5 MILLION DINARA** 1993. Dk. brown on orange and blue-gray unpt.			
	a. Issued note.	.50	2.00	7.00
	s. Specimen.	—	—	13.50

		VG	VF	UNC
R12	**10 MILLION DINARA** 1993. Deep blue on pale olive-green and m/c unpt.			
	a. Issued note.	.30	1.25	5.00
	s. Specimen.	—	—	13.50

#R13-R19 wmk: Greek design repeated. Replacement notes: Serial # prefix *Z*.

		VG	VF	UNC
R13	**20 MILLION DINARA** 1993. Olive-gray on orange and tan unpt.			
	a. Issued note.	.75	3.00	12.00
	s. Specimen.	—	—	13.50

		VG	VF	UNC
R14	**50 MILLION DINARA** 1993. Brown-violet on pink and lt. gray unpt.			
	a. Issued note.	.60	2.50	8.00
	s. Specimen.	—	—	13.50

		VG	VF	UNC
R15	**100 MILLION DINARA** 1993. Blue-black on lt. blue and gray unpt.			
	a. Issued note.	.30	1.25	5.00
	s. Specimen.	—	—	13.50

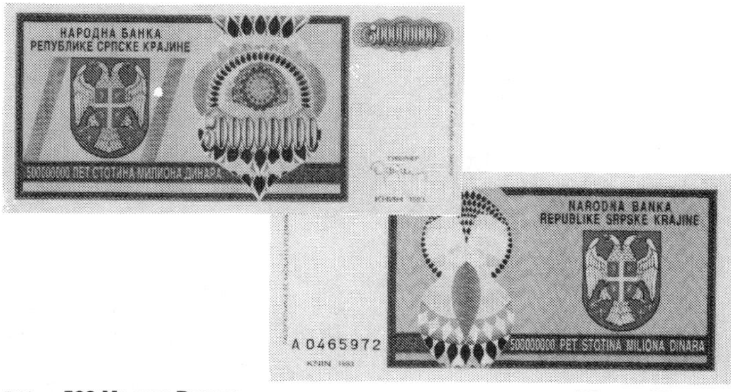

		VG	VF	UNC
R16	**500 MILLION DINARA** 1993. Orange on lilac and yellow unpt.			
	a. Issued note.	.30	1.25	7.00
	s. Specimen.	—	—	13.50

		VG	VF	UNC
R17	**1 MILLIARD DINARA** 1993. Dull brownish orange on pale blue and lt. orange unpt.			
	a. Issued note.	.30	1.25	7.00
	s. Specimen.	—	—	13.50

		VG	VF	UNC
R18	**5 MILLIARD DINARA** 1993. Purple on lilac and gray unpt.			
	a. Issued note.	.60	2.50	12.00
	s. Specimen.	—	—	13.50

		VG	VF	UNC
R19	**10 MILLIARD DINARA** 1993. Black on orange and pink unpt.			
	a. Issued note.	.75	3.00	13.50
	s. Specimen.	—	—	13.50

1993 ISSUE

#R20-R27 Knin fortress on hill at l. ctr. Serbian arms at ctr. r. on back. Wmk: Greek design repeated. Replacement notes: Serial # prefix *Z*.

		VG	VF	UNC
R20	**5000 DINARA** 1993. Red-violet and violet on blue-gray unpt.			
	a. Issued note.	.20	.75	3.00
	s. Specimen.	—	—	13.50

		VG	VF	UNC
R21	**50,000 DINARA** 1993. Brown, red and red-orange on ochre unpt.			
	a. Issued note.	.15	.75	3.00
	s. Specimen.	—	—	13.50

		VG	VF	UNC
R22	**100,000 DINARA** 1993. Violet and blue-gray on pink unpt.			
	a. Issued note.	.20	.75	3.00
	s. Specimen.	—	—	13.50

		VG	VF	UNC
R23	**500,000 DINARA** 1993. Brown and gray-green on pale green unpt.			
	a. Issued note.	.15	.75	3.00
	s. Specimen.	—	—	13.50

		VG	VF	UNC
R24	**5 MILLION DINARA** 1993. Orange and gray-green on pale orange unpt.			
	a. Issued note.	.15	.75	3.00
	s. Specimen.	—	—	13.50

		VG	VF	UNC
R25	**100 MILLION DINARA** 1993. Olive-brown and grayish green on lt. blue unpt.			
	a. Issued note.	.15	.75	3.00
	s. Specimen.	—	—	13.50

		VG	VF	UNC
R26	**500 MILLION DINARA** 1993. Chocolate brown and gray-green on pale olive-green unpt.			
	a. Issued note.	.20	.75	3.00
	s. Specimen.	—	—	13.50

R27	5 MILLIARD DINARA	VG	VF	UNC
	1993. Brown-orange and aqua on gray unpt.			
	a. Issued note.	.25	1.00	5.00
	s. Specimen.	—	—	13.50

R28	10 MILLIARD DINARA	VG	VF	UNC
	1993. Purple and red on aqua unpt.			
	a. Issued note.	.30	1.25	7.00
	s. Specimen.	—	—	13.50

R29	50 MILLIARD DINARA	VG	VF	UNC
	1993. Brown and olive-green on reddish brown unpt.			
	a. Issued note.	.25	1.00	5.00
	s. Specimen.	—	—	13.50

1994 ISSUE

#R30-R34 like #R2-R29.

Replacement notes: Serial # prefix *ZA*.

R30	1000 DINARA	VG	VF	UNC
	1994. Dk. brown and slate-gray on yellow-orange unpt.			
	a. Issued note.	.15	.50	2.00
	s. Specimen.	—	—	13.50

R31	10,000 DINARA	VG	VF	UNC
	1994. Red-brown and dull purple on ochre unpt.			
	a. Issued note.	.15	.50	2.00
	s. Specimen.	—	—	13.50

R32	500,000 DINARA	VG	VF	UNC
	1994. Dk. brown and blue-gray on grayish green unpt.			
	a. Issued note.	.20	.75	3.00
	s. Specimen.	—	—	13.50

R33	1 MILLION DINARA	VG	VF	UNC
	1994. Purple and aqua on lilac unpt.			
	a. Issued note.	.20	.75	3.00
	s. Specimen.	—	—	13.50

R34	10 MILLION DINARA	VG	VF	UNC
	1994. Gray and red-brown on pink unpt.			
	a. Issued note.	.30	1.25	6.50
	s. Specimen.	—	—	13.50

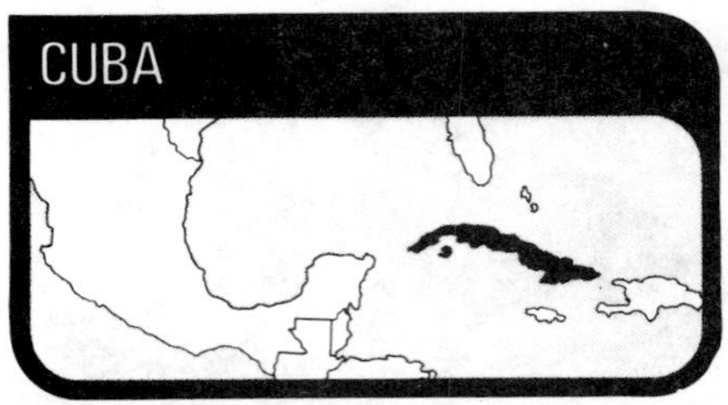

The Republic of Cuba, situated at the northern edge of the Caribbean Sea about 90 miles (145 km.) south of Florida, has an area of 44,218 sq. mi. (114,524 sq. km.) and a population of 10.95 million. Capital: Havana. The Cuban economy is based on the cultivation and refining of sugar, which provides 80 percent of export earnings.

Discovered by Columbus in 1492 and settled by Diego Velasquez in the early 1500s, Cuba remained a Spanish possession until 1898, except for a brief British occupancy in 1762-63. Cuban attempts to gain freedom were crushed, even while Spain was granting independence to its other American possessions. Ten years of warfare, 1868-78, between Spanish troops and Cuban rebels exacted guarantees of right which were never implemented. The final revolt, begun in 1895, evoked American sympathy, and with the aid of U.S. troops independence was proclaimed on May 20, 1902. Fulgencio Batista seized the government in 1952 and established a dictatorship. Opposition to Batista, led by Fidel Castro, drove him into exile on Jan. 1, 1959. A communist-type, 25-member collective leadership headed by Castro was inaugurated in March 1962.

MONETARY SYSTEM:

1 Peso = 100 Centavos
1 Peso Convertible = 1 U.S.A. Dollar, 1995-

REPUBLIC

BANCO NACIONAL DE CUBA

NATIONAL BANK OF CUBA

1961 ISSUE

#94-99 denomination at l. and r. Sign. titles: *PRESIDENTE DEL BANCO* at., *MINISTRO DE HACIENDA* at r. Printer: STC-P (w/o imprint).

94	1 PESO	VG	VF	UNC
	1961-65. Olive-green on ochre unpt. Portr. J. Martí at ctr. F. Castro w/rebel soldiers entering Havana in 1959 on back.			
	a. 1961.	1.00	2.50	13.00
	b. 1964.	.50	2.25	9.00
	c. 1965.	.40	1.75	7.00

95	5 PESOS	VG	VF	UNC
	1961-65. Dull deep green on pink unpt. Portr. A. Maceo at ctr. Invasion of 1958 on back.			
	a. 1961.	1.00	3.75	16.00
	b. 1964.	.75	3.00	12.00
	c. 1965.	.60	2.50	10.00

96	10 PESOS	VG	VF	UNC
	1961-65. Brown on tan and yellow unpt. Portr. M. Gómez at ctr. Castro addressing crowd in 1960 on back.			
	a. 1961.	1.25	5.00	22.50
	b. 1964.	1.10	4.50	18.50
	c. 1965.	1.00	4.00	16.50

97	20 PESOS	VG	VF	UNC
	1961-65. Blue on pink unpt. Portr. C. Cienfuegos at ctr. Soldiers on the beach in 1956 on back.			
	a. 1961.	2.50	10.00	45.00
	b. 1964.	2.00	8.00	32.50
	c. 1965.	1.75	7.50	30.00
	x. U.S.A. counterfeit. Series F69; F70, 1961.	3.50	15.00	85.00

NOTE: Each member of the "Bay of Pigs" invasion force was reportedly issued one hundred each of #97x.

98	50 PESOS	VG	VF	UNC
	1961. Purple on green unpt. Portr. C. García Iñiguez at ctr. Nationalization of international industries on back.	10.00	30.00	135.00

99	100 PESOS	VG	VF	UNC
	1961. Lt. red on orange unpt. Portr. C. M. de Céspedes at ctr. Attack on Moncada in 1953 on back.	25.00	75.00	250.00

NOTE: #98 and 99 were recalled shortly after release. A small hoard recently appeared in the marketplace.

1966 ISSUE

#100 and 101 denomination at l. and r. Sign titles: *PRESIDENTE DEL BANCO* at l. and r. Printer: STC-P (w/o imprint).

		VG	VF	UNC
100	**1 PESO** 1966. Deep olive-green on ochre unpt. Like #94.	.30	1.25	10.00
101	**10 PESOS** 1966. Brown on tan and yellow unpt. Like #96.	2.00	8.50	35.00

1967; 1971 ISSUE

#102-105 denomination at l. Sign. title: *PRESIDENTE DEL BANCO* at lower r. Printer: STC-P (w/o imprint).

		VG	VF	UNC
102	**1 PESO** 1967-88. Deep olive-green on ochre unpt. Similar to #94.			
	a. 1967-70; 1972.	FV	1.00	5.00
	b. 1978-85.	FV	FV	3.50
	c. 1986.	FV	FV	3.00
	d. 1988.	FV	FV	2.50

		VG	VF	UNC
103	**5 PESOS** 1967-90. Dull deep green on pink unpt. Similar to #95.			
	a. 1967-68.	FV	4.00	20.00
	b. 1970; 1972.	FV	FV	12.50
	c. 1984-87.	FV	FV	10.00
	d. 1988; 1990.	FV	FV	6.00

		VG	VF	UNC
104	**10 PESOS** 1967-89. Brown on tan and yellow unpt. Similar to #96.			
	a. 1967-71.	FV	8.00	35.00
	b. 1978.	FV	FV	25.00
	c. 1983-84; 1986-87.	FV	FV	18.00
	d. 1988-89.	FV	FV	11.00

		VG	VF	UNC
105	**20 PESOS** 1971-90. Blue on pink unpt. Similar to #97.			
	a. 1971.	FV	8.00	35.00
	b. 1978.	FV	FV	35.00
	c. 1983.	FV	FV	30.00
	d. 1987-90.	FV	FV	17.50

1975 COMMEMORATIVE ISSUE

#106, 15th Anniversary Nationalization of Banking

		VG	VF	UNC
106	**1 PESO** 1975. Olive on violet unpt. Portr. J. Martí at l., arms at r. Ship dockside on back.	.50	1.25	5.00

1983 ISSUE

		VG	VF	UNC
107	**3 PESOS** 1983-89. Red on m/c unpt. Portr. E. "Che" Guevara at ctr. Back red on orange unpt.; "Che" cutting sugar cane at ctr.			
	a. 1983-86.	FV	1.25	5.00
	b. 1988-89.	FV	FV	2.00

1990; 1991 ISSUE

Replacement notes: #108-112: *EX, DX, CX, BX, AX* series #, by denomination.

		VG	VF	UNC
108	**5 PESOS** 1991. Deep green and deep blue on m/c unpt. A. Maceo at r. Secret meeting of the rebel military in the woods at l. ctr. on back. Wmk: J. Martí.	.25	1.00	1.75

		VG	VF	UNC
109	**10 PESOS** 1991. Deep brown and deep olive-green on m/c unpt. M. Gómez at r. "Guerra de todo el Pueblo" at l. ctr. on back. Wmk: J. Martí.	.50	2.00	3.25

		VG	VF	UNC
110	**20 PESOS** 1991. Blue-black and purple on m/c unpt. Agricultural scenes at l. ctr. on back. Wmk: National heroine - Tania.	1.00	4.00	6.00

		VG	VF	UNC
111	**50 PESOS** 1990. Deep violet and dk. green on m/c unpt. Arms at ctr. C. García Iñiguez at r. Center of Genetic Engineering and Biotechnology at l. ctr. on back. Wmk: National heroine - Tania.	1.25	5.00	10.00

1995 ISSUE

#112 and 113 arms at upper ctr. r.

		VG	VF	UNC
112	**1 PESO** 1995. Dull olive-green on lt. blue and m/c unpt. J. Martí at l., arms at upper ctr. r. F. Castro w/rebel soldiers entering Havana in 1959 on back.	FV	FV	.75

		VG	VF	UNC
113	**3 PESOS** 1995. E. "Che" Guevara at l. "Che" cutting sugar cane on back.	FV	FV	1.50

BANCO CENTRAL DE CUBA

Established in 1997 to replace the Banco Nacional as issuer of coins and paper currency.

#114 and 115 held in reserve.

1997 ISSUE

		VG	VF	UNC
116	**5 PESOS** 1997. Dk. green on m/c unpt. A. Maceo at r. Back similar to #108.	FV	FV	1.65
117	**10 PESOS** 1997. Dk. brown on m/c unpt. M. Gómez at r. Back similar to #109.	FV	FV	3.25

FOREIGN EXCHANGE CERTIFICATES

The Banco Nacional de Cuba issued four types of peso certificates in series A, B, C and D. The C and D series was issued in two designs and originally required hand issue date and sign. at redemption. Resembling traveler's checks.

BANCO NACIONAL DE CUBA

SERIES A

#FX1-FX5 red-violet. Arms at l. Various Spanish colonial fortresses on back.

		VG	VF	UNC
FX1	**1 PESO** ND (1985-). Orange and olive-green unpt. Castillo San Salvador de la Punta on back.	.30	1.50	3.50

		VG	VF	UNC
FX2	**3 PESOS** ND (1985-). Orange and pink unpt. Castillo San Pedro de la Roca on back.	.60	3.50	7.00
FX3	**5 PESOS** ND (1985-). Orange and blue-green unpt. Castillo de Los Tres Reyes on back.	1.00	5.00	10.00

NOTICE

Readers with unlisted dates, signature varieties, etc. are invited to submit photocopies of their notes to: Standard Catalog of World Paper Money, 700 East State St. Iola, WI 54990-0001, fax: 1-715-445-4087, or E-Mail: thernr@krause.com.

No.	Description	VG	VF	UNC
FX4	**10 PESOS** ND (1985-). Orange and brown unpt. Castillo Nuestra Señora de Los Angeles de Jagua on back.	2.00	9.00	18.00

No.	Description	VG	VF	UNC
FX5	**20 PESOS** ND (1985-). Orange and blue unpt. Castillo de la Real Fuerza on back.	4.00	20.00	40.00

SERIES B

#FX6-FX10 dk. green. Arms at l. Various Spanish colonial fortresses on back.

No.	Description	VG	VF	UNC
FX6	**1 PESO** ND (1985-). Lt. green and olive-brown unpt. Back like #FX1.	.20	1.00	2.50
FX7	**5 PESOS** ND (1985-). Lt. green and blue-green unpt. Back like #FX3.	1.00	5.00	20.00
FX8	**10 PESOS** ND (1985-). Lt. green and brown unpt. Back like #FX4.	2.00	10.00	30.00
FX9	**20 PESOS** ND (1985-). Lt. green and blue unpt. Back like #FX5.	4.00	20.00	40.00

No.	Description	VG	VF	UNC
FX10	**50 PESOS** ND (1985-). Lt. green and dull violet unpt. Castillo de la Chorrera on back.	10.00	50.00	100.00

SERIES C FIRST ISSUE

Note: Large quantities were sold into the numismatic market.

#FX11-18 pale blue. Arms at l.

No.	Description	VG	VF	UNC
FX11	**1 PESO** ND. Lt. blue and lt. red-brown unpt.	.10	.25	1.50

No.	Description	VG	VF	UNC
FX12	**3 PESOS** ND. Lt. blue and violet unpt.	.10	.30	1.75
FX13	**5 PESOS** ND. Lt. blue and lt. olive unpt.	.10	.50	2.50
FX14	**10 PESOS** ND. Lt. blue and lilac unpt.	.10	.40	2.25
FX15	**20 PESOS** ND. Lt. blue and tan unpt.	.15	.50	3.00
FX16	**50 PESOS** ND. Lt. blue and rose unpt.	.20	.60	3.50
FX17	**100 PESOS** ND. Lt. blue and ochre unpt.	.20	.75	4.00
FX18	**500 PESOS** ND. Lt. blue and tan unpt.	3.00	10.00	30.00

SERIES C SECOND ISSUE

#FX19-FX26 blue-violet. Similar to #FX11-FX18.

No.	Description	VG	VF	UNC
FX19	**1 PESO** ND.	Reported Not Confirmed		
FX20	**3 PESOS** ND. Lt. blue and red unpt.	.15	.60	1.25
FX21	**5 PESOS** ND. Lt. blue and pale olive-green unpt.	.25	1.00	2.00

No.	Description	VG	VF	UNC
FX22	**10 PESOS** ND. Lt. blue and brown unpt.	.50	2.00	4.00
FX23	**20 PESOS** ND. Lt. blue and orange-brown unpt.	1.00	4.00	8.00

No.	Description	VG	VF	UNC
FX24	**50 PESOS** ND. Lt. blue and violet unpt.	2.00	8.00	16.00
FX25	**100 PESOS** ND. Lt. blue and gray unpt.	3.75	15.00	30.00

FX26 500 Pesos
ND. — Reported Not Confirmed

Series D First Issue

#FX27-31 pale red-brown. Arms at l.

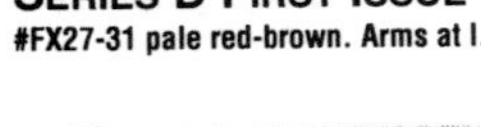

		VG	VF	Unc
FX27	**1 Peso** ND. Lt. orange and orange-brown unpt.	.30	1.50	3.50
FX28	**3 Pesos** ND. Lt. orange and pale blue unpt.	.60	3.00	7.00
FX29	**5 Pesos** ND. Lt. orange and lt. green unpt.	1.00	5.00	10.00
FX30	**10 Pesos** ND. Lt. orange and lilac unpt.	2.00	10.00	18.00

		VG	VF	Unc
FX31	**20 Pesos** ND. Lt. orange and ochre unpt.	4.00	20.00	32.00

Series D Second Issue

#FX32-FX36 dk. brown. Similar to #FX19-FX23. W/ or w/o various handstamps *ESPACIO EN BLANCO INUTILIZADO* or *ESPACIO INUTILIZADO* on back.

		VG	VF	Unc
FX32	**1 Peso** ND. Tan and pale olive-green unpt.	.10	.30	.60
FX33	**3 Pesos** ND. Tan and red unpt.	.15	.60	1.25
FX34	**5 Pesos** ND. Tan and green unpt.	.25	1.00	2.00
FX35	**10 Pesos** ND. Tan and orange unpt.	.50	2.00	4.00
FX36	**20 Pesos** ND. Tan and blue-gray unpt.	1.00	4.00	8.00

1994 Pesos Convertibles Issue

#FX37-FX43 arms at ctr. on back. Wmk: J. Martí.

		VG	VF	Unc
FX37	**1 Peso Convertible** 1994. Orange, brown and olive-green on m/c unpt. J. Martí monument at r. Arms at ctr. on back. Wmk: J. Marti.	FV	FV	2.50

		VG	VF	Unc
FX38	**3 Pesos Convertibles** 1994. Dull red, deep blue-green and brown on m/c unpt. E. "Che" Guevara monument at r.	FV	FV	7.00

		VG	VF	Unc
FX39	**5 Pesos Convertibles** 1994. Dk. green, orange and blue-black on m/c unpt. A. Maceo monument at r.	FV	FV	10.00

		VG	VF	Unc
FX40	**10 Pesos Convertibles** 1994. Brown, yellow-green and purple on m/c unpt. M. Gómez monument at r.	FV	FV	18.50

		VG	VF	Unc
FX41	**20 Pesos Convertibles** 1994. Blue, red and tan on m/c unpt. C. Cienfuegos monument at r.	FV	FV	35.00

		VG	VF	UNC
FX42	**50 Pesos Convertibles** 1994. Purple, brown and orange on m/c unpt. C. García monument at r.	FV	FV	80.00

		VG	VF	UNC
FX43	**100 Pesos Convertibles** 1994. Red-violet, brown-orange and purple on m/c unpt. C. Manuel de Céspedes monument at r.	FV	FV	150.00

Collector Series

Banco Nacional de Cuba

1961-1995 Issues

The Banco Nacional de Cuba had been selling specimen notes regularly of the 1961-1989 issues. Specimen notes dated 1961-66 have normal block # and serial # while notes from 1967 to date all have normal block # and all zero serial #.

		Issue Price	Mkt. Value
CS1	**1961 1-100 Pesos** Ovpt: *SPECIMEN* on #94a-97a, 98, 99.	—	110.00
CS2	**1964 1-20 Pesos** Ovpt: *SPECIMEN* on #94b-97b.	—	20.00
CS3	**1965 1-20 Pesos** Ovpt: *SPECIMEN* on #94c-97c.	—	14.00
CS4	**1966 1, 10 Pesos** Ovpt: *SPECIMEN* on #100, 101.	—	7.00
CS5	**1967 1-10 Pesos** Ovpt: *SPECIMEN* on #102a-104a.	—	10.00
CS6	**1968 1-10 Pesos** Ovpt: *SPECIMEN* on #102a-104a.	—	10.00
CS7	**1969 1, 10 Pesos** Ovpt: *SPECIMEN* on #102a, 104a.	—	7.00
CS8	**1970 1-10 Pesos** Ovpt: *SPECIMEN* on #102a, 103b, 104a.	—	7.00
CS9	**1971 10, 20 Pesos** Ovpt: *SPECIMEN* on #104a, 105a.	—	8.00
CS10	**1972 1, 5 Pesos** Ovpt: *SPECIMEN* on #102a, 103b.	—	7.00
CS11	**1975 1 Peso** Ovpt: *SPECIMEN* on #106.	—	10.00
CS12	**1978 1, 10, 20 Pesos** Ovpt: *SPECIMEN* on #102b, 104b, 105b.	—	11.00
CS13	**1979 1 Peso** Ovpt: *SPECIMEN* on #102b.	—	3.00
CS14	**1980 1 Peso** Ovpt: *SPECIMEN* on #102b.	—	3.00
CS15	**1981 1 Peso** Ovpt: *SPECIMEN* on #102b.	—	3.00
CS16	**1982 1 Peso** Ovpt: *MUESTRA* on #102b.	—	3.00
CS17	**1983 3, 10, 20 Pesos** Ovpt: *MUESTRA* on #104c, 105c, 107a.	—	12.00
CS18	**1984 3, 5, 10 Pesos** Ovpt: *MUESTRA* on #103c, 104c, 107a.	—	12.00
CS19	**1985 1, 3, 5 Pesos** Ovpt: *MUESTRA* on #102b, 103c, 107a.	—	12.00
CS20	**1986 1-10 Pesos** Ovpt: *MUESTRA* on #102b, 103c, 104c, 107a.	—	12.50
CS21	**1987 5, 10, 20 Pesos** Ovpt: *MUESTRA* on #103c-105c.	—	12.00
CS22	**1988 1-20 Pesos** Ovpt: *MUESTRA* on #102c, 103d-105d, 107b.	—	12.50
CS23	**1989 3, 20 Pesos** Ovpt: *MUESTRA* on #105d, 107b.	—	7.00
CS24	**1990 5, 20, 50 Pesos** Ovpt: *MUESTRA* on #103d, 105d, 111	—	10.00
CS25	**1991 5, 10, 20 Pesos** Ovpt: *SPECIMEN* on #108-110.	—	10.00
CS26	**1994 1-100 Peso Convertibles** Ovpt: *MUESTRA* on FX37-FX43.	—	60.00
CS27	**1995 1, 3 Pesos** Ovpt: *MUESTRA* on #112 and 113.	—	5.00

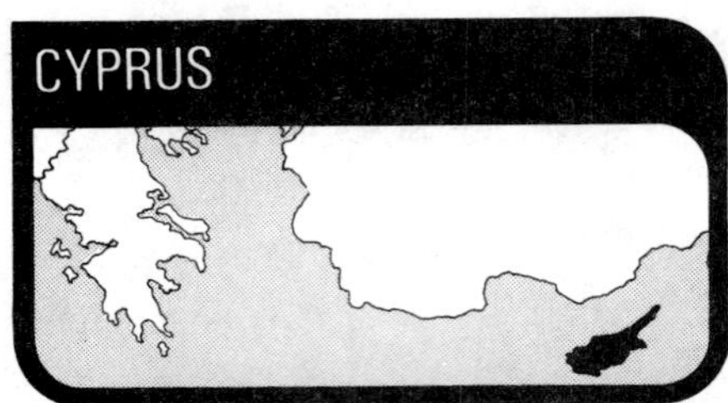

The Republic of Cyprus, a member of the European Commonwealth and Council, lies in the eastern Mediterranean Sea 44 miles (71 km.) south of Turkey and 60 miles (97 km.) west of Syria. It is the third largest island in the Mediterranean Sea, having an area if 3,572 sq. mi. (9,251 sq. km.) and a population of 729,800. Capital: Nicosia. Agriculture and mining are the chief industries. Asbestos, copper, citrus fruit, iron pyrites and potatoes are exported.

The importance of Cyprus dates from the Bronze Age when it was desired as a principal souce of copper (from which the island derived its name) and as a strategic trading center. Its role as an international marketplace made it a prime disseminator of the then prevalent cultures, a role that still influences the civilization of Western man. Because of its fortuitous position and influential role, Cyprus was conquered by a succession of empires; the Assyrian, Egyptian, Persian, Macedonian, Ptolemaic, Roman and Byzantine. It was taken from Isaac Comnenus by Richard the Lion-Hearted in 1191, sold to the Knights Templars, conquered by Venice and Turkey, and made a crown colony of Britain in 1925. Finally on Aug. 16, 1960, it became an independent republic.

In 1964, the ethnic Turks, who favor partition of Cyprus into separate Greek and Turkish states, withdrew from active participation in the government. Turkish forces invaded Cyprus in 1974 and gained control of 40 percent of the island. In 1975, Turkish Cypriots proclaimed their own Federated state in northern Cyprus. The UN held numerous discussions from 1985-92, without any results towards unification.

The president is Chief of State and Head of Government.

MONETARY SYSTEM:

1 Shilling = 9 Piastres
1 Pound = 20 Shillings to 1963
1 Shilling = 50 Mils
1 Pound = 1000 Mils, 1963-83
1 Pound = 100 Cents, 1983-

DEMOCRATIC REPUBLIC

ΚΥΠΡΙΑΚΗ ΔΗΜΟΚΡΑΤΙΑ

REPUBLIC OF CYPRUS

1961 ISSUE

#37-40 arms at r., map at lower r. Wmk: Eagle's head. Printer: BWC (w/o imprint).

		VG	VF	UNC
37	**250 MILS** 1.12.1961. Blue on m/c unpt. Fruit at l. Mine on back.	2.50	7.50	30.00
38	**500 MILS** 1.12.1961. Green on m/c unpt. Mountain road lined w/trees on back.	5.50	25.00	125.00

		VG	VF	UNC
39	**1 POUND** 1.12.1961. Brown on m/c unpt. Viaduct and pillars on back.	7.00	20.00	75.00
40	**5 POUNDS** 1.12.1961. Dk. green on m/c unpt. Embroidery and floral design on back.	15.00	40.00	175.00

ΚΕΝΤΡΙΚΗ ΤΡΑΠΕΖΑ ΤΗΣ ΚΥΠΡΟΥ

KIBRIS MERKEZ BANKASI

CENTRAL BANK OF CYPRUS

1964-66 ISSUE

#41-44 like #37-40. Various date and sign. varieties.

		VG	VF	UNC
41	**250 MILS** 1964-82. Like #37.			
	a. 1.12.1964-1.12.1969; 1.9.1971.	1.25	3.50	12.50
	b. 1.3.1971; 1.6.1972; 1.5.1973; 1.6.1974.	.75	2.00	9.00
	c. 1.7.1975-1.6.1982.	.65	1.50	6.00

		VG	VF	UNC
42	**500 MILS** 1964-79. Like #38.			
	a. 1.12.1964-1.6.1972.	2.00	5.00	20.00
	b. 1.5.1973; 1.6.1974; 1.7.1975; 1.8.1976.	1.35	3.50	12.00
	c. 1.6.1979; 1.9.1979.	1.25	2.00	7.50

		VG	VF	UNC
43	**1 POUND** 1966-78. Like #39.			
	a. 1.8.1966-1.6.1972.	2.75	7.00	27.50
	b. 1.11.1972; 1.5.1973; 1.6.1974; 1.8.1976.	2.50	4.50	17.50
	c. 1.7.1975; 1.5.1978.	2.25	3.00	12.00

		VG	VF	UNC
44	**5 POUNDS** 1966-76. Blue on m/c unpt. Like #40.			
	a. 1.8.1966; 1.9.1967; 1.12.1969.	11.50	17.50	85.00
	b. 1.6.1972; 1.11.1972; 1.7.1975.	10.50	13.50	50.00
	c. 1.5.1973; 1.6.1974; 1.8.1976.	10.00	12.50	40.00

1977-82 ISSUE

#45-48 wmk: Moufflon (ram's) head.

		VG	VF	UNC
45	**500 MILS** 1.6.1982. Brown and m/c. Woman seated at r., arms at top l. ctr. Yermasoyia Dam on back. Printer: BWC.	1.25	1.85	6.00

		VG	VF	UNC
46	**1 POUND** 1.6.1979. Dk. brown and brown on m/c unpt. Mosaic of nymph Acme at r., arms at top l. ctr. Bellapais Abbey on back. Printer: DLR.	2.25	3.50	11.00

		VG	VF	UNC
47	**5 POUNDS** 1.6.1979. Violet on m/c unpt. Limestone head from Hellenistic period at l., arms at upper ctr. r. Ancient Theater at Salamis on back. Printer: DLR.	10.00	12.50	30.00

		VG	VF	UNC
48	**10 POUNDS** 1977-85; 1993. Dk. green and blue-black on m/c unpt. Archaic bust at l., arms at r. 2 birds on back. Printer: BWC.			
	a. 1.4.1977; 1.5.1978; 1.6.1979.	20.00	28.50	60.00
	b. 1.7.1980; 1.10.1981; 1.6.1982; 1.9.1983; 1.6.1985.	20.00	25.00	50.00

1982-87 ISSUE

#49-51 wmk: Moufflon (ram's) head.

		VG	VF	UNC
49	**50 CENTS** 1.10.1983; 1.12.1984. Brown and m/c. Similar to #45. Printer BWC.	FV	1.50	4.75

		VG	VF	UNC
50	**1 POUND** 1.2.1982; 1.11.1982; 1.3.1984; 1.11.1985. Dk. brown and m/c. Like #46 but bank name in outlined (white) letters by dk. unpt. Printer: DLR.	FV	2.75	8.00

		VG	VF	UNC
51	**10 POUNDS** 1.4.1987; 1.10.1988. Dk. green and blue-black on m/c unpt. Similar to #48 but w/date above at l. of modified arms on r. Printer: DLR.	FV	22.50	40.00

1987-92 ISSUE

#53-56 enhanced designs w/micro-printing. Wmk: Moufflon (ram's) head.

		VG	VF	UNC
52	**50 CENTS** 1.4.1987; 1.10.1988; 1.11.1989. Like #49 but w/bank name in micro-printing alternately in Greek and Turkish just below upper frame. Printer: BABN.	FV	FV	3.50

53	1 POUND	VG	VF	UNC
	1987-. Like #50 but w/bank name in unbroken line of micro-printing with Greek at left and Turkish at right just below upper frame.			
	a. W/o lt. beige unpt. color on back. Micro-print line under dark bar at top.1.4.1987; Printer: DLR. 1.10.1988; 1.11.1989.	FV	FV	7.00
	b. Lt. beige color added to ctr. unpt. on back for security. Printer: F-CO. 1.11.1989; 1.2.1992.	FV	FV	5.50
	c. Dot added near upper l. corner. 1.3.1993; 1.3.1994.	FV	FV	5.00
	d. 1.9.1995.	FV	FV	4.50
	e. 1.10.1996.	FV	2.00	6.50

54	5 POUNDS	VG	VF	UNC
	1990; 1995. Violet on m/c unpt. Like #47 but w/line of micro-printing added within bank titles. Printer: DLR.			
	a. 1.10.1990.	FV	FV	22.50
	b. 1.9.1995.	FV	FV	25.00

55	10 POUNDS	VG	VF	UNC
	1989-95. Dk. green and blue-black on m/c unpt. Similar to #51 but w/enhanced security features. Printer: DLR.			
	a. 1.11.1989; 1.10.1990.	FV	FV	50.00
	b. 1.2.1992.	FV	FV	47.50
	c. 1.6.1994; 1.6.1995.	FV	FV	45.00

56	20 POUNDS	VG	VF	UNC
	1992; 1993. Deep blue on m/c unpt. Bust of Aphrodite at l., arms at upper ctr., ancient bird (pottery art) at r. Kyrenia boat at ctr., ancient pottery jugs at lower r. on back. Printer: TDLR.			
	a. Error: *YIRMI LIRA* No dot over 'i' in Yirmi. 1.2.1992.	FV	FV	120.00
	b. Corrected: *YIRMİ LIRA.* 1.2.1992; 1.3.1993.	FV	FV	95.00

1997 FIRST ISSUE

#57-60 arms at upper ctr. Wmk: Bust of Aphrodite. Thin security thread. Printer: F-CO.

57	1 POUND	VG	VF	UNC
	1.2.1997. Brown on m/c unpt. Cypriot girl at l. Handcrafts and Kato Drys village scene in background on back.	FV	FV	5.00

58	5 POUNDS	VG	VF	UNC
	1.2.1997. Purple and violet on m/c unpt. Archaic limestone head of young man at l. Peristerona church and Turkish mosque on back.	FV	FV	22.50

59	10 POUNDS	VG	VF	UNC
	1.2.1997. Olive-green and blue-green on m/c unpt. Marble head of Artemis at l. Warbler, green turtle, butterfly, moufflon, tulip and cyclamen plants on back.	FV	FV	35.00
60	20 POUNDS			
	1.2.1997. Deep blue on m/c unpt. Similar to #56.	FV	FV	75.00

1997 SECOND ISSUE

#61-64 arms at upper ctr. Wmk: Bust of Aphrodite. Thick security thread. Printer: DLR.

		VG	VF	UNC
61	1 POUND			
	1.10.1997. Brown on m/c unpt. Like #57 but w/slightly modified colors.	FV	FV	5.00
62	5 POUNDS			
	1.10.1997. Purple and violet on m/c unpt. Like #58.	FV	FV	22.50
63	10 POUNDS			
	1.10.1997. Olive-green and blue-green on m/c unpt. Like #59.	FV	FV	35.00
64 (61)	20 POUNDS			
	1.10.1997. Deep blue on m/c unpt. Like #60.	FV	FV	75.00

The Republic of Czechoslovakia (Ceskoslovensko), located in central Europe, had an area of 49,365 sq. mi. (127,859 sq. km.). Capital: Prague. Machinery was the chief export of the highly industrialized economy.

Czechoslovakia proclaimed itself a republic on Oct. 28, 1918. with T. G. Masaryk as president. Hitler provoked Czechoslovakia's German minority in the Sudentenland to agitate for autonomy. At Munich in Sept. of 1938, France and Britain forced the cession of the Sudentenland to Germany. On March 15, 1939, Germany invaded Czechoslovakia and established the Protectorate of Bohemia and Moravia. Slovakia, a province in southeastern Czechoslovakia, was constituted as a republic under Nazi influence. After the World War II defeat of the Axis powers re-established the physical integrity and independence of Czechoslovakia, while bringing it within the Russian sphere of influence. On Feb. 23-25, 1948, the Communists seized control of the government in a coup d'etat, and adopted a constitution making the country a "people's republic." A new constitution adopted June 11, 1960, converted the country into a "socialist republic" which lasted until 1989. On Nov. 17, 1989, public demonstrations against the communist government began and in Dec. of that same year, communism was overthrown and the Czech and Slovak Federal Republic was formed. On January 1, 1993 this was split to form the Czech Republic and the Republic of Slovakia.

See Czech Republic and Slovakia for additional listings.

MONETARY SYSTEM:

1 Koruna = 100 Haleru

SPECIMEN NOTES:

Large quantities of specimens were formerly made available to collectors. Most notes issued after 1945 are distinguished by a perforation consisting of a few small holes or letter S. Since the difference in price between original and specimen notes is frequently very great, both types of notes are valued. The earlier issues were recalled from circulation and perforated: *SPECIMEN* or *NEPLATNE* or with a letter *S* for collectors. Caution should be exercised while examining notes as we have been notified of examples of perforated specimen notes having the holes filled back in.

The CNB in 1997 made available to collectors uncirculated examples of #78-98, as a full set or in issue groups. As the notes were demonetized, they had no cancellation holes and regular serial #'s.

SOCIALIST REPUBLIC

CESKOSLOVENSKÁ SOCIALISTICKÁ REPUBLIKA

CZECHOSLOVAK SOCIALIST REPUBLIC

1961 ISSUE

#81 and 82 wmk: Star in circle, repeated. Printer: STC-P.

		VG	VF	UNC
81	**3 KORUN** 1961. Blue-black on blue-green unpt. Large 3 in ctr. and upper corners. Socialist arms in ctr. on back.			
	a. Issued note. Serial # prefix 2.5mm in height.	.20	.50	2.00
	b. Issued note. Serial # prefix 3mm in height.	.20	.50	2.00
	s. Perforated w/3 holes or *SPECIMEN.*	—	.50	2.00

		VG	VF	UNC
82	**5 KORUN** 1961. Dull black on pale green unpt. Text in frame. Socialist arms in ctr. on back.			
	a. Issued note. Serial # prefix 2.5mm in height.	.20	.50	2.00
	b. Issued note. Serial # prefix 3mm in height.	.20	.50	2.00
	s. Perforated w/3 holes or *SPECIMEN.*	—	.50	2.00

STÁTNÍ BANKA CESKOSLOVENSKÁ

CZECHOSLOVAK STATE BANK

1960-64 ISSUE

#88-98 printer: STC-Prague.

#88-91 Printed by wet photogravure or dry photogravure (wet printing has smaller image).

		VG	VF	UNC
88	**10 KORUN** 1960. Brown on m/c unpt. 2 girls w/flowers at r. Orava Dam on back.			
	a. Series prefix: H; F. (wet printing).	.25	1.00	7.50
	b. Series prefixes: E, J, L, M, S, X. (dry printing)	.10	.50	2.00

		VG	VF	UNC
89	**25 KORUN** 1961 (1962). Blue. Socialist arms at l. ctr. J. Zizka at r. Tabor town square on back.			
	a. Series prefix: E. (wet printing).	1.00	2.50	10.00
	b. Series prefix: Q. (dry printing)	.75	1.75	7.50
	s. Perforated: *SPECIMEN.*	—	—	2.00

		VG	VF	UNC
90	**50 KORUN** 1964 (1965). Red-brown. Russian soldier and partisan at r. Slovnaft refinery in Bratislava on back.			
	a. Series prefix: K. (wet printing).	2.00	5.00	15.00
	b. Series prefix: A; N; G; J. (dry printing)	1.00	2.50	7.50

		VG	VF	UNC
91	**100 KORUN** 1961. Deep green on m/c unpt. Factory at lower l., farm couple at r. Charles Bridge and Prague castle on back.			
	a. Wmk: Star within linden leaf, repeated. Series prefix: B01-40; C; D. (wet printing).	2.50	7.50	20.00
	b. As a. Series prefix: B41-99; P; R; T; Z; X01-24. (dry printing).	1.00	4.50	12.50
	c. Reissue wmk: Multiple stars and linden leaves. Series prefix: X25-96; G; M. (1990-92).	1.00	2.00	7.50

NOTE: #91b w/added "C-100" adhesive stamp, see Czech Republic. With *SLOVENSKÁ REPUBLIKA* adhsive stamp, see Slovakia.

1970; 1973 ISSUE

		VG	VF	UNC
92	**20 KORUN** 1970 (1971). Blue on lt. blue and m/c unpt. Arms at ctr., J. Zizka at r. Medieval procession from Kodex of Jena on back. Series prefix: F, H, L, M.	.40	1.00	2.50

		VG	VF	UNC
93	**500 KORUN** 1973. Deep brown-violet and m/c. Soldiers at r. Medieval shield at lower ctr., mountain fortress ruins at Devin at r. on back. Series prefix: U, W, Z.	4.00	10.00	30.00

NOTE: For #93 w/additional "D-500" adhesive stamp, see Czech Republic. *SLOVENSKÁ REPUBLIKA* adhesive stamp, see Slovakia.

1985-89 ISSUE

		VG	VF	UNC
94	**10 KORUN** 1986. Deep brown on m/c unpt. P. Orszagh Hviezdoslav at r. Bird at lower l., view of Orava mountains on back. Series prefix: J, P, V.	.20	.60	2.00

		VG	VF	UNC
95	**20 KORUN** 1988. Blue and m/c. J. Á. Komensky at r., alphabet at l. Tree of life growing from book at ctr., young couple at l. on back. Series prefix: E, H.	.25	.75	2.50

NOTE: For #95 and 96 w/additional *SLOVENSKÁ* adhesive stamp, see Slovakia.

		VG	VF	UNC
96	**50 KORUN** 1987. Brown-violet and blue on red and orange unpt. L. Stúr at r. Bratislava castle and town view on back. Series prefix: F, I.	.50	1.50	5.00

		VG	VF	UNC
97	**100 KORUN** 1989. Dk. green on green and red unpt. K. Gottwald at r. Prague castle on back. Series prefix: A.	.75	2.25	12.50

NOTE: #97 was withdrawn shortly after issue, apparently because of objections to the portrayal of Czech Communist Party chief secretary Klement Gottwald. In circulation from 1.10.1989 to 31.12.1990.

NOTE: For #97 w/additional *SLOVENSKÁ REPUBLIKA* adhesive stamp, see Slovakia.

		VG	VF	UNC
98	**1000 KORUN** 1985. Blue-black, blue and purple on m/c unpt. B. Smetana at r. Vysehrad Castle at l. on back. Series prefix: C, U.	7.50	27.50	60.00

NOTE: For #98 w/additional "M-1000" adhesive stamp or printed, see Czech Republic. With *SLOVENSKÁ REPUBLIKA* adhesive stamp, see Slovakia.

FOREIGN EXCHANGE CERTIFICATES

ODBERNÍ POUKAZ

These certificates were issued by the government-owned company *Tuzex*. Foreign visitors could exchange their hard currency for regular Korun or the Tuzex vouchers. These vouchers were accepted at special stores where imported or exported goods could be bought.

The common black market rate for Tuzex vouchers was 5-7 regular Korun for 1 Tuzex Koruna.

1970'S ND ISSUE

#FX11-FX18 white outer edge. *TUZEX* once in text. Dates of issue up to Dec. 1988. Several text varieties exist. Listings are for type only. Printer: STC-P.

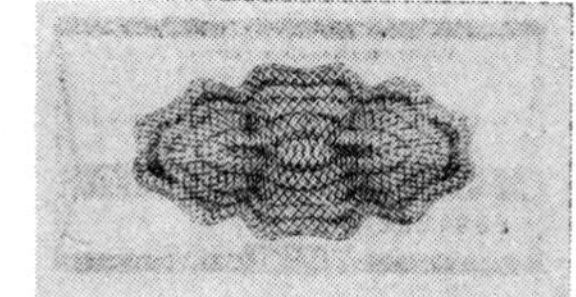

		VG	VF	UNC
FX11	**0.50 KORUNA** ND. Violet and green.	.50	1.00	2.50
FX12	**1 KORUNA** ND. Green on ochre unpt.	.50	1.00	2.50

		VG	VF	UNC
FX13	**5 KORUN** ND. Violet on blue and ochre unpt.	1.00	4.00	10.00
FX14	**10 KORUN** ND. Dk. green on green unpt.	2.00	8.00	20.00
FX15	**20 KORUN** ND. Brown on orange and green unpt.	4.00	10.00	25.00
FX16	**50 KORUN** ND. Brown on pink and orange unpt.	8.00	25.00	50.00
FX17	**100 KORUN** ND. Violet on green and violet unpt.	10.00	25.00	60.00
FX18	**500 KORUN** ND. Gray on brown unpt.	20.00	60.00	200.00

1989 ISSUE

#FX19-FX26 lg. globe w/*TUZEX* at l. and r. Colors as previous issue but outer edge w/design. Printer: STC-P.

		VG	VF	UNC
FX19	**0.50 KORUNA** 1989; 1990. Violet edge.	.30	.75	2.00
FX20	**1 KORUNA** 1989; 1990. Yellow-brown edge.	.30	.75	2.00
FX21	**5 KORUN** 1989; 1990. Blue and ochre edge.	.60	3.00	10.00

NOTE: #FX22-FX26 were redeemable 1 year from issue date.

		VG	VF	UNC
FX22	**10 KORUN** 1989; 1990. Lt. and dk. green edge.	1.50	8.00	20.00
FX23	**20 KORUN** 1989; 1990. Yellow-brown and green edge.	3.00	10.00	25.00
FX24	**50 KORUN** 1989; 1990. Pink and orange edge.	6.00	18.50	45.00
FX25	**100 KORUN** 1989; 1990. Violet and green edge.	8.00	25.00	60.00
FX26	**500 KORUN** 1989; 1990. Brown edge.	17.50	50.00	180.00

The Czech Republic is bordered in the west by Germany, to the north by Poland, to the east by Slovakia and to the south by Austria. It consists of 3 major regions: Bohemia, Moravia and Silesia. It has an area of 30,431 sq. mi. (78,864 sq. km.) and a population of 10.33 million. Capital: Prague (Praha). Agriculture and livestock are chief occupations while coal deposits are the main mineral resources.

The Czech lands in the western part were united with the Slovaks to form the Czechoslovak Republic, on Oct. 28, 1918 upon the dissolution of Austria-Hungarian Empire. This territory was broken up for the benefit of Germany, Poland and Hungary by the Munich agreement signed by the United Kingdom, France, Germany and Italy on Sept. 29, 1938. In March 1939 the German influenced Slovak government proclaimed Slovakia independent. Germany incorporated the Czech lands into the Third Reich as the "Protectorate of Bohemia and Moravia." A government-in-exile was set up in London in July 1940. The Soviets and USA forces liberated the area by May 1945. Communist influence increased steadily while pressure for liberalization culminated in the overthrow of the Stalinist leader Antonín Novotny and his associates in 1968. The Communist Party then introduced far reaching reforms which received warnings from Moscow, followed by occupation of Warsaw Pact forces resulting in stationing of Soviet forces. Mass demonstrations for reform began in Nov. 1989 and the Federal Assembly abolished the Communist Party's sole right to govern. New governments followed on Dec. 3. and Dec. 10. The Movement for Democratic Slovakia was apparent in the June 1992 elections with the Slovak National Council adopting a declaration of sovereignty, later a constitution for an independent Slovakia, with the Federal Assembly voting for the dissolution of the Czech and Slovak Federal Republic. This came into effect on Dec. 31, 1992 and both new republics came into being on Jan. 1, 1993.

MONETARY SYSTEM:

1 Czechoslovak Koruna (Kcs) = 1 Czech Koruna (Kc)
1 Koruna = 100 Haleru

REPUBLIC

CESKÁ NÁRODNÍ BANKA

CZECH NATIONAL BANK

1993 ND PROVISIONAL ISSUE

#1-3 were released 8.2.1993 having adhesive revalidation stamps affixed (later a printed *1000* was also circulated). Valid until 31.8.1993 but could be exchanged in deposits until 31.5.1994. Old Czechoslovak notes of 100 Korun and higher denominations became worthless on 7.2.1993. Smaller denominations remained in circulation until 30.11.1993.

NOTE: In 1997 the CNB made available uncirculated examples of #1-3a and 3b to collectors. The notes are without cancellation marks and have regular serial #.

		VG	VF	UNC
1	**100 KORUN** ND (1993-old date 1961). Dk. green *C-100* adhesive stamp affixed to Czechoslovakia #91b.	2.50	5.00	10.00

		VG	VF	UNC
2	**500 KORUN** ND (1993-old date 1973). Dk. green *D-500* adhesive stamp affixed to Czechoslovakia #93. Series prefixes: U, W, Z.	10.00	20.00	45.00

		VG	VF	UNC
3	**1000 KORUN** ND (1993-old date 1985). Deep green *M-1000* revalidation stamp on Czechoslovakia #98.			
	a. Adhesive stamp affixed. Series prefixes: C, U.	25.00	50.00	90.00
	b. Stamp image printed. Series prefix: U.	25.00	50.00	90.00

1993 REGULAR ISSUE

#4-9 arms at ctr. r.; value in wmk. area on back.

#4-7 replacement notes: Serial # prefix *Z*.

		VG	VF	UNC
4	**50 KORUN** 1993. Violet and black on pink and gray unpt. St. A. Ceská at r. and w/crown as wmk. Lg. A within gothic window frame at l. ctr. on back. Printer: TDLR. Serial # prefix *A*.	FV	FV	4.50

		VG	VF	UNC
5	**100 KORUN** 1993. Blue-green, green and blue-black on lilac and m/c unpt. Kg. Karel IV at r. and as wmk. Lg. seal of Charles University at l. ctr. on back. Printer: TDLR. Serial # prefix *A*.	FV	FV	8.50

		VG	VF	UNC
6	**200 KORUN** 1993. Deep brown on lt. orange and lt. green unpt. J. A. Komensky at r. and as wmk. Hands outreached at l. ctr. on back. Printer: STC-P. Serial # prefix *A*.			
	a. Security filament w/*200 KCS*.	FV	FV	15.00
	b. Security filament w/*200 KC*.	FV	FV	15.00
	x. Error. Security filament normally used in Zaïre note.	65.00	200.00	—

		VG	VF	UNC
7	**500 KORUN** 1993. Dk. brown, brown & brown-violet on pink and tan unpt. Rose in unpt. at upper ctr., Mrs. B. Nemcová at r. and as wmk. Laureate young woman's head at l. ctr. on back. Printer: TDLR. Serial # prefix *A*.	FV	FV	45.00

		VG	VF	UNC
8	**1000 KORUN** 1993. Purple and lilac on m/c unpt. F. Palacky at r. and as wmk. Eagle and Kromeriz Castle on back. Printer: STC-P. Serial # prefix *A*; *B*.	FV	FV	70.00

		VG	VF	UNC
9	**5000 KORUN** 1993. Black, blue-gray and violet on pink and lt. gray unpt. Pres. T.G. Masaryk at r. Montage of Prague Gothic and Baroque buildings on back. Printer: STC-P. Serial # prefix *A*.	FV	FV	250.00

1994-96 ISSUE

#10-16 value and stylized design in wmk. area on back. Printer: STC-P.

		VG	VF	UNC
10	**20 KORUN** 1994. Blue-black and gray on lt. blue unpt, Kg. Premysl 1 Otakar at r. and as wmk. Crown with seal above at ctr., stylized crown at lower r. on back.			
	a. Serial # prefix *A*; *B*. Security filament at ctr. (74mm from left edge). (1994).	FV	FV	2.00
	b. Serial # prefix *B*. Security filament at l. ctr. (50mm from left edge). (1995).	FV	FV	2.00

NOTICE

Readers with unlisted dates, signature varieties, etc. are invited to submit photocopies of their notes to: Standard Catalog of World Paper Money, 700 East State St. Iola, WI 54990-0001, fax: 1-715-445-4087, or E-Mail: thernr@krause.com.

		VG	VF	UNC
11	**50 KORUN** 1994. Violet and black on m/c unpt. Like #4 but w/o gray in unpt. Stylized heart at lower r. on back. Serial # prefix *B*.	FV	FV	4.00

		VG	VF	UNC
12	**100 KORUN** 1995. Blue-green, green and blue-black on lilac and m/c unpt. Like #5, but w/stylized *K* in circle at lower r. on back. Serial # prefix *B*.	FV	FV	7.50

		VG	VF	UNC
13	**200 KORUN** 1996. Deep brown on pale orange and lt. green unpt. Like #6 but w/stylized open book at lower r. on back. Serial # prefix *B*.	FV	FV	12.50

		VG	VF	UNC
14	**500 KORUN** 1995. Dk. brown, brown and brown-violet on pink and tan unpt. Like #7 but w/stylized rose at lower r. on back. Serial # prefix *B*.	FV	FV	32.50
15	**1000 KORUN** 1996. Purple and lilac on m/c unpt. Like #8 but w/stylized *P* and tree at lower r. on back. Serial # prefix *C*.	FV	FV	60.00
16	**2000 KORUN** 1996. Dk. olive-green, green and violet on tan unpt. E. Destinová at l., lyre at at upper l. in spray. Muse of music and lyric poetry Euterpe at l. ctr., violin and cello and a large *D*. , stylized lyre at lower r. on back. Serial # prefix *A*.	FV	FV	110.00

1997-99 ISSUE

#17-23;monogram changed to CR. Printer: STC-P. Ascending serial # on back.

		VG	VF	UNC
17	**50 KORUN** 1997. Violet and purple on m/c unpt. Like #11. Serial # prefix *C*.	FV	FV	3.75

		VG	VF	UNC
18	**100 KORUN** 1997. Dk. green, dk. olive-green and black on m/c unpt. Like #12. Serial # prefix *C*.	FV	FV	7.00
19	**200 KORUN** 1998. Similar to #13, but ultra-violet fibers added.	FV	FV	12.50
20	**500 KORUN** 1997. Dk. brown, brown and brown-violet on pink and tan unpt. Like #14. Serial # prefix *C*.	FV	FV	30.00

#21-23 serial # prefix: *B*. Fibers in paper.

		VG	VF	UNC
21	**1000 KORUN** 1999. Similar to #15.	Expected New Issue		

		VG	VF	UNC
22	**2000 KORUN** 1999. Similar to #16. 3 Metallic vertical bars in lyre at top ctr. on face.	FV	FV	110.00

		VG	VF	UNC
23	**5000 KORUN** 1999. Similar to #9. Metallic Hexagon emblem at top ctr. on face. Under linden leaf in wmk. area on back.	FV	FV	250.00

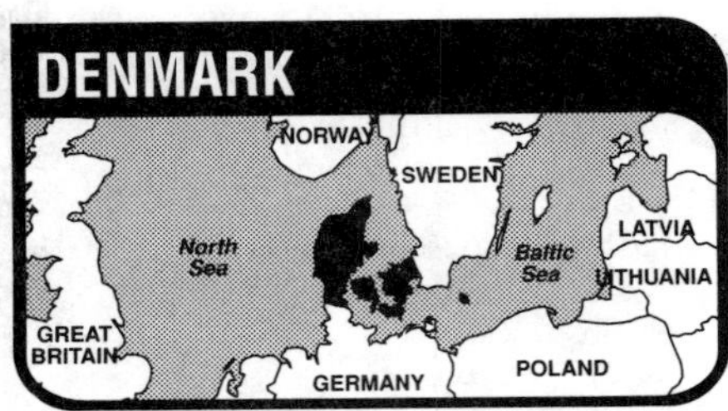

The Kingdom of Denmark, a constitutional monarchy located at the mouth of the Baltic Sea, has an area of 16,633 sq. mi. (43,069 sq. km.) and a population of 5.3 million. Capital: Copenhagen. Most of the country is arable. Agriculture, is conducted by large farms served by cooperatives. The largest industries are food processing, iron and metal, and fishing. Machinery, meats (chiefly bacon), dairy products and chemicals are exported.

Denmark, a great power during the Viking period of the 9th-11th centuries, conducted raids on western Europe and England, and in the 11th century united England, Denmark and Norway under the rule of King Canute. Despite a struggle between the crown and the nobility (13th-14th centuries) which forced the king to grant a written constitution, Queen Margrethe (1353-1412) succeeded in uniting Denmark, Norway, Sweden, Finland and Greenland under the Danish crown, placing all of Scandinavia under the rule of Denmark. Sweden and Finland were lost in 1523, and an unwise alliance with Napoleon contributed to further dismembering of the empire and fostered a liberal movement which succeeded in making Denmark a constitutional monarchy in 1849.

The present decimal system of currency was introduced in 1874.

RULERS:

Frederik IX, 1947-1972
Margrethe II, 1972-

MONETARY SYSTEM:

1 Krone = 100 Øre

KINGDOM

DANMARKS NATIONALBANK

1944-46 ISSUE

		VG	VF	UNC
41	**500 KRONER** 1944-62. Orange. Farmer w/horses at ctr. Arms on back.	110.00	160.00	225.00

1950 (1952)-63 ISSUE

Law of 7.4.1936

REPLACEMENT NOTES:

#42-47, Serial # suffix: *OJ* (for whole sheets) or *OK* (for single notes).

		VG	VF	UNC
42	**5 KRONER** (19)50; (19)52-60. Blue-green. Portr. Bentil Thorvaldsen at l., 3 Graces at r. Kalundborg city view w/5 spire church at ctr. on back. Wmk: 5 repeated.			
	a. 5 in the wmk. 10.55mm high. W/o dot after *7* in law date. (19)52. Series A0; A1; A2.	2.75	13.50	45.00
	b. As a., but w/dot after *7* in law date. (19)52-55. Series A2-A9.	1.85	9.00	30.00
	c. *5* in the wmk. 13mm high. (19)55-60. Series B0-C4.	1.50	7.50	25.00
	r. Replacement note. (19)50 (sic); (19)60. Series OJ.	1.50	7.50	25.00
	s. Specimen.	—	—	450.00

		VG	VF	UNC
43	**10 KRONER** (19)50-52. Black and olive-brown. Portr. H. C. Andersen at l., white storks in nest at r. Black and green. Landscape of Egeskov, Mølle Fyn at ctr. on back. Wmk: *5* repeated. 125 x 65mm.			
	a. Issued note. (19)51-52.	4.00	25.00	115.00
	r. Replacement note. (19)50 (sic).	5.00	30.00	125.00

		VG	VF	UNC
44	**10 KRONER** (19)50; 19(54)-74. Black and brown. Portr. H. C. Andersen at l. Black landscape at ctr. on back. Additional line in the upper and lower frame. 125 x 71mm.			
	a. Top and bottom line in frame commences w/10. Wmk: *10* repeated 11mm. (19)54. Series CO-C1.	7.00	37.50	115.00
	b. As a. Wmk: 13mm. (19)54-56. Series C1-D6.	6.00	18.50	75.00
	c. Wmk: *10* repeated 11mm. (19)56. Series D6-D8.	7.00	37.50	125.00
	d. As b. (19)56-57. Series D8-E4.	6.00	14.00	65.00
	e. As d. Top and bottom line in frame commences with *TI*. (19)61-68.	3.50	8.00	25.00
	f. As e. (19)69-72.	2.50	5.00	14.00
	g. As e. (19)73-74.	2.00	2.75	6.00
	r1. Replacement note. (19)50 (sic).	10.00	35.00	125.00
	r2. As r1. (19)60-74. Series OJ.	3.00	7.00	20.00
	r3. As r1. (19)67-74. Series OK.	4.00	12.00	30.00
	s. Specimen.	—	—	400.00

		VG	VF	UNC
45	**50 KRONER** (19)50; (19)56-70. Blue on green unpt. Portr. O. Rømer at l., Round Tower in Copenhagen at r. Back blue; Stone Age burial site Dolmen of Stenvad at Djursland at ctr.			
	a. Handmade paper. Wmk: Crowns and *50* (19)56-61.	15.00	35.00	150.00
	b. Wmk: Rhombuses and *50*. (19)62; (19)63; (19)66; (19)70.	10.00	15.00	35.00
	r1. Replacement note. (19)50 (sic). Series OJ.	15.00	45.00	135.00
	r2. Replacement note. (19)60; (19)70. Series OJ.	12.00	20.00	40.00

		VG	VF	UNC
46	**100 KRONER** (19)61-70. Red-brown on red-yellow unpt. Portr. H. C. Ørsted at l., compass card at r. Back brown. Kronborg castle in Elsinore.			
	a. Handmade paper. Wmk: Close wavy lines and compass. (19)61.	30.00	50.00	125.00
	b. Wmk: *100*. (19)61; (19)62; (19)65; (19)70.	22.50	35.00	60.00
	r. As b. Replacement note. Series OJ.	35.00	55.00	100.00

47 **500 KRONER**

	VG	VF	UNC
(19)63-67. Green. Portr. C. D. F. Reventlow at l., farmer plowing at r. Roskilde city view on back.			
a. (19)63; (19)65.	100.00	150.00	275.00
b. (19)67.	100.00	150.00	225.00
r. Replacement note. Series OJ.	125.00	—	—
s. Specimen.	—	—	1000.

1972; 1979 ISSUE

Issued under *L. 1936*. The year of issue is shown by the 2 middle numerals within the series code at lower l. or r. Sign. varieties.

#48-52 portr. at r. of all notes painted by Danish artist Jens Juel (1745-1802). Wmk: Head of J. Juel and value sometimes repeated vertically.

#48-53 printer: CB at Copenhagen (w/o imprint).

48 **10 KRONER**

	VG	VF	UNC
(19)72-78. Black on olive and m/c unpt. Portr. C. S. Kirchhoff at r. Eider bird at l. on back.			
a. (19)72-75.	FV	2.50	6.00
b. (19)76-78.	FV	FV	4.50

49 **20 KRONER**

	VG	VF	UNC
(19)79-88. Dk. blue on brown and m/c unpt. Portr. Pauline Tutein at r. Male and female House Sparrow at l. ctr. on back. Wmk: Painter's palette, brushes and *20*.	FV	FV	8.00

50 **50 KRONER**

	VG	VF	UNC
(19)72-98. Dk. gray on pale blue, dull purple and pale green unpt. Portr. F. Ryberg at r. *Carassius-Carassius* fish at l. on back.			
a. (19)72-79.	FV	FV	22.50
b. (19)82-90.	FV	FV	15.00
c. (19)92-98.	FV	FV	10.50
s. Specimen.	—	—	400.00

51 **100 KRONER**

	VG	VF	UNC
(19)72-93. Black and red on m/c unpt. Jens Juel's self-portrait (ca.1773-74) at r. Danish Red Order Ribbon moth at l. on back.			
a. Issued note.	FV	FV	30.00
s. Specimen.	—	—	500.00

52 **500 KRONER**

	VG	VF	UNC
(19)72-88. Black on green and m/c unpt. *Unknown Lady* portrait, possibly von Qualen at r. Lizard on back. Wmk: Jens Juel and *500* repeated.	FV	FV	115.00

53 **1000 KRONER**

	VG	VF	UNC
(19)72-92. Black on gray and m/c unpt. Portr. Thomasine Heiberg at r. European or Red squirrel on back. Wmk: Double portr. Jens Juel and his wife and *1000*. 1972A Issue	FV	FV	190.00

		VG	VF	UNC
54 (55)	**100 KRONER** (19)94-98. Black and orange on m/c unpt. Like #51 but w/additional security devices. Wmk: J. Jeul. Series 1972A.	FV	FV	28.50

1996-99 ISSUE

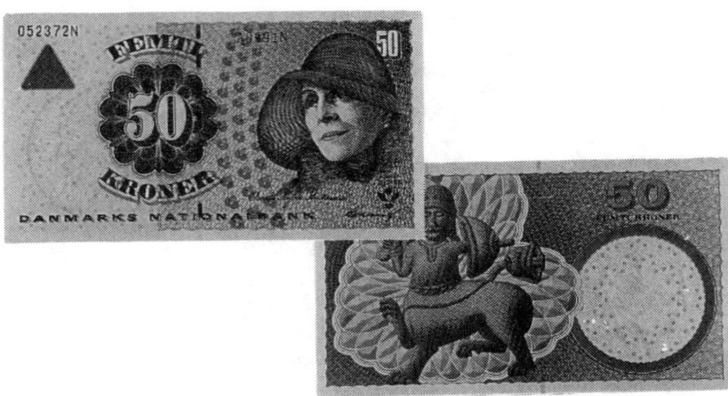

		VG	VF	UNC
55 (54)	**50 KRONER** (19)99. Black and dp. purple on m/c unpt. K. Blixen at r. and as wmk. Centaur stone relief from Landet Church, Tåsinge on back.	FV	FV	9.00

		VG	VF	UNC
56	**100 KRONER** (19)99. Black and orange. Carl Nielsen at r. Basilisk stone relief from Tømmerby Church in Thy on back.	FV	FV	20.00

		VG	VF	UNC
57	**200 KRONER** (19)97. Black on turquoise green and m/c unpt., pale red-violet latent image at upper l. J. L. Heiberg at r. Stone lion relief from Viborg Cathedral at l. ctr. on back.	FV	FV	40.00

		VG	VF	UNC
58	**500 KRONER** (19)97. Black on blue, orange and m/c unpt. N. Bohr at r. Knight and dragon relief from Lihme Church on back.	FV	FV	90.00

		VG	VF	UNC
59	**1000 KRONER** (19)98. Violet, purple and green. Purple iridescent metallic strip. A. and M. Ancher at r. Back purple, turquoise, and orange on m/c unpt. Tournament scene relief from Bislev Church at l. ctr. on back.	FV	FV	200.00

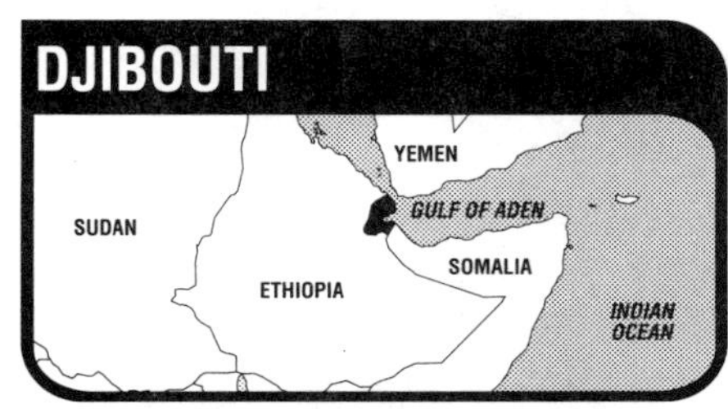

The Republic of Djibouti (formerly French Somaliland or the French Overseas Territory of Afars and Issas), located in northeast Africa at the Bab el Mandeb Strait connecting the Suez Canal and the Red Sea with the Gulf of Aden and the Indian Ocean, has an area of 8,494 sq. mi. (22,000 sq. km.) and a population of 428,000. Capital: Djibouti. The tiny nation has less than one sq. mi. of arable land, and few natural resources of salt, sand and camels. The commercial activities of the trans-shipment port of Djibouti and the Addis Ababa-Djibouti railroad are the basis of the economy. Salt, fish and hides are exported.

French interest in former French Somaliland began in 1839 with concessions obtained by a French naval lieutenant from the provincial sultans. French Somaliland was made a protectorate in 1884 and its boundaries were delimited by the Franco-British and Ethiopian accords of 1887 and 1897. It became a colony in 1896 and a territory within the French Union in 1946. In 1958, it voted to join the new French Community as an overseas territory, and reaffirmed that choice by a referendum in March 1967. Its name was changed from French Somaliland to the French Territory of Afars and Issas on July 5, 1967.

In 1977 Afars and Issas became independent under the name of the Republic of Djibouti.

NOTE: For earlier issues see French Afars and Issas.

MONETARY SYSTEM:

1 Franc = 100 Centimes

REPUBLIC OF DJIBOUTI

BANQUE NATIONALE

1979; 1984 ND ISSUE

		VG	VF	UNC
36	**500 FRANCS** ND (1979; 1988). M/c. Man at l., rocks in sea, storks at r. Stern of ship at r. on back.			
	a. Blue unpt. W/o sign. (1979).	FV	5.00	12.50
	b. Pale blue unpt. Sign title: *LE GOUVERNEUR* added. (1988).	FV	4.50	10.00

(1979)

(1988)

		VG	VF	UNC
37	**1000 FRANCS** ND (1979; 1988). M/c. Woman at l., people by diesel passenger trains at ctr. Trader w/camels at ctr. on back.			
	a. Long Arabic text on back. W/o sign. (1979).	FV	10.00	28.50
	b. Sign. title: *LE GOUVERNEUR* added above *MILLE*. Short Arabic text at top on back. (1988).	FV	8.00	21.50
	c. Long Arabic text on back. (1991).	FV	7.50	17.50
	d. As c but w/security thread. 2 sign. varieties.	FV	FV	16.50

		VG	VF	UNC
38	**5000 FRANCS** ND (1979). M/c. Man at r., forest scene at ctr. Aerial view at ctr. on back.			
	a. W/o sign.	FV	37.50	75.00
	b. W/sign.	FV	35.00	65.00
	c. As b but w/security thread.	FV	FV	55.00

		VG	VF	UNC
39	**10,000 FRANCS** ND (1984). Brown and red on yellow and green. Woman holding baby at l., goats in tree at r. Fish and harbor scene on back.			
	a. Sign. title: *TRÉSORÍEA.*	FV	75.00	120.00
	b. Sign. title: *GOUVERNEUR* . W/security thread.	FV	FV	100.00

1997 ND ISSUE

		VG	VF	UNC
40	**2000 FRANCS** ND (1997). Dk. blue, blue-black and black on m/c unpt. Young girl at r., camel caravan at ctr. Statue w/spear and shield at lower l., government bldg. at ctr. on back.	FV	FV	30.00

The Dominican Republic, occupying the eastern two-thirds of the island of Hispaniola, has an area of 18,816 sq. mi. (48,734 sq. km.) and a population of 8.1 million. Capital: Santo Domingo. The agricultural economy produces sugar, coffee, tobacco and cocoa.

Columbus discovered Hispaniola in 1492, and named it *La Isla Espanola* - "the Spanish Island." Santo Domingo, the oldest white settlement in the Western Hemisphere, was the base from which Spain conducted its exploration of the New World. Later, French buccaneers settled the western third of Hispaniola, which in 1697 was ceded to France by Spain, and in 1804 became the Republic of Haiti - "mountainous country." At this time, the Spanish called their part of Hispaniola Santo Domingo, and the French called their part Saint-Domingue. In 1822, the Haitians conquered the entire island and held it until 1844, when Juan Pablo Duarte, the national hero of the Dominican Republic, drove them out of eastern Hispaniola and established an independent Dominican Republic. The republic returned voluntarily to Spanish dominion - after being rejected by France, Britain and the United States - from 1861 to 1865, when independence was restored.

Dictatorships and democratic rule was interspersed and from 1916 to 1924 it was occupied by the U.S. from 1930 to 1961, Rafael Trujillo was dictator. In the 1994 elections, a reform government gained power.

MONETARY SYSTEM:

1 Peso Oro = 100 Centavos Oro

SPECIMEN NOTES:

In 1998 the Banco Central once again began selling various specimens over the counter to the public. Current market valuations are being reflected, subject to change.

REPUBLIC

BANCO CENTRAL DE LA REPÚBLICA DOMINICANA

1961 ND ISSUES

		VG	VF	UNC
85	**10 CENTAVOS ORO** ND (1961). Blue and black. Banco de Reservas in round frame at ctr. Back blue. Printer: ABNC.	1.00	3.50	12.50

		VG	VF	UNC
86	**10 CENTAVOS ORO** ND (1961). Black on lt. blue-green safety paper. Banco de Reservas in oval frame at ctr. Back green. Local printer.	2.00	6.00	20.00

		VG	VF	UNC
87	**25 CENTAVOS ORO** ND (1961). Red and black. Entrance to the Banco Central in rectangular frame at ctr. Back red. Printer: ABNC.	1.00	4.00	15.00

		VG	VF	UNC
88	**25 CENTAVOS ORO** ND (1961). Black. Entrance to the Banco Central in oval frame at ctr. Back green. Local printer.			
	a. Pink safety paper.	1.75	5.00	20.00
	b. Plain cream paper.	2.50	7.50	22.50

		VG	VF	UNC
89	**50 CENTAVOS ORO** ND (1961). Purple and black. Palacio Nacional in circular frame at ctr. Back purple. Printer: ABNC.	1.75	4.50	17.50

		VG	VF	UNC
90	**50 CENTAVOS ORO** ND (1961). Black on yellow safety paper. Palacio Nacional in oval frame at ctr. Back green. Local printer.	5.50	25.00	60.00

1962 ND ISSUE

#91-98 w/text over seal: *SANTO DOMINGO/DISTRITO NACIONAL/REPÚBLICA DOMINICANA.* Medallic portr. Liberty head at l., arms at r. on back. Printer: ABNC.

		VG	VF	UNC
91	**1 PESO ORO** ND (1962-63). Red. Portr. J. P. Duarte at ctr.	4.00	16.00	48.00

		VG	VF	UNC
92	**5 PESOS ORO** ND (1962). Red. Portr. J. Sánchez R. at ctr. Back purple.	6.00	24.00	72.00

		VG	VF	UNC
93	**10 PESOS ORO** ND (1962). Red. Portr. Mella at ctr. Back brown.	12.50	50.00	150.00

		VG	VF	UNC
94	**20 PESOS ORO** ND (1962). Red. *Puerta del Conde* at ctr. Back olive.	25.00	100.00	300.00
95	**50 PESOS ORO** ND (1962). Red. Tomb of Columbus at ctr. Back blue-gray.	50.00	150.00	450.00

		VG	VF	UNC
96	**100 PESOS ORO** ND (1962). Red. Woman w/coffee pot and cup at ctr. Back blue-gray.	75.00	175.00	525.00
97	**500 PESOS ORO** ND (1962). "Obelisco de Ciudad Trujillo" at ctr.	—	—	—
98	**1000 PESOS ORO** ND (1962). Minor Basilica of Santa Maria at ctr. Unique.	—	—	—

1964 ND ISSUE

#99-106 orange bank seal at r. Medallic portr. Liberty head at l., arms at r. on back. Sign. varieties. Printer: TDLR.

		VG	VF	UNC
99	**1 PESO ORO** ND (1964-73). Black on m/c unpt. Portr. J. P. Duarte at ctr. w/eyes looking l., white bow tie.			
	a. Issued note.	.50	2.50	10.00
	s. Specimen w/black ovpt: *MUESTRA.*	—	—	20.00

		VG	VF	UNC
100	**5 PESOS ORO** ND (1964-74). Brown on m/c unpt. Portr. J. Sánchez R. at ctr.			
	a. Issued note.	3.00	10.00	30.00
	s. Specimen w/black ovpt: *MUESTRA.*	—	—	20.00

		VG	VF	UNC
101	**10 PESOS ORO** ND (1964-74). Deep green on m/c unpt. Portr. Mella at ctr.			
	a. Issued note.	5.00	16.00	48.00
	s. Specimen w/black ovpt: *MUESTRA.*	—	—	22.50

		VG	VF	UNC
102	**20 PESOS ORO** ND (1964-74). Dk. brown on m/c unpt. *Altar de la Patria* at ctr.			
	a. Issued note.	8.00	30.00	75.00
	s. Specimen w/black ovpt: *MUESTRA.*	—	—	25.00

		VG	VF	UNC
103	**50 PESOS ORO** ND (1964-74). Purple on m/c unpt. Ox cart at ctr.			
	a. Issued note.	20.00	65.00	130.00
	s. Specimen w/black ovpt: *MUESTRA.*	—	—	30.00

		VG	VF	UNC
104	**100 PESOS ORO** ND (1964-74). Orange-brown on m/c unpt. Banco Central at ctr.			
	a. Issued note.	40.00	125.00	250.00
	s. Specimen.	—	—	50.00

		VG	VF	UNC
105	**500 PESOS ORO** ND (1964-74). Dk. blue on m/c unpt. Columbus tomb and cathedral at ctr.			
	a. Issued note.	100.00	400.00	750.00
	s. Specimen w/black ovpt: *MUESTRA.*	—	—	100.00

		VG	VF	UNC
106	**1000 Pesos Oro** ND (1964-74). Red and m/c unpt. National Palace at ctr. Medallic portr. Liberty at l. ctr., arms at r. ctr. on back.			
	a. Issued note.	200.00	750.00	1500.
	s. Specimen.	—	—	200.00

1973 ND Issue

		VG	VF	UNC
107	**1 Peso Oro** ND (1973-74). Black on lt. green and pinkish tan unpt. Like #99 but portr. J. P. Duarte w/eyes looking front, black bow tie.	.50	2.00	8.50

1975 Issue

#108-115 dates at ctr. in upper margin on back. Printer: TDLR.

		VG	VF	UNC
108	**1 Peso Oro** 1975-78. Black on lt. green and pinkish tan unpt. Like #107.			
	a. Issued note.	.25	1.50	4.50
	s. Specimen.	—	—	15.00

		VG	VF	UNC
109	**5 Pesos Oro** 1975-76. Brown on lt. green and lilac unpt. Like #100.	.50	5.00	15.00
110	**10 Pesos Oro** 1975-76. Green on lt. green and lilac unpt. Like #101.	1.50	9.00	27.00
111	**20 Pesos Oro** 1975-76. Brown on lt. green and blue unpt. Like #102.			
	a. Issued note.	2.50	15.00	45.00
	s. Specimen.	—	—	22.50
112	**50 Pesos Oro** 1975-76. Purple on m/c unpt. Like #103.	5.50	33.50	100.00

		VG	VF	UNC
113	**100 Pesos Oro** 1975-76. Orange-brown on m/c unpt. Like #104.			
	a. Issued note.	10.00	60.00	180.00
	s. Specimen w/black ovpt: *ESPECIMEN*. 1976.	—	—	50.00
114	**500 Pesos Oro** 1975. Dk. blue on m/c unpt. Like #105.			
	a. Issued note.	50.00	250.00	750.00
	s. Specimen.	—	—	100.00

		VG	VF	UNC
115	**1000 Pesos Oro** 1975-76. Red on m/c unpt. Like #106.			
	a. Issued note.	95.00	500.00	1500.
	s. Specimen w/black ovpt: *ESPECIMEN*. 1975.	—	—	200.00

1977-80 Issues

#116-124 dates in upper margin on back. Replacement notes: Serial # prefix and suffix *Z*.

		VG	VF	UNC
116	**1 Peso Oro** 1978-79. Black, dk. green and dk. brown on m/c unpt. J. P. Duarte at r., orange seal at l. Sugar refinery on back. Printer: ABNC.			
	a. Issued note.	.20	1.00	3.50
	s. Specimen w/red ovpt: *MUESTRA - SIN VALOR*. 1978.	—	—	15.00

NOTICE

Readers with unlisted dates, signature varieties, etc. are invited to submit photocopies of their notes to: Standard Catalog of World Paper Money, 700 East State St. Iola, WI 54990-0001, fax: 1-715-445-4087, or E-Mail: thernr@krause.com.

#117-124 orange bank seal at l. Printer: TDLR.

117	1 PESO ORO	VG	VF	UNC
	1980-82. Black, dk. green and dk. brown on m/c unpt. Like #116. Dates very lightly printed.			
	a. Issued note.	.75	1.00	3.00
	s. Specimen w/black ovpt: *ESPECIMEN*. 1980; 1981.	—	—	15.00

118	5 PESOS ORO	VG	VF	UNC
	1978-88. Deep brown, red-brown and red on m/c unpt. J. Sánchez R. at r., arms at ctr. Hydroelectric dam on back.			
	a. 1978.	.50	2.50	7.50
	b. 1980-82.	FV	2.00	6.00
	c. 1984; 1985; 1987; 1988.	FV	1.50	4.50
	s1. Specimen w/black ovpt: *ESPECIMEN*. 1978; 1980; 1981.	—	—	18.50
	s2. Specimen w/red ovpt: *MUESTRA SIN VALOR* and TDLR oval seals. 1985; 1987.	—	—	18.50
	s3. Specimen w/black ovpt: *MUESTRA SIN VALOR* and red ovpt: TDLR oval seals. 1988.	—	—	18.50

119	10 PESOS ORO	VG	VF	UNC
	1978-88. Black and green on m/c unpt. Mella at r., medallic Liberty head at ctr. Quarry mining scene on back.			
	a. 1978.	1.00	4.00	12.50
	b. 1980-82.	FV	3.00	9.00
	c. 1985; 1987; 1988.	FV	2.50	7.50
	s1. Specimen w/black ovpt: *ESPECIMEN*. 1978; 1980; 1981.	—	—	22.50
	s2. Specimen w/red ovpt: *MUESTRA SIN VALOR* and TDLR oval seals. 1985; 1987.	—	—	22.50
	s3. Specimen w/black ovpt: *MUESTRA SIN VALOR* and red ovpt: TDLR oval seals. 1988.	—	—	22.50

120	20 PESOS ORO	VG	VF	UNC
	1978-88. Black, dk. brown and olive-brown on m/c unpt. *Altar de la Patria* at ctr. *Puerta del Conde* on back.			
	a. 1978.	2.00	7.00	21.00
	b. 1980-82.	FV	5.50	17.50
	c. 1985; 1987; 1988.	FV	5.00	15.00
	s1. Specimen w/black ovpt: *ESPECIMEN*. 1978; 1980; 1981.	—	—	25.00
	s2. Specimen w/red ovpt: *MUESTRA SIN VALOR* and TDLR oval seals. 1985; 1987.	—	—	25.00
	s3. Specimen w/black ovpt: *MUESTRA SIN VALOR* and red ovpt: TDLR oval seals. 1988.	—	—	25.00

121	50 PESOS ORO	VG	VF	UNC
	1978-87. Black and purple on m/c unpt. Basilica at ctr. First cathedral in America at ctr. r. on back.			
	a. Wmk: Indian head. 1978; 1980; 1981.	5.00	22.50	45.00
	b. Wmk: J. P. Duarte. 1985; 1987.	6.00	25.00	50.00
	s1. As a. Specimen w/black ovpt: *ESPECIMEN*. 1978; 1980; 1981.	—	—	27.50
	s2. As b. Specimen w/perforated *MUESTRA SIN VALOR* and red ovpt: TDLR oval seals. 1985; 1987.	—	—	27.50

122	100 PESOS ORO	VG	VF	UNC
	1977-87. Violet, brown-orange and yellow-orange on m/c unpt. Entrance to 16th century mint at ctr. Banco Central at ctr. r. on back.			
	a. Wmk: Indian head. 1977; 1978; 1980; 1981.	10.00	42.50	125.00
	b. Wmk: J.P. Duarte. 1984; 1985; 1987.	FV	50.00	150.00
	s1. As a. Specimen w/black ovpt: *ESPECIMEN*.1978; 1980; 1981.	—	—	30.00
	s2. As b. Specimen w/perforated: *MUESTRA SIN VALOR* and red ovpt: TDLR oval seals. 1985; 1987.	—	—	30.00

123	500 PESOS ORO	VG	VF	UNC
	1978-87. Deep blue, blue and brown on m/c unpt. National Theater at ctr. Fort San Felipe at ctr. r. on back.			
	a. Wmk: Indian head. 1978; 1980; 1981.	55.00	225.00	450.00
	b. Wmk: J. P. Duarte. 1985; 1987.	50.00	200.00	400.00
	s1. As a. Specimen w/black ovpt: *ESPECIMEN*. 1978; 1980; 1981.	—	—	45.00
	s2. As b. Specimen w/perforated: *MUESTRA SIN VALOR* and red ovpt: TDLR oval seals. 1985; 1987.	—	—	45.00

		VG	VF	UNC
124	**1000 PESOS ORO**			
	1978-87. Red, purple and violet on m/c unpt. National Palace at ctr. Columbus' fortress at ctr. r. on back.			
	a. Wmk: Indian head. 1978; 1980.	100.00	275.00	550.00
	b. Wmk: J. P. Duarte. 1984; 1987.	90.00	225.00	450.00
	s1. As a. Specimen w/black ovpt: *ESPECIMEN*. 1978; 1980; 1981.	—	—	60.00
	s2. As b. Specimen w/perforated: *MUESTRA SIN VALOR* and red ovpt: TDLR oval seals. 1985; 1987.	—	—	60.00

1978 COMMEMORATIVE ISSUE

#125, Inauguration of new Banco Central bldg.

		VG	VF	UNC
125	**100 PESOS ORO**			
	15.8.1978 (- old date 1977). Special commemorative text ovpt. in black script at l. on back of #122a. Specimen in red folder.	—	—	200.00

1982 COMMEMORATIVE ISSUE

#125A, 35th Anniversary Banco Central, 1947-1982

		VG	VF	UNC
125A	**100 PESOS ORO**			
	22.10.1982 (old dates 1978, 1981). Special commemorative text ovpt. in black below bank at r. on back of #122a.			
	s1. Old date 1978. Face w/o adhesive stamp or handstamp. Specimen.	—	—	135.00
	s2. Old date 1981. Banco Central commemorative adhesive stamp affixed at l., handstamp w/date 22.10.1982 at ctr. l. Specimen.	—	—	150.00

1984 ISSUE

		VG	VF	UNC
126	**1 PESO ORO**			
	1984; 1987; 1988. Black and brown on m/c unpt. New portr. J. P. Duarte at r., otherwise like #117. Printer: TDLR.			
	a. Issued note.	FV	FV	1.00
	s1. Specimen w/red ovpt: *MUESTRA SIN VALOR* and TDLR oval seals. 1987.	—	—	15.00
	s2. Specimen w/black ovpt: *MUESTRA SIN VALOR* and red ovpt: TDLR oval seals. 1988.	—	—	15.00

1988 ISSUE

#127-130 orange bank seal at l. Wmk: Duarte (profile). Printer: USBNC.

		VG	VF	UNC
127	**50 PESOS ORO**			
	1988. Black and purple on m/c unpt. Similar to #121.			
	a. Issued note.	FV	FV	12.00
	s. Specimen w/red ovpt: *ESPECIMEN MUESTRA SIN VALOR.*	—	—	27.50

		VG	VF	UNC
128	**100 PESOS ORO**			
	1988. Violet, brown-orange and brown on m/c unpt. Similar to #122.			
	a. Issued note.	FV	FV	18.50
	s. Specimen w/red ovpt: *ESPECIMEN MUESTRA SIN VALOR.*	—	—	30.00

		VG	VF	UNC
129	**500 PESOS ORO**			
	1988. Deep blue, blue, and brown on m/c unpt. Similar to #123.			
	a. Issued note.	FV	FV	75.00
	s. Specimen w/red ovpt: *ESPECIMEN MUESTRA SIN VALOR.*	—	—	45.00

		VG	VF	UNC
130	**1000 PESOS ORO**			
	1988; 1990. Purple, red-violet and violet on m/c unpt. Similar to #124.			
	a. Issued note.	FV	FV	135.00
	s. Specimen w/red ovpt: *ESPECIMEN MUESTRA SIN VALOR.* 1988.	—	—	60.00

1990 ISSUE

#131-134 w/silver leaf-like underlays at l. and r. on face. Printer: H&S.

		VG	VF	UNC
131	**5 PESOS ORO**			
	1990. Deep brown, red-brown and red on m/c unpt. Similar to #118.	FV	FV	1.75

		VG	VF	UNC
132	**10 PESOS ORO**			
	1990. Deep green and black on m/c unpt. Similar to #119.	FV	FV	2.75

		VG	VF	UNC
133	**20 PESOS ORO** 1990. Deep brown and brown on m/c unpt. Similar to #120.	FV	FV	5.00
134	**500 PESOS ORO** 1990. Deep blue-green, black and brown on m/c unpt. Similar to #123.	FV	FV	70.00

1991 ISSUE

#135-138 orange seal at l. Printer: TDLR.

		VG	VF	UNC
135	**50 PESOS ORO** 1991; 1994. Black and purple on m/c unpt. Like #127 but wmk: Columbus.			
	a. Issued note.	FV	FV	11.00
	s. Specimen w/black ovpt: *MUESTRA SIN VALOR* and red ovpt: TDLR oval seals. 1991.	—	—	27.50
136	**100 PESOS ORO** 1991; 1994. Orange and violet on m/c unpt. Like #128.	FV	FV	17.50

		VG	VF	UNC
137	**500 PESOS ORO** 1991; 1994. Deep blue, blue and dk. brown on m/c unpt. Like #134.			
	a. Issued note.	FV	FV	65.00
	s. Specimen w/black ovpt: *MUESTRA SIN VALOR* and red ovpt: TDLR oval seals. 1991.	—	—	45.00

		VG	VF	UNC
138	**1000 PESOS ORO** 1991; 1992; 1994. Purple, red-violet and violet on m/c unpt. Like #130.			
	a. Issued note.	FV	FV	125.00
	s. Specimen w/black ovpt: *MUESTRA SIN VALOR* and red ovpt: TDLR oval seals. 1991.	—	—	60.00

1992 COMMEMORATIVE ISSUE

#139-142, Quincentennial of First Landfall by Christopher Columbus, 1992

		VG	VF	UNC
139	**20 PESOS ORO** 1992. Deep brown and brown on m/c unpt. Like #133 but w/brown commemorative text: *1492-1992 V Centenario...* at l. over orange seal. Printer: BABNC.			
	a. Issued note.	FV	FV	4.00
	s. Specimen w/red ovpt: *ESPECIMEN* and black ovpt: *ESPECIMEN SIN VALOR.*	—	—	50.00

#140-142 wmk: C. Columbus.

		VG	VF	UNC
140	**500 PESOS ORO** 1992. Brown and blue-black on m/c unpt. Sailing ships at ctr., C. Columbus at ctr. r. Arms at l., Columbus Lighthouse, placement of Cross of Christianity and map outline at ctr. on back. Printer: CBNC.			
	a. Issued note.	FV	FV	65.00
	s. Specimen w/black ovpt: *MUESTRA SIN VALOR* and red ovpt: TDLR oval seals.	—	—	110.00

		VG	VF	UNC
141	**500 PESOS ORO** 1992. Deep blue, blue and dk. brown on m/c unpt. Black commemorative text ovpt. at r. on #137. Printer: TDLR.			
	a. Issued note.	FV	FV	65.00
	s. Specimen w/black ovpt: *MUESTRA SIN VALOR* and red ovpt: TDLR oval seals.	—	—	85.00

		VG	VF	UNC
142	**1000 PESOS ORO** 1992. Purple, red-violet and violet on m/c unpt. Black commemorative text ovpt. at r. on #138. Printer: TDLR.			
	a. Issued note.	FV	FV	125.00
	s. Specimen w/black ovpt: *MUESTRA SIN VALOR* and red ovpt: TDLR oval seals.	—	—	110.00

1993 REGULAR ISSUE

		VG	VF	UNC
143	**5 PESOS ORO** 1993. Deep brown, red-brown and red on m/c unpt. Similar to #131. Printer: USBNC.	FV	FV	1.50

#144 and 145 printer: FNMT.

		VG	VF	UNC
144	**100 PESOS ORO** 1993. Orange and violet on m/c unpt. Similar to #136.	FV	FV	15.00
145	**1000 PESOS ORO** 1993. Red, purple and violet on m/c unpt. Similar to #138.	FV	FV	120.00

1994 ISSUE

		VG	VF	UNC
146	**5 PESOS ORO** 1994. Deep brown, red-brown and red on m/c unpt. Similar to #143. Printer: TDLR.	FV	FV	1.25

NOTICE

Readers with unlisted dates, signature varieties, etc. are invited to submit photocopies of their notes to: Standard Catalog of World Paper Money, 700 East State St. Iola, WI 54990-0001, fax: 1-715-445-4087, or E-Mail: thernr@krause.com.

1995 ISSUE

#147-151 orange bank seal at l. Printer: F-CO.

		VG	VF	UNC
147	**5 PESOS ORO** 1995; 1996; 1997. Deep brown, red-brown and red on m/c unpt. Similar to #146 but w/brighter colored arms at ctr.			
	a. Issued note.	FV	FV	1.35
	s. Specimen w/black ovpt: *ESPECIMEN MUESTRA SIN VALOR.* 1995.	—	—	20.00

		VG	VF	UNC
148	**10 PESOS ORO** 1995; 1996; 1997. Deep green and black on m/c unpt. Like #132.			
	a. Issued note.	FV	FV	2.50
	s. Specimen w/black ovpt: *ESPECIMEN MUESTRA SIN VALOR.* 1995.	—	—	25.00

		VG	VF	UNC
149	**50 PESOS ORO** 1995; 1997. Purple and black on m/c unpt. Like #135.			
	a. Issued note.	FV	FV	6.00
	s. Specimen w/black ovpt: *ESPECIMEN MUESTRA SIN VALOR.*	—	—	30.00

#150 and 151 w/luminescent strip of cross design w/*BCRD* in angles repeated at r. on back.

		VG	VF	UNC
150	**100 PESOS ORO** 1995. Orange, violet and brown on m/c unpt. Like #136 but w/silver overlays at l. and r., purple design w/*RD* also at r.			
	a. Issued note.	FV	FV	11.50
	s. Specimen w/black ovpt: *ESPECIMEN MUESTRA SIN VALOR.*	—	—	35.00

		VG	VF	UNC
151	**500 PESOS ORO** 1995; 1997. Deep blue, blue and brown on m/c unpt. Like #137 but w/silver overlays at l. and r., gold design w/*RD* also at r.			
	a. Issued note.	FV	FV	55.00
	s. Specimen w/black ovpt: *ESPECIMEN MUESTRA SIN VALOR.*	—	—	50.00

1997-98 ISSUE

Similar to #148-150 but printer: F-CO.

		VG	VF	UNC
152	**10 PESOS ORO** 1998. Deep green and black on m/c unpt.	FV	FV	4.00

		VG	VF	UNC
153	**20 PESOS ORO** 1998. Deep brown and brown on m/c unpt.	FV	FV	5.00
154	**50 PESOS ORO** 1997. Purple and black on m/c unpt.	FV	FV	10.00
155	**100 PESOS ORO** 1998. Orange and violet on m/c unpt.	FV	FV	16.50

COLLECTOR SERIES

BANCO CENTRAL DE LA REPÚBLICA DOMINICANA

1974 ISSUES

		ISSUE PRICE	MKT. VALUE
CS1	**1-1000 PESOS ORO** ND(1974). #99-106. Ovpt: *MUESTRA* twice on face.	—	450.00
CS2	**1-1000 PESOS ORO** ND(1974). #99-106. Ovpt: *MUESTRA* on face and back.	40.00	450.00

1978 ISSUES

		ISSUE PRICE	MKT. VALUE
CS3	**PESOS ORO** 1978. #116, 118-124. Ovpt: *MUESTRA/SIN VALOR* on face, *ESPECIMEN* on back.	40.00	235.00

		ISSUE PRICE	MKT. VALUE
CS4	**PESOS ORO** 1978. #116, 118a-120a, 121, 122a, 123, 124a. Ovpt: *SPECIMEN* w/serial # prefix Maltese cross. #122a is dated 1977.	14.00	60.00

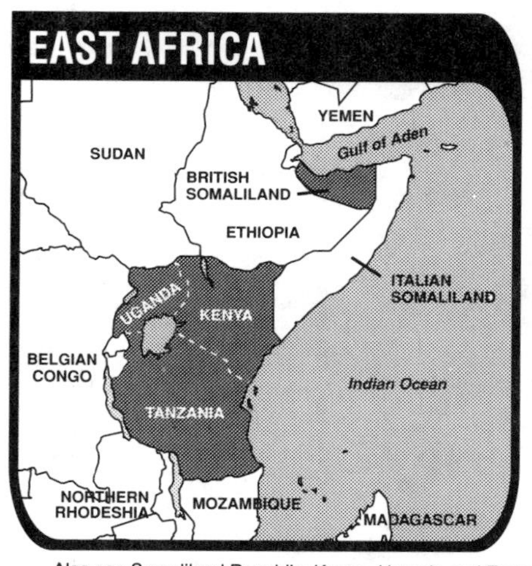

East Africa was an administrative grouping of several neighboring British territories: Kenya, Tanganyika, Uganda and Zanzibar.

The common interest of Kenya, Tanzania and Uganda invited cooperation in economic matters and consideration of political union. The territorial governors, organized as the East Africa High Commission, met periodically to administer such common activities as taxation, industrial development and education. The authority of the Commission did not infringe upon the constitution and internal autonomy of the individual colonies. The common monetary system circulated for the territories by the East African Currency Board and was also used in British Somaliland and the Aden Protectorate subsequent to the independence of India (1947) whose currency had previously circulated in these two territories.

Also see Somaliland Republic, Kenya, Uganda and Tanzania.

RULERS:
British

MONETARY SYSTEM:
1 Shilling = 100 Cents

BRITISH INFLUENCE

EAST AFRICAN CURRENCY BOARD, NAIROBI

1961 ND ISSUE

#41-44 portr. Qn. Elizabeth II at upper l. w/3 sign. at l. and 4 at r. Printer: TDLR.

		VG	VF	UNC
41	**5 SHILLINGS** ND (1961-63). Brown on m/c unpt.			
	a. Top l. sign: E. B. David. (1961).	5.00	20.00	225.00
	b. Top l. sign: A. L. Adu. (1962-63).	3.50	15.00	180.00

		VG	VF	UNC
42	**10 SHILLINGS** ND (1961-63). Green on m/c unpt.			
	a. Top l. sign: E. B. David. (1961).	9.00	25.00	350.00
	b. Top l. sign: A. L. Adu. (1962-63).	6.00	20.00	275.00

		VG	VF	UNC
43	**20 SHILLINGS** ND (1961-63). Blue on m/c unpt.			
	a. Top l. sign: E. B. David. (1961).	10.00	40.00	450.00
	b. Top l. sign: A. L. Adu. (1962-63).	7.00	30.00	300.00

		VG	VF	UNC
44	**100 SHILLINGS** ND (1961-63). Red on m/c unpt.			
	a. Top l. sign: E. B. David. (1961).	17.50	95.00	875.00
	b. Top l. sign: A. L. Adu. (1962-63).	15.00	75.00	600.00

1964 ND ISSUE

#45-48 wmk. area at l., sailboat at l. ctr. Various plants on back.

		VG	VF	UNC
45	**5 SHILLINGS** ND (1964). Brown on m/c unpt.			
	a. Issued note.	2.75	11.50	65.00
	s. Specimen. Punched hole cancelled.	—	—	—

		VG	VF	UNC
46	**10 SHILLINGS** ND (1964). Green on m/c unpt.			
	a. Issued note.	5.00	16.50	90.00
	s. Specimen. Punched hole cancelled.	—	—	—

		VG	VF	UNC
47	**20 SHILLINGS** ND (1964). Blue on m/c unpt.			
	a. Issued note.	7.50	30.00	250.00
	s. Specimen. Punched hole cancelled.	—	—	—

		VG	VF	UNC
48	**100 SHILLINGS** ND (1964). Deep red on m/c unpt.			
	a. Issued note.	9.00	45.00	165.00
	s. Specimen. Punched hole cancelled.	—	—	—

The East Caribbean States, formerly the British Caribbean Territories (Eastern Group), a currency board formed in 1950, comprised the British West Indies territories of Trinidad and Tobago; Barbados; the Leeward Islands of Anguilla, Saba, St, Christopher, Nevis and Antigua; the Windward Islands of St. Lucia, Dominica, St. Vincent and Grenada; British Guiana and the British Virgin Islands.

As time progressed, the member countries varies and this is reflected on the backs of #13-16. The first issue includes Barbados but not Grenada, while the second issue includes both Barbados and Grenada and the third issue retains Grenada while Barbados is removed. Barbados attained self-government in 1961 and independence on Nov. 30, 1966.

On May 26, 1966 British Guiana became independent as Guyana which later became a cooperative Republic on Feb. 23, 1970.

The British Virgin Islands became a largely self-governing dependent territory of the United Kingdom in 1967. United States currency is the official medium of exchange.

St. Christopher and Nevis became fully independent on Sept. 19, 1983.

Trinidad & Tobago became an independent member state of the Commonwealth on August 31, 1962.

RULERS:

British

MONETARY SYSTEM:

1 Dollar = 100 Cents

BRITISH INFLUENCE

EAST CARIBBEAN CURRENCY AUTHORITY

SIGNATURE VARIETIES

1	Chairman Director Director Director	2	Chairman Director Director Director
3	Chairman Director Director Director	4	Chairman Director Director Director
5	Chairman Director Director Director	6	Chairman Director Director Director
7	Chairman Director Director Director	8	Chairman Director Director Director
9	Chairman Director Director Director	10	Chairman Director Director Director

ISLAND PARTICIPATION

Variety I **Variety II** **Variety III**

VARIETY I: Listing of islands on back includes Barbados but not Grenada.
VARIETY II: Listing includes Barbados and Grenada.
VARIETY III: Listing retains Grenada while Barbados is deleted.

1965 ND ISSUE

#13-16 map at l., Qn. Elizabeth II at r. Coastline w/rocks and trees at l. ctr. on back. Sign. varieties. Wmk. QE II. Printer: TDLR. Replacement notes: Serial # prefix *Z1*.

Beginning in 1983, #13-16 were ovpt. with circled letters at l. indicating their particular areas of issue within the Eastern Group. Letters and their respective areas are as follows:

A, Antigua	L, St. Lucia
D, Dominica	M, Montserrat
G, Grenada	U, Anguilla
K, St. Kitts	V, St. Vincent

		VG	VF	UNC
13	**1 DOLLAR**			
	ND (1965). Red on m/c unpt. Fish at ctr.			
	a. Sign. 1; 2.	1.00	5.00	30.00
	b. Sign. 3.	.75	3.00	15.00
	c. Sign. 4.	1.00	6.00	75.00
	d. Sign. 5; 6; 7.	.50	2.00	15.00
	e. Sign. 8.	.45	1.50	10.00
	f. Sign. 9; 10. Darker red on back as previous varieties, to Series B82.	FV	.75	6.50
	g. Sign. 10. Brighter red on back. Series B83-B91.	FV	.75	7.00
	h. Ovpt: *A* in circle.	FV	.50	6.00
	i. Ovpt: *D* in circle.	FV	.50	7.00
	j. Ovpt: *G* in circle.	FV	.50	8.00
	k. Ovpt: *K* in circle.	FV	.50	6.00
	l. Ovpt: *L* in circle.	FV	.50	7.00
	m. Ovpt: *M* in circle.	FV	.50	6.00
	n. Ovpt: *V* in circle.	FV	.50	6.00

		VG	VF	UNC
14	**5 DOLLARS**			
	ND (1965). Green on m/c unpt. Flying fish at ctr.			
	a. Sign. 1.	6.00	25.00	125.00
	b. Sign. 2.	5.50	20.00	125.00
	c. Sign. 3.	Reported Not Confirmed		
	d. Sign. 4.	4.00	10.00	110.00
	e. Sign. 5; 6.	3.50	7.50	55.00
	f. Sign. 7.	4.00	10.00	75.00
	g. Sign. 8.	2.00	5.00	28.50
	h. Sign. 9; 10.	FV	3.00	15.00
	i. Ovpt: *A* in circle.	FV	2.50	15.00
	j. Ovpt: *D* in circle.	FV	2.50	15.00
	k. Ovpt: *G* in circle.	FV	2.50	15.00
	l. Ovpt: *K* in circle.	FV	2.50	15.00
	m. Ovpt: *L* in circle.	FV	7.50	100.00
	n. Ovpt: *M* in circle.	FV	2.50	15.00
	o. Ovpt: *U* in circle.	FV	2.50	15.00
	p. Ovpt: *V* in circle.	FV	2.50	15.00

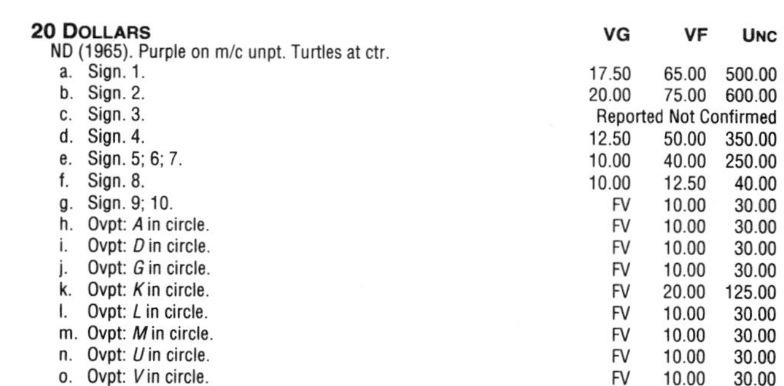

		VG	VF	UNC
15	**20 DOLLARS**			
	ND (1965). Purple on m/c unpt. Turtles at ctr.			
	a. Sign. 1.	17.50	65.00	500.00
	b. Sign. 2.	20.00	75.00	600.00
	c. Sign. 3.	Reported Not Confirmed		
	d. Sign. 4.	12.50	50.00	350.00
	e. Sign. 5; 6; 7.	10.00	40.00	250.00
	f. Sign. 8.	10.00	12.50	40.00
	g. Sign. 9; 10.	FV	10.00	30.00
	h. Ovpt: *A* in circle.	FV	10.00	30.00
	i. Ovpt: *D* in circle.	FV	10.00	30.00
	j. Ovpt: *G* in circle.	FV	10.00	30.00
	k. Ovpt: *K* in circle.	FV	20.00	125.00
	l. Ovpt: *L* in circle.	FV	10.00	30.00
	m. Ovpt: *M* in circle.	FV	10.00	30.00
	n. Ovpt: *U* in circle.	FV	10.00	30.00
	o. Ovpt: *V* in circle.	FV	10.00	30.00

		VG	VF	UNC
16	**100 DOLLARS**			
	ND (1965). Black on m/c unpt. Sea horses at ctr.			
	a. Sign. 1.	150.00	400.00	1250.
	b. Sign. 2.	Reported Not Confirmed		
	c. Sign. 5.	100.00	325.00	1350.
	d. Sign. 3; 4; 6; 7.	Reported Not Confirmed		
	e. Sign. 8.	Reported Not Confirmed		
	f. Sign. 9; 10.	FV	60.00	245.00
	g. Ovpt: *A* in circle.	FV	60.00	275.00
	h. Ovpt: *D* in circle.	50.00	125.00	500.00
	i. Ovpt: *G* in circle.	FV	85.00	300.00
	j. Ovpt: *K* in circle.	FV	95.00	550.00
	k. Ovpt: *L* in circle.	FV	60.00	225.00
	l. Ovpt: *M* in circle.	FV	50.00	200.00
	m. Ovpt: *V* in circle.	FV	55.00	245.00

EASTERN CARIBBEAN CENTRAL BANK

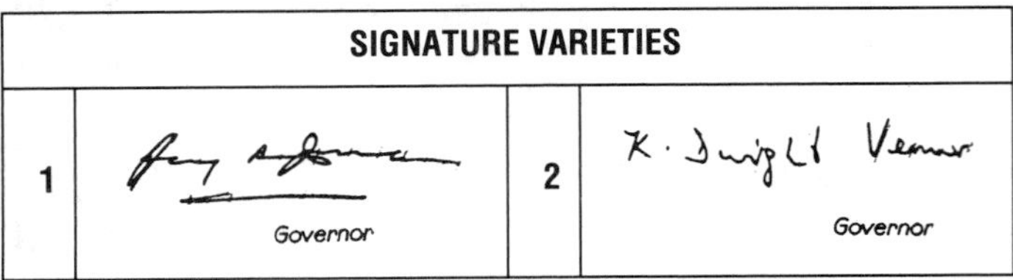

SIGNATURE VARIETIES			
1	Governor	2	Governor

1985-87 ND ISSUE

#17-25 windsurfer at l., Qn. Elizabeth II at ctr. r., map at r. Back similar to #13-16. Wmk: QEII. Printer: TDLR. Replacement notes: Serial # prefix *Z1*.

Notes w/suffix letter of serial # indicating particular areas of issue (as with ovpt. letters on previous issue).

#17-20 do not have name Anguilla at island near top of map at r. Palm tree, swordfish at ctr. r., shoreline in background on back. No $10 without Anguilla was issued.

		VG	VF	UNC
17	**1 DOLLAR** ND (1985-88). Red on m/c unpt.			
	a. Suffix letter *A*.	FV	1.00	4.50
	b. Suffix letter *D*.	FV	1.00	4.50
	c. Suffix letter *G*.	FV	1.00	4.50
	d. Suffix letter *K*.	FV	1.00	4.50
	e. Suffix letter *L*.	FV	1.00	4.50
	f. Suffix letter *M*.	FV	1.00	4.50
	g. Suffix letter *V*.	FV	1.00	4.50
	h. Ovpt: *U* in circle on suffix letter *V* issue (1988).	FV	1.00	4.50

		VG	VF	UNC
18	**5 DOLLARS** ND (1986-88). Deep green on m/c unpt.			
	a. Suffix letter *A*.	FV	FV	8.50
	b. Suffix letter *D*.	FV	FV	8.50
	c. Suffix letter *G*.	FV	FV	8.50
	d. Suffix letter *K*.	FV	FV	8.50
	e. Suffix letter *L*.	FV	FV	8.50
	f. Suffix letter *M*.	FV	FV	8.50
	g. Suffix letter *V*.	FV	FV	8.50
	h. Ovpt: *U* in circle on suffix letter *V* issue (1988).	FV	FV	8.50

		VG	VF	UNC
19	**20 DOLLARS** ND (1987-88). Purple and brown on m/c unpt.			
	a. Suffix letter *A*.	FV	FV	30.00
	b. Suffix letter *D*.	FV	FV	30.00
	c. Suffix letter *G*.	FV	FV	30.00
	d. Suffix letter *K*.	FV	FV	30.00
	e. Suffix letter *L*.	FV	FV	30.00
	f. Suffix letter *M*.	FV	12.50	32.50
	g. Suffix letter *V*.	FV	FV	30.00
	h. Ovpt: *U* in circle.	FV	FV	32.50

		VG	VF	UNC
20	**100 DOLLARS** ND (1986-88). Black and orange on m/c unpt.			
	a. Suffix letter *A*.	FV	FV	135.00
	b. Suffix letter *D*.	FV	50.00	150.00
	c. Suffix letter *G*.	FV	50.00	160.00
	d. Suffix letter *K*.	FV	FV	135.00
	e. Suffix letter *L*.	FV	FV	135.00
	f. Suffix letter *M*.	FV	FV	135.00
	g. Suffix letter *V*.	FV	FV	135.00
	h. Ovpt: *U* in circle on suffix letter *V* issue (1988).	FV	FV	135.00

1985-88 ND ISSUE

#21-25 with *ANGUILLA* island named near top of map at r.

#21, 22, 24 and 25 harbor at St. Lucia on back.

		VG	VF	UNC
21	**1 DOLLAR** ND (1988-89). Red on m/c unpt. Like #17 but Anguilla named. Sign. 1.			
	a. Suffix letter *D*.	FV	1.00	5.50
	b. Suffix letter *K*.	FV	1.00	5.50
	c. Suffix letter *L*.	FV	1.00	5.50
	d. Suffix letter *U*.	FV	1.00	5.50

		VG	VF	UNC
22	**5 DOLLARS** ND (1988-93). Deep green on m/c unpt. Like #18 but Anguilla named.			
	a. Suffix letter *A*. Sign. 1.	—	—	7.00
	b. Like a. Sign. 2.	—	—	7.00
	c. Suffix letter *D*. Sign. 1.	—	—	7.00
	g. Suffix letter *K*. Sign. 1.	—	—	7.00
	h. Like g. Sign. 2.	—	—	7.00
	i. Suffix letter *L*. Sign. 1.	—	—	7.00
	j. Like i. Sign. 2.	—	—	7.00
	k. Suffix letter *M*. Sign. 1.	—	—	7.00
	m. Suffix letter *U*. Sign. 1.	—	—	8.00
	p. Suffix letter *V*. Sign. 2.	—	—	7.00

NOTICE

Readers with unlisted dates, signature varieties, etc. are invited to submit photocopies of their notes to: Standard Catalog of World Paper Money, 700 East State St. Iola, WI 54990-0001, fax: 1-715-445-4087, or E-Mail: thernr@krause.com.

23	10 DOLLARS	VG	VF	UNC
	ND (1985-93). Blue on m/c unpt. Harbor at Grenada, sailboats at l. and ctr. on back.			
	a. Suffix letter *A*. Sign. 1.	—	—	12.00
	b. Like a. Sign. 2.	—	—	12.50
	c. Suffix letter *D*. Sign. 1.	—	—	12.00
	d. Like c. Sign. 2.	—	—	12.50
	e. Suffix letter *G*. Sign. 1.	—	—	12.00
	g. Suffix letter *K*. Sign. 1.	—	—	12.00
	h. Like g. Sign. 2.	—	—	12.50
	i. Suffix letter *L*. Sign. 1.	—	—	12.00
	j. Like i. Sign. 2.	—	—	12.00
	k. Suffix letter *M*. Sign. 1.	—	—	12.50
	m. Suffix letter *U*. Sign. 1.	—	—	12.00
	o. Suffix letter *V*. Sign. 1.	—	—	12.00
	p. Like o. Sign. 2.	—	—	12.00
24	20 DOLLARS			
	ND (1988-93). Purple and brown on m/c unpt. Like #19 but Anguilla named.			
	a. Suffix letter *A*. Sign. 1.	—	—	20.00
	b. Like a. Sign. 2.	—	—	20.00
	c. Suffix letter *D*. Sign. 1.	—	—	25.00
	d. Like c. Sign. 2.	—	—	22.50
	e. Suffix letter *G*. Sign. 1.	—	—	25.00
	g. Suffix letter *K*. Sign. 1.	—	—	23.50
	h. Like g. Sign. 2.	—	—	22.50
	i. Suffix letter *L*. Sign. 1.	—	—	25.00
	j. Like i. Sign. 2.	—	—	22.50
	k. Suffix letter *M*. Sign. 1.	—	—	22.50
	l. Like k. Sign. 2.	—	—	22.50
	m. Suffix letter *U*. Sign. 1.	—	—	25.00
	o. Suffix letter *V*. Sign. 1.	—	—	25.00

25	100 DOLLARS	VG	VF	UNC
	ND (1988-93). Black and orange on m/c unpt. Like #20 but Anguilla named.			
	a. Suffix letter *A*. Sign. 1.	—	—	120.00
	b. Like a. Sign. 2.	—	—	120.00
	c. Suffix letter *D*. Sign. 1.	—	—	120.00
	d. Like c. Sign. 2.	—	—	120.00
	e. Suffix letter *G*. Sign. 1.	—	—	120.00
	g. Suffix letter *K*. Sign. 1.	—	—	120.00
	h. Like g. Sign. 2.	—	—	120.00
	i. Suffix letter *L*. Sign. 1.	—	—	120.00
	j. Like i. Sign. 2.	—	—	120.00
	k. Suffix letter *M*. Sign. 1.	—	—	120.00
	l. Like k. Sign. 2.	—	—	120.00
	m. Suffix letter *U*. Sign. 1.	—	—	120.00
	o. Suffix letter *V*. Sign. 1.	—	—	120.00

1993 ND ISSUE

BAR CODE CHART

Antigua (A)	St. Lucia (L)
Dominica (D)	Montserrat (M)
Grenada (G)	Anguilla (U)
St. Kitts (K)	St. Vincent (V)

#26-30 Qn. Elizabeth II at ctr. r. and as wmk. (profile), turtle at lower ctr. Island map at ctr. on back. Sign. 2. Printer: TDLR.

26	5 DOLLARS	VG	VF	UNC
	ND (1993). Dk. green, black and violet on m/c unpt. Admiral's House in Antigua and Barbuda at l., Trafalgar Falls in Dominica at r. on back.			
	a. Suffix letter *A*.	FV	FV	7.50
	b. Suffix letter *D*.	FV	FV	7.50
	c. Suffix letter *G*.	FV	FV	7.50
	d. Suffix letter *K*.	FV	FV	7.50
	e. Suffix letter *L*.	FV	FV	7.50
	f. Suffix letter *M*.	FV	FV	7.50
	g. Suffix letter *U*.	FV	FV	7.50
	h. Suffix letter *V*.	FV	FV	7.50

27	10 DOLLARS	VG	VF	UNC
	ND (1993). Dk. blue, black and red on m/c unpt. Admiralty Bay in St. Vincent and Grenadines at l., sailing ship *Warspite* at r. ctr. on back.			
	a. Suffix letter *A*.	FV	FV	12.00
	b. Suffix letter *D*.	FV	FV	12.00
	c. Suffix letter *G*.	FV	FV	12.00
	d. Suffix letter *K*.	FV	FV	12.00
	e. Suffix letter *L*.	FV	FV	12.00
	f. Suffix letter *M*.	FV	FV	12.00
	g. Suffix letter *U*.	FV	FV	12.00
	h. Suffix letter *V*.	FV	FV	12.00

28 **20 DOLLARS**
ND (1993). Brown-violet, blue-gray and orange on m/c unpt. Govt. House in Montserrat at l., nutmeg in Grenada at r. on back.

	VG	VF	UNC
a. Suffix letter *A*.	FV	FV	23.50
b. Suffix letter *D*.	FV	FV	23.50
c. Suffix letter *G*.	FV	FV	23.50
d. Suffix letter *K*.	FV	FV	23.50
e. Suffix letter *L*.	FV	FV	23.50
f. Suffix letter *M*.	FV	FV	23.50
g. Suffix letter *U*.	FV	FV	23.50
h. Suffix letter *V*.	FV	FV	23.50

29 **50 DOLLARS**
ND (1993). Purple and olive-green on m/c unpt. Brimstone Hill in St. Kitts at l., Les Pitons mountains in St. Lucia at r. on back.

	VG	VF	UNC
a. Suffix letter *A*.	FV	FV	50.00
b. Suffix letter *D*.	FV	FV	60.00
c. Suffix letter *G*.	FV	FV	60.00
d. Suffix letter *K*.	FV	FV	60.00
e. Suffix letter *L*.	FV	FV	60.00
f. Suffix letter *M*.	FV	FV	60.00
g. Suffix letter *U*.	FV	FV	60.00
h. Suffix letter *V*.	FV	FV	60.00

30 **100 DOLLARS**
ND (1993). Dk. brown, dk. olive-green and tan on m/c unpt. Sir Arthur Lewis at l., E.C.C.B. Central Bank bldg. at r. on back.

	VG	VF	UNC
a. Suffix letter *A*.	FV	FV	95.00
b. Suffix letter *D*.	FV	FV	110.00
c. Suffix letter *G*.	FV	FV	110.00
d. Suffix letter *K*.	FV	FV	110.00
e. Suffix letter *L*.	FV	FV	100.00
f. Suffix letter *M*.	FV	FV	100.00
g. Suffix letter *U*.	FV	FV	100.00
h. Suffix letter *V*.	FV	FV	100.00

1994 ND ISSUE

#31-35 like #26-30 but w/clear bolder values at upper l. and lower r. Sign. 2. Replacement notes: Serial # prefix *Z*.

31 **5 DOLLARS**
ND (1994). Dk. green, black and violet on m/c unpt. Like #26.

	VG	VF	UNC
a. Suffix letter *A*.	FV	FV	6.50
b. Suffix letter *D*.	FV	FV	6.50
c. Suffix letter *G*.	FV	FV	6.50
d. Suffix letter *K*.	FV	FV	6.50
e. Suffix letter *L*.	FV	FV	6.50
f. Suffix letter *M*.	FV	9.00	12.50
g. Suffix letter *U*.	FV	FV	6.50
h. Suffix letter *V*.	FV	FV	6.50

32 **10 DOLLARS**
ND (1994). Dk. blue, black and red on m/c unpt. Like #27.

	VG	VF	UNC
a. Suffix letter *A*.	FV	FV	8.00
b. Suffix letter *D*.	FV	FV	9.00
c. Suffix letter *G*.	FV	FV	9.00
d. Suffix letter *K*.	FV	FV	9.00
e. Suffix letter *L*.	FV	FV	9.00
f. Suffix letter *M*.	FV	12.50	17.50
g. Suffix letter *U*.	FV	FV	9.00
h. Suffix letter *V*.	FV	FV	9.00

33 **20 DOLLARS**
ND (1994). Brown-violet, blue-gray and orange on m/c unpt. Like #28.

	VG	VF	UNC
a. Suffix letter *A*.	FV	FV	18.00
b. Suffix letter *D*.	FV	FV	19.00
c. Suffix letter *G*.	FV	FV	19.00
d. Suffix letter *K*.	FV	FV	19.00
e. Suffix letter *L*.	FV	FV	19.00
f. Suffix letter *M*.	FV	25.00	30.00
g. Suffix letter *U*.	FV	FV	19.00
h. Suffix letter *V*.	FV	FV	19.00

No.	Description	VG	VF	UNC
34	ND (1994). Tan, red-orange and green on m/c unpt. Like #29.			
	a. Suffix letter *A*.	FV	FV	45.00
	b. Suffix letter *D*.	FV	FV	55.00
	c. Suffix letter *G*.	FV	FV	50.00
	d. Suffix letter *K*.	FV	FV	55.00
	e. Suffix letter *L*.	FV	FV	45.00
	f. Suffix letter *M*.	FV	60.00	75.00
	g. Suffix letter *U*.	FV	FV	50.00
	h. Suffix letter *V*.	FV	FV	45.00

No.	Description	VG	VF	UNC
35	**100 DOLLARS** ND (1994). Dk. brown and dk. green on m/c unpt. Like #30.			
	a. Suffix letter *A*.	FV	FV	85.00
	b. Suffix letter *D*.	FV	FV	90.00
	c. Suffix letter *G*.	FV	FV	90.00
	d. Suffix letter *K*.	FV	FV	90.00
	e. Suffix letter *L*.	FV	FV	90.00
	f. Suffix letter *M*.	FV	100.00	150.00
	g. Suffix letter *U*.	FV	FV	90.00
	h. Suffix letter *V*.	FV	FV	90.00

1998 ND ISSUE

#36 printer: (T)DLR.

No.	Description	VG	VF	UNC
36	**100 DOLLARS** ND (1998). Dk. brown and dk. green on m/c unpt. Like #35 but w/gold foil flower enhanced colors and segmented foil over security thread.			
	a. Suffix letter *A.*	FV	FV	75.00
	b. Suffix letter *D.*	FV	FV	75.00
	c. Suffix letter *G.*	FV	FV	75.00
	d. Suffix letter *K.*	FV	FV	75.00
	e. Suffix letter *L.*	FV	FV	75.00
	f. Suffix letter *U.*	FV	FV	75.00
	g. Suffix letter *V.*	FV	FV	75.00

COLLECTOR SERIES

GOVERNMENT OF ANTIGUA AND BARBUDA

1983 ND ISSUE

This set is made with thin gold and silver foil bonded to paper.

		ISSUE PRICE	MKT. VALUE
CS1	**30 DOLLARS** ND (1983). 12 Different notes showing various flowers and animals.	—	350.00

EAST CARIBBEAN CENTRAL BANK

1988 ND ISSUE

This set is made with thin gold and silver foil bonded to paper.

		ISSUE PRICE	MKT. VALUE
CS2	**100 DOLLARS** ND (1988). 30 different notes showing various pirate ships. (20,000 sets).	1155.	1100.

The Republic of Ecuador, located astride the equator on the Pacific coast of South America, has an area of 109,484 sq. mi. (283,561 sq. km.) and a population of 11.7 million. Capital: Quito. Agriculture is the mainstay of the economy but there are appreciable deposits of minerals and petroleum. It is the world's largest exporter of bananas and balsa wood. Coffee, cacao and shrimp are also valuable exports.

Ecuador was first sighted, 1526, by Bartolome Ruiz. Conquest was undertaken by Sebastian de Benalcazar who founded Quito in 1534. Ecuador was part of the province, later Vice-royalty, of Peru until 1739 when it became part of the Vice-royalty of New Granada. After two failed attempts to attain independence in 1810 and 1812, it successfully declared its independence in October 1820, and won final victory over Spanish forces May 24, 1822. Incorporated into the Gran Colombia confederacy, it loosened its ties in 1830 and regained full independence in 1835.

MONETARY SYSTEM:

1 Condor = 25 Sucres

REPUBLIC

BANCO CENTRAL DEL ECUADOR

1944 ISSUE

#96 and 97 black on m/c unpt. Printer: ABNC.

No.	Description	VG	VF	UNC
96	**500 SUCRES** 1944-66. Mercury seated at ctr. Back deep orange.			
	a. Sign. title ovpt: *PRESIDENTE* at l. 12.5.1944; 27.6.1944.	175.00	325.00	—
	b. Sign. title ovpt: *GERENTE GENERAL* at l., *VOCAL* at r. 31.7.1944; 7.9.1944.	150.00	300.00	—
	c. Sign. title ovpt: *GERENTE GENERAL* at r. 12.1.1945-12.7.1947.	125.00	250.00	—
	d. As c. 21.4.1961-17.11.1966.	100.00	200.00	550.00
	s. Specimen. ND.	—	—	400.00

No.	Description	VG	VF	UNC
97	**1000 SUCRES** 1944-67. Woman reclining w/globe and telephone at ctr. Back greenish gray.			
	a. Sign. title ovpt: *PRESIDENTE* at l. 12.5.1944; 7.6.1944.	275.00	—	—
	b. Sign. title ovpt: *GERENTE GENERAL* at l., *VOCAL* at r. 31.7.1944; 7.9.1944.	250.00	—	—
	c. Sign. title ovpt: *PRESIDENTE* at l., *GERENTE GENERAL* at r. 12.1.1945.	225.00	—	—
	d. Sign. title ovpt: *GERENTE GENERAL* at r. 16.10.1945; 12.7.1947.	200.00	—	—
	e. As d. 21.4.1961; 27.2.1962; 4.3.1964; 23.7.1964; 17.11.1966; 6.4.1967.	100.00	—	—
	s. Specimen. ND.	—	—	400.00

NOTICE

Readers with unlisted dates, signature varieties, etc. are invited to submit photocopies of their notes to: Standard Catalog of World Paper Money, 700 East State St. Iola, WI 54990-0001, fax: 1-715-445-4087, or E-Mail: thernr@krause.com.

1950-58 ISSUE

Various dates found w/ or w/o dot after *1* in year.

		VG	VF	UNC
99	**10 SUCRES**			
	1950-74. Black on m/c unpt. Portr. S. de Benalcazar at ctr. Back blue, arms w/o flagpole stems at ctr. Printer: ABNC.			
	a. Plain background. 14.1.1950-28.11.1955.	1.50	5.00	20.00
	b. Ornate background, different background guilloches. 19.6.1956-27.4.1966.	.50	2.00	8.50
	c. Sign. title: *SUBGERENTE GENERAL*. 24.9.1957; 7.7.1959.	2.00	5.00	20.00
	d. 24.5.1968-2.1.1974.	.25	1.00	4.00
	s. Specimen. ND.	—	—	25.00

		VG	VF	UNC
102	**5 SUCRES**			

		VG	VF	UNC
	1956-73. Black on m/c unpt. Portr. A. J. de Sucre at ctr. Back red-violet; arms w/o flagpole stems at ctr. Printer: ABNC.			
	a. 19.6.1956; 29.8.1956; 2.4.1957; 2.1.1958.	.50	2.50	10.00
	b. Sign. title ovpt: *SUBGERENTE GENERAL*. 24.9.1957.	1.00	3.00	15.00
	c. 1.1.1966.	.20	.55	3.50
	d. 27.2.1970; 3.9.1973. Serial # varieties.	.15	.50	2.00

		VG	VF	UNC
103	**5 SUCRES**			
	1958-88. Portr. A. J. de Sucre at ctr. Back red-violet; arms at ctr. Printer: TDLR.			
	a. 2.1.1958-7.11.1962.	.60	2.00	7.50
	b. Sign. title ovpt: *SUBGERENTE GENERAL*. 7.7.1959.	1.00	3.00	15.00
	c. 23.5.1963-27.2.1970.	.25	.50	3.00
	d. 25.7.1979-24.5.1980.	FV	FV	1.00
	e. 22.11.1988.	FV	FV	.50
	s1. As b. Specimen. 24.5.1968.	—	—	27.50
	s2. As d. Specimen. 22.11.1988.	—	—	27.50
	s3. Specimen. ND, w/o sign. Series HA; HC.	—	—	35.00

		VG	VF	UNC
104	**50 SUCRES**			
	1957-82. National Monument w/bldgs. in background at ctr. Back green; arms at ctr. Printer: TDLR.			
	a. 2.4.1957-6.8.1965.	2.00	8.00	25.00
	b. 1.1.1966; 27.4.1966; 17.11.1966; 4.10.1967; 30.5.1969; 17.7.1974.	.50	2.00	6.00
	c. 24.5.1980; 20.8.1982.	FV	FV	1.50
	s1. Specimen. ND; 1.1.1966.	—	—	30.00
	s2. As c. Specimen. 20.8.1982.	—	—	30.00

		VG	VF	UNC
105	**100 SUCRES**			
	1957-80. Like #118 but w/different guilloches. Printer ABNC.			
	a. Sign. title: *SUBGERENTE GENERAL*. 24.9.1957.	10.00	50.00	125.00
	b. 7.7.1959-21.4.1961.	4.00	20.00	60.00
	c. 1.1.1966-7.7.1970.	2.00	4.00	15.00
	d. 1.2.1980.	1.00	2.00	5.00
	s. Specimen. ND.	—	—	32.50

1961; 1962 ISSUES

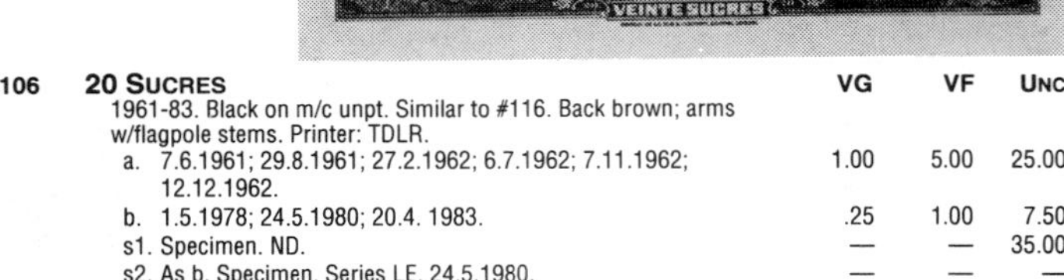

		VG	VF	UNC
106	**20 SUCRES**			
	1961-83. Black on m/c unpt. Similar to #116. Back brown; arms w/flagpole stems. Printer: TDLR.			
	a. 7.6.1961; 29.8.1961; 27.2.1962; 6.7.1962; 7.11.1962; 12.12.1962.	1.00	5.00	25.00
	b. 1.5.1978; 24.5.1980; 20.4. 1983.	.25	1.00	7.50
	s1. Specimen. ND.	—	—	35.00
	s2. As b. Specimen. Series LE. 24.5.1980.	—	—	—
	s3. Specimen. 20.4.1983.	—	—	50.00

#107 and 108 arms w/o flagpole stems at ctr. on back.

		VG	VF	UNC
107	**20 SUCRES**			
	1962-73. Black on m/c unpt. Church facade at ctr. Back brown. Printer: ABNC.			
	a. 12.12.1962-4.10.1967.	1.00	4.00	25.00
	b. 24.5.1968-3.9.1973.	.50	1.50	10.00
	s. Specimen. ND.	—	—	25.00

		VG	VF	UNC
108	**100 SUCRES**			
	29.8.1961-6.8.1965. Black on m/c unpt. Similar to #111 but crude portr. w/lt. clouds behind. Back purple. Printer: TDLR.			
	a. Issued note.	4.00	15.00	60.00
	s. Specimen. W/o sign. Series TW.	—	—	—

1965-71 ISSUES

		VG	VF	UNC
109	**10 SUCRES** 1968-83. Black on m/c unpt. Similar to #115. Back blue. Printer: TDLR.			
	a. 24.5.1968; 20.5.1971.	.25	1.50	10.00
	b. 24.5.1980; 30.9.1982; 20.4.1983.	FV	.25	6.00
	s1. As a. Specimen. 24.5.1968.	—	—	35.00
	s2. As a. Specimen. 20.5.1971. Series KY.	—	—	35.00
	s3. As b. Specimen. 30.9.1982. Series LH.	—	—	35.00
	s4. As b. Specimen. 20.4.1983. Series LJ.	—	—	35.00

		VG	VF	UNC
110	**50 SUCRES** 1968-71. Black on m/c unpt. National monument at ctr. Back green. Printer: ABNC.			
	a. 24.5.1968; 5.11.1969.	.75	5.00	22.50
	b. 20.5.1971.	.50	4.00	17.50
	s. Specimen. ND.	—	—	—
110A	**100 SUCRES** 27.4.1966-7.7.1970. Black on m/c unpt. Like #111. Back purple. Printer: ABNC.	1.00	4.00	25.00

		VG	VF	UNC
111	**100 SUCRES** 1971-80. Black on m/c unpt. Like #108 but finer portr. w/dk. clouds behind. Back purple. Printer: TDLR.			
	a. 20.5.1971; 17.7.1974.	2.00	5.00	22.50
	b. 10.8.1976; 10.8.1977.	.25	1.00	15.00
	s. Specimen. 20.5.1971.	—	—	35.00
112	**500 SUCRES** ND (ca.1971). Mercury seated at ctr. w/guilloches and other changes. Back brown. (Not issued). Printer: ABNC. Archive example.	—	—	—

		VG	VF	UNC
113	**1000 SUCRES** 17.11.1966-20.9.1973. Black on m/c unpt. Banco Central bldg. at ctr. Back olive-gray. Printer: ABNC.			
	a. Issued note.	20.00	60.00	200.00
	s. Specimen. ND.	—	—	75.00

1975-80 ISSUE

#114-118 arms on back 29mm wide, new rendition w/flagpole stems below. Printer: ABNC.

		VG	VF	UNC
114	**5 SUCRES** 1975-83. Black on m/c unpt. Portr. A. J. de Sucre at ctr. Back red-violet.			
	a. 14.3.1975; 29.4.1977.	.25	1.00	2.50
	b. 20.8.1982; 20.4.1983.	FV	FV	5.00

		VG	VF	UNC
115	**10 SUCRES** 14.3.1975; 10.8.1976; 29.4.1977; 24.5.1978. Black on m/c unpt. Portr. S. de Benalcazar at ctr. Back blue.	FV	.25	7.50

		VG	VF	UNC
116	**20 SUCRES** 10.8.1976. Black on m/c unpt. Church facade at ctr. Back brown.	FV	.50	7.50

		VG	VF	UNC
117	**50 SUCRES** 10.8.1976. Black on m/c unpt. National monument at ctr. Back green.	FV	2.00	12.50

		VF	VF	UNC
118	**100 SUCRES** 24.5.1980. Black on m/c unpt. Portr. S. Bolívar at ctr. Back purple.	FV	1.00	10.00

1976 ISSUE

#119 and 120 printer: TDLR.

		VG	VF	UNC
119	**500 SUCRES** 1976-82. Black, violet and dk. olive-brown on m/c unpt. Dr. E. de Santa Cruz y Espejo at l. Back blue on m/c unpt.; arms at ctr. and as wmk.			
	a. 24.5.1976; 10.8.1977; 9.10.1978; 25.7.1979.	2.50	10.00	35.00
	b. 20.7.1982.	2.00	7.50	25.00
	s1. Specimen. ND.	—	—	35.00
	s2. As b. Specimen.	—	—	35.00

		VG	VF	UNC
120	**1000 SUCRES** 1976-82. Dk. green and red-brown on m/c unpt. Ruminahui at r. Back dk. green on m/c unpt.; arms at ctr. and as wmk.			
	a. 24.5.1976-25.7.1979.	1.50	5.00	17.50
	b. 24.5.1980; 20.7.1982.	1.00	4.00	15.00
	s1. Specimen. ND.	—	—	35.00
	s2. Specimen. Series HP. 24.5.1980.	—	—	35.00

1984-88 ISSUES

#120A-125 w/o text: *SOCIEDAD ANONIMA* below bank title. W/o imprint.

		VG	VF	UNC
120A	**5 SUCRES** 22.11.1988. Black on m/c unpt. Portr. A. J. de Sucré at ctr. Arms on back 26mm wide. Back red-violet. Printer: TDLR.	FV	.50	4.00

		VG	VF	UNC
121	**10 SUCRES** 29.4.1986; 22.11.1988. Black on m/c unpt. Like #109. Back blue.	FV	.50	4.00

		VG	VF	UNC
121A	**20 SUCRES** 1986-88. Black on m/c unpt. Like #106. Back brown.			
	a. 29.4.1986; 22.11.1988.	FV	.75	4.00
	s. Specimen. 29.4.1986. Series LM.	—	—	50.00

		VG	VF	UNC
122	**50 SUCRES** 5.9.1984; 22.11.1988. Black on m/c unpt. Similar to #117. Back green.			
	a. Issued note.	FV	FV	7.50
	s. Specimen. 5.9.1984.	—	—	35.00

		VG	VF	UNC
123	**100 SUCRES** 29.4.1986; 20.4.1990. Black on m/c unpt. Like #111. Back purple.	FV	1.25	7.50

		VG	VF	UNC
123A	**100 SUCRES** 1988-97. Black on m/c unpt. Like #118. Serial # style varieties. Back purple.			
	a. Blue serial #. 8.6.1988; 21.6.1991; 11.10.1991.	FV	1.25	7.50
	b. 9.3.1992; 4.12.1992; 20.8.1993.	FV	.50	5.00
	c. Black serial #. 21.2.1994.	FV	.50	5.00
	d. As c. 3.4.1997.	FV	.50	5.00
	s1. As a. Specimen. 8.6.1988. Punched hole cancelled.	—	—	30.00
	s2. As b. Specimen. Series WF. 20.8.1993.	—	—	35.00

#124 and 125 wmk: Arms. W/o imprint. Sign. varieties.

		VG	VF	UNC
124	**500 SUCRES** 5.9.1984. Black, violet and dk. olive-brown on m/c unpt. Like #119.			
	a. Issued note.	FV	1.50	15.00
	s. Specimen.	—	—	35.00

		VG	VF	UNC
124A	**500 SUCRES** 8.6.1988. Black, violet and dk. olive brown on m/c unpt. Similar to #124 but many minor plate differences.	FV	1.50	15.00

		VG	VF	UNC
125	**1000 SUCRES** 1984-88. Dk. green and red-brown on m/c unpt. Like #120 but w/o EL in bank title. Serial # style varieties.			
	a. 5.9.1984; 29.9.1986.	FV	1.00	15.00
	b. 8.6.1988.	FV	1.00	12.50

NOTE: Later dates of #123A-#125 Sucres were made by different printers (w/o imprint) and vary slightly.

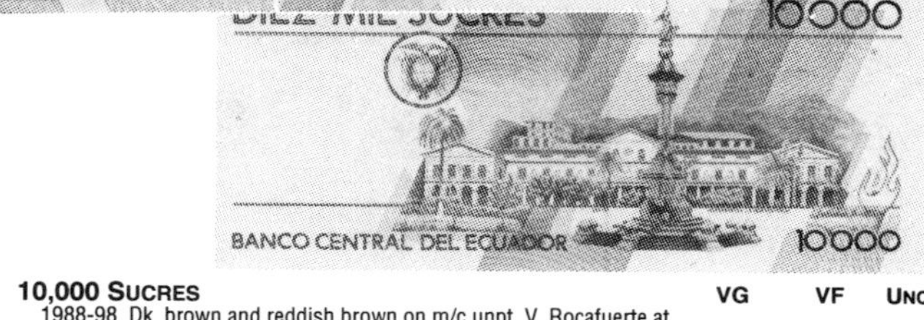

		VG	VF	UNC
126	**5000 SUCRES** 1.12.1987. Purple and brown on m/c unpt. J. Montalvo at l. and as wmk., arms at ctr. r. 2 birds and Galapagos tortoise on back. Printer: BCdE.			
	a. Issued note.	FV	5.00	20.00
	s. Specimen.	—	—	35.00

NOTE: #126 designed in Mexico.

		VG	VF	UNC
127	**10,000 SUCRES** 1988-98. Dk. brown and reddish brown on m/c unpt. V. Rocafuerte at l. and as wmk. Arms upper l. ctr., Independence monument in Quito at ctr. r. on back. Printer: BCdE. Serial # varieties exist.			
	a. 30.7.1988.	FV	5.00	15.00
	b. 21.2.1994.	FV	5.00	15.00
	c. Sign. title ovpt: *PRESIDENTE JUNTA MONETARIA*. 13.10.1994.	FV	5.00	12.50
	d. 6.2.1995.	FV	5.00	12.50
	e. Sign. titles as a. 6.3.1995; 8.8.1995; 4.1.1996.	FV	5.00	10.00
	f. Sign. title: *PRESIDENTE DEL DIRECTORIO*. 14.12.1998.	FV	FV	10.00
	s1. As a. Specimen. Series AB.	—	—	40.00
	s2. As c. Specimen. 13.10.1994 Series AH.	—	—	40.00
	s3. As e. Specimen. 6.3.1995. Series AL.	—	—	35.00

1991-99 ISSUE

		VG	VF	UNC
128	**5000 SUCRES** 1991-99. Purple and brown on m/c unpt. Like #126 but w/repositioned sign. and both serial # horizontal. Printer: BCdE.			
	a. 21.6.1991; 22.6.1992; 17.3.1992; 20.8.1993.	FV	1.50	10.00
	b. Sign. title ovpt.: *PRESIDENTE JUNTA MONETARIA*. 31.1.1995.	FV	1.50	10.00
	c. Sign. titles as a. 8.8.1995; 13.1.1996; 31.10.1996.	FV	1.50	10.00
	d. Sign. title: *PRESIDENTE DEL DIRECTORIO*. 6.3.1999.	FV	FV	7.50
	s1. Specimen. Series AG. 21.6.1991.	—	—	35.00
	s2. As a. Specimen. 17.3.1992. Series AJ.	—	—	35.00
	s3. As b. Specimen. 31.1.1995.	—	—	40.00

		VG	VF	UNC
129	**20,000 SUCRES** 31.1.1995; 20.11.1995; 2.6.1997; 8.1.1998; 26.3.1999. Brown, black and deep blue on m/c unpt. Dr. G. Garcia Moreno at r. and as wmk. Arms at ctr. on back.			
	a. Issued note.	FV	5.00	20.00
	s1. Specimen, punched hole cancelled. 31.1.1995.	—	—	35.00
	s2. Specimen. 2.6.1997. Series AD.	—	—	35.00

		VG	VF	UNC
130	**50,000 SUCRES** 31.1.1995; 2.6.1997; 20.4.1998. Gray and red-brown on m/c unpt. E. Alfaro at r. and as wmk. Arms on back. Segmented foil over security thread.			
	a. Issued note.	FV	FV	30.00
	s. Specimen. 31.1.1995. Series AB.	—	—	40.00

1999 ISSUE

Decreased security features.

		VG	VF	UNC
131	**20,000 SUCRES** 10.3.1999. As #129 w/o wide security thread.	FV	5.00	15.00

		VG	VF	UNC
132	**50,000 SUCRES** 10.3.1999. As #130 w/o security thread.	FV	5.00	15.00

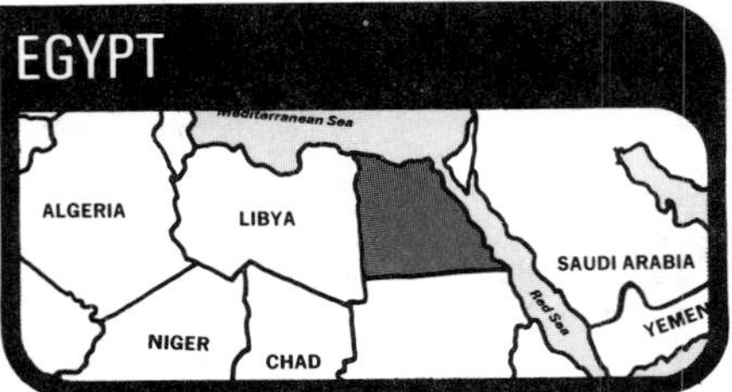

The Arab Republic of Egypt, located on the northeastern corner of Africa, has an area of 386,650 sq. mi. (1,000,000 sq. km.) and a population of 56 million. Capital: Cairo. Although Egypt is an almost rainless expanse of desert, its economy is predominantly agricultural. Cotton, rice and petroleum are exported.

Egyptian history dates back to about 4000 B.C. when the empire was established by uniting the upper and lower kingdoms. Following its "Golden Age" (16th to 13th centuries B.C.), Egypt was conquered by Persia (525 B.C.) and Alexander the Great (332 B.C.). The Ptolemies ruled until the suicide of Cleopatra (30 B.C.) when Egypt became a Roman colony. Arab caliphs ruled Egypt from 641 to 1517, when the Turks took it for their Ottoman Empire. Turkish rule, interrupted by the occupation of Napoleon (1798-1801), became increasingly casual, permitting Great Britain to inject its influence by purchasing shares in the Suez Canal. British troops occupied Egypt in 1882, becoming the de facto rulers. On Dec. 14, 1914, Egypt was made a protectorate of Britain. British occupation ended on Feb. 28, 1922, when Egypt became a sovereign, independent kingdom. The monarchy was abolished and a republic proclaimed on June 18, 1952.

On Feb. 1, 1958, Egypt and Syria formed the United Arab Republic. Yemen joined on March 8 in an association known as the United Arab States. Syria withdrew from the United Arab Republic on Sept. 29, 1961, and on Dec. 26 Egypt dissolved its ties with Yemen in the United Arab States. On Sept. 2, 1971, Egypt shed the name United Arab Republic in favor of the Arab Republic of Egypt.

MONETARY SYSTEM:

1 Pound = 100 Piastres

REPLACEMENT NOTES:

Starting in 1969, 2 types exist. Earlier system uses a single Arabic letter as series prefix instead of normal number/letter prefix. Known notes: #42. Later system has the equivalent of English "200", "300" or "400" in front of a single Arabic series letter.

SIGNATURE VARIETIES			
11	A. Elrefay, 1961-63	12	A. Zendo, 1962-66
13	A. Abdel Hamid, 1967-70	14	A. Zendo, 1972-75
15	M. Ibrahim, 1976-81	16	A. Shalabi, 1981-84
17	A. Negm, 1985	18	S. Hamed, 1986
19	I. N. Mohamad		

REPUBLIC

CENTRAL BANK OF EGYPT

1961-64 ISSUES

#35-41 sign. and date varieties.

		VG	VF	UNC
35	**25 PIASTRES** 1.11.1961-18.8.1966. Blue on m/c unpt. U. A. R. arms at r. Sign. 11; 12.	.75	2.00	6.00

		VG	VF	UNC
36	**50 PIASTRES** 1.11.1961-14.8.1966. Black on m/c unpt. U. A. R. arms at r., also in wmk. Sign. 11; 12.	.75	2.00	12.00

		VG	VF	UNC
37	**1 POUND** 1.11.1961-23.2.1967. Blue-green on lilac and m/c unpt. Tutankhamen's mask at r. Back green. Wmk: Arms. Sign. 11; 12; 13.	1.00	1.50	6.00

		VG	VF	UNC
38	**5 POUNDS** 1.11.1961-12.11.1961. Green and brown on m/c unpt. Circular guilloche at l., Tutankhamen's mask at r. Wmk: Flower. Sign. 11.	7.50	25.00	95.00

		VG	VF	UNC
39	**5 POUNDS** 13.11.1961-16.6.1964. Green and brown on m/c unpt. Similar to #38, but circular area at l. is blank. Guilloche at bottom ctr. on face and back. Wmk: Arms. Sign. 11; 12.	3.00	7.50	22.50
40	**5 POUNDS** 17.6.1964-13.2.1965. Lilac and brown on m/c unpt. Like #39. Sign. 12.	2.00	5.00	20.00

		VG	VF	UNC
41	**10 POUNDS** 1.11.1961-13.2.1965. Dk. green and dk. brown on m/c unpt. Tutankhamen's mask at r. Wmk: Arms. Sign. 11; 12.	3.50	7.50	27.50

1967-69 ISSUE

#42-46 wmk: Archaic Egyptian scribe. Replacement notes: Serial # prefix single Arabic letter.

		VG	VF	UNC
42	**25 PIASTRES** 6.2.1967-4.1.1975. Blue, green and brown on m/c unpt. Sphinx w/statue at l. ctr. U.A.R. arms at ctr. on back. Sign. 13; 14.	.15	.50	3.00

		VG	VF	UNC
43	**50 PIASTRES** 2.12.1967-28.1.1978. Red-brown and brown. Al Azhar mosque at r., University of Cairo at l. ctr. Ramses II at ctr. r. on back. Sign. 13; 14; 15.	.35	1.00	3.50

		VG	VF	UNC
44	**1 POUND** 12.5.1967-19.4.1978. Brown on m/c unpt. Sultan Quayet Bey mosque at l. ctr. Archaic statues on back. Sign. 13; 14; 15.	.50	1.00	4.00

		VG	VF	UNC
45	**5 POUNDS** 1.1.1969-78. Black on blue and m/c unpt. Ahmad ibn Tulun mosque at Cairo at ctr. r. Ruins at l., frieze at ctr. r. on back. Sign. 13; 14; 15.	2.00	3.50	18.50

		VG	VF	UNC
46	**10 POUNDS** 1.9.1969-78. Red-brown and brown on m/c unpt. Sultan Hassan Mosque at Cairo at l. ctr. Pharaoh and pyramids on back. Sign. 13; 14; 15.	3.00	5.50	22.50

1976 ISSUE

#47 and 48 replacement notes: Serial # prefix single Arabic letter.

		VG	VF	UNC
47	**25 PIASTRES** 12.4.1976-28.8.1978. Blue, green and grayish brown on blue and orange unpt. Face and wmk. like #42. A. R. E. arms on back. Sign. 15.	.30	.75	3.50
48	**20 POUNDS** 5.7.1976; 1978. Green. Mohammed Ali mosque at l., Arabic legends at r. Archaic war chariot at l. ctr., frieze at ctr. r. on back. Wmk: Egyptian scribe. Sign. 15.	6.00	9.50	35.00

1978-79 ISSUE

#49-62 no longer have conventional reading dates with Arabic day, month and year. In place of this are six Arabic numerals, the first and last making up the year of issue; next 2 digits represent the day and following 2 digits represent the month; i.e. 822119 = 22.11.(19)89. Another example including raised diamonds (= zeroes) 804107 = 4.10.(19)87. Wmk: Tutankhamen's mask.

Replacement notes: Serial # prefix. Arabic *200* or *300* before single Arabic letter.

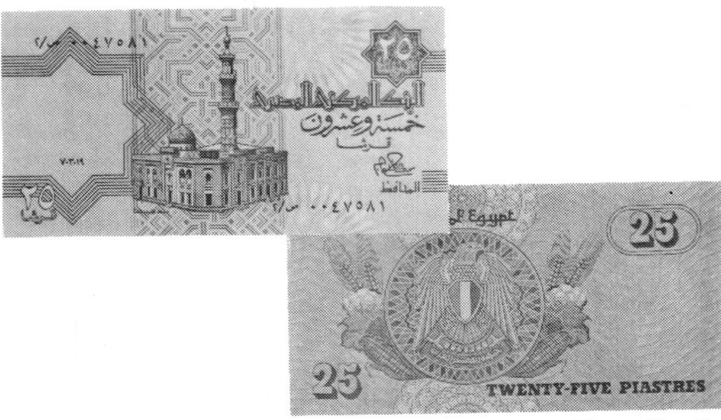

		VG	VF	UNC
49	**25 PIASTRES** 2.1.-11.5.(19)79. Black and brown on gray, pale blue and orange unpt. Al-Sayida Aisha mosque at ctr. Stylized A. R. E. arms, cotton, wheat and corn plants at ctr. on back. Sign. 15.	FV	.50	2.00

		VG	VF	UNC
50	**1 POUND** 29.5.(19)78-. Brown, purple and deep olive-green on m/c unpt. Sultan Quayet Bey mosque at l. ctr. Archaic statues on back.			
	a. Back deep brown. Solid security thread. 29.5.(19)78-10.4.(19)87. Sign. 15; 16; 17; 18.	FV	FV	1.50
	b. Back pale brown. Solid security thread. 19.11.(19)86-9.8.(19)89. Sign. 18; 19.	FV	FV	1.50
	c. Back pale brown. Segmented security thread with bank name repeated. 10.5.(19)89-28.2.(19)98. Sign. 19.	FV	FV	1.50

		VG	VF	UNC
51	**10 POUNDS** 24.6.(19)78-. Brown and brown-violet on m/c unpt. Al-Rifai mosque at ctr. Pharaoh on back. Sign. 15; 16; 17; 18; 19.	FV	FV	10.00

52 **20 POUNDS**

6.9.(19)78-. Black, gray-violet and deep green on m/c unpt. Mohammed Ali mosque at ctr. Archaic sculptures from Chapel of Sesostris I and archaic war chariot on back.

	VG	VF	UNC
a. Date below wmk. Solid security thread. 6.9.(19)78-22.4.(19)82. Sign. 15; 16.	FV	FV	30.00
b. Date at lower r. of wmk. Solid security thread. 9.12.(19)86; 4.10.(19)87. Sign. 18.	FV	FV	18.50
c. Segmented security thread w/bank name repeated. (19)88-(19)92. Sign. 19.	FV	FV	17.50

53 **100 POUNDS**

(19)78; (19)92. Blue on m/c unpt. Al-Sayida Zainab mosque at ctr. Pharaoh's mask above frieze at ctr. of vertical format on back.

	VG	VF	UNC
a. Series 1-6.(19)78. Sign. 15.	FV	40.00	120.00
b. (19)92.	FV	FV	90.00

1980-81 ISSUE

Replacement notes: Serial # prefix Arabic *200* or *300* before single Arabic series letter.

54 **25 PIASTRES**

	VG	VF	UNC
17.1.(19)80-10.1(19)84. Dk. green on lt. green, orange and blue unpt. Like #49. Sign. 15; 16.	FV	.30	1.50

55 **50 PIASTRES**

	VG	VF	UNC
1.1.(19)81-10.6.(19)83. Green and brown on m/c unpt. Al Ahzar mosque at ctr. Sculptured wall design at l., Ramses II at ctr., archaic seal at r. on back. Sign. 15; 16.	FV	.50	2.00

56 **5 POUNDS**

(19)81; (19)87. Black and blue-black on m/c unpt. Ibn Toulon mosque at ctr. Design symbolizing bounty of the Nile River at l. ctr. on back.

	VG	VF	UNC
a. 1.2.(19)81. Sign. 15.	FV	3.00	15.00
b. 6.1.(19)87. Sign. 16; 17; 18.	FV	2.50	10.00

1985 ISSUE

Replacement notes: Serial # prefix Arabic *200* or *300* before single Arabic series letter.

57 **25 PIASTRES**

(19)85-93. Purple and pale blue on pale lilac and m/c unpt. Face and wmk. like #49 and #54. Standard A.R.E. arms at l. ctr. on back.

	VG	VF	UNC
a. Solid security thread. 12.1.(19)85-30.1.(19)89. Sign. 17; 18.	FV	FV	.90
b. Segmented security thread w/bank name repeated. 5.12.(19)90-(19)98. Sign. 19.	FV	FV	.75

58 **50 PIASTRES**

(19)85-94. Black on pale orange, pink and m/c unpt. Al Azhar mosque at ctr. r. Back like #55.

	VG	VF	UNC
a. No text line at lower l. on face. Solid security thead. 2.7.(19)85- . Sign. 17; 18.	FV	.35	2.00
b. Text line added at lower l. on face. 1.2.(19)87-17.8.(19)89. Sign. 19.	FV	FV	1.25
c. Segmented security thread w/bank name repeated. 5.1.(19)90-11.8.(19)94.	FV	FV	1.00

NOTICE

Readers with unlisted dates, signature varieties, etc. are invited to submit photocopies of their notes to: Standard Catalog of World Paper Money, 700 East State St. Iola, WI 54990-0001, fax: 1-715-445-4087, or E-Mail: thernr@krause.com.

1989-94 Issue

Replacement notes: Serial # prefix Arabic *200* or *300* before single Arabic series letter.

		VG	VF	UNC
59	**5 Pounds** 2.4.(19)89-. Black and blue-black on m/c unpt. Like #56 but m/c scrollwork added in unpt. and into wmk. area. Archaic design over wmk. area at r. on back. Sign. 18.	FV	FV	5.50

		VG	VF	UNC
60	**50 Pounds** 9.2.(19)93- . Brown, violet and m/c. Mosque at r. Isis above archaic boat, ruins at l. ctr. on back. Sign. 18.	FV	FV	30.00

		VG	VF	UNC
61	**100 Pounds** 14.9.(19)94; (19)97. Dk. brown and brown-violet on m/c unpt. Sultan Hassan Mosque at lower l. ctr. Sphinx at ctr. on back. Sign. 19.	FV	FV	60.00

1995 Issue

		VG	VF	UNC
62	**50 Piastres** 6.7.(19)95-. Dull olive-gray on m/c unpt. Like #58. Sign. 19.	FV	FV	.75

Currency Notes

United Arab Republic

Law 50 of 1940

Face 4: Main heading unchanged from Face 3 but *EGYPTIAN REGION* (small line of Arabic text) is deleted.

Back 2: *UNITED ARAB REPUBLIC* in English. Various sign. Imprint: Survey Dept.

1961 ND Issue

		VG	VF	UNC
180	**5 Piastres** *L.1940.* Lilac. Qn. Nefertiti at r. Wmk: *U A R.*			
	a. Sign. Baghdady w/titles: *VICE-PRESIDENT AND MINISTER OF TREASURY.* Series 15; 16.	1.25	5.00	25.00
	b. Sign. Kaissouni w/titles: *MINISTER OF TREASURY AND PLANNING.* Series 16-18.	.25	1.00	6.00
	c. Sign. Daif w/titles: *MINISTER OF TREASURY.* Color lilac to blue. Wmk. 3mm tall. Series 18-22.	.20	.75	5.00
	d. Sign. and titles as c. Wmk. 5mm tall. Series 22-26.	.20	.75	4.00
	e. Sign. Hegazy w/titles as d. Series 26-33.	.20	.75	4.00

		VG	VF	UNC
180A	**5 Piastres** *L.1940.* Face like #180. Back w/sign. Kaissouni w/title: *MINISTER OF TREASURY* (error). Series 16.	15.00	50.00	150.00

		VG	VF	UNC
181	**10 Piastres** *L.1940.* Black. Group of militants w/flag having only 2 stars.			
	a. Sign. Baghdady w/titles: *VICE-PRESIDENT AND MINISTER OF TREASURY.* Series 16.	1.50	6.00	27.50
	b. Sign. Kaissouni w/titles: *MINISTER OF TREASURY AND PLANNING.* Series 16-18.	.40	1.50	7.50
	c. Sign. Kaissouni w/titles: *MINISTER OF TREASURY.* Series 16.	8.00	40.00	150.00
	d. Sign. Daif w/title as c. Series 18-24.	.25	1.00	6.00
	e. Sign. Hegazy w/title as c. Series 24-29.	.25	1.00	6.00

Arab Republic of Egypt

Law 50 of 1940

Face 5: *ARAB REPUBLIC OF EGYPT* in Arabic.

Back 3: *THE ARAB REPUBLIC OF EGYPT* in English. Various sign. Printer: Survey Authority or Postal Printing House.

1971 ND Issue

		VG	VF	UNC
182	**5 Piastres** *L.1940.* Lilac. Similar to #180. Imprint: Survey of Egypt.			
	a. Sign. Hegazy w/title: *MINISTER OF TREASURY.* Wmk: *U A R.* Series 33; 34.	1.00	3.50	15.00
	b. Sign. Hegazy w/title: *MINISTER OF TREASURY.* Wmk: *A R E.* Series 34-36.	.75	3.00	12.00
	c. Sign. Ibrahim w/title: *MINISTER OF FINANCE.* Wmk: *A R E.* Series 36; 37.	.35	1.50	6.00
	d. Sign. El Nashar w/title as c. Series 37.	.60	2.50	10.00
	e. Sign. Ismail. w/title as c. Series 37-40.	.20	.75	3.00
	f. Sign. M. S. Hamed. Series 40-42.	.25	1.00	4.00
	g. Sign. Loutfy. Series 42-47.	.20	.75	3.00
	h. Sign. Meguid. Series 47-50.	.15	.60	2.50
	i. Sign. Hamed. Series. 50.	2.00	6.00	25.00
	j. Like c. Printer: Postal Printing House. Sign. Hamed. Series 50-72.	.10	.35	1.50
	k. Sign. El Razaz. Series 72.	.25	1.00	5.00
183	**10 Piastres** *L.1940.* Black. Simlar to #181. Printer: Survey Authority.			
	a. Sign. Hegazy w/title: *MINISTER OF TREASURY.* Wmk: *U A R.* Series 29; 30.	2.00	8.00	35.00
	b. Sign. Hegazy w/title: *MINISTER OF TREASURY.* Wmk: *A R E.* Series 30; 31.	1.00	4.00	15.00
	c. Sign. Ibrahim w/title: *MINISTER OF FINANCE.* Wmk: *A R E.* Series 31; 32.	.45	1.75	7.00
	d. Sign. El Nashar w/titles as c. Series 32-33.	1.00	4.00	15.00
	e. Sign. Ismail w/titles as c. Series 33-35.	.25	1.00	4.00
	f. Sign. M. S. Hamed w/titles as c. Series 35-38.	.45	1.75	7.00
	g. Sign. Loutfy w/titles as c. Series 38-43.	.25	1.00	4.00
	h. Sign. Meguid w/titles as c. Series 43-46.	.20	.75	3.00
	i. Sign. Hamed w/titles as c. Series 46.	3.00	10.00	30.00

		VG	VF	UNC
184	**10 PIASTRES** *L.1940.* Black. Similar to #183 but new flag w/eagle instead of 2 stars. Sign. title: *MINISTER OF FINANCE.*			
	a. Sign. Hamed. Series 46-69.	.15	.50	2.00
	b. Sign. El Razaz. Series 69-75.	.20	.75	3.00

NOTE: Transitional series numbers from one signature to the next are generally much scarcer and command a premium. As of July, 1991 all Egyptian currency notes had been demonetized and withdrawn from circulation. In 1997 a new series was released recently due to a coinage shortage.

1997; 1998 ND ISSUE

Law 50 of 1940.

		VG	VF	UNC
185	**5 PIASTRES** *L.1940.* Green and orange. Similar to #150. El-Ghareeb w/title: *MINISTER OF FINANCE.* Arabic Series 1-2. Printer: Postal Printing House. Wmk: Kg. Tut's mask.	.10	.30	1.25
186	**5 PIASTRES** *L.1940.* Like #185 but mule issue w/sign. Salah Hamad w/title: *MINISTER OF FINANCE.*	1.00	3.00	12.50

		VG	VF	UNC
187	**10 PIASTRES** *L.1940.* Black and orange. Sphinx, pyramids at r. Mosque of Mohamed Ali at Citadel at l. on back. Sign. El Ghareeb w/title: *MINISTER OF FINANCE.* Arabic Series 1-2. Wmk: Kg. Tut's mask.	.10	.35	1.50

1998; 1999 ND ISSUE

Law 50 of 1940

#188 and 189 sign. M. Elghareeb w/title: MINISTER OF FINANCE.

		VG	VF	UNC
188	**5 PIASTRES** *L.1940.*	.10	.30	1.25

		VG	VF	UNC
189	**10 PIASTRES** *L.1940.* Dull purple on m/c unpt. Similar to #187.	.10	.30	1.00

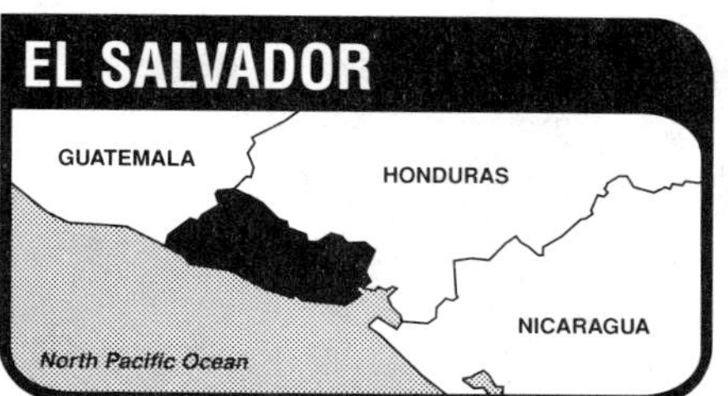

The Republic of El Salvador, a Central American country bordered by Guatemala, Honduras and the Pacific Ocean, has an area of 8,260 sq. mi. (21,041 sq. km.) and a population of 5.79 million. Capital: San Salvador. This most intensely cultivated country of Latin America produces coffee (the major crop), sugar and balsam for export. Gold, silver and other metals are largely unexploited.

The first Spanish attempt to subjugate the area was undertaken in 1523 by Pedro de Alvarado, Cortes' lieutenant. He was forced to retreat by superior Indian forces, but returned in 1525 and succeeded in bringing the region under control of the captaincy general of Guatemala, where it remained until 1821. In 1821, El Salvador and the other Central American provinces declared their independence from Spain. In 1823, the Federal Republic of Central America was formed by the five Central American States. When this federation was dissolved in 1829, El Salvador became an independent republic.

A twelve-year civil war was ended in 1992 with the signing of a UN sponsored Peace Accord. Free elections, with full participation of all political parties, were held in 1994 and 1997. Armando Calderón-Sol was elected as president in 1994 for a 5-year term.

MONETARY SYSTEM:

1 Colón = 100 Centavos

SUPERINTENDENCIA DE BANCOS Y OTRAS INSTITUCIONES FINANCIERAS:

Juan S. Quinteros	1962-1975	Marco T. Guandique	1977-Feb. 1981
Jose A. Mendoza	1968-1975	Rafael T. Carbonell	1981
Jorge A. Dowson	1975-1977	Raul Nolasco	1981-

DATING SYSTEM:

Dates listed for notes are those found on the face, regardless of the ovpt. issue dates on back which were applied practically on a daily basis as notes were needed for circulation.

REPUBLIC

BANCO CENTRAL DE RESERVA DE EL SALVADOR

1962; 1963 ISSUE

#100-146 w/various date and sign. ovpts. on back w/different shields and seals.

#100-130, 132-142, 144 and 145 portr. C. Columbus at ctr. l. on back, and later as wmk.

#100-104 printer: TDLR.

		VG	VF	UNC
100	**1 COLÓN** 12.3.1963; 25.1.1966; 23.8.1966. Black on m/c unpt. Central Bank at ctr. Back orange.	1.00	5.00	20.00

		VG	VF	UNC
101	**2 COLONES** 15.2.1962; 9.6.1964. Black on m/c unpt. Coffee bush at l., workers at l. ctr. Back red-brown.	3.00	8.00	40.00

		VG	VF	UNC
102	**5 Colones** 15.2.1962; 12.3.1963. Black on m/c unpt. Woman w/basket of fruit on her head at l. Back green.	3.00	8.00	40.00

		VG	VF	UNC
103	**10 Colones** 15.2.1962; 9.6.1964; 27.12.1966. Black on m/c unpt. Portr. M. J. Arce at ctr., serial # at lower l. and upper r. Back brown.	3.50	10.00	50.00

		VG	VF	UNC
104	**25 Colones** 1963; 1966. Black on m/c unpt. Reservoir at ctr. Back dk. blue.			
	a. 12.3.1963.	7.50	20.00	85.00
	b. 27.12.1966.	6.50	17.50	75.00
	s1. As a. Specimen.	—	—	70.00
	s2. As b. Specimen.	—	—	65.00

1964; 1965 Issue

#105-107 printer: ABNC.

		VG	VF	UNC
105	**1 Colón** 8.9.1964. Black on pink and green unpt. Farmer plowing at ctr., *SAN SALVADOR* at upper l. Black serial # and series letters. Back orange.	2.00	6.00	22.50
106	**5 Colones** 8.9.1964. Black on green and m/c unpt. Delgado addressing crowd at ctr., *SAN SALVADOR* at upper l. Black serial # at lower l. and upper r. Back deep olive-green.	2.50	7.50	32.50

		VG	VF	UNC
107	**100 Colones** 12.1.1965. Brown and green unpt. Independence monument at ctr. but *SAN SALVADOR* at upper l. Serial # at lower l. and upper r. Back olive-green.			
	a. Issued note.	20.00	65.00	200.00
	s. Specimen. Punched hole cancelled.	—	—	150.00

1967 Commemorative Issue

#108-109 printer: TDLR.

NOTE: #108 and 109 are reportedly commemoratives for the Bicentennial of the Birth of José Cañas

		VG	VF	UNC
108	**1 Colón** 20.6.1967. Black on m/c unpt. J. Cañas at r., *UN COLON* at ctr. *SAN SALVADOR* and date at r. Back orange.			
	a. Issued note.	1.00	3.00	17.50
	s. Specimen. Punched hole cancelled.	—	—	35.00

		VG	VF	UNC
109	**5 Colones** 20.6.1967. Black on pink and green unpt. Scene of J. Cañas freeing the slaves, *31.12.1823* at ctr. Back green.			
	a. Issued note.	5.00	25.00	125.00
	s. Specimen.	—	—	75.00

1968-70 Issue

#110-114 printer: USBNC.

		VG	VF	UNC
110	**1 Colón** 1968; 1970. Black on lt. orange and pale blue unpt. J. Cañas at r., *1 COLON* at ctr. Back orange.			
	a. Sign. title: *CAJERO* at r. 13.8.1968.	.75	1.50	6.00
	b. Sign. title: *GERENTE* at r. 12.5.1970.	.75	1.50	6.00
	s1. As a. Specimen.	—	—	32.50
	s2. As b. Specimen.	—	—	32.50

111 5 COLONES

1968-70. Black on green and ochre unpt. Delgado addressing crowd at ctr., *5 COLONES* at r. Back dk. green.

		VG	VF	UNC
a.	Sign. title: *CAJERO* at r. 13.8.1968; 4.2.1969.	1.25	3.50	12.50
b.	Sign. title: *GERENTE* at r. 12.5.1970.	1.25	3.50	12.50
s1.	As a. Specimen. 13.8.1968; 4.2.1969.	—	—	32.50
s2.	As b. Specimen.	—	—	32.50

112 10 COLONES

13.8.1968. Black on tan and pale blue unpt. M. J. Arce at r., *10 COLONES* at ctr. Back black.

		VG	VF	UNC
a.	Issued note.	3.00	8.00	30.00
s.	Specimen.	—	—	35.00

113 25 COLONES

12.5.1970. Black on lt. orange and pale blue unpt. Reservoir at r. Back dk. blue.

		VG	VF	UNC
a.	Issued note.	7.00	17.50	50.00
s.	Specimen.	—	—	40.00

114 100 COLONES

12.5.1970. Black on pink and pale olive-green unpt. Independence monument at ctr. Back olive-green.

		VG	VF	UNC
a.	Issued note.	17.50	45.00	145.00
s.	Specimen.	—	—	125.00

1971; 1972 ISSUE

#115-119 Printer: TDLR.

115 1 COLÓN

	VG	VF	UNC
31.8.1971; 24.10.1972. *SAN SALVADOR* and date at l., *UN COLON* at ctr., José Cañas at r. Back red.	.35	1.25	4.00

116 2 COLONES

1972-74. Black on m/c unpt. Colonial church of Panchimalco at ctr., *DOS COLONES* at r. Back red-brown.

		VG	VF	UNC
a.	24.10.1972. W/o wmk.	.35	1.50	5.00
b.	15.10.1974. W/Columbus wmk.	.35	1.50	5.00
s.	As a. Specimen.	—	—	30.00

117 5 COLONES

	VG	VF	UNC
31.8.1971-24.6.1976. Black on pale blue and m/c unpt. Face like #111 but w/o *5 COLONES* at l., Delgado addressing crowd at ctr. Back green.	FV	1.50	7.00

118 10 COLONES

31.8.1971-23.12.1976. Black on m/c unpt. *DIEZ COLONES* at ctr., M. J. Arce at r. Back dull black.

		VG	VF	UNC
a.	Issued note.	2.50	4.50	15.00
s.	Specimen. 31.8.1971; 24.10.1972.	—	—	30.00

		VG	VF	UNC
119	**25 COLONES** 31.8.1971. Black on m/c unpt. Reservoir at ctr. Similar to #106 but different design on face and back.			
	a. Issued note.	5.50	12.50	35.00
	s. Specimen.	—	—	32.50

1974 ISSUE

#120-122 black on m/c unpt. Printer: TDLR.

		VG	VF	UNC
120	**1 COLÓN** 15.10.1974. Hydroelectric dam at ctr., w/o *UN COLON* = at l. Back red; like #115.	.25	.75	4.00

		VG	VF	UNC
121	**25 COLONES** 15.10.1974; 24.6.1976; 23.12.1976. Aerial view of Acajutla port. Back blue.	5.00	8.00	25.00

		VG	VF	UNC
122	**100 COLONES** 1974-79. Indian pyramid at Tazumal at ctr., arms at lower r. Back olive-green on m/c unpt.			
	a. Regular serial #. 15.10.1974-11.5.1978.	15.00	20.00	80.00
	b. Electronic sorting serial #. 3.5.1979.	14.00	17.50	65.00
	s. As b. Specimen.	—	—	55.00

1976 ISSUE

#123 and 124 black on m/c unpt. Printer: TDLR.

		VG	VF	UNC
123	**1 COLÓN** 28.10.1976. Similar to #120 but *UN COLON* at l. Back like #125. W/o wmk.			
	a. Issued note.	.25	1.00	4.00
	s. Specimen.	—	—	30.00

		VG	VF	UNC
124	**2 COLONES** 24.6.1976. Black on m/c unpt. Like #116 but w/*DOS COLONES* at l. and r. Denomination added to face at l. Back brown-violet; w/o wmk.			
	a. Issued note.	.35	1.25	5.00
	s. Specimen.	—	—	30.00

1977-79 ISSUES

#125-130 black on m/c unpt. w/unpt. in margins.

		VG	VF	UNC
125	**1 COLÓN** 1977-80. Like #123. Printer: TDLR.			
	a. Regular style serial #. 7.7.1977; 11.5.1978.	FV	.65	4.00
	b. Electronic sorting serial #. 3.5.1979; 19.6.1980.	FV	.50	3.50

		VG	VF	UNC
126	**5 COLONES** 6.10.1977. Like #117, but *5 COLONES* at l. and r. W/o wmk. Printer: TDLR.			
	a. Issued note.	FV	1.00	5.00
	s. Specimen.	—	—	27.50

NOTE: For similar 5 Colones dated 19.6.1980, see #139.

		VG	VF	UNC
127	**10 COLONES** 7.7.1977. Black on m/c unpt. *DIEZ COLONES* at ctr., M. J. Arce at ctr. r. Back black. Printer: ABNC.	FV	2.00	8.00

		VG	VF	UNC
128	**10 COLONES** 13.10.1977. Like #127 but blue arms added to face and back. W/o wmk. Printer: ABNC.	FV	3.00	10.00

129 10 COLONES

	VG	VF	UNC
1978-80. M. J. Arce at r. Back black. Printer: TDLR.			
a. Regular serial #. 11.5.1978.	FV	2.00	7.00
b. Electronic sorting serial #. 3.5.1979; 21.7.1980.	FV	1.50	6.00
s. As b. Specimen. 3.5.1979.	—	—	27.50

130 25 COLONES

	VG	VF	UNC
1978-80. Like #121. Printer: TDLR.			
a. Regular serial #. 11.5.1978.	FV	4.00	20.00
b. Electronic sorting serial #. 3.5.1979; 19.6.1980.	FV	3.00	12.00
s. As b. Specimen. 19.6.1980.	—	—	27.50

131 50 COLONES

	VG	VF	UNC
1979; 1980. Purple on m/c unpt. Lg. bldg. and statue at l., Capt. Gen. G. Barrios at r. Ships at l., C. Columbus at ctr. on back. Printer: TDLR.			
a. 3.5.1979.	FV	6.00	20.00
b. 19.6.1980.	FV	5.00	17.50
s. As a. Specimen.	—	—	30.00

132 100 COLONES

	VG	VF	UNC
7.7.1977. Deep olive-green on m/c unpt. Independence monument at r. Printer: ABNC.	FV	16.50	55.00

1980 ISSUE

132A 5 COLONES

	VG	VF	UNC
19.6.1980 (1992). Like #134. Printer: ABNC.	FV	FV	3.00

133 100 COLONES

	VG	VF	UNC
17.7.1980. Black on m/c unpt. Like #122 but w/flag below date at upper l. Printer: TDLR.	FV	15.00	35.00

1982; 1983 ISSUE

#133A-137 w/o sign. title *GERENTE* at r.

#133A-136 black on m/c unpt. W/o unpt. in margins.

133A 1 COLÓN

	VG	VF	UNC
3.6.1982. Black on m/c unpt. Like #125. Back red. Printer: TDLR.			
a. Issued note.	FV	FV	3.50
s. Specimen.	—	—	25.00

#134-137 printer: ABNC.

134 5 COLONES

	VG	VF	UNC
1983; 1988. Black on m/c unpt. Back green.			
a. 25.8.1983.	FV	FV	4.00
b. 17.3.1988.	FV	FV	3.00
s1. As a. Specimen.	—	—	55.00
s2. As b. Specimen.	—	—	25.00

135 10 COLONES

	VG	VF	UNC
1983; 1988. Black on m/c unpt. Like #127.			
a. 25.8.1983.	FV	FV	5.50
b. 17.3.1988.	FV	FV	4.50
s1. As a. Specimen.	—	—	55.00
s2. As b. Specimen.	—	—	25.00

136 25 COLONES

	VG	VF	UNC
29.9.1983. Black on m/c unpt. Bridge and reservoir at ctr.			
a. Issued note.	FV	FV	8.00
s. Specimen.	—	—	25.00

		VG	VF	UNC
137	**100 COLONES** 1983; 1988. Deep olive-green on m/c unpt. Like #132.			
	a. 29.9.1983.	FV	FV	27.50
	b. 17.3.1988.	FV	FV	25.00
	s1. As a. Specimen.	—	—	25.00
	s2. As b. Specimen.	—	—	22.50

1990-93 ISSUES

#138 and 140 unpt. in margins.

		VG	VF	UNC
138	**5 COLONES** 16.5.1990. Black on m/c unpt. Like #126 but w/o sign., title: *GERENTE* at r., w/electronic sorting serial #. Back olive-green and dk. gray. Printer: TDLR.			
	a. Issued note.	FV	FV	2.00
	s. Specimen.	—	—	22.50

#139 *Deleted*. See #132A.

		VG	VF	UNC
140	**100 COLONES** 12.3.1993; 22.12.1994; 26.5.1995. Black, blue-green and violet on pink, blue and pale green unpt. Like #133 but w/arms at upper l., flag at lower r. Printer: TDLR.	FV	FV	25.00

1995 ISSUE

#141-143 w/ascending size serial # at upper r. Wmk: Columbus wearing cap. Printer: TDLR.

		VG	VF	UNC
141	**10 COLONES** 26.5.1995. Like #129.	FV	FV	4.50

		VG	VF	UNC
142	**25 COLONES** 26.5.1995; 9.2.1996. Similar to #130 but w/o sign., title: *GERENTE* at r.	FV	FV	8.50
143	**50 COLONES** 26.5.1995. Purple on m/c unpt. Like #131 but w/o sign., title: *GERENTE* at r.	FV	FV	12.50

1996 ISSUE

#144-146 wmk: C. Columbus wearing cap. Printer: CBNC.

		VG	VF	UNC
144	**10 COLONES** 9.2.1996. Black on m/c unpt. Similar to #141.	FV	FV	4.00

#145 and 146 w/segmented foil over security thread.

		VG	VF	UNC
145	**50 COLONES** 9.2.1996. Purple on m/c unpt. Like #143.	FV	FV	12.50

		VG	VF	UNC
146	**100 COLONES** 9.2.1996. Black, blue-green and violet on pink, blue and pale green unpt. Like #140.			
	a. Issued note.	FV	FV	22.50
	s. Specimen.	—	—	22.50

1997 ISSUE

#147-152 w/special marks for poor of sight above arms at l. ctr. C. Columbus wearing hat at l. on back and as wmk., continents over his 3 ships at ctr. Sign. titles *PRESIDENTE* and *DIRECTOR*. Date on back: 7.7.1997.

		VG	VF	UNC
147	**5 COLONES** 18.4.1997. Black, dk. green and brown on m/c unpt. National Palace at ctr. r.			
	a. Issued note. Series D.	FV	FV	1.75
	s. Specimen. Series A.	—	—	22.50

		VG	VF	UNC
148	**10 COLONES** 18.4.1997. Dk. blue-violet, brown and deep blue-green on m/c unpt. Izalco volcano at ctr. r.			
	a. Issued note. Series A.	FV	FV	3.50
	s. Specimen. Series A.	—	—	22.50

		VG	VF	UNC
149	**25 COLONES** 18.4.1997. Black, brown and blue-black on m/c unpt. San Andres pyramid at ctr. r.			
	a. Issued note. Series C.	FV	FV	7.00
	s. Specimen. Series A.	—	—	22.50

		VG	VF	UNC
150	**50 COLONES** 18.4.1997. Purple, brown and blue-black on m/c unpt. Lake Coatepeque at ctr. r.			
	a. Issued note. Series A.	FV	FV	12.50
	s. Specimen. Series A.	—	—	50.00

		VG	VF	UNC
151	**100 COLONES** 18.4.1997. Deep olive-green and dk. brown on m/c unpt. Tazumal pyramid at ctr. r.			
	a. Issued note. Series A.	FV	FV	20.00
	s. Specimen. Series A.	—	—	27.50

		VG	VF	UNC
152	**200 COLONES** 18.4.1997. Brown, red-violet and purple on m/c unpt. *EL SALVADOR DEL MUNDO* monument at ctr. r.			
	a. Issued note. Series B.	FV	FV	38.50
	s. Specimen. Series A.	—	—	35.00
153	**500 COLONES** 1997.			Expected New Issue

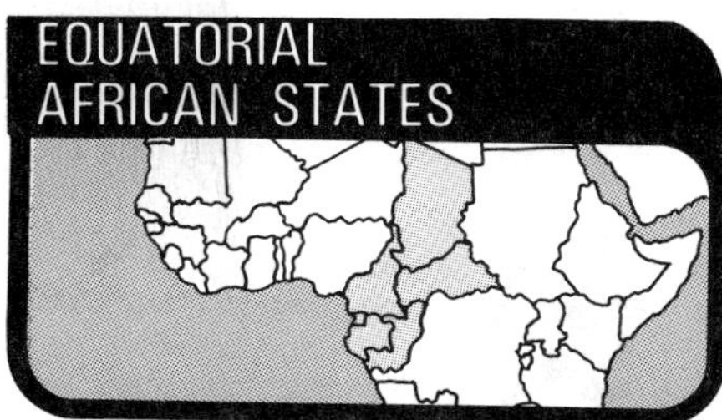

Equatorial African States (Central African States), a monetary union comprising the former French possessions and now independent states of the Republic of Congo (Brazzaville), Gabon, Central African Republic, Chad and Cameroon, issues a common currency for the member states from a common central bank. The monetary unit, the African Financial Community Franc, is tied to and supported by the French franc.

In 1960, an abortive attempt was made to form a union of the newly independent republics of Chad, Congo, Central Africa and Gabon. The proposal was discarded when Chad refused to become a constituent member. The four countries then linked into an Equatorial Customs Unit, to which Cameroon became an associate member in 1961. A more extensive cooperation of the five republics, identified as the Central African Customs and Economic Union, was entered into force at the beginning of 1966.

In 1974 the Central Bank of the Equatorial African States, which had issued coins and paper currency in its own name and with the names of the constituent member nations, changed its name to the Bank of the Central African States.

MONETARY SYSTEM:

1 Franc (C.F.A.) = 100 Centimes

EQUATORIAL AFRICAN STATES

CONTROL LETTER or SYMBOL CODE

Country	1961-72
Cameroun	*
Central African Republic	B
Chad	A
Congo	C
Equatorial Guinea	
Gabon	D

BANQUE CENTRALE DES ÉTATS DE L'AFRIQUE ÉQUATORIALE ET DU CAMEROUN

1961 ND ISSUES

		VG	VF	UNC
1	**100 FRANCS** ND (1961-62). Blue and m/c. Portr. Gov. Felix Eboue at ctr., woman w/jug at l., people in canoe at r. Cargo ships at ctr., man at r. on back.			
	a. Code letter *A*.	15.00	60.00	250.00
	b. Code letter *B*.	15.00	65.00	275.00
	c. Code letter *C*.	15.00	60.00	250.00
	d. Code letter *D*.	15.00	60.00	250.00
	e. * for Cameroun.	50.00	150.00	425.00
	f. W/o code letter.	12.50	45.00	200.00
2	**100 FRANCS** ND (1961-62). M/c. Like #1 but denomination also in English. W/* for Cameroun.	50.00	150.00	375.00

NOTE: For similar 100 Francs w/FRANÇAISE in the title see French Equatorial Africa #32. (Vol. II).

BANQUE CENTRALE DES ÉTATS DE L'AFRIQUE ÉQUATORIALE

1963 ND ISSUE

		VG	VF	UNC
3	**100 FRANCS** ND (1963). Brown and m/c. Musical instrument at l., hut at l. ctr., man at r. Elephant at l., tools at r. on back.			
	a. Code letter *A*.	8.00	30.00	85.00
	b. Code letter *B*.	8.00	30.00	95.00
	c. Code letter *C*.	8.00	30.00	85.00
	d. Code letter *D*.	8.00	30.00	85.00

		VG	VF	UNC
4	**500 FRANCS** ND (1963). Green and m/c. Girl wearing bandana at r., track mounted crane w/ore bucket in background. Radar unit at l., man on camel at r. on back.			
	a. Engraved. Code letter *A*. Block #1-4.	15.00	70.00	250.00
	b. As a. Code letter *B*.	15.00	80.00	275.00
	c. As a. Code letter *C*.	18.00	70.00	250.00
	d. As a. Code letter *D*.	15.00	70.00	250.00
	e. Lithographed. Code letter *A*. Block #5-.	10.00	55.00	225.00
	f. As e. Code letter *B*.	10.00	65.00	250.00
	g. As e. Code letter *C*.	12.00	55.00	225.00
	h. As e. Code letter *D*.	10.00	55.00	225.00

		VG	VF	UNC
5	**1000 FRANCS** ND (1963). M/c. People gathering cotton. Young men logging on back.			
	a. Engraved. Code letter *A*. Block #1-5.	15.00	80.00	275.00
	b. As a. Code letter *B*.	15.00	90.00	300.00
	c. As a. Code letter *C*.	18.00	80.00	275.00
	d. As a. Code letter *D*.	15.00	80.00	275.00
	e. Lithographed. Code letter *A*. Block #7-.	12.00	70.00	250.00
	f. As e. Code letter *B*.	12.00	80.00	275.00
	g. As e. Code letter *C*.	15.00	70.00	250.00
	h. As e. Code letter *D*.	12.00	70.00	250.00

		VG	VF	UNC
6	**5000 FRANCS** ND (1963). M/c. Girl at l., village scene at ctr. Carving at l., airplane, train crossing bridge and tractor hauling logs at ctr., man smoking a pipe at r. on back.			
	a. Code letter *A*.	125.00	350.00	650.00
	b. Code letter *B*.	125.00	325.00	650.00
	c. Code letter *C*.	125.00	350.00	650.00
	d. Code letter *D*.	125.00	350.00	650.00

		VG	VF	UNC
7	**10,000 FRANCS** ND (1968). M/c. Pres. Bokassa at r., Rock Hotel, Bangui, C.A.R. in background, arms of Central African Republic at lower l.	225.00	525.00	1250.

The Republic of Equatorial Guinea (formerly Spanish Guinea) consists of Rio Muni, located on the coast of west-central Africa between Cameroon and Gabon, and the offshore islands of Fernando Po, Annobon, Corisco, Elobey Grande and Elobey Chico. The equatorial country has an area of 10,831 sq. mi. (28,051 sq. km.) and a population of 417,000. Capital: Malabo. The economy is based on agriculture and forestry. Cacao, wood and coffee are exported.

Fernando Po was discovered between 1474 and 1496 by Portuguese navigators charting a route to the spice islands of the Far East. Portugal retained control of it and the adjacent islands until 1778 when they, together with trading rights to the African coast between the Ogooue and Niger rivers, were ceded to Spain. Fernando Po was administered, with Spanish consent, by the British from 1827 to 1844 when it was reclaimed by Spain. Mainland Rio Muni was granted to Spain by the Berlin Conference of 1885. The name of the colony was changed from Spanish Guinea to Equatorial Guinea in Dec. of 1963. Independence was attained on Oct. 12, 1968.

Additional listings can be found under Central African States.

MONETARY SYSTEM:

1 Peseta Guineana = 100 Centimos to 1975
1 Ekuele = 100 Centimos, 1975-80
1 Epkwele (pl. Bipkwele) = 100 Centimos, 1980-85
1 Franc (C.F.A.) = 100 Centimes, 1985-
1 Franco (C.F.A.) = 4 Bipkwele

REPUBLIC

BANCO CENTRAL

1969 ISSUE

#1-3 printer: FNMT.

		VG	VF	UNC
1	**100 PESETAS GUINEANAS** 12.10.1969. Red-brown on lt. tan unpt. Banana tree at l. Shoreline and man w/boat on back. Wmk: Woman's head.	1.00	3.00	9.00

		VG	VF	UNC
2	**500 PESETAS GUINEANAS** 12.10.1969. Green. Derrick loading logs at l., shoreline at ctr. Woman w/bundle on head at r. on back. Wmk: Man's head.	2.00	6.00	22.50

		VG	VF	UNC
3	**1000 PESETAS GUINEANAS** 12.10.1969. Blue. Pres. M. Nguema Biyogo at ctr. Tree at l., arms at ctr. on back. Wmk: King and queen.	2.75	7.50	25.00

BANCO POPULAR

1975 FIRST DATED ISSUE

#4-8 w/portr. Pres. M. N. Biyogo at r. and as wmk. Name under portrait: *MACIAS NGUEMA BIYOGO*. Printer: TDLR. Replacement notes: Serial # prefix *Z1*.

		VG	VF	UNC
4	**25 EKUELE** 7.7.1975. Purple on lt. orange and green unpt. Trees at ctr. Arms at l., bridge at ctr. on back. Name underneath: *PUENTE MACIAS NGUEMA BIYOGO*.	.65	1.60	3.75

		VG	VF	UNC
5	**50 EKUELE** 7.7.1975. Brown on green and pink unpt. Plants at ctr. Arms at l., logging at ctr. on back.	.65	1.60	4.00

#6-8 arms at ctr.

		VG	VF	UNC
6	**100 EKUELE** 7.7.1975. Green on pink and m/c unpt. Bridge and boats on back.	.65	1.60	4.50

		VG	VF	UNC
7	**500 EKUELE** 7.7.1975. Blue on m/c unpt. National Palace on back.	1.25	4.00	12.50

		VG	VF	UNC
8	**1000 EKUELE** 7.7.1975. Red on m/c unpt. Bank on back.	2.00	4.00	10.00

1975 SECOND DATED ISSUE

#9-13 like #4-8 but name under portrait: *MASIE NGUEMA BIYOGO NEGUE NDONG*. Different sign. Replacement notes: Serial # prefix *Z1*.

		VG	VF	UNC
9	**25 EKUELE** 7.7.1975. Like #4 except for name change on both sides.	1.00	2.00	6.50
10	**50 EKUELE** 7.7.1975. Like #5 except for name change.	1.00	2.00	6.50

		VG	VF	UNC
11	**100 EKUELE** 7.7.1975. Like #6 except for name change on both sides.	1.00	2.50	6.50
12	**500 EKUELE** 7.7.1975. Like #7 except for name change.	1.50	4.00	10.00
13	**1000 EKUELE** 7.7.1975. Like #8 except for name change.	1.50	3.50	10.00

BANCO DE GUINEA ECUATORIAL

1979 ISSUE

#14-17 wmk: T.E. Nkogo. Printer: FNMT.

		VG	VF	UNC
14	**100 BIPKWELE** 3.8.1979. Dk. olive-green and m/c. Arms at ctr., T. E. Nkogo at r. Boats along pier of Puerto de Bata on back.	1.75	4.00	10.00

		VG	VF	UNC
15	**500 BIPKWELE** 3.8.1979. Black on green and pink unpt. Arms at ctr., R. Uganda at r. Back brown and black; sailboat, shoreline and trees at l. ctr.	3.00	8.00	20.00

		VG	VF	UNC
16	**1000 BIPKWELE** 3.8.1979. Brown, black and m/c. Arms at ctr., R. Bioko at r. Back maroon and brown; men cutting food plants at l. ctr.	5.00	12.50	35.00

		VG	VF	UNC
17	**5000 BIPKWELE** 3.8.1979. Blue-gray on m/c unpt. Arms at ctr., E. N. Okenve at r. Back blue-gray and blue; logging scene at ctr.	3.00	7.50	22.50

1980 PROVISIONAL ISSUE

		VG	VF	UNC
18	**1000 BIPKWELE ON 100 PESETAS** 21.10.1980 (-old date 12.10.1969). Black ovpt. of new denomination and date on #1. (Not issued).	—	3.50	15.00

		VG	VF	UNC
19	**5000 BIPKWELE ON 500 PESETAS** 21.10.1980 (-old date 12.10.1969). Similar red ovpt. on #2. (Not issued).	—	6.00	20.00

NOTE: #18 and 19 were prepared for issue but not released to circulation. Shortly afterwards, Equatorial Guinea began the use of CFA franc currency. #3 was not ovpt. because it carries the portrait of former Pres. Biyogo.

BANQUE DES ÉTATS DE L'AFRIQUE CENTRALE

1985 ISSUE

#20-22 wmk: Carving (as printed on notes). Sign. 9. For sign. see Central African States listings.

		VG	VF	UNC
20	**500 FRANCOS** 1.1.1985. Brown on m/c unpt. Carving and jug at ctr. Man carving mask at l. ctr. on back.	1.00	2.50	5.00

		VG	VF	UNC
21	**1000 FRANCOS** 1.1.1985. Dk. blue on m/c unpt. Animal carving at lower l., map at ctr., starburst at lower r. Incomplete map of Chad at upper ctr. Elephant at l., statue at r. on back.	2.00	6.00	11.50

		VG	VF	UNC
22	**5000 FRANCOS** 1.1.1985; 1.1.1986. Brown, yellow and m/c. Carved mask at l., woman carrying bundle at r. Farmer plowing w/tractor at l., ore lift at r. on back.			
	a. 1.1.1985.	11.50	20.00	40.00
	b. 1.1.1986.	10.00	17.50	35.00

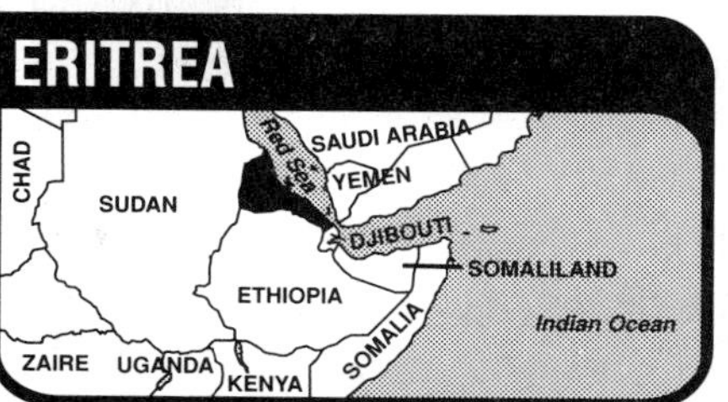

The State of Eritrea, a former Ethiopian province fronting on the Red Sea, has an area of 45,300 sq. mi. (117,600 sq. km.) and a population of 3.53 million. It was an Italian colony from 1889 until its incorporation into Italian East Africa in 1936. It was under the British Military Administration from 1941 to 1952, when the United Nations designated it an autonomous unit within the federation of Ethiopia and Eritrea. On Nov. 14, 1962, it was annexed with Ethiopia. In 1991 the Eritrean Peoples Liberation Front extended its control over the entire territory of Eritrea. Following 2 years of provisional government, Eritrea held a referendum on independence in May 1993. Overwhelming popular approval led to the proclamation of an independent Republic of Eritrea on May 24.

MONETARY SYSTEM:

1 Nakfa = 100 Cents

REPUBLIC

BANK OF ERITREA

1997 ISSUE

#1-6 flag raising at l. Wmk: Camel's head.

		VG	VF	UNC
1	**1 NAKFA** 24.5.1997. Dk. brown and black on m/c unpt. 3 girls at ctr. Back dk. green; children in bush school at ctr. r.	FV	FV	1.00

#2-6 Kinnegram vertical foil strip at l. w/camels repeated.

		VG	VF	UNC
2	**5 NAKFA** 24.5.1997. Dk. brown and black on m/c unpt. Young boy, young and old man at ctr. Back dk. green; cattle grazing under huge Jacaranda tree at ctr. r.	FV	FV	3.50

		VG	VF	UNC
3	**10 NAKFA** 24.5.1997. Dk. brown and black on m/c unpt. 3 young women at ctr. Back dk. green; truck on rails hauling box cars across viaduct over the Dogali River at ctr. r.	FV	FV	6.50

		VG	VF	UNC
4	**20 NAKFA** 24.5.1997. Dk. brown and black on m/c unpt. 3 young girls at ctr. Back dk. green; farmer plowing w/camel, woman harvesting, woman on farm tractor at ctr. r.	FV	FV	11.50

		VG	VF	UNC
5	**50 NAKFA** 24.5.1997. Dk. brown and black on m/c unpt. 3 young boys at ctr. Back dk. green; ships in Port of Masawa at ctr. r.	FV	FV	20.00

		VG	VF	UNC
6	**100 NAKFA** 24.5.1997. Dk. brown and black on m/c unpt. 3 young girls at ctr. Back dk. green; farmers plowing w/oxen at ctr. r.	FV	FV	37.50

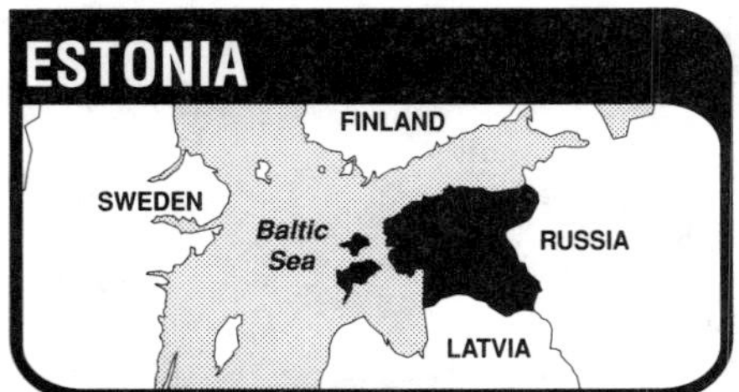

The Republic of Estonia (formerly the Estonian Soviet Socialist Republic of the U.S.S.R.) is the northernmost of the three Baltic states in eastern Europe. It has an area of 17,413 sq. mi. (45,100 sq. km.) and a population of 1.46 million. Capital: Tallinn. Agriculture and dairy farming are the principal industries. Butter, eggs, bacon, timber and petroleum are exported.

This small and ancient Baltic state has enjoyed but two decades of independence since the 13th century. After having been conquered by the Danes, the Livonian Knights, the Teutonic Knights of Germany (who reduced the people to serfdom), the Swedes, the Poles and Russia, Estonia declared itself an independent republic on Nov. 15, 1917, but was not freed until Feb. 1919. The peace treaty was signed Feb. 2, 1920. Shortly after the start of World War II, it was again occupied by Russia and incorporated as the 16th state of the U.S.S.R. Germany occupied the tiny state from 1941 to 1944, after which it was retaken by Russia. Some of the nations of the world, including the United States and Great Britain, did not recognize Estonia's incorporation as an S.S.R. into the Soviet Union.

On August 20, 1991, the Parliament of the Estonian S.S.R. voted to reassert the republic's independence.

MONETARY SYSTEM

1 Kroon = 100 Senti

REPUBLIC

EESTI PANK

BANK OF ESTONIA

1991-92 ISSUE

#69-71 replacement notes: Serial # prefix *.

#69 and 70 wmk: Fortress.

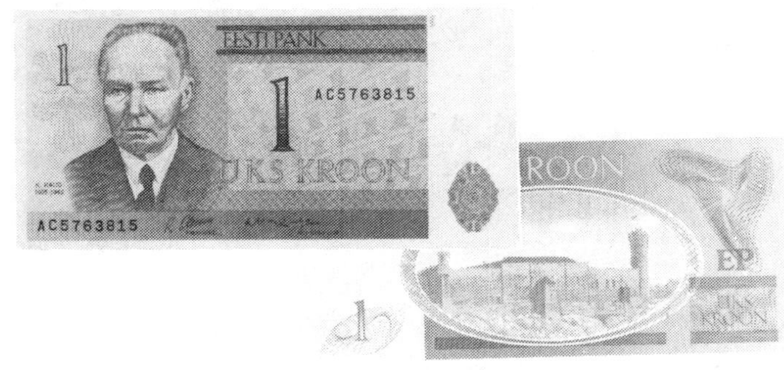

		VG	VF	UNC
69	**1 KROON** 1992. Brownish black on yellow-orange and dull violet-brown unpt. K. Raud at l. Toampea castle w/Tall Hermann (national landmarks) on back.			
	a. Issued note.	FV	FV	.75
	s. Specimen.	—	—	45.00

		VG	VF	UNC
70	**2 KROONI** 1992. Black on lt. blue-violet and grayish green unpt. K. E. von Baer at l. Tartu University bldg. at ctr. on back.			
	a. Issued note.	FV	FV	1.00
	s. Specimen.	—	—	45.00

#71-75 wmk: Arms (3 lions).

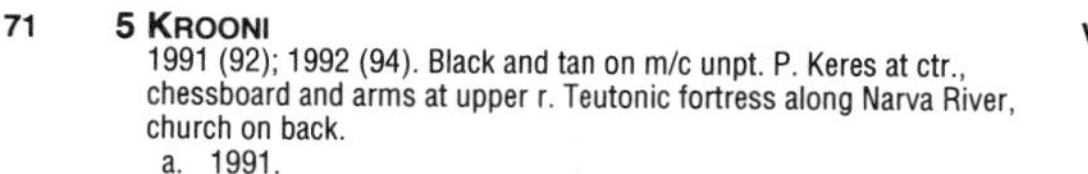

		VG	VF	UNC
71	**5 KROONI** 1991 (92); 1992 (94). Black and tan on m/c unpt. P. Keres at ctr., chessboard and arms at upper r. Teutonic fortress along Narva River, church on back.			
	a. 1991.	FV	FV	2.00
	b. 1992.	FV	FV	1.50
	s. Specimen.	—	—	60.00

		VG	VF	UNC
72	**10 KROONI** 1991 (92); 1992 (94). Purple and red-violet on m/c unpt. J. Hurt at l. ctr. Tamme-lauri oak tree at Urvaste at r. on back.			
	a. 1991.	FV	FV	4.00
	b. 1992.	FV	FV	2.50
	s. Specimen.	—	—	60.00

		VG	VF	UNC
73	**25 KROONI** 1991 (92); 1992 (94). Deep olive-green on m/c unpt. A. Hanse-Tammsaare at l. ctr., wilderness in background at r. Early rural log construction farm; view of Vargamäe on back.			
	a. 1991.	FV	FV	10.00
	b. 1992.	FV	FV	4.50
	s. Specimen.	—	—	70.00

		VG	VF	UNC
74	**100 KROONI** 1991 (92); 1992 (94). Black and deep blue on lt. blue and m/c unpt. L. Koidula at l. ctr., cuckoo bird at lower r. Waves breaking against rocky cliffs of North coast at ctr. to r. on back.			
	a. 1991.	FV	FV	25.00
	b. 1992.	FV	FV	35.00
	s. Specimen.	—	—	85.00

		VG	VF	UNC
75	**500 KROONI** 1991 (92). Blue-black and purple on m/c unpt. C. R. Jakobson at l. ctr., harvest between 2 farmers with Sakala above at r. Barn swallow in flight over rural pond at r. on back.			
	a. Issued note.	FV	FV	90.00
	s. Specimen.	—	—	200.00

1994 ISSUE

#76-80 ascending size serial # at r.

		VG	VF	UNC
76	**5 KROONI** 1994 (97). Black and tan on m/c unpt. Like #71 but w/modified design at lower r. on face and lower l. on back.			
	a. Issued note.	FV	FV	1.25
	s. Specimen.	—	—	60.00

		VG	VF	UNC
77	**10 KROONI** 1994 (97). Purple and red-violet on m/c unpt. Like #72 but w/modified design at lower r. on face and lower l. on back.			
	a. Issued note.	FV	FV	2.25
	s. Specimen.	—	—	60.00

		VG	VF	UNC
78	**50 KROONI** 1994 (95). Green and black on m/c unpt. R. Tobias at l. ctr., gates at lower ctr. r. Opera house in Tallinn at ctr. r. on back.			
	a. Issued note.	FV	FV	15.00
	s. Specimen.	—	—	80.00

		VG	VF	UNC
79	**100 KROONI** 1994 (95). Black and dk. blue on m/c unpt. Like #74 but w/gray seal at upper r.			
	a. Issued note.	FV	FV	18.50
	s. Specimen.	—	—	85.00

		VG	VF	UNC
80	**500 KROONI** 1994 (95). Blue-black and purple on m/c unpt. Like #75 but w/dk. gray bank seal at upper r.			
	a. Issued note.	FV	FV	80.00
	s. Specimen.	—	—	200.00

1996 ISSUE

		VG	VF	UNC
81	**500 KROONI** 1996 (97). Blue, black and purple on m/c unpt. Like #80 but w/hologram at upper l.			
	a. Issued note.	FV	FV	75.00
	s. Specimen.	—	—	200.00

1999 ISSUE

		VG	VF	UNC
82	**100 KROONI** 1999. Blue on lt. blue and m/c unpt. Holographic strip at l., L. Koidula at l. ctr.; cuckoo bird at lower ctr. Back blue on lt. red unpt. Waves breaking against rocky cliffs of North coast at ctr. to r.			
	a. Issued note.	FV	FV	20.00
	s. Specimen w/ovpt: *PROOV.*	—	—	45.00

COLLECTOR SERIES

EESTI PANK

BANK OF ESTONIA

1999 COLLECTOR'S SET

80th Anniversary of Bank

		ISSUE PRICE	MKT. VALUE
CS1	**100 KROONI** 1999. Set includes: 100 Krooni specimen note (#82), 5 Krooni coin, and 4 stamps. 3,000 pcs.	20.00	50.00

ETHIOPIA

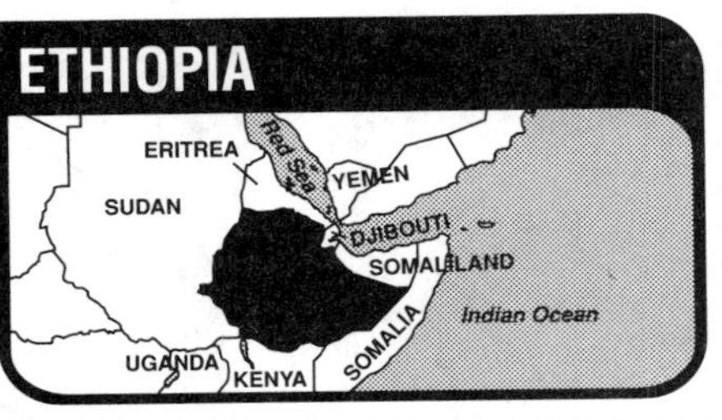

The Federal Republic of Ethiopia (formerly the Peoples Democratic Republic and the Empire of Ethiopia) is located in east-central Africa. The country has an area of 424,214 sq. mi. (1.099,900 sq. km.) and a population of 55 million people who are divided among 40 tribes that speak some 270 languages and dialects. Capital: Addis Ababa. The economy is predominantly agricultural and pastoral. Gold and platinum are mined and petroleum fields are being developed. Coffee, oilseeds, hides and cereals are exported.

Legend claims that Menelik I, the son born to Solomon, King of Israel, by the Queen of Sheba, settled in Axum in northern Ethiopia to establish the dynasty which then reigned - with only brief interruptions - until 1974. Modern Ethiopian history began with the reign of Emperor Menelik II (1889-1913) under whose guidance the country emerged from medieval isolation. Ethiopia was invaded by fascist Italy in 1935, and together with Italian Somaliland and Eritrea became part of Italian East Africa until liberated by British and Ethiopian troops in 1941. Haile Selassie I, 225th consecutive Solomonic ruler, was deposed by a military committee on Sept. 12, 1974. In July 1976, Ethiopia's military provisional government referred to the country as Socialist Ethiopia. After establishing a new regime in 1991, Ethiopia became a federated state.

Eritrea, a former Ethiopian province fronting on the Red Sea, was an Italian colony from 1890 until its incorporation into Italian East Africa in 1936. It was under British military administration from 1941 to Sept. 15, 1952, when the United Nations designated it an autonomous unit within the federation of Ethiopia and Eritrea. On Nov. 14, 1962, it was fully integrated with Ethiopia. On May 24, 1993, Eritrea became an independent nation.

RULERS:

Haile Selassie I, 1930-1936, 1941-1974

MONETARY SYSTEM:

1 Birr (Dollar) = 100 Santeems (Cents)

EMPIRE

STATE BANK OF ETHIOPIA

1961 ND ISSUE

Dollar System

#18-24 Haile Selassie at r. Arms at ctr. on back. Printer: BWC.

		VG	VF	UNC
18	**1 DOLLAR** ND (1961). Green on lilac and lt. orange unpt. Coffee bushes at l.			
	a. Issued note.	3.00	12.00	30.00
	s. Specimen. Punched hole cancelled.	—	—	25.00

		VG	VF	UNC
19	**5 DOLLARS** ND (1961). Orange on green and m/c unpt. Addis Ababa University (old palace) at l.			
	a. Issued note.	5.00	25.00	80.00
	s. Specimen. Punched hole cancelled.	—	—	50.00
20	**10 DOLLARS** ND (1961). Red on m/c unpt. Harbor at Massawa at l.			
	a. Issued note.	15.00	40.00	125.00
	s. Specimen. Punched hole cancelled.	—	—	110.00

		VG	VF	UNC
21	**20 DOLLARS** ND (1961). Brown on m/c unpt. Ancient stone monument (Axum) at l.			
	a. Issued note.	30.00	80.00	250.00
	s. Specimen. Punched hole cancelled.	—	—	125.00

		VG	VF	UNC
22	**50 DOLLARS** ND (1961). Blue on m/c unpt. Bridge over Blue Nile at l.			
	a. Issued note.	60.00	100.00	300.00
	s. Specimen. Punched hole cancelled.	—	—	175.00
23	**100 DOLLARS** ND (1961). Purple on m/c unpt. Trinity Church at Addis Ababa at l.			
	a. Sign. title: *GOVERNOR.*	90.00	150.00	400.00
	b. Sign. title: *ACTING GOVERNOR.*	70.00	125.00	350.00
	s. Specimen.	—	—	200.00
24	**500 DOLLARS** ND (1961). Dk. green on m/c unpt. Castle at Gondar at l.			
	a. Issued note.	250.00	600.00	1500.
	s. Specimen. Punched hole cancelled.	—	—	300.00

NATIONAL BANK OF ETHIOPIA

1966 ND ISSUE

#25-29 Emperor Haile Selassie at r. Arms at ctr. on back. Printer: TDLR.

		VG	VF	UNC
25	**1 DOLLAR** ND (1966). Green on m/c unpt. Aerial view of Massawa harbor, city at l.			
	a. Issued note.	2.00	6.00	20.00
	s. Specimen.	—	—	30.00

		VG	VF	UNC
26	**5 DOLLARS** ND (1966). Brown on m/c unpt. Bole Airport, Addis Ababa at l. Back orange.			
	a. Issued note.	3.00	15.00	55.00
	s. Specimen.	—	—	35.00

		VG	VF	UNC
27	**10 DOLLARS** ND (1966). Dk. red on m/c unpt. National Bank at Addis Ababa at l.			
	a. Issued note.	5.00	20.00	70.00
	s. Specimen.	—	—	50.00

		VG	VF	UNC
28	**50 DOLLARS** ND (1966). Blue on m/c unpt. Koka High Dam at l.			
	a. Issued note.	20.00	75.00	190.00
	s. Specimen.	—	—	165.00

		VG	VF	UNC
29	**100 DOLLARS** ND (1966). Purple on green and m/c unpt. Bet Giorgis in Lalibela (rock church) at l.			
	a. Issued note.	15.00	55.00	175.00
	s. Specimen.	—	—	140.00

PEOPLES DEMOCRATIC REPUBLIC

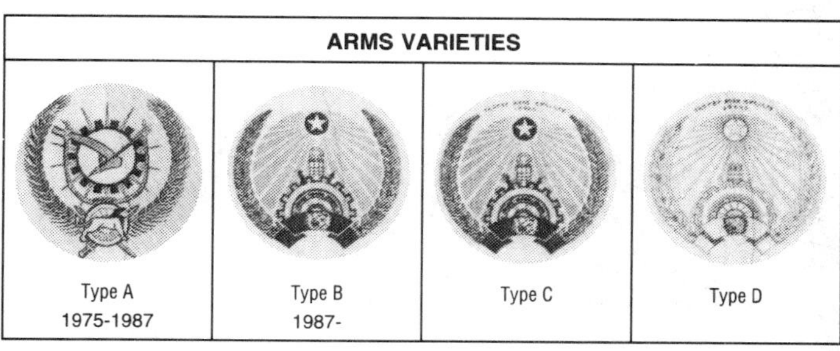

SIGNATURE VARIETIES

1	Teferra Deguefe, 1974–76 CHAIRMAN OF THE BOARD	2	Tadesse G. Kidan, 1978–87 ADMINISTRATOR
3	Bekele Tamirat, 1987–91 ADMINISTRATOR	4	Leikun Berhanu, 1991-97 GOVERNOR
5	Thbale Tala, 1997-98 GOVERNOR		Teklewold Atnafu, 1998- GOVERNOR

NATIONAL BANK OF ETHIOPIA

1976 ND ISSUE

Birr System

Law EE 1969 (1976 AD)

#30-34 have map at l., lion's head in unpt. at l. ctr. Arms Type A at r. on back. Replacement notes: Serial # prefix *ZZ*.

		VG	VF	UNC
30	**1 BIRR** *L.EE1969* (1976). Black and dk. green on lt. brown and green unpt. Young man at ctr. r., longhorns at r. Back black on m/c unpt.; birds and Tisisat waterfalls of Blue Nile on back.			
	a. Sign. 1.	.50	2.00	5.00
	b. Sign. 2.	.25	1.50	2.50

		VG	VF	UNC
31	**5 BIRR** *L.EE1969* (1976). Black and brown-orange on m/c unpt. Man picking coffee beans at ctr. r., plant at r. Kudu, caracal and Semien Mountains on back.			
	a. Sign. 1.	1.00	3.25	8.00
	b. Sign. 2.	1.25	2.75	7.00

		VG	VF	UNC
32	**10 BIRR** *L.EE1969* (1976). Brown-violet and red on m/c unpt. Woman weaving basket at ctr. r., wicker work dining table w/lid at r. Plowing w/tractor on back.			
	a. Sign. 1.	3.00	6.00	15.00
	b. Sign. 2.	2.50	4.00	12.00

		VG	VF	UNC
33	**50 BIRR** *L.EE1969* (1976). Blue-black and dk. brown on lilac and m/c unpt. Science students at ctr. r., musical instrument at r. Fasilides Castle at Gondar on back.			
	a. Sign. 1.	12.50	25.00	60.00
	b. Sign. 2.	11.50	20.00	50.00

		VG	VF	UNC
34	**100 BIRR** *L.EE1969* (1976). Purple, violet and dk. brown on m/c unpt. Menelik II standing at ctr. r., flowers at r. Young man w/microscope on back.			
	a. Sign. 1.	25.00	40.00	100.00
	b. Sign. 2.	20.00	32.50	85.00

1987 ND ISSUE

#36-40 similar to #30-34 but w/ornate tan design at l. and r. edges on back. Sign. 3. Arms Type A at r. on back. Replacement notes: Serial # prefix *ZZ*.

		VG	VF	UNC
36	**1 BIRR** *L.EE1969* (1987). Black and green on lt. brown and green unpt. Like #30.	.20	1.00	2.50
37	**5 BIRR** *L.EE1969* (1987). Black and brown-orange on m/c unpt. Like #31.	.85	2.50	6.00
38	**10 BIRR** *L.EE1969* (1987). Brown-violet and red on m/c unpt. Like #32.	1.50	3.50	10.00
39	**50 BIRR** *L.EE1969* (1987). Blue-black and dk. brown on lilac and m/c unpt. Like #33.	10.00	17.50	35.00
40	**100 BIRR** *L.EE1969* (1976). Purple, violet and dk. brown on m/c unpt. Like #34 but w/flowers and dark shield at r.	18.50	32.50	60.00

FEDERAL DEMOCRATIC REPUBLIC

NATIONAL BANK OF ETHIOPIA

1991 ND ISSUE

#41-45 like #36-40 but w/new arms Type B, C or D at r. on back.

		VG	VF	UNC
41	**1 BIRR** *L.EE1969* (1991). Dk. green on lt. brown and green unpt. Like #36. Arms Type D.			
	a. Sign. 3 w/title in Amharic script. Serial # prefix larger sanserif letters.	.25	.75	1.50
	b. Sign. 4 w/title: *GOVERNOR* and also in Amharic script.	.20	.65	1.35
	c. As b. but w/serial # prefix smaller serif letters.	.15	.60	1.25

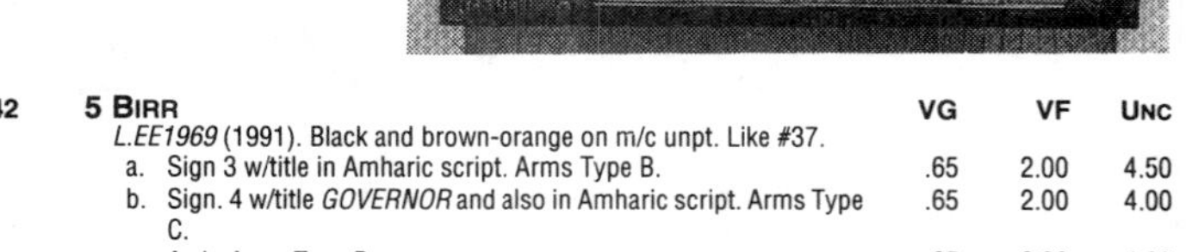

		VG	VF	UNC
42	**5 BIRR** *L.EE1969* (1991). Black and brown-orange on m/c unpt. Like #37.			
	a. Sign 3 w/title in Amharic script. Arms Type B.	.65	2.00	4.50
	b. Sign. 4 w/title *GOVERNOR* and also in Amharic script. Arms Type C.	.65	2.00	4.00
	c. As b. Arms Type B.	.65	2.00	4.00

43 **10 BIRR**
L.EE1969 (1991). Brown-violet and red on m/c unpt. Like #38. Arms Type D.

	VG	VF	UNC
a. Sign. 3 w/title in Amharic script.	1.25	3.75	7.50
b. Sign. 4 w/title: *GOVERNOR* and also in Amharic script.	1.00	3.00	6.00

44 **50 BIRR**
L.EE1969 (1991). Blue-black and dk. brown on lilac and m/c unpt. Like #39.

	VG	VF	UNC
a. Sign. 3 w/title in Amharic script. Arms Type B.	6.50	20.00	40.00
b. Sign. 4 w/title: *GOVERNOR* and also in Amharic script. Arms Type C.	6.00	17.50	35.00
c. As b. Arms Type D.	5.00	15.00	30.00

45 **100 BIRR**
L.EE1969 (1991). Purple, violet and dk. brown on m/c unpt. Like #40. Arms Type D.

	VG	VF	UNC
a. Sign. 3 w/title in Amharic script.	10.00	25.00	50.00
b. Sign. 4 w/title: *GOVERNOR* and also in Amharic script.	7.50	22.50	45.00

1997/EE1989 ISSUE

#46-50 similar to #41-45 but w/latent image (map of Ethiopia) w/value at l. W/o arms on back. Sign. 5.

46 **1 BIRR**
1997/EE1989. Black on m/c unpt. Similar to #41.

VG	VF	UNC
FV	FV	.85

#47-50 w/segmented foil over security thread.

47 **5 BIRR**
1997/EE1989. Dk. blue on m/c unpt. Similar to #42.

VG	VF	UNC
FV	FV	3.00

48 **10 BIRR**
1997/EE1989. Deep brown, red and green on m/c unpt. Similar to #43.

VG	VF	UNC
FV	FV	5.00

49 **50 BIRR**
1997/EE1989. Tan and orange-brown on m/c unpt. Farmer plowing w/oxen at ctr. and as wmk. Fasilides castle at ctr. on back.

VG	VF	UNC
FV	FV	18.50

50 **100 BIRR**
1997/EE1989. Deep blue-green, olive-green and dk. green on m/c unpt. Face like #49. Science student w/microscope at ctr. on back.

VG	VF	UNC
FV	FV	32.50

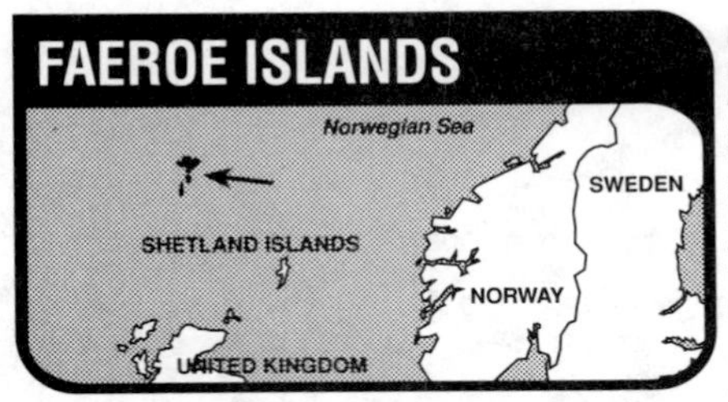

The Faroes, a self-governing community within the kingdom of Denmark, are situated in the North Atlantic between Iceland and the Shetland Islands. The 17 inhabited islets and reefs have an area of 540 sq. mi. (1,399 sq. km.) and a population of 48,000. Capital: Thorshavn. The principal industries are fishing and grazing. Fish and fish products are exported.

While it is thought that Irish hermits lived on the islands in the 7th and 8th centuries, the present inhabitants are descended from the 6th century Norse settlers. The Faroes became a Norwegian fief in 1035 and became Danish in 1380 when Norway and Denmark were united. They have ever since remained in Danish possession and were granted self-government (except for an appointed governor-general) with their own legislature, executive and flag in 1948.

The islands were occupied by British troops during World War II, after the German occupation of Denmark.

RULERS:

Danish

MONETARY SYSTEM:

1 Króne = 100 Øre

DANISH INFLUENCE

FØROYAR

1964-74 ISSUE

#16-18 have coded year dates in the l. series # (the 2 middle digits). Wmk: Anchor chain. Replacement notes: Serial # suffix *OJ; OK*.

		VG	VF	UNC
16	**10 KRÓNUR** *L.1949* (19)74. Green. Shield w/ram at l. Rural scene at ctr. on back.			
	a. Sign. L. Groth and A. P. Dam. (19)74.	FV	FV	5.50
	b. Sign. B. Klinte and J. Sundstein.	FV	FV	5.00

		VG	VF	UNC
17	**50 KRÓNUR** *L.1949* (19)67. Black, lt. blue and blue-green unpt. Portr. N. Pall at l. Back blue on green unpt. Drawing of homes and church across ctr. Sign. M. Wahl and P. M. Dam.	11.50	17.50	27.50

NOTICE

Readers with unlisted dates, signature varieties, etc. are invited to submit photocopies of their notes to: Standard Catalog of World Paper Money, 700 East State St. Iola, WI 54990-0001, fax: 1-715-445-4087, or E-Mail: thernr@krause.com.

		VG	VF	UNC
18	**100 KRÓNUR** *L.1949* (19)64; 69; 72; 75. Black on pink and gold unpt. Portr. V. U. Hammershaimb at l. Back blue on tan unpt. Drawing of house and mountains on back.			
	a. Sign. M. Wahl and H. Djurhuus. (19)64.	20.00	33.50	65.00
	b. Sign. M. Wahl and Kr. Djurhuus (19)69.	20.00	32.50	60.00
	c. Sign. as b. (19)72.	20.00	31.50	57.50
	d. Sign. L. Groth and A. P. Dam. (19)75.	20.00	30.00	50.00

1978-86 ISSUE

#19-23 have coded year dates in the l. series # (the 2 middle digits). Wmk: Anchor chain. Replacement notes: Serial # suffix *OJ; OK*.

		VG	VF	UNC
19	**20 KRÓNUR** *L.1949* (19)86; 88. Deep purple on pink and aqua unpt. Man w/ice tool at r. Back red and black; drawing of animals at ctr.			
	a. Sign. N. Bentsen and A. P. Dam. (19)86.	FV	FV	6.00
	b. Sign. B. Klinte and A. P. Dam. (19)88.	FV	FV	5.50

		VG	VF	UNC
20	**50 KRÓNUR** *L.1949* (19)78-. Black on lt. blue and gray unpt. Similar to #17 but reduced size. 140 x 72mm. Back black on gray unpt. Wmk: Chain links.			
	a. Sign. L. Groth and A. P. Dam. (19)78.	FV	FV	15.00
	b. Sign. as a. (19)87.	FV	FV	14.00
	c. Sign. N. Bentsen and A. P. Dam. (19)87.	FV	FV	13.50
	d. Sign. B. Klinte and E. Joensen (19)94.	FV	FV	13.00

21	**100 KRÓNUR**	VG	VF	UNC
	L.1949 (19)78- . Black on tan unpt. Similar to #18 but reduced size. Back black and green on ochre unpt. Wmk: Chain links.			
	a. Sign. L. Groth and A. P. Dam. (19)78.	FV	FV	40.00
	b. Sign. N. Bentsen and P. Ellefsen. (19)83.	FV	FV	37.50
	c. Sign. N. Bentsen and A. P. Dam. (19)87.	FV	FV	35.00
	d. Sign. B. Klinte and A. P. Dam. (19)88.	FV	FV	32.50
	e. Sign. B. Klinte and J. Sun Stein. (19)90.	FV	FV	30.00
	f. Sign. B. Klinte and E. Joensen. (19)94.	FV	FV	27.50

22	**500 KRÓNUR**	VG	VF	UNC
	L.1949 (19)78. Black on green and dull purple unpt. Sketch of fisherman at r. Sketch of fishermen in boat at sea on back.			
	a. Sign. L. Groth and A. P. Dam.	FV	FV	135.00
	b. Sign. B. Klinte and E. Joensen. (19)94.	FV	FV	110.00

23	**1000 KRÓNUR**	VG	VF	UNC
	L.1949 (19)78; 83; 87; 89; 94. Blue-green, black and green. H. O. Djurhuus at l. Street scene sketch on back.			
	a. Sign. L. Groth and A. P. Dam. (19)78.	FV	FV	300.00
	b. Sign. N. Bentsen and P. Ellefsen. (19)83.	FV	FV	275.00
	c. Sign. N. Bentsen and A. P. Dam. (19)87.	FV	FV	260.00
	d. Sign. B. Klinte and A. P. Dam. (19)89.	FV	FV	240.00
	e. Sign. B. Klinte and M. Petersen. (19)94.	FV	FV	225.00

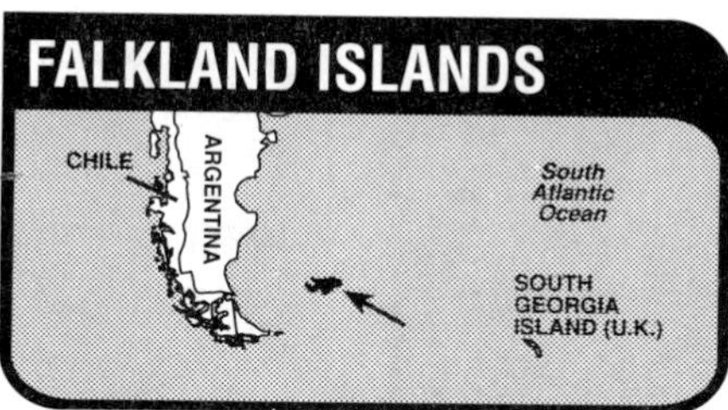

The Colony of the Falkland Islands and Dependencies, a British colony located in the South Atlantic about 500 miles northeast of Cape Horn, has an area of 4,700 sq. mi. (12,173 sq. km.) and a population of 2,100. East Falkland, West Falkland, South Georgia, and South Sandwich are the largest of the 200 islands. Capital: Stanley. Sheep grazing is the main industry. Wool, whale oil, and seal oil are exported.

The Falklands were discovered by British navigator John Davis (Davys) in 1592, and named by Capt. John Strong - for Viscount Falkland, treasurer of the British navy - in 1690. French navigator Louis De Bougainville established the first settlement, at Port Louis, in 1764. The following year Capt. John Byron claimed the islands for Britain and left a small party at Saunders Island. Spain later forced the French and British to abandon their settlements but did not implement its claim to the islands. In 1829 the Republic of Buenos Aires, which claimed to have inherited the Spanish rights, sent Louis Vernet to develop a colony on the islands. In 1831 he seized three American sailing vessels, whereupon the men of the corvette, *U.S.S. Lexington,* destroyed his settlement and proclaimed the Falklands to be "free of all governance." Britain, which had never renounced its claim, then re-established its settlement in 1833.

RULERS:

British

MONETARY SYSTEM:

1 Shilling = 12 Pence
1 Pound = 20 Shillings to 1966
1 Pound = 100 Pence, 1966-

GOVERNMENT

1960-67 ISSUE

#7-9 portr. Qn. Elizabeth II at r. Printer: TDLR.

8	**1 POUND**	VG	VF	UNC
	1967-82. Blue on gray-green and lilac unpt.			
	a. 2.1.1967.	4.00	10.00	60.00
	b. 20.2.1974.	3.50	7.00	30.00
	c. 1.12.1977.	5.00	20.00	80.00
	d. 1.1.1982.	4.00	7.50	42.50
	e. 15.6.1982.	3.50	6.00	35.00

9	**5 POUNDS**	VG	VF	UNC
	1960; 1975. Red on green unpt.			
	a. Sign: L. Gleadell: 10.4.1960.	17.50	60.00	250.00
	b. Sign: H. T. Rowlands: 30.1.1975.	15.00	50.00	200.00

1969; 1975 Issue

#10 and 11 portr. Qn. Elizabeth II at r. Printer: TDLR.

		VG	VF	UNC
10	**50 Pence** 1969; 1974. Brown on gray unpt.			
	a. Sign: L. Gleadell. 25.9.1969.	3.00	7.00	25.00
	b. Sign: H. T. Rowlands. 20.2.1974.	2.50	6.00	25.00

		VG	VF	UNC
11	**10 Pounds** 1975-82. Green on lt. orange and yellow-green unpt. Sign. H. T. Rowlands.			
	a. 5.6.1975.	17.50	25.00	225.00
	b. 1.1.1982.	18.50	35.00	285.00
	c. 15.6.1982.	16.50	20.00	180.00

1983 Commemorative Issue

#12, 150th Anniversary of English rule, 1833-1983

		VG	VF	UNC
12	**5 Pounds** 14.6.1983. Red on m/c unpt. Like #13. Commemorative legend at lower ctr.	FV	FV	20.00

1984-90 Regular Issue

#13-16 Qn. Elizabeth II at r. Penguins and shield at l., seals at r. Governor's home and church on back.

		VG	VF	UNC
13	**1 Pound** 1.10.1984. Blue on brown and yellow unpt. Like #12.	FV	FV	25.00

		VG	VF	UNC
14	**10 Pounds** 1.9.1986. Gray-green on m/c unpt. Like #12.	FV	FV	30.00

		VG	VF	UNC
15	**20 Pounds** 1.10.1984. Brown on m/c unpt. Like #12.	FV	FV	60.00

		VG	VF	UNC
16	**50 Pounds** 1.7.1990. Blue on m/c unpt. Like #12.	FV	FV	120.00

The self-declared republic of Fiji, an independent member of the British Commonwealth, consists of about 320 islands located in the southwestern Pacific 1,100 miles (1,770 km.) north of New Zealand. The islands have a combined area of 7,056 sq. mi. (18,274 sq. km.) and a population of 772,655. Capital: Suva on the island of Viti Levu. Fiji's economy is based on agriculture and mining. Sugar, coconut products, manganese and gold are exported.

The Fiji Islands were discovered by Dutch navigator Abel Tasman in 1643 and visited by British naval captain James Cook in 1774. The first complete survey of the island was conducted by the United States in 1840. Settlement by missionaries from Tonga and traders attracted by the sandalwood trade began in 1835. Following a lengthy period of intertribal warfare, the islands were unconditionally and voluntarily ceded to Great Britain in 1874 by King Cakobau. The trading center was Levuka on the island of Ovalau which was also the capital under the British from 1874-82. Fiji became an independent nation on Oct 10, 1970, the 96th anniversary of the cession of the islands to Queen Victoria. It is a member of the Commonwealth of Nations.

RULERS:

British, 1874-

MONETARY SYSTEM:

1 Shilling = 12 Pence
1 Pound = 20 Shillings to 1969
1 Dollar = 100 Cents, 1969-

GOVERNMENT

1954-57 ISSUE

Pound System

#43-47 arms at upper ctr., portr. Qn. Elizabeth II at r. Wmk: Fijian youth's bust. Printer: BWC.

		VG	VF	UNC
43	**5 SHILLINGS** 1957-65. Green and blue on lilac and green unpt.			
	a. 1.6.1957; 28.4.1961; 1.12.1962.	2.00	7.50	100.00
	b. 1.9.1964; 1.12.1964; 1.10.1965.	1.50	6.00	75.00

		VG	VF	UNC
44	**10 SHILLINGS** 1957-65. Brown on lilac and green unpt.			
	a. 1.6.1957; 28.4.1961; 1.12.1962.	3.00	22.50	200.00
	b. 1.9.1964; 1.10.1965.	2.50	20.00	150.00

		VG	VF	UNC
45	**1 POUND** 1954-67. Green on yellow and blue unpt.			
	a. 1.7.1954; 1.6.1957; 1.9.1959.	8.00	40.00	250.00
	b. 1.12.1961-1.1.1967.	3.00	30.00	200.00
46	**5 POUNDS** 1954-67. Purple on lt. orange and green unpt.			
	a. 1.7.1954; 1.9.1959; 1.10.1960.	40.00	225.00	1000.
	b. 1.12.1962; 20.1.1964; 1.12.1964; 1.1.1967.	30.00	200.00	750.00

		VG	VF	UNC
47	**10 POUNDS** 1954-64. Blue.			
	a. 1.7.1954.	100.00	375.00	1500.
	b. 1.9.1959; 1.10.1960; 20.1.1964; 11.6.1964.	65.00	300.00	850.00

1968 ND ISSUE

Decimal System

#50-55 Qn. Elizabeth at r. Arms and heading: *GOVERNMENT OF FIJI* at upper ctr. 2 sign. Ritchie and Barnes. Wmk: Fijian youth's bust. Printer: TDLR.

		VG	VF	UNC
50	**50 CENTS** ND (1968). Green on m/c unpt. Thatched roof house and palms on back.	1.00	3.00	22.50

		VG	VF	UNC
51	**1 DOLLAR** ND (1968). Brown on lilac and lt. green unpt. Scene of Yanuca in the Mamanuca Group of Islands, South Yasewas on back.	1.00	5.00	55.00

#52-55 w/o pictorial scenes on back.

		VG	VF	UNC
52	**2 DOLLARS** ND (1968). Green on yellow and lt. blue unpt.	2.00	7.50	75.00
53	**5 DOLLARS** ND (1968). Orange on lilac and gray unpt.	7.00	25.00	225.00
54	**10 DOLLARS** ND (1968). Purple on lt. orange and lilac unpt.	15.00	40.00	325.00
55	**20 DOLLARS** ND (1968). Blue on lt. green and orange unpt.	27.50	85.00	600.00

NOTICE

Readers with unlisted dates, signature varieties, etc. are invited to submit photocopies of their notes to: Standard Catalog of World Paper Money, 700 East State St. Iola, WI 54990-0001, fax: 1-715-445-4087, or E-Mail: thernr@krause.com.

1971 ND Issue

#56-61 like #50-55 but w/only 1 sign. Wmk: Fijian youth's bust. Printer: TDLR.

		VG	VF	UNC
56	**50 Cents** ND (1971). Green on m/c unpt. Like #50.			
	a. Sign. Wesley Barrett.	1.00	4.00	25.00
	b. Sign. C. A. Stinson.	1.00	3.00	22.50
57	**1 Dollar** ND (1971). Brown on lilac and lt. green unpt. Like #51.			
	a. Sign. Wesley Barrett.	1.50	5.00	80.00
	b. Sign. C. A. Stinson.	1.50	6.00	85.00
58	**2 Dollars** ND (1971). Green on yellow and lt. blue unpt. Like #52.			
	a. Sign. Wesley Barrett.	2.50	10.00	120.00
	b. Sign. C. A. Stinson.	Reported Not Confirmed		

		VG	VF	UNC
59	**5 Dollars** ND (1971). Like #53.			
	a. Sign. Wesley Barrett.	5.00	25.00	225.00
	b. Sign. C. A. Stinson.	5.00	30.00	300.00
60	**10 Dollars** ND (1971). Like #54.			
	a. Sign. Wesley Barrett.	12.50	45.00	350.00
	b. Sign. C. A. Stinson.	15.00	55.00	425.00
61	**20 Dollars** ND (1971). Like #55.			
	a. Sign. Wesley Barrett.	25.00	75.00	500.00
	b. Sign. C. A. Stinson.	25.00	100.00	600.00

Central Monetary Authority

1974 ND Issue

#62-67 like #50-55 but w/new heading: *FIJI* at top, and issuing authority name across lower ctr. 2 sign. Wmk: Fijian youth's bust. Printer: TDLR.

		VG	VF	UNC
62	**50 Cents** ND (1974). Like #50. Sign. D. J. Barnes and R. J. A. Earland. (Not issued.)	—	—	—

		VG	VF	UNC
63	**1 Dollar** ND (1974). Like #51.			
	a. Sign. D. J. Barnes and R. J. Earland.	1.00	3.00	20.00
	b. Sign. D. J. Barnes and H. J. Tomkins.	1.00	2.00	15.00

		VG	VF	UNC
64	**2 Dollars** ND (1974). Like #52.			
	a. Sign. D. J. Barnes and I. A. Craik.	4.00	20.00	160.00
	b. Sign. D. J. Barnes and R. J. Earland.	1.50	3.00	37.50
	c. Sign. D. J. Barnes and H. J. Tomkins.	1.50	3.00	35.00
65	**5 Dollars** ND (1974). Like #53.			
	a. Sign. D. J. Barnes and I. A. Craik.	7.50	40.00	225.00
	b. Sign. D. J. Barnes and R. J. Earland.	4.00	17.50	135.00
	c. Sign. D. J. Barnes and H. J. Tomkins.	4.00	15.00	110.00
66	**10 Dollars** ND (1974). Like #54.			
	a. Sign. D. J. Barnes and I. A. Craik.	20.00	65.00	575.00
	b. Sign. D. J. Barnes and R. J. Earland.	8.50	20.00	210.00
	c. Sign. D. J. Barnes and H. J. Tomkins.	7.50	17.50	175.00
67	**20 Dollars** ND (1974). Like #55.			
	a. Sign. D. J. Barnes and I. A. Craik.	35.00	150.00	950.00
	b. Sign. D. J. Barnes and R. J. Earland.	15.00	40.00	275.00
	c. Sign. D. J. Barnes and H. J. Tomkins.	15.00	65.00	350.00

1980 ND Issue

#68-72 Qn. Elizabeth II at r. ctr., arms at ctr., artifact at r. Wmk: Fijian youth's bust. Sign. D. J. Barnes and H. J. Tomkins. Printer: TDLR.

		VG	VF	UNC
68	**1 Dollar** ND (1980). Brown on m/c unpt. Open air fruit market at ctr. on back.	.65	1.00	7.50

		VG	VF	UNC
69	**2 Dollars** ND (1980). Green on m/c unpt. Harvesting sugar cane at ctr. on back.	1.25	3.00	25.00

		VG	VF	UNC
70	**5 Dollars** ND (1980). Orange on m/c unpt. Circle of fishermen w/net at ctr. on back.	3.00	7.50	55.00

71 **10 DOLLARS** | VG | VF | UNC
ND (1980). Purple on m/c unpt. Tribal dance scene at ctr. on back. | 12.50 | 20.00 | 145.00

72 **20 DOLLARS** | VG | VF | UNC
ND (1980). Blue on m/c unpt. Native hut at l. ctr. on back. | 25.00 | 50.00 | 350.00

1983; 1986 ND ISSUE

#73-77 like #54-58. Backs retouched and lithographed. Wmk: Fijian youth's bust. Sign. D. J. Barnes and S. Siwatibau.

73 **1 DOLLAR** | VG | VF | UNC
ND (1983). Black on m/c unpt. Like #68. | FV | FV | 6.00

74 **2 DOLLARS** | VG | VF | UNC
ND (1983). Green on m/c unpt. Like #69. | FV | FV | 12.50

75 **5 DOLLARS** | VG | VF | UNC
ND (1986). Orange on m/c unpt. Like #70. | FV | FV | 20.00

76 **10 DOLLARS** | VG | VF | UNC
ND (1986). Purple on m/c unpt. Like #71. | FV | FV | 55.00

77 **20 DOLLARS** | VG | VF | UNC
ND (1986). Blue on m/c unpt. Like #72. | FV | FV | 100.00

RESERVE BANK OF FIJI

1987-91 ND ISSUE

#78-82 modified portr. of Qn. Elizabeth II at r., and new banking authority. Similar to #73-77. Wmk: Fijian youth's bust. Sign. S. Siwatibau.

#78, 79, and 82 printer: BWC.

78 **1 DOLLAR** | VG | VF | UNC
ND (1987). Dk. gray on m/c unpt. Similar to #73. | FV | FV | 3.50

79 **2 DOLLARS** | VG | VF | UNC
ND (1988). Deep green on m/c unpt. Similar to #74. | FV | FV | 6.00

80 **5 DOLLARS** | VG | VF | UNC
ND (ca.1991). Brown-orange and violet on m/c unpt. Similar to #75. Printer: TDLR. | FV | FV | 20.00

		VG	VF	UNC
81	**10 DOLLARS** ND (1989). Purple, violet and brown on m/c unpt. Similar to #76. Printer: TDLR.	FV	FV	27.50

		VG	VF	UNC
82	**20 DOLLARS** ND (1988). Dk. blue, blue-green and black on m/c unpt. Similar to #77.	FV	FV	50.00

1992-95 ND ISSUE

#83-87 similar to #79-82 but w/slightly redesigned portr. Sign. Kubuabola. Printer: TDLR.

		VG	VF	UNC
83	**1 DOLLAR** ND (1993). Dk. gray on m/c unpt. Similar to #78. W/o segmented security thread.	FV	FV	2.50

		VG	VF	UNC
84	**2 DOLLARS** ND (1995). Deep green on m/c unpt. Similar to #79.	FV	FV	5.50

#85-87 vertical serial # at l., segmented foil over security thread.

		VG	VF	UNC
85	**5 DOLLARS** ND (1992). Brown-orange and violet on m/c unpt. Similar to #80.	FV	FV	11.50

		VG	VF	UNC
86	**10 DOLLARS** ND (1992). Purple, violet and brown on m/c unpt. Similar to #81.	FV	FV	18.00

		VG	VF	UNC
87	**20 DOLLARS** ND (1992). Dk. blue on m/c unpt. Similar to #82.	FV	FV	35.00

1995-96 ND ISSUE

#88-92 mature bust of Qn. Elizabeth II at r., arms at upper r. Segmented foil over security thread. Wmk: Fijian youth's bust. Printer: TDLR. Replacement notes: Serial # prefix *Z*.

		VG	VF	UNC
88	**2 DOLLARS** ND (1996). Dk. green, blue and olive-brown on m/c unpt. Kaka bird at lower l. Fijian family of 5 at l. ctr. on back.			
	a. Serial # prefix *A*.	FV	FV	7.50
	b. Serial # prefix *X*.	FV	FV	5.00
	c. Serial # prefix *AA; AB; AC*.	FV	FV	4.00

		VG	VF	UNC
89	**5 DOLLARS** ND (1995). Brown-orange on violet and m/c unpt. Bunedamu bird at lower l. Aerial view Nadi International Airport at l. ctr., ferry boat at lower ctr. r. on back.	FV	FV	10.00

90	10 DOLLARS	VG	VF	UNC
	ND (1996). Purple, violet and brown on m/c unpt. Kaka bird at lower l. Children swimming at l. in background, family in boat constructed of reeds with thatched roof shelter at l. ctr. on back.			
	a. Serial # prefix *J*.	FV	FV	30.00
	b. Serial # prefix *AA; AB; AC*.	FV	FV	17.50

91	20 DOLLARS	VG	VF	UNC
	ND (1996) Purple, blue and dk. blue on m/c unpt. Parliament House at l., Reserve Bank bldg. at ctr. r. on back.	FV	FV	30.00

92	50 DOLLARS	VG	VF	UNC
	ND (1996). Black, red, orange and violet on m/c unpt. Kaka bird at lower l. Ascending vertical serial # at l. Flag raising ceremony at l., signing of Deed of Cession over Cession Stone at ctr. on back.	FV	FV	70.00

1998 ND ISSUE

93	5 DOLLARS	VG	VF	UNC
	ND (1998). Brown and orange on m/c unpt. Like #89.	FV	FV	7.50

2000 COMMEMORATIVE ISSUE

94	2 DOLLARS	VG	VF	UNC
	2000. M/c. Sir Penaia Ganilau at r. Group portrait of islanders on back.	FV	FV	5.00
95	2000 DOLLARS			
	2000. M/c. Sir Kamisese Mara at r. Earth, rising sun; island map on back.	FV	FV	2100.

The Republic of Finland, the second most northerly state of the European continent, has an area of 130,120 sq. mi. (337,009 sq. km.) and a population of 5.12 million. Capital: Helsinki. Lumbering, shipbuilding, metal and woodworking are the leading industries. Paper, timber, wood pulp, plywood and metal products are exported.

he Finns, who probably originated in the Volga region of Russia, took Finland from the Lapps late in the 7th century. They were conquered in the 12th century by Eric IX of Sweden, and brought into contact with Western Christendom. In 1809, Sweden was conquered by Alexander I of Russia, and the peace terms gave Finland to Russia. It became a grand duchy within the Russian Empire until Dec. 6, 1917, when, shortly after the Bolshevik revolution, it declared its independence. After a brief but bitter civil war between the Russian sympathizers and Finnish nationalists in which the Whites (nationalists) were victorious, a new constitution was adopted, and on Dec. 6, 1917 Finland was established as a republic. In 1939 Soviet troops invaded Finland over disputed territorial concessions which were later granted in the peace treaty of 1940. When the Germans invaded Russia, Finland also became involved and in the Armistice of 1944 lost the Petsamo area also to the Soviets.

MONETARY SYSTEM:

1 Markka = 100 "Old" Markkaa, 1963-
1 Markka = 100 Pennis

REPUBLIC

SUOMEN PANKKI - FINLANDS BANK

1963 DATED ISSUE

#98-102 arms at ctr. or ctr. r. on back. W/o *Litt.* designation. Replacement notes: Serial # suffix *.

98	1 MARKKA	VG	VF	UNC
	1963. Lilac-brown on olive unpt. Wheat ears.			
	a. Issued note.	FV	.50	1.50
	s. Specimen.	—	—	100.00

99	5 MARKKAA	VG	VF	UNC
	1963. Blue. Conifer branch.			
	a. Issued note.	FV	1.50	5.00
	s. Specimen.	—	—	125.00

100	10 MARKKAA	VG	VF	UNC
	1963. Dk. green. Juho Kusti Paasikivi at l. (Wmk. direction varies.)			
	a. Issued note.	FV	3.00	8.00
	s. Specimen.	—	—	150.00

		VG	VF	UNC
101	**50 MARKKAA**			
	1963. Brown. Kaarlo Juho Stahlberg at l.			
	a. Issued note.	FV	15.00	40.00
	s. Specimen.	—	—	175.00

		VG	VF	UNC
102	**100 MARKKAA**			
	1963. Violet. Juhana Vilhelm Snellman at l.			
	a. Issued note.	FV	20.00	35.00
	s. Specimen.	—	—	200.00

1963 DATED ISSUE, LITT. A

#103-106 replacement notes: Serial # suffix *.

		VG	VF	UNC
103	**5 MARKKAA**			
	1963. Blue. Similar to #99, but border and date designs are more detailed.	FV	1.50	3.00

		VG	VF	UNC
104	**10 MARKKAA**			
	1963. Dk. green. Like #100. (Wmk. position varies.)	FV	3.00	5.00

		VG	VF	UNC
105	**50 MARKKAA**			
	1963. Brown. Like #101.	FV	15.00	30.00

		VG	VF	UNC
106	**100 MARKKAA**			
	1963. Violet. Like #102.	FV	20.00	35.00

1963 DATED ISSUE, LITT. B

#106A and 107 replacement notes: Serial # suffix *.

		VG	VF	UNC
106A	**5 MARKKAA**			
	1963. Blue. Like #99.	FV	1.10	2.00
107	**50 MARKKAA**			
	1963. Brown. Like #101 and #105. (Wmk. direction varies.)	FV	12.00	20.00

1975-77 ISSUE

#108-110 replacement notes: Serial # suffix *.

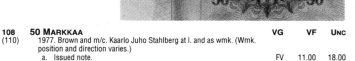

		VG	VF	UNC
108 (110)	**50 MARKKAA**			
	1977. Brown and m/c. Kaarlo Juho Stahlberg at l. and as wmk. (Wmk. position and direction varies.)			
	a. Issued note.	FV	11.00	18.00
	s. Specimen.	—	—	200.00

		VG	VF	UNC
109	**100 MARKKAA**			
	1976. Violet. Juhana Vilhelm Snellman at l. and as wmk. (Wmk. position and direction varies.)	FV	20.00	33.50

110 500 MARKKAA

1975. Blue and violet. Urho Kekkonen at l. and as wmk. Arms and 9 small shields on back. (Wmk. position varies.)

	VG	VF	UNC
a. Thin metallic security thread.	FV	100.00	170.00
b. Broad yellow plastic security thread.	FV	100.00	150.00
s. Specimen.	—	—	350.00

1980 ISSUE

#111 replacement notes: Serial # suffix *.

111 10 MARKKAA

1980. Green on brown and orange unpt. Like #100 except for color and addition of 4 raised discs at r. ctr. for denomination identification by the blind. Back green and purple. Wmk: Paasikivi.

VG	VF	UNC
FV	2.00	5.00

1980 ISSUE; LITT. A

#112 replacement notes: *W/99* as 2nd and 3rd digits in serial #.

112 10 MARKKAA

1980. Similar to #111 but date under portr., and 5 small circles at bottom. *Litt. A.*

VG	VF	UNC
FV	2.00	5.00

1986 ISSUE

#113-117 portr. as wmk. Circles above lower r. serial #.

#113-115, and 117 replacement notes: W/*99* as 2nd and 3rd digits in serial #.

113 10 MARKKAA

1986. Deep blue on blue and green unpt. Paavo Nurmi at l. and as wmk. Helsinki Olympic Stadium on back.

VG	VF	UNC
FV	FV	4.50

114 50 MARKKAA

1986. Black on red-brown and m/c unpt. Alvar Aalto at l. and as wmk. 4 raised circles at lower r. for the blind. Finlandia Hall on back.

VG	VF	UNC
FV	FV	18.50

115 100 MARKKAA

1986. Black on green and m/c unpt. Jean Sibelius at l. and as wmk. 3 raised circles at lower r. for the blind. Swans on back.

VG	VF	UNC
FV	FV	35.00

116 500 MARKKAA

1986. Black on red, brown and yellow unpt. Elias Lonnrot at l. and as wmk. Punkaharju on back.

VG	VF	UNC
FV	FV	140.00

117 1000 MARKKAA

1986. Blue and purple on m/c unpt. Anders Chydenium at l. and as wmk. King's gate, sea fortress of Suomenlinna in Helsinki harbor, seagulls on back.

VG	VF	UNC
FV	FV	275.00

1986 Dated (1991) Issue, Litt. A

#118-121 like #114-117 with w/*Litt. A* above denomination added to lower l. and optical variable device (OVD) added at upper r. to higher denominations. Circles above bank name. Port. r. as wmk.

		VG	VF	UNC
118 (119)	**50 Markkaa** 1986 (1991). Similar to #114.	FV	FV	16.00
119 (120)	**100 Markkaa** 1986 (1991). Similar to #115.	FV	FV	30.00

		VG	VF	UNC
120 (121)	**500 Markkaa** 1986 (1991). Similar to #116.	FV	FV	125.00

		VG	VF	UNC
121 (122)	**1000 Markkaa** 1986 (1991). Similar to #117.	FV	FV	235.00

1993 Issue

		VG	VF	UNC
122 (118)	**20 Markkaa** 1993. Black on blue and gold unpt. V. Linna at l. and as wmk. Optical variable device at upper r. Tampere street scene on back.	FV	FV	7.00

1993 Dated (1997) Issue; Litt. A

		VG	VF	UNC
123	**20 Markkaa** 1993 (1997). Black on blue and green unpt. Like #122 but w/optical variable device at upper r. *Litt. A.*	FV	FV	6.50

The French Republic, largest of the West European nations, has an area of 220,668 sq. mi. (547,026 sq. km.) and a population of 60 million. Capital: Paris. Agriculture, mining and manufacturing are the most important elements of France's diversified economy. Textiles and clothing, iron and steel products, machinery and transportation equipment, agricultural products and wine are exported.

France, the Gaul of ancient times, emerged from the Renaissance as a modern centralized national state which reached its zenith during the reign of Louis XIV (1643-1715) when it became an absolute monarchy and the foremost power in Europe. Although his reign marks the golden age of French culture, the domestic abuses and extravagance of Louis XIV plunged France into a series of costly wars. This, along with a system of special privileges granted the nobility and other favored groups, weakened the monarchy, brought France to bankruptcy - and laid the way for the French Revolution of 1789-94 that shook Europe and affected the whole world.

The monarchy was abolished and the First Republic formed in 1793. The new government fell in 1799 to a coup led by Napoleon Bonaparte who, after declaring himself First Consul for life, had himself proclaimed emperor of France and king of Italy. Napoleon's military victories made him master of much of Europe, but his disastrous Russian campaign of 1812 initiated a series of defeats that led to his abdication in 1814 and exile to the island of Elba. The monarchy was briefly restored under Louis XVIII. Napoleon returned to France in March 1815, but his efforts to regain power were totally crushed at the Battle of Waterloo. He was exiled to the island of St. Helena where he died in 1821.

The monarchy under Louis XVIII was again restored in 1815, but the ultrareactionary regime of Charles X (1824-30) was overthrown by a liberal revolution and Louis Philippe of Orleans replaced him as monarch. The monarchy was ousted by the Revolution of 1848 and the Second Republic proclaimed. Louis Napoleon Bonaparte (nephew of Napoleon I) was elected president of the Second Republic. He was proclaimed emperor in 1852. As Napoleon III, he gave France two decades of prosperity under a stable, autocratic regime, but led it to defeat in the Franco-Prussian War of 1870, after which the Third Republic was established.

The Third Republic endured until 1940 and ended by the capitulation of France to the swiftly maneuvering German forces. Marshal Henri Petain formed a puppet government that sued for peace and ruled unoccupied France from Vichy. Meanwhile, General Charles de Gaulle escaped to London where he formed a wartime government in exile and the Free French army. Charles de Gaulle's provisional exile government was officially recognized by the Allies after the liberation of Paris in 1944, and de Gaulle, who had been serving as head of the provisional government, was formally elected to that position. In October 1945, the people overwhelmingly rejected a return to the prewar government, thus paving the way for the formation of the Fourth Republic.

Charles de Gaulle was unanimously elected president of the Fourth Republic, but resigned in January 1946 when leftists withdrew their support. In actual operation, the Fourth Republic was remarkably like the Third, with the National Assembly the focus of power. The later years of the Fourth Republic were marked by a burst of industrial expansion unmatched in modern French history. The growth rate, however, was marred by a nagging inflationary trend that weakened the franc and undermined the competitive posture of France's export trade. This and the Algerian conflict led to the recall of de Gaulle to power, the adoption of a new constitution vesting strong powers in the executive, and establishment in 1958 of the current Fifth Republic.

MONETARY SYSTEM:

1 Nouveau Franc = 100 "old" Francs, 1960-

REPUBLIC

BANQUE DE FRANCE

1959 ISSUE

#141-145 denomination: *NOUVEAUX FRANCS* (NF).

		VG	VF	UNC
141	**5 NOUVEAUX FRANCS** 5.3.1959-5.11.1965. Blue, orange and m/c. Pantheon in Paris at l., V. Hugo at r. Village at r., V. Hugo at l. on back.	1.50	9.00	30.00
142	**10 NOUVEAUX FRANCS** 5.3.1959-4.1.1963. M/c. Skyline across, Richelieu at r. Similar scene on back, Richelieu at l.	2.50	15.00	40.00
143	**50 NOUVEAUX FRANCS** 5.3.1959-6.7.1961. M/c. Henry IV at ctr., bridge in in background. Henry IV at ctr., castle at l. on back.	12.50	37.50	125.00
144	**100 NOUVEAUX FRANCS** 5.3.1959-2.4.1964. M/c. Arch at l. Bonaparte at r. Capital bldg. at r., Bonaparte at l. on back.	20.00	33.50	110.00

		VG	VF	UNC
145	**500 NOUVEAUX FRANCS** 1959-66. M/c. Moliere at ctr.			
	a. Sign. G. Gouin d'Ambrieres, R. Tondu and P. Gargam. 2.7.1959-8.1.1965.	200.00	300.00	600.00
	b. Sign. H. Morant, R. Tondu and P. Gargam. 6.1.1966.	200.00	250.00	450.00

1962-66 ISSUE

		VG	VF	UNC
146	**5 FRANCS** 1966-70. Brown, purple and m/c. L. Pasteur at l., Pasteur Institute in Paris at r. Laboratory implements, man fighting a rabid dog, Pasteur at r. on back.			
	a. Sign. R. Tondu, P. Gargam and H. Morant. 5.5.1966-4.11.1966.	1.00	8.00	20.00
	b. Sign. R. Tondu, H. Morant and G. Bouchet. 5.5.1967-8.1.1970.	1.00	10.00	22.50

		VG	VF	UNC
147	**10 FRANCS** 1963-73. Red and m/c. Bldg. at ctr., Voltaire at r. and as wmk. Similar scene w/Voltaire at l. on back.			
	a. Sign. G. Gouin d'Ambrieres, P. Gargam and R. Tondu. 4.1.1963-2.12.1965.	FV	9.00	20.00
	b. Sign. H. Morant, P. Gargam and R. Tondu. 6.1.1966-6.4.1967.	FV	8.00	17.50
	c. Sign. G. Bouchet, H. Morant and R. Tondu. 6.7.1967-4.2.1971.	FV	8.00	17.50
	d. Sign. G. Bouchet, H. Morant and P. Vergnes. 3.6.1971-6.12.1973.	FV	7.50	14.00
	s. Specimen. Ovpt. and perforated *SPECIMEN.*	—	—	300.00

NOTICE

Readers with unlisted dates, signature varieties, etc. are invited to submit photocopies of their notes to: Standard Catalog of World Paper Money, 700 East State St. Iola, WI 54990-0001, fax: 1-715-445-4087, or E-Mail: thernr@krause.com.

148 50 FRANCS
1962-76. M/c. Bldgs. w/courtyard at ctr., Racine at r. Racine at l., bldgs across on back.

		VG	VF	UNC
a.	Sign. G. Gouin d'Ambrieres, R. Tondu and P. Gargam. 7.6.1962-4.3.1965.	FV	20.00	60.00
b.	Sign. H. Morant, R. Tondu and P. Gargam. 2.2.1967.	FV	45.00	80.00
c.	Sign. H. Morant, R. Tondu and G. Bouchet. 7.12.1967-5.11.1970.	20.00	30.00	60.00
d.	Sign. G. Bouchet, R. Tondu and H. Morant. 7.12.1967-5.11.1970.	FV	15.00	40.00
e.	Sign. G. Bouchet, P. Vergnes and H. Morant. 3.6.1971-3.10.1974.	FV	15.00	40.00
f.	Sign. G. Bouchet, J. J. Tronche and H. Morant. 6.3.1975-2.10.1975.	FV	15.00	35.00
g.	Sign. P. A. Strohl, G. Bouchet and J. J. Tronche. 2.1.1976-3.6.1976.	FV	15.00	35.00
s.	Specimen. Ovpt. and perforated specimen.	—	—	400.00

149 100 FRANCS
1964-79. M/c. P. Corneille at ctr. surrounded by arches. His bust in cartouche at ctr. on back.

		VG	VF	UNC
a.	Sign. R. Tondu. G. Gouin d'Ambrieres and P. Gargam. 2.4.1964-2.12.1965.	FV	35.00	80.00
b.	Sign. R. Tondu, H. Morant and P. Gargam. 3.2.1966-6.4.1967.	FV	25.00	55.00
c.	Sign. R. Tondu, G. Bouchet and H. Morant. 5.10.1967-1.4.1971.	FV	25.00	45.00
d.	Sign. P. Vergnes, G. Bouchet and H. Morant. 1.7.1971-3.10.1974.	FV	25.00	40.00
e.	Sign. J. J. Tronche, G. Bouchet and H. Morant. 6.2.1975-6.11.1975.	FV	25.00	40.00
f.	Sign. P. A. Strohl, G. Bouchet and J. J. Tronche. 2.1.1976-1.2.1979.	FV	25.00	40.00
s.	Specimen. Ovpt. and perforated specimen.	—	—	500.00

1968-81 ISSUE

150 10 FRANCS
1972-78. Red, brown and olive. H. Berlioz conducting at r. and as wmk. Berlioz at l., musical instrument at r. on back.

		VG	VF	UNC
a.	Sign. H. Morant, G. Bouchet and P. Vergnes. 23.11.1972-3.10.1974.	FV	4.00	10.00
b.	Sign. H. Morant, G. Bouchet and J. J. Tronche. 6.2.1975-4.12.1975.	FV	4.00	8.00
c.	Sign. P. A. Strohl, G. Bouchet and J. J. Tronche. 2.1.1976-6.7.1978.	FV	4.00	6.50
s.	Specimen. Ovpt. and perforated specimen.	—	—	300.00

151 20 FRANCS
1980-97. Dull violet, brown and m/c. C. Debussy at r. and as wmk., sea scene in background *(La Mer)*. Back similar but w/lake scene.

		VG	VF	UNC
a.	Sign. P. A. Strohl, J. J. Tronche and B. Dentaud. 1980-86.	FV	7.50	15.00
b.	Sign. P. A. Strohl, D. Ferman and B. Dentaud. 1987.	FV	5.00	10.00
c.	W/o security thread. Sign. D. Ferman, B. Dentaud and A. Charriau. 1988; 1989.	FV	5.00	10.00
d.	W/security thread. Sign. as c. 1990.	FV	FV	8.00
e.	Sign. D. Bruneel, B. Dentaud and A. Charriau. 1991.	FV	FV	8.00
f.	Sign. D. Bruneel, J. Bonnardin and A. Charriau. 1992; 1993.	FV	FV	6.00
g.	Sign. D. Bruneel, J. Bonnardin and C. Vigier. 1993.	FV	FV	6.00
h.	Sign. as g. New Ley (law) on back. 1995.	FV	FV	6.00
i.	Sign. D. Bruneel, J. Bonnardin and Y. Barroux. 1997.	FV	FV	6.00

152 50 FRANCS
1976-92. Deep blue-black on m/c unpt. M. Quentin de la Tour at ctr. r. and as wmk., and Palace of Versailles at l. ctr. in background. Q. de la Tour and St. Quentin City Hall at ctr. r. in background on back.

		VG	VF	UNC
a.	Sign. P. A. Strohl, G. Bouchet and J. J. Tronche. 1976-79.	FV	FV	17.50
b.	Sign. P. A. Strohl, J. J. Tronche and B. Dentaud. 1979-86.	FV	FV	16.00
c.	Sign. P. A. Strohl, D. Ferman and B. Dentaud. 1987.	FV	FV	15.00
d.	Sign. D. Ferman, B. Dentaud and A. Charriau. 1988; 1989.	FV	FV	14.50
e.	Sign. D. Bruneel, B. Dentaud and A. Charriau. 1990; 1991.	FV	FV	14.50
f.	Sign. D. Bruneel, J. Bonnardin and A. Charriau. 1992.	FV	FV	14.50

153 100 FRANCS

	VG	VF	UNC
1978. Brown. E. Delacroix at l. ctr. and as wmk., Marianne holding tricolor Port. of Delacroix's painting *La Liberté Guidant le Peuple at r. Sign. P. A. Strohl, G. Bouchet and J. J. Tronche.*	FV	FV	45.00

		VG	VF	UNC
154	**100 FRANCS** 1978-95. Brown. Like #153 but *100 CENT FRANCS* retouched w/heavier diagonal lines at upper l.			
	a. Sign. P. A. Strohl, G. Bouchet and J. J. Tronche. 1978-79.	FV	FV	35.00
	b. Sign. P. A. Strohl, J. J. Tronche and B. Dentaud. 1979-86.	FV	FV	32.50
	c. Sign. P. A. Strohl, D. Ferman and B. Dentaud. 1987.	FV	FV	30.00
	d. Sign. D. Ferman, B. Dentaud and A. Charriau. 1988-90.	FV	FV	32.50
	e. Sign. D. Bruneel, B. Dentaud and A. Charriau. 1991.	FV	FV	30.00
	f. Sign. D. Bruneel, J. Bonnardin and C. Vigier. 1993.	FV	FV	27.50
	g. Sign. as f. New Ley (law) on back. 1994; 1995.	FV	FV	27.50

		VG	VF	UNC
155	**200 FRANCS** 1981-94. Blue-green, yellow and m/c. Figure w/staff at l., Baron de Montesquieu at r. and as wmk. Similar but w/Castle of Labrède on back (Montesquieu's birthplace).			
	a. Sign. P. A. Strohl, J. J. Tronche and B. Dentaud. 1981-86.	FV	FV	65.00
	b. Sign. P. A. Strohl, D. Ferman and B. Dentaud. 1987.	FV	FV	60.00
	c. Sign. D. Ferman, B. Dentaud and A. Charriau. 1988; 1989.	FV	FV	57.50
	d. Sign. D. Bruneel, B. Dentaud and A. Charriau. 1990; 1991.	FV	FV	55.00
	e. Sign. D. Bruneel, J. Bonnardin and A. Charriau. 1992.	FV	FV	50.00
	f. Sign. D. Bruneel, J. Bonnardin and C. Vigier. New Ley (law) on back. 1994.	FV	FV	47.50

		VG	VF	UNC
156	**500 FRANCS** 1968-93. Yellow-brown and dk. brown. Tower of St. Jacques Church in Paris at l., B. Pascal at ctr. B. Pascal at l., abbey of Port Royal on back.			
	a. Sign. G. Bouchet, R. Tondu and H. Morant. 4.1.1968-8.1.1970.	FV	115.00	160.00
	b. Sign. G. Bouchet, P. Vergnes and H. Morant. 5.8.1971-5.9.1974.	FV	110.00	150.00
	c. Sign. G. Bouchet, J. J. Tronche and H. Morant. 5.12.1974-6.11.1975.	FV	FV	135.00
	d. Sign. P. A. Strohl, G. Bouchet and J. J. Tronche. 1.4.1976-7.6.1979.	FV	FV	130.00
	e. Sign. P. A. Strohl, J. J. Tronche and B. Dentaud. 7.6.1979-6.2.1986.	FV	FV	130.00
	f. Sign. P. A. Strohl, D. Ferman and B. Dentaud. 8.1.1987; 22.1.1987; 5.11.1987.	FV	FV	125.00
	g. Sign. of D. Ferman, B. Dentaud and A. Charriau. 3.3.1988-1.2.1990.	FV	FV	125.00
	h. Sign. D. Bruneel, B. Dentaud and A. Charriau. 5.7.1990-2.5.1991.	FV	FV	125.00
	i. Sign. D. Bruneel, J. Bonnardin and A. Charriau. 3.10.1991-7.1.1993.	FV	FV	125.00
	j. Sign. D. Bruneel, J. Bonnardin and C. Vigier. 2.9.1993.	FV	FV	125.00
	s. Specimen. Ovpt. and perforated *SPECIMEN.*	—	—	400.00

1993-97 ISSUE

Many technical anti-counterfeiting devices used on these notes.

		VG	VF	UNC
157	**50 FRANCS** 1992 (1993). Purple and dk. blue on blue, green and m/c unpt. Drawing of *le Petit Prince* at l. Old airplane at top l., topographical map of Africa at ctr., Antoine de Saint-Exupéry at r. and as wmk. Breguet XIV biplane on back. Name as Éxupéry, old law clause on back.			
	a. Sign. D. Bruneel, J. Bonnardin and A. Charriau. 1992.	FV	FV	15.00
	b. Sign. D. Bruneel, J. Bonnardin and C. Vigier. 1993.	FV	FV	15.00
157A	**50 FRANCS** 1994-. As 157 but corrected to Exupéry, new law clause on back.			
	a. Sign. D. Bruneel, J. Bonnardin and C. Vigier. 1994-97.	FV	FV	12.50
	b. Sign. D. Bruneel, J. Bonnardin and Y. Barroux. 1997.	FV	FV	10.00

		VG	VF	UNC
158	**100 FRANCS** 1997; 1998. Deep brown on orange, pink and lt. green unpt. P. Cézanne at r. and as wmk. Painting of fruit at l. on back. Sign. as #157d.	FV	FV	25.00

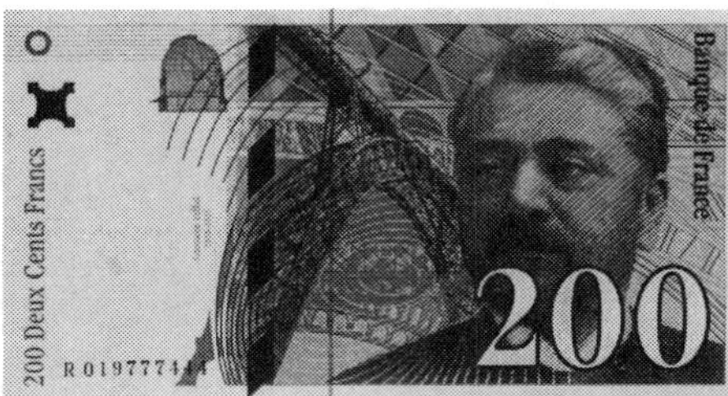

		VG	VF	UNC
159	**200 FRANCS** 1995-. Brown and pink on m/c unpt. G. Eiffel at r. and as wmk., observatory at upper l. ctr., Eiffel tower truss at ctr. View through tower base across exhibition grounds at l. ctr. on back. Sign. as #157c.			
	a. Sign. D. Bruneel, J. Bonnardin and C. Vigier. 1995; 1996.	FV	FV	50.00
	b. Sign. D. Bruneel, J. Bonnardin and J. Barroux. 1996; 1997.	FV	FV	48.50

		VG	VF	UNC
160	**500 FRANCS** 1994-96. Dk. green and black on m/c unpt. M. and P. Curie at ctr. r. Segmented foil strip at l. Laboratory utensils at l. ctr. on back. Wmk: M. Curie. Sign. as #157b.			
	a. 1994-96.	FV	FV	130.00
	b. 1998. Sign. as #157d.	FV	FV	120.00

FRENCH AFARS & ISSAS

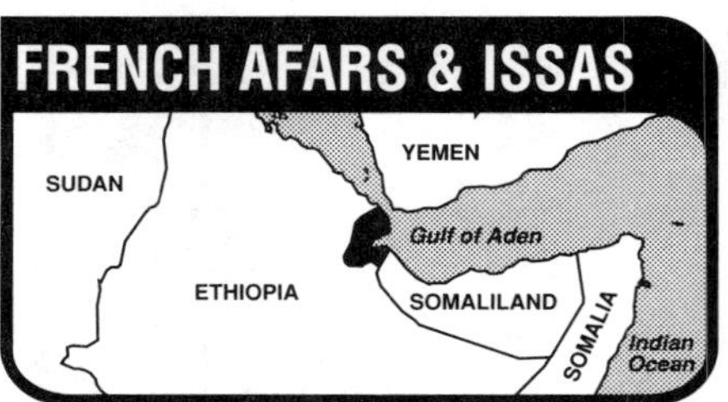

The French Overseas Territory of Afars and Issas (formerly French Somaliland, later to be independent as Djibouti) is located in northeast Africa at the Bab el Mandeb Strait connecting the Suez Canal and the Red Sea with the Gulf of Aden and the Indian Ocean, has an area of 8,494 sq. mi. (22,000 sq. km.) and a population of 542,000. Capital: Djibouti. The tiny nation has less than one sq. mi. of arable land, and no natural resources except salt, sand and camels. The commercial activities of the trans-shipment port of Djibouti and the Addis Ababa-Djibouti railroad are the basis of the economy. Salt, fish and hides are exported.

French interest in former French Somaliland began in 1839 with concessions obtained by a French naval lieutenant from the provincial sultans. French Somaliland was made a protectorate in 1884 and its boundaries were delimited by the Franco-British and Ethiopian accords of 1887 and 1897. It became a colony in 1896 and a territory within the French Union in 1946. In 1958, it voted to join the new French Community as an overseas territory, and reaffirmed that choice by a referendum in March 1967. Its name was changed from French Somaliland to the French Territory of Afars and Issas on July 5, 1967.

The French Tricolor, which had flown over the strategically important territory for 115 years, was lowered for the last time on June 27, 1977, when French Afars and Issas became Djibouti.

NOTE: For later issues see Djibouti.

RULERS:

French to 1977

MONETARY SYSTEM:

1 Franc = 100 Centimes

TRÉSOR PUBLIC, TERRITOIRE FRANÇAIS DES AFARS ET DES ISSAS

1969 ND ISSUE

		VG	VF	UNC
30	**5000 FRANCS** ND (1969). M/c. Aerial view of Djibouti harbor at ctr. Ruins at ctr. on back.	55.00	175.00	425.00

1973; 1974 ND ISSUE

		VG	VF	UNC
31	**500 FRANCS** ND (1973). M/c. Ships at l. ctr. Rearing antelope at ctr. on back.	8.50	20.00	120.00

		VG	VF	UNC
32	**1000 FRANCS** ND (1974). M/c. Woman holding jug at l. ctr. on face. Reversed image as face on back.	16.50	50.00	225.00

1975 ND ISSUE

		VG	VF	UNC
33	**500 FRANCS** ND (1975). M/c. Man at l., rocks in sea, storks at r. Stern of ship at r. on back.	5.00	15.00	60.00

		VG	VF	UNC
34	**1000 FRANCS** ND (1975). M/c. Woman at l., people by diesel passenger trains at ctr. Trader w/camels on back.	8.00	17.50	95.00

		VG	VF	UNC
35	**5000 FRANCS** ND (1975). M/c. Man at r., forest scene at ctr. Aeriel view at ctr. on back.	35.00	65.00	175.00

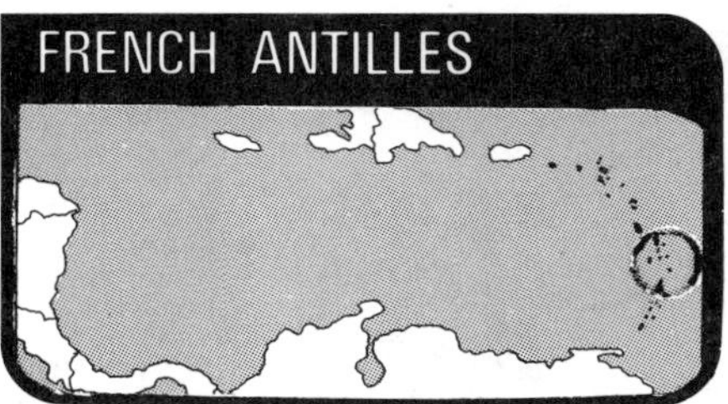

Three French overseas departments, Guiana, Guadeloupe and Martinique which issued a common currency from 1961-1975. Since 1975 Bank of France notes have circulated.

RULERS:
French

MONETARY SYSTEM:
1 Nouveau Franc = 100 "old" Francs
1 Franc = 100 Centimes

FRENCH INFLUENCE

SIGNATURE VARIETIES		
	Le Directeur Général	**Le Président du Conseil de Surveillance**
1	André POSTEL-VINAY	Pierre CALVET 1959-1965
2	André POSTEL-VINAY	Bernard CLAPPIER 1966-1972

INSTITUT D'EMISSION DES DÉPARTEMENTS D'OUTRE-MER

1961 ND PROVISIONAL ISSUE

Nouveau Franc System

#1-3 ovpt: *GUADELOUPE, GUYANE, MARTINIQUE.* Sign. 1.

		VG	VF	UNC
1	**1 NOUVEAU FRANC ON 100 FRANCS** ND (1961). M/c. La Bourdonnais at l. Woman at r. on back.	10.00	40.00	200.00

		VG	VF	UNC
2	**10 NOUVEAUX FRANCS ON 1000 FRANCS** ND (1961). M/c. Fishermen from the Antilles.	35.00	175.00	800.00

		VG	VF	UNC
3	**50 NOUVEAUX FRANCS ON 5000 FRANCS** ND (1961). M/c. Woman w/fruit bowl at ctr. r.	125.00	450.00	1500.

SECOND 1961 ND PROVISIONAL ISSUE

#4, ovpt: *DÉPARTEMENT DE LA GUADELOUPE - DÉPARTEMENT DE LA GUYANE - DÉPARTEMENT DE LA MARTINIQUE.* Sign. 1.

		VG	VF	UNC
4	**5 NOUVEAUX FRANCS ON 500 FRANCS** ND (1961). Brown on m/c unpt. Sailboat at l., 2 women at r. Men w/carts containing plants and wood on back.	35.00	150.00	625.00

INSTITUT D'EMISSION DES DÉPARTEMENTS D'OUTRE-MER RÉPUBLIQUE FRANCAISE

1963 ND ISSUE

#5-10 ovpt: *DÉPARTEMENT DE LA GUADELOUPE - DÉPARTEMENT DE LA GUYANE - DÉPARTEMENT DE LA MARTINIQUE.* Sign. 1.

		VG	VF	UNC
5	**10 NOUVEAUX FRANCS** ND (1963). Brown and green on m/c unpt. Girl at r., coastal scenery in background. People cutting sugar cane on back.			
	a. Issued note.	3.00	15.00	160.00
	s. Specimen.	—	—	125.00

		VG	VF	UNC
6	**50 NOUVEAUX FRANCS** ND (1963). Green on m/c unpt. Banana harvest. Shoreline w/houses at l., man and woman at r. on back.			
	a. Issued note.	12.50	45.00	275.00
	s. Specimen.	—	—	185.00

1964 ND ISSUE

		VG	VF	UNC
7	**5 FRANCS** ND (1964). Like #4, but smaller size.			
	a. Sign. 1.	15.00	40.00	450.00
	b. Sign. 2.	7.50	20.00	250.00

		VG	VF	UNC
8	**10 FRANCS** ND (1964). Like #5.			
	a. Sign. 1.	4.50	18.50	100.00
	b. Sign. 2.	3.00	12.50	75.00
9	**50 FRANCS** ND (1964). Like #6.			
	a. Sign. 1.	10.00	32.50	240.00
	b. Sign. 2.	7.50	22.00	185.00

		VG	VF	UNC
10	**100 FRANCS** ND (1964). Brown and m/c. Gen. Schoelcher at ctr. r. Schoelcher at l. ctr., various arms and galleon around on back.			
	a. Sign. 1.	50.00	100.00	475.00
	b. Sign. 2.	25.00	50.00	285.00

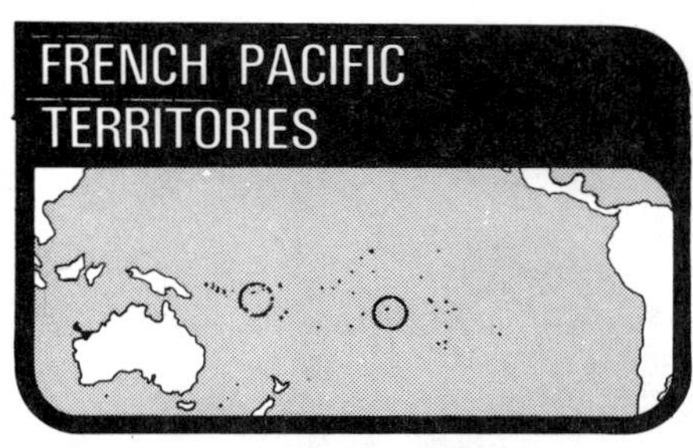

The French Pacific Territories include French Polynesia, New Caledonia and formerly the New Hebrides Condominium. For earlier issues also refer to French Oceania and Tahiti.

INSTITUT D'EMISSION D'OUTRE-MER

1985-96 ND ISSUE

NOTE: For #1 w/ovpt: *NOUMEA* on back see New Caledonia #45.

		VG	VF	UNC
1	**500 FRANCS** ND (1992). M/c. Sailboat at ctr., fisherman at r., Man at l., objects at r. on back.			
	a. 2 sign. W/o security thread. Sign. 2.	FV	FV	15.00
	b. 3 sign. W/security thread. Sign. 3.	FV	FV	12.50
2	**1000 FRANCS** ND (1996). M/c. Hut in palm trees at l., girl at r.			
	a. Sign. 3.	FV	FV	22.50
	b. Sign. 4.	FV	FV	20.00
3	**5000 FRANCS** ND (1996). M/c. Bougainville at l., sailing ships at ctr. Sign. 3.	FV	FV	92.50

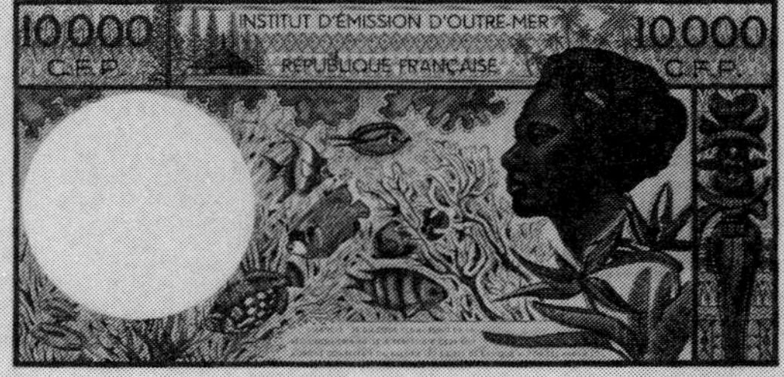

		VG	VF	UNC
4	**10,000 FRANCS** ND (1985). M/c. Tahitian girl w/floral headdress at upper l. topuristic bungalows at ctr. Fish at ctr., Melanesian girl wearing flower at r. on back. Wmk: 2 ethnic heads.			
	a. 2 sign. W/o security thread. Sign. 1.	FV	FV	180.00
	b. 3 sign. W/security thread. (New Ley on back.) Sign. 5.	FV	FV	160.00

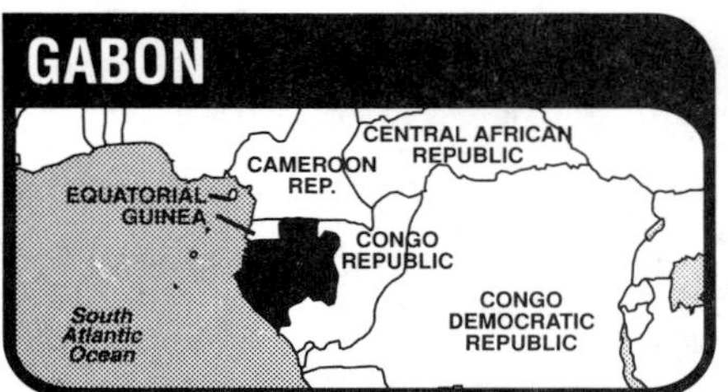

The Gabonese Republic, a member of the French Community, straddles the equator on the west coast of Africa. The hot and humid rain forest country has an area of 103,347 sq. mi. (267,667 sq. km.) and a population of 1.01 million, almost all of Bantu origin. Capital: Libreville. Extravagantly rich in resources, Gabon exports crude oil, manganese ore, gold and timbers.

Gabon was first visited by Portuguese navigator Diego Cam in the 15th century. Dutch, French and British traders, lured by the rich stands of hard woods and oil palms, quickly followed. The French founded their first settlement on the left bank of the Gabon River in 1839 and established their presence by signing treaties with the tribal chiefs. After gradually extending their influence into the interior during the last half of the 19th century, France occupied Gabon in 1885 and, in 1910, organized it as one of the four territories of French Equatorial Africa. It became an autonomous republic within the French Union in 1946, and on Aug. 17, 1960, became a completely independent republic within the new French Community.

NOTE: For related currency, see the Equatorial African States.

MONETARY SYSTEM:

1 Franc = 100 Centimes

SIGNATURE VARIETIES:

Refer to introduction to Central African States.

REPUBLIC

BANQUE CENTRALE

1971 ND ISSUE

		VG	VF	UNC
1	**10,000 FRANCS** ND (1971). M/c. Pres. O. Bongo at r., mask at l., mine elevator at ctr. Statue at l. and r., tractor plowing at ctr. on back. Sign. 1.	40.00	100.00	275.00

BANQUE DES ÉTATS DE L'AFRIQUE CENTRALE

1974 ND ISSUE

		VG	VF	UNC
2	**500 FRANCS** ND (1974); 1978. Lilac-brown on m/c unpt. Woman wearing kerchief at l., logging at ctr. Mask at l., students and chemical testing at ctr., statue at r. on back.			
	a. Engraved. Sign. 6. ND (1974).	1.75	4.50	12.50
	b. Lithographed. Sign. 9. 1.4.1978.	1.10	2.75	8.00

		VG	VF	UNC
3	**1000 FRANCS** ND (1974; 1978); 1978-84. Red and blue on m/c unpt. Ship and oil refinery at ctr., Pres. O. Bongo at r. Mask at l., trains, planes and bridge at ctr., statue at r. on back.			
	a. Sign. 4 w/titles: *LE DIRECTEUR GÉNÉRAL* and *UN CENSEUR.* Engraved. Wmk: Antelope head in half profile. ND (1974).	45.00	125.00	215.00
	b. Like a. Sign. 6.	4.00	10.00	27.50
	c. Sign. 6 w/titles: *LE DIRECTEUR GÉNÉRAL* and *UN CENSEUR.* Lithographed. Wmk. Antelope head in profile. ND (1978).	3.50	9.00	25.00
	d. Sign. 9 w/titles: *LE GOUVERNEUR* and *UN CENSEUR.* Lithographed. Wmk. like b. 1.4.1978; 1.1.1983; 1.6.1984.	3.25	8.00	20.00

		VG	VF	UNC
4	**5000 FRANCS** ND (1974; 1978). Brown. Oil refinery at l., open pit mining and Pres. O. Bongo at r. Mask at l., bldgs. at ctr., statue at r. on back.			
	a. Sign. 4 w/titles: *LE DIRECTEUR GENERAL* and *UN CENSEUR.* ND (1974).	35.00	85.00	210.00
	b. Like a. Sign. 6.	16.50	40.00	110.00
	c. Sign. 9 w/titles: *LE GOUVERNEUR* and *UN CENSEUR.* ND (1978).	10.00	25.00	70.00
	x1. Error. As a. W/o sign.	25.00	60.00	180.00
	x2. Error. As c. W/o sign.	20.00	50.00	155.00

		VG	VF	UNC
5	**10,000 FRANCS** ND (1974; 1978). M/c. Similar to #1 except for new bank name on back.			
	a. Sign. 6 w/titles: *LE DIRECTEUR GÉNÉRAL* and *UN CENSEUR.* ND (1974).	27.50	65.00	130.00
	b. Sign. 9 w/titles: *LE GOUVERNEUR* and *UN CENSEUR.* ND (1978).	20.00	50.00	95.00

1983; 1984 ND ISSUE

		VG	VF	UNC
6	**5000 FRANCS** ND (1984-91). Brown on m/c unpt. Mask at l., woman w/fronds at r. Plowing and mine ore conveyor on back. Sign. 9; 14.			
	a. Sign. 9. (1984).	FV	15.00	35.00
	b. Sign. 14. (1991).	FV	13.50	32.50

		VG	VF	UNC
7	**10,000 FRANCS** ND (1983-91). Brown and green on m/c unpt. Stylized antelope heads at l., woman at r. Loading fruit onto truck at l. on back. Sign. 9; 14.			
	a. Sign. 9. (1984).	FV	27.50	70.00
	b. Sign. 14. (1991).	FV	25.00	65.00

1985 ISSUE

#8-10 wmk: Carving (same as printed on notes).

		VG	VF	UNC
8	**500 FRANCS** 1.1.1985. Brown on orange and m/c unpt. Carving and jug at ctr. Man carving mask at l. ctr. on back. Sign. 9.	1.25	2.25	5.50

		VG	VF	UNC
9	**1000 FRANCS** 1.1.1985. Deep blue on m/c unpt. Carving at l., map at ctr., Pres. O. Bongo at r. Incomplete outline map of Chad at top ctr. Elephant at l., animals at ctr., man carving at r. on back. Sign. 9.	FV	9.50	20.00

1986 ISSUE

		VG	VF	UNC
10	**1000 FRANCS** 1986-91. Deep blue on m/c unpt. Like #9 but w/outline map of Chad at top completed.			
	a. Sign. 9. 1.1.1986; 1.1.1987; 1.1.1990.	FV	7.00	12.50
	b. Sign. 14. 1.1.1991.	FV	6.50	11.50

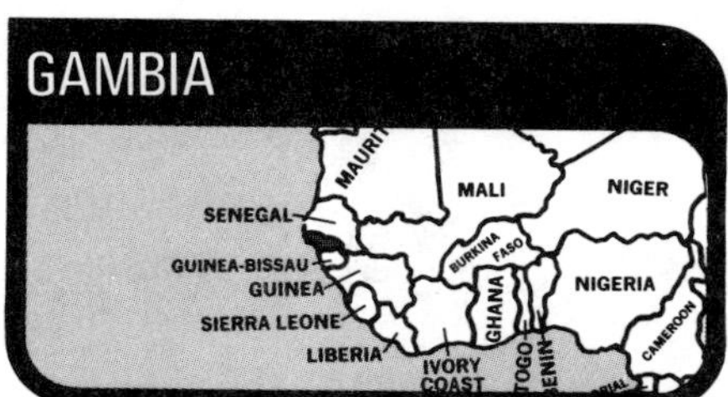

The Republic of The Gambia, an independent member of the British Commonwealth, occupies a strip of land 7 miles (11 km.) to 20 miles (32 km.) wide and 200 miles (322 km.) long encompassing both sides of West Africa's Gambia River, and completely surrounded by Senegal. The republic, one of Africa's smallest countries, has an area of 4,361 sq. mi. (11,295 sq. km.) and a population of 1.09 million. Capital: Banjul. Agriculture and tourism are the principal industries. Peanuts constitute 95 per cent of export earnings.

The Gambia was once part of the great empires of Ghana and Songhay. When Portuguese gold seekers and slave traders visited The Gambia in the 15th century, it was part of the Kingdom of Mali. In 1588 the territory became, through purchase, the first British colony in Africa. English slavers established Fort James, the first settlement, on a small island a dozen miles up the Gambia River in 1664. After alternate periods of union with Sierra Leone and existence as a separate colony, The Gambia became a British colony in 1888. On Feb. 18, 1965, The Gambia achieved independence as a constitutional monarchy within the Commonwealth of Nations, with Elizabeth II as Head of State as Queen of The Gambia. It became a republic on April 24, 1970, remaining a member of the Commonwealth, but with the president as Chief of State and Head of Government.

RULERS:

British to 1970

MONETARY SYSTEM:

1 Shilling = 12 Pence
1 Pound = 20 Shillings to 1970
1 Dalasi = 100 Bututs 1970-

SIGNATURE VARIETIES

1	CHAIRMAN	DIRECTOR	7		
2	GENERAL MANAGER	GOVERNOR	8		
3			9	GENERAL MANAGER	ACTING GOVERNOR
4			10	GENERAL MANAGER	GOVERNOR
5			11		
6			12		

BRITISH INFLUENCE

GAMBIA CURRENCY BOARD

1965 ND ISSUE

Pound System

#1-3 sailboat at l. Wmk. Crocodile's head. Sign. 1.

		VG	VF	UNC
1	**10 SHILLINGS** ND (1965-70). Green and brown on m/c unpt. Workers in field on back.	5.00	12.50	30.00

		VG	VF	UNC
2	**1 POUND** ND (1965-70). Red and brown on m/c unpt. Loading sacks at dockside on back.	8.00	22.50	65.00

		VG	VF	UNC
3	**5 POUNDS** ND (1965-70). Blue and green on m/c unpt. Back blue; man and woman operating agricultural machine at ctr. r.	15.00	35.00	95.00

REPUBLIC

CENTRAL BANK OF THE GAMBIA

1971; 1972 ND ISSUE

Dalasi System

#4-8 sailboat at l., Pres. D. Kairaba Jawara at r. Sign. varieties. Wmk: Crocodile's head.

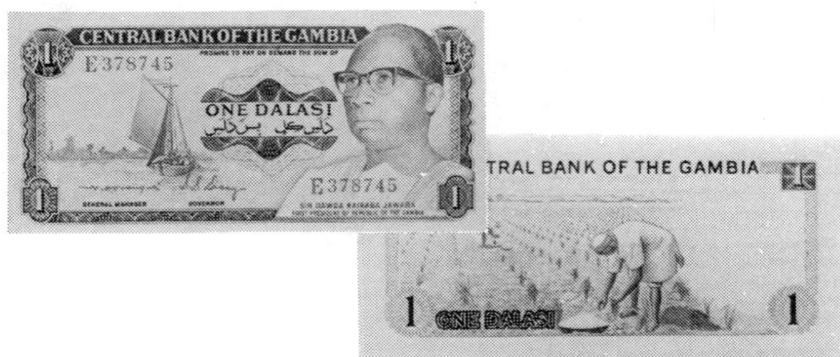

		VG	VF	UNC
4	**1 DALASI** ND (1971-87). Purple on m/c unpt. Back similar to #1.			
	a. Sign. 2.	3.00	10.00	50.00
	b. Sign. 3.	4.50	15.00	60.00
	c. Sign. 4.	1.00	3.00	20.00
	d. Sign. 5.	.50	2.00	10.00
	e. Sign. 6.	.25	.75	2.00
	f. Sign. 7.	.25	.75	2.00
	g. Sign. 8.	.50	2.00	5.00

NOTICE

Readers with unlisted dates, signature varieties, etc. are invited to submit photocopies of their notes to: Standard Catalog of World Paper Money, 700 East State St. Iola, WI 54990-0001, fax: 1-715-445-4087, or E-Mail: thernr@krause.com.

		VG	VF	UNC
5	**5 DALASIS** ND (1972-86). Red on m/c unpt. Back similar to #2.			
	a. Sign. 2.	12.50	30.00	125.00
	b. Sign. 4.	2.00	6.00	25.00
	c. Sign. 6.	1.50	4.00	10.00
	d. Sign. 7.	FV	2.00	5.50

		VG	VF	UNC
6	**10 DALASIS** ND (1972-86). Green on m/c unpt. Fishermen in boat w/net on back.			
	a. Sign. 3.	3.00	12.00	32.50
	b. Sign. 4.	Reported	Not	Confirmed
	c. Sign. 6.	2.25	4.50	12.50
	d. Sign. 7.	1.35	3.50	7.50

		VG	VF	UNC
7	**25 DALASIS** ND (1972-83). Blue on m/c unpt. Back similar to #3 but design is at l. ctr.			
	a. Sign. 2.	35.00	80.00	225.00
	b. Sign. 6.	17.50	40.00	100.00

1978 ND COMMEMORATIVE ISSUE

#8, Opening of Central Bank on 18.2.1978

		VG	VF	UNC
8	**1 DALASI** ND (1978). Purple on m/c unpt. Central bank bldg. on back; commemorative legend beneath. Sign. 5.	4.00	10.00	40.00

1987 ND ISSUE

#9-11 w/line of microprinting under text: *PROMISE TO PAY....* Wmk: Crocodile's head.

		VG	VF	UNC
9	**5 DALASIS** ND (1987-90). Red on m/c unpt. Like #5 but back red and orange.			
	a. Sign. 8.	.75	2.00	6.00
	b. Sign. 10.	.65	1.50	5.50

		VG	VF	UNC
10	**10 DALASIS** ND (1987-90). Green on m/c unpt. Like #6 but back green and lt. olive.			
	a. Sign. 8 w/title: *GOVERNOR* at r.	1.25	3.00	9.00
	b. Sign. 9 w/title: *ACTING GOVERNOR* at r.	1.25	3.00	9.50

		VG	VF	UNC
11	**25 DALASIS** ND (1987-90).Blue on m/c unpt. Like #7 but back blue, black and aqua.			
	a. Sign. 8 w/title: *GOVERNOR* at r.	3.00	8.00	30.00
	b. Sign. 9 w/title: *ACTING GOVERNOR* at r.	3.00	7.00	22.50
	c. Sign. 10.	3.00	6.00	20.00

1989-91 ND ISSUE

#12-15 Pres. Jawara at r. Microprinting of bank name above and below title. Wmk: Crocodile's head.

		VG	VF	UNC
12	**5 DALASIS** ND (1991-95). Red and orange on m/c unpt. Giant Kingfisher at ctr. Herding cattle on back.			
	a. Sign. 10.	FV	FV	2.50
	b. Sign. 11.	FV	FV	2.25

		VG	VF	UNC
13	**10 DALASIS** ND (1991-95). Dk. green, green and olive-green on m/c unpt. Sacred Ibis at ctr. Abuko Earth satellite station at l. ctr. on back.			
	a. Sign. 10.	FV	FV	4.00
	b. Sign. 11.	FV	FV	4.00

		VG	VF	UNC
14	**25 DALASIS** ND (1991-95). Dk. blue-violet, black and blue on m/c unpt. Carmine Bee Eater at ctr. Govt. house at l. ctr. on back. Sign. 10.	FV	FV	8.00

		VG	VF	UNC
15	**50 DALASIS** ND (1989-95). Purple and violet on m/c unpt. Crested birds at ctr. Stone circles at Wassu on back. Sign. 10.	FV	FV	15.00

1996 ND ISSUE

#16-19 backs similar to #12-15. Wmk: Crocodile's head. W/o imprint. Sign. 12. Replacement notes: Serial # prefix *Z*.

		VG	VF	UNC
16	**5 DALASIS** ND (1996). Red, orange and dk. brown on m/c unpt. Giant Kingfisher at ctr., young girl at r. Back like #12.	FV	FV	2.00

17 **10 DALASIS**
ND (1996). Dk. green, bright green and olive-green on m/c unpt. Sacred Ibis at ctr., young boy at r. Back like #13.

VG	VF	UNC
FV	FV	3.50

18 **25 DALASIS**
ND (1996). Deep blue-violet, black and blue on m/c unpt. Carmine Bee Eater at ctr., man at r. Back like #14.

VG	VF	UNC
FV	FV	7.00

19 **50 DALASIS**
ND (1996). Purple and violet on m/c unpt. Crested bird at ctr., woman at r. Back like #15.

VG	VF	UNC
FV	FV	12.50

Georgia (formerly the Georgian Social Democratic Republic under the U.S.S.R.), is bounded by the Black Sea to the west and by Turkey, Armenia and Azerbaijan. It occupies the western part of Transcaucasia covering an area of 26,900 sq. mi. (69,700 sq. km.) and a population of 5.16 million. Capital: Tbilisi. Hydro-electricity, minerals, forestry and agriculture are the chief industries.

The Georgian dynasty first emerged after the Macedonian victory over the Achaemenid Persian empire in the 4th century B.C. Roman "friendship" was imposed in 65 B.C. after Pompey's victory over Mithradates. The Georgians embraced Christianity in the 4th century A.D. During the next three centuries Georgia was involved in the ongoing conflicts between the Byzantine and Persian empires. The latter developed control until Georgia regained its independence in 450-503 A.D. but then it reverted to a Persian province in 533 A.D., Then restored as a kingdom by the Byzantines in 562 A.D. It was established as an Arab emirate in the 8th century. The Seljuk Turks invaded but the crusades thwarted their interests. Over the following centuries Turkish and Persian rivalries along with civil strife divided the area under the two influences.

Czarist Russian interests increased and a treaty of alliance was signed on July 24, 1773 whereby Russia guaranteed Georgian independence and it acknowledged Russian suzerainty. Persia invaded again in 1795 leaving Tiflis in ruins. Russia slowly took over annexing piece by piece and soon developed total domination. After the Russian Revolution the Georgians, Armenians and Azerbaijanis formed the short- lived Transcaucasian Federal Republic on Sept. 20, 1917 which broke up into three independent republics on May 26, 1918. A Germano-Georgian treaty was signed on May 28, 1918, followed by a Turko-Georgian peace treaty on June 4. The end of WW I and the collapse of the central powers allowed free elections.

On May 20, 1920, Soviet Russia concluded a peace treaty recognizing its independence, but later invaded on Feb. 11, 1921 and a soviet republic was proclaimed. On March 12, 1922 Stalin included Georgia in a newly formed Transcaucasian Soviet Federated Socialist Republic. On Dec. 5, 1936 the T.S.F.S.R. was dissolved and Georgia became a direct member of the U.S.S.R. The collapse of the U.S.S.R. allowed full transition to independence and on April 9, 1991 a unanimous vote declared the republic an independent state based on its original treaty of independence of May 1918.

MONETARY SYSTEM:

1 Lari = 1,000,000 'old' Laris, 1995-
1 Lari = 100 Thetri to 1995

REPUBLIC

GEORGIAN NATIONAL BANK

FIRST 1993 *KUPONI* ND ISSUE

#25-32, view of Tbilisi at ctr. r. w/equestrian statue of Kg. V. Gorgosal in foreground, Mt. Tatzminda in background. Cave dwellings at l. ctr. on back. Fractional serial # prefix w/1 as denominator. Wmk: Hexagonal design repeated.

#25-28 w/o ornate triangular design at l. and r. of lg. value in box at l. ctr. on face, or at sides of value at r. on back.

#23 and 24 not used.

25 **5 (LARIS)**
ND (1993). Dull brown on lilac unpt. W/rosettes at sides of value on face and back.

VG	VF	UNC
.05	.20	1.00

26 **10 (LARIS)**
ND (1993). Yellow-brown on lilac unpt.

VG	VF	UNC
.05	.30	1.50

27 **50 (LARIS)**
ND (1993). Lt. blue on lilac unpt.

VG	VF	UNC
.10	.50	1.75

		VG	VF	UN
28	**100 (LARIS)** ND (1993). Greenish gray and lt. brown on lilac unpt.	.15	.75	3.00

		VG	VF	UNC
29	**500 (LARIS)** ND (1993). Purple on lilac unpt.	.20	.75	4.50

		VG	VF	UNC
30	**1000 (LARIS)** ND (1993). Blue-gray and brown on lilac unpt.	.30	1.50	7.50

		VG	VF	UNC
31	**5000 (LARIS)** ND (1993). Green and brown on lilac unpt. Back green on pale brown-orange.	.20	1.00	3.00
32	**10,000 (LARIS)** ND (1993). Violet on lilac and brown unpt.	.60	3.00	15.00

SECOND 1993 *KUPONI* ND ISSUE

#33-38 like #25-28 but w/ornate triangular design at l. and r. of lg. value in box at l. ctr. on face, and at sides of value at r. on back. Fractional serial # prefix w/2 as denominator. Wmk: Hexagonal design repeated.

		VG	VF	UNC
33	**1 (LARIS)** ND (1993). Red-orange and lt. brown on lilac unpt. Similar to #25.	—	.05	.25

		VG	VF	UNC
34	**3 (LARIS)** ND (1993). Purple and lt. brown on lilac unpt. Similar to #25.	.05	.10	.35
35	**5 (LARIS)** ND (1993). Like #25.	.05	.10	.50

		VG	VF	UNC
36	**10 (LARIS)** ND (1993). Like #26.	.05	.10	.75

		VG	VF	UNC
37	**50 (LARIS)** ND (1993). Like #27.	.05	.20	1.25
38	**100 (LARIS)** ND (1993). Like #28.	.10	.50	3.50

THIRD 1993 DATED ISSUE

#39-42 similar to first 1993 issue but fractional serial # prefix w/3 as denominator.

		VG	VF	UNC
39	**10,000 (LARIS)** 1993. Violet on lilac and brown unpt.	.15	.60	3.25
40	**25,000 (LARIS)** 1993. Orange and dull brown on lilac unpt.	.20	1.00	4.50
41	**50,000 (LARIS)** 1993. Pale red-brown and tan on lilac unpt. Back dull red-brown on pale brown-orange unpt.	.20	1.00	4.50

		VG	VF	UNC
42	**100,000 (LARIS)** 1993. Olive-green and brown on lilac unpt. Back pale olive-green on dull brown-orange unpt.	.20	1.00	5.00

FOURTH 1993 DATED ISSUE

#43-46 griffin at l. and r. of ornate round design at ctr. on face. 2 bunches of grapes w/vine above and below value on vertical format back. Wmk: Isometric rectangular design.

		VG	VF	UNC
43	**250 (LARIS)** 1993. Dk. blue on green, lilac and lt. blue unpt.			
	a. W/security thread.	.05	.15	1.25
	b. W/o security thread. (Easily removeable by hand.)	—	—	—

		VG	VF	UNC
44	**2000 (LARIS)** 1993. Green and blue on gold and green unpt.	.10	.50	2.50

		VG	VF	UNC
45	**3000 (LARIS)** 1993. Brown and yellow on lt. brown unpt.	.10	.45	2.25

		VG	VF	UNC
46	**20,000 (LARIS)** 1993; 1994. Purple on lt. red and blue unpt.			
	a. Lg. wmk. 1993.	.10	.50	3.00
	b. W/security foil printing at l. edge of design. Sm. wmk. 1994.	.10	.50	2.75

1994 ISSUE

#47-52 similar to #43-46 but w/security foil printing at l. edge of design. Wmk: Isometric rectangular design repeated.

		VG	VF	UNC
47	**30,000 (LARIS)** 1994. Dull red-brown on pale orange and lt. gray unpt.	.10	.50	2.75

		VG	VF	UNC
48	**50,000 (LARIS)** 1994. Dk. olive-green and dull black on pale olive-green and tan unpt.	.15	.50	2.75

		VG	VF	UNC
48A	**100,000 (LARIS)** 1994. Dk. gray on lt. blue and lt. gray unpt.			
	a. Lg. wmk.	.20	1.00	5.50
	b. Sm. wmk.	.20	1.00	5.00

		VG	VF	UNC
49	**150,000 (LARIS)** 1994. Dk. blue-green on pale blue, lt. gray and lilac unpt.	.20	1.00	5.50

		VG	VF	UNC
50	**250,000 (LARIS)** 1994. Brown-orange on pale orange and lt. green unpt.	.20	.75	3.50

		VG	VF	UNC
51	**500,000 (LARIS)** 1994. Deep violet on pale purple and pink unpt.	.20	1.00	7.50

		VG	VF	UNC
52	**1 MILLION (LARIS)** 1994. Red on pink and pale yellow-brown unpt.	.50	2.25	14.00

1994 PRIVATIZATION CHECK VOUCHER ISSUE

		VG	VF	UNC
52A	VARIOUS DENOMINATIONS 1994. Orange, black and m/c.	—	—	55.00

1995 ISSUE

#57-59 wmk: Griffin.

#53-59 arms at l. to ctr.

		VG	VF	UNC
53	1 LARI 1995. Deep purple on m/c unpt. N. Pirosmani between branches at ctr. View of Tbilisi, painting of deer at ctr. r. on back.	FV	FV	3.00

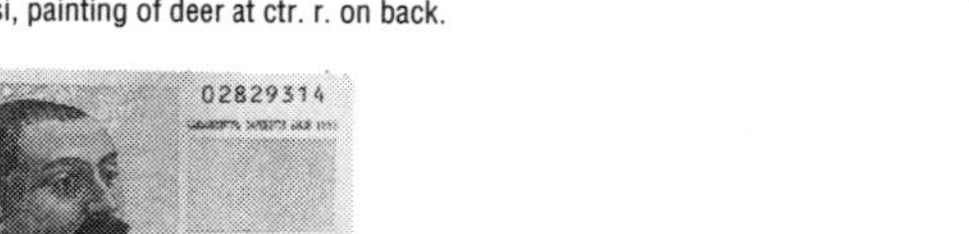

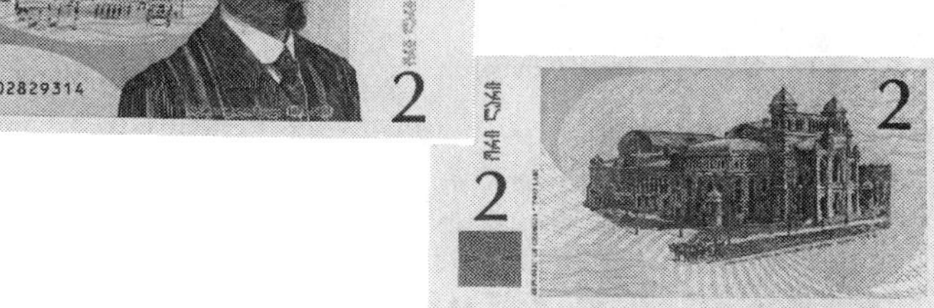

		VG	VF	UNC
54	2 LARI 1995. Deep olive-green on m/c unpt. Bars of music at l., Z. Paliashvili at ctr. r. Opera House in Tbilisi at ctr. r. on back.	FV	FV	5.50

		VG	VF	UNC
55	5 LARI 1995. Brown on m/c unpt. I. Javakhishvili at ctr. Map above ornate lion statue at l. ctr., Tbilisi State University above open book at r.	FV	FV	10.00

		VG	VF	UNC
56	10 LARI 1995. Blue-black on m/c unpt. Flowers at l., A. Tsereteli and swallow at ctr. r. Woman seated on stump while spinning yarn with a crop spindle between ornamental branches at ctr. r. on back. Wmk: Arms repeated vertically.	FV	FV	18.50

		VG	VF	UNC
57	20 LARI 1995. Dk. brown on m/c unpt. Open book and newspaper at upper l., I. Chavchavadze at ctr. Statue of Kg. V. Gorgosal between views of Tbilisi at ctr. r. on back.	FV	FV	35.00

		VG	VF	UNC
58	50 LARI 1995. Dk. brown and deep blue-green on m/c unpt. Griffin at l., Princess Tamara at ctr. r. Mythical figure at ctr. r. on back.	FV	FV	65.00

		VG	VF	UNC
59	100 LARI 1995. Dk. brown, purple and black on m/c unpt. Carved bust of S. Rustaveli at ctr. r. Frieze at upper ctr. r. on back.	FV	FV	125.00
60	500 LARIS 1995. Deep purple on m/c unpt. Kg. David "The Builder" w/bldg. at ctr. Early Georgian inscriptions, cross on back. (Not issued).	—	—	—

REGIONAL

REPUBLIC OF ABKHAZIA

The Republic of Abkhazia is bounded by the Black Sea to the west, on the east by Russia, and Georgia to the southeast. The war between the Georgian and Abkhazia Republics took place June, 1991 to November, 1992.

ABKHAZIAN GOVERNMENT

1991-92 ND PROVISIONAL ISSUE

Soviet rubles circulated in Abkhazia December, 1991 to February, 1992 and also June, 1992 to October, 1992 w/o remarks. Other times they were accepted as general currency, but with parallel circulation notes.

These provisional issues were issued to help the Abkhazia war refugees from Georgian occupied territories.

		VG	VF	UNC
R1	**250 RUBLES** ND(1991-92). Green on white adhesive 25 stamp (Georgian map) on Russia #234.	10.00	15.00	20.00
R2	**250 RUBLES** ND(1991-92). Green on white adhesive 25 stamp (Georgian map) on Russia #234.	10.00	15.00	20.00

		VG	VF	UNC
R3	**500 RUBLES** ND(1991-92). Brown on white adhesive 50 stamp (Georgian map) on Russia #235.	10.00	15.00	25.00

		VG	VF	UNC
R4	**500 RUBLES** ND(1991-92). Brown on white adhesive 50 stamp (Georgian map) on Russia #241.	10.00	15.00	25.00

		VG	VF	UNC
R6	**1000 RUBLES** ND(1991-92). Dk. blue on white adhesive 100 stamp (Georgian map) on Russia #242.	10.00	15.00	25.00

		VG	VF	UNC
R5	**1000 COUPONS** ND(1991-92). Dk. blue on white adhesive 100 stamp (Georgian map) on Russia #236.	10.00	15.00	25.00

NOTICE

Readers with unlisted dates, signature varieties, etc. are invited to submit photocopies of their notes to: Standard Catalog of World Paper Money, 700 East State St. Iola, WI 54990-0001, fax: 1-715-445-4087, or E-Mail: thernr@krause.com.

MILITARY

GEORGIAN MILITARY

These provisional issues were released to the Georgian Military forces in lieu of a salary for personal use only in the garrison's shops, canteens, etc. It was limited special circulation money for buying provisions at reduced garrison prices.

FIRST 1993 ND PROVISIONAL ISSUE

First coupon issue on Georgian #29-32 w/Georgian stamps. These were issued under Georgia's first president, Zviad Gamsakhurdija.

		VG	VF	UNC
M1	**500 COUPONS** ND(1993). Red on white adhesive 0.50 stamp w/*GRUZIJA* on Georgia #29.	15.00	30.00	40.00

		VG	VF	UNC
M2	**1000 COUPONS** ND(1993). M/c adhesive 1.00 stamp w/*GRUZIJA* on Georgia #30.	20.00	35.00	50.00

SECOND 1993 ND PROVISIONAL ISSUE

		VG	VF	UNC
M3	**5000 COUPONS** ND(1993). Red and brown on blue adhesive 0.50 stamp w/GRUZIJA on Georgia #31.	15.00	25.00	35.00

		VG	VF	UNC
M4	**10,000 COUPONS** ND(1993). M/c on brown adhesive 1.00 stamp w/*GRUZIJA* on Georgia #32.	20.00	30.00	45.00

THIRD 1993 ND PROVISIONAL ISSUE

First & Third coupon issues on Georgian #31, 32, 39 w/Georgian stamps, ovpt: denomination.

		VG	VF	UNC
M5	**5000 COUPONS** ND(1993). Red on white adhesive 0.50 stamp w/*GRUZIJA* and ovpt: *5000* on Georgia #31. ND(1993). Red and brown on blue adhesive 0.50 stamp w/*GRUZIJA* and ovpt: *5000* on Georgia #31.	15.00	20.00	30.00

THIRD 1993 ND PROVISIONAL ISSUE

First & Third coupon issues on Georgian #31, 32, 39 w/Georgian stamps, ovpt: denomination.

		VG	VF	UNC
M5	**5000 COUPONS** ND(1993). Red on white adhesive 0.50 stamp w/*GRUZIJA* and ovpt: *5000* on Georgia #31. ND(1993). Red and brown on blue adhesive 0.50 stamp w/*GRUZIJA* and ovpt: *5000* on Georgia #31.	15.00	20.00	30.00

		VG	VF	UNC
M7	**10,000 COUPONS** ND(1993). M/c adhesive 1.00 stamp w/*GRUZIJA* and ovpt: *10000* on Georgia #32 or #39.	15.00	25.00	35.00

		VG	VF	UNC
M8	**10,000 COUPONS** ND(1993). M/c on brown adhesive 1.00 stamp w/*GRUZIJA* and ovpt: *10000* on Georgia #32 or #39.	15.00	20.00	30.00

The Federal Republic of Germany (formerly West Germany), located in north-central Europe, since 1990 with the unification of East Germany, has an area of 137.82 sq. mi. (356,854 sq. km.) and a population of 81.9 million. Capital: Berlin. The economy centers about one of the world's foremost industrial establishments. Machinery, motor vehicles, iron, steel, chemicals, yarns and fabrics are exported.

During the post-Normandy phase of World War II, Allied troops occupied the western German provinces of Schleswig-Holstein, Hamburg, Lower Saxony, Bremen, North Rhine-Westphalia, Hesse, Rhineland-Palatinate, Baden-Wurttemberg, Bavaria and Saarland. The conquered provinces were divided into American, British and French occupation zones. Five eastern German provinces were occupied and administered by the forces of the Soviet Union.

The western occupation forces restored the civil status of their zones on Sept. 21, 1949, and resumed diplomatic relations with the provinces on July 2, 1951. On May 5, 1955, nine of the ten western provinces, organized as the Federal Republic of Germany, became fully independent. The tenth province, Saarland, was restored to the republic on Jan. 1, 1957.

The post-WW II division of Germany ended on Oct. 3, 1990, when the German Democratic Republic (East Germany) ceased to exist and its five constituent provinces were formally admitted to the Federal Republic of Germany. An election Dec. 2, 1990, chose representatives to the united federal parliament (Bundestag), which then conducted its opening session in Berlin in the old Reichstag building.

MONETARY SYSTEM:

1 Deutsche Mark (DM) = 100 Pfennig

FEDERAL REPUBLIC

DEUTSCHE BUNDESBANK

1960 ISSUE

#18-24 portr. as wmk. Replacement notes: Serial # prefix *Y, Z, YA-, ZA-*.

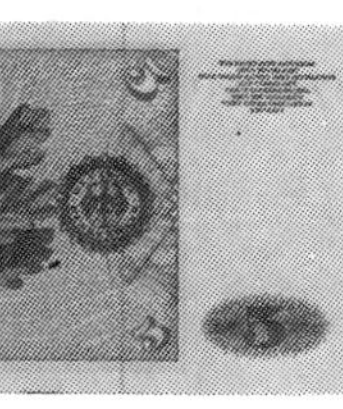

		VG	VF	UNC
18	**5 DEUTSCHE MARK** 2.1.1960. Green on m/c unpt. Young Venetian woman by A. Dürer at r. Oak sprig at l. ctr. on back.	3.50	7.00	30.00
	#19-23 w/ or w/o ultraviolet sensitive features.			
19	**10 DEUTSCHE MARK** 2.1.1960. Blue on m/c unpt. Young man by A. Dürer at r. Sailing ship *Gorch Fock* on back.	7.00	17.50	45.00
20	**20 DEUTSCHE MARK** 2.1.1960. Black and green on m/c unpt. E. Tucher by A. Dürer at r. Violin, bow and clarinet on back.	14.00	25.00	75.00

		VG	VF	UNC
21	**50 DEUTSCHE MARK** 2.1.1960. Brown and olive-green on m/c unpt. Chamberlain H. Urmiller at r. Holsten-Tor gate in Lübeck on back.	35.00	42.50	90.00
22	**100 DEUTSCHE MARK** 2.1.1960. Blue on m/c unpt. *Master Seb. Münster* by C. Amberger at r. Eagle on back.	65.00	80.00	135.00

		VG	VF	UNC
23	**500 DEUTSCHE MARK** 2.1.1960. Brown-lilac on m/c unpt. Male portrait by Hans Maler zu Schwaz. Eltz Castle on back.	FV	400.00	550.00
24	**1000 DEUTSCHE MARK** 2.1.1960. Dk. brown on m/c unpt. Astronomer J. Schöner by Lucas Cranach the Elder at r. Cathedral of Limburg on the Lahn on back.	FV	800.00	950.00

BUNDESKASSENSCHEIN

1960's ND ISSUE

#25, 26, 28 and 29 small change notes. Replacement notes: Serial # prefix 4 petals (+).

		VG	VF	UNC
25	**5 PFENNIG** ND. Black and dk. green on lilac unpt. (Not issued).	—	—	100.00

		VG	VF	UNC
26	**10 PFENNIG** ND. Dk. brown on tan unpt. (Not issued).	—	—	25.00

#27 held in reserve.

		VG	VF	UNC
28	**1 DEUTSCHE MARK** ND. Black and blue on m/c unpt. (Not issued).	—	—	150.00

		VG	VF	UNC
29	**2 DEUTSCHE MARK** ND. Purple and tan on m/c unpt. (Not issued).	—	—	30.00

DEUTSCHE BUNDESBANK (CONT.)

1970-80 ISSUE

#30-36 portr. as wmk. Replacement notes: Serial # prefix *Y, Z, YA-, ZA-*.

		VG	VF	UNC
30	**5 DEUTSCHE MARK** 1970; 1980. Green on m/c unpt. Like #18.			
	a. 2.1.1970.	4.00	7.50	40.00
	b. W/ © *DEUTSCHE BUNDESBANK 1963* on back. 2.1.1980.	FV	5.00	6.00

#31a-34a letters of serial # either 2.8 or 3.3mm in height.

		VG	VF	UNC
31	**10 DEUTSCHE MARK** 1970-80. Blue on m/c unpt. Like #19.			
	a. 2.1.1970.	FV	10.00	32.50
	b. 1.6.1977.	FV	10.00	25.00
	c. W/o © notice. 2.1.1980.	FV	12.50	35.00
	d. W/ © *DEUTSCHE BUNDESBANK 1963* on back. 2.1.1980.	FV	FV	11.00

		VG	VF	UNC
32	**20 DEUTSCHE MARK** 1970-80. Black and green on m/c unpt. Like #20.			
	a. 2.1.1970.	FV	18.50	50.00
	b. 1.6.1977.	FV	22.50	80.00
	c. W/o © notice. 2.1.1980.	FV	FV	60.00
	d. W/ © *DEUTSCHE BUNDESBANK 1961* on back. 2.1.1980.	FV	FV	20.00
33	**50 DEUTSCHE MARK** 1970-80. Brown and olive-green on m/c unpt. Like #21.			
	a. 2.1.1970.	FV	30.00	80.00
	b. 1.6.1977.	FV	FV	45.00
	c. W/o © notice. 2.1.1980.	FV	FV	75.00
	d. W/ © *DEUTSCHE BUNDESBANK 1962* on back. 2.1.1980.	FV	FV	50.00

		VG	VF	UNC
34	**100 DEUTSCHE MARK** 1970-80. Blue on m/c unpt. Like #22.			
	a. 2.1.1970.	FV	65.00	100.00
	b. 1.6.1977.	FV	FV	90.00
	c. W/o © notice. 2.1.1980.	FV	FV	95.00
	d. W/ © *DEUTSCHE BUNDESBANK 1962* on back. 2.1.1980.	FV	FV	90.00
35	**500 DEUTSCHE MARK** 1970-80. Brown-lilac on m/c unpt. Male portr. by H. Maler zu Schwaz at r. Castle Eltz on back.			
	a. 2.1.1970.	FV	FV	400.00
	b. 1.6.1977.	FV	FV	375.00
	c. 2.1.1980.	FV	FV	400.00

		VG	VF	UNC
36	**1000 DEUTSCHE MARK** 1977-80. Dk. brown on m/c unpt. Astronomer J. Schöner by L. Cranach "the elder" at r. and as wmk. Cathedral of Limburg on the Lahn on back.			
	a. 1.6.1977.	FV	FV	800.00
	b. 2.1.1980.	FV	FV	775.00

1989-91 ISSUE

#37-44 replacement notes: Serial # prefix *ZA; YA*.

		VG	VF	UNC
37	**5 DEUTSCHE MARK** 1.8.1991. Green and olive-green on m/c unpt. B. von Arnim at r. Bank seal and Brandenburg Gate in Berlin at l. ctr., script on open envelope at lower r. in wmk. area on back. Sign. Schlesinger-Tietmeyer.	FV	FV	5.00

		VG	VF	UNC
38	**10 DEUTSCHE MARK** 1989-93. Bluish purple and blue. C. F. Gauss at r. Sextant at l. ctr., mapping at lower r. in wmk. area on back.			
	a. Sign. Pöhl-Schlesinger. 2.1.1989.	FV	FV	15.00
	b. Sign. Schlesinger-Tietmeyer. 1.8.1991.	FV	FV	11.00
	c. Sign. Tietmeyer-Gaddum. 1.10.1993.	FV	FV	9.00

		VG	VF	UNC
39	**20 DEUTSCHE MARK** 1991; 1993. Green, black and red-violet on m/c unpt. A. von Droste-Hülshoff at r. Quill pen and tree at l. ctr., open book at lower r. in wmk. area on back.			
	a. Sign. Schlesinger-Tietmeyer. 1.8.1991.	FV	FV	16.50
	b. Sign. Tietmeyer-Gaddum. 1.10.1993.	FV	FV	15.00

		VG	VF	UNC
40	**50 DEUTSCHE MARK** 1989-93. Dk. brown and violet on m/c unpt. B. Neuman at r. Architectural drawing of Bishop's residence in Würzburg at l. ctr., bldg. blueprint at lower r. in wmk. area on back.			
	a. Sign. Pöhl-Schlesinger. 2.1.1989.	FV	FV	50.00
	b. Sign. Schlesinger-Tietmeyer. 1.8.1991.	FV	FV	42.50
	c. Sign. Tietmeyer-Gaddum. 1.10.1993.	FV	FV	37.50

		VG	VF	UNC
41	**100 DEUTSCHE MARK** 1989-93. Deep blue and violet on m/c unpt. C. Schumann at ctr. r. Bldg. at l. in background, grand piano at ctr., multiple tuning forks at lower r. in wmk. area on back.			
	a. Sign. Pöhl-Schlesinger. 2.1.1989.	FV	FV	110.00
	b. Sign. Schlesinger-Tietmeyer. 1.8.1991.	FV	FV	80.00
	c. Sign. Tietmeyer-Gaddum. 1.10.1993.	FV	FV	75.00

		VG	VF	UNC
42	**200 DEUTSCHE MARK** 2.1.1989. Red-orange and blue on m/c unpt. P. Ehrlich at r. Microscope at l. ctr., medical science symbol at lower r. in wmk. area on back. Sign. Pöhl-Schlesinger.	FV	FV	150.00

		VG	VF	UNC
43	**500 DEUTSCHE MARK** 1991; 1993. Red-violet and blue on m/c unpt. M. S. Merian at r. Dandelion w/butterfly and caterpillar at ctr., flower at lower r. in wmk. area on back.			
	a. Sign. Schlesinger-Tietmeyer. 1.8.1991.	FV	FV	375.00
	b. Sign. Tietmeyer-Gaddum. 1.10.1993.	FV	FV	350.00

		VG	VF	UNC
44	**1000 DEUTSCHE MARK** 1.8.1991; 1.10.1993. Deep brown-violet and blue-green on m/c unpt. City drawing at ctr., Wilhelm and Jacob Grimm at ctr. r. Bank seal at l., book frontispiece of "Deutches Wörterbuch" over entry for freedom at l. ctr., child collecting falling stars at lower r. in wmk. area on back.			
	a. Sign. Schlesinger-Tietmeyer. 1.8.1991.	FV	FV	750.00
	b. Sign. Tietmeyer-Gaddum. 1.10.1993.	FV	FV	700.00

1996 ISSUE

#45-47 like #40-42 but w/Kinegram foil added at l. ctr.

		VG	VF	UNC
45	**50 DEUTSCHE MARK** 2.1.1996. Dk. brown and violet on m/c unpt. Diamond-shaped Kinegram foil.	FV	FV	35.00
46	**100 DEUTSCHE MARK** 2.1.1996. Deep blue and violet on m/c unpt. Lyre-shaped Kinegram foil.	FV	FV	68.50
47	**200 DEUTSCHE MARK** 2.1.1996. Red-orange and blue on m/c unpt. Double hexagon-shaped Kinegram foil.	FV	FV	135.00

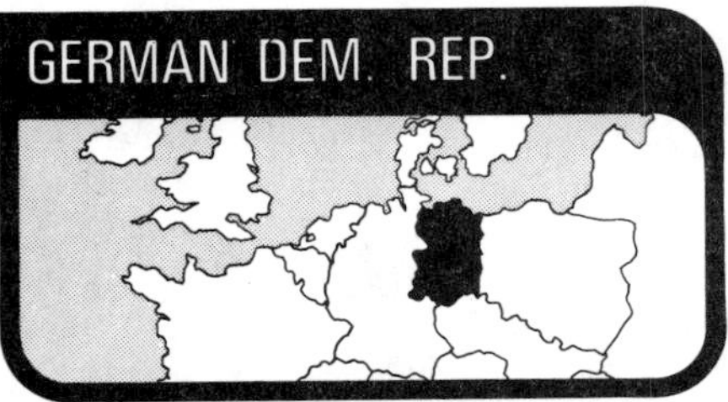

The German Democratic Republic (East Germany), located on the great north European plain ceased to exist in 1990. During the closing days of World War II in Europe, Soviet troops advancing into Germany from the east occupied the German provinces of Mecklenburg, Brandenburg, Saxony-Anhalt, Saxony and Thuringia. These five provinces comprised the occupation zone administered by the Soviet Union after the cessation of hostilities. The other three zones were administered by the U.S., Great Britain and France. Under the Potsdam agreement, questions affecting Germany as a whole were to be settled by the commanders in chief of the occupation zones acting jointly and by unanimous decision. When Soviet intransigence rendered the quadripartite commission inoperable, the three western zones were united to form the Federal Republic of Germany, May 23, 1949. Thereupon the Soviet Union dissolved its occupation zone and established it as the Democratic Republic of Germany, Oct. 7, 1949. East and West Germany became reunited as one country on Oct. 3, 1990.

MONETARY SYSTEM:

1 Mark = 100 Pfennig

DEMOCRATIC REPUBLIC

DEUTSCHE NOTENBANK

1964 ISSUE

#22-26 replacement notes: Serial # prefix *XA-XZ; YA-YZ; ZA-ZZ*.

#22 and 25 arms at l. on back.

#23, 24 and 26 arms at upper ctr. r.

		VG	VF	UNC
22	**5 MARK** 1964. Brown on m/c unpt. A. von Humboldt at r. Humboldt University in Berlin at l. ctr. on back. Wmk: Hammer and compass.	1.25	3.00	8.00

		VG	VF	UNC
23	**10 MARK** 1964. Green on m/c unpt. F. von Schiller at r. Zeiss Factory in Jena at l. ctr. on back. Wmk: Hammer and compass.	3.00	6.00	13.50

		VG	VF	UNC
24	**20 MARK** 1964. Red-brown on m/c unpt. J .W. von Goethe at r. and as wmk. National Theater in Weimar at l. ctr. on back.	2.00	8.50	15.00

		VG	VF	UNC
25	**50 MARK** 1964. Blue-green on m/c unpt. F. Engels at r. and as wmk. Wheat threshing at l. ctr. on back.	5.00	10.00	30.00

		VG	VF	UNC
26	**100 MARK** 1964. Blue on m/c unpt. K. Marx at r. and as wmk. Brandenburg Gate in Berlin at l. ctr. on back.	4.00	12.00	45.00

STAATSBANK DER DDR

1971-85 ISSUE

#27-31 arms at upper l. on face. Arms at l. on back. Portr. as wmk. Replacement notes: Serial # prefix *YA-YI, YZ, ZA-ZQ.*

		VG	VF	UNC
27	**5 MARK** 1975. Purple on m/c unpt. T. Müntzer at r. Harvesting on back.			
	a. 6 digit wide serial #.	.40	1.00	2.50
	b. 6 digit narrow serial #. (1987).	.50	1.25	3.00

		VG	VF	UNC
28	**10 MARK** 1971. Brown on m/c unpt. C. Zetkin at r. Woman at radio station on back.			
	a. 6 digit wide serial #.	.75	1.85	4.50
	b. 7 digit narrow serial #. (1985).	.40	1.00	3.50

		VG	VF	UNC
29	**20 MARK** 1975. Green on m/c unpt. J. W. von Goethe at r. Children leaving school on back.			
	a. 6 digit wide serial #.	.85	2.00	5.00
	b. 7 digit narrow serial #. (1986).	1.25	3.00	7.50

		VG	VF	UNC
30	**50 MARK** 1971. Red on m/c unpt. F. Engels at r. Oil refinery on back.			
	a. 7 digit wide serial #.	1.35	4.50	15.00
	b. 7 digit narrow serial #. (1986).	1.35	3.50	10.00

		VG	VF	UNC
31	**100 MARK** 1975. Blue on m/c unpt. K. Marx at r. Street scene in East Berlin on back.			
	a. 7 digit wide serial #.	1.85	4.50	20.00
	b. 7 digit narrow serial #. (1986).	1.85	4.50	11.00

		VG	VF	UNC
32	**200 MARK** 1985. Dk. olive-green and dk. brown on m/c unpt. Family at r. Teacher dancing w/children in front of modern school bldg. at ctr. on back. Wmk: Dove. (Not issued.)	—	—	75.00

		VG	VF	UNC
33	**500 MARK** 1985. Dk. brown on m/c unpt. Arms at r. and as wmk. Govt. bldg. Staatsrat (in Berlin) at ctr. on back. (Not issued.)	—	—	75.00

FOREIGN EXCHANGE CERTIFICATES

FORUM-AUSSENHANDELSGESELLSCHAFT M.B.H.

1979 ISSUE

Certificates issued by state-owned export-import company. These were in the form of checks for specified amounts for purchase of goods.

1 Mark = 1 DM (West German Mark)

#FX1-FX7 replacement notes: Serial # prefix *ZA, ZB*.

		VG	VF	UNC
FX1	**50 PFENNIG** 1979. Violet on m/c unpt. Back violet and orange.	1.00	3.50	8.50

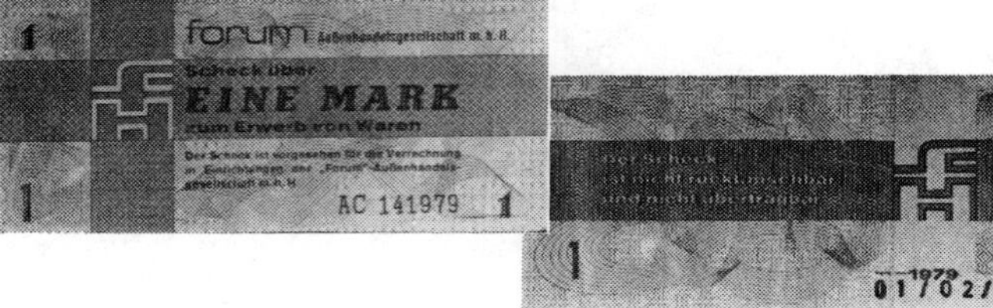

		VG	VF	UNC
FX2	**1 MARK** 1979. Brown and rose.	1.00	2.50	6.00
FX3	**5 MARK** 1979. Green and peach.	1.50	6.00	15.00
FX4	**10 MARK** 1979. Blue and lt. green.	2.00	8.00	20.00
FX5	**50 MARK** 1979. Pinkish red and orange.	3.00	8.00	20.00
FX6	**100 MARK** 1979. Olive and green. Back olive and yellow..	4.00	8.00	20.00
FX7	**500 MARK** 1979. Gray-brown, and purple. Back gray-brown and blue.	15.00	37.50	75.00

COLLECTOR SERIES

STAATSBANK DER DDR

1989 COMMEMORATIVE ISSUE

#CS1, Opening of Brandenburg Gate, 1989

		ISSUE PRICE	MKT. VALUE
CS1 (34)	**22.12.1989 20 MARK** Black and purple on m/c unpt. Brandenburg Gate in Berlin at ctr.	—	675.00

NOTE: As stated on the actual note, #CS1 was never intended to be legal tender.

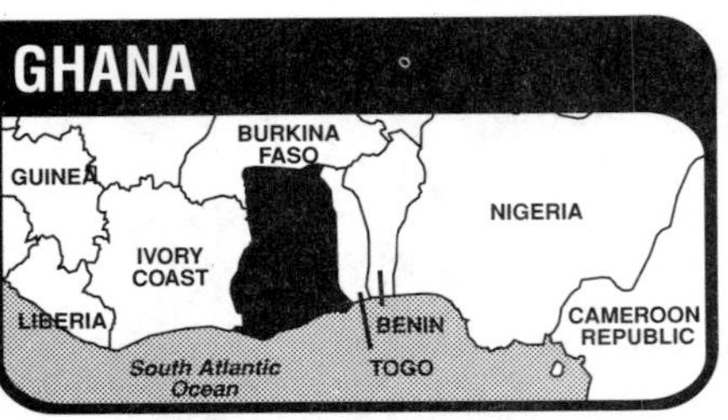

The Republic of Ghana, a member of the British Commonwealth situated on the West Coast of Africa between the Ivory Coast and Togo, has an area of 92,098 sq. mi. (238,537 sq. km.) and a population of 15.6 million, almost entirely African. Capital: Accra. Cocoa (the major crop), coconuts, palm kernels and coffee are exported. Mining, second in importance to agriculture, is concentrated on gold, manganese and industrial diamonds.

Ghana was first visited by Portuguese traders in 1470, and through the 17th century was used by various European powers - England, Denmark, Holland, Germany - as a center for their slave trade. Britain achieved control of the Gold Coast in 1821, and established the colony of Gold Coast in 1874. In 1901, Britain annexed the neighboring Ashanti Kingdom; the same year a northern region known as the Northern Territories became a British protectorate. Part of the former German colony of Togoland was mandated to Britain by the League of Nations and administered as part of the Gold Coast. The state of Ghana, comprising the Gold Coast and British Togoland, obtained independence on March 6, 1957, becoming the first black African colony to do so. On July 1, 1960, Ghana adopted a republican constitution, changing from a ministerial to a presidential form of government. The government was overthrown, the constitution suspended and the National Assembly dissolved by the Ghanaian Army and police on Feb. 24, 1966. The government was returned to civilian authority in Oct. 1969, but was again seized by military officers in a bloodless coup on Jan. 13, 1972. Ghana remains a member of the Commonwealth of Nations, with executive authority vested in the Supreme Military Council.

Ghana's monetary denomination of "cedi" is derived from the word "sedie" meaning cowrie, a shell money commonly employed by coastal tribes.

MONETARY SYSTEM:

1 Shilling = 12 Pence
1 Pound = 20 Shillings to 1965
1 Cedi = 100 Pesewas, 1965-

REPLACEMENT NOTES

#10-16: *Z/99* prefix. #17-22 dated 1979-80: *ZZ* prefix; 1982 date: *XX* prefix. #23-28: *Z/1* prefix.

REPUBLIC

BANK OF GHANA

1958-63 ISSUE

#1-3 various date and sign. varieties. Wmk: *GHANA* in star.

		VG	VF	UNC
1	**10 SHILLINGS** 1958-63. Green and brown. Bank of Ghana bldg. in Accra at ctr r. Star on back.			
	a. 2 sign. Printer: TDLR. 1.7.1958.	2.00	7.50	30.00
	b. W/o imprint. 1.7.1961; 1.7.1962.	1.00	5.00	25.00
	c. 1 sign. 1.7.1963.	.75	3.00	15.00

		VG	VF	UNC
2	**1 POUND** 1958-62. Red-brown and blue. Bank of Ghana bldg. in Accra at ctr. Cocoa pods in 2 heaps on back.			
	a. Printer: TDLR. 1.7.1958; 1.4.1959.	1.25	4.00	20.00
	b. W/o imprint. 1.7.1961; 1.7.1962.	1.00	3.00	15.00

		VG	VF	UNC
3	**5 POUNDS** 1.7.1958-1.7.1962. Purple and orange. Bank of Ghana bldg. in Accra at ctr. Cargo ships, logs in water on back.	6.00	18.00	55.00

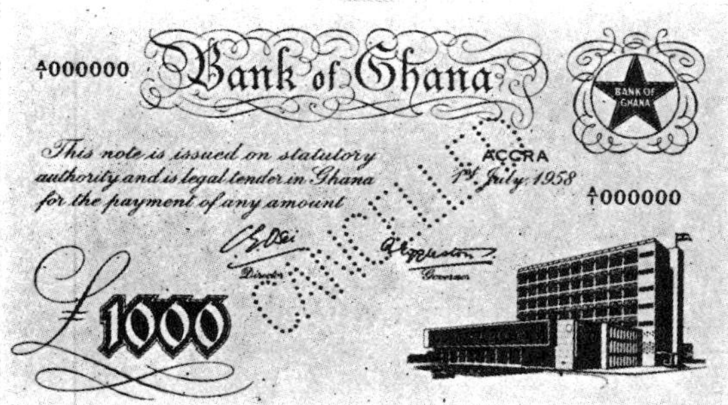

		VG	VF	UNC
4	**1000 POUNDS** 1.7.1958. Blackish brown. Bank of Ghana bldg. in Accra at lower r.	—	85.00	275.00

NOTE: #4 was used in interbank transactions.

1965 ISSUE

#5-9 wmk: Kwame Nkrumah.

		VG	VF	UNC
5	**1 CEDI** ND (1965). Blue on m/c unpt. Portr. K. Nkrumah at upper r. Bank on back.	.75	2.50	7.00

		VG	VF	UNC
6	**5 CEDIS** ND (1965). Dk. brown on m/c unpt. Portr. K. Nkrumah at upper r. Parliament House at l. ctr. on back.	1.00	3.50	8.00

		VG	VF	UNC
7	**10 CEDIS** ND (1965). Green on m/c unpt. Portr. K. Nkrumah at upper l. Independence Square at ctr. on back.	3.00	7.00	17.50

		VG	VF	UNC
8	**50 CEDIS** ND (1965). Red on m/c unpt. Portr. K. Nkrumah at upper l. Island and coconut trees on back.	6.00	15.00	45.00

		VG	VF	UNC
9	**100 CEDIS** ND (1965). Purple on m/c unpt. Portr. K. Nkrumah at upper r. Hospital on back.	12.00	30.00	70.00

		VG	VF	UNC
9A	**1000 CEDIS** ND(1965). Black. Lg. star at upper l. Bank of Ghana bldg. in Accra at r. on back.	—	—	500.00

1967 ISSUE

Various date and sign. varieties.

#10-16 wmk: Arms - Eagle's head above star. Replacement notes: Serial # prefix *Z/99*.

		VG	VF	UNC
10	**1 CEDI** 23.2.1967; 8.1.1969; 1.10.1970; 1.10.1971. Blue on m/c unpt. Cacao tree with pods at r. Shield and ceremonial sword on back.	.50	1.50	5.00

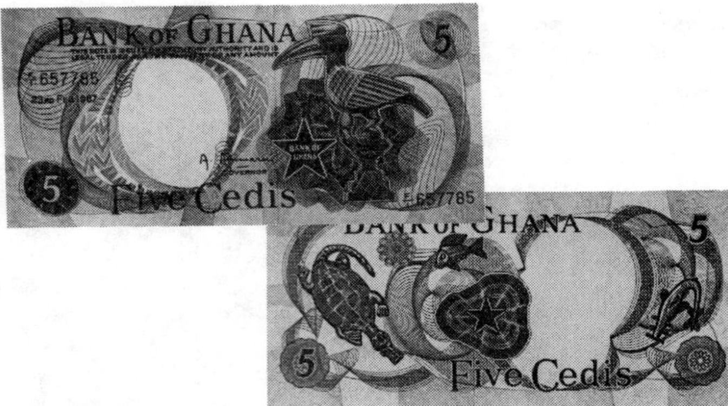

		VG	VF	UNC
11	**5 CEDIS** 23.2.1967; 8.1.1969. Dk. brown on m/c unpt. Wood carving of a bird at r. Animal carvings on back.	2.50	8.00	30.00

		VG	VF	UNC
12	**10 CEDIS** 23.2.1967; 8.1.1969; 1.10.1970. Red on m/c unpt. Art products at r. Small statuettes on back.	3.00	8.00	35.00

1972-73 ISSUE

#13-16 wmk: Arms - Eagle's head above star.

		VG	VF	UNC
13	**1 CEDI** 1973-78. Dk. blue, deep green, and purple on m/c unpt. Young boy w/slingshot at r. Man cutting Cacao pods from tree at l. ctr. on back.			
	a. 2.1.1973.	.25	.75	2.50
	b. 2.1.1975; 2.1.1976.	.15	.45	1.25

NOTE: Date 2.1.1976 has two minor varieties in length of *"2nd"* as part of date.

		VG	VF	UNC
14	**2 CEDIS** 1972-78. Green on m/c unpt. Young man w/hoe at r. Workers in field at l. ctr. on back.			
	a. 21.6.1972. Sign. 1. J. J. Ansah.	.25	.75	2.50
	b. 21.6.1972. Sign. 2. G. Rikes.	.25	.75	2.50
	c. 2.1.1977; 2.1.1978.	.15	.45	1.25

		VG	VF	UNC
15	**5 CEDIS** 1973-78. Brown on m/c unpt. Woman wearing lg. hat at r. Huts on back.			
	a. 2.1.1973; 2.1.1975.	.35	.85	3.00
	b. 2.1.1977; 4.7.1977; 2.1.1978.	.25	.75	1.75

		VG	VF	UNC
16	**10 CEDIS** 1973-78. Red, violet and dk. brown on m/c unpt. Elderly man smoking a pipe at r. Dam on back.			
	a. 2.1.1973. Sign. 1. Serial # prefix *A/1*.	.50	1.50	5.00
	b. 2.1.1973. Sign. 2. Serial # prefix *B/1-*.	.50	1.50	5.00
	c. 2.1.1975.	.50	2.00	7.50
	d. 2.1.1976; 2.1.1977; 2.1.1978.	.25	.75	1.75

1979 ISSUE

#17-22 wmk: Arms - Eagle's head above star. Replacement notes: Serial # prefix *XX; ZZ*.

#17-21, 2 serial # varieties.

		VG	VF	UNC
17	**1 CEDI** 7.2.1979; 6.3.1982. Green and m/c. Young man at r. Man weaving at ctr. r. on back.	.15	.30	1.25

		VG	VF	UNC
18	**2 CEDIS** 7.2.1979; 2.1.1980; 2.7.1980; 6.3.1982. Blue and m/c. School girl at r. Workers tending plants in field at ctr. r. on back.	.20	.50	1.75

19 **5 CEDIS**
7.2.1979; 2.1.1980; 6.3.1982. Red and m/c. Elderly man at r. Men cutting log at l. ctr. on back.

VG	VF	UNC
.25	.75	2.50

20 **10 CEDIS**
7.2.1979; 2.1.1980; 6.3.1982. Purple and m/c. Young woman at r. Fishermen w/long net at l. ctr. on back.

VG	VF	UNC
.50	1.75	6.00

21 **20 CEDIS**
7.2.1979; 2.7.1980; 6.3.1982. Green and m/c. Miner at r. Man weaving at ctr. r. on back.

VG	VF	UNC
.35	1.00	10.00

22 **50 CEDIS**
7.2.1979; 2.7.1980. Brown and m/c. Old man at r. Men splitting cacao pods on back.

VG	VF	UNC
.20	.60	3.50

1983-91 ISSUE

#23-31 Replacement notes: Serial # prefix *Z/1*.

#23-27 arms at top ctr. r.

23 **10 CEDIS**
15.5.1984. Purple and m/c. W. Larbi, F. Otoo, E. Nukpor at l. People going to rural bank at ctr. on back. W/o security thread.

VG	VF	UNC
FV	.25	.75

#24-28 wmk: Arms - Eagle's head above star.

24 **20 CEDIS**
15.5.1984; 15.7.1986. Shades of green and aqua. Qn. Mother Yaa Asantewa at l. Workers and flag procession on back.

VG	VF	UNC
FV	.50	1.75

25 **50 CEDIS**
1.4.1983; 15.5.1984; 15.7.1986. Brown, violet and m/c. Boy w/hat at l. ctr. Drying grain at ctr. on back.

VG	VF	UNC
FV	.60	2.00

NOTICE

Readers with unlisted dates, signature varieties, etc. are invited to submit photocopies of their notes to: Standard Catalog of World Paper Money, 700 East State St. Iola, WI 54990-0001, fax: 1-715-445-4087, or E-Mail: thernr@krause.com.

		VG	VF	UNC
26	**100 CEDIS** 1983-91. Purple, blue and m/c. Woman at l. ctr. Loading produce onto truck at ctr. on back.			
	a. Sign. J. S. Addo. 1.4.1983; 15.5.1984; 15.7.1986.	FV	.75	3.50
	b. Sign. G. K. Agama. 19.7.1990; 19.9.1991.	FV	FV	2.50

		VG	VF	UNC
27	**200 CEDIS** 1983-93. Lt. brown, orange and m/c. Old man at l. ctr. Children in classroom at ctr. on back.			
	a. Sign. J. S. Addo. 1.4.1983; 15.5.1984; 15.7.1986.	FV	1.25	4.00
	b. Sign. G. K. Agama. 20.4.1989; 19.7.1990; 19.9.1991; 14.10.1992; 10.8.1993.	FV	FV	2.50

		VG	VF	UNC
28	**500 CEDIS** 1986-94. Purple and blue-green on m/c unpt. Arms at r. Cacao trees w/cacao pods and miner at ctr. on back.			
	a. Sign. J. S. Addo. 31.12.1986.	FV	2.00	10.00
	b. Sign. G. K. Agama. 20.4.1989; 19.7.1990.	FV	FV	5.00
	c. Sign. as a. 19.9.1991; 14.10.1992; 10.8.1993; 10.6.1994.	FV	FV	3.75

#29-31 arms at lower l. and as wmk. Sign. G. K. Agama.

		VG	VF	UNC
29	**1000 CEDIS** 1991-. Dk. brown, dk. blue and dk. green on m/c unpt. Jewels at r. Harvesting, splitting cacao pods at l. ctr. on back.			
	a. 22.2.1991.	FV	2.00	7.00
	b. Segmented foil security thread. 22.7.1993; 10.6.1994; 6.1.1995; 23.2.1996.	FV	FV	4.50

		VG	VF	UNC
30	**2000 CEDIS** 15.6.1994; 6.1.1995. 23.2.1996. Red-brown, violet and black on m/c unpt. Suspension bridge at r. Fisherman loading nets into boat at l. ctr. on back.	FV	FV	9.00

		VG	VF	UNC
31	**5000 CEDIS** 29.6.1994; 6.1.1995; 23.2.1996. Green and red-orange on m/c unpt. Lg. stars in unpt. at ctr., supported shield of arms at upper r. Map at l. ctr., freighter in harbor at ctr., log flow in foreground on back.	FV	FV	22.00

1996 ISSUE

#32-34 like #29-31 but reduced size.

		VG	VF	UNC
32	**1000 CEDIS** 5.12.1996; 1.12.1997. Dk. brown, dk. blue and dk. green on m/c unpt.	FV	FV	2.50
33	**2000 CEDIS** 5.12.1996. Red-brown, violet and black on m/c unpt.	FV	FV	4.50
34	**5000 CEDIS** 5.12.1996; 1.12.1997. Green and red-orange on m/c unpt.	FV	FV	10.00

COLLECTOR SERIES

BANK OF GHANA

1977 ISSUE

		ISSUE PRICE	MKT. VALUE
CS1	**1977 1-10 CEDIS** #13b, 14c, 15b, 16d. w/ovpt: *SPECIMEN* and Maltese cross prefix serial #.	14.00	25.00

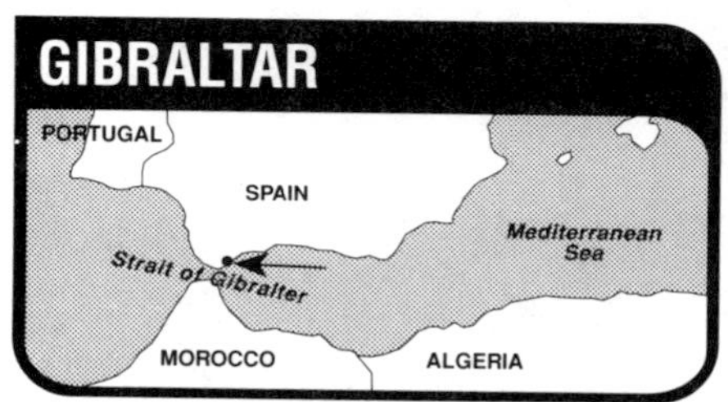

The British Colony of Gibraltar, located at the southernmost point of the Iberian Peninsula, has an area of 2.25 sq. mi. (5.8 sq. km.) and a population of 29,048 Capital (and only town): Gibraltar. Aside from its strategic importance as guardian of the western entrance to the Mediterranean Sea, Gibraltar is also a free port and a British naval base.

Gibraltar, rooted in Greek mythology as one of the Pillars of Hercules, has long been a coveted stronghold. Moslems took it from Spain and fortified it in 711. Spain retook it in 1309, lost it again to the Moors in 1333, and retook it in 1462. After Barbarossa sacked Gibraltar in 1540, Spain strengthened its defenses and held it until the War of the Spanish Succession when it was captured by a combined British and Dutch force, 1704. Britain held it against the Franco-Spanish attacks of 1704-05 and through the historic "Great Siege" of 1779-83. Recently Spain has attempted to discourage British occupancy by harassment and economic devices. In 1967, Gibraltar's inhabitants voted 12,138 to 44 to remain under British rule.

RULERS:

British

MONETARY SYSTEM:

1 Shilling = 12 Pence
1 Pound = 20 Shillings to 1971
1 Pound = 100 New Pence, 1971-

GOVERNMENT OF GIBRALTAR

1934 ORDINANCE; 1958 ISSUE

#17-19 printer: TDLR.

		VG	VF	UNC
17	**10 SHILLINGS** 3.10.1958; 1.5.1965. Blue on yellow-brown unpt. Rock of Gilbraltar at l.	4.50	25.00	175.00

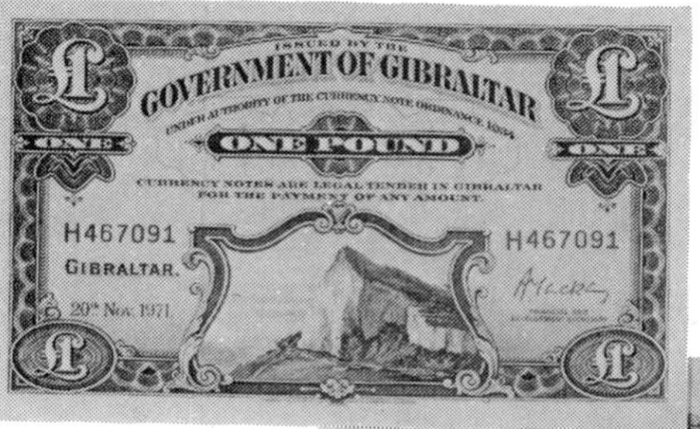

		VG	VF	UNC
18	**1 POUND** 1958-75. Green on yellow-brown unpt. Rock of Gibraltar at bottom ctr.			
	a. Sign. title: *FINANCIAL SECRETARY.* 3.10.1958; 1.5.1965.	2.50	10.00	65.00
	b. Sign. title: *FINANCIAL AND DEVELOPMENT SECRETARY.* 20.11.1971.	2.00	7.50	32.50
	c. 20.11.1975.	3.00	20.00	165.00

		VG	VF	UNC
19	**5 POUNDS** 1958-75. Brown. Rock of Gibraltar at bottom ctr.			
	a. Sign. title: *FINANCIAL SECRETARY.* 3.10.1958; 1.5.1965.	12.50	50.00	275.00
	b. Sign. title: *FINANCIAL AND DEVELOPMENT SECRETARY.* 1.5.1965; 20.11.1971; 20.11.1975.	10.00	30.00	250.00

ORDINANCE CAP 39; 1975; 1986 ISSUE

#20-24 Qn. Elizabeth II at ctr. and as wmk. Sign. varieties. Printer: TDLR.

		VG	VF	UNC
20	**1 POUND** 1975-88. Brown and red on m/c unpt. The Covenant of Gibraltar at l. ctr. on back. 3 sign. varieties.			
	a. 20.11.1975 (1978).	FV	3.00	15.00
	b. 15.9.1979.	FV	2.00	12.50
	c. 10.11.1983.	FV	FV	17.50
	d. 21.10.1986;4.8.1988	FV	FV	5.00

		VG	VF	UNC
21	**5 POUNDS** 1975; 1988. Green on m/c unpt. Back like #20.			
	a. 20.11.1975.	FV	10.00	20.00
	b. 4.8.1988.	FV	FV	17.50

		VG	VF	UNC
22	**10 POUNDS** 1975; 1986. Deep violet, dk. brown and deep blue-green on m/c unpt. Governor's house on back.			
	a. 20.11.1975 (1977).	FV	20.00	50.00
	b. 21.10.1986.	FV	17.50	35.00

		VG	VF	UNC
23	**20 POUNDS** 1975-86. Lt. brown on m/c unpt. Back similar to #22.			
	a. 20.11.1975 (1978).	FV	50.00	225.00
	b. 15.9.1979.	FV	60.00	400.00
	c. 1.7.1986.	FV	FV	67.50

		VG	VF	UNC
24	**50 POUNDS** 27.11.1986. Purple on m/c unpt. Rock of Gibraltar on back.	FV	FV	150.00

1995 ISSUE

#25-28 Qn. Elizabeth at r. and as wmk., shield of arms at l.

		VG	VF	UNC
25	**5 POUNDS** 1.7.1995. Green and purple on m/c unpt. Urn above gateway at l. ctr. Tavik ibn Zeyad w/sword at r., Moorish castle at upper l. on back.	FV	FV	15.00

		VG	VF	UNC
26	**10 POUNDS** 1.7.1995. Orange-brown and violet on m/c unpt. Lighthouse above cannon at l. ctr. Portr. Gen. Eliott at r., scene of "The Great Siege, 1779-85" at upper l. ctr. on back.	FV	FV	30.00

		VG	VF	UNC
27	**20 POUNDS** 1.7.1995. Purple and violet on m/c unpt. Bird above cannon at l. ctr. Portr. Admiral Nelson at r., H.M.S. Victory at upper l. ctr. on back.	FV	FV	55.00

		VG	VF	UNC
28	**50 POUNDS** 1.7.1995. Red and violet on m/c unpt. Gibraltar monkey above horse and carriage at l. ctr. Portr. W. Churchill at upper r., Spitfire airplanes at the North Front, 1942 at upper l. ctr. on back.	FV	FV	125.00

COLLECTOR SERIES

GOVERNMENT OF GIBRALTAR

1975 ISSUE

		ISSUE PRICE	MKT. VALUE
CS1	**1975 1-20 POUNDS** #20a, 21a, 22, 23a. w/ovpt: *SPECIMEN* and serial # prefix: Maltese cross.	14.00	45.00

NOTICE

Readers with unlisted dates, signature varieties, etc. are invited to submit photocopies of their notes to: Standard Catalog of World Paper Money, 700 East State St. Iola, WI 54990-0001, fax: 1-715-445-4087, or E-Mail: thernr@krause.com.

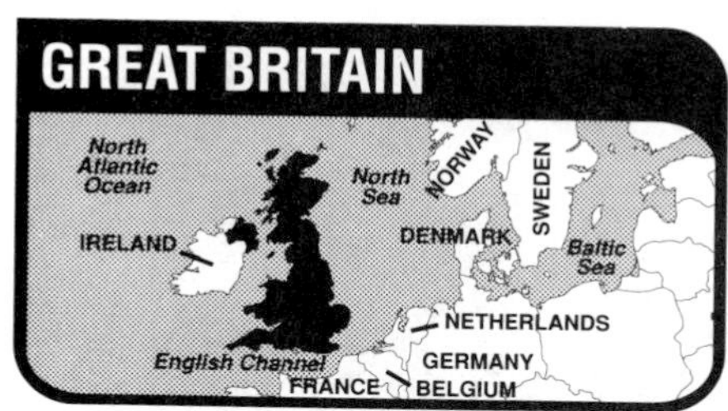

The United Kingdom of Great Britain and Northern Ireland, (including England, Scotland, Wales and Norhtern Ireland) is located off the northwest coast of the European continent, has an area of 94,227 sq. mi. (244,046 sq. km.), and a population of 58.5 million. Capital: London.

The economy is based on industrial activity and trading. Machinery, motor vehicles, chemicals, and textile yarns and fabrics are exported.

After the departure of the Romans, who brought Britain into an active relationship with Europe, Britain fell prey to invaders from Scandinavia and the Low Countries who drove the original Britons into Scotland and Wales, and established a profusion of kingdoms that finally united in the 11th century under the Danish King Canute. Norman rule, following the conquest of 1066, stimulated the development of those institutions which have since distinguished British life. Henry VIII (1509-47) turned Britain from continental adventuring and faced it to the sea - a decision that made Britain a world power during the reign of Elizabeth I (1558-1603). Strengthened by the Industrial Revolution and the defeat of Napoleon, 19th century Britain turned to the remote parts of the world and established a colonial empire of such extent and prosperity that the world has never seen its like. World Wars I and II sealed the fate of the Empire and relegated Britain to a lesser role in world affairs by draining her resources and inaugurating a worldwide movement toward national self-determination in her former colonies.

By the mid-20th century, most of the former British Empire had gained independence and had evolved into the Commonwealth of Nations. This association of equal and and autonomous states, set out to agree views and special relationships with one another (appointing High Commissioners rather than Ambassadors) for mutual benefit, trade interests, etc. The Commonwealth is presently (1999) composed of 54 member nations, including the United Kingdom. All recognize the monarch as Head of the Commonwealth; 16 continue to recognize Queen Elizabeth II as Head of State. In addition to the United Kingdom, they are: Antigua & Barbuda, Australia, The Bahamas, Barbados, Belize, Canada, Grenada, Paupa New Guinea, St. Christopher & Nevis, St. Lucia, St. Vincent & the Grenadines, Solomon Islands.

RULERS:

Elizabeth II, 1952-

MONETARY SYSTEM:

1 Shilling = 12 Pence
1 Pound = 20 Shillings to 1971
1 Pound = 100 New Pence, 1971-

KINGDOM

BANK OF ENGLAND

1957 ND ISSUE

		VG	VF	UNC
371	**5 POUNDS** ND (1957-67). Blue and m/c. Helmeted Britannia hd. at l., St. George and dragon at lower ctr., denomination *£5* in blue print on back. Sign. L. K. O'Brien.	10.00	30.00	50.00
372	**5 POUNDS** ND (1961-63). Blue and m/c. Like #371 but denomination *£5* recessed in white on back.	10.00	30.00	50.00

1960-64 ND ISSUE

#373-376 portr. Qn. Elizabeth II at r.

#373-375 wmk: Laureate heads in continuous vertical row at l.

		VG	VF	UNC
373	**10 SHILLINGS** ND (1960-70). Brown on m/c unpt. Britannia seated w/shield in circle at ctr. r. on back.			
	a. Sign. L. K. O'Brien. (1960-61).	2.00	4.00	12.00
	b. Sign. J. Q. Hollom. (1962-66).	1.50	3.00	10.00
	c. Sign. J. S. Fforde. (1966-70).	1.50	2.50	7.00

		VG	VF	UNC
374	**1 POUND** ND (1960-77). Deep green on m/c unpt. Back similar to #373.			
	a. Sign. L. K. O'Brien. (1960-61).	2.00	4.00	12.00
	b. Sign. as a. Small letter *R* (for Research) at lower l. ctr. on back. (Notes printed on reel-fed web press.) Serial # prefixes A01N; A05N; A06N.	80.00	150.00	250.00
	c. Sign. J. Q. Hollom. (1962-66).	2.00	4.00	9.00
	d. Sign. as c. Letter *G* at lower l. ctr. on back. (Printed on experimental German Goebel Press.)	6.00	15.00	25.00
	e. Sign. J. S. Fforde. (1966-70).	2.00	4.00	8.00
	f. Sign. as e. Letter *G* at lower ctr. on back.	6.00	15.00	25.00
	g. Sign. J. B. Page. (1970-77).	2.00	4.00	7.00

		VG	VF	UNC
375	**5 POUNDS** ND (1963-72). Deep blue on m/c unpt. Britannia seated w/shield in 8-petalled pattern at ctr. on back.			
	a. Sign. J. Q. Hollom. (1962-66).	9.00	17.50	32.50
	b. Sign. J. S. Fforde. (1966-70).	9.00	15.00	30.00
	c. Sign. J. B. Page. (1970-71).	9.00	15.00	30.00

		VG	VF	UNC
376	**10 POUNDS** ND (1964). Deep brown on m/c unpt. Lion facing l. at ctr. on back. Wmk: Qn. Elizabeth II.			
	a. Sign. J. Q. Hollom. (1964-66).	18.00	25.00	50.00
	b. Sign. J. S. Fforde. (1966-70).	18.00	22.50	45.00
	c. Sign. J. B. Page. (1970-77).	18.00	22.50	45.00

1971-82 ND ISSUE

#377-381 Qn. Elizabeth II in court robes at r.

		VG	VF	UNC
377	**1 POUND** ND (1978-82). Deep green on m/c unpt. Back guilloches gray at lower l. and r. corners. Sir I. Newton at ctr. r. on back and in wmk.			
	a. Green sign. J. B. Page. (1978-82).	2.00	3.00	6.00
	b. Back guilloches lt. green at lower l. and r. Black sign. D. H. F. Somerset. (1982-84).	2.00	3.00	5.00

		VG	VF	UNC
378	**5 POUNDS** ND (1971-90). Blue-black and blue on m/c unpt. Duke of Wellington at ctr. r., battle scene of Waterloo at l. ctr. on back and in wmk.			
	a. Blue-gray sign. J. B. Page. (1971-72).	FV	FV	35.00
	b. Black sign. J. B. Page. Litho back w/small *L* at lower l. (1973-82).	FV	FV	27.50
	c. Black sign. D. H. F. Somerset. (1982-88). Thin security thread.	FV	FV	20.00
	d. Sign. D. H. F. Somerset. Thick security thread.	FV	FV	35.00
	e. Sign. G. M. Gill (1988-91).	FV	FV	20.00

		VG	VF	UNC
379	**10 POUNDS** ND (1975-91). Deep brown on m/c unpt. F. Nightingale at ctr. r., hospital scene w/F. Nightingale as the "Lady w/lamp" at l. ctr. on back and as wmk.			
	a. Brown sign. J. B. Page. (1978-82).	FV	20.00	50.00
	b. Black sign. D. H. F. Somerset (1982-88).	FV	FV	50.00
	c. Black sign. D. H. F. Somerset. W/segmented security thread. (1982-88).	FV	FV	50.00
	d. Sign. G. M. Gill (1988-91).	FV	FV	40.00
	e. Sign. G. E. A. Kentfield (1991).	FV	FV	40.00

		VG	VF	UNC
380	**20 POUNDS** ND (1970-91). Purple on m/c unpt. Shakespeare statue at ctr. r. on back.			
	a. Wmk: Qn. Elizabeth II. Sign. J. S. Fforde. (1970).	35.00	70.00	225.00
	b. Wmk. as a. Sign. J. B. Page. (1970-82).	35.00	50.00	90.00
	c. Wmk. as a. Sign. D. H. F. Somerset. (1982-84).	FV	FV	85.00
	d. Wmk: Shakespeare. Modified background colors. Segmented security thread. D. H. F. Somerset. (1984-88).	FV	FV	80.00
	e. Sign. G. M. Gill (1988-91).	FV	FV	80.00

		VG	VF	UNC
381	**50 POUNDS** ND (1981-93). Olive-green and brown on m/c unpt. Wmk: Qn. Elizabeth II at l., w/o imprint. View and plan of St. Paul's Cathedral at l., Sir C. Wren at ctr. r. on back.			
	a. Black sign. D. H .F. Somerset (1981-88).	FV	FV	200.00
	b. Modified background and guilloche colors. Segmented foil on security thread on surface. Sign. G. M. Gill (1988-91).	FV	FV	165.00
	c. Sign. G. E. A. Kentfield (1991-93).	FV	FV	165.00

1990-92 ISSUE

#382-384 Qn. Elizabeth II at r. and as wmk.

		VG	VF	UNC
382	**5 POUNDS** ©1990 (1990-93). Dk. brown and deep blue-green on m/c unpt. Britannia seated at upper l. Rocket locomotive at l., G. Stephenson at r. on back.			
	a. Lt. blue sign. G. M. Gill (1990-91).	FV	FV	20.00
	b. Blue-black sign. G. M. Gill, darker brownish black portr. of Qn. Elizabeth II (1991).	FV	FV	16.00
	c. Like b. Sign. G. E. A. Kentfield (1991).	FV	FV	13.50

		VG	VF	UNC
383	**10 POUNDS** ©1992 (1992-93). Black, brown and red on m/c unpt. Britannia at l. Cricket match at l., Charles Dickens at r. on back. Sign. G. E. A. Kentfield (1992).	FV	FV	26.50

		VG	VF	UNC
384	**20 POUNDS** ©1991 (1991-93). Black, teal-violet and purple on m/c unpt. Britannia at l. Broken vertical foil strip and purple optical device at l. ctr. M. Faraday w/students at l., portr. at r. on back. Serial # olive-green to maroon at upper l. and dk. blue at r.			
	a. Sign. G. M. Gill (1990-91).	FV	FV	55.00
	b. Sign. G. E. A. Kentfield (1991).	FV	FV	52.50

1993 MODIFIED ISSUE

#385-388 Qn. Elizabeth II at r. and as wmk.

		VG	VF	UNC
385	**5 POUNDS** ©1990 (1993-99). Like #382 but w/dk. value symbol at upper l. corner, also darker shading on back.			
	a. Sign. G. E. A. Kentfield (1993).	FV	FV	12.50
	b. Sign. M. Lowther (1999).	FV	FV	12.50

		VG	VF	UNC
386	**10 POUNDS** ©1993 (1993-). Like #383 but w/enhanced symbols for value and substitution of value £10 for crown at upper r. on face. Additional value symbol at top r. on back.			
	a. Sign. G. E. A. Kentfield (1993).	FV	FV	25.00
	b. Sign. M. Lowther (1999).	FV	FV	21.50

		VG	VF	UNC
387	**20 POUNDS** ©1993 (1993-99). Like #384 but w/dk. value symbol at upper l. corner and substitution of value symbol for crown at upper r. corner on face. Additional value symbol at top r. on back.			
	a. Sign. G. E. A. Kentfield (1993).	FV	FV	45.00
	b. Sign. M. Lowther (1999).	FV	FV	40.00

		VG	VF	UNC
388	**50 POUNDS** ©1994 (1994-). Brownish-black, red and violet on m/c unpt. Allegory in oval in unpt. at l. Bank gatekeeper at lower l., his house at l. and Sir J. Houblon at r. on back.			
	a. Sign. G. E. A. Kentfield (1993).	FV	FV	120.00
	b. Sign. M. Lowther (1999).	FV	FV	110.00

1999 Issue

		VG	VF	UNC
389	**5 Pounds** 1999.	Expected New Issue		
390	**10 Pounds** 1999.	Expected New Issue		

		VG	VF	UNC
391	**20 Pounds** © 1999. Brown and purple on red and green unpt. Worchester Cathedral at l., Sir E. Elgar at r. on back. 20 and Britannia in OVD, modified top l. and r. value numerals.	FV	FV	40.00
392	**50 Pounds** 1999.	Expected New Issue		

Military

British Armed Forces, Special Vouchers

NOTE: The Ministry of Defense sold large quantities of remainders including #M32 and M35 w/2-hole punch cancelled w/normal serial # some years ago. Original specimens of #M35 have one punched hole and special serial # 123456 and 789012.

1962 ND Fourth Series

#M30-M36 w/o imprint. (Not issued).

		VG	VF	UNC
M30	**3 Pence** ND (1962). Slate on violet and lt. green unpt. Specimen.	—	Rare	—

		VG	VF	UNC
M31	**6 Pence** ND (1962). Blue on violet and lt. green unpt. Specimen.	—	Rare	—
M32	**1 Shilling** ND. Dk. brown on olive and orange unpt.			
	a. Normal serial #, but w/o punch cancellations.	6.00	25.00	100.00
	b. Cancelled remainder w/2 punched holes.	—	—	3.50
	c. Specimen w/1 punched hole.	—	Rare	—
M33	**2 Shillings - 6 Pence** ND (1962). Red-orange on violet and lt. green unpt. Specimen.	—	Rare	—

		VG	VF	UNC
M34	**5 Shillings** ND. Green on lt. brown unpt. Specimen only.	—	Rare	—

		VG	VF	UNC
M35	**10 Shillings** ND. Violet on blue and green unpt.			
	a. Normal serial # but w/o punch cancellations.	5.00	25.00	125.00
	b. Cancelled remainder w/normal serial # and 2 punched holes.	—	—	5.50
	c. Specimen w/special serial # and 1 punched hole.	—	Rare	—

		VG	VF	UNC
M36	**1 Pound** ND. Violet on pale green and lilac unpt.			
	a. Normal serial #, w/o punch cancellations.	—	—	1.00
	b. Specimen w/special serial # and 1 punched hole.	—	Rare	—

1960s Fifth Series

#M37-M43 known only as specimens.

		VG	VF	UNC
M37	**3 Pence** ND. Red-brown, purple and green. Specimen.	—	Rare	—
M38	**6 Pence** ND. Green, turquoise and lt. brown. Specimen.	—	Rare	—
M39	**1 Shilling** ND. Lilac and green. Specimen.	—	Rare	—
M40	**2 Shillings - 6 Pence** ND. Purple, turquoise and lt. brown. Specimen.	—	Rare	—
M41	**5 Shillings** ND. Blue, red and turquoise. Specimen.	—	Rare	—
M42	**10 Shillings** ND. Orange, green and slate. Specimen.	—	Rare	—
M43	**1 Pound** ND. Olive and red-brown. Specimen.	—	Rare	—

1972 Sixth Series

#M44-M46 printer: TDLR.

		VG	VF	UNC
M44	**5 New Pence** ND (1972). Brown and green.	—	—	2.00

		VG	VF	UNC
M45	**10 New Pence** ND (1972). Violet and green.	—	—	3.00

M46 **50 NEW PENCE**
ND (1972). Green.

	VG	VF	UNC
M46	—	—	4.00

1972 SIXTH SERIES SECOND ISSUE

#M47-M49 printer: BWC.

		VG	VF	UNC
M47	**5 NEW PENCE** ND (1972). Like #M44.	—	—	.40
M48	**10 NEW PENCE** ND (1972). Like #M45.	—	—	.60
M49	**50 NEW PENCE** ND (1972). Like #M46.	—	—	.75

COLLECTOR SERIES

BANK OF ENGLAND

1995 ISSUE

#CS1 and CS2, 200th Anniversary of the First 5 Pound Note

		ISSUE PRICE	MKT. VALUE
CS1	**5 POUNDS** Uncut sheet of 3 notes #385 in folder. Serial #AB16-AB18. Last sheet printing.	68.00	100.00
CS2	**5 POUNDS** Uncut sheet of 3 notes #385 in folder. Serial #AC01-AC03. First web printing.	68.00	100.00
CS4	**5 POUNDS** As #385a w/serial # prefix HK issued commemorating the Return of Hong Kong to the People's Republic of China.		
	a. Single note in a special card.	—	—
	b. Uncut sheet of 12.	—	—
	c. Uncut sheet of 35.	—	—
CS5	**5, 10, 20 POUNDS** As #385b, 386b, 387b w/serial # prefix BE98 with matching numbers. Limited to 1888.	—	100.00
CS3	**10 POUNDS** As #386 w/serial #HM70. 70th Birthday of Queen Elizabeth II. Issued in a case w/£5 Proof coin. 2,000 sets.	—	—

The Hellenic Republic of Greece is situated in southeastern Europe on the southern tip of the Balkan Peninsula. The republic includes many islands, the most important of which are Crete and the Ionian Islands. Greece (including islands) has an area of 50,949 sq. mi. (131,957 sq. km.) and a population of 10.3 million. Capital: Athens. Greece is still largely agricultural. Tobacco, cotton, fruit and wool are exported.

Greece, the Mother of Western civilization, attained the peak of its culture in the 5th century BC, when it contributed more to government, drama, art and architecture than any other people to this time. Greece fell under Roman domination in the 2nd and 1st centuries BC, becoming part of the Byzantine Empire until Constantinople fell to the Crusaders in 1202. With the fall of Constantinople to the Turks in 1453, Greece became part of the Ottoman Empire. Independence from Turkey was won with the revolution of 1821-27. In 1833, Greece was established as a monarchy, with sovereignty guaranteed by Britain, France and Russia. After a lengthy power struggle between the monarchist forces and democratic factions, Greece was proclaimed a republic in 1925. The monarchy was restored in 1935 and reconfirmed by a plebiscite in 1946. The Italians invaded Greece via Albania on Oct. 28, 1940 but were driven back well within the Albanian border. Germany began its invasion on April 6, 1941 and quickly overran the entire country, driving off a British Expeditionary force by the end of April. King George II and his new government went into exile. The German - Italian occupation of Greece lasted until Oct. 1944. On April 21, 1967, a military junta took control of the government and suspended the constitution. King Constantine II made an unsuccessful attempt against the junta in the fall of 1968 and consequently fled to Italy. The monarchy was formally abolished by plebiscite, Dec. 8, 1974, and Greece established as the "Hellenic Republic," the third republic in Greek history.

The island of Crete (Kreti), located 60 miles southeast of the Peloponnesus, was the center of a brilliant civilization that flourished before the advent of Greek culture. After being conquered by the Romans, Byzantines, Moslems and Venetians, Crete became part of the Turkish Empire in 1669. As a consequence of the Greek Revolution of the 1820s, it was ceded to Egypt. Egypt returned the island to the Turks in 1840, and they ceded it to Greece in 1913, after the Second Balkan War.

The Ionian Islands, situated in the Ionian Sea to the west of Greece, is the collective name for the islands of Corfu, Cephalonia, Zante, Santa Maura, Ithaca, Cthera and Paxo, with their minor dependencies. Before Britain acquired the islands, 1809-1814, they were at various times subject to the authority of Venice, France, Russia and Turkey. They remained under British control until their cession to Greece on March 29, 1864.

RULERS:

Paul I, 1947-1964
Constantine II, 1964-1973

MONETARY SYSTEM:

1 Drachma = 100 Lepta

GREEK ALPHABET											
Α	α	Alpha	(ä)	Ι	ι	Iota	(ē)	Ρ	ρ	Rho	(r)
Β	β	Beta	(b)	Κ	κ	Kappa	(k)	Σ	σ	Sigma	(s)6
Γ	γ	Gamma	(g)	Λ	λ	Lambda	(l)	Τ	τ	Tau	(t)
Δ	δ	Delta	(d)	Μ	μ	Mu	(m)	Υ	υ	Upsilon	(o͞o)
Ε	ε	Epsilon	(e)	Ν	ν	Nu	(n)	Φ	φ	Phi	(f)
Ζ	ζ	Zeta	(z)	Ξ	ξ	Xi	(ks)	Χ	χ	Chi	(H)
Η	η	Eta	(ā)	Ο	ο	Omicron	(o)	Ψ	ψ	Psi	(ps)
Θ	θ	Theta	(th)	Π	π	Pi	(p)	Ω	ω	Omega	(ō)

KINGDOM

ΤΡΑΠΕΖΑ ΤΗΣ ΕΛΛΑΔΟΣ

BANK OF GREECE

1964-70 ISSUE

#195-197 wmk: Head of Ephebus.

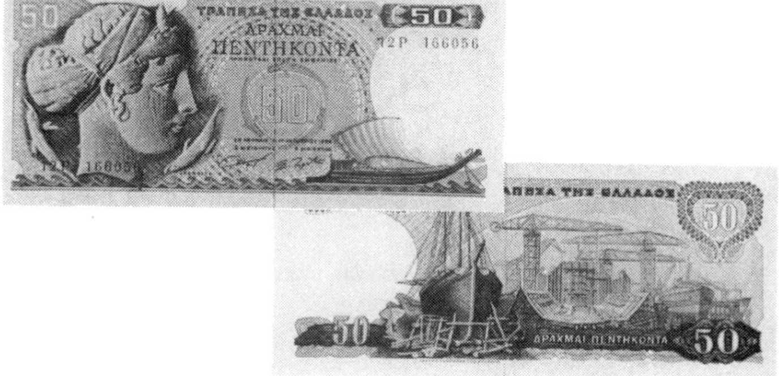

		VG	VF	UNC
195	**50 DRACHMAI** 1.10.1964. Blue on m/c unpt. Arethusa at l., galley at bottom r. Shipyard on back.	.45	.85	2.00

		VG	VF	UNC
196	**100 DRACHMAI** 1966-67. Red-brown on m/c unpt. Demokritos at l., bldg. and atomic symbol at r. University at ctr. on back.			
	a. Sign. Zolotas as Bank President. 1.7.1966.	8.00	20.00	65.00
	b. Sign. Galanis as Bank President. 1.10.1967.	.90	1.50	4.00

		VG	VF	UNC
197	**500 DRACHMAI** 1.11.1968. Olive on m/c unpt. Relief of Elusis at ctr. Relief of animals at bottom l., fruit at bottom ctr. on back.	FV	FV	9.00

		VG	VF	UNC
198	**1000 DRACHMAI** 1.11.1970. Brown on m/c unpt. Zeus at l., stadium at bottom ctr. Back brown and green; woman at l. and view of city Hydra on the Isle of Hydra.			
	a. Wmk: Head of Aphrodite of Knidnidus in 3/4 profile (1970).	FV	20.00	50.00
	b. Wmk: Head of Ephebus of Anticyicythera in profile (1972).	FV	FV	15.00

REPUBLIC

ΤΡΑΠΕΖΑ ΤΗΣ ΕΛΛΑΔΟΣ

BANK OF GREECE

1978 ISSUE

#199 and 200 wmk: Head of Charioteer Polyzalos of Delphi.

		VG	VF	UNC
199	**50 DRACHMAI** 8.12.1978. Blue on m/c unpt. Poseidon at l. Sailing ship at l. ctr., man and woman at r. on back.	FV	FV	1.00

		VG	VF	UNC
200	**100 DRACHMAI** 8.12.1978. Brown and violet on m/c unpt. Athena at l. Back maroon, green and orange; A. Kora at l., Church of Arkadios Convent at bottom r.	FV	FV	1.75

1983-87 ISSUE

#201-203 wmk: Head of Charioteer Polyzalos of Delphi.

		VG	VF	UNC
201	**500 DRACHMAI** 1.2.1983. Deep green on m/c unpt. I. Capodistrias at l. ctr., his birthplace at lower r. Fortress overlooking Corfu on back.	FV	FV	4.50

		VG	VF	UNC
202	**1000 DRACHMAI** 1.7.1987. Brown on m/c unpt. Apollo at ctr. r., ancient coin at bottom l. ctr. Discus thrower and Hera Temple ruins on back.	FV	FV	8.00
203	**5000 DRACHMAI** 23.3.1984. Deep blue on m/c unpt. T. Kolokotronis at l., Church of the Holy Apostles at Calamata at bottom ctr. r. Landscape and view of town of Karytaina at ctr. r. on back.	FV	FV	35.00

1995-98 ISSUE

#204 and 205 wmk: Bust of Philip of Macedonia.

		VG	VF	UNC
204	**200 DRACHMAI** 2.9.1996. Brown-orange on m/c unpt. R. Velestinlis-Ferios at l. Velestinlis-Ferios singing his patriotic song at lower r. Secret school run by Greek priests (during the Ottoman occupation) at ctr. r. on back.	FV	FV	3.25
205	**5000 DRACHMAI** 1.6.1998. Purple and yellow-green on m/c unpt. Similar to #203 but reduced size.	FV	FV	33.50

		VG	VF	UNC
206	**10,000 DRACHMAI** 16.1.1995. Deep purple on m/c unpt. Dr. G. Papanikolaou at l. ctr., microscope at lower ctr. r. Medical care frieze at bottom ctr., statue of Asclepius at ctr. r. on back.	FV	FV	65.00

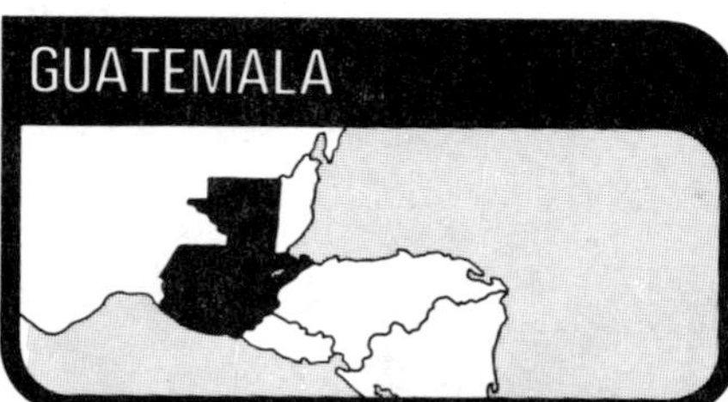

The Republic of Guatemala, the northernmost of the five Central American republics, has an area of 42,042 sq. mi. (108,889 sq. km.) and a population of 11.69 million. Capital: Guatemala City. The economy of Guatemala is heavily dependent on resources which are being developed. Coffee, cotton and bananas are exported.

Guatemala, once the site of the ancient Mayan civilization, was conquered by Pedro de Alvarado, the lieutenant of Cortes who undertook the conquest from Mexico. Skilled in strategy and cruelty, he progressed rapidly along the Pacific coastal lowlands to the highland plain of Quezaltenango where the decisive battle for Guatemala was fought. After routing the Mayan forces, he established the first capital of Guatemala in 1524.

Guatemala of the colonial period included all of Central America but Panama. Guatemala declared its independence of Spain in 1821 and was absorbed into the short-lived Mexican empire of Augustin Iturbide, 1822-23. From 1823 to 1839 Guatemala was a constituent state of the Central American Republic. Upon dissolution of the federation, Guatemala became an independent republic.

MONETARY SYSTEM:

1 Peso = 100 Centavos to 1924
1 Quetzal = 100 Centavos, 1924-

REPUBLIC

BANCO DE GUATEMALA

1957-58 ISSUE

		VG	VF	UNC
35	**1/2 QUETZAL** 22.1.1958. Brown on m/c unpt. Hermitage of Cerro del Carmen at l. Two Guatemalans on back.	3.00	9.00	45.00
36	**1 QUETZAL** 16.1.1957; 22.1.1958. Green on m/c unpt. Palace of the Captains General at l. Lake Atitlan on back.	3.00	6.00	35.00
37	**5 QUETZALES** 22.1.1958. Purple vase (Vasija de Uaxactum)at l. Mayan-Spanish battle scene on back.	8.00	30.00	100.00
38	**10 QUETZALES** 22.1.1958; 12.1.1962; 9.1.1963; 8.1.1964. Red. Round stone carving (Ara de Tikal) at l. Founding of old Guatemala on back.	10.00	50.00	145.00

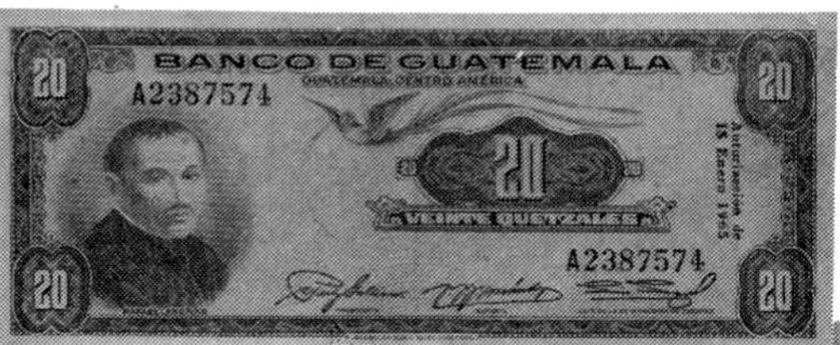

		VG	VF	UNC
39	**20 QUETZALES** 1958(?); 9.1.1963; 8.1.1964; 15.1.1965. Blue. R. Landivar at l. Meeting of Independence on back.	20.00	75.00	235.00

1959-60 ISSUES

#40-50 sign. varieties. Sign. title: *JEFE DE...* at r. Printer: W&S.

		VG	VF	UNC
40	**1/2 QUETZAL** 18.2.1959. Like #29. Lighter brown shadings around value guilloche at l. Printed area 2mm smaller than #41. 6-digit serial #.	2.00	7.00	45.00
41	**1/2 QUETZAL** 18.2.1959; 13.1.1960; 18.1.1961. Similar to #40 but darker brown shadings around value guilloche at l. 7-digit serial #.	1.00	3.00	25.00
42	**1 QUETZAL** 18.2.1959. Green palace. Like #30. Dull green back. 6-digit serial #.	2.00	6.00	45.00
43	**1 QUETZAL** 18.2.1959-8.1.1964. Black and green. Like #42, but black palace. Back bright green. 7-digit serial #.	1.00	4.50	22.50
44	**5 QUETZALES** 18.2.1959. Like #31. Vase in purple.	8.00	25.00	90.00
45	**5 QUETZALES** 18.2.1959-8.1.1964. Similar to #44 but redesigned guilloche. Vase in brown.	5.00	20.00	80.00
46	**10 QUETZALES** 18.2.1959. Like #32. Stone in red.	15.00	40.00	135.00

#	Denomination	VG	VF	UNC
47	**10 QUETZALES** 18.2.1959; 13.1.1960; 18.1.1961. Similar to #46 but redesigned guilloche. Stone in brown.	12.50	30.00	110.00
48	**20 QUETZALES** 13.1.1960-15.1.1965. Blue. Similar to #33, but portr. R. Landivar at r.	20.00	65.00	180.00
49	**100 QUETZALES** 18.2.1959. Dk. blue. Like #34, w/Indio de Nahuala in blue at ctr.	115.00	250.00	500.00

#	Denomination	VG	VF	UNC
50	**100 QUETZALES** 13.1.1960-15.1.1965. Dk. blue. Indio de Nahuala in brown at r.	115.00	250.00	450.00

1964-67 ISSUE

#51-57 sign. varieties. Printer: TDLR.

#	Denomination	VG	VF	UNC
51	**1/2 QUETZAL** 8.1.1964-5.1.1972. Brown on m/c unpt. Hermitage of Cerro del Carmen at l. Two natives at ctr. on back.	1.00	3.00	15.00

#	Denomination	VG	VF	UNC
52	**1 QUETZAL** 8.1.1964-5.1.1972. Black and green on m/c unpt. Palace of the Captains General at ctr. r. Lake Atitlan on back.	1.50	3.50	17.50

#53-57 two wmk. varieties.

#	Denomination	VG	VF	UNC
53	**5 QUETZALES** 8.1.1964-6.1.1971. Purple on m/c unpt. Vase "Vasija de Uaxactum" at r.	3.00	7.50	30.00
54	**10 QUETZALES** 15.1.1965-7.1.1970. Red on m/c unpt. Round carved stone "Arade Tikal" at r. Mayan-Spanish battle scene on back.	8.00	25.00	85.00
55	**20 QUETZALES** 15.1.1965-6.1.1971. Blue on m/c unpt. R. Landivar at r. Founding of Guatemala on back.	17.50	45.00	165.00

#	Denomination	VG	VF	UNC
56	**50 QUETZALES** 13.1.1967-5.1.1973. Orange and blue on m/c unpt. Gen. J. M. Orellana at r. Back orange; bank at ctr.	50.00	165.00	375.00

#	Denomination	VG	VF	UNC
57	**100 QUETZALES** 21.1.1966; 13.1.1967; 3.1.1969; 7.1.1970. Blue-black and brown on pale green and m/c unpt. Indio de Nahuala at r. City and mountain in valley Antihua on back.	75.00	140.00	300.00

1969-75 ISSUE

#58-64 Quetzal bird at upper ctr. Various date and sign. varieties. Printer: TDLR.

#60-64 wmk: Tecun Uman.

#	Denomination	VG	VF	UNC
58	**1/2 QUETZAL** 1972-83. Brown on m/c unpt. Tecun Uman (national hero) at r. Tikal temple on back.			
	a. W/o security (flourescent) imprint. 5.1.1972; 5.1.1973.	.30	1.50	5.00
	b. Security (flourescent) imprint on back. 2.1.1974; 3.1.1975; 7.1.1976; 20.4.1977.	.25	.60	3.50
	c. Date at r. 4.1.1978; 3.1.1979; 2.1.1980; 7.1.1981; 6.1.1982; 6.1.1983.	.20	.50	3.50

#	Denomination	VG	VF	UNC
59	**1 QUETZAL** 1972-83. Green on m/c unpt. Gen. J. M. Orellana at r. Banco de Guatemala bldg. on back.			
	a. Security (flourescent) imprint on face. Date at lower r. 5.1.1972; 5.1.1973.	.50	1.50	5.50
	b. Security imprint as a. on face and back. 2.1.1974; 3.1.1975; 7.1.1976.	.40	1.00	4.50
	c. Date at r. 5.1.1977; 20.4.1977; 4.1.1978; 3.1.1979; 2.1.1980; 7.1.1981; 6.1.1982; 6.1.1983; 30.12.1983.	.35	.60	3.00

#	Denomination	VG	VF	UNC
60	**5 QUETZALES** 1969-83. Purple on m/c unpt. Gen. (later Pres.) J. R. Barrios at r. Classroom scene on back.			
	a. 3.1.1969; 6.1.1971; 5.1.1972; 5.1.1973.	1.25	3.75	17.50
	b. 2.1.1974; 3.1.1975; 7.1.1976; 5.1.1977; 20.4.1977.	1.10	2.50	12.50
	c. Date at r. 4.1.1978; 3.1.1979; 2.1.1980; 7.1.1981; 6.1.1982; 6.1.1983.	1.00	2.00	10.00

#	Denomination	VG	VF	UNC
61	**10 QUETZALES** 1971-83. Red on m/c unpt. Gen. M. G. Granados at r. National Assembly session of 1872 on back.			
	a. 6.1.1971; 5.1.1972; 3.1.1973.	2.50	5.00	30.00
	b. 2.1.1974; 3.1.1975; 7.1.1976; 5.1.1977; 20.4.1977.	2.25	4.50	20.00
	c. 3.1.1979; 2.1.1980; 7.1.1981; 6.1.1982; 6.1.1983.	2.00	3.75	17.00

		VG	VF	UNC
62	**20 QUETZALES** 1972-83; 1988. Blue on m/c unpt. Dr. M. Galvez at r. Granting of Independence to Central America on back.			
	a. 5.1.1972; 5.1.1973.	4.00	7.50	32.50
	b. 2.1.1974; 3.1.1975; 7.1.1976; 5.1.1977; 20.4.1977.	3.75	6.00	25.00
	c. 4.1.1978; 2.1.1979; 2.1.1980; 7.1.1981; 6.1.1982; 6.1.1983.	3.50	5.00	20.00
	d. 6.1.1988.	FV	4.50	18.50

		VG	VF	UNC
63	**50 QUETZALES** 1974; 1981-83. Orange on m/c unpt. C. O. Zachrisson at r. Crop workers on back.			
	a. 2.1.1974.	10.00	18.50	75.00
	b. 7.1.1981; 6.1.1982; 6.1.1983.	9.00	15.00	60.00

		VG	VF	UNC
64	**100 QUETZALES** 1975-83. Brown on m/c unpt. F. Marroquin at r. University of San Carlos de Borromeo on back.			
	a. 5.1.1972.	22.50	37.50	125.00
	b. 3.1.1975; 7.1.1976; 3.1.1979.	20.00	32.50	110.00
	c. 6.1.1982; 6.1.1983.	18.50	30.00	100.00

1983 ISSUE

#65-71 similar to #58-64. Wmk: Tecun Uman. Printer: G&D.

		VG	VF	UNC
65	**1/2 QUETZAL** 6.1.1983-4.1.1989. Brown on m/c unpt. Tecun Uman at r. Tikal temple on back. Similar to #58.	FV	FV	2.00

		VG	VF	UNC
66	**1 QUETZAL** 30.12.1983-4.1.1989. Blue-green and green on m/c unpt. Gen. J. Orellana at r. Banco de Guatemala bldg. on back. Similar to #59.	FV	FV	3.50
67	**5 QUETZALES** 6.1.1983-6.1.1988. Purple on m/c unpt. J. R. Barrios at r. Classroom scene on back. Similar to #60.	FV	FV	7.50

		VG	VF	UNC
68	**10 QUETZALES** 30.12.1983-6.1.1988. Red-violet and red-brown on m/c unpt. Gen. M. G. Granados at r. National Assembly session of 1872 on back. Similar to #61.	FV	3.50	12.50
69	**20 QUETZALES** 6.1.1983-7.1.1987. Blue on m/c unpt. Dr. M. Galvez at r. Similar to #62.	FV	3.00	19.00

		VG	VF	UNC
70	**50 QUETZALES** 30.12.1983-7.1.1987. Orange and yellow-orange on m/c unpt. C. O. Zachrisson at r. Crop workers on back. Similar to #63.	FV	16.50	32.50
71	**100 QUETZALES** 30.12.1983-7.1.1987. Brown on m/c unpt. F. Marroquin at r. Similar to #64.	FV	25.00	55.00

1989; 1990 ISSUE

#72-74 printer: CBN. Sign. varieties.

		VG	VF	UNC
72	**1/2 QUETZAL** 14.2.1992. Brown on m/c unpt. Similar to #65. W/o wmk.	FV	FV	1.50

		VG	VF	UNC
73	**1 QUETZAL** 3.1.1990; 6.3.1991; 22.1.1992; 14.2.1992. Blue-green on m/c unpt. Similar to #66. W/o wmk.	FV	FV	2.00

		VG	VF	UNC
74	**5 QUETZALES** 3.1.1990; 6.3.1991; 22.1.1992. Purple on m/c unpt. Similar to #67.	FV	FV	4.50

#75-78 similar to #68-71. Vertical serial # at l. Wmk: Tecun Uman. Printer: TDLR. Sign. varieties.

		VG	VF	UNC
75	**10 QUETZALES** 3.1.1990; 22.1.1992. Brown-violet and red on m/c unpt. Similar to #68.	FV	FV	7.00

		VG	VF	UNC
76	**20 QUETZALES** 4.1.1989; 3.1.1990; 22.1.1992. Blue-black, purple and blue on m/c unpt. Similar to #69.	FV	FV	12.50

		VG	VF	UNC
77	**50 QUETZALES** 4.1.1989; 3.1.1990. Orange and green on m/c unpt. Similar to #70.	FV	FV	25.00

		VG	VF	UNC
78	**100 QUETZALES** 4.1.1989; 3.1.1990; 22.1.1992. Brown and red-brown on m/c unpt. Similar to #71. Back lilac and m/c.	FV	16.50	40.00

1992 ISSUE

#79-82 similar to #65-68 but more colorful backs. Printer: Oberthur F-CO.

		VG	VF	UNC
79	**1/2 QUETZAL** 16.7.1992. Brown on m/c unpt. Similar to #65.	FV	FV	1.00
80	**1 QUETZAL** 16.7.1992. Blue-green on m/c unpt. Similar to #66.	FV	FV	1.50

		VG	VF	UNC
81	**5 QUETZALES** 16.7.1992. Purple on m/c unpt. Similar to #67.	FV	FV	3.50

#82-85 wmk: Tecun Uman.

		VG	VF	UNC
82	**10 QUETZALES** 16.7.1992. Brown-violet and red on m/c unpt. Similar to #68.	FV	FV	6.00

#83-85 similar to #69-71 but more colorful backs. Printer: BABN.

		VG	VF	UNC
83	**20 QUETZALES** 12.8.1992. Blue-black, purple and blue on m/c unpt. Similar to #69.	FV	FV	10.00
84	**50 QUETZALES** 12.8.1992. Orange and green on m/c unpt. Similar to #70.	FV	FV	22.50

		VG	VF	UNC
85	**100 QUETZALES** 27.5.1992. Brown on m/c unpt. Date at lower l., gold colored device at r. Back lt. brown and m/c. Similar to #71.	FV	FV	35.00

1993; 1995 ISSUE

#86-89 printer: CBNC.

		VG	VF	UNC
86	**1/2 QUETZAL** 27.10.1993; 27.9.1994; 6.9.1995. Brown on m/c unpt. Similar to #79 but w/colorful back.	FV	FV	1.00

		VG	VF	UNC
87	**1 QUETZAL** 27.10.1993; 6.9.1994; 6.9.1995. Dk. green on green and m/c unpt. Similar to #80 but w/colorful back.	FV	FV	1.25

		VG	VF	UNC
88	**5 QUETZALES** 1993; 1995. Purple on m/c unpt. Similar to #81 but w/colorful back.			
	a. 27.10.1993; 16.6.1995.	FV	FV	3.00
	b. W/o imprint. 16.6.1995.	FV	FV	2.75

		VG	VF	UNC
89	**10 QUETZALES** 16.6.1995. Brown-violet and red on m/c unpt. Similar to #82 but w/colorful back. Large and small, printer imprint on back.	FV	FV	5.00

1994 ISSUE

#90 and 91 printer: F-CO.

		VG	VF	UNC
90	**1 QUETZAL** 27.9.1994. Dk. green on green and m/c unpt. Similar to #73 but w/colorful back.	FV	FV	1.00
91	**10 QUETZALES** 29.6.1994. Brown-violet and red on m/c unpt. Similar to #75 but w/colorful back.	FV	FV	4.50

1994; 1995 ISSUE

#92-94 Printer: TDLR.

		VG	VF	UNC
92	**5 QUETZALES** 29.6.1994. Purple on m/c unpt. Similar to #74 but w/colorful back.	FV	FV	2.50

		VG	VF	UNC
93	**50 QUETZALES** 16.6.1995. Orange and green on m/c unpt. Similar to #77 but w/colorful back.	FV	FV	15.00

		VG	VF	UNC
94	**100 QUETZALES** 29.6.1994; 16.6.1995. Brown on m/c unpt. Similar to #78 but w/colorful back.	FV	FV	30.00

1995 ISSUE

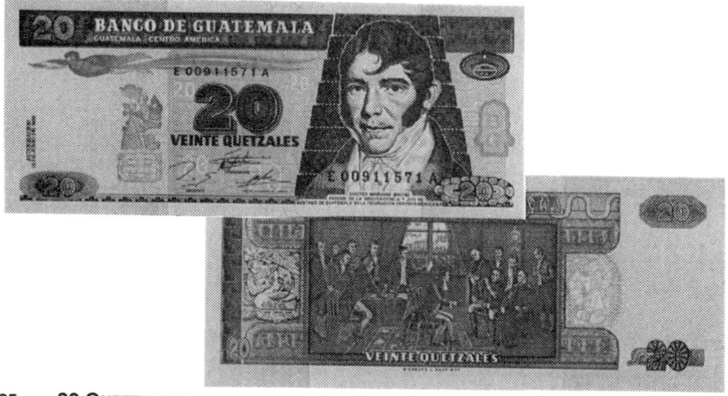

		VG	VF	UNC
95	**20 QUETZALES** 16.6.1995. Blue-black, purple and blue on m/c unpt. Similar to #69 but w/colorful back. Printer: G&D.	FV	FV	7.50

1996 ISSUE

		VG	VF	UNC
96	**1/2 QUETZAL** 28.8.1996. Brown on m/c unpt. Similar to #86. Printer: H&S.	FV	FV	.75
97	**1 QUETZAL** 28.8.1996.	FV	FV	1.50

1998 ISSUE

#97 and 98 printer: DLR.

		VG	VF	UNC
98	**1/2 QUETZAL** 9.1.1998. Brown on m/c unpt. Similar to #96.	FV	FV	.75
99	**1 QUETZAL** 9.1.1998. Dk. green and green on m/c unpt. Similar to #90.	FV	FV	1.00

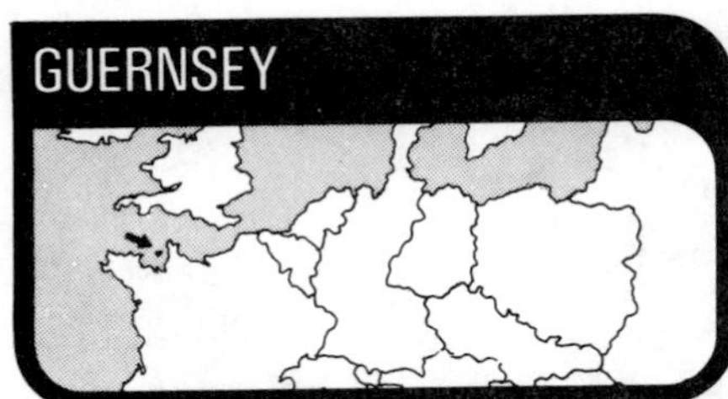

The Bailiwick of Guernsey, a British crown dependency located in the English Channel 30 miles (48 km.) west of Normandy, France, has an area of 30 sq. mi. (78 sq. km.), including the Isles of Alderney, Jethou, Herm, Brechou and Sark, and a population of 53,794. Capital: St. Peter Port. Agriculture and cattle breeding are the main occupations.

Militant monks from the Duchy of Normandy established the first permanent settlements on Guernsey prior to the Norman invasion of England, but the prevalence of prehistoric monuments suggests an earlier occupancy. The island, the only part of the Duchy of Normandy belonging to the British crown, has been a possession of Britain since the Norman Conquest of 1066. During the Anglo-French Wars, the harbors of Guernsey were employed in the building and outfitting of ships for the English privateers preying on French shipping. Guernsey is administered by its own laws and customs. Acts passed by the British Parliament are not applicable to Guernsey unless the island is specifically mentioned. During World War II, German troops occupied the island from 1940 to 1944.

United Kingdom bank notes and coinage circulate concurrently with Guernsey money as legal tender.

RULERS:

British to 1940, 1944-

MONETARY SYSTEM:

1 Penny = 8 Doubles
1 Shilling = 12 Pence
1 Pound = 20 Shillings to 1971
1 Pound = 100 New Pence 1971-

STATES OF GUERNSEY

1945; 1956 ISSUE

#42-44 printer: PBC.

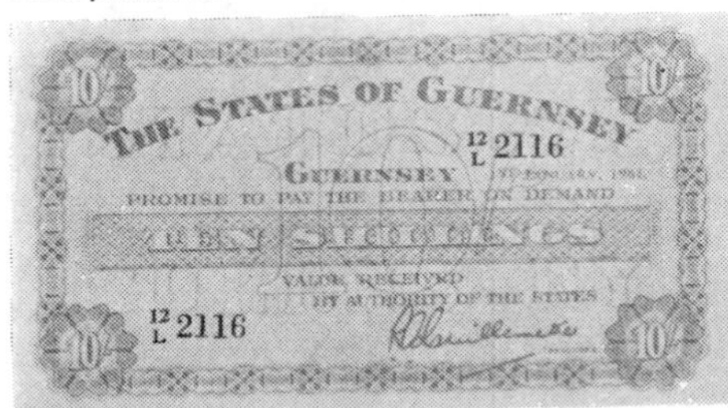

		VG	VF	UNC
42	**10 SHILLINGS** 1945-66. Lilac on lt. green unpt. Back purple.			
	a. 1.8.1945-1.9.1957.	20.00	75.00	300.00
	b. 1.7.1958-1.3.1965.	6.00	50.00	120.00
	c. 1.7.1966.	7.50	25.00	85.00

		VG	VF	UNC
43	**1 POUND** 1945-66. Purple on green unpt. Harbor entrance across ctr. Back green.			
	a. 1.8.1945-1.3.1957.	10.00	60.00	450.00
	b. 1.9.1957-1.3.1962; 1.6.1963; 1.3.1965.	7.50	60.00	250.00
	c. 1.7.1966.	8.00	30.00	125.00

		VG	VF	UNC
44	**5 POUNDS** 1.12.1956; 1.3.1965; 1.7.1966. Green and blue. Flowers at l.	60.00	300.00	750.00

1969; 1975 ND ISSUE

#45-47 printer: BWC. Replacement notes: Serial # prefix *Z*.

		VG	VF	UNC
45	**1 POUND** ND (1969-75). Olive on pink and yellow unpt. Arms at ctr. Castle Cornet on back.			
	a. Sign. Guillemette.	2.00	5.50	45.00
	b. Sign. Hodder.	2.00	5.00	25.00
	c. Sign. Bull.	2.00	4.50	20.00

		VG	VF	UNC
46	**5 POUNDS** ND (1969-75). Purple on lt. brown unpt. Arms at r. City view and harbor wall on back.			
	a. Sign. Guillemette.	10.00	30.00	175.00
	b. Sign. Hodder.	9.00	25.00	110.00
	c. Sign. Bull.	9.00	20.00	80.00

		VG	VF	UNC
47	**10 POUNDS** ND (1975-80). Blue, green and m/c. Britannia w/lion and shield at l. Sir I. Brock and Battle of Queenston Hgts. on blue back. Sign. Hodder.	20.00	75.00	265.00

1980 ND ISSUE

#48-51 Guernsey States seal at lower l. on face and as wmk. Printer: BWC. Replacement notes: Serial # prefix *Z*.

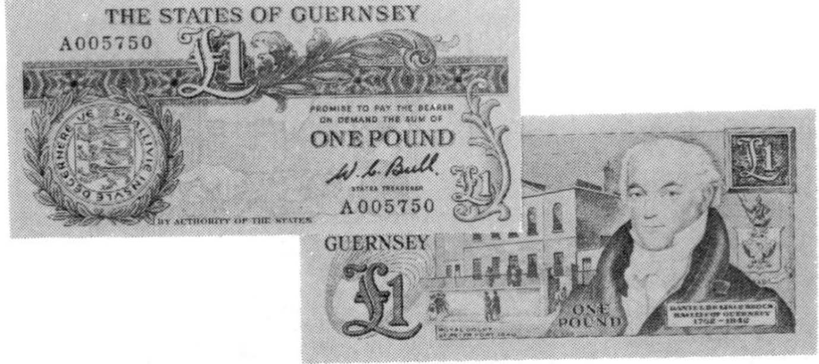

		VG	VF	UNC
48	**1 POUND** ND (1980-89). Dk. green and black on m/c unpt. Market square scene of 1822 at lower ctr. in unpt. D. De Lisle Brock and Royal Court of St. Peter Port on back. 135 x 67mm.			
	a. Black sign. W. C. Bull.	FV	3.00	6.00
	b. Sign. M. J. Brown.	FV	3.00	6.00

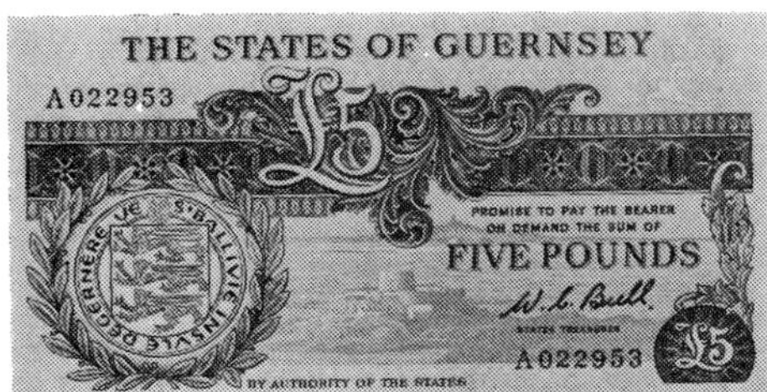

		VG	VF	UNC
49	**5 POUNDS** ND (1980-89). Purple, dk. brown and olive-brown on m/c unpt. Fort Grey at lower ctr. in unpt. T. De La Rue and Fountain St. at ctr., workers at envelope making machine at lower r. on back. Black sign. W. C. Bull. 146 x 78mm.	FV	9.00	22.50

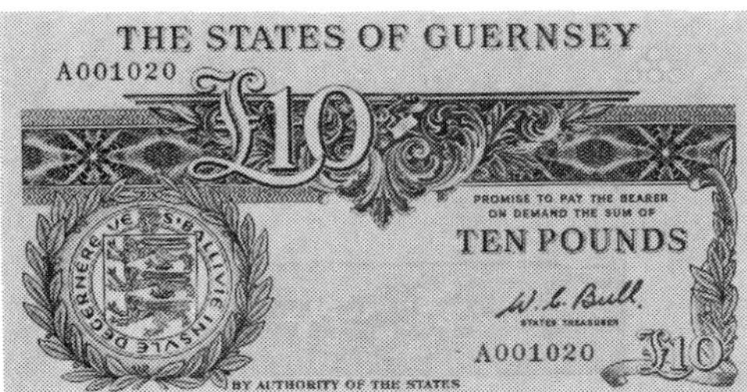

		VG	VF	UNC
50	**10 POUNDS** ND (1980-89). Purple, blue and blue-black on m/c unpt. Castle Cornet at lower ctr. Maj. Sir Isaac Brock and battle of Queenston Hgts. on back. 151 x 85mm.			
	a. Black sign. W. C. Bull.	FV	18.50	60.00
	b. Sign. M. J. Brown.	FV	17.50	45.00

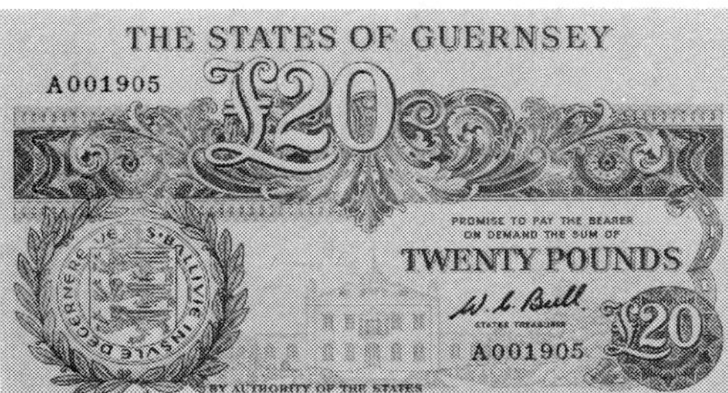

		VG	VF	UNC
51	**20 POUNDS** ND (1980-89). Red, red-violet, brown and orange on m/c unpt. 1815 scene of Saumarez Park at lower ctr. in unpt. Adm. Lord de Saumarez and ships on back. 161 x 90mm.			
	a. Black sign. W. C. Bull.	FV	37.50	100.00
	b. Sign. M. J. Brown.	FV	35.00	90.00

1990; 1991 ND ISSUE

#52-55 similar to #48-51 but reduced size. Wmk: Guernsey States seal. Printer: (T)DLR. Replacement notes: Serial # prefix *Z*.

		VG	VF	UNC
52	**1 POUND** ND (ca.1991-). Dk. green and black on m/c unpt. Similar to #48. 128 x 65mm.			
	a. Green sign. M. J. Brown.	FV	FV	4.00
	b. Sign. D. P. Trestain.	FV	FV	3.50

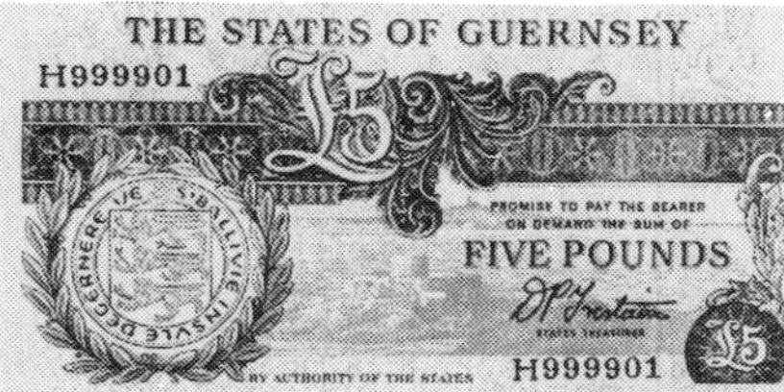

		VG	VF	UNC
53	**5 POUNDS** ND (1990-95). Purple, dk. brown and olive-brown on m/c unpt. Similar to #49. 136 x 70mm.			
	a. Brown sign. M. J. Brown.	FV	FV	15.00
	b. Sign. D. P. Trestain.	FV	FV	13.50
54	**10 POUNDS** ND (ca.1991-95). Purple, blue and blue-black on m/c unpt. Similar to #50. 142 x 75mm.			
	a. Blue sign. M. J. Brown.	FV	FV	30.00
	b. Sign. D. P. Trestain.	FV	FV	30.00

		VG	VF	UNC
55	**20 POUNDS** ND (ca.1991-95). Red, red-violet, brown and orange on m/c unpt. Similar to #51. 149 x 80mm.			
	a. Red-orange sign. M. J. Brown.	FV	FV	57.50
	b. Sign. D. P. Trestain.	FV	FV	50.00

1994-96 ND Issue

#56-59 Qn. Elizabeth II at r. and as wmk., Guernsey States seal at bottom ctr. r. Sign. D. P. Trestain. Printer: TDLR.

		VG	VF	Unc
56	**5 Pounds** ND (1996). Dk. brown and purple on m/c unpt. St. Peter Port Town Church at lower l. Fort Grey at upper l. ctr., Hanois Lighthouse at ctr. r. on back.	FV	FV	15.00

		VG	VF	Unc
57	**10 Pounds** ND (1995). Violet, blue and dk. blue on m/c unpt. Elizabeth College at lower l. Saumarez Park above Le Niaux Watermill and Le Trepid Dolmen at l. ctr. on back.	FV	FV	28.50

		VG	VF	Unc
58	**20 Pounds** ND (1996). Pink, dk. brown and orange on m/c unpt. St. James Concert Hall at lower l. Flowers at lower l., St. Sampson's Church at l. ctr., sailboats below Vale Castle at ctr. r., ship at upper r. on back.	FV	FV	50.00

		VG	VF	Unc
59	**50 Pounds** ND (1994). Dk. brown, dk. green and blue-black on m/c unpt. Royal Court House at lower l. Stone carving, letter of Marque at lower l., St. Andrew's Church at ctr. r. on back.	FV	FV	120.00

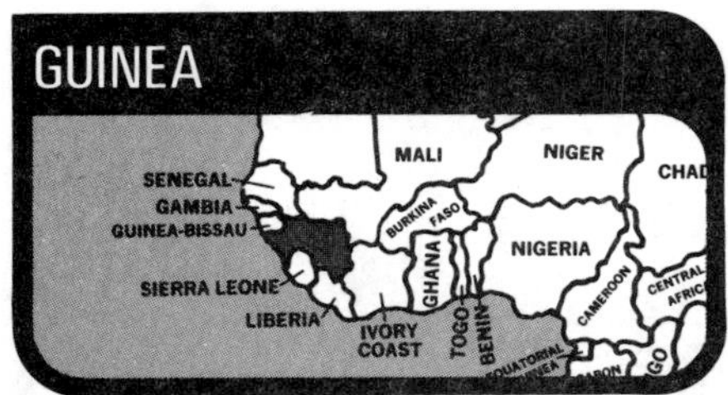

The Republic of Guinea (formerly French Guinea), situated on the Atlantic coast of Africa between Sierra Leone and Guinea-Bissau, has an area of 94,964 sq. mi. (245,957 sq. km.) and a population of 7.4 million. Capital: Conakry. Although Guinea contains one-third of the world's reserves of bauxite and significant deposits of iron ore, gold and diamonds, the economy is still dependent on agriculture. Aluminum, bananas, copra and coffee are exported.

The coast of Guinea was known to Portuguese navigators of the 15th century but was seldom visited by European traders of the 16th-18th centuries because of its dangerous coastal waters. French penetration of the area began in the mid-19th century with the entering into of protectorate treaties with several of the coastal chiefs. After a long struggle with Guinea's native leader Samory Toure, France secured the area and until 1890 administered it as a part of Senegal. In 1895 the colony (Guinee Francaise) became an autonomous part of the federation of French West Africa. The inhabitants were extended French citizenship in 1946 when the colony became an overseas territory of the French Union. Guinea became an independent republic on Oct. 2, 1958, when it declined to enter the new French Community.

MONETARY SYSTEM:

1 Franc = 100 Centimes to 1971
1 Syli = 10 Francs, 1971-1980
Franc System, 1985-

Republic

Banque Centrale de la République de Guinée

1960 Issue

		VG	VF	Unc
12	**50 Francs** 1.3.1960. Brown on m/c unpt. Heavy machinery on back.	1.00	4.00	25.00

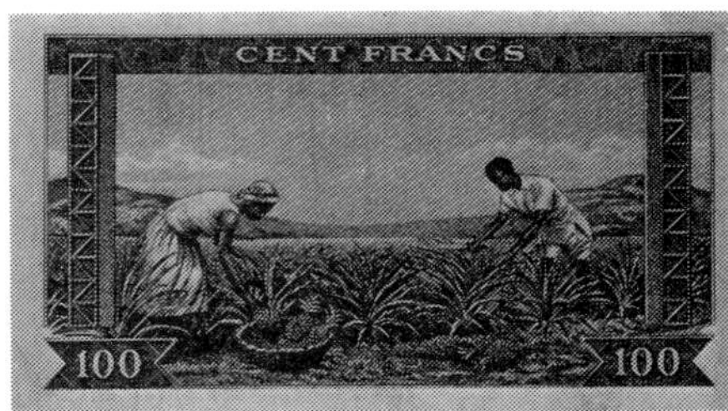

		VG	VF	Unc
13	**100 Francs** 1.3.1960. Brown-violet on m/c unpt. Pineapple harvesting on back.	2.00	6.00	40.00
14	**500 Francs** 1.3.1960. Blue on m/c unpt. Men pulling long boats ashore on back.	5.00	25.00	150.00

		VG	VF	UNC
15	**1000 FRANCS** 1.3.1960. Green on m/c unpt. Banana harvesting on back.	3.50	17.50	90.00

1971 ISSUE

		VG	VF	UNC
16	**10 SYLIS** 1971. Brown on m/c unpt. Patrice Lumumba at r. People w/bananas on back.	.20	.60	1.75

		VG	VF	UNC
17	**25 SYLIS** 1971. Dk. brown on m/c unpt. Man smoking a pipe at r. Man and cows on back.	.30	.85	3.00

		VG	VF	UNC
18	**50 SYLIS** 1971. Green on m/c unpt. Bearded man at l. Landscape w/large dame and reservoir on back.	1.00	3.00	10.00

		VG	VF	UNC
19	**100 SYLIS** 1971. Purple on m/c unpt. A. S. Toure at l. Steam shovel and two dump trucks on back.	.75	2.25	10.00

1980; 1981 ISSUE

		VG	VF	UNC
20	**1 SYLI** 1981. Olive on green unpt. Mafori Bangoura at r.			
	a. Issued note.	.05	.15	.50
	s. Specimen.	—	—	6.00

		VG	VF	UNC
21	**2 SYLIS** 1981. Black and brown on orange unpt. Green guilloche at ctr. Kg. Mohammed V of Morocco at l.			
	a. Issued note.	.05	.25	.75
	s. Specimen.	—	—	7.00

		VG	VF	UNC
22	**5 SYLIS** 1980. Blue on pink unpt. Kwame Nkrumah at r. Back like #16.			
	a. Issued note.	.20	.65	2.00
	s. Specimen.	—	—	8.00

		VG	VF	UNC
23	**10 SYLIS** 1980. Red and red-orange on m/c unpt. Like #16.			
	a. Issued note.	.25	.75	2.50
	s. Specimen.	—	—	9.00

		VG	VF	UNC
24	**25 SYLIS** 1980. Dk. green on m/c unpt. Like #17. Back green and m/c.			
	a. Issued note.	.40	1.20	4.00
	s. Specimen.	—	—	10.00

		VG	VF	UNC
25	**50 SYLIS** 1980. Dk. red and brown on m/c unpt. Like #18.			
	a. Issued note.	.65	2.00	7.00
	s. Specimen.	—	—	11.00

		VG	VF	UNC
26	**100 SYLIS** 1980. Blue on m/c unpt. Like #19.			
	a. Issued note.	1.75	6.00	15.00
	s. Specimen.	—	—	15.00

NOTICE

Readers with unlisted dates, signature varieties, etc. are invited to submit photocopies of their notes to: Standard Catalog of World Paper Money, 700 East State St. Iola, WI 54990-0001, fax: 1-715-445-4087, or E-Mail: thernr@krause.com.

		VG	VF	UNC
27	**500 SYLIS** 1980. Dk. brown on m/c unpt. J. Broz Tito at l. Modern bldg. on back.			
	a. Issued note.	.85	2.50	12.50
	s. Specimen.	—	—	20.00

NOTE: #27 is purported to commemorate Marshal Tito's visit to Guinea.

1985 ISSUE

		VG	VF	UNC
28	**25 FRANCS** 1985. Blue on m/c unpt. Young boy at l. Girl by huts at ctr. r. on back.			
	a. Issued note.	FV	.20	1.25
	s. Specimen.	—	—	3.00

		VG	VF	UNC
29	**50 FRANCS** 1985. Red-violet on m/c unpt. Bearded man at l. Plowing w/water buffalo at ctr. on back.			
	a. Issued note.	FV	.75	1.50
	s. Specimen.	—	—	5.00

		VG	VF	UNC
30	**100 FRANCS** 1985. Purple on m/c unpt. Young woman at l. Harvesting bananas at ctr. on back.			
	a. Issued note.	FV	.50	1.75
	s. Specimen.	—	—	7.50

31	500 FRANCS	VG	VF	UNC
	1985. Green on m/c unpt. Woman at l. Minehead at ctr. on back.			
	a. Issued note.	FV	1.25	4.50
	s. Specimen.	—	—	8.50

32	1000 FRANCS	VG	VF	UNC
	1985. Brown and blue on m/c unpt. Girl at l. Shovel loading ore into open end dump trucks at ctr., mask at r. on back.			
	a. Issued note.	FV	1.85	6.50
	s. Specimen.	—	—	10.00

33	5000 FRANCS	VG	VF	UNC
	1985. Blue and brown on m/c unpt. Woman at l. Dam at ctr., mask at r. on back.			
	a. Issued note.	FV	6.00	20.00
	s. Specimen.	—	—	22.50

The Republic of Guinea-Bissau, a former Portuguese overseas province on the west coast of Africa between Senegal and Guinea, has an area of 13,948 sq. mi. (36,125 sq. km.) and a population of 1.18 million. Capital: Bissau. The country has undeveloped deposits of oil and bauxite. Peanuts, oil-palm kernels and hides are exported.

The African Party for the Independence of Guinea-Bissau was founded in 1956, and several years later began a guerrilla warfare that grew in effectiveness until 1974, when the rebels controlled most of the colony. Portugal's costly overseas wars in her African territories resulted in a military coup in Portugal in April 1974, that appreciably brightened the prospects for freedom for Guinea-Bissau. In August 1974, the Lisbon government signed an agreement granting independence to Portuguese Guinea effective Sept. 10, 1974. The new republic took the name of Guinea-Bissau.

On Jan. 1, 1997, Guinea-Bissau became a member of the West African States, and has issued CFA currency notes with the code letter 'S'. Refer to West African States listings.

RULERS:

Portuguese until 1974

MONETARY SYSTEM:

1 Peso = 100 Centavos, 1975-1997
1 Franc = 65 Pesos, 1997-

REPUBLIC

BANCO NACIONAL DA GUINÉ-BISSAU

1975 ISSUE

#1-3 wmk: A. Cabral.

1	50 PESOS	VG	VF	UNC
	24.9.1975. Blue and brown on m/c unpt. P. Nalsna at l., group at ctr. Field workers at ctr., woman at r. on back.	1.00	2.50	12.50

2	100 PESOS	VG	VF	UNC
	24.9.1975. Brown (shades) on m/c unpt. D. Ramos at l., group in open hut at lower l. ctr. Objects and woman on back.	1.50	3.50	17.50

		VG	VF	UNC
3	**500 PESOS** 24.9.1975. Green, black and brown on m/c unpt. Pres. A. Cabral at l., arms at ctr., soldier at r. Carving and two youths on back.	8.00	20.00	70.00

#4 *Deleted.* See #8.

1978-84 ISSUE

#5-9 arms at lower r. on face. Wmk: A. Cabral. Replacement notes: Serial # prefix *Z*.

		VG	VF	UNC
5	**50 PESOS** 28.2.1983. Orange on blue and m/c unpt. Artifact at l. ctr., P. Nalsna at r. Local scene on back. Printer: BWC.	.25	1.00	3.50

		VG	VF	UNC
6	**100 PESOS** 28.2.1983. Red on m/c unpt. Carving at l., D. Ramos at r. Bldg. at l. ctr. on back. W/o imprint.	.30	1.25	4.50

		VG	VF	UNC
7	**500 PESOS** 28.2.1983. Deep blue on m/c unpt. Carving at l., F. Mendes at r. Slave trade scene on back. W/o imprint.	.40	2.00	5.50

		VG	VF	UNC
8	**1000 PESOS** 24.9.1978. Green on brown and m/c unpt. Weaver and loom at lower l. ctr., Pres. A. Cabral at r. Allegory w/title: *Apoteose ao Triunfo* on back. Printer: BWC.			
	a. Sign. titles: *COMISSARIO PRINCIPAL, COMISSARIO DE ESTADO DES FINANCAS* and *GOVERNADOR.*	7.50	20.00	62.50
	b. Sign. titles: *PRIMEIRO MINISTRO, MINISTRO DE ECONOMIA E FINANCAS* and *GOVERNADOR.*	.75	3.00	7.00

		VG	VF	UNC
9	**5000 PESOS** 12.9.1984. Brown and black on m/c unpt. Map at l. ctr., Pres. A. Cabral at r. Harvesting grain at ctr. on back. W/o imprint.	1.00	4.00	10.00

1990 ISSUE

#10-15 sign. titles: *MINISTRO-GOVERNADOR* and *VICE-GOVERNADOR*. Printer: TDLR.

Replacement notes: Serial # prefixes *AZ; BZ; CZ; DZ; ZA* or *ZZ*.

#10-12 wmk: *BCG*.

		VG	VF	UNC
10	**50 PESOS** 1.3.1990. Red on m/c unpt. Similar to #5 but reduced size w/o wmk. area.	.05	.25	1.00

		VG	VF	UNC
11	**100 PESOS** 1.3.1990. Olive-gray on m/c unpt. Similar to #6 but reduced size w/o wmk. area.	.05	.20	.75

12 **500 Pesos**
1.3.1990. Deep blue on m/c unpt. Similar to #7 but reduced size w/o wmk. area.

VG	VF	UNC
.15	.60	2.50

#13-15 wmk: Portr. A. Cabral.

13 **1000 Pesos**
1990; 1993. Dk. brown, brown-violet and orange on m/c unpt. Similar to #8.

		VG	VF	UNC
a.	Sign. titles: *MINISTRO-GOVERNADOR* and *VICE-GOVERNADOR.* 1.3.1990.	.20	.75	3.00
b.	Sign. titles: *GOVERNADOR* and *VICE-GOVERNADOR.* 1.3.1993.	.10	.50	2.00

14 **5000 Pesos**
1990; 1993. Purple, violet and brown on m/c unpt. Similar to #9.

		VG	VF	UNC
a.	Sign. titles: *MINISTRO-GOVERNADOR* and *VICE-GOVERNADOR.* 1.3.1990.	.25	1.00	4.25
b.	Sign. titles: *GOVERNADOR* and *VICE-GOVERNADOR.* 1.3.1993.	.20	.90	3.75

15 **10,000 Pesos**
1990; 1993. Green, olive-brown and blue on m/c unpt. Statue at lower l. ctr., outline map at ctr., A. Cabral at r. Local people fishing w/nets in river at ctr. on back.

		VG	VF	UNC
a.	Sign titles: *MINISTRO-GOVERNADOR* and *VICE-GOVERNADOR.* 1.3.1990.	.50	2.00	8.00
b.	Sign. titles: *GOVERNADOR* and *VICE-GOVERNADOR.* 1.3.1993.	.40	1.75	7.00

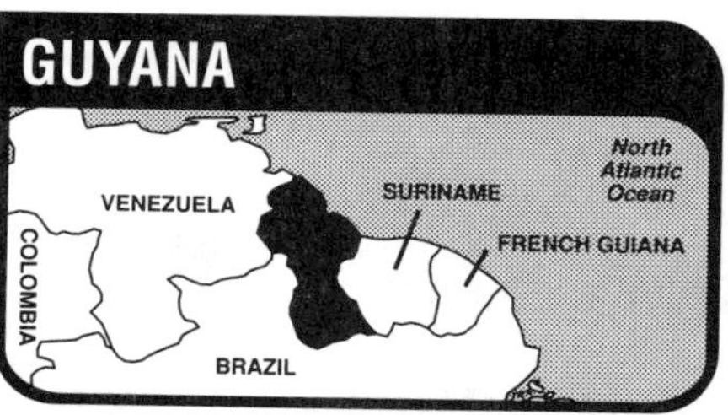

The Cooperative Republic of Guyana, (formerly British Guiana) an independent member of the British Commonwealth situated on the northeast coast of South America, has an area of 83,000 sq. mi. (214,969 sq. km.) and a population of 706,000. Capital: Georgetown. The economy is basically agrarian. Sugar, rice and bauxite are exported.

The original area of Guyana, which included present-day Surinam, French Guiana, and parts of Brazil and Venezuela, was sighted by Columbus in 1498. The first European settlement was made late in the 16th century by the Dutch. For the next 150 years, possession alternated between the Dutch and the British, with a short interval of French control. The British exercised de facto control after 1796, although the area, which included the Dutch colonies of Essequebo, Demerary and Berbice, wasn't ceded to them by the Dutch until 1814. From 1803 to 1831, Essequebo and Demerary were administered separately from Berbice. The three colonies were united in the British Crown Colony of British Guiana in 1831. British Guiana won internal self-government in 1952 and full independence, under the traditional name of Guyana, on May 26, 1966.

Notes of the British Caribbean Currency Board circulated from 1950-1965.

RULERS:

British to 1966

MONETARY SYSTEM:

1 Dollar = 4 Shillings 2 Pence, 1837-1965
1 Dollar = 100 Cents, 1966-

SIGNATURE VARIETIES

No.	Signatures	No.	Signatures
1	GOVERNOR — MINISTER OF FINANCE	2	GOVERNOR — MINISTER OF FINANCE
3	GOVERNOR — MINISTER OF FINANCE	4	GOVERNOR — MINISTER OF FINANCE
4A	GOVERNOR — MINISTER OF FINANCE	5	GOVERNOR — MINISTER OF FINANCE
6	GOVERNOR — VICE PRESIDENT ECONOMIC PLANNING AND FINANCE	7	GOVERNOR — MINISTER OF FINANCE
8	GOVERNOR (ag.) — MINISTER OF FINANCE	9	GOVERNOR — MINISTER OF FINANCE
10	GOVERNOR — MINISTER OF FINANCEI		

Republic

Bank of Guyana

1966 ND Issue

#21-29 wmk: Macaw's (parrot) head. Printer: TDLR.
#21-27 arms at ctr., Kaieteur Falls at r.

		VG	VF	UNC
21	**1 DOLLAR** ND (1966-). Red-brown on m/c unpt. Black bush polder at l., rice harvesting at r. on back.			
	a. Sign. 1; 2.	.60	3.00	15.00
	b. Sign. 3; 4.	1.25	6.00	30.00
	c. Sign. 4A.	.05	.30	1.50
	d. Sign. 5.	.20	1.00	4.00
	e. Sign. 6 (1983).	.10	.40	1.50
	f. Serial # prefix *B/1* or higher. Sign. 7 (1989).	FV	FV	1.00
	g. Sign. 8 (1992); 9.	FV	FV	.75

		VG	VF	UNC
22	**5 DOLLARS** ND (1966-). Dk. green on m/c unpt. Cane sugar harvesting at l., conveyor at r. on back.			
	a. Sign. 1; 2.	1.65	8.00	40.00
	b. Sign. 3.	2.00	10.00	50.00
	c. Sign. 5.	.20	1.00	5.00
	d. Sign. 6 (1983).	.15	.60	3.00
	e. Serial # prefix *A/27* or higher. Sign. 7 (1989).	FV	FV	1.00
	f. Sign. 8 (1992); 9.	FV	FV	.75

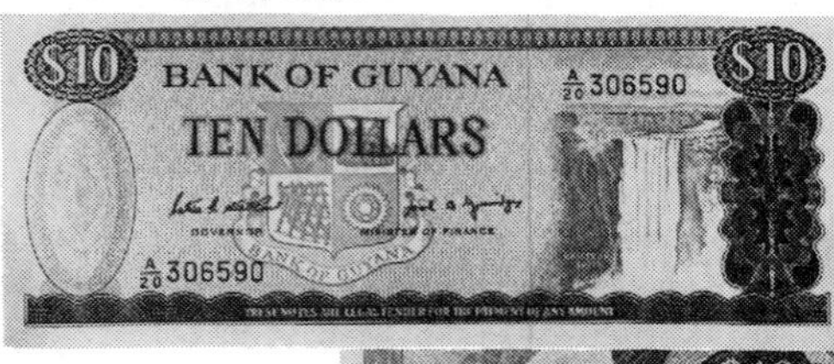

		VG	VF	UNC
23	**10 DOLLARS** ND (1966-). Dk. brown on m/c unpt. Bauxite mining at l., aluminum plant at r. on back.			
	a. Sign. 1; 2; 3.	2.00	10.00	50.00
	b. Sign. 4; 5.	.50	2.50	12.50
	c. Sign. 6 (1983).	.30	1.25	6.00
	d. Serial # prefix *A/16* or higher. Sign. 7 (1989).	FV	FV	1.00
	e. Sign. 8 (1992).	FV	FV	1.50
	f. Sign. 9.	FV	FV	1.00

		VG	VF	UNC
24	**20 DOLLARS** ND (1966-88). Brown and purple m/c unpt. Shipbuilding at l., ferry vessel "Malali" at r. on back.			
	a. Sign. 1; 4A.	2.00	10.00	50.00
	b. Sign. 5.	FV	3.00	15.00
	c. Sign. 6 (1983).	FV	2.50	12.50
	d. Serial # prefix *A/42* or higher. Sign. 7 (1989).	FV	FV	1.50

#25 and 26 not used.

1989; 1992 ND ISSUE

#27-29 printer: TDLR.

		VG	VF	UNC
27	**20 DOLLARS** ND (1989). Brown and purple on m/c unpt. Similar to #24, but design element at l. and r. Sign. 7; 9.	FV	FV	2.50

#28 and 29 map of Guyana at r., bank arms at ctr.

		VG	VF	UNC
28	**100 DOLLARS** ND (1989). Blue on m/c unpt. Cathedral at ctr. on back. Sign. 7; 8.	FV	FV	6.00

		VG	VF	UNC
29	**500 DOLLARS** ND (ca. 1992). Lilac-brown and purple on m/c unpt. Public bldgs. in Georgetown on back.			
	a. Sign. 8.	FV	FV	35.00
	b. Sign. 9.	FV	FV	10.00

1996; 1999 ND ISSUE

#30-33 map of Guyana at r., bank arms at ctr. Ascending serial # at upper r. Wmk: Macaw's (parrot) head.

		VG	VF	UNC
30	**20 DOLLARS** ND (1996). Brown and purple on m/c unpt. Like #27. Sign. 10; 11.	FV	FV	1.00
31	**100 DOLLARS** ND (1999). Like #28. Sign. 10; 11.	FV	FV	4.00
32	**500 DOLLARS** ND (1996). Lilac-brown and purple on m/c unpt. Segmented foil over security thread. Like #29. Sign. 10.	FV	FV	8.50

		VG	VF	UNC
33	**1000 DOLLARS** ND (1996). Dk. green, deep red and brown on m/c unpt. Bank bldg. at ctr. on back. Segmented foil over security thread. Sign. 10.	FV	FV	15.00

The Republic of Haiti, which occupies the western one third of the island of Hispañola in the Caribbean Sea between Puerto Rico and Cuba, has an area of 10,714 sq. mi. (27,750 sq. km.) and a population of 7 million. Capital: Port-au-Prince. The economy is based on agriculture, light manufacturing and tourism which is becoming increasingly important. Coffee, bauxite, sugar, essential oils and handicrafts are exported.

Columbus discovered Hispañola in 1492. Spain colonized the island, making Santo Domingo the base for exploration of the Western Hemisphere. Later French buccaneers settled the western third of Hispañola which was ceded to France by Spain in 1697. Slaves brought over from Africa to work the coffee and sugar cane plantations made it one of the richest colonies of the French Empire. The Republic of Haiti was established in 1804 after the slave revolts of the 1790's.

As a republic from 1915-1934 it was occupied by the U.S. Francois Duvalier was president 1957-1981, and his son 1981-1986, when a quick succession of governments continued with U.N. and U.S. intervention through the 1990's.

MONETARY SYSTEM:

1 Gourde = 100 Centimes
5 Gourdes = 1 U.S. Dollar, 1919-89

REPUBLIC

BANQUE NATIONALE DE LA RÉPUBLIQUE D'HAITI

CONVENTION DU 12 AVRIL 1919

SIXTH ISSUE (CA.1951-64)

#178-181, 183 and 184 arms at ctr. on back. First sign. title: *Le President*. Printer: ABNC.

No.	Denomination	VG	VF	UNC
178	**1 GOURDE** *L.1919.* Dk. brown on lt. blue and m/c. unpt. Citadel rampart at ctr. Prefix letters AS-BM. 5 sign. varieties.	.75	2.00	17.50
179	**2 GOURDES** *L.1919.* Blue and m/c. lt. green in unpt. Like #178. Prefix letters Z-AF. 6 sign. varieties.	1.00	3.00	22.00
180	**5 GOURDES** *L.1919.* Orange on green unpt. Woman harvesting coffee beans at l. Prefix letters G-M. 3 sign. varieties.	1.50	4.50	20.00

No.	Denomination	VG	VF	UNC
181	**10 GOURDES** *L.1919.* Green on m/c unpt. Coffee plant at ctr. Prefix letters B-D. 2 sign. varieties.	3.00	10.00	50.00
183	**50 GOURDES** *L.1919.* Olive-green on m/c unpt. Cotton bolls at ctr. Specimen.	—	—	225.00

No.	Denomination	VG	VF	UNC
184	**100 GOURDES** *L.1919.* Purple on m/c unpt. Field workers at l. Prefix letter A.			
	a. Issued note.	20.00	50.00	200.00
	s. Specimen, punched hole cancelled.	—	—	175.00

CONVENTION DU 12 AVRIL 1919
SEVENTH ISSUE (CA.1964)

#185-189 like #178-180 but new guilloche patterns, w/o green in unpt. Arms at ctr. on back. Printer: ABNC.

No.	Denomination	VG	VF	UNC
185	**1 GOURDE** *L.1919.* Dk. brown on lt. blue and m/c unpt. Citadel rampart at ctr. Prefix letters BK-BT.	.50	1.50	8.50

No.	Denomination	VG	VF	UNC
186	**2 GOURDES** *L.1919.* Blue on lt. blue and m/c unpt. Citadel rampart at ctr. Prefix letters AE-AJ.	.75	2.50	15.00

No.	Denomination	VG	VF	UNC
187	**5 GOURDES** *L.1919.* Orange on lt. blue and m/c unpt. Woman harvesting coffee beans at l. Prefix letter N.	.50	1.00	7.00

NOTE: It is reported that the entire shipment of #187 was stolen and never officially released.

No.	Denomination	VG	VF	UNC
188	**50 GOURDES** *L.1919.* Olive-green on blue and magenta unpt. Cotton bolls at ctr. (Not issued.) Archive example.	—	—	—
189	**100 GOURDES** *L.1919.* Purple on m/c unpt. Field workers at l. (Not issued.) Archive example.	—	—	—

CONVENTION DU 12 AVRIL 1919

EIGHTH ISSUE (CA.1967)

#190-195 arms at ctr. on back. Printer: TDLR.

#190-193 second sign. title: *LE DIRECTEUR*.

No.	Denomination	VG	VF	UNC
190	**1 GOURDE** *L.1919.* Brown on m/c unpt. Similar to #185. Prefix letters DA-DL.			
	a. Issued note.	.30	1.00	7.50
	s. Specimen.	—	—	27.50

No.	Denomination	VG	VF	UNC
191	**2 GOURDES** *L.1919.* Grayish blue on m/c unpt. Similar to #186. Prefix letters DA-DF.			
	a. Issued note.	.50	1.50	9.00
	s. Specimen.	—	—	27.50

No.	Denomination	VG	VF	UNC
192	**5 GOURDES** *L.1919.* Orange on lt. blue and m/c unpt. Similar to #187. Prefix letters DA-DK.	1.00	4.00	13.50

		VG	VF	Unc
193	**10 Gourdes** *L.1919.* Green on m/c unpt. Coffee plant at ctr. Prefix letters DA.			
	a. Issued note.	3.00	8.00	30.00
	s. Specimen.	—	—	35.00

		VG	VF	Unc
194	**50 Gourdes** *L.1919.* Olive-green on m/c unpt. Cotton bolls at ctr. Prefix letters DA. Second sign. title: *UN DIRECTEUR.*			
	a. Issued note.	10.00	17.50	80.00
	s. Specimen.	—	—	170.00

		VG	VF	Unc
195	**100 Gourdes** *L.1919.* Purple on m/c unpt. Similar to #205. Prefix letters DA.	20.00	35.00	150.00

Convention du 12 Avril 1919

Ninth Issue

#196-198 Pres. Dr. F. Duvalier at ctr. or l. Arms at ctr. on back. Printer: TDLR.

		VG	VF	Unc
196	**1 Gourde** *L.1919.* Dk. brown on m/c unpt. Prefix letters DK-DT.			
	a. Issued note.	.25	.60	3.50
	s. Specimen.	—	—	20.00

		VG	VF	Unc
197	**2 Gourdes** *L.1919.* Grayish blue on m/c unpt. Like #196. Prefix letters DG-DJ.			
	a. Issued note.	.50	1.25	4.50
	s. Specimen.	—	—	25.00

		VG	VF	Unc
198	**5 Gourdes** *L.1919.* Orange on m/c unpt. Portr. Pres. Duvalier at l. Prefix letters DJ-DK.			
	a. Issued note.	1.00	2.50	7.50
	s. Specimen.	—	—	25.00

Convention du 13 Avril 1919

Tenth Issue

#200-203 arms at ctr. on back. Printer: ABNC.

		VG	VF	Unc
200	**1 Gourde** *L.1919.* Dk. brown on m/c unpt. Portr. Pres. Dr. F. Duvalier at ctr. Prefix letters A-Z; AA-CR. 3 sign. varieties.			
	a. Issued note.	.25	.60	2.00
	s. Specimen.	—	—	20.00

#201-207 w/4 lines of text on back (like previous issues).

		VG	VF	Unc
201	**2 Gourdes** *L.1919.* Blue on m/c unpt. Like #200. First issued w/o prefix, then letters A-Q.	.50	1.25	3.50

		VG	VF	Unc
202	**5 Gourdes** *L.1919.* Orange on m/c unpt. Portr. Pres. Dr. F. Duvalier at l. First issued w/o prefix, then letters A-Z; AA-AP. 3 sign. varieties.	1.00	2.00	4.50
203	**10 Gourdes** *L.1919.* Dk. green on m/c unpt. Portr. Pres. Dr. F. Duvalier at ctr. First issued w/o prefix, then letter A.			
	a. Issued note.	2.50	5.00	12.50
	s. Specimen.	—	—	30.00

		VG	VF	Unc
204	**50 Gourdes** *L.1919.* Dk. gray on m/c unpt. Portr. Pres. L. F. Salomon Jeune at ctr. First issued w/o prefix, then letters A-C. 2 sign. varieties.			
	a. Issued note.	10.00	17.50	30.00
	s. Specimen.	—	—	40.00

		VG	VF	UNC
205	**100 GOURDES** *L.1919.* Purple on m/c unpt. Portr. H. Christophe (Pres., later Kg.) at l. W/o prefix letter. 2 sign. varieties.	20.00	40.00	70.00

		VG	VF	UNC
206	**250 GOURDES** *L.1919.* Dk. yellow-green on m/c unpt. J. J. Dessalines at r. W/o prefix letter.			
	a. Issued note.	55.00	110.00	200.00
	s. Specimen.	—	—	225.00

		VG	VF	UNC
207	**500 GOURDES** *L.1919.* Red on m/c unpt. Similar to #203. W/o prefix letter.			
	a. Issued note.	82.50	165.00	300.00
	s. Specimen.	—	—	350.00

#208 and 209 held in reserve.

ELEVENTH ISSUE (CA.1973)

Lois des 21 Mai 1935 et 15 Mai 1953 et au Décret du 22 Novembre 1973 (issued 1979)

#210-214 arms at ctr. on back. Printer: ABNC.

		VG	VF	UNC
210	**1 GOURDE** *L.1973, etc.* Dk. brown on m/c unpt. Like #200. Prefix letters A-Z; AA-AC.	.30	.60	2.00

#211-214 w/3 lines of text on back.

		VG	VF	UNC
211	**2 GOURDES** *L.1973, etc.* Blue on m/c unpt. Like #201. Prefix letters A-J.	.60	1.25	3.00
212	**5 GOURDES** *L.1973, etc.* Orange on m/c unpt. Like #202. Prefix letters A-AA.	1.00	2.00	4.00

		VG	VF	UNC
213	**50 GOURDES** *L.1973, etc.* Dk. gray on m/c unpt. Like #204. Prefix letter A.	10.00	17.50	27.50
214	**100 GOURDES** *L.1973, etc.* Purple on m/c unpt. Like #205. W/o prefix letter. Two serial # varieties.	20.00	35.00	70.00

#215-217 held in reserve.

TWELFTH ISSUE

Lois des 21 Mai 1935 et 15 Mai 1953 et au Décret du 22 Novembre 1973

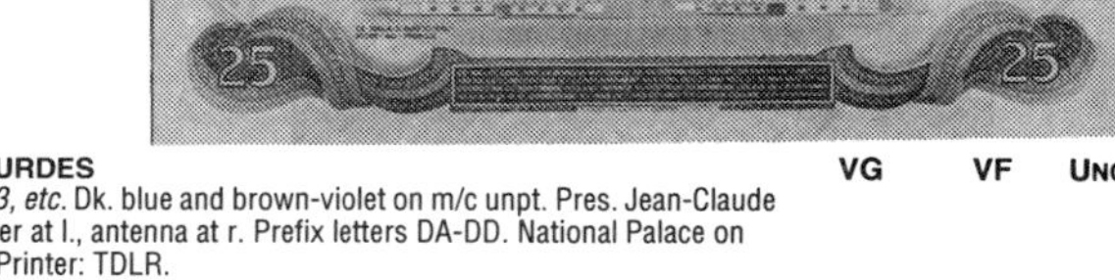

		VG	VF	UNC
218	**25 GOURDES** *L.1973, etc.* Dk. blue and brown-violet on m/c unpt. Pres. Jean-Claude Duvalier at l., antenna at r. Prefix letters DA-DD. National Palace on back. Printer: TDLR.			
	a. Issued note.	3.00	7.50	15.00
	s. Specimen.	—	—	30.00

#219-229 held in reserve.

BANQUE DE LA RÉPUBLIQUE D'HAITI

LOI DU 17 AOUT 1979 (1980-82)

#230-232, 235-238 sign. titles: *LE GOUVERNEUR, LE GOUVERNEUR ADJOINT* and *LE DIRECTEUR*. Arms at ctr. on back. Printer: ABNC.

		VG	VF	UNC
230	**1 GOURDE** *L.1979.* Dk. brown on m/c unpt. Like #210. W/ or w/o prefix letter.			
	a. Printed on paper w/planchettes. Smaller size numerals in serial #.	FV	.20	.75
	b. Printed on Tyvek. Larger size numerals in serial #.	FV	.50	1.50
	s. As b. Specimen.	—	—	25.00

		VG	VF	UNC
231	**2 GOURDES** *L.1979.* Blue on m/c unpt. Like # 230 W/o or w/prefix letter.			
	a. Printed on paper w/planchettes. Smaller size numerals in serial #.	FV	.50	1.50
	b. Printed on Tyvek. Larger size numerals in serial #.	FV	.75	2.00
232	**5 GOURDES** *L.1979.* Orange on m/c unpt. Like #212. Prefix letters A-T, AA-.	FV	1.00	3.00

#233 and 234 held in reserve.

		VG	VF	UNC
235	**50 GOURDES** *L.1979.* Dk. brown on green and m/c unpt. Like #213.			
	a. Printed on dull white paper w/planchettes. W/o prefix letter or letter A; B; G.	FV	12.00	25.00
	b. Printed on Tyvek. Prefix letter C. Wmk: American bald eagle symbol of ABNC.	FV	12.00	27.50
	c. Printed on Tyvek but w/o wmk. Prefix letter D; F.	FV	12.00	25.00
	s1. As a. Specimen.	—	—	35.00
	s2. As c. Specimen.	—	—	40.00

		VG	VF	Unc
236	**100 Gourdes**			
	L.1979. Purple on m/c unpt. Like #205.			
	a. Printed on paper w/planchettes. Prefix letters A; B.	FV	16.00	40.00
	b. Printed on Tyvek. Prefix letter C; D.	FV	16.00	40.00
	s. As a. Specimen.	—	—	35.00
237	**250 Gourdes**			
	L.1979. Dk. yellow-green on m/c unpt. Similar to #206. Printed on Tyvek.			
	a. Issued note.	FV	45.00	100.00
	s. Specimen.	—	—	100.00
238	**500 Gourdes**			
	L.1979. Red on m/c unpt. Similar to #207. Printed on Tyvek.			
	a. Issued note.	FV	90.00	200.00
	s. Specimen.	—	—	300.00

1984; 1985 Issue

#239-240 arms at ctr. on back. Printer: TDLR. Replacement notes: Serial # prefix *ZZ*.

		VG	VF	Unc
239	**1 Gourde**			
	L.1979 (1984). Dk. brown on m/c unpt. Like #196. Double prefix letters. Sign. titles like #230.	FV	.20	.60
240	**2 Gourdes**			
	L.1979 (1985). Grayish blue on m/c unpt. Similar to #191.	FV	.50	1.50

#241-243 sign. title at r: *LE DIRECTEUR GENERAL*. Arms at ctr. on back.

		VG	VF	Unc
241	**5 Gourdes**			
	L.1979 (1985). Orange on m/c unpt. Portr. Pres. Jean-Claude Duvalier at l. and as wmk. Printer: G&D.			
	a. Issued note.	FV	1.00	4.00
	s. Specimen.	—	—	35.00

		VG	VF	Unc
242	**10 Gourdes**			
	L.1979 (1984). Green on m/c unpt. Similar to #203, but portr. Jean-Claude Duvalier at ctr. Printer: ABNC.			
	a. Issued note.	FV	2.00	6.00
	s. Specimen.	—	—	27.50

		VG	VF	Unc
243	**25 Gourdes**			
	L.1979 (1985). Blue on pink and m/c unpt. Like #241. Printer: G&D.			
	a. Issued note.	FV	4.50	15.00
	s. Specimen.	—	—	30.00

#244 *Deleted*. See #240.

1986-88 Issue

#245-252 sign. title at r: *LE DIRECTEUR GENERAL*. Arms at ctr. on back.

		VG	VF	Unc
245	**1 Gourde**			
	1987. Dk. brown and brown-black on m/c unpt. Toussaint L'Ouverture at ctr. Printer: G&D.			
	a. Issued note.	FV	FV	.50
	s. Specimen.	—	—	22.50

		VG	VF	Unc
245A (240b)	**2 Gourdes**			
	L.1979. Grayish blue on m/c unpt. Like #240.	FV	.35	1.25

		VG	VF	UNC
246	**5 GOURDES** 1987. Orange and brown on m/c unpt. Statue of Combat de Vertiéres at upper ctr. Wmk: Palm tree. Printer: G&D.			
	a. Issued note.	FV	FV	2.50
	s. Specimen.	—	—	25.00

		VG	VF	UNC
247	**10 GOURDES** 1988. Green, red and blue on m/c unpt. Catherine Flon Arcahaie seated sewing the first flag of the Republic at r. Back green. Printer: ABNC.			
	a. Issued note.	FV	FV	4.50
	s. Specimen.	—	—	27.50

		VG	VF	UNC
248	**25 GOURDES** 1988. Dk. blue and purple on m/c unpt. Palace of Justice at ctr. Wmk: Palm tree. Printer: G&D.			
	a. Issued note.	FV	FV	9.00
	s. Specimen.	—	—	28.50

NOTICE

Readers with unlisted dates, signature varieties, etc. are invited to submit photocopies of their notes to: Standard Catalog of World Paper Money, 700 East State St. Iola, WI 54990-0001, fax: 1-715-445-4087, or E-Mail: thernr@krause.com.

		VG	VF	UNC
249	**50 GOURDES** 1986. Dk. brown on green and m/c unpt. Design and sign. titles like #235. Printer: ABNC.	FV	FV	30.00
250	**100 GOURDES** 1986. Purple on m/c unpt. Similar to #236 (but more colorful). Printer: TDLR.			
	a. Issued note.	FV	FV	45.00
	s. Specimen.	—	—	35.00
251	**250 GOURDES** 1988. Tan on m/c unpt. Similar to #237. Printer: ABNC.			
	a. Issued note.	FV	FV	80.00
	s. Specimen.	—	—	70.00
252	**500 GOURDES** 1988. Red on m/c unpt. Pres. A. Pétion at r. Printer: ABNC.	FV	FV	150.00

1989-91 ISSUE

#253-255 arms at ctr. on back. Printer: USBC.

		VG	VF	UNC
253	**1 GOURDE** 1989. Dk. brown and brown-black on m/c unpt. Toussaint L'Ouverture w/short hair at ctr.			
	a. Issued note.	FV	FV	.60
	s. Specimen.	—	—	22.50

		VG	VF	UNC
254	**2 GOURDES** 1990. Blue-black on m/c unpt. Citadel rampart at ctr.			
	a. Issued note.	FV	.50	3.00
	s. Specimen.	—	—	25.00

		VG	VF	UNC
255	**5 GOURDES** 1989. Orange and brown on m/c unpt. Like #246.	FV	FV	1.75

#256-258 legal clause on face and back w/o reference to the United States. Arms at ctr. on back. Wmk: Palm tree. Printer: G&D.

256	10 GOURDES	VG	VF	UNC
	1991. Dk. green, red and blue on m/c unpt. Similar to #247, but w/C. F. Arcahaie at ctr.			
	a. Issued note.	FV	FV	4.00
	s. Specimen.	—	—	25.00

257	50 GOURDES	VG	VF	UNC
	1991. Dk. olive-green on m/c unpt. Portr. Pres. L. F. Salomon Jeune at ctr.			
	a. Issued note.	FV	FV	10.00
	s. Specimen.	—	—	50.00

258	100 GOURDES	VG	VF	UNC
	1991. Purple on m/c unpt. Portr. H. Christophe at l.			
	a. Issued note.	FV	FV	20.00
	s. Specimen.	—	—	25.00

1992-94 ISSUE

#259-264 w/o laws. Shortened clause on face and back: *CE BILLET EST EMIS CONFORMEMENT...* Arms at ctr. on back.

#259-261 printer: TDLR. Replacement notes: Serial # prefix *ZZ*.

259	1 GOURDE	VG	VF	UNC
	1992; 1993. Dk. brown and brown-black on m/c unpt. Like #245.	FV	FV	.50

260	2 GOURDES	VG	VF	UNC
	1992. Blue-black on m/c unpt. Like #254.	FV	FV	.75

261	5 GOURDES	VG	VF	UNC
	1992. Orange and brown on m/c unpt. Like #246.			
	a. Issued note.	FV	FV	1.50
	s. Specimen.	—	—	22.50

262	25 GOURDES	VG	VF	UNC
	1993. Dk. blue and purple on m/c unpt. Like #248. Printer: G&D.			
	a. Issued note.	FV	FV	4.00
	s. Specimen.	—	—	25.00

263	250 GOURDES	VG	VF	UNC
	1994. Olive-brown and dk. brown on m/c unpt. Portr. J. J. Dessalines at l.			
	a. Issued note.	FV	FV	33.50
	s. Specimen.	—	—	100.00

		VG	VF	UNC
264	**500 GOURDES** 1993. Red-violet on m/c unpt. Portr. Pres. A. Pétion at l. Printer: G&D.			
	a. Issued note.	FV	FV	60.00
	s. Specimen.	—	—	200.00

1998 SERIES

		VG	VF	UNC
265	**10 GOURDES** 1998. Like #256. Printer: G&D.	FV	FV	4.00

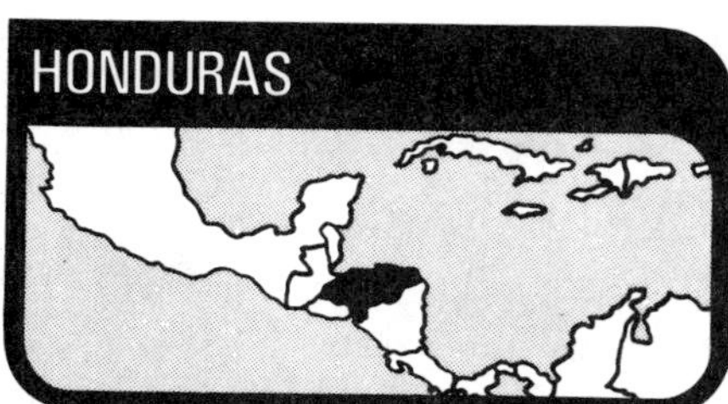

The Republic of Honduras, situated in Central America between El Salvador, Nicaragua and Guatemala, has an area of 43,277 sq. mi. (112,088 sq. km.) and a population of 5.6 million. Capital: Tegucigalpa. Tourism, agriculture, mining (gold and silver), and logging are the chief industries. Bananas, timber and coffee are exported.

Honduras, a site of the ancient Mayan Empire, was claimed for Spain by Columbus in 1502, during his last voyage to the Americas. The first settlement was made by Cristobal de Olid under orders of Hernan Cortes, then in Mexico. The area, regarded as one of the most promising sources of gold and silver in the New World, was a part of the Captaincy General of Guatemala throughout the colonial period. After declaring its independence from Spain in 1821, Honduras fell briefly to the Mexican Empire of Agustin de Iturbide, and then joined the Central American Federation (1823-39). Upon dissolution of the federation, Honduras became an independent republic.

MONETARY SYSTEM:

I Peso = 100 Centavos, 1871-1926
1 Lempira = 100 Centavos, 1926-

REPÚBLICA DE HONDURAS

BANCO CENTRAL DE HONDURAS

Established July 1, 1950 by merger of Banco Atlantida and Banco de Honduras. Various date and sign. varieties.

1950-51 ISSUE

		VG	VF	UNC
49	**100 LEMPIRAS** 1951-73. Yellow on m/c unpt. Valle at l., arms at r. Village and bridge on back.			
	a. W/o security thread, lilac-pink unpt. Printer: W&S. 16.3.1951; 8.3.1957.	85.00	225.00	—
	b. W/o security thread, w/fibers at r. ctr., lt. green and lt. orange unpt. Printer: W&S. 5.2.1964; 22.3.1968; 10.12.1969.	65.00	150.00	—
	c. W/security thread, yellow unpt. 13.10.1972; 23.3.1973.	55.00	125.00	225.00
	d. As c. but w/o security thread. 13.10.1972.	55.00	125.00	225.00
	s. Specimen, punched hole cancelled.	—	—	200.00

1953-56 ISSUE

		VG	VF	UNC
51	**5 LEMPIRAS** 1953-68. Gray on m/c unpt. Morazan at l., arms at r. Serial # at upper l. and upper r. Battle of Trinidad on back. Printer: ABNC.			
	a. Date horizontal. 17.3.1953; 19.3.1954; 7.5.1954.	6.00	27.50	100.00
	b. As a. 21.2.1958-7.1.1966.	4.00	20.00	75.00
	c. Date vertical. 15.4.1966; 29.9.1967; 22.3.1968.	3.50	17.50	60.00

		VG	VF	UNC
52	**10 LEMPIRAS** 1954-69. Brown on m/c unpt. Cabañas at l., arms at r. Old bank on back. Date and sign. style varieties. Printer: TDLR.			
	a. R. sign. title: *MINISTRO DE HACIENDA...* 19.11.1954.	15.00	60.00	125.00
	b. R. sign. title: *MINISTRO DE ECONOMIA...* 19.2.1960-10.1.1969.	10.00	25.00	75.00

53	20 LEMPIRAS	VG	VF	UNC
	1954-72. Green. D. de Herrera at l., arms at r. Waterfalls on back. Printer: TDLR.			
	a. 4.6.1954; 5.4.1957; 6.3.1959.	21.50	52.50	175.00
	b. 27.4.1962-6.3.1964.	18.00	45.00	150.00
	c. 7.1.1966-18.2.1972.	15.00	37.50	125.00

1961 ISSUE

54A	1 LEMPIRA	VG	VF	UNC
	10.2.1961; 30.7.1965. Red on m/c unpt. Lempira at l., modified design of #45 w/black serial #. Dios del Maiz/Idolo Maya and Mayan artifacts on back. 2 sign. varieties. Printer: TDLR.			
	a. Issued note.	1.00	4.00	18.50
	s. Specimen. Punched hole cancelled. 10.2.1961.	—	—	50.00

1968; 1970 ISSUE

55	1 LEMPIRA	VG	VF	UNC
	1968; 1972. Red on green and pink unpt. Lempira at l., design different from #50 and 45. *Ruinas de Copan Juego de Pelota* on back. Printer: TDLR.			
	a. R. sign. title: *MINISTRO DE ECONOMIA...* 25.10.1968.	.80	2.50	8.00
	b. R. sign. title: *MINISTRO DE HACIENDA...* 21.1.1972.	.75	1.00	3.50

56	5 LEMPIRAS	VG	VF	UNC
	1968-74. Black on m/c unpt. Morazan at l., arms at r. Serial # at lower l. and upper r. Battle scene of Trinidad at ctr. on back. Printer: ABNC.			
	a. Date horizontal. 29.11.1968; 11.4.1969.	5.00	30.00	65.00
	b. Date vertical. 11.4.1969-24.8.1974.	2.50	8.00	40.00

57	10 LEMPIRAS	VG	VF	UNC
	18.12.1970-13.11.1975. Brown on m/c unpt. Cabañas at l., arms at r. Ruins and new bank on back. Printer: ABNC.	3.50	12.50	35.00

1973; 1974 ISSUE

58	1 LEMPIRA	VG	VF	UNC
	11.3.1974. Red on green and lilac unpt. Lempira w/o feather at l., arms at r. Different view of Ruinas de Copan on back. Printer: TDLR.	.50	.70	1.50

59	5 LEMPIRAS	VG	VF	UNC
	1974-78. Black on m/c unpt. Morazan at l., arms at r. Battle of Trinidad at l. on back. Printer: ABNC.			
	a. Date vertical. 24.10.1974.	2.50	7.50	27.50
	b. Date horizontal. 12.12.1975-13.2.1978.	2.00	4.00	18.00

60	20 LEMPIRAS	VG	VF	UNC
	2.3.1973-3.6.1977. Green on m/c unpt. D. de Herrera at l., arms at r. Presidential residence on back. Date placement varieties. Printer: TDLR.	12.50	37.50	80.00

1976 COMMEMORATIVE ISSUE

#61, Centennial of the Marco Aurelio Soto Government

#	Denomination	VG	VF	UNC
61	**2 LEMPIRAS** 23.9.1976. Purple on m/c unpt. Arms at l., M. A. Soto at r. Island and Port of Amapala on back. Printer: TDLR.	FV	.60	2.00

1975-78 REGULAR ISSUE

#	Denomination	VG	VF	UNC
62	**1 LEMPIRA** 30.6.1978. Red. Like #58 but Indian symbols added below bank name on back. Printer: TDLR.	FV	.35	1.50

#	Denomination	VG	VF	UNC
63	**5 LEMPIRAS** 1978-94. Black, dk. blue, and deep olive-green on m/c unpt. Arms at l., Morazán at r. Battle of Trinidad Nov. 11, 1827 on back. Printer: TDLR.			
	a. 4.10.1978; 8.5.1980.	FV	1.25	3.50
	b. 8.12.1985; 30.3.1989.	FV	1.00	2.50
	c. Red serial # at upper l. in ascending size. 14.1.1993; 25.2.1993.	FV	FV	2.25
	d. Brown serial # as c. 12.5.1994.	FV	FV	2.00

#	Denomination	VG	VF	UNC
64	**10 LEMPIRAS** 1976-89. Brown on m/c unpt. Cabañas at l. Scene of City University on back. Printer: ABNC.			
	a. 18.3.1976-10.5.1979.	FV	2.50	6.50
	b. 8.9.1983; 3.7.1986; 24.11.1987; 5.10.1989.	FV	2.00	5.50

#	Denomination	VG	VF	UNC
65	**20 LEMPIRAS** 1978-93. Green on m/c unpt. D. de Herrera at r. and as wmk. Port of Puerto Cortes on back. Date placement varieties. Printer: ABNC.			
	a. 2.11.1978; 10.11.1979.	FV	5.00	10.00
	b. Vertical date at r. 23.6.1982; 18.3.1983; 5.1.1984; 9.4.1987.	FV	4.00	8.50
	c. Horizontal date at upper l. 5.10.1989; 1.3.1990; 29.11.1990; 24.1.1991; 9.5.1991; 29.8.1991.	FV	3.50	7.50
	d. 10.12.1992; 1.7.1993.	FV	FV	5.50

#	Denomination	VG	VF	UNC
66	**50 LEMPIRAS** 1976-93. Deep blue on m/c unpt. J. M. Galvez D. at l. National Development Bank on back. Wmk: tree. Printer: ABNC.			
	a. Vertical date at r. 29.1.1976-10.9.1979.	FV	12.50	20.00
	b. 3.7.1986-24.9.1987; 10.11.1989.	FV	8.00	16.50
	c. Horizontal date at upper l. 13.12.1990-29.8.1991.	FV	7.00	13.50
	d. 18.3.1993; 1.7.1993.	FV	FV	9.00

#	Denomination	VG	VF	UNC
67	**100 LEMPIRAS** 16.1.1975; 29.1.1976; 18.3.1976; 13.1.1977; 12.1.1978; 10.9.1979. Brown-orange on m/c unpt. Valle at l. Signatepeque school of forestry on back. Printer: TDLR.	FV	20.00	45.00

1980-81 ISSUE

#	Denomination	VG	VF	UNC
68	**1 LEMPIRA** 1980; 1984; 1989. Red on m/c unpt. Arms at l., Lempira at r. Ruins of Copan on back. Printer: TDLR.			
	a. W/o security thread. 29.5.1980; 18.10.1984.	FV	.30	1.00
	b. W/security thread. 30.3.1989.	FV	FV	.75

#	Denomination	VG	VF	UNC
69	**100 LEMPIRAS** 1981-94. Brown-orange, dk. olive-green, and deep purple on m/c unpt. J. C. del Valle at r. and as wmk. Different view of forestry school on back. Printer: TDLR.			
	a. Regular serial #. 8.1.1981; 23.6.1982; 8.9.1983.	FV	15.00	28.50
	b. 3.7.1986; 10.12.1987; 21.12.1989.	FV	12.50	25.00
	c. 13.12.1989-12.5.1994.	FV	FV	22.50

1989 ISSUE

		VG	VF	UNC
70	**10 LEMPIRAS** 21.9.1989. Dk. brown and red on m/c unpt. (of vertical stripes). Arms at l., Cabañas at r. City University on back. Printer: TDLR.	FV	1.50	3.75

1992-93 ISSUE

		VG	VF	UNC
71	**1 LEMPIRA** 10.9.1992. Dk. red on m/c unpt. Similar to #47a but back in paler colors. Printer: CBNC.	FV	FV	.65

#72-75 printer: TDLR. Pre-1994 dates have red serial #; 1994 dates have brown serial #.

		VG	VF	UNC
72	**2 LEMPIRA** 14.1.1993; 25.2.1993; 12.5.1994. Purple on m/c unpt. Like #61 but w/lt. blue unpt. at l. Ascending size serial # at upper l.	FV	FV	1.00

NOTICE

Readers with unlisted dates, signature varieties, etc. are invited to submit photocopies of their notes to: Standard Catalog of World Paper Money, 700 East State St. Iola, WI 54990-0001, fax: 1-715-445-4087, or E-Mail: thernr@krause.com.

		VG	VF	UNC
73	**20 LEMPIRAS** 14.1.1993 (1994); 25.2.1993 (1995); 12.5.1994; 12.12.1996. Deep green and dk. brown on m/c unpt. D. de Herrera at r. and as wmk. Back vertical; Presidential House at ctr.	FV	FV	5.00

		VG	VF	UNC
74	**50 LEMPIRAS** 14.1.1993 (1994); 25.2.1993 (1995); 12.5.1994. Blue-black and dk. brown on m/c unpt. J. M. Galvez D. at r. and as wmk. Back vertical; Central Bank Annex at ctr.	FV	FV	11.00

		VG	VF	UNC
75	**100 LEMPIRAS** 14.1.1993; 12.5.1994. Brown-orange, dk. olive-green and dk. brown on m/c unpt. Like #69 but w/engraved date. Serial # at upper l. in ascending size. Enhanced unpt. in wmk. area on back. Black sign. Red serial #.	FV	FV	20.00

1994; 1995 ISSUE

		VG	VF	UNC
76 (77)	**1 LEMPIRA** 12.5.1994. Red on m/c unpt. Similar to #71 but w/brown ascending size serial # at upper l. Printer: TDLR.	FV	FV	.50

		VG	VF	UNC
77	**100 LEMPIRAS** 12.5.1994. Brown-orange, black and olive-green on m/c unpt. J. C. del Valle at ctr. r. and as wmk., bridge over the Choluteca river at r. Valle's house at l. on back. Brown serial #. (W/o imprint).	FV	FV	15.00
78 (76)	**500 LEMPIRAS** 16.11.1995 (1997). Violet and purple on m/c unpt. Dr. R. Rosa at r. and as wmk., National Gallery of Art in background. View of Rosario de San Juancito at l. ctr. on back.	FV	FV	65.00

1996-98 ISSUE

#79-81 brown serial # w/ascending serial # at upper l.

#79-80 printer. F-CO.

		VG	VF	UNC
79	**1 LEMPIRA** 1996-98. Dk. red on m/c unpt. Like #71.			
	a. 12.12.1996.	FV	FV	.50
	b. 18.9.1997. (W/o imprint).	FV	FV	.50
	c. 12.12.1998.	FV	FV	.50

		VG	VF	UNC
80	**5 LEMPIRAS** 12.12.1996. Black, dk. blue and deep olive-green on m/c unpt. Like #63.	FV	FV	1.65

		VG	VF	UNC
81	**10 LEMPIRAS** 12.12.1996. Dk. brown and red on m/c unpt. Like #70. Printer: TDLR.	FV	FV	3.50

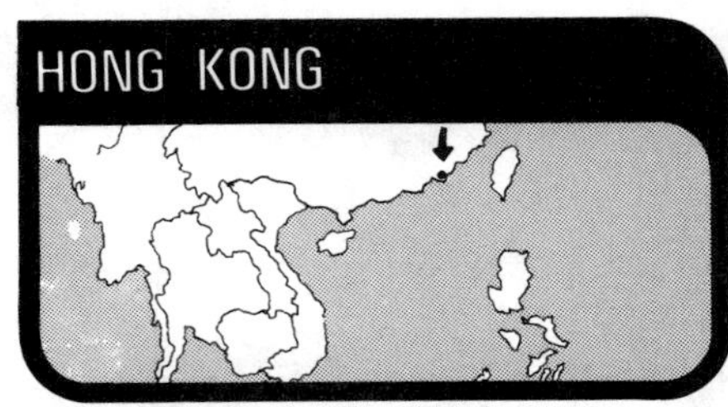

Hong Kong S.A.R., the former British Colony reverted to control of the Peoples Republic of China on July 1, 1997 as a Special Administrative Region. It is situated at the mouth of the Canton or Pearl River 90 miles (145 km.) southeast of Canton, has an area of 409 sq. mi. (1,091 sq. km.) and an estimated population of 6.5 million. Capital: Central (formerly Victoria). The port of Hong Kong had developed as the comercial center of the Far East, a transshipment point for goods destined for China and the countries of the Pacific rim. Light manufacturing and tourism are important components of the economy.

Long a haven for fishermen-pirates and opium smugglers, the island of Hong Kong was ceded to Britain at the conclusion of the first Opium War (1839-1842). At the time, the acquisition of "a barren rock" was ridiculed by both London and English merchants operating in the Far East. The Kowloon Peninsula and Stonecutter's Island were ceded in 1860 and the so-called New Territories, comprising most of the mainland of the colony, were leased to Britain for 99 years in 1898.

Hong Kong was returned to the Peoples Republic of China in 1997 and was made a Special Autonomous Region. Enjoying a high degree of autonomy and vested with executive, legislative and independent judicial power.

RULERS:

British (1845-1997)

MONETARY SYSTEM:

1 Dollar = 100 Cents

COMMERCIAL BANKS:

Chartered Bank - #68-81
Hong Kong & Shanghai Banking Corporation - #184-205
Mercantile Bank Limited - #244-245
Standard Chartered Bank - #278-289
Government of Hong Kong - #325-327
Bank of China - #329-333

BRITISH INFLUENCE

CHARTERED BANK

行銀 打 渣[1]

Cha Ta Yin Hang

Prior to December 1956, it was in business as The Chartered Bank of India, Australia & China. In the 1980s it became the Standard Bank, which later became the Standard Chartered Bank.

1961; 1967 ND ISSUES

#68-72 wmk: Helmeted warrior's head. Printer: TDLR.

		VG	VF	UNC
68	**5 DOLLARS** 1961-62; ND. Black and green on m/c unpt. Arms at lower l. Chinese junk and sampan at ctr. on back.			
	a. 1.7.1961.	30.00	100.00	350.00
	b. 3.3.1962.	37.50	120.00	525.00
	c. ND (1962-70).	15.00	50.00	200.00

		VG	VF	UNC
69	**5 DOLLARS** ND (1967). Black and yellow-brown on m/c unpt. Like #C8.	11.00	35.00	175.00
70	**10 DOLLARS** 1961-62; ND. Black and red-violet on red unpt. Arms at l. Chartered Bank bldg. at ctr. on back.			
	a. 1.7.1961.	40.00	110.00	365.00
	b. 3.3.1962.	25.00	80.00	185.00
	c. ND (1962-70).	10.00	30.00	100.00

		VG	VF	UNC
71	**100 DOLLARS** 1961; ND. Dk. green and brown on m/c unpt. Arms at ctr. Harbor view on back.			
	a. 1.7.1961.	250.00	700.00	1650.
	b. ND (1961-70).	150.00	425.00	900.00

		VG	VF	UNC
72	**500 DOLLARS** 1961-77. Black and dk. brown on m/c unpt. Male portr. at l. Ship, harbor view at ctr. on back.			
	a. Sign. titles: *ACCOUNTANT* and *MANAGER*. 1.7.1961.	600.00	1600.	3250.
	b. Sign. titles as a. ND (1962-?).	175.00	600.00	1650.
	c. Sign. titles: *ACCOUNTANT* and *CHIEF MANAGER IN HONG KONG*. ND (?-1975).	175.00	600.00	1650.
	d. Sign. titles as c. 1.1.1977.	110.00	400.00	1100.

1970 ND; 1975-77 ISSUE

#73-76 bank bldg. at l., bank crest at ctr. Wmk: Helmeted warrior's head. Printer: TDLR.

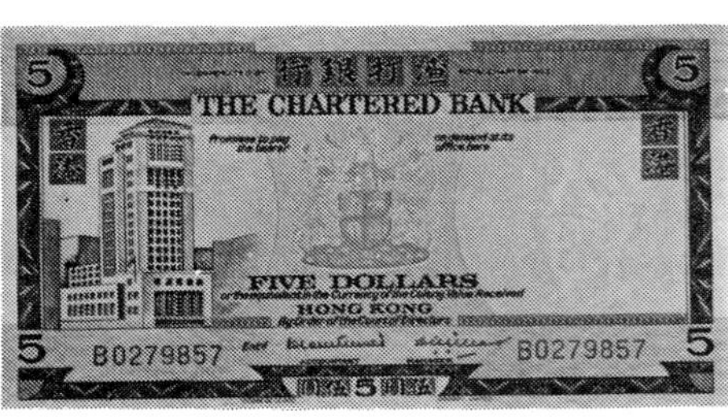

		VG	VF	UNC
73	**5 DOLLARS** ND (1970-75); 1975. Dk. brown on m/c unpt. City Hall at ctr. r. on back.			
	a. Sign. titles: *ACCOUNTANT* and *MANAGER*. ND (1970-75).	.85	3.00	13.50
	b. Sign. titles: *ACCOUNTANT* and *CHIEF MANAGER IN HONG KONG* at r. ND; 1.6.1975.	1.65	6.50	26.50

		VG	VF	UNC
74	**10 DOLLARS** ND; 1975; 1977. Dk. green on m/c unpt. Ocean terminal at ctr. r.			
	a. Sign. titles: *ACCOUNTANT* and *MANAGER*. ND (1970-75).	3.25	9.00	45.00
	b. Sign. titles: *ACCOUNTANT* and *CHIEF MANAGER IN HONG KONG*. ND; 1.6.1975.	2.75	11.00	40.00
	c. Sign. titles as b. 1.1.1977.	1.50	5.50	22.50

		VG	VF	UNC
75	**50 DOLLARS** ND (1970-75). Blue on m/c unpt. City Hall at ctr. r. on back.	50.00	150.00	425.00
76	**100 DOLLARS** ND; 1977. Red on m/c unpt.			
	a. ND (1970-75).	47.50	175.00	465.00
	b. 1.1.1977.	30.00	60.00	150.00

1979; 1980 ISSUE

#77-81 bank bldg. at l., arms at ctr. on back. Wmk: Helmeted warrior's head. Printer: TDLR (w/o imprint).

		VG	VF	UNC
77	**10 DOLLARS** 1.1.1980; 1.1.1981. Green on m/c unpt. Stylistic carp at r.	FV	FV	10.00

		VG	VF	UNC
78	**50 DOLLARS** 1979-82. Blue on m/c unpt. Chinze at r.			
	a. 1.1.1979.	FV	FV	110.00
	b. 1.1.1981; 1.1.1982.	FV	FV	80.00

		VG	VF	UNC
79	**100 DOLLARS** 1979-82. Red on m/c unpt. Mythical horse *Qilin* at r.			
	a. 1.1.1979.	FV	FV	110.00
	b. 1.1.1980.	FV	FV	80.00
	c. 1.1.1982.	FV	FV	62.50

		VG	VF	UNC
80	**500 DOLLARS** 1979; 1982. Brown on m/c unpt. Mythical phoenix at r.			
	a. 1.1.1979.	FV	FV	265.00
	b. 1.1.1982.	FV	FV	200.00

		VG	VF	UNC
81	**1000 DOLLARS** 1979; 1982. Yellow-orange on m/c unpt. Dragon at r.			
	a. 1.1.1979.	FV	FV	475.00
	b. 1.1.1982.	FV	FV	325.00

HONG KONG & SHANGHAI BANKING CORPORATION

Hsiang K'ang Shang Hai Hui Li Yin Hang

Formerly The Hong Kong and Shanghai Banking Company, Limited.

HONG KONG BRANCH

1932-35 ISSUE

179	500 Dollars	VG	VF	Unc
	1935-69. Brown and blue. Arms at top ctr., Sir T. Jackson at r. Back blue; allegorical female head at l., bank bldg. at ctr.			
	a. Handsigned. 1.6.1935-1.7.1937.	250.00	1300.	4000.
	b. Printed sign. 1.4.1941-1.8.1952.	170.00	450.00	1500.
	c. 11.7.1960-1.8.1966.	FV	250.00	1200.
	d. 31.7.1967.	FV	225.00	1000.
	e. 11.2.1968.	FV	125.00	450.00
	f. 27.3.1969.	FV	150.00	600.00

1959 Issue

#181-183 wmk: Helmeted warrior's head. Printer: BWC.

181	5 Dollars	VG	VF	Unc
	1959-75. Brown on m/c unpt. Woman seated at r. New bank bldg. at ctr. on back.			
	a. Sign. titles: *CHIEF ACCOUNTANT* and *CHIEF MANAGER*. 2.5.1959-29.6.1960.	3.75	15.00	60.00
	b. 1.5.1963.	50.00	175.00	475.00
	c. 1.5.1964-27.3.1969.	1.50	5.00	25.00
	d. Sign. titles: *CHIEF ACCOUNTANT* and *GENERAL MANAGER*. 1.4.1970-18.3.1971.	1.00	4.50	22.00
	e. 13.3.1972; 31.10.1972.	.85	3.00	11.00
	f. Sm. serial #. 31.10.1973; 31.3.1975.	.75	1.25	7.00

182	10 Dollars	VG	VF	Unc
	1959-83. Dk. green on m/c unpt. Portr. woman w/sheaf of grain at upper l., arms below. Back similar to #184.			
	a. Sign. titles: *CHIEF ACCOUNTANT* and *CHIEF MANAGER*. 21.5.1959-12.2.1960.	4.50	17.50	62.50
	b. 1.5.1963; 1.9.1963.	5.50	22.50	80.00
	c. 1.5.1964; 1.9.1964.	5.00	20.00	72.50
	d. 1.10.1964.	40.00	165.00	575.00
	e. 1.2.1965; 1.8.1966; 31.7.1967.	2.00	8.50	30.00
	f. 20.3.1968; 23.11.1968; 27.3.1969; 18.3.1971.	1.75	7.50	26.50
	g. Sign. titles: *CHIEF ACCOUNTANT* and *GENERAL MANAGER*. 1.4.1970-31.3.1977.	1.65	3.75	13.50
	h. Sign. titles: *CHIEF ACCOUNTANT* and *EXECUTIVE DIRECTOR*. 31.3.1978; 31.3.1979.	1.50	3.00	12.00
	i. Sign. titles: *CHIEF ACCOUNTANT* and *GENERAL MANAGER*. 31.3.1980; 31.3.1981.	1.50	2.00	8.00
	j. Sign. titles: *MANAGER* and *GENERAL MANAGER*. 31.3.1982; 31.3.1983.	1.50	2.00	8.00

183	100 Dollars	VG	VF	Unc
	1959-72. Red on m/c unpt. Woman seated at l. w/open book, arms at upper ctr. Wmk: Helmeted warrior's head and denomination.			
	a. Sign. titles: *CHIEF ACCOUNTANT* and *CHIEF MANAGER*. 12.8.1959-1.10.1964.	37.50	90.00	225.00
	b. 1.2.1965-27.3.1969.	30.00	65.00	165.00
	c. Sign. titles: *CHIEF ACCOUNTANT* and *GENERAL MANAGER*. 1.4.1970; 18.3.1971; 13.3.1972.	15.00	50.00	135.00

1968-73 Issue

#184-186 printer: BWC.

184	50 Dollars	VG	VF	Unc
	1968-83. Dk. blue on lt. blue and m/c unpt. Arms at r. New bank bldg. at l. ctr. on back. Wmk: Helmeted warrior's head and denomination.			
	a. Sign. titles: *CHIEF ACCOUNTANT* and *CHIEF MANAGER*. 31.5.1968; 27.3.1969.	8.50	35.00	110.00
	b. Sign. titles: *CHIEF ACCOUNTANT* and *GENERAL MANAGER*. 31.10.1973; 31.3.1975; 31.3.1978.	8.00	30.00	95.00
	c. Sign. titles as b. 31.3.1977.	8.00	30.00	95.00
	d. Sign. titles: *CHIEF ACCOUNTANT* and *EXECUTIVE DIRECTOR*. 31.3.1977.	8.00	30.00	95.00
	e. 31.3.1979.	30.00	120.00	300.00
	f. Sign. titles: *CHIEF ACCOUNTANT* and *GENERAL MANAGER*. 31.3.1980.	FV	FV	45.00
	g. 31.3.1981.	FV	11.00	40.00
	h. Sign. titles: *MANAGER* and *GENERAL MANAGER*. 31.3.1982; 31.3.1983.	FV	9.00	36.50

185	100 Dollars	VG	VF	Unc
	1972-76. Red on m/c unpt. Arms at l. Facing lions at lower l. and r., bank bldg. at ctr., dragon in medallion at r. on back.			
	a. W/4 lg. serial # on back. 13.3.1972; 31.10.1972.	16.50	47.50	120.00
	b. Smaller electronic sorting serial # on face. W/o serial # on back. 31.10.1972.	22.50	70.00	175.00
	c. 31.10.1973.	15.00	35.00	82.50
	d. 31.3.1975; 31.3.1976.	15.00	25.00	62.50

		VG	VF	UNC
186	**500 DOLLARS**			
	1973-76. Brown on m/c unpt. Arms at l. Bank bldg. at l., lion's head at r. on back.			
	a. 31.10.1973.	FV	165.00	375.00
	b. 31.3.1975.	FV	185.00	410.00
	c. 31.3.1976.	FV	150.00	385.00

1977; 1978 ISSUE

#187, 189 and 190 wmk: Lion's head. Printer: BWC.

		VG	VF	UNC
187	**100 DOLLARS**			
	1977-83. Red on lighter m/c unpt. Similar to #185.			
	a. Sign. titles: *CHIEF ACCOUNTANT* and *EXECUTIVE DIRECTOR*. 31.3.1977; 31.3.1978.	FV	16.00	80.00
	b. Sign. titles as a. 31.3.1979.	30.00	60.00	175.00
	c. 31.3.1980; 31.3.1981.	FV	FV	60.00
	d. Sign. titles: *MANAGER* and *GENERAL MANAGER*. 31.3.1982; 31.3.1983.	FV	FV	35.00

#188 *Deleted*. See #186.

		VG	VF	UNC
189	**500 DOLLARS**			
	1978-83. Brown and black on m/c unpt. Similar to #186 but w/modified frame designs.			
	a. 31.3.1978; 31.3.1980; 31.3.198 1981.	FV	FV	150.00
	b. 31.3.1983.	FV	FV	115.00

		VG	VF	UNC
190	**1000 DOLLARS**			
	1977-83. Gold and black on m/c unpt. Arms at r. Lion at l., bank bldg. at ctr. r. on back.			
	a. 31.3.1977.	FV	FV	325.00
	b. 31.3.1979; 31.3.1980; 31.3.1981; 31.3.1983.	FV	FV	240.00

1985-87 ISSUE

#191-196 arms at l. Facing lions at lower l. and r. w/new bank bldg. at ctr. on back. Sign. varieties. Wmk: Lion's head. Printer: TDLR. Replacement notes: Serial # prefix *ZZ*.

		VG	VF	UNC
191	**10 DOLLARS**			
	1985-92. Deep green on m/c unpt. Sampan and ship at r. at r. on back.			
	a. Sign. title: *GENERAL MANAGER*. 1.1.1985; 1.1.1986; 1.1.1987.	FV	FV	4.50
	b. Sign. title: *EXECUTIVE DIRECTOR*. 1.1.1988.	FV	FV	4.00
	c. Sign. title: *GENERAL MANAGER*. 1.1.1989; 1.1.1990; 1.1.1991; 1.1.1992.	FV	FV	3.50

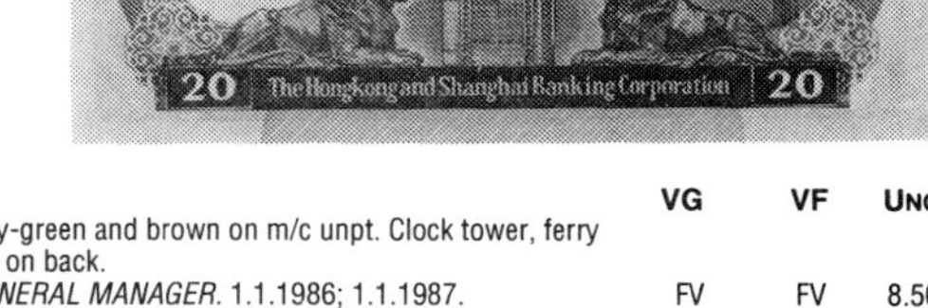

		VG	VF	UNC
192	**20 DOLLARS**			
	1986-89. Deep gray-green and brown on m/c unpt. Clock tower, ferry in harbor view at r. on back.			
	a. Sign. title: *GENERAL MANAGER*. 1.1.1986; 1.1.1987.	FV	FV	8.50
	b. Sign. title: *EXECUTIVE DIRECTOR*. 1.1.1988.	FV	FV	7.50
	c. Sign. title: *GENERAL MANAGER*. 1.1.1989.	FV	FV	6.50

		VG	VF	UNC
193	**50 DOLLARS**			
	1985-92. Purple on m/c unpt. Men in boats at r. on back.			
	a. Sign. title: *GENERAL MANAGER*. 1.1.1985; 1.1.1986; 1.1.1987.	FV	FV	17.50
	b. Sign. title: *EXECUTIVE DIRECTOR*. 1.1.1988.	FV	FV	15.00
	c. Sign. title: *GENERAL MANAGER*. 1.1.1989; 1.1.1990; 1.1.1991; 1.1.1992.	FV	FV	12.50
194	**100 DOLLARS**			
	1985-88. Red on m/c unpt. Tiger Balm Garden pagoda at r.			
	a. Sign. title: *GENERAL MANAGER*. 1.1.1985; 1.1.1986; 1.1.1987.	FV	FV	27.50
	b. Sign. title: *EXECUTIVE DIRECTOR*. 1.1.1988.	FV	FV	25.00

		VG	VF	Unc
195	**500 Dollars** 1987-92. Brown on m/c unpt. Old tower at r. on back.			
	a. Sign. title: *GENERAL MANAGER.* 1.1.1987.	FV	FV	100.00
	b. Sign. title: *EXECUTIVE DIRECTOR.* 1.1.1988.	FV	FV	95.00
	c. Sign. title: *GENERAL MANAGER.* 1.1.1989; 1.1.1990; 1.1.1991; 1.1.1992.	FV	FV	90.00
196	**1000 Dollars** 1.1.1985; 1.1.1986; 1.1.1987. Red, brown and orange on m/c unpt. Old Supreme Court bldg. at r. on back.	FV	FV	175.00

1988-90 Issue

#197-199 printer: TDLR. Replacement notes: Serial # prefix *ZZ*.

		VG	VF	Unc
197	**20 Dollars** 1.1.1990; 1.1.1991; 1.1.1992. Like #192 but gray on orange, pink and m/c unpt. Sign. title: *GENERAL MANAGER.*	FV	FV	6.00
198	**100 Dollars** 1.1.1989; 1.1.1990; 1.1.1991; 1.1.1992. Similar to #194. Sign. title: *GENERAL MANAGER.* Back red and black on m/c unpt.	FV	FV	22.50
199	**1000 Dollars** 1988-1991. Similar to #196. Back orange, brown and olive-brown on m/c unpt.			
	a. Sign. title: *EXECUTIVE DIRECTOR.* 1.1.1988.	FV	FV	175.00
	b. Sign title: *GENERAL MANAGER.* 1.1.1989; 1.1.1990; 1.1.1991.	FV	FV	170.00

Hong Kong & Shanghai Banking Corporation Limited

1993; 1995 Issue

#201-205 lion's head at l. and as wmk., city view in unpt. at ctr. New bank bldg. at ctr. between facing lions on back. Printer: TDLR. Notes dated 1.1.1996 and after w/o imprint. Replacement notes: Serial # prefix *ZZ*.

#200 not used.

		VG	VF	Unc
201	**20 Dollars** 1993-. Gray on m/c unpt.			
	a. Sign. title: *EXECUTIVE DIRECTOR.* 1.1.1993; 1.1.1994.	FV	FV	8.00
	b. Sign. titles as a. Copyright clause on both sides. 1.1.1995; 1.1.1996.	FV	FV	7.00
	c. Sign. title: *GENERAL MANAGER.* 1.1.1997; 1.7.1997.	FV	FV	6.00

		VG	VF	Unc
202	**50 Dollars** 1993-. Purple and violet on m/c unpt.			
	a. Sign. title: *EXECUTIVE DIRECTOR.* 1.1.1993; 1.1.1994.	FV	FV	15.00
	b. Sign. title as a. Copyright clause on both sides. 1.1.1995; 1.1.1996.	FV	FV	13.50
	c. Sign. title: *GENERAL MANAGER.* 1.1.1997; 1.7.1997.	FV	FV	11.50

		VG	VF	Unc
203	**100 Dollars** 1993-. Red, orange and black on m/c unpt. Ten Thousand Buddha Pagoda at Shatin at r. on back.			
	a. Sign. title: *EXECUTIVE DIRECTOR.* 1.1.1993; 1.1.1994; 1.1.1996.	FV	FV	27.50
	b. Sign. title: *GENERAL MANAGER.* 1.1.1997; 1.7.1997.	FV	FV	22.50
204	**500 Dollars** 1993-. Brown and red-orange on m/c unpt. Government house at upper r. on back.			
	a. Sign. title: *EXECUTIVE DIRECTOR.* 1.1.1993; 1.1.1994.	FV	FV	100.00
	b. Sign. title as a. Copyright clause on both sides. 1.1.1995; 1.1.1996.	FV	FV	95.00
	c. Sign. title: *GENERAL MANAGER.* 1.1.1997; 1.7.1997.	FV	FV	90.00
205	**1000 Dollars** 1993-. Orange, red-brown and olive-green on pink and m/c unpt. Legislative Council bldg. at r. on back.			
	a. Sign. title: *EXECUTIVE DIRECTOR.* 1.1.1993; 1.1.1994.	FV	FV	190.00
	b. Sign. title: *GENERAL MANAGER.* 1.1.1997; 1.7.1997.	FV	FV	175.00

Mercantile Bank Limited

行銀利有港香

Hsiang K'ang Yu Li Yin Hang

Formerly The Mercantile Bank of India Limited. In 1978 this bank was absorbed by the Hong Kong & Shanghai Banking Corp.

1964 Issue

		VG	VF	Unc
244	**100 Dollars** 1964-73. Red-brown on m/c unpt. Aerial view of coastline. Woman standing w/pennant and shield at ctr. on back. Wmk: Dragon. Printer: TDLR.			
	a. 28.7.1964.	275.00	900.00	2700.
	b. 5.10.1965.	165.00	500.00	1550.
	c. 27.7.1968.	175.00	600.00	1800.
	d. 16.4.1970.	90.00	375.00	1350.
	e. 1.11.1973.	85.00	325.00	1175.

1974 Issue

		VG	VF	Unc
245	**100 Dollars** 4.11.1974. Red, purple and brown on m/c unpt. Woman standing w/pennant and shield at l. Back red on m/c unpt., city view at ctr. Wmk: Dragon. Printer: TDLR.	16.50	55.00	240.00

STANDARD CHARTERED BANK

Hong Kong Cha Ta Yin Hang

1985-89 ISSUES

#278 -283 bank bldg. at l., bank arms at ctr. on back. Wmk: Helmeted warrior's head.

#		VG	VF	UNC
278	**10 DOLLARS** 1985-91. Dk. green on yellow-green and m/c unpt. Similar to #77.			
	a. Sign. titles: *FINANCIAL CONTROLLER* and *AREA GENERAL MANAGER*. 1.1.1985.	FV	FV	7.00
	b. Sign. titles: *AREA FINANCIAL CONTROLLER* and *AREA GENERAL MANAGER*. 1.1.1986; 1.1.1987; 1.1.1988; 1.1.1989.	FV	FV	6.00
	c. Sign. titles: *AREA FINANCIAL CONTROLLER* and *GENERAL MANAGER*. 1.1.1990.	FV	FV	5.00
	d. Sign. titles: *CHIEF FINANCIAL OFFICER* and *GENERAL MANAGER*. 1.1.1991.	FV	FV	5.00

#		VG	VF	UNC
279	**20 DOLLARS** 1985; 1992. Dk. gray, orange and brown on m/c unpt. Turtle at r.			
	a. Sign. titles: *FINANCIAL CONTROLLER* and *AREA GENERAL MANAGER*. 1.1.1985.	FV	FV	9.00
	b. Sign. titles: *CHIEF FINANCIAL OFFICER* and *AREA GENERAL MANAGER*. 1.1.1992.	FV	FV	7.00

#		VG	VF	UNC
280	**50 DOLLARS** 1985-91. Purple, violet and dk. gray on m/c unpt. Similar to #78.			
	a. Sign. titles: *FINANCIAL CONTROLLER* and *AREA GENERAL MANAGER*. 1.1.1985.	FV	FV	27.50
	b. Sign. titles: *AREA FINANCIAL CONTROLLER* and *AREA GENERAL MANAGER*. 1.1.1987; 1.1.1988.	FV	FV	23.50
	c. Sign. titles: *AREA FINANCIAL CONTROLLER* and *GENERAL MANAGER*. 1.1.1990.	FV	FV	20.00
	d. Sign. titles: *CHIEF FINANCIAL OFFICER* and *GENERAL MANAGER*. 1.1.1991.	FV	FV	20.00

#		VG	VF	UNC
281	**100 DOLLARS** 1985-92. Red on m/c unpt. Similar to #79.			
	a. Sign. titles: *FINANCIAL CONTROLLER* and *AREA GENERAL MANAGER*. 1.1.1985.	FV	FV	45.00
	b. Sign. titles: *FINANCIAL CONTROLLER* and *AREA GENERAL MANAGER*. 1.1.1986-1.1.1989.	FV	FV	35.00
	c. Sign. titles: *FINANCIAL CONTROLLER* and *AREA GENERAL MANAGER*. 1.1.1990.	FV	FV	30.00
	d. Sign. titles: *FINANCIAL CONTROLLER* and *AREA GENERAL MANAGER*. 1.1.1991; 1.1.1992.	FV	FV	27.50
282	**500 DOLLARS** 1988-92. Maroon, gray and green on m/c unpt. Similar to #80.			
	a. Sign. titles: *FINANCIAL CONTROLLER* and *AREA GENERAL MANAGER*. 1.1.1988; 1.1.1989.	FV	FV	125.00
	b. Sign. titles: *FINANCIAL CONTROLLER* and *AREA GENERAL MANAGER*. 1.1.1990.	FV	FV	120.00
	c. Sign. titles: *FINANCIAL CONTROLLER* and *AREA GENERAL MANAGER*. 1.1.1991; 1.1.1992.	FV	FV	110.00

#		VG	VF	UNC
283	**1000 DOLLARS** 1985-92. Yellow-orange on m/c unpt. Similar to #81.			
	a. Sign. titles: *FINANCIAL CONTROLLER* and *AREA GENERAL MANAGER*. 1.1.1985.	FV	FV	225.00
	b. Sign. titles: *AREA FINANCIAL CONTROLLER* and *AREA GENERAL MANAGER*. 1.1.1987.	FV	FV	285.00
	c. Sign. titles as b. 1.1.1988.	FV	FV	175.00
	d. Sign. titles: *FINANCIAL CONTROLLER* and *AREA GENERAL MANAGER*. 1.1.1992.	FV	FV	175.00

1993 ISSUE

#284-289 Bauhinia flower blossom replaces bank arms at ctr. on back. Wmk: *SCB* above helmeted warrior's head.

#		VG	VF	UNC
284	**10 DOLLARS** 1993-95. Dk. green on yellow-green unpt. Face like #278.			
	a. Sign. titles: *CHIEF FINANCIAL OFFICER* and *AREA GENERAL MANAGER*. 1.1.1993.	FV	FV	4.50
	b. Sign. titles: *HEAD OF FINANCE* and *GENERAL MANAGER*. 1.1.1994; 1.1.1995.	FV	FV	3.50

		VG	VF	UNC
285	**20 DOLLARS** 1993-. Dk. gray, orange and brown on m/c unpt. Face like #279.			
	a. Sign. titles: *CHIEF FINANCIAL OFFICER* and *AREA GENERAL MANAGER.* 1.1.1993.	FV	FV	8.00
	b. Sign. titles: *HEAD OF FINANCE* and *GENERAL MANAGER.* 1.1.1994; 1.1.1995; 1.1.1996; 1.1.1997; 1.7.1997.	FV	FV	6.00
	c. Sign. titles: *HEAD OF FINANCE* and *CHIEF EXECUTIVE.* 1.1.1998.	FV	FV	6.00

		VG	VF	UNC
286	**50 DOLLARS** 1993-. Purple, violet and dk. gray on m/c unpt. Face like #280.			
	a. Sign. titles: *CHIEF FINANCIAL OFFICER* and *AREA GENERAL MANAGER.* 1.1.1993.	FV	FV	15.00
	b. Sign. titles: *HEAD OF FINANCE* and *GENERAL MANAGER.* 1.1.1994; 1.1.1995; 1.1.1997; 1.7.1997.	FV	FV	11.50
	c. Sign. titles: *HEAD OF FINANCE* and *CHIEF EXECUTIVE.* 1.1.1998.	FV	FV	11.50

		VG	VF	UNC
287	**100 DOLLARS** 1993-. Red and purple on m/c unpt. Face like #281.			
	a. Sign. titles: *CHIEF FINANCIAL OFFICER* and *AREA GENERAL MANAGER.* 1.1.1993.	FV	FV	27.50
	b. Sign. titles: *HEAD OF FINANCE* and *GENERAL MANAGER.* 1.1.1994; 1.1.1995; 1.1.1996; 1.1.1997; 1.7.1997.	FV	FV	22.50
	c. Sign. titles: *HEAD OF FINANCE* and *CHIEF EXECUTIVE.* 1.1.1998.	FV	FV	22.50

		VG	VF	UNC
288	**500 DOLLARS** 1993-. Brown and blue-green on m/c unpt. Face like #282.			
	a. Sign. titles: *CHIEF FINANCIAL OFFICER* and *AREA GENERAL MANAGER.* 1.1.1993.	FV	FV	100.00
	b. Sign. titles: *HEAD OF FINANCE* and *GENERAL MANAGER.* 1.1.1994; 1.1.1995; 1.1.1996; 1.1.1997; 1.7.1997; 1.1.1998.	FV	FV	90.00
289	**1000 DOLLARS** 1993-. Yellow-orange on m/c unpt. Face like #283.			
	a. Sign. titles: *CHIEF FINANCIAL OFFICER* and *AREA GENERAL MANAGER.* 1.1.1993.	FV	FV	190.00
	b. Sign. titles: *HEAD OF FINANCE* and *GENERAL MANAGER.* 1.1.1994; 1.1.1995; 1.1.1997; 1.7.1997.	FV	FV	175.00

GOVERNMENT OF HONG KONG

府政港香

Hsiang K'ang Cheng Fu

Signature Chart:

1	J.J. Cowperthwaite, 1961-71	4	Sir Piers Jacobs, 1986-92
2	C.P. Haddon-Cave, 1971-81	5	Sir Hamish Macleod, 1992-95
3	Sir J.H. Bremridge, 1981-86		

1961 ND ISSUE

#325-327 portr. Qn. Elizabeth II at r. Uniface.

		VG	VF	UNC
325	**1 CENT** ND (1961-95). Brown on lt. blue unpt.			
	a. Sign. 1. (1961-71).	.05	.10	.25
	b. Sign. 2. (1971-81).	.05	.25	.50
	c. Sign. 3. (1981-86).	.50	1.75	5.00
	d. Sign. 4. (1986-92).	.05	.10	.25
	e. Sign. 5. (1992-95).	.05	.10	.25

		VG	VF	UNC
326	**5 CENTS** ND (1961-65). Green on lilac unpt.	.35	1.75	10.00

		VG	VF	UNC
327	**10 CENTS** ND (1961-65). Red on grayish unpt.	.20	.90	7.00

PEOPLES REPUBLIC INFLUENCE

BANK OF CHINA

行銀國中

Chung Kuo Yin Hang

1994 ISSUE

#329-#333 Bank of China Tower at l. Wmk: Chinze. Printer: TDLR (HK) Ltd. (W/o imprint).

		VG	VF	UNC
329	**20 DOLLARS** 1.5.1994; 1.1.1996; 1.7.1997. Blue-black, blue and violet on m/c unpt. Narcissus flowers at lower ctr. r. Aerial view of Wanchai and Central Hong Kong at ctr. r. on back.	FV	FV	4.50

330	50 DOLLARS	VG	VF	UNC
	1.5.1994; 1.1.1996; 1.7.1997. Purple and blue on violet and m/c unpt. Chrysanthemum flowers at lower ctr. r. Aerial view of cross-harbor tunnel at ctr. r. on back.	FV	FV	10.00

331	100 DOLLARS	VG	VF	UNC
	1.5.1994; 1.1.1996; 1.7.1997. Red-violet, orange and red on m/c unpt. Lotus flowers at lower ctr. r. Aerial view of Tsimshatsui, Kowloon Peninsula at ctr. r. on back.	FV	FV	18.00

332	500 DOLLARS	VG	VF	UNC
	1.5.1994; 1.1.1995; 1.1.1996; 1.7.1997. Dk. brown and blue on m/c unpt. Peony flowers at lower ctr. r. Hong Kong Container Terminal in Kwai Chung at ctr. r. on back.	FV	FV	80.00

333	1000 DOLLARS	VG	VF	UNC
	1.5.1994; 1.1.1995; 1.1.1996; 1.7.1997. Reddish brown, orange and pale olive-green on m/c unpt. Bauhinia flowers at lower ctr. r. Aerial view overlooking the Central district at ctr. r. on back.	FV	FV	155.00

The Hungarian Republic, located in central Europe, has an area of 35,919 sq. mi. (93,030 sq. km.) and a population of 10.21 million. Capital: Budapest. The economy is based on agriculture and a rapidly expanding industrial sector. Machinery, chemicals, iron and steel, and fruits and vegetables are exported.

The ancient kingdom of Hungary, founded by the Magyars in the 9th century, expanded its greatest power and authority in the mid-14th century. After suffering repeated Turkish invasions, Hungary accepted Habsburg rule to escape Turkish occupation, regaining independence in 1867 with the Emperor of Austria as king of a dual Austro-Hungarian Empire.

Sharing the defeat of the Central Powers in World War I, Hungary lost the greater part of its territory and population and underwent a period of drastic political revision. The short-lived republic of 1918 was followed by a chaotic interval of communist rule during 1919, and the restoration of the kingdom in 1920 with Admiral Horthy as regent of a kingdom without a king. Although a German ally in World War II, Hungary was occupied by German troops who imposed a pro-Nazi dictatorship in 1944. Soviet armies drove out the Germans in 1945 and assisted the communist minority in seizing power. A revised constitution published on Aug. 20, 1949, had established Hungary as a "People's Republic" of the Soviet type, but it is once again a republic as of Oct. 23, 1989.

MONETARY SYSTEM:

1 Forint = 100 Fillér 1946-

PEOPLES REPUBLIC

MAGYAR NEMZETI BANK

HUNGARIAN NATIONAL BANK

1957-83 ISSUE

168	10 FORINT	VG	VF	UNC
	1957-75. Deep green on m/c unpt. Value at l., portr. S. Petőfi at r. Trees and river, "Birth of (Hungarian) Song" by János Jankó at ctr. on back.			
	a. 23.5.1957.	.30	2.50	7.50
	b. 24.8.1960.	.25	.75	5.00
	c. 12.10.1962.	.10	.50	3.50
	d. 30.6.1969.	.10	.40	2.00
	e. Serial # varieties. 28.10.1975.	FV	.25	1.50
	s. As a, c, d, e. Specimen w/red ovpt. and perforated: *MINTA*.	—	—	25.00

169	20 FORINT	VG	VF	UNC
	1957-80. Deep blue on m/c unpt. Value at l., portr. G. Dózsa at r. Nude penthathlete male Csaba Hegedüs with hammer and wheat at ctr. on back.			
	a. 23.5.1957.	.30	3.00	6.00
	b. 24.8.1960.	1.00	5.00	25.00
	c. 12.10.1962.	.20	1.50	5.00
	d. 3.9.1965.	.20	1.00	5.00
	e. 30.6.1969.	.20	.75	3.50
	f. Serial # varieties. 28.10.1975.	.15	.50	2.50
	g. 30.9.1980.	FV	.40	2.00
	s. As a - g. Specimen w/red ovpt. and perforated: *MINTA*.	—	—	25.00

#170, 172 and 173 arms of 3-bar shield w/star in grain spray.

		VG	VF	UNC
170	**50 FORINT** 1965-89. Deep brown and brown on m/c unpt. Value at l., portr. Prince F. Rákóczi II at r. Battle of the Hungarian insurrectionists "kuruc" against pro-Austrian soldiers "labanc" scene at ctr. on back.			
	a. 3.9.1965.	.35	1.50	7.50
	b. 30.6.1969.	.35	1.50	7.50
	c. Serial # varieties. 28.10.1975.	1.00	2.00	4.00
	d. Serial # prefix D. 30.9.1980.	.20	1.00	10.00
	e. Serial # prefix H. 30.9.1980.	.15	.75	4.00
	f. 10.11.1983.	.10	.50	2.50
	g. 4.11.1986.	.10	.50	2.50
	h. 10.1.1989.	.10	.40	2.00
	s. As a - h. Specimen. Ovpt *MINTA*.	—	—	25.00

		VG	VF	UNC
171	**100 FORINT** 1957-89. Violet on m/c unpt. Value at l., portr. L. Kossuth at r. Horse drawn wagon in "Took Refuge from the Storm" by K. Lotz at ctr. on back.			
	a. 23.5.1957.	1.00	3.00	6.00
	b. 24.8.1960.	2.00	4.00	6.50
	c. 12.10.1962.	1.50	3.00	4.50
	d. 24.10.1968.	FV	3.00	4.50
	e. 28.10.1975. Serial # varieties.	FV	3.00	4.00
	f. 30.9.1980.	FV	FV	3.00
	g. 30.10.1984.	FV	FV	3.00
	h. 10.1.1989.	FV	FV	2.00
	s. As a - h. As b, h. Specimen w/red ovpt. and perforted: *MINTA*.	—	—	25.00

		VG	VF	UNC
172	**500 FORINT** 1969-80. Purple on m/c unpt. Portr. E. Ady at r. Aerial view of Budapest and Danube River on back.			
	a. 30.6.1969.	FV	FV	6.00
	b. Serial # varieties. 28.10.1975.	FV	FV	4.50
	c. 30.9.1980.	FV	FV	4.50
	s. As c. Specimen.	—	—	25.00

		VG	VF	UNC
173	**1000 FORINT** 1983. Deep green and olive-green on m/c unpt. Portr. B. Bartók at r. Back green on m/c unpt.; Anya Statue - mother nursing baby by F. Medgyessy at ctr.			
	a. Serial # prefix: *A*. 25.3.1983.	FV	FV	8.00
	b. Serial # prefix: *B; C; D*. 10.11.1983.	FV	FV	8.00
	s. As a, b. Specimen w/red ovpt. and perforated: *MINTA*.	—	—	25.00

REPUBLIC

MAGYAR NEMZETI BANK

1990; 1992 ISSUE

#174-177 St. Stephan's Crown over Hungarian Arms replaces 3-bar shield.

#174-177 numerous photocopy counterfeits began appearing in mid-1999.

		VG	VF	UNC
174	**100 FORINT** 1992-95. Violet on m/c unpt. Like # 171 but w/new arms.			
	a. 15.1.1992.	FV	FV	1.50
	b. 16.12.1993.	FV	FV	1.50
	c. 20.12.1995.	FV	FV	1.50
	s. As a, b, c. Specimen w/red. ovpt. and perforated *MINTA*.	—	—	25.00

		VG	VF	UNC
175	**500 FORINT** 31.7.1990. Purple on m/c unpt. Like #172 but w/new arms.	FV	FV	4.50
176	**1000 FORINT** 1992-96. Deep green and olive-green on m/c unpt. Like #173 but w/new arms.			
	a. Serial # prefix: *D*. 30.10.1992.	FV	FV	9.00
	b. Serial # prefix: *D*. 16.12.1993.	FV	FV	7.50
	c. Serial # prefix: *E; F*. 15.1.1996.	FV	FV	7.50

		VG	VF	UNC
177	**5000 FORINT** 1990-95. Deep brown and brown on orange and m/c unpt. Portr. Count I. Széchenyi at r. Academy of Science at ctr. on back.			
	a. Serial # prefix: *H*. 31.7.1990.	FV	FV	30.00
	b. Serial # prefix: *J*. 30.10.1992.	FV	FV	30.00
	c. Serial # prefix: *J*. 16.12.1993.	FV	FV	30.00
	d. Serial # prefix: *J*; *K*. 31.8.1995.	FV	FV	30.00
	s. As a. Specimen w/red ovpt. and perforated: *MINTA*.	—	—	35.00

1997-99 ISSUE

#178-183 crowned arms at lower ctr.

		VG	VF	UNC
178	**200 FORINT** 1998. Dk. green and grayish purple on m/c unpt. Kg. R. Károly at r. and as wmk. Diósgyóri Vár castle ruins at l. on back.	FV	FV	2.00

		VG	VF	UNC
179	**500 FORINT** 1998. Brown-violet and violet on m/c unpt. Ferenc Rákóczi II at r. and as wmk. Sárospatak Castle on back.	FV	FV	4.00

		VG	VF	UNC
180	**1000 FORINT** 1998; 1999. Dk. blue-green and violet on m/c unpt. Kg. Mátyas at r. and as wmk. Fountain in the palace at Visegrád on back.	FV	FV	7.50

#181-183 w/hologram.

		VG	VF	UNC
181	**2000 FORINT** 1998. Dk. brown and brown on m/c unpt. Prince G. Bethlen at r. and as wmk. Prince G. Bethlen amongst scientists at l. ctr. on back.	FV	FV	12.50

		VG	VF	UNC
182	**5000 FORINT** 1999. Dp. violet and purple on m/c unpt. István Széchenyi at r. and as wmk. Széchenyi's home at Nagycenk on back. Serial # prefixes: *BA, BB, BC, BD, BF*.	FV	FV	30.00

		VG	VF	UNC
183	**10,000 FORINT** 1997-. Violet, dull purple and blue-black on m/c unpt. Kg. St. Stephan at r. and as wmk. View of Esztergom at l. ctr. on back.			
	a. Serial # prefixes: *AA, AB, AC*. 1997.	FV	FV	60.00
	b. Serial # prefixes: *AA, AB, AC* w/additional security devices. 1998.	FV	FV	60.00

NOTICE

Readers with unlisted dates, signature varieties, etc. are invited to submit photocopies of their notes to: Standard Catalog of World Paper Money, 700 East State St. Iola, WI 54990-0001, fax: 1-715-445-4087, or E-Mail: thernr@krause.com.

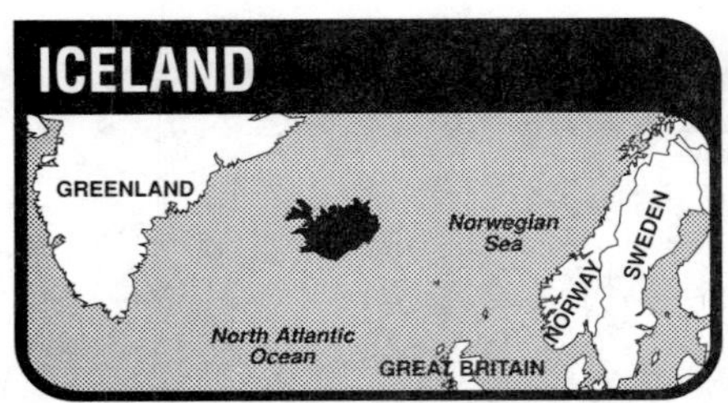

The Republic of Iceland, an island of recent volcanic origin in the North Atlantic east of Greenland and immediately south of the Arctic Circle, has an area of 39,768 sq. mi. (103,000 sq. km.) and a population of 269,700. Capital: Reykjavík. Fishing is the chief industry and accounts for more than 70 percent of the exports.

Iceland was settled by Norwegians in the 9th century and established as an independent republic in 930. The Icelandic assembly called the "Althing," also established in 930, is the oldest parliament in the world. Iceland came under Norwegian sovereignty in 1262, and passed to Denmark when Norway and Denmark were united under the Danish crown in 1384. In 1918, it was established as a virtually independent kingdom in union with Denmark. On June 17, 1944, while Denmark was still under occupation by troops of the Third Reich, Iceland was established by plebiscite as an independent republic.

MONETARY SYSTEM:

1 Krona = 100 Aurar, 1874-

SIGNATURE VARIETIES

SIGNATURE VARIETIES			
31	V. Thor – J. G. Mariasson, 1961–1964	32	J. Nordal - V. Thor, 1961-64
33	J.G. Mariasson - J. Nordal, 1961-67	34	J. Nordal - J.G. Mariasson, 1961-67
35	S. Klemenzson - J.G. Mariasson, 1966-67	36	J. Nordal - S. Klemenzson, 1966-67
37	J. Nordal - D. Olafsson, 1967-86	38	D. Olafsson - J. Nordal, 1967-86
39	S. Klemenzson - D. Olafsson, 1967-71	40	S. Frimannsson - D. Olafsson, 1971-73
41	J. Nordal - S. Frimannsson, 1971-73	42	G. Hjartarson - D. Olafsson, 1974-84
43	J. Nordal - G. Hjartarson, 1974-84	44	G. Hjartarson - T. Arnason, 1984
45	T. Arnason - J. Nordal, 1984-93	46	T. Arnason - D. Olafsson, 1984-93
47	J. Nordal - T. Arnason, 1984-93	48	G. Halmgrimsson - T. Arnason, 1986-90
49	J. Nordal - G. Hallgrimsson, 1986-90	50	B.I Gunnarsson - T. Arnason, 1991-93
51	J. Nordal - B.I. Gunnarsson, 1991-1993	52	J. Sigurthsson - B.I. Gunnarsson, 1994
53	B.I. Gunnarsson - J. Sigurthsson, 1994	54	E. Gudnason - S. Hermansson, 1994-
55	S. Hermansson - B.I. Gunnarsson, 1994	56	E. Gudnason, 199x

REPUBLIC

SEDLABANKI ÍSLANDS

CENTRAL BANK OF ICELAND

LAW OF 29.3.1961

#42-47 printer: BWC (w/o imprint).

#43-47 wmk: S. Bjornsson.

		VG	VF	UNC
42	**10 KRÓNUR** *L.1961.* Brown-violet on green and orange unpt. J. Eiriksson at l., ships in Port of Reykjavík at lower ctr. Back green; ships moored at pier. Sign. 33; 34.	1.50	3.00	6.00

		VG	VF	UNC
43	**25 KRÓNUR** *L.1961.* Purple on m/c unpt. M. Stephensen at l. Fjord at ctr. Fishing boats near Westmen Islands on back. Sign. 34.	1.00	2.00	5.00

		VG	VF	UNC
44	**100 KRÓNUR** *L.1961.* Dk. blue-green on m/c unpt. T. Gunnarsson at l. Sheepherders on horseback, sheep in foreground, Mt. Mekla in background on back. Sign. 31-33; 35; 36; 38-43.	.50	1.50	3.00

		VG	VF	UNC
45	**500 KRÓNUR** *L.1961.* Green on lilac and m/c unpt. H. Hafstein at l. Sailors on back. Sign. 36; 38-43.	1.00	2.00	6.00

46 **1000 Krónur**

	VG	VF	Unc
L.1961. Blue on m/c unpt. J. Sigurthsson at r., bldg. at lower ctr. Rock formations on back. Sign. 31-34; 36; 38-43.	2.50	5.00	10.00

47 **5000 Krónur**

	VG	VF	Unc
L.1961. Brown on m/c unpt. Similar to #41. E. Benediktsson at l., dam at lower ctr. Man overlooking waterfalls on back. Sign. 36; 38-43.	5.00	12.00	27.50

Law 29 March 1961 (1981-86) Issue

#48-52 Printer: BWC (w/o imprint), then later by TDLR (w/o imprint). These made after takeover of BWC by TDLR.

#48-53 wmk: J. Sigurthsson.

48 **10 Krónur**

	VG	VF	Unc
L.1961 (1981). Blue on m/c unpt. A. Jónsson at r. Old Icelandic household scene on back. Sign. 37; 38; 42; 43.	FV	FV	1.00

49 **50 Krónur**

	VG	VF	Unc
L.1961 (1981). Brown on m/c unpt. Bishop Guthbranthur Thorlaksson at l. 2 printers on back. Sign. 37; 38; 42; 43.	FV	FV	2.00

50 **100 Krónur**

	VG	VF	Unc
L.1961 (1981). Dk. green on m/c unpt. Prof. Magnússon at r. Monk w/illuminated manuscript on back. Sign. 37; 38; 42; 43; 45-53.	FV	FV	4.00

51 **500 Krónur**

	VG	VF	Unc
L.1961 (1981). Red on m/c unpt. J. Sigurthsson at l. ctr. Sigurthsson working at his desk on back. Sign. 37; 38; 42; 43; 45; 48-53.	FV	FV	15.00

52 **1000 Krónur**

	VG	VF	Unc
L.1961 (1984-91). Purple on m/c unpt. Bishop B. Sveinsson w/book at r. Church at ctr. on back. Sign. 38; 42; 43; 45; 48-51.	FV	FV	25.00

53 **5000 Krónur**

	VG	VF	Unc
L.1961 (1986-). Blue on m/c unpt. R. Jónsdór at ctr. Bishop G. Thorláksson w/two previous wives at r. Jónsdottir and two girls examining embroidery on back.			
a. Sign. 38; 46; 47.	FV	FV	145.00
b. Sign. 54-56. (1997).	FV	FV	125.00

Law 5 Mai 1986 (1994-) Issue

#54-56 like #50-52 but w/new sign. and law date.

		VG	VF	Unc
54	**100 Krónur** *L.1986* (1994). Sign 52; 53.	FV	FV	3.00
55	**500 Krónur** *L.1986* (1994). Sign. 45; 50-53.	FV	FV	13.50

		VG	VF	Unc
56	**1000 Krónur** *L.1986* (1994). Sign. 45; 50; 51; 54-56.	FV	FV	22.50

		VG	VF	Unc
57	**2000 Krónur** *L.1986* (1995). Brown and blue-violet on m/c unpt. Painting "Inside, Outside" at ctr., J. S. Kajarval at r. Painting "Yearning for Flight" (Leda and the Swan) and "Woman with Flower" on back. Sign. 54-56.	FV	FV	45.0C

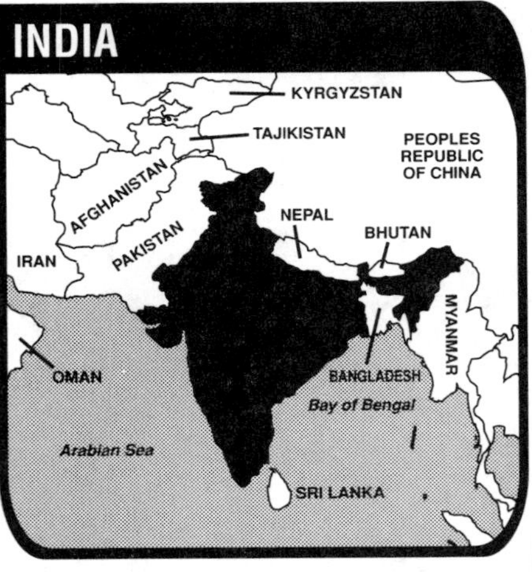

The Republic of India, a subcontinent jutting southward from the mainland of Asia, has an area of 1,266,595 sq. mi. (3,287,590 sq. km.) and a population of 913.2 million, second only to that of the Peoples Republic of China. Capital: New Delhi. India's economy is based on agriculture and industrial activity. Engineering goods, cotton apparel and fabrics, handicrafts, tea, iron and steel are exported.

The people of India have had a continuous civilization since about 2500 BC, when an urban culture based on commerce and trade, and to a lesser extent, agriculture, was developed by the inhabitants of the Indus River Valley. The origins of this civilization are uncertain, but it declined about 1500 B.C., when the region was conquered by the Aryans. Over the following 2,000 years, the Aryans developed a Brahmanic civilization and introduced the caste system. Several successive empires flourished in India over the following centuries, notably those of the Mauryans, Guptas and Mughals. In the 7th and 8th centuries AD, the Arabs expanded into western India, bringing with them the Islamic faith. A Muslim dynasty (the Mughal Empire) controlled virtually the entire subcontinent during the period preceding the arrival of the Europeans; an Indo-Islamic style of art and architecture evolved, of which the Taj Mahal is a splendid example.

The Portuguese were the first to arrive, off Calicut in May 1498. It was not until 1612, after Portuguese and Spanish power began to wane, that the English East India Company established its initial settlement at Surat. By the end of the century, English traders were firmly established in Bombay, Madras and Calcutta, as well as in some parts of the interior, and Britain was implementing a policy to create the civil and military institutions that would insure British dominion over the country. By 1757, following the successful conclusion of a war of colonial rivalry with France, the British were firmly established in India not only as traders, but as conquerors. During the next 60 years, the English East India Company acquired dominion over most of India by bribery and force, and ruled directly or through puppet princelings.

The Indian Mutiny (also called Sepoy Mutiny) of 1857-59, begun by Indian troops in the service of the British East India Company, revealed the intensity of the growing resentment against British domination. The widespread rebellion against British rule was unsuccessful, but resulted in the transfer of government from the company to the British crown.

Following World War I, in which India sent six million troops to fight at the side of the Allies, Indian nationalism intensified under the banner of the Indian National Congress and the leadership of Mohandas Gandhi, who called the non-violent revolt against British authority. The Government of India Act of 1935 proposed a federal status linking the British India provinces with the many princely states; in addition, provincial legislatures were to be created. The federal status was never implemented, but the legislatures were created after the election of 1937, with the National Congress winning majorities in most of the provinces.

When Britain declared war on Germany in Sept., 1939, the viceroy declared India also to be at war with a common enemy. The Congress, however, demanded independence as a condition for cooperation. Britain refused. But as the Japanese advanced into Asia, Britain offered to transfer to Indians power over all but military affairs during the war, and set forth a plan for postwar independence. Congress was willing to accept the wartime transfer of power, but both Congress and the Muslim League rejected Britain's plan for independence; Congress because it did not sufficiently safeguard Indian unity, the Muslims (who wanted a separate Muslim state) because of fears of what would happen to Muslims within a united India.

Early in 1947, Prime Minister Clement Attlee announced that Britain would leave India "by a date not later than June 1948," even though the Hindus and Muslims could not agree among themselves on a plan for self-government. The National Congress, aware that the Muslim League would revolt rather than accept an all-India government, reluctantly agreed to the formation of a separate Muslim state. The Muslim-populated provinces of the northwest frontier, Sindh and West Punjab in the west, and East Bengal in the east were separated from India to form the Muslim state of Pakistan, which became independent on August 14, 1947. India became independent on the following day. Initially, Pakistan consisted of East and West Pakistan, two areas separated by 1,000 miles of Indian territory. East Pakistan seceded from Pakistan on March 26, 1971, and with the support of India established itself as the independent Peoples Republic of Bangladesh.

The Republic of India is a member of the Commonwealth of Nations. The president is the Chief of State. The prime minister is the Head of Government.

NOTE: Since March 1994, 1, 2 and 5 Rupee notes are no longer issued. They have been replaced by coins.

MONETARY SYSTEM:

1 Rupee = 100 Naye Paise, 1957-1964
1 Rupee = 100 Paise, 1964-

NOTE: STAPLE HOLES AND CONDITION:

Perfect uncirculated notes are rarely encountered without having at least two tiny holes made by staples, stick pins or stitching having been done during age old accounting practices before and after a note is released to circulation.

SIGNATURE VARIETIES			
Governors, Reserve Bank of India (all except 1 Rupee notes)			
71	C. D. Deshmukh February 1943–June 1949	72	B. Rama Rau July 1949-January 1957
73	K. G. Ambegaokar January 1957-February 1957	74	H. V. R. Iengar July 1949-January 1957

75	P. C. Bhattacharyya March 1962-June 1967	76	L. K. Jha July 1967-May 1970
77	B. N. Adarkar May 1970-June 1970	78	S. Jagannathan June 1970-May 1975
79	N. C. Sen Gupta May 1975-August 1975	80	K. R. Puri August 1975-May 1977
81	M. Narasimham May 1975-August 1975	82	I. G. Patel December 1977-1981
83	Manmohan Singh 1981-1983	84	R. N. Malhotra 1983-1984
85	Abhitam Ghosh, 1984 (in office 20 days)	86	S. Venkitaramanan 1984-
87	C. Rangarajan	88	R. N. Malhotra

REPUBLIC OF INDIA

RESERVE BANK OF INDIA

FIRST SERIES

#27-47 Asoka column at r. Lg. letters in unpt. beneath serial #. Wmk: Asoka column.

Error singular Hindi = *RUPAYA* Corrected plural Hindi = *RUPAYE*

VARIETIES: #27-28, 33, 38, 42, 46, 48 and 50 have large headings in Hindi expressing value incorrectly in the singular form Rupaya.

NOTE: For similar notes but in different colors, please see Haj Pilgrim and Persian Gulf listings at the end of this country listing.

		VG	VF	UNC
27	**2 RUPEES** ND. Red-brown on violet and green unpt. Tiger head at l. on back. Value in English and error Hindi on face and back. Gujarati numberal 2 at upper r. 8 value text lines on back. Sign. 72.	.50	2.50	8.00
28	**2 RUPEES** ND. Similar to #27 but English 2 at upper l. and r. Redesigned panels on face. 7 value text lines on back; third 18mm long. Sign 72.	.50	2.50	8.00
29	**2 RUPEES** ND. Red-brown on violet and green unpt. Like #28 but Hindi corrected. Tiger head at l. looking to l., third value text line on back 24mm long.	VG	VF	UNC
	a. Sign. 72.	1.25	5.00	20.00
	b. Sign. 74.	1.00	4.00	12.00

		VG	VF	UNC
30	**2 RUPEES** ND. Red-brown on green unpt. Face like #29. Tiger head at l. looking to r., w/13 value text lines at ctr. on back. Sign. 75.	1.50	6.50	18.00

		VG	VF	UNC
31	**2 RUPEES** ND. Olive on tan unpt. Like #30. Sign. 75.	2.00	6.50	17.50
32	**5 RUPEES** ND. Green on brown unpt. English value only on face, serial # at ctr. *Rs. 5* and antelope on back. Sign 72.	1.00	4.00	15.00
33	**5 RUPEES** ND. Like #32 but value in English and error Hindi on face, serial # at r. 8 value lines on back, fourth line 21mm long. Sign. 72.	.75	2.00	9.00

		VG	VF	UNC
34	**5 RUPEES** ND. Like #33 but Hindi corrected. Fourth value text line on back 26mm long. Sign. 72.	.75	3.00	9.00
35	**5 RUPEES** ND. Green on brown unpt. Like #34 but redesigned panels at l. and r.	VG	VF	UNC
	a. W/o letter. Sign. 74.	1.00	5.00	15.00
	b. Letter A. Sign. 74.	1.00	5.00	15.00

NOTE: For similar note but in orange, see #R2 (Persian Gulf listings).

		VG	VF	UNC
36	**5 RUPEES** ND (1962-67). Green on brown unpt. Like #35 but sign. title: *GOVERNOR* centered. 13 value text lines on back.	VG	VF	UNC
	a. Letter A. Sign. 75.	2.00	7.00	20.00
	b. Letter B. Sign. 75.	1.25	6.00	20.00
37	**10 RUPEES** ND. Violet on m/c unpt. English value only on face. *Rs. 10* at lower ctr. 1 serial #. English in both lower corners, dhow at ctr. on back.	VG	VF	UNC
	a. Sign. 71.	6.50	16.50	50.00
	b. Sign. 72.	4.00	10.00	30.00
38	**10 RUPEES** ND. Like #37 but value in English and error Hindi on face and back. 2 serial #. Third value text line on back. 24mm long. Sign. 72.	.75	3.00	15.00

		VG	VF	UNC
39	**10 RUPEES** ND. Violet on m/c unpt. Like #38 but Hindi corrected. Dhow at ctr. on back. Third value text line on back 29mm long.	VG	VF	UNC
	a. W/o letter. Sign. 72.	2.00	6.00	15.00
	b. W/o letter. Sign. 74.	2.00	6.00	15.00
	c. Letter A. Sign. 74.	2.00	6.00	15.00

NOTE: For similar note but in red, see #R3 (Persian Gulf listings); in blue, see #R5 (Haj Pilgrim listings).

		VG	VF	UNC
40	**10 RUPEES** ND. Green on brown unpt. Like #39 but sign. title: *GOVERNOR* centered. 13 value text lines on back.	VG	VF	UNC
	a. Letter A. Sign. 75.	2.00	5.00	15.00
	b. Letter B. Sign. 75.	2.00	5.00	15.00
41	**100 RUPEES** ND. Blue on m/c unpt. English value only on face. Two elephants at ctr. w/8 value text lines below and bank emblem at l. on back.	VG	VF	UNC
	a. Dk. blue. Sign. 72.	30.00	60.00	135.00
	b. Lt. blue. Sign. 72.	25.00	55.00	110.00

		VG	VF	UNC
42	**100 RUPEES** ND. Purplish-blue on m/c unpt. Like #41 but value in English and error Hindi on face and back. 7 value text lines on back; third 27mm long.			
	a. Black serial #. Sign. 72.	16.00	40.00	100.00
	b. Red serial #. Sign. 72.	16.00	40.00	100.00

		VG	VF	UNC
43	**100 RUPEES** ND. Purplish blue on m/c unpt. Like #42 but Hindi corrected. Third value text line 40mm long.			
	a. W/o letter, thin paper. Sign. 72.	15.00	35.00	85.00
	b. W/o letter, thin paper. Sign. 74.	15.00	35.00	85.00
	c. Letter A, thick paper. Sign. 74.	Reported Not Confirmed		

NOTE: For similar note but in green, see #R4 (Persian Gulf listings); in red, see #R6 (Haj Pilgrim listings).

		VG	VF	UNC
44	**100 RUPEES** ND. Violet and m/c. Heading in rectangle at top, serial # at upper l. and lower r. Title: *GOVERNOR* at ctr. r. Dam at ctr. w/13 value text lines at l. on back. Sign. 74.	15.00	35.00	85.00
45	**100 RUPEES** ND. Violet and m/c. Like #44 but sign. title: *GOVERNOR* centered. Sign. 75.	12.50	25.00	65.00

		VG	VF	UNC
46	**1000 RUPEES** ND. Brown on green and blue unpt. Value in English and error Hindi on face and back. Tanjore Temple at ctr. w/7 value text lines at l. on back.			
	a. BOMBAY. Sign. 72.	50.00	125.00	—
	b. CALCUTTA. Sign. 72.	50.00	125.00	—
	c. DELHI. Sign. 72.	50.00	125.00	—
	d. MADRAS. Sign. 72.	50.00	125.00	—

		GOOD	FINE	XF
47	**1000 RUPEES** ND. Brown on green and blue unpt. Like #46 but Hindi corrected. Tanjore Temple at ctr. 13 value text lines on back. *BOMBAY*.			
	a. Sign. 75.	35.00	75.00	125.00
	b. Sign. 79.	35.00	75.00	125.00
	c. Sign. 80.	35.00	75.00	125.00
48	**5000 RUPEES** ND. Green, violet and brown. Asoka column at l. Value in English and error Hindi on face and back. Gateway of India on back.			
	a. *BOMBAY*. Sign. 72.	—	Rare	—
	b. *CALCUTTA*. Sign. 72.	—	Rare	—
	c. *DELHI*. Sign. 72.	—	Rare	—
49	**5000 RUPEES** ND. Green, violet and brown. Like #48 but Hindi corrected. Gateway of India on back. *BOMBAY*. Sign. 74.	200.00	325.00	800.00

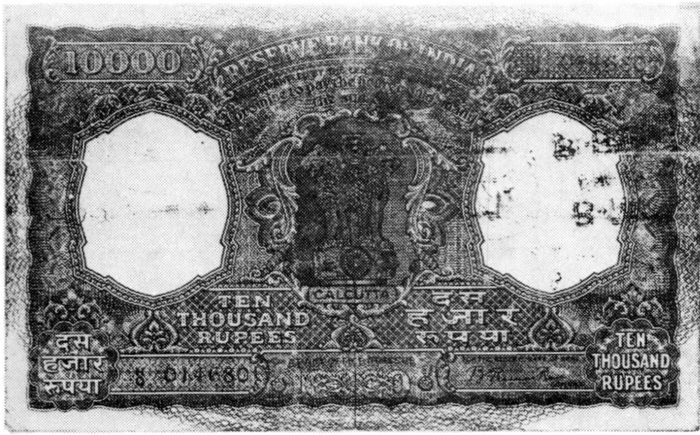

		GOOD	FINE	XF
50	**10,000 RUPEES** ND. Blue, violet and brown. Asoka column at ctr. Value in English and error Hindi on face and back.			
	a. *BOMBAY*. Sign. 72.	400.00	650.00	1250.
	b. *CALCUTTA*. Sign. 72.	400.00	650.00	1250.
50A	**10,000 RUPEES** ND. Like #50 but Hindi corrected.			
	a. *BOMBAY*. Sign. 74.	400.00	650.00	1250.
	b. *MADRAS*. Sign. 74.	500.00	800.00	1250.
	c. *NEW DELHI*. Sign. 74.	500.00	800.00	1250.
	d. *BOMBAY*. Sign. 76.	500.00	800.00	1250.

SECOND SERIES

Most notes of reduced size. Large letters found in unpt. beneath serial #.

#51-65 Asoka column at r.

Urdu Incorrect (actually Farsi)

Corrected Urdu

		VG	VF	UNC
51	**2 RUPEES** ND. Brown and m/c. Numeral *2* at ctr. 7mm high. Tiger at ctr. on back.			
	a. Sign. 75 w/title: *GOVERNOR* centered at bottom.	.75	2.50	12.00
	b. Sign. 76 w/title: *GOVERNOR* at ctr. r.	.75	2.50	12.00

		VG	VF	UNC
52	**2 RUPEES** ND. Deep pink and m/c. Numeral *2* at ctr. 15mm high. Tiger at ctr. on back. Sign. 78.	.50	2.00	10.00
53	**2 RUPEES** ND. Deep pink and m/c. English text at l. on face. Like #52 but corrected Urdu at bottom l. on back.			
	a. W/o letter. Sign. 78.	.50	2.50	10.00
	b. W/o letter. Sign. 80.	.50	2.50	10.00

	VG	VF	UNC
c. Letter A. Sign. 80.	.75	3.00	12.00
d. Letter A. Sign. 82.	.20	1.00	4.00
e. Letter B. Sign. 82.	.20	1.00	4.00
f. Letter C. Sign. 82.	.20	1.00	4.00
g. Letter C. Sign. 83.	.20	1.00	4.00

53A 2 RUPEES

ND. Deep pink and m/c. English text at r. on face. Similar to #53 but tiger at ctr. on back.

	VG	VF	UNC
a. W/o letter. Sign. 83.	.30	1.00	4.00
b. Letter A. Sign. 85.	.30	1.00	4.00
c. Letter B. Sign. 85.	.30	1.00	4.00
d. W/o letter. Sign. 84.	.40	1.50	7.00
e. Letter B. Sign. 86.	.25	1.00	3.00

54 5 RUPEES

ND. Green and m/c. Numeral *5* at ctr. 11mm high. Antelope at ctr. on back.

	VG	VF	UNC
a. Sign. 75 w/title: *GOVERNOR* centered at bottom.	.50	2.50	10.00
b. Sign. 76 w/title: *GOVERNOR* at ctr. r.	.50	2.50	10.00

55 5 RUPEES

	VG	VF	UNC
ND. Dk. green on m/c unpt. Numeral *5* at ctr. 17mm high. Antelope at ctr. on back. Sign. 78.	.50	2.50	10.00

56 5 RUPEES

ND. Dk. green on m/c unpt. Like #55 but antelope at ctr., corrected Urdu at bottom l. on back.

	VG	VF	UNC
a. W/o letter. Sign. 78.	.50	2.00	7.50
b. Letter A. Sign. 78.	.50	2.00	7.50

57 10 RUPEES

ND. Purple and m/c. Numeral *10* at ctr. 30mm broad. Dhow at ctr. on back.

	VG	VF	UNC
a. Sign. 75 w/title: *GOVERNOR* centered at bottom.	1.00	2.50	10.00
b. Sign. 76 w/title: *GOVERNOR* at ctr. r.	1.00	2.50	10.00

58 10 RUPEES

	VG	VF	UNC
ND. Black on brown and pale green unpt. Numeral *10* at ctr. 18mm broad. Heading in English and Hindi on back. Sign. 76.	2.50	10.00	25.00

59 10 RUPEES

ND. Dk. brown on m/c unpt. Like #58. Heading only in Hindi on back.

	VG	VF	UNC
a. W/o letter. Sign. 78.	.75	2.50	10.00
b. Letter A. Sign. 78.	.75	2.50	10.00

60 10 RUPEES

ND. Dk. brown on m/c unpt. Like #59 but corrected Urdu at bottom l. on back.

	VG	VF	UNC
a. Letter A. Sign. 78.	1.00	3.00	10.00
b. Letter B. Sign. 78.	1.00	5.00	20.00
c. Letter B. Sign. 80.	1.00	3.00	10.00
d. Letter B. Sign. 81.	1.00	5.00	30.00
e. Letter C. Sign. 81.	.75	3.00	9.00
f. Letter C. Sign. 82.	.75	3.00	9.00
g. Letter D. Sign. 82.	.75	3.00	9.00
h. Letter D. Sign. 83.	.75	3.00	9.00
i. Letter E. Sign. 83.	.75	3.00	9.00
j. Letter E. Sign. 85.	.75	3.00	9.00
k. Letter F. Sign. 85.	.75	3.00	9.00
l. Letter G. Sign. 85.	.75	3.00	9.00
m. Letter E. Sign. 84.	1.00	4.00	14.00

60A 10 RUPEES

ND. Dk. brown on m/c unpt. but w/Hindi title above *RESERVE BANK OF INDIA* and Hindi text at l. of *10* and *I PROMISE...* at r. Sanskrit title added under Asoka column at r.

	VG	VF	UNC
a. Sign. 85.	.50	2.00	6.00
b. Sign. 86. Lg. serial #.	.50	2.00	6.00
c. Sign. 86. Sm. serial #.	.50	2.00	6.00
d. Sign. 88.	.50	2.00	6.00

Incorrect Kashmiri (actually Farsi)

Corrected Kashmiri

61 20 RUPEES

ND. Orange and m/c. Parliament House at ctr. on back. Sign. 78.

	VG	VF	UNC
a. Dk. colors under sign., error in Kashmiri in fifth line on back.	2.00	6.00	17.50
b. Lt. colors under sign., error in Kashmiri in fifth line on back.	1.50	5.00	12.00

61A 20 RUPEES

	VG	VF	UNC
ND. Orange and m/c. Like #61b but corrected Kashmiri in fifth line on back.	1.50	5.00	12.00

		VG	VF	UNC
62	**100 RUPEES** ND. Blue and m/c. Numeral *100* at ctr. 43mm broad. Dam at ctr. w/only English heading on back.			
	a. Sign. 75.	6.00	15.00	50.00
	b. Sign. 76.	6.00	15.00	50.00

		VG	VF	UNC
63	**100 RUPEES** ND. Blue and m/c. Numeral *100* at ctr. 28mm broad. Dam at ctr. w/only Hindi heading on back. Sign. 78.	6.00	15.00	40.00

		VG	VF	UNC
64	**100 RUPEES** ND. Like #63 but corrected Urdu value line on back.			
	a. W/o letter. Sign. 78.	5.00	15.00	45.00
	b. W/o letter. Sign. 80.	5.00	14.00	35.00
	c. W/o letter. Sign. 81.	5.00	14.00	35.00
	d. Letter A. Sign. 82.	5.00	14.00	40.00

		VG	VF	UNC
65	**1000 RUPEES** ND. Brown on m/c unpt. Text in English and Hindi on face. Temple at ctr. on back. *BOMBAY.*			
	a. Sign. 79.	35.00	75.00	125.00
	b. Sign. 80.	35.00	75.00	125.00

GOVERNMENT OF INDIA

1969 ND COMMEMORATIVE ISSUE

#66, Centennial - Birth of M. K. Gandhi

		VG	VF	UNC
66	**1 RUPEE** ND (1969-70). Violet and m/c. Coin w/Gandhi and *1869-1948* at r. Reverse of Gandhi coin on back at l. Sign. 82.	.75	2.50	7.50

RESERVE BANK OF INDIA

1969 ND COMMEMORATIVE ISSUE

#67-70, Centennial - Birth of M. K. Gandhi

		VG	VF	UNC
67	**2 RUPEES** ND (1969-70). Red-violet and m/c. Face like #52. Gandhi seated at ctr. on back.			
	a. Sign. 76.	1.00	3.00	10.00
	b. Sign. 77.	1.00	3.00	10.00

		VG	VF	UNC
68	**5 RUPEES** ND (1969-70). Dk. green on m/c unpt. Face like #55. Back like #67.			
	a. Sign. 76.	.75	3.00	10.00
	b. Sign. 77.	1.00	4.00	12.50

		VG	VF	UNC
69	**10 RUPEES** ND (1969-70). Brown and m/c. Face like #59. Back like #68.			
	a. Sign. 76.	1.00	4.00	12.50
	b. Sign. 77.	1.50	6.00	15.00

70 **100 RUPEES**

	VG	VF	UNC
ND (1969-70). Blue and m/c. Face like #63. Back like #68.			
a. Sign. 76.	7.50	25.00	70.00
b. Sign. 77.	7.50	25.00	70.00

GOVERNMENT OF INDIA

SIGNATURE VARIETIES			
Various Secretaries, (1 Rupee notes only)			
33	H. M. Patel, 1951–1957	34	A.K. Roy, 1957
35	L.K. Jha, 1957-1963	36	S. Boothalingam, 1964–1966
NOTE: The sign. H. M. Patel is often misread as "Mehta." There was never any such individual serving as Secretary. Do not confuse H. M. Patel with I. G. Patel who served later.			
37	S. Jagannathan, 1967–1968	38	I.G. Patel, 1968-19725
39	M.G. Kaul, 1973-1976	40	Manomohan Singh, 1976-1980
41	R.N. Malhotra, 1980-1981	42	M. Narasimham, 1981-1985
43	Pratap Kishen Kaul, 1983-1985	44	S. Venkitaramanan, 1985-1988
45	Gopi Arora, 1989	46	Bimal Jalan, 1990
47	S.B. Shukla, 1991	48	Montek Singh Ahluwalia, 1991

1957; 1963 ISSUE

#75-78A wmk: Asoka column.

75 **1 RUPEE**

	VG	VF	UNC
1957. Violet on m/c unpt. Redesigned coin w/Asoka column at r. Coin dated 1957, *100 Naye Paise* in Hindi, 7 value text lines on back.			
a. Letter A. Sign. 33 w/sign. title: *SECRETARY...*	.75	3.00	10.00
b. Letter A. Sign. 33 w/sign. title: *PRINCIPAL SECRETARY...*	.50	2.00	8.00
c. Letter B. Sign. 34 w/sign. title: *SECRETARY...*	1.00	4.00	20.00
d. Letter B. Sign. 35.	1.50	6.00	50.00
e. Letter C. Sign. 35.	.30	1.25	5.00
f. Letter D. Sign. 35.	.30	1.25	5.00

NOTE: For similar note but in red, see #R1 in Persian Gulf listings.

76 **1 RUPEE**

	VG	VF	UNC
1963-65. Violet on m/c unpt. Redesigned note. Coin w/various dates and *1 Rupee* in Hindi, 13 value text lines on back.			
a. Letter A. Sign. 35. 1963.	.20	.75	3.00
b. Letter B. Sign. 36. 1964.	2.00	10.00	75.00
c. Letter B. Sign. 36. 1965.	.30	1.25	5.00

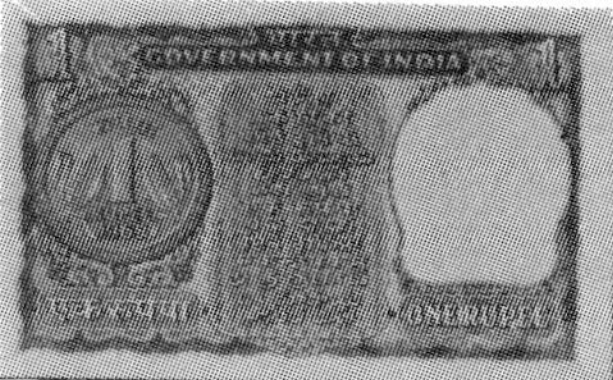

77 **1 RUPEE**

	VG	VF	UNC
1966-80. Violet on m/c unpt. Redesigned note, serial # at l. Coin w/various dates on back.			
a. W/o letter. Sign. 36. 1966.	.20	.75	3.00
b. Letter A. Sign. 37. 1967.	.35	1.25	5.00
c. Letter A. Sign. 37. 1968.	.20	.75	3.00
d. Letter B. Sign. 38 w/sign. title: *SPECIAL SECRETARY...* 1968.	.20	.75	3.00
e. Letter B. Sign. 38 w/sign. title: *SPECIAL SECRETARY...* 1969.	.20	.75	3.00
f. Letter C. Sign. 38 w/title: *SPECIAL SECRETARY...* 1969.	.15	.60	2.50
g. Letter C. Sign. 38. 1970.	.20	.75	3.00
h. Letter C. Sign. 38. 1971.	.20	.75	3.00
i. Letter D. Sign. 38. 1971.	.20	.75	3.00
j. Letter D. Sign. 38. 1972.	.20	.75	3.00
k. Letter E. Sign. 38. 1972.	.20	.75	3.00
l. Letter E. Sign. 39. 1973.	.20	.75	3.00
m. Letter F. Sign. 39. 1973.	.20	.75	3.00
n. Letter F. Sign. 39. 1974.	.20	.75	3.00
o. Letter G. Sign. 39. 1974.	.20	.75	3.00
p. Letter G. Sign. 39. 1975.	.20	.75	3.00
q. Letter H. Sign. 39. 1975.	.20	.75	3.00
r. Letter H. Sign. 39. 1976.	.20	.75	3.00
s. Letter I. Sign. 39. 1976.	.30	1.00	4.00
t. W/o letter. Sm. serial #. Sign. 40. 1976.	.15	.60	2.50
u. Sm. serial #. Sign. 40. 1977.	.15	.60	2.50
v. Letter A. Sign. 40. 1978.	.15	.60	2.50
w. Letter A. Sign. 40. 1979.	.15	.60	2.50
x. Letter A. Sign. 40. 1980.	.15	.60	2.50
y. W/o letter. Sign. 41. 1980.	.20	.75	3.00
z. Letter A. Sign. 41. 1980.	.20	.75	3.00
aa. Letter B. Sign. 41. 1980.	.10	.50	2.00

78 **1 RUPEE**

	VG	VF	UNC
1981-82. Purple and violet on lt. blue, brown and m/c unpt. Coin w/Asoka column at upper r. Offshore oil drilling platform and reverse of coin w/date on back.			
a. Sign. 41. 1981.	.10	.25	1.00
b. Sign. 42. 1981.	.10	.25	1.00

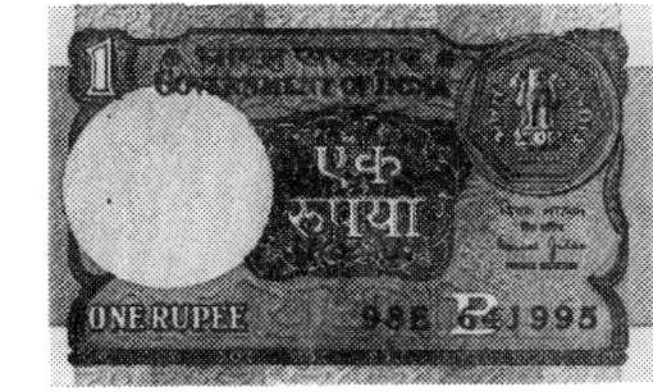

78A **1 RUPEE**

	VG	VF	UNC
1983-1994. Similar to #78 but w/new coin design.			
a. Sign. 43 w/title: *SECRETARY...* 1983-85.	.10	.20	1.00
b. Sign. 44 w/title: *FINANCE SECRETARY...* 1985.	.10	.20	1.00
c. Letter A. Sign. 44. 1986-89.	.10	.20	1.00
d. Letter B. Sign. 45. 1989.	.20	.50	2.00
e. Letter B. Sign. 46. 1990.	.20	.50	2.00
f. Letter B. Sign. 47. 1991.	.20	.75	2.50
g. Letter B. Sign. 48 w/title: *SECRETARY...* 1991.	.20	.75	2.50

	VG	VF	UNC
h. Letter B. Sign. 48. 1992.	.20	.75	2.50
i. Letter B. Sign. 48 w/title: *FINANCE SECRETARY...* 1993.	2.00	4.00	15.00
j. Letter B. Sign. 48. 1994.	.25	1.00	3.00

RESERVE BANK OF INDIA

THIRD SERIES

Lg. letters in unpt. beneath serial #.
#79-88 Asoka column at r. and as wmk.

79 2 RUPEES

ND(1976). Orange on m/c unpt. Space craft at ctr. on back.

	VG	VF	UNC
a. Sign. 80.	.50	1.50	4.00
b. Sign. 81.	.60	2.50	5.00
c. W/o letter. W/o wmk. Sign. 82.	.50	1.50	4.00
d. W/o letter. W/wmk: 6 wheels surrounding Asoka column. Sign. 82.	.50	1.50	4.00
e. Letter A. Sign. 82.	.50	1.50	4.00
f. Letter A. Sign. 83.	.50	1.50	4.00
g. Letter B. Sign. 83.	Reported Not Confirmed		
h. W/o letter. Sign. 85.	.50	1.50	4.00
i. Letter A. Sign. 85.	.50	1.50	4.00
j. Letter B. Sign. 85.	.50	1.50	4.00
k. Letter A. Sign. 84.	1.00	2.50	5.00
l. Letter B. Sign. 86.	.40	1.50	4.00
m. Letter B. Sign. 87.	.40	1.50	4.00

	VG	VF	UNC
a.			
b. W/o letter. Sign. 80.	.50	2.00	4.00
c. Letter A. Sign. 80.	.50	2.00	4.00
d. Letter A. Sign. 81.	.50	2.00	4.00
e. Letter A. Sign. 82.	.50	2.00	4.00
f. Letter B. Sign. 82.	.50	1.25	3.00
g. Letter C. Sign. 82.	.50	1.25	3.00
h. Letter C. Sign. 83.	.25	.75	3.00
i. Letter D. Sign. 83.	.25	.75	3.00
j. W/o letter. New seal in Hindi and English. Sign. 85.	.25	.75	3.00
k. Letter A. New seal. Sign. 85.	.25	.75	3.00
l. Letter E. Sign. 84.	.75	1.50	4.00
m. Letter F. Sign. 85.	.25	.75	3.00
n. Letter G. Sign. 85.	.25	.75	3.00
o. Letter D. Sign. 85.	.50	2.00	5.00
p. Letter B. Sign. 86.	.25	.75	2.50
q. Letter B. Sign. 87.	.15	.50	2.00

81 10 RUPEES

ND. Brown on m/c unpt. Tree w/peacocks at ctr. on back.

	VG	VF	UNC
a. W/o letter. Sign. 78.	1.00	2.50	6.00
b. W/o letter. Sign. 80.	1.00	2.50	6.00
c. W/o letter. Sign. 81.	1.25	3.00	7.50
d. Letter A. Sign. 82.	.75	3.00	4.00
e. W/o letter. Sign. 82.	.75	3.00	4.00
f. Letter A. Sign. 83.	.50	1.25	4.00
g. Letter B. Sign. 85.	.50	1.00	4.00
h. Letter C. Sign. 85.	.50	1.00	4.00

82 20 RUPEES

ND. Red and purple on m/c unpt. Back orange on m/c unpt.; Hindu Wheel of Sun God at lower ctr.

	VG	VF	UNC
a. Sign. 78.	1.00	2.50	7.50
b. Sign. 80.	1.00	2.50	7.50
c. Sign. 81.	1.50	4.00	9.00
d. W/o letter. Sign. 82.	1.00	2.50	7.50
e. Letter A. Sign. 82.	1.00	2.50	7.50
f. Letter A. Sign. 83.	1.00	2.50	5.00
g. Letter A. Sign. 84.	1.00	2.50	5.00
h. Letter B. Sign. 84.	1.00	2.50	5.00
i. Letter B. Sign. 87.	.75	2.00	4.00
j. Letter C. Sign. 87.	.50	1.25	2.75
k. Letter C. Sign. 89.	.50	1.25	2.75

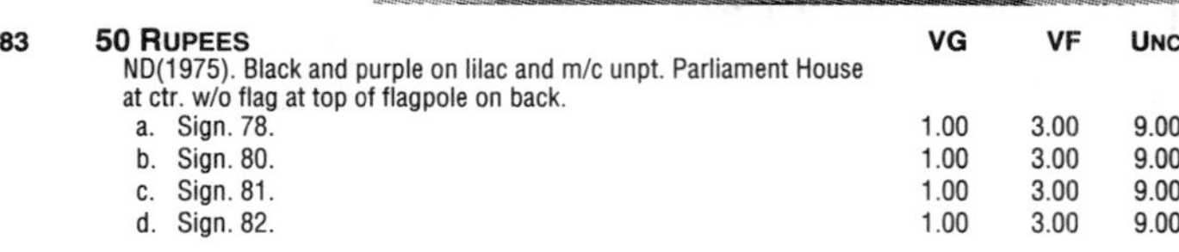

83 50 RUPEES

ND(1975). Black and purple on lilac and m/c unpt. Parliament House at ctr. w/o flag at top of flagpole on back.

	VG	VF	UNC
a. Sign. 78.	1.00	3.00	9.00
b. Sign. 80.	1.00	3.00	9.00
c. Sign. 81.	1.00	3.00	9.00
d. Sign. 82.	1.00	3.00	9.00

84 50 RUPEES

ND(1978). Black and purple on orange, lilac and m/c unpt. Similar to #83 but w/flag at top of flagpole on back.

	VG	VF	UNC
a. Sign. 85.	1.25	3.00	8.00
b. Sign. 85.	1.25	3.00	8.00
c. Sign. 84.	1.25	2.50	8.00
d. Letter A. Sign. 84.	1.25	2.50	8.00
e. Letter B. Sign. 84.	1.25	2.50	8.00
f. Letter A. Sign. 86.	1.25	2.50	6.00
g. Letter B. Sign. 86.	1.25	2.50	6.00
h. Letter A. Sign. 87.	1.25	2.50	6.00
i. Letter B. Sign. 87.	1.25	2.50	5.00
j. Letter C. Sign. 87.	1.25	2.50	5.00

85	100 RUPEES	VG	VF	UNC
	ND(1975). Black and blue-violet on brown and m/c unpt. (tan at ctr.). Dam, agricultural work at ctr. on back. Denomination above bar at lower r. Black sign.			
	a. Sign. 78.	4.50	7.00	22.50
	b. Sign. 80.	3.00	6.00	20.00
	c. Sign. 81.	3.00	6.00	20.00
	d. Sign. 84.	3.00	6.00	15.00

85A	100 RUPEES	VG	VF	UNC
	ND. Like #85 but w/o bar under denomination at lower r. Sign. 84.	3.50	6.00	17.50

86	100 RUPEES	VG	VF	UNC
	ND(1979). Black, deep red and purple on m/c unpt. (pink at ctr.). Like #85A. Deep red sign.			
	a. Sign. 82.	2.50	4.00	17.50
	b. Sign. 83.	2.50	4.00	17.50
	c. Sign. 84.	2.50	4.00	17.50
	d. Sign. 86.	2.50	4.00	17.50
	e. Letter A. Sign. 86.	2.50	4.00	12.00
	f. W/o letter. Sign. 87.	2.50	4.00	12.00
	g. Letter A. Sign. 87.	2.50	4.00	12.00
	h. Letter B. Sign. 87.	2.50	4.00	8.50

87	500 RUPEES	VG	VF	UNC
	ND (1987). Brown, deep blue-green and deep blue on m/c unpt. M. K. Gandhi at ctr. r. Electronic sorting marks at lower l. Gandhi leading followers across back. Wmk: Asoka column.			
	a. Sign. 84.	FV	20.00	40.00
	b. Sign. 86.	FV	FV	37.50
	c. Sign. 87.	FV	FV	36.00

1992 ISSUE

88	10 RUPEES	VG	VF	UNC
	ND (1992). Dull brown-violet on orange, green and m/c unpt. Back red-violet; rural temple at l. ctr.			
	a. Sign. 86.	.50	1.25	3.00
	b. Letter A. Sign. 86.	.50	1.25	3.00
	c. Letter A. Sign. 87.	.50	1.25	3.00
	d. Letter B. Sign. 87.	.50	1.25	3.00
	e. Letter C. Sign. 87.	.50	1.25	3.00
	f. Letter D. Sign. 87.	.25	1.25	2.50
	g. Letter E. Sign. 87.	.25	1.25	2.50

1996-99 ND ISSUE

#89-91 M. K. Gandhi at r. and as wmk. Reserve Bank seal at lower r. In 1999 the name was spelled out as Mahatma Gandhi.

89	10 RUPEES	VG	VF	UNC
	ND (1996). Pale brown-violet on m/c unpt. Ornamented rhinoceros and elephant heads behind tiger at l. ctr. on back.			
	a. Sign. 87.	FV	.50	2.00
	b. Letter L; M. Sign. 87.	FV	.50	2.00
	c. Letter N; R. Sign. 88.	FV	.50	2.00

		VG	VF	UNC
90	**50 RUPEES** ND (1997). Black and purple on m/c unpt. Parliament house at l. ctr. on back.			
	a. W/o letter. Sign. 87.	FV	FV	4.00
	b. W/o letter. Sign. 88.	FV	FV	4.00
	c. Letter A. Sign. 88.	FV	FV	4.00
	d. Letter M. Sign. 87.	FV	FV	1.25
	e. Letter R. Sign. 88.	FV	FV	1.25
	f. Letter N. Sign. 88.	FV	FV	1.25
	g. Letter A. Sign. 88.	FV	FV	1.25
	h. Letter P. Sign. 88.	FV	FV	1.25

		VG	VF	UNC
91	**100 RUPEES** ND (1996). Black, purple and dk. olive-green on pale blue-green and m/c unpt. Himalaya mountains at l. ctr. on back. Segmented foil over security thread.			
	a. W/o letter. Sign. 87.	FV	2.50	9.00
	b. Letter E. Sign. 87.	FV	2.50	9.00
	c. Letter L. Sign. 87.	FV	2.50	9.00
	d. Letter A. Sign. 87.	FV	FV	7.00
	e. Letter L. Sign. 88.	FV	FV	7.00
	f. Letter E. Sign. 88.	FV	FV	7.00
	g. W/o letter. Sign. 88.	FV	FV	7.00

		VG	VF	UNC
92	**500 RUPEES** ND (1997). Dk. brown, olive-green and purple on m/c unpt. Similar to #87. Segmented foil over security thread.			
	a. W/o letter. Sign. 87.	FV	FV	50.00
	b. W/o letter. Sign. 88.	FV	FV	50.00
	c. Letter A. Sign. 88.	FV	FV	50.00

PERSIAN GULF

Intended for circulation in areas of Oman, Bahrain, Qatar and Trucial States during 1950's and early 1960's.

GOVERNMENT OF INDIA

ND ISSUE

		VG	VF	UNC
R1	**1 RUPEE** ND. Red. Like #75c. Sign. 34.	3.00	15.00	50.00

NOTE: Sign. L. K. Jha and H. V. R. Iengar are reliably reported.

RESERVE BANK OF INDIA

ND ISSUE

		VG	VF	UNC
R2	**5 RUPEES** ND. Orange. Like #35a. Sign. 74.	20.00	75.00	225.00

		VG	VF	UNC
R3	**10 RUPEES** ND. Red. Like #39c. Letter A. Sign. 74.	25.00	100.00	300.00

		VG	VF	UNC
R4	**100 RUPEES** ND. Green. Like #43b. Sign. 74.	50.00	300.00	1200.

HAJ PILGRIM

Intended for use by Moslem pilgrims in Mecca, Saudi Arabia.

RESERVE BANK OF INDIA

(ND) ISSUE

#R5 and R6 Asoka column at r. Letters *HA* near serial #, and *HAJ* at l. and r. of bank title at top.

		VG	VF	UNC
R5	**10 RUPEES** ND. Blue. Like #39c. Sign. 74.	25.00	75.00	400.00
R6	**100 RUPEES** ND. Red. Like #43b. Sign. 74.	125.00	500.00	—

The Republic of Indonesia, the world's largest archipelago, extends for more than 3,000 miles (4,827 km.) along the equator from the mainland of southeast Asia to Australia. The more than 17,500 islands comprising the archipelago have a combined area of 735,268 sq. mi. (2,042,005 sq. km.) and a population of 195 million, including East Timor. Capital: Jakarta. Petroleum, timber, rubber and coffee are exported.

Had Columbus succeeded in reaching the fabled Spice Islands, he would have found advanced civilizations a millennium old, and temples still ranked among the finest examples of ancient art. During the opening centuries of the Christian era, the islands were influenced by Hindu priests and traders who spread their culture and religion. Moslem invasions began in the 13th century, fragmenting the island kingdoms into small states which were unable to resist Western colonial infiltration. Portuguese traders established posts in the 16th century, but they were soon outnumbered by the Dutch who arrived in 1602 and gradually asserted control over the islands comprising present-day Indonesia. Dutch dominance, interrupted by British incursions during the Napoleonic Wars, established the Netherlands East Indies as one of the richest colonial possessions in the world.

The Indonesian independence movement, which began between the two world wars, was encouraged by the Japanese during their 3-year occupation during World War II. Indonesia proclaimed its independence on Aug. 17, 1945, three days after the surrender of Japan, and was established on Dec. 28, 1949, after four years of Dutch military efforts to reassert control. West Irian, formerly Netherlands New Guinea, came under the administration of Indonesia on May 1, 1963.

MONETARY SYSTEM:

1 Rupiah = 100 Sen, 1945-

REPUBLIC

REPUBLIK INDONESIA

1961 ISSUE

78	1 RUPIAH	VG	VF	UNC
	1961. Dk. green. Rice field workers at l. Farm produce on back.	.10	.25	.60

79	2 1/2 RUPIAH	VG	VF	UNC
	1961. Black, dk. blue and brown on blue-green unpt. Corn field work at l.	.10	.25	.75

1961 BORNEO ISSUE

#79A and 79B Pres. Sukarno at l. Javanese dancer at r. on back.

79A	1 RUPIAH	VG	VF	UNC
	1961. Green on orange unpt.	1.50	4.00	10.00

79B	2 1/2 RUPIAH	VG	VF	UNC
	1961. Blue on gray-brown unpt.	1.50	4.00	10.00

1964 ISSUE

#80 and 81 Pres. Sukarno at l. Wmk: Arms at ctr.

80	1 RUPIAH	VG	VF	UNC
	1964. Red and brown.			
	a. Imprint: *Pertjetakan Kebajoran* at bottom ctr. on face.	.75	2.00	6.00
	b. W/o imprint.	.30	1.00	3.00

81	2 1/2 RUPIAH	VG	VF	UNC
	1964. Blue and brown.			
	a. Imprint like #80a.	1.00	2.50	7.50
	b. W/o imprint.	1.00	2.50	7.50

#82-88 Pres. Sukarno at l. Javanese dancers on most backs.

82	5 RUPIAH	VG	VF	UNC
	1960. Lilac.			
	a. Wmk: Sukarno.	.50	1.50	5.00
	b. Wmk: Water buffalo.	.40	1.00	4.00
83	10 RUPIAH			
	1960. Lt. brown. Wmk: Sukarno.	.50	2.00	6.00

84	25 RUPIAH	VG	VF	UNC
	1960. Green.			
	a. Printer: TDLR. Wmk: Sukarno.	1.00	4.00	10.00
	b. Printer: Pertjetakan. Wmk: Water buffalo.	1.00	4.00	10.00

85	50 RUPIAH	VG	VF	UNC
	1960. Dk. blue.			
	a. Printer: TDLR. Wmk: Sukarno.	2.00	8.00	20.00
	b. Printer: Pertjetakan. Wmk: Water buffalo.	1.50	4.50	12.50

86	100 RUPIAH	VG	VF	UNC
	1960. Red-brown. Man and woman on back.			
	a. Wmk: Sukarno.	2.50	10.00	22.50
	b. Wmk: Water buffalo.	Reported Not Confirmed		

87	500 RUPIAH	VG	VF	UNC
	1960. Dk. blue-green.			
	a. Printer: TDLR. Wmk: Sukarno.	5.00	12.50	37.50
	b. Printer: Pertjetakan. Wmk: Sukarno.	5.00	12.50	37.50
	c. Printer Pertjetakan b. Wmk: Water buffalo.	5.00	12.50	37.50
	d. Printer Pertjetakan b. Wmk: Coat of arms.	7.00	15.00	42.50

88	1000 RUPIAH	VG	VF	UNC
	1960. Green.			
	a. Printer: TDLR. Wmk: Sukarno.	15.00	35.00	100.00
	b. Printer: Pertjetakan. Wmk: Water buffalo.	7.00	20.00	50.00

NOTICE

Readers with unlisted dates, signature varieties, etc. are invited to submit photocopies of their notes to: Standard Catalog of World Paper Money, 700 East State St. Iola, WI 54990-0001, fax: 1-715-445-4087, or E-Mail: thernr@krause.com.

BANK INDONESIA

1963 ISSUE

89	10 RUPIAH	VG	VF	UNC
	1963. Blue and brown on m/c unpt. A Balinese wood carver at l. Balinese huts, shrine at ctr., mythical figure at r. on back. Wmk: Water buffalo.	.15	.50	1.50

1964 ISSUE

#95-96, 98 and 101 have printed Indonesian arms in wmk. area at r.

90	1 SEN	VG	VF	UNC
	1964. Green-blue and brown. Peasant w/straw hat at r.	—	.05	.10

91	5 SEN	VG	VF	UNC
	1964. Lilac-brown. Female volunteer in uniform at r.	—	.05	.10

92	10 SEN	VG	VF	UNC
	1964. Blue on yellow-green unpt. Like #91.	—	.05	.10

93	25 SEN	VG	VF	UNC
	1964. Red on yellow-green unpt. A volunteer in uniform at r.	—	.05	.15

94	50 SEN	VG	VF	UNC
	1964. Purple and red. Like #93.	—	.10	.25

		VG	VF	UNC
95	**25 RUPIAH** 1964. Dull green on lt. brown unpt. Batak woman weaver at l. Batak house at ctr. on back.	.20	.65	2.00

		VG	VF	UNC
96	**50 RUPIAH** 1964. Dk. brown and green on aqua unpt. Timor woman spinner at l. Rice barns at ctr. on back.	.15	.50	1.50

		VG	VF	UNC
97	**100 RUPIAH** 1964. Brown and red on lt. tan unpt. Rubber tapper at l. Kalimantan house at ctr. on back. Wmk: Water buffalo.			
	a. Printer's name: *P. T. Pertjetakan Kebajoran Imp.* 16mm. long at r. on back.	.65	2.00	6.00
	b. Printer's name: *PN Pertjetakan Kebajoran Imp.* 22mm. long at r. on back.	.40	1.25	4.00

		VG	VF	UNC
98	**100 RUPIAH** 1964. Blue on lt. tan unpt. Like #97.	.50	1.50	5.00
99	**10,000 RUPIAH** 1964. Red and dk. brown on m/c unpt. Two fishermen at l. Floating houses at ctr. on back. Wmk: Water buffalo.	1.50	4.00	20.00
100	**10,000 RUPIAH** 1964. Green. Like #99.	.65	2.00	6.00

		VG	VF	UNC
101	**10,000 RUPIAH** 1964. Green. Like #100, but w/wmk. arms.			
	a. Wmk. at ctr.	.80	3.00	8.00
	b. Wmk. at l. and r.	.65	2.50	7.50

1968 ISSUE

#102-112 Gen. Sudirman at l.

#102 and 103 wmk: Arms at ctr.

		VG	VF	UNC
102	**1 RUPIAH** 1968. Red on lt. blue and purple unpt. Arms at r. Woman collecting copra at l. on back.	.25	.75	2.25

		VG	VF	UNC
103	**2 1/2 RUPIAH** 1968. Dk. blue. Arms at r. Woman gathering paddy rice stalks at l. on back.	.25	.75	2.25

#104-110 wmk: Arms at r.

		VG	VF	UNC
104	**5 RUPIAH** 1968. Pale violet on m/c unpt. Dam construction on back.	.50	1.50	4.50

		VG	VF	UNC
105	**10 RUPIAH** 1968. Lt. brown on m/c unpt. Oil refinery on back.	.30	1.00	3.00

		VG	VF	UNC
106	**25 RUPIAH** 1968. Green on lt. brown and m/c unpt. Back brown; Ampra lift bridge over Musi River at ctr. r.	.50	1.50	4.50

		VG	VF	UNC
107	**50 RUPIAH** 1968. Violet and dk. blue on m/c unpt. Airplanes in repair hangar at ctr. r. on back.	.80	2.50	7.50

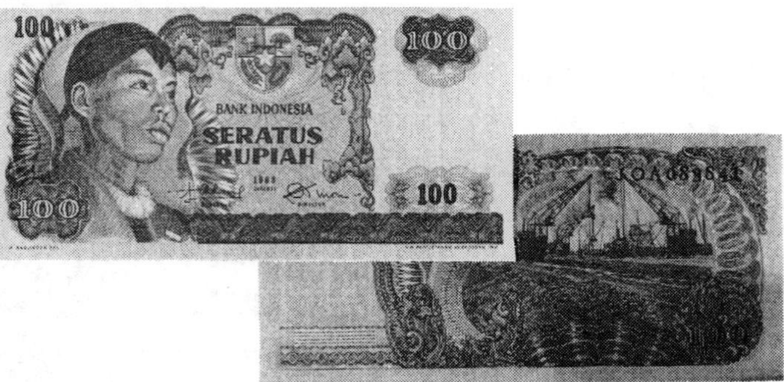

		VG	VF	UNC
108	**100 RUPIAH** 1968. Deep red on m/c unpt. Coal facility at the port of Tanjung Priok at ctr. r. on back.	.50	1.50	5.00

		VG	VF	UNC
109	**500 RUPIAH** 1968. Brown and dk. green on m/c unpt. Yarn spinning in cotton mill on back.	.80	2.50	10.00
110	**1000 RUPIAH** 1968. Orange and dk. brown on m/c unpt. Fertilizer plant at ctr. r. on back.	1.00	3.00	12.00

NOTE: Deceptive forgeries of #110 exist.

#111 and 112 wmk: Prince Diponegoro. Two serial # varieties.

		VG	VF	UNC
111	**5000 RUPIAH** 1968. Blue-green on m/c unpt. Cement plant at ctr. r. on back.	5.50	22.50	70.00

		VG	VF	UNC
112	**10,000 RUPIAH** 1968. Red-brown and dk. brown on m/c unpt. Back purple; tin facility at ctr. r.	5.00	20.00	60.00

1975; ND ISSUE

#112 A, B, 113A, 114A wmk: Prince Diponegoro.

		VG	VF	UNC
112A	**100 RUPIAH** ND. Red on m/c unpt. Prince Diponegoro at l. Mountain scenery at l. ctr. on back. (Not issued.)			
	a. Normal serial #.	—	—	—
	s. Specimen.	—	—	—

		VG	VF	UNC
112B	**500 RUPIAH** ND. Green on m/c unpt. Prince Diponegoro at l. Terraced rice fields in Sianok Gorge on back. (Not issued.)			
	a. Normal serial #.	Reported Not Confirmed		
	s. Specimen.	—	—	—

		VG	VF	UNC
113	**1000 RUPIAH** ND; 1975. Blue-green and blue on m/c unpt. Prince Diponegoro at l. Farmer plowing in terraced rice fields on back.			
	a. 1975. Wmk: Majapahit statue.	.50	2.00	7.50
	s. ND. Specimen. (Not issued.)	—	—	—

		VG	VF	UNC
113A	**5000 RUPIAH** ND. Brown on m/c unpt. Prince Diponegoro at r. Three sailing ships on back. (Not issued.)			
	a. Normal serial #.	—	—	—
	s. Specimen.	—	—	—

114 **5000 Rupiah**

	VG	VF	Unc
1975. Brown on m/c unpt. Fisherman w/net at r. Back like #113A. Wmk: Tjut Njak Din's head.	2.50	7.50	25.00

114A **10,000 Rupiah**

	VG	VF	Unc
ND. Green and red on m/c unpt. Face like #113A. Peasants at ctr. on back. (Not issued.)			
a. Normal serial #.	—	—	—
s. Specimen.	—	—	—

115 **10,000 Rupiah**

	VG	VF	Unc
1975. Brown, red and m/c. Stone relief at Borobudur Temple. Large mask from Bali at l. on back. Wmk: Gen. Sudirman.	7.50	25.00	75.00

1977 Issue

116 **100 Rupiah**

	VG	VF	Unc
1977. Red on m/c unpt. Rhinoceros at l. Rhinoceros in jungle scene at ctr. on back. Wmk: Arms.	.20	.60	2.00

117 **500 Rupiah**

	VG	VF	Unc
1977. Green on pink and m/c unpt. Woman w/orchids at l. Bank of Indonesia at ctr. on back and as wmk.	.40	1.00	3.50

1979 Issue

118 **10,000 Rupiah**

	VG	VF	Unc
1979. Purple on m/c unpt. Javanese Gamelan Orchestra at ctr. Prambanan Temple on back. Wmk: Dr. Soetomo.	3.00	9.00	25.00

1980 Issue

119 **1000 Rupiah**

	VG	VF	Unc
1980. Blue on m/c unpt. Dr. Soetomo at ctr. r. Mountain scene in Sianok Valley on back. Wmk: Sultan Hasanudin.	.30	1.00	3.50

120 **5000 Rupiah**

	VG	VF	Unc
1980. Brown on m/c unpt. Diamond cutter at ctr. Back brown, green and m/c. 3 Torajan houses from Celebes at ctr.			
a. Wmk: D. Sartika.	2.00	6.00	20.00
p. Proof. Wmk: Prince Diponegoro.	—	—	—

1982 Issue

#	Denomination	VG	VF	UNC
121	**500 Rupiah** 1982. Dk. green on m/c unpt. Man standing by Amorphophallus Titanum giant flower at l. Bank of Indonesia on back. Wmk: Gen. A. Yani.	.25	.75	2.50

1984-88 Issue

#	Denomination	VG	VF	UNC
122	**100 Rupiah** 1984. Red on m/c unpt. Goura Victoria at l. Asahan Dam on back. Wmk: Arms.			
	a. Engraved.	.10	.40	1.25
	b. Litho.	.05	.25	.75

#	Denomination	VG	VF	UNC
123	**500 Rupiah** 1988. Brown and dk. green on m/c unpt. Stag at l. Bank of Indonesia Cirebon branch at r. on back. Wmk: Gen. A. Yani.	.20	.60	1.50

#	Denomination	VG	VF	UNC
124	**1000 Rupiah** 1987. Blue-black on m/c unpt. Raja Sisingamangaraja XII at ctr., arms at l. Yogyakarta Court at ctr. on back. Wmk: Sultan Hasanuddin.	.30	1.00	2.00

#	Denomination	VG	VF	UNC
125	**5000 Rupiah** 1986. Dk. brown on m/c unpt. Teuku Umar at ctr. Minaret of Kudus mosque at r. on back. Wmk: C. Martha Tijahahu.	2.25	3.50	10.00

#	Denomination	VG	VF	UNC
126	**10,000 Rupiah** 1985. Purple on m/c unpt. R. A. Kartini at l. Prambanan Temple at ctr. Female graduate at ctr. r. on back. Wmk: Dr. T. Mangoenkoesoemo.	3.00	6.00	15.00

1992 Issue

#127-132 arms at upper r. area. Printer: Perum Percetakan Uang.

#127-129 second date appears after imprint.

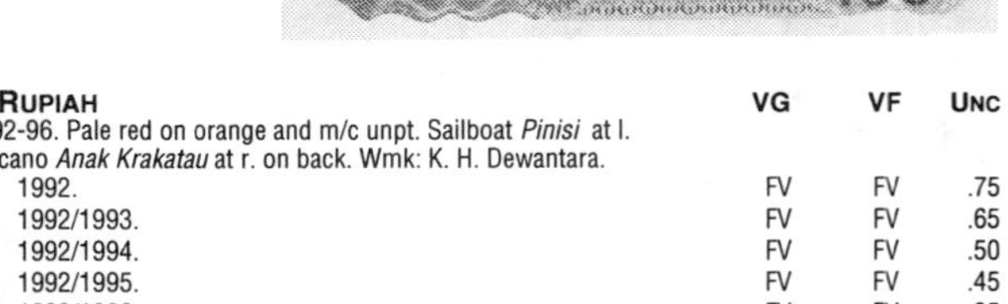

#	Denomination	VG	VF	UNC
127	**100 Rupiah** 1992-96. Pale red on orange and m/c unpt. Sailboat *Pinisi* at l. Volcano *Anak Krakatau* at r. on back. Wmk: K. H. Dewantara.			
	a. 1992.	FV	FV	.75
	b. 1992/1993.	FV	FV	.65
	c. 1992/1994.	FV	FV	.50
	d. 1992/1995.	FV	FV	.45
	e. 1992/1996.	FV	FV	.35
	f. 1992/1999.	FV	FV	.25

NOTICE

Readers with unlisted dates, signature varieties, etc. are invited to submit photocopies of their notes to: Standard Catalog of World Paper Money, 700 East State St. Iola, WI 54990-0001, fax: 1-715-445-4087, or E-Mail: thernr@krause.com.

128 500 RUPIAH
1992-. Brown and green on m/c unpt. Orangutan resting on limb at l. Native huts at E. Kalimanoan at r. on back. Wmk: H. O. S. Tjokroaminoto.

	VG	VF	UNC
a. 1992.	FV	FV	1.25
b. 1992/1993.	FV	FV	1.10
c. 1992/1994.	FV	FV	1.00
d. 1992/1995.	FV	FV	.90
e. 1992/1996.	FV	FV	.50
f. 1992/1997.	FV	FV	.40
g. 1992/1998.	FV	FV	.30
h. 1992/1999.	FV	FV	.20

129 1000 RUPIAH
1992-. Deep blue on lt. blue and m/c unpt. Aerial view of Lake Toba at l. ctr. Native huts, stone monument at Nias Island at ctr. on back. Wmk: Tjut Njak Meutia.

	VG	VF	UNC
a. 1992.	FV	FV	2.00
b. 1992/1993.	FV	FV	1.85
c. 1992/1994.	FV	FV	1.75
d. 1992/1995.	FV	FV	1.50
e. 1992/1996.	FV	FV	1.00
f. 1992/1997.	FV	FV	.75
g. 1992/1998.	FV	FV	.65
h. 1992/1999.	FV	FV	.55

130 5000 RUPIAH
1992-. Black, brown and dk. brown on m/c unpt. Sa Sando musical instrument, tapestry at ctr. Volcano w/3-color Lake Kelimutu at ctr. on back. Wmk: Tjut Njak Din.

	VG	VF	UNC
a. 1992.	FV	FV	7.50
b. 1992/1993.	FV	FV	7.00
c. 1992/1994.	FV	FV	6.75
d. 1992/1995.	FV	FV	6.50
e. 1992/1996.	FV	FV	3.50
f. 1992/1997.	FV	FV	2.50
g. 1992/1998.	FV	FV	1.50
h. 1992/1999.	FV	FV	1.25

131 10,000 RUPIAH
1992-. Purple and red on m/c unpt. Sri Sultan Hamengku Buwono IX at l., girl scouts at ctr. r. Borobudur Temple on hillside on back. Wmk: W. R. Soepratman.

	VG	VF	UNC
a. 1992.	FV	FV	12.50
b. 1992/1993.	FV	FV	12.00
c. 1992/1994.	FV	FV	11.50
d. 1992/1995.	FV	FV	11.00
e. 1992/1996.	FV	FV	6.00
f. 1992/1997.	FV	FV	4.00
g. 1992/1998 & letter prefix.	FV	FV	15.00

132 20,000 RUPIAH
1992-95. Black, dk. grayish green and red on m/c unpt. Red Cenderawasih bird at ctr. Cloves flower at ctr., map of Indonesian Archipelago at r. on back. Wmk: K. H. Dewantara.

	VG	VF	UNC
a. 1992.	FV	FV	21.50
b. 1992/1993.	FV	FV	20.00
c. 1992/1994.	FV	FV	19.00
d. 1992/1995.	FV	FV	25.00

1993 COMMEMORATIVE ISSUES

#133 and 134, 25 Years of Economic Development

133 50,000 RUPIAH
1993-94. Greenish blue, tan and gray on m/c unpt. Pres. Soeharto at l. ctr., surrounded by various scenes of development activities. Anti-counterfeiting design at r. Jet plane over Soekarno-Hatta International Airport at ctr. on back. Wmk: W. R. Soepratman.

	VG	VF	UNC
a. 1993.	FV	FV	50.00
b. 1993/1994.	FV	FV	45.00

		VG	VF	UNC
134	**50,000 RUPIAH** 1993. Design like #133, but pale gray. Plastic. Pres. Soeharto in OVD at r.			
	a. Note alone.	—	—	40.00
	b. Included in souvenir folder.	—	—	125.00

1995 ISSUE

		VG	VF	UNC
135	**20,000 RUPIAH** 1995-. Back., dark grayish green and red on m/c unpt. Like #132 but w/new engraved date, new sign. and segmented foil over security thread.			
	a. 1995.	FV	FV	18.50
	b. 1995/1996.	FV	FV	10.00
	c. 1995/1997.	FV	FV	6.00
136	**50,000 RUPIAH** 1995-. Greenish blue, tan tan and gray on m/c unpt. Like #133 but w/new engraved date, new sign. and segmented foil over security thread.			
	a. 1995.	FV	FV	42.50
	b. 1995/1996.	FV	FV	25.00
	c. 1995/1997.	FV	FV	15.00

1998-99 ISSUE

#137 and 138 printer: PPU.

		VG	VF	UNC
137	**10,000 RUPIAH** 1998. Deep purple and black on m/c unpt. Tjut Njak Dhien at r., arms at upper r., bank monogram at lower r. Segara Anak Volcanic Lake at ctr. r. on back.	FV	FV	3.00

		VG	VF	UNC
138	**20,000 RUPIAH** 1998. Deep green and dk. brown on m/c unpt. Ki Hadjar Dewantara at ctr. and as wmk., arms at upper l., Ganesha at l., bank monogram at r.	FV	FV	5.50

		VG	VF	UNC
140	**100,000 RUPIAH** 1999. Soekarno and Hatta busts at ctr. Bank Indonesia bldg. on back. Plastic polymer.	FV	FV	45.00

REGIONAL - IRIAN BARAT

REPUBLIC INDONESIA

1963 ND PROVISIONAL ISSUE

#R1 and R2 Pres. Sukarno at l. w/ovpt: *IRIAN BARAT* at lower r. on Republik Indonesia issue.

		VG	VF	UNC
R1	**1 RUPIAH** ND (1963 - old date 1961). Orange.	3.50	10.00	25.00
R2	**2 1/2 RUPIAH** ND (1963 - old date 1961). Violet.	3.50	10.00	30.00

BANK INDONESIA

1963 ND PROVISIONAL ISSUE

#R3-R5 Pres. Sukarno at l. w/ovpt: *IRIAN BARAT* on Bank Indonesia issue.

		VG	VF	UNC
R3	**5 RUPIAH** ND (1963 - old date 1960). Gray-olive.	6.50	20.00	50.00

R4 **10 RUPIAH**
ND (1963 - old date 1960). Red.

VG	VF	UNC
6.00	18.50	40.00

R5 **100 RUPIAH**
ND (1963 - old date 1960). Green.

VG	VF	UNC
12.50	37.50	90.00

REGIONAL - RIAU

REPUBLIC INDONESIA

1963 ND PROVISIONAL ISSUE

#R6 and R7 Pres. Sukarno at l. w/ovpt: *RIAU* at lower r. on Republik Indonesia issue.

R6 **1 RUPIAH**
ND (1963 - old date 1961). Orange.

VG	VF	UNC
6.50	20.00	50.00

R7 **2 1/2 RUPIAH**
ND (1963 - old date 1961). Blue.

VG	VF	UNC
7.50	22.50	60.00

NOTE: Contemporary counterfeit on fragile paper w/artificial blue fibers exist.

BANK INDONESIA

1963 ND PROVISIONAL ISSUE

#R8-R10 Pres. Sukarno at l. w/ovpt: *RIAU* on Bank Indonesia issue.

R8 **5 RUPIAH**
ND (1963 - old date 1960). Violet. Ovpt. on #82a, w/prefix *X* in serial #.

VG	VF	UNC
7.00	21.50	55.00

NOTE: Counterfeits on #82a but w/o prefix X on serial # exist.

R9 **10 RUPIAH**
ND (1963 - old date 1960). Red.

VG	VF	UNC
6.00	18.50	45.00

R10 **100 RUPIAH**
ND (1963 - old date 1960). Green.

VG	VF	UNC
20.00	60.00	150.00

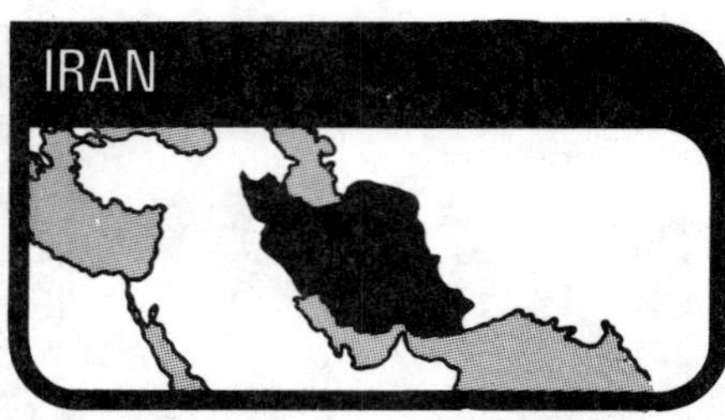

The Islamic Republic of Iran, located between the Caspian Sea and the Persian Gulf in southwestern Asia, has an area of 636,296 sq. mi. (1,648,000 sq. km.) and a population of 60.1 million. Capital: Tehran. Although predominantly an agricultural state, Iran depends heavily on oil for foreign exchange. Crude oil, carpets and agricultural products are exported.

Iran (historically known as Persia) is one of the world's most ancient and resilient nations. Strategically astride the lower land gate to Asia, it has been conqueror and conquered, sovereign nation and vassal state, ever emerging from its periods of glory or travail with its culture and political individuality intact. Iran (Persia) was a powerful empire under Cyrus the Great (600-529 B.C.), its borders extending from the Indus to the Nile. It has also been conquered by the predatory empires of antique and recent times - Assyrian, Medean, Macedonia, Seljuq, Turk, Mongol - and more recently been coveted by Russia, Germany and Great Britain. Revolts against the absolute power of the Shahs resulted in the establishment of a constitutional monarchy in 1906. In 1931 the Kingdom of Persia became known as the Kingdom of Iran. In 1979, the Pahlavi monarchy was toppled and an Islamic Republic proclaimed.

RULERS:

Mohammad Reza Pahlavi, SH1320-58/1941-79AD

PRESIDENTS:

Islamic Republic of Iran
Abolhassan Bani Sadr, SH1358-60 (AD1979-Jun 81)
Mohammad Ali Rajai, SH1360 (AD-1981 Jun-Oct)
Hojjatoleslam Ali Khamene'i, SH1360-(AD1981-)

MONETARY SYSTEM:

1 Rial 100 Dinars = 20 Shahis
1 Toman = 10 Rials SH1310- (1932-)

SIGNATURE AND TITLE VARIETIES

Kingdom: Mohammad Reza Pahlavi

	GENERAL DIRECTOR	MINISTER OF FINANCE
7	Ebrahim Kashani	Abdolbagi Shoaii
8	Dr. Ali Asghar Pourhomayoun	Abdul Hossein Behnia
9	Mehdi Samii	Abdul Hossein Behnia
10	Mehdi Samii	Amir Abbas Hoveyda
11	Mehdi Samii	Dr. Jamshid Amouzegar
12	Khodadad Farmanfarmaian	Dr. Jamshid Amouzegar
13	Abdol Ali Jahanshahi	Dr. Jamshid Amouzegar
14	Mohammad Yeganeh	Dr. Jamshid Amouzegar
	GENERAL DIRECTOR	MINISTER OF ECONOMIC AND FINANCIAL AFFAIR
15	Mohammad Yeganeh	Hushang Ansary
16	Hassan Ali Mehran	Hushang Ansary
17	Hassan Ali Mehran	Mohammad Yeganeh

NOTE: Some signers used more than one signature (Jamshid Amouzegar), some held more than one term of office (Mehdi Samii) and others held the office of both General Director and Minister of Finance (Mohammad Yeganeh) at different times.

Shah Mohammad Reza Pahlavi, SH1323-58/1944-79 AD

Type V. Imperial Iranian Army (IIA) uniform. Full face. SH1337-40.

Type VI. Imperial Iranian Air Force (IIAF) uniform. Three quarter face. SH1341-44.

Type VII. Imperial Iranian Army (IIA) uniform. Full face. SH1347-48.

Type VIII. Commander in Chief of Iran's Armed Forces. Three quarter face. Large portrait. MS2535 to SH1358.

Type IX. Shah Pahlavi in CinC uniform and his father Shah Reza in Imperial Iranian Army (IIA) uniform. MS2535.

KINGDOM OF IRAN

BANK MARKAZI IRAN

1961; 1962 ISSUE

#71 and 72 fifth portr. of Shah Pahlavi in army uniform at r. Wmk: Young Shah Pahlavi. Yellow security security thread runs vertically. Sign. 7. Printer: Harrison (w/o imprint).

#73-75 sixth portr. of Shah Pahlavi in air force uniform. Wmk: Young Shah Pahlavi. Yellow security thread runs vertically. Sign. 8. Printer: Harrison (w/o imprint).

		VG	VF	UNC
71	**10 RIALS** SH1340 (1961). Blue on green and orange unpt. Geometric design at ctr. Amir Kabir dam near Karaj on back.	.50	1.00	2.75

		VG	VF	UNC
72	**20 RIALS** SH1340 (1961). Dk. brown on lt. brown and orange unpt. Geometric design at ctr. Statue of Shah and Ramsar Hotel on back.	.60	1.50	3.50

		VG	VF	UNC
73	**50 RIALS** SH1341 (1962). Green on orange and blue unpt. Shah Pahlavi at r. Koohrang dam and tunnel on back.			
	a. Sm. date 2.5mm high.	1.00	2.00	5.00
	b. Lg. date 4.0mm high.	1.00	2.00	5.00

		VG	VF	UNC
74	**500 RIALS** SH1341 (1962). Black on pink and purple unpt. Shah Pahlavi at ctr. Winged horses on back.	7.50	20.00	70.00

		VG	VF	UNC
75	**1000 RIALS** SH1341 (1962). Brown on red and blue unpt. Shah Pahlavi at ctr. Tomb of Hafez in Shiraz on back.	12.00	45.00	145.00

1963; 1964 ISSUE

#76 and 77 sixth portr. of Shah Pahlavi in armed forces uniform at r. Wmk: Young Shah Pahlavi. Yellow security thread. Printer: Harrison (w/o imprint).

		VG	VF	UNC
76	**50 RIALS** SH1343 (1964). Dk. green on orange and blue unpt. Ornate design at ctr. Koohrang Dam and tunnel on back. Sign. 9.	1.00	3.50	9.00
77	**100 RIALS** SH1342 (1963). Maroon on lt. green unpt. Ornate design at ctr. Oil refinery at Abadan on back. Sign. 9.	.75	2.25	5.00

1965 ND ISSUE

#78-82 sixth portr. of Shah Pahlavi in armed forces uniform at r. Wmk: Young Shah Pahlavi. Yellow security thread. Printer: Harrison (w/o imprint).

		VG	VF	UNC
78	**20 RIALS** ND (1965). Dk. brown on pink and green unpt. Ornate design at ctr. Oriental hunters on horseback on back.			
	a. Sign. 9.	.35	.85	2.25
	b. Sign. 10.	.50	1.50	4.00
79	**50 RIALS** ND (1965). Dk. green on orange and blue unpt. Ornate design at ctr. Koohrang Dam and tunnel on back.			
	a. Sign. 9.	1.75	5.00	15.00
	b. Sign. 10.	1.75	5.00	15.00
80	**100 RIALS** ND (1965). Maroon on olive-green unpt. M/c ornate design. Oil refinery at Abadan on back. Sign. 10.	1.50	4.50	12.50
81	**200 RIALS** ND (1965). Dk. blue on orange and lavender unpt. M/c ornate design at ctr. Railroad bridge on back. Sign. 9.	2.00	8.00	25.00
82	**500 RIALS** ND (1965). Black on pink and purple unpt. Shah at ctr. Winged horses on back. Sign. 9.	6.00	20.00	70.00
83	**1000 RIALS** ND (1965). Brown on red and blue unpt. Shah at ctr. Tomb of Hafez at Shiraz on back. Sign. 9.	10.00	35.00	115.00

1969 ND ISSUE

#84-87 seventh portr. of Shah Pahlavi in army uniform at r. Wmk: Young Shah Pahlavi. Yellow security thread runs vertically. Sign. 11 or 12. Printer: Harrison (w/o imprint).

#84-89 are called "Dark Panel" notes. The bank name is located on a contrasting dk. ornamental panel at the top ctr.

#88- 89A seventh portr. of Shah Pahlavi in army uniform at ctr. Sign. 11.

		VG	VF	UNC
84	**20 RIALS** ND (1969). Dk. brown on pink and green unpt. Ornate design at ctr. Oriental hunters on horseback on back.	.35	.85	2.25

NOTICE

Readers with unlisted dates, signature varieties, etc. are invited to submit photocopies of their notes to: Standard Catalog of World Paper Money, 700 East State St. Iola, WI 54990-0001, fax: 1-715-445-4087, or E-Mail: thernr@krause.com.

		VG	VF	UNC
85	**50 RIALS** ND (1969-71). Green on orange and blue unpt. Ornate design at ctr. Koohrang Dam and tunnel on back.			
	a. Sign. 11.	.35	.85	2.25
	b. Sign. 12.	.75	1.50	4.00
86	**100 RIALS** ND (1969-71). Maroon on lt. green and m/c unpt. Ornate design at ctr. Oil refinery at Abadan on back.			
	a. Sign. 11.	1.00	2.00	5.00
	b. Sign. 12.	1.00	2.00	5.00
87	**200 RIALS** ND (1969-71). Dk. blue on orange and purple unpt. M/c ornate design. Railroad bridge on back.			
	a. Sign. 11.	3.00	8.00	20.00
	b. Sign. 12.	4.00	11.00	25.00
88	**500 RIALS** ND (1969). Black on pink and purple unpt. Ornate frame at ctr. Winged horses on back.	4.00	12.00	40.00

		VG	VF	UNC
89	**1000 RIALS** ND (1969). Brown on red and blue unpt. Ornate frame at ctr. Tomb of Hafez at Shiraz on back.	6.00	18.00	60.00
89A	**5000 RIALS** ND (1969). Purple on red and m/c unpt. Ornate frame at ctr. Golestan Palace in Tehran on back. Printed in Pakistan.	200.00	550.00	1500.

1971 ND ISSUE

#90-96 are called "Light Panel" notes. The bank name is located on a contrasting lt. ornamental background panel at the top ctr.

#90-92 seventh portr. of Shah Pahlavi in army uniform at r. Wmk: Young Shah Pahlavi. Yellow security thread runs vertically. Printer: Harrison (w/o imprint).

		VG	VF	UNC
90	**50 RIALS** ND (1971). Dk. green on orange and blue unpt. Like #79 but w/light panel. Sign. 13.	1.00	2.75	7.00

		VG	VF	UNC
91	**100 RIALS** ND (1971-73). Maroon on olive-green unpt. Like #80 but w/light panel.			
	a. Sign. 11.	1.00	2.50	6.00
	b. Sign. 12.	1.00	4.00	9.00
	c. Sign. 13.	.50	1.65	4.50

		VG	VF	UNC
92	**200 RIALS** ND (1971-73). Dk. blue on orange and lavender unpt. Like #81 but w/light panel.			
	a. Sign. 11.	2.00	8.00	20.00
	b. Sign. 12.	3.00	10.00	30.00
	c. Sign. 13.	1.50	4.00	10.00

#93-96 seventh portr. of Shah Pahlavi in army uniform at ctr. Wmk: Young Shah Pahlavi.

		VG	VF	UNC
93	**500 RIALS** ND (1971-73). Black on pink and purple unpt. Like #82 but w/light panel.			
	a. Sign. 11.	3.00	10.00	30.00
	b. Sign. 12.	6.00	15.00	60.00
	c. Sign. 13.	5.00	15.00	40.00

		VG	VF	UNC
94	**1000 RIALS** ND (1971-73). Brown on red and blue unpt. Like #83 but w/light panel.			
	a. Sign. 11.	7.50	20.00	70.00
	b. Sign. 12.	6.50	17.50	65.00
	c. Sign. 13.	5.00	15.00	40.00

		VG	VF	UNC
95	**5000 RIALS** ND (1971-72). Purple on red and m/c unpt. Ornate frame at ctr. Golestan Palace in Tehran on back.			
	a. Sign. 12.	35.00	100.00	300.00
	b. Sign. 13.	28.50	85.00	250.00

		VG	VF	UNC
96	**10,000 RIALS** ND (1972-73). Dk. green and brown. Ornate frame at ctr. National Council of Ministries in Tehran on back.			
	a. Sign. 11.	75.00	150.00	500.00
	b. Sign. 13.	60.00	125.00	400.00

1971 ND COMMEMORATIVE ISSUE

2,500th Anniversary of the Persian Empire

#97 and 98 lg. eighth portr. of Shah Pahlavi in the "Commander in Chief" of Iranian armed forces uniform at r. Wmk: Young Shah Pahlavi. Yellow security thread runs vertically. Sign. 11 or 12. Printer: TDLR.

		VG	VF	UNC
97	**50 RIALS** SH1350 (1971). Green on blue, brown and m/c unpt. Floral design at ctr. Shah Pahlavi giving land deeds to villager on back.			
	a. Sign. 11.	1.00	2.50	6.00
	b. Sign. 13.	1.00	2.50	6.00

		VG	VF	UNC
98	**100 RIALS** SH1350 (1971). Maroon on orange and m/c unpt. M/c geometric and floral design. 3 vignettes labeled: *HEALTH, AGRICULTURE* and *EDUCATION* on back.	.50	1.50	4.50

***#99 Deleted.* See #101a.**

1974 ND ISSUE

#100-107 lg. eighth portr. of Shah Pahlavi at r. Wmk: Young Shah Pahlavi. Yellow security thread runs vertically. Printer: TDLR. Replacement notes: Serial # prefix *01/X; 02/X; 03/X; 99/9; 98/9; 97/9.*

		VG	VF	UNC
100	**20 RIALS** ND (1974-79). Brown on orange, lilac and m/c unpt. Persian carpet design, shepherd and ram. Amir Kabir Dam near Karaj on back.			
	a. Sign. 16.	.50	1.00	2.50
	b. Sign. 17.	.50	1.00	3.00
	c. Sign. 18.	.50	1.00	2.50

		VG	VF	UNC
101	**50 RIALS** ND (1974-79). Green on brown, blue and m/c unpt. Persian carpet design. Tomb of Cyrus the Great at Persepolis at l. ctr. on back.			
	a. Yellow security thread. Sign. 14.	.50	1.00	2.50
	b. Yellow security thread. Sign. 15.	.20	.50	1.25
	c. Yellow security thread. Sign. 16.	.50	1.00	2.50
	d. Black security thread. Sign: 17.	.50	1.00	3.00
	e. Black security thread. Sign. 18.	.50	1.00	3.00

		VG	VF	UNC
102	**100 RIALS** ND (1974-79). Maroon on orange and m/c unpt. Persian carpet design. Marmar Palace at l. ctr. on back.			
	a. Yellow security thread. Sign. 15.	1.00	2.50	6.50
	b. Yellow security thread. Sign. 16.	.50	1.25	3.00
	c. Black security thread. Sign. 17.	.50	1.25	3.00
	d. Black security thread. Sign. 18.	.50	1.25	3.00

		VG	VF	UNC
103	**200 RIALS** ND (1974-79). Blue on green and m/c unpt. Persian carpet design. Shahyad Square in Tehran on back.			
	a. 6 point star in design on back. Yellow security thread. Monument name as Maidane Shahyad at lower l. on back. Sign. 15.	2.50	6.00	15.00
	b. 12 point star in design on back. Yellow security thread. Monument name as Maidane Shahyad. Sign. 16.	1.00	4.00	9.00

		VG	VF	UNC
	c. 12 point star in design on back. Yellow security thread. Monument name changed to Shahyad Aryamer. Sign. 16.	1.00	3.50	8.00
	d. 12 point star in design on back. Black security thread and Shahyad Aryamer monument. Sign. 17.	1.00	4.00	9.00
	e. 12 point star in design on back. Black security thread and Shahyad Aryamer monument. Sign. 18.	1.00	2.00	5.00

		VG	VF	UNC
104	**500 RIALS** ND (1974-79). Black on green, orange and m/c unpt. Persian carpet design. Winged horses on back.			
	a. 6 point star in design below Shah Pahlavi. Yellow security thread. Sign. 15.	1.50	4.00	15.00
	b. 6 point star in design below Shah Pahlavi. Yellow security thread. Sign. 16.	1.00	3.00	10.00
	c. Diamond design below Shah Pahlavi. Black security thread. Sign. 17.	1.00	3.50	10.00
	d. Diamond design below Shah Pahlavi. Black security thread. Sign. 18.	1.00	3.00	10.00

		VG	VF	UNC
105	**1000 RIALS** ND (1974-79). Brown on green, yellow and m/c unpt. Persian carpet design. Tomb of Hafez in Shiraz on back.			
	a. Yellow security thread. Sign. 15.	4.00	11.00	30.00
	b. Yellow security thread. Sign. 16.	1.00	3.00	10.00
	c. Black security thread. Sign. 17.	1.00	3.00	9.00
	d. Black security thread. Sign. 18.	1.50	4.00	13.50

		VG	VF	UNC
106	**5000 RIALS** ND (1974-79). Purple on pink, green and m/c unpt. Persian carpet design. Golestan Palace in Tehran on back.			
	a. Yellow security thread. Sign. 15.	26.50	80.00	200.00
	b. Yellow security thread. Sign. 16.	1.50	6.50	25.00
	c. Black security thread. Sign. 17.	16.50	50.00	125.00
	d. Black security thread. Sign. 18.	20.00	60.00	150.00

		VG	VF	UNC
107	**10,000 RIALS** ND (1974-79). Green on brown and m/c unpt. Persian carpet design. National Council of Ministries in Tehran on back.			
	a. Yellow security thread. Sign. 15.	40.00	120.00	350.00
	b. Yellow security thread. Sign. 16.	7.50	20.00	75.00
	c. Black security thread. Sign. 17.	20.00	60.00	200.00
	d. Black security thread. Sign. 18.	20.00	60.00	200.00

1976 ND COMMEMORATIVE ISSUE

50th Anniversary of the Founding of the Pahlavi Dynasty

#108, ninth portr. of Shah Pahlavi w/Shah Reza at r. Wmk: Young Shah Pahlavi. Yellow security thread runs vertically. Sign. 16. Printer: TDLR.

		VG	VF	UNC
108	**100 RIALS** ND (1976). Maroon on orange, green and m/c unpt. Persian carpet design w/old Bank Melli at bottom ctr. 50th anniversary design in purple and lavender consisting of 50 suns surrounding Pahlavi Crown on back.	.50	1.50	4.50

ISLAMIC REPUBLIC

REVOLUTIONARY OVERPRINTS

After the Islamic Revolution of 1978-79, the Iranian government used numerous overprints on existing stocks of unissued paper money to obliterate Shah Pahlavi's portrait. There were many unauthorized and illegal crude stampings such as a lg. "X" and hand obliterations used by zealous citizens which circulated freely, but only three major types of official overprints were used by the government.

PROVISIONAL ISSUES

All provisional government ovpt. were placed on existing notes of Shah Pahlavi already printed. Overprinting was an interim action meant to discredit and disgrace the deposed Shah as well as to publicize and give credence to the new Islamic Republic. The overprints themselves gave way to more appropriate seals and emblems, changes of watermarks and finally to a complete redesigning of all denominations of notes.

In all cases the Shah's portr. was covered by an arabesque design. Eight different styles and varieties of this ovpt. were used. Watermark ovpt., when used, are either the former Iranian national emblem of Lion and Sun or the calligraphic Persian text of *JUMHURI-YE-ISLAMI-YE-IRAN* (Islamic Republic of Iran) taken from the obverse of the country's new emblem. All ovpt. colors are very dark and require careful scrutiny to distinguish colors other than black.

MEASUREMENTS OF OVERPRINTS:

At times there are variances in size of the ovpt. on the Shah's portr. The place to measure for the correct mm. size is across the widest part of the top of the ovpt., approximately a position from "ear to ear".

GOVERNMENT

TYPE 1 ND PROVISIONAL ISSUE

#110-116 Type I ovpt: Arabesque design over Shah at r. Wmk. area at l. w/o ovpt. Replacement notes: Refer to #100-107.

		VG	VF	UNC
110	**20 RIALS** ND.			
	a. Black 27mm ovpt. on #100a.	.75	2.50	7.50
	b. Black 27mm ovpt. on #100b.	—	Rare	—
111	**50 RIALS** ND. Ovpt. on #101b.			
	a. Black 27mm ovpt.	.75	2.00	5.00
	b. Green 27mm ovpt.	1.00	2.50	7.00
112	**100 RIALS** ND. Ovpt. on #102c.			
	a. Black 27mm ovpt.	1.00	3.00	10.00
	b. Maroon 27mm ovpt.	2.50	10.00	25.00

		VG	VF	UNC
113	**200 RIALS** ND. Ovpt. on #103.			
	a. Black 28mm ovpt. on #103a.	—	Rare	—
	b. Black 28mm ovpt. on #103b.	—	Rare	—
	c. Black 28mm ovpt on #103d.	1.50	8.00	20.00
	d. Black 32mm ovpt on #103d.	2.50	10.00	30.00
114	**500 RIALS** ND. Ovpt. on #104.			
	a. Black 28mm ovpt. on #104b.	4.00	12.00	40.00
	b. Black 28mm ovpt. on #104c.	—	Rare	—
	c. Black 28mm ovpt. on #104d.	4.00	11.00	35.00
115	**1000 RIALS** ND. Ovpt. on #105.			
	a. Black 32mm ovpt. on #105b.	4.00	12.00	45.00
	b. Black 32mm ovpt. on #105d.	7.00	20.00	65.00
	c. Brown 32mm ovpt. on #105d.	7.00	20.00	65.00
116	**5000 RIALS** ND. Black 32mm ovpt. on #106.	100.00	200.00	350.00

TYPE 2 ND PROVISIONAL ISSUE

#117-122 Type II ovpt: Arabesque design over Shah at r. and lion and sun national emblem over wmk. area at l.

		VG	VF	UNC
117	**50 RIALS** ND. Ovpt. on #101.			
	a. Black 27mm ovpt. on #101c.	2.50	7.00	20.00
	b. Black 27mm ovpt. on #101d.	—	Rare	—
	c. Black 27mm ovpt. on #101e.	—	Rare	—
118	**100 RIALS** ND. Ovpt. on #102.			
	a. Black 28mm ovpt. on #102c.	2.00	5.00	15.00
	b. Black 33mm ovpt. on #102d.	.35	1.00	3.00
119	**200 RIALS** ND. Ovpt. on #103.			
	a. Black 28mm ovpt. on #103d.	4.00	12.00	35.00
	b. Black 33mm ovpt. on #103d.	5.00	15.00	40.00
120	**500 RIALS** ND. Ovpt. on #104.			
	a. Black ovpt. on #104b.	—	Rare	—
	b. Black 28mm ovpt. on #104d.	7.00	20.00	65.00
	c. Black 22mm ovpt. on #104d.	7.00	20.00	70.00
121	**1000 RIALS** ND. Ovpt. on #105.			
	a. Black 32mm ovpt. on #105b.	—	Rare	—
	b. Black 32mm ovpt. on #105d.	4.00	12.50	45.00
122	**5000 RIALS** ND. Ovpt. on #106.			
	a. Black 32mm ovpt. on #106b.	25.00	70.00	200.00
	b. Black 32mm ovpt. on #106c.	—	Rare	—
	c. Black 32mm ovpt. on #106d.	200.00	400.00	700.00

TYPE 3 ND PROVISIONAL ISSUE

#123-126 Type III ovpt: Arabesque design over Shah at r. and calligraphic Persian text *JUMHURI-YE ISLAMI-YE-IRAN* (Islamic Republic of Iran) over wmk. area at l.

		VG	VF	UNC
123	**50 RIALS** ND. Ovpt. on #101.			
	a. Black 28mm ovpt., dk. green script on #101c.	2.00	6.00	20.00
	b. Black 33mm ovpt., black script on #101e.	.35	1.00	3.25
124	**500 RIALS** ND. Ovpt. on #104.			
	a. Black 28mm ovpt., black script on #104b.	3.00	10.00	35.00
	b. Black 33mm ovpt., black script on #104d.	2.50	7.50	22.50
125	**1000 RIALS** ND. Ovpt. on #105.			
	a. Black 32mm ovpt., black script on #105b.	5.00	15.00	50.00
	b. Black 32mm ovpt., black script on #105d.	4.50	14.00	45.00
	c. Brown 32mm ovpt., violet script on #105b.	7.50	20.00	75.00

NOTICE

Readers with unlisted dates, signature varieties, etc. are invited to submit photocopies of their notes to: Standard Catalog of World Paper Money, 700 East State St. Iola, WI 54990-0001, fax: 1-715-445-4087, or E-Mail: thernr@krause.com.

		VG	VF	UNC
126	**5000 RIALS** ND. Ovpt. on #106.			
	a. Purple 32mm. ovpt., purple script on #106b.	125.00	250.00	600.00
	b. Black 32mm. ovpt., purple script on #106d.	20.00	60.00	200.00

NOTE: Some notes w/Shah portr. are found w/unofficial ovpts., i.e. large purple or black stamped *X* on portr. and wmk. area.

1980 EMERGENCY CIRCULATING CHECK ISSUE

		VG	VF	UNC
126A	**10,000 RIALS** ND (1980). Dk. blue w/black text on green unpt. Drawings of modern bldgs. at l. and ctr. Wmk: Bank name repeated. Uniface.	20.00	80.00	200.00

BANK MARKAZI IRAN

	Notes of the Islamic Republic of Iran	
18	Yousef Khoshkish (on ovpt.)	Mohammad Yeganeh (on ovpt.)
19	Mohammad Ali Mowlavi	Ali Ardalan
20	Ali Reza Nobari	Abol Hassan Bani-Sadr
21	Dr. Mohsen Nourbakhsh	Hossein Nemazi
22	Dr. Mohsen Nourbakhsh	Iravani
23	Ghasemi	Iravani
24	Ghasemi	Dr. Mohsen Nourbakhsh
25	Mohammad Hossein Adeli	Dr. Mohsen Nourbakhsh
26	Mohammad Hosein Adeli	Mohammad Khan
27	Dr. Mohsen Nourbakhsh	Mohammad Khan

#127-131 calligraphic Persian (Farsi) text from circular republic seal at l., Iman Reza mosque at r. W/o wmk. Yellow security thread w/*BANK MARKAZI IRAN* in black runs through vertically. Back has circular shield w/stars and points at r. Sign. 19. Printer: TDLR (w/o imprint).

#127 and #130 have calligraphic seal printed in the same color as the note (blue and lavender, respectively) and with no variation. #128, 129 and 131 had the calligraphic seal applied locally after notes were printed. Numerous color varieties, misplacement or total omission can be seen on face or back, or both.

		VG	VF	UNC
127	**200 RIALS** ND (1981). Blue on green and m/c unpt. Tomb of Ibn-E-Sina in Hamadan at l. on back.			
	a. Ovpt. lion and sun on face.	.75	2.00	5.50
	b. Ovpt. dk. brown seal.	—	—	—

		VG	VF	UNC
127A	**200 RIALS** ND (1981). Blue, blue-violet and deep green on m/c unpt. Face like #127 w/ovpt. lion and sun. Victory Monument renamed *Banaye Azadi* at l. on back. Sign. 19.	—	Rare	—

		VG	VF	UNC
128	**500 RIALS** ND (1981). Dk. brown on orange, green and m/c unpt. Winged horses on back.	.30	1.50	5.00

		VG	VF	UNC
129	**1000 RIALS** ND (1981). Rust and brown on green and m/c unpt. Tomb of Hafez in Shiraz on back.	2.00	6.00	15.00

		VG	VF	UNC
130	**5000 RIALS** ND (1981). Lavender on green and m/c unpt. Oil refinery at Tehran on back.			
	a. Security thread.	4.00	10.00	35.00
	b. W/o security thread.	10.00	35.00	100.00

		VG	VF	UNC
131	**10,000 RIALS** ND (1981). Deep green, olive-brown and dk. brown on m/c unpt. National Council of Ministries in Tehran on back.			
	a. Dk. brown circular seal at l. Dk. brown circular shield seal at r. on back.	8.00	25.00	80.00
	b. W/o shield seal on back.	10.00	35.00	100.00
	c. W/o circular seal on face.	10.00	35.00	100.00
	d. W/o seals on face or back.	10.00	35.00	100.00

NOTE: #131 first ovpt. w/circular gray-yellow lion and sun on both sides, then additional ovpt. regular black calligraphic seal on top of first ovpt. Notes w/o black seal, or misplaced seal, are errors.

1981 ND SECOND ISSUE

#132-134 Islamic motifs. White security thread w/*BANK MARKAZI IRAN* in black Persian script runs vertically. Sign. 20 unless otherwise noted. Printer: TDLR (w/o imprint). Replacement notes: Serial # prefix *99/99; 98/99; 97/99;* etc.

		VG	VF	UNC
132	**100 RIALS** ND (1981). Maroon on lt. brown and m/c unpt. Imam Reza shrine at Mashad at r. Madressa Chahr-Bagh in Isfahan on back. Wmk: Republic seal.	.50	1.00	3.50

		VG	VF	UNC
133	**5000 RIALS** ND (1981). Violet, red-orange and brown on m/c unpt. Mullahs leading marchers carrying posters of Ayatollah Khomeini at ctr. Hazrat Masoumeh shrine at l. ctr. on back.			
	a. Wmk: Republic seal.	5.00	12.00	30.00
	b. Wmk: Arms.	5.00	12.00	30.00

		VG	VF	UNC
134	**10,000 RIALS** ND (1981). Deep blue-green on yellow and m/c unpt. Face like #133. Imam Reza shrine in Mashad at ctr. on back.			
	a. Sign. 20. Wmk: Republic seal.	6.00	15.00	50.00
	b. Sign. 21. Wmk: Arms.	6.00	15.00	50.00
	c. Sign. 22. Wmk: Arms.	6.00	15.00	50.00

1982; 1983 ND ISSUE

#135-139 Islamic motifs. White security thread w/black *BANK MARKAZI IRAN* in Persian letters repeatedly runs vertically. Printer: TDLR.

#	Denomination	VG	VF	UNC
135	**100 RIALS** ND (1982). Maroon on lt. brown and m/c unpt. Like #132 except for wmk.	.40	1.00	2.00

#	Denomination	VG	VF	UNC
136	**200 RIALS** ND (1982-). Blue-black on m/c unpt. Mosque at ctr. Back gray-green on m/c unpt.; farmers and farm tractor at l. ctr.			
	a. Sign. 21. Wmk: Arms.	.30	.75	2.50
	b. Sign. 23.	FV	FV	2.25
	c. Sign. 21. Wmk: Khomeini.	FV	FV	2.00

#	Denomination	VG	VF	UNC
137	**500 RIALS** ND (1982-). Gray and olive. Feyzieh Madressa Seminary at lower l., lg. prayer gathering at ctr. Tehran University on back.			
	a. Sign. 21. Wmk: Arms.	FV	FV	7.50
	b. Sign. 22.	FV	5.00	25.00
	c. Sign. 23.	FV	FV	7.00
	d. Sign. 23. Wmk: Mohd. H. Fahmideh (youth).	FV	FV	5.00
	e. Sign. 24.	FV	FV	4.50
	f. Sign. 25.	FV	FV	4.25
	g. Sign. 26.	FV	FV	4.00

Wmk:

#	Denomination	VG	VF	UNC
138	**1000 RIALS** ND (1982-). Dk. olive-green, red-brown and brown on m/c unpt. Feyzieh Madressa Seminary at ctr. Mosque of Omar (Dome of the Rock) in Jerusalem on back.			
	a. Sign. 21. Additional short line of text under mosque on back. Wmk: Arms.	FV	FV	12.50
	b. Sign. like a. No line of text under bldg. on back.	FV	FV	30.00
	c. Sign. 22.	FV	FV	15.00
	d. Sign. 23.	FV	FV	10.00
	e. Sign. 23. Wmk: Mohd. H. Fahmideh (youth).	FV	FV	7.00
	f. Sign. 24.	FV	FV	6.00
	g. Sign. 25.	FV	FV	5.00
	h. Sign. 26.	FV	FV	5.00
	i. Sign. 27.	FV	FV	5.00

#	Denomination	VG	VF	UNC
139	**5000 RIALS** ND (1983-). Red and m/c. Similar to #133; reduced crown. Radiant sun removed from upper l. on face. 2 small placards of Khomeini added to crowd.			
	a. Sign. 21.	FV	FV	24.00
	b. Sign. 22. Wmk: Arms.	FV	FV	24.00

NOTE: #139 exists w/2diff. sign. 21 style of Nemazi.

CENTRAL BANK OF THE ISLAMIC REPUBLIC OF IRAN

1985; 1986 ND ISSUE

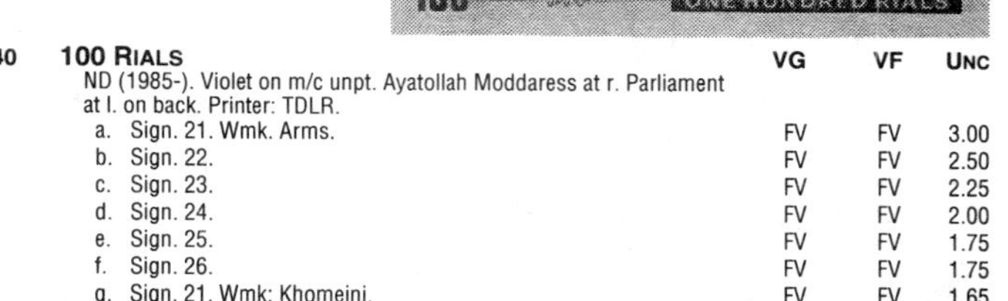

#	Denomination	VG	VF	UNC
140	**100 RIALS** ND (1985-). Violet on m/c unpt. Ayatollah Moddaress at r. Parliament at l. on back. Printer: TDLR.			
	a. Sign. 21. Wmk. Arms.	FV	FV	3.00
	b. Sign. 22.	FV	FV	2.50
	c. Sign. 23.	FV	FV	2.25
	d. Sign. 24.	FV	FV	2.00
	e. Sign. 25.	FV	FV	1.75
	f. Sign. 26.	FV	FV	1.75
	g. Sign. 21. Wmk: Khomeini.	FV	FV	1.65

#	Denomination	VG	VF	UNC
141	**2000 RIALS** ND(1986-). Violet, olive-green and dk. brown on m/c unpt. Revolutionists before mosque at ctr. r. Kaabain Mecca on back.			
	a. Sign. 21. Wmk: Arms.	FV	FV	7.50
	b. Sign. 22.	FV	FV	7.50
	c. Sign. 23.	FV	FV	10.00
	d. Sign.23. Wmk: Mohd. H. Fahmideh (youth).	FV	FV	6.50
	e. Sign. 24.	FV	FV	6.00
	f. Sign. 25.	FV	FV	5.50
	g. Sign. 26.	FV	FV	5.00
	h. Sign. 27.	FV	FV	5.00

1992; 1993 ND Issue

#142 Held in reserve.

#143-146 Khomeini at r. Sign. 25.

		VG	VF	Unc
143	**1000 Rials** ND (1992-). Brown and deep olive-green on m/c unpt. Mosque of Omar (Dome of the Rock) in Jerusalem at ctr. on back. Wmk: Mohd. A. Fahmideh.			
	a. Sign. 25.	FV	FV	5.50
	b. Sign. 27.	FV	FV	4.50
144	**2000 Rials** ND.	Expected New Issue		

#145 and 146 wmk: Khomeini.

		VG	VF	Unc
145	**5000 Rials** ND (1993-). Dk. brown, brown and olive-green on m/c unpt. Back red-violet and pale olive-green on m/c unpt., flowers and birds at ctr. r.			
	a. Sign. 21.	FV	FV	15.00
	b. Sign. 25.	FV	FV	14.50
	c. Sign. 27	FV	FV	15.00

		VG	VF	Unc
146	**10,000 Rials** ND (1992-). Deep blue-green, blue and olive-green on m/c unpt. Mount Damavand at ctr. r. on back.			
	a. Sign. 25.	FV	FV	23.50
	b. Sign. 26.	FV	FV	22.50
	c. Sign. 27.	FV	FV	20.00

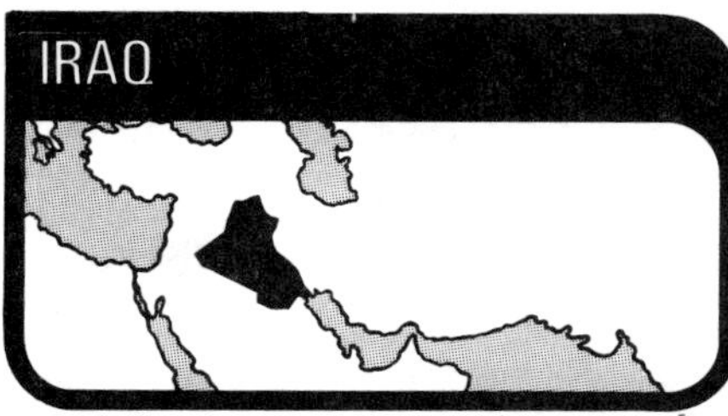

The Republic of Iraq, historically known as Mesopotamia, is located in the Near East and is bordered by Kuwait, Iran, Turkey, Syria, Jordan and Saudi Arabia. It has an area of 167,925 sq. mi. (434,924 sq. km.) and a population of 22.2 million. Capital: Baghdad. The economy of Iraq is based on agriculture and petroleum. Crude oil accounts for 94 percent of the exports before the war with Iran began in 1980.

Iraq was the site of a number of flourishing civilizations of antiquity - Sumerian, Assyrian, Babylonian, Parthian, Persian - and of the Biblical cities of Ur, Nineveh and Babylon. Desired because of its favored location which embraced the fertile alluvial plains of the Tigris and Euphrates Rivers, Mesopotamia - "land between the rivers" - was conquered by Cyrus the Great of Persia, Alexander of Macedonia and by Arabs who made the legendary city of Baghdad the capital of the ruling caliphate. Suleiman the Great conquered Mesopotamia for Turkey in 1534, and it formed part of the Ottoman Empire until 1623, and from 1638 to 1917. Great Britain, given a League of Nations mandate over the territory in 1920, recognized Iraq as a kingdom in 1922. Iraq became an independent constitutional monarchy presided over by the Hashemite family, direct descendants of the prophet Mohammed, in 1932. In 1958, the army-led revolution of July 14 overthrew the monarchy and proclaimed a republic. After several military coups, Saddam Hussein became president in 1979.

MONETARY SYSTEM:

1 Dinar = 1000 Fils

Republic

Central Bank of Iraq

1958 Issue

#51-55 new Republic arms w/1958 at r. and as wmk. Sign. varieties.

		VG	VF	Unc
51	**1/4 Dinar** 1958. Green on m/c unpt. Palm tree at ctr. on back.	1.00	5.00	15.00
52	**1/2 Dinar** 1958. Brown on m/c unpt. Fortress and minaret at ctr. on back.	2.00	8.00	30.00

53 **1 Dinar**
1958. Blue on m/c unpt. Ornate harp-like piece w/strings on back.

VG	VF	Unc
1.50	6.50	20.00

54 **5 Dinars**
1958. Lt. purple on m/c unpt. Two ancient figures at ctr., *FIVE DINARS* at l. on back.

VG	VF	Unc
2.50	12.50	35.00

55 **10 Dinars**
1958. Dk. blue on m/c unpt. Ancient carvings of winged creatures at ctr. on back.

VG	VF	Unc
6.00	30.00	90.00

1971 ND Issue

#56-60 wmk: Falcon's head. Sign. varieties.

56 **1/4 Dinar**
ND (1971). Green and brown on m/c unpt. Harbor at ctr. *1/4 Dinar* at l, palm tree at ctr. on back.

VG	VF	Unc
1.00	3.00	9.00

57 **1/2 Dinar**
ND (1971). Brown and blue on m/c unpt. Oil refinery at ctr. *1/2 Dinar* at l., walled fort and minaret at ctr. on back.

VG	VF	Unc
2.50	8.00	25.00

58 **1 Dinar**
ND (1971). Blue and brown on m/c unpt. Factory at ctr. Doorway at ctr., *1 Dinar* at l. on back.

VG	VF	Unc
2.00	6.00	18.50

59 **5 Dinars**
ND (1971). Lilac on brown and m/c unpt. Parliament bldg. across face. King Hummorabi on throne giving court minister first law (eye for eye...), *5 Dinars* at l. on back.

VG	VF	Unc
5.00	15.00	45.00

60 **10 DINARS** ND (1971). Purple, blue and brown on m/c unpt. Coffer dam at ctr. Ancient carvings of winged creatures at ctr., *10 Dinars* at l. on back. VG 5.00 VF 15.00 UNC 45.00

1973 ND; 1978 ISSUE

#61-66 wmk: Falcon's head. Sign. varieties.

61 **1/4 DINAR** ND (1973). Green and black on m/c unpt. Similar to #56. *Quarter Dinar* at bottom r. on back. VG .50 VF 1.50 UNC 5.00

62 **1/2 DINAR** ND (1973). Brown on m/c unpt. Face design similar to #57. *Half Dinar* below Minaret of the Great Mosque at Samarra at ctr. on back. VG 1.25 VF 4.00 UNC 12.50

63 **1 DINAR** ND (1973). Blue on green and m/c unpt. Similar to #58. *One Dinar* at bottom r. on back.

	VG	VF	UNC
a. 1 line of Arabic caption (factory name) below.	1.00	4.50	32.50
b. W/o Arabic caption below factory.	1.00	3.25	10.00

64 **5 DINARS** ND (1973). Lilac on m/c unpt. Similar to #59. *Five Dinars* at bottom on back. VG .75 VF 2.50 UNC 7.50

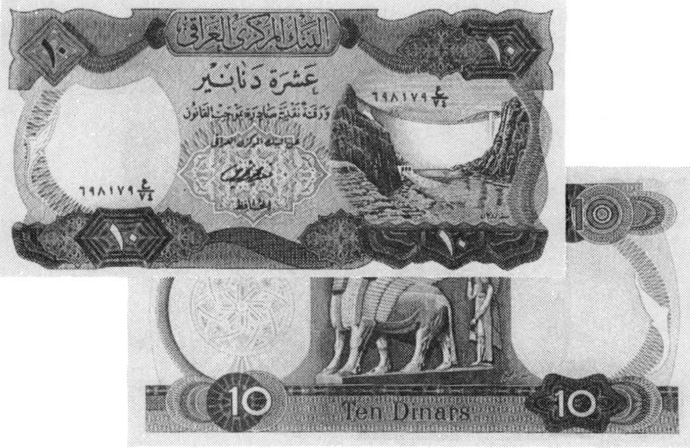

65 **10 DINARS** ND (1973). Purple on blue and m/c unpt. Coffer dam at r. Back similar to #60, but *Ten Dinars* at bottom. VG 1.50 VF 4.50 UNC 13.50

66 **25 DINARS** 1978/AH1398; 1980/AH1400. Green and brown on m/c unpt. 3 Arabian horses at ctr., date below sign. at lower r. Abbaside Palace on back. 182 x 88mm. VG 2.50 VF 7.50 UNC 22.50

1979-86 ISSUE

#67-72 wmk: Arabian horse's head. Sign. varieties.

67 **1/4 DINAR** 1979/AH1399. Green and m/c. Palm trees at ctr. Bldg. on back. VG .15 VF 1.00 UNC 4.50

68 **1/2 DINAR**
1980/AH1400; 1985/AH1405. Brown and m/c. Astrolabe at r. Minaret of Samarra on back. VG .15 VF .75 UNC 3.00

69 **1 DINAR**
1979/AH1399; 1980/AH1400; 1984/AH1404. Olive-green and deep blue on m/c unpt. Coin design at ctr. Musan-2teriah School in Baghdad on back. VG .25 VF .75 UNC 2.25

70 **5 DINARS**
1980/AH1400; 1981/AH1401; 1982/AH1402. Brown-violet on deep blue and m/c unpt. Waterfalls at ctr. Walled city on back. VG .30 VF 1.25 UNC 5.50

71 **10 DINARS**
1980/AH1400; 1981/AH1401; 1982/AH1402; 1983/AH1403. Purple on blue, violet and m/c unpt. A. Abulhasan ibn al Hisham at r. Tower on back. VG .65 VF 2.00 UNC 4.50

72 **25 DINARS**
1981/AH1401; 1982/AH1402. Green and brown. Similar to #66 but date below horses. Reduced size, 175 x 80mm. VG .35 VF 1.25 UNC 4.00

73 **25 DINARS**
1986. Brown and black on green, blue and m/c unpt. Medieval horsemen charging at ctr., S. Hussein at r. and as wmk. City gate at l., monument at ctr. on back. VG .75 VF 1.50 UNC 5.50

NOTE: In a sudden economic move during summer of 1993, it was announced that all previous 25 Dinar notes issued before #74 had become worthless.

1990; 1991 EMERGENCY GULF WAR ISSUE

#74-76 local printing.

74 **25 DINARS**
1990/AH1411; 1991/AH1411. Similar to #72 but green and gray on lt. green unpt. Litho. VG FV VF FV UNC 5.00

		VG	VF	UNC
75	**50 DINARS** 1991/AH1411. Brown and blue-green on peach and m/c unpt. S. Hussein at r. Minaret of the Great Mosque at Samarra at ctr. r. on back.	.75	2.50	7.50

		VG	VF	UNC
76	**100 DINARS** 1991/AH1411. Dk. blue-green on lilac and m/c unpt. S. Hussein at r. Crossed swords below Iraqi flag at ctr. on back.	1.00	3.00	9.00

1992-93 EMERGENCY ISSUE

#77-79 dull lithograph printing. W/faint indelible ink wmk.

		VG	VF	UNC
77	**1/4 DINAR** 1993/AH1413. Green on m/c unpt. Like #67.	FV	FV	.75

		VG	VF	UNC
78	**1/2 DINAR** 1993/AH1413. Brown on m/c unpt. Like #68.	FV	FV	1.00

		VG	VF	UNC
79	**1 DINAR** 1992/AH1412. Green and blue-black on m/c unpt. Like #69.	FV	FV	1.65

#80 and 81 S. Hussein at r. Printed in China.

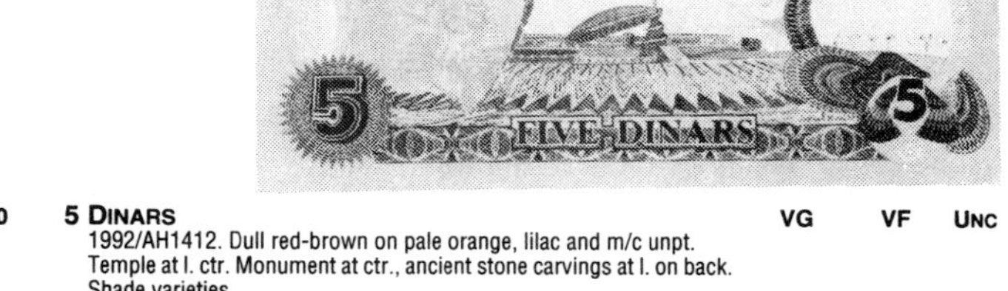

		VG	VF	UNC
80	**5 DINARS** 1992/AH1412. Dull red-brown on pale orange, lilac and m/c unpt. Temple at l. ctr. Monument at ctr., ancient stone carvings at l. on back. Shade varieties.			
	a. W/border around embossed text at ctr.	FV	FV	3.50
	b. W/o border around embossed text at ctr.	FV	FV	3.50
	c. As b. w/o embossed text at ctr.	FV	FV	3.00

		VG	VF	UNC
81	**10 DINARS** 1992/AH1412. Deep purple, blue-green and m/c. Winged lion sculpture at l. on back.	FV	FV	5.50

#82 Not assigned.

1994-95 Issue

#83-85 S. Hussein at r.

		VG	VF	Unc
83	**50 Dinars** 1994/AH1414. Brown and pale green on m/c unpt. Ancient statuette, monument at l. ctr. Modern Saddam bridge at ctr. on back.	FV	FV	4.00

		VG	VF	Unc
84	**100 Dinars** 1994/AH1414. Blue-black on lt. blue and pale ochre unpt. Walled compound at ctr. Modern bldg. at ctr. on back. Printed wmk: Falcon's head.	FV	FV	5.50

NOTE: Shade varieties exist.

		VG	VF	Unc
85	**250 Dinars** 1995/AH1415. Lavender on blue and m/c unpt. Hydroelectric dam at l. ctr. Archaic frieze across back.	FV	FV	6.50

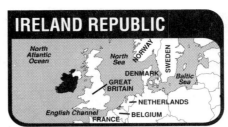

IRELAND REPUBLIC

North Atlantic Ocean · North Sea · NORWAY · SWEDEN · DENMARK · Baltic Sea · GREAT BRITAIN · NETHERLANDS · BELGIUM · English Channel · FRANCE

The Republic of Ireland, which occupies five-sixths of the island of Ireland located in the Atlantic Ocean west of Great Britain, has an area of 27,136 sq. mi. (70,283 sq. km.) and a population of 3.6 million. Capital: Dublin.

Agriculture and dairy farming are the principal industries. Meat, livestock, dairy products and textiles are exported.

The Irish Free State was established as a dominion on Dec. 6, 1921. Ireland withdrew from the Commonwealth and proclaimed itself a republic on April 18, 1949. The government, however, does not use the term "Republic of Ireland," which tacitly acknowledges the partitioning of the island into Ireland and Northern Ireland, but refers to the country simply as 'Eire' "Ireland".

RULERS:

British to 1921

MONETARY SYSTEM:

1 Shilling = 12 Pence
1 Pound = 20 Shillings to 1971
1 Pound = 100 Pence, 1971-2001
1 Euro = 100 Cent

Republic

Banc Ceannais na hÉireann

Central Bank of Ireland

1961-63 Issue

#63-69 representation of river gods at ctr. on back. Replacement notes: From 1974-1976 single letter prefix plus 6-digit serial number for 1£ - 20£. For 1£ and 5£ dated 1975 a "00" was used in front of the prefix letter.

#63-65 portr. Lady Hazel Lavery at l., denomination at bottom ctr.

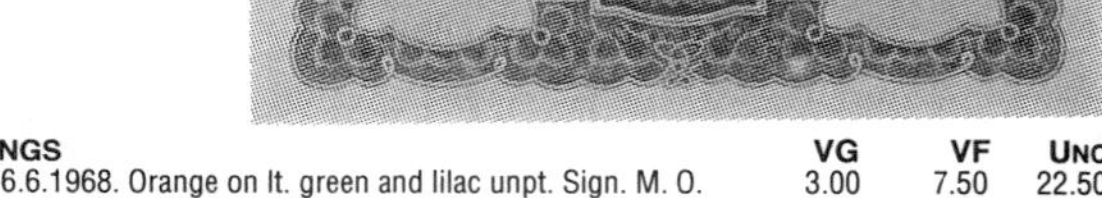

		VG	VF	Unc
63	**10 Shillings** 3.1.1962-6.6.1968. Orange on lt. green and lilac unpt. Sign. M. O. Muimhneachain and T. K. Whitaker.	3.00	7.50	22.50

		VG	VF	Unc
64	**1 Pound** 1962-76. Green on pale gold unpt.			
	a. Sign. M. O. Muimhneachain and T. K. Whitaker. 16.3.1962-8.10.1968.	FV	6.00	25.00
	b. Sign. T. K. Whitaker and C. H. Murray. 1.3.1969-17.9.1970.	FV	5.00	22.00
	c. Sign. like b, but metallic security thread at l. of ctr. 8.7.1971-21.4.1975.	FV	4.00	18.00
	d. Sign. C. H. Murray and M. O. Murchu. 30.9.1976.	FV	3.00	12.00

Note: Replacement notes: Serial # prefix *S* or *00A*.

	65 5 POUNDS	VG	VF	UNC
	1961-75. Brown on lt. gold and orange unpt.			
a.	Sign. M. O. Muimhneachain and T. K. Whitaker. 15.8.1961-12.8.1968.	FV	25.00	125.00
b.	Sign. T. K. Whitaker and C. H. Murray. 12.5.1969; 27.2.1970.	FV	20.00	85.00
c.	Sign. like b., but metallic security thread at l. of ctr. 18.1.1971-5.9.1975.	FV	12.50	60.00

NOTE: Replacement notes: Serial # prefix *R* or *OOK*.

#66-69 Lady Hazel Lavery in Irish national costume w/chin resting on her hand and leaning on an Irish harp.

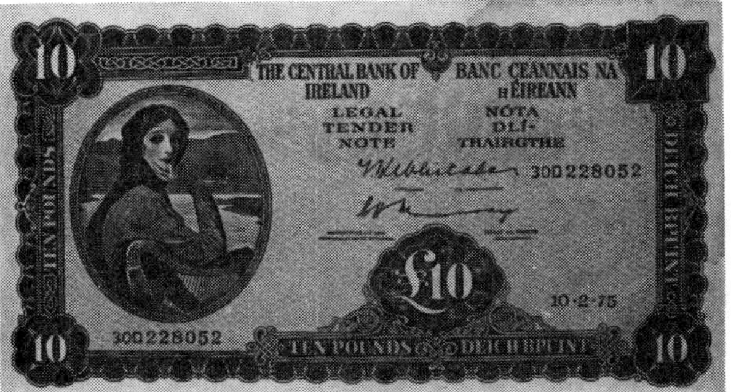

	66 10 POUNDS	VG	VF	UNC
	1962-76. Blue on m/c unpt.			
a.	Sign. M. O. Muimhneachain and T. K. Whitaker. 2.5.1962-16.7.1968.	FV	45.00	150.00
b.	Sign. T. K. Whitaker and C. H. Murray. 5.5.1969; 9.3.1970.	FV	35.00	100.00
c.	Sign. like b, but metallic security thread at l. of ctr. 19.5.1971-10.2.1975.	FV	25.00	85.00
d.	Sign. C. H. Murray and M. O. Murchu. 2.12.1976.	FV	22.50	80.00

NOTE: Replacement notes: Serial # prefix *T*.

	67 20 POUNDS	VG	VF	UNC
	1961-76. Red on m/c unpt.			
a.	Sign. M. O. Muimhneachain and T. K. Whitaker. 1.6.1961-15.6.1965.	FV	85.00	300.00
b.	Sign. T. K. Whitaker and C. H. Murray. 3.3.1969-6.1.1975.	FV	60.00	225.00
c.	Sign. C. H. Murray and M. O. Murchu. 24.3.1976.	FV	50.00	175.00

NOTE: Replacement notes: Serial # prefix *V*.

	68 50 POUNDS	VG	VF	UNC
	1962-77. Purple on m/c unpt.			
a.	Sign. M. O. Muimhneachain and T. K. Whitaker. 1.2.1962-6.9.1968.	FV	150.00	375.00
b.	Sign. T. K. Whitaker and C. H. Murray. 4.11.1970-16.4.1975.	FV	125.00	300.00
c.	Sign. C. H. Murray and M. O. Murchu. 4.4.1977.	FV	100.00	270.00

	69 100 POUNDS	VG	VF	UNC
	1963-77. Green on m/c unpt.			
a.	Sign. M. O. Muimhneachain and T. K. Whitaker. 16.1.1963-9.9.1968.	FV	275.00	575.00
b.	Sign. T. K. Whitaker and C. H. Murray. 26.10.1970; 3.3.1972; 26.2.1973; 10.4.1975.	FV	225.00	500.00
c.	Sign. C. H. Murray and M. O. Murchu. 4.4.1977.	FV	200.00	425.00

1976-82 ISSUE

#70-74 replacement notes: Serial # prefixes *AAA; BBB;* etc.

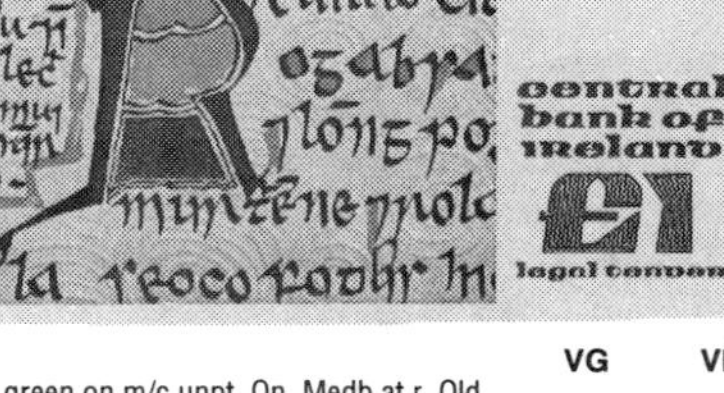

	70 1 POUND	VG	VF	UNC
	1977-89. Dk. olive-green and green on m/c unpt. Qn. Medb at r. Old writing on back. Wmk: Lady Lavery.			
a.	Sign. C. H. Murray and M. O. Murchu. 10.6.1977-29.11.1977.	2.00	3.00	10.00
b.	Sign. C. H. Murray and T. F. O'Cofaigh. 30.8.1978-30.10.1981.	FV	2.50	8.00
c.	Sign. T. F. O'Cofaigh and M. F. Doyle. 30.6.1982-24.4.1987.	FV	2.00	7.00
d.	Sign. M. F. Doyle and S. P. Cromien. 23.3.1988-17.7.1989.	FV	2.00	6.50

	71 5 POUNDS	VG	VF	UNC
	1976-93. Brown and red on m/c unpt. J. S. Eriugena at r. Old writing on back.			
a.	Sign. T. K. Whitaker and C. H. Murray. 26.2.1976.	FV	FV	30.00
b.	Sign. C. H. Murray and M. O. Murchu. 18.5.1976-17.10.1977.	FV	FV	27.50
c.	Sign. C. H. Murray and T. F. O'Cofaigh. 25.4.1979-29.10.1981.	FV	FV	25.00
d.	Sign. T. F. O'Cofaigh and M. F. Doyle. 1982; 17.10.1983-22.4.1987.	FV	FV	22.50
e.	Sign. M. F. Doyle and S. P. Cromien. 12.8.1988-7.5.1993.	FV	FV	20.00

		VG	VF	UNC
72	**10 POUNDS** 1978-92. Violet and purple on m/c unpt. J. Swift at r. Old street map on back.			
	a. Sign. C. H. Murray and T. F. O'Cofaigh. 1.6.1978-28.10.1981.	FV	FV	50.00
	b. Sign. T. F. O'Cofaigh and M. F. Doyle. 1982; 25.2.1983-9.2.1987.	FV	FV	42.50
	c. Sign. M. F. Doyle and S. P. Cromien. 22.12.1987-15.4.1992.	FV	FV	37.50

		VG	VF	UNC
73	**20 POUNDS** 1980-92. Blue on m/c unpt. W. B. Yeats at r., Abbey Theatre symbol at ctr. Map on back.			
	a. Sign. C. H. Murray and T. F. O'Cofaigh. 7.1.1980-28.10.1981.	FV	FV	75.00
	b. Sign. T. F. O'Cofaigh and M. F. Doyle. 11.7.1983-28.8.1986.	FV	FV	65.00
	c. Sign. M. F. Doyle and S. P. Cromien. 12.8.1987-14.2.1992.	FV	FV	60.00

		VG	VF	UNC
74	**50 POUNDS** 1982; 1991. Red and brown on m/c unpt. Carolan playing harp in front of group. Musical instruments on back.			
	a. Sign. T. F. O'Cofaigh and M. F. Doyle. 1.11.1982.	FV	FV	150.00
	b. Sign. M. F. Doyle and S. P. Cromien. 5.11.1991.	FV	FV	120.00

1992-95 ISSUE

#75-78 wmk: Lady Lavery and value. Replacement notes: Serial # prefixes *BBB; CCC,* etc.

		VG	VF	UNC
75	**5 POUNDS** 1994-. Dk. brown, reddish brown, and grayish purple on m/c unpt. Mater Misericordiae Hospital at bottom l. ctr., Sister C. McAuley at r. School children at ctr. on back.			
	a. Sign. M. F. Doyle and S. P. Cromien. 15.3.1994-28.4.1994.	FV	FV	18.50
	b. Sign. M. O'Connell and P. H. Mullarkey. 21.12.1994-14.9.1998.	FV	FV	15.00

		VG	VF	UNC
76	**10 POUNDS** 1993-. Dk. green and brown on m/c unpt. Aerial view of Dublin at ctr., J. Joyce at r. Sculpted head representing Liffey River at l., map in unpt. on back.			
	a. Sign. M. F. Doyle and S. P. Cromien. 14.7.1993-27.4.1994.	FV	FV	30.00
	b. Sign. M. O'Connell and P. H. Mullarkey. 13.3.1995-28.4.1999.	FV	FV	25.00

		VG	VF	UNC
77	**20 POUNDS** 1992-. Violet, brown and dk. grayish blue on m/c unpt. Derryname Abbey at l. ctr., D. O'Connell at r. Writings and bldg. on back.			
	a. Sign. M. F. Doyle and S. P. Cromien. 10.9.1992-29.4.1994.	FV	FV	55.00
	b. Sign. M. O'Connell and P. H. Mullarkey. 14.6.1995-12.8.1999.	FV	FV	45.00

		VG	VF	UNC
78	**50 POUNDS** 6.10.1995; 14.2.1996; 19.3.1999. Dk. blue and violet on m/c unpt. D. Hyde at r., Áras an Uachtaráin bldg. in background at ctr. Back dk. gray and deep olive-green on m/c unpt.; Parnell statue at l., crest of Conradh na Gaeilge at upper ctr. r. Sign. M. O'Connell and P. H. Mullarkey.	FV	FV	110.00
79	**100 POUNDS** 22.8.1996. C. D. Parnell at r., Avondale House and gardens in Rathdrum at lower l. ctr., Irish Wolfhound at lower l. Parts of the Parnell monument in Dublin on back. Sign. M. O'Connell and P. H. Mullarkey.	FV	FV	200.00

NORTHERN IRELAND

From 1800 to 1921 Ireland was an integral part of the United Kingdom. The Anglo-Irish treaty of 1921 established the Irish Free State of 26 counties within the Commonwealth of Nations and recognized the partition of Ireland. The six predominantly Protestant counties of northeast Ulster chose to remain a part of the United Kingdom with a limited self-government.

Up to 1928 the notes of the private or commerical banks were circulating in the whole of Ireland. After the establishment of the Irish Free State, the private or commercial notes were only issued for circulation in Northern Ireland.

NOTE: For notes of the Irish Republic see Ireland - Republic (Éire).

RULERS:

British

MONETARY SYSTEM:

1 Shilling = 12 Pence
1 Pound = 20 Shillings to 1971
1 Pound = 100 New Pence, 1971-

BRITISH INFLUENCE

ALLIED IRISH BANKS LTD.

Formerly Provincial Bank of Ireland Ltd., later became First Trust Bank.

1982 ISSUE

#1-5 designs similar to Provincial Bank of Ireland Ltd. (#247-251) except for bank title and sign. Printer: TDLR.

		VG	VF	UNC
1	**1 POUND** 1.1.1982; 1.7.1983; 1.12.1984. Green on m/c unpt. Young girl at r. Sailing ship *Girona* at ctr. on back.	FV	6.00	22.50

		VG	VF	UNC
2	**5 POUNDS** 1.1.1982. Blue and purple on m/c unpt. Young woman at r. Dunluce Castle at ctr. on back.	FV	12.50	45.00

#	Denomination / Description	VG	VF	UNC
3	**10 POUNDS** 1.1.1982; 1.12.1984. Brown and gray-green on m/c unpt. Young man at r. Wreck of the *Girona* at ctr. on back.	FV	22.50	65.00
4	**20 POUNDS** 1.1.1982. Purple and green. Elderly woman at r. Chimney at Lacada Pt. at ctr. on back.	FV	42.50	120.00
5	**100 POUNDS** 1.1.1982. Black, olive and green. Elderly man at r. The *Armada* at ctr. on back.	FV	185.00	400.00

ALLIED IRISH BANKS PUBLIC LIMITED COMPANY

Formerly Allied Irish Banks Ltd., later became First Trust Bank.

1987-88 ISSUE

#6-9 like #2-5 except for bank title and sign. Printer: TDLR.

#	Denomination / Description	VG	VF	UNC
6	**5 POUNDS** 1.1.1987; 1.1.1990. Similar to #2.	FV	FV	30.00

#	Denomination / Description	VG	VF	UNC
7	**10 POUNDS** 1.3.1988; 1.1.1990; 18.5.1993. Similar to #3.	FV	FV	47.50
8	**20 POUNDS** 1.4.1987. Similar to #4.	FV	FV	87.50

#	Denomination / Description	VG	VF	UNC
9	**100 POUNDS** 1.12.1988. Similar to #5.	FV	FV	350.00

BANK OF IRELAND

BELFAST BRANCH

1967 ND ISSUE

#56-64 Mercury at l., woman w/harp at r. Airplane, bank bldg. and boat on back. Sign. title as Agent.

#	Denomination / Description	VG	VF	UNC
56	**1 POUND** ND (1967). Black on green and lilac unpt. 151 x 72mm. Sign. W. E. Guthrie.	2.00	5.00	22.50
57	**5 POUNDS** ND (1967-68). Brown-violet.			
	a. Sign. W. E. Guthrie. (1967). .	9.00	17.50	70.00
	b. Sign. H. H. M. Chestnutt. (196 1968).	8.00	15.00	55.00
58	**10 POUNDS** ND (1967). Brown and yellow. Sign. W. E. Guthrie.	18.00	35.00	135.00

#59 and 60 *Deleted*.

1971-74 ND ISSUES

W/o word *Sterling* after Pound.

#61-63 replacement notes: Serial # prefix *Z*.

#	Denomination / Description	VG	VF	UNC
61	**1 POUND** ND (1972-77). Black on lt. green and lilac unpt. Like #56 but smaller size. 134 x 66mm.			
	a. Sign. H. H. M. Chestnutt. (1972).	FV	3.00	16.50
	b. Sign. A. S. J. O'Neill. (1977).	FV	FV	13.50
62	**5 POUNDS** ND (1971-77). Blue on lt. green and lilac unpt. 146 x 78mm.			
	a. Sign. H. H. M. Chestnutt. (1971).	FV	13.50	40.00
	b. Sign. A. S. J. O'Neill. (1977).	FV	12.50	27.50
63	**10 POUNDS** ND (1971-77). Brown on lt. green and pale orange unpt.			
	a. Sign. H. H. M. Chestnutt. (1971).	FV	25.00	75.00
	b. Sign. A. S. J. O'Neill. (1977).	FV	20.00	45.00
64	**100 POUNDS** ND (1974-78). Red on m/c unpt.			
	a. Sign. H. H. M. Chestnutt. (1974).	FV	FV	375.00
	b. Sign. A. S. J. O'Neill. (1978).	FV	FV	300.00

1980S ND ISSUE

Word *Sterling* added after Pound.

#	Denomination / Description	VG	VF	UNC
65	**1 POUND** ND. Black on lt. green and lilac unpt. Like #61 but w/*STERLING* added below value. Wmk: Bank name repeated. Sign. A. S. J. O'Neill.	FV	2.25	6.50
66	**5 POUNDS** ND. Blue on lt. green and lilac unpt. Like #62 but w/£ signs added in corners.			
	a. Sign. A. S. J. O'Neill.	FV	11.50	25.00
	b. Sign. D. F. Harrison.	FV	13.50	30.00

#	Denomination / Description	VG	VF	UNC
67	**10 POUNDS** ND (1984). Dk. brown on lt. green and pale orange unpt. Like #63.			
	a. Sign. A. S. J. O'Neill.	FV	22.50	45.00
	b. Sign. D. F. Harrison.	FV	25.00	50.00
67A	**20 POUNDS** ND. Dk. olive-green on m/c unpt.			
	a. Sign. A. S. J. O'Neill.	FV	42.50	85.00
	b. Sign. D. F. Harrison.	FV	47.50	95.00
68	**100 POUNDS** ND. Red on m/c unpt. Similar to #64 but w/£ sign at upper r. and lower l. corners on face and back. *Sterling* added at lower ctr. on face.			
	a. Sign. A. S. J. O'Neill.	FV	FV	285.00
	b. Sign. D. F. Harrison.	FV	FV	210.00

1983 COMMEMORATIVE ISSUE

#69, Bank of Ireland Bicentenary, 1783-1983

#	Denomination / Description	VG	VF	UNC
69	**20 POUNDS** 1983. Dk. olive-green on m/c on unpt. Like #67A but commemorative text below bank title. Sign. A. S. J. O'Neill.	75.00	175.00	400.00

1990-95 ISSUE

#70-74 bank seal (Hibernia seated) at l., six county shields at upper ctr. Queen's University in Belfast on back. Sign. D. F. Harrison. Wmk: Medusa head.

#	Denomination / Description	VG	VF	UNC
70	**5 POUNDS** 28.8.1990; 16.1.1992. Blue and purple on m/c unpt.	FV	FV	15.00

#	Denomination / Description	VG	VF	UNC
71	**10 POUNDS** 14.5.1991. Purple and maroon on m/c unpt.	FV	FV	27.50

#	Denomination / Description	VG	VF	UNC
72	**20 POUNDS** 9.5.1991. Green and brown on m/c unpt.	FV	FV	52.50
73 (74)	**100 POUNDS** 28.8.1992. Red on m/c unpt.	FV	FV	225.00

NOTE: Specimens and 3-subject sheets were sold to collectors. Low numbers were also available to special folders.

1995; 1997 ISSUE

#	Denomination / Description	VG	VF	UNC
74	**5 POUNDS** 1997. M/c.	FV	FV	15.00
75	**10 POUNDS** 1995. M/c.	FV	FV	27.50
76	**20 POUNDS** 1995. M/c.	FV	FV	52.50
77 (74)	**50 POUNDS** 1.7.1995. M/c.	FV	FV	110.00
78	**100 POUNDS** 1995. M/c.	FV	FV	225.00

BELFAST BANKING COMPANY LIMITED

NOTE: See also Ireland.

BELFAST BRANCH

1922-23 ISSUE

#126-131 arms at top or upper ctr. w/payable text: *. . . at our Head Office, Belfast.*

#	Denomination / Description	VG	VF	UNC
127	**5 POUNDS** 1923-66. Black on red unpt.			
	a. Black serial #. 3.1.1923; 3.5.1923; 7.9.1927.	17.50	45.00	150.00
	b. Red serial #. 8.3.1928-2.10.1942.	12.50	35.00	80.00
	c. Red serial #. 6.1.1966.	10.00	20.00	50.00

#	Denomination / Description	VG	VF	UNC
128	**10 POUNDS** 1923-65. Black on green unpt.			
	a. Black serial #. 3.1.1923.	40.00	65.00	225.00
	b. Green serial #. 9.1.1929-1.1.1943.	30.00	55.00	150.00
	c. Green serial #. 3.12.1963; 5.6.1965.	18.00	30.00	75.00

129 20 Pounds
1923-65. Black on purple unpt.

		VG	VF	Unc
a.	Black serial #. 3.1.1923.	45.00	100.00	300.00
b.	Mauve serial #. 9.11.1939; 10.8.1940.	40.00	90.00	250.00
c.	Black serial #. 3.2.1943.	37.50	65.00	180.00
d.	Black serial #. 5.6.1965.	35.00	50.00	150.00

130 50 Pounds
1923-63. Black on orange unpt.

		VG	VF	Unc
a.	Black serial #. 3.1.1923; 3.5.1923.	150.00	275.00	500.00
b.	Yellow serial #. 9.11.1939; 10.8.1940.	125.00	150.00	375.00
c.	Black serial #. 3.2.1943.	95.00	150.00	300.00
d.	Black serial #. 3.12.1963.	85.00	125.00	250.00

131 100 Pounds
1923-68. Black on red unpt.

		VG	VF	Unc
a.	3.1.1923; 3.5.1923.	170.00	350.00	600.00
b.	9.11.1939; 3.2.1943.	FV	200.00	450.00
c.	3.12.1963.	FV	185.00	350.00
d.	8.5.1968.	FV	175.00	300.00

First Trust Bank

Formerly Allied Irish Banks PLC, which acquired the Trustee Savings Bank. Member AIB Group Northern Ireland PLC.

1994 Issue

#132-135 five shields at bottom ctr. Printer: TDLR. Sign. title: GROUP MANAGING DIRECTOR. Wmk: Young woman.

132 10 Pounds

	VG	VF	Unc
10.1.1994. Dk. brown and violet. Face similar to #3. Sailing ship Girona at ctr. on back.	FV	FV	25.00

133 20 Pounds

	VG	VF	Unc
10.1.1994. Violet, dk. brown and red-brown on m/c unpt. Face similar to #4. Chimney at Lacada Pt. at ctr. on back.	FV	FV	50.00

134 50 Pounds

	VG	VF	Unc
10.1.1994. Black, dk. olive-green and blue on m/c unpt. Face similar to #5. Cherubs holding armada medallion at ctr. on back.	FV	FV	110.00

135 100 Pounds

	VG	VF	Unc
10.1.1994. Black and olive-brown on m/c unpt. Elderly couple at r. The *Armada* at ctr. on back.	FV	FV	200.00

1998 Issue

#	Denomination	VG	VF	Unc
136	**10 Pounds** 1.1.1998. M/c.	FV	FV	37.50
137	**20 Pounds** 1.1.1998. M/c.	FV	FV	75.00
138	**50 Pounds** 1.1.1998. M/c.	FV	FV	155.00
139	**100 Pounds** 1.1.1998. M/c.	FV	FV	285.00

NORTHERN BANK LIMITED

1929 REGULAR ISSUE

#178 sailing ship, plow and man at grindstone at upper ctr.

		VG	VF	UNC
178	**1 POUND** 1929-68. Black. Blue guilloche.			
	a. Red serial #. 6.5.1929; 1.7.1929; 1.8.1929.	15.00	35.00	90.00

		VG	VF	UNC
	b. Black prefix letters and serial #. 1.1.1940.	6.00	15.00	45.00
	c. 1.10.1968.	3.00	12.00	35.00

1930-43 ISSUE

#181 sailing ship, plow and man at grindstone at upper ctr.

		VG	VF	UNC
181	**10 POUNDS** 1930-68. Black on red unpt.			
	a. Red serial #. 1.1.1930-1.1.1940.	40.00	80.00	150.00
	b. Black serial #. 1.8.1940; 1.9.1940.	30.00	70.00	120.00
	c. Red serial #. 1.1.1942-1.11.1943.	25.00	50.00	100.00
	d. Imprint on back below central design. 1.10.1968.	FV	25.00	60.00

1968 ISSUE

		VG	VF	UNC
184	**5 POUNDS** 1.10.1968. Black on green unpt.	10.00	20.00	47.50
185	**50 POUNDS** 1.10.1968. Black on dk. blue unpt. *NBLD* monogram on back.	85.00	150.00	300.00
186	**100 POUNDS** 1.10.1968. Black on dk. blue unpt. *NBLD* monogram on back.	175.00	300.00	500.00

1970 ISSUE

#187-192 cows at l., shipyard at bottom ctr., loom at r. Stylized arms at ctr. on back. Sign. varieties.

NOTICE

Readers with unlisted dates, signature varieties, etc. are invited to submit photocopies of their notes to: Standard Catalog of World Paper Money, 700 East State St. Iola, WI 54990-0001, fax: 1-715-445-4087, or E-Mail: thernr@krause.com.

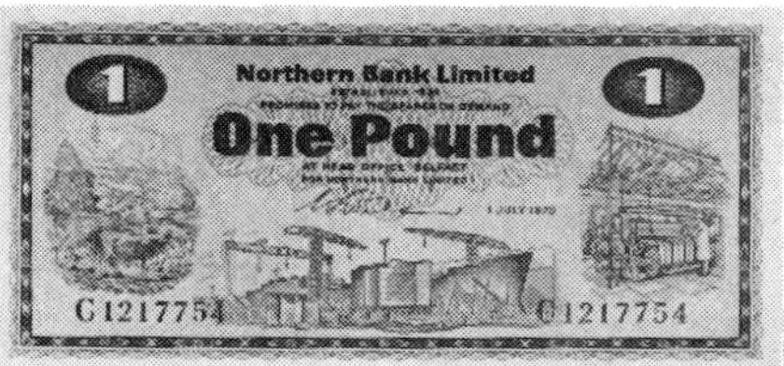

		VG	VF	UNC
187	**1 POUND** 1970-82. Green on pink unpt. Printer: BWC.			
	a. 1.7.1970; 1.10.1971; 1.1.1976.	FV	2.50	17.50
	b. 1.8.1978; 1.7.1979; 1.4.1982.	FV	2.25	12.50
188	**5 POUNDS** 1.7.1970-1.4.1982. Lt. blue.	FV	11.00	32.50
189	**10 POUNDS** 1970-88. Brown.			
	a. 1.7.1970; 1.10.1971.	FV	22.50	60.00
	b. 1.1.1976; 1.4.1982; 15.6.1988.	FV	20.00	50.00
190	**20 POUNDS** 1.7.1970; 1.3.1981; 15.6.1988. Purple.	FV	37.50	110.00
191	**50 POUNDS** 1.7.1970. Orange.	FV	87.50	200.00
192	**100 POUNDS** 1.7.1970; 1.10.1971; 1.1.1975; 1.1.1980. Red.	FV	175.00	350.00

1988-90 ISSUE

#193-197 dish antenna at l., stylized *N* at ctr. and computer on back. Printer: TDLR.

		VG	VF	UNC
193	**5 POUNDS** 24.8.1988; 24.8.1989; 24.8.1990. Blue and m/c. Station above trolley car at ctr., W. A. Traill at r.	FV	FV	15.00

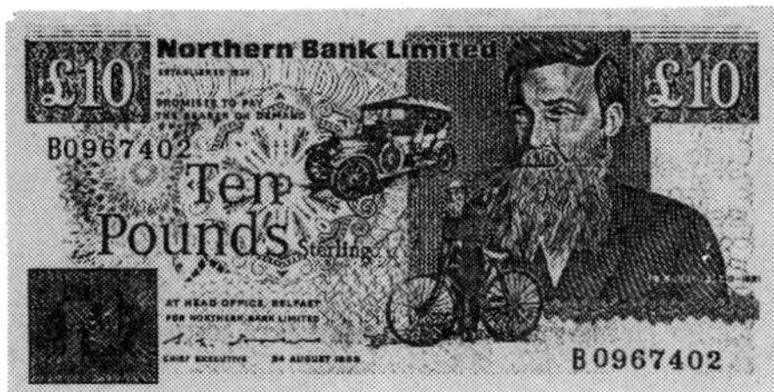

		VG	VF	UNC
194	**10 POUNDS** 24.8.1988; 14.5.1991; 24.8.1993. Red and brown on m/c unpt. Early automobile above bicyclist at ctr., J. B. Dunlop at r.	FV	FV	45.00

		VG	VF	UNC
195	**20 POUNDS** 24.8.1988; 24.8.1989; 24.8.1990; 9.5.1991; 30.3.1992. Purple-brown, red and m/c. Airplane at ctr., H. G. Ferguson at r., tractor at bottom r.	FV	FV	60.00

		VG	VF	UNC
196	**50 POUNDS** 1.11.1990. Bluish green, black and m/c. Tea dryer, centrifugal machine at ctr, Sir S. Davidson at r.	FV	FV	150.00

		VG	VF	UNC
197	**100 POUNDS** 1.11.1990. Lilac, black, blue and m/c. Airplanes and ejection seat at ctr., Sir J. Martin at r.	FV	FV	300.00

1997 ISSUE

#198 and 199 city hall in Belfast at ctr., bldgs. and architectural drawings in unpt. on back.

		VG	VF	UNC
198	**10 POUNDS** 1997. Dk. brown and violet on m/c unpt. J. B. Dunlop at r. and as wmk., bicycle at lower l.	FV	FV	28.50
199	**20 POUNDS** 24.2.1997. Violet and dk. brown on m/c unpt. H. Ferguson at r. and as wmk., farm tractor at lower l.	FV	FV	55.00
200	**50 POUNDS** 1997.	Expected New Issue		
201	**100 POUNDS** 1997.	Expected New Issue		

2000 COMMEMORATIVE ISSUE

		VG	VF	UNC
202	**5 POUNDS** (1999).	FV	FV	15.00

PROVINCIAL BANK OF IRELAND LIMITED

See also Ireland-Republic and Northern - Allied Irish Banks Ltd.

1965 ISSUE

#243 and 244 cameo portr. archaic woman at upper ctr. Bank bldg. at ctr. on back.

#243-246 printer: TDLR.

		VG	VF	UNC
243	**1 POUND** 1.12.1965. Green. Woman at ctr.	6.00	15.00	40.00
244	**5 POUNDS** 6.12.1965. Similar to #242A.	11.00	25.00	60.00

1968 ISSUE

		VG	VF	UNC
245	**1 POUND** 1.1.1968-1.1.1972. Green. Like #241. 150 x 71mm.	4.00	10.00	27.50
246	**5 POUNDS** 5.1.1968; 5.1.1970; 5.1.1972. Brown. Like #243. 139 x 84mm.	10.00	15.00	45.00

1977; 1981 ISSUE

#247-251 designs similar to Allied Irish Banks Ltd. issues except for bank title and sign. Printer: TDLR. Replacement notes: Serial # prefix *ZZ; ZY*.

		VG	VF	UNC
247	**1 POUND** 1977; 1979. Green on m/c unpt. Young girl at r. Sailing ship *Girona* at ctr. on back.			
	a. Sign. J. G. McClay. 1.1.1977.	2.00	7.00	17.50
	b. Sign. F. H. Hollway. 1.1.1979.	FV	6.00	15.00

		VG	VF	UNC
248	**5 POUNDS** 1977; 1979. Blue and purple on m/c unpt. Young woman at r. Dunluce Castle at ctr. on back.			
	a. Sign. J. G. McClay. 1.1.1977.	10.00	18.50	50.00
	b. Sign. F. H. Hollway. 1.1.1979.	10.00	13.50	45.00

		VG	VF	UNC
249	**10 POUNDS** 1977; 1979. Brown and gray-green on m/c unpt. Young man at r. Wreck of the *Girona* at ctr. on back.			
	a. Sign. J. G. McClay. 1.1.1977.	20.00	30.00	70.00
	b. Sign. F. H. Hollway. 1.1.1979.	20.00	25.00	65.00

		VG	VF	UNC
250	**20 POUNDS** 1.3.1981. Purple and green. Elderly woman at r. Chimney at Lacada Pt. at ctr. on back.	FV	50.00	110.00
251	**100 POUNDS** 1.3.1981. Black, olive and green. Elderly man at r. The *Armada* at ctr. on back.	FV	175.00	385.00

ULSTER BANK LIMITED

BELFAST BRANCH

1966-70 ISSUE

#321-324 view of Belfast at lower l. and r., port w/bridge at lower ctr. below sign., date to r. Arms at ctr. on back. Sign. Jno. J. A. Leitch. Printer: BWC.

		VG	VF	UNC
321	**1 POUND** 4.10.1966. Blue-black on m/c unpt. 151 x 72mm.	4.00	8.50	22.50
322	**5 POUNDS** 4.10.1966. Brown on m/c unpt. 140 x 85mm.	10.00	25.00	65.00
323	**10 POUNDS** 4.10.1966. Green on m/c unpt. 151 x 93mm.	20.00	40.00	100.00
324	**20 POUNDS** 1.7.1970. Lilac on m/c unpt. 161 x 90mm. Specimen.	—	—	—

1971-82 ISSUE

#325-330 printer: BWC.

#325-328 similar to #321-324 but date at l., sign. at ctr. r.

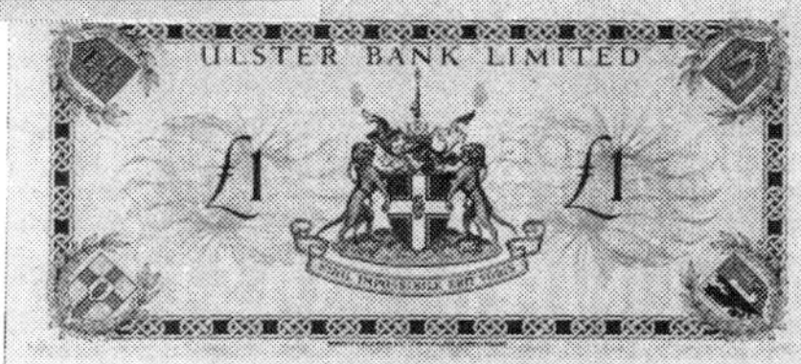

		VG	VF	UNC
325	**1 POUND** 1971-76. Blue-black on m/c unpt. Wmk: Bank name repeated. 135 x 67mm.			
	a. Sign. H. E. O'B. Traill. 15.2.1971.	4.00	8.50	17.50
	b. Sign. R. W. Hamilton. 1.3.1973; 1.3.1976.	3.00	4.50	9.00
326	**5 POUNDS** 1971-86. Brown on m/c unpt. 146 x 78mm.			
	a. Sign. H. E. O'B. Traill. 15.2.1971.	9.00	20.00	60.00
	b. Sign R. W. Hamilton. 1.3.1973; 1.3.1976.	8.50	13.50	32.50
	c. Sign. V. Chambers. 1.10.1982; 1.10.1983; 1.9.1986.	FV	10.00	28.50

		VG	VF	UNC
327	**10 POUNDS** 1971-88. Green on m/c unpt. 151 x 86mm.			
	a. Sign. H. E. O'B. Traill. 15.2.1971.	18.50	35.00	90.00
	b. Sign. R. W. Hamilton. 1.3.1973; 1.3.1976; 2.6.1980.	17.50	25.00	65.00
	c. Sign. V. Chambers. 1.10.1982; 1.10.1983; 1.2.1988.	FV	22.50	50.00
328	**20 POUNDS** 1.10.1982; 1.10.1983. Violet on m/c unpt. Sign. V. Chambers.	FV	47.50	90.00
329	**50 POUNDS** 1.10.1982. Brown on m/c unpt. Sign. V. Chambers.	FV	90.00	150.00
330	**100 POUNDS** 1.3.1973. Red on m/c unpt. Sign. R. W. Hamilton.	FV	FV	350.00

1989-90 ISSUE

#331-334 similar to previous issue but smaller size notes. Sign. J. Wead. Printer: TDLR.

NOTE: The Bank of Ireland sold to collectors matched serial # sets of £5-10-20 notes as well as 100 sets of replacement serial # prefix *Z*.

		VG	VF	UNC
331	**5 POUNDS** 1.12.1989; 1.1.1992; 4.1.1993. Brown on m/c unpt. Similar to #326.	FV	FV	20.00

		VG	VF	UNC
332	**10 POUNDS** 1.12.1990. Green on m/c unpt. Similar to #327.	FV	FV	35.00
333	**20 POUNDS** 1.11.1990. Violet on m/c unpt. Similar to #328.	FV	FV	70.00
334	**100 POUNDS** 1.12.1990. Red on m/c unpt. Similar to #330.	FV	FV	250.00

1996; 1998 ISSUE

		VG	VF	UNC
335	**5 POUNDS** 1.7.1998.	—	—	—

		VG	VF	UNC
336 (335)	**10 POUNDS** 1.1.1997. Blue and green on m/c unpt. Like #332.	FV	FV	30.00

		VG	VF	UNC
337 (336)	**20 POUNDS** 1.1.1996. Purple and violet on m/c unpt. Like #333 but w/hologram at upper ctr. r.	FV	FV	55.00

		VG	VF	UNC
338 (337)	**50 POUNDS** 1.1.1997. Brown on m/c unpt. Like #329 but w/hologram at upper ctr. r.	FV	FV	140.00

COLLECTOR SERIES

BANK OF IRELAND

NOTE: The Bank of Ireland sold to collectors matched serial # sets of £5-10-20 notes as well as 100 sets of replacement serial # prefix *Z*.

1978 ND ISSUE

		ISSUE PRICE	MKT. VALUE
CS1	**ND (1978). 1, 5, 10, 100 POUNDS** #61b-64b ovpt: *SPECIMEN* and Maltese cross prefix serial #.	7.00	90.00

1995 ND ISSUE

		ISSUE PRICE	MKT. VALUE
CS3	**ND (1995). 5, 10, 100 POUNDS** #62b-64b ovpt: *SPECIMEN.*	—	250.00

PROVINCIAL BANK OF IRELAND LIMITED

1978 ISSUE

		ISSUE PRICE	MKT. VALUE
CS2	**1978 1, 5, 10 POUNDS** #247a-249a dated 1.1.1977. Ovpt: *SPECIMEN* and Maltese cross prefix serial #.	7.00	55.00

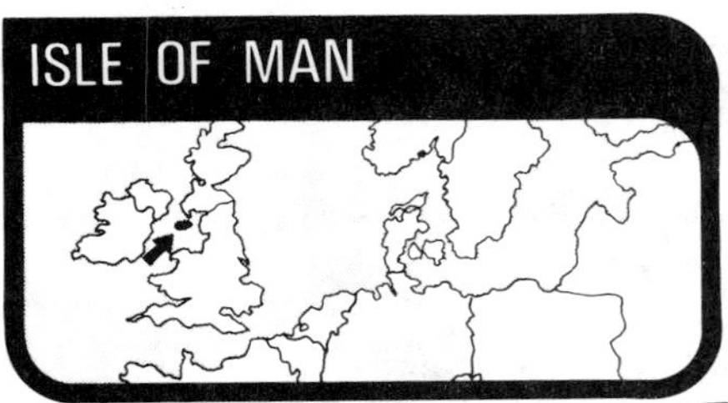

The Isle of Man, a dependency of the British Crown located in the Irish Sea equidistant from Ireland, Scotland and England, has an area of 227 sq. mi. (588 sq. km.) and a population of 61,000. Capital: Douglas. Agriculture, dairy farming, fishing and tourism are the chief industries.

The prevalence of prehistoric artifacts and monuments on the island gives evidence that its mild, almost sub-tropical climate was enjoyed by mankind before the dawn of history. Vikings came to the Isle of Man during the 9th century and remained until ejected by Scotland in 1266. The island came under the protection of the English Crown in 1288, and in 1406 was granted, in perpetuity, to the Earls of Derby. In 1736 it was inherited by the Duke of Atholl. Rights and title were purchased from the Duke of Atholl in 1765 by the British Crown; the remaining privileges of the Atholl family were transferred to the crown in 1829. The Sovereign of the United Kingdom (currently Queen Elizabeth II) holds the title Lord of Man. The Isle of Man is ruled by its own legislative council and the House of Keys, one of the oldest legislative assemblies in the world. Acts of Parliament passed in London do not affect the island unless it is specifically mentioned.

United Kingdom bank notes and coinage circulate concurrently with Isle of Man money as legal tender.

RULERS:
British

MONETARY SYSTEM:
1 Pound = 20 Shillings to 1971
1 Pound = 100 New Pence, 1971-

BRITISH INFLUENCE

LLOYDS BANK LIMITED

1955 ISSUE

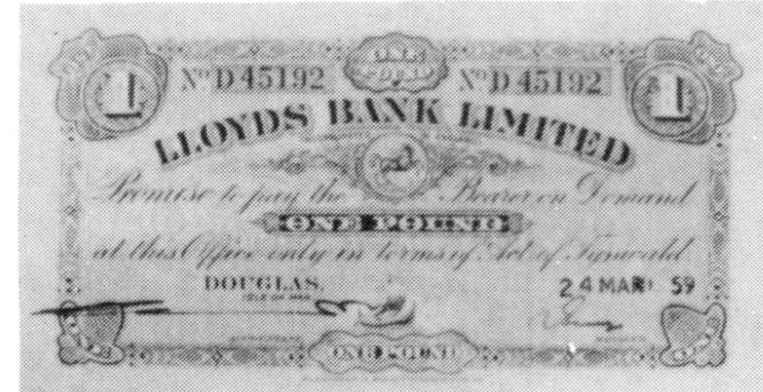

		GOOD	FINE	XF
13	**1 POUND** 21.1.1955-14.3.1961. Black on green unpt. Bank arms at upper ctr.			
	a. Issued note.	90.00	180.00	400.00
	r. Unsigned remainder. ND.	—	—	120.00

WESTMINSTER BANK LIMITED

Formerly the London County Westminster and Parr's Bank Limited.

1955 ISSUE

#23A, various date and sign. varieties.

		GOOD	FINE	XF
23A	**1 POUND** 1955-61. Black on lt. yellow unpt. Crowned Triskele supported by lion and unicorn at upper ctr. W/text: *INCORPORATED IN ENGLAND* added below bank name. Printer: W&S.			
	a. 23.11.1955.	150.00	300.00	600.00
	b. 4.4.1956-10.3.1961.	75.00	150.00	300.00

NOTICE

Readers with unlisted dates, signature varieties, etc. are invited to submit photocopies of their notes to: Standard Catalog of World Paper Money, 700 East State St. Iola, WI 54990-0001, fax: 1-715-445-4087, or E-Mail: thernr@krause.com.

GOVERNMENT

SIGNATURE VARIETIES

1961 ND ISSUE

#24-27 Triskele arms at lower ctr.and as wmk., young portr. Qn. Elizabeth II at r. Printer: BWC.

SIGNATURE VARIETIES			
1	Garvey	2	Stallard
3	Paul (26mm)	4	Paul(20mm)
5	Dawaon	6	Cashen

24	10 SHILLINGS	VG	VF	UNC
	ND (1961). Red on m/c unpt. Old sailing boat on back.			
	a. Sign. 1.	10.00	20.00	45.00
	b. Sign. 2.	10.00	20.00	45.00
	s. Sign. 1. Specimen.	—	—	150.00

25	1 POUND	VG	VF	UNC
	ND (1961). Purple on m/c unpt. Tynwald Hill on back.			
	a. Sign. 1.	15.00	30.00	80.00
	b. Sign. 2.	15.00	30.00	80.00
	s. Sign. 1. Specimen.	—	—	100.00

26	5 POUNDS	VG	VF	UNC
	ND (1961). Green and blue on m/c unpt. Castle Rushen on back.			
	a. Sign. 1.	40.00	175.00	750.00
	b. Sign. 2.	30.00	100.00	450.00
	s. Sign. 1. Specimen w/normal serial # blocked out.	—	—	200.00

1969 ND ISSUE

27	50 NEW PENCE	VG	VF	UNC
	ND (1969). Blue on m/c unpt. Back like #24. 139 x 66mm. Sign. 2.	3.00	10.00	25.00

1972 ND ISSUE

#28-31 Triskele arms at ctr. and as wmk., mature portr. Qn. Elizabeth II at r. Sign. title: *LIEUTENANT GOVERNOR.* Printer: BWC.

28	50 NEW PENCE	VG	VF	UNC
	ND (1972). Blue on m/c unpt. Back like #24. 126 x 62mm.			
	a. Sign. 2.	2.00	7.50	50.00
	b. Sign. 3.	1.50	4.00	25.00
	c. Sign. 4.	1.00	2.00	15.00
	s. As a. Specimen. Punched hole cancelled.	—	—	30.00

29	1 POUND	VG	VF	UNC
	ND (1972). Purple on m/c unpt. Back similar to #25.			
	a. Sign. 2.	3.00	25.00	100.00
	b. Sign. 3.	5.00	30.00	115.00
	c. Sign. 4.	2.00	6.00	20.00
	s. As a. Specimen. Punched hole cancelled.	—	—	55.00

30	5 POUNDS	VG	VF	UNC
	ND (1972). Blue-black and violet on m/c unpt. Back gray-green; similar to #26.			
	a. Sign. 2.	20.00	50.00	4000.00
	b. Sign. 3.	10.00	25.00	200.00
	s. As a. Specimen. Punched hole cancelled.	—	—	165.00

		VG	VF	UNC
31	**10 POUNDS** ND (1972). Brown and dk. green on m/c unpt. Back brown and orange; Peel Castle ca.1830 at ctr.			
	a. Sign. 2.	150.00	350.00	1000.
	b. Sign. 3.	50.00	150.00	500.00
	s. As a. Specimen, punched hole cancelled.	—	—	500.00

1979 COMMEMORATIVE ISSUE

#32, Millennium Year 1979

		VG	VF	UNC
32	**20 POUNDS** 1979. Red-orange, orange and dk. brown on m/c unpt. Triskele at ctr. Qn. Elizabeth II at r. Island outline at upper r. Commemorative text at lower r. of triskele. Laxey wheel ca. 1854, crowd of people w/ hills in background on back. Printer: BWC.	40.00	100.00	350.00

1979 ND ISSUE

#33-37 Qn. Elizabeth II at r., arms at ctr. Sign. title: *TREASURER OF THE ISLE OF MAN.* Wmk: Triskele arms. Printer: BWC.

#33s-38s were mounted on a board for bank display.

		VG	VF	UNC
33	**50 PENCE** ND. Blue on m/c unpt. Like #28. Sign. 5.			
	a. Issued note.	FV	FV	5.00
	s. Specimen. Normal serial #, punched hole cancelled.	—	—	—

		VG	VF	UNC
34	**1 POUND** ND. Purple on m/c unpt. Like #29. Sign. 5.			
	a. Issued note.	FV	FV	10.00
	s. Specimen. Normal serial #, punched hole cancelled.	—	—	—

		VG	VF	UNC
35	**5 POUNDS** ND. Blue-black and violet on m/c unpt. Like #30. Sign. 5. Series A-C.	15	40.00	100.00

		VG	VF	UNC
35A	**5 POUNDS** ND. Blue-black and violet on m/c unpt. Like #35 but w/modified guilloche. Series D.			
	a. Issued note.	FV	13.50	55.00
	s. Specimen. Normal serial #, punched hole cancelled.	—	—	—

		VG	VF	UNC
36	**10 POUNDS** ND. Brown and dk. green on m/c unpt. Like #31. Sign. 5.			
	a. Issued note. Prefix A.	20.00	50.00	275.00
	b. Issued note. Prefix B.	250.00	500.00	1000.
	s. Specimen. Prefix A, normal serial #, punched hole cancelled.	—	—	350.00

		VG	VF	UNC
37	**20 POUNDS** ND (1979). Red-orange, orange and dk. brown on m/c unpt. Like #32 but w/o commemorative text.			
	a. Issued note.	FV	40.00	200.00
	s. Specimen. Normal serial #, punched hole cancelled.	—	—	350.00

1983 ND ISSUE

		VG	VF	UNC
38 (39)	**1 POUND** ND (1983). Green on m/c unpt. Like #25 but printed on Bradvek, a special plastic.	2.00	4.50	15.00

39 (38) **50 POUNDS**
ND (1983). Blue gray, deep green and olive-green on m/c unpt. Douglas Bay on back.

	VG	VF	UNC
a. Issued note.	FV	100.00	175.00
s. Specimen. Normal serial #, punched hole cancelled.	—	—	—

1983 ND REDUCED SIZE ISSUE

#40-44 smaller format. Qn. Elizabeth II at r., arms at ctr. Wmk: Triskele. Printer: TDLR. Replacement notes: Serial # prefix *Z*.

40 **1 POUND**
ND. Purple on m/c unpt. Back like #25.

	VG	VF	UNC
a. Sign. 5.	FV	FV	8.00
b. Sign. 6.	FV	FV	6.00

41 **5 POUNDS**
ND. Greenish blue and lilac-brown on m/c unpt. Back like #30.

	VG	VF	UNC
a. Sign. 5.	FV	FV	30.00
b. Sign. 6.	FV	FV	17.50

42 **10 POUNDS**
ND. Brown and green on m/c unpt. Like #31. Back brown, orange and m/c. Sign. 6.

VG	VF	UNC
—	—	25.00

43 **20 POUNDS**
ND. Brown and red-orange on m/c unpt. Back like #32.

	VG	VF	UNC
a. Sign. 5.	FV	FV	110.00
b. Sign. 6.	FV	FV	70.00

44 **50 POUNDS**
ND. Blue-gray, bright green and olive on m/c unpt. Back like #38.

VG	VF	UNC
FV	FV	125.00

1998 ND ISSUE

#45 like #40-44 but w/*LIMITED* deleted from payment clause.

45 (47) **10 POUNDS**
ND (1998). Brown and green on m/c unpt. Like #41 but w/*LIMITED* deleted from payment clause.

VG	VF	UNC
FV	FV	30.00

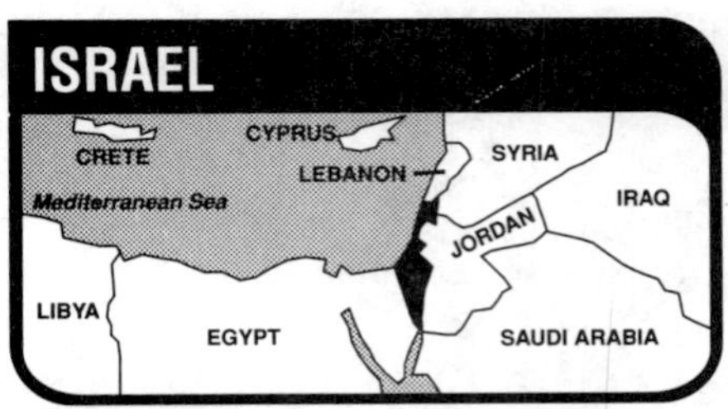

The State of Israel, at the eastern end of the Mediterranean Sea, bounded by Lebanon on the north, Syria on the northeast, Jordan on the east, and Egypt on the southwest, has an area of 7,847 sq. mi. (23,309 sq. km.) and a population of 5.53 million. Capital: Jerusalem. Diamonds, chemicals, citrus, textiles, and minerals are exported.

Palestine, which corresponds to Canaan of the Bible, was settled by the Philistines about the 12th century B.C. and shortly thereafter was invaded by the Jews who established the kingdoms of Israel and Judah. Because of its position as part of the land bridge connecting Asia and Africa, Palestine was invaded and conquered by nearly all of the historic empires of ancient Europe and Asia. In the 16th century it became a Turkish satrap. After falling to the British in World War I, it, together with Transjordan, was mandated to Great Britain by the League of Nations, 1922.

For more than half a century prior to the termination of the British mandate over Palestine, 1948, Zionist leaders had sought to create a Jewish homeland for Jews dispersed throughout the world. For almost as long, Jews fleeing persecution had immigrated to Palestine. The Nazi persecutions of the 1930s and 1940s increased the Jewish movement to Palestine and generated international support for the creation of a Jewish state, first promulgated by the Balfour Declaration of 1917 which asserted British support for the endeavor. The dream of a Jewish homeland was realized on May 14, 1948 when Palestine was proclaimed the State of Israel.

MONETARY SYSTEM:

1 Lira = 100 Agorot, 1958-1980
1 Sheqel = 10 "old" Lirot, 1980-85
1 Sheqel = 100 New Agorot, 1980-1985
1 New Sheqel = 1000 "old" Sheqalim, 1985-
1 New Sheqel = 100 Agorot, 1985-

STATE OF ISRAEL

BANK OF ISRAEL

1958-60 / 5718-20 ISSUE

#29, 30 and 33 printer: JEZ (w/o imprint).

#		VG	VF	UNC
29	**1/2 LIRA** 1958/5718. Green. Woman soldier w/basket full of oranges at l. and as wmk. Tombs of the Sanhedrin on back.	.50	1.25	5.00

#		VG	VF	UNC
30	**1 LIRA** 1958/5718. Blue and m/c. Fisherman w/net and anchor at l. and as wmk. Wreath on back.			
	a. Paper w/security thread at l. Black serial #.	.25	.75	3.00
	b. Red serial #.	.25	.75	3.00
	c. Paper w/security thread and morse tape, brown serial #.	.15	.50	2.00

#31 and 32 printer: TDLR (w/o imprint).

#		VG	VF	UNC
31	**5 LIROT** 1958/5718. Brown and m/c. Worker w/hammer in front of factory at l. and as wmk. Seal of Shema on back.	.50	1.50	7.50

#		VG	VF	UNC
32	**10 LIROT** 1958/5718. Lilac and violet. Scientist w/microscope and test tube at l. and as wmk. Dead Sea scroll and vases on back.			
	a. Paper w/security thread. Black serial #.	.35	1.00	4.00
	b. Paper w/security thread and morse tape. Red serial #.	.35	1.00	4.00
	c. Paper w/security thread and morse tape. Blue serial #.	.35	1.00	4.00
	d. Paper w/security thread and morse tape. Brown serial #.	.35	1.00	4.00

#		VG	VF	UNC
33	**50 LIROT** 1960/5720. Brown and m/c. Boy and girl at l. and as wmk. Mosaic of menorah on back.			
	a. Paper w/security thread. Black serial #.	1.25	4.00	16.00
	b. Paper w/security thread. Red serial #.	1.25	4.00	16.00
	c. Paper w/security thread and morse tape. Blue serial #.	1.00	3.00	12.50
	d. Paper w/security thread and morse tape. Green serial #.	1.00	3.00	12.50
	e. Paper w/security thread and morse tape. Brown serial #.	.85	2.50	10.00

NOTICE

Readers with unlisted dates, signature varieties, etc. are invited to submit photocopies of their notes to: Standard Catalog of World Paper Money, 700 East State St. Iola, WI 54990-0001, fax: 1-715-445-4087, or E-Mail: thernr@krause.com.

1968 / 5728 ISSUE

#34-37 printer: JEZ (w/o imprint).

#	Denomination	VG	VF	UNC
34	**5 LIROT** 1968/5728. Gray-green and blue on m/c unpt. A. Einstein at r. and as wmk. Atomic reactor at Nahal Sorek on back.			
	a. Black serial #.	.75	2.50	15.00
	b. Red serial #.	.75	2.50	15.00

#	Denomination	VG	VF	UNC
35	**10 LIROT** 1968/5728. Brown, violet and m/c. C. Nahman Bialik at r. and as wmk. Bialik's house in Tel Aviv on back.			
	a. Black serial #.	.50	1.50	5.00
	b. Green serial #.	.50	1.50	6.00
	c. Blue serial #.	.50	1.50	5.00

#	Denomination	VG	VF	UNC
36	**50 LIROT** 1968/5728. Lt. brown and green on m/c unpt. Pres. C. Weizmann at r. and as wmk. Knesset bldg. in Jerusalem on back.			
	a. Black serial #.	.70	2.00	10.00
	b. Blue serial #.	.60	1.75	8.50

#	Denomination	VG	VF	UNC
37	**100 LIROT** 1968/5728. Blue and green on m/c unpt. Dr. B. Zeev Herzl at r. and as wmk. Menorah and symbols of the 12 tribes of Israel at l. ctr. on back.			
	a. Wmk: Profile. Black serial #. 3.5mm.	1.50	5.00	15.00
	b. Wmk: 3/4 profile r. Red serial #.	1.50	5.00	15.00
	c. Wmk: Profile. Black serial #. 2.8mm. W/o series letter.	1.50	5.00	15.00
	d. Wmk: Profile. Brown serial #.	1.50	5.00	15.00

1973-75 / 5733-35 ISSUE

#38-51 printer: JEZ (w/o imprint).

All the following notes except #41 and 45 have marks for the blind on the face. #38-46 have barely discernible bar code strips at lower l. and upper r. on back. All have portr. as wmk. Various gates in Jerusalem on backs.

#	Denomination	VG	VF	UNC
38	**5 LIROT** 1973/5733. Lt. and dk. brown. H. Szold at r. Lion's Gate on back.	.15	.50	3.50

#	Denomination	VG	VF	UNC
39	**10 LIROT** 1973/5733. Purple on lilac unpt. Sir M. Montefiore at r. Jaffa Gate on back.	.15	.50	3.50

		VG	VF	UNC
40	**50 LIROT** 1973/5733. Green on olive-green unpt. C. Weizmann at r. Sichem Gate on back.	.50	1.50	5.00

		VG	VF	UNC
41	**100 LIROT** 1973/5733. Blue on blue and brown unpt. Dr. B. Zeev Herzl at r. Zion Gate on back.	.50	1.50	5.00

		VG	VF	UNC
42	**500 LIROT** 1975/5735. Black on tan and brown unpt. D. Ben-Gurion at r. Golden Gate on back.	2.50	8.50	35.00

1978-84 / 5738-44 ISSUE

		VG	VF	UNC
43	**1 SHEQEL** 1978/5738 (1980). Purple on lilac unpt. Like #39.	.15	.50	2.00

		VG	VF	UNC
44	**5 SHEQALIM** 1978/5738 (1980). Green on olive-green unpt. Like #40.	.25	.75	3.00

		VG	VF	UNC
45	**10 SHEQALIM** 1978/5738 (1980). Blue on blue and brown unpt. Like #41.	.50	1.50	5.00

NOTE: Colored bars were used to identify various surface-coated papers, used experimentally.

		VG	VF	UNC
46	**50 SHEQALIM** 1978/5738 (1980). Black on tan and brown unpt. Like #42.			
	a. W/o small bars below serial # or barely discernible bar code strips on back.	.15	.50	2.00
	b. W/o small bars below serial #, but w/bar code strips on back.	.50	1.50	6.00
	c. 2 green bars below serial # on back.	6.00	20.00	85.00
	d. 4 black bars below serial # on back.	6.00	20.00	85.00
	e. As a. 12-subject sheet.	—	—	25.00

NOTE: Colored bars were used to identify various surface-coated papers, used experimentally.

NOTICE

Readers with unlisted dates, signature varieties, etc. are invited to submit photocopies of their notes to: Standard Catalog of World Paper Money, 700 East State St. Iola, WI 54990-0001, fax: 1-715-445-4087, or E-Mail: thernr@krause.com.

47	100 SHEQALIM	VG	VF	UNC
	1979/5739. Red-brown. Ze'ev Jabotinsky at r. Herod's Gate on back.			
	a. W/o bars below serial # on back.	.50	1.50	5.00
	b.2 bars below serial # on back.	6.00	20.00	75.00

48	500 SHEQALIM	VG	VF	UNC
	1982/5742. Red on m/c unpt. Farm workers at ctr., Baron E. de Rothschild at r. Vine leaves on back.	.50	1.50	7.00

49	1000 SHEQALIM	VG	VF	UNC
	1983/5743. Green on m/c unpt. Rabbi M. B. Maimon-Maimonides at r. View of Tiberias at l. on back.			
	a. Error in first letter *he* of second word at r. in vertical text (right to left), partly completed letter resembling 7.	1.50	4.00	15.00
	b. Corrected letter resembling *17.*	.75	2.50	10.00
	c. As a. Uncut sheet of 3. (3,610).	—	—	45.00
	d. As b. Uncut sheet of 3. (3.365).	—	—	30.00

50	5000 SHEQALIM	VG	VF	UNC
	1984/5744. Blue on m/c unpt. City view at ctr., L. Eshkol at r. Water pipe and modern design on back.			
	a. Issued note.	1.50	5.00	15.00
	b. Uncut sheet of 3. (2,755)	—	—	45.00

51	10,000 SHEQALIM	VG	VF	UNC
	1984/5744. Brown, black, orange and dk. green on m/c unpt. Stylized tree at ctr., G. Meir at r. and as wmk. Gathering in front of Moscow synagogue on back.			
	a. Issued note.	3.00	10.00	30.00
	b. Uncut sheet of 3. (2,720)	—	—	100.00

1985-92 / 5745-52 ISSUE

#51A-56 portr. as wmk. Printer: JEZ (w/o imprint). All with marks for the blind.

SIGNATURE VARIETIES			
5	Mandelbaum, 1986	6	Shapira and Mandelbaum, 1985
7	Lorincz and Bruno, 1987–91	8	Lorincz and Frankel, 1992

51A	1 NEW SHEQEL	VG	VF	UNC
	1986/5746. Like #49 except for denomination. Sign. 5.			
	a. Issued note.	.25	.75	4.50
	b. Uncut sheet of 3. (2,017).	—	—	7.00
	c. Uncut sheet of 12. (1,416).	—	—	27.50
	d. Uncut sheet of 18. (1.503).	—	—	42.50

52	5 NEW SHEQALIM	VG	VF	UNC
	1985/5745; 1987/5747. Like #50 except for denomination.			
	a. Sign. 6. 1985/5745.	.75	2.00	12.00
	b. Sign. 7. 1987/5747.	.50	1.50	10.00
	c. Uncut sheet of 3. (1,630).	—	—	40.00

53	10 NEW SHEQALIM	VG	VF	UNC
	1985/5745; 1987/5747; 1992/5752. Like #51 except for denomination.			
	a. Sign. 6. 1985/5745.	1.00	5.00	25.00
	b. Sign. 7. 1987/5747.	.75	2.00	15.00
	c. Sign. 8. 1992/5752.	.65	1.75	12.50
	d. Uncut sheet of 3. (1,571).	—	—	50.00

54	20 NEW SHEQALIM	VG	VF	UNC
	1987/5747; 1993/5753. Dk. gray on m/c unpt. M. Sharett standing holding flag at ctr., his bust at r. and as wmk. Herzlya High School at ctr. on back.			
	a. W/o sm. double circle w/dot in wmk. area face and back. Sign. 7. 1987/5747.	FV	FV	25.00
	b. W/sm. double circle w/dot in wmk. area face and back. Sign. 7. 1987/5747.	FV	FV	20.00
	c. Sign. 8. 1993/5753.	FV	FV	20.00

55	50 NEW SHEQALIM	VG	VF	UNC
	1985/5745-1992/5752. Purple on m/c unpt. S. J. Agnon at r. and as wmk. Various bldgs. and book titles on back.			
	a. Sign. 6. 1985/5745.	FV	FV	50.00
	b. Sign. 7. Slight color variations. 1988/5748.	FV	FV	45.00
	c. Sign. 8. 1992/5752.	FV	FV	40.00

56	100 NEW SHEQALIM	VG	VF	UNC
	1986/5746; 1989/5749; 1995/5755. Brown on m/c unpt. Y. Ben-Zvi at r. and as wmk. Stylized village of Perui'im and carob tree on back.			
	a. Sign. 5. Plain security thread and plain white paper. 1986/5746.	FV	FV	85.00
	b. Sign. 6. W/security thread inscribed: *Bank Israel,* paper w/colored threads. 1989/5749.	FV	FV	70.00
	c. Sign. 8. 1995/5755.	FV	FV	65.00

57	200 NEW SHEQALIM	VG	VF	UNC
	1991/5751-. Deep red, purple and blue-green on m/c unpt. Z. Shazar at r. and as wmk. School girl writing at ctr. on back.			
	a. Sign. 7. 1991/5751.	FV	FV	135.00
	b. Sign. 8. 1994/5754.	FV	FV	120.00

NOTICE

Readers with unlisted dates, signature varieties, etc. are invited to submit photocopies of their notes to: Standard Catalog of World Paper Money, 700 East State St. Iola, WI 54990-0001, fax: 1-715-445-4087, or E-Mail: thernr@krause.com.

1998 ISSUE

#58, 50th Anniversary - State of Israel

		VG	VF	UNC
58	**50 NEW SHEQALIM** 1998/5758. Purple on m/c unpt. Like #55 but w/OVI *50* at upper l., serial # below. Sign. 8.	FV	FV	25.00

NOTE: #58 was issued in a special folder. (10,001 pcs.).

1998 DATED 1999 ISSUE

#59-62 vertical format.

		VG	VF	UNC
59	**20 NEW SHEQALIM** 1998 (1999). Dk. green on m/c unpt. M. Sharett at bottom, flags in background. Scenes of his life and work on back.	FV	FV	12.50

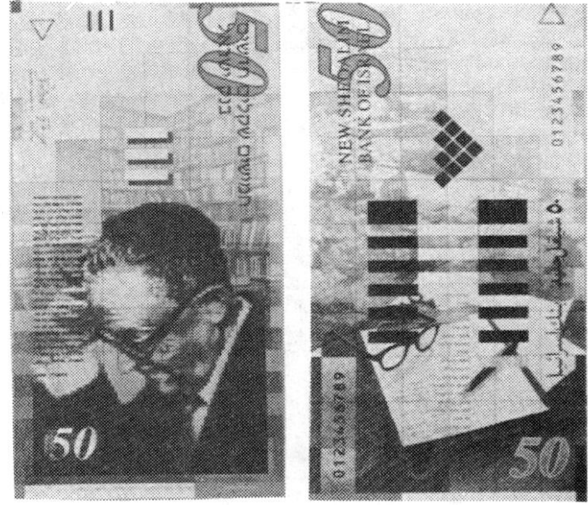

		VG	VF	UNC
60	**50 NEW SHEQALIM** 1998. Purple on m/c unpt. S. Y. Agnon at bottom, library shelves in background. Scenes of his life and work on back.	FV	FV	30.00

		VG	VF	UNC
61	**100 NEW SHEQALIM** 1998. Dk. brown on m/c unpt. I. Ben-Zvi at bottom. Scenes of his life and work on back.	FV	FV	55.00

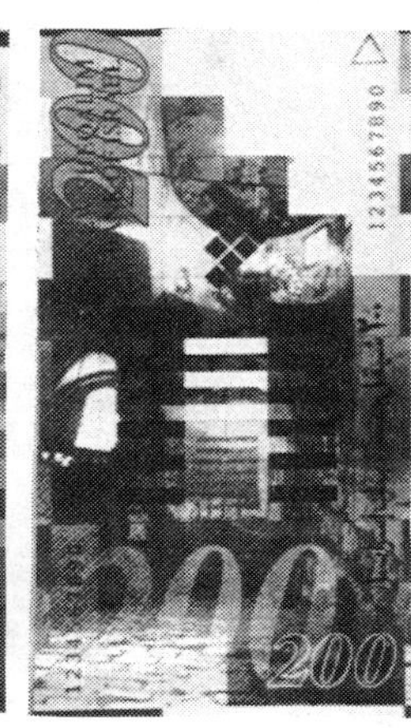

		VG	VF	UNC
62	**200 NEW SHEQALIM** 1998. Red and red-orange on m/c unpt. Z. Shazar at bottom, classroom in background. Scenes of his life and work on back.	FV	FV	110.00

COLLECTOR SERIES

BANK OF ISRAEL

1990 ISSUE

		ISSUE PRICE	MKT. VALUE
CS1	**(1990). 1-50 NEW SHEQALIM** 1985-87. #51Aa-55a w/matching serial #. Issued in special packaging. (2,000).	75.00	95.00

1991 ISSUE

		ISSUE PRICE	MKT. VALUE
CS2	**(1991). 100, 200 NEW SHEQALIM** 1985-86. #56a and 57a w/matching serial # issued in special packaging. (2,000).	149.00	150.00

The Italian Republic, a 700-mile-long peninsula extending into the heart of the Mediterranean Sea, has an area of 116,304 sq. mi. (301,255 sq. km.) and a population of 54.5 million. Captal: Rome. The economy centers about agriculture, manufacturing, forestry and fishing. Machinery, textiles, clothing and motor vehicles are exported.

From the fall of Rome until modern times, "Italy" was little more than a geographical expression. Although nominally included in the Empire of Charlemagne and the Holy Roman Empire, it was in reality divided into a number of independent states and kingdoms presided over by wealthy families, soldiers of fortune or hereditary rulers. The 19th century unification movement fostered by Mazzini, Garibaldi and Cavor attained fruition in 1860-1870 with the creation of the Kingdom of Italy and the installation of Victor Emanuele, King of Italy. Benito Mussolini came to power during the post-World War I period of economic and political unrest, installed a Fascist dictatorship with a figurehead king as titular Head of State.

Mussolini entered Italy into the German-Japanese anti-Comintern pact (Tri-Partite Pact) and withdrew from the League of Nations. The war did not go well for Italy and Germany was forced to assist Italy in its failed invasion of Greece. The Allied invasion of Sicily on July 10, 1943 and bombing Rome brought the Fascist council to a no vote of confidence on July 24, 1943. Mussolini was arrested but soon escaped and set up a government in Saló. Rome fell to the Allied forces in June 1944 and the country was allowed the status of co-belligerent against Germany. The Germans held northern Italy for another year. Mussolini was eventually captured and executed by partisans. Following the defeat of the Axis powers the Italian monarchy was dissolved by plebiscite, and the Italian Republic proclaimed on June 10, 1946.

MONETARY SYSTEM:

1 Lira = 100 Centesimi

DECREES:

There are many different dates found on the following notes of the Banca d'Italia. These include ART. DELLA LEGGE (law date) and the more important DECRETO MINISTERIALE (D. M. date). The earliest D.M. date is usually found on the back of the note while later D.M. dates are found grouped together. The actual latest date (of issue) is referred to in the following listings.

FACE SEAL VARIETIES:

Type B
Facing head of Medusa

Type C
Winged lion of St. Mark of Venice above 3 shields of Genoa, Pisa and Amalfi

REPUBLIC

REPUBBLICA ITALIANA - BIGLIETTO DI STATO

1966 ISSUE

#	Denomination	VG	VF	UNC
93	**500 LIRE** 1966-75. Dk. gray on m/c unpt. Eagle w/snake at l., Arethusa at r. 3 sign. varieties.			
	a. 20.6.1966; 20.10.1967; 23.2.1970.	1.00	2.00	10.00
	b. 23.4.1975.	10.00	30.00	240.00

DECRETO MINISTERIALE 14.2.1974

#	Denomination	VG	VF	UNC
94	**500 LIRE** 14.2.1974; 2.4.1979. Green-blue. Mercury at r. 3 sign. varieties.	.50	1.00	2.00

DECRETO MINISTERIALE 5.6.1976

#	Denomination	VG	VF	UNC
95	**500 LIRE** 20.12.1976. Like #94.	.50	1.50	3.50

BANCA D'ITALIA

BANK OF ITALY

1962 ISSUE

Decreto Ministeriale 12.4. 1962; Decreto Ministeriale 28.6.1962.

#	Denomination	VG	VF	UNC
96	**1000 LIRE** 1962-68. Blue on red and brown unpt. G. Verdi at r. Wmk: Laureate head.			
	a. Sign. Carli and Ripa. 14.7.1962; 14.1.1964.	FV	1.50	25.00
	b. Sign. Carli and Ripa. 5.7.1963; 25.7.1964.	FV	4.00	65.00
	c. Sign. Carli and Febbraio. 10.8.1965; 20.5.1966.	FV	1.50	30.00
	d. Sign. Carli and Pacini. 4.1.1968.	FV	4.00	80.00

#	Denomination	VG	VF	UNC
97	**10,000 LIRE** 1962-73. Brown, purple, orange and red-brown w/dk. brown text on m/c unpt. Michaelangelo at r. Piazza del Campidoglio in Rome. Wmk: Roman head.			
	a. Sign. Carli and Ripa. 3.7.1962; 14.1.1964; 27.7.1964.	FV	10.00	30.00
	b. Sign. Carli and Febbraio. 20.5.1966.	FV	10.00	30.00
	c. Sign. Carli and Pacini. 4.1.1968.	FV	10.00	35.00
	d. Sign. Carli and Lombardo. 8.6.1970.	FV	10.00	30.00
	e. Sign. Carli and Barbarito. 15.2.1973; 27.11.1973.	FV	FV	30.00

NOTICE

Readers with unlisted dates, signature varieties, etc. are invited to submit photocopies of their notes to: Standard Catalog of World Paper Money, 700 East State St. Iola, WI 54990-0001, fax: 1-715-445-4087, or E-Mail: thernr@krause.com.

1964 ISSUE

Decreto Ministeriale 20.8.1964.

98	5000 LIRE	VG	VF	UNC
	1964-70. Green on pink unpt. Columbus at r. Ship at l. ctr. on back.			
	a. Sign. Carli and Ripa. 3.9.1964.	4.00	10.00	140.00
	b. Sign. Carli and Pacini. 4.1.1968.	4.00	10.00	140.00
	c. Sign. Carli and Lombardo. 20.1.1970.	4.00	10.00	140.00

1967 ISSUE

Decreto Ministeriale 27.6.1967.

99	50,000 LIRE	VG	VF	UNC
	1967-74. Brownish black, dk. brown and reddish brown w/black text on m/c unpt. Leonardo da Vinci at r. City view at ctr. on back. Wmk: bust of Madonna.			
	a. Sign. Carli and Febbraio. 4.12.1967.	FV	80.00	350.00
	b. Sign. Carli and Lombardo. 19.7.1970.	FV	50.00	280.00
	c. Sign. Carli and Barbarito. 16.5.1972; 4.2.1974.	FV	50.00	280.00

100	100,000 LIRE	VG	VF	UNC
	1967-74. Brownish black, brown and deep olive-green on m/c unpt. A. Manzoni at r. Mountain lake scene at ctr. on back. Wmk: Archaic female bust. Seal: Type B.			
	a. Sign. Carli and Febbraio. 3.7.1967.	FV	100.00	400.00
	b. Sign. Carli and Lombardo. 19.7.1970.	FV	90.00	300.00
	c. Sign. Carli and Barbarito. 6.2.1974.	FV	90.00	300.00

1969; 1971 ISSUE

Decreto Ministeriale 26.2.1969; Decreto Ministeriale 15.5.1971.

101	1000 LIRE	VG	VF	UNC
	1969-81. Black and brown on lt. blue and lilac unpt. Harp at l. ctr., G. Verdi at r. Paper w/security thread. La Scala opera house at l. ctr. on back. Wmk: Vertical row of laureate heads. Seal: Type B.			
	a. Sign. Carli and Lombardo. 25.3.1969; 11.3.1971.	FV	1.00	4.00
	b. Sign. Carli and Barbarito. 15.2.1973.	FV	1.25	10.00
	c. Sign. Carli and Barbarito. 5.8.1975.	FV	1.00	4.00
	d. Sign. Baffi and Stevani. 10.1.1977; 10.5.1979.	FV	2.00	12.50
	e. Sign. Ciampi and Stevani. 20.2.1980; 6.9.1980; 30.5.1981.	FV	1.00	4.00

102	5000 LIRE	VG	VF	UNC
	1971-77. Olive. Mythical seahorse at ctr., Columbus at r. 3 sailing ships of Columbus' at l. ctr. on back. Seal: Type C.			
	a. Sign. Carli and Lombardo. 20.5.1971.	FV	4.00	20.00
	b. Sign. Carli and Barbarito. 11.4.1973.	FV	5.00	30.00
	c. Sign. Baffi and Stevani. 10.11.1977.	FV	5.00	30.00

1973; 1974 ISSUE

Decreto Ministeriale 10.9.1973; Decreto Ministeriale 20.12.1974.

103	2000 LIRE	VG	VF	UNC
	1973; 1976; 1983. Brown and green on lt. tan and olive unpt. Galileo at ctr., ornate arms at l., bldgs. and leaning tower of Pisa at r. Signs of the Zodiac on back. Wmk: Man's head. Seal: Type C.			
	a. Sign. Carli and Barbarito. 8.10.1973.	FV	3.00	20.00
	b. Sign. Baffi and Stevani. 20.10.1976.	FV	2.50	12.50
	c. Sign. Ciampi and Stevani. 24.10.1983.	FV	FV	5.00

104 20,000 LIRE

	VG	VF	UNC
21.2.1975. Brownish black and dk. brown on red-brown and pale olive-green unpt. Titian at ctr. Painting at l. ctr. on back. Wmk: Woman's head. Seal: Type C. Sign. Carli and Barbarito.	FV	35.00	125.00

1976-79 ISSUE

Decreto Ministeriale 2.3.1979; Decreto Ministeriale 25.8.1976; Decreto Ministeriale 20.6.1977; Decreto Ministeriale 16.6.1978.

105 5000 LIRE

	VG	VF	UNC
1979-83. Brown and green. Man at l. Bldg. and statuary at ctr. r. on back. Wmk: Man w/cap. Seal: Type C.			
a. Sign. Baffi and Stevani. 9.3.1979.	FV	5.50	10.00
b. Sign. Ciampi and Stevani. 1.7.1980; 3.11.1982; 19.10.1983.	FV	5.00	10.00

106 10,000 LIRE

	VG	VF	UNC
1976-84. Black and m/c. Man at l. and as wmk. Column at r. on back. Seal: Type C.			
a. Sign. Baffi and Stevani. 30.10.1976; 29.12.1978.	FV	11.00	18.50
b. Sign. Ciampi and Stevani. 6.9.1980; 3.11.1982; 8.3.1984.	FV	10.00	12.50

107 50,000 LIRE

	VG	VF	UNC
1977-82. Blue, red and green. Young women and lion of St. Mark at l. Modern design of arches on back. Seal: Type C.			
a. Sign. Baffi and Stevani. 20.6.1977; 12.6.1978; 23.10.1978.	FV	30.00	40.00
b. Sign. Ciampi and Stevani. 11.4.1980.	FV	30.00	40.00
c. Sign. Ciampi and Stevani. 2.11.1982.	FV	35.00	100.00

108 100,000 LIRE

	VG	VF	UNC
D.1978. Red-violet and black on m/c unpt. Woman's bust at l. and as wmk. Modern bldg. design at r. on back. Seal: Type C.			
a. Sign. Ciampi and Stevani. 20.6.1978.	FV	65.00	100.00
b. Sign. Ciampi and Stevani. 1.7.1980-10.5.1982.	FV	65.00	135.00

1982; 1983 ISSUE

Decreto Ministeriale 6.1.1982; Decreto Ministeriale 1.9.1983.

109 1000 LIRE

	VG	VF	UNC
D.1982. Dk. green and tan. Marco Polo at r. and as wmk. Bldg. at bottom of vertical format on back. Printer: ODBI. Seal: Type C.			
a. Sign. Ciampi and Stevani. 6.1.1982.	FV	FV	3.00
b. Sign. Ciampi and Speziali. 6.1.1982.	FV	FV	2.75

110 100,000 LIRE

	VG	VF	UNC
D.1983. Dk. brown and brown on green and olive-green unpt. Couple at ctr., Caravaggio at r. and as wmk. Fruit basket at l., castle at upper ctr. on back. Seal: Type C.			
a. Sign. Ciampi and Stevani. 1.9.1983.	FV	FV	125.00
b. Sign. Ciampi and Speziali. 1.9.1983.	FV	FV	110.00

1984; 1985 ISSUE

Decreto Ministeriale 4.1.1985; Decreto Ministeriale 3.9.1984; Decreto Ministeriale 6.2.1984.

111 5000 LIRE

	VG	VF	UNC
D.1985. Olive-green and blue on m/c unpt. Coliseum at ctr., V. Bellini at r. and as wmk. Scene from opera *Norma* at l. ctr. on back. Seal: Type C.			
a. Sign. Ciampi and Stevani.	FV	FV	8.50
b. Sign. Ciampi and Speziali.	FV	FV	7.50
c. Sign. Fazco and Amici.	FV	FV	7.50

		VG	VF	UNC
112	**10,000 LIRE** *D.1984.* Dk. blue on m/c unpt. Lab instrument at ctr. A. Volta at r. and as wmk. Mausoleum at l. ctr. on back. Seal: Type C.			
	a. Sign. Ciampi and Stevani. 3.9.1984.	FV	FV	14.00
	b. Sign. Ciampi and Speziali. 3.9.1984.	FV	FV	12.50
	c. Sign. Fazio and Speziali. 3.9.1984.	FV	FV	12.50

		VG	VF	UNC
113	**50,000 LIRE** *D.1984.* Red-violet and m/c. Figurine at ctr., G.L. Bernini at r. and as wmk. Equestrian statue at l. ctr. on back. Seal: Type C.			
	a. Sign. Ciampi and Stevani. 5.12.1984; 28.10.1985; 1.12.1986.	FV	FV	60.00
	b. Sign. Ciampi and Speziali. 25.1.1990.	FV	FV	55.00
	c. Sign. Fazio and Speziali.	FV	FV	55.00

1990-94 ISSUE

Decreto Ministeriale 3.10.1990; Decreto Ministeriale 27.5.1992; Decreto Ministeriale 6.5.1994.

		VG	VF	UNC
114	**1000 LIRE** *D.1990.* Red-violet and m/c. M. Montessori at r. and as wmk. Teacher and student at l. ctr. on back. Seal: Type C.			
	a. Sign. Ciampi and Speziali.	FV	FV	3.00
	b. Sign. Fazio and Speziali.	FV	FV	2.75
	c. Sign. Fazio and Amici.	FV	FV	2.75

		VG	VF	UNC
115	**2000 LIRE** *D.1990.* Dk. brown on m/c unpt. Arms at l. ctr.; G. Marconi at r. and as wmk. Liner *Elettra* at upper l. ctr., radio towers at l., early radio set at ctr. on back. Seal: Type C. Sign. Ciampi and Speziali.	FV	FV	4.50

		VG	VF	UNC
116	**50,000 LIRE** *D.1992.* Violet and dull green on m/c unpt. Similar to #113. Seal: Type C.			
	a. Sign. Ciampi and Speziali.	FV	FV	60.00
	b. Sign. Fazio and Amici.	FV	FV	55.00

		VG	VF	UNC
117	**100,000 LIRE** *D.1994.* Dk. brown, reddish brown and pale green on m/c unpt. Similar to #110. Seal: Type C.			
	a. Sign. Fazio and Speziali. 6.5.1994.	FV	FV	100.00
	b. Sign. Fazio and Amici.	FV	FV	90.00

1997 ISSUE

Decreto Ministeriale 6.5.1997.

		VG	VF	UNC
118	**500,000 LIRE** *D.1997.* Deep purple, dk. blue and bright green on m/c unpt. Raphaël at r., painting of *Triumph of Galatée* at ctr. *The School of Athens* at l. ctr. on back. Seal: Type C. Sign. Fazio and Amici.	FV	FV	350.00

NOTICE

Readers with unlisted dates, signature varieties, etc. are invited to submit photocopies of their notes to: Standard Catalog of World Paper Money, 700 East State St. Iola, WI 54990-0001, fax: 1-715-445-4087, or E-Mail: thernr@krause.com.

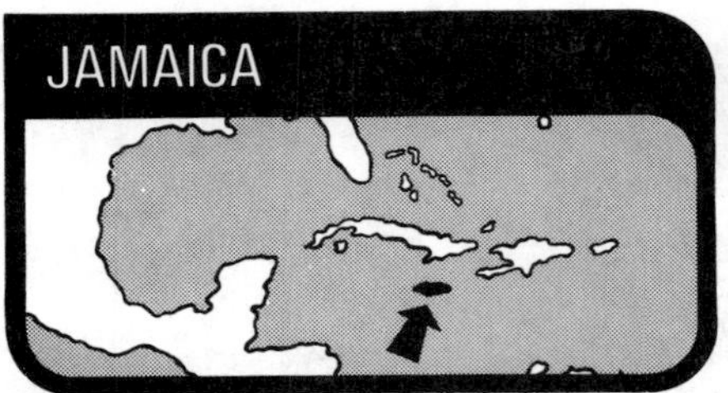

Jamaica, a member of the British Commonwealth situated in the Caribbean Sea 90 miles south of Cuba, has an area of 4,232 sq. mi. (10,991 sq. km.) and a population of 2.5 million. Capital: Kingston. The economy is founded chiefly on mining, tourism and agriculture. Alumina, bauxite, sugar, rum and molasses are exported.

Jamaica was discovered by Columbus on May 3, 1494, and settled by Spain in 1509. The island was captured in 1655 by a British naval force under the command of Admiral William Penn, and ceded to Britain by the Treaty of Madrid in 1670. For more than 150 years, the Jamaican economy of sugar, slaves and piracy was one of the most prosperous in the New World. Dissension between the property-oriented island legislature and the home government prompted Parliament to establish a crown colony government for Jamaica in 1866. From 1958 to 1961 Jamaica was a member of the West Indies Federation, withdrawing when Jamaican voters rejected the association. The colony attained independence on Aug. 6, 1962.

Jamaica is a member of the Commonwealth of Nations. Elizabeth II is the Head of State, as Queen of Jamaica.

A decimal standard currency system was adopted on Sept. 8, 1969 and notes were issued during 1970.

RULERS:

British

MONETARY SYSTEM:

1 Shilling = 12 Pence
1 Pound = 20 Shillings to 1969
1 Dollar = 100 Cents, 1969-

BRITISH INFLUENCE

BANK OF JAMAICA

SIGNATURE VARIETIES			
1	Stanley W. Payton, 1960–64	2	Richard T. P. Hall, **Acting Governor** – 1964–66
3	Richard T. P. Hall **Governor** – 1966–67	4	G. Arthur Brown, 1967–77
5	Herbert Samuel Walker, 1977–81	6	Dr. Owen C. Jefferson, **Acting Governor** – 1981-83
7	Horace G. Barber, 1983-86	8	Headley A. Brown, 1986-89
9	Dr. Owen C. Jefferson **Acting Governor**, 1989-90	10	G. A Brown, 1990-93
11	R. Rainsford, 1993	12	J. Bussieres, 1994–

LAW 1960

1961 ND ISSUE

Pound System

#49-51 Qn. Elizabeth II at l. Latin motto below arms. Sign. S. W. Payton. Printer: TDLR.

		VG	VF	UNC
49	**5 SHILLINGS** *L.1960.* (1961). Red on m/c unpt. River rapids on back.	5.50	16.50	90.00
50	**10 SHILLINGS** *L.1960.* (1961). Purple on m/c unpt. Men w/bananas on back.	7.50	35.00	275.00

		VG	VF	UNC
51	**1 POUND** *L.1960.* (1961). Green on m/c unpt. Harvesting on back.	7.50	35.00	250.00

1964 ND ISSUE

#51A-51C like previous issue, but English motto below arms. Printer: TDLR.

		VG	VF	UNC
51A	**5 SHILLINGS** *L.1960.* (1964). Red on m/c unpt.			
	a. Sign. 1. Gothic serial #.	3.00	15.00	85.00
	b. Sign. 1. Roman numeral serial #.	3.50	20.00	100.00
	c. Sign. 2.	2.50	10.00	90.00
	d. Sign. 4.	2.00	7.50	65.00
51B	**10 SHILLINGS** *L.1960.* (1964). Purple on m/c unpt.			
	a. Sign. 1. Gothic serial #.	3.50	10.00	150.00
	b. Sign. 1. Roman numeral serial #.	3.50	12.50	160.00
	c. Sign. 2.	3.50	10.00	175.00
	d. Sign. 3.	5.00	17.50	200.00
	e. Sign. 4.	3.00	8.50	120.00

		VG	VF	UNC
51C	**1 POUND** *L.1960.* (1964). Green on m/c unpt.			
	a. Sign. 1. Gothic serial #.	5.00	20.00	200.00
	b. Sign. 1. Roman numeral serial #.	10.00	50.00	300.00
	c. Sign. 2.	5.50	20.00	200.00
	d. Sign. 3.	7.50	30.00	285.00
	e. Sign. 4.	4.00	17.50	185.00

		VG	VF	UNC
52	**5 POUNDS** *L.1960.* Blue on m/c unpt. Storage plant at ctr., woman w/fruit basket at r. on back.			
	a. Sign. 1. Gothic serial #.	35.00	200.00	1000.
	b. Sign. 1. Roman numeral serial #.	40.00	225.00	1100.
	c. Sign. 3.	30.00	175.00	1000.
	d. Sign. 4.	30.00	150.00	850.00

LAW 1960

1970 ND ISSUE

Dollar System

#53-58 wmk: Pineapple. Sign. 4. Printer: TDLR.

		VG	VF	UNC
53	**50 CENTS** *L.1960* (1970). Red on m/c unpt. M. Garvey at l., arms in unpt. at ctr. National shrine on back.	1.00	3.00	8.50

		VG	VF	UNC
54	**1 DOLLAR** *L.1960* (1970). Purple on m/c unpt. Sir A. Bustamante at l., arms at bottom ctr. r. Tropical harbor on back.	1.00	3.00	8.50

		VG	VF	UNC
55	**2 DOLLARS** *L.1960* (1970). Dk. green on m/c unpt. P. Bogle, arms at l., bird at ctr. Group of people on back.	1.25	4.00	13.50

NOTE: For #54 and 55 w/red serial # see #CS1-CS3.

		VG	VF	UNC
56	**5 DOLLARS** *L.1960* (1970). Dk. brown, green and blue-gray on m/c unpt. N. Manley at l., arms at bottom ctr. Old Parliament at ctr. r. on back.	2.50	10.00	45.00

		VG	VF	UNC
57	**10 DOLLARS** *L.1960* (1970). Blue-black and black on m/c unpt. G. W. Gordon at l., arms in unpt. at ctr. Bauxite mining scene at ctr. r. on back.	5.00	22.50	100.00

1973 FAO COMMEMORATIVE ISSUE

#58, 25th Anniversary Declaration of Human Rights 1948-73

		VG	VF	UNC
58	**2 DOLLARS** 1973. Like #55 but *Universal Declaration of Human Rights/1948 - 10 December - 1973. Toward Food Education Employment for All/Articles 23-26* added on back. Serial # double prefix FA-O. Sign. 4.	1.00	3.25	16.00

1976; 1977 ND ISSUE

#59-63 new guilloches in corners and some larger denomination numerals on face and back. Wmk: Pineapple. Printer: TDLR. Replacement notes: Serial # prefix *ZY* or *ZZ*.

		VG	VF	UNC
59	**1 DOLLAR** *L.1960* (1976). Purple on m/c unpt. Like #54 but w/corner design modifications.			
	a. Sign. 4.	.35	1.50	6.00
	b. Sign. 5.	.25	1.00	3.00
60	**2 DOLLARS** *L.1960* (1976). Dk. green on m/c unpt. Like #55 but w/corner design modifications.			
	a. Sign. 4.	.50	2.00	8.50
	b. Sign. 5.	.50	2.00	5.50

		VG	VF	UNC
61	**5 DOLLARS** *L.1960* (1976). Dk. brown, green and blue-green on m/c unpt. Like #56 but w/corner design modifications.			
	a. Sign. 4.	1.25	5.00	25.00
	b. Sign. 5.	.85	3.50	20.00
62	**10 DOLLARS** *L.1960* (1976). Blue-black and black on m/c unpt. Like #57 but w/corner design modifications. Sign. 4.	3.00	15.00	95.00

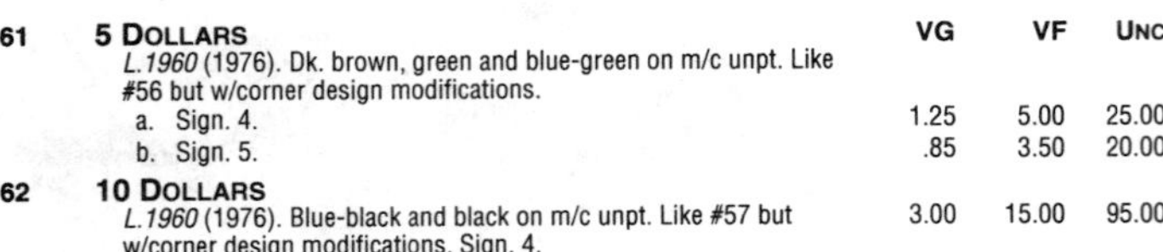

		VG	VF	UNC
63	**20 DOLLARS** *L.1960* (1977). Maroon on m/c unpt. N. Nethersole at l., flag in unpt. at ctr., arms below. Bank of Jamaica on back. Sign. 4.	4.00	17.50	100.00

1978-84 ISSUE

Bank of Jamaica Act

#64-68 wmk: Pineapple. Printer: TDLR. Replacement notes: Serial # prefix *ZY* or *ZZ*.

		VG	VF	UNC
64	**1 DOLLAR** ND (1982-86). Purple on m/c unpt. Like #59.			
	a. Sign. 6.	.15	.50	2.50
	b. Sign. 7.	.10	.35	1.50
65	**2 DOLLARS** ND (1982-86). Dk. green on m/c unpt. Like #60.			
	a. Sign. 6.	.25	1.25	7.50
	b. Sign. 7.	.20	1.00	6.00
66	**5 DOLLARS** ND (1984). Dk. brown, green and blue-gray on m/c unpt. Similar to #61. Sign. 7.	.15	.60	6.00

		VG	VF	UNC
67	**10 DOLLARS** 1978-81. Bluish purple on m/c unpt. Like #62.			
	a. Sign. 5. 1.10.1978; 1.10.1979.	.50	2.50	25.00
	b. Sign. 9. 1.12.1981.	.40	1.00	7.50

		VG	VF	UNC
68	**20 DOLLARS** 1978-83. Red on m/c unpt. Like #63.			
	a. Sign. 5. 1.10.1978; 1.10.1979; 1.10.1981.	1.00	3.00	30.00
	b. Sign. 6. 1.12.1981.	.85	2.00	20.00
	c. Sign. 7. 1.12.1983.	.75	1.25	16.50

1985 REDUCED SIZE ISSUE

#68A-72 note size: 144 x 68mm. Wmk: Pineapple. Printer: TDLR. Replacement notes: Serial # prefix *ZY* or *ZZ*.

#70-72 arms at bottom ctr.

		VG	VF	UNC
68A	**1 DOLLAR** 1985-90. Purple on m/c unpt. Similar to #64; lower corner guilloches modified.			
	a. Sign. 7. 1.1.1985.	FV	FV	2.50
	b. Sign. 8. 1.3.1986; 1.2.1987; 1.9.1987.	FV	FV	2.25
	c. Sign. 9. 1.7.1989.	FV	FV	2.00
	d. Sign. 10. 1.1.1990.	FV	FV	1.50

		VG	VF	UNC
69	**2 DOLLARS** 1985-93. Dk. green and violet on m/c unpt. Similar to #65 but lithographed. Horizontal sorting bar at r.			
	a. Sign. 7. 1.1.1985.	FV	FV	3.00
	b. Sign. 8. 1.3.1986; 1.2.1987; 1.9.1987.	FV	FV	2.25
	c. Sign. 9. 1.7.1989.	FV	FV	2.00
	d. Sign. 10. 1.1.1990; 29.5.1992.	FV	FV	1.25
	e. Sign. 11. 1.2.1993.	FV	FV	1.25

70	5 DOLLARS	VG	VF	UNC
	1985-92. Dk. brown, green and blue-gray on m/c unpt. Similar to #66 but w/2 horizontal blue-green sorting bars at l. and r.			
	a. Sign. 7. 1.1.1985.	FV	FV	4.25
	b. Sign. 8. 1.9.1987.	FV	FV	3.25
	c. Sign. 9. 1.5.1989.	FV	FV	2.25
	d. Sign. 10. 1.7.1991; 1.8.1992.	FV	FV	1.75

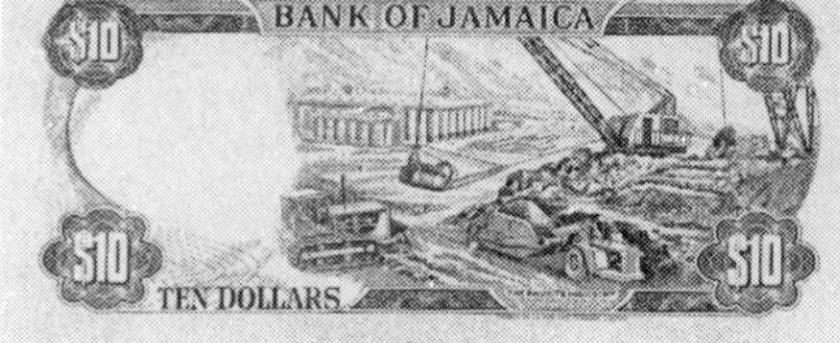

71	10 DOLLARS	VG	VF	UNC
	1985-. Bluish purple on m/c unpt. Similar to #67 but 3 horizontal sorting bars at l. and r.			
	a. Sign. 7. 1.1.1985.	FV	FV	7.50
	b. Sign. 8. 1.9.1987.	FV	FV	6.00
	c. Sign. 9. 1.8.1989.	FV	FV	3.00
	d. Sign. 10. 1.5.1991; 1.8.1992.	FV	FV	1.75
	e. Sign. 12. 1.3.1994.	FV	FV	1.50

72	20 DOLLARS	VG	VF	UNC
	1985-. Red-orange, violet and black on m/c unpt. Similar to #68 but circular electronic sorting mark at l.			
	a. Sign. 7. 1.1.1985.	FV	FV	10.00
	b. Sign. 8. 1.3.1986; 1.2.1987; 1.9.1987.	FV	FV	8.00
	c. Sign. 9. 1.9.1989.	FV	FV	7.00
	d. Sign. 10. 1.10.1991.	FV	FV	4.50
	e. Sign. 12. 1.2.1995.	FV	FV	3.50
	f. Sign. 13. 24.5.1996.	FV	FV	3.00

1986-91 ISSUE

#73-75 wmk: Pineapple. Printer: TDLR. Replacement notes: Serial # prefix *ZZ; ZY*.

73	50 DOLLARS	VG	VF	UNC
	1988-95. Brown, purple and red-violet on m/c unpt. S. Sharpe at l. Doctor's Cave Beach on back.			
	a. Sign. 8. 1.8.1988.	FV	FV	7.50
	b. Sign. 11. 1.2.1993.	FV	FV	6.50
	c. Sign. 12. 1.2.1995.	FV	FV	5.50

74	100 DOLLARS	VG	VF	UNC
	1.12.1986; 1.9.1987. Black and purple on m/c unpt. Sir D. Sangster at l. Dunn's River Falls at r. on back. Sign. 8.	FV	5.00	22.50

75	100 DOLLARS	VG	VF	UNC
	1991-93. Black and purple on licac unpt. Like #74. 2 circles at r., each w/vertical orange bar. More silver waves added to both *$100* on back.			
	a. Sign. 10. 1.7.1991.	FV	FV	13.00
	b. 1.6.1992.	FV	FV	11.00
	c. Sign. 11. 1.2.1993.	FV	FV	10.00

1994 Issue

#76-78 printer: TDLR. Replacement notes: Serial # prefix *ZY* or *ZZ*.

		VG	VF	Unc
76	**100 Dollars** 1.3.1994. Black and purple on lilac unpt. Like #75 but w/ascending size serial # and segmented foil over security thread.	FV	FV	7.00

		VG	VF	Unc
77	**500 Dollars** 1.5.1994. Purple, violet and brown on m/c unpt. Nanny of the Maroons at l. Map of islands above Fort Royal at ctr. r. on back. Sign. 12.	FV	FV	35.00

Collector Series

Bank of Jamaica

1976 Issue

		Issue Price	Mkt. Value
CS1	**1976 1-10 Dollars** #54-57 w/matching red star prefix serial # and *SERIES 1976.* (5000 sets issued).	30.00	20.00

1977 Issue

		Issue Price	Mkt. Value
CS2	**1977 1-10 Dollars** #59a-61a, 62 w/matching red star prefix serial # and *SERIES 1977.* (7500 sets issued).	29.50	15.00

1978 Issue

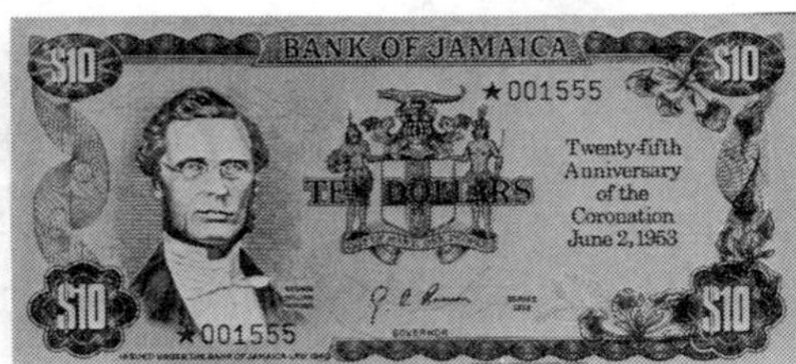

		Issue Price	Mkt. Value
CS3	**1978 1-10 Dollars** #54-57 in double set. One is like #CS1-2 w/ *SERIES 1978* and the other w/additional ovpt: *Twenty-fifth Anniversary of the Coronation June 2, 1953* and *SERIES 1978* at r. All w/matching red star prefix serial #. (6250 sets issued).	61.00	30.00

JAPAN

Japan, a constitutional monarchy situated off the east coast of Asia, has an area of 145,856 sq. mi. (377,819 sq. km.) and a population of 126 million. Capital: Tokyo. Japan, one of the three major industrial nations of the free world, exports machinery, motor vehicles, textiles and chemicals.

Japan, founded (so legend holds) in 660 BC by a direct descendant of the Sun Goddess, was first brought into contact with the west by a storm-blown Portuguese ship in 1542. European traders and missionaries proceeded to enlarge the contact until the Shogunate, sensing a military threat in the foreign presence, expelled all foreigners and severed relations with the outside world in the 17th century. (Except for one Dutch outpost in Nagasaki.) After contact was reestablished by Commodore Perry of the U.S. Navy in 1854, Japan rapidly industrialized, abolished the Shogunate and established a parliamentary form of government, and by the end of the 19th century achieved the status of a modern economic and military power. A series of wars with China and Russia, and participation with the Allies in World War I, enlarged Japan territorially but brought its interests into conflict with the Far Eastern interests of the United States and Britain, causing it to align with the Axis powers for the pursuit of World War II. After its defeat in World War II, Japan renounced military aggression as a political instrument, established democratic self-government, and quickly reasserted its position as an economic world power.

RULERS:

Hirohito (Showa), 1926-1989
Akihito (Heisei), 1989-

MONETARY SYSTEM:

1 Sen = 10 Rin
1 Yen = 100 Sen

Constitutional Monarchy

Bank of Japan

日 本 銀 行 券

Nip-pon Gin-ko Ken

1963-69 ND Issue

		VG	VF	Unc
95	**500 Yen** ND (1969). Blue on m/c unpt. Tomomi Iwakura at r. Back steel blue; Mt. Fuji at l. ctr. Wmk: 5-petaled flowers.			
	a. Single letter serial # prefix	FV	10.00	25.00
	b. Double letter serial # prefix.	FV	6.00	10.00

		VG	VF	UNC
96	**1000 YEN** ND (1963). Dk. green on m/c unpt. Hirobumi Ito at r. and as wmk. Back brown; Bank of Japan at ctr.			
	a. Single letter serial # prefix. Black serial #.	FV	25.00	90.00
	b. As a., but w/double letter serial # prefix.	FV	15.00	30.00
	c. Single letter serial # prefix. Blue serial #.	FV	17.50	45.00
	d. As c., but w/double letter serial # prefix.	FV	12.00	20.00

1984 ND ISSUE

#97-99 wmk. same as portr.

#97s-99s were released in a special booklet by Printing Bureau, Ministry of Finance.

		VG	VF	UNC
97	**1000 YEN** ND (1984-93). Blue on m/c unpt. Soseki Natsume at r. and as wmk. Crane at l. and r. on back.			
	a. Single letter serial # prefix. Black serial #	FV	12.50	30.00
	b. As a., but w/double letter serial # prefix.	FV	FV	18.00
	c. Single letter serial # prefix. Blue serial #.	FV	12.00	30.00
	d. As c., but w/double letter serial # prefix.	FV	FV	18.00
	s. As b. Specimen. Perforated *mihon*.	—	—	2250.

		VG	VF	UNC
98	**5000 YEN** ND (1984-93). Violet on m/c unpt. Inazo Nitobe at r. and as wmk. Lake and Mt. Fuji at ctr. on back.			
	a. Single letter serial # prefix. Black serial #.	FV	60.00	85.00
	b. As a., but w/double letter serial # prefix.	FV	FV	75.00
	s. As b. Specimen. Perforated *mihon*.	—	—	2250.

		VG	VF	UNC
99	**10,000 YEN** ND (1984-93). Lt. brown on m/c unpt. Yukichi Fukuzawa at r. and as wmk. Pheasant at l. and r. on back.			
	a. Single letter serial # prefix.	FV	120.00	175.00
	b. As a., but w/double letter serial # prefix.	FV	FV	140.00
	s. As b. Specimen. Perforated *mihon.*	—	—	2250.

1993 ND ISSUE

#100-102 microprinting added to upper or lower r. corner.

		VG	VF	UNC
100	**1000 YEN** ND (1993-). Blue on m/c unpt. Like #97.			
	a. Single letter serial # prefix. Brown serial # (1993).	FV	12.00	20.00
	b. As a., but w/double letter serial # prefix.	FV	FV	13.00
101	**5000 YEN** ND (1993-). Violet on m/c unpt. Like #98.			
	a. Single letter serial # prefix. Brown serial # (1993).	FV	60.00	85.00
	b. As a., but w/double letter serial # prefix.	FV	FV	65.00
102	**10,000 YEN** ND (1993-). Lt. brown on m/c unpt. Like #99.			
	a. Single letter serial # prefix. Brown serial # (1993).	FV	120.00	160.00
	b. As a., but w/double letter serial # prefix.	FV	FV	125.00

2000 COMMEMORATIVE ISSUE

#103 G9 Conference in Okinawa

		VG	VF	UNC
103	**2000 YEN** ND (2000). Okinawa's Shuri Gate. Scene from *Genji Monogolari* (Tale of Genji) on back.	Expected New Issue		

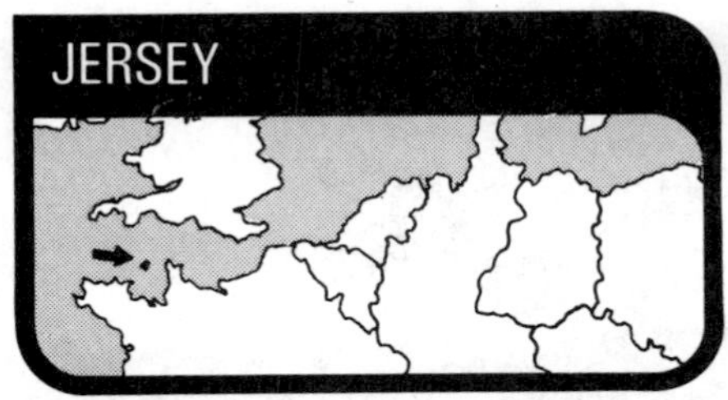

The Bailiwick of Jersey, a British Crown dependency located in the English Channel 12 miles (19 km.) west of Normandy, France, has an area of 45 sq. mi. (117 sq. km.) and a population of 72,691. Capital: St. Helier. The economy is based on agriculture and cattle breeding - the importation of cattle is prohibited to protect the purity of the island's world-famous strain of milk cows.

Jersey was occupied by Neanderthal man 100,000 years B.C., and by Iberians of 2000 B.C. who left their chamber tombs in the island's granite cliffs. Roman legions almost certainly visited the island although they left no evidence of settlement. The country folk of Jersey still speak an archaic form of Norman-French, lingering evidence of the Norman annexation of the island in 933 B.C. Jersey was annexed to England in 1206, 140 years after the Norman Conquest. The dependency is administered by its own laws and customs; laws enacted by the British Parliament do not apply to Jersey unless it is specifically mentioned. During World War II, German troops occupied the island from 1940 until 1944.

United Kingdom bank notes and coinage circulate concurrently with Jersey money as legal tender.

RULERS:

British

MONETARY SYSTEM:

1 Shilling = 12 Pence
1 Pound = 20 Shillings to 1971
1 Pound = 100 New Pence, 1971-

BRITISH INFLUENCE

STATES OF JERSEY, TREASURY

SIGNATURE VARIETIES			
1	F.N. Padgham, 1963–72	2	J. Clennett, 1972-83
3	Leslie May, 1983-93	4	Baird, 1993-

1963 ND ISSUE

#7-10 Qn. Elizabeth II at r. looking l., wearing cape. Wmk: Jersey cow's head. Sign. 3. Printer: TDLR. Replacement notes: Serial # prefix *Z*.

		VG	VF	UNC
7	**10 SHILLINGS** ND (1963). Brown on m/c unpt. St. Ouen's Manor on back.	2.00	4.50	15.00

		VG	VF	UNC
8	**1 POUND** ND (1963). Green on m/c unpt. Mont Orgueil Castle on back. 2 sign. varieties.			
	a. Sign. 1.	3.00	10.00	75.00
	b. Sign. 2.	3.00	6.00	35.00
	c. W/o sign.	15.00	35.00	120.00
	s. Specimen.	—	—	20.00

		VG	VF	UNC
9	**5 POUNDS** ND (1963). Dk. red on m/c unpt. St. Aubin's Fort on back.			
	a. Sign. 1.	10.00	35.00	300.00
	b. Sign. 2.	8.50	20.00	50.00
	s. Specimen.	—	—	35.00

		VG	VF	UNC
10	**10 POUNDS** ND (1972). Purple on m/c unpt. Back similar to #7.			
	a. Sign. 2.	18.00	25.00	60.00
	s. Specimen.	—	—	40.00

1976 ND ISSUE

#11-14 Qn. Elizabeth at ctr. r. looking l., wearing a tiara. Wmk: Jersey cow's head. Printer: TDLR. Replacement notes: Serial # prefixes *ZB; ZC*.

		VG	VF	UNC
11	**1 POUND** ND (1976-88). Blue on m/c unpt. Battle of Jersey scene on back.			
	a. Sign. 2.	FV	2.00	7.50
	b. Sign. 3.	FV	1.75	7.00
	s. Specimen.	—	—	5.00

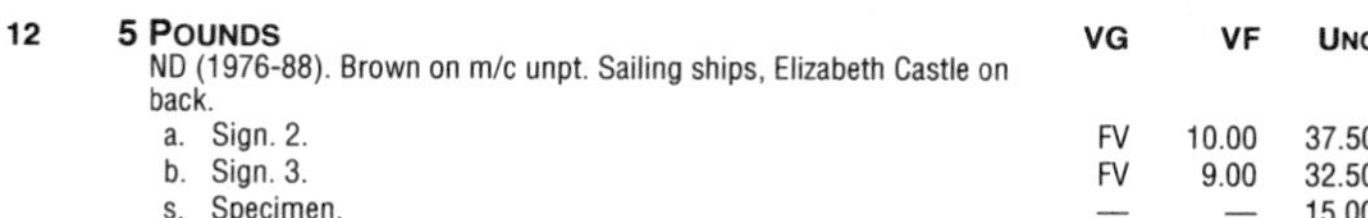

		VG	VF	UNC
12	**5 POUNDS** ND (1976-88). Brown on m/c unpt. Sailing ships, Elizabeth Castle on back.			
	a. Sign. 2.	FV	10.00	37.50
	b. Sign. 3.	FV	9.00	32.50
	s. Specimen.	—	—	15.00

		VG	VF	UNC
13	**10 POUNDS** ND (1976-88). Green on m/c unpt. Victoria College on back.			
	a. Sign. 2.	FV	22.50	55.00
	b. Sign. 3.	FV	20.00	50.00
	s. Specimen.	—	—	25.00

		VG	VF	UNC
14	**20 POUNDS** ND (1976-88). Red-brown on m/c unpt. Sailing ship, Gorey Castle on back.			
	a. Sign. 2.	FV	42.50	115.00
	b. Sign. 3.	FV	35.00	120.00
	s. Specimen.	—	—	35.00

1989 ND ISSUE

#15-19 birds at l. corner, arms at ctr., Qn. Elizabeth II at r. facing, wearing cape. Wmk: Jersey cow's head. Sign. 3. Replacement notes: Serial # prefix *CZ*.

		VG	VF	UNC
15	**1 POUND** ND (1989). Dk. green and violet on m/c unpt. Church at l. ctr. on back.			
	a. Issued note.	FV	FV	4.50
	s. Specimen.	—	—	5.00

		VG	VF	UNC
16	**5 POUNDS** ND (1989). Rose on m/c unpt. La Corbiere lighthouse on back.			
	a. Issued note.	FV	FV	20.00
	s. Specimen.	—	—	10.00

		VG	VF	UNC
17	**10 POUNDS** ND (1989). Orange-brown on m/c unpt. Battle of Jersey on back.			
	a. Issued note.	FV	FV	37.50
	s. Specimen.	—	—	15.00

		VG	VF	UNC
18	**20 POUNDS** ND (1989). Blue on m/c unpt. St. Ouen's Manor on back.			
	a. Issued note.	FV	FV	70.00
	s. Specimen.	—	—	25.00

NOTICE

Readers with unlisted dates, signature varieties, etc. are invited to submit photocopies of their notes to: Standard Catalog of World Paper Money, 700 East State St. Iola, WI 54990-0001, fax: 1-715-445-4087, or E-Mail: thernr@krause.com.

		VG	VF	UNC
19	**50 POUNDS** ND (1989). Dk. gray on m/c unpt. Government House on back.			
	a. Issued note.	FV	FV	150.00
	s. Specimen.	—	—	50.00

1993 ND ISSUE

#20-24 like #15-19 but w/solid color denomination at upper r. Wmk: Jersey cow's head. Sign. 4.

		VG	VF	UNC
20	**1 POUND** ND (1993). Dk. green on m/c unpt. Like #15.			
	a. Issued note.	FV	FV	5.00
	s. Specimen.	—	—	4.00

		VG	VF	UNC
21	**5 POUNDS** ND (1993). Rose on m/c unpt. Like #16.			
	a. Issued note.	FV	FV	20.00
	s. Specimen.	—	—	8.00

		VG	VF	UNC
22	**10 POUNDS** ND (1993). Orange-brown on m/c unpt. Like #17.			
	a. Issued note.	FV	FV	35.00
	s. Specimen.	—	—	15.00

		VG	VF	UNC
23	**20 POUNDS** ND (1993). Blue on m/c unpt. Like #18.			
	a. Issued note.	FV	FV	70.00
	s. Specimen.	—	—	25.00
24	**50 POUNDS** ND (1993). Dk. gray on m/c unpt. Like #19.			
	a. Issued note.	FV	FV	130.00
	s. Specimen.	—	—	45.00

1995 COMMEMORATIVE ISSUE

#25, 50th Anniversary - Liberation of Jersey

		VG	VF	UNC
25	**1 POUND** 9.5.1995. Dk. green and purple on m/c unpt. Face like #20 w/island outline at upper r., w/text: *50th Anniversary...* at l. in wmk. area. Face and back of German Occupation 1 Pound #6 on back. Wmk: Cow's head. Sign. 4. Printer: TDLR.			
	a. Issued note.	FV	FV	5.00
	s. Specimen.	—	—	6.00

NOTE: #25 also issued in a special wallet w/commemorative 2£ coin. (6000 pcs.). Current market value: $20.00.

COLLECTOR SERIES

STATES OF JERSEY, TREASURY

1978 ISSUE

		ISSUE PRICE	MKT. VALUE
CS1	**ND (1978) 1-20 POUNDS** #11a-14a w/ovpt: *SPECIMEN* and Maltese cross prefix serial #.	14.00	45.00

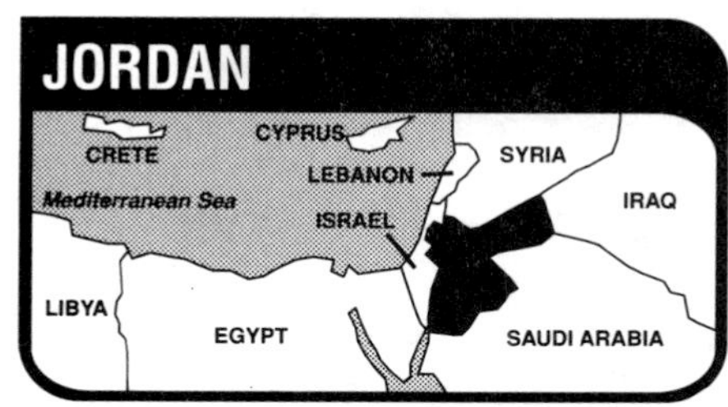

The Hashemite Kingdom of Jordan, a constitutional monarchy in southwest Asia, has an area of 37,738 sq. mi. (97,740 sq. km.) and a population of 4.3 million. Capital: Amman. Agriculture and tourism comprise Jordan's economic base. Chief exports are phosphates, tomatoes and oranges.

Jordan is the Edom and Moab of the time of Moses. It became part of the Roman province of Arabia in 106 AD, was conquered by the Arabs in 633-36, and was part of the Ottoman Empire from the 16th century until World War I. At that time, the regions presently known as Jordan and Israel were mandated to Great Britain by the League of Nations as Transjordan and Palestine. In 1922 Transjordan was established as the semi-autonomous Emirate of Transjordan, ruled by the Hashemite Prince Abdullah but still nominally a part of the British mandate. The mandate over Transjordan was terminated in 1946, the country becoming the independent Hashemite Kingdom of Transjordan. The kingdom was renamed The Hashemite Kingdom of The Jordan in 1950.

RULERS:

Hussein I, 1952-1999
Abdullah, 1999-

MONETARY SYSTEM:

1 Dirham = 100 Fils
1 Dinar = 10 Dirhams, until 1993
1 Dinar = 10 Piastres, 1993-

KINGDOM

CENTRAL BANK OF JORDAN

SIGNATURE VARIETIES					
9			10		
11			12A		
12			13		
14			15		
16			17		
18			19		
20			21		
22			23		

LAW 1959

FIRST ND ISSUE

#9-12 Kg. Hussein at l. w/law date 1959 in Arabic (*1909*).

#	Denomination	VG	VF	UNC
9	**500 FILS** *L.1959.* Brown on m/c unpt. Forum Jerash on back. w/*FIVE HUNDRED FILS* at bottom margin on back. Sign. 10-12.	3.50	15.00	42.50

#	Denomination	VG	VF	UNC
10	**1 DINAR** *L.1959.* Green on m/c unpt. al-Aqsa Mosque "Dome of the Rock" at ctr. w/columns at r. on back. Sign. 10-12.	3.00	10.00	40.00

#	Denomination	VG	VF	UNC
11	**5 DINARS** *L.1959.* Red-brown on m/c unpt. Al-Hazne, Treasury of Pharaoh at Petra at ctr. r. on back. Sign. 10-12.	10.00	25.00	90.00

#	Denomination	VG	VF	UNC
12	**10 DINARS** *L.1959.* Blue-gray on m/c unpt. Baptismal site on River Jordan on back. Sign. 10; 11.	25.00	65.00	185.00

SECOND ND ISSUE

#13-16 Kg. Hussein I at l., w/o law date *1959* (in Arabic 1909). Wmk: Kg. Hussein wearing turban.

#	Denomination	VG	VF	UNC
13	**1/2 DINAR** ND. Like #9, but w/*HALF DINAR* at bottom margin on back.			
	a. Sign. 12.	1.75	5.00	26.50
	b. Sign. 12A.	—	—	—
	c. Sign. 14.	1.50	4.50	13.50
14	**1 DINAR** ND. Like #10.			
	a. Sign. 13.	3.00	9.00	40.00
	b. Sign. 14.	2.50	8.00	35.00

15 5 DINARS
ND. Like #11.

a. Sign. 12.	4.00	12.50	57.50
b. Sign. 15.	3.25	10.00	55.00

16 10 DINARS ND. Like #12.	VG	VF	UNC
a. Sign. 12.	8.50	25.00	100.00
b. Sign. 12A.	—	—	—
c. Sign. 13.	7.50	22.50	90.00
d. Sign. 14.	7.00	21.50	85.00
e. Sign. 15.	6.00	18.50	65.00

1975; 1977 ND ISSUE

#17-21 Kg. Hussein at l. Wmk: Kg. Hussein wearing turban.

17 1/2 DINAR	VG	VF	UNC
ND (1975-92). Brown on m/c unpt. Jerash at r. on back. Sign. 15-18.	FV	.60	3.25

18 1 DINAR ND (1975-92). Dk. green on m/c unpt. Al-Aqsa Mosque "Dome of the Rock" behind columns at r. on back.	VG	VF	UNC
a. Sign. 15.	FV	FV	10.00
b. Sign. 16.	FV	FV	8.50
c. Sign. 17.	FV	FV	7.50
d. Sign. 18.	FV	FV	6.50
e. Sign. 19.	FV	FV	5.00

NOTICE

Readers with unlisted dates, signature varieties, etc. are invited to submit photocopies of their notes to: Standard Catalog of World Paper Money, 700 East State St. Iola, WI 54990-0001, fax: 1-715-445-4087, or E-Mail: thernr@krause.com.

19 5 DINARS ND (1975-92). Red on m/c unpt. Al-Hazne, Treasury of the Pharaoh at Petra at r. on back.	VG	VF	UNC
a. Sign. 15.	FV	FV	30.00
b. Sign. 16.	FV	FV	27.50
c. Sign. 18.	FV	FV	22.50
d. Sign. 19.	FV	FV	27.50

20 10 DINARS ND (1975-92). Blue on m/c unpt. Cultural palace above and amphitheater at ctr. r. on back.	VG	VF	UNC
a. Sign. 15.	FV	FV	85.00
b. Sign. 16.	FV	FV	65.00
c. Sign. 18.	FV	FV	45.00
d. Sign. 19.	FV	FV	35.00

21 20 DINARS	VG	VF	UNC
1977; 1981; 1985; 1987; 1988. Deep brown on m/c unpt. Electric power station of Zerga on back. Sign. 16-18.	FV	FV	75.00

1991 ISSUE

22 20 DINARS	VG	VF	UNC
1977 (1991); 1982 (1991); 1985 (1992). Blue on m/c unpt. Like #21. (Sign. 16; 15; 17, respectively.)	FV	FV	100.00

1992 ISSUE

#23-27 Kg. Hussein wearing headdress at ctr. r. and as wmk. Sign. 19.

		VG	VF	UNC
23	**1/2 DINAR** AH1412/1992-AH1413/1993. Lilac-brown and dk. brown on m/c unpt. Qusayr Amra fortress at r. on back.			
	a. AH1412/1992.	FV	FV	4.25
	b. AH1413/1993.	FV	FV	3.50
	s. Specimen.	—	—	—

		VG	VF	UNC
24	**1 DINAR** AH1412/1992-AH1413/1993. Green on olive and m/c unpt. Ruins of Jerash at ctr. r. on back.			
	a. AH1412/1992.	FV	FV	6.50
	b. AH1413/1993.	FV	FV	5.00
	s. Specimen.	—	—	—

		VG	VF	UNC
25	**5 DINARS** AH1412/1992-AH1413/1993. Red and violet-brown on m/c unpt. Treasury at Petra on back.			
	a. AH1412/1992.	FV	FV	30.00
	b. AH1413/1993.	FV	FV	25.00
	s. Specimen.	—	—	—

		VG	VF	UNC
26	**10 DINARS** AH1412/1992. Blue, gray-violet and green on m/c unpt. al-Rabadh Castle ruins on back.	FV	FV	45.00

		VG	VF	UNC
27	**20 DINARS** AH1412/1992. Dk. brown, green and red-brown on m/c unpt. Dome of the Rock at l. ctr. on back.	FV	FV	95.00

1995-96 ISSUE

#28-32 w/title: *THE HASHEMITE KINGDOM OF JORDAN* on back.

		VG	VF	UNC
28	**1/2 DINAR** AH1415/1995-. Lilac-brown and dk. brown on m/c unpt. Like #23.			
	a. AH1415/1995. Sign. 19.	FV	FV	3.50
	b. AH1417/1997. Sign. 21.	FV	FV	3.00

		VG	VF	UNC
29	**1 DINAR** AH1415/1995-. Green and olive on m/c unpt. Like #24.			
	a. AH1415/1995. Sign. 19.	FV	FV	5.50
	b. AH1416/1996. Sign. 21.	FV	FV	5.00
	c. AH1417/1997. Sign. 21.	FV	FV	5.00

		VG	VF	UNC
30	**5 DINARS** AH1415/1995-. Red-violet, purple and orange on m/c unpt. Like #25.			
	a. AH1415/1995. Sign. 19.	FV	FV	17.50
	b. AH1417/1997. Sign. 22.	FV	FV	16.50

		VG	VF	UNC
31	**10 DINARS** AH1416/1996. Purple, dk. blue and black on m/c unpt. Like #26 but castle ruins renamed *Aljourn*. Sign. 20.	FV	FV	35.00

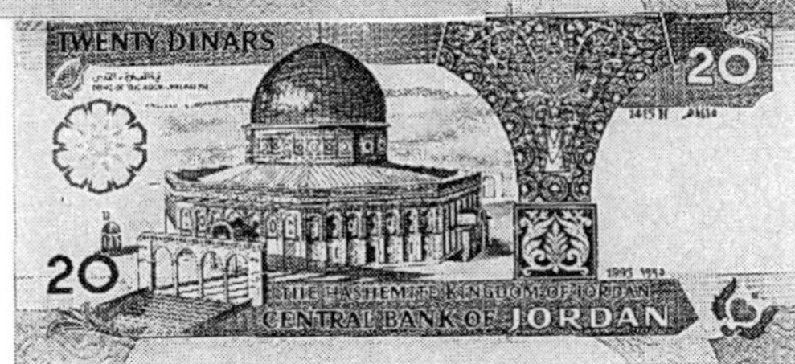

		VG	VF	UNC
32	**20 DINARS** AH1415/1995. Dk. brown, green and red-brown on m/c unpt. Like #27. Sign. 19.	FV	FV	65.00

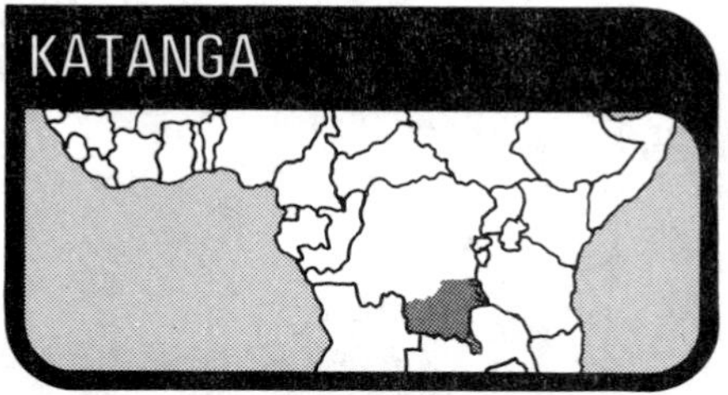

Katanga, the southern province of the former Zaïre extends northeast to Lake Tanganyika, east and south to Zambia, and west to Angola. It was inhabited by Luba and Bantu peoples, and was one of Africa's richest mining areas.

In 1960, Katanga, under the leadership of provincial president Moise Tshombe and supported by foreign mining interests, seceded from newly independent Republic of the Congo. A period of political confusion and bloody fighting involving Congolese, Belgian and United Nations forces ensued. At the end of the rebellion in 1962, Katanga was reintegrated into the republic, and is known as the Shaba region.

For additional history, see Zaïre.

MONETARY SYSTEM:

1 Franc = 100 Centimes

INDEPENDENT

GOVERNMENT

1961 ND PROVISIONAL ISSUE

#1-4 w/red ovpt: *GOUVERNEMENT KATANGA* on face and back of Banque D'Emission du Rwanda et du Burundi notes.

		GOOD	FINE	XF
1	**5 FRANCS** ND (1961 - old date 15.5.1961). Ovpt. on Rwanda & Burundi #1.	—	—	—
2	**10 FRANCS** ND (1961 - old date 15.9.1960; 5.10.1960). Ovpt. on Rwanda & Burundi #2.	—	—	—

		GOOD	FINE	XF
3	**20 FRANCS** ND (1961 - old date/15.9.1960; 5.10.1960). Ovpt. on Rwanda & Burundi #3.	—	—	—

		GOOD	FINE	XF
4	**50 FRANCS** ND (1961 - old date 1.10.1960). Ovpt. on Rwanda & Burundi #4.	—	—	—

BANQUE NATIONALE DU KATANGA

1960 ISSUE

#5-10 Moise Tshombe at r. Bldg. at l. on back.
#5A and 6A Moise Tshombe at l., flag at r. Printer: W&S (Not issued).

		VG	VF	UNC
5	**10 FRANCS** 1.12.1960; 15.12.1960. Lilac and yellow.			
	a. Issued note.	8.50	20.00	50.00
	r. Remainder, no serial #.	—	—	60.00
	s. Specimen.	—	60.00	75.00

		VG	VF	UNC
5A	**10 FRANCS** 1.12.1960. Green, brown and red. Reservoir at ctr. Foundry at ctr. on back.			
	r. Remainder w/o date or serial #.	—	—	500.00
	s. Specimen.	—	—	—

		VG	VF	UNC
6	**20 FRANCS** 1960. Blue-green.			
	a. 21.11.1960.	17.50	40.00	75.00
	b. 1.12.1960.	25.00	60.00	120.00
	r. Remainder, w/o serial #.	—	—	80.00
	s. Specimen.	—	80.00	100.00

		VG	VF	UNC
6A	**20 FRANCS** 1.12.1960. M/c. Aerial view at ctr. Miners at ctr. on back. Specimen.	—	—	—

		VG	VF	UNC
7	**50 FRANCS** 10.11.1960. Brown and salmon.			
	a. Issued note.	20.00	50.00	90.00
	r. Remainder, w/o serial #.	—	—	125.00
	s. Specimen.	—	100.00	125.00

		VG	VF	UNC
8	**100 FRANCS** 31.10.1960. Brown, green and yellow.			
	a. Issued note.	25.00	60.00	100.00
	r. Remainder, w/o serial #.	—	—	150.00

		VG	VF	UNC
9	**500 FRANCS** 31.10.1960. Green, violet and olive.			
	a. Issued note.	90.00	175.00	250.00
	r. Remainder, w/o serial #.	—	—	200.00
	s. Specimen.	—	150.00	225.00

NOTICE

Readers with unlisted dates, signature varieties, etc. are invited to submit photocopies of their notes to: Standard Catalog of World Paper Money, 700 East State St. Iola, WI 54990-0001, fax: 1-715-445-4087, or E-Mail: thernr@krause.com.

#	Denomination	VG	VF	UNC
10	**1000 FRANCS** 31.10.1960. Blue and brown.			
	a. Issued note.	100.00	200.00	300.00
	r. Remainder, w/o serial #.	—	—	300.00
	s. Specimen.	—	275.00	325.00

1962 ISSUE

#12-14 wheel of masks and spears on back. Wmk: Elephant.

#	Denomination	VG	VF	UNC
12	**100 FRANCS** 18.5.1962; 15.8.1962; 15.9.1962; 14.1.1963. Dk. green and brown on m/c unpt. Woman carrying ears of corn at r.			
	a. Issued note.	8.50	20.00	60.00
	s. Specimen.	—	—	100.00

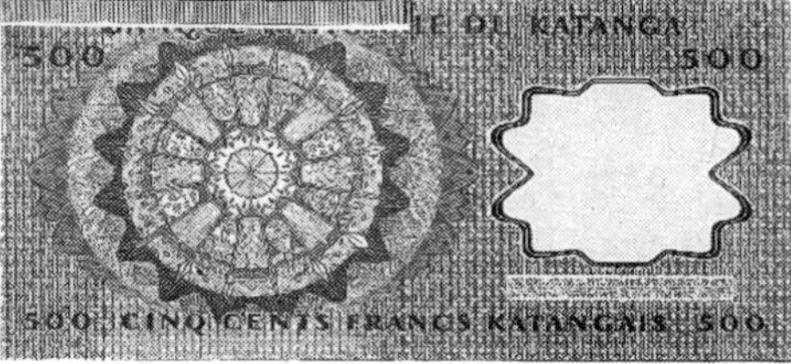

#	Denomination	VG	VF	UNC
13	**500 FRANCS** 17.4.1962. Purple and m/c. Man w/fire at r.			
	a. Issued note.	80.00	200.00	325.00
	s. Specimen.	—	425.00	525.00

#	Denomination	VG	VF	UNC
14	**1000 FRANCS** 26.2.1962. Dk. blue, red and brown on m/c unpt. Woman carrying child on back while picking cotton at r. Ornate wheel at l.			
	a. Issued note.	40.00	150.00	225.00
	s. Specimen.	—	—	300.00

KAZAKHSTAN

The Republic of Kazakhstan is bordered to the west by the Caspian Sea and Russia, to the north by Russia, in the east by the Peoples Republic of China and in the south by Uzbekistan and Kirghizia. It has an area of 1,049,155 sq. mi. (2,717,300 sq. km.) and a population of 16.5 million. Capital: Alma-Ata (formerly Verny). The country is rich in mineral resources including coal, tungsten, copper, lead, zinc and manganese with huge oil and natural gas reserves; while agriculture is important, as it was once. 20 percent of the total acreage of the combined U.S.S.R. Non-ferrous metallurgy, heavy engineering and chemical industries are leaders in its economy.

The Kazakhs are a branch of the Turkic peoples which led the nomadic life of herdsman until WW I. In the 13th century they come under Genghis Khan's eldest son Juji and later became a part of the Golden Horde, a western Mongol empire. Around the beginning of the 16th century they were divided into 3 confederacies, known as zhuz or hordes, in the steppes of Turkistan. At the end of the 17th century an incursion by the Kalmucks, a remnant of the Oirat Mongol confederacy, resulted in heavy losses on both sides which facilitated Russian penetration. Resistance to Russian settlements varied throughout the 1800's, but by 1900 over 100 million acres was declared Czarist state property and used for a planned peasant colonization. After a revolution in 1905 Kazakh deputies were elected. In 1916 the Czarist government ordered mobilization of all males, between 19 and 43 for auxiliary service. The Kazakhs rose in defiance which led the governor general of Turkestan to send troops against the rebels. Shortly after the Russian revolution Kazakh nationalists asked for full autonomy. The Communist coup d'état of Nov. 1917 led to civil war. In 1919-20 the Red army defeated the "White" Russian forces and occupied Kazakhstan and fought against the Nationalist government formed on Nov. 17, 1917 by Ali Khan Bukey Khan. The Kazakh Autonomous Soviet Socialist Republic was proclaimed on Aug. 26, 1920 within the R.S.F.S.R. Russian and Ukrainian colonization continued while 2 purges in 1927 and 1935 quelled any Kazakh feelings of priority in the matters of their country. On Dec. 5, 1936, Kazakhstan qualified for full status as an S.S.R. and held its first congress in 1937. Independence was declared on Dec. 16, 1991 and the new Republic joined the C.I.S.

MONETARY SYSTEM:

1 Tengé = 100 Tyin = 500 Rubles (Russian), 1993 -

REPUBLIC

КАЗАКСТАН УЛТТЫК БАНКІ

KAZAKHSTAN NATIONAL BANK

1993-96 ISSUE

#1-6 ornate denomination in circle at r. Circular arms at l. on back. Serial # at l. or lower l. Wmk. paper.

#	Denomination	VG	VF	UNC
1	**1 TYIN** 1993. Violet and blue-violet on yellow and m/c unpt. 2 wmk. varieties.	FV	FV	.50

#	Denomination	VG	VF	UNC
2	**2 TYIN** 1993. Blue-violet on lt. blue and m/c unpt.			
	a. 2 wmk. varieties.	FV	FV	.50
	b. W/o wmk.	FV	FV	.45

#	Denomination	VG	VF	UNC
3	**5 TYIN** 1993. Violet on lt. blue and m/c unpt.	FV	FV	.60

4 **10 TYIN**

1993. Deep red on pink and m/c unpt.

VG	VF	UNC
FV	FV	.75

5 **20 TYIN**

1993. Black and blue-gray on m/c unpt.

VG	VF	UNC
FV	FV	.75

6 **50 TYIN**

1993. Dk. brown and black on m/c unpt.

VG	VF	UNC
FV	FV	2.75

#7-15 arms at upper ctr. r. on back.

#7-9 wmk: symmetrical design repeated.

7 **1 TENGÉ**

1993. Dk. blue on m/c unpt. Al-Farabi at ctr. r. Back lt. blue on m/c unpt; architectural drawings of mosque at l. ctr., arms at upper r.

VG	VF	UNC
FV	FV	2.50

8 **3 TENGÉ**

1993. Dk. green on m/c unpt. Suinbai at ctr. r. Mountains, forest, and river at l. ctr. on back.

VG	VF	UNC
FV	FV	3.00

9 **5 TENGÉ**

1993. Dk. brown-violet on m/c unpt. Kurmanfazy at ctr. r. Cemetery at l. ctr. on back.

VG	VF	UNC
FV	FV	2.25

10 **10 TENGÉ**

1993. Dk. green on m/c unpt. Shoqan Valikhanov at ctr. r. and as wmk. Mountains, forest, and lake at l. ctr. on back.

VG	VF	UNC
FV	FV	2.00

11 **20 TENGÉ**

1993. Brown on m/c unpt. A. Kunanbrev at ctr. r. and as wmk. Equestrian hunter at l. ctr. on back.

VG	VF	UNC
FV	FV	15.00

12 **50 TENGÉ**

1993. Red-brown and deep violet on m/c unpt. Abilkhair Khan at ctr. r. and as wmk. Native artwork at l. ctr. on back.

VG	VF	UNC
FV	FV	7.00

		VG	VF	UNC
13	**100 TENGÉ** 1993. Purple and dk. blue on m/c unpt. Abylai Khan at ctr. r. and as wmk. Domed bldg. at l. ctr. on back.	FV	FV	5.50

#14-17 al-Farabi at r. and as wmk.

		VG	VF	UNC
14	**200 TENGÉ** 1993. Red and brown on m/c unpt. Back blue and m/c; domes of bldg. at l. on back.	FV	FV	11.00

		VG	VF	UNC
15	**500 TENGÉ** 1994. Blue-black and violet on m/c unpt. Ancient bldg. on back.	FV	FV	17.50

		VG	VF	UNC
16	**1000 TENGÉ** 1994. Deep green, red and orange on m/c unpt. Ancient bldg. on back.	FV	FV	32.50

		VG	VF	UNC
17	**2000 TENGÉ** 1996. Dk. brown on m/c unpt. Gate on back.	FV	FV	60.00

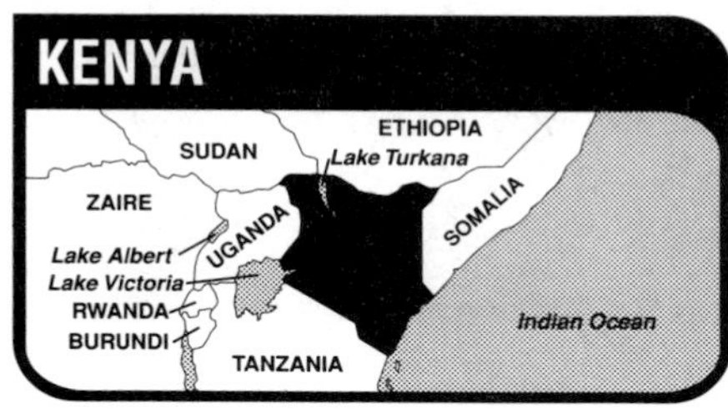

The Republic of Kenya, located on the east coast of Central Africa, has an area of 224,961 sq. mi. (582,646 sq. km.) and a population of 26.4 million. Capital: Nairobi. The predominantly agricultural country exports coffee, tea and petroleum products.

The Arabs came to the coast of Kenya in the 8th century and established posts to conduct an ivory and slave trade. The Portuguese, the inveterate wanderers of the Age of Exploration, followed in the 16th century. After a lengthy and bitter struggle with the sultans of Zanzibar who controlled much of the southeastern coast of Africa, the Portuguese were driven away (late 17th century) and for many years Kenya was simply a port of call on the route to India. German and British interests in the 19th century produced agreements defining their respective spheres of influence. The British sphere was administered by the Imperial East Africa Co. until 1895, when the British government purchased the company's rights in the East Africa Protectorate which in 1920 was designated as Kenya Colony and protectorate - the latter being a 10-mile wide coastal strip together with Mombasa, Lamu and other small islands nominally retained by the Sultan of Zanzibar. Kenya achieved self-government in June of 1963 as a consequence of the 1952-60 Mau Mau terrorist campaign to secure land reforms and political rights for Africans. Independence was attained on Dec. 12, 1963. Kenya became a republic in 1964. It is a member of the Commonwealth of Nations. The president is Chief of State and Head of Government.

Notes of the East African Currency Board were in use during the first years.

RULERS:

British to 1964

MONETARY SYSTEM:

1 Shilling (Shilingi) = 100 Cents

REPUBLIC

CENTRAL BANK OF KENYA

1966 ISSUE

#1-5 M. Jomo Kenyatta at l., arms at ctr. in unpt. Values also in Arabic numerals and letters. Wmk: Lion's head.

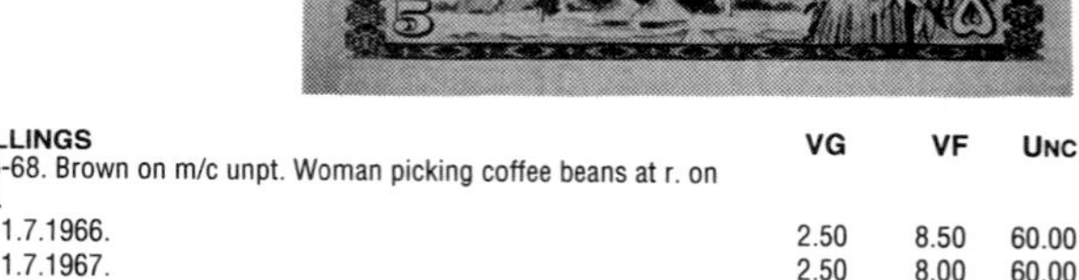

		VG	VF	UNC
1	**5 SHILLINGS** 1966-68. Brown on m/c unpt. Woman picking coffee beans at r. on back.			
	a. 1.7.1966.	2.50	8.50	60.00
	b. 1.7.1967.	2.50	8.00	60.00
	c. 1.7.1968.	2.50	8.00	65.00
	s. As a. Specimen, punched hole cancelled.	—	—	40.00

		VG	VF	UNC
2	**10 SHILLINGS** 1966-68. Green on m/c unpt. Tea pickers in field on back.			
	a. 1.7.1966.	3.00	15.00	85.00
	b. 1.7.1967.	4.50	18.50	100.00
	c. 1.7.1968.	4.00	17.50	100.00
	s. As a. Specimen, punched hole cancelled.	—	—	80.00

		VG	VF	UNC
3	**20 SHILLINGS** 1966-68. Blue on m/c unpt. Plants and train w/sisal on back.			
	a. 1.7.1966.	5.00	22.50	185.00
	b. 1.7.1967.	5.00	25.00	185.00
	c. 1.7.1968.	5.00	25.00	200.00
	s. As a. Specimen, punched hole cancelled.	—	—	140.00

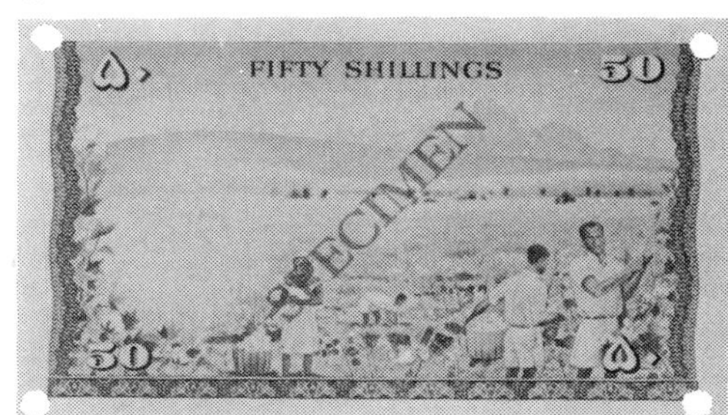

		VG	VF	UNC
4	**50 SHILLINGS** 1966-68. Dk. brown on m/c unpt. Cotton picking below Mt. Kenya on back.			
	a. 1.7.1966.	50.00	250.00	650.00
	b. 1.7.1967.	55.00	300.00	750.00
	c. 1.7.1968.	50.00	300.00	700.00
	s. As a. Specimen, punched hole cancelled.	—	—	525.00

		VG	VF	UNC
5	**100 SHILLINGS** 1966; 1968. Purple on m/c unpt. Workers at pineapple plantation on back.			
	a. 1.7.1966.	12.50	50.00	400.00
	b. 1.7.1968.	12.50	55.00	450.00
	s. As a. Specimen, punched hole cancelled.	—	—	325.00

1969 ISSUE

#6-10 M. Jomo Kenyatta at l., values w/o Arabic numerals and letters. Different text at lower ctr. Wmk: Lion's head.

		VG	VF	UNC
6	**5 SHILLINGS** 1.7.1969-1.7.1973. Brown on m/c unpt. Similar to #1.	1.00	4.00	17.50
7	**10 SHILLINGS** 1.7.1969-1.7.1974. Green on m/c unpt. Similar to #2.	2.00	6.00	42.50
8	**20 SHILLINGS** 1.7.1969-1.7.1973. Blue on m/c unpt. Similar to #3.	3.00	20.00	140.00
9	**50 SHILLINGS** 1969; 1971. Dk. brown on m/c unpt. Similar to #4.			
	a. 1.7.1969.	70.00	275.00	800.00
	b. 1.7.1971.	150.00	500.00	—
10	**100 SHILLINGS** 1.7.1969-1.7.1973. Purple on m/c unpt. Similar to #5.	5.00	35.00	250.00

1974 ISSUE

#11-14 M. Jomo Kenyatta at l., values in latent images at bottom l. Wmk: Lion's head.

		VG	VF	UNC
11	**5 SHILLINGS** 12.12.1974; 1.1.1975; 1.7.1976; 1.7.1977. Brown-orange on m/c unpt. Woman picking coffee beans at r. on back.	.50	1.75	7.00

		VG	VF	UNC
12	**10 SHILLINGS** 1.1.1975; 1.7.1976; 1.7.1977. Dk. green and dk. brown on m/c unpt. Back green; cattle at ctr. r. on back.	1.00	3.00	12.50

		VG	VF	UNC
13	**20 SHILLINGS** 1974-77. Dk. blue on m/c unpt. Lions on back.			
	a. 12.12.1974.	3.00	10.00	50.00
	b. 1.1.1975; 1.7.1976; 1.7.1977.	2.00	5.50	27.50

14	100 SHILLINGS	VG	VF	UNC
	1974-77. Purple on lt. green and m/c unpt. Kenyatta statue and tower on back. 153 x 79mm.			
	a. 12.12.1974.	7.50	20.00	150.00
	b. 1.1.1975; 1.7.1976.	5.00	15.00	115.00
	c. 1.7.1977.	5.00	17.50	130.00

1978 ISSUE

#15-18 M. Jomo Kenyatta at l., w/English value in 3rd line only on face. Wmk: Lion's head.

NOTE: #15-18 were withdrawn soon after Kenyatta's death. A shortage of currency resulted in a limited re-issue during Dec. 1993 - Jan. 1994 of mostly circulated notes.

15	5 SHILLINGS	VG	VF	UNC
	1.7.1978. Brown-orange on m/c unpt. Similar to #11. W/English value on face in third line only.	.40	1.25	3.50

16	10 SHILLINGS	VG	VF	UNC
	1.7.1978. Dk. green and dk. brown on m/c unpt. Similar to #12.	.65	2.00	5.50

17	20 SHILLINGS	VG	VF	UNC
	1.7.1978. Blue-black and blue on m/c unpt. Similar to #13.	1.25	3.75	11.50

18	100 SHILLINGS	VG	VF	UNC
	1.7.1978. Purple, dk. brown and dk. blue on m/c unpt. Similar to #14 but w/different colors in guilloches. 157 x 81mm.	2.50	7.50	22.50

1980-81 ISSUE

#19-23 arms at ctr., Pres. Daniel T.A. Moi at r. Wmk: Lion's head.

19	5 SHILLINGS	VG	VF	UNC
	1.1.1981; 1.1.1982; 1.7.1984. Lt. brown on m/c unpt. 3 rams w/giraffes and mountain in background on back.	FV	.75	3.50

20	10 SHILLINGS	VG	VF	UNC
	1.1.1981-1.7.1988. Green on m/c unpt. 2 cows at l., 2 school children drinking milk at ctr. on back.	FV	1.00	4.00

21	20 SHILLINGS	VG	VF	UNC
	1.1.1981-1.7.1987. Blue on m/c unpt. 4 women reading newspaper at ctr. on back.	FV	1.50	9.00

22	50 SHILLINGS	VG	VF	UNC
	1.6.1980; 1.7.1985; 14.9.1986; 1.7.1987; 1.7.1988. Dk. red and m/c. Back olive; jet aircraft flying over Jomo Kenyatta airport.	FV	1.50	7.50

23	100 SHILLINGS	VG	VF	UNC
	1.6.1980-1.7.1988. Purple and m/c. Kenyatta statue, tower and mountains on back.	3.00	10.00	40.00

23A	200 SHILLINGS	VG	VF	UNC
	14.9.1986; 1.7.1987; 1.7.1988. Dk. brown on m/c unpt. Triangle in lower l. border. No silvering on value at upper r. Fountain at ctr. on back.			
	a. 14.9.1986.	FV	6.50	40.00
	b. 1.7.1987.	FV	10.00	85.00
	c. 1.7.1988.	FV	15.00	100.00

1986-90 ISSUE

#24-30 Pres. Daniel T. A. Moi at r., arms at l. ctr. Vertical serial # at l. Wmk: Lion's head. Replacement notes: Serial # prefix *ZZ*.

NOTE: The small date of 2.1.1992 were printed by H&S.

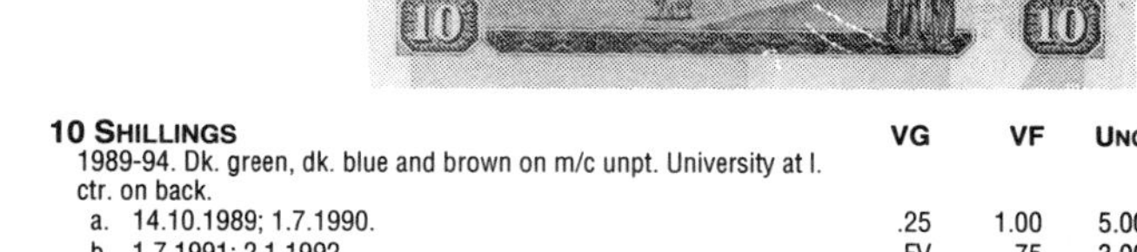

24	10 SHILLINGS	VG	VF	UNC
	1989-94. Dk. green, dk. blue and brown on m/c unpt. University at l. ctr. on back.			
	a. 14.10.1989; 1.7.1990.	.25	1.00	5.00
	b. 1.7.1991; 2.1.1992.	FV	.75	3.00
	c. 1.7.1993; 1.1.1994.	FV	FV	1.35

25	20 SHILLINGS	VG	VF	UNC
	1988-92. Dk. blue and m/c. Moi International Sports Complex on back.			
	a. 12.12.1988.	1.35	4.00	15.00
	b. 1.7.1989; 1.7.1990.	.50	2.00	7.50
	c. 1.7.1991; 2.1.1992.	FV	2.00	5.00

NOTE: #25 dated 12.12.1988 is believed to be a commemorative for the 25th Anniversary of Independence.

26	50 SHILLINGS	VG	VF	UNC
	1990; 1992. Red-brown on m/c unpt. Back green; modern bldgs. at l., flag at r.			
	a. 10.10.1990.	1.00	3.00	12.50
	b. 1.7.1992.	1.50	5.00	15.00

27	100 SHILLINGS	VG	VF	UNC
	1989-95. Purple, dk. green and red on m/c unpt. Monument to 25th Anniversary of Independence w/Mt. Kenya on back.			
	a. 14.10.1989; 1.7.1990; 1.7.1991.	2.75	5.00	25.00
	b. 2.1.1992.	FV	4.00	17.50
	c. 2.7.1992; 1.1.1994; 1.1.1995.	FV	3.00	12.50

#28 *Deleted.* See #23A.

29	200 SHILLINGS	VG	VF	UNC
	1989-94. Similar to #23A but rose replaces colored triangle to r. of *200* at lower l. Additional silver diamond design under 200 at upper r. Vertical serial # at l.			
	a. 1.7.1989; 1.7.1990.	FV	4.50	27.50
	b. 2.1.1992.	FV	5.00	25.00
	c. 1.7.1992; 14.9.1993; 1.1.1994.	FV	4.00	16.50

30	500 SHILLINGS	VG	VF	UNC
	1988-95. Black, deep green and red on m/c unpt. Roses at l. Modern bldg., Mt. Kenya on back.			
	a. 14.10.1988.	10.00	30.00	150.00
	b. 1.7.1989.	FV	18.50	75.00
	c. 1.7.1990.	FV	15.00	50.00
	d. 2.1.1992.	9.00	22.00	75.00
	e. 1.7.1992; 14.9.1993.	FV	15.00	50.00
	f. 1.1.1995.	9.00	20.00	65.00

1993 ISSUE

#31 Pres. Daniel T. A. Moi at ctr. r.

31	20 SHILLINGS	VG	VF	UNC
	14.9.1993; 1.1.1994. Similar to #25 but w/roses added to l. border, vertical red serial #. Male runner and other artistic enhancements added on back.	FV	FV	3.00

1995; 1996 ISSUE

#32-37 Pres. Daniel T. A. Moi at l. ctr., arms at upper ctr. r. Ascending size serial #. Wmk: Facing lion's head.

32	20 SHILLINGS	VG	VF	UNC
	1.7.1995. Dk. blue, brown and blue-green on m/c unpt. Baton at l., Moi Int'l Sports Complex at l. ctr., runner at ctr. r. on back.	FV	FV	2.25

33	50 SHILLINGS	VG	VF	UNC
	1.1.1996; 1.1.1997; 1.7.1998. Brown-violet and blue-black on m/c unpt. Dromedary caravan on back.	FV	FV	4.50

34	100 SHILLINGS	VG	VF	UNC
	1.7.1996; 1.7.1997; 1.7.1998. Purple, red and deep green on m/c unpt. People by Monument to 25th Anniversary of Independence at ctr., branch of fruit at l. on back.	FV	FV	6.50

35 **200 SHILLINGS**

	VG	VF	UNC
1.7.1996; 1.1.1998. Dk. brown, blue-gray and dk. green on m/c unpt. Unity monument at ctr., women harvesting at l. on back.	FV	FV	12.50

36 **500 SHILLINGS**

	VG	VF	UNC
1.7.1995. Black, green and red on m/c unpt. Modern bldg. at l. ctr. on back.	FV	FV	21.00

37 **1000 SHILLINGS**

	VG	VF	UNC
12.12.1994; 1.7.1995. Brown-violet on m/c unpt. Water buffalo, elephants and bird on back.	FV	FV	55.00

1996; 1997 ISSUE

#38 and 40 Pres. Daniel T. A. Moi at l. ctr. Wmk: Facing lion's head. W/segmented foil over security thread and ascending serial #.

38 **20 SHILLINGS**

	VG	VF	UNC
1.1.1996; 1.1.1997; 1.7.1998. Dk. blue on m/c unpt. Like #25. W/security thread.	FV	FV	2.00

39 **500 SHILLINGS**

	VG	VF	UNC
1997. Black, green and red on m/c unpt. Like #36.	FV	FV	22.50

40 **1000 SHILLINGS**

	VG	VF	UNC
1.7.1997. Brown-violet and olive-green on m/c unpt. Like #37.	FV	FV	37.50

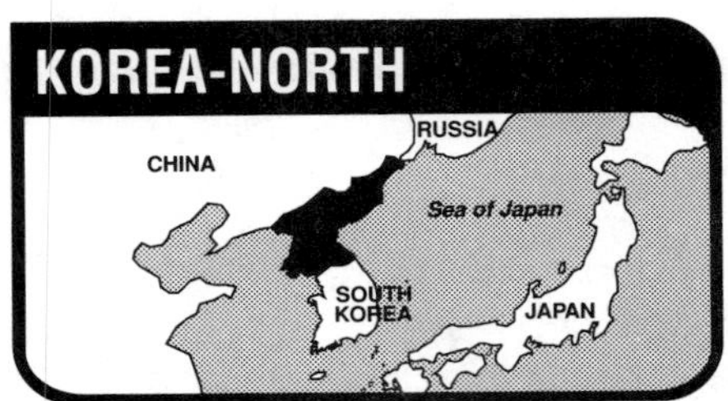

The Democratic Peoples Republic of Korea, situated in in northeastern Asia on the northern half of the Korean peninsula between the Peoples Republic of China and the Republic of Korea, has an area of 46,540 sq. mi. (120,538 sq. km.) and a populati on of 23.26 million. Capital: Pyongyang. The economy is based on heavy based on heavy industry and agriculture. Metals, minerals and farm produce are exported.

Japan replaced China as the predominant foreign influence in Korea in 1895 and annexed the peninsular country in 1910. Defeat in World War II brought an end to Japanese rule. U.S. troops entered Korea from the south and Soviet forces entered from the north. The Cairo conference (1943) had established that Korea should be "free and independent." The Potsdam conference (1945) set the 38th parallel as the line dividing the occupation forces of the United States and Russia. When Russia refused to permit a U.N. commission designated to supervise reunification elections to enter North Korea, an election was held in South Korea which established the Republic of Korea on Aug. 15, 1948. North Korea held an unsupervised election on Aug. 25, 1948, and on the following day proclaimed the establishment of the Democratic Peoples Republic of Korea.

MONETARY SYSTEM:

1 Won = 100 Chon

Democratic Peoples Republic

Korean Central Bank

1959 Issue

#12-17 arms at l. or upper l. Wmk. paper.

		VG	VF	UNC
12	**50 Chon** 1959. Blue on m/c unpt. Arms at upper l.	.15	.50	2.00

		VG	VF	UNC
13	**1 Won** 1959. Red-brown on m/c unpt. Fishing boat at ctr.	.15	.50	2.00

		VG	VF	UNC
14	**5 Won** 1959. Green on m/c unpt. Lg. bldg. at ctr.	.15	.40	2.00

		VG	VF	UNC
15	**10 Won** 1959. Red on m/c unpt. Fortress gateway at ctr. r. Woman picking fruit on back.	.20	.50	2.00

		VG	VF	UNC
16	**50 Won** 1959. Purple on m/c unpt. Bridge and city at ctr. Woman w/wheat on back.	.20	.50	2.00

		VG	VF	UNC
17	**100 Won** 1959. Green on m/c unpt. Steam freight train in factory area at ctr. River w/cliffs on back.	.25	.75	3.00

1978 Issue

#18-22 arms at upper l.

NOTE: Circulation of varieties #18-21:

a. For general circulation.
b. For Socialist visitors.
c. For non-Socialist visitors.
d. Replaced a.
e. Not known.

		VG	VF	UNC
18	**1 Won** 1978. Olive-green on m/c unpt. 2 adults and 2 children at ctr. Back purple and m/c; soldier at l., woman w/flowers at ctr., woman at r.			
	a. Red and black serial #. No seal on back.	.25	.75	3.00
	b. Black serial #. Green seal at l. on back.	.20	.60	2.50
	c. Red serial #. Red seal at l. on back.	.20	.60	2.50
	d. Red serial #. Lg. numeral *1* in red guilloche on back.	.20	.60	2.50
	e. Black serial #. Lg. numeral *1* in blue guilloche on back.	.20	.60	2.50

		VG	VF	UNC
19	**5 WON** 1978. Blue-gray on m/c unpt. Worker w/book and gear, and woman w/wheat at ctr. Mt. Gumgang on back.			
	a. Red and black serial #. No seal on back.	.25	.75	3.00
	b. Black serial #. Green seal at l. on back.	.25	.85	3.50
	c. Red serial #. Red seal at l. on back.	.25	.85	3.50
	d. Red serial #. Lg. numeral *5* in red guilloche on back.	.25	.85	3.50
	e. Black serial #. Lg. numeral *5* in blue guilloche on back.	.25	.85	3.50

		VG	VF	UNC
20	**10 WON** 1978. Brown on m/c unpt. Winged equestrian statue "Chonllima" at ctr. Waterfront factory on back.			
	a. Red and black serial #. No seal on back.	.40	1.25	7.50
	b. Black serial #. Green seal at upper r. on back.	.30	1.00	4.00
	c. Red serial #. Red seal at upper r. on back.	.30	1.00	4.00
	d. Red serial #. Lg. numeral *10* in red guilloche on back.	.30	1.00	4.00
	e. Black serial #. Lg. numeral *10* in blue guilloche on back.	.30	1.00	4.00

		VG	VF	UNC
21	**50 WON** 1978. Olive-green on m/c unpt. Soldier w/man holding torch, woman w/wheat, man w/book at ctr. Lake scene on back.			
	a. Red and black serial #. No seal on back.	.50	1.50	6.00
	b. Black serial #. Green seal at lower r. on back.	.35	1.10	4.50
	c. Red serial #. Red seal at lower r. on back.	.35	1.10	4.50
	d. Red serial #. Lg. numeral *50* in red guilloche on back.	.50	1.10	4.50
	e. Black serial #. Lg. numeral *50* in blue guilloche on back.	.50	1.10	4.50

		VG	VF	UNC
22	**100 WON** 1978. Brown on lilac and m/c unpt. Kim Il Sung at ctr. r. House w/trees on back. Red and black serial #. No seal on back.	.75	2.50	10.00

1988 "CAPITALIST VISITOR" ISSUE

#23-26 arms at upper l. on face; red serial #. "Value" backs.

		VG	VF	UNC
23	**1 CHON** 1988. Blue on purple unpt.	.10	.20	.40
24	**5 CHON** 1988. Blue on pink unpt.	.15	.25	.50
25	**10 CHON** 1988. Blue and black on green-yellow unpt.	.20	.40	.75
26	**50 CHON** 1988. Blue on yellow unpt.	.25	.50	1.00

#27-30 dk. green on blue and pink unpt. w/winged equestrian statue "Chonllima" at ctr., arms at upper r. Red serial #.

		VG	VF	UNC
27	**1 WON** 1988.	.30	.75	2.50

		VG	VF	UNC
28	**5 WON** 1988.	.40	1.50	7.50
29	**10 WON** 1988.	.75	3.00	12.50
30	**50 WON** 1988.	1.50	8.00	40.00

1988 "SOCIALIST VISITOR" ISSUE

#31-38 arms at upper r. Denomination on back. Black serial #.

		VG	VF	UNC
31	**1 CHON** 1988. Red-brown on pink and blue unpt.	FV	FV	1.25

		VG	VF	UNC
32	**5 CHON** 1988. Purple on pink and blue unpt.	FV	FV	1.75

		VG	VF	UNC
33	**10 CHON** 1988. Olive-green on pink and blue unpt.	FV	FV	2.50
34	**50 CHON** 1988. Brown-violet on pink and blue unpt.	FV	FV	3.00

#35-38 red on blue and ochre unpt. Temple at ctr., olive sprig on globe at r. Olive sprig on globe on back.

		VG	VF	UNC
35	**1 WON** 1988.	FV	FV	3.50
36	**5 WON** 1988.	FV	FV	12.50
37	**10 WON** 1988.	FV	FV	25.00
38	**50 WON** 1988.	FV	FV	100.00

1992 ISSUE

#39-42 arms at upper l. Wmk: Winged equestrian statue "Chonllima".

		VG	VF	UNC
39	**1 WON** 1992. Grayish olive-green and olive-brown on m/c unpt. Young woman w/flower basket at ctr. r. Mt. Gumgang on back.	FV	FV	1.50

		VG	VF	UNC
40	**5 WON** 1992. Blue-black and deep purple on m/c unpt. Students at ctr. r. w/modern bldg. and factory in background. Palace on back.	FV	FV	4.00

		VG	VF	UNC
41	**10 WON** 1992. Deep brown and red-brown on m/c unpt. Factory worker, winged equestrian statue "Chonllima" at ctr., factories in background at r. Flood gates on back.	FV	FV	6.00

		VG	VF	UNC
42	**50 WON** 1992. Deep brown and deep olive-brown on m/c unpt. Monument to 5 year plan at l. and as wmk., young professionals at ctr. r., arms at upper r. Landscape of pine trees and mountains on back.	FV	FV	25.00

		VG	VF	UNC
43	**100 WON** 1992. Deep brown and brown-violet on m/c unpt. Arms at lower l. ctr., Kim Il Sung at r. Rural home at ctr. on back. Wmk: Arched gateway.	FV	FV	50.00

1998 ISSUE

		VG	VF	UNC
44	**1 WON** 1998.	Expected New Issue		
45	**5 WON** 1998.	—	—	.75
46	**10 WON** 1998.	—	—	1.75
47	**50 WON** 1998.	Expected New Issue		
48	**100 WON** 1998.	Expected New Issue		

		VG	VF	UNC
49 (44)	**500 WON** 1998. Slate gray on lt. blue and purple unpt. Assembly Hall. Back red and black. Suspension bridge.	FV	FV	325.00

COLLECTOR SERIES

KOREAN CENTRAL BANK

1978 ISSUE

		ISSUE PRICE	MKT. VALUE
CS1	**1978 1-100 WON.** Red ovpt. Korean characters for specimen on #18a-21a, 22 (w/all zero serial #).	—	30.00

1992 ISSUE

		ISSUE PRICE	MKT. VALUE
CS2	**1992 1-100 WON.** Red, rectangular ovpt. Korean characters for specimen on #39-43. (39, 42 and 43 w/all zero serial #, 40-41 w/normal serial #).	—	20.00

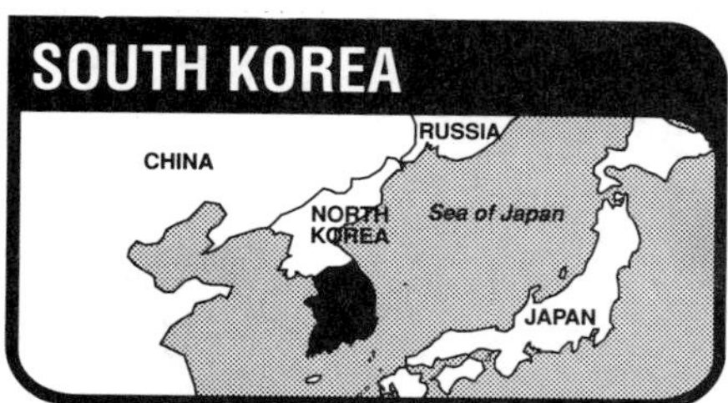

The Republic of Korea, situated in northeastern Asia on the southern half of the Korean peninsula between North Korea and the Korean Strait, has an area of 38,025 sq. mi. (98,484 sq. km.) and a population of 44.61 million. Capital: Seoul. The economy is based on agriculture and textiles. Clothing, plywood and textile products are exported. Japan replaced China as the predominant foreign influence in Korea in 1895 and annexed the peninsular country in 1910. Defeat in World War II brought an end to Japanese rule. U.S. troops entered Korea from the south and Soviet forces entered from the north. The Cairo Conference (1943) had established that Korea should be "free and independent." The Potsdam Conference (1945) set the 38th parallel as the line dividing the occupation forces of the United States and Russia. When Russia refused to permit a U.N. commission designated to supervise reunification elections to enter North Korea, an election was held in South Korea on May 10, 1948. By its determination, the Republic of Korea was inaugurated on Aug. 15, 1948.

MONETARY SYSTEM:

1 Won (Hwan) = 100 Chon
1 new Won = 10 old Hwan, 1962-

DATING:

The modern notes of Korea are dated according to the founding of the first Korean dynasty, that of the house of Tangun, in 2333 BC.

REPUBLIC

BANK OF KOREA

1958-60 ISSUE

Hwan System.

		VG	VF	UNC
25	**1000 HWAN** 4293 (1960); 4294 (1961); 1962. Black on olive unpt. Kg. Sejong the Great at r. Back blue-green and lt. brown; flaming torch at ctr.			
	a. 4293 (1960).	2.50	16.50	125.00
	b. 4294 (1961).	1.50	10.00	75.00
	c. 1962.	1.65	11.00	85.00

1961-62 ISSUE

		VG	VF	UNC
26	**100 HWAN** 1962. Green on orange and m/c unpt. Woman reading to child at r. Archway at l., date at bottom r. margin on back.	12.50	50.00	275.00

		VG	VF	UNC
27	**500 HWAN** 4294 (1961). Blue-green on m/c unpt. Kg. Sejong the Great at r. Back green; bldg. at r. 8-character imprint.	10.00	60.00	450.00

1962 ND Issues

Won System.

		VG	VF	UNC
28	**10 Jeon** 1962. Deep blue on pale blue and pink unpt.	.05	.10	.40

		VG	VF	UNC
29	**50 Jeon** 1962. Black on pale green and ochre unpt. Back brown.	.05	.10	.50

		VG	VF	UNC
30	**1 Won** ND (1962). Violet on brown unpt.	.05	.10	1.00

		VG	VF	UNC
31	**5 Won** ND (1962). Black on gray-green unpt.	.10	.25	2.00

		VG	VF	UNC
32	**10 Won** ND (1962). Brown on green unpt.	.35	1.00	6.00

		VG	VF	UNC
33	**10 Won** 1962-65; ND. Brown on lilac and green unpt. Tower at l. Medieval tortoise warship (and date) at ctr. on back.			
	a. 1962.	2.50	8.00	50.00
	b. 1963.	2.75	8.50	52.50
	c. 1964.	1.50	4.50	28.50
	d. 1965.	1.00	3.00	20.00
	e. ND.	.15	.50	3.00

		VG	VF	UNC
34	**50 Won** ND (1962). Red-brown on blue and lilac unpt. Rock in the sea at l. Torch at ctr. on back.	4.00	12.50	85.00

		VG	VF	UNC
35	**100 Won** 1962-69. Green on olive unpt. Archway at l. Unpt: *100* Won at ctr. Pagoda and date on back.			
	a. 1962.	5.50	16.50	110.00
	b. 1963.	4.50	13.50	80.00
	c. 1964.	4.00	12.50	75.00
	d. 1965.	4.00	12.50	75.00
	e. 1969.	5.00	15.00	90.00

		VG	VF	UNC
36	**100 Won** ND (1962). Green on blue and gold unpt. Archway similar to #35 at l. 5-petaled blossom at ctr. in unpt. Back similar to #34.	2.00	10.00	75.00
37	**500 Won** ND (1962). Blue on lilac and green unpt. Pagoda portal at l. Back similar to #34.	4.00	17.50	110.00

1965; 1966 ND Issue

		VG	VF	UNC
38	**100 Won** ND (1965). Dk. green and blue on m/c unpt. Bank name and denomination in red. Kg. Sejong the Great at r. Bldg. on back.	.65	1.75	5.50

		VG	VF	UNC
38A	**100 WON** ND (1965). Dk. blue-green. Bank name and denomination in maroon. Like #38.	.75	2.25	10.00

		VG	VF	UNC
39	**500 WON** ND (1966). Black on m/c unpt. City gate at l. Medieval tortoise warships on back.	.75	1.50	9.00

1969-73 ND ISSUE

		VG	VF	UNC
40	**50 WON** ND (1969). Black on green and brown unpt. Pavilion at l. Back blue; torch at ctr.	.25	1.00	4.00

		VG	VF	UNC
41	**5000 WON** ND (1972). Brown on green and m/c unpt. Yi I at r. and as wmk. Lg. bldg. on back.	7.50	12.50	40.00

		VG	VF	UNC
42	**10,000 WON** ND (1973). Dk. brown on m/c unpt. Kg. Sejong the Great at l. ctr. Bldgs. and pavilion on back. Wmk: Woman w/headdress.	15.00	25.00	60.00

1973-79 ND ISSUE

		VG	VF	UNC
43	**500 WON** ND (1973). Blue and green on m/c unpt. Adm. Yi Sun-shin at l., medieval tortoise warship at ctr. Bldg. w/steps on back.	FV	1.00	3.50

		VG	VF	UNC
44	**1000 WON** ND (1975). Purple on m/c unpt. Yi Hwang at r. Do-San Academy in black on back. Wmk: Flowers.	FV	2.00	5.00
45	**5000 WON** ND (1977). Brown on m/c unpt. Yi I at r. and as wmk. Sm. bldg. w/steps on back.	FV	8.50	20.00

		VG	VF	UNC
46	**10,000 WON** ND (1979). Black and dk. green on m/c unpt. Monument at l., Kg. Sejong at r. and as wmk. Pavilion at ctr. on back.	FV	20.00	40.00

1983 ND ISSUE

		VG	VF	UNC
47	**1000 WON** ND (1983). Purple on m/c unpt. Yi Hwang at r. and as wmk. One raised colored dot for blind at lower l. Bldgs. in courtyard on back.	FV	FV	4.00

		VG	VF	UNC
48	**5000 WON** ND (1983). Brown on m/c unpt. Yi I at r. and as wmk. Two raised colored dots for blind at lower l. Sm. bldg. w/steps on back.	FV	FV	11.00

		VG	VF	UNC
49	**10,000 WON** ND (1983). Dk. green on m/c unpt. Monument at l; Kg. Sejong at r. and as wmk. Three raised colored dots for blind at lower l. Pavilion at ctr. on back.	FV	FV	22.50
50	**10,000 WON** ND (1994). Like #49 but pale green in wmk. area. Microprinting security features.	FV	FV	20.00

AUXILIARY MILITARY PAYMENT CERTIFICATE COUPONS

Issued to Korean troops in Vietnam to facilitate their use of United States MPC. These coupons could not be used as currency by themselves.

SERIES I

#M1-M8 were issued on Dec. 29, 1969, and were valid only until June or Oct. 7, 1970. Anchor on glove crest. Validation stamp on back. Uniface.

		VG	VF	UNC
M1	**5 CENTS** ND (1969). Maroon, red-brown and yellow ctr. Flowering branch at l., lg. *5* at r.	90.00	225.00	—
M2	**10 CENTS** ND (1969). Dk. blue w/lt. blue-green ctr. Flowers at l., lg. *10* at. r.	90.00	225.00	—
M3	**25 CENTS** ND (1969). Brown and yellow ctr. Flower at l., lg. *25* at r.	—	—	—
M4	**50 CENTS** ND (1969). Green and yellow ctr. Flower at l., lg. *50* at r.	—	—	—
M5	**1 DOLLAR** ND (1969). Brown and yellow ctr. Korean flag at l., lg. *1* at r.	—	—	—
M6	**5 DOLLARS** ND (1969). Blue and turquoise ctr. Flowers at l., lg. *5* at r.	—	—	—
M7	**10 DOLLARS** ND (1969). Brown and yellow ctr. Flowers at l.	—	—	—
M8	**20 DOLLARS** ND (1969). Green and yellow ctr. Flowers at l.	—	—	—

SERIES II

#M9-M16 were issued June (or Oct.) 1970. Anchor symbol ctr., 702 at l., lg. denomination numerals r. Face and back similar.

		VG	VF	UNC
M9	**5 CENTS** ND (1970). Maroon and violet on ochre unpt. Space capsule at l.	20.00	65.00	200.00

		VG	VF	UNC
M10	**10 CENTS** ND (1970). Red and yellow on green paper. Flowers at l. Back red.	30.00	90.00	275.00

		VG	VF	UNC
M11	**25 CENTS** ND (1970). Green and blue. Crown at l.	90.00	225.00	—

		VG	VF	UNC
M12	**50 CENTS** ND (1970). Blue and green. Pottery w/legs at l.	90.00	225.00	—
M13	**1 DOLLAR** ND (1970). Maroon and red on lt. green paper. Torch at l.	—	—	—
M14	**5 DOLLARS** ND (1970). Red, ochre and yellow on lt. blue paper. Holed coin at l.	—	—	—
M15	**10 DOLLARS** ND (1970). Blue on yellow paper. Pagoda at l.	—	—	—
M16	**20 DOLLARS** ND (1970). Green on pink paper. Vignette at l.	—	—	—

Series III

#M17-M24, military symbol in circle at ctr. on face.

		VG	VF	Unc
M17	**5 Cents** ND. Brown and maroon on yellow paper. "5" at l., clam shell and pearl at ctr. Kettle on back.	20.00	65.00	200.00
M18	**10 Cents** ND. Blue w/green tint. "10" at l., snail at ctr. Candle holder on back.	30.00	75.00	275.00

		VG	VF	Unc
M19	**25 Cents** ND. Red. lilac and ochre. "25" at l., crest seal on turtle at r. Back pink; archway at ctr.	90.00	225.00	—
M20	**50 Cents** ND. Green and blue. "50" at l., tiger at ctr. Balancing rock on back.	90.00	225.00	—

		VG	VF	Unc
M21	**1 Dollar** ND. Brown and maroon. Flowers at l. Shrine on back.	—	—	—

		VG	VF	Unc
M22	**5 Dollars** ND. Blue and lt. blue on yellow paper. Bush at l., crest seal on rayed cloud at r. Tower at ctr. on back.	—	—	—
M23	**10 Dollars** ND. Yellow and maroon. Pagoda on face. Turtle boat on back.	—	—	—
M24	**20 Dollars** ND. 2 dragons at ctr. Korean house on back.	—	—	—

Series IV

#M25-M32, Korean warrior at ctr. on face.

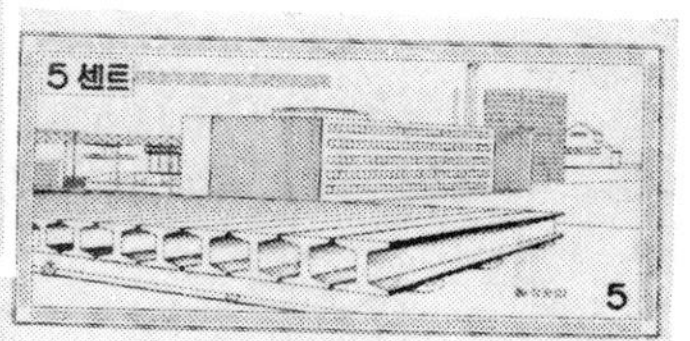

		VG	VF	Unc
M25	**5 Cents** ND. Pink, deep green and lt. blue. Beams and steel mill at ctr. on back.	20.00	40.00	185.00

		VG	VF	Unc
M26	**10 Cents** ND. Deep green on yellow-green. Modern city complex on back. Thick or thin paper.	20.00	40.00	185.00
M27	**25 Cents** ND. Yellow and maroon. 2 bridges on back.	60.00	200.00	—
M28	**50 Cents** ND. Blue-green and maroon. Back blue-green and red; dam.	90.00	225.00	—

		VG	VF	Unc
M29	**1 Dollar** ND. Green on lt. green unpt. Oil refinery on back.	35.00	100.00	250.00

		VG	VF	Unc
M30	**5 Dollars** ND. Brown on gold unpt. Back red-orange; natural gas tank.	350.00	700.00	—

		VG	VF	Unc
M31	**10 Dollars** ND. Pink and green. Back pink and blue; loading area at docks.	60.00	200.00	—
M32	**20 Dollars** ND. Blue and purple. Back green; 4-lane superhighway.	—	—	—

NOTICE

Readers with unlisted dates, signature varieties, etc. are invited to submit photocopies of their notes to: Standard Catalog of World Paper Money, 700 East State St. Iola, WI 54990-0001, fax: 1-715-445-4087, or E-Mail: thernr@krause.com.

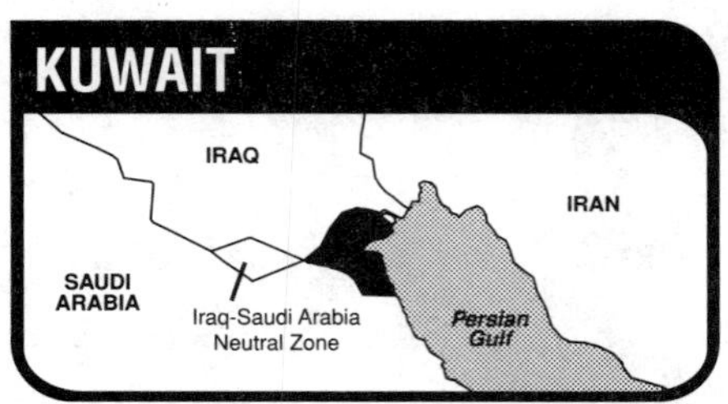

The State of Kuwait, a constitutional monarchy located on the Arabian Peninsula at the northwestern corner of the Persian Gulf, has an area of 6,880 sq. mi. (17,818 sq. km.) and a population of 2.02 million. Capital: Kuwait. Petroleum, the basis of the economy, provides 95 per cent of the exports.

The modern history of Kuwait began with the founding of the men who wandered northward from the region of the Qatar Peninsula of eastern Arabia. Fearing that the Turks would take over the sheikhdom, Shaikh Mubarak entered into an agreement with Great Britain, 1899, placing Kuwait under the protection of Britain and empowering Britain to conduct its foreign affairs. Britain terminated the protectorate on June 19, 1961, giving Kuwait its independence (by a simple exchange of notes) but agreeing to furnish military aid on request.

The Kuwait dinar, one of the world's strongest currencies, is backed 100 percent by gold and foreign exchange holdings.

On Aug. 2, 1990 Iraqi forces invaded and rapidly overran Kuwaiti forces. Annexation by Iraq was declared on Aug. 8. The Kuwaiti government established itself in exile in Saudi Arabia. The United Nations forces attacked on Feb. 24, 1991 and Kuwait City was liberated on Feb. 26. Iraq quickly withdrew remaining forces.

RULERS:

British to 1961
Abdullah, 1961-1965
Sabah Ibn Salim Al Sabah, 1965-1977
Jabir Ibn Ahmad Al Sabah, 1977-

MONETARY SYSTEM:

1 Dinar = 1000 Fils

SIGNATURE VARIETIES					
1	Amir H. Sheik Jaber Al-Ahmad				
	BANK GOVERNOR	FINANCE MINISTER		BANK GOVERNOR	FINANCE MINISTER
2	Hamza Abbas	Abdul Rehman Al Atiquei	3	Hamza Abbas	Abdul Latif Al-Hamad
4	Abdul Wahab Al-Tammar	Ali Khalifa Al-Sabah	5	Abdul Wahab Al-Tammar	Jassem Mohammad Al-Kharafi
6	Salem Abdul Aziz Al-Sabah	Jassem Mohammad Al-Kharafi	7	Salem Abdul Aziz Al-Sabah	
8	Salem Abdul Aziz Al-Sabah				

ST2ATE

Kuwait Currency Board

Law of 1960, 1961 ND Issue

#1-5 Amir Shaikh Abdullah at r. and as wmk. Sign. 1.

		VG	VF	UNC
1	**1/4 Dinar** *L.1960* (1961). Brown on m/c unpt. Aerial view, Port of Kuwait at ctr. on back.	4.00	15.00	37.50

		VG	VF	UNC
2	**1/2 Dinar** *L.1960* (1961). Purple on m/c unpt. School at ctr. on back.	4.50	20.00	70.00

		VG	VF	UNC
3	**1 Dinar** *L.1960* (1961). Red-brown on m/c unpt. Cement plant at ctr. on back.	7.50	30.00	125.00

		VG	VF	UNC
4	**5 Dinars** *L.1960* (1961). Blue on m/c unpt. Street scene on back.	50.00	175.00	450.00

		VG	VF	UNC
5	**10 Dinars** *L.1960* (1961). Green on m/c unpt. Dhow on back.	60.00	200.00	475.00

Central Bank of Kuwait

Law #32 of 1968, First ND Issue

#6-10 Amir Shalkh Sabah at r. and as wmk. Sign. #2.

#	Denomination	VG	VF	UNC
6	**1/4 DINAR** *L.1968.* Brown on m/c unpt. Back similar to #1.	1.00	4.00	18.00

#	Denomination	VG	VF	UNC
7	**1/2 DINAR** *L.1968.* Purple on m/c unpt. Back similar to #2.	1.75	3.50	20.00

#	Denomination	VG	VF	UNC
8	**1 DINAR** *L.1968.* Red-brown and blue on m/c unpt. Oil refinery on back.	3.50	6.00	30.00

#	Denomination	VG	VF	UNC
9	**5 DINARS** *L.1968.* Blue and aqua on m/c unpt. View of Kuwait on back.	12.50	30.00	90.00

#	Denomination	VG	VF	UNC
10	**10 DINARS** *L.1968.* Green and brown on m/c unpt. Back similar to #5.	20.00	50.00	125.00

LAW #32 OF 1968, SECOND ND ISSUE

#11-16 arms at r. Black serial #. #11-15 wmk.: Dhow.

NOTE: During the 1991 war with Iraq, Iraqi forces stole the following groups of notes:

#11 - 1/4 Dinar, Prefix denominators 54-68. #14 - 5 Dinar, Prefix denominators #18-20.

#12 - 1/2 Dinar, Prefix denominators 30-37. #15 - 10 Dinar, Prefix denominators #70-87.

#13 - 1 Dinar, Prefix denominators #47-53. #16 - 20 Dinar, Prefix denominators #9-13.

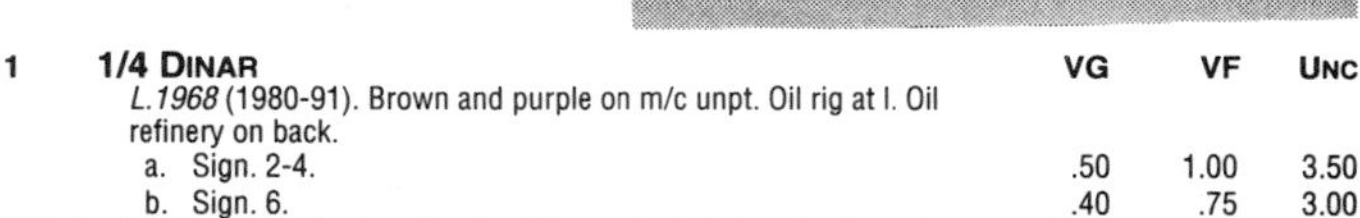

#	Denomination	VG	VF	UNC
11	**1/4 DINAR** *L.1968* (1980-91). Brown and purple on m/c unpt. Oil rig at l. Oil refinery on back.			
	a. Sign. 2-4.	.50	1.00	3.50
	b. Sign. 6.	.40	.75	3.00

NOTE: Contraband stolen by invading Iraqi forces included prefix denominators #54-68.

#	Denomination	VG	VF	UNC
12	**1/2 DINAR** *L.1968* (1980). Purple on m/c unpt. Tower at l. Harbor scene on back.			
	a. Sign. 2-4.	.60	1.25	6.00
	b. Sign. 6.	.50	1.00	4.00

NOTE: Contraband stolen by invading Iraqi forces include prefix denominators #30-37.

#	Denomination	VG	VF	UNC
13	**1 DINAR** *L.1968* (1980-91). Red-violet and purple on on m/c unpt. Modern bldg. at l. Old fortress on back.			
	a. Overall ornate unpt. Sign. 2.	1.00	2.50	12.50
	b. As a. Sign. 3.	.85	2.00	6.50
	c. As a. Sign. 4.	.75	1.75	6.00
	d. Plain colored unpt. at top and bottom. Sign. 6.	.75	1.50	5.50

NOTE: Contraband stolen by invading Iraqi forces include prefix denominators #47-53.

		VG	VF	UNC
14	**5 DINARS** *L.1968* (1980-91). Deep blue and black on m/c unpt. Minaret at l. Lg. bldg. on back.			
	a. Overall ornate unpt. Sign. 2, 4.	3.00	8.00	30.00
	b. Clear margins at top and at bottom. Sign. 6.	2.50	7.00	17.50

NOTE: Contraband stolen by invading Iraqi forces include prefix denominators #18-20.

		VG	VF	UNC
15	**10 DINARS** *L.1968* (1980-91). Green on m/c unpt. Falcon at l. Sailing boat on back.			
	a. Overall ornate unpt. Sign. 2-4.	4.00	10.00	40.00
	b. Clear margins at top and at bottom. Sign. 6.	3.00	8.00	32.50

NOTE: Contraband stolen by invading Iraqi forces include prefix denominators #70-87.

		VG	VF	UNC
16	**20 DINARS** *L.1968* (1986-91). Brown and olive-green on m/c unpt. Bldg. at l. Central Bank at l. ctr. on back. Wmk: Eagle's head.			
	a. Sign. 5.	12.50	35.00	125.00
	b. Sign. 6.	3.00	8.00	32.50

NOTE: Contraband stolen by invading Iraqi forces include prefix denominators #9-13.

LAW #32 OF 1968, 1992 ND POST LIBERATION ISSUE

Note: After the 1991 Gulf War, Kuwait declared all previous note issues worthless.

#17-22 like previous issue. Red serial # at top r. Wmk: Dhow. Sign. 7.

		VG	VF	UNC
17	**1/4 DINAR** *L.1968* (1992). Violet and black on silver and m/c unpt. Back brown on m/c unpt. Like #11.	FV	FV	3.00

		VG	VF	UNC
18	**1/2 DINAR** *L.1968* (1992). Deep blue, blue-green and deep violet on silver and m/c unpt. Like #12.	FV	FV	5.00

		VG	VF	UNC
19	**1 DINAR** *L.1968* (1992). Deep olive-green, green and deep blue on silver and m/c unpt. Like #13.	FV	FV	6.50

		VG	VF	UNC
20	**5 DINARS** *L.1968* (1992). Olive-brown, green and pink on m/c unpt. Like #14.	FV	FV	35.00

		VG	VF	UNC
21	**10 DINARS** *L.1968* (1992). Orange-red, olive-brown on m/c unpt. Like #15. Sign. 7, 8.	FV	FV	62.50

		VG	VF	UNC
22	**20 DINARS** *L.1968* (1992). Violet-brown on m/c unpt. Like #16. Sign. 7, 8.	FV	FV	115.00

LAW #32 OF 1968, 1994 ND ISSUE

#23-28 near value.

#23-28 segmented silver vertical thread at ctr. r. Wmk: Falcon's head. Sign. 8.

		VG	VF	UNC
23	**1/4 DINAR** *L.1968* (1994). Brown, grayish purple and deep orange on m/c unpt. Ship at bottom ctr. r. Girls playing game on back.	FV	FV	2.25

		VG	VF	UNC
24	**1/2 DINAR** *L.1968* (1994). Brown and dk. grayish green on m/c unpt. Souk shops at lower r. Boys playing game on back.	FV	FV	5.00

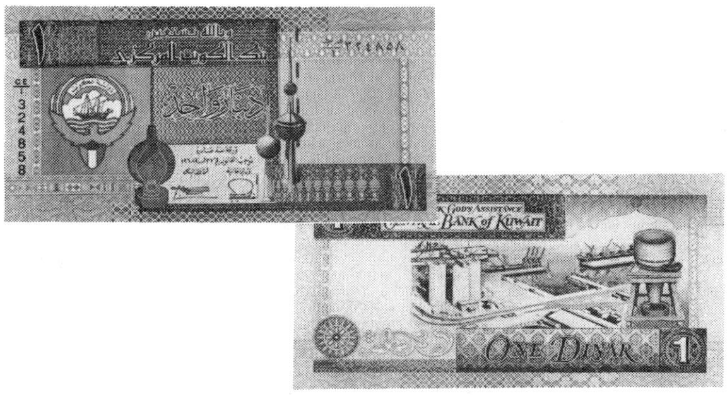

		VG	VF	UNC
25	**1 DINAR** *L.1968* (1994). Deep brown, purple and dk. gray on m/c unpt. Pinnacles at ctr. r. Aerial view of harbor docks on back.	FV	FV	9.00

#26-28 silver foiling of falcon's head at l. ctr.

		VG	VF	UNC
26	**5 DINARS** *L.1968* (1994). Red-violet and grayish green on m/c unpt. Pinnacle at r. Oil refinery at ctr. on back.	FV	FV	28.50

		VG	VF	UNC
27	**10 DINARS** *L.1968* (1994). Purple, violet and dk. brown on m/c unpt. Mosque at lower r. Pearl fisherman at l. ctr., dhow at r. on back.	FV	FV	52.50

NOTE: #23-27 were reported as withdrawn in early 1995 due to the word *Allah* being present.

		VG	VF	UNC
28	**20 DINARS** *L.1968* (1994). Dk. olive-green, orange and olive-brown on m/c unpt. Fortress at lower r. Central bank at bottom l. ctr., old fortress gate, pinnacle at r. on back.	FV	FV	100.00

COLLECTOR SERIES

CENTRAL BANK OF KUWAIT

1993 ISSUE

Note: Issued in special folder for "Second Anniversary of Liberation of Kuwait."

		ISSUE PRICE	MKT. VALUE
CS1	**26.2.1993 1 DINAR** Orange-red, violet-blue and blue. Plastic w/silver on window. Text on back includes: "THIS IS NOT LEGAL TENDER."	—	15.00

The Republic of Kyrgyzstan, independent state since Aug. 31, 1991, is a member of the UN and of the C.I.S. It was the last state of the Union Republics to declare its sovereignty. Capital: Bishkek (formerly Frunze). Population of 4.51 million.

Originally part of the Autonomous Turkestan S.S.R. founded on May 1, 1918, the Kyrgyz ethnic area was established on October 14, 1924 as the Kara-Kirghiz Autonomous Region within the R.S.F.S.R. Then on May 25, 1925 the name Kara (black) was dropped. It became an A.S.S.R. on Feb. 1, 1926 and a Union Republic of the U.S.S.R. in 1936. On Dec. 12, 1990, the name was then changed to the Republic of Kyrgyzstan.

MONETARY SYSTEM:

1 COM = 100 ТЫЙЫН
1 SOM = 100 Tyiyn

REPUBLIC

КЫРГЫЗ РЕСПУБЛИКАСЫ

KYRGYZ REPUBLIC

1993 ND ISSUE

#1-3 bald eagle at ctr. Ornate design at ctr. on back. Wmk: Eagle in repeating pattern.

		VG	VF	UNC
1	**1 TYIYN** ND (1993). Dk. brown on pink and brown-orange unpt.	FV	FV	.75

		VG	VF	UNC
2	**10 TYIYN** ND (1993). Brown on pale green and brown-orange unpt.	FV	FV	.85

		VG	VF	UNC
3	**50 TYIYN** ND (1993). Gray on blue and brown-orange unpt.	FV	FV	1.25

NOTICE

Readers with unlisted dates, signature varieties, etc. are invited to submit photocopies of their notes to: Standard Catalog of World Paper Money, 700 East State St. Iola, WI 54990-0001, fax: 1-715-445-4087, or E-Mail: thernr@krause.com.

КЫРГЫЗСТАН БАНКЫ
KYRGYZSTAN BANK
1993; 1994 ND ISSUE

#4-6 Equestrian statue of Manas the Noble at ctr. r. Manas Mausoleum at l. ctr. on back. Wmk: Eagle in repeating pattern.

4	**1 SOM**	VG	VF	UNC
	ND (1993). Red on m/c unpt.	FV	FV	1.75

5	**5 SOM**	VG	VF	UNC
	ND (1993). Deep grayish green on m/c unpt.	FV	FV	7.50

6	**20 SOM**	VG	VF	UNC
	ND (1993). Purple on m/c unpt.	FV	FV	25.00

КЫРГЫЭ БАНКЫ
KYRGYZ BANK
1994 ND ISSUE

Replacement notes: Serial # prefix *ZZ*.

7	**1 SOM**	VG	VF	UNC
	ND (1994). Brown on yellow and m/c unpt. A. Maldybayev at r. and as wmk. String musical instruments, Bishkek's Philharmonic Society and Manas Architectural Ensemble at l. ctr. on back.	FV	FV	1.35

8	**5 SOM**	VG	VF	UNC
	ND (1994). Dk. blue on yellow and m/c unpt. B. Beishenaliyeva at r. and as wmk. National Opera Theatre at l. ctr. on back.	FV	FV	3.25

		VG	VF	UNC
9	**10 SOM** ND (1994). Green and brown on m/c unpt. Kassim at r. and as wmk. Mountains on back.	FV	FV	5.50
10	**20 SOM** ND (1994). Red-orange on m/c unpt. T. Moldo at r. and as wmk. Manas Mausoleum on back.	FV	FV	6.00
11	**50 SOM** ND (1994). Reddish brown on m/c unpt. Czarina Kurmanjan-datka at r. and as wmk., Uzgen Architectural Ensemble, mausoleum and minaret on back.	FV	FV	12.50
12	**100 SOM** ND (1994). Dk. brown on m/c unpt. Toktogul at r. and as wmk. Hydroelectric Dam at l. ctr. on back.	FV	FV	25.00

1997 ISSUE

Replacement notes: Serial # prefix *XX*.

13	**5 SOM**	VG	VF	UNC
	1997. Dk. blue and violet on m/c unpt. Similar to #8.	FV	FV	1.25

14	**10 SOM**	VG	VF	UNC
	1997. Dk. green, purple and red on m/c unpt. Similar to #9.	FV	FV	3.25

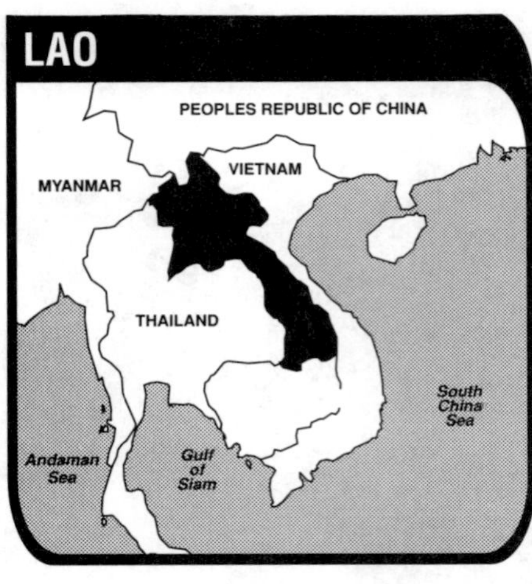

The Lao People's Democratic Republic, located on the Indo-Chinese Peninsula between the Socialist Republic of Vietnam and the Kingdom of Thailand, has an area of 91,429 sq. mi. (236,800 sq. km.) and a population of 5.12 million. Captial: Vientiane. Agriculture employs 95 percent of the people. Tin, lumber and coffee are exported.

The first United Kingdom of Laos was established in the mid-14th century by King Fa Ngum who ruled an area including present Laos, northeastern Thailand, and the southern part of China's Yunnan province from his capital at Luang Prabang. Thailand and Vietnam obtained control over much of the present Lao territory in the 18th century and remained dominant until France established a protectorate over the area in 1893 and incorporated it into the Union of Indo-China. The Independence of Laos was proclaimed in March of 1945, during the last days of the Japanese occupation of World War II. France reoccupied Laos in 1946, and established it as a constitutional monarchy within the French Union in 1949. In 1953, war erupted between the government and the Pathet Lao, a Communist movement supported by the Vietnamese Communist forces. Peace was declared in 1954 with Laos becoming fully independent in 1955 and the Pathet Lao being permitted to occupy two northern provinces. Civil war broke out again in 1960 with the United States supporting the government of the Kingdom of Laos and the North Vietnamese helping the Communist Pathet Lao, and continued, with intervals of truce and political compromise, until the formation of the Lao People's Democratic Republic on Dec. 2, 1975.

RULERS:

Sisavang Vong, 1949-1959
Savang Vatthana, 1959-1975

MONETARY SYSTEM:

1 Kip = 100 At, 1955-1978
1 new Kip = 100 old Kip, 1979-

Kingdom

Banque Nationale du Laos

SIGNATURE VARIETIES		
	LE GOUVERNEUR ຜູ້ອໍານວຍການ	UN CENSEUR (ຜູ້ກວດກາຜູ້ນຶ່ງ)
1		
2		
3		
4		
5		
6		

1962-63 Issue

		VG	VF	Unc
8	**1 Kip** ND (1962). Brown on pink and bue unpt. Stylized figure at l. Tricephalic elephant arms at ctr. on back.			
	a. Sign. 3; 4.	.10	.20	.50
	s. Sign. 3. Specimen.	—	—	75.00

#9; 11-14 wmk: Tricephalic elephant arms.

		VG	VF	Unc
9	**5 Kip** ND (1962). Green on m/c unpt. S. Vong at r. Temple at l., man on elephant at ctr. on back.			
	a. Sign. 2.	4.50	17.50	42.50
	b. Sign. 5.	.15	.35	1.25
	s. As a. Specimen.	—	—	150.00

		VG	VF	Unc
10	**10 Kip** ND (1962). Blue on yellow and green unpt. Woman at l. (like back of Fr. Indochina #102). Stylized sunburst on back (like face of #102). Wmk: Elephant's head.			
	a. Sign. 1.	15.00	75.00	—
	b. Sign. 5.	.15	.35	1.65
	s. As a. Specimen.	—	—	150.00

#11-14 Kg. Savang Vatthana at l. Replacement notes: Serial # prefix *S9* (=*Z9* in English).

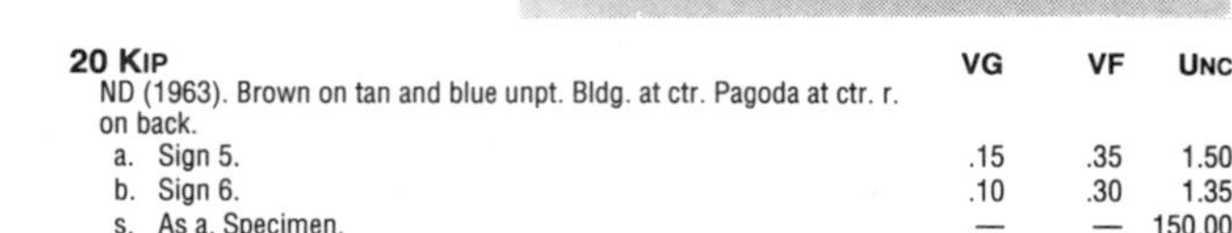

		VG	VF	Unc
11	**20 Kip** ND (1963). Brown on tan and blue unpt. Bldg. at ctr. Pagoda at ctr. r. on back.			
	a. Sign 5.	.15	.35	1.50
	b. Sign 6.	.10	.30	1.35
	s. As a. Specimen.	—	—	150.00

NOTICE

Readers with unlisted dates, signature varieties, etc. are invited to submit photocopies of their notes to: Standard Catalog of World Paper Money, 700 East State St. Iola, WI 54990-0001, fax: 1-715-445-4087, or E-Mail: thernr@krause.com.

12 **50 KIP**

	VG	VF	UNC
ND (1963). Purple on brown and blue unpt. Pagoda at ctr. Back purple; bldg. at r.			
a. Sign. 5; 6.	.10	.25	1.50
s. Sign. 5. Specimen.	—	—	150.00

13 **200 KIP**

	VG	VF	UNC
ND (1963). Blue on green and gold unpt. Temple of That Luang at ctr. Waterfalls on back.			
a. Sign. 4.	.40	1.25	5.00
b. Sign. 6.	.20	.50	2.50
s. As a. Specimen.	—	—	150.00

14 **1000 KIP**

	VG	VF	UNC
ND (1963). Brown on blue and gold unpt. Temple at ctr. 3 long canoes on back.			
a. Sign. 5.	.40	1.00	5.00
b. Sign. 6.	.25	.75	4.25
s. As a. Specimen.	—	—	150.00

1974; 1975 ND ISSUE

15 **10 KIP**

	VG	VF	UNC
ND (1974). Blue on m/c unpt. Kg. Savang Vatthana at ctr. r. Back blue and brown; ox cart. Sign. 6.			
a. Normal serial #. (Not issued).	—	—	125.00
s. Specimen.	—	—	150.00

#16-19 Kg. Savang Vatthana at l. Wmk: Tricephalic elephant arms. Sign. 6.

16 **100 KIP**

	VG	VF	UNC
ND (1974). Brown on blue, green and pink unpt. Pagoda at ctr. Ox cart on back.			
a. Issued note.	.15	.35	1.75
s. Specimen.	—	—	150.00

17 **500 KIP**

	VG	VF	UNC
ND (1974). Red on m/c unpt. Pagoda at ctr. Dam on back.			
a. Issued note.	.20	.65	2.75
s. Specimen.	—	—	150.00

18 **1000 KIP**

	VG	VF	UNC
ND. Black on m/c unpt. Elephant on back.			
a. Normal serial #. (Not issued.)	—	—	150.00
s. Specimen.	—	—	175.00

#	Denomination	VG	VF	UNC
19	**5000 KIP** ND (1975). Blue-gray on m/c unpt. Pagoda at ctr. Musicians w/instruments on back.			
	a. Issued note.	.75	2.25	7.50
	s. Specimen.	—	—	150.00

STATE OF LAOS

PATHET LAO GOVERNMENT

ND ISSUE

#19A-24 printed in Peoples Republic of China and circulated in areas under control of Pathet Lao insurgents. Later these same notes became the accepted legal tender for the entire country.

#	Denomination	VG	VF	UNC
19A	**1 KIP** ND. Green on yellow and blue unpt. Threshing grain at ctr. Medical clinic scene on back.			
	a. Issued note.	—	—	40.00
	s. Specimen.	—	—	150.00

#	Denomination	VG	VF	UNC
20	**10 KIP** ND. Lilac and red on m/c unpt. Medical examination scene. Fighters in the brush on back.			
	a. Wmk: Temples.	.10	.25	1.00
	b. Wmk: 5-pointed stars.	.05	.15	.75
	s. As b. Specimen.	—	—	50.00

#	Denomination	VG	VF	UNC
21	**20 KIP** ND. Brown on lt. green unpt. Rice distribution. Forge workers on back.			
	a. Wmk: Temples.	.10	.25	1.25
	b. Wmk: 5-pointed stars.	.10	.25	1.10
	s. As b. Specimen.	—	—	50.00

#	Denomination	VG	VF	UNC
22	**50 KIP** ND. Purple on m/c unpt. Factory workers. Plowing ox on back.			
	a. Wmk: Temples.	.05	.35	1.65
	b. Wmk: 5-pointed stars.	.10	.25	1.35
	s. As b. Specimen.	—	—	50.00

#	Denomination	VG	VF	UNC
23	**100 KIP** ND. Blue on m/c unpt. Long boats on lake. Scene in textile store on back. Wmk: Temples.			
	a. Issued note.	.10	.35	2.25
	s. Specimen.	—	—	50.00

#	Denomination	VG	VF	UNC
23A	**200 KIP** ND. Green on m/c unpt. Road and trail convoys. Factory scene on back. Wmk: Temples.			
	a. Issued note.	.15	.50	2.75
	s. Specimen.	—	—	50.00
	x. Lithograph counterfeit (1974) on plain paper, w/o serial #. Ho Chi Minh at r. on back.	25.00	75.00	175.00

24 **500 KIP**

ND. Brown on m/c unpt. Armed field workers in farm scene. Soldiers shooting down planes on back. Wmk: Temples.

	VG	VF	UNC
a. Issued note.	.35	1.25	5.00
s. Specimen.	—	—	50.00

LAO PEOPLES DEMOCRATIC REPUBLIC

GOVERNMENT

1979 PROVISIONAL ISSUE

		VG	VF	UNC
24A	**50 KIP ON 500 KIP** ND. New legends and denomination ovpt. on #24. (Not issued).	15.00	100.00	300.00

BANK OF THE LAO PDR

1979 ND; 1988-97 ISSUE

#25-32 wmk: Stars, hammer and sickles.

#25-29 replacement notes: Serial # prefixes *ZA; ZB; ZC*.

25 **1 KIP**

ND (1979). Blue-gray on m/c unpt. Militia unit at l., arms at upper r. Schoolroom scene on back.

	VG	VF	UNC
a. Issued note.	.05	.15	1.00

26 **5 KIP**

ND (1979). Green on m/c unpt. Shoppers at a store, arms at upper r. Logging elephants on back.

	VG	VF	UNC
a. Issued note.	.05	.15	.65
s. Specimen.	—	—	15.00

27 **10 KIP**

ND (1979). Dk. brown on m/c unpt. Lumber mill at l., arms at upper r. Medical scenes on back.

	VG	VF	UNC
a. Issued note.	.10	.20	.60
s. Specimen.	—	—	15.00

28 **20 KIP**

ND (1979). Brown on m/c unpt. Arms at l., tank w/troop column at ctr. Back brown and maroon; textile mill at ctr.

	VG	VF	UNC
a. Issued note.	.10	.20	.75
s. Specimen.	—	—	15.00

29 **50 KIP**

ND (1979). Violet on m/c unpt. Rice planting at l. ctr., arms at upper r. Back red and brown; hydroelectric dam.

	VG	VF	UNC
a. Issued note.	.10	.20	.75
s. Specimen.	—	—	15.00

#30-32 replacement notes: Serial # prefixes *AM; ZL; ZK*.

30 **100 KIP**

ND (1979). Deep blue-green and deep blue on m/c unpt. Grain harvesting at l., arms at upper r. Bridge, storage tanks, and soldier on back.

	VG	VF	UNC
a. Issued note.	FV	FV	1.00
s. Specimen.	—	—	17.50

31 **500 KIP**

1988. Dk. brown, purple and deep blue on m/c unpt. Modern irrigation systems at ctr., arms above. Harvesting fruit at ctr. on back.

	VG	VF	UNC
a. Issued note.	FV	FV	2.00
s. Specimen.	—	—	20.00

		VG	VF	UNC
32	**1000 KIP** 1992-96. Dk. green, deep purple and green on m/c unpt. 3 women at l., temple at ctr. r., arms at upper r. Cattle at ctr. on back. Red serial #.			
	a. W/o security thread. 1992.	FV	FV	4.00
	b. W/security thread. 1994.	FV	FV	3.50
	c. As b. 1995.	FV	FV	3.50
	d. As b. 1996.	FV	FV	3.50
	s. As a. Specimen.	—	—	30.00

#33 and 34 Kaysone Phomvihane at l. and as wmk., arms at upper r.

		VG	VF	UNC
33	**2000 KIP** 1997. Dk. brown and blue-black on m/c unpt. Temple in unpt. at ctr. r. Cement factory at ctr. on back.			
	a. Issued note.	FV	FV	2.25
	s. Specimen.	—	—	25.00

		VG	VF	UNC
34	**5000 KIP** 1997. Black and purple on m/c unpt. Temple in unpt. at ctr. r. Hydroelectric complex at ctr. on back.			
	a. Issued note.	FV	FV	5.00
	s. Specimen.	—	—	25.00

1998 ISSUE

		VG	VF	UNC
35	**1000 KIP** 1998. Dk. green, deep purple and green on m/c unpt. Similar to #32. Red and green serial #. Wmk: Stars, hammer and sickle repeated.			
	a. Issued note.	FV	FV	3.00
	s. Specimen.	—	—	15.00

LATVIA

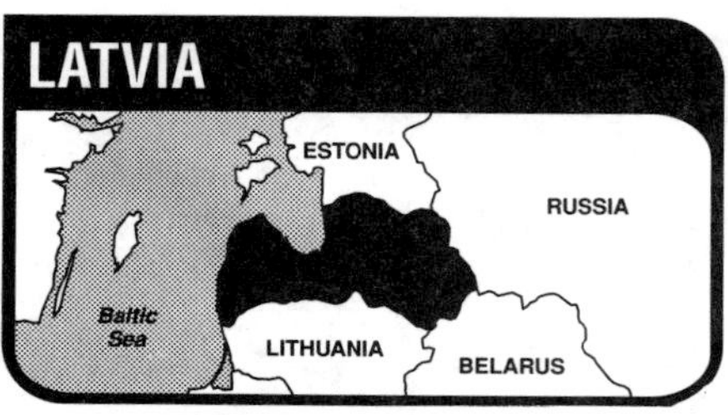

The Republic of Latvia, the central Baltic state in east Europe, has an area of 24,595 sq. mi. (43,601 sq. km.) and a population of 2.48 million. Capital: Riga. Livestock raising and manufacturing are the chief industries. Butter, bacon, fertilizers and telephone equipment are exported.

The Latvians, of Aryan descent, were nomadic tribesmen who settled along the Baltic prior to the 13th century. Lacking a central government, they were easily conquered by the German Teutonic knights, Russia, Sweden and Poland. Following the third partition of Poland by Austria, Prussia and Russia in 1795, Latvia came under Russian domination and did not experience autonomy until the Russian Revolution of 1917 provided an opportunity for freedom. The Latvian republic was established on Nov. 18, 1918. It was occupied by Soviet troops in 1939 and annexed to the Soviet Union in 1940. Following the German occupation of 1941-44, it was retaken by Russia and reestablished as a member S.S. Republic of the Soviet Union. Western countries, including the United States, did not recognize Latvia's incorporation into the Soviet Union. Latvia declared its independence from the former U.S.S.R. on Aug. 22, 1991.

MONETARY SYSTEM:

1 Lats = 100 Santimu, 1923-40; 1992
1 Lats = 200 Rublu, 1993
1 Rublis = 1 Russian Ruble, 1992

REPUBLIC

GOVERNMENT

1992 ISSUE

#35-40 wmk: Symmetrical design.

		VG	VF	UNC
35	**1 RUBLIS** 1992. Violet on yellow and ochre unpt. Back violet-brown on lt. green and yellow unpt.	—	.10	.30

		VG	VF	UNC
36	**2 RUBLI** 1992. Purple on brown-orange and yellow unpt.	—	.10	.35

		VG	VF	UNC
37	**5 RUBLI** 1992. Deep blue on lt. blue and lt. yellow-orange unpt. Back blue-black on blue and lt. blue unpt.	—	.15	.50

38 **10 RUBLU**

1992. Purple on red-orange and pale orange unpt.

VG	VF	UNC
.10	.25	.75

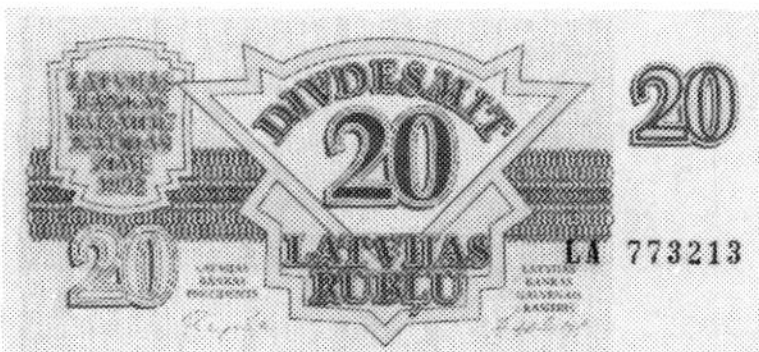

39 **20 RUBLU**

1992. Violet on lilac and pink unpt.

VG	VF	UNC
.15	.60	1.75

40 **50 RUBLU**

1992. Gray-green on lt. blue and pink unpt.

VG	VF	UNC
.20	.85	2.75

41 **200 RUBLU**

1992. Greenish black on yellow and blue-green unpt. Back greenish black on lt. blue and pink unpt.

VG	VF	UNC
.50	2.00	5.00

42 **500 RUBLU**

1992. Violet-brown on gray and dull orange unpt.

VG	VF	UNC
1.35	4.00	10.00

1992 DATED 1993-98 ISSUE

#43-48 Lielvarde woven belt vertically at r. Metalized belt at l., arms at lower r. on back. Wmk: Young woman in national costume.

43 **5 LATI**

1992 (1993). Varied shades of green on tan and pale green unpt. Oak tree at ctr. r. Local art at ctr. on back.

VG	VF	UNC
FV	FV	13.50

44 **10 LATU**

1992 (1993). Violet and purple on m/c unpt. Landscape of Daugava River at ctr. National bow broach at ctr. on back.

VG	VF	UNC
FV	FV	25.00

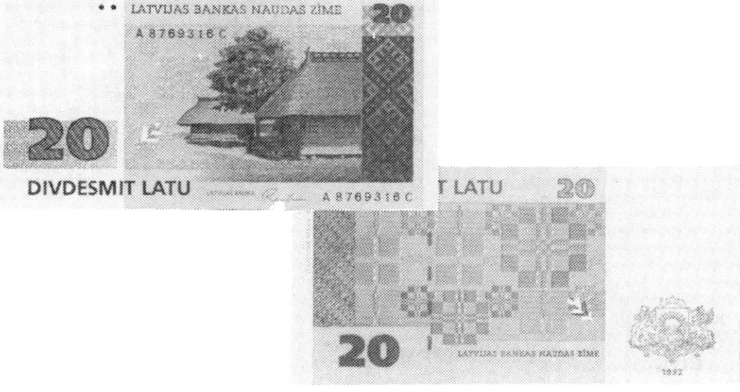

45 **20 LATU**

1992 (1993). Brown and dk. brown on m/c unpt. Rural house at r. National ornamented woven linen at l. ctr. on back.

VG	VF	UNC
FV	FV	47.50

		VG	VF	Unc
46	**50 Latu** 1992 (1994). Deep blue on m/c unpt. Sailing ship at r. Two crossed keys and a cross on back.	FV	FV	115.00

		VG	VF	Unc
47	**100 Latu** 1992 (1994). Red and dk. brown on m/c unpt. K. Barons at r. Ornaments of the woven national belt on back.	FV	FV	225.00

		VG	VF	Unc
48	**500 Latu** 1992 (1998). Purple on m/c unpt. Young woman in national costume at r. Small ornamental brass crowns on back.	FV	FV	750.00

LEBANON

The Republic of Lebanon, situated on the eastern shore of the Mediterranean Sea between Syria and Israel, has an area of 4,015 sq. mi. (10,400 sq. km.) and a population of 3.45 million. Capital: Beirut. The economy is based on agriculture, trade and tourism. Fruit, other foodstuffs and textiles are exported.

Almost at the beginning of recorded history, Lebanon appeared as the well-wooded hinterland of the Phoenicians who exploited its famous forests of cedar. The mountains were a Christian refuge and a Crusader stronghold. Lebanon, the history of which is essentially the same as that of Syria, came under control of the Ottoman Turks early in the 16th century. Following the collapse of the Ottoman Empire after World War I, Lebanon, along with Syria, became a French mandate. The French drew a border around the predominantly Christian Lebanon Sanjak or administrative subdivision and on Sept. 1, 1920 proclaimed the area the State of Grand Lebanon (Etat du Grand Liban), a republic under French control. France announced the independence of Lebanon during WWII after Vichy control was deposed on Nov. 26, 1941. It became fully independent on Jan. 1, 1944, but the last British and French troops did not leave until the end of Aug. 1946.

Since the late 1950's the independent Palestinian movement caused government friction. By 1976 large-scale fighting broke out, which continued thru 1990. In April 1996, Israel staged a 17 day bombardment of the southern areas.

MONETARY SYSTEM

1 Livre (Pound) = 100 Piastres

République Libanaise

1952; 1956 Issue

#55-60 all dated 1st of January. Sign. varieties. Printer: TDLR.

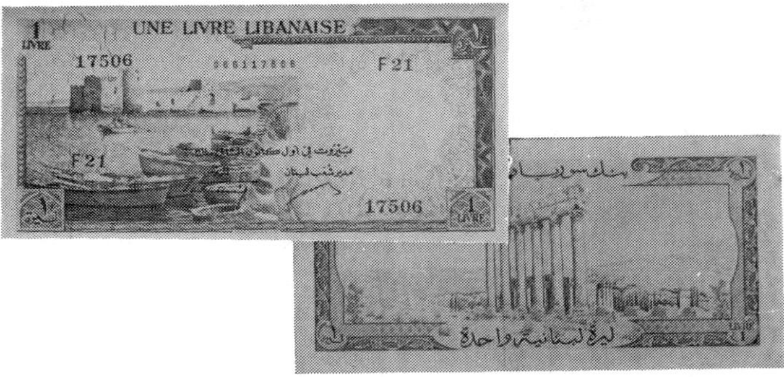

		VG	VF	Unc
55	**1 Livre** 1.1.1952-64. Brown on m/c unpt. Boats at dockside (Saida) at l. Columns of Baalbek on back. W/ or w/o security strip.	.50	5.00	20.00

		VG	VF	Unc
56	**5 Livres** 1.1.1952-64. Blue on m/c unpt. Courtyard of the Palais de Beit-Eddine. Snowy mountains w/trees on back. W/ or w/o security strip.	2.00	17.50	90.00

		VG	VF	Unc
57	**10 Livres** 1.1.1956; 1.1.1961; 1.1.1963. Green on m/c unpt. Ruins of pillared temple. Shoreline w/city in hills on back.	6.00	30.00	135.00

58 **25 LIVRES** 1.1.1952; 1.1.1953. Blue-gray on m/c unpt. Harbor town. stone arch bridge at ctr. r. on back. Wmk: Lion's head.

VG	VF	UNC
30.00	85.00	325.00

59 **50 LIVRES** 1.1.1952; 1.1.1953; 1.1.1964. Deep brown on m/c unpt. Coast landscape. Lg. rock formations in water on back. Wmk: Lion's head.

VG	VF	UNC
45.00	115.00	450.00

60 **100 LIVRES** 1.1.1952; 1.1.1953; 1.1.1958; 1.1.1963. Blue on m/c unpt. View of Beyrouth. Cedar tree at ctr. on back and as wmk.

VG	VF	UNC
12.50	35.00	125.00

REPUBLIC

BANQUE DU LIBAN

1964; 1978 ISSUE

#61-67 printer: TDLR.

61 **1 LIVRE** 1964-80. Brown on lt. blue unpt. Columns of Baalbek. Cavern on back. Wmk: 2 eagles.

	VG	VF	UNC
a. 1964; 1968.	.85	2.50	12.50
b. 1971; 1972; 1973; 1974.	.65	2.00	9.00
c. 1978; 1980.	.40	1.00	3.00

62 **5 LIVRES** 1964-88. Green on blue and lt. yellow unpt. Bldgs. Footbridge at ctr. r. on back. Wmk: Ancient galley.

	VG	VF	UNC
a. 1964.	1.65	5.00	15.00
b. 1967; 1968.	1.00	3.00	11.50
c. 1972; 1974; 1978.	.45	1.25	4.00
d. 1986; 1988.	.10	.25	1.00

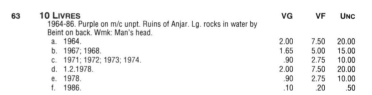

63 **10 LIVRES** 1964-86. Purple on m/c unpt. Ruins of Anjar. Lg. rocks in water by Beint on back. Wmk: Man's head.

	VG	VF	UNC
a. 1964.	2.00	7.50	20.00
b. 1967; 1968.	1.65	5.00	15.00
c. 1971; 1972; 1973; 1974.	.90	2.75	10.00
d. 1.2.1978.	2.00	7.50	20.00
e. 1978.	.90	2.75	10.00
f. 1986.	.10	.20	.50

64 **25 LIVRES** 1964-83. Brown on gold unpt. Citadel on the sea (Saida). Ruin on rocks on back. Wmk: Lion's head.

	VG	VF	UNC
a. 1964; 1967; 1968.	4.00	12.50	35.00
b. 1972; 1973; 1974; 1978.	2.50	8.50	27.50
c. 1983.	.15	.30	1.00

		VG	VF	UNC
65	**50 LIVRES** 1964-88. Dk. gray, purple and dk. olive-green on m/c unpt. Ruins of Temple of Bacchus on face. Bldg. on back. Wmk: Cedar tree.			
	a. 1964; 1967; 1968.	4.50	15.00	45.00
	b. 1972; 1973; 1974; 1978.	3.50	10.00	30.00
	c. Guilloche added above temple ruins w/10-petaled rosette at l. in unpt. Clear wmk. area on back. 1983; 1985.	.25	.30	1.50
	d. W/o control # above ruins on face. 1988.	FV	FV	1.25

		VG	VF	UNC
66	**100 LIVRES** 1964-88. Blue on lt. pink and lt. blue unpt. Palais Beit-Eddine w/inner courtyard. Snowy trees in mountains on back. Wmk: bearded male elder.			
	a. 1964; 1967; 1968.	5.50	13.50	40.00
	b. 1973; 1974; 1977; 1978; 1980.	4.00	8.50	25.00
	c. Guilloche added under bank name on face and back. Clearer wmk. area on back. 1983; 1985.	.15	.60	2.50
	d. W/o control # at upper ctr. 1988.	.10	.30	1.00

		VG	VF	UNC
67	**250 LIVRES** 1978-88. Deep gray-green and blue-black on m/c unpt. Ruins at Tyras on face and back. Wmk: Ancient circular sculpture w/head at ctr. from the Grand Temple Podium.			
	a. 1978.	3.00	16.50	50.00
	b. 1983. Control # at top ctr.	1.25	5.00	15.00
	c. 1985.	.20	1.00	5.00
	d. 1986; 1987.	.15	1.00	4.50
	e. W/o control # above sign. at archway on face. 1986; 1988.	FV	.50	4.00

1988; 1993 ISSUE

Law of 1988

#68 and 69 printer: TDLR.

		VG	VF	UNC
68	**500 LIVRES** 1988. Brown and olive-green on m/c unpt. Beirut city view at ctr. Back brown on m/c unpt.; ruins at l. ctr. Wmk: Lion's head.	.50	.85	2.00

		VG	VF	UNC
69	**1000 LIVRES** 1988; 1990-92. Dk. blue, blue-black and green on m/c unpt. Map at r. Ruins at ctr., modern bldg. at ctr. back. Wmk: Cedar tree.			
	a. 1988.	.85	1.50	3.00
	b. 1990; 1991.	.50	1.00	2.50
	c. 1992.	FV	FV	2.00

		VG	VF	UNC
70	**10,000 LIVRES** 1993. Violet, olive-brown and purple on m/c unpt. Ancient ruins at Tyros at ctr. City ruins w/5 archaic statues on back. Wmk: Ancient circular sculpture w/head at ctr. from the Grand Temple Podium.	FV	FV	17.50

NOTICE

Readers with unlisted dates, signature varieties, etc. are invited to submit photocopies of their notes to: Standard Catalog of World Paper Money, 700 East State St. Iola, WI 54990-0001, fax: 1-715-445-4087, or E-Mail: thernr@krause.com.

1994 ISSUE

#71-74 ornate block designs as unpt. Arabic serial # and matching bar code, #. Wmk: Cedar tree. Printer: BABN.

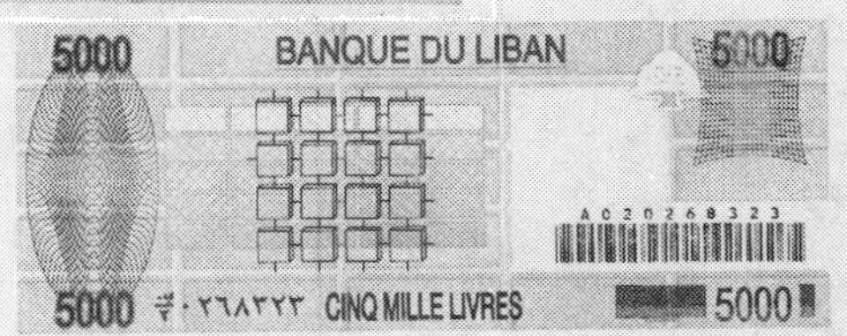

		VG	VF	UNC
71	**5000 LIVRES** 1994; 1995. Red and purple on pink and m/c unpt. Geometric designs on back.			
	a. 1994.	FV	FV	6.50
	b. 1995.	FV	FV	5.50

		VG	VF	UNC
72	**20,000 LIVRES** 1994; 1995. Red-brown and orange on yellow and m/c unpt. Geometric designs w/lg. *LIBAN* l. ctr. on back.	FV	FV	30.00

		VG	VF	UNC
73	**50,000 LIVRES** 1994; 1995. Blue-black and brown-violet on m/c unpt. Cedar tree at upper l., artistic boats at lower l. ctr. Lg. diamond w/BDL at l. ctr., cedar tree at lower l. on back.	FV	FV	70.00

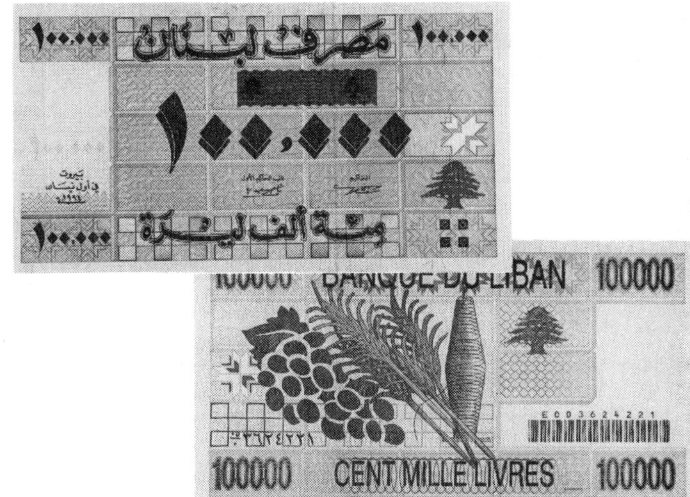

		VG	VF	UNC
74	**100,000 LIVRES** 1994; 1995. Dk. blue-green and dk. green on m/c unpt. Cedar tree at lower r. Artistic bunch of grapes and grain stalks at l. ctr. on back.	FV	FV	100.00

1998 ISSUE

		VG	VF	UNC
75	**10,000 LIVRES** 1998. Green, yellow and orange on m/c unpt. Patrotic Monument, stylized landscape on back. Embedded iridescent planchets in paper.	FV	FV	17.50

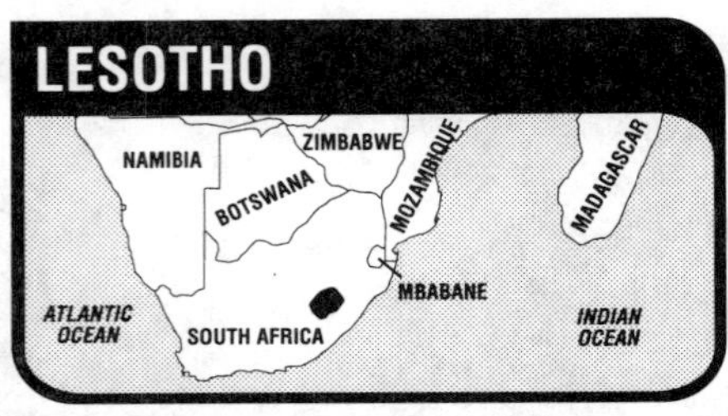

The Kingdom of Lesotho, a constitutional monarchy located within the east-central part of the Republic of South Africa, has an area of 11,716 sq. mi. (30,355 sq. km.) and a population of 2.0 million. Capital: Maseru. The economy is based on subsistence agriculture and livestock raising. Wool, mohair, water through Katse Dam, and cattle are exported. Lesotho (formerly Basutoland) was sparsely populated until the end of the 16th century. Between the 16th and 19th centuries an influx of refugees from tribal wars led to the development of a distinct Basotho group. During the reign of tribal chief Moshoeshoe I (1823-70), a series of wars with the Orange Free State resulted in the loss of large areas of territory to South Africa. Moshoeshoe II appealed to the British for help, and Basutoland was constituted a native state under British protection. In 1871 it was annexed to Cape Colony, but was restored to direct control by the Crown in 1884. From 1884 to 1959 legislative and executive authority was vested in a British High Commissioner. The constitution of 1959 recognized the expressed wish of the people for independence, which was attained on Oct. 4, 1966, when Lesotho became a monarchy under King Moshoeshoe II. Following his death in an automobile accident in Jan. 1996 his eldest son Prince Bereng Seeiso became King Letsie III on Oct. 17, 1997. Lesotho is a member of the Commonwealth of Nations. The king of Lesotho is Chief of State.

RULERS:

King Motlotlehi Moshoeshoe II, 1966-1996
King Letsi III, 1997-

MONETARY SYSTEM:

1 Loti = 100 Lisente

KINGDOM

LESOTHO MONETARY AUTHORITY

1979 ISSUE

#1-3A arms at ctr., military bust of Kg. Moshoeshoe II at r. Wmk: Basotho hat. Sign. 1.
Replacement notes: Partial date given in the 2 numbers of the serial # prefix for #1-8.

		VG	VF	UNC
1	**2 MALOTI** (19)79. Dk. brown on m/c unpt. Bldg. and Lesotho flag at l. on back.			
	a. Blue and brown unpt. at r. of Kg.	1.00	5.00	15.00
	x. Error. Brown unpt. at r. of Kg.	—	—	—

		VG	VF	UNC
2	**5 MALOTI** (19)79. Deep blue on m/c unpt. Craftsmen weaving at l. ctr. on back.	2.50	8.00	25.00

		VG	VF	UNC
3	**10 MALOTI** (19)79. Red and purple on m/c unpt. Basotho horseman in maize field at ctr. on back.	5.50	18.50	95.00

		VG	VF	UNC
3A	**20 MALOTI** (19)79. Herdsmen w/cattle at l. ctr. on back. Printer's specimen. (Not issued.)	—	—	—

CENTRAL BANK OF LESOTHO

SIGNATURE CHART

	Minister of Finance	Governor
1	E.R, Sekhonyana	E.K. Molemohi
2	K. Rakhetla	S. Schoenberg
1985-1988	K. Rakhetla	Mr. E.L. Karlsson
3	E.R. Sekhonyana	Dr. A.M. Maruping
4	E.L. Thoahlane	Dr. A.M. Maruping
5	Dr. L.V. Ketso	Dr. A.M. Maruping

1981; 1984 ISSUE

#4-8 arms at ctr., military bust of Kg. Moshoeshoe II at r. Partial year date given as the denominator of the serial # prefix. Wmk: Basotho hat.

		VG	VF	UNC
4	**2 MALOTI** (19)81; 84. Like #1.			
	a. Sign. 1 (19)81.	1.10	3.00	11.00
	b. Sign. 2 (19)84.	1.00	2.50	10.00

		VG	VF	UNC
5	**5 MALOTI** (19)81. Face like #2. Waterfalls at ctr. on back. Sign 1.	1.50	7.50	32.50

		VG	VF	UNC
6	**10 MALOTI** (19)81. Like #3.			
	a. Sign. 1 (19)81.	3.00	8.50	40.00
	b. Sign. 2 (19)81 (issued 1984).	3.00	6.00	22.50

		VG	VF	UNC
7	**20 MALOTI** (19)81; 84. Dk. green and olive-green on m/c unpt. Mosotho herdsboy w/cattle at l. ctr. on back.			
	a. Sign. 1 (19)81.	6.00	20.00	75.00
	b. Sign. 2 (19)84.	6.00	10.00	32.50

		VG	VF	UNC
8	**50 MALOTI** (19)81. Purple and deep blue on m/c unpt. "Qiloane" mountain at l. on back. Sign. 1.	15.00	50.00	225.00

1989 ISSUE

#9-13 arms at ctr., civilian bust of Kg. Moshoeshoe II in new portr. at r. Designs similar to #4-8 but w/Kg. also as wmk. Sign. 3.

		VG	VF	UNC
9	**2 MALOTI** 1989. Similar to #4.	.75	1.50	2.00

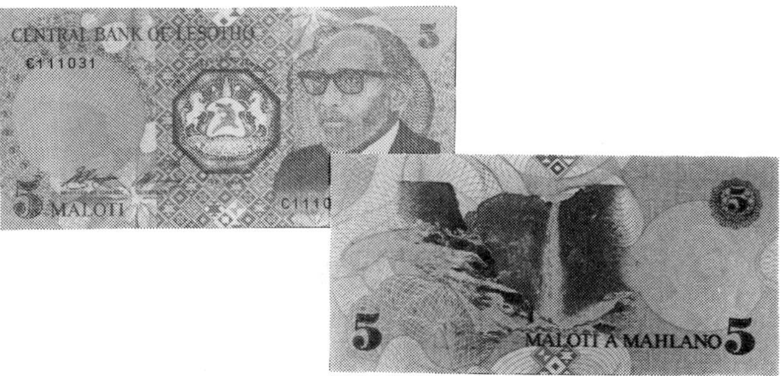

		VG	VF	UNC
10	**5 MALOTI** 1989. Similar to #5.	1.00	2.00	5.00

		VG	VF	UNC
11	**10 MALOTI** 1989; 1990. Similar to #6.	1.00	3.00	8.00

		VG	VF	UNC
12	**20 MALOTI** 1989; 1990. Dk. green and blue-black on m/c unpt. Similar to #7.	FV	6.00	17.50
13	**50 MALOTI** 1989. Purple and deep blue on m/c unpt. Similar to #18.			
	a. Issued note.	10.00	25.00	75.00
	s. Specimen.	—	—	—

1992 ISSUE

		VG	VF	UNC
14	**50 MALOTI** 1992. Purple, dk. olive-green and dk. blue on m/c unpt. Seated Kg. Moshoeshoe I at r. "Qiloane" mountain at l. ctr. on back. Sign. 4.	8.50	15.00	60.00

1994 ISSUE

#15-18 seated Kg. Moshoeshoe II at l., arms at ctr. and as wmk. Sign. 5.

		VG	VF	UNC
15	**20 MALOTI** 1994. Deep olive-green and blue-black on m/c unpt. Mosotho herdsboy w/cattle near huts at ctr. r. on back.	FV	FV	12.50
16	**50 MALOTI** 1994; 1997. Purple, olive-green and dk. blue on m/c unpt. Herdsman on horseback w/pack mule at ctr., "Qiloane" mountain at r. on back.	FV	FV	30.00

		VG	VF	UNC
17	**100 MALOTI** 1994; 1997. Dk. olive-green, orange and brown on m/c unpt. Sheep by shed and home at ctr. r. on back.	FV	FV	50.00

		VG	VF	UNC
18	**200 MALOTI** 1994. Dk. brown, brown and orange on m/c unpt. Herdsman w/sheep on back. Kinogram strip vertically at r.	FV	FV	85.00

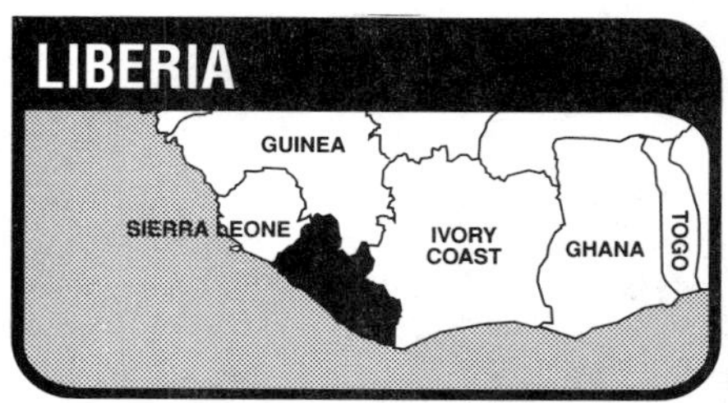

The Republic of Liberia, located on the southern side of the west African bulge between Sierra Leone and the Ivory Coast, has an area of 38,250 sq. mi. (111,369 sq. km.) and a population of 2.6 million. Capital: Monrovia. The major industries are agriculture, mining and lumbering. Iron ore, diamonds, rubber, coffee and cocoa are exported.

The Liberian coast was explored and chartered by Portuguese navigator Pedro de Cintra in 1461. For the following three centuries Portuguese traders visited the area regularly to trade for gold, slaves and pepper. The modern country of Liberia, Africa's first republic, was settled in 1822 by the American Colonization Society as a homeland for American freed slaves, with the U.S. government furnishing funds and assisting in negotiations for procurement of land from the native chiefs. The various settlements united in 1839 to form the Commonwealth of Liberia, and in 1847 established the country as a republic with a constitution modeled after that of the United States.

Notes were issued from 1857 through 1880; thereafter the introduction of dollar notes of the United States took place. U.S. money was declared legal tender in Liberia in 1943, replacing British West African currencies. Not until 1989 was a distinctive Liberian currency again issued.

MONETARY SYSTEM:

1 Dollar = 100 Cents

REPUBLIC

NATIONAL BANK OF LIBERIA

1989 ISSUE

#19 replacement note: Serial # prefix *ZZ*.

		VG	VF	UNC
19	**5 DOLLARS** 12.4.1989. Black and deep green on m/c unpt. Portr. J. J. Roberts at ctr., tapping trees at r. Back deep green on m/c unpt.; National Bank bldg. at ctr. Printer: TDLR.	1.00	2.50	7.00

1991 ISSUE

#20 replacement note: Serial # prefix *ZZ*.

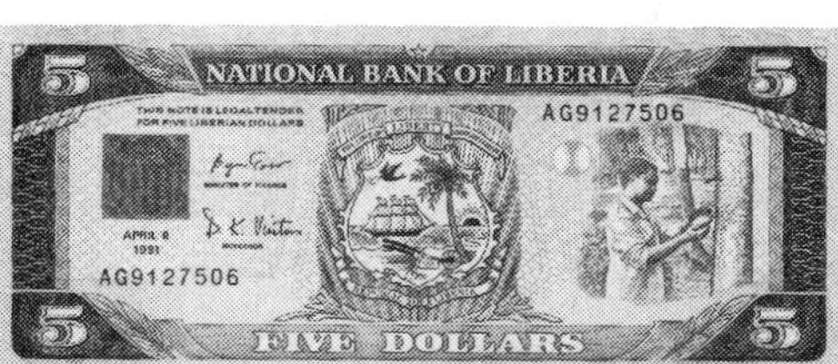

		VG	VF	UNC
20	**5 DOLLARS** 6.4.1991. Similar to #19 but w/arms at ctr. Printer: TDLR.	FV	FV	3.00

1998 ISSUE

		VG	VF	UNC
21	**20 DOLLARS** 1998.		Expected New Issue	
22	**50 DOLLARS** 1998.		Expected New Issue	
23	**100 DOLLARS** 1998.		Expected New Issue	

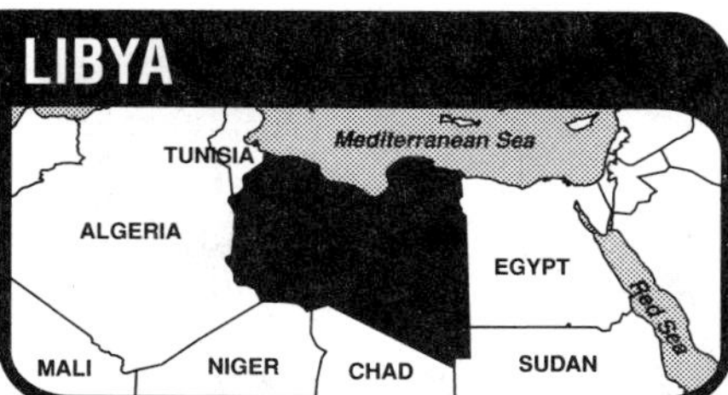

The Socialist People's Libyan Arab Jamahiriya, located on the north central coast of Africa between Tunisia and Egypt, has an area of 679,359 sq. mi. (1,759,540 sq. km.) and a population of 5.59 million. Capital: Tripoli. Crude oil, which accounts for 90 percent of the export earnings, is the mainstay of the economy.

Libya has been subjected to foreign rule throughout most of its history, various parts of it having been ruled by the Phoenicians. Carthaginians, Vandals, Byzantines, Greeks, Romans, Egyptians, and in the following centuries the Arab's language, culture and religion were adopted by the indigenous population. Libya was conquered by the Ottoman Turks in 1553, and remained under Turkish domination, becoming a Turkish vilayet in 1835, until it was conquered by Italy and made into a colony in 1911. The name "Libya", the ancient Greek name for North Africa exclusive of Egypt, was given to the colony by Italy in 1934. Libya came under Allied administration after the fall of Tripoli on Jan. 23, 1943 and was divided into zones of British and French control. On Dec. 24, 1951, in accordance with a United Nations resolution, Libya proclaimed its independence as a constitutional monarchy, thereby becoming the first country to achieve independence through the United Nations. The monarchy was overthrown by a coup d'etat on Sept. 1, 1969, and Libya was established as a republic.

RULERS:

Idris I, 1951-1969

MONETARY SYSTEM:

1 Piastre = 10 Milliemes
1 Pound = 100 Piastres = 1000 Milliemes, 1951-1971
1 Dinar = 1000 Dirhams, 1971-

CONSTITUTIONAL MONARCHY

BANK OF LIBYA

LAW OF 5.2.1963 - FIRST ISSUE

Pound System

#23-27 crowned arms at l. Wmk: Arms.

		VG	VF	UNC
23	**1/4 POUND** *L.1963/AH1382*. Red on m/c unpt.	3.50	15.00	100.00
24	**1/2 POUND** *L.1963/AH1382*. Purple on m/c unpt.	5.00	25.00	125.00
25	**1 POUND** *L.1963/AH1382*. Blue on m/c unpt.	8.00	35.00	250.00

		VG	VF	UNC
26	**5 POUNDS** *L.1963/AH1382*. Green on m/c unpt.	15.00	85.00	—

		VG	VF	UNC
27	**10 POUNDS** *L.1963/AH1382.* Brown on m/c unpt.	20.00	120.00	—

LAW OF 5.2.1963 - SECOND ISSUE

#28-32 crowned arms at l. Reduced size notes. Wmk: Arms.

		VG	VF	UNC
28	**1/4 POUND** *L.1963/AH1382.* Red on m/c unpt.	4.00	17.50	150.00
29	**1/2 POUND** *L.1963/AH1832.* Purple on m/c unpt.	5.00	27.50	200.00
30	**1 POUND** *L.1963/AH1382.* Blue on m/c unpt.	7.00	35.00	275.00

		VG	VF	UNC
31	**5 POUNDS** *L.1963/AH1382.* Green on m/c unpt.	15.00	65.00	400.00
32	**10 POUNDS** *L.1963/AH1382.* Brown on m/c unpt.	25.00	100.00	700.00

SOCIALIST PEOPLES REPUBLIC

CENTRAL BANK OF LIBYA

SIGNATURE VARIETIES			
1	[signature]	2	[signature]
3	[signature]	4	[signature]

1971 ISSUE

Dinar System

#33-37 w/ or w/o Arabic inscription at lower r. on face. Wmk: Arms (Heraldic eagle).

		VG	VF	UNC
33	**1/4 DINAR** ND. Orange-brown on m/c unpt. Arms at l. Doorway on back.			
	a. W/o inscription (1971).	5.00	20.00	140.00
	b. W/ inscription (1972).	1.00	3.50	30.00

		VG	VF	UNC
34	**1/2 DINAR** ND. Purple on m/c unpt. Arms at l. Oil refinery on back.			
	a. W/o inscription (1971).	7.50	35.00	220.00
	b. W/inscription (1972).	2.00	5.00	40.00

		VG	VF	UNC
35	**1 DINAR** ND. Blue on m/c unpt. Gate and minaret at l. Hilltop on back.			
	a. W/o inscription (1971).	10.00	40.00	375.00
	b. W/ inscription (1972).	3.00	7.50	60.00

36	5 DINARS	VG	VF	UNC
	ND. Olive on m/c unpt. Arms at l. Fortress at ctr. on back.			
	a. W/o inscription (1971).	20.00	65.00	400.00
	b. W/ inscription (1972).	5.00	15.00	140.00

37	10 DINARS	VG	VF	UNC
	ND. Blue-gray on m/c unpt. Omar El Mukhtar at l. 3 horsemen at ctr. on back.			
	a. W/o inscription (1971).	35.00	100.00	575.00
	b. W/ inscription (1972).	4.00	12.50	90.00

#38-42 ***Deleted.*** **See #33b-37b.**

1980; 1981 ISSUE

#42A-46 wmk: Heraldic falcon.

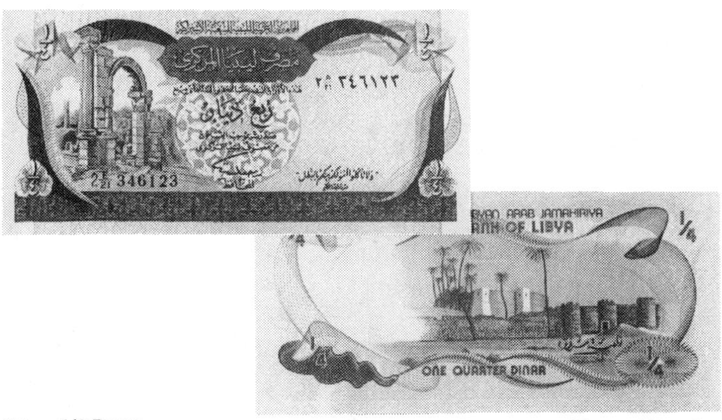

42A	1/4 DINAR	VG	VF	UNC
	ND (1981). Green on m/c unpt. Ruins at l. Fortress and palms at ctr. r. on back.			
	a. Sign. 1.	.45	1.75	6.00
	b. Sign. 2.	.40	1.50	4.50

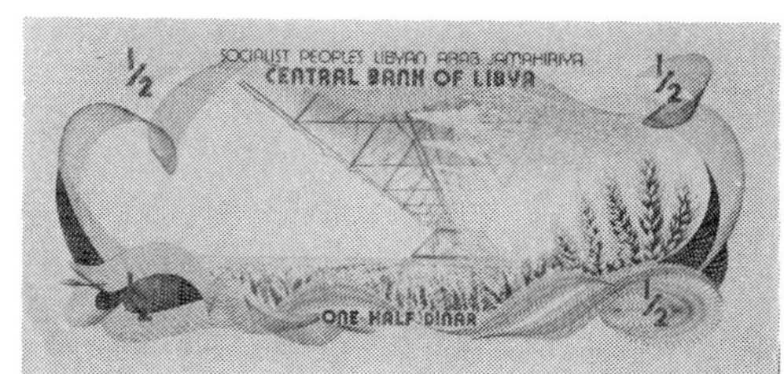

43	1/2 DINAR	VG	VF	UNC
	ND (1981). Green on m/c unpt. Petroleum refinery at l. Irrigation system above wheat field on back.			
	a. Sign. 1.	.75	3.00	7.50
	b. Sign. 2.	.50	2.25	6.00

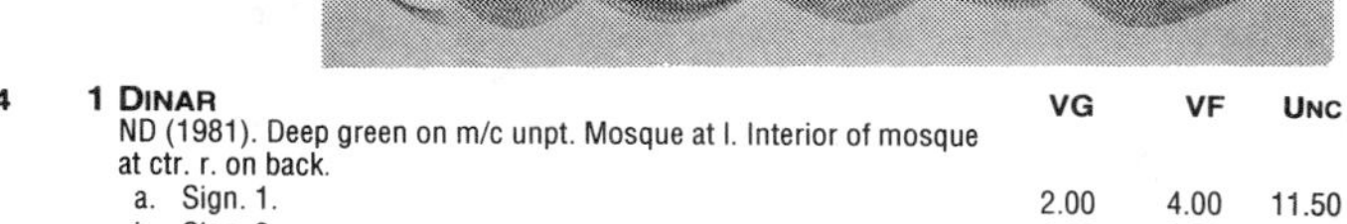

44	1 DINAR	VG	VF	UNC
	ND (1981). Deep green on m/c unpt. Mosque at l. Interior of mosque at ctr. r. on back.			
	a. Sign. 1.	2.00	4.00	11.50
	b. Sign. 2.	1.65	3.00	10.00

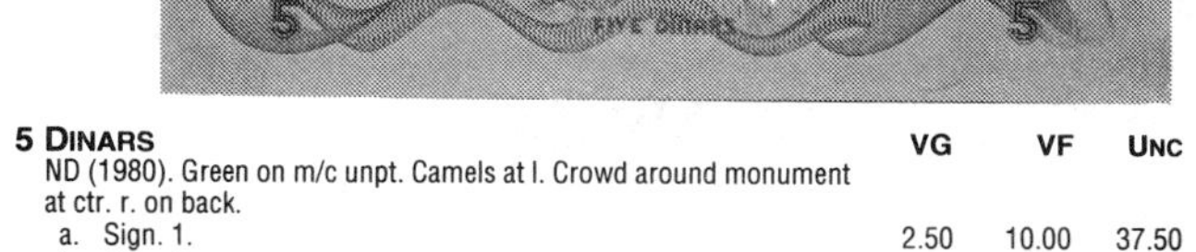

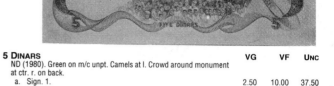

45	5 DINARS	VG	VF	UNC
	ND (1980). Green on m/c unpt. Camels at l. Crowd around monument at ctr. r. on back.			
	a. Sign. 1.	2.50	10.00	37.50
	b. Sign. 2.	2.25	9.00	20.00

		VG	VF	UNC
46	**10 DINARS** ND (1980). Green on m/c unpt. Omar El Mukhtar at l. Lg. crowd below hilltop fortress at ctr. on back.			
	a. Sign. 1.	5.50	22.00	85.00
	b. Sign. 2.	5.00	20.00	45.00

1984 ISSUE

#47-51 designs generally similar to previous issue. Sign. 2.

		VG	VF	UNC
47	**1/4 DINAR** ND (1984). Green and brown on m/c unpt. Similar to #42A.	FV	1.50	4.00

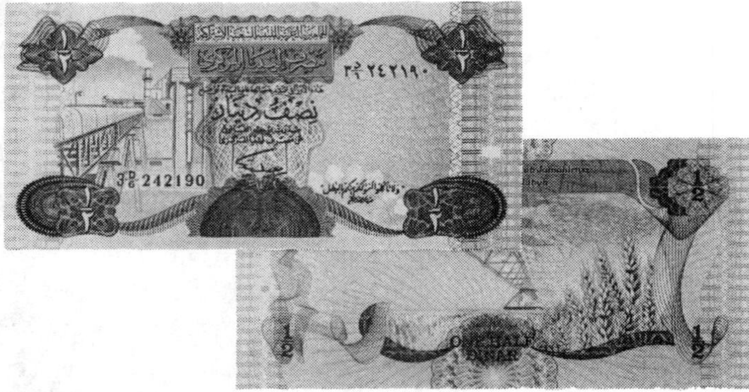

		VG	VF	UNC
48	**1/2 DINAR** ND (1984). Green and purple on m/c unpt. Similar to #43.	FV	2.00	4.00

		VG	VF	UNC
49	**1 DINAR** ND (1984). Green and dk. blue on m/c unpt. Similar to #44.	FV	4.00	12.50

		VG	VF	UNC
50	**5 DINARS** ND (1984). Dk. green and lt. green on m/c unpt. Similar to #45.	FV	8.50	25.00

		VG	VF	UNC
51	**10 DINARS** ND (1984). Dk. green on m/c unpt. Similar to #46.	FV	15.00	40.00

1988-90 ISSUE

#52-58 wmk: Heraldic falcon. Sign. 3.

		VG	VF	UNC
52	**1/4 DINAR** ND (ca.1990). Green, blue and black on m/c unpt. Ruins at ctr. Back brown; English text at top, fortress w/palm trees at l. ctr. Design features similar to #47.	FV	1.00	2.00

NOTICE

Readers with unlisted dates, signature varieties, etc. are invited to submit photocopies of their notes to: Standard Catalog of World Paper Money, 700 East State St. Iola, WI 54990-0001, fax: 1-715-445-4087, or E-Mail: thernr@krause.com.

53 **1/2 DINAR** VG VF UNC
ND (ca.1990). Deep purple and blue on m/c unpt. Oil refinery at l ctr. Back purple; English text at top, irrigation system at l. ctr. Similar to #48. FV 1.75 3.00

54 **1 DINAR** VG VF UNC
ND (1988). Blue and green on m/c unpt. M. Kadaffy at l. ctr. Temple at lower ctr. r. on back. FV 2.00 7.50

55 **5 DINARS**
ND (ca.1991). Gray and violet on m/c unpt. Camel at ctr. Crowd and monument on back. English text at top. FV 7.50 22.50

56 **10 DINARS**
ND (1989). Green on m/c unpt. Omar el-Mukhtar at l. Arabic text; lg. crowd before hilltop fortress at ctr. Octagonal frame w/o unpt. at upper r. on back. FV 14.00 40.00

1991-93 ISSUE

57 **1/4 DINAR** VG VF UNC
ND (ca.1991). Green, blue and black on m/c unpt. Like #52, but w/all Arabic text on back. More pink in unpt. on face.
a. Sign. 3. FV FV 4.00
b. Sign. 4. FV FV 3.00

58 **1/2 DINAR** VG VF UNC
ND (ca. 1991). Deep purple and blue on m/c unpt. Like #53, but w/all Arabic text on back. More pinkish unpt. at upper corners.
a. Sign. 3. FV FV 3.00
b. Sign. 4. FV FV 3.00

59 **1 DINAR** VG VF UNC
ND (1993). Blue and green on m/c unpt. Like #54, but w/modified green and pink unpt.
a. Sign. 4. FV FV 4.50
b. Sign. 5. FV FV 4.00

60 **5 DINARS** VG VF UNC
ND (ca. 1991). Gray and violet on m/c unpt. Like #55, but w/all Arabic text on back.
a. Sign. 3. FV FV 15.00
b. Sign. 4. FV FV 14.00
c. Sign. 5. FV FV 12.50

61 **10 DINARS** VG VF UNC
ND (1991). Green on m/c unpt. Like #56, but w/unpt. in octagonal frame at upper r. on back. Sign. 4; 5. FV FV 37.50

The Republic of Lithuania (formally the Lithuanian Soviet Federated Socialist Republic), southernmost of the Baltic states in east Europe, has an area of 26,173 sq. mi. (65,201 sq. km.) and a population of 3.72 million. Capital: Vilnius. The economy is based on livestock raising and manufacturing. Hogs, cattle, hides and electric motors are exported.

Lithuania emerged as a grand duchy joined to Poland through the Lublin Union in 1569. In the 15th century it was a major power of central Europe, stretching from the Baltic to the Black Sea. Following the third partition of Poland by Austria, Prussia and Russia, 1795, Lithuania came under Russian domination and did not regain its independence until shortly before the end of World War I when it declared itself a sovereign republic. The republic was occupied by Soviet troops in June of 1940 and annexed to the U.S.S.R. Following the German occupation of 1941-44, it was retaken by Russia and reestablished as a member republic of the Soviet Union. Western countries, including the United States, did not recognize Lithuania's incorporation into the Soviet Union.

Lithuania declared its independence March 11, 1990, and it was recognized by the United States on Sept. 2, 1991, followed by the Soviet government in Moscow on Sept. 6. It was seated in the UN General Assembly on Sept. 17, 1991.

MONETARY SYSTEM:

1 Litas = 100 Centu

REPUBLIC

LIETUVOS BANKAS

BANK OF LITHUANIA

1991 ISSUE

Talonas System

#29-31 plants on face, arms at ctr. in gray on back. W/ and w/o counterfeiting clause at bottom. Wmk. paper.

		VG	VF	UNC
29	**0.10 TALONAS** 1991. Brown on green and gold unpt.			
	a. W/o 3 lines of black text at ctr.	.05	.15	.35
	b. W/3 lines of black text at ctr.	.05	.10	.25
	x. Error. As b. but w/ text: *PAGAL ISTATYMA* repeated.	1.00	2.50	5.00

		VG	VF	UNC
30	**0.20 TALONAS** 1991. Lilac on green and gold unpt. W/3 lines of black text at ctr.	.05	.10	.25

		VG	VF	UNC
31	**0.50 TALONAS** 1991. Blue-green on green and gold unpt.			
	a. W/o 3 lines of black text at ctr.	.10	.20	.50
	b. W/3 lines of black text at ctr.	.05	.15	.25
	x1. As b. but first word of text: *VALSTYBINIS.* (error).	1.00	2.50	7.50
	x2. As x1 but w/inverted text. (contemporary fake).	—	—	—

#32-38 value w/plants at ctr., arms in gray at r. Animals or birds on back. Wmk: Lg. squarish diamond w/symbol of the republic throughout paper. W/ and w/o counterfeiting clause at bottom of face.

		VG	VF	UNC
32	**1 (TALONAS)** 1991. Brown on yellow-gold unpt. Numeral w/cranberry branch at ctr. 2 lizards on back.			
	a. W/o text.	.10	.20	.50
	b. W/ text.	.10	.20	.50

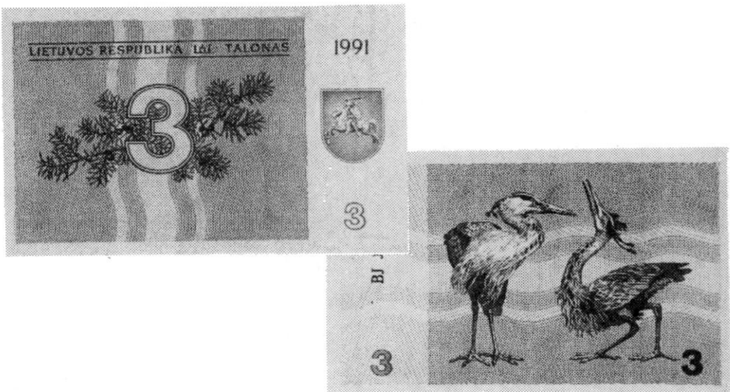

		VG	VF	UNC
33	**3 (TALONU)** 1991. Dk. green and gray on blue-green, ochre and brown unpt. Numeral w/juniper branch at ctr. 2 birds (pewits) on back.			
	a. W/o text.	.10	.20	.50
	b. W/ text.	.10	.20	.50

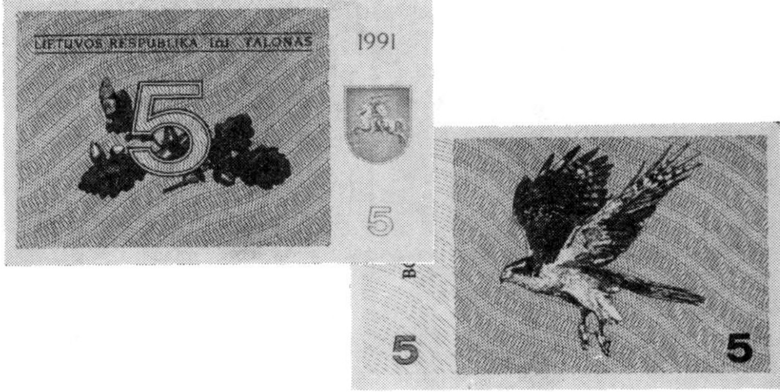

		VG	VF	UNC
34	**5 (TALONU)** 1991. Dk. purple and gray on blue and gray unpt. Numeral w/oak tree branch at ctr. Hawk at ctr. on back.			
	a. W/o text.	.75	1.25	3.50
	b. W/ text.	.50	.75	1.00

		VG	VF	UNC
35	**10 (TALONU)** 1991. Brown on pinkish unpt. Numerals w/walnut tree branch at ctr. 2 martens on back.			
	a. W/o text.	.50	1.35	4.00
	b. W/ text.	.50	1.00	2.00

		VG	VF	UNC
36	**25 (TALONU)** 1991. Purplish gray on blue and orange unpt. Numerals w/pine tree branch at ctr. Lynx on back.			
	a. W/o text.	3.00	8.00	15.00
	b. W/ text.	.40	1.00	3.00

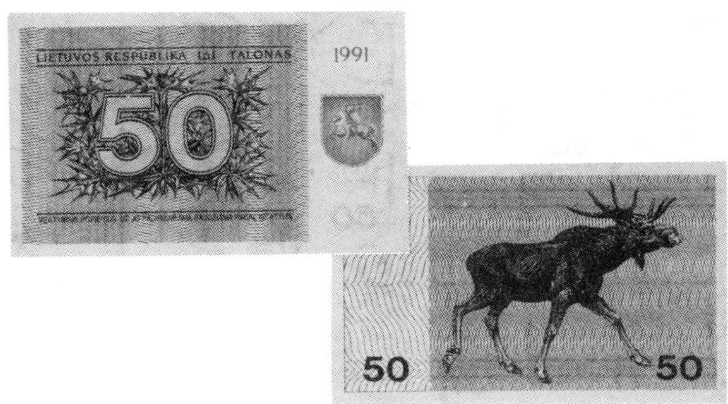

		VG	VF	UNC
37	**50 (TALONU)** 1991. Green and orange on orange unpt. Numerals w/seashore plant at ctr. Moose on back.			
	a. W/o text.	1.50	4.50	10.00
	b. W/ text.	.50	1.00	3.00

		VG	VF	UNC
38	**100 (TALONU)** 1991. Green and brown on brown unpt. Numerals and dandelions at ctr. European bison on back.			
	a. W/o text.	1.50	5.00	12.00
	b. W/ text.	.50	1.50	4.00

1992 ISSUE

#39-44 value on plant at ctr., shield of arms at r. on face. Wmk. as #32-38. Smaller size than #32-38.

		VG	VF	UNC
39	**1 (TALONAS)** 1992. Brown on orange and ochre unpt., dk. brown shield. 2 birds on back.	.05	.10	.20

		VG	VF	UNC
40	**10 (TALONU)** 1992. Brown on tan and ochre unpt., gray shield. Nest w/birds on back.	.10	.25	.75

		VG	VF	UNC
41	**50 (TALONU)** 1992. Dk. grayish green on lt. green and gray unpt., dk. gray-green shield. 2 birds on back.	1.00	2.00	6.00

		VG	VF	UNC
42	**100 (TALONU)** 1992. Grayish purple on blue and red-orange unpt., gray shield. 2 martens on back.	.10	.35	1.00

		VG	VF	UNC
43	**200 (TALONU)** 1992. Dk. brown on red and brown unpt., gray shield. 2 elk on back.			
	a. Issued note.	.40	1.00	3.00
	x. Error. W/o gray shield at r.	—	—	—

		VG	VF	UNC
44	**500 (TALONU)** 1992. Brown-violet on blue unpt., brown shield. Bear on back.	1.00	2.25	5.00

1993 ISSUE

#45 and 46 arms in brown at l., value w/branches at ctr. Animals on back. Wmk: Pattern repeated, circle w/design inside.

		VG	VF	UNC
45	**200 TALONU** 1993. Brown and red on blue unpt. 2 elk on back.	.65	1.75	4.00

		VG	VF	UNC
46	**500 TALONU** 1993. Brown on blue and brown unpt. 2 wolves on back.	.20	.65	1.50

NOTE: #46 was withdrawn after 6 weeks.

1991 DATED ISSUE (1993)

Litu System

#47-49 arms "Vytis" at upper r. on back and as wmk. Printer: USBNC (w/o imprint).

		VG	VF	UNC
47	**10 LITU** 1991 (1993). Brownish black and brown on tan unpt. Aviators S. Darius and S. Girénas at ctr. Monoplane "Lituanica" at upper ctr. on back.			
	a. *GIRENAS* name w/o accent on E (error).	FV	4.00	11.00
	b. *GIRÉNAS* name w/accent on E.	FV	3.00	8.00

		VG	VF	UNC
48	**20 LITU** 1991 (1993). Dk. brown and green on violet and tan unpt. J. Maironis at r. Liberty at l., Museum of History in Kaunas at ctr. on back.	FV	7.00	15.00

		VG	VF	UNC
49	**50 LITU** 1991 (1993). Yellowish black and brown on ochre and tan unpt. J. Basanavicius at r. Cathedral at Vilnius at l. on back.	FV	13.50	25.00

		VG	VF	UNC
50	**100 LITU** 1991 (1993). Deep green, blue and brown on m/c unpt. Arms "Vytis" at ctr., S. Daukantas at r. Aerial view of University of Vilnius at l. ctr. on back.	FV	25.00	70.00
51	**500 LITU** 1991. Arms "Vytis" at ctr., V. Kudirka at r. Liberty bell on back. (Not issued).	—	—	—
52	**1000 LITU** 1991. Arms "Vytis" at ctr., M. Ciurlionis at r. 2 people on back. (Not issued).	—	—	—

1993; 1994 ISSUE

#53-58 wmk: Arms "Vytis." Shield w/"Vytis" at ctr. r. on back. Printer: TDLR (w/o imprint).

		VG	VF	UNC
53	**1 LITAS** 1994. Black and dk. brown on orange and m/c unpt. J. Zemaite at r. Old church at l. on back.			
	a. Issued note.	FV	FV	1.25
	b. Uncut sheet of 40.	—	—	25.00

		VG	VF	UNC
54	**2 LITAI** 1993. Black and dk. green on pale green and m/c unpt. Samogitian Bishop M. Valancius at r. Trakai castle at l. on back.			
	a. Issued note.	FV	FV	2.50
	b. Uncut sheet of 40.	—	—	50.00

		VG	VF	UNC
55	**5 LITAI** 1993. Purple, violet and dk. blue-green on m/c unpt. J. Jablonskis at ctr. r. Mother and daughter at spinning wheel at l. ctr. on back.			
	a. Issued note.	FV	FV	3.50
	b. Uncut sheet of 40.	—	—	100.00

		VG	VF	UNC
56	**10 LITU** 1993. Dk. blue, dk. green, and brown-violet on m/c unpt. Similar to #47 but pilots at r.	FV	FV	8.00

		VG	VF	UNC
57	**20 LITU** 1993. Dk. brown, purple and deep blue-green on m/c unpt. Similar to #48.	FV	FV	12.50
58	**50 LITU** 1993. Dk. brown, red-brown and blue-black on m/c unpt. Similar to #49.	FV	FV	22.50

1997-98 ISSUE

#59-63 printer: G&D (w/o imprint).

		VG	VF	UNC
59	**10 LITU** 1997. Dk. blue, dk. green and brown-violet on m/c unpt. Like #56 but w/1 sign. Wmk: Arms "Vytis".	FV	FV	7.50

		VG	VF	UNC
60	**20 LITU** 1997. Dk. brown, purple and deep green on m/c unpt. Like #57 but w/1 sign. Wmk: J. Maironis.	FV	FV	10.00

		VG	VF	UNC
61	**50 LITU** 1998. Brown and green on ochre and m/c unpt. J. Basanavicius at r. Cathedral and bell tower at Vilnius on back.	FV	FV	18.00
62	**100 LITU** Similar to #58.			Expected New Issue

		VG	VF	UNC
63 (61)	**200 LITU** 1997. Dk. blue on blue and m/c unpt. Vydúnas at r., "Vytis" at lower l. ctr. Klaipéda Lighthouse at l. on back.	FV	FV	65.00

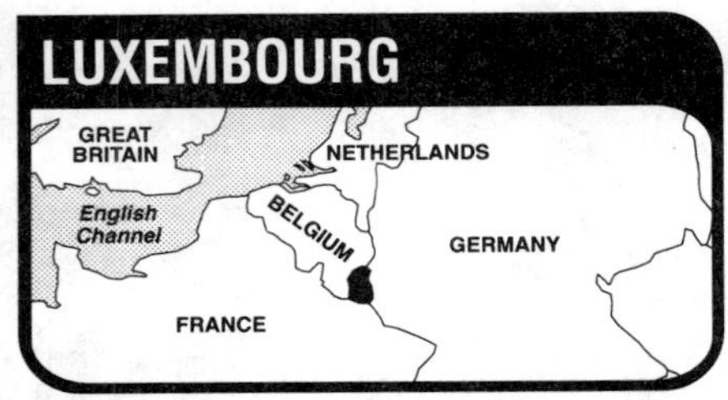

The Grand Duchy of Luxembourg is located in western Europe between Belgium, Germany and France. It has an area of 998 sq. mi. (2,586 sq. km.) and a population of 418,300. Capital: Luxembourg. The economy is based on steel - Luxembourg's per capita production of 16 tons is the highest in the world.

Founded about 963, Luxembourg was a prominent country of the Holy Roman Empire; one of its sovereigns became Holy Roman Emperor as Henry VII, 1308. After being made a duchy by Emperor Charles IV, 1534, Luxembourg passed under the domination of Burgundy, Spain, Austria and France in 1443-1815. It regained autonomy under the Treaty of Vienna, 1815, as a grand duchy in union with the Netherlands, though ostensibly a member of the German Confederation. When Belgium seceded from the Kingdom of the Netherlands, in 1830, Luxembourg was forced to cede its greater western section to Belgium. The tiny duchy left the German Confederation in 1867 when the Treaty of London recognized it as an independent state and guaranteed its perpetual neutrality. Luxembourg was occupied by Germany and liberated by American forces in both world wars.

RULERS:

Charlotte, 1919-1964
Jean, 1964-

MONETARY SYSTEM:

1 Franc = 100 Centimes

GRAND DUCHY

BANQUE INTERNATIONALE A LUXEMBOURG

INTERNATIONAL BANK IN LUXEMBOURG

1968 ISSUE

		VG	VF	UNC
14	**100 FRANCS** 1.5.1968. Green-blue and blue on m/c unpt. Tower at l., Portr. Grand Duke Jean at r. Steelworks and dam on back. Wmk: *BIL*. Printer: F-CO.	1.25	4.00	15.00

1981 ISSUE

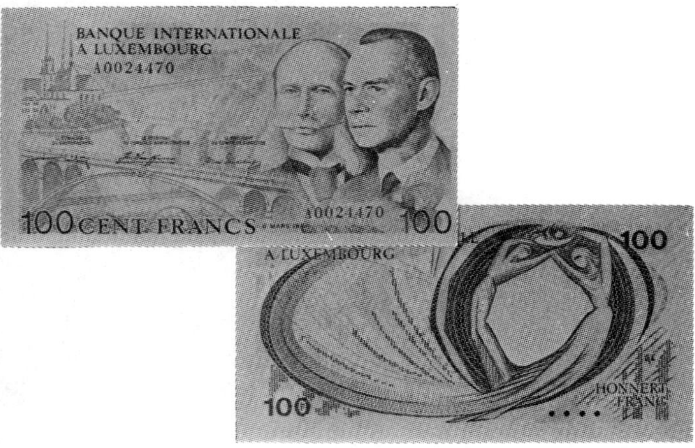

		VG	VF	UNC
14A	**100 FRANCS** 8.3.1981. Brown and tan on m/c unpt. Bridge to Luxembourg City at l., Grand Duke Jean at r., Henry in background. Back purple on m/c unpt; 2 stylized female figures swirling around wmk. area. Wmk: *BIL*.	1.00	3.50	12.50

GRAND DUCHÉ DE LUXEMBOURG

1961; 1963 ISSUE

#51 and 52 Grand Duchess Charlotte at r.

		VG	VF	UNC
51	**50 FRANCS** 6.2.1961. Brown on m/c unpt. Landscape w/combine harvester on back.			
	a. Issued note.	2.00	4.00	10.00
	s. Specimen, punched hole cancelled.	—	—	45.00
52	**100 FRANCS** 18.9.1963. Red-brown on m/c unpt. Hydroelectric dam on back.			
	a. Issued note.	5.00	10.00	30.00
	s. Specimen, punched hole cancelled.	—	—	65.00

1966-72 ISSUE

#53-56 Grand Duke Jean at l. ctr.

		VG	VF	UNC
53	**10 FRANCS** 20.3.1967. Green on m/c unpt. Grand Duchess Charlotte Bridge in city on back.			
	a. Issued note.	.75	2.25	5.00
	s. Specimen, punched hole cancelled.	—	—	25.00

		VG	VF	UNC
54	**20 FRANCS** 7.3.1966. Blue on m/c unpt. Moselle River w/dam and lock on back.			
	a. Issued note.	1.00	2.25	5.50
	s. Specimen, punched hole cancelled.	—	—	35.00

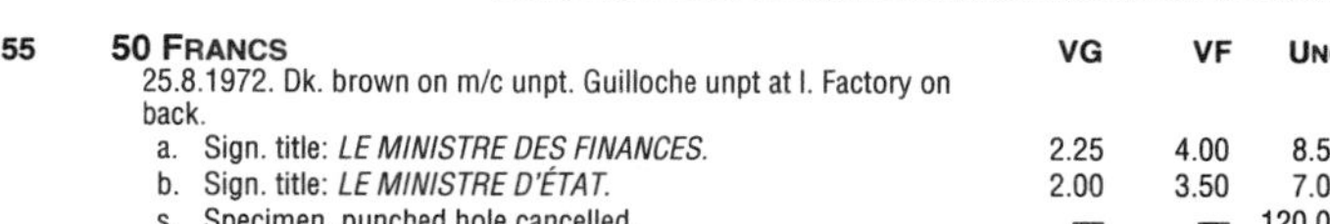

55	50 FRANCS	VG	VF	UNC
	25.8.1972. Dk. brown on m/c unpt. Guilloche unpt at l. Factory on back.			
	a. Sign. title: *LE MINISTRE DES FINANCES.*	2.25	4.00	8.50
	b. Sign. title: *LE MINISTRE D'ÉTAT.*	2.00	3.50	7.00
	s. Specimen, punched hole cancelled.	—	—	120.00

56	100 FRANCS	VG	VF	UNC
	15.7.1970. Red on m/c unpt. View of Adolphe Bridge on back.			
	a. Issued note.	FV	4.00	12.50
	s. Specimen, punched hole cancelled.	—	—	50.00

1980 ISSUE

57	100 FRANCS	VG	VF	UNC
	14.8.1980. Brownish red on m/c unpt. Grand Duke Jean at ctr. r., bldg. at l. Back gold and red; city of Luxembourg scene. Sign. varieties.	FV	4.50	7.50

INSTITUT MONETAIRE LUXEMBOURGEOIS

SIGNATURE VARIETIES			
MINISTRE DU TRESOR			
1	J. Poos	2	J. Santer

1985-93 ND ISSUE

#58-60 Grand Duke Jean at ctr. r. and as wmk.

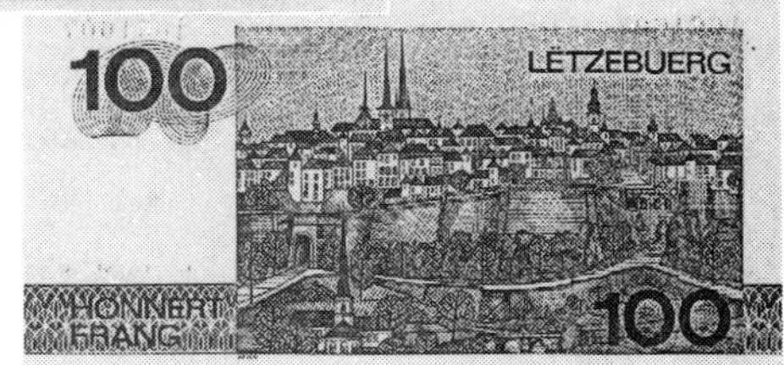

58	100 FRANCS	VG	VF	UNC
	ND (1986). Red on m/c unpt. Like #57, but w/new issuer's name.			
	a. W/o © symbol. Sign. 1. Series A-K.	FV	FV	6.50
	b. W/© symbol. Sign. 2. Series L-.	FV	FV	4.50

59	1000 FRANCS	VG	VF	UNC
	ND (1985). Brown on m/c unpt. Castle of Vianden at l., Grand Duke Jean at ctr. Bldg. sketches at ctr. r. on back.	FV	FV	45.00

60	5000 FRANCS	VG	VF	UNC
	ND(1993; 1996). Green, orange and olive-green on brown and m/c unpt. Chateau de Clevaux at l. 17th century map, European Center at Luxembourg-Kirchberg at ctr. r. on back. 2 sign. varieties.			
	a. Serial # prefix A. ND.	FV	200.00	300.00
	b. Serial # Prefix B. 10.1996.	FV	FV	225.00

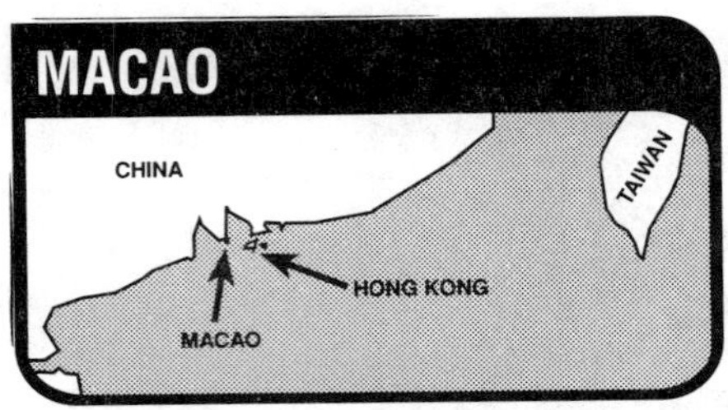

The Province of Macao, a Portuguese overseas province located in the South China Sea 35 miles southwest of Hong Kong, consists of the peninsula and the islands of Taipa and Coloane. It has an area of 6 sq. mi. (16. sq. km.) and a population of 433,000. Capital: Macao. Macao's economy is based on tourism, gambling, commerce and gold trading - Macao is one of the few entirely free markets for gold in the world. Cement, textiles, vegetable oils and metal products are exported.

Established by the Portuguese in 1557, Macao is the oldest European settlement in the Far East. The Chinese, while agreeing to Portuguese settlement, did not recognize Portuguese sovereign rights and the Portuguese remained largely under control of the Chinese until 1849, when the Portuguese abolished the Chinese custom house and declared the independence of the port. The Manchu government formally recognized the Portuguese right to "perpetual occupation" of Macao in 1887, but its boundaries are still not delimited. In Mar. 1940 the Japanese army demanded recognition of the nearby "puppet" government at Changshan. In Sept. 1943 they demanded installation of their "advisors" in lieu of a military occupation.

Macao became a special administrative area under The Peoples Republic of China on Dec. 20, 1999.

RULERS:
Portuguese

MONETARY SYSTEM:
1 Pataca = 100 Avos

PORTUGUESE INFLUENCE

BANCO NACIONAL ULTRAMARINO

大西洋國海外滙理銀行

Ta Hsi Yang Kuo Hai Wai Hui Li Yin Hang

1963-68 ISSUE

#49, 50, and 52 portr. Bishop D. Belchior Carneiro at lower r. and as wmk. Bank seal w/sailing ship at l. Woman and sailing ships at ctr. on back. Printer: BWC.

49	5 PATACAS	VG	VF	UNC
	21.3.1968. Brown on m/c unpt. Sign. varieties.			
	a. Issued note.	4.50	15.00	60.00
	s. Specimen.	—	—	110.00

50	10 PATACAS	VG	VF	UNC
	8.4.1963. Deep blue-violet on m/c unpt. Sign. varieties.			
	a. Issued note.	4.00	12.50	50.00
	s. Specimen.	—	—	120.00

51	100 PATACAS	VG	VF	UNC
	1.8.1966. Brown on m/c unpt. Portr. M. de Arriaga Brum da Silveira at r. Arms at l., flag atop archway at ctr. on back. Printer: TDLR.			
	a. Issued note.	50.00	235.00	800.00
	s. Specimen.	—	—	650.00

52	500 PATACAS	VG	VF	UNC
	8.4.1963. Green on m/c unpt.			
	a. Issued note.	100.00	225.00	650.00
	s. Specimen.	—	—	450.00

1973 ISSUE

53	100 PATACAS	VG	VF	UNC
	13.12.1973. Deep blue-violet on m/c unpt. Ruins of S. Paulo Cathedral at r. and as wmk. Junk at l., bank seal w/sailing ship at ctr. on back. Sign. titles: *GOVERNADOR and ADMINISTRADOR* above signs.			
	a. Issued note.	40.00	125.00	400.00
	s. Specimen.	—	—	350.00

1976-79 ISSUE

#54-57 w/text: *CONSELHO DE GESTAO* at ctr.

54	5 PATACAS	VG	VF	UNC
	18.11.1976. Brown on m/c unpt. Like #49. Sign. varieties.			
	a. Issued note.	2.50	10.00	40.00
	s. Specimen.	—	—	100.00

55	10 PATACAS	VG	VF	UNC
	7.12.1977. Deep blue-violet on m/c unpt. Like #50.			
	a. Issued note.	2.50	10.00	40.00
	s. Specimen.	—	—	120.00

NOTICE

Readers with unlisted dates, signature varieties, etc. are invited to submit photocopies of their notes to: Standard Catalog of World Paper Money, 700 East State St. Iola, WI 54990-0001, fax: 1-715-445-4087, or E-Mail: thernr@krause.com.

		VG	VF	UNC
56	**50 PATACAS** 1.9.1976. Greenish-gray on m/c unpt. Portr. L. de Camoes at r. Bank seal w/sailing ship at l., woman and sailing ships at ctr. on back.			
	a. Issued note.	30.00	90.00	300.00
	s. Specimen.	—	—	225.00

		VG	VF	UNC
57	**100 PATACAS** 8.6.1979. Blue on m/c unpt. Like #53. Sign. title: *PRESIDENTE* at l. sign.			
	a. Issued note.	35.00	110.00	450.00
	s. Specimen.	—	—	350.00
57A	**500 PATACAS** 24.4.1979. Green on m/c unpt. Like #52.			
	a. Issued note.	100.00	250.00	500.00
	s. Specimen.	—	—	500.00

1981; 1988 ISSUE

#58-62 bank seal w/sailing ship at l., 19th century harbor scene on back.

		VG	VF	UNC
58	**5 PATACAS** 8.8.1981. Green on m/c unpt. Temple at r.			
	a. W/sign. title: *PRESIDENTE* at l.	1.65	5.00	15.00
	b. W/o sign. title: *PRESIDENTE* at l. 2 sign. varieties.	1.35	4.00	12.00
	s. As b. Specimen.	—	—	80.00

		VG	VF	UNC
59	**10 PATACAS** 8.8.1981; 12.5.1984. Brown on m/c unpt. Lighthouse w/flag at r.			
	a. W/sign. title: *PRESIDENTE* at l.	3.00	9.00	27.50
	b. W/sign. title: *VICE-PRESIDENTE* at l.	2.00	6.00	18.00
	c. W/o sign. title at l. 2 sign. varieties.	1.65	5.00	15.00
	d. 3 decrees at upper l. 12.5.1984.	1.35	4.00	12.00
	s1. As a. Specimen.	—	—	100.00
	s2. As d. Specimen.	—	—	80.00

		VG	VF	UNC
60	**50 PATACAS** 8.8.1981. Purple on m/c unpt. Portr. L. de Camoes at r. and as wmk.			
	a. W/sign. title: *PRESIDENTE* at l.	10.00	17.50	60.00
	b. W/o sign. title: *PRESIDENTE* at l.	6.50	13.50	40.00
	s1. As a. Specimen.	—	—	150.00
	s2. As b. Specimen.	—	—	130.00

		VG	VF	UNC
61	**100 PATACAS** 1981; 1984. Blue and purple on m/c unpt. Portr. C. Pessanha at r.			
	a. W/sign. title: *PRESIDENTE* at l. 8.8.1981; 12.5.1984.	13.50	18.50	55.00
	b. W/o sign. title: *PRESIDENTE* at l. 8.8.1981; 12.5.1984.	13.00	16.50	35.00
	s1. As a. Specimen.	—	—	200.00
	s2. As b. Specimen.	—	—	175.00

		VG	VF	UNC
62	**500 PATACAS** 1981; 1984. Olive-green on m/c unpt. Portr. V. de Morais at r. Peninsula on back.			
	a. 8.8.1981. 2 sign. varieties.	65.00	85.00	250.00
	b. 12.5.1984.	67.50	90.00	300.00
	s1. As a. Specimen.	—	—	350.00
	s2. As b. Specimen.	—	—	350.00

63 **1000 PATACAS**
1988. Brown and yellow-orange on m/c unpt. Stylized dragon at r. Modern view of bridge to Macao on back.

	VG	VF	UNC
a. Issued note.	130.00	175.00	450.00
b. Specimen.	—	—	600.00

1988 COMMEMORATIVE ISSUE

#64, 35th Anniversary Grand Prix

64 **10 PATACAS**
11.26-27.1988 (- old date 1984). Black ovpt. at l. on face, at ctr. on back of #59a.

	VG	VF	UNC
	3.00	10.00	25.00

1990-96 ISSUE

#65-69 bank seal w/sailing ship at l., bridge and city view on back. Wmk: Junk.

65 **10 PATACAS**
8.7.1991. Brown and olive-green on m/c unpt. Bldg. at r.

	VG	VF	UNC
a. Issued note.	FV	4.00	7.50
s. Specimen.	—	—	150.00

66 **20 PATACAS**
1.9.1996. Lilac and purple on lt. green and m/c unpt. B.N.U. bldg. at r., facing dragons in border at l. and r.

	VG	VF	UNC
a. Issued note.	FV	FV	8.50
s. Specimen.	—	—	250.00

67 **50 PATACAS**
13.7.1992. Olive-brown on m/c unpt. Holiday marcher w/dragon costume at ctr. r., man at r.

	VG	VF	UNC
a. Issued note.	FV	FV	22.50
s. Specimen.	—	—	300.00

68 **100 PATACAS**
13.7.1992. Black on m/c unpt. Early painting of settlement at ctr., junk at r.

	VG	VF	UNC
a. Issued note.	FV	FV	30.00
s. Specimen.	—	—	400.00

69 **500 PATACAS**
3.9.1990. Olive-green on m/c unpt. Bldg. at r. 2 sign. varieties.

	VG	VF	UNC
a. Issued note.	FV	FV	120.00
s. Specimen.	—	—	500.00

70 **1000 PATACAS**
8.7.1991. Brown and yellow-orange on m/c unpt. Like #63. 2 sign. varieties.

	VG	VF	UNC
a. Issued note.	FV	FV	200.00
s. Specimen.	—	—	500.00

BANCO DA CHINA

中國銀行

Chung Kuo Yin Hang

1995; 1996 ISSUE

#90-95 Bank of China-Macao bldg. at l., lotus blossom at lower ctr. on back. Wmk: Lotus blossom(s).

		VG	VF	UNC
90	**10 PATACAS** 16.10.1995. Dk. brown and deep green on m/c unpt. Farel de Guia lighthouse at r.	FV	FV	5.50

		VG	VF	UNC
91	**20 PATACAS** 1.9.1996. Purple and violet on m/c unpt. Ama Temple at r.	FV	FV	7.50

		VG	VF	UNC
92	**50 PATACAS** 16.10.1995. Black, dk. brown and brown on m/c unpt. University of Macao at r.	FV	FV	17.50

		VG	VF	UNC
93	**100 PATACAS** 16.10.1995. Black, brown and purple on m/c unpt. New terminal of Port Exterior at r.	FV	FV	32.50

		VG	VF	UNC
94	**500 PATACAS** 16.10.1995. Dk. green and dk. blue on m/c unpt. Ponte de Amizade bridge at r.	FV	FV	100.00

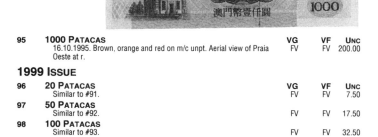

		VG	VF	UNC
95	**1000 PATACAS** 16.10.1995. Brown, orange and red on m/c unpt. Aerial view of Praia Oeste at r.	FV	FV	200.00

1999 ISSUE

		VG	VF	UNC
96	**20 PATACAS** Similar to #91.	FV	FV	7.50
97	**50 PATACAS** Similar to #92.	FV	FV	17.50
98	**100 PATACAS** Similar to #93.	FV	FV	32.50
99	**500 PATACAS** Similar to #94.	FV	FV	100.00
100	**1000 PATACAS** Similar to #95.	FV	FV	200.00

The Republic of Macedonia is land-locked, and is bordered in the north by Yugoslavia, to the east by Bulgaria, in the south by Greece and to the west by Albania. It has an area of 9,923 sq. mi. (25,713 sq. km.) and its population at the 1991 census was 2,038,847, of which the predominating ethnic groups were Macedonians. The capital is Skopje.

The Slavs, settled in Macedonia since the 6th century, who had been Christianized by Byzantium, were conquered by the non-Slav Bulgars in the 7th century and in the 9th century formed a Macedo-Bulgarian empire, the western part of which survived until Byzantine conquest in 1014. In the 14th century it fell to Serbia, and in 1355 to the Ottomans. After the Balkan Wars of 1912-13 Turkey was ousted, and Serbia received the greater part of the territory, the balance going to Bulgaria and Greece. In 1918, Yugoslav Macedonia was incorporated into Serbia as "South Serbia," becoming a republic in the S.F.R. of Yugoslavia. Claims to the historical Macedonian territory have long been a source of contention between Bulgaria and Greece.

On Nov. 20, 1991 parliament promulgated a new constitution, and declared its independence on Nov. 20, 1992 and was admitted to the UN on April 8, 1993.

MONETARY SYSTEM:

1 ДЕНАР (Denar) = 100 ДЕНИ (Deni)

REPUBLIC

НАРОДНА БАНКА НА МАКЕДОНИЈА

NATIONAL BANK OF MACEDONIA

1992 ISSUE

#1-8 wmk. paper.

#1-6 farmers harvesting at l. Ilenden monument in Krushevo at l. on back.

		VG	VF	UNC
1	**10 (DENAR)** 1992. Pale blue on lilac unpt.	.10	.20	.75

		VG	VF	UNC
2	**25 (DENAR)** 1992. Red on lilac unpt.	.10	.20	1.00

		VG	VF	UNC
3	**50 (DENAR)** 1992. Brown on ochre unpt.	.10	.20	1.00

		VG	VF	UNC
4	**100 (DENAR)** 1992. Blue-gray on lt. blue unpt.	.10	.20	1.00

		VG	VF	UNC
5	**500 (DENAR)** 1992. Bright green on ochre unpt.	.15	.40	1.25

		VG	VF	UNC
6	**1000 (DENAR)** 1992. Dull blue-violet on pink unpt.	.35	.65	1.75

		VG	VF	UNC
7	**5000 (DENAR)** 1992. Deep brown and dull red on m/c unpt. Woman at desk top computer at ctr. Ilenden monument at l. on back.	.35	1.50	6.00

		VG	VF	UNC
8	10,000 (DENAR) 1992. Blue-black on pink and gray unpt. Bldgs. at ctr. r. Musicians at l. of Ilenden monument at ctr. r. on back.	.65	2.50	8.50

НАРОДНА БАНКА НА РЕПУБЛИКА МАКЕДОНИЈА

NATIONAL BANK OF THE REPUBLIC OF MACEDONIA

1993 ISSUE

Currency Reform

1 "New" Denar = 100 "Old" Denari

#9-12 wmk: Ilenden monument in Krushevo.

		VG	VF	UNC
9	10 DENARI 1993. Lt. blue on m/c unpt. Houses on mountainside in Krushevo at ctr. r. Ilenden monument at l. ctr. on back.			
	a. Issued note.	FV	FV	1.50
	s. Specimen.	—	—	15.00

		VG	VF	UNC
10	20 DENARI 1993. Wine-red on m/c unpt. Tower in Skopje in vertical format on face. Turkish bath in Skopje at l. ctr. on back.			
	a. Issued note.	FV	FV	2.50
	s. Specimen.	—	—	15.00

		VG	VF	UNC
11	50 DENARI 1993. Lt. red on m/c unpt. National Bank bldg. in Skopje at r. Church of St. Pantaleimon at l. on back.			
	a. Issued note.	FV	FV	4.00
	s. Specimen.	—	—	15.00

		VG	VF	UNC
12	100 DENARI 1993. Brown on m/c unpt. National Museum in Ohrid at r. St. Sophia church in Ohrid at l. on back.			
	a. Issued note.	FV	FV	8.00
	s. Specimen.	—	—	15.00

		VG	VF	UNC
13	500 DENARI 1993. Greenish gray on m/c unpt. City wall at upper ctr. r. Orthodox church at l. and as wmk. on back.			
	a. Issued note.	FV	FV	35.00
	s. Specimen.	—	—	15.00

1996 ISSUE

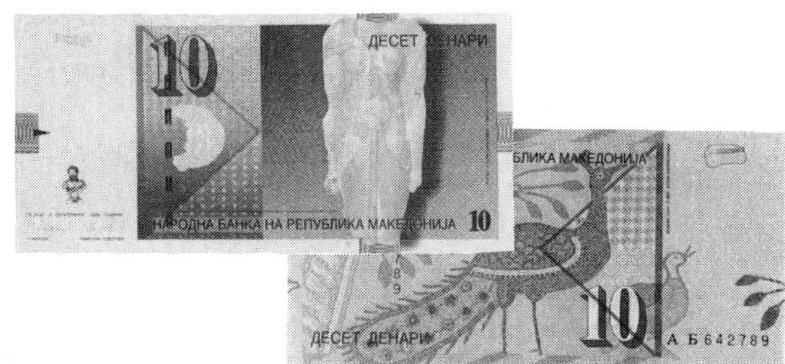

		VG	VF	UNC
14	10 DENARI 8.9.1996. Deep olive-green w/black text on pink, violet, purple and m/c unpt. Statue torso of Goddess Isida at ctr. r. and as wmk. Back blue-green, deep olive-green w/black text on tan and m/c unpt. Mosaic of branch over peacock and duck.			
	a. Issued note.	FV	FV	1.50
	s. Specimen.	—	—	20.00

		VG	VF	UNC
15	**50 DENARI**			
	8.9.1996. Brown w/black text on m/c unpt. Byzantine copper follis of Anastasia at ctr. r. and as wmk. Archangel Gabriel at l. ctr. on back.			
	a. Issued note.	FV	FV	2.75
	s. Specimen.	—	—	20.00

		VG	VF	UNC
16	**100 DENARI**			
	8.9.1996. Brown w/purple text on m/c unpt. Lg. baroque wooden ceiling rosette in Debar town house at ctr. r. and as wmk. J. Harevin's engraving of Skopje "seen" through town house window frame at l. ctr.			
	a. Issued note.	FV	FV	5.00
	s. Specimen.	—	—	25.00

		VG	VF	UNC
17	**500 DENARI**			
	8.9.1996. Black and violet on m/c unpt. 6th century golden death mask, Trebenista, Ohrid at r. and as wmk. Violet poppy flower and plant at l. ctr. on back.			
	a. Issued note.	FV	FV	22.50
	s. Specimen.	—	—	25.00
18	**1000 DENARI**			
	8.9.1996. Brown and orange on m/c unpt. 14th century icon of Madonna Episkepsis and Christ Child, church of St. Vrach-Mali, Ohrid at ctr. r. Partial view of the St. Sophia church in Ohrid at l. ctr. Wmk: Madonna.			
	a. Issued note.	FV	FV	40.00
	s. Specimen.	—	—	30.00
19	**5000 DENARI**			
	8.9.1996. Black and violet on olive-green and m/c unpt. 6th century bronze figurine of Tetovo Maenad VI (horizontally) at ctr. r. and as wmk. 6th century mosaic of Cerberus the Dog tied to a fig tree, representing the watcher of Heaven (horizontally) at l. ctr. on back.			
	a. Issued note.	FV	FV	175.00
	s. Specimen.	—	—	60.00

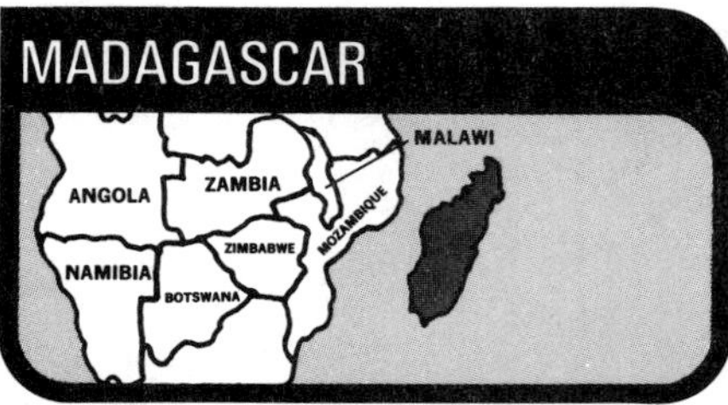

The Democratic Republic of Madagascar, an independent member of the French Community located in the Indian Ocean 250 miles (402 km.) off the southeast coast of Africa, has an area of 226,658 sq. mi. (587,041 sq. km.) and a population of 14.1 million. Capital: Antananarivo. The economy is primarily agricultural; large bauxite deposits are presently being developed. Coffee, vanilla, graphite and rice are exported.

Diago Diaz, a Portuguese navigator, sighted the island of Madagascar on Aug. 10, 1500, when his ship became separated from an India-bound fleet. Attempts at settlement by the British during the reign of Charles I and by the French during the 17th and 18th centuries were of no avail, and the island became a refuge and supply base for Indian Ocean pirates. Despite considerable influence on the island, the British accepted the imposition of a French protectorate in 1886 in return for French recognition of Britain's sphere of influence in Zanzibar. Madagascar was made a French colony in 1896 after absolute control had been established by military force. Britain occupied the island after the fall of France in 1942, to prevent its seizure by the Japanese, and gave it to the Free French in 1943. On Oct. 14, 1958, following a decade of intermittent but bitter warfare, Madagascar, as the Malagasy Republic, became an autonomous state within the French Community. On June 27, 1960, it became a sovereign independent nation, though remaining nominally within the French Community. The Malagasy Republic was renamed the Democratic Republic of Madagascar in 1976.

MONETARY SYSTEM:

1 CFA Franc = 0.02 French Franc, 1959-1961
5 Malagasy Francs (F.M.G.) = 1 Ariary, 1961-

MALAGASY

INSTITUT D'EMISSION MALGACHE

1961 ND PROVISIONAL ISSUE

#51-55 new bank name and new Ariary denominations ovpt. on previous issue of Banque de Madagascar et des Comores. Wmk: Woman's head.

		VG	VF	UNC
51	**50 FRANCS = 10 ARIARY**			
	ND (1961). M/c. Woman w/hat at ctr. r. Man at ctr. on back. Ovpt. on #45.			
	a. Sign. title: *LE CONTROLEUR GENERAL.*	3.00	12.50	50.00
	b. Sign. title: *LE DIRECTEUR GENERAL ADJOINT.*	3.00	15.00	60.00

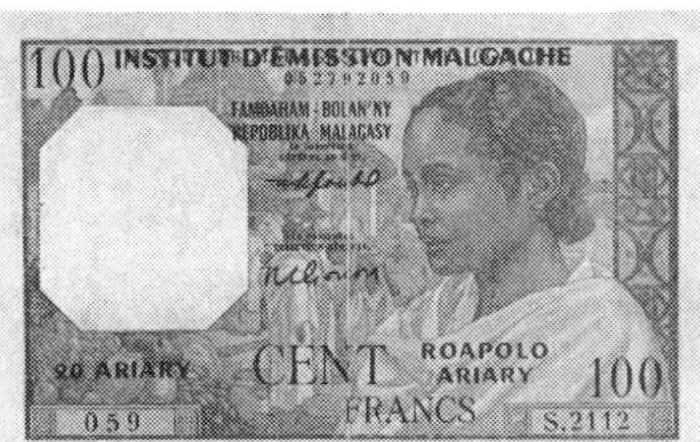

		VG	VF	UNC
52	**100 FRANCS = 20 ARIARY**			
	ND (1961). M/c. Woman at ctr. r., palace of the Qn. of Tananariva in background. Woman, boats and animals on back. Ovpt. on #46b.	4.00	20.00	65.00

53 **500 FRANCS = 100 ARIARY**

	VG	VF	UNC
ND (1961). M/c. Man w/fruit at ctr. Ovpt. on #47.	15.00	75.00	250.00

54 **1000 FRANCS = 200 ARIARY**

	VG	VF	UNC
ND (1961 - old date 9.10.1952). M/c. Man and woman at l. ctr. Ox cart at ctr. r. on back. Ovpt. on #48.	20.00	140.00	375.00

55 **5000 FRANCS = 1000 ARIARY**

	VG	VF	UNC
ND (1961). M/c. Gallieni at upper l., woman at r. Woman and baby on back. Ovpt. on #49.	50.00	300.00	800.00

NOTE: #53-55 some notes also have old dates of intended or original issue (1952-55).

1963 ND REGULAR ISSUE

56 **1000 FRANCS = 200 ARIARY**

	VG	VF	UNC
ND (1963). M/c. Portr. Pres. P. Tsiranana, people in canoes at l. Ox cart at ctr. r. on back. Wmk: Woman's head.			
a. W/o sign. and title.	50.00	375.00	600.00
b. W/sign. and title.	40.00	250.00	550.00

1966 ND ISSUE

#57-60 wmk: Woman's head.

57 **100 FRANCS = 20 ARIARY**

	VG	VF	UNC
ND (1966). M/c. 3 women spinning. Trees on back. 2 sign. varieties.	2.50	12.50	40.00

58 **500 FRANCS = 100 ARIARY**

	VG	VF	UNC
ND (1966). M/c. Woman at l., landscape in background. River scene on back. 2 sign. varieties.	7.50	60.00	200.00

59 **1000 FRANCS = 200 ARIARY**

	VG	VF	UNC
ND (1966). M/c. Woman and man at l. Similar to #48 and #54 but size 150 x 80mm.	8.50	75.00	250.00

60 **5000 FRANCS = 1000 ARIARY**

	VG	VF	UNC
ND (1966). M/c. Portr. Pres. P. Tsiranana at l., workers in rice field at r. Woman and boy on back.	12.50	90.00	300.00

1969-ISSUE

61 **50 FRANCS = 10 ARIARY**
ND (1969). M/c. Like #51. Different sign. title.

VG	VF	UNC
2.25	7.50	25.00

MADAGASCAR DEMOCRATIC REPUBLIC

BANKY FOIBEN'NY REPOBLIKA MALAGASY

BANQUE CENTRALE DE LA RÉPUBLIQUE MALGACHE

1974 ND ISSUE

#62-66 replacement notes: Serial # prefix *Z/*.

62 **50 FRANCS = 10 ARIARY**
ND (1974-75). Purple on m/c unpt. Young man at ctr. r. Fruit stand under umbrella at l. ctr. on back.

VG	VF	UNC
1.50	4.00	12.50

63 **100 FRANCS = 20 ARIARY**
ND. Brown on m/c unpt. Old man at r. Rice planting on back.

VG	VF	UNC
1.00	3.00	10.00

#64-66 wmk: Zebu's head.

64 **500 FRANCS = 100 ARIARY**
ND. Green on m/c unpt. Butterfly at l., young woman at ctr. r. holding ornate bag on head. Dancers at ctr. on back.

VG	VF	UNC
2.50	6.00	30.00

65 **1000 FRANCS = 200 ARIARY**
ND. Blue on m/c unpt. Lemurs at l., man in straw hat at r. Trees and designs on back.

VG	VF	UNC
3.50	8.00	45.00

66 **5000 FRANCS = 1000 ARIARY**
ND. Red and violet on m/c unpt. Oxen at l., young woman at ctr. r. Back violet and orange; tropical plants and African carving at ctr.

VG	VF	UNC
15.00	35.00	90.00

BANKY FOIBEN'I MADAGASIKARA

1983 ND ISSUE

#67-70 wmk: Zebu's head. Sign. varieties. Replacement notes: Serial # prefix *Z/*.

		VG	VF	UNC
67	**500 FRANCS = 100 ARIARY** ND (1983-87). Brown and red on m/c unpt. Boy w/fish in net at ctr. Aerial view of port at r. on back.	FV	1.50	5.00

		VG	VF	UNC
68	**1000 FRANCS = 200 ARIARY** ND (1983-87). Violet on m/c unpt. Man w/hat playing flute at ctr. Fruits and vegetables at r. on back.	FV	2.00	7.50

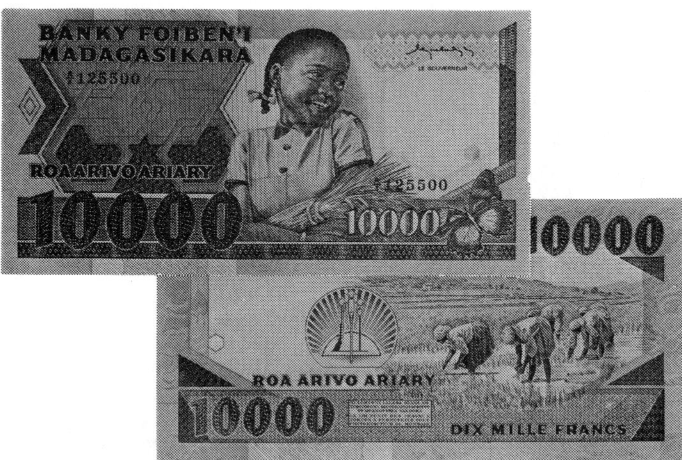

		VG	VF	UNC
69	**5000 FRANCS = 1000 ARIARY** ND (1983-87). Blue on m/c unpt. Woman and child at ctr. Book at upper ctr., school at ctr. r., monument at lower r. on back.	FV	10.00	35.00
70	**10,000 FRANCS = 2000 ARIARY** ND (1983-87). Green on m/c unpt. Young girl w/sheaf at ctr. Harvesting rice at ctr. r. on back.	FV	20.00	65.00

1988 ND ISSUE

#71-74 vertical serial # at r. Sign. varieties. Wmk: Zebu's head. Replacement notes: Serial # prefix *ZZ*.

		VG	VF	UNC
71	**500 FRANCS = 100 ARIARY** ND (1988-93). Similar to #67, but modified unpt.	FV	1.50	5.00

		VG	VF	UNC
72	**1000 FRANCS = 200 ARIARY** ND (1988-93). Similar to #68, but modified unpt.	FV	2.00	7.50

		VG	VF	UNC
73	**5000 FRANCS = 1000 ARIARY** ND (1988-94). Similar to #69, but modified unpt.	FV	4.00	15.00

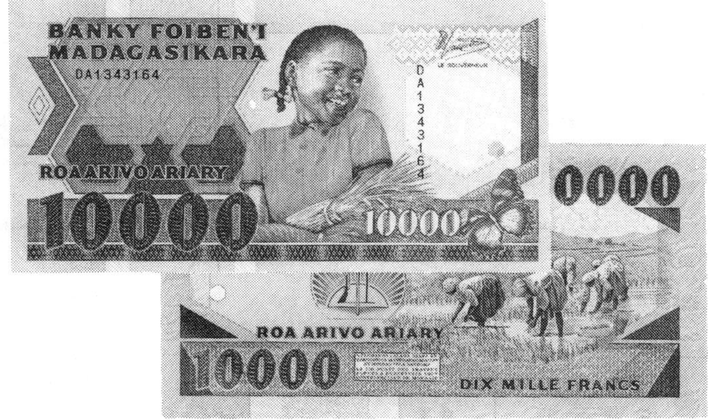

		VG	VF	UNC
74	**10,000 FRANCS = 2000 ARIARY** ND (1988-94). Similar to #70, but modified unpt.	FV	10.00	30.00

1993-95 ND ISSUE

#75-80 wmk: Zebu's head.

		VG	VF	UNC
75	**500 FRANCS = 100 ARIARY** ND (1994). Dk. brown and dk. green on m/c unpt. Girl at ctr. r., village in unpt. at upper ctr. Herdsmen w/Zebus at ctr. l., village in upper background at l. ctr. on back.	FV	FV	1.65

		VG	VF	UNC
76	**1000 FRANCS = 200 ARIARY** ND (1994). Dk. brown and dk. blue on m/c unpt. Young man at ctr. r., boats in background. Young woman w/basket of shellfish at ctr., fisherman w/net at l. ctr. on back.	FV	FV	1.25

		VG	VF	UNC
77	**2500 FRANCS = 500 ARIARY** ND (1993). Red, green, blue and black on m/c unpt. Older woman at ctr. Heron, tortoise, lemur, and butterfly in foliage on vertical format back.	FV	FV	2.50

NOTICE

Readers with unlisted dates, signature varieties, etc. are invited to submit photocopies of their notes to: Standard Catalog of World Paper Money, 700 East State St. Iola, WI 54990-0001, fax: 1-715-445-4087, or E-Mail: thernr@krause.com.

		VG	VF	UNC
78	**5000 FRANCS = 1000 ARIARY** ND (1995). Dk. brown and violet on lilac and m/c unpt. Young male head at r., ox cart, cane cutters at ctr. Animals, birds and seashells on back.	FV	FV	5.50

		VG	VF	UNC
79	**10,000 FRANCS = 2000 ARIARY** ND (1995). Dk. brown on tan and m/c unpt. Old man at r., statuette, local artifacts at ctr. Artisans at work on back.	FV	FV	10.00

		VG	VF	UNC
80	**25,000 FRANCS = 5000 ARIARY** ND (1993) Olive-green and green on m/c unpt. Old man at ctr., island outline at l. Scene of traditional bullfighting at r. on back.	FV	FV	17.50

1998 ND Issue

		VG	VF	UNC
81	**2500 Francs = 500 Ariary** ND (1998). M/c. Woman at r., village in background. Woman weaving at l. ctr. on back.	FV	FV	3.50

		VG	VF	UNC
82	**25,000 Francs = 5000 Ariary** ND (1998). M/c. Mother w/child at ctr. r., fruit trees in background. Woman harvesting at ctr. on back.	FV	FV	25.00

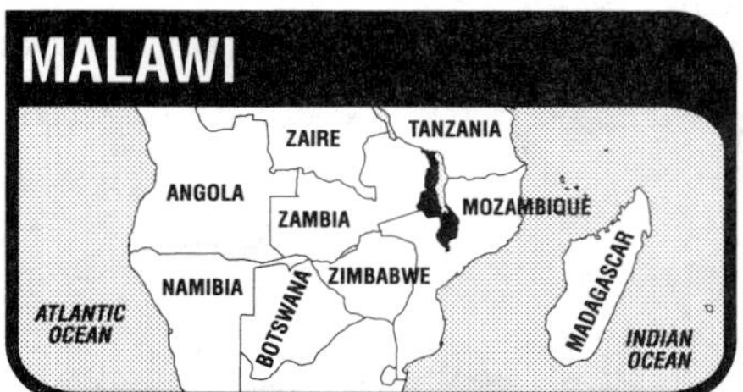

The Republic of Malawi (formerly Nyasaland), located in southeastern Africa to the west of Lake Malawi (Nyasa), has an area of 45,747 sq. mi. (118,484 sq. km.) and a population of 11 million. Capital: Lilongwe. The economy is predominantly agricultural. Tobacco, tea, peanuts and cotton are exported.

Although the Portuguese, heirs to the restless spirit of Prince Henry, were the first Europeans to reach the Malawi area, the first meaningful contact was made by missionary-explorer Dr. David Livingstone who arrived at Lake Malawi on Sept. 16, 1859, and remained to make extensive explorations in the 1860s. Subsequent clashes between settlements of Scottish missionaries and Arab slave traders, and the procurement of development rights by Cecil Rhodes, 1884, stimulated British interest and brought about the establishment of the Nyasaland protectorate in 1891. In 1953, Nyasaland reluctantly joined the Federation of Rhodesia and Nyasaland and, after prolonged protest, was granted self-government within the federation. Nyasaland became the independent nation of Malawi on July 6, 1964, and became a republic two years later. As a one party dictatorship lasting 30 years until 1994 when elections returned Malawi to a multi-party democracy. Malawi is a member of the Commonwealth of Nations. The president is the Chief of State and Head of Government.

Also see Rhodesia, Rhodesia and Nyasaland.

RULERS:

British to 1964

MONETARY SYSTEM:

1 Pound = 20 Shillings to 1971
1 Kwacha = 100 Tambala 1971-

Republic

Reserve Bank of Malawi

1964 Reserve Bank Act; First Issue

Pound System

#1-4 portr. Dr. H. K. Banda at l., fishermen in boat on Lake Malawi at ctr. Sign. title: *GOVERNOR* only. Wmk: Rooster.

		VG	VF	UNC
1	**5 Shillings** *L.1964.* Blue-gray on m/c unpt. Arms w/bird on back.	7.50	18.50	95.00
2	**10 Shillings** *L.1964.* Brown on m/c unpt. Workers in tobacco field on back.	10.00	60.00	275.00

		VG	VF	UNC
3	**1 Pound** *L.1964.* Green on m/c unpt. Workers picking cotton at ctr. r. on back.	10.00	75.00	325.00

		VG	VF	UNC
4	**5 Pounds** *L.1964.* Blue and brown on m/c unpt. Tea pickers below Mt. Mulanje on back.	40.00	300.00	950.00

1964 Reserve Bank Act; Second Issue

#1A-3A portr. Dr. H. K. Banda at l., fishermen at ctr. Sign. titles: *GOVERNOR* and *GENERAL MANAGER*.

		VG	VF	UNC
1A	**5 SHILLINGS** *L.1964*. Blue-gray on m/c unpt. Like #1.	10.00	12.50	70.00

		VG	VF	UNC
2A	**10 SHILLINGS** *L.1964*. Brown on m/c unpt. Like #2.	5.00	20.00	95.00

		VG	VF	UNC
3A	**1 POUND** *L.1964*. Green on m/c unpt. Like #3.	6.00	32.50	150.00

1964 Reserve Bank Act; 1971 Issue

Kwacha System

		VG	VF	UNC
5	**50 TAMBALA** *L.1964* (1971). Blue-gray on m/c unpt. Face like #1A. Independence Arch in Blantyre at r. on back.	10.00	40.00	175.00

		VGCHAVG	VF	UN
6	**1 KWA** *L.1964* (1971). Brown on m/c unpt. Like #2A.	15.00	60.00	250.00

		VG	VF	UNC
7	**2 KWACHA** *L.1964* (1971). Green on m/c unpt. Like #3A.	17.50	70.00	280.00

		VG	VF	UNC
8	**10 KWACHA** *L.1964* (1971). Blue and brown on m/c unpt. Like #4 but 2 signs.	30.00	120.00	495.00

1973-74 Issue

#9-12 portr. Dr. H. K. Banda as Prime Minister at r., fishermen in boat on Lake Malawi and palm tree at ctr. W/ or w/o dates. Wmk: Rooster.

		VG	VF	UNC
9	**50 TAMBALA** *L.1964* (ND); 1974-75. Blue-gray on m/c unpt. Sugar cane harvesting on back.			
	a. ND (1973).	6.00	20.00	140.00
	b. 30.6.1974.	3.00	10.00	55.00
	c. 31.1.1975.	2.00	5.00	37.50

		VG	VF	UNC
10	**1 KWACHA** *L.1964* (ND); 1974-75. Red-brown on m/c unpt. Plantation worker, hill in background on back.			
	a. ND (1973).	5.00	20.00	135.00
	b. 30.6.1974.	4.00	14.00	95.00
	c. 31.1.1975.	3.00	6.00	75.00

		VG	VF	UNC
11	**5 KWACHA** *L.1964* (ND); 1974-75. Red-orange on m/c unpt. Worker w/basket at ctr., *K5* at upper l. on back.			
	a. ND (1973).	11.50	55.00	350.00
	b. 30.6.1974.	Reported Not Confirmed		
	c. 31.1.1975.	8.00	30.00	195.00
12	**10 KWACHA** *L.1964* (ND); 1974-75. Blue and brown on m/c unpt. Plantation workers w/mountains in background on back.			
	a. ND (1973).	15.00	90.00	375.00
	b. 30.6.1974.	13.50	100.00	400.00
	c. 31.1.1975.	9.00	65.00	245.00

1976; 1983 ISSUE

#13-17 portr. Dr. H. K. Banda as President at r. Wmk: Rooster. Sign. varieties.

		VG	VF	UNC
13	**50 TAMBALA** 1976-84. Blue-gray on m/c unpt. Cotton harvest on back.			
	a. 31.1.1976.	1.00	3.00	25.00
	b. 1.7.1978.	1.50	4.50	35.00
	c. 1.1.1981.	1.00	3.75	30.00
	d. 1.5.1982.	.50	1.00	8.50
	e. 1.1.1983.	1.50	5.00	40.00
	f. 1.11.1984.	2.50	10.00	85.00
	s. As. a. Specimen.	—	—	35.00

		VG	VF	UNC
14	**1 KWACHA** 1976-84. Red-brown on m/c unpt. Workers harvesting, mountains in background on back.			
	a. 31.1.1976.	.75	3.00	22.50
	b. 1.7.1978.	.75	3.00	25.00
	c. 30.6.1979.	1.65	6.50	65.00
	d. 1.1.1981.	.50	2.00	17.50
	e. 1.5.1982.	.35	1.50	12.50
	f. 1.1.1983.	.75	3.00	25.00
	g. 1.4.1984.	.35	1.50	12.50
	h. 1.11.1984.	.50	2.00	15.00
	s. Specimen. 31.1.1976.	—	—	40.00

		VG	VF	UNC
15	**5 KWACHA** 1976-84. Red on m/c unpt. Field workers, *K5* at upper r. on back.			
	a. 31.1.1976.	3.00	15.00	100.00
	b. 1.7.1978.	3.00	15.00	100.00
	c. 30.6.1979.	3.50	17.50	150.00
	d. 1.1.1981.	2.50	7.50	50.00
	e. 1.1.1983.	1.75	5.00	35.00
	f. 1.11.1984.	3.00	8.00	120.00
	s. Specimen. 31.1.1976.	—	—	50.00

		VG	VF	UNC
16	**10 KWACHA** 1976-85. Deep blue and brown on m/c unpt. Capital bldg. at Lilongwe on back.			
	a. 31.1.1976.	7.50	25.00	350.00
	b. 1.7.1978.	7.50	25.00	350.00
	c. 30.6.1979.	8.50	30.00	450.00
	d. 1.1.1981.	7.50	25.00	350.00
	e. 1.1.1983.	6.50	22.50	300.00
	f. 1.11.1984.	8.00	27.50	400.00
	g. 1.8.1985.	7.50	26.50	375.00
	s. Specimen. 31.1.1976.	—	—	45.00

		VG	VF	UNC
17	**20 KWACHA** 1983; 1984. Green, brown-violet on m/c unpt. Back green; Reserve Bank at ctr.			
	a. 1.7.1983.	4.50	15.00	100.00
	b. 1.11.1984.	9.00	35.00	250.00

1986 ISSUE

#18-22 portr. Pres. Dr. H. K. Banda at r. Wmk: Rooster.

NOTICE

Readers with unlisted dates, signature varieties, etc. are invited to submit photocopies of their notes to: Standard Catalog of World Paper Money, 700 East State St. Iola, WI 54990-0001, fax: 1-715-445-4087, or E-Mail: thernr@krause.com.

		VG	VF	UNC
18	**50 TAMBALA** 1.3.1986. Black and dk. brown on m/c unpt. Picking corn on back.	.25	1.00	8.00

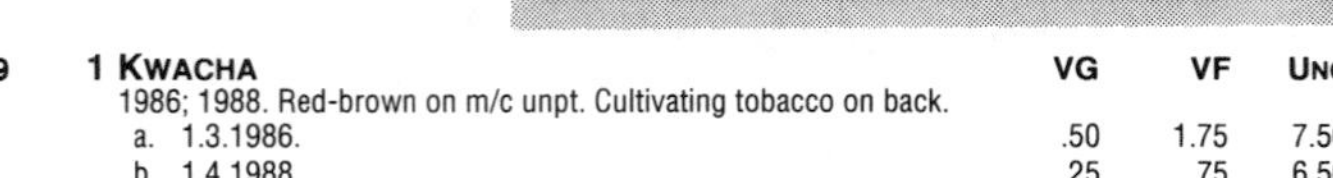

		VG	VF	UNC
19	**1 KWACHA** 1986; 1988. Red-brown on m/c unpt. Cultivating tobacco on back.			
	a. 1.3.1986.	.50	1.75	7.50
	b. 1.4.1988.	.25	.75	6.50

		VG	VF	UNC
20	**5 KWACHA** 1986; 1988. Red-orange on m/c unpt. University of Malawi on back.			
	a. 1.3.1986.	1.85	6.50	35.00
	b. 1.4.1988.	.90	5.00	30.00

		VG	VF	UNC
21	**10 KWACHA** 1986; 1988. Deep blue and brown on m/c unpt. Lilongwe, capital city, on back.			
	a. 1.3.1986.	3.00	12.50	75.00
	b. 1.4.1988.	2.00	8.50	40.00

		VG	VF	UNC
22	**20 KWACHA** 1986; 1988. Deep green on m/c unpt. Kamuzu International Airport on back.			
	a. 1.3.1986.	6.00	25.00	150.00
	b. 1.4.1988.	3.00	15.00	100.00

1989 ACT; 1990; 1993 ISSUE

#23-28 palm tree, man in dugout canoe, and rayed silver circle at ctr., portr. Dr. H. K. Banda as President at r. Ascending size vertical serial # at l. and lower r. Wmk: Rooster.

		VG	VF	UNC
23	**1 KWACHA** 1990; 1992. Red-brown on m/c unpt. Back similar to #19.			
	a. 1.12.1990.	FV	FV	5.00
	b. 1.5.1992.	FV	FV	2.00

		VG	VF	UNC
24	**5 KWACHA** 1990; 1994. Red-orange and olive-green on m/c unpt. University of Malawi at l. ctr. on back.			
	a. 1.12.1990.	FV	FV	7.50
	b. 1.1.1994.	FV	FV	4.50

		VG	VF	UNC
25	**10 KWACHA** 1990-94. Blue-gray, blue-violet and dk. brown on m/c unpt. Lilongwe City municipal bldg. at l. ctr. on back.			
	a. 1.12.1990.	FV	FV	13.50
	b. 1.9.1992.	FV	FV	6.00
	c. Smaller sign. as b. 1.1.1994.	FV	FV	4.00
26	**20 KWACHA** 1.9.1990. Green, orange and blue on m/c unpt. Kamazu International Airport at l. ctr. on back.	FV	FV	35.00

		VG	VF	UNC
27	**20 KWACHA** 1.7.1993. Like #26 but w/larger airplane on back.	FV	FV	10.00

		VG	VF	UNC
28	**50 KWACHA** 1990; 1994. Pale purple, violet and blue on m/c unpt. Independence Arch at Blantyre at ctr. on back.			
	a. 1.6.1990.	FV	12.50	55.00
	b. 1.1.1994.	FV	FV	30.00

		VG	VF	UNC
29	**100 KWACHA** 1993; 1994. Blue, green and dk. brown on m/c unpt. Trucks hauling maize to storage facility at ctr. on back.			
	a. 1.4.1993.	FV	30.00	65.00
	b. 1.1.1994.	FV	FV	40.00

1995 ISSUE

#30-35 Pres. Muluzi at r., bird(s) at upper l., sunrise above fisherman in boat on Lake Malawi at ctr., bird over silver segmented sunburst at l. Wmk: Fish.

		VG	VF	UNC
30	**5 KWACHA** 1.6.1995. Red and orange-brown on m/c unpt. Zebras at l. on back.	FV	FV	1.75

		VG	VF	UNC
31	**10 KWACHA** 1.6.1995. Black, dk. blue and dk. brown on m/c unpt. Capital Hill, Lilongwe at l. ctr. on back.	FV	FV	4.00

		VG	VF	UNC
32	**20 KWACHA** 1.6.1995. Deep green and dk. brown on m/c unpt. Harvesting tea leaves at l. ctr. on back.	FV	FV	7.50

		VG	VF	UNC
33	**50 KWACHA** 1.6.1995. Purple and violet on m/c unpt. Independence Arch in Blantyre at l. ctr. on back.	FV	FV	8.00

34 **100 KWACHA** | VG | VF | UNC
1.6.1995. Purple and deep ultramarine on m/c unpt. Trucks hauling maize to storage facility at l. ctr. on back. | FV | FV | 15.00

35 **200 KWACHA** | VG | VF | UNC
1.6.1995. Brown-violet and blue-green and silver on m/c unpt. Elephants on back. | FV | FV | 35.00

1989 ACT; 1997 ISSUE

#36-41 J. Chilembwe at r. and as wmk., sunrise, fishermen at ctr., bank stylized logo at lower l.

#36-39 bank seal at top ctr. r. on back.

36 **5 KWACHA** | VG | VF | UNC
1.7.1997. Deep olive-green, green and olive-brown on m/c unpt. Villagers mashing grain at l. on back. | FV | FV | 1.05

37 **10 KWACHA** | VG | VF | UNC
1.7.1997. Dk. brown and brown-violet on m/c unpt. Children in "bush" school at l. ctr. on back. | FV | FV | 1.50

38 **20 KWACHA** | VG | VF | UNC
1.7.1997. Blackish purple, purple and violet on m/c unpt. Workers harvesting tea leaves, mountains in background at l. on back. | FV | FV | 3.25

39 **50 KWACHA** | VG | VF | UNC
1.7.1997. Dk. green, deep blue and aqua on m/c unpt. Independence arch in Blantyre at l. ctr. on back. | FV | FV | 5.00

40 **100 KWACHA** | VG | VF | UNC
1.7.1997. Purple, red and violet on m/c unpt. Circular kinogram bank seal at r. Capital Hill Lilongwe at l. ctr. on back. | FV | FV | 15.00

41 **200 KWACHA** | VG | VF | UNC
1.7.1997. Dk. gray, dull blue and deep blue-green on m/c unpt. Oval kinogram bank seal at r. Reserve Bank bldg. in Lilongwe at l. ctr. on back. | FV | FV | 17.50

42 **500 KWACHA**
1.7.1997. Expected New Issue

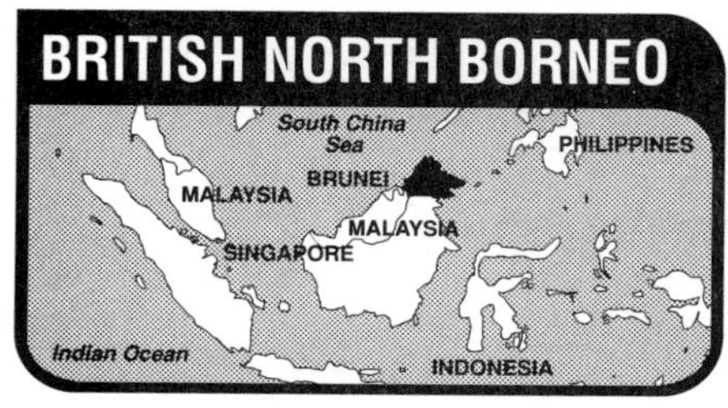

Malaya and British Borneo, a Currency Commission named the Board of Commissioners of Currency, Malaya and British North Borneo, was initiated on Jan. 1, 1952, for the purpose of providing a common currency for use in Johore, Kelantan, Kedah, Perlis, Trengganu, Negri Sembilan, Pahang, Perak, Salangor, Penang, Malacca, Singapore, North Borneo, Sarawak and Brunei.

For later issues see Brunei, Malaysia and Singapore.

RULERS:

British

MONETARY SYSTEM:

1 Dollar = 100 Cents

Board of Commissioners of Currency

1959-61 Issue

 # 8-9 arms of 5 states on back. Wmk: Tiger's head.

		VG	VF	Unc
8	**1 Dollars** 1.3.1959. Blue on m/c unpt. Sailing boat at l. Men w/boat on back.			
	a. Printer: W & S.	7.50	20.00	80.00
	b. Printer: TDLR.	3.00	10.00	40.00

		VG	VF	Unc
9	**10 Dollars** 1.3.1961. Red and dk. brown on m/c unpt. Farmer plowing w/ox at r. Printer: TDLR.			
	a. Sm. serial #. Series A.	17.50	50.00	200.00
	b. Lg. serial #. Series A.	17.50	55.00	225.00
	c. Lg. serial #. Series B.	20.00	62.50	250.00

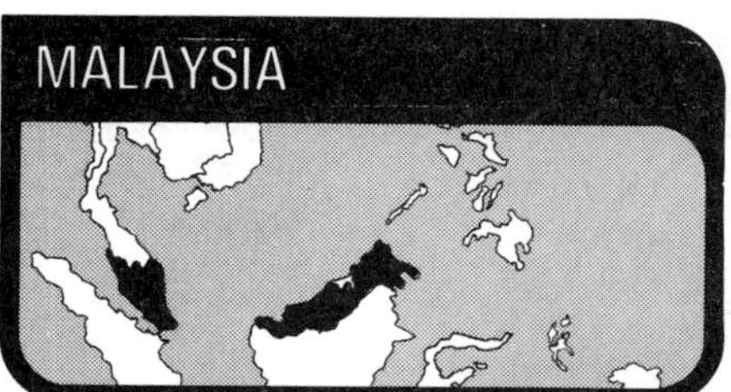

Malaysia, an independent federation of southeast Asia consisting of 11 states of West Malaysia on the Malay Peninsula and two states of East Malaysia on the island of Borneo, has an area of 127,316 sq. mi. (329,747 sq. km.) and a population of 21.7 million. Capital: Kuala Lumpur. The federation came into being on Sept. 16, 1963. Rubber, timber, tin, iron ore and bauxite are exported.

The constituent states of Malaysia are Johore, Kedah, Kelantan, Malacca, Negri Sembilan, Pahang, Penang, Perak, Perlis, Selangor and Trengganu of West Malaysia; and Sabah and Sarawak of East Malaysia. Singapore joined the federation in 1963, but broke away on Aug. 9, 1965, to become an independent republic. Malaysia is a member of the Commonwealth of Nations. The "Paramount Ruler" is Chief of State. The prime minister is Head of Government.

MONETARY SYSTEM:

1 Ringgit (Dollar) = 100 Sen

DEMONITIZED NOTES:

All 500 and 1000 Ringgitt notes will cease to be legal tender on July 1, 1999.

Federation

Bank Negara Malaysia

All notes w/Yang Di-Pertuan Agong, Tunku Abdul Rahman, first Head of State of Malaysia (died 1960).

1967 ND Issue

#1-6 old spelling of *DI-PERLAKUKAN*. Arms on back. Wmk: Tiger's head. Sign. of Ismail Md. Ali w/title: *GABENOR*.

#1, 2, and 6 printer: BWC.

		VG	VF	Unc
1	**1 Ringgit** ND (1967-72). Blue on m/c unpt.			
	a. Solid security thread.	.75	2.50	7.00
	b. Segmented foil over security thread.	1.00	4.00	8.00

		VG	VF	Unc
2	**5 Ringgit** ND (1967-72). Green on m/c unpt.			
	a. Solid security thread.	2.00	7.00	35.00
	b. Segmented foil security thread.	2.00	7.00	40.00

#3-5 printer: TDLR. Replacement notes: Serial # prefix *Z/*.

		VG	VF	Unc
3	**10 Ringgit** ND (1967-72). Red-orange on m/c unpt. *(SA-PULOH)*.			
	a. Solid security thread.	5.00	12.00	45.00
	b. Segmented foil security thread.	5.00	12.00	50.00
4	**50 Ringgit** ND (1967-72). Blue on m/c unpt. *(LIMA PULOH)*.			
	a. Solid security thread.	FV	40.00	130.00
	b. Segmented foil security thread.	FV	40.00	130.00

		VG	VF	Unc
5	**100 Ringgit** ND (1967-72). Violet on m/c unpt. *(SA-RATUS)*.			
	a. Solid security thread.	FV	80.00	220.00
	b. Segmented foil over security thread.	FV	80.00	230.00

		VG	VF	UNC
6	**1000 Ringgit** ND (1967-72). Brown-violet on m/c unpt. *(SA-RIBU)*. Printer: BWC.	FV	600.00	1550.

1972; 1976 ND Issue

#7-12 new spelling *DIPERLAKUKAN*. Arms on back. Wmk: Tiger's head. Sign. of Ismail Md. Ali w/title: *GABENUR*.

#7, 8, 11 and 12 printer: BWC.

		VG	VF	UNC
7	**1 Ringgit** ND (1972-76). Blue on m/c unpt. Like #1.	FV	1.00	5.00

		VG	VF	UNC
8	**5 Ringgit** ND (1976). Green on m/c unpt. Like #2.	FV	3.00	14.00

#9 and 10 printer: TDLR.

		VG	VF	UNC
9	**10 Ringgit** ND (1972-76). Red-orange and brown on m/c unpt. *(SEPULUH)*. Like #3.			
	a. Solid security thread.	FV	5.00	30.00
	b. Segmented foil over security thread.	FV	5.00	30.00

		VG	VF	UNC
10	**50 Ringgit** ND (1972-76). Blue on m/c unpt.*(LIMA PULUH)*. Like #4.			
	a. Solid security thread.	FV	30.00	95.00
	b. Segmented foil over security thread.	FV	35.00	100.00

		VG	VF	UNC
11	**100 Ringgit** ND (1972-76). Violet on m/c unpt. *(SERATUS)*. Like #5.	FV	60.00	180.00
12	**1000 Ringgit** ND (1972-76). Brown-violet on m/c unpt. *(SERIBU)*. Like #6.	FV	500.00	1200.

1976; 1981 ND Issues

#13-18 arms on back. Wmk: Tiger's head.

#13-16 different guilloche w/latent image numeral at lower l.

#13-15 printer: BWC.

		VG	VF	UNC
13	**1 Ringgit** ND (1976-81). Blue on m/c unpt. Like #7.			
	a. Sign. Ismail Md. Ali. (1976).	FV	.75	5.00
	b. Sign. Abdul Aziz Taha. (1981).	FV	.70	4.00
14	**5 Ringgit** ND (1976-81). Green on m/c unpt. Like #8.			
	a. Sign. Ismail Md. Ali. (1976).	FV	3.25	12.00
	b. Sign. Abdul Aziz Taha. (1981).	FV	3.00	11.00
15	**10 Ringgit** ND (1976-81). Red-orange and brown on m/c unpt. Like #9. Sign. Ismail Md. Ali. (1976).	FV	8.00	20.00

#15A, 16A and 17b replacement notes: Serial # prefix *X/*.

		VG	VF	UNC
15A	**10 Ringgit** ND (1976-81). Like #15 but printer: TDLR. Sign. Abdul Aziz Taha.	FV	6.00	17.50

		VG	VF	UNC
16	**50 Ringgit** ND (1976-81). Blue on m/c unpt. Like #10. Sign. Ismail Md. Ali (1976). Printer: BWC.	FV	30.00	75.00
16A	**50 Ringgit** ND (1981-83). Blue on m/c unpt. Like #16 but printer: TDLR. Sign. Abdul Aziz Taha (1981).	FV	30.00	75.00
17	**100 Ringgit** ND (1976-81). Purple on m/c unpt. Like #11. Printer: TDLR.			
	a. Sign. Ismail Md. Ali. (1976).	FV	45.00	125.00
	b. Sign. Abdul Aziz Taha. (1981).	FV	50.00	130.00
18	**1000 Ringgit** ND (1976-81). Purple and green on m/c unpt. Face like #12. Parliament bldg. in Kuala Lumpur on back. Sign. Ismail Md. Ali. Printer: BWC.	—	425.00	1100.

1981-83 ND Issues

#19-26 new design w/marks for the blind. Sign. of Abdul Aziz Taha. Wmk: T. A. Rahman. Replacement notes: Serial # prefixes *BA; WA; UZ; ZZ*.

		VG	VF	UNC
19	**1 Ringgit** ND (1982-84). Dk. blue and brown on pink and m/c unpt. National Monument Kuala Lumpurate at ctr. on back. Printer: BWC.	FV	1.00	3.00

		VG	VF	UNC
19A	**1 RINGGIT** ND (1981-83). Like #19 except for printer: TDLR.	FV	.75	3.00

		VG	VF	UNC
20	**5 RINGGIT** ND (1983-84). Dk. green and blue on m/c unpt. King's Palace at Kuala Lumpur on back. Printer: TDLR.	FV	3.00	9.00

		VG	VF	UNC
21	**10 RINGGIT** ND (1983-84). Red and brown on m/c unpt. Railway station at Kuala Lumpur on back. Printer: TDLR.	FV	6.00	15.00

		VG	VF	UNC
22	**20 RINGGIT** ND (1982-84). Deep brown and dk. blue on m/c unpt. Bank Negara Malaysia bldg. in Kuala Lumpur on back. Printer: BWC.	FV	10.00	22.50

		VG	VF	UNC
23	**50 RINGGIT** ND (1983-84). Black and blue-gray on m/c unpt. National Museum at Kuala Lumpur on back. Printer: TDLR.	FV	30.00	55.00

		VG	VF	UNC
24	**100 RINGGIT** ND (1983-84). Red-brown and violet on m/c unpt. National Mosque in Kuala Lumpur on back. Printer: TDLR.	FV	50.00	110.00

		VG	VF	UNC
25	**500 RINGGIT** ND (1982-84). Dk. red and purple on m/c unpt. High Court bldg. in Kuala Lumpur on back. Printer: BWC.	FV	220.00	350.00

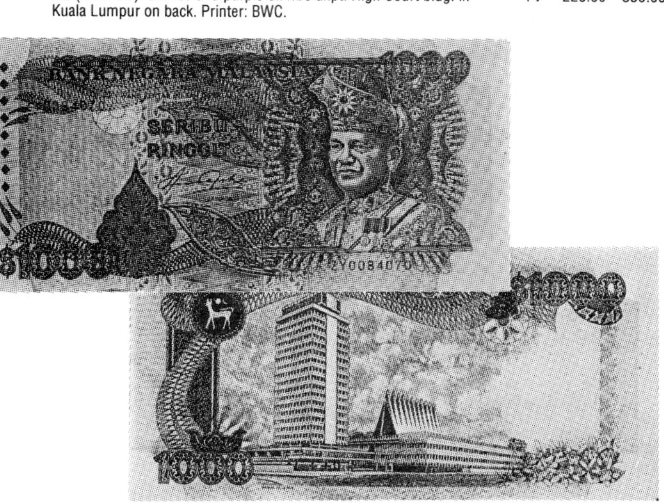

		VG	VF	UNC
26	**1000 RINGGIT** ND (1983-84). Gray-green on m/c unpt. Parliament bldg. in Kuala Lumpur on back. Printer: TDLR.	FV	440.00	700.00

NOTICE

Readers with unlisted dates, signature varieties, etc. are invited to submit photocopies of their notes to: Standard Catalog of World Paper Money, 700 East State St. Iola, WI 54990-0001, fax: 1-715-445-4087, or E-Mail: thernr@krause.com.

1986-95 ND Issues

#27-34 similar to #19-26 but no mark for the blind, white space for wmk. (both sides), and vertical serial #. Sign. Datuk Jaafar Hussein. Wmk: T. A. Rahman.

#27-31, 32, 33 and 34 printer: TDLR. Replacement notes: Serial # prefixes *BA; WA; UZ or ZZ.*

		VG	VF	UNC
27	**1 Ringgit** ND (1986; 1989). Dk. blue on m/c unpt.			
	a. Usual security thread (1986).	FV	FV	3.00
	b. Segmented foil over security thread (1989).	FV	FV	2.50

		VG	VF	UNC
28	**5 Ringgit** ND (1986-91). Dk. green and green on m/c unpt.			
	a. Usual security thread (1986).	FV	FV	6.00
	b. Segmented foil over security thread (1989).	FV	FV	5.00
	c. Flagpole w/o crossbar at top of back (1991).	FV	FV	4.00

		VG	VF	UNC
29	**10 Ringgit** ND (1989). Brown, red-orange and violet on m/c unpt. Segmented foil over security thread. Railway station at Kuala Lumpur at l. ctr. on back.	FV	FV	8.50
29A	**10 Ringgit** ND (1989). Brown, red-orange and violet on m/c unpt. Segmented foil over security thread. Railway station at Kuala Lumpur at l. ctr. on back. Printer: BABN.	FV	FV	8.50

		VG	VF	UNC
30	**20 Ringgit** ND (1989). Deep brown and olive on m/c unpt.	FV	FV	15.00

		VG	VF	UNC
31	**50 Ringgit** ND (1989). Blue and black on m/c unpt. Segmented foil over security thread.	FV	FV	35.00
31A	**50 Ringgit** ND (1991-92). Like #31, but printer: BABN.	FV	FV	32.50
31B	**50 Ringgit** ND (1991-92). Like #31, but printer: F-CO.	FV	FV	32.50

		VG	VF	UNC
32	**100 Ringgit** ND (1989). Purple on m/c unpt. Segmented foil over security thread. Printer: TDLR.	FV	FV	60.00
32A	**100 Ringgit** ND (1991-93). Like #32, but printer: USBNC.	FV	FV	68.00
32B	**100 Ringgit** ND (1991-93). Like #32, but printer: BABN.	FV	FV	68.00
33	**500 Ringgit** ND (1989). Red and brown on yellow and m/c unpt. Segmented foil over security thread.	FV	FV	275.00
34	**1000 Ringgit** ND (1989). Blue, green and purple on m/c unpt. Segmented foil over security thread.	FV	FV	525.00

1995 ND Issues

#35-38 sign. Ahmed Mohd. Don. Wmk: T.A. Rahman.

		VG	VF	UNC
35	**5 Ringgit** ND (1995). Dk. blue on m/c unpt. Like #28. Printer: TDLR.	FV	FV	3.50

		VG	VF	UNC
35A	**5 RINGGIT** ND (1995). Dk. green. Like #35. Segmented security thread. Printer: CBN.	FV	FV	3.50

		VG	VF	UNC
36	**10 RINGGIT** ND (1995). Dk. brown, red-orange and violet on m/c unpt. Like #29. Printer: F-CO.	FV	FV	6.50

		VG	VF	UNC
37	**10 RINGGIT** ND (1995). Dk. brown, red-orange and violet on m/c unpt. Like #29. Printer: BABN.	FV	FV	10.00
38	**10 RINGGIT** ND (1995). Dk. brown, red-orange and violet on m/c unpt. Like #29. Printer: G&D.	FV	FV	6.50

1996-99 ND ISSUE

#39-44 T. A. Rahman at r. and as wmk. 2 sign. varieties.

		VG	VF	UNC
39	**2 RINGGIT** ND (1996). Purple and red-violet on m/c unpt. Modern tower at l., communications satellite at upper ctr. Printer: NBM (w/o imprint).	FV	FV	1.50

NOTICE

Readers with unlisted dates, signature varieties, etc. are invited to submit photocopies of their notes to: Standard Catalog of World Paper Money, 700 East State St. Iola, WI 54990-0001, fax: 1-715-445-4087, or E-Mail: thernr@krause.com.

		VG	VF	UNCT
40	**5 RINGGI** ND (1998). M/c. Printer: CBNC.	FV	FV	2.75

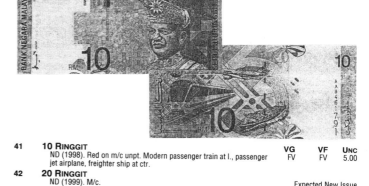

		VG	VF	UNC
41	**10 RINGGIT** ND (1998). Red on m/c unpt. Modern passenger train at l., passenger jet airplane, freighter ship at ctr.	FV	FV	5.00
42	**20 RINGGIT** ND (1999). M/c.	Expected New Issue		
43	**50 RINGGIT** ND (1998). M/c. Offshore oil platform at l. on back.	FV	FV	30.00
44	**100 RINGGIT** ND (1999). M/c.	FV	FV	50.00

1998 COMMEMORATIVE ISSUE

#45, XVI Commonwealth Games, Kuala Lumpur, 1998

		VG	VF	UNC
45	**50 RINGGIT** (19)98. Black and purple on m/c unpt. T. A. Rahman at r., Petronas Towers at ctr., multimedia corridor in unpt. at r. Utama Bukit Jalil Stadium at ctr., games logo at l. on back. Serial # prefix: *KL/98.*	FV	FV	60.00

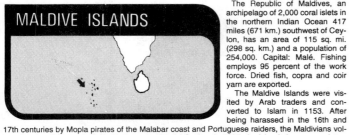

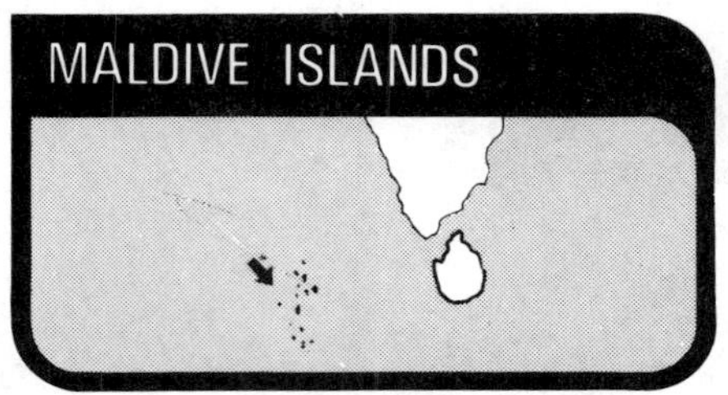

The Republic of Maldives, an archipelago of 2,000 coral islets in the northern Indian Ocean 417 miles (671 km.) southwest of Ceylon, has an area of 115 sq. mi. (298 sq. km.) and a population of 254,000. Capital: Malé. Fishing employs 95 percent of the work force. Dried fish, copra and coir yarn are exported.

The Maldive Islands were visited by Arab traders and converted to Islam in 1153. After being harassed in the 16th and 17th centuries by Mopla pirates of the Malabar coast and Portuguese raiders, the Maldivians voluntarily placed themselves under the suzerainty of Ceylon. In 1887, the islands became an internally self-governing British protectorate and a nominal dependency of Ceylon. Traditionally a sultanate, the Maldives became a republic in 1953 but restored the sultanate in 1954. The Sultanate of the Maldive Islands attained complete internal and external autonomy within the Commonwealth on July 26, 1965, and on Nov. 11, 1968 again became a republic.

RULERS:

British to 1965

MONETARY SYSTEM:

1 Rufiyya (Rupee) = 100 Lari

REPUBLIC

MALDIVIAN STATE, GOVERNMENT TREASURER

1951-80 ISSUE

		VG	VF	UNC
7	**50 RUPEES** 1951-80. Blue on m/c unpt. Waterfront bldg. at ctr. on back.			
	a. 1951/AH1371.	35.00	90.00	250.00
	b. 4.6.1960/AH1379.	5.00	15.00	45.00
	c. Litho. 1.8.1980/AH17.7.1400.	6.00	17.50	50.00

MALDIVES MONETARY AUTHORITY

1983 ISSUE

#9-14 dhow at r. Wmk: Arms. Printer: BWC.

		VG	VF	UNC
9	**2 RUFIYAA** 7.10.1983/AH1404. Black on olive-brown and m/c unpt. Shoreline village on back.	FV	FV	3.00

		VG	VF	UNC
10	**5 RUFIYAA** 7.10.1983/AH1404. Deep purple on green and m/c unpt. Fishing boats at ctr. on back.	FV	FV	3.50

		VG	VF	UNC
11	**10 RUFIYAA** 7.10.1983/AH1404. Brown on m/c unpt. Villagers working at ctr. on back.	FV	FV	3.00

		VG	VF	UNC
12	**20 RUFIYAA** 7.10.1983/AH1404. Red-violet on m/c unpt. Fishing boats at dockside in Malé Harbour on back.			
	a. 7.10.1983/AH1404.	FV	FV	5.00
	b. 1987/AH1408.	FV	FV	6.00

		VG	VF	UNC
13	**50 RUFIYAA** 1983; 1987. Blue-violet on m/c unpt. Village Market in Malé at ctr. on back.			
	a. Imprint at bottom ctr. on back. 7.10.1983/AH1404.	FV	FV	17.50
	b. W/o imprint. 1987/AH1408.	FV	FV	13.00

		VG	VF	UNC
14	**100 RUFIYAA** 1983; 1987. Dk. green and brown on m/c unpt. Tomb of Medhuziyaaraiy at ctr. on back.			
	a. Imprint at bottom ctr. on back. 7.10.1983/AH1404.	FV	FV	27.50
	b. W/o imprint. 1987/AH1408.	FV	FV	25.00

1990 ISSUE

#15-17 wmk: Arms. Printer: TDLR.

		VG	VF	UNC
15	**2 RUFIYAA** 1990/AH1411. Like #9, but darker dhow and trees, also slightly diff. unpt. colors.	FV	FV	1.25
16	**5 RUFIYAA** 1990/AH1411. Like #10, but brown unpt. at ctr., also darker boats on back.	FV	FV	2.50
17	**500 RUFIYAA** 1990/AH1411. Orange and green on m/c unpt. Grand Friday Mosque and Islamic Center on back.	FV	FV	95.00

1995; 1996 ISSUE

#18 and 19 w/design into borders. Ascending size serial # at l. and lower r. Wmk: Arms. Printer: TDLR.

		VG	VF	UNC
18	**100 RUFIYAA** 1995/AH1416. Dk. green and brown on m/c unpt. Like #14 but lt. blue unpt. at l.	FV	FV	23.00
19	**500 RUFIYAA** 1996/AH1416. Orange and green on m/c unpt. Like #17 but ship in dark color.	FV	FV	90.00

1998 ISSUE

		VG	VF	UNC
20	**5 RUFIYAA** 1998/AH1419. Deep purple, dk. blue and violet on m/c unpt. Like #10.	FV	FV	2.00

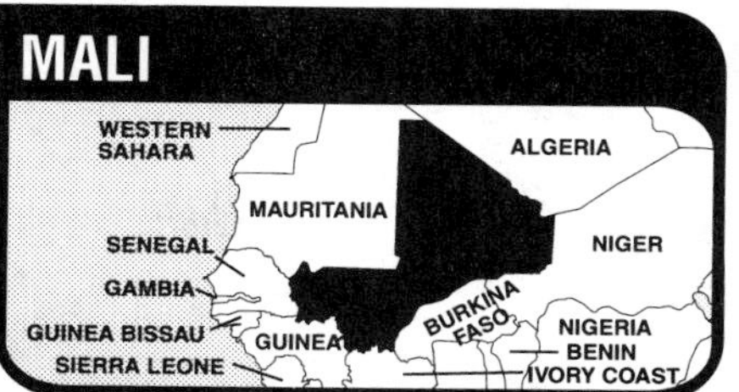

The Republic of Mali, a landlocked country in the interior of West Africa southwest of Algeria, has an area of 478,764 sq. mi. (1,240,000 sq. km.) and a population of 9.79 million. Capital: Bamako. Livestock, fish, cotton and peanuts are exported.

Malians are descendants of the ancient Malinke Kingdom of Mali that controlled the middle Niger from the 11th to the 17th centuries. The French penetrated the Sudan (now Mali) about 1880, and established their rule in 1898 after subduing fierce native resistance. In 1904 the area became the colony of Upper Senegal-Niger (changed to French Sudan in 1920), and became part of the French Union in 1946. In 1958 French Sudan became the Sudanese Republic with complete internal autonomy. Senegal joined with the Sudanese Republic in 1959 to form the Mali Federation which, in 1960, became a fully independent member of the French Community. Upon Senegal's subsequent withdrawal from the Federation, the Sudanese, on Sept. 22, 1960, proclaimed their nation the fully independent Republic of Mali and severed all ties with France.

Mali seceded from the African Financial Community in 1962, then rejoined in 1984. Issues specially marked with letter *D* for Mali were made by the Banque des Etats de l'Afrique de l'Ouest. See also French West Africa, and West African States.

MONETARY SYSTEM:

1 Franc = 100 Centimes

SIGNATURE VARIETIES

SIGNATURE VARIETIES			
1	Ministre Des Finances		Gouverneur de La Banque
2	Ministre d'Etat	Ministre Des Finances	Gouverneur de La Banque
3	Le Président du Counseil d'Administration		Le Directeur Général
4	Le Président du Counseil d'Administration		Le Directeur Général
5	Le Président du Counseil d'Administration		Le Directeur Général
6	Le Président du Counseil d'Administration		Le Directeur Général
7	Le Président du Counseil d'Administration		Le Directeur Général
8	Le Président du Counseil d'Administration		Le Directeur Général
9	Le Président du Counseil d'Administration		Le Directeur Général

REPUBLIC

BANQUE DE LA RÉPUBLIQUE DU MALI

FIRST 1960 (1962) ISSUE

NOTE: Post-dated on Day of Independence.

#1-5 Pres. Modibo Keita at l. Sign. 1.

		VG	VF	UNC
1	**50 FRANCS** 22.9.1960. Purple on m/c unpt. Village on back.	5.00	25.00	100.00

		VG	VF	UNC
2	**100 FRANCS** 22.9.1960. Brown on yellow unpt. Cattle on back.	5.00	30.00	165.00
3	**500 FRANCS** 22.9.1960. Red on lt. blue and orange unpt. Woman and tent on back.	55.00	200.00	875.00

		VG	VF	UNC
4	**1000 FRANCS** 22.9.1960. Blue on lt. green and orange unpt. Farmers w/oxen at lower r. Back blue; man and huts.	20.00	85.00	350.00
5	**5000 FRANCS** 22.9.1960. Green on m/c unpt. 2 farmers plowing w/oxen at r. Market scene and bldg. on back.	150.00	400.00	—

SECOND 1960 (1967) ISSUE

NOTE: Post-dated on Day of Independence.

#6-10 Modibo Keita at r. Sign 2. Printer: TDLR.

		VG	VF	UNC
6	**50 FRANCS** 22.9.1960 (1967). Purple on blue and lt. green unpt. Dam at lower l. Back purple; woman and village.	17.50	50.00	220.00

		VG	VF	UNC
7	**100 FRANCS** 22.9.1960 (1967). Brown on green and lilac unpt. Tractors at lower l. Back brown; old man at r., canoes at ctr., city view behind.	12.50	40.00	215.00
8	**500 FRANCS** 22.9.1960 (1967). Green on yellow, blue and red unpt. Bldg. at lower l. Longhorn cattle on back.	30.00	125.00	385.00

		VG	VF	UNC
9	**1000 FRANCS** 22.9.1960 (1967). Blue on lilac and brown unpt. Bank at lower l. Back blue; people and Djenne mosque.	25.00	135.00	660.00

		VG	VF	UNC
10	**5000 FRANCS** 22.9.1960 (1967). Dk. red on green unpt. Farmers at ctr. Market scene and bldgs. on back.	65.00	250.00	600.00

BANQUE CENTRALE DU MALI

1970-73 ND ISSUES

#12-15 wmk: Man's head. Sign. varieties.

		VG	VF	UNC
11	**100 FRANCS** ND (1972-73). Brown and m/c. Woman at l., hotel at r. Woman at l., boats docking at ctr. on back. Sign. 4.	6.00	25.00	82.50

12	500 FRANCS	VG	VF	UNC
	ND (1973-84). Brown and m/c. Soldier at l., tractors at r. Men and camels on back.			
	a. Sign. 4.	1.50	5.00	17.50
	b. Sign. 5.	1.50	5.00	17.50
	c. Sign. 6.	1.50	5.00	17.50
	d. Sign. 7.	1.50	5.00	17.50
	e. Sign. 8.	1.50	5.00	17.50
	f. Sign. 9.	5.00	20.00	67.50

13	1000 FRANCS	VG	VF	UNC
	ND (1970-84). Brownish black, purple and m/c. Bldg. at l., older man at r. Carvings at l., mountain village at ctr. on back.			
	a. Sign. 4.	2.50	6.00	22.50
	b. Sign. 5.	2.50	6.00	22.50
	c. Sign. 6.	2.50	6.00	20.00
	d. Sign. 7.	2.50	6.00	17.50
	e. Sign. 8.	2.50	6.00	17.50

14	5000 FRANCS	VG	VF	UNC
	ND (1972-84). Blue, brown and m/c. Cattle at lower l., man w/turban at r. Woman and flowers at l. ctr., woman at textile machinery at r. on back.			
	a. Sign. 4.	8.50	25.00	85.00
	b. Sign. 5.	8.50	25.00	80.00
	c. Sign. 6.	8.50	25.00	75.00
	d. Sign. 7.	8.50	25.00	75.00
	e. Sign. 8.	8.50	25.00	75.00

15	10,000 FRANCS	VG	VF	UNC
	ND (1970-84). M/c. Man w/fez at l., factory at lower r. Weaver at l., young woman w/coin headband at r. on back.			
	a. Sign. 3.	20.00	50.00	145.00
	b. Sign. 4.	15.00	35.00	100.00
	c. Sign. 5.	15.00	35.00	100.00
	d. Sign. 6.	15.00	35.00	110.00
	e. Sign. 7.	15.00	35.00	100.00
	f. Sign. 8.	15.00	35.00	95.00
	g. Sign. 9.	15.00	35.00	110.00

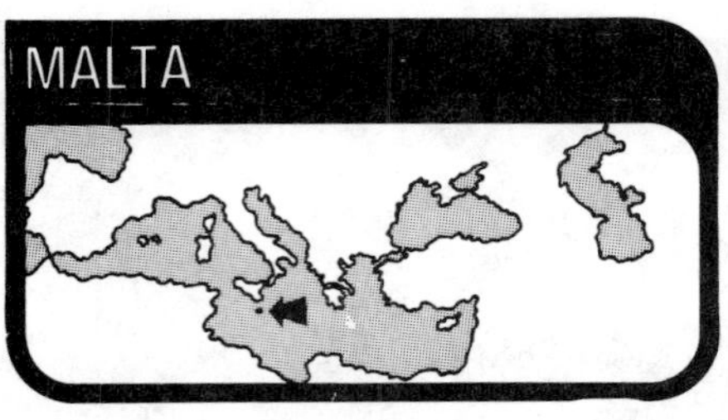

The Republic of Malta, an independent parliamentary democracy within the British Commonwealth, is situated in the Mediterranean Sea between Sicily and North Africa. With the islands of Gozo and Comino, Malta has an area of 122 sq. mi. (316 sq. km.) and a population of 374,700. Capital: Valletta. With the islands of Gozo (Ghawdex), Comino, Cominetto and Filfla, Malta has no proven mineral resources, an agriculture insufficient to its needs and a small but expanding, manufacturing facility. Clothing, textile yarns and fabrics, and knitted wear are exported.

For more than 3,500 years Malta was ruled, in succession, by Phoenicians, Carthaginians, Romans, Arabs, Normans, the Knights of Malta, France and Britain. Napoleon seized Malta by treachery in 1798. The French were ousted by a Maltese insurrection assisted by Britain, and in 1814, Malta, of its own free will, became part of the British Empire. The island was awarded the George Cross for conspicuous corrage during World War II. Malta obtained full independence in September 1964, electing to remain within the Commonwealth with Elizabeth II as Head of State as Queen of Malta.

RULERS:

British to 1974

MONETARY SYSTEM:

1 Cent = 10 Mils

1 Lira (Pound) = 100 Cents, 1971-

REPUBLIC

GOVERNMENT

1949 ORDINANCE; 1963 ND ISSUE

#25-27 Qn. Elizabeth II at r. Printer: BWC.

		VG	VF	UNC
25	**10 SHILLINGS** *L.1949* (1963). Green and blue on m/c unpt. Cross at ctr. Mgarr Harbor, Gozo on back.	6.00	30.00	165.00

		VG	VF	UNC
26	**1 POUND** *L.1949* (1963). Brown and violet on m/c unpt. Cross at ctr. Industrial Estate, Marsa on back.	6.00	30.00	165.00

		VG	VF	UNC
27	**5 POUNDS** *L.1949* (1961). Blue on m/c unpt. Cross at ctr. Grand Harbor on back.			
	a. Sign. D. A. Shepherd (1961).	30.00	160.00	750.00
	b. Sign. R. Soler (1963).	30.00	150.00	700.00

BANK CENTRALI TA' MALTA

CENTRAL BANK OF MALTA

1967 CENTRAL BANK ACT; 1968-69 ND ISSUE

#28-30 designs similar to #25-27. Printer: BWC.

		VG	VF	UNC
28	**10 SHILLINGS** *L.1967* (1968). Red on m/c unpt. Similar to #25.	5.00	20.00	90.00

		VG	VF	UNC
29	**1 POUND** *L.1967* (1969). Olive-green on m/c unpt. Similar to #26.	7.50	20.00	150.00

		VG	VF	UNC
30	**5 POUNDS** *L.1967* (1968). Brown and violet on m/c unpt. Similar to #27.	10.00	50.00	300.00

1967 CENTRAL BANK ACT; 1973 ND ISSUE

#31-33 arms at r., map at ctr. Wmk: Allegorical head of Malta. Printer: TDLR. Replacement notes: Serial # prefix *X/1, Y/1* or *Z/1* (by denomination).

		VG	VF	UNC
31	**1 LIRA** *L.1967* (1973). Green on m/c unpt. War Memorial at l. Prehistoric Temple in Tarxien at l., old capital city of Medina at ctr. on back.			
	a. Sign. J. Sammut and A. Camilleri.	FV	4.00	35.00
	b. Sign. H. de Gabriele and J. Laspina.	FV	4.00	35.00
	c. Sign. H. de Gabriele and A. Camilleri.	FV	4.00	35.00
	d. Sign. J. Laspina and J. Sammut.	FV	4.00	35.00
	e. Sign. A. Camilleri and J. Laspina.	FV	4.00	35.00
	f. Sign. J. Sammut and H. de Gabriele.	FV	4.00	35.00

		VG	VF	UNC
32	**5 LIRI** *L.1967* (1973). Blue on m/c unpt. Neptune at l. Marina at l., boats at ctr. r. on back.			
	a. Sign. H. de Gabriele and J. Laspina.	FV	15.00	85.00
	b. Sign. H. de Gabriele and A. Camilleri.	FV	15.00	85.00
	c. Sign. J. Laspina and J. Sammut.	FV	15.00	85.00
	d. Sign. A. Camilleri and J. Laspina.	FV	15.00	85.00
	e. Sign. J. Sammut and H. de Gabriele.	FV	15.00	85.00
	f. Sign. J. Sammut and A. Camilleri.	FV	15.00	85.00

		VG	VF	UNC
33	**10 LIRI** *L.1967* (1973). Brown on m/c unpt. Like #32. View of Grand Harbour and boats on back.			
	a. Sign. H. de Gabriele and A. Camilleri.	FV	30.00	145.00
	b. Sign. J. Laspina and J. Sammut.	FV	35.00	220.00
	c. Sign. A. Camilleri and J. Laspina.	FV	35.00	220.00
	d. Sign. J. Sammut and H. de Gabriele.	FV	35.00	220.00
	e. Sign. L. Spiteri w/title: *DEPUTAT GOVERNATUR.*	FV	35.00	145.00

1979 ND ISSUE

Central Bank Act, 1967

#34-36 map at upper l., arms at upper r. Wmk: Allegorical head of Malta. Printer: TDLR. Replacement notes: Serial prefix *X/2, Y/2* or *Z/2* (by denomination).

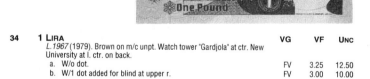

		VG	VF	UNC
34	**1 LIRA** *L.1967* (1979). Brown on m/c unpt. Watch tower "Gardjola" at ctr. New University at l. ctr. on back.			
	a. W/o dot.	FV	3.25	12.50
	b. W/1 dot added for blind at upper r.	FV	3.00	10.00

		VG	VF	UNC
35	**5 LIRI** *L.1967* (1979). Purple and violet on m/c unpt. Statue of "Culture" at ctr. Aerial view of Marsa Industrial Estate at l. ctr. on back.			
	a. W/o 2 dots.	FV	14.00	50.00
	b. W/2 dots added for blind at upper r.	FV	13.00	45.00

NOTICE

Readers with unlisted dates, signature varieties, etc. are invited to submit photocopies of their notes to: Standard Catalog of World Paper Money, 700 East State St. Iola, WI 54990-0001, fax: 1-715-445-4087, or E-Mail: thernr@krause.com.

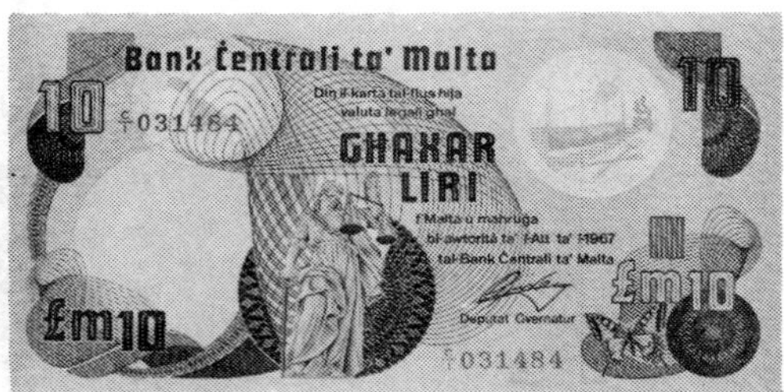

		VG	VF	UNC
36	**10 LIRI** *L.1967* (1979). Gray and pink on m/c unpt. Statue of "Justice" at ctr. Aerial view of Malta drydocks at l. ctr. on back.			
	a. W/o 3 dots.	FV	28.00	70.00
	b. W/3 dots added for blind at upper r.	FV	28.00	85.00

1986 ND ISSUE

#37-40 sailing craft and map of Malta at ctr., A. Barbara at r. Wmk: Allegorical head of Malta. Printer: TDLR. Replacement notes: Serial # prefix *W/2*, *X/2*, *Y/2* or *Z/2* (by denomination).

		VG	VF	UNC
37	**2 LIRI** *L.1967* (1986). Red-orange on m/c unpt. Dockside crane at l., aerial harbor view at r. on back.	FV	FV	18.50

		VG	VF	UNC
38	**5 LIRI** *L.1967* (1986). Gray-green and blue on m/c unpt. w/2 black horizontal accounting bars at lower r. Sailboats in harbor and repairing of fishing nets on back.	FV	FV	35.00

		VG	VF	UNC
39	**10 LIRI** *L.1967* (1986). Olive and dk. green on m/c unpt. w/3 dk. green horizontal accounting bars at lower r. Shipbuilding on back.	FV	FV	60.00

		VG	VF	UNC
40	**20 LIRA** *L.1967* (1986). Brown and red-brown on m/c unpt. w/4 brown horizontal accounting bars at lower r. Statue and govt. bldg. at ctr. on back.	FV	FV	150.00

1989 ND ISSUE

#41-44 doves at l., Malta standing w/rudder at ctr. r. Wmk: Turreted head of Malta. Printer: TDLR. Replacement notes: Serial # prefix *W/2*, *X/2*, *Y/2* or *Z/2* (by denomination).

		VG	VF	UNC
41	**2 LIRI** *L.1967* (1989). Purple on m/c unpt. Bldgs. in Malta and Gozo on back.	FV	FV	15.00
42	**5 LIRI** *L.1967* (1989). Blue on m/c unpt. Historical tower on back.	FV	FV	35.00
43	**10 LIRI** *L.1967* (1989). Green on m/c unpt. Wounded people being brought into National Assembly on back.	FV	FV	65.00
44	**20 LIRA** *L.1967* (1989). Brown on m/c unpt. Prime Minister Dr. G. B. Olivier on back.	FV	FV	125.00

1994 ND ISSUE

#45-48 like #41-44 but w/enhanced colors and segmented foil over security threads.

		VG	VF	UNC
45	**2 LIRI** *L.1967* (1994). Purple on m/c unpt.	FV	FV	15.00
46	**5 LIRI** *L.1967* (1994). Blue on m/c unpt.	FV	FV	30.00
47	**10 LIRI** *L.1967* (1994). Green on m/c unpt.	FV	FV	50.00
48	**20 LIRA** *L.1967* (1994). Brown on m/c unpt.	FV	FV	100.00

COLLECTOR SERIES

BANK CENTRALI TA' MALTA

1979 ISSUE

		ISSUE PRICE	MKT. VALUE
CS1	**ND (1979) 1-10 LIRI** #34a-36a w/ovpt: *SPECIMEN* and Maltese cross prefix serial #.	14.00	30.00

MARTINIQUE

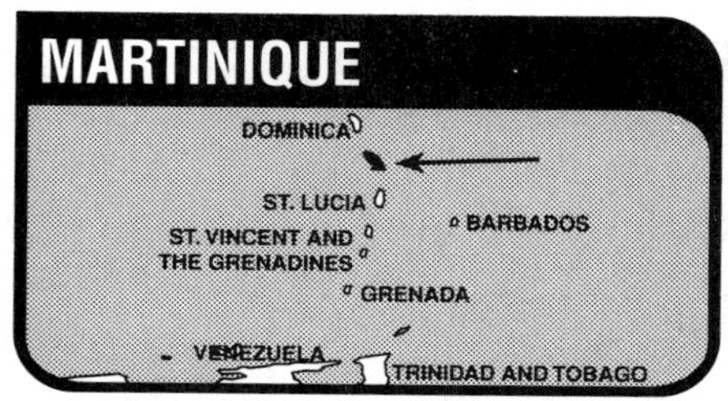

The French Overseas Department of Martinique, located in the Lesser Antilles of the West Indies between Dominica and Saint Lucia, has an area of 425 sq. mi. (1,101 sq. km.) and a population of 329,000. Capital: Fort-de-France. Agriculture and tourism are the major sources of income. Bananas, sugar and rum are exported.

Christopher Columbus discovered Martinique, probably on June 15, 1502. France took possession on June 25, 1635, and has maintained possession since that time except for three short periods of British occupation during the Napoleonic Wars. A French department since 1946, Martinique voted a reaffirmation of that status in 1958, remaining within the new French Community. Martinique was the birthplace of Napoleon's Empress Josephine, and the site of the eruption of Mt. Pelee in 1902 that claimed over 40,000 lives.

RULERS:

French

MONETARY SYSTEM:

1 Franc = 100 Centimes

FRENCH INFLUENCE

NOTE: For later issues see French Antilles.

CAISSE CENTRALE DE LA FRANCE D'OUTRE-MER

1960 ND PROVISIONAL ISSUE

#37-41 ovpt: *MARTINIQUE* and new denominations on previous "old" Franc issues.

		VG	VF	UNC
37	**1 NOUVEAU FRANC ON 100 FRANCS** ND (1960). M/c. La Bourdonnais at l., native couple at r.	10.00	85.00	300.00

		VG	VF	UNC
38	**5 NOUVEAUX FRANCS ON 500 FRANCS** ND (1960). M/c. 2 women at r., sailboat at l. Farmers w/ox carts on back.	20.00	160.00	525.00

		VG	VF	UNC
39	**10 NOUVEAUX FRANCS ON 1000 FRANCS** ND (1960). M/c. Fisherman. Woman w/box of produce on her head at l. ctr. on back.	35.00	200.00	700.00
40	**50 NOUVEAUX FRANCS ON 5000 FRANCS** ND (1960). M/c. Woman holding fruit bowl at ctr. Harvesting scene on back.	150.00	700.00	—
41	**50 NOUVEAUX FRANCS ON 5000 FRANCS** ND (1960). M/c. Gen. Schoelcher. Specimen.	—	—	—

MAURITANIA

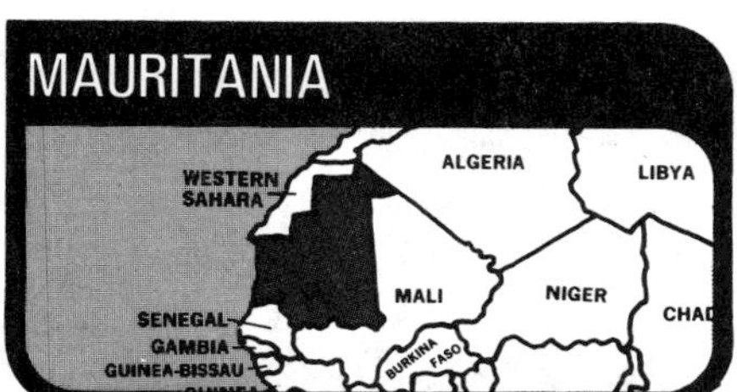

The Islamic Republic of Mauritania, located in northwest Africa bounded by Spanish Sahara, Mali, Algeria, Senegal and the Atlantic Ocean, has an area of 397,955 sq. mi. (1,030,700 sq. km.) and a population of 2.33 million. Capital: Nouakchott. The economy centers on herding, agriculture, fishing and mining. Iron ore, copper concentrates and fish products are exported.

The indigenous Negroid inhabitants were driven out of Mauritania by Berber invaders of the Islamic faith in the 11th century. The Berbers in turn were conquered by Arab invaders, the Beni Hassan, in the 16th century. Arab traders carried on a gainful trade in gum arabic, gold and slaves with Portuguese, Dutch, English and French traders until late in the 19th century when France took control of the area, and in 1920 made it a part of French West Africa. Mauritania became a part of the French Union in 1946 and was made an autonomous republic within the new French Community in 1958, when the Islamic Republic of Mauritania was proclaimed. The republic became independent on November 28, 1960, and withdrew from the French Community in 1966.

On June 28, 1973, in a move designed to emphasize its non-alignment with France, Mauritania converted its currency from the old French-supported CFA franc unit to a new unit called the Ouguiya.

MONETARY SYSTEM:

1 Ouguiya = 5 Khoum

100 Ouguiya = 500 CFA Francs, 1973-

NOTE: Issues specially marked with letter *E* for Mauritania were made by the Banque Centrale des Etats de l'Afrique de l'Ouest. These issues were used before Mauritania seceded from the French Community of the West African States in 1973. For listing see West African States.

REPUBLIC

BANQUE CENTRALE DE MAURITANIE

1973 ISSUE

#1-3 printed in Algeria.

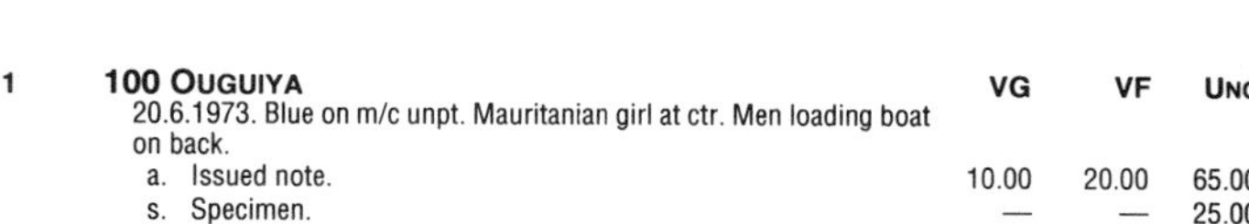

		VG	VF	UNC
1	**100 OUGUIYA** 20.6.1973. Blue on m/c unpt. Mauritanian girl at ctr. Men loading boat on back.			
	a. Issued note.	10.00	20.00	65.00
	s. Specimen.	—	—	25.00

		VG	VF	UNC
2	**200 OUGUIYA** 20.6.1973. Brown on m/c unpt. Bedouin woman at l., tents in background. Camels and huts on back.			
	a. Issued note.	11.00	25.00	75.00
	s. Specimen.	—	—	27.50

NOTICE

Readers with unlisted dates, signature varieties, etc. are invited to submit photocopies of their notes to: Standard Catalog of World Paper Money, 700 East State St. Iola, WI 54990-0001, fax: 1-715-445-4087, or E-Mail: thernr@krause.com.

3	1000 OUGUIYA	VG	VF	UNC
	20.6.1973. Green and m/c. Woman weaving on loom at l., metal worker at r. ctr. Local musicians and scenes on back.			
	a. Issued note.	15.00	35.00	120.00
	s. Specimen.	—	—	30.00

1974; 1979 ISSUE

#4-7 wmk: Old man w/beard. Sign. varieties. Printer: G&D (w/o imprint).

4	100 OUGUIYA	VG	VF	UNC
	1974-. Purple, violet and brown on m/c unpt. Musical instruments at l., cow and tower at r. on back.			
	a. 28.11.1974. Thin security thread.	4.00	10.00	25.00
	b. 28.11.1983.	7.50	15.00	35.00
	c. 28.11.1985.	2.00	7.50	15.00
	d. 28.11.1989. Thick security thread.	1.50	5.00	12.50
	e. 28.11.1992.	FV	4.00	10.00
	f. 28.11.1993.	FV	3.00	9.00
	g. 28.11.1995.	FV	2.50	6.00
	h. 28.11.1996.	FV	2.50	5.50
	s. As a. Specimen.	—	—	20.00

5	200 OUGUIYA	VG	VF	UNC
	1974-. Brown, dk. olive-green and brown-orange on m/c unpt. Bowl and rod at l., dugout canoe and palm tree at r. on back.			
	a. 28.11.1974. Thin security thread.	6.00	15.00	30.00
	b. 28.11.1985.	4.00	10.00	25.00
	c. 28.11.1989. Thick security thread.	3.00	6.00	22.50
	d. 28.11.1992.	FV	5.00	21.50
	e. 28.11.1993.	FV	5.00	15.00
	f. 28.11.1995.	FV	5.00	10.00
	g. 28.11.1996.	FV	5.00	8.50
	s. As a. Specimen.	—	—	25.00

6	500 OUGUIYA	VG	VF	UNC
	1979-. Green, brown and dk. green on m/c unpt. Back brown, green and black; field workers at l., mine entrance complex at r.			
	a. 28.11.1979. Thin security thread.	18.00	40.00	90.00
	b. 28.11.1983.	16.00	35.00	90.00
	c. 28.11.1985.	8.50	15.00	40.00
	d. 28.11.1989. Thick security thread.	6.50	12.00	36.00
	e. 28.11.1991.	FV	10.00	30.00
	f. 28.11.1992.	FV	8.00	25.00
	g. 28.11.1993.	FV	8.00	22.50
	h. 28.11.1995.	FV	8.00	20.00
	i. 28.11.1996.	FV	8.00	18.50
	s. As a. Specimen.	—	—	40.00

7	1000 OUGUIYA	VG	VF	UNC
	1974-. Blue, violet and blue-black on m/c unpt. Bowl of fish at l., camel, hut and tower at r. back.			
	a. 28.11.1974. Thin security thread.	18.00	40.00	85.00
	b. 28.11.1985.	11.50	30.00	55.00
	c. 28.11.1989. Thick security thread.	10.00	25.00	45.00
	d. 28.10.1991.	FV	20.00	40.00
	e. 28.11.1992.	FV	15.00	40.00
	f. 28.11.1993.	FV	15.00	35.00
	g. 28.11.1995.	FV	15.00	27.50
	s. As a. Specimen.	—	—	50.00

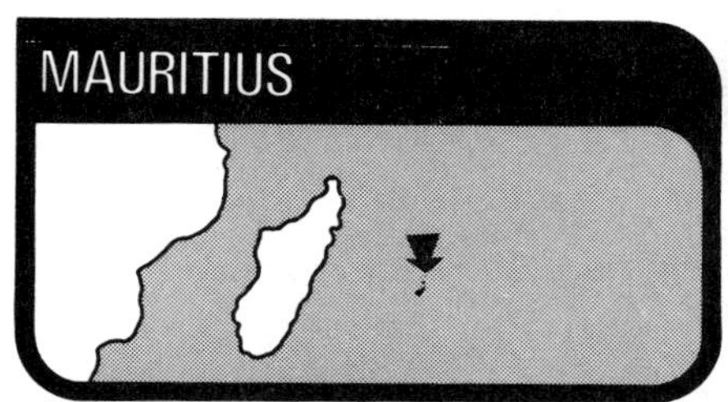

The island of Mauritius, a member of the British Commonwealth located in the Indian Ocean 500 miles (805 km.) east of Madagascar, has an area of 790 sq. mi. (2,045 sq. km.) and a population of 1.13 million. Capital: Port Louis. Sugar provides 90 percent of the export revenue.

Cartographic evidence indicates that Arabs and Malays arrived at Mauritius during the Middle Ages. Domingo Fernandez, a Portuguese navigator, visited the island in the early 16th century, but Portugal made no attempt at settlement. The Dutch took possession, and named the island, in 1598. Their colony failed to prosper and was abandoned in 1710. France claimed Mauritius in 1715 and developed a strong and prosperous colony that endured until the island was captured by the British in 1810, during the Napoleonic Wars. British possession was confirmed by the Treaty of Paris, 1814. Mauritius became independent on March 12, 1968, with Elizabeth II as Head of State as Queen of Mauritius. Mauritius became a Republic on March 12, 1992, with a President as Head of State.

RULERS:

British

MONETARY SYSTEM:

1 Rupee = 100 Cents, 1848-

BRITISH INFLUENCE
BANK OF MAURITIUS

SIGNATURE VARIETIES

	GOVERNOR OF THE BANK	MANAGING DIRECTOR		GOVERNOR OF THE BANK	MANAGING DIRECTOR
1	[signature]	[signature]	2	[signature]	[signature]
3	[signature]	[signature]	4	[signature]	[signature]
5	GOVERNOR [signature]	[signature]			

1967 ND ISSUE

#30-33 Qn. Elizabeth II at r. Wmk: Dodo bird. Printer: TDLR. Replacement notes: Serial # prefix Z/#.

#		VG	VF	UNC
30	**5 RUPEES** ND (1967). Blue on m/c unpt. Sailboat on back.			
	a. Sign. 1.	.75	1.75	9.50
	b. Sign. 3.	1.00	3.00	25.00
	c. Sign. 4.	.50	1.25	6.50

#		VG	VF	UNC
31	**10 RUPEES** ND (1967). Red on m/c unpt. Government bldg. on back.			
	a. Sign. 1.	.85	2.00	13.50
	b. Sign. 2.	1.00	3.00	22.50
	c. Sign. 4.	.75	1.25	8.50

#		VG	VF	UNC
32	**25 RUPEES** ND (1967). Green on m/c unpt. Ox cart on back.			
	a. Sign. 1.	2.50	5.50	45.00
	b. Sign. 4.	2.00	5.00	37.50

#		VG	VF	UNC
33	**50 RUPEES** ND (1967). Purple on m/c unpt. Ships docked at Port Louis harbor on back.			
	a. Sign. 1.	10.00	27.50	135.00
	b. Sign. 2.	7.50	25.00	125.00
	c. Sign. 4.	4.00	10.00	57.50

1985-91 ND ISSUE

#34-41 replacement notes: Serial # prefix Z/#.

#34-36 outline of Mauritius map on back. Wmk: Dodo bird. Printer: TDLR. Sign. 5.

#		VG	VF	UNC
34	**5 RUPEES** ND (1985). Dk. brown. Arms at lower l. ctr., bldg. w/flag at r. Bank on back.	FV	FV	1.25

		VG	VF	UNC
35	**10 RUPEES** ND (1985). Green on m/c unpt. Arms at lower l. ctr., bldg. w/flag at ctr. r. Bridge on back.			
	a. Dk. green printing.	FV	FV	3.00
	b. Lt. green printing.	FV	FV	1.75

		VG	VF	UNC
36	**20 RUPEES** ND. Bluish purple, blue-green, blue and orange on m/c unpt. Lady Jugnauth at l., arms at ctr., bldg. w/flag at lower r. Satellite dishes at ctr. on back.	FV	FV	3.50

#37 and 38 arms at lower l. to lower ctr., bldg. w/flag at r. Wmk: Dodo bird. Printer: BWC w/o imprint.

		VG	VF	UNC
37	**50 RUPEES** ND (1986). Dk. blue on m/c unpt. 2 deer and butterfly on back.	FV	FV	7.00

		VG	VF	UNC
38	**100 RUPEES** ND (1986). Red on m/c unpt. Landscape on back.	FV	FV	14.50

		VG	VF	UNC
39	**200 RUPEES** ND (1985). Blue on m/c unpt. Sir Seewoodsagur Ramgoolam at l. Lg. home (Le Réduit) on back. Printer: TDLR.	FV	FV	27.50

		VG	VF	UNC
40	**500 RUPEES** ND (1988). Brown and orange on m/c unpt. Bldg. w/flag at ctr., arms below, Sir A. Jugnaurh (Prime Minister) at r. Sugar cane field workers loading wagon w/mountains in background on back. Wmk: Dodo bird. Printer: BWC.	FV	FV	65.00

		VG	VF	UNC
41	**1000 RUPEES** ND (1991). Blue and purple on m/c unpt. Sir V. Ringadoo at l., palm trees and bldg. w/flag at ctr. Port Louis harbor on back. Wmk: Dodo bird.	FV	FV	120.00

1998 ISSUE

#42-48 arms at lower l., bldg. facades at ctr., standing Justice w/scales at lower r. in unpt. Wmk: Dodo bird's head. Ascending serial #.

#42-48 raised much public controversy being printed w/the values in English/ Sanskrit/ Tamil instead of the normal English/ Tamil/ Sanskrit order. They are being withdrawn and a new issue is being prepared for release.

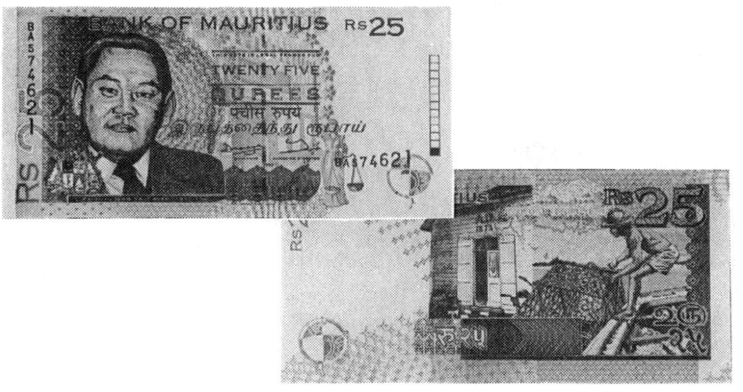

		VG	VF	UNC
42	**25 RUPEES** 1998. Black, violet and brown on m/c unpt. Sir M. J. Ah-chuen at l. Bldg. facade at ctr., worker at r. on back.	FV	FV	4.00

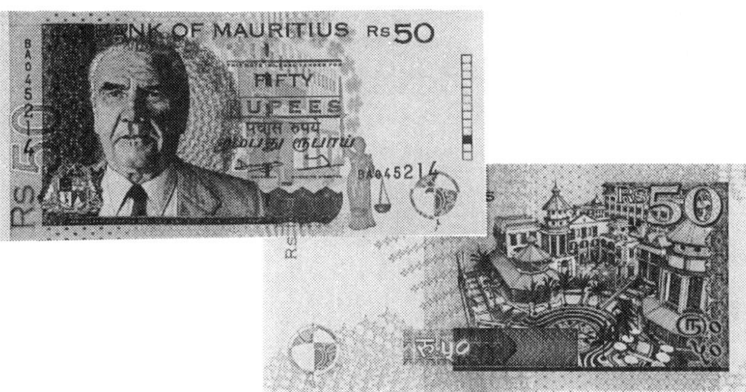

		VG	VF	UNC
43	**50 RUPEES** 1998. Black, purple and deep blue on m/c unpt. J. M. Paturau at l. Bldg. complex at ctr. r. on back.	FV	FV	7.00

		VG	VF	UNC
44	**100 RUPEES** 1998. Black, blue and deep blue-green on m/c unpt. R. Seeneevassen at r. Bldg. at r. on back.	FV	FV	13.50

		VG	VF	UNC
45	**200 RUPEES** 1998. Black, deep green and violet on m/c unpt. Sir A. R. Mohamed at l. Market street scene.	FV	FV	27.50

		VG	VF	UNC
46	**500 RUPEES** 1998. Black, brown and orange on m/c unpt. S. Bissoondoyal at l. University of Mauritius at ctr. r. on back.	FV	FV	60.00

		VG	VF	UNC
47	**1000 RUPEES** 1998. Black and blue on m/c unpt. Sir C. G. Duval at l. Women dancing at ctr. r. on back.	FV	FV	110.00
48	**2000 RUPEES** 1998. Rose, orange, black, yellow-brown on m/c unpt. Seewoosagur Ramgoolam at l. Ox cart on back.	FV	FV	190.00

1999 ISSUE

#49-55 as 42-48 but w/corrected language text English/Tamil/Hindi.

		VG	VF	UNC
49	**25 RUPEES** 1999. Similar to #42.	FV	FV	4.00
50	**50 RUPEES** 1999. Similar to #43.	FV	FV	6.50
51	**100 RUPEES** 1999. Similar to #44.	FV	FV	12.50
52	**200 RUPEES** 1999. Similar to #45.	FV	FV	25.00
53	**500 RUPEES** 1999. Similar to #46.	FV	FV	55.00

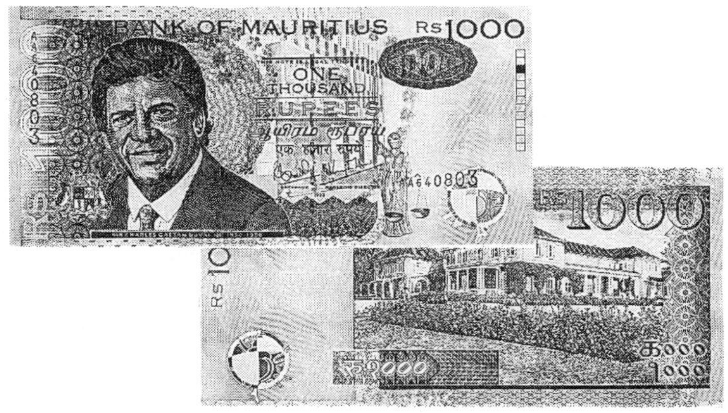

		VG	VF	UNC
54	**1000 RUPEES** 1999. Slate black, lt. blue and red unpt. Sir Charles Duval. Back lt. blue and red. Bldg. at ctr.	FV	FV	105.00
55	**2000 RUPEES** 1999. Similar to #48.	FV	FV	215.00

Collector Series

Bank of Mauritius

1978 ND Issue

		Issue Price	Mkt. Value
CS1	**ND (1978) 5-50 Rupees** #30c, 31c, 32b, 33c w/ovpt.: *SPECIMEN* and Maltese cross prefix serial #.	14.00	30.00

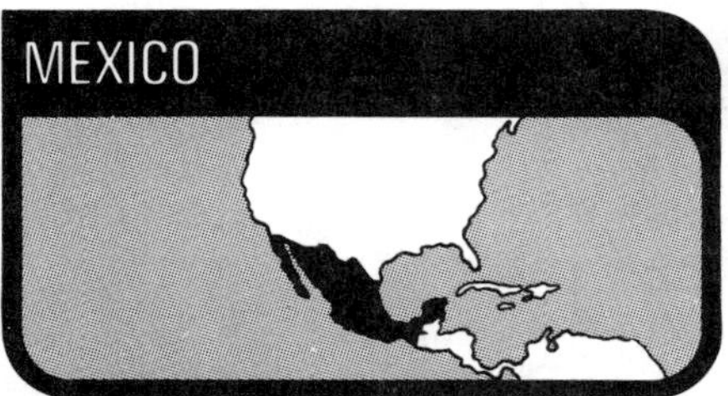

The United Mexican States, located immediately south of the United States, has an area of 759,529 sq. mi. (1,967,183 sq. km.) and a population of 95.5 million. Capital: Mexico City. The economy is based on agriculture, manufacturing and mining. Cotton, sugar, coffee and shrimp are exported.

Mexico was the site of highly advanced Indian civilizations 1,500 years before conquistador Hernando Cortes conquered the wealthy Aztec empire of Montezuma. 1519-1521, and founded a Spanish colony which lasted for nearly 300 years. During the Spanish period, Mexico, then called New Spain, stretched from Guatemala to the present states of Wyoming and California, its present northern boundary having been established by the secession of Texas during (1836) and the war of 1846-1848 with the United States.

Independence from Spain was declared by Father Miguel Hidalgo on Sept. 16, 1810, Mexican Independence Day and was achieved by General Agustin de Iturbide in 1821. Iturbide became emperor in 1822 but was deposed when a republic was established a year later. For more than half a century following the birth of the republic, the political scene of Mexico was characterized by turmoil which saw two emperors (including the unfortunate Maximilian), several dictators and an average of one new government every nine months passing swiftly from obscurity to oblivion. The land, social, economic and labor reforms promulgated by the Reform Constitution of Feb. 5, 1917 established the basis for a sustained economic development and participative democracy that have made Mexico one of the most politically stable countries of modern Latin America.

MONETARY SYSTEM:

1 Peso = 100 Centavos
1 Nuevo Peso = 1000 "old" Pesos, 1992-1996
1 Peso = 1 Nuevo Peso, 1996-

Estados Unidos Mexicanos

United States of Mexico

El Banco de México, S.A.

1948 Issue

#49, 51 and 52 sign. varieties. Printer: ABNC.

		VG	VF	Unc
49	**50 Pesos** 1948-72. Deep blue on m/c unpt. Portr. I. de Allende at l. Middle sign. title: *INTERVENTOR DE LA COM. NAC. BANCARIA.* Engraved dates. Back blue; Independence Monument at ctr.			
	a. 22.12.1948. Black series letters. Series: BM-BD.	3.00	6.00	15.00
	b. 23.11.1949. Series: BU-BX.	3.00	6.00	15.00
	c. 26.7.1950. Series: BY-CF.	3.00	5.00	13.50
	d. 27.12.1950. Series: CS-DH.	3.00	5.00	13.50
	e. 19.1.1953. Series: DK-DV.	2.00	4.00	12.00
	f. 10.2.1954. Series: DW-EH.	2.00	4.00	10.00
	g. 8.9.1954. Series: EI-FF.	2.00	4.00	10.00
	h. 11.1.1956. Series: FK-FV.	2.00	4.00	10.00
	i. 19.6.1957. Series: FW-GP.	2.00	4.00	10.00
	j. 20.8.1958. Series: HC-HR.	2.00	4.00	10.00
	k. 18.3.1959. Red series letters. Series: HS-IP.	2.00	4.00	10.00
	l. 20.5.1959. Series: IQ-JN.	2.00	4.00	10.00
	m. 25.1.1961. Series: JO-LB.	1.50	3.00	8.00
	n. 8.11.1961. Series: LC-AID.	1.50	3.00	8.00
	o. 24.4.1963. Series: AIE-BAP.	1.50	3.00	8.00
	p. 17.2.1965. Series: BAQ-BCD.	1.00	2.50	5.50
	q. 10.5.1967. Series: BCY-BEG.	1.00	2.50	5.00
	r. 19.11.1969. Series: BGK-BIC.	1.00	2.50	4.50
	s. 22.7.1970. Series: BIG-BKN.	1.00	2.50	4.50
	t. 27.6.1972. Series: BLI-BMG.	1.00	2.50	4.50
	u. 29.12.1972. Series: BNG-BRB.	1.00	2.00	4.50
	v. Specimen, punched hole cancelled.	—	—	125.00

		VG	VF	Unc
51	**500 Pesos** 1948-78. Black on m/c unpt. Portr. J. M. Morelos y Pavon at r. W/o "No" above serial #. Middle sign. title: *INTERVENTOR DE LA COM. NAC. BANCARIA.* Back green; Palace of Mining at ctr.			
	a. 22.12.1948. Series: BA.	15.00	40.00	150.00
	b. 27.12.1950. Series: CS; CT.	15.00	40.00	150.00
	c. 3.12.1951. Series: DI; DJ.	15.00	40.00	150.00
	d. 19.1.1953. Series: DK-DN.	12.00	25.00	60.00
	e. 31.8.1955. Series: FG-FJ.	12.00	20.00	50.00
	f. 11.1.1956. Series: FK-FL.	12.00	20.00	50.00
	g. 19.6.1957. Series: FW-GB.	12.00	20.00	50.00

51	500 PESOS	VG	VF	UNC
	h. 20.8.1958. Series: HC-HH.	10.00	20.00	40.00
	i. 18.3.1959. Series: HS-HX.	10.00	20.00	40.00
	j. 20.5.1959. Series: IQ-IV.	10.00	20.00	40.00
	k. 25.1.1961. Series: JO-JT.	10.00	20.00	40.00
	l. 8.11.1961. Series: LC-MP.	10.00	20.00	40.00
	m. 17.2.1965. Series: BAQ-BCN.	6.00	12.00	25.00
	n. 24.3.1971. Series: BKD-BKT.	2.50	5.00	12.50
	o. 27.6.1972. Series: BLI-BLT.	2.50	5.00	12.50
	p. 29.12.1972. Series: BNG-BNP.	2.50	5.00	12.50
	q. 18.7.1973. Series: BUY-BWB.	1.75	5.00	12.50
	r. 2.8.1974. Series: BXV-BZI.	1.75	3.50	10.00
	s. 18.2.1977. Series: BZJ-CCK.	1.00	3.50	8.50
	t. 18.1.1978. Series: CCL-CDY.	1.00	3.50	8.50

52	1000 PESOS 1948-77. Black on m/c unpt. Portr. Cuauhtemoc at l. Middle sign. title: *INTERVENTOR DE LA COM. NAC. BANCARIA.* Back brown; Chichen Itza pyramid at ctr.	VG	VF	UNC
	a. 22.12.1948. Series: BA.	25.00	45.00	150.00
	b. 23.11.1949. Series: BU.	25.00	45.00	150.00
	c. 27.12.1950. Series: CS.	25.00	45.00	125.00
	d. 3.12.1951. Series: DI; DJ.	25.00	45.00	125.00
	e. 19.1.1953. Series: DK; DL.	25.00	45.00	125.00
	f. 31.8.1955. Series: FG; FH.	20.00	40.00	75.00
	g. 11.1.1956. Series: FK; FL.	20.00	40.00	75.00
	h. 19.6.1957. Series: FN-FX.	20.00	35.00	60.00
	i. 20.8.1958. Series: HC-HE.	20.00	35.00	60.00
	j. 18.3.1959. Series: HS-HU.	18.00	30.00	50.00
	k. 20.5.1959. Series: IQ-IS.	18.00	30.00	50.00
	l. 25.1.1961. Series: JO-JQ.	18.00	30.00	45.00
	m. 8.11.1961. Series: LC-LV.	15.00	25.00	40.00
	n. 17.2.1965. Series: BAQ-BCN.	7.00	15.00	30.00
	o. 24.3.1971. Series: BKO-BKT.	2.00	4.50	15.00
	p. 27.6.1972. Series: BLI-BLM.	2.00	4.50	12.00
	q. 29.12.1972. Series: BNG-BNK.	2.00	4.50	12.00
	r. 18.7.1973. Series: BUY-BWB.	2.00	4.50	12.00
	s. 2.8.1974. Series: BXV-BYY.	2.00	4.50	12.00
	t. 18.2.1977. Series: BZL-CBQ.	2.00	4.00	12.00

1950 IS8SUE

#54 and 55 sign. varieties. Printer: ABNC.

54	20 PESOS 1950-70. Black on m/c unpt. Portr. J. Ortiz de Dominguez at l. W/o "No" above serial #. Back olive-green; Federal Palace courtyard at ctr.	VG	VF	UNC
	a. 27.12.1950. Black series letters. Series: CS; CT.	1.10	3.00	15.00
	b. 19.1.1953. Series: DK.	1.10	3.00	15.00
	c. 10.2.1954. Red series letters. Series: DW.	1.10	2.50	12.50
	d. 11.1.1956. Series: FK.	1.10	2.50	12.50
	e. 19.6.1957. Series: FW.	1.10	2.50	12.00
	f. 20.8.1958. Series: HC, HD.	1.10	2.50	12.00
	g. 18.3.1959. Series: HS, HT.	1.10	2.00	10.00
	h. 20.5.1959. Series: IQ, IR.	1.10	2.00	10.00
	i. 25.1.1961. Series: JO, JP.	.75	1.50	8.00
	j. 8.11.1961. Series: LC-LG.	.75	1.50	8.00
	k. 24.4.1963. Series: AIE-AIH.	.50	1.25	8.00
	l. 17.2.1965. Series: BAQ-BAV.	.50	1.25	8.00
	m. 10.5.1967. Series: BCY-BDB.	.50	1.25	7.50
	n. 27.8.1969. Series: BGA; BGB.	.50	1.25	7.50
	o. 18.3.1970. Series: BID-BIF.	.50	1.25	7.50
	p. 22.7.1970. Series: BIG-BIK.	.50	1.25	7.50
	s. Specimen, punched hole cancelled.	—	—	125.00

55	100 PESOS 1950-61. Brown on m/c unpt. Portr. M. Hidalgo at l. Middle sign. title: *INTERVENTOR DE LA COM. NAC. BANCARIA.* Engraved dates. Back olive-green; coin w/national seal at ctr.			
	a. 27.12.1950. Black series letters. Series: CS-CZ.	6.00	10.00	25.00
	b. 19.1.1953. Series: DK-DP.	3.50	7.00	20.00
	c. 10.2.1954. Series: DW-DZ.	3.50	7.00	20.00
	d. 8.9.1954. Series: EI-ET.	3.50	7.00	20.00
	e. 11.1.1956. Series: FK-FV.	3.50	7.00	20.00
	f. 19.6.1957. Series: FW-GH.	3.50	7.00	20.00
	g. 20.8.1958. Series: HC-HR.	3.50	7.00	17.50
	h. 18.3.1959. Series: HS-IH.	3.50	7.00	17.50
	i. 20.5.1959. Series: IQ-JF.	3.50	7.00	17.50
	j. 25.1.1961. Series: JO-KL.	3.50	7.00	17.50

1954 ISSUE

58	10 PESOS 1954-67. Black on m/c unpt. Portr. E. Ruiz de Valezquez at r. Text: *MEXICO D.F.* above series letters. Back brown; road to Guanajuato at ctr. Printer: ABNC.	VG	VF	UNC
	a. 10.2.1954. Series: DW, DX.	.60	2.50	8.00
	b. 8.9.1954. Series: EI-EN.	.60	2.50	8.00
	c. 19.6.1957. Series: FW, FX.	.60	2.50	8.00
	d. 24.7.1957. Series: GQ.	.60	2.50	8.00
	e. 20.8.1958. Series: HC-HF.	.25	1.50	5.00
	f. 18.3.1959. Series: HS-HU.	.25	1.50	5.00
	g. 20.5.1959. Series: IQ-IS.	.25	1.50	5.00
	h. 25.1.1961. Series: JO-JT.	.25	1.00	4.00
	i. 8.11.1961. Series: LC-LV.	.25	1.00	4.00
	j. 24.4.1963. Series: AIE-AIT.	.25	1.00	4.00
	k. 17.2.1965. Series: BAQ-BAX.	.25	1.00	4.00
	l. 10.5.1967. Series: BCY-BDA.	.25	1.00	4.00
	s. Specimen, punched hole cancelled.	—	—	150.00

1957; 1961 ISSUE

#59-61 printer: ABNC.

59	1 PESO 1957-70. Black on m/c unpt. Aztec calendar stone at ctr. Text: *MEXICO D.F.* added above date at lower l. Back red. Independence monument at ctr.	VG	VF	UNC
	a. 19.6.1957. Series: FW-GF.	.10	1.00	3.00
	b. 24.7.1957. Series: GH-GR. (Do not exist).	—	—	—
	c. 4.12.1957. Series: GS-HB.	.10	.75	2.50
	d. 20.8.1958. Series: HC-HL.	.10	.75	2.50
	e. 18.3.1959. Series: HS-IB.	.10	.50	2.00
	f. 20.5.1959. Series: IQ-IZ.	.10	.50	2.00
	g. 25.1.1961. Series: JO-KC.	.10	.25	1.50
	h. 8.11.1961. Series: LC; LD.	.10	.25	1.50
	i. 9.6.1965. Series: BCO-BCX.	.10	.25	1.75
	j. 10.5.1967. Series: BCY-BEB.	.10	.25	1.25
	k. 27.8.1969. Series: BGA-BGJ.	.10	.25	1.25
	l. 22.7.1970. Series: BIG-BIP.	.10	.20	1.00

60	5 PESOS 1957-70. Black on m/c unpt. Portr. G. Faure at ctr. Text: *MEXICO D.F.* before date. Back gray; Independence Monument at ctr.	VG	VF	UNC
	a. 19.6.1957. Series: FW, FX.	.40	2.00	6.00
	b. 24.7.1957. Series: GQ, GR.	.40	2.00	6.00
	c. 20.8.1958. Series: HC-HJ.	.25	1.50	5.00
	d. 18.3.1959. Series: HS-HV.	.25	1.50	5.00
	e. 20.5.1959. Series: IQ-IT.	.25	1.50	5.00
	f. 25.1.1961. Series: JO-JV.	.15	.75	3.00
	g. 8.11.1961. Series: LC-MP.	.15	.75	3.00
	h. 24.4.1963. Series: AIE-AJJ.	.15	.50	2.00
	i. 19.11.1969. Series: BGK-BGT.	.15	.50	2.00
	j. 22.7.1970. Series: BIG-BII.	.15	.50	2.00

NOTICE

Readers with unlisted dates, signature varieties, etc. are invited to submit photocopies of their notes to: Standard Catalog of World Paper Money, 700 East State St. Iola, WI 54990-0001, fax: 1-715-445-4087, or E-Mail: thernr@krause.com.

61 **100 PESOS**
1961-73. Brown on m/c unpt. Like #55 but series letters below serial #.

	VG	VF	UNC
a. 8.11.1961. Red series letters. Series: LN-YL, AAP-ADW.	2.00	5.00	15.00
b. 24.4.1963. Series: AIS-ASX.	2.00	5.00	15.00
c. 17.2.1965. Series: BAQ-BBU.	2.00	5.00	15.00
d. 10.5.1967. Series: BDE-BFI.	2.00	5.00	10.00
e. 22.7.1970. Series: BIG-BKO.	2.00	5.00	10.00
f. 24.3.1971. Series: BKP-BLH.	2.00	5.00	10.00
g. 27.6.1972. Series: BLP-BMO.	2.00	5.00	10.00
h. 29.12.1972. Series: BPI-BUM.	1.00	2.00	7.50
i. 18.7.1973. Series: BVG-BXS.	1.00	2.00	7.50

1969-74 ISSUE

#62-66 bank title w/*S.A.* 3 sign. and sign. varieties. Printer: BdM.

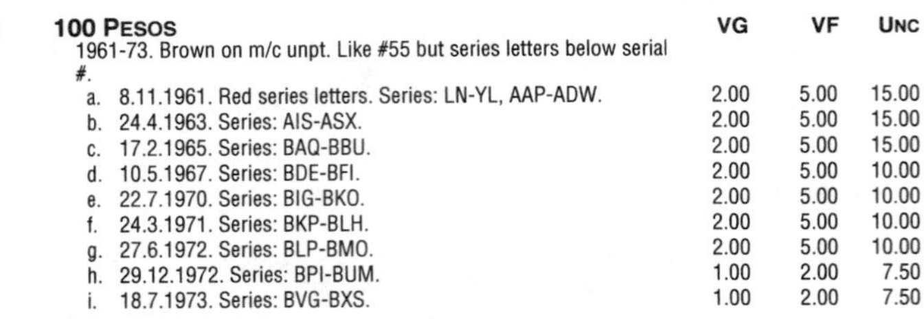

62 **5 PESOS**
1969-72. Black on m/c unpt. J. Ortiz de Dominguez at r. Yucca plant, aqueduct, village of Queretaro and national arms on back.

	VG	VF	UNC
a. 3.12.1969.	.15	.25	2.00
b. 27.10.1971.	.15	.25	1.25
c. 27.6.1972.	.15	.25	1.00

63 **10 PESOS**
1969-77. Dk. green on m/c unpt. Bell at l., M. Hidalgo y Castilla at r. National arms and Dolores Cathedral on back.

	VG	VF	UNC
a. 16.9.1969.	.25	.50	4.00
b. 3.12.1969.	.15	.25	1.50
c. 22.7.1970.	.15	.25	1.25
d. 3.2.1971.	.15	.25	1.00
e. 29.12.1972.	.15	.25	1.00
f. 18.7.1973.	.10	.20	1.00
g. 16.10.1974.	.10	.20	1.00
h. 15.5.1975.	.10	.20	.75
i. 18.2.1977.	.10	.20	.75

64 **20 PESOS**
1972-77. Red and black on m/c unpt. J. Morelos y Pavon at r. w/bldg. in background. Pyramid of Quetzalcoatl on back.

	VG	VF	UNC
a. 29.12.1972.	.25	.50	2.00
b. 18.7.1973.	.10	.30	1.25
c. 8.7.1976.	.10	.20	1.00
d. 8.7.1977.	.10	.20	1.00

65 **50 PESOS**
1973-78. Blue on m/c unpt. Gov't. palace at l., B. Juárez at r. Red and black series letters and serial #. Temple and Aztec god on back.

	VG	VF	UNC
a. 18.7.1973.	.30	1.00	4.00
b. 8.7.1976.	.20	.50	2.00
c. 5.7.1978.	.20	.50	2.00

66 **100 PESOS**
1974; 1978. Purple on m/c unpt. V. Carranza at l., "La Trinchera" painting at ctr. Red and black series letters and serial #. Stone figure on back.

	VG	VF	UNC
a. 30.5.1974.	.30	1.00	3.00
b. 5.7.1978.	.30	1.00	2.50

1978-80 ISSUE

#67-71 bank title w/*S.A.* Printer: BdM.

		VG	VF	UNC
67	**50 PESOS**			
	1978; 1979. Blue on m/c unpt. Like #65 but only red series letters and a black serial #.			
	a. 5.7.1978.	.30	1.00	2.00
	b. 17.5.1979.	.20	.40	1.00
68	**100 PESOS**			
	1978-79. Purple on m/c unpt. Like #66 but only red series letters and a black serial #.			
	a. 5.7.1978.	.20	.40	1.00
	b. 17.5.1979. Engraved. Litho back. Series before LL.	—	—	—
	c. 17.5.1979. Litho back. Series LS and later.	—	—	—

		VG	VF	UNC
69	**500 PESOS**			
	29.6.1979. Black on dk. olive-green on m/c unpt. F. I. Madero at l. and as wmk. Aztec calendar stone on back. Pink paper.	1.00	3.00	9.00

		VG	VF	UNC
70	**1000 PESOS**			
	1978-79. Dk. brown and brown on m/c unpt. J. de Asbaje at r. and as wmk. Santo Domingo plaza at l. ctr. on back. Lt. tan paper.			
	a. 5.7.1978.	2.00	4.50	15.00
	b. 17.5.1979.	1.00	4.00	10.00
	c. 29.6.1979.	1.00	3.00	9.00

		VG	VF	UNC
71	**5000 PESOS**			
	25.3.1980. Red on m/c unpt. Cadets at l. ctr., one of them as wmk. Chapultepec castle on back. Lt. blue paper.	5.00	12.50	42.50
72	**10,000 PESOS**			
	18.1.1978. Purple on m/c unpt. Portr. M. Romero at l. Back green; National Palace at ctr. Printer: ABNC. Series CCL-CES.	5.00	20.00	75.00

1981 ISSUE

#73-78 bank title w/*S.A.* W/4 sign. and sign. varieties. Printer: BdM.

		VG	VF	UNC
73	**50 PESOS**			
	27.1.1981. Blue on m/c unpt. Like #67 but 4 sign.	.10	.25	1.00

		VG	VF	UNC
74	**100 PESOS**			
	1981-82. Purple on m/c unpt. Like #68 but 4 sign.			
	a. 27.1.1981.	.10	.20	1.00
	b. 3.9.1981.	.10	.20	1.00
	c. 25.3.1982.	.10	.20	.75

		VG	VF	UNC
75	**500 PESOS**			
	1981-82. Green on m/c unpt. Like #69 but 4 sign. and narrower serial #.			
	a. 27.1.1981.	.25	1.00	4.50
	b. 25.3.1982.	.25	1.00	4.00

		VG	VF	UNC
76	**1000 PESOS**			
	1981-82. Dk. brown and brown on m/c unpt. Like #70 but 4 sign. and narrower serial #.			
	a. Engraved bldgs. on back. 27.1.1981.	.50	2.00	9.00
	b. Litho. bldgs. on back. 27.1.1981.	.50	2.00	9.00
	c. 3.9.1981.	.50	2.00	8.00
	d. 25.3.1982.	.50	2.00	8.00

		VG	VF	UN
77	**5000 PESOS** 1981; 1982. Red and black on m/c unpt., lt. blue paper. Like #71 but 4 sign. and narrower serial #.			
	a. 27.1.1981.	1.00	5.00	25.00
	b. 25.3.1982.	1.00	5.00	25.00

		VG	VF	UNC
78	**10,000 PESOS** 1981-82. Blue-black, brown and deep blue-green on m/c unpt. Power plant at ctr., Gen. Lazaro Cardenas at r. and as wmk. Back dk. green, red and blue; Coyolxauhqui stone carving at ctr. Lt. green paper.			
	a. 8.12.1981.	10.00	25.00	50.00
	b. 25.3.1982.	2.00	10.00	45.00
	c. Red and blue serial #. 30.9.1982.	2.00	10.00	45.00
	d. Green and red serial #. 30.9.1982.	—	—	—

1983-84 ISSUES

#79-84 *S.A.* removed from bank title. W/4 sign. Printer: BdM.

		VG	VF	UNC
79	**500 PESOS** 1983; 1984. Green on m/c unpt. Similar to #75 but w/silk threads and w/o wmk. Design continued over wmk. area on both sides. White paper.			
	a. 14.3.1983.	.20	.85	3.00
	b. 7.8.1984.	.20	.75	2.50

		VG	VF	UNC
80	**1000 PESOS** 1983; 1984. Dk. brown and brown on m/c unpt. Like #76 but *S.A.* removed from title.			
	a. 13.5.1983.	.75	2.25	5.50
	b. 7.8.1984.	.65	2.00	5.00

		VG	VF	UN
81	**1000 PESOS** 30.10.1984. Dk. brown and brown on m/c unpt. Similar to #80 but rayed quill pen printed over wmk. area at l.	.35	.85	2.50

		VG	VF	UNC
82	**2000 PESOS** 1983-84. Black, dk. green and brown on m/c unpt. J. Sierra at l. ctr., University bldg. at r. 19th century courtyard on back.			
	a. 26.7.1983.	1.00	3.00	10.00
	b. 7.8.1984.	.75	1.25	4.00
	c. 30.10.1984.	.75	1.25	4.00

		VG	VF	UNC
83	**5000 PESOS** 1983. Red and black on m/c unpt. Like #77 but *S.A.* removed from title.			
	a. 13.5.1983.	1.25	3.50	10.00
	b. 26.7.1983.	1.00	3.00	9.00
	c. 5.12.1983.	.90	2.75	8.50
84	**10,000 PESOS** 1983. Blue-black, brown and deep blue-green on m/c unpt. Similar to #78 but *S.A.* removed from bank title.			
	a. 13.5.1983.	2.00	4.50	17.50
	b. Red and dk. blue serial #. 26.7.1983.	2.00	4.50	17.50
	c. Green and blue serial #. 26.7.1983.	2.00	4.00	17.50
	d. Purple and blue serial #. 26.7.1983.	—	—	—
	e. 5.12.1983.	2.00	4.50	17.50

1985 ISSUES

#85-94 w/3 sign. *S.A.* removed from bank title. Printer: BdM.

		VG	VF	UNC
85	**1000 PESOS** 19.7.1985. Dk. brown and brown on m/c unpt. Like #81 but only 3 sign.	.35	.65	2.00

		VG	VF	UNC
86	**2000 PESOS** 1985-89. Black, dk. green and brown on m/c unpt. Like #82 but only 3 sign.			
	a. W/*SANTANA* at lower l. 2 date positions. 19.7.1985.	.60	1.25	3.00
	b. As a. 24.2.1987.	.60	1.25	3.00
	c. W/o *SANTANA*. 28.3.1989.	.60	1.25	1.50

		VG	VF	UNC
87	**5000 PESOS** 19.7.1985. Red on m/c unpt. Blue tint paper. Like #83 but only 3 sign.	1.75	2.25	7.50

		VG	VF	UNC
88	**5000 PESOS** 1985-89. Purple and brown-orange on m/c unpt. Similar to #87 but design continued over wmk. area. W/o wmk. Lt. tan paper.			
	a. W/*SANTANA* vertically at lower l. 19.7.1985.	.65	2.00	5.00
	b. As a. 24.2.1987.	.60	1.75	4.00
	c. W/o *SANTANA*. 28.3.1989.	.50	1.50	3.00

		VG	VF	UNC
89	**10,000 PESOS** 19.7.1985; 24.2.1987. Blue-black, brown and deep blue-green on m/c unpt. Like #84 but only 3 sign.			
	a. Purple and blue serial #. 19.7.1985.	1.50	3.00	9.00
	b. Green and blue serial #. 19.7.1985.	1.50	2.50	8.00
	c. Red and blue serial #. 24.2.1987.	1.50	2.50	7.00
	d. Green and blue serial #. 24.7.1987.	1.25	2.00	6.00

		VG	VF	UNC
90	**10,000 PESOS** 1987-91. Deep blue-black on brown and blue-green unpt. Similar to #89 but wmk. area filled in. Lt. tan paper.			
	a. W/*SANTANA*. at lower l. under refinery design. 24.2.1987.	1.50	3.00	9.00
	b. W/o *SANTANA*. 1.2.1988.	1.50	2.50	8.00
	c. 28.3.1989.	1.50	2.50	7.00
	d. 16.5.1991.	1.25	2.00	6.00

		VG	VF	UNC
91	**20,000 PESOS** 1985-87. Deep blue on blue and m/c unpt. Fortress above coastal cliffs at ctr. Don A. Quintana Roo at r. and as wmk. Artwork on back.			
	a. 19.7.1985.	4.00	7.00	20.00
	b. 24.2.1987.	3.50	6.50	18.50
	c. 27.8.1987.	3.00	5.50	16.50

		VG	VF	UNC
92	**20,000 PESOS** 1988; 1989. Blue-black on blue and pink unpt. Similar to #91 but design continued over wmk. area.			
	a. 1.2.1988.	3.50	5.00	12.50
	b. 28.3.1989.	3.25	4.50	11.50

		VF	VF	UNC
93	**50,000 PESOS** 1986-90. Purple on m/c unpt. Aztec symbols at ctr., Cuauhtémoc at r. and as wmk. Aztec and Spaniard fighting at l. ctr. on back. Pink paper.			
	a. 12.5.1986; 24.2.1987; 27.8.1987; 1.2.1988.	7.50	13.50	70.00
	b. 28.3.1989; 10.1.1990; 20.12.1990.	7.00	12.50	50.00

		VG	VF	UNC
94	**100,000 PESOS** 1988; 1991. Blue-black and maroon on m/c unpt. P. E. Calles at l. and as wmk, Banco de Mexico at ctr. Deer, cactus, lake and mountain at ctr. r. on back.			
	a. 4.1.1988.	15.00	22.50	100.00
	b. 2.9.1991.	13.50	20.00	90.00

1992 First Issue

Nuevos Pesos System

1000 "old" Pesos = 1 Nuevo Peso

#95-98 similar to #91-94. 3 sign. and sign. varieties. Printer: BdM.

		VG	VF	UNC
95	**10 Nuevos Pesos** 31.7.1992. Blue-black, brown and deep blue-green on m/c unpt. Similar to #90. Series A-Y.	FV	FV	6.00

		VG	VF	UNC
96	**20 Nuevos Pesos** 31.7.1992. Deep blue on blue and m/c unpt. Similar to #92. Series A-Q.	FV	FV	12.00

		VG	VF	UNC
97	**50 Nuevos Pesos** 31.7.1992. Purple on m/c unpt. Similar to #93. Series A-P.	FV	FV	26.50

		VG	VF	UNC
98	**100 Nuevos Pesos** 31.7.1992. Blue-black and maroon on m/c unpt. Similar to #94. Series A-Q.	FV	FV	50.00

1992 (1994) Second Issue

#99-104 printer: BdM.

		VG	VF	UNC
99	**10 Nuevos Pesos** 10.12.1992 (1994). Deep blue-green and gold on m/c unpt. E. Zapata at r., hands holding of corn at ctr. Machinery at lower l., statue of Zapata on horseback near peasant at ctr. r., bldg. in background. Series A-T.	FV	FV	4.00
100	**20 Nuevos Pesos** 10.12.1992 (1994). Purple and dk. blue on m/c unpt. B. Juárez at r., heraldic eagle at ctr. Monument, statues "Hemiciclo a Juárez" on back. Series A-T.	FV	FV	6.50
101	**50 Nuevos Pesos** 10.12.1992 (1994). Red-violet and black on m/c unpt. J. M. Morelos at r., crossed cannons on outlined bow and arrow below his flag at l. ctr. Butterflies at l., boat fishermen at ctr. on back. Series A-AF.	FV	FV	15.00
102	**100 Nuevos Pesos** 10.12.1992 (1994). Red and brown on m/c unpt. Nezahualcóyotl at r. and as wmk., Aztec figure at ctr. Xochipilli statue on back. Series A-V.	FV	FV	23.50

		VG	VF	UNC
103	**200 NUEVOS PESOS** 10.12.1992 (1994). Dk. olive-green, dk. brown and olive-brown on m/c unpt. J. de Asbaje at r. and as wmk., open book and quill pen at ctr. Temple de San Jerónimo on back. Series A-E.	FV	FV	45.00

		VG	VF	UNC
104	**500 NUEVOS PESOS** 10.12.1992 (1994). Red-brown, deep purple and dk. brown-violet on m/c unpt. I. Zaragoza at ctr. r. and as wmk., Battle of Puebla at l. ctr. Cathedral at Puebla at ctr. on back. Series A-C.	FV	FV	100.00

1994; 1995 (1996) ISSUE

#105-116 similar to #99-104 but *EL* omitted from bank title, *NUEVOS* and *PAGARÁ A LA VISTA AL PORTADOR* are omitted. 2 sign. Printer: BdM.

		VG	VF	UNC
105	**10 PESOS** 1994 (1996); 1996. Deep blue-green and gold on m/c unpt. Similar to #99. Series A-.			
	a. 6.5.1994.	FV	FV	3.00
	b. 10.5.1996.	FV	FV	2.75

		VG	VF	UNC
106	**20 PESOS** 1994 (1996); 1996. Purple and dk. blue on m/c unpt. Similar to #100. Series A-.			
	a. 6.5.1994.	FV	FV	6.00
	b. 10.5.1996.	FV	FV	5.50

		VG	VF	UNC
107	**50 PESOS** 1994-98 (1996). Red-violet and black on m/c unpt. Similar to #101. Series A-.			
	a. 6.5.1994.	FV	FV	13.50
	b. 10.5.1996.	FV	FV	12.50
	c. 17.3.1998.	FV	FV	11.50

		VG	VF	UNC
108	**100 PESOS** 6.5.1994 (1996); 1996. Red and brown-orange on m/c unpt. Similar to #102. Series A-.			
	a. 6.5.1994.	FV	FV	22.50
	b. 10.5.1996.	FV	FV	20.00

		VG	VF	UNC
109	**200 PESOS** 1995-98 (1996). Dk. olive-green, dk. brown and olive-brown on m/c unpt. Similar to #103. Series A-.			
	a. 7.2.1995.	FV	FV	40.00
	b. 10.5.1996.	FV	FV	38.50
	c. 17.3.1998.	FV	FV	37.50

		VG	VF	UNC
110	**500 PESOS** 1995 (1996); 1996. Red-brown, deep purple and dk. brown-violet on m/c unpt. Similar to #104. Series A-.			
	a. 7.2.1995.	FV	FV	95.00
	b. 10.5.1996.	FV	FV	90.00

COLLECTOR SERIES

Matched serial # sets of ABNC 1-100 Pesos and BdM 5-1000 Pesos Series A were released at the International Coin Convention in México City. Unc. set $30.00.

The Republic of Moldova is bordered in the north, east, and south by the Ukraine and on the west by Romania. It has an area of 13,000 sq. mi. (33,700 sq. km.) and a population of 4.5 million. Capital: Chisinau. Agriculture products grown are mainly cereals, grapes, tobacco, sugar beets and fruit. Industry is dominated by food processing, clothing, building materials and agricultural machinery.

The historical Romanian principality of Moldova was established in the 14th century. It fell under Turkish suzerainty in the 16th century. From 1812 to 1918, Russians occupied the eastern portion of Moldova which they named Bessarabia. In March 1918, the Bessarabian legislature voted in favor of reunification with Romania. At the Paris Peace Conference of 1920, the union was officially recognized by the United States, France, U.K., Italy and several other nations. The new Soviet government did not accept the union. In 1924, to pressure Romania, a Moldavian Autonomous Soviet Socialist Republic (A.S.S.R.) was established within the USSR on the border, consisting of a strip extending east of the Nistru River. Today it is Transdniestria (or Transdniester).

Following the Molotov-Ribbentrop Pact (1939), the Soviet-German agreement which divided eastern Europe, the Soviet forces reoccupied the region in June 1940 and the Moldavian S.S.R. was proclaimed. Transdniestria was transferred to the new republic. Ukrainian S.S.R. obtained possession of the southern part of Bessarabia. The region was liberated by the Romanian army in 1941. The Soviets reconquered the territory in 1944, enforcing Russification.

A declaration of republican sovereignty was adopted in June 1990 and the area was renamed Moldova. It became an independent republic in August 1991. In December 1991, Moldova became a member of the C.I.S. In 1992, supporting the Russian involvement, Transdniestria seceded from Moldova. In May 1992, bloody fighting ensued involving Moldavians (Romanians) and rebels aided by contingents of Cossacks and the Russian 14th army. The Moldavian government made several futile requests for United Nations intervention, but was forced to accept the presence of Russian forces in eastern Moldova (Transdniestria) until the region is recognized with special political status.

MONETARY SYSTEM:

100 Rubles = 1000 Cupon, 1992
1 Leu = 1000 Cupon, 1993-

REPUBLIC

MINISTER OF FINANCE

RUBLE CONTROL COUPONS

		VG	VF	UNC
A11	**VARIOUS AMOUNTS** 1992.			
	a. Full sheet.	—	.50	1.00
	b. Coupon.	—	—	.10

BANCA NATIONALA A MOLDOVEI

1992; 1993 "CUPON" ISSUE

#1-4 arms at l. Castle at r. on back. Wmk. paper (varies).

		VG	VF	UNC
1	**50 CUPON** 1992. Gray-green on gray unpt.	.10	.40	2.25

		VG	VF	UNC
2	**200 CUPON** 1992. Blue-black on gray unpt. Back purple on lilac unpt.	.10	.40	2.25

		VG	VF	UNC
3	**1000 CUPON** 1993. Brown on pale blue-green and ochre unpt. Bank monogram at upper l.	.15	.65	3.00

		VG	VF	UNC
4	**5000 CUPON** 1993. Pale brown-violet, orange and pale olive-green unpt. Bank monogram at upper l. Back pale brown-violet on pale brown-orange unpt.	.45	1.35	5.00

1992 (1993) ISSUE

#5-7 Kg. Stefan at l., arms at upper ctr. r. Soroca Fortress at ctr. r. on back. Wmk. paper.

		VG	VF	UNC
5	**1 LEU** 1992 (1993). Brown and dk. olive-green on ochre unpt.	FV	.45	2.00

6 **5 Lei** VG VF Unc
1992 (1993). Purple on lt. blue and ochre unpt. FV 1.00 5.00

7 **10 Lei** VG VF Unc
1992 (1993). Red brown and olive-green on pale orange unpt. FV 1.75 7.50

1992; 1994 Issue

#8-16 Kg. Stefan at l. and as wmk., arms at upper ctr. r.

#8-14 bank monogram at upper r. corner.

8 **1 Leu** VG VF Unc
1994; 1995. Brown on ochre, pale yellow-green and m/c unpt. Monastery at Capriana at ctr. r. on back. FV FV 1.75

9 **5 Lei** VG VF Unc
1994; 1995. Blue-green on lilac and pale aqua unpt. Basilica of St. Dumitru in Orhei at ctr. r. on back. FV FV 3.00

10 **10 Lei** VG VF Unc
1994; 1995. Red-brown on pale blue and gold unpt. Monastery at Hîrjauca at ctr. r. on back. FV FV 5.50

#11 and 12 held in reserve.

13 **20 Lei** VG VF Unc
1992 (1994); 1994; 1995. Blue-green on lt. green, aqua and ochre unpt. Soroca Fortress at ctr. r. on back. FV 2.75 10.00

14 **50 Lei** VG VF Unc
1992 (1994); 1994. Red-violet on lilac and m/c unpt. Monastery at Hîrbovet at ctr. r. on back. FV FV 18.50

15 **100 Lei**
1992 (1995). Brown on m/c unpt. Tighina Fortress on back. FV FV 35.00

16 **200 Lei** VG VF Unc
1992 (1995). Purple on m/c unpt. Chisinau City Hall on back. FV FV 65.00

1992 (1999) Issue

17 **500 Lei** VG VF Unc
1992 (1999). Church. FV FV 135.00

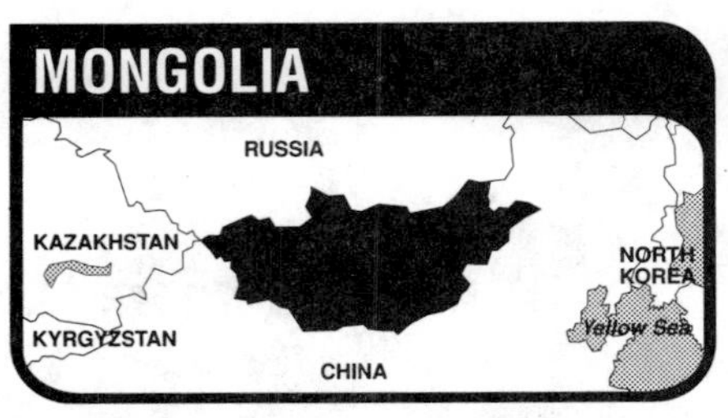

The State of Mongolia (formerly the Mongolian Peoples Republic), a landlocked country in central Asia between the Soviet Union and the Peoples Republic of China, has an area of 604,247 sq. mi. (1,565,000 sq. km.) and a population of 2.4 million. Capital: Ulan Bator. Animal herds and flocks are the chief economic asset. Wool, cattle, butter, meat and hides are exported.

Mongolia (often referred to as Outer Mongolia), one of the world's oldest countries, attained its greatest power in the 13th century when Genghis Khan and his successors conquered all of China and extended their influence westward as far as Hungary and Poland. The empire dissolved in later centuries and in 1691 was brought under suzerainty of the Manchus, who had conquered China in 1644. Later the Chinese republican movement led by Sun Yat-sen overthrew the Manchus and set up the Chinese Republic in 1911. Mongolia, with the support of Russia, proclaimed its independence from China on March 13, 1921, when the Provisional Peoples Government was established. Later, on Nov. 26, 1924, the government proclaimed the Mongolian Peoples Republic. Opposition to the communist party developed in late 1989 and after demonstrations and strikes the Politburo resigned on Mar. 12, 1990 and the new State of Mongolia was organized.

RULERS:

Chinese to 1921

MONETARY SYSTEM:

1 Tugrik (Tukhrik) = 100 Mongo

STATE

УЛСЫН БАНК

STATE BANK

1966 ISSUE

#35-41 Socialist arms at upper l. Backs are m/c. Wmk: Circles forming a 6-petaled flower-like pattern.

#36-41 portr. Sukhe-Bataar at r.

		VG	VF	UNC
35	**1 TUGRIK** 1966. Brown on pale green and yellow unpt.	.20	.35	.75
36	**3 TUGRIK** 1966. Dk. green on lt. green and pink unpt.	.25	.50	1.00
37	**5 TUGRIK** 1966. Dk. blue on lt. blue and pale green unpt.	.25	.50	1.00
38	**10 TUGRIK** 1966. Red on pale red and blue unpt.	.25	.75	1.25
39	**25 TUGRIK** 1966. Brown-violet.	.50	1.00	1.50
40	**50 TUGRIK** 1966. Dk. green on lt. green and gold unpt. Govt. bldg. at Ulan-Bator on back.	1.00	2.50	3.00

		VG	VF	UNC
41	**100 TUGRIK** 1966. Dk. brown on ochre and blue-green unpt. Back like #40.	2.00	4.00	7.50

1981-83 ISSUE

#42-45 and 47-48 like #36-41. Replacement notes: Serial # prefix ЯАЧ

		VG	VF	UNC
42	**1 TUGRIK** 1983. Brown on pale green and yellow unpt. Like #35.	FV	FV	1.00

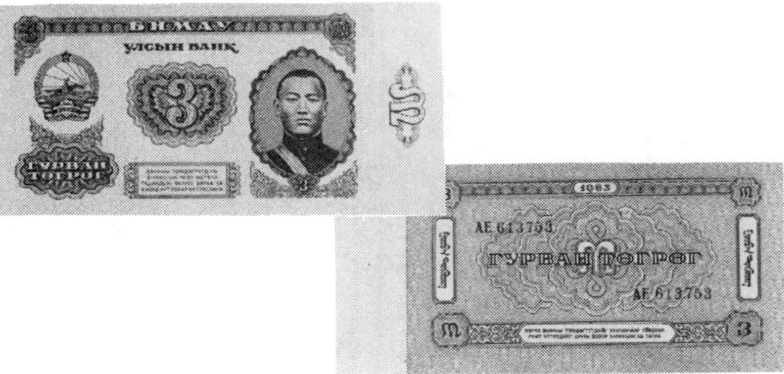

		VG	VF	UNC
43	**3 TUGRIK** 1983. Dk. green on lt. green and pink unpt. Like #36.	FV	FV	1.25
44	**5 TUGRIK** 1981. Blue on lt. blue and pale green unpt. Like #37.	FV	FV	1.75

		VG	VF	UNC
45	**10 TUGRIK** 1981. Red on pale red and blue unpt. Like #38.	FV	FV	2.00

		VG	VF	UNC
46	**20 TUGRIK** 1981. Yellow-green on lt. green and brown unpt. Sukhe-Bataar at ctr., arms at l. Power station at Ulan-Bator at ctr. r. on back.	FV	FV	2.25

47	**50 TUGRIK**	VG	VF	UNC
	1981. Dk. green on lt. green and gold unpt. Like #40.	FV	FV	5.00

48	**100 TUGRIK**	VF	VF	UNC
	1981. Dk. brown on ochre and blue-green unpt. Like #41.	FV	FV	9.00

МОНГОЛ БАНК

MONGOL BANK

1993 ND; 1994-95 ISSUE

#49-51 "Soemba" arms at upper ctr. Replacement notes: Serial # prefix *ZZ*.

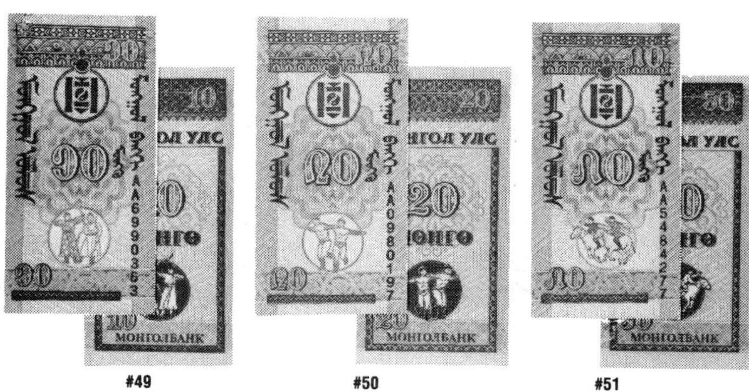

#49 #50 #51

		VG	VF	UNC
49	**10 MONGO** ND (1993). Red-violet on pale red-orange unpt. 2 archers at lower ctr. on face and back.	FV	FV	.65
50	**20 MONGO** ND (1993). Brown on ochre and yellow-brown unpt. 2 athletes at lower ctr. on face and back.	FV	FV	.65
51	**50 MONGO** ND (1993). Greenish-black on blue and pale green unpt. 2 horsemen at lower ctr. on face and back.	FV	FV	.65

#52-60 wmk: Genghis Khan.

52	**1 TUGRIK**	VG	VF	UNC
	ND (1993). Dull olive-green and brown-orange on ochre unpt. Chinze at l. "Soemba" arms at ctr. r. on back.	FV	FV	1.00

#53-57 youthful portr. Sukhe-Bataar at l., "Soemba" arms at ctr. Horses grazing in mountainous landscape at ctr. r. on back.

53	**5 TUGRIK**	VG	VF	UNC
	ND (1993). Deep orange, ochre and brown on m/c unpt.	FV	FV	1.25

54	**10 TUGRIK**	VG	VF	UNC
	ND (1993). Green, blue and lt. green on m/c unpt.	FV	FV	1.25

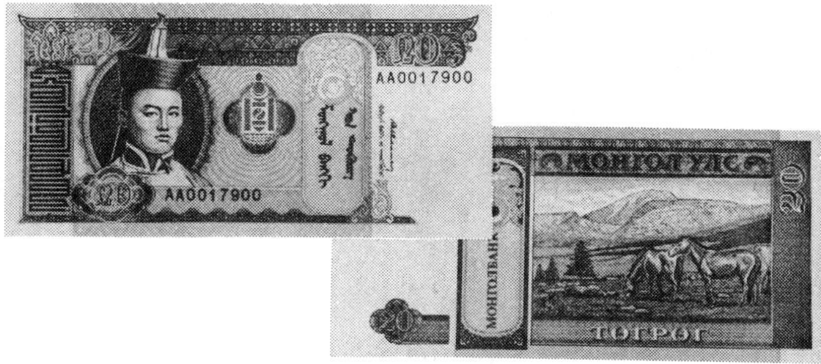

55	**20 TUGRIK**	VG	VF	UNC
	ND (1993). Violet, orange and red on m/c unpt.	FV	FV	1.25

56	**50 TUGRIK**	VG	VF	UNC
	ND (1993). Dk. brown on m/c unpt.	FV	FV	1.50

		VG	VF	UNC
57	**100 TUGRIK** ND (1993); 1994. Purple, brown and dk. blue on m/c unpt.	FV	FV	2.00

#58-61 Genghis Khan at l. and as wmk., "Soemba" arms at ctr. Ox drawn yurte, village at ctr. r. on back.

		VG	VF	UNC
58	**500 TUGRIK** ND (1993; 1997). Dk. green, brown and yellow-green on m/c unpt.	FV	FV	5.00

		VG	VF	UNC
59	**1000 TUGRIK** ND (1993; 1997). Blue-gray, brown and blue on m/c unpt.	FV	FV	10.00
60	**5000 TUGRIK** 1994. Purple, violet and red on m/c unpt. Bldg. complex, tree, people on back.	FV	FV	17.50
61	**10,000 TUGRIK** 1995. Black, dk. olive-green and orange on m/c unpt. Bldg. complex, tree, people on back.	FV	FV	35.00

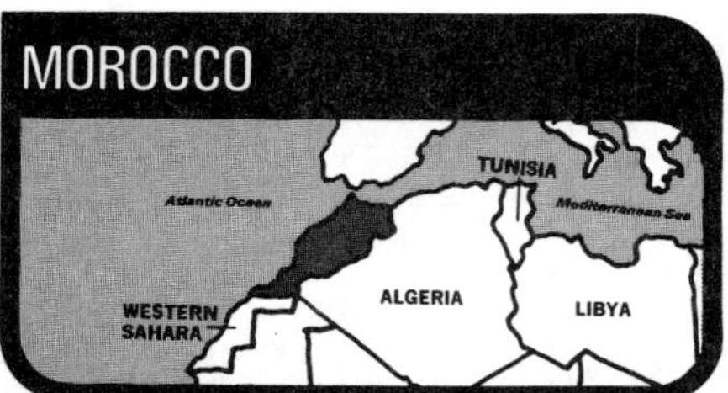

The Kingdom of Morocco, situated on the northwest corner of Africa south of Spain, has an area of 172,413 sq. mi. (712,550 sq. km.) and a population of 28.3 million. Capital: Rabat. The economy is essentially agricultural. Phosphates, fresh and preserved vegetables, canned fish and raw material are exported.

Morocco's strategic position at the gateway to western Europe has been the principal determinant of its violent, frequently unfortunate history. Time and again the fertile plain between the rugged Atlas Mountains and the sea has echoed the battle's trumpet as Phoenicians, Romans, Vandals, Visigoths, Byzantine Greeks and Islamic Arabs successively conquered and occupied the land. Modern Morocco is a remnant of an early empire formed by the Arabs at the close of the 7th century which encompassed all of northwest Africa and most of the Iberian Peninsula. During the 17th and 18th centuries, while under the control of native dynasties, it was the headquarters of the famous Sale pirates. Morocco's strategic position involved it in the competition of 19th century European powers for political influence in Africa, and resulted in the division of Morocco into French and Spanish spheres of interest which were established as protectorates in 1912. Morocco became independent on March 2, 1956, after France agreed to end its protectorate. Spain signed similar agreements on April 7 of the same year.

RULERS:

Muhammad V, AH1346-1380/1927-1961AD
Hassan II, AH1380-1420 /1961-1999AD
Muhammad VI AH 1420/1999AD

MONETARY SYSTEM:

1 Dirham = 100 Francs, 1921-1974
1 Dirham = 100 Centimes = 100 Santimat, 1974-

SIGNATURE VARIETIES	
GOVERNMENT COMISSIONER	**GOVERNOR**
Mohamed Tahiri, 1960	M'hamed Zeghari
Ahmed Ben Nani, 1963-65	M'Hamed Zeghari
	Driss Slaovi
Mohamed Lemniai, 1966	Driss Slaovi
Abdelaziz El Alami, 1967	Driss Slaovi
Abdelkrim Lazrek, 1968	M'hamed Zeghari
Abdelkrim Lazrek, 1969	Prince Moulay Hassan Ben Mehdi El Alaovi
Mohamed El Mdaghri, 1970	Prince Moulay Hassan Ben Mehdi El Alaovi
Hassan Lukash, 1985-89	Ahmed Ben Nani
	Mohamed Es Sakat
	Mohamed Es Sakat (modified sign.)
1996	Mohamed Es Sakat (modified sign.)

KINGDOM

BANQUE DU MAROC

Established June 30, 1959

1960 (ND); 1965 ISSUE

#53-55 wmk: Lion's head. French printing.

		VG	VF	UNC
53	**5 DIRHAMS** ND (1960); 1965-69. Brown and m/c. Kg. Muhammad V wearing a fez at r. Harvesting at l., man holding sheaf at r. on back.			
	a. Sign. 1. ND (1960).	2.00	8.50	35.00
	b. Sign. 2. ND (1963).	1.75	7.50	32.50
	c. Sign. 3. 1965/AH1384.	1.50	6.00	30.00
	d. Sign. 4. 1966/AH1386.	1.35	5.75	28.50
	e. Sign. 6. 1968/AH1387.	1.25	5.50	27.50
	f. Sign. 7. 1969/AH1389.	1.25	5.50	27.50

		VG	VF	UNC
54	**10 DIRHAMS** ND (1960); 1965-69. Brown and m/c. Kg. Muhammad V wearing a fez at l. Orange picking on back.			
	a. Sign. 1. ND (1960).	2.75	11.50	45.00
	b. Sign. 2. ND (1963).	2.50	10.00	40.00
	c. Sign. 3. 1965/AH1384.	2.00	8.50	35.00
	d. Sign. 6. 1968/AH1387.	2.00	8.00	32.50
	e. Sign. 7. 1969/AH1389.	1.75	7.50	30.00

		VG	VF	UNC
55	**50 DIRHAMS** 1965-69. Brown and m/c. Kg. Hassan II at r. Miners at work on back.			
	a. Sign. 3. 1965/AH1385.	15.00	60.00	360.00
	b. Sign. 5. 1966/AH1386.	13.50	55.00	325.00
	c. Sign. 6.	11.50	46.50	275.00
	d. Sign. 7.	10.00	42.50	260.00

1970 ISSUE

#56-59 Kg. Hassan II at l. and as wmk. Printer: TDLR.

		VG	VF	UNC
56	**5 DIRHAMS** 1970/AH1390. Purple on lt. blue and m/c unpt. Castle at ctr. Industrial processing on back. Sign. 8. Replacement notes: Serial # prefix *Z*.	FV	1.50	4.50

		VG	VF	UNC
57	**10 DIRHAMS** 1970; 1985. Brown on lt. green and m/c unpt. Villa at ctr. Processing oranges on back. Replacement notes: Serial # prefix *Y*.			
	a. Sign. 8. 1970/AH1390.	FV	2.00	6.50
	b. Sign. 9. 1985/AH1405.	FV	FV	5.50
58	**50 DIRHAMS** 1970; 1985. Green and brown on m/c unpt. City at ctr. Dam on back. Replacement notes: Serial # prefix *X*.			
	a. Sign. 8. 1970/AH1390.	FV	12.00	22.50
	b. Sign. 9. 1985/AH1405.	FV	FV	20.00

		VG	VF	UNC
59	**100 DIRHAMS** 1970; 1985. Brown and blue on lt. green and m/c unpt. Bldg. at ctr. Oil refinery on back. Replacement notes: Serial # prefix *W*.			
	a. Sign. 8. 1970/AH1390.	FV	20.00	37.50
	b. Sign. 9. 1985/AH1405.	FV	FV	35.00

BANK AL-MAGHRIB

1987 ISSUE

#60-62 Kg. Hassan II facing at r. and as wmk. 2 sign. varieties.

		VG	VF	UNC
60	**10 DIRHAMS** 1987/AH1407. Red-brown and red on m/c unpt. Musical instrument and pillar at l. ctr. on back.			
	a. Sign. 9.	FV	FV	7.50
	b. Sign. 10.	FV	FV	6.00

		VG	VF	UNC
61	**50 Dirhams** 1987/AH1407. Green on m/c unpt. Mounted militia charging, flowers at ctr. on back.			
	a. Sign. 9.	FV	FV	17.50
	b. Sign. 10.	FV	FV	16.50
62	**100 Dirhams** 1987/AH1407. Brown on m/c unpt. Demonstration on back.			
	a. Sign. 9.	FV	FV	30.00
	b. Sign. 10.	FV	FV	28.00

1987 (1991) Issue

#63-66 older bust of Kg. Hassan II at r. facing half l. Wmk: Kg. facing.

		VG	VF	UNC
63	**10 Dirhams** 1987/AH407 (ca.1991). Brown-violet and purple on m/c unpt. Back like #60, but diff. colors of unpt.			
	a. Sign. 10.	FV	FV	6.00
	b. Sign. 11.	FV	FV	3.00
64	**50 Dirhams** 1987/AH1407 (ca.1991). Green on m/c unpt. Back like #61.			
	a. Sign. 10.	FV	FV	15.00
	b. Sign. 11.	FV	FV	12.50
	c. Sign. 12.	FV	FV	10.00
65	**100 Dirhams** 1987/AH1407 (ca.1991). Brown and blue on m/c unpt. Back like #62.			
	a. Sign. 10.	FV	FV	25.00
	b. Sign. 11.	FV	FV	20.00
	c. Sign. 12.	FV	FV	18.50

		VG	VF	UNC
66	**200 Dirhams** 1987/AH1407 (ca.1991). Blue-violet and blue on m/c unpt. Mausoleum of Kg. Muhammad V at ctr. Sailboat, shell and coral on back.			
	a. Sign. 10.	FV	FV	45.00
	b. Sign. 11.	FV	FV	42.50
	c. Sign. 12.	FV	FV	35.00

1996 Issue

		VG	VF	UNC
67	**20 Dirhams** 1996. M/c. Kg. Hassan II at l., mosque at ctr. Fountain on back. Sign. 12.	FV	FV	5.50

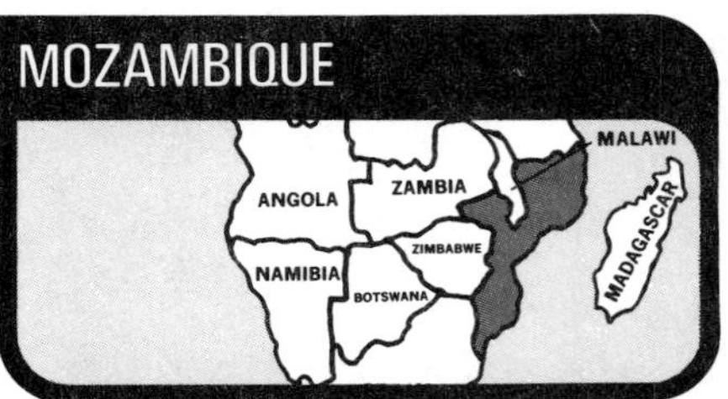

The People's Republic of Mozambique, a former overseas province of Portugal stretching for 1,430 miles (2,301 km.) along the southeast coast of Africa, has an area of 309,494 sq. mi. (783,030 sq. km.) and a population of 16 million, 99 percent of whom are native Africans of the Bantu tribes. Capital: Maputo. Agriculture is the chief industry. Cashew nuts, cotton, sugar, copra and tea are exported.

Vasco da Gama explored all the coast of Mozambique in 1498 and found Arab trading posts already along the coast. Portuguese settlement dates from the establishment of the trading post of Mozambique in 1505. Within five years Portugal absorbed all the former Arab sultanates along the east African coast. The area was organized as a colony in 1907 and became an overseas province in 1952. In Sept. of 1974, after more than a decade of guerrilla warfare with the forces of the Mozambique Liberation Front and Portugal agreed to the independence of Mozambique, effective June 25, 1975. Mozambique became a member of the Commonwealth of Nations in November 1995. The President is Head of State; the Prime Minister is Head of Government.

RULERS:

Portuguese to 1975

MONETARY SYSTEM:

1 Escudo = 100 Centavos, 1911-1975
1 Escudo = 1 Metica = 100 Centimos, 1975-

Banco Nacional Ultramarino

Moçambique Branch

1961; 1967 Issue

#109 and 110 printer: BWC.

		VG	VF	UNC
109	**100 Escudos** 27.3.1961. Green on m/c unpt. Portr. A. de Ornelas at r., arms at upper ctr. Bank steamship seal at l. on back.			
	a. Wmk: Arms.	1.50	3.50	8.00
	b. W/o wmk.	1.00	3.00	7.00

		VG	VF	UNC
110	**500 Escudos** 22.3.1967. Purple on m/c unpt. Portr. C. Xavier at r., arms at upper ctr.	4.00	15.00	60.00

NOTICE

Readers with unlisted dates, signature varieties, etc. are invited to submit photocopies of their notes to: Standard Catalog of World Paper Money, 700 East State St. Iola, WI 54990-0001, fax: 1-715-445-4087, or E-Mail: thernr@krause.com.

1970 ISSUE

Sign. varieties.

		VG	VF	UNC
111	**50 ESCUDOS** 27.10.1970. Black on m/c unpt. J. de Azevedo Coutinho at l. ctr., arms at upper ctr. r. Back green; bank steamship seal at l. Wmk: Arms.	1.00	3.00	12.50

FIRST 1972 ISSUE

		VG	VF	UNC
112	**1000 ESCUDOS** 16.5.1972. Black-blue on m/c unpt. Kg. Afonso V at r. and as wmk., arms at upper ctr. Allegorical woman w/ships at l. on back, bank steamship seal at upper ctr. 3 sign. varieties.	10.00	21.50	85.00

NOTE: #112 has 2 1/2mm. serial # w/o prefix or 3mm. serial # and 3-letter prefix.

SECOND 1972 ISSUE

		VG	VF	UNC
113	**100 ESCUDOS** 23.5.1972. Blue on m/c unpt. G. Coutinho and S. Cabral at l. ctr. Surveyor at ctr. on back. Wmk: Coutinho.	2.00	7.50	40.00

		VG	VF	UNC
114	**500 ESCUDOS** 23.5.1972. Purple on m/c unpt. G. Coutinho at l. ctr. and as wmk. Cabral and airplane on back.	4.00	15.00	55.00

		VG	VF	UNC
115	**1000 ESCUDOS** 23.5.1972. Green on m/c unpt. Face similar to #114. 2 men in cockpit of airplane at l. ctr. on back.	5.00	25.00	100.00

PEOPLES REPUBLIC

BANCO DE MOÇAMBIQUE

1976 ND PROVISIONAL ISSUE

#116-119 black ovpt. of new bank name.

		VG	VF	UNC
116	**50 ESCUDOS** ND (1976 - old date 27.10.1970). Black on m/c unpt. Ovpt. on #111.	.10	.20	.85

		VG	VF	UNC
117	**100 ESCUDOS** ND (1976 - old date 27.3.1961). Green on m/c unpt. Ovpt. on #109.	.10	.30	1.00

		VG	VF	UNC
118	**500 ESCUDOS** ND (1976 - old date 22.3.1967). Purple on m/c unpt. Ovpt. on #110.	.25	.75	4.00

		VG	VF	UNC
119	**1000 ESCUDOS** ND (1976 - old date 23.5.1972). Green on m/c unpt. Ovpt. on #115.	.25	1.00	8.00

1976 ISSUE

#120-124 Pres. S. Machel at l. ctr. Printer: TDLR.

NOTE: #120-124 appear to be unadopted designs.

		VG	VF	UNC
120	**5 METICAS** 25.6.1976. Brown and m/c. Kudo on back. Specimen, punched hole cancelled.	—	—	—
121	**10 METICAS** 25.6.1976. Blue on m/c. Lions on back. Specimen, punched hole cancelled.	—	—	—
122	**20 METICAS** 25.6.1976. Red and m/c. Giraffes on back. Specimen, punched hole cancelled.	—	—	—
123	**50 METICAS** 25.6.1976. Purple and m/c. Cape buffalo on back. Specimen, punched hole cancelled.	—	—	—

		VG	VF	UNC
124	**100 METICAS** 25.6.1976. Green and m/c. Elephants on back. Specimen, punched hole cancelled.	—	—	—

NOTICE

Readers with unlisted dates, signature varieties, etc. are invited to submit photocopies of their notes to: Standard Catalog of World Paper Money, 700 East State St. Iola, WI 54990-0001, fax: 1-715-445-4087, or E-Mail: thernr@krause.com.

REPÚBLICA POPULAR DE MOÇAMBIQUE

1980 ISSUE

#125-128 arms at ctr.

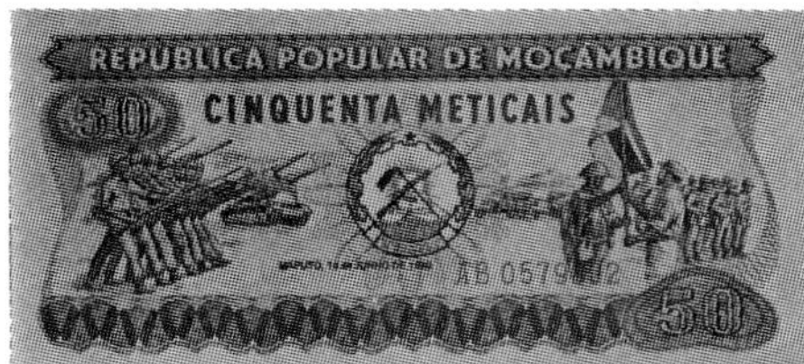

		VG	VF	UNC
125	**50 METICAIS** 16.6.1980. Dk. brown and brown on m/c unpt. Soldiers at l., flag ceremony at r. Soldiers in training on back.	.15	.40	1.25

		VG	VF	UNC
126	**100 METICAIS** 16.6.1980. Green on m/c unpt. Soldiers at flagpole at l., E. Mondlane at r. Public ceremony on back.	.20	.65	2.00

		VG	VF	UNC
127	**500 METICAIS** 16.6.1980. Deep blue-violet and dk. blue-green on m/c unpt. Government assembly at l., chanting crowd at r. Chemists and school scene on back.	.30	.75	4.00

		VG	VF	UNC
128	**1000 METICAIS** 16.6.1980. Deep red on m/c unpt. Pres. S. Machel w/3 young boys at r., revolutionary monument at l. Mining and harvesting scenes on back.	.75	1.75	4.00

1983-88 ISSUE

#129-132 modified arms at ctr. Smaller size serial #.

		VG	VF	UNC
129	**50 METICAIS** 16.6.1983; 16.6.1986. Similar to #125 except for arms.	.10	.35	1.50

		VG	VF	UNC
130	**100 METICAIS** 16.6.1983; 16.6.1986; 16.6.1989. Similar to #126 except for arms.	.15	.50	1.75

		VG	VF	UNC
131	**500 METICAIS** 16.6.1983; 16.6.1986; 16.6.1989. Similar to #127 except for arms.	.25	.75	6.00

		VG	VF	UNC
132	**1000 METICAIS** 16.6.1983; 16.6.1986; 16.6.1989. Similar to #128 except for arms.	.60	1.50	7.50

		VG	VF	UNC
133	**5000 METICAIS** 3.2.1988; 3.2.1989. Purple, brown and violet on m/c unpt. Carved statues at l., painting at r. Dancers and musicians on back. Wmk: Pres. Machel.	.60	1.75	10.00

1991-93 ISSUE

#134-137 arms at upper ctr. r. printed on silver or gold underlay. Bank seal at lower l. on back. Wmk: J. Chissano. Printer: TDLR.

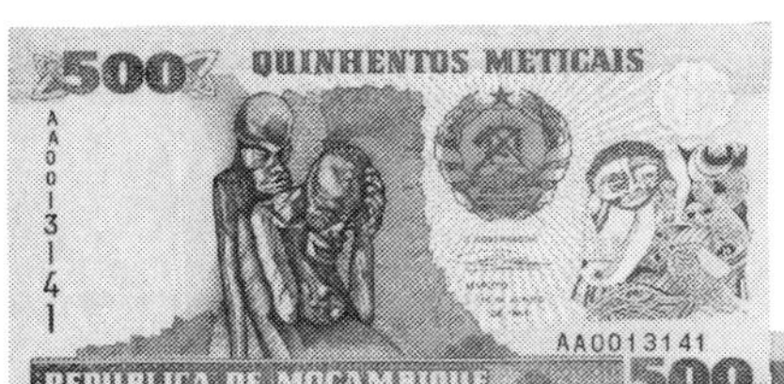

		VG	VF	UNC
134	**500 METICAIS** 16.6.1991. Brown and blue on m/c unpt. Native carving of couple in grief at l. ctr., native art at r. Dancing warriors at ctr. on back.	FV	.35	1.75

		VG	VF	UNC
135	**1000 METICAIS** 16.6.1991. Brown and red on m/c unpt. E. Mondlane at l. ctr., military flag raising ceremony at r. Monument at l. ctr. on back.	FV	.65	2.75

136 **5000 Meticais** — VG / VF / Unc
16.6.1991. Purple, violet and orange-brown on m/c unpt. S. Machel at l. ctr., monument to the Socialist vanguard at r. Foundry workers at ctr. on back. — FV / 1.00 / 4.50

137 **10,000 Meticais** — VG / VF / Unc
16.6.1991. Blue-green, brown and orange on m/c unpt. J. Chissano at l. ctr., high tension electrical towers at r. w/farm tractor in field and high-rise city view in background at r. Plowing with oxen at ctr. on back. — FV / 1.50 / 6.00

#138 and 139 Bank of Mozambique bldg. at l. ctr. arms at upper r. Cabora Bassa hydroeletric dam on back. Wmk: Bank monogram.

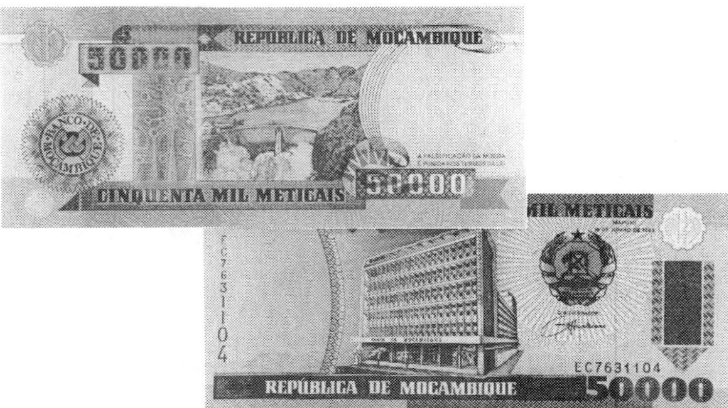

138 **50,000 Meticais** — VG / VF / Unc
16.6.1993 (1994). Dk. brown, red-brown on m/c unpt. — FV / FV / 8.00

139 **100,000 Meticais** — VG / VF / Unc
16.6.1993 (1994). Red, brown-orange and olive-brown on m/c unpt. — FV / FV / 15.00

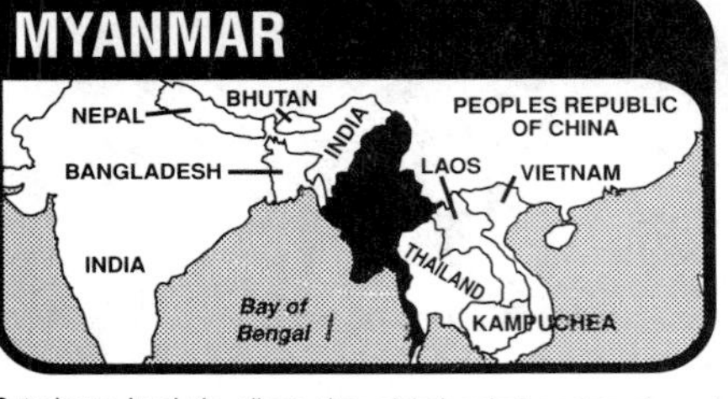

The Socialist Republic of the Union of Myanmar (formally called Burma), a country of Southeast Asia fronting on the Bay of Bengal and the Andaman Sea, has an area of 261,789 sq. mi. (676,552 sq. km.) and a population of 44.7 million. Capital: Ranggon. Myanmar is an agricultural country heavily dependent on its leading product (rice) which embodies two-thirds of the cultivated area and accounts for 40 percent of the value of exports. Petroleum, lead, tin, silver, zinc, nickel, cobalt and precious stones are exported.

The first European to reach Burma, about 1435, was Nicolo Di Conti, a merchant of Venice. During the beginning of the reign of Bodawpaya (1782-1819AD) the kingdom comprised most of the same area as it does today including Arakan which was taken over in 1784-85. The British East India Company, while unsuccessful in its 1612 effort to establish posts along the Bay of Bengal, was enabled by the Anglo-Burmese Wars of 1824-86 to expand to the whole of Burma and to secure its annexation to British India. In 1937, Burma was separated from India, becoming a separate British colony with limited self-government. The Japanese occupied Burma in 1942, and on Aug. 1, 1943 Burma became an "independent and sovereign state" under Dr. Ba Maw who was appointed the Adipadi (head of state) which collpased with the surrender of Japanese forces. Burma became an independent nation outside the British Commonwealth on Jan. 4, 1948, the constitution of 1948 providing for a parliamentary democracy and the nationalization of certain industries. However, political and economic problems persisted, and on March 2, 1962, Gen. Ne Win took over the government, suspended the constitution, installed himself as chief of state, and pursued a socialistic program with nationalization of nearly all industry and trade. On Jan. 4, 1974, a new constitution adopted by referendum established Burma as a "socialist republic" under one-party rule. The country name in English was changed to Union of Myanmar in 1989.

MONETARY SYSTEM:

1 Kyat = 100 Pya, 1943-1945, 1952-

Republic

Central Bank of Myanmar

1990 ND Issue

67 **1 Kyat** — VG / VF / Unc
ND (1990). Pale brown and orange on m/c unpt. Gen. Aung San at l. and as wmk. Dragon carving at l. on back. — FV / FV / .30

1991-98 ND Issue

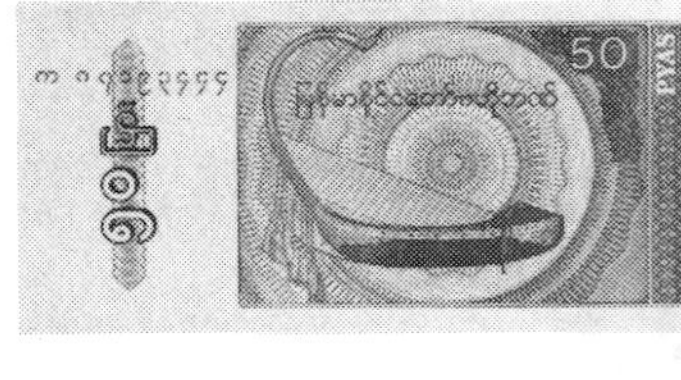

68 **50 Pyas** — VG / VF / Unc
ND (1994). Dull purple and dull brown on gray and tan unpt. Musical string instrument at ctr. Wmk: *OM.* — FV / FV / .30

69 **1 Kyat** — VG / VF / Unc
ND (1996). Gray, blue and purple on m/c unpt. Chinze at r. Wmk: B/CM. — FV / FV / .30

		VG	VF	UNC
70	**5 KYATS** ND (1996). Dk. brown and blue-green on m/c unpt. Chinze at l. ctr. Ball game scene on back.			
	a. Wmk: Chinze. (1996).	FV	FV	.75
	b. Wmk: Chinze bust over value. (1997).	FV	FV	.50

		VG	VF	UNC
71	**10 KYATS** ND (1996). Deep purple and violet on m/c unpt. Chinze at r. ctr. Elaborate barge on back.			
	a. Wmk: Chinze. (1996).	FV	FV	1.00
	b. Wmk: Chinze bust over value. (1997).	FV	FV	.60

		VG	VF	UNC
72	**20 KYATS** ND (1994). Deep olive-green, brown and blue-green on m/c unpt. Chinze at l. Fountain of elephants in park at ctr. r. on back. Wmk: Chinze bust over value.	FV	FV	1.00

		VG	VF	UNC
73	**50 KYATS** ND (1994-). Red-brown, tan and dk. brown on m/c unpt. Chinze at r. and as wmk. Coppersmith at l. ctr. on back.			
	a. Wmk: Chinze. (1994).	FV	FV	2.75
	b. Wmk: Chinze bust over value. (1997).	FV	FV	2.50

		VG	VF	UNC
74	**100 KYATS** ND (1994). Blue-violet, blue-green and dk. brown on m/c unpt. Chinze at l. Workers restoring temple and grounds at ctr. r. on back. Wmk: Chinze bust over value.			
	a. Security thread in positive script.	FV	FV	4.00
	b. Security thread in negative script.	FV	FV	4.00

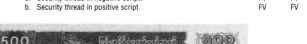

		VG	VF	UNC
75	**200 KYATS** ND (ca.1991). Dk. blue and green on m/c unpt. Chinze at r., his head as wmk. Elephant pulling log at ctr. r. on back. Wmk: Chinze.			
	a. Security thread in negative script.	FV	FV	8.00
	b. Security thread in positive script.	FV	FV	6.00

		VG	VF	UNC
76	**500 KYATS** ND (1994). Purple, brown-violet and brown-orange on m/c unpt. Chinze at l. Workers restoring medieval statue, craftsman and water hauler at ctr. r. on back. Wmk: Chinze bust over value.			
	a. Security thread in negative script.	FV	FV	14.00
	b. Security thread in positive script.	FV	FV	10.00

NOTICE

Readers with unlisted dates, signature varieties, etc. are invited to submit photocopies of their notes to: Standard Catalog of World Paper Money, 700 East State St. Iola, WI 54990-0001, fax: 1-715-445-4087, or E-Mail: thernr@krause.com.

77	1000 KYATS	VG	VF	UNC
	ND (1998). Deep green and purple on m/c unpt. Chinze at r. Central Bank bldg. at l. ctr. on back. Wmk: Chinze bust.			
	a. Security thread in negative script.	FV	FV	15.00
	b. Security thread in positive script.	FV	FV	15.00

FOREIGN EXCHANGE CERTIFICATES

CENTRAL BANK

1993 ND ISSUE

FX1	1 DOLLAR (USA)	VG	VF	UNC
	ND (1993). Blue, brown, yellow and green.	—	—	4.00

FX2	5 DOLLARS (USA)	VG	VF	UNC
	ND (1993). Maroon, yellow and blue.	—	—	13.50

FX3	10 DOLLARS (USA)	VG	VF	UNC
	ND (1993). Blue, green and gray.	—	—	27.50
FX4	20 DOLLARS (USA)			
	ND (1997). Maroon, yellow and brown.	—	—	35.00

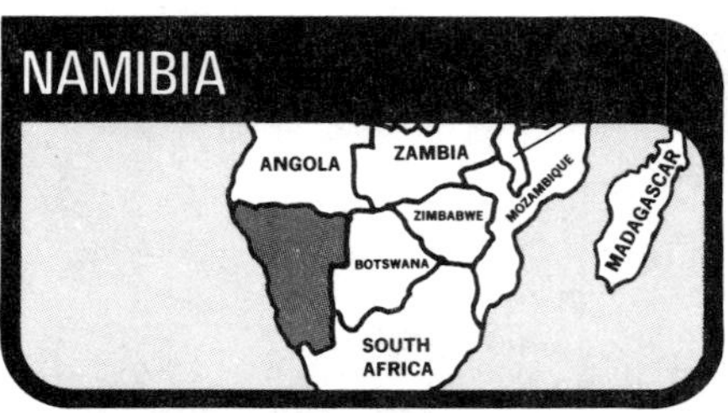

The Republic of Namibia, once the German colonial territory of German South West Africa, is situated on the Atlantic coast of southern Africa, bounded on the north by Angola, on the east by Botswana, and on the south by South Africa. It has an area of 318,261 sq. mi. (824, 290 sq. km.) and a population of 1.7 million. Capital: Windhoek. Diamonds, copper, lead, zinc and cattle are exported.

South Africa undertook the administration of South West Africa under the terms of a League of Nations mandate on Dec. 17, 1920. When the League of Nations was dissolved in 1946, its supervisory authority for South West Africa was inherited by the United Nations. In 1946 the UN denied South Africa's request to annex South West Africa. South Africa responded by refusing to place the territory under a UN trusteeship. In 1950 the International Court of Justice ruled that South Africa could not unilaterally modify the international status of South West Africa. A 1966 UN resolution declaring the mandate terminated was rejected by South Africa, and the status of the area remained in dispute. In June 1968 the UN General Assembly voted to rename the territory Namibia. In 1971 the International Court of Justice ruled that South Africa's presence in Namibia was illegal. In Dec. 1973 the UN appointed a UN Commissioner, and a multi-racial Advisory Council was also appointed. An interim government was formed in 1977 and independence was to be declared by Dec. 31, 1978. This resolution was rejected by major UN powers. In April 1978 South Africa accepted a plan for UN-supervised elections which led to political abstention by the South West Africa People's Organization (SWAPO) party. The result was the dissolution of the Minister's Council and National Assembly in Jan. 1983. A Multi-Party Conference (MPC) was formed in May 1984 which held talks with SWAPO. The MPC petitioned South Africa for Namibian self-government and on June 17, 1984 the Transitional Government of National Unity was installed. Negotiations were held in 1988 between Angola, Cuba and South Africa reaching a peaceful settlement on Aug. 5, 1988. By April 1, 1989, Cuban troops were to withdraw from Angola and South African troops from Namibia. The Transitional Government resigned on Feb. 28, 1988 for the upcoming elections of the constituent assembly in Nov. 1989. Independence was finally achieved on March 21, 1990, within the Commonwealth of Nations. The President is Head of State; the Prime Minister is Head of Government.

MONETARY SYSTEM:

1 Namibia Dollar = 100 Cents

NOTE: For notes of the 3 commercial banks circulating until 1963 see Southwest Africa listings in Vol. 2.

SIGNATURE VARIETIES			
1	GOVERNOR Mr. Erik L. Karlsson	2	GOVERNOR Dr. Jaafar B. Ahmad
3	Mr. T. Alwendo		

REPUBLIC

BANK OF NAMIBIA

1993 ND ISSUE

#1-3 Capt. H. Wittbooi at l. ctr. and as wmk. Printer: Tumba Bruk A.B. (Sweden - w/o imprint). Sign. 1. Replacement notes: Serial # prefix *X; Y; Z* for #1, 2 and 3 respectively.

1	10 NAMIBIA DOLLARS	VG	VF	UNC
	ND (1993). Blue-black on m/c unpt. Arms at upper l. Springbok at r. on back.			
	a. Sign. 1.	FV	FV	5.00
	s. Specimen. Serial # prefix *S*.	—	—	110.00

		VG	VF	UNC
2	**50 NAMIBIA DOLLARS** ND (1993). Blue-green and dk. brown on m/c unpt. Arms at upper ctr. Kudu at r. on back.			
	a. Sign. 1.	FV	FV	25.00
	s. Specimen. Serial # prefix *S*.	—	—	110.00

		VG	VF	UNC
3	**100 NAMIBIA DOLLARS** ND (1993). Red, brown and red-brown on m/c unpt. Arms at upper ctr. r. Oryx at r. on back.			
	a. Sign. 1.	FV	FV	45.00
	s. Specimen. Serial # prefix *S*.	—	—	110.00

1996 ND ISSUE

#4-7 Capt. H. Wittbooi at l. ctr. and as wmk. Segmented foil over security thread and ascending serial #. Sign. 2. Printer: TDLR. Replacement notes: Serial # prefix *V; Y; Z; W* respectively for #5, 6, 7 and 8.

		VG	VF	UNC
4	**10 NAMIBIA DOLLARS** ND (1996).	Expected New Issue		

		VG	VF	UNC
5 (4)	**20 NAMIBIA DOLLARS** ND (1996). Orange and violet on m/c unpt. Arms at upper l. Red hartebeest at ctr. r. on back.			
	a. Sign. 2.	FV	FV	9.00
	s. Specimen. Serial # prefix *H*.	—	—	100.00

		VG	VF	UNC
6	**50 NAMIBIA DOLLARS** ND (1999). Blue-green and dk. brown on m/c unpt. Arms at upper ctr. Kudu at r. on back.			
	a. Sign. 3. Similar to #2.	FV	FV	25.00
	s. Specimen. Serial # prefix *P*.	—	—	100.00
7	**100 NAMIBIA DOLLARS** ND (1999). Red, brown and red-brown on m/c unpt. Arms at upper ctr. r. Oryx at r. on back.			
	a. Sign. 3.	FV	FV	45.00
	s. Specimen. Serial # prefix *T*.	—	—	100.00

		VG	VF	UNC
8 (5)	**200 NAMIBIA DOLLARS** ND (1996). Purple and violet on m/c unpt. Arms at upper ctr. Roan antelope at ctr. r. on back.			
	a. Sign. 2.	FV	FV	70.00
	s. Specimen. Serial # prefix *V*.	—	—	100.00

COLLECTOR SERIES

BANK OF NAMIBIA

1993 ND ISSUE

		ISSUE PRICE	MKT. VALUE
CS1	**10, 50, 100 DOLLARS** ND (1993). #1-3 w/matched serial # mounted in a special plexiglass frame.	150.00	165.00

1996; 1999 ND ISSUE

		ISSUE PRICE	MKT. VALUE
CS2	**20, 50, 100, 200 DOLLARS** ND (1996; 1999). #5, 6, 7, 8 w/matched serial #.	—	350.00

NOTE: Issued only to current owners of #CS1 to complete matched serial sets.

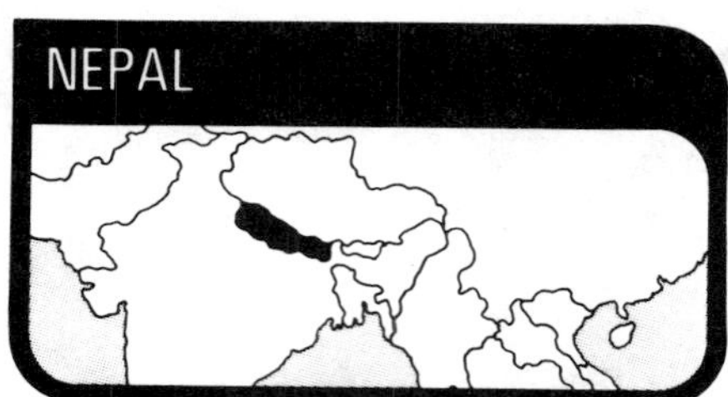

The Kingdom of Nepal, the world's only Hindu kingdom, is a landlocked country located in central Asia along the southern slopes of the Himalayan Mountains. It has an area of 56,136 sq. mi. (140,797 sq. km.) and a population of 23.1 million. Capital: Kathmandu. Nepal has substantial deposits of coal, copper, iron and cobalt but they are largely unexploited. Agriculture is the principal economic activity. Livestock, rice, timber and jute are exported.

Prithvi Narayan Shah, ruler of the principality of Gurkha, formed Nepal from a number of independent mountain states in the latter half of the 18th century. After his death a period of political instability ensued which lasted until the 1840's when the Rana family reduced the monarch to a figurehead and established itself as hereditary Prime Ministers. A popular revolution (1950-51) toppled the Rana family and reconstituted the power in the throne. In 1959 King Mahendra declared Nepal a constitutional monarchy. A new constitution promulgated in 1962 instituted a system of panchayat (village council) democracy from the village to the national levels. In 1990, following political unrest, the king's powers were reduced, and the country adopted a system of parliamentary democracy.

RULERS:

Mahendra Vira Vikrama Shahi Deva, 1955-1972
Birendra Bir Bikram Shahi Deva, 1972-

MONETARY SYSTEM:

1 Rupee = 100 Paisa, 1961-

SIGNATURE VARIETIES			
1	Janak Raj	2	Bharat Raj
3	Narendra Raj	4	Himalaya Shamsher (J.B. Rama)
5	Lakshmi Nath Gautam	6	Pradhumna Lal (Rajbhandari)
7	Bekh Bahadur Thapa	8	Yadav Prasad Pant
9	Kul Shekhar Sharma	10	Kalyan Dikram Adhikary
11	Ganesh Bahadur Thapa	12	Harishankar Tripathi
13	Satyendra Pyara Shrestha		

KINGDOM

STATE BANK

1961; 1965 ND ISSUE

#12-15 denominations in Nepalese language changed from "Mohru" on previous issue to "Rupees" on both face and back. Wmk: Plumed crown.

		VG	VF	UNC
12	**1 RUPEE** ND (1965). Violet and olive-green. Coin at l., temple at ctr. Back lilac and green; arms at ctr., coin at r. Sign. 8.	.20	.85	3.50

#13-15 portr. Kg. Mahendra Vira Vikrama at upper l.

		VG	VF	UNC
13	**5 RUPEES** ND (1961). Purple and aqua. Stupa at ctr. Himalayas on back. Sign. 5; 7; 8.	.50	1.35	4.00

		VG	VF	UNC
14	**10 RUPEES** ND (1961). Dk. brown and red. Temple at ctr. Arms at ctr. on back. Sign. 5; 6; 7; 8.	.90	2.75	8.00

		VG	VF	UNC
15	**100 RUPEES** ND (1961). Green and brown. Temple at Lalitpor at ctr. Rhinoceros at ctr. on back. Sign. 6; 7; 8.	3.00	10.00	35.00

1972 ND ISSUE

#16-21 Kg. Mahendra Vira Vikrama wearing military uniform w/white cap at l. Wmk: Plumed crown. Sign. 8.

		VG	VF	UNC
16	**1 RUPEE** ND (1972). Lt. brown on blue unpt. Back brown and purple; 4-chair rotary swing at ctr. r., arms at upper r. on back.	.20	.65	1.75

		VG	VF	UNC
17	**5 RUPEES** ND (1972). Lt. green on lilac unpt. Back green and blue; terraced hillside w/Himalayas in background.	.30	.85	2.50

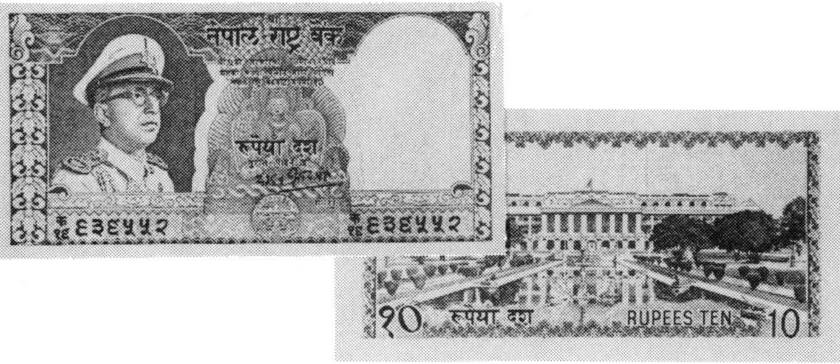

		VG	VF	UNC
18	**10 RUPEES** ND (1972). Lt. brown on dull olive-green and lt. blue unpt. Back green and brown; Singha Dunbar at Kathmandu at ctr.	.35	1.00	2.50
19	**100 RUPEES** ND (1972). Green on lilac unpt. Himalayas at ctr. Ornate bldg., temple and arms at r. on back.	3.00	7.00	18.00
20	**500 RUPEES** ND (1972). Brown and violet. 2 tigers on back.	25.00	75.00	200.00

		VG	VF	UNC
21	**1000 RUPEES** ND (1972). Blue and m/c. Great Stupa at Bodhnath. House and mountains on back.	26.50	75.00	200.00

1974 ND ISSUE

#22-28 Kg. Birendra Bir Bikram in military uniform w/dk. cap at l. Wmk: Plumed crown.

		VG	VF	UNC
22	**1 RUPEE** ND (1974). Blue on purple and gold unpt. Temple at ctr. Back blue and brown; 2 musk deer at ctr., arms at upper r. Sign. 9; 10; 11; 12.	.05	.25	1.00

		VG	VF	UNC
23	**5 RUPEES** ND (1974). Red, brown and green. Temple at ctr. Back red and brown; 2 yaks at ctr. r. Sign. 9; 10; 11.	.15	.40	3.25

		VG	VF	UNC
24	**10 RUPEES** ND (1974). Dk. and lt. brown on m/c unpt. Vishnu on Garnda at ctr. Back brown and green; 2 antelopes at ctr., arms at r. Sign. 9; 10; 11.	.30	.85	3.25

		VG	VF	UNC
25	**50 RUPEES** ND (1974). Purple and green on m/c unpt. Bldg. at ctr. Back blue and brown; mountain goat standing facing r. at ctr., arms at r. Sign. 9.	1.50	3.50	10.00

		VG	VF	UNC
26	**100 RUPEES** ND (1974). Green and purple on m/c unpt. Mountains at ctr., temple at r. Back green; rhinoceros walking l., "eye" at upper l. corner, arms at upper r. Sign. 9.	3.00	7.00	20.00
27	**500 RUPEES** ND (1974). Brown on m/c unpt. Monastery at ctr. Back brown and gold; 2 tigers at ctr. r., arms at upper r. Sign. 9; 10.	25.00	75.00	200.00
28	**1000 RUPEES** ND (1974). Blue on m/c unpt. Temple and Great Stupa at ctr. Elephant at ctr., arms at upper r. on back. Sign. 9.	25.00	80.00	225.00

1981-87 ND ISSUE

#29-36 Kg. Birendra Bir Bikram wearing plumed crown at l. Wmk: Plumed crown.

		VG	VF	UNC
29	**2 RUPEES** ND (1981-). Green on lt. blue and lilac unpt. Temple at ctr. Back m/c; leopard at ctr.			
	a. Line from king's lower lip extending downward. Serial # 24mm long. Sign. 10.	FV	FV	2.00
	b. No line from king's lower lip. Sign. 10; 11; 13.	FV	FV	.65
	c. As b. Serial # 20mm long. Sign. 12.	FV	FV	.85

		VG	VF	UNC
30	**5 RUPEES** ND (1987-). Brown on red and m/c unpt. Temple at ctr. Back similar to #23.			
	a. Serial # 24mm long. Sign. 11; 12; 13.	FV	FV	1.25
	b. Serial # 20mm long. Sign. 12.	FV	FV	1.25

		VG	VF	UNC
31	**10 RUPEES** ND (1985-87). Dk. brown and orange on lilac and m/c unpt. Vishnu on Garnda at ctr. Antelopes at ctr., arms at r. on back.			
	a. Serial # 24mm long. Sign. 11; 12.	FV	FV	2.00
	b. Segmented foil over security thread. Sign. 13.	FV	FV	1.75

		VG	VF	UNC
32	**20 RUPEES** ND (1982-87). Orange on m/c unpt. Janakpur Temple at ctr. Back orange and m/c; deer at ctr., arms at r. Serial # 24mm long. Sign. 10; 11.	FV	FV	5.00

		VG	VF	UNC
33	**50 RUPEES** ND (1983-). Blue on m/c unpt. Palace at ctr. Mountain goat at ctr., arms at r. on back.			
	a. W/title at r. Serial # 24mm long. Sign. 10. (1983).	FV	FV	5.50
	b. W/title at ctr. Serial # 20mm long. Sign. 11; 12.	FV	FV	3.50
	c. Segmented foil over security thread. Sign. 13.	—	—	3.00

		VG	VF	UNC
34	**100 RUPEES** ND (1981). Green on pale lilac and m/c unpt. Temple at r. Rhinoceros walking l., arms at upper r. on back. Similar to #26, but w/o "eye" at upper l. Sign. 10; 11.			
	a. Line from king's lower lip extending downward. W/security thread. Serial # 24mm long. Sign. 10.	FV	FV	6.50
	b. No line from king's lower lip. Serial # at lower l. Sign. 10.	FV	FV	6.00
	c. Serial # 20mm long. Sign. 11.	FV	FV	5.50
	d. As b. Segmented foil over security thread. Sign. 12.	FV	FV	5.00
	e. As c and d.	FV	FV	4.50

		VG	VF	UNC
35	**500 RUPEES** ND (1981). Brown and blue-violet on m/c unpt. Temple at ctr. Back brown and gold on blue unpt.; 2 tigers at ctr. r., arms at upper r.			
	a. Line from King's lip extending downwards. Serial # 24mm long. Sign. 10.	FV	FV	45.00
	b. Serial # 20mm long. Sign. 11.	FV	FV	20.00
	c. Segmented foil over security thread. Sign. 12.	FV	FV	18.50

		VG	VF	UNC
36	**1000 RUPEES** ND (1981). Brown and gray on m/c unpt. Stupa and temple on face. Elephant at ctr., arms at upper r. on back. Sign. 10, 11.			
	a. Line from King's lip extending downwards. Serial # 24mm long. Sign. 10.	FV	FV	85.00
	b. Serial # 20mm long. Sign. 11.	FV	FV	37.50
	c. Segmented foil over security thread. Sign. 12.	FV	FV	36.00

1988-96 ND ISSUE

#37 and 38 Kg. Birendra Bir Bikram wearing plumed crown at l. Wmk: Crown.

		VG	VF	UNC
37	**1 RUPEE** ND (1991-) Purple and dull blue on m/c unpt. Back like #22. Sign.12; 13.	FV	FV	.40

		VG	VF	UNC
38	**20 RUPEES** ND (1988-). Orange on m/c unpt. Like #32, but m/c border on face and back.			
	a. Serial # 24mm long. Sign. 11; 12.	FV	FV	2.25
	b. Segmented foil over security thread. Serial # 20mm long. Sign. 13.	FV	FV	2.00

1996 ND ISSUE

#39 and 40 Kg. Birendra Bir Bikram wearing plumed crown at l. Wmk: Crown.

		VG	VF	UNC
39	**500 RUPEES** ND (1996). Brown, blue-violet and silver on m/c unpt. Like #35. Sign. 13.	FV	FV	18.00
40	**1000 RUPEES** ND (1996). Blue, brown and silver on m/c unpt. Like #36. Sign. 13.	FV	FV	35.00

1997 ND COMMEMORATIVE ISSUE

#41 and 42, Silver Jubilee of Accession, 1972-1997

#41 and 42 portr. Kg. Birenda Bir Bikram wearing plumed crown at l. Wmk: Plumed crown.

		VG	VF	UNC
41	**25 RUPEES** ND (1997). Black and dk. brown on m/c unpt. Royal palace at ctr. r. Back dull green and orange; pillars w/chinze at l., steer at ctr., arms at r.	FV	FV	2.25

		VG	VF	UNC
42	**250 RUPEES** ND (1997). Dk. gray and blue-gray on m/c unpt. House of Representatives in unpt. at ctr., royal palace at ctr. r. Back blue and orange on green unpt.; pillars w/chinze at l., steer at ctr., arms at r.	FV	FV	17.50

#42 was also issued in a special folder.

NOTICE

Readers with unlisted dates, signature varieties, etc. are invited to submit photocopies of their notes to: Standard Catalog of World Paper Money, 700 East State St. Iola, WI 54990-0001, fax: 1-715-445-4087, or E-Mail: thernr@krause.com.

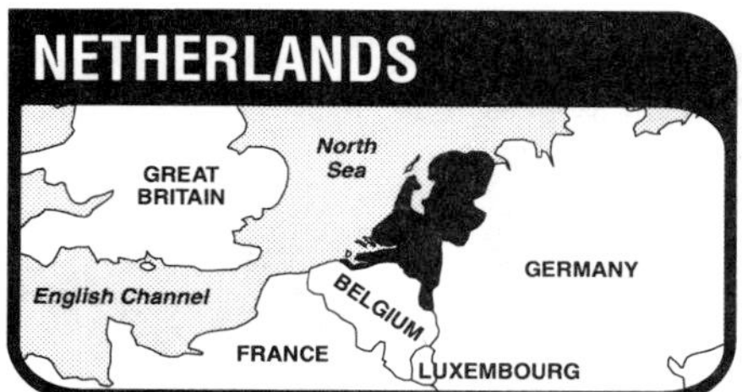

The Kingdom of the Netherlands, a country of western Europe fronting on the North Sea and bordered by Belgium and Germany, has an area of 15,770 sq. mi. (40,844 sq. km.) and a population of 15.5 million. Capital: Amsterdam, but the seat of government is at The Hague. The economy is based on dairy farming and a variety of industrial activities. Chemicals, yarns and fabrics, and meat products are exported.

After being a part of Charlemagne's empire in the 8th and 9th centuries, the Netherlands came under the control of Burgundy and the Austrian Hapsburgs, and finally were subjected to Spanish domination in the 16th century. Lead by William of Orange, the Dutch revolted against Spain in 1568. The seven northern provinces formed the Union of Utrecht and declared their independence in 1581, becoming the Republic of the United Netherlands. In the following century, the "Golden Age" of Dutch history, the Netherlands became a great sea and colonial power, a patron of the arts and a refuge for the persecuted. In 1814, all the provinces of Holland and Belgium were merged into the Kingdom of the United Netherlands under William I. The Belgians withdrew in 1830 to form their own kingdom, the last substantial change in the configuration of European Netherlands. German forces invaded in 1940 and the royal family fled to England where a government in exile was formed. German High Commissioner Arthur Seyss-Inquart was placed in command until 1945 when the arrival of Allied military forces ended the occupation. Reigning since 1948, in 1981 Queen Juliana abdicated in favor of her daughter, Beatrix.

RULERS:

Juliana, 1948-1981
Beatrix, 1981-

MONETARY SYSTEM:

1 Gulden = 100 Cents

KONINKRIJK - KINGDOM

DE NEDERLANDSCHE BANK

NETHERLANDS BANK

1966-72 ISSUE

		VG	VF	UNC
90	**5 GULDEN** 26.4.1966. Green on m/c unpt. J. V. D. Vondel at r. Modern design of Amsterdam Play-house on back. Wmk: Inkwell, quill pen and scroll.			
	a. Serial # at upper l. and lower r. Gray paper w/clear wmk.	FV	FV	10.00
	b. Serial # at upper l. and lower r. White paper w/vague wmk. Series XA/XM.	FV	FV	12.50
	c. Serial # at upper l. and ctr. r. in smaller type. (Experimental issue; only circulated in the province of Utrecht.) Series 6AA.	25.00	75.00	175.00

		VG	VF	UNC
91	**10 GULDEN** 25.4.1968. Dk. blue on violet and m/c unpt. Stylized self-portrait of F. Hals at r. Modern design on back. Wmk: Cornucopia.			
	a. *O* in "bullseye" at upper l. on back.	FV	6.00	12.00
	b. Plain "bullseye" at upper l. on back.	FV	FV	10.00

		VG	VF	UNC
92	**25 GULDEN** 10.2.1971. Red on m/c unpt. J. Pietersz Sweelinck at r. Modern design on back. Wmk: Rectangular wave design.	FV	FV	22.50

		VG	VF	UNC
93	**100 GULDEN** 14.5.1970. Dk. brown on m/c unpt. M. Adriaensz de Ruyter at r. Compass-card or rhumbcard design at ctr. on back.	FV	FV	110.00

		VG	VF	UNC
94	**1000 GULDEN** 30.3.1972. Black and dk. green on m/c unpt. B. d' Espinoza at r. Wmk: Pyramid in bowl on slab.	FV	FV	900.00

1973 ISSUE

		VG	VF	UNC
95	**5 GULDEN** 28.3.1973. Dk. green on green and m/c unpt. J. V. D. Vondel at r. Wmk. like #90.	FV	FV	8.00

1977-85 ISSUE

		VG	VF	UNC
96	**50 GULDEN** 4.1.1982. Orange and yellow on m/c unpt. Sunflower w/bee at lower ctr. Vertical format. Map and flowers on back. Wmk: Bee.	FV	FV	40.00

		VG	VF	UNC
97	**100 GULDEN** 28.7.1977 (1981). Dk. brown on m/c unpt. Water-snipe bird at r. Head of great snipe bird on back and as wmk.	FV	FV	80.00

		VG	VF	UNC
98	**250 GULDEN** 25.7.1985 (1986). Violet on m/c unpt. Lighthouse. Vertical format. Lighthouse and map on back. Wmk: Rabbit and *VHP*.	FV	FV	185.00

1989-97 ISSUE

		VG	VF	UNC
99	**10 GULDEN** 1.7.1997. Purple and blue-violet on m/c unpt. Value and geometric designs on face and back. Wmk: Bird.	FV	FV	9.00

		VG	VF	UNC
100	**25 GULDEN** 5.4.1989. Red on m/c unpt. Value and geometric designs on face and back. Wmk: Robin.	FV	FV	20.00

#101 Held in reserve.

		VG	VF	UNC
102	**100 GULDEN** 9.1.1992 (7.9.1993). Dk. and lt. brown, gray and gold on m/c unpt. Value and geometric designs on face and back. Wmk: Little owl.	FV	FV	77.50

#103 Held in reserve.

104	**1000 GULDEN** 2.6.1994. Dk. gray and green. Geometric designs on face and back. Wmk: Lapwing's head.	FV	FV	675.00

NETHERLANDS ANTILLES

The Netherlands Antilles, part of the Netherlands realm, comprise two groups of islands in the West Indies: Bonaire and Curacao near the Venezuelan coast; and St. Eustatius, Saba and the southern part of St. Martin (St. Maarten) southeast of Puerto Rico. The island group has an area of 385 sq. mi. (961 sq. km.) and a population of 191,000. Capital: Willemstad. Chief industries are the refining of crude oil, and tourism. Petroleum products and phosphates are exported.

On Dec. 15, 1954, the Netherlands Antilles were given complete domestic autonomy and granted equality within the Kingdom with Surinam and the Netherlands.

RULERS:
Dutch

MONETARY SYSTEM:
1 Gulden = 100 Cents

BANK VAN DE NEDERLANDSE ANTILLEN

1962 ISSUE

#1-7 woman seated w/scroll and flag in oval at l. Crowned arms at ctr. on back. Wmk: *NA* monogram. Printer: JEZ.

		VG	VF	UNC
1	**5 GULDEN** 2.1.1962. Blue on m/c unpt. View of Curacao at ctr.	4.00	10.00	60.00
2	**10 GULDEN** 2.1.1962. Green on m/c unpt. High-rise bldg. (Aruba) at ctr.	7.50	18.00	90.00
3	**25 GULDEN** 2.1.1962. Black-gray on m/c unpt. View of Bonaire at ctr.	20.00	40.00	140.00

		VG	VF	UNC
4	**50 GULDEN** 2.1.1962. Brown on m/c unpt. City by the seaside (St. Maarten) at ctr.	35.00	85.00	260.00
5	**100 GULDEN** 2.1.1962. Violet on m/c unpt. Monument (St. Eustatius) at ctr.	70.00	125.00	325.00
6	**250 GULDEN** 2.1.1962. Olive-green on m/c unpt. Boats on the beach (Saba) at ctr.	175.00	350.00	600.00

		VG	VF	UNC
7	**500 GULDEN** 2.1.1962. Red on m/c unpt. Oil refinery (Curacao) at ctr.	350.00	425.00	700.00

1967 ISSUE

#8-13 monument *Steunend op eigen Kracht...* at l. Crowned arms at ctr. on back. Wmk: *NA* monogram. Printer: JEZ.

		VG	VF	UNC
8	**5 GULDEN** 1967; 1972. Dk. blue and green on m/c unpt. View of Curacao at ctr.			
	a. 28.8.1967.	3.50	6.00	25.00
	b. 1.6.1972.	3.50	5.00	17.50

		VG	VF	UNC
9	**10 GULDEN** 1967; 1972. Green on m/c unpt. View of Aruba at ctr.			
	a. 28.8.1967.	7.00	10.00	32.50
	b. 1.6.1972.	6.50	6.50	27.50
10	**25 GULDEN** 1967; 1972. Black-gray on m/c unpt. View of Bonaire at ctr.			
	a. 28.8.1967.	14.00	27.50	90.00
	b. 1.6.1972.	13.00	20.00	70.00
11	**50 GULDEN** 1967; 1972. Brown on m/c unpt. Beach (St. Maarten) at ctr.			
	a. 28.8.1967.	28.00	65.00	165.00
	b. 1.6.1972.	26.00	45.00	100.00

		VG	VF	UNC
12	**100 GULDEN** 1967; 1972. Violet on m/c unpt. Boats and fishermen on the beach (St. Eustatius) at ctr.			
	a. 28.8.1967.	75.00	100.00	275.00
	b. 1.6.1972.	70.00	85.00	180.00
13	**250 GULDEN** 28.8.1967. Olive-green on m/c unpt. Mountains (Saba) at ctr.	175.00	200.00	425.00

#14 *Deleted.* See #A1 in Vol. II.

1979; 1980 ISSUE

#15-19 like #8-13. Printer: JEZ.

		VG	VF	UNC
15	**5 GULDEN** 1980; 1984. Purplish blue on m/c unpt. Like #8.			
	a. 23.12.1980.	FV	4.50	22.50
	b. 1.6.1984.	FV	6.00	30.00

		VG	VF	UNC
16	**10 GULDEN** 1979; 1984. Green and blue-green on m/c unpt. Like #9.			
	a. 14.7.1979.	FV	8.50	35.00
	b. 1.6.1984.	FV	11.00	45.00
17	**25 GULDEN** 14.7.1979. Blue and blue-green on m/c unpt. Like #10.	FV	50.00	200.00
18	**50 GULDEN** 23.12.1980. Red on m/c unpt. Like #11.	FV	65.00	325.00
19	**100 GULDEN** 14.7.1979. Red-brown and violet on m/c unpt. Like #12.	FV	90.00	450.00

1970 MUNTBILJET ISSUE

#20 and 21 crowned arms at r. on back. Printer: JEZ.

		VG	VF	UNC
20	**1 GULDEN** 8.9.1970. Red and orange. Aerial view of harbor at l. ctr.	FV	1.00	2.00

		VG	VF	UNC
21	**2 1/2 GULDEN** 8.9.1970. Blue. Jetliner at l. ctr.	FV	3.00	5.00

1986 ISSUE

#22-27 back and wmk: Shield-like bank logo. Sign. and sign. title varieties. Printer: JEZ.

		VG	VF	UNC
22	**5 GULDEN** 1986; 1990; 1994. Dk. blue on m/c unpt. *Troepiaal* (Tropical bird) at ctr.			
	a. 31.3.1986.	FV	FV	8.50
	b. 1.1.1990.	FV	FV	10.00
	c. 1.5.1994.	FV	FV	7.50

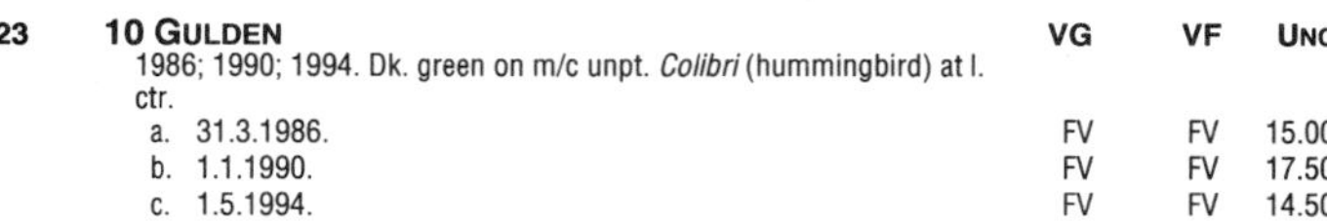

		VG	VF	UNC
23	**10 GULDEN** 1986; 1990; 1994. Dk. green on m/c unpt. *Colibri* (hummingbird) at l. ctr.			
	a. 31.3.1986.	FV	FV	15.00
	b. 1.1.1990.	FV	FV	17.50
	c. 1.5.1994.	FV	FV	14.50

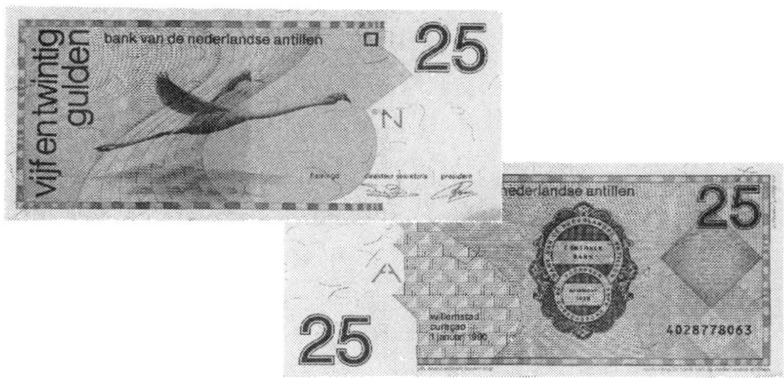

		VG	VF	UNC
24	**25 GULDEN** 1986; 1990; 1994. Red on m/c unpt. Flamingo at l. ctr.			
	a. 31.3.1986.	FV	FV	35.00
	b. 1.1.1990.	FV	FV	45.00
	c. 1.5.1994.	FV	FV	28.50

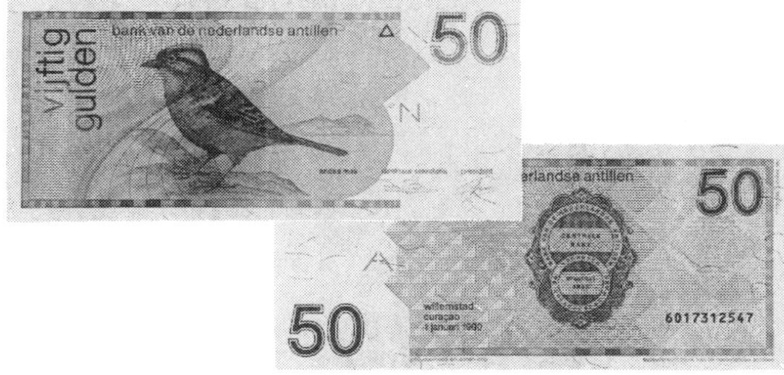

		VG	VF	UNC
25	**50 GULDEN** 1986; 1990; 1994. Brown-orange on m/c unpt. Rufous (collard sparrow) at l. ctr.			
	a. 31.3.1986.	FV	FV	67.50
	b. 1.1.1990.	FV	FV	70.00
	c. 1.5.1994.	FV	FV	55.00

		VG	VF	UNC
26	**100 GULDEN** 1986; 1990; 1994. Brown on m/c unpt. Bananaquit at l. ctr.			
	a. 31.3.1986.	FV	FV	120.00
	b. 1.1.1990.	FV	FV	130.00
	c. 1.5.1994.	FV	FV	85.00

		VG	VF	UNC
27	**250 GULDEN** 1986; 1990. Purple and red-violet on m/c unpt. Caribbean mockingbird at l. ctr.			
	a. 31.3.1986.	FV	FV	245.00
	b. 1.1.1990.	FV	FV	225.00

1998 ISSUE

#28-31 similar to #23-26 but w/gold foil at lower r. and small gold circles and pearl ink object at r. in wmk. area.

		VG	VF	UNC
28	**10 GULDEN** 1.1.1998. Purplish blue on m/c unpt.	FV	FV	12.50

		VG	VF	UNC
29	**25 GULDEN** 1.1.1998. Red on m/c unpt.	FV	FV	22.50

		VG	VF	UNC
30	**50 GULDEN** 1.1.1998. Brown-orange on m/c unpt.	FV	FV	50.00

		VG	VF	UNC
31	**100 GULDEN** 1.1.1998. Brown on m/c unpt.	FV	FV	100.00

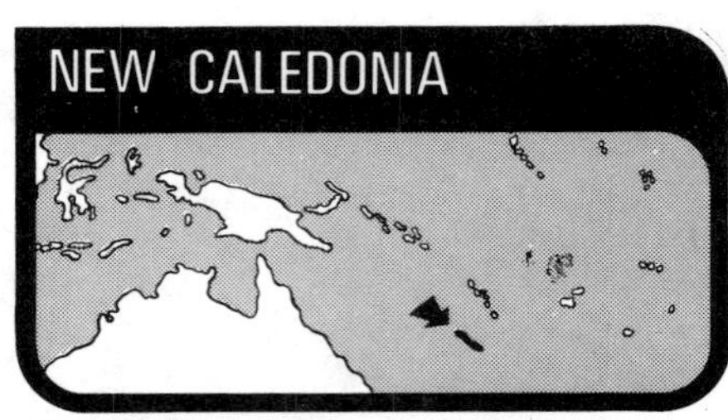

The French Overseas Territory of New Caledonia, a group of about 25 islands in the South Pacific, is situated about 750 miles (1,207 km.) east of Australia. The territory, which includes the dependencies of Ile des Pins, Loyalty Islands, Ile Huon, Isles Belep, Isles Chesterfield, and Ile Walpole, has a total land area of 6,530 sq. mi. (19,058 sq. km.) and a population of 152,000. Capital: Noumea. The islands are rich in minerals; New Caledonia has the world's largest known deposit of nickel. Nickel, nickel castings, coffee and copra are exported.

British navigator Capt. James Cook discovered New Caledonia in 1774. The French took possession in 1853, and established a penal colony on the island in 1854. The European population of the colony remained disproportionately convict until 1894. New Caledonia became an overseas territory within the French Community in 1946, and in 1958 and 1972 chose to remain affiliated with France.

RULERS:

French

MONETARY SYSTEM:

1 Franc = 100 Centimes

SIGNATURE/TITLE VARIETIES

	DIRECTEUR GÉNÉRAL	PREÉSIDENT DU CONSEIL DE SURVEILLANCE
1	André Postel-Vinay, 1967-1972	Bernard Clappier, 1966-1972
2	Claude Panouillot, 1972-1978	André De Lattre,1973
3	Claude Panouillot, 1972-1978	Marcel Theron, 1974-1979
4	Yves Roland-Billecart, 1979-	Gabriel Lefort, 1980-1984
5	Yves Roland-Billecart, 1985-	Jacques Waitzenegger, 1985-

INSTITUT D'EMISSION D'OUTRE-MER

NOUMÉA BRANCH

1969 ND ISSUE

		VG	VF	UNC
59	**100 FRANCS** ND (1969). Brown on m/c unpt. Girl wearing wreath and playing guitar at r. W/o ovpt: *REPUBLIQUE FRANÇAISE* at lower ctr. Girl at l., harbor scene at ctr. on back. Intaglio. Sign. 1.	3.00	12.50	45.00

		VG	VF	UNC
60	**500 FRANCS** ND (1969-92). M/c. Dugout canoe w/sail at ctr., fisherman at r. Man at l., rock formation at l. ctr., native art at r. on back.			
	a. Sign. 1.	7.50	12.50	35.00
	b. Sign. 2.	7.00	11.50	32.50
	c. Sign. 3.	6.50	10.00	30.00
61	**1000 FRANCS** ND (1969). M/c. Hut under palm tree at l., girl at r. W/o ovpt: *RÉPUBLIQUE FRANÇAISE* at lower l. Bldg., bird at l., deer near hut at r. on back. Sign. 1.	13.50	25.00	100.00

#62 Deleted. See #65.

1971 ND ISSUE

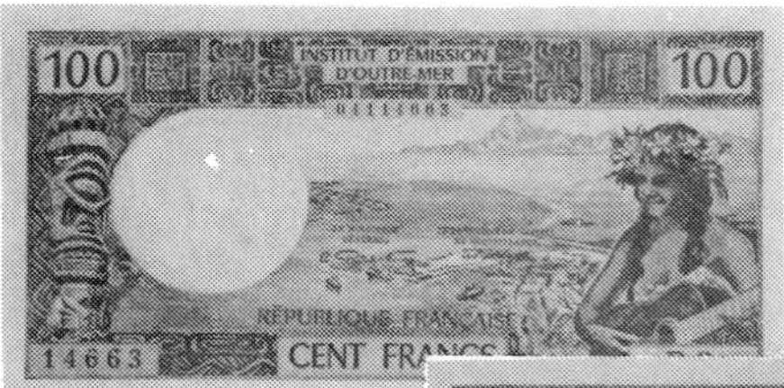

		VG	VF	UNC
63	**100 FRANCS** ND (1971; 1973). Brown on m/c unpt. Like #59 but w/ovpt: *RÉPUBLIQUE FRANÇAISE* at lower ctr.			
	a. Intaglio. Sign. 1 (1971).	2.00	5.00	28.50
	b. Lithographed. Series beginning #H2, from #51,000. Sign. 1 (1973).	1.75	4.00	25.00
	c. As. b. Sign. 2 (1975).	1.65	3.50	20.00
	d. As b. Sign. 3 (1977).	1.50	3.00	17.50
64	**1000 FRANCS** ND (1971; 1983). M/c. Like #46 but w/ovpt: *RÉPUBLIQUE FRANÇAISE* ovpt. at lower l.			
	a. Sign. 1 (1971).	12.50	17.50	35.00
	b. Sign. 4 (1983).	11.50	16.50	32.50

		VG	VF	UNC
65	**5000 FRANCS** ND (1971-84). M/c. Bougainville at l., sailing ships at ctr. Ovpt: *RÉPUBLIQUE FRANÇAISE.* Admiral Febvrier-Despointes at r., sailboat at ctr. r. on back.			
	a. Sign. 1 (1971).	60.00	100.00	200.00
	b. Sign. 2 (1975).	57.50	95.00	190.00
	c. Sign. 4 (1982-84).	55.00	87.50	175.00
	s. As a. Specimen.	—	—	150.00

NOTE: For current 500 and 10,000 Francs see French Pacific Territories.

NOTICE

Readers with unlisted dates, signature varieties, etc. are invited to submit photocopies of their notes to: Standard Catalog of World Paper Money, 700 East State St. Iola, WI 54990-0001, fax: 1-715-445-4087, or E-Mail: thernr@krause.com.

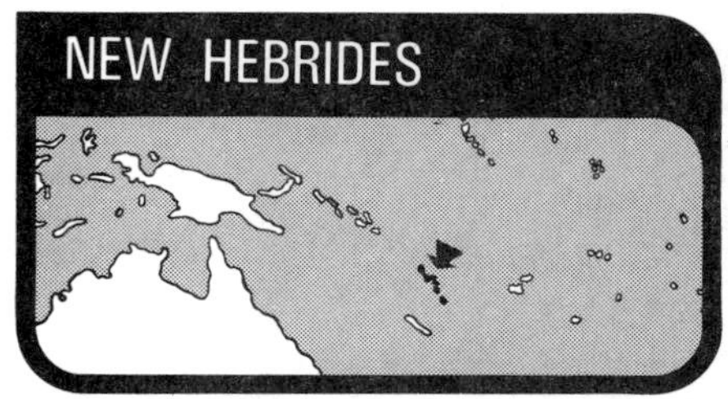

New Hebrides Condominium, a group of islands located in the South Pacific 500 miles (800 km.) west of Fiji, were under the joint sovereignty of Great Britain and France. The islands have an area of 5,700 sq. mi. (14,763 sq. km.) and a population of mainly Melanesians of mixed blood. Capital: Port-Vila. The volcanic and coral islands, while material and subject to frequent earthquakes, are extremely fertile, and produce copra, coffee, tropical fruits and timber for export.

The New Hebrides were discovered by Portuguese navigator Pedro de Quiros in 1606, visited by French explorer Bougainville in 1768, and named by British navigator Capt. James Cook in 1774. Ships of all nations converged on the islands to trade for sandalwood, prompting France and Britain to relinquish their individual claims and declare the islands a neutral zone in 1878. The New Hebrides were placed under the control of a mixed Anglo-French commission of naval officers during the native uprisings of 1887, and established as a condominium under the joint sovereignty of France and Great Britain in 1906.

NOTE: For later issues see Vanuatu.

RULERS:

British and French to 1980

MONETARY SYSTEM:

1 Franc = 100 Centimes

SIGNATURE/TITLE VARIETIES

	DIRECTEUR GÉNÉRAL	PREÉSIDENT DU CONSEIL DE SURVEILLANCE
1	André Postel-Vinay, 1967-1972	Bernard Clappier, 1966-1972
2	Claude Panquillot, 1972-1973	André De Lattre,1973
3	Claude Panquillot, 1974-1978	Marcel Theron, 1974-1979
4	Yves Roland-Billecart, 1979-1984	Gabriel Lefort, 1980-1984
5	Yves Roland-Billecart, 1985-	Jacques Waitzenegger, 1985-

INSTITUT D'EMISSION D'OUTRE-MER, NOUVELLES HÉBRIDES

1965; 1967 ND ISSUE

		VG	VF	UNC
16	**100 FRANCS** ND (1965-71). M/c. Black on yellow and green unpt. Girl w/guitar at r. Girl at l., harbor scene at ctr. w/ovpt: *NOUVELLES-HÉBRIDES* in capital letters on back. Sign. 1.	5.00	25.00	75.00

		VG	VF	UNC
17	**1000 FRANCS** ND (1967-71). Red. Hut under palm tree at l., girl at r. Bldg., bird at l., deer near hut at r. w/ovpt: *NOUVELLES HÉBRIDES* in capital letters at upper ctr. on back. Sign. 1.	15.00	50.00	175.00

1970 ND ISSUE

		VG	VF	UNC
18	**100 FRANCS** ND (1970; 1972; 1977). M/c. Like #16, but red and blue unpt. *Nouvelles Hébrides* in script on face and back.			
	a. Intaglio plates. Sign. 1. (1970).	2.00	5.00	28.50
	b. Lithographed Series beginning E1, from no. 51,000. Sign. 1. (1972).	1.75	4.00	25.00
	c. As b. Sign. 2. (1975).	1.65	3.50	20.00
	d. As b. Sign. 3. (1977).	1.50	3.00	17.50

		VG	VF	UNC
19	**500 FRANCS** ND (1970-80). Blue, green and m/c. Dugout canoe w/sail at ctr., fisherman at. r. Man at l., rock formation at l. ctr., native art at r. on back.			
	a. Sign. 1. (1970).	7.50	12.50	35.00
	b. Sign. 3. (1979).	7.00	11.50	32.50
	c. Sign. 4. (1980).	6.50	10.00	30.00

		VG	VF	UNC
20	**1000 FRANCS** ND (1970-80). Orange and brown. Like #17. *Nouvelles Hébrides* in script on face and back.			
	a. Sign. 1. (1970).	15.00	25.00	75.00
	b. Sign. 2. (1975).	13.50	21.50	65.00
	c. Sign. 3. (1980).	12.50	18.50	55.00

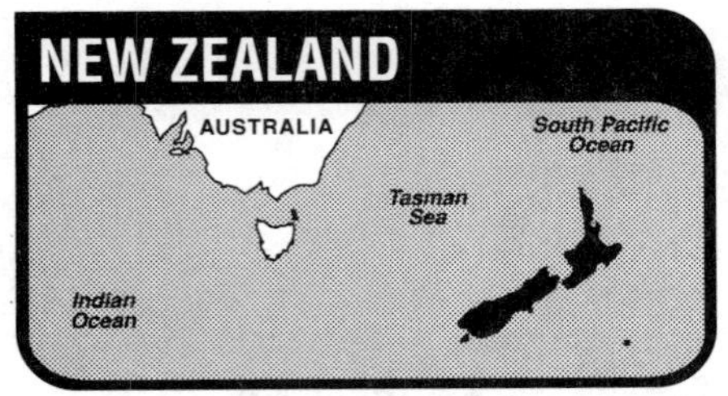

New Zealand, a parliamentary state located in the southwestern Pacific 1,250 miles (2,011 km.) east of Australia, has an area of 103,736 sq. mi. (269,056 sq. km.) and a population of 3.77 million. Capital: Wellington. Wool, meat, dairy products and some manufactured items are exported.

New Zealand was discovered and named by Dutch navigator Abel Tasman in 1642, and explored by British navigator Capt. James Cook who surveyed it in 1769 and annexed the land to Great Britain. The British government disavowed the annexation and for the next 70 years the only white settlers to arrive were adventurers attracted by the prospects of lumbering, sealing and whaling. Great Britain annexed the land in 1840 by treaty with the native chiefs and made it a dependency of New South Wales. The colony was granted self-government in 1852, a ministerial form of government in 1856, and full dominion status on Sept. 26, 1907. Full internal and external autonomy, which New Zealand had in effect possessed for many years, was formally extended in 1947. New Zealand is a member of the Commonwealth of Nations. Elizabeth II is Head of State as Queen of New Zealand.

RULERS:

British

MONETARY SYSTEM:

1 Shilling = 12 Pence
1 Pound = 20 Shillings to 1967
1 Pound = 20 Shillings (also 2 Dollars) to 1967
1 Dollar = 100 Cents, 1967-

RESERVE BANK OF NEW ZEALAND

1940 ND ISSUE

#158-162 portr. Capt. J. Cook at lower r. Sign. title: *CHIEF CASHIER.* Wmk: Maori chief. Printer: TDLR.

		VG	VF	UNC
158	**10 SHILLINGS** ND (1940-67). Brown on m/c unpt. Arms at upper ctr. Kiwi at l., treaty signing at ctr. on back.			
	a. Sign. T. P. Hanna. (1940-55).	2.50	15.00	125.00
	b. Sign. G. Wilson. (1955-56).	4.50	30.00	200.00
	c. Sign. R. N. Fleming. W/o security thread. (1956-67).	1.50	5.00	75.00
	d. As c. W/security thread. (1967).	1.50	4.00	35.00

		VG	VF	UNC
159	**1 POUND** ND (1940-67). Purple on m/c unpt. Arms at upper ctr. Sailing ship on sea at l. on back.			
	a. Sign. T. P. Hanna. (1940-55).	3.00	9.00	150.00
	b. Sign. G. Wilson. (1955-56).	4.00	15.00	175.00
	c. Sign. R. N. Fleming. W/o security thread. (1956-67).	3.00	25.00	150.00
	d. As c. W/security thread. (1967).	2.00	5.00	40.00

		VG	VF	UNC
160	**5 POUNDS** ND (1940-67). Blue on m/c unpt. Crowned arms at upper ctr. Island, water and mountains on back.			
	a. Sign. T. P. Hanna. (1940-55).	9.00	20.00	160.00
	b. Sign. G. Wilson. (1955-56).	9.00	25.00	200.00
	c. Sign. R. N. Fleming. W/o security thread. (1956-67).	9.00	17.50	150.00
	d. As c. W/security thread. (1967).	6.50	10.00	75.00

		VG	VF	UNC
161	**10 POUNDS** ND (1940-67). Green on m/c unpt. Crowned arms, sailing ship at l. Herd of animals at l. ctr. on back.			
	a. Sign. T. P. Hanna. (1940-55).	30.00	55.00	375.00
	b. Sign. G. Wilson. (1955-56).	35.00	70.00	425.00
	c. Sign. R. N. Fleming. (1956-67).	17.50	30.00	150.00
	d. As c. W/security thread. (1967).	10.00	18.50	125.00

		VG	VF	UNC
162	**50 POUNDS** ND (1940-67). Red on m/c unpt. Crowned arms, sailing ship at l. Dairy farm and mountain on back.			
	a. Sign. T. P. Hanna. (1940-55).	220.00	450.00	2000.
	b. Sign. G. Wilson. (1955-56).	220.00	450.00	2250.
	c. Sign. R. N. Fleming. (1956-67).	125.00	400.00	850.00

NOTICE

Readers with unlisted dates, signature varieties, etc. are invited to submit photocopies of their notes to: Standard Catalog of World Paper Money, 700 East State St. Iola, WI 54990-0001, fax: 1-715-445-4087, or E-Mail: thernr@krause.com.

1967 ND ISSUE

#163-168 Qn. Elizabeth II at r. on face. Birds and plants on back. Wmk: Capt. J. Cook. Printer: TDLR.

#163b-168b replacement notes: Special serial # prefix and * suffix.

		VG	VF	UNC
163	**1 DOLLAR** ND (1967-81). Brown on m/c unpt.			
	a. Sign. R. N. Fleming. (1967-68).	1.50	5.00	55.00
	b. Sign. D. L. Wilks. (1968-75).	1.50	3.00	17.50
	c. Sign. R. L. Knight. (1975-77).	1.00	1.50	8.50
	d. Sign. H. R. Hardie. (1977-81).	1.00	1.50	8.50

		VG	VF	UNC
164	**2 DOLLARS** ND (1967-81). Purple on m/c unpt.			
	a. Sign. R. N. Fleming. (1967-68).	2.00	5.00	40.00
	b. Sign. D. L. Wilks. (1968-75).	2.00	4.00	22.50
	c. Sign. R. L. Knight. (1975-77).	1.50	2.50	15.00
	d. Sign. H. R. Hardie. (1977-81).	1.50	2.50	15.00

		VG	VF	UNC
165	**5 DOLLARS** ND (1967-81). Orange on m/c unpt.			
	a. Sign. R. N. Fleming. (1967-68).	4.00	8.00	50.00
	b. Sign. D. L. Wilks. (1968-75).	10.00	20.00	100.00
	c. Sign. R. L. Knight. (1975-77).	3.00	5.00	32.50
	d. Sign. H. R. Hardie. (1977-81).	3.00	6.00	37.50

		VG	VF	UNC
166	**10 DOLLARS** ND (1967-81). Blue on m/c unpt.			
	a. Sign. R. N. Fleming. (1967-68).	7.50	12.50	100.00
	b. Sign. D. L. Wilks. (1968-75.)	8.00	15.00	140.00
	c. Sign. R. L. Knight. (1975-77).	7.50	12.50	100.00
	d. Sign. H. R. Hardie. (1977-81).	7.50	12.50	110.00

		VG	VF	UNC
167	**20 DOLLARS** ND (1967-81). Green on m/c unpt.			
	a. Sign. R. N. Fleming. (1967-68).	15.00	22.50	125.00
	b. Sign. D. L. Wilks. (1968-75).	15.00	25.00	200.00
	c. Sign. R. L. Knight. (1975-77).	12.00	17.50	150.00
	d. Sign. H. R. Hardie. (1977-81).	12.00	15.00	95.00
168	**100 DOLLARS** ND (1967-77). Red on m/c unpt.			
	a. Sign. R. N. Fleming. (1967-68).	85.00	150.00	750.00
	b. Sign. R. L. Knight. (1975-77).	65.00	100.00	600.00

1981-83 ND ISSUE

#169-175 new portr. of Qn. Elizabeth II on face. Birds and plants on back. Wmk: Capt. J. Cook. Printer: BWC.

#169a, 170a, 171a, 171b, 172b and 173a replacement notes: Special serial # prefix and * suffix.

		VG	VF	UNC
169	**1 DOLLAR** ND (1981-92). Dk. brown on m/c unpt. Back similar to #163.			
	a. Sign. H. R. Hardie w/title: *CHIEF CASHIER.* (1981-85).	FV	1.00	4.00
	b. Sign. S. T. Russell w/title: *GOVERNOR.* (1985-89).	FV	1.00	3.00
	c. Sign. D. T. Brash. (1989-92).	FV	1.00	3.00

		VG	VF	UNC
170	**2 DOLLARS** ND (1981-92). Purple on m/c unpt. Back similar to #164.			
	a. Sign. H. R. Hardie w/title: *CHIEF CASHIER.* (1981-85).	FV	1.75	5.00
	b. Sign. S.T. Russell w/title: *GOVERNOR.* (1985-89).	FV	1.50	4.50
	c. Sign. D. T. Brash. (1989-92).	FV	1.50	4.00

		VG	VF	UNC
171	**5 DOLLARS** ND (1981-92). Orange on m/c unpt. Back similar to #165.			
	a. Sign. H. R. Hardie w/title: *CHIEF CASHIER.* (1981-85).	FV	4.50	12.50
	b. Sign. S.T. Russell w/title: *GOVERNOR.* (1985-89).	FV	4.50	12.50
	c. Sign. D. T. Brash. (1989-92).	FV	3.75	8.50

		VG	VF	UNC
172	**10 DOLLARS** ND (1981-92). Blue on m/c unpt. Back similar to #166.			
	a. Sign. H. R. Hardie w/title: *CHIEF CASHIER.* (1981-85).	FV	8.50	20.00
	b. Sign. S.T. Russell w/title: *GOVERNOR.* (1985-89).	FV	7.50	17.50
	c. Sign. D. T. Brash. (1989-92).	FV	7.50	17.50

		VG	VF	UNC
173	**20 DOLLARS** ND (1981-92). Green on m/c unpt. Back similar to #167.			
	a. Sign. H. R. Hardie w/title: *CHIEF CASHIER.* (1981-85).	FV	16.50	40.00
	b. Sign. S.T. Russell w/title: *GOVERNOR.* (1985-89).	FV	15.00	35.00
	c. Sign. D. T. Brash. (1989-92).	FV	15.00	32.50

		VG	VF	UNC
174	**50 DOLLARS** ND (1981-92). Yellow-orange on m/c unpt. Owl at ctr. on back.			
	a. Sign. H. R. Hardie, w/title: *CHIEF CASHIER.* (1981-85).	FV	35.00	110.00
	b. Sign. D. T. Brash, w/title: *GOVERNOR* (1989-92).	FV	32.50	90.00

		VG	VF	UNC
175	**100 DOLLARS** ND (1981-89). Red on m/c unpt.			
	a. Sign. H. R. Hardie w/title: *CHIEF CASHIER.* (1981-85).	FV	70.00	175.00
	b. Sign. S.T. Russell w/title: *GOVERNOR.* (1985-89).	FV	70.00	150.00

1990 COMMEMORATIVE ISSUE

#176, 150th Anniversary - Treaty of Waitangi, 1840-1990

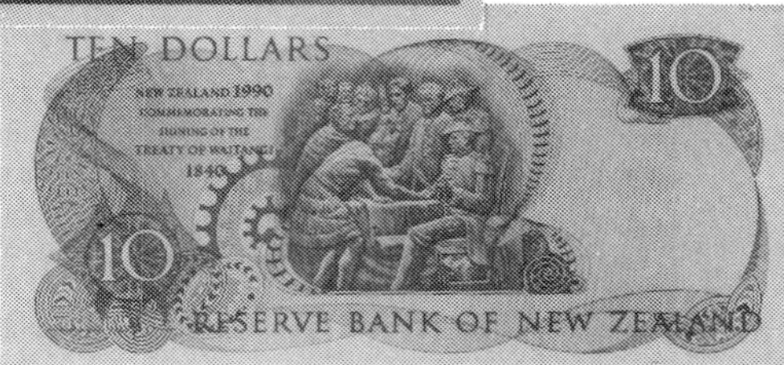

		VG	VF	UNC
176	**10 DOLLARS** 1990. Blue-violet and pale blue on m/c unpt. Face design like #172, w/addition of 1990 Commission logo, the White Heron (in red and white w/date 1990) at r. of Qn. Special inscription and scene of treaty signing on back. Wmk: Capt. J. Cook. Serial # prefix *BBB; CCC; DDD.* Printer: BWC.	FV	FV	20.00

NOTE: #176 w/prefix letters *AAA* was issued in 2, 4, 8, 16 and 32 subject panes. Market value is 10% over face value.

NOTE: #176 w/serial # prefix *BBB* was also issued in a special folder.

1992 ND ISSUE

#177-181 wmk: Qn. Elizabeth II. Sign. D.T. Brash. Replacement notes: Serial # prefix *ZZ.* Printer: TDLR.

		VG	VF	UNC
177	**5 DOLLARS** ND (1992-). Red-brown, brown and brown-orange on m/c unpt. Mt. Everest at l., Sir Edmund Hillary at ctr. Flora w/Hoiho penguin at ctr. r. on back.			
	a. Issued note.	FV	FV	6.50
	b. Uncut block of 4 in special folder.	FV	FV	16.00
	c. Uncut block of 8 in special folder.	FV	FV	30.00

178	10 DOLLARS	VG	VF	UNC
	ND (1992). Blue and purple on m/c unpt. Camellia flowers at l., K. Sheppard at ctr. r. Pair of Whio ducks at ctr. r. on back.			
	a. Issued note.	FV	FV	16.00
	b. Uncut pair in special folder.	FV	FV	17.50
	c. Uncut block of 4 in special folder.	FV	FV	30.00

179	20 DOLLARS	VG	VF	UNC
	ND (1992). Green on m/c unpt. Qn. Elizabeth II at r., gov't. bldg. at l. in unpt. Back pale green and blue; Karearea falcons at ctr.			
	a. Issued note.	FV	FV	32.50
	b. Uncut block of 4 in special folder.	FV	FV	60.00

180	50 DOLLARS	VG	VF	UNC
	ND (1992). Purple, violet and deep blue on m/c unpt. Sir A. Ngata at r., Maori meeting house at l. in unpt. Kokako crow at r. on back.			
	a. Issued note.	FV	FV	60.00
	b. Uncut block of 4 in special folder.	FV	FV	150.00

NOTICE

Readers with unlisted dates, signature varieties, etc. are invited to submit photocopies of their notes to: Standard Catalog of World Paper Money, 700 East State St. Iola, WI 54990-0001, fax: 1-715-445-4087, or E-Mail: thernr@krause.com.

181	100 DOLLARS	VG	VF	UNC
	ND (1992). Violet-brown and red on m/c unpt. Lord Rutherford of Nelson at ctr., Nobel prize medal in unpt. at l. Mohua yellowhead bird on tree trunk at ctr. r., moth at lower l. on back.			
	a. Issued note.	FV	FV	100.0
	b. Uncut block of 4 in special folder.	FV	FV	300.00

1994 ND ISSUE

#182 and 183 replacement notes: Serial # prefix *ZZ*.

		VG	VF	UNC
182	**10 DOLLARS** ND (1994). Like #178 but bright blue at ctr. behind Whio ducks on back.	FV	FV	12.00
183	**20 DOLLARS** ND (1994). Like #179 but bright green at ctr. behind Karearea falcon on back.	FV	FV	20.00

1996 COMMEMORATIVE ISSUE

#184, 70th Birthday - Qn. Elizabeth II

184	20 DOLLARS	VG	VF	UNC
	ND (1996). Green on m/c unpt. Commemorative ovpt. on #183. Serial # prefix *ER*.	FV	FV	125.00

NOTE: Issued in a special folder w/a $5 Commemorative coin (3000).

1999 ISSUE

#185-189 w/o imprint. Printer: NPA.

185	5 DOLLARS	VG	VF	UNC
	ND(1999). Similar to #177 but polymer plastic.	FV	FV	6.50

		VG	VF	UNC
186	**10 DOLLARS** ND(1999). Similar to #178 but polymer plastic.	FV	FV	12.00

		VG	VF	UNC
187	**20 DOLLARS** ND(1999). Similar to #179 but polymer plastic.	FV	FV	22.50
188	**50 DOLLARS** ND(1999).	Expected New Issue		
189	**100 DOLLARS** ND(1999). Similar to #181 but polymer plastic.	FV	FV	95.00

1999 COMMEMORATIVE ISSUE

#190, Millennium Commemorative

#190 printer: NPA.

		VG	VF	UNC
190	**10 DOLLARS** 1999. M/c. Earth, map of New Zealand at l. Ceremonial boat in ctr. Extreme sport activities on back. Polymer plastic.	FV	FV	15.00

COLLECTOR SERIES

RESERVE BANK OF NEW ZEALAND

1990 ND COMMEMORATIVE ISSUE

		ISSUE PRICE	MKT. VALUE
CS176	**10 DOLLARS** 1990. W/special serial # prefix.		
	a. Serial # prefix *CWB* (for Country Wide Bank).	—	9.00
	b. Serial # prefix *FTC* (for Farmers Trading Co.).	—	9.00
	c. Serial # prefix *MBL* (for Mobil Oil Co.).	—	9.00
	d. Serial # prefix *RNZ* (for Radio New Zealand).	—	9.00
	e. Serial # prefix *RXX* (for Rank Xerox Co.).	—	9.00
	f. Serial # prefix *TNZ* (for Toyota New Zealand).	—	9.00

1992 ISSUE

		ISSUE PRICE	MKT. VALUE
CS180	**50 DOLLARS** ND (1993). Red serial #.	—	65.00

NOTE: Issued w/$50 phone card.

1993 ND ISSUE

		IP	MKT. VALUE
CS183	**20 DOLLARS** As #183.		
	a. Uncut pair. W/serial # prefix: *TRBNZA* on back in folder.	—	—
	b. In folder w/$20 phone card. 2500 sets.	—	35.00

1999 ISSUE

		ISSUE PRICE	MKT. VALUE
CS185	**5 DOLLARS** As #185. Serial # prefix: *AA*.		
	a. Uncut pair.	12.50	20.00
	b. Uncut sheet of 40 notes. 150 sheets.	130.00	150.00
CS186	**10 DOLLARS** As #186. Serial # prefix: *AA*.		
	a. Uncut pair. 2,000 pairs.	19.00	25.00
	b. Uncut sheet of 40 notes. 150 sheets.	255.00	300.00
CS187	**20 DOLLARS** As #187. Serial # prefix: *AA*.		
	a. Uncut pair. 4,000 pairs.	38.00	50.00
	b. Uncut sheet of 40. 150 sheets.	500.00	600.00

CS188 50 DOLLARS

	ISSUE PRICE	MKT. VALUE
	Expected New Issue	

CS189 100 DOLLARS
As #189. Serial # prefix: *AA*.

	ISSUE PRICE	MKT. VALUE
a. Uncut pair. 1,000 pairs.	130.00	150.00
b. Uncut sheet of 28. 100 sheets.	1720.	1800.

1999 COMMEMORATIVE ISSUE

#CS190 Millenium Commemorative

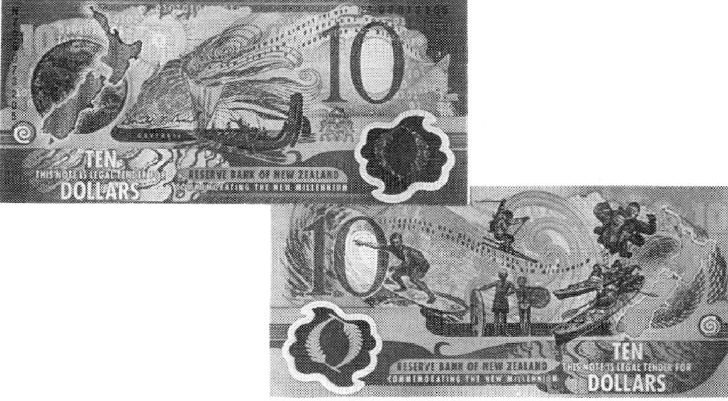

CS190 10 DOLLARS
As #190 but w/bank ovpt. in red under 10 on face.

	ISSUE PRICE	MKT. VALUE
a. Single note in folder w/serial # prefix: *NZ*.	18.00	15.00
b. Uncut pair in folder w/serial # prefix: *NZ*.	19.00	25.00
c. Uncut sheet of 20 w/serial # prefix: *NZ*.	175.00	225.00

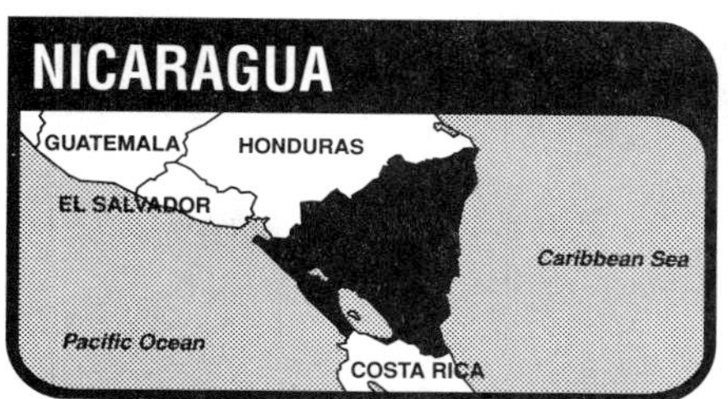

The Republic of Nicaragua, situated in Central America between Honduras and Costa Rica, has an area of 50,193 sq. mi (130,000 sq. km.) and a population of 4.39 million. Capital: Managua. Agriculture, mining (gold and silver) and hardwood logging are the principal industries. Cotton, meat, coffee, tobacco and sugar are exported.

Columbus sighted the coast of Nicaragua in 1502 during the course of his last voyage of discovery. It was first visited in 1522 by conquistadors from Panama, under command of Gonzalez Davila. After the first settlements were established in 1524 at Granada and Leon, Nicaragua was incorporated, for administrative purpose, in the Captaincy General of Guatemala, which included every Central American state but Panama. The Captaincy General declared its independence from Spain on Sept. 15, 1821. The next year Nicaragua united with the Mexican Empire of Agustin de Iturbide, then in 1823 with the Central American Republic. When the federation was dissolved, Nicaragua declared itself an independent republic in 1838.

MONETARY SYSTEM:

1 Peso = 100 Centavos to 1912
1 Córdoba = 100 Centavos, 1912-1987
1 New Córdoba = 1000 Old Córdobas, 1988-90
1 Córdoba Oro = 100 Centavos, 1990-

NOTE: See Collector Series for special sets.

REPUBLIC

BANCO CENTRAL DE NICARAGUA

DECRETO 26.4.1962

Series A

#107-114 portr. F. Hernandez Córdoba at ctr. on back. Printer: ABNC.

		VG	VF	UNC
107	**1 CÓRDOBA** *D.1962*. Blue on m/c unpt. Banco Central at upper ctr.	.15	.75	4.00
108	**5 CÓRDOBAS** *D.1962*. Green on m/c unpt. C. Nicarao at upper ctr. Similar to #100.	.75	2.50	10.00

		VG	VF	UNC
109	**10 CÓRDOBAS** *D.1962*. Red on m/c unpt. Portr. M. de Larreynaga at upper ctr.	1.50	4.50	20.00

		VG	VF	UNC
110	**20 CÓRDOBAS** *D.1962.* Orange-brown on m/c unpt. Portr. T. Martinez at upper ctr.	3.00	10.00	40.00

		VG	VF	UNC
111	**50 CÓRDOBAS** *D.1962.* Purple on m/c unpt. Portr. M. Jerez at upper ctr.	6.00	25.00	75.00

		VG	VF	UNC
112	**100 CÓRDOBAS** *D.1962.* Red-brown on m/c unpt. Portr. J. D. Estrada at upper ctr.	4.00	12.50	50.00
113	**500 CÓRDOBAS** *D.1962.* Black on m/c unpt. Portr. R. Dario at upper ctr.	50.00	175.00	400.00
114	**1000 CÓRDOBAS** *D.1962.* Brown on m/c unpt. Portr. A. Somoza at upper ctr.	60.00	200.00	500.00

DECRETO 25.5.1968

Series B

#115-120 portr. F. Hernandez Córdoba on back. Printer: TDLR.

		VG	VF	UNC
115	**1 CÓRDOBA** ND. Blue on m/c unpt. Like #107.			
	a. W/3 sign.	.10	.35	1.00
	b. Pres. A. Somoza hand sign. at l.	—	—	—

		VG	VF	UNC
116	**5 CÓRDOBAS** *D.1968.* Green on m/c unpt. Like #108.	.50	1.50	4.00
117	**10 CÓRDOBAS** *D.1968.* Red on m/c unpt. Like #109.	.75	2.00	6.00

NOTE: Some of #118-120 were apparently released w/o r.h. sign. after the Managua earthquake of 1972 damaged the Central Bank building.

		VG	VF	UNC
118	**20 CÓRDOBAS** *D.1968.* Orange-brown on m/c unpt. Like #110.			
	a. W/3 sign.	1.00	3.00	10.00
	b. W/o r.h. sign.	—	—	—
119	**50 CÓRDOBAS** *D.1968.* Purple on m/c unpt. Like #111.			
	a. W/3 sign.	4.00	7.50	27.50
	b. W/o r.h. sign.	—	—	—
120	**100 CÓRDOBAS** *D.1968.* Red-brown on m/c unpt. Like #112.			
	a. W/3 sign.	3.00	6.00	17.50
	b. W/o r.h. sign.	—	—	—

DECRETO 27.4.1972

Series C

#121-128 printer: TDLR.

		VG	VF	UNC
121	**2 CÓRDOBAS** *D.1972.* Olive-green on m/c unpt. Banco Central at r. Furrows at l. on back.			
	a. W/3 sign.	.10	.25	2.00
	b. W/o l.h. sign.	—	—	350.00

		VG	VF	UNC
122	**5 CÓRDOBAS** *D.1972.* Dk. green on m/c unpt. C. Nicarao standing at r. w/bow. Fruitseller at l. on back.	.25	.75	2.50

		VG	VF	UNC
123	**10 CÓRDOBAS** *D.1972.* Red on m/c unpt. A. Castro standing at r. atop rocks. Hacienda at l. on back.	.30	.85	2.50

		VG	VF	UNC
124	**20 CÓRDOBAS** *D.1972.* Orange-brown on m/c unpt. R. Herrera igniting cannon at r. Signing ceremony of abrogation of Chamorro-Bryan Treaty of 1912, Somoza at ctr. on back.	.50	1.25	3.50

		VG	VF	UNC
125	**50 CÓRDOBAS** *D.1972.* Purple on m/c unpt. M. Jerez at r. Cows at l. on back.	10.00	30.00	80.00

		VG	VF	UNC
126	**100 CÓRDOBAS** *D.1972.* Violet on m/c unpt. J. Dolores Estrada at r. Flower at l. on back.	.50	1.50	4.00

		VG	VF	UNC
127	**500 CÓRDOBAS** *D.1972.* Black on m/c unpt. R. Darío at r. National Theater at l. on back.	10.00	25.00	85.00

		VG	VF	UNC
28	**1000 CÓRDOBAS** *D.1972.* Brown on m/c unpt. A. Somoza G. at r. View of Managua at l. on back.			
	a. 3 sign.	12.00	30.00	100.00
	b. 2 sign. (w/o r.h. sign.).	—	—	110.00

DECRETO 20.2.1978

Series D

#129-130 printer: TDLR.

		VG	VF	UNC
129	**20 CÓRDOBAS** *D.1978.* Like #124.	.30	1.00	5.00

		VG	VF	UNC
130	**50 CÓRDOBAS** *D.1978.* Like #125.	.30	1.00	6.50

DECRETO 16.8.1979

Series E, first issue

#131-133 w/frame. Printer: TDLR.

		VG	VF	UNC
131	**50 CÓRDOBAS** *D.1979.* Purple on m/c unpt. Comdt. C. F. Amador at r. Liberation of 19.7.1979 on back.	.50	1.50	4.00

132	100 CÓRDOBAS *D.1979.* Dk. brown on m/c unpt. Like #126.	VG .50	VF 1.50	UNC 4.00

133	500 CÓRDOBAS *D.1979.* Deep blue on m/c unpt. Like #127.	VG .50	VF 1.25	UNC 5.00

1979 ND SECOND ISSUE

Series E, second issue

#134-139 w/o frame. Wmk: Sandino. Printer: TDLR.

134	10 CÓRDOBAS *D.1979.* Red on m/c unpt. A. Castro standing atop rocks at r. Miners on back.	VG .25	VF .60	UNC 2.50

135	20 CÓRDOBAS *D.1979.* Orange-brown on m/c unpt. Comdt. G. P. Ordoñez at r. Marching troops on back.	VG .30	VF .75	UNC 3.00

136	50 CÓRDOBAS *D.1979.* Purple on m/c unpt. Comdt. C. F. Amador at r. Liberation of 19.7.1979 on back.	VG .35	VF .85	UNC 3.50

137	100 CÓRDOBAS *D.1979.* Brown on m/c unpt. J. D. Estrada at r. Flower on back. Sign. varieties.	VG .50	VF 1.00	UNC 4.00

138	500 CÓRDOBAS *D.1979.* Deep olive-green on m/c unpt. Engraved. R. Darío at r. Teatro Popular at l. on back. Sign. varieties.	VG .65	VF 1.65	UNC 6.50

139	1000 CÓRDOBAS *D.1979.* Blue-gray on m/c unpt. Engraved. Gen. A. C. Sandino at r. Hut (Sandino's birthplace) on back. Sign. varieties.	VG 2.50	VF 10.00	UNC 40.00

RESOLUTION OF 6.8.1984

Series F

#140-143 wmk: Sandino. Printer: TDLR.

		VG	VF	UNC
140	**50 CÓRDOBAS** *L.1984* (1985). Purple on m/c unpt. Like #136.	.20	.50	3.00
141	**100 CÓRDOBAS** *L.1984* (1985). Brown on m/c unpt. Like #137.	.30	1.00	4.00
142	**500 CÓRDOBAS** *L.1984* (1985). Deep olive-green on m/c unpt. Like #138.	.20	1.00	6.00
143	**1000 CÓRDOBAS** *L.1984* (1985). Blue-gray on m/c unpt. Like #139.	.50	2.00	11.00

RESOLUTION OF 11.6.1985

Series G

#144-146 wmk: Sandino. Replacement notes: Serial # prefix *ZA; ZB*. Printer: TDLR.

		VG	VF	UNC
144	**500 CÓRDOBAS** *L.1985* (1987). Deep olive-green on m/c unpt. Like #142. Lithographed.	.20	.50	3.00

		VG	VF	UNC
145	**1000 CÓRDOBAS** *L.1985* (1987). Dk. gray on m/c unpt. Like #143.			
	a. Engraved.	.35	1.00	4.00
	b. Lithographed.	.15	.50	2.75

		VG	VF	UNC
146	**5000 CÓRDOBAS** *L.1985* (1987). Brown, orange and black on m/c unpt. Map at upper ctr., Gen. B. Zeledon at r. National Assembly bldg. on back.	.15	.50	2.50

A.P.E. DEL 26 OCT.

1987 ND PROVISIONAL ISSUE

#147-149 black ovpt. new denomination on face and back of old Series F and G notes printed by TDLR.

		VG	VF	UNC
147	**20,000 CÓRDOBAS ON 20 CÓRDOBAS** *D.1987* (1987). Ovpt. on unissued 20 Cordobas Series F. Colors and design like #135.	.20	.75	2.75

		VG	VF	UNC
148	**50,000 CÓRDOBAS ON 50 CÓRDOBAS** *D.1987* (1987). Ovpt. on #140.	.25	.60	3.00

		VG	VF	UNC
149	**100,000 CÓRDOBAS ON 500 CÓRDOBAS** *D.1987* (1987). Ovpt. on #144.	.30	.75	3.00

		VG	VF	UNC
150	**500,000 CÓRDOBAS ON 1000 CÓRDOBAS** *D.1987* (1987). Ovpt. on #145b. (Not issued).	.50	1.25	5.00

1985 (1988) Issue

#151-156 wmk: Sandino. Replacement notes: Serial # prefix *ZA*.

		VG	VF	Unc
151	**10 Córdobas** 1985 (1988). Green and olive on m/c unpt. Comdt. C. F. Amador at r. Troop formation marching at l. on back.	.10	.35	1.25

		VG	VF	Unc
152	**20 Córdobas** 1985 (1988). Blue-black and blue on m/c unpt. Comdt. G. P. Ordoñez at r. Demonstration for agrarian reform at l. on back.	.10	.35	1.25

		VG	VF	Unc
153	**50 Córdobas** 1985 (1988). Brown and dk. red on m/c unpt. Gen. J. D. Estrada at r. Medical clinic scene at l. on back.	.10	.35	1.00

		VG	VF	Unc
154	**100 Córdobas** 1985 (1988). Deep blue, blue and gray on m/c unpt. R. Lopez Perez at r. State council bldg. at l. on back.	.20	.50	2.00

		VG	VF	Unc
155	**500 Córdobas** 1985 (1988). Purple, blue and brown on m/c unpt. R. Dario at r. Classroom w/students at l. on back.	.25	.60	2.50

		VG	VF	Unc
156	**1000 Córdobas** 1985 (1988). Brown on m/c unpt. Gen. A. C. Sandino at r. Liberation of 19.7.1979 on back.			
	a. Engraved w/wmk. at l. Serial # prefix FA.	.25	.60	2.00
	b. Lithographed w/o wmk. at l. Serial # prefix FC.	.25	.50	1.25

		VG	VF	Unc
157	**5000 Córdobas** ND (1988). Ovpt. elements in black on face and back of #146. Face ovpt.: sign. and title: *PRIMER VICE PRESIDENTE BANCO CENTRAL DE NICARAGUA* at l., 2 lines of text at lower ctr. blocked out, guilloche added at r. Ovpt: guilloche at l. and r., same sign. title as ovpt. on face at r. on back.	.25	.60	1.75

#158 and 159 black ovpt. of new denominations on face and back of earlier notes. Ovpt. errors exist and are rather common.

		VG	VF	Unc
158	**10,000 Córdobas on 10 Córdobas** ND (1989). Ovpt. on #151.	.25	.75	2.25

159 **100,000 CÓRDOBAS ON 100 CÓRDOBAS**

	VG	VF	UNC
ND (1989). Ovpt. on #154.	.40	1.00	3.50

1989 ND EMERGENCY ISSUE

#160 and 161 grid map of Nicaragua at ctr. on face and back. Wmk: Sandino.

160 **20,000 CÓRDOBAS**

	VG	VF	UNC
ND (1989). Black on blue, yellow and m/c unpt. Comdt. G. P. Ordoñez at r. Church of San Francisco Granada at l., map at ctr. on back.	.35	.85	3.50

161 **50,000 CÓRDOBAS**

	VG	VF	UNC
ND (1989). Brown on purple, orange and m/c unpt. Gen. J. D. Estrada at r. Hacienda San Jacinto at l., map at ctr. on back.	.25	.60	2.50

1990 ND PROVISIONAL ISSUE

#162-164, black ovpt. new denomination on face and back of earlier notes.

NOTE: Ovpt. errors exist and are rather common.

162 **200,000 CÓRDOBAS ON 1000 CÓRDOBAS**

	VG	VF	UNC
ND (1990). Ovpt on #156b.	.15	.40	1.75

163 **500,000 CÓRDOBAS ON 20 CÓRDOBAS**

	VG	VF	UNC
ND (1990). Ovpt. on #152.	.40	1.00	3.50

164 **1 MILLION CÓRDOBAS ON 1000 CÓRDOBAS**

	VG	VF	UNC
ND (1990). Ovpt. on #156b.	.40	1.00	3.50

1990 ND EMERGENCY ISSUE

#165 and 166 wmk: Sandino head, repeated.

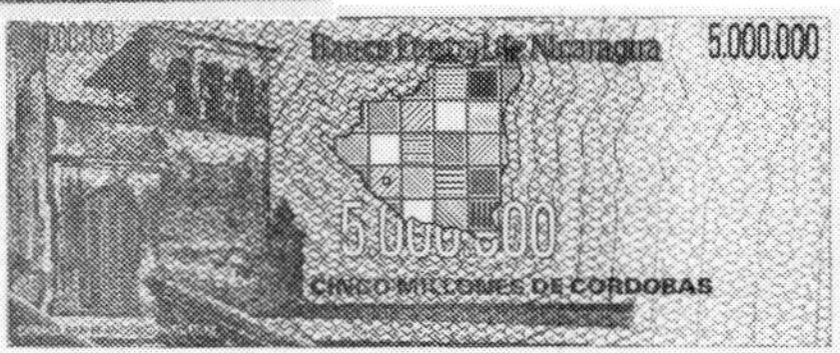

165 **5 MILLION CÓRDOBAS**

	VG	VF	UNC
ND (1990). Purple and orange on red and m/c unpt. Like #160.	.20	.50	2.00

166 **10 MILLION CÓRDOBAS**

	VG	VF	UNC
ND (1990). Purple and lilac on blue and m/c unpt. Like #161.	.25	.60	2.50

1990; 1991-92 ND ISSUES

#167-170, F. H. Córdoba at r. Arms at l., flower at r. on back. Printer: Harrison.

		VG	VF	UNC
167	**1 CENTAVO** ND (1991). Purple on pale green and m/c unpt.	FV	.05	.15

		VG	VF	UNC
168	**5 CENTAVOS** ND (1991). Red-violet on pale green and m/c unpt. 2 sign. varieties.	FV	.05	.20

		VG	VF	UNC
169	**10 CENTAVOS** ND (1991). Olive-green on lt. green and m/c unpt. 2 sign. varieties.	FV	.10	.25

		VG	VF	UNC
170	**25 CENTAVOS** ND (1991). Blue on pale green and m/c unpt. 2 sign. varieties.	FV	.15	.35

#171 and 172 printer: CBNC.

		VG	VF	UNC
171	**1/2 CÓRDOBA** ND (1991). Brown and green on m/c unpt. F. H. de Córdoba at l., plant at r. Arms at ctr. on green back.	FV	FV	.50

		VG	VF	UNC
172	**1/2 CÓRDOBA** ND (1992). Face like #171. Arms at l., national flower at r. on green back.	FV	FV	.65

#173-177, 2 sign. varieties.

		VG	VF	UNC
173	**1 CÓRDOBA** 1990. Blue on purple and m/c unpt. Sunrise over field of maize at l., F. H. Córdoba at r. Back green and m/c; arms at ctr. Printer: TDLR. 2 sign. varieties.	FV	FV	.75

		VG	VF	UNC
174	**5 CÓRDOBAS** ND (1991). Red-violet and deep olive-green on m/c unpt. Indian Chief Diriangén at l., sorghum plants at r. R. Herrera firing cannon at British warship on green back. Printer: CBNC. 2 sign. varieties.	FV	FV	2.00

		VG	VF	UNC
175	**10 CÓRDOBAS** 1990. Green on blue and m/c unpt. Sunrise over rice field at l., M. de Larreynaga at r. Back dk. green and m/c; arms at ctr. Printer: TDLR.	FV	FV	3.50

		VG	VF	UNC
176	**20 CÓRDOBAS** ND (1990). Pale red-orange and dk. brown on m/c unpt. Sandino at l., coffee plant at r. E. Mongalo at l., fire in the Mesón de Rivas (1854) at ctr. on green back. 2 sign. varieties. Printer: CBNC.	FV	FV	6.00

		VG	VF	UNC
177	**50 CÓRDOBAS** ND (1991). Purple and violet on m/c unpt. Dr. P. J. Chamorro at l., banana plants at r. Toppling of Somoza's statue and scene at polling place on green back. 2 sign. varieties. Printer: CBNC.	FV	FV	12.50

		VG	VF	UNC
178	**100 CÓRDOBAS** 1990. Blue and red on m/c unpt. Sunrise over cotton field at l., R. Darío at r. Back green and m/c; arms at ctr. Printer: TDLR. 3 sign. Series A.	FV	FV	22.50

1992-96 ISSUE

		VG	VF	UNC
179	**1 CÓRDOBA** 1995. Blue on purple and m/c unpt. Similar to #173. Printer: BABN. Series B.	FV	FV	.65

		VG	VF	UNC
180	**5 CÓRDOBAS** 1995. Red, deep olive-green and brown on m/c unpt. Similar to #174. Printer: F-CO.	FV	FV	1.75

		VG	VF	UNC
181	**10 CÓRDOBAS** 1996. Green on blue and m/c unpt. Similar to #175. Printer: G & D.	FV	FV	3.00
182	**20 CÓRDOBAS** 1995. Pale red-orange and dk. brown on m/c unpt. Similar to #176. Printer: F-CO.	FV	FV	5.50

		VG	VF	UNC
183	**50 CÓRDOBAS** 1995. Purple and violet on m/c unpt. Similar to #177 but w/2 sign. Printer: F-CO.	FV	FV	11.00

		VG	VF	UNC
184	**100 CÓRDOBAS** 1992. Blue and red on m/c unpt. Like #178 but w/2 sign. Series B.	FV	FV	20.00

1997 ISSUE

		VG	VF	UNC
185	**20 CÓRDOBAS** 1997. Series C.	FV	FV	5.00
186 (185)	**50 CÓRDOBAS** 1997.	FV	FV	8.50
187 (186)	**100 CÓRDOBAS** 1997.	FV	FV	16.50
188 (187)	**500 CÓRDOBAS** 199x.			Expected New Issue
189 (188)	**1000 CÓRDOBAS** 199x.			Expected New Issue

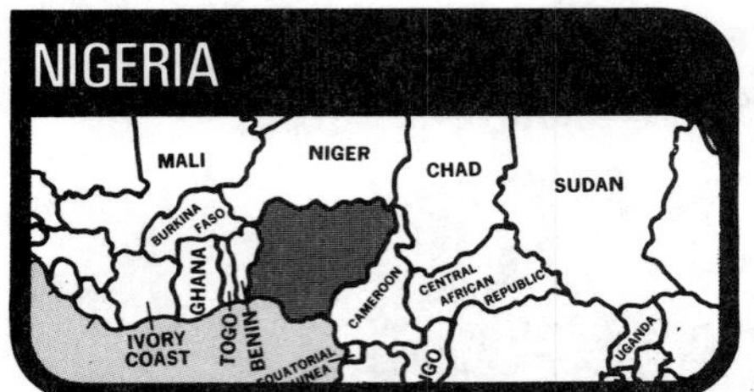

The Federal Republic of Nigeria, situated on the Atlantic coast of Africa between Benin and Cameroon, has an area of 356,667 sq. mi. (923,768 sq. km.) and a population of 107.1 million. Capital: Lagos. The economy is based on petroleum and agriculture. Crude oil, cocoa, tobacco and tin are exported.

Following the Napoleonic Wars, the British expanded their trade with the interior of Nigeria. British claims to a sphere of influence in that area were recognized by the Berlin Conference of 1885, and in the following year the Royal Niger Company was chartered. Direct British control of the territory was initiated in 1900, and in 1914 the amalgamation of northern and southern Nigeria into the Colony and Protectorate of Nigeria was effected. In 1960, following a number of territorial and constitutional changes, Nigeria was granted independence within the British Commonwealth as a federation of the northern, western and eastern regions. Nigeria altered its political relationship with Great Britain on Oct. 1, 1963, by proclaiming itself a republic. It did, however, elect to remain a member of the Commonwealth. The Supreme Commander of Armed Forces is the Head of the Federal Military Government.

On May 30, 1967, the Eastern Region of the republic - an area occupied principally by the proud and resourceful Ibo tribe - seceded from Nigeria and proclaimed itself the independent Republic of Biafra. Civil war erupted and raged for 31 months. Casualties, including civilian, were about two million, the majority succumbing to malnutrition and disease. Biafra surrendered to the federal government on January 15, 1970. After military coups in 1983 and 1985 the government was assumed by an Armed Forces Ruling Council. A transitional civilian council was formed in 1993. Nigeria was suspended from the Commonwealth in November 1995, but was re-admitted on May 29, 1999.

RULERS:

British to 1963

MONETARY SYSTEM:

1 Shilling = 12 Pence
1 Pound = 20 Shillings to 1973
1 Naira (10 Shillings) = 100 Kobo, 1973-

SIGNATURE/TITLE VARIETIES

1	GOVERNOR — CHIEF OF BANKING OPERATIONS	2	GOVERNOR — CHIEF OF BANKING OPERATIONS
3		4	DIRECTOR OF DOMESTIC OPERATIONS
5		6	
7	GOVERNOR — DIRECTOR OF CURRENCY OPERATIONS	8	DIRECTOR OF CURRENCY OPERATIONS
9		10	

FEDERAL REPUBLIC OF NIGERIA

CENTRAL BANK OF NIGERIA

1967 ND ISSUE

Pound System

#6-13 bank bldg. at l. Wmk: Lion's head.

		VG	VF	UNC
6	**5 SHILLINGS** ND (1967). Lilac and blue. Back lilac; log cutting.	5.00	20.00	140.00
7	**10 SHILLINGS** ND (1967). Green and brown. Back green; stacking grain sacks.	9.00	45.00	300.00

		VG	VF	UNC
8	**1 POUND** ND (1967). Red and dk. brown. Back red; man beating cluster from date palm at r.	.75	2.00	8.00
9	**5 POUNDS** ND (1967). Blue-gray and blue-green on m/c unpt. Back blue-gray; food preparation.	10.00	40.00	375.00

1968 ND ISSUE

#10-13 designs similar to previous issue. Wmk: Lion's head.

		VG	VF	UNC
10	**5 SHILLINGS** ND (1968). Green and orange. Back green.			
	a. R. sign. title: *GENERAL MANAGER.*	4.00	20.00	175.00
	b. R. sign. title: *CHIEF OF BANKING OPERATIONS.*	5.00	25.00	200.00

		VG	VF	UNC
11	**10 SHILLINGS** ND (1968). Blue on m/c unpt.			
	a. R. sign. title: *GENERAL MANAGER.*	7.50	35.00	250.00
	b. R. sign. title: *CHIEF OF BANKING OPERATIONS.*	10.00	50.00	375.00
12	**1 POUND** ND (1968). Olive-brown and violet. Back olive-brown.			
	a. R. sign. title: *GENERAL MANAGER.*	7.50	35.00	250.00
	b. R. sign. title: *CHIEF OF BANKING OPERATIONS.*	10.00	50.00	375.00
13	**5 POUNDS** ND (1968). Red-brown and blue. Back red-brown.			
	a. R. sign. title: *GENERAL MANAGER.*	20.00	75.00	500.00
	b. R. sign. title: *CHIEF OF BANKING OPERATIONS.*	25.00	100.00	550.00

1973; 1977 ND ISSUE

Naira System

#14-17 bank bldg. at l. ctr. Wmk: Heraldic eagle. Replacement notes: Serial # prefix *DZ/*.

14	50 KOBO	VG	VF	UNC
	ND (1973-78). Blue and purple on m/c unpt. Back brown; logging at r.			
	a. Sign. 1.	1.00	4.00	8.00
	b. Sign. 2.	1.50	5.00	35.00
	c. Sign. 3.	.50	2.00	15.00
	d. Sign. 4.	.65	2.00	15.00
	e. Sign. 5.	.50	2.00	15.00
	f. Sign. 6.	.25	1.75	10.00
	g. Sign. 7; 8; 9.	FV	FV	1.50

15	1 NAIRA	VG	VF	UNC
	ND (1973-78). Red and brown on m/c unpt. Back red; stacking grain sacks.			
	a. Sign. 1.	2.00	5.00	12.50
	b. Sign. 2.	1.50	4.00	12.50
	c. Sign. 3.	1.50	4.00	12.50
	d. Sign. 4.	4.00	17.50	50.00

16	5 NAIRA	VG	VF	UNC
	ND (1973-). Blue-gray and olive-green on m/c unpt. Back blue-gray; man beating cluster from date palm at r.			
	a. Sign. 1.	7.00	15.00	70.00
	b. Sign. 2.	4.00	10.00	50.00
	c. Sign. 3.	15.00	60.00	275.00
	d. Sign. 4.	20.00	75.00	325.00

17	10 NAIRA	VG	VF	UNC
	ND (1973-78). Carmine and dk. blue on m/c unpt. Back carmine; dam at ctr.			
	a. Sign. 1.	15.00	35.00	110.00
	b. Sign. 2.	7.00	22.50	85.00
	c. Sign. 3.	35.00	125.00	400.00
	d. Sign. 4.	40.00	150.00	485.00

18	20 NAIRA	VG	VF	UNC
	ND (1977-84). Yellow-green and black on red and m/c unpt. Gen M. Muhammed at l. Arms at ctr. r. on back.			
	a. Sign. 2.	30.00	100.00	325.00
	b. Sign. 3.	20.00	60.00	200.00
	c. Sign. 4.	8.00	20.00	65.00
	d. Sign. 5.	6.00	15.00	45.00
	e. Sign. 6.	4.00	10.00	35.00

1979 ND ISSUE

#19-22 sign. titles: *GOVERNOR* and *DIRECTOR OF DOMESTIC OPERATIONS*. Wmk: Heraldic eagle.

19	1 NAIRA	VG	VF	UNC
	ND (1979-84). Red on orange and m/c unpt. H. Macaulay at l. Mask at ctr. r. on back.			
	a. Sign. 4.	.50	2.00	7.50
	b. Sign. 5.	.30	1.00	5.00
	c. Sign. 6.	.25	.75	3.00

20	5 NAIRA	VG	VF	UNC
	ND (1979-84). Green on m/c unpt. Alhaji Sir Abubakar Tafawa Balewa at l. Dancers at ctr. r. on back.			
	a. Sign. 4.	2.00	5.00	15.00
	b. Sign. 5.	1.50	4.00	12.50
	c. Sign. 6.	1.00	3.00	10.00

21	10 NAIRA	VG	VF	UNC
	ND (1979-84). Brown, purple and violet on m/c unpt. A. Ikoku at l. 2 women w/bowls on heads at ctr. r. on back.			
	a. Sign. 4.	4.00	12.00	30.00
	b. Sign. 5.	3.00	8.00	25.00
	c. Sign. 6.	7.00	20.00	—

1984; 1991 ND ISSUE

#23-27 new colors and sign. Like #18-21 but reduced size. Wmk: Heraldic eagle.

23	1 NAIRA	VG	VF	UNC
	ND (1984-). Red, violet and green. Like #19. Back olive and lt. violet.			
	a. Sign. title at r.: *DIRECTOR OF DOMESTIC OPERATIONS.* Sign. 6.	FV	1.00	3.00
	b. Sign. title at r.: *DIRECTOR OF CURRENCY OPERATIONS.* Sign. 7.	FV	FV	2.50
	c. Titles as b. Sign. 8.	FV	FV	2.50
	d. Titles as b. Sign. 9.	FV	FV	2.50

		VG	VF	UNC
24	**5 NAIRA**			
	ND (1984-). Purple and brown-violet on m/c unpt. Like #20.			
	a. Sign. title at r.: *DIRECTOR OF DOMESTIC OPERATIONS.* Sign. 6.	FV	2.00	6.50
	b. Sign. title at r.: *DIRECTOR OF CURRENCY OPERATIONS.* Sign. 7.	FV	1.00	4.00
	c. Titles as b. Sign. 8.	FV	FV	2.00
	d. Titles as b. Sign. 9.	FV	FV	2.00
	e. Titles as b. Sign. 10.	FV	FV	1.75

		VG	VF	UNC
25	**10 NAIRA**			
	ND (1984-). Red-violet and orange on m/c unpt. Back red. Like #21.			
	a. Sign. title at r.: *DIRECTOR OF DOMESTIC OPERATIONS.* Sign. 6.	FV	2.50	9.00
	b. Sign. title at r.: *DIRECTOR OF CURRENCY OPERATIONS.* Sign. 7.	FV	2.50	5.50
	c. Titles as b. Sign. 8.	FV	FV	3.25
	d. Titles as b. Sign. 9.	FV	FV	3.00
	e. Titles as b. Sign. 10.	FV	FV	3.00

		VG	VF	UNC
26	**20 NAIRA**			
	ND (1984-). Dk. blue-green, dk. green and green on m/c unpt. Like #18.			
	a. Sign. title at r.: *DIRECTOR OF DOMESTIC OPERATIONS.* Sign. 6.	FV	5.00	20.00
	b. Sign. title at r.: *DIRECTOR OF CURRENCY OPERATIONS.* Sign. 7.	FV	FV	6.00
	c. Titles as b. Sign. 8.	FV	FV	4.00
	d. Titles as b. Sign. 9.	FV	FV	4.00
	e. Titles as b. Sign. 10.	FV	FV	3.00

		VG	VF	UNC
27	**50 NAIRA**			
	ND (1991-). Dk. blue, black and gray on m/c unpt. Four busts reflecting varied citizenry at l. ctr. Three farmers in field at ctr. r., arms at lower r. on back.			
	a. Sign. 8.	FV	3.50	12.50
	b. Sign. 9.	FV	FV	7.50
	c. Sign. 10.	FV	FV	6.50

1999 ISSUE

		VG	VF	UNC
28	**100 NAIRA** (1999).	Expected New Issue		
29	**200 NAIRA** (2000).	Expected New Issue		
30	**500 NAIRA** (2000).	Expected New Issue		

NORWAY

NORWAY
ICELAND
Norwegian Sea
North Atlantic Ocean
GREAT BRITAIN
North Sea
DENMARK
SWEDEN
FINLAND
RUSSIA
ESTONIA
LATVIA

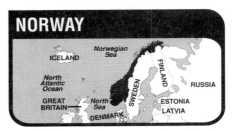

The Kingdom of Norway, a constitutional monarchy located in northwestern Europe, has an area of 150,000 sq. mi. (388,500 sq. km.) including the island territories of Spitzbergen (Svalbard) and Jan Mayen, and a population of 4.4 million. Capital: Oslo (Christiania until 1924). The diversified economic base of Norway includes shipping, fishing, forestry, agriculture, and manufacturing. Nonferrous metals, paper and paperboard, paper pulp, iron, steel and oil are exported.

A United Norwegian kingdom was established in the 9th century, the era of the indomitable Norse Vikings who ranged far and wide, visiting the coasts of northwestern Europe, the Mediterranean, Greenland and North America. In the 13th century, the Norse kingdom was united briefly with Sweden, then passed, through the Union of Kalmar, 1397, to the rule of Denmark which was maintained until 1814. In 1814, Norway fell again under the rule of Sweden. The union lasted until 1905 when the Norwegian Parliament arranged a peaceful separation and invited a Danish prince (King Haakon VII) to occupy the throne of an independent Kingdom of Norway.

RULERS:

Olav V, 1957-1991
Harald V, 1991-

MONETARY SYSTEM:

1 Krone = 100 Øre, 1873-

KINGDOM

NORGES BANK

1948-55 ISSUE

#30-33 Replacement notes: Serial # prefix *Z*.

		VG	VF	UNC
30	**5 KRONER**			
	1955-63. Blue. Portr. F. Nansen at l. Fishing scene on back.			
	a. Sign. Brofoss - Thorp. 1955-57.	5.00	20.00	50.00
	b. Sign. Brofoss - Ottesen. 1959-63.	4.00	11.00	45.00

#31 replacement notes: Serial # prefix *X*.

		VG	VF	UNC
31	**10 KRONER**			
	1954-73. Yellow-brown. Portr. C. Michelsen at l. Mercury w/ships on back.			
	a. Sign. Jahn - Thorp. 1954.	3.00	8.50	40.00
	b. Sign. Brofoss - Thorp. 1954.	3.00	8.50	35.00
	c. Sign. Brofoss - Ottesen. 1959-65.	2.00	4.00	20.00
	d. Sign. Brofoss - Petersen. 1965-69.	FV	3.00	14.00
	e. Sign. Brofoss - Odegaard. 1970.	FV	2.50	11.00
	f. Sign. Wold - Odegaard. 1971-73.	FV	2.00	8.00

32 **50 KRONER**
1950-65. Dk. green. Portr. B. Bjornson at upper l. and as wmk., crowned arms at upper ctr. Harvesting on back.

		VG	VF	UNC
a.	Sign. Jahn - Thorp. 1950-54.	17.00	60.00	200.00
b.	Sign. Brofoss - Thorp. 1954-58.	17.00	50.00	175.00
c.	Sign. Brofoss - Ottesen. 1959-65.	14.00	40.00	140.00

33 **100 KRONER**
1949-62. Red. Portr. H. Wergel at upper l. and as wmk., crowned arms at upper ctr. Logging on back.

		VG	VF	UNC
a.	Sign. Jahn - Thorp. 1949-54.	22.50	50.00	200.00
b.	Sign. Brofoss - Thorp. 1954-58.	20.00	50.00	175.00
c.	Sign. Brofoss - Ottesen. 1959-62.	20.00	40.00	140.00

#34 and 35 replacement notes: Serial # prefix G.

34 **500 KRONER**
1948-76. Dk. green. Portr. N. Henrik Abel at upper l. and as wmk., crowned supported arms at upper ctr. Factory workers on back.

		VG	VF	UNC
a.	Sign. Jahn - Thorp. 1948; 1951.	150.00	300.00	—
b.	Sign. Brofoss - Thorp. 1954; 1956; 1958.	120.00	250.00	—
c.	Sign. Brofoss - Ottesen. 1960-64.	105.00	225.00	—
d.	Sign. Brofoss - Petersen. 1966-69.	100.00	200.00	—
e.	Sign. Brofoss - Odegaard. 1970.	100.00	175.00	—
f.	Sign. Wold - Odegaard. 1971-76.	80.00	150.00	300.00
s.	Specimen.	—	—	—

35 **1000 KRONER**
1949-74. Red-brown. Portr. H. Ibsen at l. and as wmk., crowned supported arms at upper ctr. Old man and child on back.

		VG	VF	UNC
a.	Sign. Jahn - Thorp. 1949; 1951; 1953.	225.00	350.00	650.00
b.	Sign. Brofoss - Thorp. 1955; 1958.	225.00	350.00	—
c.	Sign. Brofoss - Ottesen. 1961; 1962.	200.00	300.00	—
d.	Sign. Brofoss - Petersen. 1965-70.	185.00	275.00	425.00
e.	Sign. Brofoss - Odegaard. 1971-74.	185.00	250.00	350.00

1962-78 ISSUE

#36-40 arms at ctr.

#36 and 41 replacement notes: Serial # prefix *H* or *Q*.

		VG	VF	UNC
36	**10 KRONER** 1972-84. Blue-black on m/c unpt. F. Nansen at l. Fisherman and cargo ship at r. on back. Wmk: Value *10* repeated.			
	a. Sign. Wold and Odegaard. 1973-76.	FV	2.00	7.00
	b. Sign. Wold and Sagård. 1977-79; 1981-84.	FV	FV	4.00

#37-40 replacement notes: Serial # prefix *X* or *Z*.

		VG	VF	UNC
37	**50 KRONER** 1966-83. Green on m/c unpt. B. Björnson at l. and as wmk. Old church at r. on back.			
	a. Sign. Brofoss and Petersen. 1966-67; 1969.	FV	20.00	75.00
	b. Sign. Wold and Odegaard. 1971-73.	FV	15.00	50.00
	c. As b. W/security thread. 1974-75.	FV	10.00	30.00
	d. Sign. Wold and Sagård. 1976-83.	FV	10.00	28.50

		VG	VF	UNC
38	**100 KRONER** 1962-77. Red-violet on m/c unpt. H. Wergeland at l. and as wmk. Establishment of Constitution in 1814 at r. on back.			
	a. Sign. Brofoss and Ottesen. 1962-65.	FV	20.00	80.00
	b. Sign. Brofoss and Petersen. 1965-69.	FV	18.50	80.00
	c. Sign. Brofoss and Odegaard. 1970.	FV	18.50	55.00
	d. Sign. Wold and Odegaard. 1971-76.	FV	18.50	50.00
	e. Sign. Wold and Sagård. 1977.	FV	FV	40.00

		VG	VF	UNC
39	**500 KRONER** 1978-85. Green on brown unpt. N. Henrik Abel at l. and as wmk. University of Oslo at r. on back.			
	a. Sign. Skånland and Sagård. 1978; 1982.	FV	100.00	200.00
	b. Sign. Wold and Sagård. 1985.	FV	100.00	170.00

		VG	VF	UNC
40	**1000 KRONER** 1975-87. Brown and violet on m/c unpt. H. Ibsen at l. and as wmk. Scenery on back.			
	a. Sign. Wold and Odegaard. 1975.	FV	200.00	275.00
	b. Sign. Wold and Sagård. 1978; 1980; 1982-85.	FV	FV	250.00
	c. Sign. Skånland and Sagård. 1985-87.	FV	FV	225.00

1977 ISSUE

		VG	VF	UNC
41	**100 KRONER** 1977-82. Purple on pink and m/c unpt. C. Collett at l. and as wmk. Date at top l. ctr. Filigree design on back. Sign. Wold and Sagård.			
	a. Brown serial #. 1977.	FV	FV	50.00
	b. Black serial #. 1979; 1980.	FV	FV	40.00
	c. 1981; 1982.	FV	FV	40.00

1983-91 ISSUE

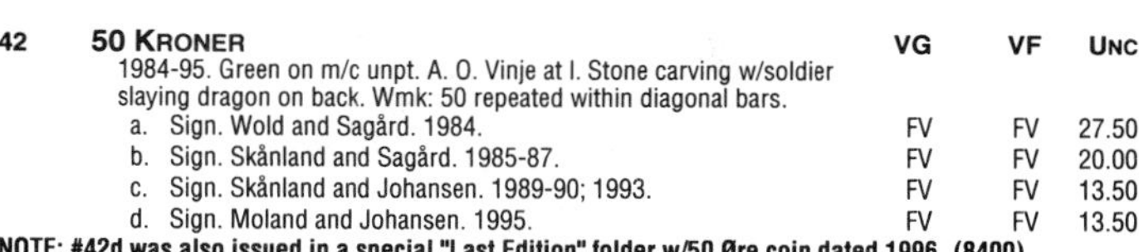

42	**50 KRONER**	VG	VF	UNC
	1984-95. Green on m/c unpt. A. O. Vinje at l. Stone carving w/soldier slaying dragon on back. Wmk: 50 repeated within diagonal bars.			
	a. Sign. Wold and Sagård. 1984.	FV	FV	27.50
	b. Sign. Skånland and Sagård. 1985-87.	FV	FV	20.00
	c. Sign. Skånland and Johansen. 1989-90; 1993.	FV	FV	13.50
	d. Sign. Moland and Johansen. 1995.	FV	FV	13.50

NOTE: #42d was also issued in a special "Last Edition" folder w/50 Øre coin dated 1996. (8400).

43	**100 KRONER**	VG	VF	UNC
	1983-94. Red-violet on pink and m/c unpt. Similar to #41 but smaller printing size, and date at lower r.			
	a. Wold and Sagård. 1983.	FV	FV	40.00
	b. As a. but lg. date. 1984.	FV	FV	40.00
	c. Sign. Skånland and Sagård. 1985-87.	FV	FV	35.00
	d. Sign. Skånland and Johansen. 1988-93.	FV	FV	27.50
	e. Sign. Moland and Johansen. 1994.	FV	FV	27.50

NOTE: #43e was also issued in a special "Last Edition" folder w/1 Krone coin dated 1996. (6000).

44	**500 KRONER**	VG	VF	UNC
	1991; 1994; 1996; 1997. Blue-violet on m/c unpt. E. Grieg at l. Floral mosaic at ctr. on back. Wmk: Multiple portr. of Grieg vertically.			
	a. Sign. Skånland and Johansen. 1991.	FV	FV	115.00
	b. Sign. Moland and Johansen. 1994.	FV	FV	100.00
	c. Sign. Storvik and Johansen. 1996; 1997.	FV	FV	90.00

45	**1000 KRONER**	VG	VF	UNC
	1989; 1990. Purple and dk. blue on m/c unpt. C. M. Falsen at l. 1668 royal seal on back. Sign. Skånland and Johansen.	FV	FV	200.00

1994-96 ISSUE

#46 and 47 sign. K. Storvik and S. Johansen.

46	**50 KRONER**	VG	VF	UNC
	1996; 1998. Dark green on pale green and m/c unpt. P. C. Asbjörnsen at r. and as repeated vertical wmk. Water lilies and dragonfly on back.	FV	FV	13.00

47	**100 KRONER**	VG	VF	UNC
	1995; 1997-99. Deep brown-violet and brown-violet on m/c unpt. K. Flagstad at r. and as repeated vertical wmk. Theatre layout on back.			
	a. 1995; 1997; 1998.	FV	FV	27.50
	b. 1999.	FV	FV	25.00

48	**200 KRONER**	VG	VF	UNC
	1994; 1998. Blue-black and dk. blue on m/c unpt. Birkeland at r. and as repeated vertical wmk. Map of the North Pole; North America and Northern Europe at l. ctr. on back.			
	a. Sign. T. Moland and S. Johansen. 1994.	FV	FV	50.00
	b. Sign. Storvik and Johansen. 1998.	FV	FV	50.00
49	**500 KRONER**			
	1999. Foil strip at r.	FV	FV	110.00
50	**1000 KRONER**			
	199x.			Expected New Issue

Listings for
Nouméa, see New Caledonia

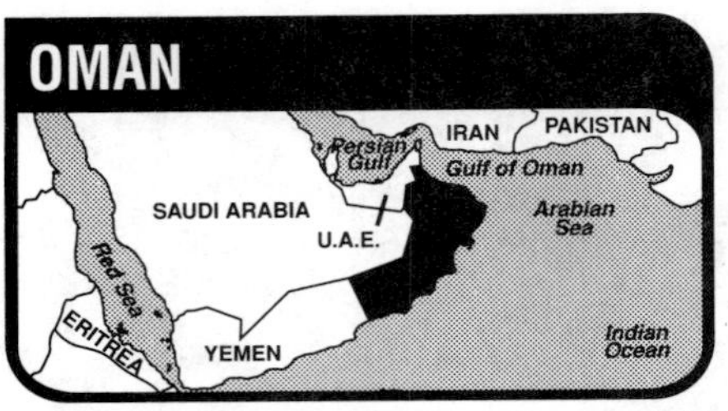

The Sultanate of Oman (formerly Muscat and Oman), an independent monarchy located in the southeastern part of the Arabian Peninsula, has an area of 82,030 sq. mi. (212,457 sq. km.) and a population of 2.14 million. Capital: Muscat. The economy is based on agriculture, herding and petroleum. Petroleum products, dates, fish and hides are exported.

The first European contact with Muscat and Oman was made by the Portuguese who captured Muscat, the capital and chief port, in 1508. They occupied the city, utilizing it as a naval base and factory and holding it against land and sea attacks by Arabs and Persians until finally ejected by local Arabs in 1650. It was next occupied by the Persians who maintained control until 1741, when it was taken by Ahmed ibn Sa'id of the present ruling family. Muscat and Oman was the most powerful state in Arabia during the first half of the 19th century, until weakened by the persistent attack of interior nomadic tribes. British influence, initiated by the signing of a treaty of friendship with the Sultanate in 1798, remains a dominant fact of the civil and military phases of the government, although Britain recognizes the Sultanate as a sovereign state and there is no colonial relationship between them.

Sultan Sa'id bin Taimur was overthrown by his son, Qaboos bin Sa'id, on July 23, 1970. He changed the nation's name to the Sultanate of Oman.

RULERS:

Sa'id bin Taimur, AH1351-1390/1932-1970 AD
Qaboos bin Sa'id, AH1390-/-1419/1970-1999 AD

MONETARY SYSTEM:

1 Rial Omani = 1000 Baiza (Baisa)
1 Rial Saidi = 1000 Baiza (Baisa)

MUSCAT AND OMAN

SULTANATE OF MUSCAT AND OMAN

1970 ND ISSUE

#1-6 arms at r. and as wmk.

		VG	VF	UNC
1	**100 BAIZA** ND (1970). Brown on blue-green and m/c unpt.			
	a. Issued note.	.30	.80	3.00
	s. Specimen.	—	—	15.00

		VG	VF	UNC
2	**1/4 RIAL SAIDI** ND (1970). Blue and brown on m/c unpt. Jalali Fortress on back.			
	a. Issued note.	.70	1.00	4.00
	s. Specimen.	—	—	20.00

		VG	VF	UNC
3	**1/2 RIAL SAIDI** ND (1970). Green and purple on m/c unpt. Sumail Fortress on back.			
	a. Issued note.	1.25	2.00	8.00
	s. Specimen.	—	—	25.00

		VG	VF	UNC
4	**1 RIAL SAIDI** ND (1970). Red and olive-green on m/c unpt. Sohar Fort on back.			
	a. Issued note.	2.50	4.00	15.00
	s. Specimen.	—	—	30.00

		VG	VF	UNC
5	**5 RIALS SAIDI** ND (1970). Purple and blue on m/c unpt. Nizwa Fort on back.			
	a. Issued note.	13.00	20.00	60.00
	s. Specimen.	—	—	50.00

		VG	VF	UNC
6	**10 RIALS SAIDI** ND (1970). Dk. brown and blue on m/c unpt. Mirani Fort on back.			
	a. Issued note.	25.00	45.00	100.00
	s. Specimen.	—	—	90.00

OMAN

OMAN CURRENCY BOARD

1973 ND ISSUE

#7-12 arms at r. and as wmk. Like #1-6.

		VG	VF	UNC
7	**100 BAIZA** ND (1973). Brown on blue-green and m/c unpt.			
	a. Issued note.	.50	.85	2.25
	s. Specimen.	—	—	20.00

#8-12 different fortresses on back.

		VG	VF	UNC
8	**1/4 RIAL OMANI** ND (1973). Blue and brown on m/c unpt.			
	a. Issued note.	.40	1.00	3.75
	s. Specimen.	—	—	25.00

		VG	VF	UNC
9	**1/2 RIAL OMANI** ND (1973). Green and purple on m/c unpt.			
	a. Issued note.	1.75	2.75	7.00
	s. Specimen.	—	—	30.00

		VG	VF	UNC
10	**1 RIAL OMANI** ND (1973). Red and olive-green on m/c unpt.			
	a. Issued note.	2.75	6.50	15.00
	s. Specimen.	—	—	35.00

		VG	VF	UNC
11	**5 RIALS OMANI** ND (1973). Purple and blue on m/c unpt.			
	a. Issued note.	15.00	27.50	60.00
	s. Specimen.	—	—	60.00

		VG	VF	UNC
12	**10 RIALS OMANI** ND (1973). Dk. brown and blue on m/c unpt.			
	a. Issued note.	25.00	45.00	85.00
	s. Specimen.	—	—	85.00

CENTRAL BANK OF OMAN

1977; 1985 ND ISSUE

#13-19 arms at r. and as wmk.

		VG	VF	UNC
13	**100 BAISA** ND (1977). Lt. brown on m/c unpt. Port of Qaboos on back.	FV	FV	1.50

		VG	VF	UNC
14	**200 BAISA** ND (1985). Purple on m/c unpt. Rustaq Fortress on back.	FV	FV	2.25

15 **1/4 RIAL**
ND (1977). Blue and brown on m/c unpt. Back similar to #2.

VG	VF	UNC
FV	FV	2.50

16 **1/2 RIAL**
ND (1977). Green and violet on m/c unpt. Back similar to #3.

VG	VF	UNC
FV	FV	3.75

17 **1 RIAL**
ND (1977). Red and brown on m/c unpt. Back similar to #14.

VG	VF	UNC
FV	FV	7.00

18 **5 RIALS**
ND (1977). Lilac and blue on m/c unpt. Back similar to #15.

VG	VF	UNC
FV	14.00	28.50

19 **10 RIALS**
ND (1977). Brown and blue on m/c unpt. Back similar to #16.

VG	VF	UNC
FV	30.00	65.00

20 **20 RIALS**
ND (1977). Gray-blue and orange on m/c unpt. Sultan Qaboos bin Sa'id at r. Central Bank at l. ctr. on back. Wmk: Arms.

VG	VF	UNC
FV	60.00	125.00

21 **50 RIALS**
ND. Olive-brown, blue and dk. brown on m/c unpt. Sultan at r. Jabreen Fort at l. ctr. on back.

VG	VF	UNC
FV	145.00	225.00

NOTICE

Readers with unlisted dates, signature varieties, etc. are invited to submit photocopies of their notes to: Standard Catalog of World Paper Money, 700 East State St. Iola, WI 54990-0001, fax: 1-715-445-4087, or E-Mail: thernr@krause.com.

1985-90 ISSUE

#22-30 Sultan Qaboos bin Sa'id at r. and as wmk.

22	**100 BAISA**	VG	VF	UNC
	AH1408-1414/1987-1994AD. Lt. brown on m/c unpt. Port of Qaboos on back.			
	a. 1987/AH1408.	FV	FV	1.50
	b. 1989/AH1409.	FV	FV	1.00
	c. 1992/AH1413.	3.00	7.50	20.00
	d. 1994/AH1414.	FV	FV	.75

23	**200 BAISA**	VG	VF	UNC
	AH1407-1414/1987-1994AD. Purple on m/c unpt. Rustaq Fort on back.			
	a. 1987/AH1407.	FV	FV	2.00
	b. 1993/AH1413.	FV	FV	1.75
	c. 1994/AH1414.	FV	FV	1.50

24	**1/4 RIAL**	VG	VF	UNC
	1989/AH1409. Blue and brown on m/c unpt. Modern fishing industry on back.	FV	FV	2.25

25	**1/2 RIAL**	VG	VF	UNC
	1987/AH1408. Green on m/c unpt. Aerial view of Sultan Qaboos University on back.	FV	FV	3.50

26	**1 RIAL**	VG	VF	UNC
	AH1407-1414/1987-1994AD. Red, black and olive-brown on m/c unpt. Sohar Fort at l. on back.			
	a. 1987/AH1407.	FV	FV	8.00
	b. 1989/AH1409.	FV	FV	7.50
	c. 1994/AH1414.	FV	FV	6.00

27	**5 RIALS**	VG	VF	UNC
	1990/AH1411. Dk. rose, brown-violet and m/c unpt. Fort Nizwa on back.	FV	FV	28.50

28	**10 RIALS**	VG	VF	UNC
	AH1408/1987AD; AH1413/1993AD. Dk. brown, red-brown and blue on m/c unpt. Fort Mirani at l. ctr. on back.			
	a. 1987/AH1408.	FV	FV	50.00
	b. 1993/AH1413.	FV	FV	45.00

29	**20 RIALS**	VG	VF	UNC
	AH1407/1987AD; AH1414/1994AD. Brown, dk. olive-brown and blue-gray on m/c unpt. Similar to #20.			
	a. 1987/AH1408.	FV	FV	90.00
	b. 1994/AH1414.	FV	FV	87.50

		VG	VF	UNC
30	**50 RIALS** AH1405/1985AD; AH1413/1992AD. Olive-brown, blue and dk. brown on m/c unpt. Like #21 but w/*Jabreen Fort* added at lower r. on back.			
	a. 1985/AH1405.	FV	FV	215.00
	b. 1992/AH1413.	FV	FV	210.00

1995 ISSUE

#31-38 Sultan Qaboos at r. and as wmk.

#31-36, 38 arms at upper l.

		VG	VF	UNC
31	**100 BAISA** 1995/AH1416. Deep olive-green, dk. green-blue and purple on m/c unpt. Faslajs irrigation system at ctr. Oryx, and wildlife at l. ctr. on back.	FV	FV	1.00

		VG	VF	UNC
32	**200 BAISA** 1995/AH1416. Black, deep blue and green on m/c unpt. Seeb & Salalah Airports at l. ctr. Raysut Port and Marine Science & Fisheries Center at lower l., aerial view of Sultan Qaboos port ctr. on back.	FV	FV	1.25

		VG	VF	UNC
33	**1/2 RIAL** 1995/AH1416. Dk. brown and gray on m/c unpt. Bahla Castle at ctr. Nakhl Fort and Al-Hazm castle at lower l., Nakhl Fort at ctr. on back.	FV	FV	3.00

		VG	VF	UNC
34	**1 RIAL** 1995/AH1416. Deep purple, purple and blue-green on m/c unpt. Sultan Qaboos Sports Complex, Burj al-Sahwa, road overpass at ctr. Omani Khanjar, traditional silver bracelets and ornaments w/shipbuilding in background unpt. on back.	FV	FV	4.50

		VG	VF	UNC
35	**5 RIALS** 1995/AH1416. Red on pale blue and m/c unpt. Sultan Qaboos University bldg. w/clock tower at ctr. Nizwa city view at l. ctr. on back.	FV	FV	20.00

		VG	VF	UNC
36	**10 RIALS** 1995/AH1416. Dk. brown on pale blue and m/c unpt. al-Nahdha in Salalah Tower, Jabreen coconut palm and frankincense tree at ctr. Mutrah Fort and Corniche at l. ctr. on back.	FV	FV	37.50

NOTICE

Readers with unlisted dates, signature varieties, etc. are invited to submit photocopies of their notes to: Standard Catalog of World Paper Money, 700 East State St. Iola, WI 54990-0001, fax: 1-715-445-4087, or E-Mail: thernr@krause.com.

37 **20 RIALS**
1995/AH1416. Dk. blue-green and olive-green on m/c unpt. Central Bank of Oman bldg. at ctr., minaret at r. Muscat Security Market at l., aerial view of Rysayl Industrial Area at ctr., Oman Chamber of Commerce bldg. at upper r. on back.

VG	VF	UNC
FV	FV	70.00

38 **50 RIALS**
1995/AH1416. Purple and violet on m/c unpt. Ministry of Finance and Economy bldg. at ctr., Mirani Fort at r. Cabinet Bldg. at l., Ministry of Commerce and Industry bldg. at ctr. r. on back.

VG	VF	UNC
FV	FV	175.00

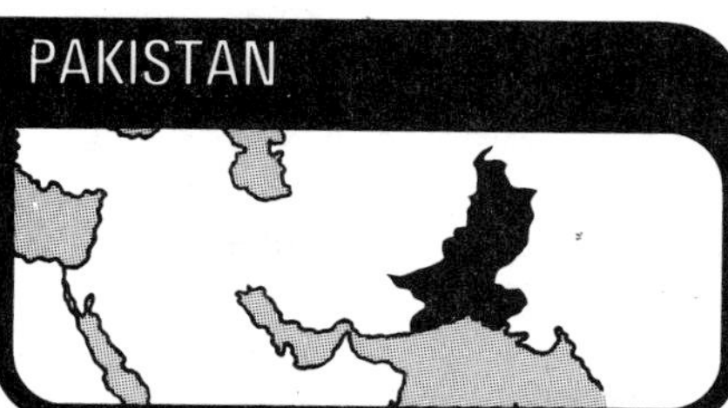

The Islamic Republic of Pakistan, located on the Indian subcontinent between India and Afghanistan, has an area of 310,404 sq. mi. (803,943 sq. m.) and a population of 137.4 million. Capital: Islamabad. Pakistan is mainly an agricultural land. Yarn, cotton, rice and leather are exported.

Afghan and Turkish intrusions into northern India between the 11th and 18th centuries resulted in large numbers of Indians being converted to Islam. The idea of a separate Moslem state independent of Hindu India developed in the 1930's and was agreed to by Britain in 1946. The Islamic majority areas of India, consisting of the separate geographic entities known as East and West Pakistan, achieved self-government as Pakistan, with dominion status in the British Commonwealth, when the British withdrew from India on Aug. 14, 1947. Pakistan became a republic in 1956. When a basic constitutional crisis initiated by the election of Dec. 1, 1970 - the first direct general election in Pakistani history - could not be resolved by the leaders of East and West Pakistan, the East Pakistanis seceded from the Islamic Republic of Pakistan (March 26, 1971) and formed the independent People's Republic of Bangladesh.

Pakistan was expelled from the Commonwealth on January 20, 1972 and re-admitted again on October 1, 1989.

MONETARY SYSTEM:

1 Rupee = 16 Annas to 1961
1 Rupee = 100 Paisa (Pice), 1961-

REPUBLIC

GOVERNMENT OF PAKISTAN

1969 ND ISSUE

9A (9) **1 RUPEE**
ND (1969). Blue on m/c unpt. Arms at r. and as wmk. Back violet on lt. blue unpt.; archway at l. ctr. 5 sign. varieties.

VG	VF	UNC
.50	1.50	4.25

1973 ND ISSUE

10 **1 RUPEE**
ND (1973). Brown on m/c unpt. Like #9A. 2 sign. varieties.

	VG	VF	UNC
a. Sign. 1. *Aftab Qazi.*	.50	1.25	3.50
b. Sign. 2. *Abdul Rauf.*	.40	1.00	2.75

STATE BANK OF PAKISTAN

CITY OVERPRINT VARIETIES

Dacca	Karachi	Lahore
ঢাকা ڈھاکہ	করাচী کراچی	লাহোর لاہور

Some notes exist w/Urdu and some w/Bengali ovpt. denoting city of issue, Dacca, Karachi or Lahore. These are much scarcer than the regular issues. Sign. varieties.

NOTICE

Readers with unlisted dates, signature varieties, etc. are invited to submit photocopies of their notes to: Standard Catalog of World Paper Money, 700 East State St. Iola, WI 54990-0001, fax: 1-715-445-4087, or E-Mail: thernr@krause.com.

1964 ND Issue

#28-31 portr. of M. Ali Jinnah at ctr. or r. and as wmk. Serial # and sign. varieties

		VG	VF	UNC
19	**500 Rupees** ND (1964). Red on gold and lt. green unpt. M. Ali Jinnah at ctr. Bank on back. Sign. in Urdu (b) or Latin (a, b, c) letters.			
	a. Ovpt: *Dacca.*	3.50	10.00	55.00
	b. Ovpt: *Karachi.* 2 sign. varieties.	4.00	12.00	60.00
	c. Ovpt: *Lahore.*	4.00	12.00	60.00

1973 ND Issue

#20-23 M. Ali Jinnah and as wmk.

		VG	VF	UNC
20	**5 Rupees** ND (1973). Orange-brown on pale blue and dull green unpt. M. Ali Jinnah at ctr. Terraces on back. 3 sign. varieties. 2 paper varieties.			
	a. Serial # prefix double letters.	.50	2.00	6.75
	b. Serial # prefix fractional w/double letters over numerals.	.40	1.75	5.50

		VG	VF	UNC
21	**10 Rupees** ND (1973). Green on m/c unpt. Jinnah at l. Park scene on back. 2 sign. varieties.	.75	3.00	10.00
22	**50 Rupees** ND (1973). Blue on m/c unpt. Jinnah at ctr. Back green; sailing ships. 3 sign. varieties.	2.00	8.00	25.00

		VG	VF	UNC
23	**100 Rupees** ND (1973). Dk. blue on m/c unpt. M. Ali Jinnah at l. Mosque on back. 2 sign. varieties.	4.00	15.00	55.00

Government of Pakistan

SIGNATURE VARIETIES

1	Abdur Rauf	2	Aftab Ahmed Khan
3	Habibullah Baig	4	Izhar ul-Hag
5	Saeed Ahmad Quresh	6	Rafiq Akhind
7	Qazi Alimullah Marfi	8	Khalid Javed
9	Javed Talat	10	Mian Tayeb Hasan
11	Moeen Afzal	12	

1975 ND Issue

		VG	VF	UNC
24	**1 Rupee** ND (1975). Blue on lt. green and lilac unpt. Arms at r. and as wmk. Tower at l. on back. Lower border on face is 14mm high and includes text in 4 languages. Sign. 1.	5.00	10.00	35.00

		VG	VF	UNC
24A (24)	**1 Rupee** ND (1975-81). Blue on lt. green and lilac unpt. Like #24, but lower border is 22mm high on face. Sign. 1-3.	.50	1.00	2.50

1981-83 ND Issue

حصولِ رزقِ حلال عبادت ہے

URDU TEXT LINE A

رزقِ حلال عین عبادت ہے

URDU TEXT LINE B

		VG	VF	UNC
25	**1 RUPEE** ND (1981-82). Dull brown on m/c unpt. Arms at r. and as wmk. Tomb of Allama Iqbal on back. No Urdu text line at bottom on back. Serial # at upper ctr. Sign. 3.	.20	.40	1.00

		VG	VF	UNC
26	**1 RUPEE** ND (1982). Dull brown on m/c unpt. Like #25 but w/Urdu text line A at bottom on back.			
	a. Serial # at upper ctr. Sign. 3.	.10	.40	1.00
	b. Serial # at lower r. Sign. 3.	.10	.30	.75

		VG	VF	UNC
27	**1 RUPEE** ND (1983-). Like #26 but w/Urdu text line B at bottom on back.			
	a. Serial # at upper ctr. Sign. 3.	FV	.10	.50
	b. Serial # at lower r. Sign. 3.	FV	.10	.50
	c. As a. Sign. 4.	FV	.10	.50
	d. As b. Sign. 4.	FV	.10	.50
	e. As a. Sign. 5.	FV	.10	.50
	f. As b. Sign. 5.	FV	.10	.50
	g. As a. Sign. 6.	FV	.10	.50
	h. As b. Sign. 6.	FV	.10	.50
	i. As b. Sign. 7.	FV	.10	.50
	j. As a. Sign. 7.	FV	.10	.50
	k. As b. Sign. 8.	FV	.10	.50
	l. As b. Sign. 9.	FV	.10	.50
	m. As b. Sign. 10.	FV	.10	.50
	n. As b. Sign. 11.	FV	.10	.50

STATE BANK OF PAKISTAN

1975-78 ND ISSUE

#28-31 M. Ali Jinnah at r. and as wmk. Serial # and sign. varieties.

		VG	VF	UNC
28	**5 RUPEES** ND (1975-84). Dk. brown on tan and pink unpt. Khajak railroad tunnel on back. No Urdu text line beneath upper title on back. 2 sign. varieties.	FV	.40	2.00

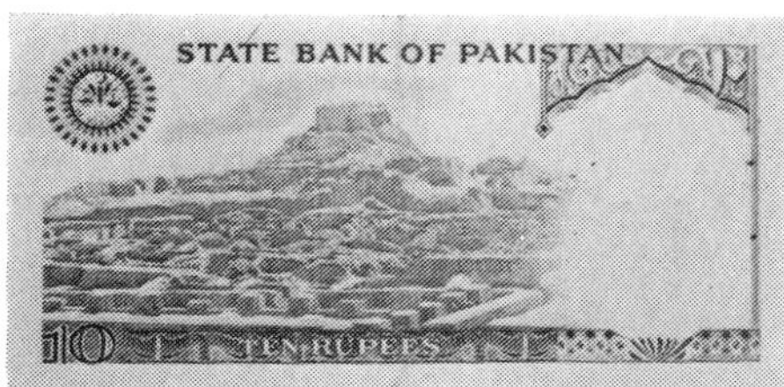

		VG	VF	UNC
29	**10 RUPEES** ND (1975-84). Pale olive-green on m/c unpt. View of Mohanjodaro on back. No Urdu text line beneath upper title on back. 2 sign. varieties.	FV	.75	3.00
30	**50 RUPEES** ND (1978-84). Purple on m/c unpt. Gate of Lahore fort on back. No Urdu text line beneath upper title on back. 2 sign. varieties.	FV	3.00	10.00

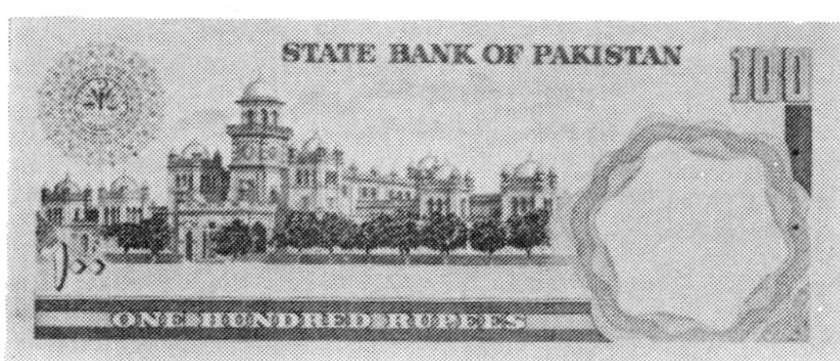

		VG	VF	UNC
31	**100 RUPEES** ND (1975-84). Red and orange on m/c unpt. Islamic College, Peshawar, on back. No Urdu text line beneath upper title on back. 2 sign. varieties.	FV	7.50	20.00

1985 ND ISSUE

#33-36 M. Ali Jinnah at r. and as wmk.

#32 Deleted.

		VG	VF	UNC
33	**5 RUPEES** ND (1985). Dk. brown on tan and pink unpt. Like #28 but w/Urdu text line A beneath upper title on back.	FV	1.00	3.00
34	**10 RUPEES** ND (1985). Pale olive-green on m/c unpt. Like #29 but w/Urdu text line A beneath upper title on back.	FV	1.00	4.00

		VG	VF	UNC
35	**50 RUPEES** ND (1985). Purple on m/c unpt. Like #30 but w/Urdu text line A beneath upper title on back.	FV	3.25	12.00
36	**100 RUPEES** ND (1985). Red and orange on m/c unpt. Like #31 but w/Urdu text line A beneath upper title on back.	FV	8.50	25.00

1986-87 ND ISSUE

		VG	VF	UNC
37	**2 RUPEES** ND (1986-). Pale purple on m/c unpt. Arms at r. and as wmk. Badshahi mosque on back. Urdu text line B beneath upper title on back. 5 sign. varieties.	FV	FV	.50

NOTE: #37 shade varieties exist.

#38-43 M. Ali Jinnah at r. and as wmk.

		VG	VF	UNC
38	**5 RUPEES** ND (1986). Dk. brown on tan and pink unpt. Like #28 but w/Urdu text line B beneath upper title on back. 5 sign. varieties.	FV	FV	1.00

		VG	VF	UNC
39	**10 RUPEES** ND (1986). Pale olive-green on m/c unpt. Like #29 but w/Urdu text line B beneath upper title on back. 5 sign. varieties.	FV	FV	1.50

		VG	VF	UNC
40	**50 RUPEES** ND (1986). Purple on m/c unpt. Like #30 but w/Urdu text line B beneath upper title on back. 5 sign. varieties.	FV	FV	6.00
41	**100 RUPEES** ND (1986). Red and orange on m/c unpt. Like #31 but w/Urdu text line B beneath upper title on back. 5 sign. varieties.	FV	FV	8.50

		VG	VF	UNC
42	**500 RUPEES** ND (1986-). Deep blue-green and olive-green on m/c unpt. State Bank of Pakistan bldg. at ctr. on back. 5 sign. varieties.	FV	FV	30.00

		VG	VF	UNC
43	**1000 RUPEES** ND (1987-). Deep purple and blue-black on m/c unpt. Tomb of Jahangir on back. 3 sign. varieties.	FV	FV	70.00

1997 COMMEMORATIVE ISSUE

#44, Golden Jubilee of Independence, 1947-1997

		VG	VF	UNC
44	**5 RUPEES** 1997. Dull violet on lt. green and pale orange-brown unpt. M. Ali Jinnah at r. and as wmk. Tomb of Shah Rukn-e-Alam at l. ctr., bank seal at upper r. on back.	FV	FV	1.25

REGIONAL

STATE BANK OF PAKISTAN

CA. 1960S ND HAJ PILGRIM ISSUES

#R3-R5 ovpt: *FOR HAJ PILGRIMS FROM PAKISTAN/FOR USE IN SAUDI ARABIA ONLY.*

NOTE: All Haj Pilgrim notes were discontinued or destroyed in 1994.

		VG	VF	UNC
R3	**10 RUPEES** ND. Green on m/c unpt. Like #16 but w/ovpt. 2 sign. varieties.	7.50	16.50	50.00

		VG	VF	UNC
R4	**10 RUPEES** ND. Purple on m/c unpt. Like #16 and #21 but w/ovpt.	1.50	3.50	7.00

		VG	VF	UNC
R5	**100 RUPEES** ND. Brown on m/c unpt. Like #23; black ovpt.	25.00	100.00	225.00

CA. 1970S ND HAJ PILGRIM ISSUE

#R6 and R7 ovpt: *FOR HAJ PILGRIMS FROM PAKISTAN/FOR USE IN SAUDI ARABIA ONLY* and Urdu for "Haj Note."

		VG	VF	UNC
R6	**10 RUPEES** ND. Blue-black on m/c unpt. Like #34; black ovpt.	.50	1.00	5.50

		VG	VF	UNC
R7	**100 RUPEES** ND. Gold on m/c unpt. Like #31; dk. brown ovpt. 2 sign. varieties.	3.00	7.50	25.00

Listings for

Papeete see Tahiti

Papua New Guinea, an independent member of the British Commonwealth, occupies the eastern half of the island of New Guinea. It lies north of Australia near the equator and borders on West Irian. The country, which includes nearby Bismarck Archipelago, Buka and Bougainville, has an area of 176,280 sq. mi. (461,691 sq. km.) and a population of 3.85 million who are divided into more than 1,000 separate tribes speaking more than 700 mutually unintelligible languages. Capital: Port Moresby. The economy is agricultural, and exports include copra, rubber, cocoa, coffee, tea, gold and copper.

New Guinea, the world's largest island after Greenland, was discovered by Spanish navigator Jorge de Menezes, who landed on the northwest shore in 1527. European interests, attracted by exaggerated estimates of the resources of the area, resulted in the island being claimed in whole or part by Spain, the Netherlands, Great Britain and Germany.

Papua (formerly British New Guinea), situated in the southeastern part of the island of New Guinea, has an area of 90,540 sq. mi. (234,499 sq. km.) and a population of 740,000. It was temporarily annexed by Queensland in 1883 and by the British Crown in 1888. Papua came under control of the Australian Commonwealth in 1901 and became the Territory of Papua in 1906. Japan invaded New Guinea and Papua early in 1942, but Australian control was restored before the end of the year in Papua and in 1945 in New Guinea.

In 1884 Germany annexed the area known as German New Guinea (also Neu-Guinea or Kaiser Wilhelmsland) comprising the northern section of eastern New Guinea, and granted its administration and development to the New-Guinea Compagnie. Administration reverted to Germany in 1889 following the failure of the company to exercise adequate administration. While a German protectorate, German New Guinea had an area of 92,159 sq. mi. (238,692 sq. km.) and a population of about 250,000. Capital: Herbertshohe, later named Rabaul. Copra was the chief crop. Australian troops occupied German New Guinea in Aug. 1914, shortly after Great Britain declared war on Germany. It was mandated to Australia by the League of Nations in 1920 and known as the Territory of New Guinea. The territory was invaded and occupied by Japan in 1942. Following the Japanese surrender, it came under U.N. trusteeship, Dec. 13, 1946, with Australia as the administering power.

The Papua and New Guinea Act, 1949, provided for the government of Papua and New Guinea as one administrative unit. On Dec. 1, 1973, Papua New Guinea became self-governing with Australia retaining responsibility for defense and foreign affairs. Full independence was achieved on Sept. 16, 1975 and Papua New Guinea is now a member of the Commonwealth of Nations. The Queen of England is Chief of State.

RULERS:

British

MONETARY SYSTEM:

1 Kina = 100 Toea, 1975-

BANK OF PAPUA NEW GUINEA

SIGNATURE VARIETIES			
1		2	
3		4	
5			

1975 ISSUE

#1-4 stylized Bird of Paradise at l. ctr. and as wmk.

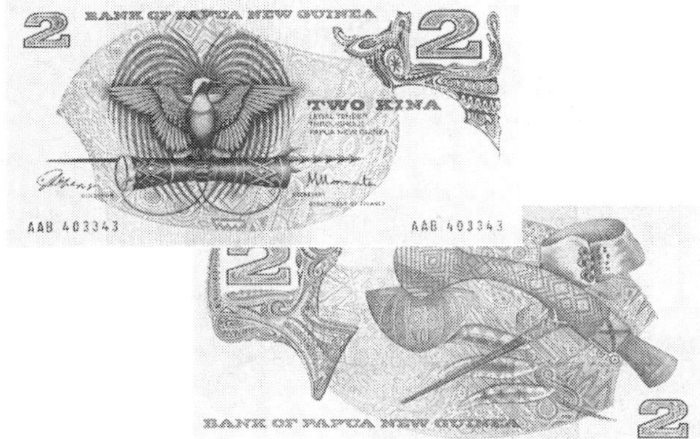

		VG	VF	UNC
1	**2 KINA** ND (1975). Black on lt green and m/c unpt. Artifacts on back. Sign. 1.	1.65	3.50	12.50

		VG	VF	UNC
2	**5 KINA** ND (1975). Violet and purple on m/c unpt. Mask at ctr. r. on back. Sign. 1.	3.75	7.00	32.50

		VG	VF	UNC
3	**10 KINA** ND (1975). Dk. blue-green and purple on m/c unpt. Bowl, ring and other artifacts on back. Sign. 1.	7.00	14.00	60.00

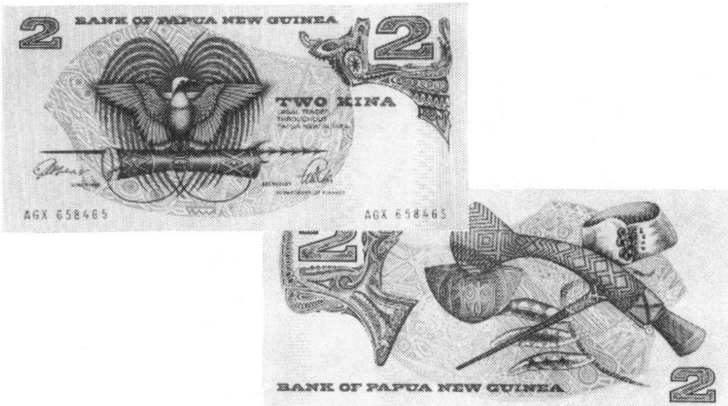

		VG	VF	UNC
4	**20 KINA** ND (1977). Dk. brown and deep red on m/c unpt. Boar's head at r. on back. Sign. 1.	14.00	22.00	90.00

1981-85 ISSUES

		VG	VF	UNC
5	**2 KINA** ND (1981). Black and dk. green on lt. green and m/c unpt. Like #1. White strip 16mm wide at r.			
	a. Sign. 1.	FV	FV	8.00
	b. Sign. 2.	FV	5.00	25.00
	c. Sign. 3.	FV	FV	5.00

		VG	VF	UNC
6	**5 KINA** ND (1981). Violet and purple on m/c unpt. Like #2. White strip 22mm wide at r.			
	a. Sign. 1.	FV	6.50	22.50
	b. Sign. 2.	FV	7.00	27.50
7	**10 KINA** ND (1985). Dk. blue, purple and green on m/c unpt. Like #3. White strip 18mm wide at r. Sign. 1.	FV	10.00	50.00

#8 Held in Reserve.

		VG	VF	UNC
9	**10 KINA** ND (1988). Dk. blue, dk. green and brown-violet on m/c unpt. Similar to #7 but different design elements in unpt. representing a modern bldg. Ornate corner designs omitted on face and back.			
	a. Sign. 2.	FV	15.00	85.00
	b. Sign. 3.	FV	FV	22.50

		VG	VF	UNC
10	**20 KINA** ND. Dk. brown and deep red on m/c unpt. Similar to #4 but different design elements in unpt. Sign. 3.	FV	FV	45.00

		VG	VF	UNC
11	**50 KINA** ND (1989). Black and red on orange, yellow and m/c unpt. National Parliament bldg. at ctr. Foreign Affairs Minister M. Somare at l. ctr., ceremonial masks at r. on back. Wmk: Central Bank logo. Sign. 3.	FV	FV	82.50

1991 COMMEMORATIVE ISSUE

#12, 9th South Pacific Games 1991

		VG	VF	UNC
12	**2 KINA** 1991. Black and dk. green on lt. green and m/c unpt. Similar to #5 but w/stylized Bird of Paradise in clear circle at lower r. Polymer. Sign. 3. Printer: NPA (w/o imprint).	FV	FV	6.50

1992; 1993 ND REGULAR ISSUES

#12A, 13 and 14 wmk: Stylized Bird of Paradise at l. ctr.

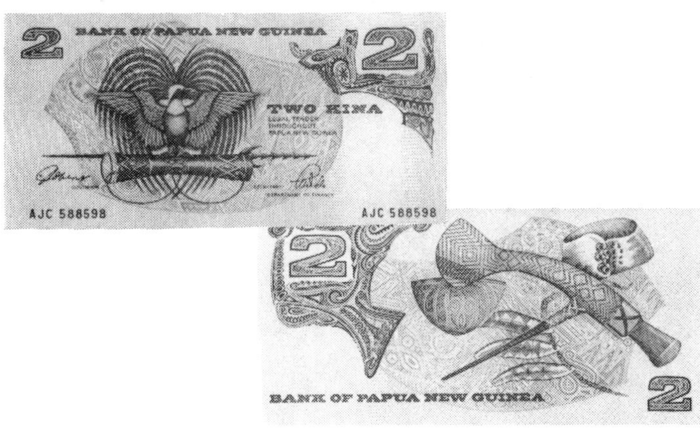

		VG	VF	UNC
12A	**2 KINA** ND (1992). Black and dk. green on lt. green and m/c unpt. Like #5 but most design elements much lighter. Serial # darker and heavier type face. Sign. 3.	FV	FV	5.00

		VG	VF	UNC
13	**5 KINA** ND (1992). Violet and purple on m/c unpt. Like #6 but most design elements much lighter. Serial # darker, heavier type face. Sign. 3.	FV	FV	15.00

		VG	VF	UNC
14	**5 KINA** ND (1993). Violet and purple on m/c unpt. Like #13 but w/segmented security thread and new sign. title: *Secretary for Finance and Planning.* Sign. 4.	FV	FV	12.50

1995 ND COMMEMORATIVE ISSUE

#15, 20th Anniversary Bank of Papua New Guinea

		VG	VF	UNC
15	**2 KINA** ND (1995). Black and dk. green on lt. green and m/c unpt. Similar to #12 but w/ornate *20 ANNIVERSARY* logo at l. Sign 4. Polymer. Printer: NPA (w/o imprint).	FV	FV	6.50

1996 ND REGULAR ISSUE

		VG	VF	UNC
16	**2 KINA** ND (1996). Black and dk. green on lt. green and m/c unpt. Similar to #12A and 15. Sign. 5.	FV	FV	4.50

1998 COMMEMORATIVE ISSUE

#17, Bank's 25th Anniversary

		VG	VF	UNC
17	**5 KINA** 1998. M/c.	FV	FV	30.00

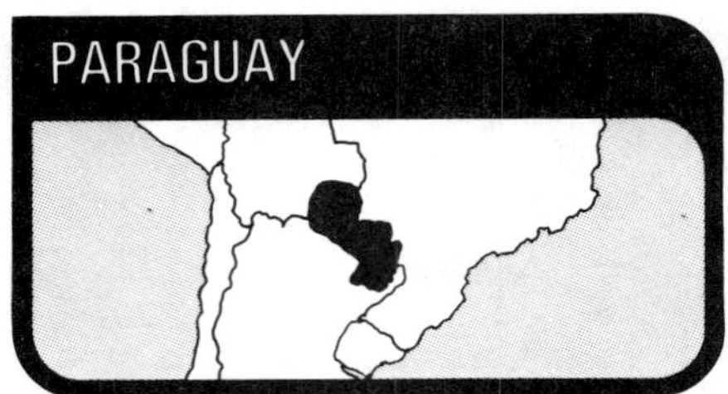

The Republic of Paraguay, a landlocked country in the heart of South America surrounded by Argentina, Bolivia and Brazil, has an area of 157,048 sq. mi. (406,752 sq. km.) and a population of 5.65 million, 95 percent of whom are of mixed Spanish and Indian descent. Capital: Asunción. The country is predominantly agrarian, with no important mineral deposits or oil reserves. Meat, timber, oilseeds, tobacco and cotton account for 70 percent of Paraguay's export revenue.

Paraguay was first visited by Alejo Garcia, a shipwrecked Spaniard, in 1520. The interior was explored by Sebastian Cabot in 1526 and 1529, when he sailed up the Paraná and Paraguay Rivers. Asunción, which would become the center of a province embracing much of southern South America, was established by the Spanish explorer Juan de Salazar on Aug. 15, 1537. For a century and a half the history of Paraguay was largely the history of the agricultural colonies established by the Jesuits in the south and east to Christianize the Indians. In 1811, following the outbreak of the South American wars of independence, Paraguayan patriots overthrew the local Spanish authorities and proclaimed their country's independence.

MONETARY SYSTEM:

1 Guaraní = 100 Centimos, 1944-

REPUBLIC

BANCO CENTRAL DEL PARAGUAY

DECRETO LEY DE NO. 18 DEL 25 DE MARZO DE 1952 (FROM AUG. 1963)

#192-201 arms at l. Sign. size and name varieties. Replacement notes: Serial # prefix *Z*. Printer: TDLR.

		VG	VF	UNC
192	**1 GUARANÍ** *L.1952.* Green on m/c unpt. Soldier at r. Black serial # at lower l. and lower r. Banco Central on back.	.25	1.00	4.00

		VG	VF	UNC
193	**1 GUARANÍ** *L.1952.* Green on m/c unpt. Soldier at r. Palacio Legislativo on back.			
	a. Black serial # at lower l. and lower r.	.10	.35	1.75
	b. Black serial # at upper l. and lower r.	.10	.25	1.25

NOTICE

Readers with unlisted dates, signature varieties, etc. are invited to submit photocopies of their notes to: Standard Catalog of World Paper Money, 700 East State St. Iola, WI 54990-0001, fax: 1-715-445-4087, or E-Mail: thernr@krause.com.

		VG	VF	UNC
194	**5 GUARANÍES** *L.1952.* Blue on m/c unpt. Girl holding jug at r., black serial # at lower l. and lower r. Hotel Guarani on back.	.25	1.50	6.00

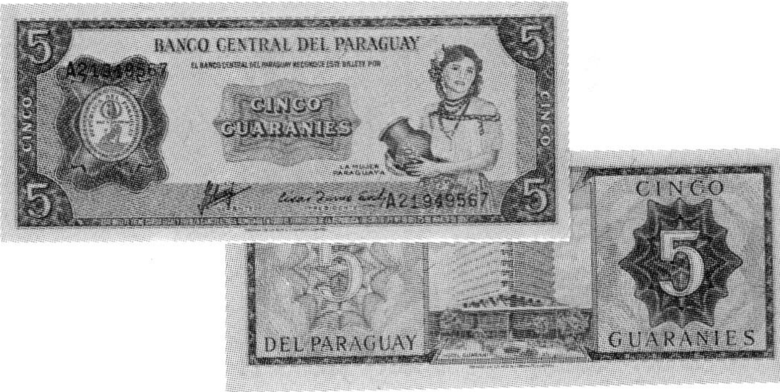

		VG	VF	UNC
195	**5 GUARANÍES** *L.1952.* Black on m/c unpt. Like #194.			
	a. Red serial # at lower l. and lower r.	.10	.30	1.50
	b. Red serial # at upper l. and lower r.	.10	.30	1.25

		VG	VF	UNC
196	**10 GUARANÍES** *L.1952.* Deep red on m/c unpt. Gen. E. A. Garay at r. International bridge on back.			
	a. Black serial # at lower l. and lower r.	.15	.40	2.25
	b. Black serial # at upper l. and lower r.	.15	.40	2.00

		VG	VF	UNC
197	**50 GUARANÍES** *L.1952.* Brown on m/c unpt. M. J. F. Estigarribia at r. Country road on back.			
	a. Black serial # at lower l. and lower r.	.75	1.75	7.00
	b. Black serial # at upper l. and lower r.	.20	.75	4.00

		VG	VF	UNC
198	**100 GUARANÍES** *L.1952.* Green on m/c unpt. Gen. J. E. Diaz at r. Black serial # at lower l. and lower r. Ruins of Humaita on back.	.75	3.00	15.00

NOTE: Do not confuse green #198 w/later issue #205 also in green. #198 w/value: *CIEN GUARANIES* at bottom on back.

		VG	VF	UNC
199	**100 GUARANÍES** *L.1952.* Orange on m/c unpt. Like #198.			
	a. Black serial # at lower l. and lower r.	1.25	2.50	7.00
	b. Black serial # at upper l. and lower r.	.50	1.00	3.00

		VG	VF	UNC
200	**500 GUARANÍES** *L.1952.* Blue-gray on m/c unpt. Gen. B. Caballero at r. Federal merchant ship on back.			
	a. Black serial # at lower l. and lower r.	1.50	4.00	10.00
	b. Black serial # at upper l. and lower r.	1.00	2.00	6.00

		VG	VF	UNC
201	**1000 GUARANÍES** *L.1952.* Purple on m/c unpt. Mariscal F. S. Lopez at r. National shrine on back.			
	a. Black serial # at lower l. and lower r.	4.00	8.00	20.00
	b. Black serial # at upper l. and lower r.	2.00	6.00	15.00

#202-204 printer: TDLR.

		VG	VF	UNC
202	**5000 GUARANÍES** *L.1952.* Red-orange on m/c unpt. Arms at ctr., D. C. A. López at r. López Palace on back.			
	a. Black serial # at lower l. and lower r.	7.50	20.00	60.00
	b. Black serial # at upper l. and lower r.	5.00	15.00	45.00

		VG	VF	UNC
203	**10,000 GUARANÍES** *L.1952.* Dk. brown on m/c unpt. Arms at ctr., Dr. J. Caspar Rodriguez de Francia at r., black serial # at lower l. and lower r. Historical scene from 14.5.1811 on back.	9.00	30.00	80.00
204	**10,000 GUARANÍES** *L.1952.* Dk. brown on m/c unpt. Like #203 but *CASPAR* changed to *GASPAR* below Francia.			
	a. Black serial # at lower l. and lower r.	9.00	30.00	80.00
	b. Black serial # at upper l. and lower r.	FV	20.00	50.00

1982; 1990 ND ISSUE

#205-210 replacement notes: Serial # prefix *Z*.

#205-209 like #199-203 except expression of values changed on back from Spanish to native Guaraní. Printer: TDLR.

		VG	VF	UNC
205	**100 GUARANÍES** *L.1952* (1982). Green on m/c unpt. Like #199 but value on back stated: *SA GUARANI*. 4 sign. varieties.	.10	.25	1.25

		VG	VF	UNC
206	**500 GUARANÍES** *L.1952* (1982). Blue-gray on m/c unpt. Like #200 but value on back stated: *PO SA GUARANI*. 6 sign. varieties.	FV	FV	1.85

		VG	VF	UNC
207	**1000 GUARANÍES** *L.1952* (1982). Purple on m/c unpt. Like #201 but value on back stated: *SU GUARANI*. 6 sign. varieties.	FV	FV	2.00

		VG	VF	UNC
208	**5000 Guaraníes** *L.1952* (1982). Red-orange on m/c unpt. Like #202 but value on back stated: *PO SU GUARANI*. 6 sign. varieties.	FV	FV	6.50

		VG	VF	UNC
209	**10,000 Guaraníes** *L.1952* (1982). Dk. brown on m/c unpt. Like #203 but value on back stated: *PA SU GUARANI*. 5 sign. varieties.	FV	FV	11.00

		VG	VF	UNC
210	**50,000 Guaraníes** *L.1952* (1990). Deep purple and lt. blue on m/c unpt. Soldier at r., outline map of Paraguay at ctr. Back purple and olive-green on m/c unpt. House of Independence at ctr. Wmk: Bust of soldier. 3 sign. varieties. Printer: TDLR.	FV	FV	45.00

1994 ND Issue

		VG	VF	UNC
211	**50,000 Guaraníes** *L.1952* (1994). Purple and lt. blue on m/c unpt. Like #210 but w/segmented foil over security thread. 3 sign. varieties.	FV	FV	40.00

1995 ND Issue

#212 and 213 printer: F-CO.

		VG	VF	UNC
212	**500 Guaraníes** *L.1952* (1995). Blue-gray on m/c unpt. Like #206. 2 sign. varieties.	FV	FV	1.25
213	**1000 Guaraníes** *L.1952* (1995). Purple on m/c unpt. Like #207.	FV	FV	2.00

Ley 489 del 29.6.1995; 1997-98 Issue

		VG	VF	UNC
214 (215)	**1000 Guaraníes** 1998. Purple on m/c unpt. Like #213. Printer: CC,SA.	FV	FV	1.75
215 (214)	**5000 Guaraníes** *L.1995* (1997). Red-orange on m/c unpt. Like #208. Silver foil over security thread. Printer: TDLR. 2 sign. varieties.	FV	FV	5.00
216	**10,000 Guaraníes** 1998.	FV	FV	8.50

		VG	VF	UNC
217 (216)	**50,000 Guaraníes** 1998. Purple and lt. blue on m/c unpt. Like #211. Printer: TDLR. Series A, B.	FV	FV	28.50

		VG	VF	UNC
218 (217)	**100,000 GUARANÍES** 1998. M/c. San R. González de Santa Cruz at r. *Represa de Haipú* Hydroelectric Dam on back. Printer: TDLR.	FV	FV	50.00

COLLECTOR SERIES

BANCO CENTRAL DEL PARAGUAY

1979 ISSUE

		ISSUE PRICE	MKT. VALUE
CS1	**100-10,000 GUARANÍES** *L.1972* (1979). 199b-202b, 204b ovpt: *SPECIMEN* and w/serial # prefix Maltese cross.	14.00	25.00

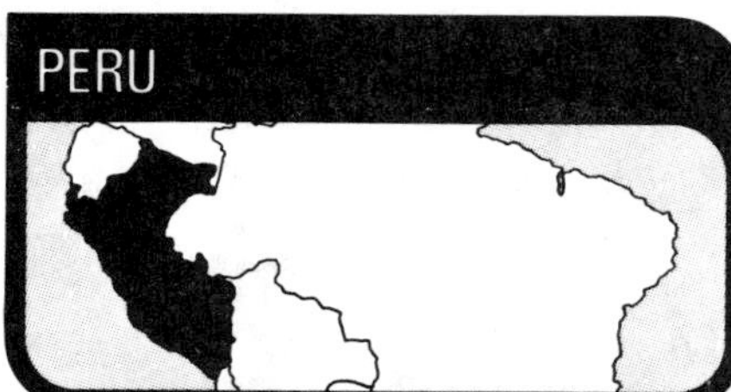

The Republic of Perú, located on the Pacific coast of South America, has an area of 496,222 sq. mi. (1,285,216 sq. km.) and a population of 24.4 million. Capital: Lima. The diversified economy includes mining, fishing and agriculture. Fish meal, copper, sugar, zinc and iron ore are exported.

Once part of a great Inca Empire that reached from northern Ecuador to Central Chile, Perú was conquered in 1531-33 by Francisco Pizarro. Desirable as the richest of the Spanish viceroyalties, it was torn by warfare between avaricious Spaniards until the arrival in 1569 of Francisco de Toledo, who initiated 2 1/2 centuries of efficient colonial rule which made Lima the most aristocratic colonial capital and the stronghold of Spain's South American possessions. José de San Martín of Argentina proclaimed Perú's independence on July 28, 1821; Simón Bolívar of Venezuela secured it in Dec. of 1824 when he defeated the last Spanish army in South America. After several futile attempts to re-establish its South American empire, Spain recognized Perú's independence in 1879.

MONETARY SYSTEM:

1 Sol = 1 Sol de Oro = 100 Centavos, 1879-1985
1 Inti = 1000 Soles de Oro, 1986-1991
1 Nuevo Sol = 100 Centimes = 1 Million Intis, 1991-

REPUBLIC

BANCO CENTRAL DE RESERVA DEL PERÚ

1960 ISSUE

		VG	VF	UNC
82A	**10 SOLES** 8.7. 1960; 1.2. 1961. Orange on m/c unpt. Liberty seated holding shield and staff at ctr. Serial # and series at lower l. and upper r. Printer: TDLR.	.75	1.50	5.00

LEY 13958, 1962; 1964 ISSUE

#83-87 Liberty seated holding shield and staff at ctr. Arms at ctr. on back. Printer: TDLR.

		VG	VF	UNC
83	**5 SOLES DE ORO** 9.2.1962; 20.9.1963; 18.6.1965; 18.11.1966; 23.2.1968. Green on m/c unpt. Serial # at lower l. and upper r. Series J.	.30	1.00	3.00

		VG	VF	UNC
84	**10 SOLES DE ORO** 8.6.1962; 20.9.1963; 20.5.1966; 25.5.1967; 23.2.1968. Orange on m/c unpt. Series I.	.30	1.00	3.75

		VG	VF	UNC
85	**50 SOLES DE ORO** 9.2.1962; 20.9.1963; 23.2.1968. Blue on m/c unpt. Serial # at lower l. and upper r. Series H.	.75	3.00	10.00

		VG	VF	UNC
86	**100 Soles de Oro** 13.3.1964; 23.2.1968. Black on lt. blue and m/c unpt. Series G.	2.00	6.00	18.50

		VG	VF	UNC
87	**500 Soles de Oro** 9.2.1962; 20.9.1963; 20.5.1966; 23.2.1968. Brown on lt. brown and m/c unpt. Series L.	2.75	9.00	35.00

1962; 1965 Issue

#88-91 like #84-87. *Pagará al Portador* added under bank name at top ctr. Printer: ABNC.

		VG	VF	UNC
88	**10 Soles de Oro** 26.2.1965. Red-orange on lt. green and m/c unpt. Series C.	.50	1.50	4.00

		VG	VF	UNC
89	**50 Soles de Oro** 20.8.1965. Blue on m/c unpt. Series B.	1.00	5.00	15.00
90	**100 Soles de Oro** 12.9.1962; 20.8.1965. Black on lt. blue and m/c unpt. Series A.	2.00	6.00	18.00

		VG	VF	UNC
91	**500 Soles de Oro** 26.2.1965. Brown on m/c unpt. Series P.	8.00	25.00	60.00

1968 Issue

#92-98 arms at ctr. 3 sign. Printer: TDLR.

Replacement notes: Serial # *Z999 . . .*

		VG	VF	UNC
92	**5 Soles de Oro** 23.2.1968. Green on m/c unpt. Artifacts at l., Inca Pachacútec at r. Fortaleza de Sacsahuaman on back. Series J.	.25	.50	2.50
93	**10 Soles de Oro** 23.2.1968. Red-orange on m/c unpt. Bldg. at l., G. Inca de la Vega at r. Lake Titicaca, boats on back. Series I.	.20	.65	1.75
94	**50 Soles de Oro** 23.2.1968. Blue-gray on m/c unpt. Workers at l., Tupac Amaru II at r. Scene of historic town of Tinta on back. Series H.	.25	.75	4.50
95	**100 Soles de Oro** 23.2.1968. Black on m/c unpt. Dock workers at l., H. Unanue at r. Church, site of first National Congress on back. Series G.	.50	1.50	6.00

		VG	VF	UNC
96	**200 Soles de Oro** 23.2.1968. Purple on m/c unpt. Fishermen at l., R. Castilla at r. Frigate Amazonas at ctr. on back. Series Q.	1.00	3.50	10.00
97	**500 Soles de Oro** 23.2.1968. Brown on m/c unpt., tan near ctr. Builders at l., N. de Pierola at r. National mint on back. Series L.	2.00	5.00	15.00
98	**1000 Soles de Oro** 23.2.1968. Violet on m/c unpt. M. Grau at l., Francisco Bolognesi (misspelled BOLOGÑESI) at r. Scene of Machu Picchu on back. Series R.	4.00	12.00	25.00

1969 Issue

#99-105 like #92-98. 2 sign. Printer: TDLR.

Replacement notes: Serial # *Z999 . . .*

		VG	VF	UNC
99	**5 Soles de Oro** 1969-74. Like #92. Series J.			
	a. 20.6.1969.	.10	.30	2.00
	b. 16.10.1970; 9.9.1971; 4.5.1972.	.10	.30	1.50
	c. 24.5.1973; 16.5.1974; 15.8.1974.	.10	.25	1.25

		VG	VF	UNC
100	**10 SOLES DE ORO**			
	1969-74. Like #93. Series I.			
	a. 20.6.1969.	.10	.30	1.50
	b. 16.10.1970; 9.9.1971.	.10	.30	1.25
	c. 4.5.1972; 24.5.1973; 16.5.1974.	.10	.25	1.00
101	**50 SOLES DE ORO**			
	1969-74. Like #94. Series H.			
	a. 20.6.1969.	.25	.75	4.00
	b. 16.10.1970; 9.9.1971; 4.5.1972.	.20	.60	3.00
	c. 24.5.1973; 16.5.1974; 15.8.1974.	.20	.50	2.00

		VG	VF	UNC
102	**100 SOLES DE ORO**			
	1969-74. Like #95. Series G.			
	a. 20.6.1969.	.25	.75	4.00
	b. 16.10.1970; 9.9.1971; 4.5.1972.	.20	.60	3.00
	c. 24.5.1973; 16.5.1974; 15.8.1974.	.20	.50	2.50
103	**200 SOLES DE ORO**			
	1969-74. Like #96. Series Q.			
	a. 20.6.1969.	.60	2.50	8.00
	b. 24.5.1973; 16.5.1974; 15.8.1974.	.50	1.75	6.50

		VG	VF	UNC
104	**500 SOLES DE ORO**			
	1969-74. Like #97. Series L.			
	a. 20.6.1969.	1.25	4.00	15.00
	b. 20.6.1969; 16.10.1970; 9.9.1971; 4.5.1972; 24.5.1973.	1.00	3.50	12.00
	c. 16.5.1974; 15.8.1974.	.60	2.50	8.00

		VG	VF	UNC
105	**1000 SOLES DE ORO**			
	1969-73. Like #98 but *BOLOGNESI* correctly spelled at r. Series R.			
	a. 20.6.1969; 16.10.1970.	1.75	6.00	25.00
	b. 9.9.1971; 4.5.1972; 24.5.1973.	1.50	5.00	22.50

1975 ISSUE

#106-111 3 sign. Printer: TDLR.

Replacement notes: Serial # ***Z999 . . .***

		VG	VF	UNC
106	**10 SOLES DE ORO**			
	2.10.1975. Like #93. Series I.	.10	.25	1.25

		VG	VF	UNC
107	**50 SOLES DE ORO**			
	2.10.1975. Like #94. Series H.	.10	.30	1.25
108	**100 SOLES DE ORO**			
	2.10.1975. Like #95. Series G.	.20	.50	2.00

#109 Not assigned.

		VG	VF	UNC
110	**500 SOLES DE ORO**			
	2.10.1975. Like #97. Pale green unpt. near ctr. Series L.	1.00	3.00	10.00
111	**1000 SOLES DE ORO**			
	2.10.1975. Like #98. Name correctly spelled. Series R.	2.00	5.00	22.50

1976-77 Issues

#112 and 113 w/o *Pagará al Portador* at top. W/o security thread. 3 sign. Printer: TDLR. Replacement notes: Serial # *Z999...*

		VG	VF	UNC
112	**10 Soles de Oro** 17.11.1976. Like #106. Series I.	.10	.25	1.50

		VG	VF	UNC
113	**50 Soles de Oro** 15.12.1977. Like #107. Series H.	.10	.30	1.25

#114-115 printer: IPS-Roma.

		VG	VF	UNC
114	**100 Soles de Oro** 22.7.1976. Green, brown and m/c. Arms at l., Tupac Amaru II at r. Machu Picchu on back.	.10	.30	1.25

		VG	VF	UNC
115	**500 Soles de Oro** 22.7.1976. Green, blue and yellow. Arms at ctr., J. Quiñones at r. Logging scene on back.	.05	.15	.85

#116 and 117 printer: BDDK. Replacement notes: Serial # prefix *Y*, and suffix letters *YA*; none reported for 117b.

		VG	VF	UNC
116	**1000 Soles de Oro** 22.7.1976. Green, brown and m/c. Arms at ctr., M. Grau at r. Fishermen on back.	.50	2.00	6.00

		VG	VF	UNC
117	**5000 Soles de Oro** 1976-85. Brown and maroon on m/c unpt. Arms at ctr., Col. Bolognesi at r. and as wmk. 2 miners in mine on back.			
	a. 22.7.1976.	1.00	2.50	7.00
	b. 5.11.1981.	.15	.50	1.50
	c. 21.6.1985.	.05	.20	1.00

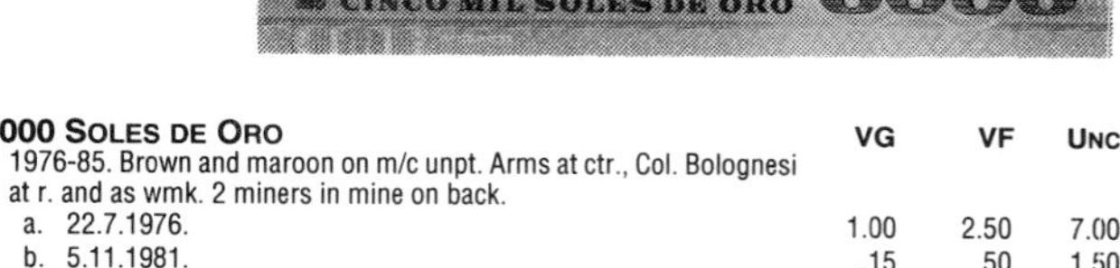

1979 Issue

#117A *Deleted*. See #125A.

#118-120 denominations below coat-of-arms. Printer: TDLR. Replacement notes: Serial # prefix *Y* and suffix letters *AY*.

		VG	VF	UNC
118	**1000 Soles de Oro** 1.2.1979; 3.5.1979. Black, green and m/c. Adm. Grau at r. and as wmk., arms at ctr. Fishermen and boats on back.	.50	1.00	3.00

		VG	VF	UNC
119	**5000 SOLES DE ORO** 1.2.1979. Brown-violet and m/c. Similar to #117 but *CINCO MIL* added at bottom on face. Miners on back.	.50	1.50	5.00

		VG	VF	UNC
120	**10,000 SOLES DE ORO** 1.2.1979; 5.11.1981. Black, blue-violet and purple on m/c unpt. Garcilaso Inca de la Vega at r. and as wmk. Indian digging at l., woman w/flowers at ctr. on back.	.65	2.00	10.00

1981 ISSUE

#121 *Deleted.* See #125B.

#122-125 portr. as wmk. Printer: ABNC.

		VG	VF	UNC
122	**1000 SOLES DE ORO** 5.11.1981. Black, green and m/c. Similar to #118 but slightly modified guilloche in unpt. at ctr.	.10	.20	1.00

		VG	VF	UNC
123	**5000 SOLES DE ORO** 5.11.1981. Black and red-brown on m/c unpt. Similar to #119 but denomination is above signs. at ctr.	.35	1.00	4.00

		VG	VF	UNC
124	**10,000 SOLES DE ORO** 5.11.1981. Black, blue-violet and purple on m/c unpt. Similar to #120 but slight variations on borders.	.50	1.50	6.00

		VG	VF	UNC
125	**50,000 SOLES DE ORO** 5.11.1981; 2.11.1984. Black and orange on m/c unpt. Arms at ctr., N. de Pierola at r. Drilling rig at l. on back, helicopter approaching.	1.00	3.00	11.50

1982; 1985 ISSUE

Replacement notes: Serial # prefix *YA* and *ZZ* respectively.

		VG	VF	UNC
125A	**500 SOLES DE ORO** 18.3.1982. Like #115 but printer: (T)DLR.	.25	.50	3.00
125B	**50,000 SOLES DE ORO** 23.8.1985. Black, orange and m/c. Like #125. Printer: TDLR.	.75	2.25	6.50

1985 ND PROVISIONAL ISSUE

		VG	VF	UNC
126	**100,000 SOLES DE ORO** ND (ca.1985). Ovpt. bank name and new denomination in red on #122.	30.00	90.00	235.00

#127 Held in reserve.

1985-91 ISSUES

During the period from around 1984 and extending beyond 1990, Perú suffered from a hyperinflation that saw the Sol depreciate in value dramatically and drastically. A sudden need for new Inti banknotes caused the government to approach a number of different security printers in order to satisfy the demand for new notes.

#128-150 involve 7 different printers: BdM, BDDK, CdM-B, FNMT, G&D, IPS-Roma and TDLR. Listings proceed by denomination and in chronological order. All portr. appear also as wmk., and all notes have arms at ctr. on face.

Replacement notes:

BdM - Serial # prefix *Y; Z.*
BDDK - Serial # prefix *Y.*
FNMT - Serial # prefix *Y.*
IPS-Roma - Serial # prefix *Y; Z.*
TDLR - Serial # prefix *Y; Z.*

		VG	VF	UNC
128	**10 INTIS** 3.4.1985; 17.1.1986. Black, dk. blue and purple on m/c unpt. R. Palma at r. Back aqua and purple; Indian farmer digging at l. and another picking cotton at ctr. Printer: TDLR.	.05	.15	.40

		VG	VF	UNC
129	**10 INTIS** 26.6.1987. Black, dk. blue and purple on m/c unpt. Like #128. Printer: IPS-Roma.	.05	.10	.35

		VG	VF	UNC
130	**50 INTIS** 3.4.1985. Black, orange and green on m/c unpt. N. de Pierola at r. Drilling rig at l. on back, helicopter approaching. Printer: TDLR.	.15	.30	1.00

		VG	VF	UNC
131	**50 INTIS** 1986; 1987. Black, orange and green on m/c unpt. Like #130. Printer: CdM-Brazil.			
	a. 6.3.1986.	.05	.20	.50
	b. 26.6.1987.	.05	.10	.40

		VG	VF	UNC
132	**100 INTIS** 1985-86. Black and dk. brown on m/c unpt. R. Castilla at r. Women workers by cotton spinning frame at l. ctr. on back. Printer: CdM-Brazil.			
	a. 1.2.1985; 1.3.1985.	1.00	2.00	10.00
	b. 6.3.1986. W/add'l pink and lt. green vertical unpt. at r.	.15	.40	1.75

		VG	VF	UNC
133	**100 INTIS** 26.6.1987. Black and dk. brown on m/c unpt. Like #132b. Printer: BDDK.	.05	.10	.35

		VG	VF	UNC
134	**500 INTIS** 1985; 1987. Deep brown-violet and olive-brown on m/c unpt. J. G. Condorcanqui Tupac Amaru II at r. Mountains and climber at ctr. on back. Printer: BDDK.			
	a. 1.3.1985.	.15	.30	1.00
	b. 26.6.1987. Ornate red-orange vertical strip at l. end of design w/added security thread underneath.	.05	.10	.40

		VG	VF	UNC
135	**500 INTIS** 6.3.1986. Deep brown-violet and olive-brown on m/c unpt. Similar to #134b. Printer: FNMT.	1.00	3.50	10.00

		VG	VF	UNC
136	**1000 INTIS** 1986-88. Deep green, olive-brown and red on m/c unpt. Mariscal A. Avelino C. at r. Ruins off Chan Chan on back. Printer: TDLR.			
	a. 6.3.1986.	.15	.30	1.00
	b. 26.6.1987; 28.6.1988.	.05	.10	.40

		VG	VF	UNC
137	**5000 INTIS** 28.6.1988. Purple, deep brown and red-orange on m/c unpt. Adm. M. Grau at r. Fishermen repairing nets on back. Printer: G&D.	.05	.15	.60
138	**5000 INTIS** 28.6.1988. Purple, deep brown and red-orange on m/c unpt. Like #137. Printer: IPS-Roma.	.25	.80	2.50
139	**5000 INTIS** 9.9.1988. Purple, deep brown and red-orange on m/c unpt. Like #137. W/o wmk. Printer: TDLR.	.25	.80	2.50

		VG	VF	UNC
140	**10,000 INTIS** 28.6.1988. Aqua, blue and orange on lt. green and m/c unpt. C. Vallejo at r. Black and red increasing size serial # (anti-counterfeiting device). Santiago de Chuco street scene on back. Printer IPS-Roma.	.05	.25	.75

		VG	VF	UNC
141	**10,000 INTIS** 28.6.1988. Dk. blue and orange on lt. green and m/c unpt. Like #140 but w/broken silver security thread. Printer: TDLR.	.25	.60	2.50

		VG	VF	UNC
142	**50,000 INTIS** 28.6.1988. Red, violet and dk. blue on m/c unpt. Victor Raul Haya de la Torre at r. Chamber of National Congress on back. Printer: IPS-Roma.	.25	.75	3.00
143	**50,000 INTIS** 28.6.1988. Red, violet and dk. blue on m/c unpt. Like #142 but w/segmented foil security thread. Printer: TDLR.	.50	2.00	5.00

#144-150 arms at ctr. Various printers.

		VG	VF	UNC
144	**100,000 INTIS** 21.11.1988. Brown and black on m/c unpt. F. Bolognesi at r. Local boats in Lake Titicaca on back. Bolognesi's printed image on wmk. area at l. Printer: TDLR.	.25	.75	2.25

		VG	VF	UNC
144A	**100,000 INTIS** 21.12.1988. Brown and black on m/c unpt. Like #144 but w/wmk: *F. Bolognesi*. Segmented foil over security thread.	.25	.75	2.25
145	**100,000 INTIS** 21.12.1989. Like #144b, but w/black security thread at r. of arms. Printer: BdeM.	.25	.75	3.00

146 500,000 INTIS | VG .30 | VF 1.50 | UNC 4.50

21.11.1988. Blue and blue-violet on m/c unpt. Face like #128. Church of *La Caridád* (charity), site of first National Congress, on back. R. Palma's printed image on wmk. area at l. Printer: TDLR.

146A 500,000 INTIS | VG .35 | VF 1.65 | UNC 5.00

21.12.1988. Blue and blue-violet on m/c unpt. Like #146 but w/wmk: *R. Palma*. Segmented foil over security thread.

147 500,000 INTIS | VG .30 | VF 1.25 | UNC 4.50

21.12.1989. Blue and blue-violet on m/c unpt. Like #146b, but w/black security thread at r. Printer: BdeM.

148 1,000,000 INTIS | VG .25 | VF 1.00 | UNC 4.50

5.1.1990. Dk. red, green and m/c. H. Unanue at r. and as wmk. Medical college at San Fernando at l. ctr. on back. Printer: TDLR.

149 5,000,000 INTIS | VG 2.25 | VF 7.00 | UNC 20.00

5.1.1990. Brown, red and m/c. A. Raimondi at r. and as wmk. Indian comforting Raimundi on back. Printer: BdeM.

150 5,000,000 INTIS | VG .65 | VF 2.00 | UNC 6.00

16.1.1991. Similar to #149 but plants printed on wmk. area at l. on face. Old bldg. at r. on back. Printer: IPS-Roma.

1991; 1992 ISSUES

MONETARY REFORM:

1 Nuevo Sol = 1 Million Intis. arms at upper r.

#151-155 arms at upper r.

151 10 NUEVOS SOLES | VG FV | VF FV | UNC 8.50

1.2.1991. Dk. green and blue-green on m/c unpt. WW II era fighter plane as monument at upper ctr., José Abelardo Quiñones at r. and as wmk. Biplane inverted (signifying pilot's death) at l. ctr. on back. Printer: TDLR.

151A 10 NUEVOS SOLES | VG FV | VF FV | UNC 8.50

10.9.1992. Dk. green and blue-green on m/c unpt. Like #151 but printer: IPS-Roma.

152 20 NUEVOS SOLES | VG FV | VF FV | UNC 20.00

1.2.1991. Black, brown and orange on m/c unpt. Patio of San Marcos University at ctr. Raul Porras B. at r. and as wmk. Palace of Torre Tagle at l. ctr. on back. Printer: TDLR.

#153-155 printer: IPS-Roma.

153 20 NUEVOS SOLES | VG FV | VF FV | UNC 16.00

25.6.1992. Black, brown and orange on m/c unpt. Like #152.

154 50 NUEVOS SOLES — VG / VF / UNC
1.2.1991; 25.6.1992. Red-brown, blue-violet and black on m/c unpt. Bldg. at ctr., Abraham Valdelomar at r. and as wmk. Laguna de Huacachina at l. ctr. on back. — FV / FV / 40.00

155 100 NUEVOS SOLES — VG / VF / UNC
1.2.1991; 25.6.1992; 10.9.1992. Black, blue-black, red-violet and deep green on m/c unpt. Arch monument at ctr., Jorge Basadre (Grohmann) at r. and as wmk., arms at upper r. National Library at l. ctr. on back.

		VG	VF	UNC
a.	W/Jorge Basadre. 1.2.1991.		FV	75.00
b.	W/Jorge Basadre Grohmann. 10.9.1992.		FV	70.00

1994; 1995 ISSUE

#156-161 similar to #151-155 but w/clear wmk. area.

156 10 NUEVOS SOLES — VG / VF / UNC
16.6.1994. Dk. green and blue-green on m/c unpt. Like #151. Printer: TDLR. — FV / FV / 7.50

157 10 NUEVOS SOLES — VG / VF / UNC
20.4.1995. Dk. green and blue-green on m/c unpt. Like #156. Printer: G&D. — FV / FV / 7.00

158 20 NUEVOS SOLES — VG / VF / UNC
16.6.1994. Black, brown and orange on m/c unpt. Like #152. Printer: TDLR. — FV / FV / 14.00

159 20 NUEVOS SOLES
20.4.1995. Similar to #158. — FV / FV / 13.50

#160-162 printer: IPS-Roma.

160 50 NUEVOS SOLES — VG / VF / UNC
16.6.1994; 20.4.1995. Brown, deep blue and black on m/c unpt. Like #154. — FV / FV / 32.50

161 100 NUEVOS SOLES — VG / VF / UNC
20.4.1995. Black, blue-black, red-violet and deep green on m/c unpt. Like #155b. — FV / FV / 65.00

162 200 NUEVOS SOLES — VG / VF / UNC
20.4.1995. Red, brown-violet and dk. blue on m/c unpt. Isabel Flores de Oliva, St. Rose of Lima at r. and as wmk., well in unpt. at ctr. Convent of Santo Domingo at l. on back. — FV / FV / 120.00

1996 Issue

#163-165 printer: IPS-Roma.

		VG	VF	Unc
163	**10 Nuevos Soles** 25.4.1996. Like #156.	FV	FV	9.50
164	**20 Nuevos Soles** 25.4.1996. Like #158.	FV	FV	13.50
165	**100 Nuevos Soles** 25.4.1996. Like #161.	FV	FV	65.00

1997 Issue

		VG	VF	Unc
166	**10 Nuevos Soles** 11.6.1997. Dk. green and blue-green on m/c unpt. Like #157. Printer: BABN.	FV	FV	7.50
167	**20 Nuevos Soles** 11.6.1997. Like #158. Printer: BABN.	FV	FV	13.50
168	**50 Nuevos Soles** 11.6.1997. Like #154. Printer: IPS-Roma.	FV	FV	32.50

Banco de Credito del Perú/Banco Central de Reserva del Perú

1985 Emergency Check Issue

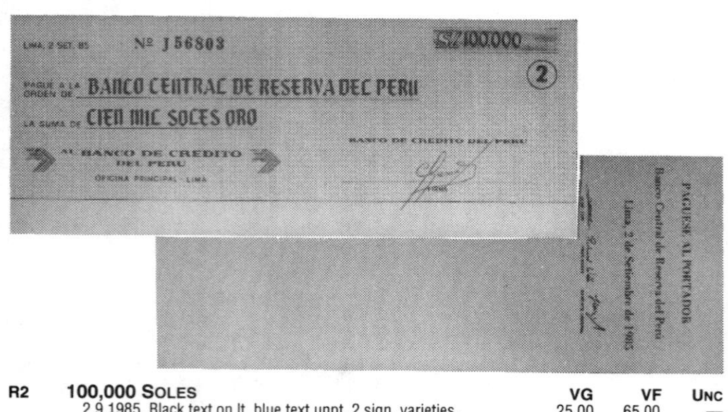

		VG	VF	Unc
R2	**100,000 Soles** 2.9.1985. Black text on lt. blue text unpt. 2 sign. varieties.	25.00	65.00	—

Banco de la Nación/Banco Central de Reserva del Perú

1985 Cheques Circulares de Gerencia Issue

#R6-R8 bank monogram at upper l.

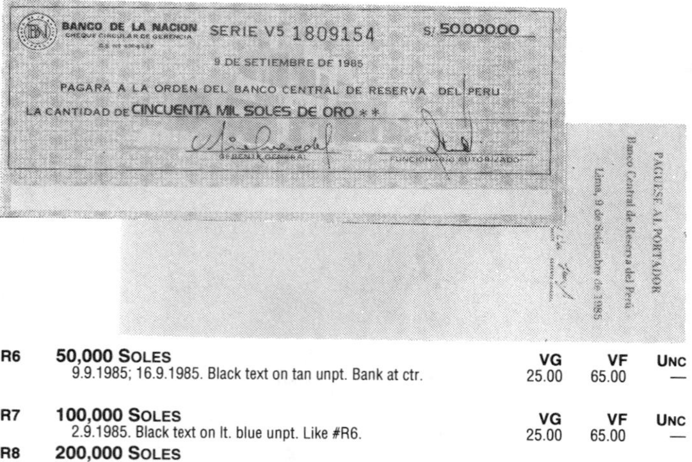

		VG	VF	Unc
R6	**50,000 Soles** 9.9.1985; 16.9.1985. Black text on tan unpt. Bank at ctr.	25.00	65.00	—
R7	**100,000 Soles** 2.9.1985. Black text on lt. blue unpt. Like #R6.	25.00	65.00	—
R8	**200,000 Soles** 2.9.1985. Black text on pink unpt. Like #R6.	25.00	65.00	—

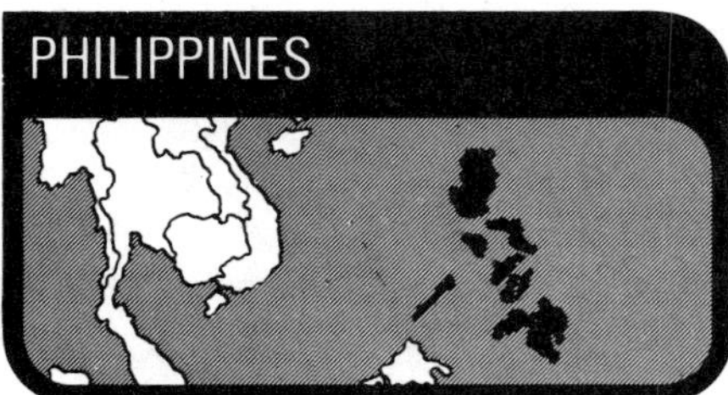

The Republic of the Philippines, an archipelago in the western Pacific 500 miles (805 km.) from the southeast coast of Asia, has an area of 115,830 sq. mi. (300,000 sq. km.) and a population of 73.36 million. Capital: Manila. The economy of the 7,000-island group is based on agriculture, forestry and fishing. Timber, coconut products, sugar and hemp are exported.

Migration to the Philippines began about 30,000 years ago when land bridges connected the islands with Borneo and Sumatra. Ferdinand Magellan claimed the islands for Spain in 1521. The first permanent settlement was established by Miguel de Legazpi at Cebu in April of 1565; Manila was established in 1572. A British expedition captured Manila and occupied the Spanish colony in Oct. of 1762, but it was returned to Spain by the treaty of Paris, 1763. Spain held the Philippines amid a growing movement of Filipino nationalism until 1898 when they were ceded to the United States at the end of the Spanish-American War. The Filipinos then fought unsuccessfully against the United States to maintain their independent Republic proclaimed by Emilio Aguinaldo. The country became a self-governing Commonwealth of the United States in 1935, and attained independence as the Republic of the Philippines on July 4, 1946. During World War II the Japanese had set up a puppet republic, but this quasi-government failed to achieve worldwide recognition. The occupation lasted from late 1941 to 1945. Ferdinand Marcos lost to Corazón Aquino in elections of 1986. Marcos then fled the country. In 1992 Fidel Ramos was elected president. In 1998, J. E. Estrada was elected president.

MONETARY SYSTEM:

1 Peso = 100 Centavos to 1967
1 Piso = 100 Sentimos, 1967-

Republic

Central Bank of the Philippines

1949 ND "English" Issues

#125, 127, and 129 sign. E. Quirino and M. Cuaderno. Printer: SBNC.

		VG	VF	Unc
125	**5 Centavos** ND. Red on tan unpt. Back red.	.25	.50	1.75

		VG	VF	Unc
126	**5 Centavos** ND. LIke #125. Sign. R. Magsaysay and M. Cuaderno. Printer: W&S.	.10	.25	1.50
127	**10 Centavos** ND. Brownish purple on tan unpt. Back brownish purple.			
	a. Issued note.	.25	.50	2.50
	r. Remainder w/o serial #.	—	100.00	250.00
128	**10 Centavos** ND. LIke #126. Sign. R. Magsaysay and M. Cuaderno. Printer: W&S.	.25	.50	1.50
129	**20 Centavos** ND. Green on lt. green unpt. Back green.			
	a. Issued note.	.30	.60	3.50
	r. Remainder w/o serial # (error).	—	100.00	250.00

#130-141 printr: TDLR.

		VG	VF	Unc
130	**20 Centavos** ND. Green on lt. green unpt. Back green.			
	a. Sign. R. Magsaysay and M. Cuaderno.	.20	.50	2.00
	b. Sign. C. Garcia and M. Cuaderno.	.20	.50	1.75

		VG	VF	UNC
131	**50 CENTAVOS** ND. Blue on lt. blue unpt. Back blue. Sign. R. Magsaysay and M. Cuaderno.	.20	.50	2.50

		VG	VF	UNC
132	**1/2 PESO** ND. Green on yellow and blue unpt. Ox-cart w/Mt. Mayon in background at ctr. Back green. Sign. C. Garcia and M. Cuaderno.	.20	.75	2.50

#133-141 bank seal at lower r.

		VG	VF	UNC
133	**1 PESO** ND. Black on lt. gold and blue unpt. A. Mabini at l. Back black; Barasoain Church at ctr.			
	a. Sign. E. Quirino and M. Cuaderno. *GENUINE* in very lt. tan letters just beneath top heading on face.	7.00	22.00	85.00
	b. Sign. E. Quirino and M. Cuaderno w/o *GENUINE* on face.	.50	1.50	5.00
	c. Sign. R. Magsaysay and M. Cuaderno.	.25	.75	3.00
	d. Sign. C. Garcia and M. Cuaderno.	.25	.75	2.50
	e. Sign. C. Garcia and A. Castillo w/title: *Acting Governor.*	.50	1.00	3.50
	f. Sign. D. Macapagal and A. Castillo w/title: *Governor.*			
	g. Sign. F. Marcos and A. Castillo.	.25	.75	2.00
	h. Sign. F. Marcos and A. Calalang.	.10	.30	1.50
	s. Sign. as f. Specimen.	—	—	55.00

		VG	VF	UNC
134	**2 PESOS** ND. Black on blue and gold unpt. Portr. J. Rizal at l. Back blue; landing of Magellan in the Philippines.			
	a. Sign. E. Quirino and M. Cuaderno.	1.00	4.00	15.00
	b. Sign. R. Magsaysay and M. Cuaderno.	.75	2.00	5.00
	c. Sign. C. Garcia and A. Castillo w/title: *Acting Governor.*	.75	1.50	4.00
	d. Sign. D. Macapagal and A. Castillo w/title: *GOVERNOR.*	.15	.75	2.00
	s. Sign. as b. Specimen.	—	—	60.00
	s. Sign. as d. Specimen.	—	—	60.00

NOTICE

Readers with unlisted dates, signature varieties, etc. are invited to submit photocopies of their notes to: Standard Catalog of World Paper Money, 700 East State St. Iola, WI 54990-0001, fax: 1-715-445-4087, or E-Mail: thernr@krause.com.

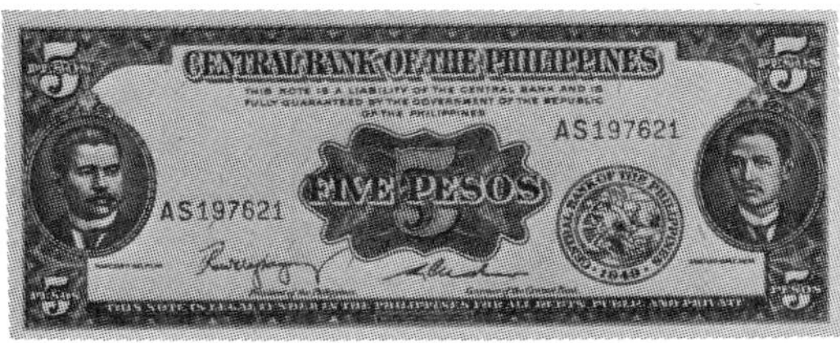

		VG	VF	UNC
135	**5 PESOS** ND. Black on yellow and gold unpt. Portr. M. H. del Pilar at l., Lopez Jaena at r. Back gold; newspaper "La Solidaridad".			
	a. Sign. E. Quirino and M. Cuaderno.	2.00	7.50	25.00
	b. Sign. R. Magsaysay and M. Cuaderno.	1.00	3.50	10.00
	c. Sign. C. Garcia and M. Cuaderno.	1.50	4.00	15.00
	d. Sign. C. Garcia and A. Castillo w/title: *Acting Governor.*	1.25	3.00	12.00
	e. Sign. D. Macapagal and A. Castillo w/title: *Governor.*	.20	.40	1.50
	f. Sign. F. Marcos and G. Licaros.	.20	.40	2.00
	s. Sign. as e. Specimen.	—	—	65.00

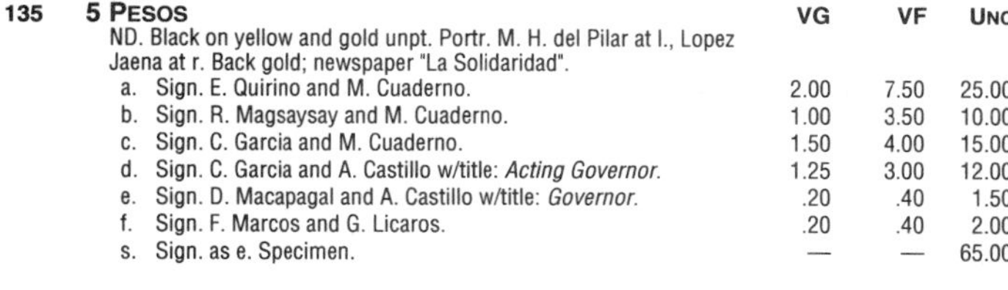

		VG	VF	UNC
136	**10 PESOS** ND. Black on tan and lt. red unpt. Fathers Burgos, Gomez and Zamora at l. Back brown; monument.			
	a. Sign. E. Quirino and M. Cuaderno.	8.00	25.00	75.00
	b. Sign. R. Magsaysay and M. Cuaderno.	2.50	7.00	20.00
	c. Sign. C. Garcia and M. Cuaderno.	3.00	7.50	22.50
	d. Sign. C. Garcia and A. Castillo w/title: *Acting Governor.*	2.50	7.00	17.50
	e. Sign. D. Macapagal and A. Castillo w/title: *Governor.*	.25	.75	2.50
	f. Sign. F. Marcos and G. Licaros.	1.00	2.50	7.50
	s. Sign. as b. Specimen.	—	—	70.00
	s. Sign. as d. Specimen.	—	—	70.00

		VG	VF	UNC
137	**20 PESOS** ND. Black on yellow unpt. Portr. A. Bonifacio at l., E. Jacinto at r. Back brownish orange; flag and monument.			
	a. Sign. E. Quirino and M. Cuaderno.	10.00	30.00	85.00
	b. Sign. R. Magsaysay and M. Cuaderno.	2.75	8.00	25.00
	c. Sign. C. Garcia and A. Castillo w/title: *Acting Governor.*	2.25	7.00	20.00
	d. Sign. D. Macapagal and A. Castillo w/title: *Governor.*	.50	1.50	5.00
	e. Sign. F. Marcos and G. Licaros.	.35	1.00	3.50
	s. Sign. as a. Specimen.	—	—	100.00
	s. Sign. as d. Specimen.	—	—	75.00

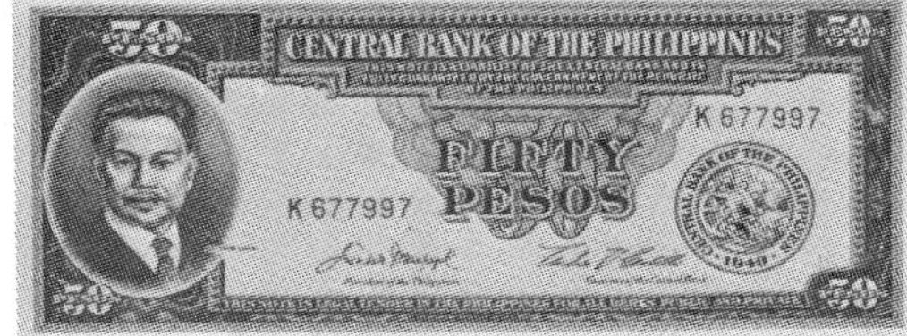

		VG	VF	UNC
138	**50 PESOS** ND. Black on pink and lt. tan unpt. Portr. A. Luna at l. Back red; scene of blood compact of Sikatuna and Legaspi.			
	a. Sign. E. Quirino and M. Cuaderno.	50.00	170.00	—
	b. Sign. R. Magsaysay and M. Cuaderno.	20.00	45.00	90.00
	c. Sign. C. Garcia and M. Cuaderno.	8.00	20.00	40.00
	d. Sign. D. Macapagal and A. Castillo.	.65	3.00	7.50
	s. Sign. as d. Specimen.	—	—	85.00

		VG	VF	UNC
139	**100 PESOS** ND. Black on gold unpt. T. Sora at l. Back yellow; regimental flags. Sign. E. Quirino and M. Cuaderno.	3.00	10.00	25.00

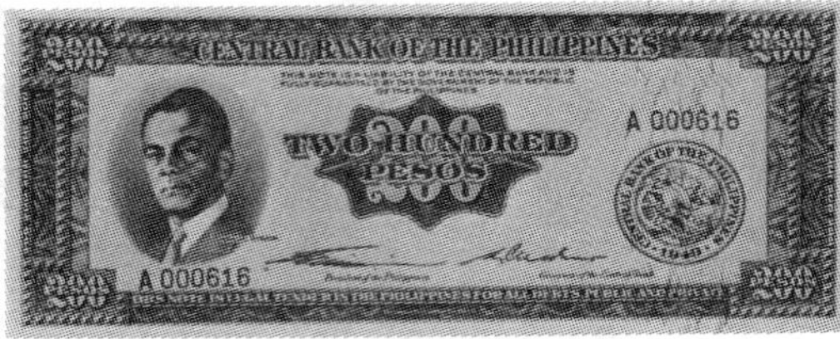

		VG	VF	UNC
140	**200 PESOS** ND. Green on pink and lt. blue unpt. Pres. Manuel Quezon at l. Back green; Legislative bldg. Sign. E. Quirino and M. Cuaderno.	5.00	17.50	40.00

		VG	VF	UNC
141	**500 PESOS** ND. Black on purple and lt. tan unpt. Pres. Manuel Roxas at l. Back purple; Central Bank. Sign. E. Quirino and M. Cuaderno.	10.00	40.00	95.00

BANGKO SENTRAL NG PILIPINAS

1969 ND "PILIPINO" ISSUE

#142-147 heading at top in double outline. Replacement notes: Serial # prefix "+".

		VG	VF	UNC
142	**1 PISO** ND (1969). Blue and black on m/c unpt. J. Rizal at l. and as wmk. Scene of Aguinaldo's Independence Declaration of June 12, 1898 on back.			
	a. Sign. F. Marcos and A. Calalang.	.20	.60	1.75
	b. Sign. F. Marcos and A. Licaros.	.15	.50	1.25
	s. Sign. as b. Specimen.	—	—	45.00

#143-145 printer: G&D (w/o imprint).

		VG	VF	UNC
143	**5 PISO** ND (1969). Green and brown on m/c unpt. A. Bonifacio at l. in brown and as wmk. Scene of the Katipunan organization on back.			
	a. Sign. F. Marcos and A. Calalang.	.50	1.50	4.50
	b. Sign. F. Marcos and G. Licaros.	.20	1.00	3.50
	s. Sign. as b. Specimen.	—	—	25.00

		VG	VF	UNC
144	**10 PISO** ND (1969). Brown on m/c unpt. A. Mabini at l. and as wmk. Barasoain Church on back.			
	a. Sign. F. Marcos and A. Calalang.	.50	1.50	5.00
	b. Sign. F. Marcos and G. Licaros.	.50	1.50	4.00
	s1. Sign. as a. Specimen.	—	—	125.00
	s2. Sign. as b. Specimen.	—	—	20.00

		VG	VF	UNC
145	**20 PISO** ND (1969). Orange and brown on m/c unpt. M. L. Quezon at l. in brown and as wmk. Malakanyang Palace on back.			
	a. Sign. F. Marcos and A. Calalang.	.75	2.00	5.00
	b. Sign. F. Marcos and G. Licaros.	.75	2.00	5.00
	s1. Sign. as a. Specimen.	—	—	125.00
	s2. Sign. as b. Specimen.	—	—	25.00

		VG	VF	UNC
146	**50 PISO** ND (1969). Red on m/c unpt. S. Osmeña at l. and as wmk. Legislative bldg. on back.			
	a. Sign. F. Marcos and A. Calalang.	1.00	3.00	7.50
	b. Sign. F. Marcos and G. Licaros.	1.00	3.00	7.50
	s1. Sign. as a. Specimen. De La Rue.	—	—	400.00
	s2. Sign. as b. Specimen.	—	—	30.00

147	100 PISO	VG	VF	UNC
	ND (1969). Purple on m/c unpt. M. Roxas at l. and as wmk. Old Central Bank on back.			
	a. Sign. F. Marcos and A. Calalang.	3.00	9.00	22.50
	b. Sign. F. Marcos and G. Licaros.	2.50	7.50	20.00

1970'S ND FIRST ISSUE

#148-151 heading at top in single outline. Sign. F. Marcos and G. Licaros. Replacement notes: Serial # prefix "+".

148	5 PISO	VG	VF	UNC
	ND. Green on m/c unpt. Like #143 but A. Bonifacio in green.			
	a. Issued note.	.25	.75	2.00
	s. Specimen.	—	—	20.00
149	10 PISO			
	ND. Brown on m/c unpt. Like #144 but w/o white paper showing at sides on face or back.			
	a. Issued note.	.50	2.00	7.50
	s. Specimen.	—	—	40.00

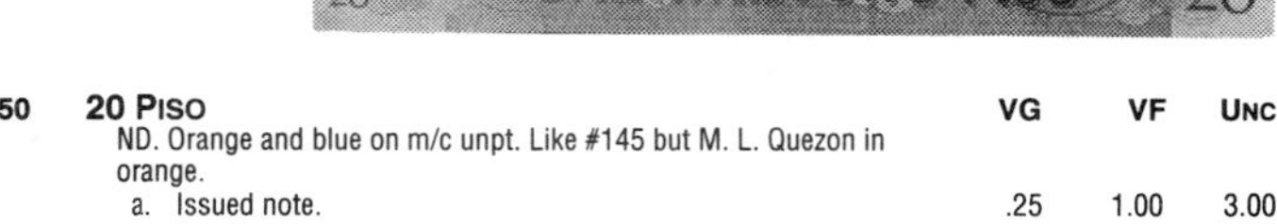

150	20 PISO	VG	VF	UNC
	ND. Orange and blue on m/c unpt. Like #145 but M. L. Quezon in orange.			
	a. Issued note.	.25	1.00	3.00
	s. Specimen.	—	—	45.00

151	50 PISO	VG	VF	UNC
	ND. Red on m/c unpt. Similar to #146. Seal under denomination instead of over, sign. closer, *LIMAMPUNG PISO* in one line, and other modifications.			
	a. Issued note.	1.50	5.00	10.00
	s. Specimen.	—	—	60.00

1970'S ND SECOND ISSUE

#152-158 light, fully detailed bank seal. Ovpt: *ANG BAGONG LIPUNAN* (New Society) on wmk. area, 1974-85. Replacement notes: Serial # prefix "+".

#152-156, 158 sign. F. Marcos and G. Licaros.

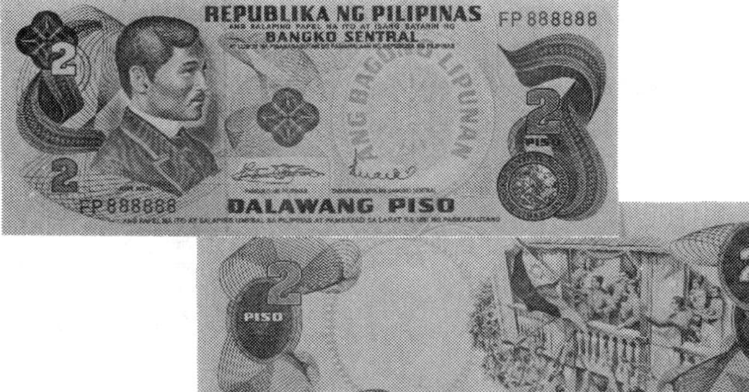

152	2 PISO	VG	VF	UNC
	ND. Blue on m/c unpt. J. Rizal at l. and as wmk. Scene of Aguinaldo's Independence Declaration of June 12, 1898 on back.			
	a. Issued note.	.20	.40	1.25
	s1. Specimen.	—	—	12.00
	s2. Specimen. De La Rue.	—	—	225.00

153	5 PISO	VG	VF	UNC
	ND. Green on m/c unpt. Like #148.			
	a. Dark ovpt.	.30	.80	3.00
	b. Light ovpt.	.30	.80	3.00
	s1. Specimen.	—	—	20.00
	s2. Specimen. De La Rue.	—	—	225.00
154	10 PISO			
	ND. Brown on m/c unpt. Like #149.			
	a. Issued note.	.30	.75	2.00
	s1. Specimen.	—	—	25.00
	s2. Specimen. De La Rue.	—	—	225.00
155	20 PISO			
	ND. Orange on m/c unpt. Like #150.			
	a. Issued note.	.75	2.00	5.00
	s1. Specimen.	—	—	35.00
	s2. Specimen. De La Rue.	—	—	225.00
156	50 PISO			
	ND. Red on m/c unpt. Like #151.			
	a. Brown sign. title.	3.00	5.00	15.00
	b. Red sign. title.	3.00	10.00	30.00
	s. Sign. as b. Specimen.	—	—	45.00

157	100 PISO	VG	VF	UNC
	ND. Purple on m/c unpt. Like #147. Bank seal in purple at l.			
	a. Sign. F. Marcos and A. Calalang.	5.00	20.00	50.00
	b. Sign. F. Marcos and G. Licaros.	1.50	3.00	15.00
	s1. Sign. as a. Specimen.	—	—	200.00
	s2. Sign. as b. Specimen.	—	—	65.00

158	100 Piso	VG	VF	Unc
	ND. Purple on m/c unpt. Face resembling #157 but heading at top solid letters, green bank seal at lower r., and denomination near upper r. Back similar to #157 but denomination at bottom.			
	a. Issued note.	10.00	35.00	100.00
	s. Specimen.	—	—	175.00

1978 ND Issue

#159-167 w/dk. silhouette bank seal. Replacement notes: Serial # prefix "+".

159	2 Piso	VG	VF	Unc
	ND. Blue on m/c unpt. Like #152.			
	a. Sign. F. Marcos and G. Licaros.	.10	.30	2.00
	b. Sign. F. Marcos and J. Laya. Black serial #.	.10	.30	1.50
	c. Sign. F. Marcos and J. Laya. Red serial #.	.10	.30	1.50
	d. Sign. as b. Uncut sheet of 4.	—	—	15.00
	s. Sign. as b. Specimen.	—	—	15.00

160	5 Piso	VG	VF	Unc
	ND. Green on m/c unpt. Like #153.			
	a. Sign. F. Marcos and G. Licaros.	.15	.50	2.50
	b. Sign. F. Marcos and J. Laya. Black serial #.	.15	1.50	5.00
	c. Sign. F. Marcos and J. Laya. Red serial #.	.15	.40	3.00
	d. Sign. F. Marcos and J. Fernandez.	.15	.40	1.50
	e. Sign. as b. Uncut sheet of 4.	—	—	30.00
	f. Sign. as d. Uncut sheet of 4.	—	—	30.00
	s. Sign. as b. Specimen.	—	—	20.00

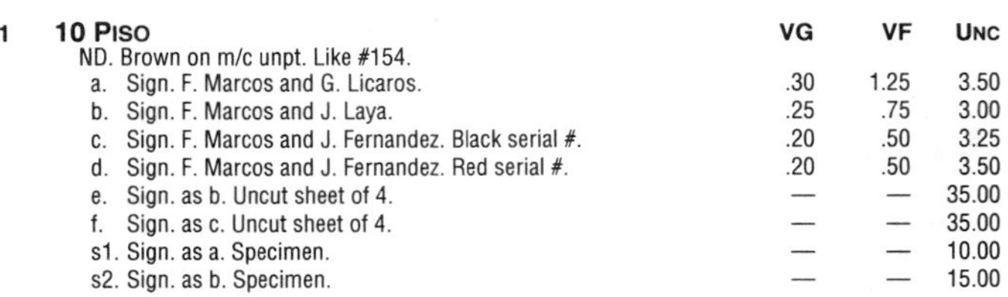

161	10 Piso	VG	VF	Unc
	ND. Brown on m/c unpt. Like #154.			
	a. Sign. F. Marcos and G. Licaros.	.30	1.25	3.50
	b. Sign. F. Marcos and J. Laya.	.25	.75	3.00
	c. Sign. F. Marcos and J. Fernandez. Black serial #.	.20	.50	3.25
	d. Sign. F. Marcos and J. Fernandez. Red serial #.	.20	.50	3.50
	e. Sign. as b. Uncut sheet of 4.	—	—	35.00
	f. Sign. as c. Uncut sheet of 4.	—	—	35.00
	s1. Sign. as a. Specimen.	—	—	10.00
	s2. Sign. as b. Specimen.	—	—	15.00

162	20 Piso	VG	VF	Unc
	ND. Orange and blue on m/c unpt. Like #155.			
	a. Sign. F. Marcos and G. Licaros.	.30	1.50	4.00
	b. Sign. F. Marcos and J. Laya.	.30	1.25	4.00
	c. Sign. F. Marcos and J. Fernandez.	.30	1.00	3.00
	d. Sign. as b. Uncut sheet of 4.	—	—	40.00
	e. Sign. as d. Uncut sheet of 4.	—	—	40.00
	s1. Sign. as a. Specimen.	—	—	25.00
	s2. Sign. as b. Specimen.	—	—	30.00

163	50 Piso	VG	VF	Unc
	ND. Red on m/c unpt. Like #156.			
	a. Sign. F. Marcos and G. Licaros.	.50	2.00	10.00
	b. Sign. F. Marcos and J. Laya.	.50	2.00	6.00
	c. Sign. F. Marcos and J. Fernandez.	.50	1.50	6.00
	s. Sign. as b. Specimen.	—	—	35.00

164	100 PISO	VG	VF	UNC
	ND. Purple and deep olive-green on m/c unpt. Face like #158. New Central Bank complex w/ships behind on back.			
	a. Sign. F. Marcos and G. Licaros.	2.00	6.00	15.00
	b. Sign. F. Marcos and J. Laya.	1.50	5.00	10.00
	c. Sign. F. Marcos and J. Fernandez. Black serial #.	.80	2.50	7.50
	s. Sign. as b. Specimen.	—	—	40.00

1978 COMMEMORATIVE ISSUE

#165, Centennial - Birth of Pres. Osmeña, 1978

165	50 PISO	VG	VF	UNC
	1978. Black circular commemorative ovpt. at l. on #163a.	2.00	5.00	15.00

1981 COMMEMORATIVE ISSUES

#166, Papal Visit of John Paul II, 1981

166	2 PISO	VG	VF	UNC
	1981. Black commemorative ovpt. at ctr. r. on #159b.			
	a. Regular prefix letters before serial #.	.10	.35	1.75
	b. Special prefix letters *JP* and all zero numbers (presentation).	—	—	—

NOTICE

Readers with unlisted dates, signature varieties, etc. are invited to submit photocopies of their notes to: Standard Catalog of World Paper Money, 700 East State St. Iola, WI 54990-0001, fax: 1-715-445-4087, or E-Mail: thernr@krause.com.

#167, Inauguration of Pres. Marcos, 1981

167	10 PISO	VG	VF	UNC
	1981. Black commemorative ovpt. at ctr. r. on #161b.			
	a. Regular prefix letters before serial #. Wide and narrow collar varieties.	.25	.75	3.50
	b. Special prefix letters *FM* and all zero numbers (presentation).	—	—	15.00
	s. As a. Specimen. Wide or narrow collar.	—	—	50.00

1985-91 ND ISSUE

#168-173 replacement notes: Serial # prefix "+".

168	5 PISO	VG	VF	UNC
	ND (1985-94). Deep green and brown on m/c unpt. Aguinaldo at l. ctr. and as wmk., plaque w/cannon at r. Aguinaldo's Independence Declaration of June 12, 1898 on back.			
	a. Sign. F. Marcos and J. Fernandez. Black serial #.	FV	.65	2.00
	b. Sign. C. Aquino and J. Fernandez. Black serial #.	FV	FV	1.50
	c. Sign. as b. Red serial # (1990).	FV	FV	1.00
	d. Sign. C. Aquino and J. Cuisia Jr. Red serial #.	FV	FV	1.00
	e. Sign. M. Ramos and J. Cuisia Jr. Red serial #.	FV	FV	.75
	f. Sign. as b. Uncut sheet of 4.	—	—	30.00
	g. Sign. as d. Uncut sheet of 4.	—	—	30.00
	h. Sign. as e. Uncut sheet of 4.	—	—	15.00
	s1. Sign. as b. Specimen.	—	—	15.00
	s2. Sign. as c. Specimen.	—	—	15.00
	s3. Sign. as d. Specimen.	—	—	20.00

169	10 PISO	VG	VF	UNC
	ND (1985-94). Dk. brown, brown and blue-gray on m/c unpt. Mabini at l. ctr. and as wmk., handwritten scroll at r. Barasoain church on back.			
	a. Sign. F. Marcos and J. Fernandez.	FV	1.00	4.00
	b. Sign. C. Aquino and J. Fernandez.	FV	FV	1.75
	c. Sign. C. Aquino and J. Cuisia Jr. Black serial #.	FV	FV	2.00
	d. Sign. as c. Red serial #.	FV	FV	2.50
	e. Sign. M. Ramos and J. Cuisia Jr.	—	—	2.50
	f. Sign. as b. Uncut sheet of 4.	—	—	38.50
	g. Sign. as b. Uncut sheet of 32.	—	—	—
	s. Sign. as b. Specimen.	—	—	25.00

		VG	VF	UNC
170	**20 PISO**			
	ND (1986-94). Orange and blue on m/c unpt. Pres. M. Quezon at l. ctr. and as wmk., arms at r. Malakanyang Palace on back.			
	a. Sign. F. Marcos and J. Fernandez. Black serial #.	FV	2.00	8.00
	b. Sign. C. Aquino and J. Fernandez. Black serial #.	FV	1.00	4.00
	c. Sign. C. Aquino and J. Cuisia Jr. Black serial #.	FV	FV	3.00
	d. Sign. as c. Red serial #.	FV	1.00	5.00
	e. Sign. M. Ramos and J. Cuisia Jr. Red serial #.	FV	FV	1.35
	f. Sign. M. Ramos and J. Cuisia Jr. Black serial #.	—	2.00	8.00
	g. Sign. as b. Uncut sheet of 4.	—	—	45.00
	s. Sign. as b. Specimen.	—	—	35.00

		VG	VF	UNC
171	**50 PISO**			
	ND (1987-94). Red and purple on m/c unpt. Pres. S. Osmeña at l. ctr. and as wmk., gavel at r. Legislative bldg. on back.			
	a. Sign. C. Aquino and J. Fernandez. Black serial #.	FV	1.00	5.00
	b. Sign. C. Aquino and J. Cuisia Jr. Black serial #.	FV	1.00	4.50
	c. Sign. M. Ramos and J. Cuisia Jr. Black serial #.	FV	FV	4.00
	s1. Sign. as a. Specimen.	—	—	75.00
	s2. Sign. as b. Specimen.	—	—	65.00
	s3. Sign. as b. Uncut sheet of 4. Specimen.	—	—	30.00
	s4. Sign. as c. Specimen.	—	—	65.00

		VG	VF	UNC
172	**100 PISO**			
	ND (1987-94). Purple on m/c unpt. Pres. M. Roxas at l. ctr. and as wmk. USA and Philippine flags at r. New Central Bank complex at l. ctr. w/old bldg. facade above on back.			
	a. Sign. C. Aquino and J. Fernandez.	FV	FV	9.00
	b. Sign. C. Aquino and J. Cuisia Jr. Black serial #.	FV	FV	9.00
	c. Sign. as b. Red serial #.	FV	FV	10.00
	d. Sign. M. Ramos and J. Cuisia Jr. Red serial #.	FV	FV	5.00
	e. Sign. as d. Blue serial #.	FV	FV	10.00
	s1. Sign. as a. Specimen.	—	—	15.00
	s2. Sign. as b. Specimen.	—	—	13.50
	s3. Sign. as c. Specimen.	—	—	15.00
	s4. Sign. as d. Specimen.	—	—	70.00
	s5. Sign. as d. Specimen. Uncut sheet of 4.	—	—	25.00
	s6. Sign. as b. Specimen. Uncut sheet of 4.	—	—	75.00
	s7. Sign. as b. Specimen. Uncut sheet of 32.	—	—	200.00
	s8. Sign. as e. Specimen. Blue serial #.	—	—	75.00

		VG	VF	UNC
173	**500 PISO**			
	ND (1987-94). Black and brown on m/c unpt. Aquino at l. ctr. and as wmk., flag in unpt. at ctr., typewriter at lower r. Various scenes and gatherings of Aquino's career on back.			
	a. Sign. C. Aquino and J. Fernandez.	FV	FV	45.00
	b. Sign. C. Aquino and J. Cuisia Jr.	FV	FV	40.00
	c. Sign. M. Ramos and J. Cuisia Jr.	FV	FV	30.00
	s1. Sign. as a. Specimen.	—	—	90.00
	s2. Sign. as b. Specimen.	—	—	80.00
	s3. Sign. as b. Specimen. Uncut sheet of 4.	—	—	90.00
174	**1000 PISO**			
	ND (1991-94). Dk. blue and blue-black on m/c unpt. J. A. Santos, J. L. Escoda and V. Lim at l. ctr. and as wmk., flaming torch at r. Banawe rice terraces at l. to ctr., local carving and hut at ctr. r. on back.			
	a. Sign. C. Aquino and J. Cuisia Jr.	FV	FV	85.00
	b. Sign. M. Ramos and J. Cuisia Jr.	FV	FV	60.00

1986-91 COMMEMORATIVE ISSUES

Commemorative ovpt. not listed were produced privately in the Philippines.

#175, Visit of Pres. Aquino to the United States

		VG	VF	UNC
175	**5 PISO**			
	1986. Deep green and brown on on m/c unpt. Like #168 but w/commemorative text, seal and visit dates on wmk. area. Prefix letters CA. Sign. C. Aquino and J. Cuisia Jr.			
	a. Serial #1-20,000 in special folder.	FV	FV	9.00
	b. Serial # above 20,000.	FV	FV	1.00
	c. Uncut sheet of 4.	—	—	30.00

#176, Canonization of San Lorenzo Ruiz

		VG	VF	UNC
176	**5 PISO**			
	18.10.1987. Deep green and brown on m/c unpt. Like #168 but w/commemorative design, text and date on wmk. area.			
	a. Issued note.	FV	FV	3.00
	b. Uncut sheet of 8 in special folder.	—	—	20.00

#177, 40th Anniversary of Central Bank

		VG	VF	UNC
177	**5 PISO** 1989. Deep green and brown on m/c unpt. Like #168 but w/red commemorative design, text and date on wmk. area.			
	a. Issued note.	FV	FV	1.25
	b. Uncut sheet of 8 in special folder.	—	—	20.00

#178, Women's Rights, 1990

		VG	VF	UNC
178	**5 PISO** 1990. Deep green and brown on m/c unpt. Like #168 but w/black commemorative design on wmk. area.	FV	FV	1.00

#179, II Plenary Council, 1991

		VG	VF	UNC
179	**5 PISO** 1991. Deep green and brown on m/c unpt. Like #168 but w/black commemorative design and date on wmk. area.	FV	FV	2.00

1995 ND; 1998-99 ISSUE

#180-186 like #168-174 but w/redesigned Central Bank seal w/date 1993 at r.

#180 and 181 sign. M. Ramos and G. Singson.

		VG	VF	UNC
180	**5 PISO** ND (1995). Deep green and brown on m/c unpt.	FV	FV	1.50
181	**10 PISO** ND (1995-97). Dk. brown and blue-gray on m/c unpt.			
	a. Red serial #.	FV	FV	2.00
	b. Sign. as a. Black serial #.	FV	FV	2.50

		VG	VF	UNC
182	**20 PISO** ND (1995-97); 1998; 1999. Orange and blue on m/c unpt.			
	a. Sign. M. Ramos and G. Singson. Red serial #. ND.	FV	FV	3.00
	b. Sign. as a. Black serial #.	FV	FV	3.00
	c. Sign. J. E. Estrada and G. C. Singson. 1998; 1999.	FV	FV	3.00
	s1. Specimen. Sign. as a.	—	—	80.00
	s2. Specimen. Uncut sheet of 4.	FV	FV	100.00

		VG	VF	UNC
183	**50 PISO** ND (1995-). Red and purple on m/c unpt.			
	a. Issued note.	FV	FV	5.00
	b. Red serial #. 1998.	FV	FV	8.00

		VG	VF	UNC
184	**100 PISO** ND (1995-97); 1998. Purple on m/c unpt.			
	a. Sign. M. Ramos and G. Singson. ND; 1998.	FV	FV	10.00
	b. Sign. J. E. Estrada and G. C. Singson. 1998.	FV	FV	7.00
	s. As a. Specimen.	—	—	25.00

		VG	VF	UNC
185	**500 PISO** ND (1995); 1998. Black on m/c unpt.			
	a. Sign. M. Ramos and G. Singson. ND.	FV	FV	35.00
	b. Sign. J. E. Estrada and G. C. Singson. 1998.	FV	FV	35.00
	s. As a. Specimen.	—	—	75.00

		VG	VF	UNC
186	**1000 Piso**			
	ND (1995); 1998. Dk. blue on m/c unpt.			
	a. Sign. M. Ramos and G. Singson. ND; 1998.	FV	FV	47.50
	b. Sign. J. E. Estrada and G. C. Singson. 1998.	FV	FV	40.00
	s. As a. Specimen.	—	—	85.00

1997 Issue

		VG	VF	UNC
187	**10 Piso**			
	1997; 1998. Dk. brown and blue-gray on m/c unpt. A. Mabini and A. Bonifacio at l. ctr.; flag, book, declaration and quill pen at r. Wmk: A. Mabini. Barasoain church at l., blood "Pacto de Sangre" meeting at lower r. on back.			
	a. 1997.	FV	FV	3.00
	b. Single figure wmk. 1998.	FV	FV	3.00
	c. Double figures wmk. 1998.	FV	FV	4.00

1998 Commemorative Issue

#188-190, Centennial of First Republic, 1898-1998

		VG	VF	UNC
188	**100 Piso**			
	1998 (1997). Purple on m/c unpt. Like #184 but w/centennial design and inscription in rectangular frame at l. on wmk. area.			
	a. ND.	FV	FV	10.00
	b. 1998 in upper l.	FV	FV	10.00

NOTICE

Readers with unlisted dates, signature varieties, etc. are invited to submit photocopies of their notes to: Standard Catalog of World Paper Money, 700 East State St. Iola, WI 54990-0001, fax: 1-715-445-4087, or E-Mail: thernr@krause.com.

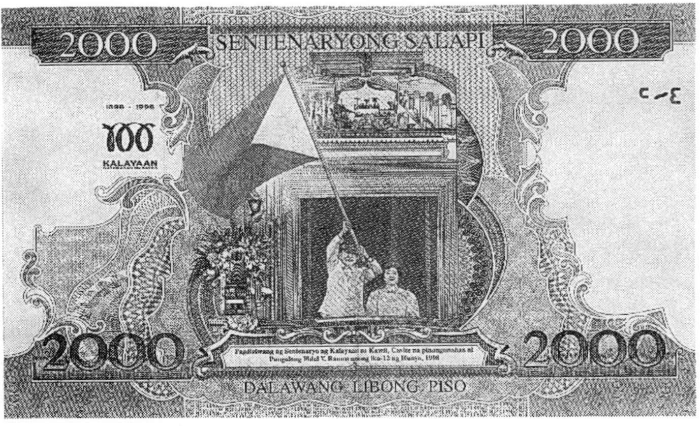

		VG	VF	UNC
189	**2000 Piso**			
	1998. M/c. Pres. J. E. Estrada taking his oath of office on June 30, 1998 in the Barasoain Church at ctr. Re-enactment of the declaration of Philippine Independence at the Aguinaldo Shrine in Kawif, Cavite on June 12, 1998 by Pres. F. V. Ramos at ctr. on back. Wmk: Estrada and Ramos. 216 x 133mm, issued in folder.	—	—	175.00
190	**100,000 Piso**			
	1998. Green, yellow and brown. Pres. F. V. Ramos.	—	—	—

NOTE: #190 issued at twice face value, then lowered to $800.00. (1,000 pcs.).

1999 Commemorative Issue

#191, 50th Anniversary Bangko Sentral

		VG	VF	UNC
191	**50 Piso**			
	1999. Red and purple on m/c unpt. Ovpt. on #183.	FV	FV	9.00

Collector Series

Bangko Sentral ng Pilipinas

1978 ND Issue

		Issue Price	Mkt. Value
CS1	**1978 ND 2-100 Piso**		
	#159a-164a ovpt: *SPECIMEN* and w/serial # prefix Maltese cross.	14.00	60.00

The Republic of Poland, formerly the Polish Peoples Republic, located in central Europe, has an area of 120,725 sq. mi. (312,677 sq. km.) and a population of 38.6 million. Capital: Warsaw. The economy is essentially agricultural, but industrial activity provides the products for foreign trade. Machinery, coal, coke, iron, steel and transport equipment are exported.

Poland, which began as a Slavic duchy in the 10th century and reached its peak of power between the 14th and 16th centuries, has had a turbulent history of invasion, occupation or partition by Mongols, Turkey, Hungary, Sweden, Austria, Prussia and Russia.

The first partition took place in 1772. Prussia took Polish Pomerania. Russia took part of the eastern provinces. Austria took Galicia, in which lay the fortress city of Krakow (Cracow). The second partition occurred in 1793 when Russia took another slice of the eastern provinces and Prussia took what remained of western Poland. The third partition, 1795, literally removed Poland from the map. Russia took what was left of the eastern provinces. Prussia seized most of central Poland, including Warsaw. Austria took what was left of the south. Napoleon restored to Poland much of the territory lost to Prussia and Austria, but after his defeat another partition returned the Duchy of Warsaw to Prussia, made Kracow into a tiny republic, and declared what remained to be the Kingdom of Poland under the czar and in permanent union with Russia.

Poland re-emerged as an independent state recognized by the Treaty of Versailles on June 28, 1919, and maintained its independence until 1939 when it was invaded by Germany, then partitioned between Germany and Russia. Poland's present boundaries were determined by the U.S.-British-Russian agreement of Aug. 16, 1945. The Government of National Unity was replaced when the Polish Communist-Socialist faction won a decisive victory at the polls in 1947 and established a "People's Democratic Republic" of the Soviet type. In Dec. 1989, Poland became a republic once again.

MONETARY SYSTEM:

1 Zloty = 100 Groszy, 1919-

PEOPLES REPUBLIC

NARODOWY BANK POLSKI

POLISH NATIONAL BANK

1962; 1965 ISSUE

		VG	VF	UNC
140A	**20 ZLOTYCH** 2.1.1965. M/c. Man at r., arms at upper l. ctr. (Not issued).	—	—	—

		VG	VF	UNC
141	**1000 ZLOTYCH** 1962; 1965. Orange, red and green on m/c unpt. Copernicus at ctr. r. and as wmk., arms at upper r. Zodiac signs in ornate sphere at l. on back.			
	a. Issued note. 29.10.1965.	1.50	5.00	20.00
	s1. Specimen ovpt: *WZOR.* 24.5.1962. (Not issued).	—	—	225.00
	s2. Specimen ovpt: *WZOR* w/regular serial #. 29.10.1965.	—	—	25.00

1974-77 ISSUE

#142-146 eagle arms at lower ctr. or lower r. and as wmk. Sign. varieties.

		VG	VF	UNC
142	**50 ZLOTYCH** 1975-88. Olive-green on m/c unpt. K. Swierczewski at ctr. Order of Grunwald at l. on back.			
	a. 9.5.1975.	.50	2.00	10.00
	b. 1.6.1979; 1.6.1982.	.10	.30	2.75
	c. 1.6.1986; 1.12.1988.	.10	.20	.75
	s1. Specimen ovpt: *WZOR.* 1975; 1986; 1988.	—	—	8.50
	s2. Specimen ovpt: *WZOR.* 1979.	—	—	7.00
	s3. Specimen ovpt: *WZOR.* 1982.	—	—	11.50

		VG	VF	UNC
143	**100 ZLOTYCH** 1975-88. Brown on lilac and m/c unpt. L. Warynski at r. Old paper at l. on back.			
	a. 15.1.1975; 17.5.1976.	.50	2.00	10.00
	b. 1.6.1979; 1.6.1982.	.10	.30	3.00
	c. 1.6.1986; 1.12.1988.	.10	.20	.75
	s1. Specimen ovpt: *WZOR.* 1975; 1982.	—	—	8.50
	s2. Specimen ovpt: *WZOR.* 1976.	—	—	7.00
	s3. Specimen ovpt: *WZOR.* 1979.	—	—	11.50

		VG	VF	UNC
144	**200 ZLOTYCH** 1976-88. Purple on orange and m/c unpt. J. Dabrowski at r. standing woman at wall on back.			
	a. 25.5.1976.	.50	2.00	12.00
	b. 1.6.1979; 1.6.1982.	.10	.30	4.50
	c. 1.6.1986; 1.12.1988.	.10	.25	1.00
	s1. Specimen ovpt: *WZOR.* 1976; 1986.	—	—	8.50
	s2. Specimen ovpt: *WZOR.* 1979.	—	—	7.00
	s3. Specimen ovpt: *WZOR.* 1982.	—	—	11.50

145	500 ZLOTYCH	VG	VF	UNC
	1974-82. Brown on tan and m/c unpt. T. Kosciuszko at ctr. Arms and flag at l. ctr. on back.			
	a. 16.12.1974; 15.6.1976.	.75	2.25	13.50
	b. 1.6.1979.	.20	.65	7.00
	c. 1.6.1982.	.10	.25	1.00
	s1. Specimen ovpt: *WZOR*. 1974; 1976.	—	—	8.50
	s2. Specimen ovpt: *WZOR*. 1979.	—	—	7.00
	s3. Specimen ovpt: *WZOR*. 1982.	—	—	11.50

146	1000 ZLOTYCH	VG	VF	UNC
	1975-82. Blue on olive-green and m/c unpt. Copernicus at r. Atomic symbols on back.			
	a. 2.7.1975.	.75	2.25	17.50
	b. 1.6.1979.	.40	1.35	9.00
	c. 1.6.1982.	.15	.40	1.50
	s1. Specimen ovpt: *WZOR*. 1975; 1982.	—	—	11.50
	s2. Specimen ovpt: *WZOR*. 1979.	—	—	7.00

POLSKA RZECZPOSPOLITA LUDOWA

PEOPLES REPUBLIC OF POLAND

NARODOWY BANK POLSKI

POLISH NATIONAL BANK

1977 ISSUE

147	2000 ZLOTYCH	VG	VF	UNC
	1977-82. Dk. green and dk. brown on m/c unpt. Mieszko I at r., arms at lower ctr. and as wmk. B. Chrobry on back.			
	a. 1.5.1977.	.75	2.25	37.50
	b. 1.6.1979.	.30	1.00	13.50
	c. 1.6.1982.	.20	.60	3.00
	s1. Specimen ovpt: *WZOR*. 1977.	—	—	11.50
	s2. Specimen ovpt: *WZOR*. 1979.	—	—	7.00
	s3. Specimen ovpt: *WZOR*. 1982.	—	—	15.00

1982 ISSUE

#148-150 wmk: Arms.

148	10 ZLOTYCH	VG	VF	UNC
	1.6.1982. Blue and green on m/c unpt. J. Bem at l. ctr., arms at lower r. Large value on back.			
	a. Issued note.	.10	.25	.75
	s. Specimen ovpt: *WZOR*.	—	—	11.50

149	20 ZLOTYCH	VG	VF	UNC
	1.6.1982. Brown and purple on m/c unpt. R. Traugutt at l. ctr., arms at lower r. Large value on back.			
	a. Issued note.	.10	.25	.75
	s. Specimen ovpt: *WZOR*.	—	—	11.50

150	5000 ZLOTYCH	VG	VF	UNC
	1982-88. Black, purple and dk. green on m/c unpt. F. Chopin at r., arms at lower ctr. *Polonaise* music score at ctr. on back.			
	a. 1.6.1982.	.25	1.00	4.00
	b. 1.6.1986.	FV	.75	3.00
	c. 1.12.1988.	FV	FV	2.50
	s. Specimen ovpt: *WZOR*.	—	—	13.50

1987-90 ISSUE

#151-158 arms at lower ctr. or lower r. and as wmk.

		VG	VF	UNC
151	**10,000 ZLOTYCH** 1.2.1987; 1.12.1988. Black and red on green and m/c unpt. S. Wyspianski at l. ctr. Trees and city scene on back.			
	a. 1.2.1987.	.75	2.25	11.00
	b. 1.12.1988.	FV	.50	3.00
	s. Specimen ovpt: *WZOR.*	—	—	8.50

		VG	VF	UNC
152	**20,000 ZLOTYCH** 1.2.1989. Dk. brown on tan and gold unpt. M. Curie at r. Scientific instrument on back.			
	a. Issued note.	FV	1.35	4.25
	s. Specimen ovpt: *WZOR.*	—	—	7.00

		VG	VF	UNC
153	**50,000 ZLOTYCH** 1.12.1989. Dk. brown and greenish black on m/c unpt. S. Staszic at l. ctr. Staszic Palace in Warsaw on back.			
	a. Issued note.	FV	2.50	6.50
	s. Specimen ovpt: *WZOR.*	—	—	8.50

		VG	VF	UNC
154	**100,000 ZLOTYCH** 1.2.1990. Black and grayish purple on m/c unpt. S. Moniuszko at r. Warsaw Theatre at l. on back.			
	a. Issued note.	FV	5.50	10.00
	s. Specimen ovpt: *WZOR.*	—	—	11.50

		VG	VF	UNC
155	**200,000 ZLOTYCH** 1.12.1989. Dk. purple on red, tan and m/c unpt. Coin of Sigismund III at lower ctr., arms at r. Back purple on brown unpt.; Warsaw shield at l., view of Warsaw. Wmk: Geometric design repeated.			
	a. Issued note.	FV	11.00	30.00
	s. Specimen ovpt: *WZOR.*	—	—	15.00

RZECZPOSPOLITA POLSKA

REPUBLIC OF POLAND

NARODOWY BANK POLSKI

POLISH NATIONAL BANK

1990-92 ISSUE

		VG	VF	UNC
156	**500,000 ZLOTYCH** 20.4.1990. Dk. blue-green and black on m/c unpt. H. Sienkiewicz at l. ctr. Shield w/3 books, also 4 flags on back.			
	a. Issued note.	FV	25.00	67.50
	s. Specimen ovpt: *WZOR.*	—	—	37.50
157	**1,000,000 ZLOTYCH** 15.2.1991. Brown-violet, purple and red on m/c unpt. W. Reymont at r. Tree w/rural landscape in background on back.			
	a. Issued note.	FV	45.00	175.00
	s. Specimen ovpt: *WZOR.*	—	—	70.00

158	2,000,000 ZLOTYCH	VG	VF	UNC
	14.8.1992. Black and deep brown-violet on m/c unpt. I. Paderewski at l. ctr. Imperial eagle at l. on back.			
	a. Issued note, misspelling *KONSTYTUCYJY* on back. Series A.	—	—	250.00
	b. As a., but corrected spelling *KONSTYTUCYJNY* on back. Series B.	FV	90.00	200.00
	s. Specimen ovpt: *WZOR*.	—	—	135.00

1993 ISSUE

#159-163 similar to #153, 154, 156-158 but modified w/color in wmk. area, eagle w/crown at lower ctr. Wmk: Eagle's head.

159	50,000 ZLOTYCH	VG	VF	UNC
	16.11.1993. Dk. blue-green and black on m/c unpt. Similar to #153.			
	a. Issued note.	FV	3.00	6.50
	s. Specimen ovpt: *WZOR*.	—	—	8.50

160	100,000 ZLOTYCH	VG	VF	UNC
	16.11.1993. Black and grayish purple on m/c unpt. Similar to #154.			
	a. Issued note.	FV	5.00	9.00
	s. Specimen ovpt: *WZOR*.	—	—	11.50
161	500,000 ZLOTYCH			
	16.11.1993. Dk. blue-green and black on m/c unpt. Similar to #156.			
	a. Issued note.	FV	27.50	40.00
	s. Specimen ovpt: *WZOR*.	—	—	37.50

162	1,000,000 ZLOTYCH	VG	VF	UNC
	16.11.1993. Brown-violet, purple and red on m/c unpt. Similar to #157.			
	a. Issued note.	FV	47.50	100.00
	s. Specimen ovpt: *WZOR*.	—	—	70.00
163	2,000,000 ZLOTYCH			
	16.11.1993. Black and deep brown on m/c unpt. Similar to #158.			
	a. Issued note.	FV	95.00	200.00
	s. Specimen ovpt: *WZOR*.	—	—	135.00

1990 (1996) "CANCELLED" ISSUE

Currency Reform

1 "new" Zloty = 10,000 "old" Zlotych

#164-172 arms at l. and as wmk.

NOTE: #164-172 were printed in Germany (w/o imprint). Before their release, it was decided a more sophisticated issue of notes should be prepared and these notes were later ovpt: *NIEOBIEGOWY* (non-negotiable) in red and released to the public. Specimens also have been reported.

164	1 ZLOTY	VG	VF	UNC
	1.3.1990. Blue-gray and brown on m/c unpt. Bldg. in Gdynia at r. Sailing ship at l. on back.			
	a. Cancelled note.	—	—	3.00
	s. Specimen ovpt: *WZOR*.	—	—	35.00

165	2 ZLOTE	VG	VF	UNC
	1.3.1990. Dk. brown and brown on m/c unpt. Mining conveyor tower at Katowice at r. Battle of Upper Silesia (1921) monument at l. on back.			
	a. Cancelled note.	—	—	3.00
	s. Specimen ovpt: *WZOR*.	—	—	35.00

166 5 ZLOTYCH

1.3.1990. Deep green on m/c unpt. Bldg. in Zamosc at r. Order of Grunwald at l. on back.

	VG	VF	UNC
a. Cancelled note.	—	—	3.00
s. Specimen ovpt: *WZOR*.	—	—	35.00

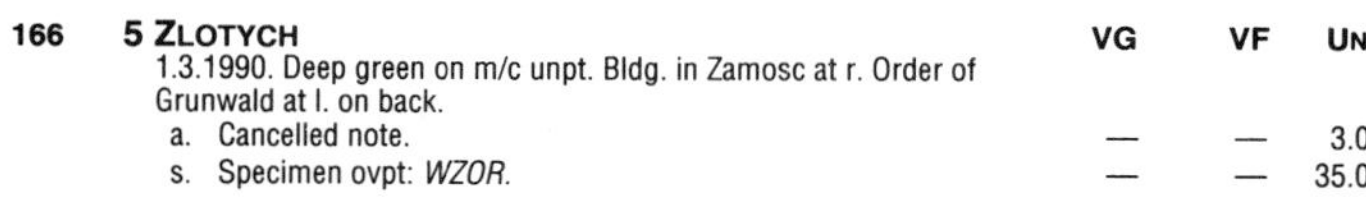

167 10 ZLOTYCH

1.3.1990. Red and purple on m/c unpt. Bldg. in Warsaw at r. Statue of Warszawa at l. on back.

	VG	VF	UNC
a. Cancelled note.	—	—	3.00
s. Specimen ovpt: *WZOR*.	—	—	35.00

168 20 ZLOTYCH

1.3.1990. Brownish black and deep violet on m/c unpt. Grain storage facility in Gdansk at r. Male statue at l. on back.

	VG	VF	UNC
a. Cancelled note.	—	—	3.00
s. Specimen ovpt: *WZOR*.	—	—	35.00

169 50 ZLOTYCH

1.3.1990. Purple on lilac and m/c unpt. Church in Wroclaw at r. Medallion at l. on back.

	VG	VF	UNC
a. Cancelled note.	—	—	3.00
s. Specimen ovpt: *WZOR*.	—	—	35.00

NOTICE

Readers with unlisted dates, signature varieties, etc. are invited to submit photocopies of their notes to: Standard Catalog of World Paper Money, 700 East State St. Iola, WI 54990-0001, fax: 1-715-445-4087, or E-Mail: thernr@krause.com.

170 100 ZLOTYCH

1.3.1990. Dk. brown and black on orange and m/c unpt. Bldg. in Poznan at r. Medieval seal at l. on back.

	VG	VF	UNC
a. Cancelled note.	—	—	3.00
s. Specimen ovpt: *WZOR*.	—	—	35.00

171 200 ZLOTYCH

1.3.1990. Black and deep purple on m/c unpt. Bldgs. in Krakow at r. Medieval coin at l. on back.

	VG	VF	UNC
a. Cancelled note.	—	—	3.00
s. Specimen ovpt: *WZOR*.	—	—	35.00

172 500 ZLOTYCH

1.3.1990. Black on green and m/c unpt. Church in Gniezno at r. Medieval seal at l. on back.

	VG	VF	UNC
a. Cancelled note.	—	—	3.00
s. Specimen ovpt: *WZOR*.	—	—	35.00

1994 (1995) REGULAR ISSUE

#173-177 replacement notes: Serial # prefix *ZA*.

#173-175 arms at upper l. ctr.

173 10 ZLOTYCH

25.3.1994 (1995). Dk. brown, brown and olive-green on m/c unpt. Prince Mieszko I at ctr. r. Medieval denar of Mieszko I at l. ctr. on back.

	VG	VF	UNC
a. Issued note.	FV	FV	6.50
s. Specimen ovpt: *WZOR*.	—	—	7.50

		VG	VF	UNC
174	**20 Zlotych** 25.3.1994 (1995). Purple and deep blue on m/c unpt. Kg. Boleslaw Chroby I at ctr. r. Medieval denar of Boleslaw II at l. ctr. on back.			
	a. Issued note.	FV	FV	10.00
	s. Specimen ovpt: *WZOR.*	—	—	13.50

		VG	VF	UNC
175	**50 Zlotych** 25.3.1994 (1995). Blue-violet and deep blue and green on m/c unpt. Kg. Kazimierz Wielki IIIat ctr. r. Eagle from seal, orb and sceptre at l. ctr., town views of Cracow and Kazimierz on back.			
	a. Issued note.	FV	FV	22.50
	s. Specimen ovpt.: *WZOR.*	—	—	35.00

		VG	VF	UNC
176	**100 Zlotych** 25.3.1994 (1995). Olive-green on m/c unpt. Wladyslaw Jagiello II. Arms and Teutonic Knights' castle in Malbork on back.			
	a. Issued note.	FV	FV	45.00
	s. Specimen ovpt: *WZOR.*	—	—	67.50

		VG	VF	UNC
177	**200 Zlotych** 25.3.1994. Brown on m/c unpt. Kg. Zygmunt I the old arms and eagle in hexagon from the Zygmunt's chapel in the Wawel Cathedral and Wawel's court on back.			
	a. Issued note.	FV	FV	85.00
	s. Specimen ovpt: *WZOR.*	—	—	130.00

Foreign Exchange Certificates

Pekao Trading Co. (P.K.O.)/Bank Polska

Bon Towarowy (Trade Voucher)

1969 Series

#FX21-FX33 serial # prefix *E; F; G.*

		VG	VF	UNC
FX21	**1 Cent** 1969. Black and blue on pale blue unpt. Back brown on pale blue unpt.	1.25	3.00	5.00

		VG	VF	UNC
FX22	**2 Cents** 1969. Black and green on orange and pink unpt. Back red on pink unpt.	1.25	3.00	5.00

		VG	VF	UNC
FX23	**5 Cents** 1969. Black on orange unpt. Back brown on orange unpt.	1.75	4.50	7.50

		VG	VF	UNC
FX24	**10 Cents** 1969. Blue and black on orange and yellow unpt. Back olive on yellow unpt.	2.50	6.00	10.00
FX25	**20 Cents** 1969.	3.50	9.00	15.00
FX26	**50 Cents** 1969.	4.00	10.00	17.50
FX27	**1 Dollar** 1969. Brown and green on lilac and violet unpt.	5.00	12.50	20.00
FX28	**2 Dollars** 1969.	9.00	15.00	25.00
FX29	**5 Dollars** 1969.	10.00	25.00	—
FX30	**10 Dollars** 1969.	13.50	35.00	—
FX31	**20 Dollars** 1969.	17.50	45.00	—
FX32	**50 Dollars** 1969.	35.00	85.00	—
FX33	**100 Dollars** 1969.	100.00	175.00	—

1979 Series

#FX34-FX46 serial # prefix *H; I*.

		VG	VF	UNC
FX34	**1 Cent** 1979.	.60	1.50	2.50

		VG	VF	UNC
FX35	**2 Cents** 1979. Brown on pink and tan unpt.	.75	1.75	3.00

		VG	VF	UNC
FX36	**5 Cents** 1979. Brown-violet on pale green and yellow unpt. Back lilac on lt. green unpt.	1.00	2.50	4.00

		VG	VF	UNC
FX37	**10 Cents** 1979. Deep green on pink and lilac unpt.	1.10	2.75	4.50

		VG	VF	UNC
FX38	**20 Cents** 1979.	1.20	3.00	5.00

		VG	VF	UNC
FX39	**50 Cents** 1979. Brown on orange and yellow unpt. Back red-brown on yellow unpt.	1.75	4.50	7.50
FX40	**1 Dollar** 1979. Olive-green on lt. blue and lilac unpt.	3.00	7.50	12.50
FX41	**2 Dollars** 1979.	5.00	12.00	20.00

		VG	VF	UNC
FX42	**5 Dollars** 1979.	5.50	14.00	35.00
FX43	**10 Dollars** 1979.	12.00	30.00	50.00
FX44	**20 Dollars** 1979.	18.50	47.50	80.00
FX45	**50 Dollars** 1979.	30.00	75.00	125.00
FX46	**100 Dollars** 1979.	50.00	125.00	200.00

Marynarski Bon Towarowy

Seamen's Trade Vouchers

1973 Series

#FX47-FX52 winged anchor w/knot at l.

		VG	VF	UNC
FX47	**1 Cent** 1.7.1973.	4.00	10.00	—
FX48	**2 Cents** 1.7.1973.	5.00	12.50	—
FX49	**5 Cents** 1.7.1973.	6.00	15.00	—
FX50	**10 Cents** 1.7.1973.	7.00	17.50	—
FX51	**20 Cents** 1.7.1973.	8.00	20.00	—
FX52	**50 Cents** 1.7.1973. Blue and green on green unpt. Anchor at l. Back black on green unpt.	12.00	30.00	—
FX53	**1 Dollar** 1.7.1973.	20.00	50.00	—
FX54	**2 Dollars** 1.7.1973.	32.50	80.00	—
FX55	**5 Dollars** 1.7.1973.	45.00	110.00	—

NOTE: Higher denominations may have been issued.

Collector Series

Narodowy Bank Polski

1948; 1965 Issue

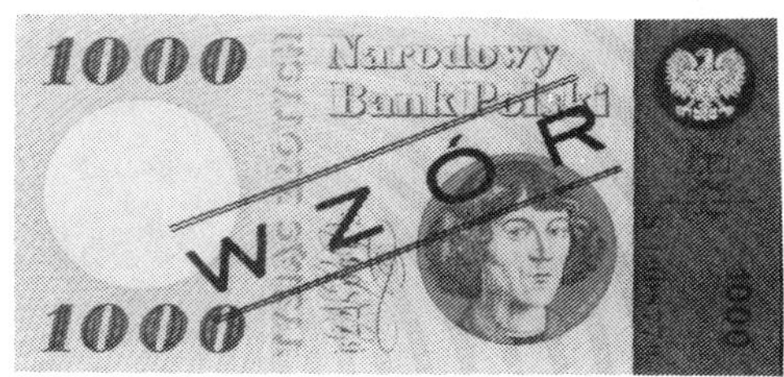

		Issue Price	Mkt. Value
CS1	**1948; 1965 20-1000 Zlotych** #137, 138, 139a, 140 and 141a w/deep red ovpt: *WZOR* on face; normal serial #.	—	75.00

1974 Issue

		Issue Price	Mkt. Value
CS2	**1974; 50 Grozy-500 Zlotych** #104b-118b.	12.50	15.00

1978 Issue

		Issue Price	Mkt. Value
CS3	**1978 20,100 Zlotych** #137, 139a w/dk. blue ovpt: *150 LAT BANKU POLSKIEGO 1828-1978* on face.	—	25.00

1979-92 Issue

		Issue Price	Mkt. Value
CS4	**1979-92; 20-2 Million Zlotych** #142-157a, 148a w/red ovpt: *WZOR* on face; all zero serial # and additional black specimen # w/star suffix. Red ovpt: *SPECIMEN* on back.	—	300.00

NOTE: Originally #CS4 was sold in a special booklet by Pekao Trading Company at its New York City, NY, and Warsaw offices. Currently available only from the Polish Numismatic Society.

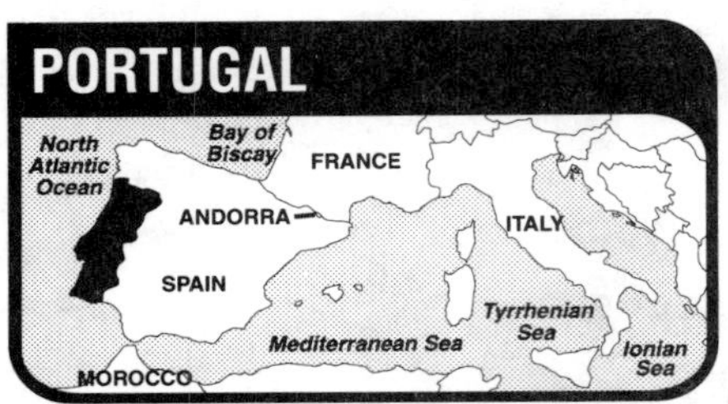

The Portuguese Republic, located in the western part of the Iberian Peninsula in southwestern Europe, has an area of 35,553 sq. mi. (92,080 sq. km.) and a population of 9.93 million. Capital: Lisbon. Portugal's economy is based on agriculture and a small but expanding industrial sector. Textiles, machinery, chemicals, wine and cork are exported.

After centuries of domination by Romans, Visigoths and Moors, Portugal emerged in the 12th century as an independent kingdom financially and philosophically prepared for the great period of exploration that would follow. Attuned to the inspiration of Prince Henry the Navigator (1394-1460), Portugal's daring explorers of the 14th and 15th centuries roamed the world's oceans from Brazil to Japan in an unprecedented burst of energy and endeavor that culminated in 1494 with Portugal laying claim to half the transoceanic world. Unfortunately for the fortunes of the tiny kingdom, the Portuguese proved to be inept colonizers. Less than a century after Portugal laid claim to half the world, English, French and Dutch trading companies had seized the lion's share of the world's colonies and commerce, and Portugal's place as an imperial power was lost forever. The monarchy was overthrown in 1910 and a republic established.

On April 25, 1974, the government of Portugal was seized by a military junta which reached agreements providing for independence for the Portuguese overseas provinces of Portuguese Guinea (Guinea-Bissau), Mozambique, Cape Verde Islands, Angola, and St. Thomas and Prince Islands (Sao Tome e Principe).

MONETARY SYSTEM

1 Escudo = 100 Centavos, 1910-

REPUBLIC

BANCO DE PORTUGAL

1960; 1961 ISSUE

		VG	VF	UNC
163	**20 ESCUDOS** 26.7.1960. Ch. 6A. Dk. green and purple on m/c unpt. Portr. of Dom Luiz de Menezes at r. and as wmk. Bank seal at l. on back. 8 sign. varieties.	2.50	7.50	30.00

		VG	VF	UNC
164	**50 ESCUDOS** 24.6.1960. Ch. 7A. Blue on m/c unpt. Arms at upper ctr. F. Pereira de Mello at r. and as wmk. Back dk. green and m/c; bank seal at l., statue "The Thinker" at ctr. 8 sign. varieties.	10.00	20.00	40.00

NOTICE

Readers with unlisted dates, signature varieties, etc. are invited to submit photocopies of their notes to: Standard Catalog of World Paper Money, 700 East State St. Iola, WI 54990-0001, fax: 1-715-445-4087, or E-Mail: thernr@krause.com.

		VG	VF	UNC
165	**100 ESCUDOS** 19.12.1961. Ch. 6A. Black and deep violet on pink and m/c unpt. P. Nunes at r. and as wmk., arms at upper ctr. Fountain and arches at l., bank seal at ctr. on back. 7 sign. varieties.	7.50	25.00	65.00

		VG	VF	UNC
166	**1000 ESCUDOS** 30.5.1961. Ch. 8A. Purple on m/c unpt. Qn. F. de Lancastre at r. and as wmk. Back blue. Printer: BWC (w/o imprint). 8 sign. varieties.	15.00	50.00	175.00

1964-66 ISSUE

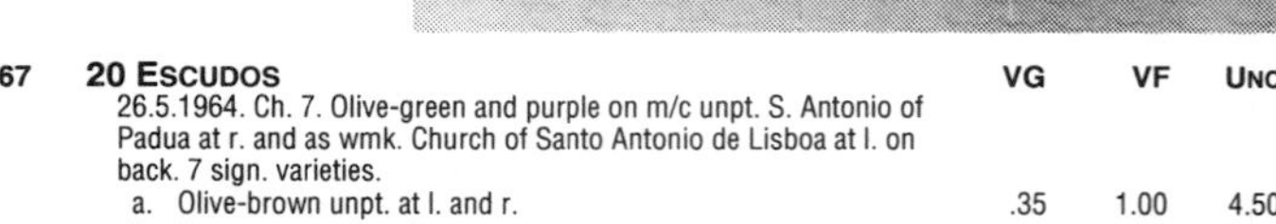

		VG	VF	UNC
167	**20 ESCUDOS** 26.5.1964. Ch. 7. Olive-green and purple on m/c unpt. S. Antonio of Padua at r. and as wmk. Church of Santo Antonio de Lisboa at l. on back. 7 sign. varieties.			
	a. Olive-brown unpt. at l. and r.	.35	1.00	4.50
	b. Green unpt. at l. and r.	.35	1.00	2.50

		VG	VF	UNC
168	**50 ESCUDOS** 28.2.1964. Ch. 8. Dk. brown on m/c unpt. Qn. Isabella at r. and as wmk. Old city Conimbria on back. 15 sign. varieties.	.50	1.50	4.50

		VG	VF	UNC
169	**100 ESCUDOS** 1965; 1978. Ch. 7. Blue on lt. tan and m/c unpt. C. Castello Branco at r. and as wmk. City of Porto in 19th century at l. on back.			
	a. 22 sign. varieties. 30.11.1965.	1.00	1.75	7.50
	b. 6 sign. varieties. 20.9.1978.	1.00	1.50	6.50

		VG	VF	UNC
170	**500 ESCUDOS** 1966; 1979. Ch. 10. Brown on m/c unpt. Old map at ctr., João II at r. and as wmk. Compass-card or Rhumb-card and double statue on back. Printer: JEZ (w/o imprint).			
	a. 7 sign. varieties. 25.1.1966.	5.00	10.00	25.00
	b. 9 sign. varieties. 6.9.1979.	4.00	7.50	17.50

		VG	VF	UNC
171	**1000 ESCUDOS** 2.4.1965. Ch. 9. Gray-blue on red-brown and m/c unpt. Pillar at l., arms at upper ctr., Dom Diniz at r. and as wmk. Scene of founding of University of Lisbon in 1290 on back. Printer: JEZ (w/o imprint). 7 sign. varieties.	110.00	200.00	500.00

1967 ISSUE

		VG	VF	UNC
172	**1000 ESCUDOS** 19.5.1967. Ch. 10. Blue and violet on m/c unpt. Flowers at l., Qn. Maria II at r. and as wmk. Her medallion portr. at l., Banco de Portugal in 1846 bldg. at lower r. on back. Printer: JEZ (w/o imprint). 24 sign. varieties.	8.00	15.00	37.50

1968; 1971 ISSUE

		VG	VF	UNC
173	**20 ESCUDOS** 27.7.1971. Ch. 8. Green (shades) on m/c unpt. G. de Orta at r. and as wmk. 16th century market in Goa on back. 15 sign. varieties.	FV	.75	2.50

		VG	VF	UNC
174	**50 ESCUDOS** 1968; 1980. Ch. 9. Dk. brown on m/c unpt. Arms at l., infante Dona Maria at r. and as wmk. Sintra in 1507 on back.			
	a. 7 sign. varieties. 28.5.1968.	FV	1.00	4.00
	b. 9 sign. varieties. 1.2.1980.	FV	1.00	3.75

		VG	VF	UNC
175	**1000 Escudos** 1968-82. Ch. 11. Blue on m/c unpt. Dom Pedro V at ctr. and as wmk. Conjoined busts at l., ceremonial opening of the first railway at bottom ctr. and r. on back. Printer: BWC (w/o imprint).			
	a. 24 sign. varieties. 28.5.1968.	FV	8.50	20.00
	b. 8 sign. varieties. 16.9.1980	FV	8.50	20.00
	c. 9 sign. varieties. 3.12.1981.	FV	8.00	20.00
	d. 9 sign. varieties. 21.9.1982.	10.00	15.00	40.00
	e. 11 sign. varieties. 26.10.1982.	FV	8.00	20.00

1978; 1979 Issue

		VG	VF	UNC
176	**20 Escudos** 1978. Ch. 9. Green (shades) on m/c unpt. Admiral Coutinho at r. and as wmk. Airplane on back. Lg. or sm. size numerals in serial #.			
	a. 6 sign. varieties. 13.9.1978.	FV	.50	2.25
	b. 6 sign. varieties. 4.10.1978.	FV	.50	2.00

		VG	VF	UNC
177	**500 Escudos** 4.10.1979 (1982). Ch. 11. Brown on m/c unpt. Old street layout of part of Braga at ctr., F. Sanches at r. and as wmk. 17th century street scene in Braga on back. Printer: JEZ (w/o imprint). 9 sign. varieties.	FV	5.00	15.00

NOTICE

Readers with unlisted dates, signature varieties, etc. are invited to submit photocopies of their notes to: Standard Catalog of World Paper Money, 700 East State St. Iola, WI 54990-0001, fax: 1-715-445-4087, or E-Mail: thernr@krause.com.

1980-89 Issues

		VG	VF	UNC
178	**100 Escudos** 1980-85. Ch. 8. Dk. blue on m/c unpt. Manuel M. B. du Bocage seated at r. and as wmk. Early 19th century scene of Rossio Square in Lisbon on back.			
	a. 8 sign. varieties. Darker imprint through ctr. 2.9.1980.	FV	1.35	5.00
	b. 8 sign. varieties. Light imprint through ctr. 24.2.1981.	FV	1.25	4.50
	c. 7 sign. varieties. 31.1.1984.	FV	1.25	4.50
	d. 6 sign. varieties. 12.3.1985.	FV	1.25	4.50
	e. 6 sign. varieties. 4.6.1985.	FV	1.25	4.50

		VG	VF	UNC
179	**100 Escudos** 1986-88. Ch. 9. Blue (shades) on m/c unpt. F. Pessoa at ctr. r. and as wmk. Rosebud on back.			
	a. 5 sign. varieties. 16.10.1986.	FV	1.00	4.50
	b. 8 sign. varieties. 12.2.1987.	FV	1.00	4.00
	c. Prefix letters *FIL*. 12.2.1987.	—	—	50.00
	d. 8 sign. varieties. 3.12.1987.	FV	1.00	3.75
	e. 6 sign. varieties. 26.5.1988.	FV	1.00	3.50
	f. 6 sign. varieties. 24.11.1988.	FV	1.00	3.50

NOTE: #179c was issued in a special folder w/an adhesive postage stamp affixed on the upper r. corner of the folder commemorating the 300th Anniversary of Portuguese Paper Money.

		VG	VF	UNC
180	**500 Escudos** 1987-94. Ch. 12. Brown and m/c. J. X. M. da Silveira at ctr. r. and as wmk., arms at upper l. Sheaf on back.			
	a. 8 sign. varieties. 20.11.1987.	FV	FV	10.00
	b. 6 sign. varieties. 4.8.1988.	FV	FV	9.00
	c. 6 sign. varieties. 4.10.1989.	FV	FV	8.50
	d. 5 sign. varieties. 13.2.1992.	FV	FV	8.00
	e. 7 sign. varieties. 18.3.1993.	FV	FV	7.50
	f. 6 sign. varieties. 4.11.1993.	FV	FV	7.00
	g. 5 sign. varieties. 29.4.1994.	FV	FV	6.50

181	1000 ESCUDOS	VG	VF	UNC
	1983-94. Ch. 12. Purple and dk. brown on m/c unpt. T. Braga at ctr. r. and as wmk. Museum artifacts on back.			
	a. 9 sign. varieties. 2.8.1983.	FV	FV	15.00
	b. 5 sign. varieties. 12.6.1986.	FV	FV	18.50
	c. 8 sign. varieties. 26.2.1987.	FV	FV	18.00
	d. 8 sign. varieties. 3.9.1987.	FV	FV	17.50
	e. 6 sign. varieties. 22.12.1988.	FV	FV	17.00
	f. 6 sign. varieties. 9.11.1989.	FV	FV	16.50
	g. 5 sign. varieties. 26.7.1990.	FV	FV	16.00
	h. 5 sign. varieties. 20.12.1990.	FV	FV	16.00
	i. 5 sign. varieties. 6.2.1992.	FV	FV	16.00
	j. 6 sign. varieties. 17.6.1993.	FV	FV	16.00
	k. 6 sign. varieties. 3.3.1994.	FV	FV	16.00
182	5000 ESCUDOS			
	1980-86. Ch. 1. Brown and m/c. A. Sergio at l. ctr. and as wmk. A. Sergio walking at ctr. on back. Printer: TDLR (w/o imprint).			
	a. 8 sign. varieties. 10.9.1980.	FV	40.00	80.00
	b. 8 sign. varieties. 27.1.1981.	FV	FV	77.50
	c. 10 sign. varieties. 24.5.1983.	FV	FV	75.00
	d. 6 sign. varieties. 4.6.1985.	FV	FV	72.50
	e. 6 sign. varieties. 7.1.1986.	FV	FV	70.00
183	5000 ESCUDOS			
	1987. Ch. 2. Olive-green and brown on m/c unpt. A. de Quental at ctr. r. and as wmk. Six hands w/rope and chain at ctr. on back.			
	a. 8 sign. varieties. 12.2.1987.	FV	FV	55.00
	b. 8 sign. varieties. 3.12.1987.	FV	FV	55.00

184	5000 ESCUDOS	VG	VF	UNC
	1988-93. Ch. 2A. Olive-green and brown on m/c unpt. Like #183.			
	a. 6 sign. varieties. 28.10.1988.	FV	FV	52.50
	b. 6 sign. varieties. 6.7.1989.	FV	FV	60.00
	c. 6 sign. varieties. 19.10.1989.	FV	FV	57.50
	d. 5 sign. varieties. 31.10.1991.	FV	FV	55.00
	e. 7 sign. varieties. 18.3.1993.	FV	FV	52.50
	f. 7 sign. varieties. 2.9.1993.	FV	FV	52.50
185	10,000 ESCUDOS			
	1989-91. Ch. 1. Orange, lt. brown and yellow. Dr. E. Moniz by human brain at ctr. and as wmk. Nobel Prize medal, snakes, tree at ctr. on back.			
	a. 6 sign. varieties. 12.1.1989.	FV	FV	100.00
	b. 6 sign. varieties. 14.12.1989.	FV	FV	97.50
	c. 5 sign. varieties. 16.5.1991.	FV	FV	95.00

1991 ISSUE

186	2000 ESCUDOS	VG	VF	UNC
	1991-93. Ch. 1. Dk. brown and blue on m/c unpt. B. Dias at l. and as wmk., astrolabe at ctr. Sailing ship at ctr., arms at r. on back.			
	a. 5 sign. varieties. 23.5.1991.	FV	FV	35.00
	b. 5 sign. varieties. 29.8.1991.	FV	FV	32.50
	c. 6 sign. varieties. 16.7.1992.	FV	FV	28.50
	d. 6 sign. varieties. 21.10.1993.	FV	FV	25.00

1995-97 ISSUE

NOTE: #187-191, Quincentenary of Portuguese Discoveries Series

187	500 ESCUDOS	VG	VF	UNC
	1997. Ch. 13. Violet and brown on m/c unpt. J. de Barros at r. and as wmk., crowned shields on global view at upper ctr., angels below at l. and r. in unpt. Allegory of the Portuguese Discoveries at l. ctr., illustrations from the "Grammer" at l. in unpt. on back.			
	a. 6 sign. varieties. 17.4.1997.	FV	FV	7.50
	b. 6 sign. varieties. 11.9.1997.	FV	FV	6.50

188	1000 ESCUDOS	VG	VF	UNC
	1996; 1998. Ch. 13. Purple and brown on m/c unpt. P. Alvares Cabral wearing helmet at r. and as wmk., Brazilian arms at ctr. Old sailing ship at ctr., birds and animals of Brazilian jungle in unpt. on back. Sign. varieties.			
	a. 6 sign. varieties. 18.4.1996.	FV	FV	15.00
	b. 6 sign. varieties. 31.10.1996.	FV	FV	13.50
	c. 6 sign. varieties. 12.3.1998.	FV	FV	11.50

		VG	VF	UNC
189	**2000 ESCUDOS** 1995-. Ch. 2. Blue-violet and deep blue-green on m/c unpt. B. Dias at r. and as wmk., cruzado coin of Dom João II at upper ctr., sailing instrument below. Old sailing ship at ctr. r., compass, map at l. ctr. on back.			
	a. 5 sign. varieties. 21.9.1995.	FV	FV	27.50
	b. 6 sign. varieties. 1.2.1996.	FV	FV	22.50
	c. 31.7.1997.	—	—	—

		VG	VF	UNC
190	**5000 ESCUDOS** 1995-. Ch. 3. Deep olive-green and brown-violet on unpt. V. da Gama at r. and as wmk., medallion at upper ctr. Old sailing ship at ctr. r., V. da Gama w/kg. and court at l. on back.			
	a. 5 sign. varieties. 5.1.1995.	FV	FV	67.50
	b. 6 sign. varieties. 12.9.1996.	FV	FV	65.00
	c. 6 sign. varieties. 20.2.1997.	FV	FV	65.00
	d. 6 sign. varieties. 11.9.1997.	FV	FV	62.50

		VG	VF	UNC
191	**10,000 ESCUDOS** 1996. Ch. 2. Violet and dk. brown on m/c unpt. Infante Dom Henrique at r. and as wmk., arms at ctr. Old sailing ship at ctr. on back. 6 sign. varieties.			
	a. 2.5.1996.	FV	FV	100.00
	b. 10.7.1997.	FV	FV	95.00

Portuguese Guinea (now Guinea-Bissau), a former Portuguese province of the west coast of Africa bounded on the north by Senegal and on the east and southeast by Guinea, had an area of 13,948 sq. mi. (36,125 sq. km.). Capital: Bissau. The province exported peanuts, timber and beeswax.

Portuguese Guinea was discovered by Portuguese navigator Nuno Tristao in 1446. Trading rights in the area were granted to Cape Verde islanders but few prominent posts were established before 1851, and they were principally coastal installations. The chief export of this colony's early period was slaves for South America, a practice that adversely affected trade with the native people and retarded subjection of the interior. Territorial disputes with France delayed final demarcation of the colony's frontiers until 1905.

The African Party for the Independence of Guinea-Bissau was founded in 1956, and several years later began a guerrilla warfare that grew in effectiveness until 1974, when the rebels controlled most of the colony. Portugal's costly overseas wars in her African territories resulted in a military coup in Portugal in April 1974, that appreciably brightened the prospects for freedom for Guinea-Bissau. In August, 1974, the Lisbon government signed an agreement granting independence to Portuguese Guinea effective Sept. 10, 1974. The new republic took the name of Guinea-Bissau.

RULERS:

Portuguese to 1974

MONETARY SYSTEM:

1 Escudo = 100 Centavos, 1910-1975

NOTE: For later issues see Guinea-Bissau.

BANCO NACIONAL ULTRAMARINO, GUINÉ

DECRETOS - LEI 39221 E 44891; 1964 ISSUE

#40-42 J. Teixeira Pinto at l., bank ship seal at r. Woman sitting, ships through the ages in background at ctr. on back.

		VG	VF	UNC
40	**50 ESCUDOS** 30.6.1964. Dk. green on lilac and m/c unpt.	10.00	25.00	60.00

		VG	VF	UNC
41	**100 ESCUDOS** 30.6.1964. Blue-green on m/c unpt.	14.00	35.00	95.00
42	**500 ESCUDOS** 30.6.1964. Brown on m/c unpt.	32.50	80.00	225.00

43	1000 ESCUDOS	VG	VF	UNC
	30.4.1964. Red-orange on m/c unpt. Portr. H. Barreto at r., bank ship seal at upper ctr. Woman standing, ships through the ages in background at l. ctr. on back. Printer: BWC.	25.00	60.00	165.00

DECRETOS - LEI 39221 E 44891; 1971 ISSUE

#44-46 Portuguese arms at upper ctr. Woman standing, ships through the ages in background at l. ctr., bank ship seal at lower l. on back.

44	50 ESCUDOS	VG	VF	UNC
	17.12.1971. Olive-green on m/c unpt. N. Tristao at r. and as wmk.	5.00	15.00	35.00

45	100 ESCUDOS	VG	VF	UNC
	17.12.1971. Blue on m/c unpt. Portr. N. Tristao at r. and as wmk.	6.50	20.00	55.00
46	500 ESCUDOS			
	27.7.1971. Purple on m/c unpt. Portr. H. Barreto at r.	13.50	40.00	135.00

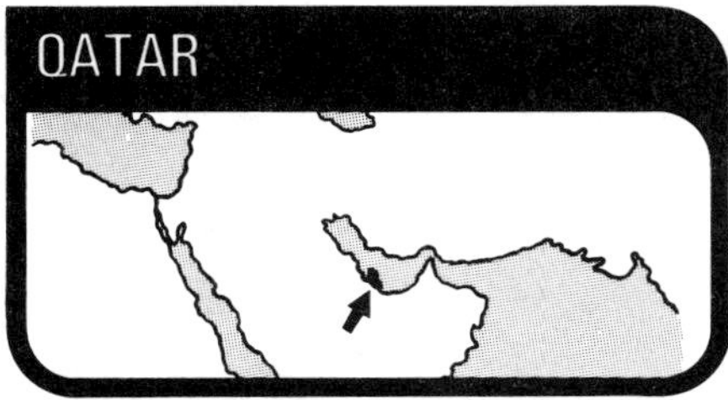

The State of Qatar, an emirate in the Persian Gulf between Bahrain and Trucial Oman, has an area of 4,247 sq. mi. (11,000 sq. km.) and a population of 548,000. Capital: Doha. Oil is the chief industry and export.

Qatar was under Turkish control from 1872 until the beginning of World War I when the Ottoman Turks evacuated the Qatar Peninsula. In 1916 Sheikh Abdullah placed Qatar under the protection of Great Britain and gave Britain responsibility for its defense and foreign relations. Qatar joined with Dubai in a monetary union and issued coins and paper money in 1966 and 1969. When Britain announced in 1968 that it would end treaty relationships with the Persian Gulf sheikhdoms in 1971, this union was dissolved. Qatar joined Bahrain and the seven trucial sheikhdoms (the latter now called the United Arab Emirates) in an effort to form a union of Arab emirates. However, the nine sheikhdoms were unable to agree on terms of union, and Qatar declared its independence as the State of Qatar on Sept. 3, 1971.

Also see Qatar and Dubai.

MONETARY SYSTEM:

1 Riyal = 100 Dirhem

EMIRATE

QATAR MONETARY AGENCY

1973 ND ISSUE

#1-6 arms in circle at r. Wmk: Falcon's head.

1	1 RIYAL	VG	VF	UNC
	ND (1973). Red on lilac and m/c unpt. Port of Doha at l. on back.			
	a. Issued note.	.75	2.50	12.00
	s. Specimen.	—	—	35.00

2	5 RIYALS	VG	VF	UNC
	ND (1973). Dk. brown on lilac and m/c unpt. Qatar National Museum at l. on back.			
	a. Issued note.	2.00	5.00	20.00
	s. Specimen.	—	—	40.00

3	10 RIYALS	VG	VF	UNC
	ND (1973). Green on m/c unpt. Qatar Monetary Agency bldg. at l. on back.			
	a. Issued note.	3.75	7.50	25.00
	s. Specimen.	—	—	50.00

4 **50 RIYALS** — VG / VF / UNC
ND (1976). Blue on m/c unpt. Offshore oil drilling platform at l. on back.

	VG	VF	UNC
a. Issued note.	60.00	225.00	725.00
s. Specimen.	—	—	500.00

5 **100 RIYALS**
ND (1973). Olive-green and lt. brown on m/c unpt. Ministry of Finance bldg. at l. on back.

	VG	VF	UNC
a. Issued note.	FV	90.00	250.00
s. Specimen.	—	—	225.00

6 **500 RIYALS**
ND (1973). Blue-green on m/c unpt. Mosque of the Sheikhs and minaret at l. on back.

	VG	VF	UNC
a. Issued note.	FV	350.00	750.00
s. Specimen.	—	—	700.00

NOTICE

Readers with unlisted dates, signature varieties, etc. are invited to submit photocopies of their notes to: Standard Catalog of World Paper Money, 700 East State St. Iola, WI 54990-0001, fax: 1-715-445-4087, or E-Mail: thernr@krause.com.

1980's ND Issue

#7-13 arms at r. Wmk: Falcon's head.

#		VG	VF	UNC
7	**1 RIYAL** ND. Brown on m/c unpt. City street scene in Doha at l. ctr. on back.	FV	.80	4.00

8 **5 RIYALS**
ND. Dk. red and purple on m/c unpt. Back red-brown, green and brown; sheep and plants at l. ctr.

	VG	VF	UNC
a. Wmk: Hawk, nostril visible, and top bill overlaps bottom.	FV	2.25	6.00
b. Wmk: Hawk, w/o nostril, beak even.	FV	FV	3.25

#		VG	VF	UNC
9	**10 RIYALS** ND. Green on blue and m/c unpt. National Museum at l. ctr. on back.	FV	3.00	7.50

#		VG	VF	UNC
10	**50 RIYALS** ND (1989). Blue on m/c unpt. Furnace at a steel factory on back.	FV	15.00	27.50

		VG	VF	UNC
11	**100 RIYALS** ND. Green on m/c unpt. Qatar Monetary Agency bldg. at l. ctr. on back.	FV	27.50	40.00

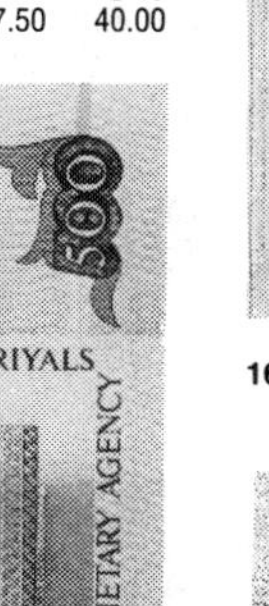

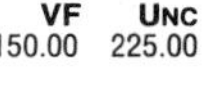

		VG	VF	UNC
12	**500 RIYALS** ND. Blue and green on m/c unpt. Offshore oil drilling platform on vertical back.	FV	150.00	225.00

1985 ND ISSUE

		VG	VF	UNC
13	**1 RIYAL** ND (1985). Brown on m/c unpt. Face like #7. Back purple; boat beached at l., Ministry of Finance, Emir's Palace in background at ctr.			
	a. Wmk: Hawk, nostril visible, and top bill overlaps bottom.	FV	FV	1.25
	b. Wmk: Hawk, w/o nostril, beak even.	FV	FV	.80

QATAR CENTRAL BANK

1996 ND ISSUE

#14-19 similar to #8-13 but w/two sign. Wmk: Falcon's head.

		VG	VF	UNC
14	**1 RIYAL** ND (1996). Brown on m/c unpt. Similar to #13.	FV	FV	.75

		VG	VF	UNC
15	**5 RIYALS** ND (1996). Red and purple on m/c unpt. Similar to #8.	FV	FV	2.50

		VG	VF	UNC
16	**10 RIYALS** ND (1996). Green and blue on m/c unpt. Similar to #9.	FV	FV	3.50

		VG	VF	UNC
17	**50 RIYALS** ND (1996). Blue on m/c unpt. Similar to #10.	FV	FV	20.00

		VG	VF	UNC
18	**100 RIYALS** ND (1996). Green on m/c unpt. Similar to #11.	FV	FV	35.00

		VG	VF	UNC
19	**500 RIYALS** ND (1996). Blue on m/c unpt. Silver foil emblem at upper l. Similar to #12.	FV	FV	150.00

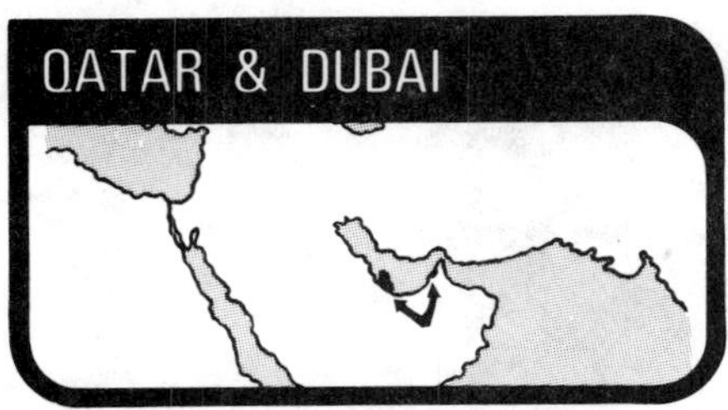

The State of Qatar, which occupies the Qatar Peninsula jutting into the Persian Gulf from eastern Saudi Arabia, has an area of 4,247 sq. mi. (11,000 sq. km.) and a population of 382,000. Capital: Doha. The traditional occupations of pearling, fishing and herding have been replaced in economics by petroleum-related industries. Crude oil, petroleum products, and tomatoes are exported.

Dubai is one of the seven sheikhdoms comprising the United Arab Emirates (formerly Trucial States) located along the southern shore of the Persian Gulf. It has a population of about 60,000. Capital (of the United Arab Emirates): Abu Dhabi.

Qatar, which initiated protective treaty relations with Great Britain in 1820, achieved independence on Sept. 3, 1971, upon withdrawal of the British military presence from the Persian Gulf, and replaced its special treaty arrangement with Britain with a treaty of general friendship. Dubai attended independence on Dec. 1, 1971, upon termination of Britain's protective treaty with the trucial sheikhdoms, and on Dec. 2, 1971, entered into the union of the United Arab Emirates.

Despite the fact that the sultanate of Qatar and the sheikhdom of Dubai were merged under a monetary union, the two territories were governed independently from each other. Qatar now uses its own currency while Dubai uses the United Arab Emirates currency and coins.

MONETARY SYSTEM:

1 Riyal = 100 Dirhem

SULTANATE AND SHEIKHDOM

QATAR AND DUBAI CURRENCY BOARD

1960S ND ISSUE

#1-6 dhow, derrick and palm tree at l. Wmk: Falcon's head.

		VG	VF	UNC
1	**1 RIYAL**			
	ND. Dk. green on m/c unpt.			
	a. Issued note.	3.00	20.00	85.00
	s. Specimen.	—	—	75.00

		VG	VF	UNC
2	**5 RIYALS**			
	ND. Purple on m/c unpt.			
	a. Issued note.	7.50	50.00	275.00
	s. Specimen.	—	—	150.00

		VG	VF	UNC
3	**10 RIYALS**			
	ND. Gray-green on m/c unpt.			
	a. Issued note.	15.00	60.00	450.00
	s. Specimen.	—	—	200.00
4	**25 RIYALS**			
	ND. Blue on m/c unpt.			
	a. Issued note.	100.00	600.00	—
	s. Specimen.	—	—	1350.

		VG	VF	UNC
5	**50 RIYALS**			
	ND. Red on m/c unpt.			
	a. Issued note.	175.00	650.00	—
	s. Specimen.	—	—	1100.

		VG	VF	UNC
6	**100 RIYALS**			
	ND. Olive on m/c unpt.			
	a. Issued note.	100.00	450.00	1500.
	s. Specimen.	—	—	1000.

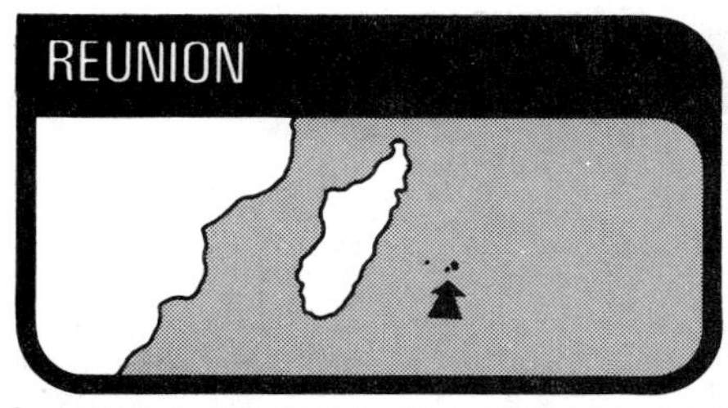

The Department of Reunion, an overseas department of France located in the Indian Ocean 400 miles (640 km.) east of Madagascar, has an area of 969 sq. mi. (2,510 sq. km.) and a population of 556,000. Capital: Saint-Denis. The island's volcanic soil is extremely fertile. Sugar, vanilla, coffee and rum are exported.

Although first visited by Portuguese navigators in the 16th century, Reunion was uninhabited when claimed for France by Capt. Goubert in 1638. It was first colonized as Isle de Bourbon by the French in 1662 as a layover station for ships rounding the Cape of Good Hope to India. It was renamed Reunion in 1793. The island remained in French possession except for the period of 1810-15, when it was occupied by the British. Reunion became an overseas department of France in 1946, and in 1958 voted to continue that status within the new French Union. Bauque du France notes were introduced 1.1.1973.

MONETARY SYSTEM:

1 Franc = 100 Centimes
1 Nouveau Franc = 50 Old Francs, 1967

INSTITUT D'EMISSION DES DÉPARTEMENTS D'OUTRE-MER, RÉPUBLIQUE FRANÇAISE

1964; 1965 ND PROVISIONAL ISSUE

#51-53 ovpt: DÉPARTEMENT DE LA RÉUNION.

		VG	VF	UNC
51	**500 FRANCS** ND (1964). M/c. 2 girls at r., sailboat at l. Farmers w/ox-carts on back.			
	a. Sign. A. Postel-Vinay and P. Calvet.	9.00	42.50	225.00
	b. Sign. A. Postel-Vinay and B. Clappier.	8.50	40.00	200.00
	s. Specimen.	—	—	175.00

		VG	VF	UNC
52	**1000 FRANCS** ND (1964). M/c. 2 women (symbol of the "Union Française") at r. Sign. A. Postel-Vinay and P. Calvet.			
	a. Issued note.	15.00	60.00	300.00
	s. Specimen.	—	—	250.00

		VG	VF	UNC
53	**5000 FRANCS** ND (1965). Brown on m/c unpt. Gen. Schoelcher at ctr. r. Sign. A. Postel-Vinay and P. Calvet.			
	a. Issued note.	35.00	130.00	550.00
	s. Specimen.	—	—	450.00

1967 ND PROVISIONAL ISSUE

		VG	VF	UNC
54	**10 NOUVEAUX FRANCS ON 500 FRANCS** ND (1967-71). M/c. Ovpt. on #51.			
	a. Sign. A. Postel-Vinay and P. Calvet. (1967).	5.00	30.00	135.00
	b. Sign. A. Postel-Vinay and B. Clappier. (1971).	5.00	27.50	110.00

		VG	VF	UNC
55	**20 NOUVEAUX FRANCS ON 1000 FRANCS** ND (1967-71). M/c. Ovpt. on #52.			
	a. Sign. A. Postel-Vinay and P. Calvet. (1967).	7.50	35.00	150.00
	b. Sign. A. Postel-Vinay and B. Clappier. (1971).	7.50	32.50	135.00

56	**100 NOUVEAUX FRANCS ON 5000 FRANCS**	**VG**	**VF**	**UNC**
	ND (1967-71). M/c. Ovpt. on #53.			
	a. Sign. A. Postel-Vinay and P. Calvet. (1967).	22.50	80.00	300.00
	b. Sign. A. Postel-Vinay and B. Clappier. (1971).	22.50	75.00	250.00

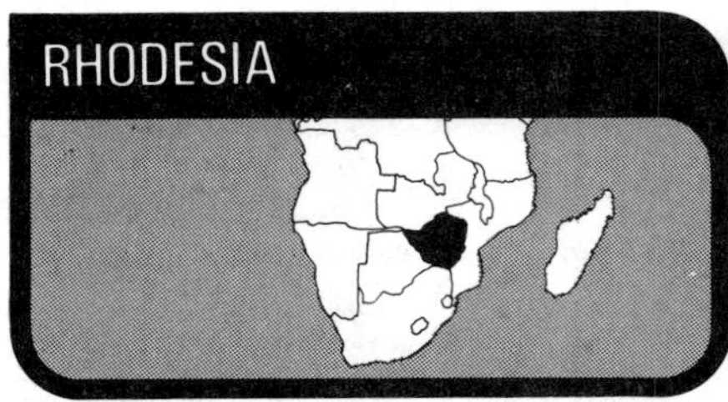

The "Republic of" Rhodesia (never recognized by the British government and was referred to as Southern Rhodesia, now Zimbabwe) located in the east-central part of southern Africa, has an area of 150,804 sq. mi. (390,580 sq. km.) and a population of 9.9 million. Capital: Harare. The economy is based on agriculture and mining. Tobacco, sugar, asbestos, copper and chrome ore and coal are exported.

The Rhodesian area, the habitat of paleolithic man, contains extensive evidence of earlier civilizations, notably the world-famous ruins of Zimbabwe, a gold-trading center that flourished about the 14th or 15th century AD. The Portuguese of the 16th century were the first Europeans to attempt to develop south-central Africa, but it remained for Cecil Rhodes and the British South Africa Co. to open the hinterlands. Rhodes obtained a concession for mineral rights from local chiefs in 1888 and administered his African empire (named Southern Rhodesia in 1895) through the British South Africa Co. until 1923, when the British government annexed the area after the white settlers voted for existence as a separate entity, rather than for incorporation into the Union of South Africa.

From Sept. of 1953 through 1963 Southern Rhodesia was joined with the British protectorates of Northern Rhodesia and Nyasaland into a multiracial federation. When the federation was dissolved at the end of 1963, Northern Rhodesia and Nyasaland became the independent states of Zambia and Malawi.

Britain was prepared to grant independence to Southern Rhodesia but declined to do so when the politically dominant white Rhodesians refused to give assurances of representative government. In November 1965, the white minority government of Southern Rhodesia unilaterally declared Southern Rhodesia an independent dominion. The United Nations and the British Parliament both proclaimed this unilateral declaration of independence null and void. Following a conference in London in December 1979, the opposition government conceded and it was agreed that the British government should resume control. In 1970, the government proclaimed a republic, but this too received no recognition. In 1979, the government purported to change the name of the Colony to Zimbabwe Rhodesia, but again this was never recognized. A British governor soon returned to Southern Rhodesia. One of his first acts was to affirm the nullification of the purported declaration of independence. On April 18, 1980, pursuant to an act of the British Parliament, the colony of Southern Rhodesia became independent within the commonwealth as the Republic of Zimbabwe.

NOTE: For later issues see Zimbabwe.

RULERS:

British to 1970 (1980)

MONETARY SYSTEM:

1 Shilling = 12 Pence
1 Pound = 20 Shillings to 1970
1 Dollar = 100 Cents, 1970-80

RESERVE BANK OF RHODESIA

1964 ISSUE

Pound System

#24-26 arms at upper ctr., Qn. Elizabeth II at r. Various date and sign. varieties. Wmk: C. Rhodes. Printer: BWC. Printed in England from engraved plates.

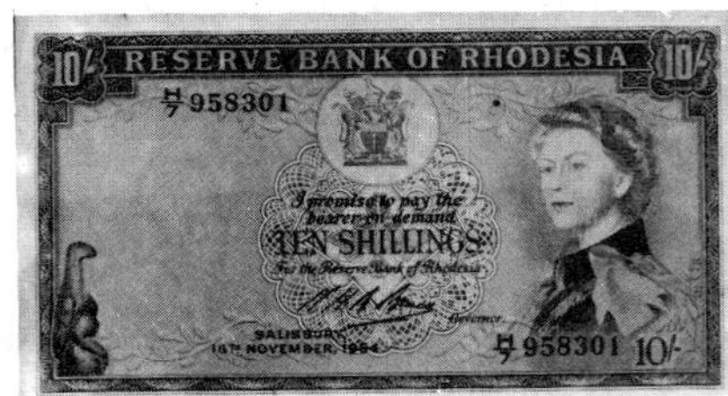

24	**10 SHILLINGS**	**VG**	**VF**	**UNC**
	30.9.1964-16.11.1964. Blue on m/c unpt. Blue portr. w/black serial #. Tobacco field at l. ctr. on back.	7.50	45.00	225.00

25	**1 POUND**	**VG**	**VF**	**UNC**
	3.9.1964-16.11.1964. Red on m/c unpt. Red portr., black serial #. Victoria Falls at l. ctr. on back.	5.00	35.00	175.00

26	5 POUNDS	VG	VF	UNC
	10.11.1964; 12.11.1964; 16.11.1964. Blue-green on m/c unpt. Lilac portr., black serial #. Zimbabwe ruins at l. ctr. on back.	12.50	50.00	200.00

1966 ISSUE

#27-29 arms at upper ctr., Qn. Elizabeth II at r. Various date and sign. varieties. Wmk: C. Rhodes. Printed in Rhodesia (w/o imprint). Lithographed.

27	10 SHILLINGS	VG	VF	UNC
	1.6.1966; 10.9.1968. Blue on m/c unpt. Similar to #24 but w/black portr. Red serial #.	2.50	20.00	110.00

28	1 POUND	VG	VF	UNC
	15.6.1966-14.10.1968. Pale red on m/c unpt. Similar to #25 but brown portr. Red serial #.	7.50	40.00	200.00

29	5 POUNDS	VG	VF	UNC
	1.7.1966. Blue-green on m/c unpt. Similar to #26 but purple portr. Red serial #.	15.00	60.00	300.00

NOTE: Before the issue of #25, 27 and 29, a series of Rhodesian banknotes was printed in Germany by Giesecke and Devrient, Munich. An injunction prevented delivery of this issue and it was never released. Subsequently it was destroyed.

REPUBLIC

RESERVE BANK OF RHODESIA

1970-72 ISSUE

Dollar System

#30-33 bank logo at upper ctr., arms at r. Replacement notes: Serial # prefixes *W/1, X/1, Y/1, Z/1* respectively.

30	1 DOLLAR	VG	VF	UNC
	1970-79. Blue on m/c unpt. Back like #27. 2 sign. varieties.			
	a. Wmk: C. Rhodes. 17.2.1970-18.8.1971.	1.50	5.00	25.00
	b. Wmk. as a. 14.2.1973-18.4.1978.	1.00	2.50	12.50
	c. Wmk: Zimbabwe bird. 2.8.1979.	.50	1.50	8.50

31	2 DOLLARS	VG	VF	UNC
	1970-79. Red on m/c unpt. Back like #28. 2 sign. varieties.			
	a. Wmk: C. Rhodes. 17.2.1970-4.1.1972.	2.00	5.00	22.50
	b. Wmk. as a. 29.6.1973-5.8.1977.	1.50	3.00	15.00
	c. Wmk. as a. 10.4.1979.	10.00	40.00	135.00
	d. Wmk: Zimbabwe bird. 10.4.1979; 24.5.1979.	1.00	2.50	10.00

32	5 DOLLARS	VG	VF	UNC
	1972-79. Brown on m/c unpt. Giraffe at lower l. 2 lions on back. 2 sign. varieties.			
	a. Wmk: C. Rhodes. 16.10.1972.	3.00	7.00	27.50
	b. Wmk. as a. 1.3.1976; 20.10.1978.	2.75	6.00	22.50
	c. Wmk: Zimbabwe bird. 15.5.1979. (1980).	2.50	5.00	25.00

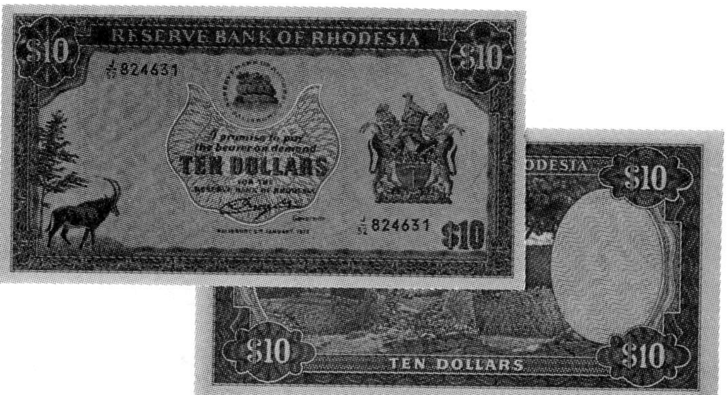

33	10 DOLLARS	VG	VF	UNC
	1970-79. Black on blue-green and m/c unpt. Antelope at lower l. Back like #29. 2 sign. varieties.			
	a. Wmk: C. Rhodes. 17.2.1970-8.5.1972.	7.00	20.00	85.00
	b. Wmk. as a. 20.11.1973-1.3.1976.	5.00	10.00	30.00
	c. Wmk: Zimbabwe bird. 2.1.1979.	4.00	8.00	22.50

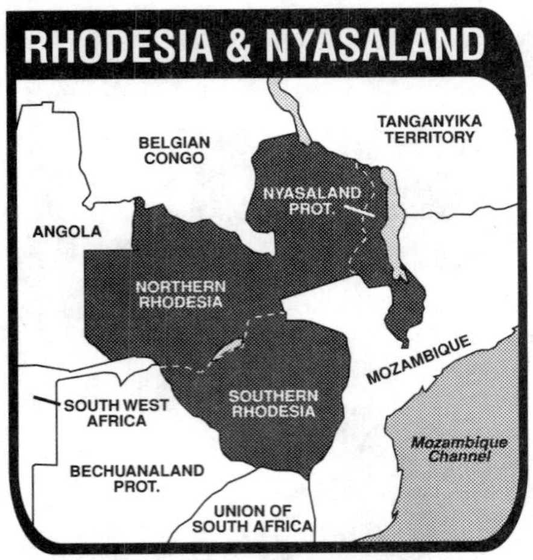

Rhodesia and Nyasaland (now the Republic of Zimbabwe) located in the east-central part of southern Africa, has an area of 150,804 sq. mi. (390,580 sq. km.) and a population of 6.9 million. Capital: Salisbury. The economy is based on agriculture and mining, Tobacco, sugar, asbestos, copper and chrome ore and coal are exported.

The Rhodesian area, the habitat of paleolithic man, contains extensive evidence of earlier civilizations, notably the world-famous ruins of Zimbabwe, a gold-trading center that flourished about the 14th or 15th century AD. The Portuguese of the 16th century were the first Europeans to attempt to develop south-central Africa, but it remained for Cecil Rhodes and the British South Africa Co. to open the hinterlands. Rhodes obtained a concession for mineral rights from local chiefs in 1888 and administered his African empire (named Southern Rhodesia in 1895) through the British South Africa Co. until 1923, when the British government annexed the area after the white settlers voted for existence as a separate entity, rather than for incorporation into the Union of South Africa. From Sept. of 1953 through 1963 Southern Rhodesia was joined with the British protectorates of Northern Rhodesia and Nyasaland into a multiracial federation. When the federation was dissolved at the end of 1963, Northern Rhodesia and Nyasaland became the independent states of Zambia and Malawi.

For earlier issues refer to Southern Rhodesia in Volume 2. For later issues refer to Malawi, Zambia, Rhodesia and Zimbabwe in Volume 3.

RULERS:

British to 1963

MONETARY SYSTEM:

1 Shilling = 12 Pence
1 Pound = 20 Shillings to 1963

BANK OF RHODESIA AND NYASALAND

1956 ISSUE

#20-23 portr. Qn. Elizabeth II at r. Various date and sign. varieties. Wmk: C. Rhodes. Printer: BWC.

		VG	VF	UNC
20	**10 SHILLINGS** 1956-61. Reddish brown on m/c unpt. River scene on back.			
	a. Sign. Graffery-Smith. 3.4.1956-6.5.1960.	15.00	100.00	300.00
	b. Sign. H. J. Richards. 30.12.1960-30.1.1961.	12.50	75.00	250.00
	s. As a. Specimen punched hole cancelled. 3.4.1956.	—	—	150.00

		VG	VF	UNC
21	**1 POUND** 1956-61. Green on m/c unpt. Zimbabwe ruins at ctr. on back.			
	a. Sign. Graffery-Smith. 22.5.1956-17.6.1960.	15.00	125.00	350.00
	b. Sign. H. J. Richards. 23.11.1960-23.1.1961.	10.00	100.00	325.00
	s. As a. Specimen punched hole cancelled. 2.5.1956.	—	—	200.00

		VG	VF	UNC
22	**5 POUNDS** 1956-61. Blue on m/c unpt. Victoria Falls on back.			
	a. Sign. Graffery-Smith. 3.4.1956-19.6.1959.	20.00	150.00	550.00
	b. Sign. H. J. Richards. 30.1.1961; 1.2.1961.	15.00	140.00	450.00
	s. As a. Specimen punched hole cancelled. 3.4.1956.	—	—	275.00
23	**10 POUNDS** 1956-61. Brown on m/c unpt. Back gray-green; elephants at ctr.			
	a. Sign. Graffery-Smith. 3.4.1956; 15.4.1957; 3.7.1959; 3.6.1960.	150.00	500.00	1750.
	b. Sign. H. J. Richards. 1.2.1961.	125.00	450.00	1500.
	s. As a. Specimen punched hole cancelled. 3.4.1956.	—	—	1000.

Romania (formerly the Socialist Republic of Romania), a country in southeast Europe, has an area of 91,699 sq. mi. (237,500 sq. km.) and a population of 22.7 million. Capital: Bucharest. Machinery, foodstuffs, raw minerals and petroleum products are exported. Heavy industry and oil have become increasingly important to the economy since 1959.

The area of Romania, generally referred to as Dacia, inhabited by Dacians or Getae, a people of Thracian stock. The kingdom of Dacia existed as early as 200 BC. In the reign of Emperor Augustus, the Dacians began to provoke the Romans. In a series of campaigns 101-102AD and 105-106AD, Emperor Trajan conquered Dacia and converted it into a Roman province. During the third century AD, raids by the Goths became so grave a menace that the Roman legions were withdrawn across the Danube in 271AD. While successive waves of invaders, including Goths, Huns, Gepidae, Avars and Slavs, made the country a battleground although the Romanized population preserved a Latin speech and identity and its Christianity (on Orthodox line after eleventh century). Through gradual assimilation of the Slavonic tribes, these people developed into a distinct ethnic group called Wallachians (Valachs or Vlachs).

During 900-1200AD, the Romanian dukedoms of Transylvania were unable to resist the Hungarian infiltration and the region became an autonomous principality under suzerainty of the king of Hungary. Some Romanian State structures, later under Byzantine influence, begin in the eleventh century in Dobruja.

In the thirteenth century, small countries crystallized south of the Carpathian Mountains. These were the base of principality of Wallachia established in 1310. The early years involved Wallachia in struggles with Hungary. It became an independent state in 1330. Since 1369, Wallachia has supported many wars, losing Dobruja and recognizing suzerainty of the Sultan, in the early fifteenth century. The autonomy of the country was insured by payment of an annual tribute.

Moldavia, established in 1359 had a similar evolution. For 150 years this principality successfully defended itself against attacks by foreign powers. Stefan the Great (1457-1504) was a champion of Christendom against the Turks. In the sixteenth century, Moldavia acknowledged Ottoman suzerainty, having a large autonomy.

With defeat in 1526, Hungary came under Turkish rule. Transylvania became a separate principality under the protection of the Sultan (1541).

At the close of the sixteenth century, the three principalities were united (Transylvania in 1599 and Moldavia in 1600) by Prince Mihai Viteazul of Wallachia, who made continual war on the Turks in an attempt to gain and maintain independence. The Ottomans restored, their control of the principalities after Michael's death, imposing political restrictions. More so, the Turks imposed a Phanariot regime in Moldavia (1711) and Wallachia (1716). These rulers were usually Orthodox members of noble Greek families from Istanbul.

The last Turkish vassal was eliminated in 1699 and Austria obtained the possession of Transylvania by the Treaty of Karlowitz. Under Hapsburg's administration, the region was made into a grand principality in 1765.

Because of the decline of Turkish power during the eighteenth century, the Austrian and later Russian influence became preeminent in the area. Between 1718-1734, the Hapsburgs annexed the region of Oltenia, in western Wallachia. In 1775 Moldavia lost its northern region Bukovina to Austria and in 1812 Russia annexed its eastern portion, Bessarabia.

The erosion of Turkish influence became more evident after the national movement of Tudor Vladimirescu in 1821 in Wallachia. The Phanariot system was ended, Romanian rulers were reestablished. The principalities, although remaining under Sultan control, were more autonomous. As such, in 1829, the Turkish monopoly of commerce was abolished. Important institutional reforms were adopted.

The European insurrectionist movements of 1848 reached the area. In Moldova and Wallachia the provisional revolutionary governments were put down by a Russo-Turkish military intervention. In Transylvania the Romanians, as native and majority of the population, continued to fight for social and national emancipation, which went unrecognized by the Hungarian revolutionary government. In 1867, Transylvania was incorporated under Hungarian administration during the Austro-Hungarian Empire. After the Russian defeat in the Crimean War, the European powers ended the Russian protectorate and returned regions south of Bessarabia to Moldavia. The question of the union of Wallachia and Moldavia was resolved in 1859. The union was voted in unanimously on January 5 at Iasi, the Moldavian capital; and on January 24 at Bucharest. The two assemblies elected a single prince, Alexandru Ioan Cuza, establishing the fruition of Romania. Prince Cuza was deposed by a conspiracy in 1866. A provisional government then elected Prince Karl of Hohenzollern-Sigmaringen, who took office as Carol I and was vested as hereditary prince. A constitution was adopted on his arrival. A rapid modernization of the country was perceived. Romania was successfully in a war against Turkey (1877-78) and proclaimed itself to be independent. The Congress of Berlin (1878) recognized this fact. The historical region of Dobruja, was returned, but Romania was forced to cede Bessarabia to Russia.

In 1881, Carol I became king. In 1888, Romania became a constitutional monarchy with a bicameral legislature.

Neutral during the First Balkan War (1912), Romania joined Serbia and Greece in the Second Balkan War (1913) against Bulgaria. The intervention and deployment of Romanian troops into Bulgaria resulted in the acquisition of southern Dobruja.

When WW I began, the kingdom was officially neutral in 1916, the Romanian army invaded Transylvania, but Austro-German, Turkish and Bulgarian forces occupied the south of the country. The Romanians persisted in keeping Moldavia. In March 1918, the Bessarabian legislature voted in favor of reunification with Romania. With the triumph of the Allies in October, the Romanian army liberated the southern region and reoccupied Transylvania. Bukovina (Oct. 28, 1918) and Transylvania (Dec. 1) proclaimed their reunification with Romania. In 1919, the Romanian army shattered the Bolshevik forces, which were in Hungary.

A new constitution was adopted in 1923. During this period in history, the Romanian government struggled with domestic problems, agrarian reform and economic reconstruction.

In the background of WW II, in 1940, after the defeat of France, following the Soviet-Nazi agreement of August 1939, the Red army occupied Bessarabia and northern Bukovina (June). Later, northern Transylvania was annexed by Hungary (August) and southern Dobruja was returned to Bulgaria (September). In this context, King Carol II abdicated in favor of his son Mihai.

The government was reorganized along Fascist lines between September 14, 1940 - January 23, 1941. A military dictatorship followed. Marshal Ion Antonescu installed himself as chief of state. When the Germans invaded the Soviet Union, Romania also became involved in recovering the regions of Bessarabia and northern Bukovina annexed by Stalin in 1940.

On August 23, 1944, King Mihai I proclaimed an armistice with the Allied Forces. The Romanian army drove out the Germans and Hungarians in northern Transylvania, but the country was subsequently occupied by the Soviet army. That monarchy was abolished on December 30, 1947, and Romania became a "People's Republic" based on the Soviet regime. The process of sovietization included frequent purges of dissidents: politicians, military personnel, clergy, cultural leaders and peasants. Romanian elite disappeared into the concentration camps. The anti-Communist combative resistance movement developed in spite of the Soviet army presence until 1956. The partisans remained in the mountains until 1964. With the accession of N. Ceausescu to power, Romania began to exercise a considerable degree of independence, refusing to participate in the invasion of Czechoslovakia (August 1968). In 1965, it was proclaimed a "Socialist Republic". After 1977, an oppressed and impoverished domestic scene worsened.

On December 17, 1989, an anti-Communist revolt began in Timisoara. On December 22, 1989 the Communist government was overthrown by organized freedom fighters in Bucharest. Ceausescu and his wife were arrested and later executed. The new government has established a republic, the official and constitutional name being Romania.

MONETARY SYSTEM:

1 Leu = 100 Bani

SOCIALIST REPUBLIC

BANCA NATIONALA A REPUBLICII SOCIALISTE ROMÂNIA

1966 ISSUE

#91-94 arms at ctr. Wmk: Rhombuses.

		VG	VF	UNC
91	**1 LEU** 1966. Olive-brown and tan.			
	a. Issued note.	.10	.40	1.50
	s. Specimen.	—	—	10.00

		VG	VF	UNC
92	**3 LEI** 1966. Blue on orange and m/c unpt.			
	a. Issued note.	.20	.50	2.50
	s. Specimen.	—	—	10.00

		VG	VF	UNC
93	**5 LEI** 1966. Brown and dk. blue on m/c unpt. Cargo ships at dockside on back.			
	a. Issued note.	.20	.50	2.50
	s. Specimen.	—	—	10.00

		VG	VF	UNC
94	**10 LEI** 1966. Purple on m/c unpt. Harvest scene on back.			
	a. Issued note.	.20	.50	3.50
	s. Specimen.	—	—	10.00

#95-97 arms at ctr. r. Wmk: Rhombuses.

		VG	VF	UNC
95	**25 LEI** 1966. Dk. green on m/c unpt. Portr. T. Vladimirescu at l. Large refinery on back.			
	a. Issued note.	.25	.50	4.00
	s. Specimen.	—	—	15.00

		VG	VF	UNC
96	**50 LEI** 1966. Dk. green on m/c unpt. A. I. Cuza at l. Culture Palace in Iasi at ctr. r. on back.			
	a. Issued note.	.40	1.50	5.00
	s. Specimen.	—	—	15.00

		VG	VF	UNC
97	**100 LEI** 1966. Dk. blue and purple on m/c unpt. Portr. N. Balcescu at l. The Athenaeum in Bucharest at ctr. r. on back.			
	a. Issued note.	.25	1.25	6.00
	s. Specimen.	—	—	20.00

NOTICE

Readers with unlisted dates, signature varieties, etc. are invited to submit photocopies of their notes to: Standard Catalog of World Paper Money, 700 East State St. Iola, WI 54990-0001, fax: 1-715-445-4087, or E-Mail: thernr@krause.com.

REPUBLIC

BANCA NATIONALA A ROMÂNIEI

1991 ISSUE

		VG	VF	UNC
98	**500 LEI** 1991. Dk. brown on m/c unpt. C. Brâncusi at r. and as wmk. Brâncusi seated w/statue at l. ctr. on back. 1 sign. Wmk: Bust facing.			
	a. Jan. 1991.	.65	2.00	10.00
	b. April 1991.	.30	.90	2.75
	x. As b, w/*APRILIED* (error).	Reported Not Confirmed		

		VG	VF	UNC
99	**1000 LEI** Sept. 1991. Red-brown, blue-green and brown-orange on m/c unpt. Circular shield at l. ctr., sails of sailing ships at lower ctr., M. Eminescu at r. and as wmk. Putna monastery at l. ctr. on back. 2 sign.	.50	1.00	3.50

1992; 1993 ISSUE

		VG	VF	UNC
100	**200 LEI** Dec. 1992. Dull deep brown and brown-violet on m/c unpt. Square-topped shield at l. ctr., steamboat *Tudor Vladimirescu* above heron and Sulina Lighthouse in unpt. at ctr., G. Antipa at r. Herons, fish, and net on outline of Danube Delta in at l. ctr. on back. Wmk: Bank monogram repeated.	.10	.50	2.00

101 500 LEI
Dec. 1992. Dull deep green, reddish-brown and violet on m/c unpt. Square topped shield at l. ctr., sculptures at ctr., C. Brâncusi at r. Sculptures at l. ctr. on back. Wmk: Bust right.

		VG	VF	UNC
	a. Wmk: Bust facing as #98.	.15	2.00	6.00
	b. Wmk: Bust to r.	.10	.50	1.75

102 1000 LEI
May 1993. Similar to #99 but square-topped shield of arms at l. ctr. .20 .50 2.00

		VG	VF	UNC
103	**5000 LEI** March 1992. Pale purple on m/c unpt. Round seal at l. ctr., church at ctr., A. Iancu at r. and as wmk. Church at l., the gate of Alba Iulia stronghold at l. ctr., seal at ctr. r. on back.	.75	2.25	10.00

1993; 1994 ISSUE

		VG	VF	UNC
104	**5000 LEI** May 1993. Similar to #103 but square-topped shield at l. ctr.	.25	.75	2.50

		VG	VF	UNC
105	**10,000 LEI** Feb. 1994. Dull violet and reddish brown on m/c unpt. N. Iorga at r. and as wmk., snake god Glycon at ctr. Statue of Fortuna at l., historical museum in Bucharest at ctr. The Thinking Man of Hamangia at lower ctr. r. on back.	FV	FV	4.00

1996-98 ISSUE

#106-110 arms at top l., bank monogram at upper ctr. r. Bank monogram at top r. on back.

		VG	VF	UNC
106	**1000 LEI** 1998. Blue-violet, dk. green and olive-brown on m/c unpt. M. Eminescu at r. and as wmk., lily flower and quill pen at ctr. Lime and blue flowers at l. ctr., ruins of ancient fort of Histria at ctr. on back.	FV	FV	1.50

		VG	VF	UNC
107	**5000 LEI** 1998. Violet, dk. brown and brown-orange on m/c unpt. L. Blaga at r. and as wmk., daffodil at ctr. Vine leaf at l. ctr., roadside crucifix at ctr. on back.	FV	FV	3.00

		VG	VF	UNC
108	**10,000 LEI** 1999. Green-yellow on m/c unpt. N. Iorga at r. and as wmk., gentian flower at ctr. The church of Curtea de Arges monastery at ctr., Wallachian arms of prince Constantin Brancoveanu (1686-1714) at l. on back.	FV	FV	4.50

		VG	VF	UNC
109	**50,000 LEI** Nov. 1996. Purple and red-violet on lilac and m/c unpt. G. Enescu at r. and as wmk., floral ornament, musical notes at ctr., arms at upper l. Sphinx of Carpathian mountains at l. ctr., musical chord from "Oedip Rege" above on back.	FV	FV	12.50

		VG	VF	UNC
110	**100,000 LEI** 1998. Dull red on olive-green and m/c unpt. N. Grigorescu at r. and as wmk., mallow flowers and artist's brush at ctr. Peasant girl w/ewe at l., cottage at ctr. on back.	FV	FV	20.00

1999 COMMEMORATIVE ISSUE

#111, Total Solar Eclipse, August 11, 1999

		VG	VF	UNC
111	**2000 LEI** 1999. Blue on m/c unpt. Imaginative reproduction of the Solar System at r., with the mention of the event. The map of Romania having the colors of the national flag, (blue, yellow, red) marking the area where the phenomenon of the solar eclipse was total at ctr. on back. Polymer plastic.			
	a. Issued note.	FV	FV	2.00
	b. Collector series with the prefix 001A.	—	—	7.50

RUSSIA

Russia, (formerly the central power of the Union of Soviet Socialist Republics and now of the Commonwealth of Independent States) which occupies the northern part of Asia and the far eastern part of Europe, has an area of 8,649,538 sq. mi. (17,075,450 sq. km.) and a population of 147.5 million. Capital: Moscow. Exports include machinery, iron and steel, crude oil, timber and nonferrous metals.

The first Russian dynasty was founded in Novgorod by the Viking Rurik in 862 AD. Under Yaroslav the Wise (1019-54) the subsequent Kievan state became one of the great commercial and cultural centers of Europe before falling to the Mongols of the Batu Khan, 13th century, who ruled Russia until late in the 15th century when Ivan III threw off the Mongol yoke. The Russian Empire was enlarged, and solidified during the reigns of Ivan the Terrible, Peter the Great and Catherine the Great, and by 1881 extended to the Pacific and into Central Asia.

Assignats, the first government paper money of the Russian Empire, were introduced in 1769, and gave way to State Credit Notes in 1843. Russia was put on the gold standard in 1897 and reformed its currency at that time.

All pre-1898 notes were destroyed as they were turned in to the Treasury, accounting for their uniform scarcity today.

The last Russian Czar, Nicholas II (1894-1917), was deposed by the provisional government under Prince Lvov and later Alexander Kerensky during the military defeat in World War I. This government rapidly lost ground to the Bolshevik wing of the Socialist Democratic Labor Party which attained power following the Bolshevik Revolution. During the Russian Civil War (1917-1922) many regional governments, national states and armies in the field were formed which issued their own paper money. (See Vol. I).

After the victory of the Red armies, many of these areas became federal republics of the Russian Socialist Federal Soviet Republic (РСфСР), or autonomous soviet republics which united on Dec. 30, 1922, to form the Union of Soviet Socialist Republics (СССР). Beginning with the downfall of the communist government in Poland, other European countries occupied since WW II, began democratic elections which spread into Russia itself, leaving the remaining states united in a newly founded Commonwealth of Independent States (C.I.S.). The USSR Supreme Soviet voted a formal end to the treaty of union signed in 1922 and dissolved itself.

MONETARY SYSTEM:

1 Ruble = 100 Kopeks, until 1997
1 Ruble = 1000 "old" Rubles, Jan. 1, 1998-

CYRILLIC ALPHABET

А	а	А	а	A	С	с	С	с	S
Б	б	Б	б	B	Т	т	Т	т	T
В	в	В	в	V	У	у	У	у	U
Г	г	Г	г	G	Ф	ф	Ф	ф	F
Д	д	Д	д, g	D	Х	х	Х	х	Kh
Е	е	Е	е	ye	Ц	ц	Ц	ц	C
Ё	ё	Ё	ё	yo	Ч	ч	Ч	ч	ch
Ж	ж	Ж	ж	zh	Ш	ш	Ш	ш	sh
З	з	З	з	Z	Щ	щ	Щ	щ	shch
И	и	И	и	I	Ъ*)	ъ*)	—	ъ	'
Й	й	Й	й	J	Ы	ы	—	ы	
К	к	К	k, к	K	Ь**)	ь**)	—	ь	'
Л	л	Л	л	L	Э		Э		E
М	м	М	м	M	Ю	ю	Ю	ю	yu
Н	н	Н	н	N	Я	я	Я	я	ya
О	о	О	о	O	І	і	І	і	I
П	п	П	п	P	Ѣ	ѣ	Ѣ	ѣ	ye
Р	р	Р	р	R					

*) "hard", and **) "soft" signs; both soundless. I and Ѣ were dropped in 1918.

С.С.С.Р. - СОЮЗ СОВЕТСКИХ ТИЧЕСКИХ РЕСПУБЛИК

U.S.S.R. - Union Of Soviet Socialist Republics

ГОСУДАРСТВЕННЫЙ КАЗНАЧЕЙСКИЙ БИЛЕТ

State Treasury Note

1961 Issue

#222-224 arms at upper l. Wmk: Stars.

		VG	VF	Unc
222	**1 Ruble** 1961. Brown on pale green unpt. Back red on m/c unpt.			
	a. Issued note.	.05	.10	.25
	s. Specimen.	—	—	15.00

		VG	VF	Unc
223	**3 Rubles** 1961. Dk. green on m/c unpt. View of Kremlin at ctr. Back lt. blue on green and m/c unpt.			
	a. Issued note.	.05	.10	.50
	s. Specimen.	—	—	15.00

		VG	VF	Unc
224	**5 Rubles** 1961. Blue on peach unpt. Kremlin Spasski tower at l. Back blue on m/c unpt.			
	a. Issued note.	.05	.15	.75
	s. Specimen.	—	—	15.00

БИЛЕТ ГОСУДАРСТВЕННОГО БАНКА С.С.С.Р.

State Bank Note U.S.S.R.

1961 Issue

		VG	VF	Unc
233	**10 Rubles** 1961. Red-brown on pale gold unpt. Arms at upper l., portr. V. I. Lenin at r. Wmk: St ars.			
	a. Issued note.	.10	.25	1.00
	s. Specimen.	—	—	15.00

#234-236 portr. V. I. Lenin at upper l., arms at upper ctr.

		VG	VF	Unc
234	**25 Rubles** 1961. Purple on pale lt. green unpt. Wmk: Stars.			
	a. Lilac tinted paper.	.25	1.00	5.00
	b. White paper.	.10	.25	1.00
	s. Specimen.	—	—	15.00

		VG	VF	Unc
235	**50 Rubles** 1961. Dk. green and green on green and pink unpt. Kremlin at upper ctr. on back.			
	a. Issued note.	.25	.75	3.00
	s. Specimen.	—	—	15.00

		VG	VF	Unc
236	**100 Rubles** 1961. Brown on lt. blue unpt. Kremlin tower at ctr. on back. Date on back. Wmk: Lenin.			
	a. Issued note.	.35	1.00	4.00
	s. Specimen.	—	—	15.00

1991 Issue

#237-243 similar to #222-236.

#237-239 wmk: Star in circle repeated.

		VG	VF	Unc
237	**1 Ruble** 1991. Dk. green and red-brown on tan unpt. Similar to #222.			
	a. Issued note.	.05	.10	.25
	s. Specimen.	—	—	15.00

238 3 RUBLES
1991. Green on blue and m/c unpt. Similar to #223.

	VG	VF	UNC
a. Issued note.	.10	.25	.75
s. Specimen.	—	—	15.00

239 5 RUBLES
1991. Blue-gray on lt. blue, pale green and pink unpt. Similar to #224.

	VG	VF	UNC
a. Issued note.	.05	.15	.60
s. Specimen.	—	—	15.00

240 10 RUBLES
1991. Red-brown and green on m/c unpt. Similar to #233.

	VG	VF	UNC
a. Issued note.	.15	.25	.75
s. Specimen.	—	—	15.00

241 50 RUBLES
1991. Dk. brown, green and red on m/c unpt. Similar to #235.

	VG	VF	UNC
a. Issued note.	.20	.75	6.00
s. Specimen.	—	—	15.00

242 100 RUBLES
1991. Deep red-brown and blue on m/c unpt. Similar to #236. Date on face at r. Wmk: Lenin.

	VG	VF	UNC
a. Issued note.	.25	.75	4.00
s. Specimen.	—	—	15.00

243 100 RUBLES
1991. Like #242 but w/added pink and green guilloche at r. in wmk. area, blue guilloche added at upper l. on back. Wmk: Stars.

	VG	VF	UNC
a. Issued note.	.30	.75	3.00
s. Specimen.	—	—	15.00

#244-246 portr. V. I. Lenin at upper l. and as wmk., arms at upper ctr. Different views of the Kremlin on back.

244 200 RUBLES
1991. Green and brown on m/c unpt.

VG	VF	UNC
.50	2.00	15.00

245 500 RUBLES
1991. Red and green on m/c unpt.

VG	VF	UNC
1.00	3.00	20.00

		VG	VF	UNC
246	**1000 RUBLES** 1991. Brown and blue on green and m/c unpt.	1.00	3.00	20.00

C.I.S. - COMMONWEALTH OF INDEPENDENT STATES

РОССИЙСКАЯ ФЕДЕРАЦИЯ

RUSSIAN FEDERATION

1992 ISSUE

		VG	VF	UNC
247	**50 RUBLES** 1992. Brown and gray on green and m/c unpt. Similar to #241. Wmk: Star in circle repeated.			
	a. Issued note.	.15	.35	1.50
	s. Specimen.	—	—	15.00

		VG	VF	UNC
248	**200 RUBLES** 1992. Green and brown on m/c unpt. Similar to #244, but guilloche added in wmk. area on back. Wmk. as #247.			
	a. Issued note.	.25	.75	2.50
	s. Specimen.	—	—	15.00

		VG	VF	UNC
249	**500 RUBLES** 1992. Red, violet and dk. green on m/c unpt. Similar to #245, but guilloche added in wmk. area on back. Wmk: Stars.			
	a. Issued note.	.15	.50	4.00
	s. Specimen.	—	—	15.00

		VG	VF	UNC
250	**1000 RUBLES** 1992. Dk. brown and deep green on m/c unpt. Similar to #246, but guilloche added in wmk. area on back. Wmk: Stars.			
	a. Issued note.	.15	.50	1.50
	s. Specimen.	—	—	15.00

1992 GOVERNMENT PRIVATIZATION CHECK ISSUE

		VG	VF	UNC
251	**10,000 RUBLES** 1992. Dk. brown on m/c unpt. Parliament White House in Moscow. Text indicating method of redemption into shares of govt.-owned property on back. Handstamp from bank added at bottom. Valid until Dec. 31, 1993.	10.00	20.00	45.00

NOTE: While not a regular banknote, #251 was easily negotiable and was widely distributed by the govt. It was to provide funds to allow citizens to "buy into" a business. Worth about $35 at time of issue (early 1992), inflation since then has cut its real value dramatically.

БАНК РОССИЙ

BANK OF RUSSIA

1992 ISSUE

		VG	VF	UNC
252	**5000 RUBLES** 1992. Blue and maroon on m/c unpt. St. Basil's Cathedral at l. Kremlin on back. Wmk: Stars.			
	a. Issued note.	.25	.50	1.50
	s. Specimen.	—	—	15.00

		VG	VF	UNC
253	**10,000 RUBLES** 1992. Brown, black and red on m/c unpt. Kremlin w/new tricolor flag at l. ctr. and as wmk. Kremlin towers at ctr. r. on back.			
	a. Issued note.	.25	.75	2.00
	s. Specimen.	—	—	15.00

1993 ISSUE

at or near ctr. on back. #254-260 new tricolor flag over stylized Kremlin at l., monogram at upper r. or near ctr. on back.

#254-256 wmk: Stars within wavy lines repeated.

		VG	VF	UNC
254	**100 RUBLES** 1993. Blue-black on pink and lt. blue unpt. Kremlin, Spasski Tower at ctr. r. on back.	.05	.10	.50

		VG	VF	UNC
255	**200 RUBLES** 1993. Brown on pink and m/c unpt. Kremlin gate at ctr. on back.	.10	.50	1.50

		VG	VF	UNC
56	**500 RUBLES** 1993. Green, blue and purple on m/c unpt. Kremlin at l. ctr. on back.	.05	.15	1.25

		VG	VF	UNC
257	**1000 RUBLES** 1993. Green, olive-green and brown on m/c unpt. Kremlin at ctr. on back. Wmk: Stars.	.15	.50	2.00

#258-260 new flag over Kremlin at l. and as wmk. Kremlin at or near ctr. on back.

		VG	VF	UNC
258	**5000 RUBLES** 1993; 1993/94. Blue, brown and violet on m/c unpt.			
	a. 1993.	—	2.50	10.00
	b. 1993//94.	—	2.00	6.50

		VG	VF	UNC
259	**10,000 RUBLES** 1993; 1993//94. Violet, greenish blue, brownish purple and m/c.			
	a. 1993.	—	4.00	15.00
	b. 1993//94.	—	2.00	7.50

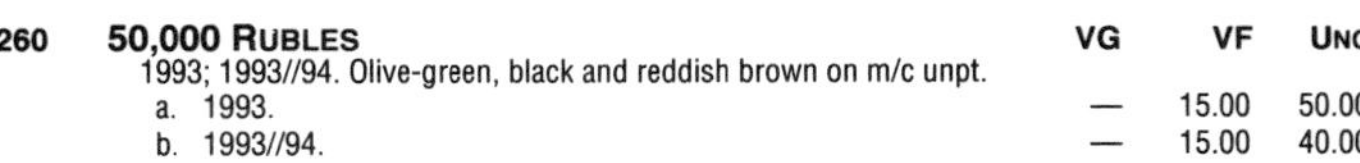

		VG	VF	UNC
260	**50,000 RUBLES** 1993; 1993//94. Olive-green, black and reddish brown on m/c unpt.			
	a. 1993.	—	15.00	50.00
	b. 1993//94.	—	15.00	40.00

1995 ISSUE

		VG	VF	UNC
261	**1000 RUBLES** 1995. Dk. brown and brown on m/c unpt. Seaport of Vladivostok at l. ctr., memorial column at ctr. r. and as wmk. Entrance to Vladivostok Bay at ctr. on back. Wmk: *1000* and memorial column.	—	.50	2.00

		VG	VF	UNC
262	**5000 RUBLES** 1995. Deep blue-green and dk. olive-green on m/c unpt. Monument of the Russian Millennium in Novgorod at l. ctr. Cathedral of St. Sophia at ctr. and as wmk. Old towered city wall at upper l. ctr. on back.	FV	1.00	4.00

		VG	VF	UNC
263	**10,000 RUBLES** 1995. Dk. brown and dk. gray on m/c unpt. Arch bridge over Yenisei River in Krasnoyarsk at l. ctr., steeple at ctr. r. and as. wmk. Hydroelectric dam at ctr. on back.	FV	2.00	6.00

		VG	VF	UNC
264	**50,000 RUBLES** 1995. Dk. brown, grayish purple and black on m/c unpt. Monument at ctr. Fountain in St. Petersburg at upper ctr. on back. Wmk: Bldg. w/steeple.	FV	FV	25.00

		VG	VF	UNC
265	**100,000 RUBLES** 1995. Purple and brown on m/c unpt. Chariot monument at ctr. Bolshoi (Great) Theatre in Moscow on back. Wmk: Bldg. over value.	—	20.00	45.00
266	**500,000 RUBLES** 1995 (1997). Brown-violet on m/c unpt. Statue of Peter the Great, sailing ship dockside in port of Arkhangelsk at ctr. Monastery in Solovetsky Island on back.	—	50.00	175.00

1997 (1998) "NEW RUBLE" ISSUE

1 Ruble = 1000 "old" Rubles

#267-271 like #262-266.

		VG	VF	UNC
267	**5 RUBLES** 1997 (1998). Deep blue-green and dk. olive-green on m/c unpt. Like #262.	FV	FV	.65

		VG	VF	UNC
268	**10 RUBLES** 1997 (1998). Dk. brown and dk. gray on m/c unpt. Like #263.	FV	FV	1.25

269 **50 RUBLES** 1997 (1998). Dk. brown, grayish purple and black on m/c unpt. Like #264.

VG	VF	UNC
FV	FV	4.00

270 **100 RUBLES** 1997 (1998). Violet and brown on m/c unpt. Like #265.

VG	VF	UNC
FV	FV	7.50

271 **500 RUBLES** 1997 (1998). Brown-violet on m/c unpt. Like #266.

VG	VF	UNC
FV	FV	35.00

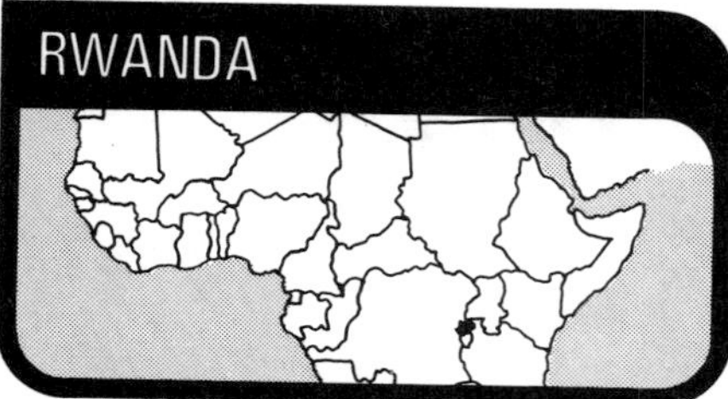

The Republic of Rwanda, located in central Africa between the Republic of the Congo and Tanzania, has an area of 10,169 sq. mi. (26,340 sq. km.) and a population of 5.1 million. Capital: Kigali. The economy is based on agriculture and mining. Coffee and tin are exported.

German lieutenant Count von Goetzen was the first European to visit Rwanda, 1894. Four years later the court of the Mwami (the Tutsi king of Rwanda) willingly permitted the kingdom to become a protectorate of Germany. In 1916, during the African campaigns of World War I, Belgian troops from the Congo occupied Rwanda. After the war it, together with Burundi, became a Belgian League of Nations mandate under the name of the Territory of Ruanda-Urundi. Following World War II, Ruanda-Urundi became a Belgian administered U.N. trust territory. The Tutsi monarchy was deposed by the U.N. supervised election of 1961, after which Belgium granted Rwanda internal autonomy. On July 1, 1962, the U.N. terminated the Belgian trusteeship and granted full independence to both Rwanda and Burundi. Banknotes were used in common with the Belgian Congo, and later with Burundi.

A coup in 1973 established a military government in the 1980's. There was increasing tension with refugees from neighboring Uganda, culminating in a 1990 Tutsi invasion. U.N. forces were posted in 1994-96 but civil strife continues.

Also see Belgian Congo, Rwanda-Burundi.

MONETARY SYSTEM:

1 Franc (Amafranga, Amafaranga) = 100 Centimes

REPUBLIC

BANQUE NATIONALE DU RWANDA

BANKI NASIYONALI Y'U RWANDA

1962 PROVISIONAL ISSUE

#1-5 ovpt: *BANQUE NATIONALE DU RWANDA* and sign. title: *LE GOUVERNEUR* on Banque d'Emission du Rwanda et du Burundi notes.

#1-3 stamped ovpt.

1 **20 FRANCS** ND (1962 -old date 5.10.1960). Green on tan and pink unpt. Maroon or black ovpt. on Rwanda-Burundi #3.

GOOD	FINE	XF
70.00	175.00	400.00

2 **50 FRANCS** ND (1962 -old dates 15.9.1960; 1.10.1960). Red on m/c unpt. Maroon ovpt. on Rwanda-Burundi #4.

GOOD	FINE	XF
75.00	225.00	500.00

NOTICE

Readers with unlisted dates, signature varieties, etc. are invited to submit photocopies of their notes to: Standard Catalog of World Paper Money, 700 East State St. Iola, WI 54990-0001, fax: 1-715-445-4087, or E-Mail: thernr@krause.com.

		Good	Fine	XF
3	**100 Francs** ND (1962 -old dates 15.9.1960; 1.10.1960; 31.7.1962). Blue on lt. green and tan unpt. Ovpt. on Rwanda-Burundi #5.			
	a. Black ovpt.	75.00	135.00	300.00
	b. Purple ovpt.	75.00	135.00	300.00
4	**500 Francs** ND (1962 -old dates 15.9.1960; 15.9.1961). Lilac-brown on m/c unpt. Embossed ovpt. and blind embossed facsimile sign. on Rwanda-Burundi #6.	300.00	800.00	1200.
5	**1000 Francs** ND (1962 -old dates 15.5.1961; 1.7.1962). Green on m/c unpt. Embossed ovpt. and blind facsimile sign. on Rwanda-Burundi #7.	250.00	750.00	1100.

1964 Issue

#6-10 various date and sign. title varieties. Replacement notes: Serial # prefix *ZZ*.

		VG	VF	Unc
6	**20 Francs** 1964-76. Brown on m/c unpt. Flag of Rwanda at l. 4 young boys at l. ctr. w/pipeline in background at ctr. on back.			
	a. Sign. titles: *VICE GOUVERNEUR* and *GOUVERNEUR*, w/security thread. 1.7.1964; 31.3.1966; 15.3.1969; 1.9.1969.	2.50	7.50	15.00
	b. Sign. titles: *VICE GOUVERNEUR* and *ADMINISTRATEUR*, w/security thread. 1.7.1965.	3.50	8.50	20.00
	c. Sign. titles: *GOUVERNEUR* and *ADMINISTRATEUR*, w/security thread. 1.7.1971.	1.25	3.00	7.50
	d. Sign. titles: *ADMINISTRATEUR* and *ADMINISTRATEUR*, w/security thread. 30.10.1974.	.50	1.50	6.00
	e. Sign. titles: *ADMINISTRATEUR* and *GOUVERNEUR*, w/o security thread. 1.1.1976.	.50	.75	1.35
	s1. As a. Specimen. 1.7.1964; 31.3.1966; 15.3.1969.	—	—	5.00
	s2. As b. Specimen. 1.7.1965.	—	—	3.50
	s3. As c. Specimen. 1.7.1971.	—	—	3.50
	s4. As d. Specimen. 30.10.1974.	—	—	6.00

		VG	VF	Unc
7	**50 Francs** 1964-76. Blue on green unpt. Map of Rwanda at l. ctr. Miner at l. w/miners digging at ctr.			
	a. Sign. titles: *VICE GOUVERNEUR* and *GOUVERNEUR*, w/security thread. 1.7.1964; 31.1.1966; 1.9.1969.	3.00	10.00	20.00
	b. Sign. titles: *ADMINISTRATEUR* and *GOUVERNEUR*, w/security thread. 1.7.1971; 30.10.1974.	.75	2.00	7.00
	c. Sign. titles: *ADMINISTRATEUR* and *GOUVERNEUR*, w/o security thread. 1.1.1976.	.50	1.00	2.50
	s1. As a. Specimen. 1.7.1964; 31.1.1966; 1.9.1969.	—	—	4.00
	s2. As b. Specimen. 1.7.1971; 30.10.1974.	—	—	4.00

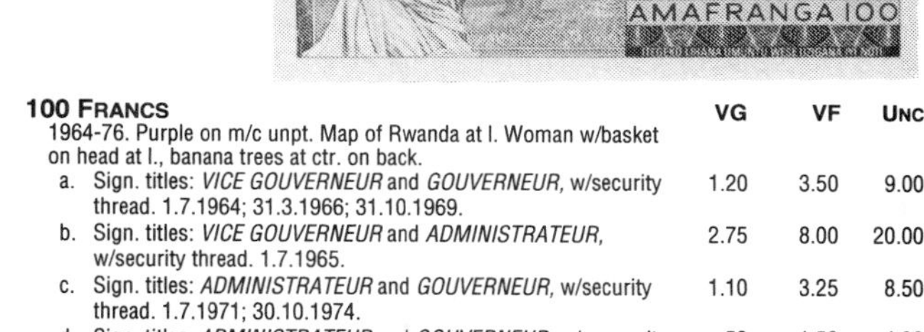

		VG	VF	Unc
8	**100 Francs** 1964-76. Purple on m/c unpt. Map of Rwanda at l. Woman w/basket on head at l., banana trees at ctr. on back.			
	a. Sign. titles: *VICE GOUVERNEUR* and *GOUVERNEUR*, w/security thread. 1.7.1964; 31.3.1966; 31.10.1969.	1.20	3.50	9.00
	b. Sign. titles: *VICE GOUVERNEUR* and *ADMINISTRATEUR*, w/security thread. 1.7.1965.	2.75	8.00	20.00
	c. Sign. titles: *ADMINISTRATEUR* and *GOUVERNEUR*, w/security thread. 1.7.1971; 30.10.1974.	1.10	3.25	8.50
	d. Sign. titles: *ADMINISTRATEUR* and *GOUVERNEUR*, w/o security thread. 1.1.1976.	.50	1.50	4.00
	s1. As a. Specimen. 1.7.1964; 31.10.1969.	—	—	6.00
	s2. As c. Specimen. 1.7.1971; 30.10.1974.	—	—	6.00

		VG	VF	Unc
9	**500 Francs** 1964-76. Dk. green and m/c. Arms of Rwanda at l. Man w/basket on head at l., rows of plants in background on back.			
	a. Sign. titles: *VICE GOUVERNEUR* and *GOUVERNEUR*. 1.7.1964; 31.3.1966; 31.10.1969.	3.50	10.00	42.50
	b. Sign. titles: *ADMINISTRATEUR* and *GOUVERNEUR*. 1.7.1971; 30.10.1974; 1.1.1976.	2.50	7.50	25.00
	s1. As a. Specimen. 1.7.1964; 31.3.1966.	—	—	12.50
	s2. As b. Specimen. 1.7.1971; 30.10.1974	—	—	12.50

		VG	VF	Unc
10	**1000 Francs** 1964-76. Red and m/c. Arms of Rwanda at l. Man and terraced hills at ctr. on back.			
	a. Sign. titles: *VICE GOUVERNEUR* and *GOUVERNEUR*. 1.7.1964; 31.3.1966; 15.3.1969.	8.00	25.00	80.00
	b. Sign. titles: *ADMINISTRATEUR* and *GOUVERNEUR*. 1.7.1971; 30.10.1974.	7.00	20.00	45.00
	c. Printed sign. titles like b. 1.1.1976.	5.00	15.00	30.00
	s1. As a. Specimen. 31.3.1966; 15.3.1969.	—	—	17.50
	s2. As b. Specimen. 1.7.1971.	—	—	17.50

1974 Issue

		VG	VF	Unc
11	**500 Francs** 19.4.1974. Green and m/c. Gen. Habyarimana at l. Back like #9.			
	a. Issued note.	5.00	10.00	25.00
	s. Specimen.	—	—	10.00

1978 Issue

		VG	VF	Unc
12	**100 Francs** 1.1.1978. Gray on lt. blue and m/c unpt. Zebras. Woman carrying child at l., mountains in background at ctr. r. on back.			
	a. Issued note.	.85	2.50	7.00
	s. Specimen.	—	—	12.50

		VG	VF	Unc
13	**500 Francs** 1.1.1978. Orange and m/c. Impalas. 8 drummers at l., strip mining at r. on back.			
	a. Wmk: Impala's head.	2.50	7.50	15.00
	b. W/o wmk.	21.50	65.00	150.00
	s. As a. Specimen.	—	—	20.00

		VG	VF	Unc
14	**1000 Francs** 1.1.1978. Green and m/c. Boy picking tea leaves at l. Tribal dancer at r. on back. Wmk: Impala's head.			
	a. Issued note.	4.00	12.50	27.50
	s. Specimen.	—	—	25.00

		VG	VF	Unc
15	**5000 Francs** 1.1.1978. Green, blue and m/c. Female w/basket on her head at l., field workers at ctr. Lake and mountains on back. Wmk: Impala's head.			
	a. Issued note.	45.00	65.00	150.00
	s. Specimen.	—	—	100.00

1981 Issue

		VG	VF	Unc
16	**500 Francs** 1.7.1981. Brown and m/c. Arms at l., 3 gazelle at r. Men working in field at l. on back. Wmk: Crowned crane's head.			
	a. Issued note.	2.25	8.00	22.50
	s. Specimen.	—	—	20.00

		VG	VF	Unc
17	**1000 Francs** 1.7.1981. Green, brown and m/c. 2 Watusi warriors at r. 2 gorillas at l., canoe in lake at r. on back. Wmk: Crowned crane's head.			
	a. Issued note.	4.00	12.00	30.00
	s. Specimen.	—	—	32.50

1982 Issue

		VG	VF	Unc
18	**100 Francs** 1.8.1982. Black on lilac and m/c unpt. Zebras at ctr. and r. Back purple and m/c; woman carrying baby at l., view of mountains at ctr. Wmk: Impala's head.	.50	1.60	4.00

1988-89 ISSUE

#19, 21 and 22 similar to #18, #17 and #15, but new spelling *AMAFARANGA* on back. Slight color differences and new sign. titles: *2E VICE-GOUVERNEUR and GOUVERNEUR.*

		VG	VF	UNC
19	**100 FRANCS** 24.4.1989. Similar to #18.	.40	1.25	3.50

#20 Deleted.

		VG	VF	UNC
21	**1000 FRANCS** 1.1.1988; 24.4.1989. Similar to #17.	2.75	8.00	15.00
22	**5000 FRANCS** 1.1.1988; 24.4.1989. Similar to #15.	16.50	50.00	90.00

1994 ISSUE

#23-25 mountainous landscape at ctr. r. Wmk: Impala's head. Printer: G&D (w/o imprint).

		VG	VF	UNC
23	**500 FRANCS** 1.12.1994. Blue-black, black and dk. blue-green on m/c unpt. Antelope at l. ctr. on back.	FV	FV	7.50

		VG	VF	UNC
24	**1000 FRANCS** 1.12.1994. Purple, red-brown and dk. brown on m/c unpt. Vegetation at l., water buffalo at ctr. on back.	FV	FV	18.50

		VG	VF	UNC
25	**5000 FRANCS** 1.12.1994. Dk. brown, violet and purple on m/c unpt. Reclining lion at l. ctr. on back.	FV	FV	50.00

1998 ISSUE

		VG	VF	UNC
26	**500 FRANCS** 1.12.1998. M/c. Gorillas on back.	FV	FV	10.00
27	**1000 FRANCS** 1.12.1998. M/c.	FV	FV	20.00
28	**5000 FRANCS** 1.12.1998. M/c.	FV	FV	62.50

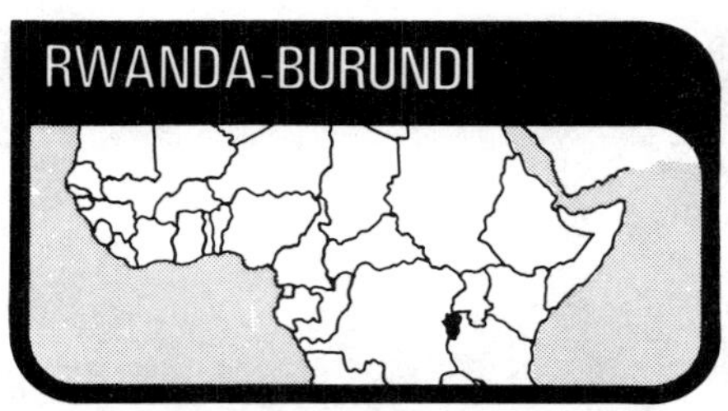

Rwanda-Burundi, a Belgian League of Nations mandate and United Nations trust territory comprising the provinces of Rwanda and Burundi of the former colony of German East Africa, was located in central Africa between the present Republic of the Congo, Uganda and mainland Tanzania. The mandate-trust territory had an area of 20,916 sq. mi. (54,272 sq. km.).

For specific statistics and history of Rwanda and Burundi see individual entries.

When Rwanda and Burundi were formed into a mandate for administration by Belgium, their names were changed to Ruanda and Urundi and they were organized as an integral part of the Belgian Congo, during which time they used a common banknote issue with the Belgian Congo. After the Belgian Congo acquired independence as the Republic of the Congo, the provinces of Ruanda and Urundi reverted to their former names of Rwanda and Burundi and issued notes with both names on them. In 1962, both Rwanda and Burundi became separate independent states.

Also see Belgian Congo, Burundi and Rwanda.

MONETARY SYSTEM:

1 Franc = 100 Centimes

MANDATE - TRUST TERRITORY

BANQUE D'EMISSION DU RWANDA ET DU BURUNDI

1960 ISSUE

		VG	VF	UNC
1	**5 FRANCS** 1960-63. Lt. brown on green unpt. Antelope at l.			
	a. 15.9.1960; 15.5.1961.	10.00	32.50	125.00
	b. 15.4.1963.	10.00	32.50	125.00

		VG	VF	UNC
2	**10 FRANCS** 15.9.1960; 5.10.1960. Dull gray on pale blue and pale orange unpt. Hippopotamus at l. Printer: TDLR.	20.00	60.00	225.00

		VG	VF	UNC
3	**20 FRANCS** 15.9.1960; 5.10.1960. Green on tan and pink unpt. Crocodile at r. Printer: TDLR.	22.50	70.00	300.00

		GOOD	FINE	XF
4	**50 FRANCS** 15.9.1960; 1.10.1960. Red on m/c unpt. Lioness at ctr. r.	15.00	40.00	160.00

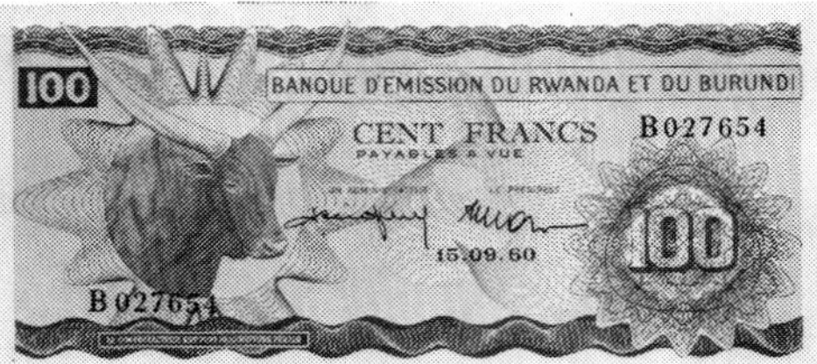

		GOOD	FINE	XF
5	**100 FRANCS** 15.9.1960; 1.10.1960; 31.7.1962. Blue on lt. green and tan unpt. Zebu at l.	12.50	28.50	110.00

		GOOD	FINE	XF
6	**500 FRANCS** 15.9.1960; 15.5.1961; 15.9.1961. Lilac-brown on m/c unpt. Rhinoceros at ctr. r.	150.00	450.00	—

		GOOD	FINE	XF
7	**1000 FRANCS** 15.9.1960; 15.5.1961; 31.7.1962. Green on m/c unpt. Zebra at r.	135.00	425.00	—

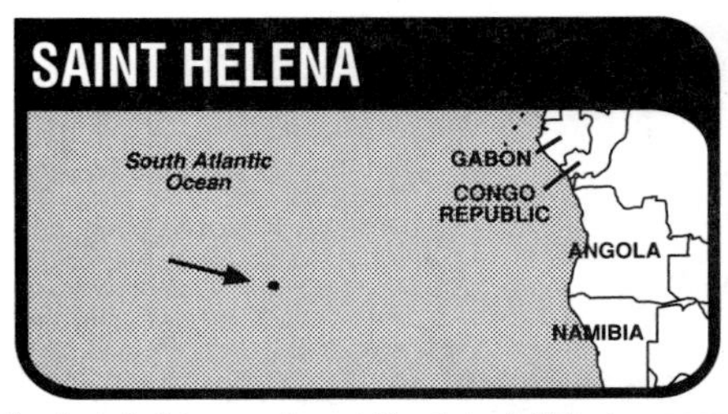

The Colony of St. Helena, a British colony located about 1,150 miles (1,850 km.) from the west coast of Africa, has an area of 47 sq. mi. (122 sq. km.) and a population of 5,700. Capital: Jamestown. Flax, lace and rope are produced for export. Ascension and Tristan da Cunha are dependencies of St. Helena.

The island was discovered and named by the Portuguese navigator João da Nova Castella in 1502. The Portuguese imported livestock, fruit trees and vegetables but established no permanent settlement. The Dutch occupied the island temporarily, 1645-1651. The original European settlement was founded by representatives of the British East India Company sent to annex the island after the departure of the Dutch. The Dutch returned and captured St. Helena from the British on New Year's Day, 1673, but were in turn ejected by a British force under Sir Richard Munden. Thereafter St. Helena was the undisputed possession of Great Britain. The island served as the place of exile for Napoleon, several Zulu chiefs, and an ex-sultan of Zanzibar.

RULERS:

British

MONETARY SYSTEM:

1 Pound = 20 Shillings to 1971

1 Pound = 100 New Pence, 1971-

SIGNATURE VARIETIES	
1	
2	
3	

GOVERNMENT OF ST. HELENA

1976; 1979 ND ISSUE

#5-8 views of the island at l., Qn. Elizabeth II at r.

#5-7 Royal arms w/motto at l., shield w/ship at ctr. r. on back.

		VG	VF	UNC
5	**50 PENCE** ND (1979). Purple on pink and pale yellow-green unpt. correctly spelled *ANGLIAE* in motto. Sign. 2.	1.00	1.50	4.50

NOTE: #5 w/serial #170,001-200,000 are non-redeemable.

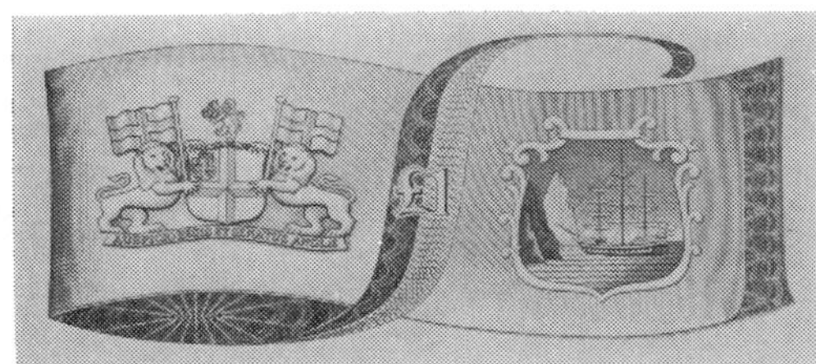

		VG	VF	UNC
6	**1 POUND** ND (1976). Deep olive-green on pale orange and ochre unpt. Incorrect spelling *ANGLAE* in motto. 153 x 67mm.	2.00	6.00	20.00

		VG	VF	UNC
7	**5 POUNDS** ND (1976). Blue on lt. brown unpt. Sign. 1.			
	a. Incorrect spelling *ANGLAE* in motto.	FV	10.00	30.00
	b. Corrected spelling *ANGLIAE* in motto.	FV	FV	20.00

		VG	VF	UNC
8	**10 POUNDS** ND (1979). Pale red on m/c unpt. Arms on back, correctly spelled *ANGLIAE* in motto. Sign. varieties.			
	a. Sign. 2.	FV	FV	52.50
	b. Sign. 3.	—	—	30.00
	c. As a. Uncut sheet of 3.	—	—	275.00
	r. Remainder w/o sign. or serial #.	—	—	100.00

1982; 1986 ND ISSUE

#9 and 10 Qn. Elizabeth II at r.

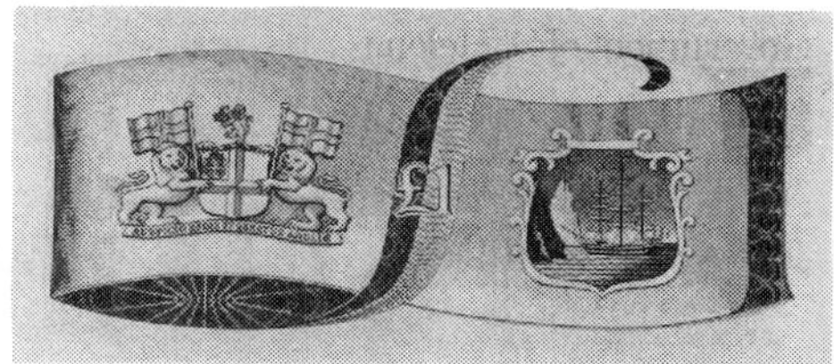

		VG	VF	UNC
9	**1 POUND** ND (1982). Deep olive-green on pale orange and ochre unpt. Like #6 but corrected spelling *ANGLIAE* in motto. Reduced size, 147 x 66mm. Sign. 2.	FV	FV	4.50

NOTE: #9 w/serial #*A/1* 350,000 - *A/1* 400,000 are non-redeemable.

		VG	VF	UNC
10	**20 POUNDS** ND (1986). Dk. brown on m/c unpt. Harbor view at l. ctr. Back lt. green; arms at ctr. 4 signs. in block form.	FV	FV	60.00

1999 ND ISSUE

		VG	VF	UNC
11	**5 POUNDS** ND. Similar to #7. 4 signs. in block form.	FV	FV	27.50

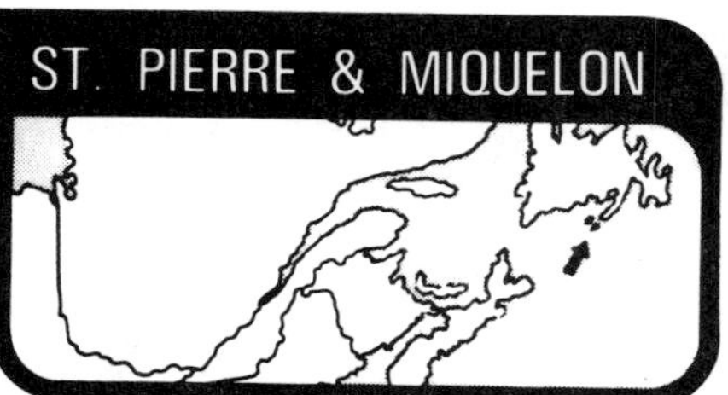

The Territorial Collectivity of St. Pierre and Miquelon, a French overseas territory located 10 miles (16 km.) off the south coast of Newfoundland, has an area of 93 sq. mi. (242 sq. km.) and a population of *6,000. Capital: St. Pierre. The economy of the barren archipelago is based on cod fishing and fur farming Fish and fish products, and mink and silver fox pelts are exported.

The islands, occupied by the French in 1604, were captured by the British in 1702 and held until 1763 when they were returned to the possession of France and employed as a fishing station. They passed between France and England on six more occasions between 1778 and 1814 when they were awarded permanently to France by the Treaty of Paris. The rugged, soil-poor granite islands, which will support only evergreen shrubs, are all that remain to France of her extensive colonies in North America. In 1958 St. Pierre and Miquelon voted in favor of the new constitution of the Fifth Republic of France, thereby choosing to remain within the French Community.

Notes of the Banque de France circulated 1937-1942; afterwards notes of the Caisse Centrale de la France Libre and the Caisse Centrale de la France d'Outre-Mer.

RULERS:

French

MONETARY SYSTEM:

1 Franc = 100 Centimes
1 Nouveau Franc = 100 "old" Francs, 1960-

CAISSE CENTRALE DE LA FRANCE D'OUTRE-MER

SAINT-PIERRE-ET-MIQUELON

1960 ND PROVISIONAL ISSUE

#30-35 ovpt: *SAINT-PIERRE-ET-MIQUELON* and new denomination.

		VG	VF	UNC
30	**1 NOUVEAU FRANC ON 50 FRANCS** ND (1960). M/c. Ovpt. on Reunion #25.			
	a. Special series *A.1-Y.1* w/3 digit serial # and 5 digit control #.	7.50	30.00	125.00
	b. Normal series w/5 digit serial # and 9 digit control #.	3.00	10.00	65.00

1961; 1963 ND PROVISIONAL ISSUE

		VG	VF	UNC
31	**1 NOUVEAU FRANC ON 50 FRANCS** ND (1961). M/c. B. d'Esnambuc at l., ship at r. Woman on back.	35.00	200.00	600.00

		VG	VF	UNC
32	**2 NOUVEAUX FRANCS ON 100 FRANC** ND (1963). M/c. La Bourdonnais at l., 2 women at r. Woman looking at mountains on back.	4.00	15.00	70.00

		VG	VF	UNC
33	**10 NOUVEAUX FRANCS ON 500 FRANCS** ND (1964). M/c. Bldgs. and sailboat at l., 2 women at r. Ox-carts w/wood and plants on back.	12.00	50.00	250.00

		VG	VF	UNC
34	**20 NOUVEAUX FRANCS ON 1000 FRANCS** ND (1964). M/c. 2 women at r. Women at r., 2 men in small boat on back.	35.00	100.00	325.00

		VG	VF	UNC
35	**100 NOUVEAUX FRANCS ON 5000 FRANCS** ND (1961). M/c. Gen. Schoelcher at ctr. r. Family on back.	85.00	450.00	2000.

The Democratic Republic of Sao Tomé and Príncipe (formerly the Portuguese overseas province of St. Thomas and Prince Islands) is located in the Gulf of Guinea 150 miles (241 km.) off the west African coast. It has an area of 372 sq. mi. (960 sq. km.) and a population of *121,000. Capital: Sao Tomé. The economy of the islands is based on cocoa, copra and coffee.

St. Thomas and St. Prince were uninhabited when discovered by Portuguese navigators Joao de Santarem and Pedro de Escobar in 1470. After the failure of their initial settlement, 1485, the Portuguese successfully colonized St. Thomas with a colony of prisoners and exiled Jews, 1493. An initial prosperity based on the sugar trade gave way to a time of misfortune, 1567-1709, that saw the colony attacked and occupied or plundered by the French and Dutch; ravaged by the slave revolt of 1595; and finally rendered destitue by the transfer of the world sugar trade to Brazil. In the late 1800s, the colony turned from the production of sugar to cocoa, the basis of its present prosperity.

The islands were designated a Portuguese overseas province in 1951. On April 25, 1974, the government of Portugal was seized by a military junta which reached agreements providing for independence for the Portuguese overseas provinces of Portuguese Guinea (Guinea-Bissau), Mozambique, Cape Verde Islands, Angola, and St. Thomas and Prince Islands. The Democratic Republic of Sao Tomé and Príncipe was declared on July 12, 1975.

RULERS:

Portuguese to 1975

MONETARY SYSTEM:

1 Escudo = 100 Centavos, 1911-1976
1 Dobra = 100 Centimos, 1977-

BANCO NACIONAL ULTRAMARINO

S. TOMÉ E PRÍNCIPE BRANCH

1964 ISSUE

		VG	VF	UNC
40	**1000 ESCUDOS** 11.5.1964. Green on m/c unpt. J. de Santarem at r., bank arms at upper ctr. Woman, sailing ships at l. ctr., arms at upper r. on back.			
	a. Issued note.	25.00	60.00	135.00
	s. Specimen.	—	—	125.00

1974 CIRCULATING BEARER CHECK ISSUE

		VG	VF	UNC
41	**100 ESCUDOS** 31.3.1974.	—	—	—
42	**500 ESCUDOS** 28.4.1974.	—	—	—
43	**500 ESCUDOS** 31.12.1974.	20.00	50.00	125.00

		VG	VF	UNC
43A	**1000 ESCUDOS** 23.12.1974; 31.12.1974. Red.	45.00	85.00	150.00

DEMOCRATIC REPUBLIC

BANCO NACIONAL DE S. TOMÉ E PRÍNCIPE

1976 PROVISIONAL ISSUE

#44-48 new bank name ovpt. in red on both sides of Banco Nacional Ultramarino notes.

#44-46 bank seal at l., Portuguese arms at lower ctr., Kg. D. Afonso V at r. Printer: BWC.

		VG	VF	UNC
44	**20 ESCUDOS** 1.6.1976 (- old date 20.11.1958). Brown on m/c unpt. Ovpt. on #36.	2.00	5.00	12.50

		VG	VF	UNC
45	**50 ESCUDOS** 1.6.1976 (- old date 20.11.1958). Brown-viole-on m/c unpt. Ovpt. on #37.	2.00	5.00	12.50

		VG	VF	UNC
46	**100 ESCUDOS** 1.6.1976 (- old date 20.11.1958). Purple on m/c unpt. Ovpt. on #38.	4.00	10.00	20.00

		VG	VF	UNC
47	**500 ESCUDOS** 1.6.1976 (- old date 18.4.1956). Blue on m/c unpt. Ovpt. on #39.	15.00	37.50	100.00
48	**1000 ESCUDOS** 1.6.1976 (- old date 11.5.1964). Green on m/c unpt. Ovpt. on #40.	1.50	40.00	120.00

#49 Deleted. See #43A.

1976 CIRCULATING BEARER CHECK ISSUE

BANCO NACIONAL DE S. TOMÉ E PRÍNCIPE

S. Tomé, 21 de Junho de 1976

№ 9020013 Esc.=500$00=

Pague contra este original de cheque (não o tendo feito pelo duplicado) à ordem de AO PORTADOR

a quantia de QUINHENTOS ESCUDOS

Pagável em S. TOMÉ E PRINPICE

P. P. BANCO NACIONAL DE S. TOMÉ E PRÍNCIPE

		VG	VF	UNC
50	**500 ESCUDOS** 21.6.1976. Black on pink and lt. aqua unpt. 167 x 75mm.	10.00	27.50	85.00
51	**1000 ESCUDOS** 21.6.1976. 167 x 75mm.	13.50	33.00	100.00

DECRETO-LEI NO. 50/76; 1977 ISSUE

#52-55 Rei Amador at r. and as wmk., arms at lower l. Sign. titles: *O MINISTRO DA COORDENACÃO ECONOMICA* and *O GOVERNADOR*. Printer: BWC.

		VG	VF	UNC
52	**50 DOBRAS** 12.7.1977. Red and m/c. Parrot at ctr. in unpt. Scene w/2 fishermen in boats on back.	.65	2.00	6.00

		VG	VF	UNC
53	**100 DOBRAS** 12.7.1977. Green and m/c. Flower at ctr. in unpt. Group of people preparing food on back.	1.50	4.00	7.50

NOTICE

Readers with unlisted dates, signature varieties, etc. are invited to submit photocopies of their notes to: Standard Catalog of World Paper Money, 700 East State St. Iola, WI 54990-0001, fax: 1-715-445-4087, or E-Mail: thernr@krause.com.

		VG	VF	UNC
54	**500 DOBRAS** 12.7.1977. Purple and m/c. Turtle at ctr. in unpt. Waterfall on back.	3.00	10.00	22.50
55	**1000 DOBRAS** 12.7.1977. Blue and m/c. Bananas at ctr. in unpt. Fruit gatherer on back.	7.00	20.00	75.00

DECRETO-LEI NO. 6/82; 1982 ISSUE

#56-59 like #52-55 but w/sign. titles: *O MINISTRO DO PLANO* and *O GOVERNADOR*. Printer: BWC.

		VG	VF	UNC
56	**50 DOBRAS** 30.9.1982. Like #52.	.40	1.25	5.00

		VG	VF	UNC
57	**100 DOBRAS** 30.9.1982. Like #53.	.50	1.50	7.00
58	**500 DOBRAS** 30.9.1982. Like #54.	1.75	5.50	20.00

		VG	VF	UNC
59	**1000 DOBRAS** 30.9.1982. Like #55.	3.00	10.00	30.00

DECRETO-LEI NO. 1/88; 1989 ISSUE

#60-62 designs like #57-59 except sign. title at l.: *O MINISTRO DA ECONOMIA E FINANÇAS*. Printer: TDLR.

		VG	VF	UNC
60	**100 DOBRAS** 4.1.1989. Green and m/c. Like #57.	.40	1.25	4.00

		VG	VF	UNC
61	**500 DOBRAS** 4.1.1989. Violet, red, orange and tan on m/c unpt. Like #58.	.90	2.00	6.00

		VG	VF	UNC
62	**1000 DOBRAS** 4.1.1989. Blue, green and m/c unpt. Like #59.	1.75	5.00	15.00

BANCO CENTRAL DE S.TOMÉ E PRÍNCIPE

DECRETO LEI NO. 29/93; 1993 ISSUE

#63 and 64 like #61 and 62. Serial # at l. black, at r. lt. blue. Printer: TDLR.

		VG	VF	UNC
63	**500 DOBRAS** 26.8.1993. Violet, red, orange and tan on blue and m/c unpt. Like #61 but arms at lower l. is blue.	FV	FV	3.50

		VG	VF	UNC
64	**1000 DOBRAS** 26.8.1993. Violet and deep blue and blue-green on m/c unpt. Similar to #62.	FV	FV	8.50

DECRETO LEI NO. 42/96; 1996 ISSUE

#65-68 Rei Amador at r. and as wmk., arms at upper ctr. r. Printer: TDLR.

		VG	VF	UNC
65	**5000 DOBRAS** 22.10.1996. Purple, lilac and olive-green on m/c unpt. Papa Figo bird at l. ctr. Esplanade, modern bldg. at l. ctr. on back.	FV	FV	8.00

		VG	VF	UNC
66	**10,000 DOBRAS** 22.10.1996. Dk. green, blue-violet and tan on m/c unpt. Ossobo bird at l. ctr. Bridge over river at l. ctr. on back.	FV	FV	14.00

		VG	VF	UNC
67	**20,000 DOBRAS** 22.10.1996. Red, olive-brown and blue-black on m/c unpt. Cammussela bird at l. ctr. Beach scene at l. ctr. on back.	FV	FV	22.50

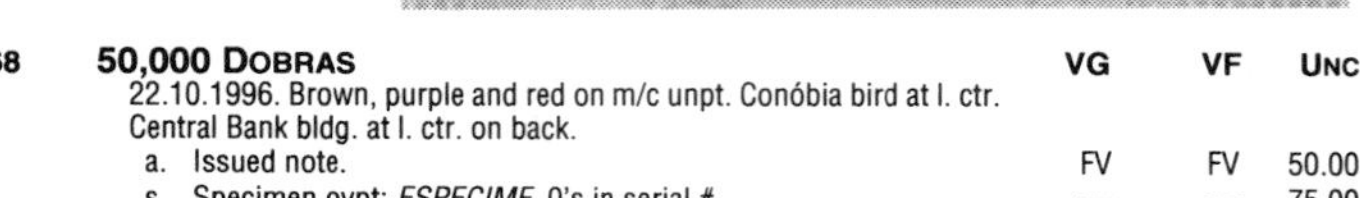

		VG	VF	UNC
68	**50,000 DOBRAS** 22.10.1996. Brown, purple and red on m/c unpt. Conóbia bird at l. ctr. Central Bank bldg. at l. ctr. on back.			
	a. Issued note.	FV	FV	50.00
	s. Specimen ovpt: *ESPECIME*, 0's in serial #.	—	—	75.00

Listings for

Samoa, see Western Samoa

The Kingdom of Saudi Arabia, an independent and absolute hereditary monarchy comprising the former sultanate of Nejd, the old kingdom of Hejaz, Asir and El Jasa, occupies four-fifths of the Arabian peninsula. The kingdom has an area of 830,000 sq. mi. (2,149,690 sq. km.) and a population of 17.8 million. Capital: Riyadh. The economy is based on oil, which provides 85 percent of Saudi Arabia's revenue.

Mohammed united the Arabs in the 7th century and his followers founded a great empire with its capital at Medina. The Turks established nominal rule over much of Arabia in the 16th and 17th centuries, and in the 18th century divided it into principalities. The Kingdom of Saudi Arabia was created by King Ibn-Saud (1882-1953), a descendant of earlier Wahabi rulers of the Arabian peninsula. In 1901 he seized Riyadh, capital of the Sultanate of Nejd, and in 1905 established himself as Sultan. In 1913 he captured the Turkish province of Hasa; took the Hejaz in 1925 and by 1926 most of Asir. In 1932 he combined Nejd and Hejaz into the single kingdom of Saudi Arabia. Asir was incorporated into the kingdom a year later.

One of the principal cities, Mecca, is the Holy center of Islam and is the scene of an annual Pilgrimage from the entire Moslem world.

RULERS:

Sa'ud Ibn Abdul Aziz, AH1373-1383/1953-1964AD
Faisal, AH1383-1395/1964-1975AD
Khaled, AH1395-1402/1975-1982AD
Fahd, AH1402-/1982AD-

MONETARY SYSTEM:

1 Riyal = 20 Ghirsh

KINGDOM

SAUDI ARABIAN MONETARY AGENCY

SIGNATURE VARIETIES			
1		2	
3		4	

LAW OF 1.7.AH1379; 1961 ND ISSUE

#6-10 arms (palm tree and crossed swords) on back and as wmk.

		VG	VF	UNC
6	**1 RIYAL** *L. AH1379* (1961). Brown on lt. blue and green unpt. Hill of Light at ctr. Back violet-brown and green. Sign. #1.	2.00	10.00	40.00

		VG	VF	UNC
7	**5 RIYALS** *L. AH1379* (1961). Blue and green on m/c unpt. Fortress at ctr.			
	a. Sign. #1.	15.00	60.00	250.00
	b. Sign. #2.	20.00	85.00	325.00

		VG	VF	UNC
8	**10 RIYALS** *L. AH1379* (1961). Green on pink and m/c unpt. Dhows in Jedda harbor.			
	a. Sign. #1.	15.00	65.00	250.00
	b. Sign. #2.	20.00	100.00	350.00

		VG	VF	UNC
9	**50 RIYALS** *L. AH1379* (1961). Violet and olive-green on m/c unpt. Derrick at ctr. r.			
	a. Sign. #1.	60.00	200.00	750.00
	b. Sign. #2.	60.00	200.00	750.00

		VG	VF	UNC
10	**100 RIYALS** *L. AH1379* (1961). Red on m/c unpt. Bldg. at l., archway in background at ctr., bldg. at r.			
	a. Sign. #1.	200.00	750.00	2000.
	b. Sign. #2.	175.00	650.00	1750.

LAW OF 1.7.AH1379; 1966 ND ISSUE

#11-15 wmk: Arms.

		VG	VF	UNC
11	**1 RIYAL** *L. AH1379* (1966). Purple on m/c unpt. Gov't. bldg. at ctr. r. Saudi arms on back.			
	a. Sign. #2.	.50	2.50	10.00
	b. Sign. #3.	.50	2.50	12.50

		VG	VF	UNC
12	**5 RIYALS** *L. AH1379* (1966). Green on m/c unpt. Airport. Oil loading on ships at dockside on back.			
	a. Sign. #2.	2.00	7.50	35.00
	b. Sign. #3.	5.00	25.00	65.00

		VG	VF	UNC
13	**10 RIYALS** *L. AH1379* (1966). Gray-blue on m/c unpt. Mosque. Al-Masa Wall w/arches on back. Sign. #2.	2.50	9.00	35.00

		VG	VF	UNC
14	**50 RIYALS** *L. AH1379* (1966). Brown on m/c unpt. Courtyard of mosque at r. Saudi arms at l., row of palms at ctr. on back.			
	a. Sign. #2.	20.00	60.00	250.00
	b. Sign. #3.	18.00	55.00	225.00

		VG	VF	UNC
15	**100 RIYALS** *L. AH1379* (1966). Red on m/c unpt. Gov't. bldg. at ctr. r. Derricks at l. ctr. on back.			
	a. Sign. #2.	30.00	100.00	350.00
	b. Sign. #3.	25.00	90.00	300.00

LAW OF 1.7.AH1379; 1976; 1977 ND ISSUE

#16-19 portr. Kg. Faisal at r. and as wmk. Sign. 4.

		VG	VF	UNC
16	**1 RIYAL** *L. AH1379* (1977). Red-brown on m/c unpt. Hill of Light at ctr. Airport at l. ctr. on back.	.25	.50	2.00

INCORRECT

CORRECTED

		VG	VF	UNC
17	**5 RIYALS** *L. AH1379* (1977). Green and brown on m/c unpt. Irrigation canal at ctr. Dam at l. ctr. on back.			
	a. Incorrect Khamsa (five) in lower ctr. panel of text.	1.50	5.00	15.00
	b. Correct Khamsa (five) in lower ctr. panel of text.	1.00	2.00	6.50

		VG	VF	UNC
18	**10 RIYALS** *L. AH1379* (1977). Lilac and brown on m/c unpt. Oil drilling platform at ctr. Oil refinery on back.	FV	4.00	15.00

		VG	VF	UNC
19	**50 RIYALS** *L. AH1379* (1976). Green, purple and brown on m/c unpt. Arches of mosque at ctr. Courtyard of mosque at l. ctr. on back.	FV	16.00	40.00

		VG	VF	UNC
20	**100 RIYALS** *L. AH1379* (1976). Blue and turquoise on m/c unpt. Mosque at ctr., Kg. 'Abd al-'Aziz Ibn Saud at r. Long bldg. w/arches on back.	FV	30.00	75.00

LAW OF 1.7.AH1379; 1983; 1984 ND ISSUE

#21-26 wmk: Kg. Fahd.

#21-24 upper l. panel also exists w/unnecessary upper accent mark in "Monetary."

INCORRECT

CORRECTED

		VG	VF	UNC
21	**1 RIYAL** *L. AH1379* (1984). Dk. brown on m/c unpt. 7th century gold dinar at l., Portr. Kg. Fahd at ctr. r. Flowers and landscape on back. 2 sign. varieties.			
	a. Incorrect text. Sign. 5.	FV	1.00	2.00
	b. Correct "Monetary." Sign. 5; 6.	FV	FV	1.25

NOTICE

Readers with unlisted dates, signature varieties, etc. are invited to submit photocopies of their notes to: Standard Catalog of World Paper Money, 700 East State St. Iola, WI 54990-0001, fax: 1-715-445-4087, or E-Mail: thernr@krause.com.

		VG	VF	UNC
22	**5 RIYALS** *L. AH1379* (1983). Purple, brown, and blue-green on m/c unpt. Dhows at l., portr. Kg. Fahd at ctr. r. Oil refinery at ctr. r. on back.			
	a. Incorrect text. Sign. 5.	FV	1.50	4.50
	b. Correct "Monetary." Sign. 5.	FV	FV	3.25

		VG	VF	UNC
23	**10 RIYALS** *L. AH1379* (1983). Black, brown and purple on m/c unpt. Fortress at l., portr. Kg. Fahd at ctr. r. Palm trees at ctr. r. on back.			
	a. Incorrect text. Sign. 5.	FV	4.00	9.00
	b. Correct "Monetary." Sign. 5.	FV	FV	7.00

		VG	VF	UNC
24	**50 RIYALS** *L. AH1379* (1983). Dk. green and dk. brown on m/c unpt. Mosque of Omar (Dome of the Rock) in Jerusalem at l., portr. Kg. Fahd at ctr. r. Mosque at ctr. on back.			
	a. Incorrect text. Sign. 5.	FV	FV	30.00
	b. Correct "Monetary." Sign. 5.	FV	FV	25.00

#25-26 Saudi arms in blind embossed latent image area at l. ctr.

		VG	VF	UNC
25	**100 RIYALS** *L. AH1379* (1984). Brown-violet and olive-green on m/c unpt. Mosque at l., portr. Kg. Fahd at ctr. r. Mosque at ctr. on back. Sign. 5.	FV	FV	45.00

INCORRECT CORRECTED

		VG	VF	UNC
26	**500 Riyals** *L. AH1379* (1983). Purple and green on m/c unpt. Courtyard at l., portr. Kg. 'Abd al-'Aziz Ibn Saud at ctr. r. Courtyard of Great Mosque at ctr. on back.			
	a. Incorrect "Five Hundred Riyals" in lower ctr. panel of text. Sign. 5.	FV	150.00	250.00
	b. Correct "Five Hundred Riyals" in lower ctr. panel of text. Sign. 5.	FV	FV	185.00

SCOTLAND

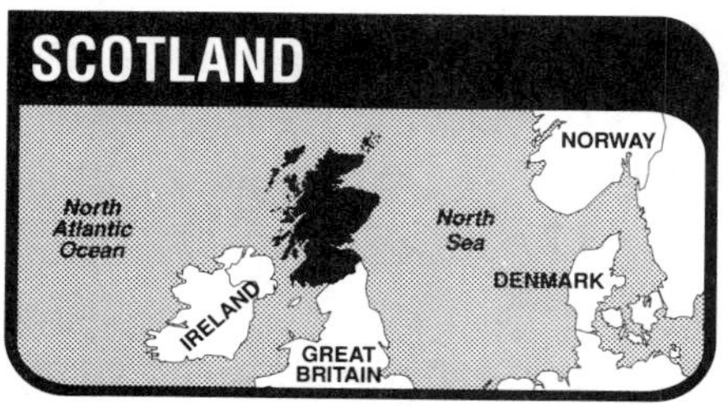

Scotland, a part of the United Kingdom of Great Britain and Northern Ireland, consists of the northern part of the island of Great Britain. It has an area of 30,414 sq. mi. (78,772 sq. km.). Capital: Edinburgh. Principal industries are agriculture, fishing, manufacturing and ship-building.

In the 5th century, Scotland consisted of four kingdoms; that of the Picts, the Scots, Strathclyde, and Northumbria. The Scottish kingdom was united by Malcolm II (1005-34), but its ruler was forced to do homage to the English crown in 1174. Scotland won independence under Robert Bruce at Bannockburn in 1314 and was ruled by the house of Stuart from 1371 to 1688. The personal union of the kingdoms of England and Scotland was achieved in 1603 by the accession of King James VI of Scotland as James I of England. Scotland was united with England by Parliamentary act in 1707.

RULERS:

British

MONETARY SYSTEM:

1 Shilling = 12 Pence
1 Pound = 20 Shillings to 1971
1 Pound = 100 New Pence, 1971-1981
1 Pound = 100 Pence, 1982-

Bank of Scotland

1935; 1938 Issue

		VG	VF	UNC
93	**10 Pounds** 1938-63. Scottish arms in panel at l., medallion of Goddess of fortune below arms at r. Bank bldg. on back.			
	a. Sign. Lord Elphinstone and A. W. M. Beveridge.	50.00	140.00	300.00
	b. Sign. Lord Elphinstone and J. B. Crawford.	40.00	100.00	240.00
	c. Sign. Lord Bilsland and Sir Wm. Watson. 27.9.1963.	25.00	70.00	150.00

		VG	VF	UNC
94	**20 Pounds** 1935-65. Like #93.			
	a. Sign. Lord Elphinstone and A. W. M. Beveridge.	80.00	110.00	210.00
	b. Sign. Lord Elphinstone and J. Macfarlane.	70.00	100.00	190.00
	c. Sign. Lord Elphinstone and J. B. Crawford.	65.00	92.50	165.00
	d. Sign. Lord Elphinstone and Sir Wm. Watson.	55.00	85.00	150.00
	e. Sign. Sir J. Craig and Sir Wm. Watson.	50.00	77.50	135.00
	f. Sign. Lord Bilsland and Sir Wm. Watson.	45.00	70.00	120.00

1961 Issue

		VG	VF	UNC
102	**1 Pound** 1961-65. Lt. brown and pale blue. Medallion at ctr. Date below.			
	a. Imprint ends: *LD.* Sign. Lord Bilsland and Sir Wm. Watson. 10.5.1961-13.2.1964.	4.00	12.00	27.50
	b. Imprint ends: *LTD.* Sign. Lord Bilsland and Sir Wm. Watson. 4.5.1965; 11.5.1965.	3.50	10.00	25.00

		VG	VF	UNC
103	**5 POUNDS** 14.9.1961-22.9.1961. Lt. brown and pale blue. Reduced size. Sign. Lord Bilsland and Sir Wm. Watson.	15.00	35.00	75.00

1961; 1966 ISSUE

		VG	VF	UNC
105	**1 POUND** 1966; 1967. Lt. brown and pale blue. Similar to #102 but *EDINBURGH* and date at r. Sign. Lord Polwarth and J. Letham w/titles: *GOVERNOR* and *TREASURER & GENERAL MANAGER*. 2 wmk. varieties.			
	a. W/o electronic sorting marks on back. 1.6.1966.	4.00	12.00	30.00
	b. W/electronic sorting marks on back. 3.3.1967.	4.00	12.00	27.50

		VG	VF	UNC
106	**5 POUNDS** 1961-67. Blue and lt. brown. Medallion of fortune at ctr., numerals of value filled in at base. Arms at l., ship at r. on back.			
	a. Sign. Lord Bilsland and Sir Wm. Watson w/titles: *GOVERNOR* and *TREASURER*. 25.9.1961-12.1.1965.	15.00	30.00	60.00
	b. Sign. Lord Polwarth and Sir Wm. Watson. 7.3.1966-8.3.1966.	20.00	35.00	75.00
	c. Lighter shades of printing. Sign. Lord Polwarth and J. Letham w/titles: *GOVERNOR* and *TREASURER & GENERAL MANAGER*. 1.2.1967; 2.2.1967.	15.00	30.00	60.00
	d. Sign. titles as b. W/electronic sorting marks on back. 1.11.1967.	20.00	35.00	75.00

1968; 1969 ISSUE

		VG	VF	UNC
109	**1 POUND** 1968; 1969. Ochre on m/c unpt. Arms at ctr. flanked by 2 women. Arms at upper l., shield at upper ctr., sailing ship at upper r. on back.			
	a. *EDINBURGH* 19mm in length. 17.7.1968.	6.00	15.00	35.00
	b. *EDINBURGH* 24mm in length. 18.8.1969.	6.00	15.00	35.00

		VG	VF	UNC
110	**5 POUNDS** 1968-69. Green on m/c unpt. Similar to #109.			
	a. *EDINBURGH* 19mm in length. 1.11.1968.	30.00	70.00	140.00
	b. *EDINBURGH* 24mm in length. 8.12.1969.	30.00	70.00	140.00

		VG	VF	UNC
110A	**20 POUNDS** 5.5.1969. Scottish arms in panel at l., medallion of Goddess of Fortune below arms at ctr. r. Lord Polwarth and J. Letham. W/security thread. Wmk: Thistle.	60.00	125.00	300.00

NOTE: #110A was an emergency printing of 25,000 examples.

1970-74 ISSUE

#111-115 arms at ctr. flanked by 2 women. Sir W. Scott at r.

#111-113 replacement notes: #111 - Serial # prefix *Z/1*, *Z/2* or *Z/3*; #112 - Serial # prefix *ZA* or *ZB*; #113 - Serial # prefix *ZB*.

		VG	VF	UNC
111	**1 POUND** 1970-88. Green on m/c unpt. Sailing ship at l., arms at upper ctr., medallion of Pallas seated at r. on back.			
	a. Sign. Lord Polwarth and T. W. Walker. 10.8.1970; 31.8.1971.	5.00	12.00	35.00
	b. Sign. Lord Clydesmuir and T. W. Walker. 1.11.1972; 30.8.1973.	5.00	10.00	35.00
	c. Sign. Lord Clydesmuir and A. M. Russell. 28.10.1974-3.10.1978.	3.00	5.00	22.50
	d. Sign. Lord Clydesmuir and D. B. Pattullo. 15.10.1979; 4.11.1980.	3.00	5.00	15.00
	e. Sign. T. N. Risk and D. B. Pattullo. 30.7.1981.	4.00	7.00	18.00
	f. W/o sorting marks on back. Sign. like e. 7.10.1983; 9.11.1984; 12.12.1985; 18.11.1986.	2.00	3.00	10.00
	g. Sign. T. N. Risk and L. P. Burt. 19.8.1988.	2.00	3.00	8.00
	s. As a. Specimen. 10.8.1970.	—	—	85.00

112 5 POUNDS
1970-88. Blue on m/c unpt. Back similar to #111.

		VG	VF	UNC
a.	Sign. Lord Polwarth and T. W. Walker. 10.8.1970; 2.9.1971.	15.00	35.00	80.00
b.	Sign. Lord Clydesmuir and T. W. Walker. 4.12.1972; 5.9.1973.	15.00	35.00	75.00
c.	Sign. Lord Clydesmuir and A. M. Russell. 4.11.1974; 1.12.1975; 21.11.1977; 19.10.1978.	12.00	25.00	60.00
d.	Sign. Lord Clydesmuir and D. B. Pattullo. 28.9.1979; 28.11.1980.	12.00	20.00	55.00
e.	Sign. T. N. Risk and D. B. Pattullo. 27.7.1981; 25.6.1982.	10.00	15.00	45.00
f.	W/o encoding marks. 13.10.1983; 29.2.1988.	FV	12.00	30.00
s.	As a. Specimen. 10.8.1970.	—	—	100.00

113 10 POUNDS
1974-90. Brown on m/c unpt. Medallions of sailing ship at lower l., Pallas seated at upper l. ctr., arms at r. on back.

		VG	VF	UNC
a.	Sign. Lord Clydesmuir and A. M. Russell. 1.5.1974-10.10.1979.	20.00	35.00	100.00
b.	Sign. Lord Clydesmuir and D. B. Pattullo. 5.2.1981.	20.00	30.00	100.00
c.	Sign. T. N. Risk and D. B. Pattullo. 22.7.1981; 16.6.1982; 14.10.1983; 17.9.1984; 20.10.1986; 6.8.1987.	FV	20.00	70.00
d.	Sign. T. N. Risk and P. Burt. 1.9.1989; 31.10.1990.	FV	20.00	50.00

114 20 POUNDS
1970-87. Purple on m/c unpt. Arms at upper l. above sailing ship w/medallion of Pallas seated below, head office bldg. at ctr. on back.

		VG	VF	UNC
a.	Sign. Lord Polwarth and T. W. Walker. 1.10.1970.	40.00	90.00	225.00
b.	Sign. Lord Clydesmuir and T. W. Walker. 3.1.1973.	40.00	70.00	175.00
c.	Sign. Lord Clydesmuir and A. M. Russell. 8.11.1974; 14.1.1977.	40.00	60.00	160.00
d.	Sign. Lord Clydesmuir and D. B. Pattullo. 16.7.1979; 2.2.1981.	FV	50.00	140.00
e.	Sign. T. N. Risk and D. B. Pattullo. 4.8.1981-5.12.1987.	FV	45.00	120.00
s.	As a. Specimen. 1.10.1970.	—	—	125.00

115 100 POUNDS
1971-90. Red on m/c unpt. Arms at upper l., medallions of sailing ship at lower l., Pallas seated at lower r., head office bldg. at ctr. on back.

		VG	VF	UNC
a.	Sign. Lord Clydesmuir and T. W. Walker. 6.12.1971; 6.9.1973.	225.00	300.00	500.00
b.	Sign. T. N. Risk and D. B. Pattullo. 26.11.1986; 18.12.1995.	FV	FV	300.00
s.	As a. Specimen.	—	—	300.00

1990-92 STERLING ISSUE

#116-118 similar to previous issue but w/*STERLING* added below value. Smaller size notes.

116 5 POUNDS
1990-94. Blue on m/c unpt. Similar to #112, but 135 x 70mm.

		VG	VF	UNC
a.	Sign. T. N. Risk and P. Burt. 20.6.1990.	FV	12.00	20.00
b.	Sign. D. B. Pattullo and P. Burt. 6.11.1991; 18.1.1993; 7.1.1994.	FV	10.00	18.00

	VG	VF	UNC
117 10 POUNDS 7.5.1992; 9.3.1993; 13.4.1994. Deep brown on m/c unpt. Similar to #113, but 142 x 75mm. Sign. D. B. Pattullo and P. Burt.	FV	20.00	37.50

	VG	VF	UNC
118 20 POUNDS 1.7.1991; 3.2.1992; 12.1.1993. Purple on m/c unpt. Similar to #114 but reduced size, 148 x 81mm. Sign. D. B. Pattullo and P. Burt.	FV	40.00	65.00

		VG	VF	UNC
118A	**100 POUNDS**			
	14.2.1990; 2.12.1992; 9.2.1994. Red on m/c unpt. Similar to #115 but in Sterling added to denomination. Sign. D. B. Pattullo and P. Burt.	FV	210.00	325.00

1995 COMMEMORATIVE ISSUE

#119-122, Tercentenary - Bank of Scotland

#119-123 Sir W. Scott at l. and as wmk., bank arms at ctr. Bank head office bldg. at lower l., medallion of Pallas seated, arms and medallion of sailing ships at r. on back. Printer: TDLR (W/o imprint).

		VG	VF	UNC
119	**5 POUNDS**			
	1995-. Dk. blue and purple on m/c unpt. Oil well riggers working w/drill at ctr. on back.			
	a. Sign. D. B. Pattullo and P. Burt. 4.1.1995.	FV	FV	18.50
	b. Sign. Bruce Pattullo and G. Masterton. 13.9.1996.	FV	FV	13.50
	c. Sign. A. Grant and G. Masterton. 5.8.1998.	FV	FV	12.50

		VG	VF	UNC
120	**10 POUNDS**			
	1995-. Dk. brown and deep olive-green on m/c unpt. Workers by distilling equipment at ctr. on back.			
	a. Sign. D. B. Pattullo and P. Burt. 1.2.1995.	FV	FV	35.00
	b. Sign. Bruce Pattullo and G. Masterton. 5.8.1997.	FV	FV	27.50
	c. Sign. A. Grant and G. Masterton. 18.8.1998.	FV	FV	25.00

		VG	VF	UNC
121	**20 POUNDS**			
	1995-. Violet and brown on m/c unpt. Woman researcher at laboratory station at ctr. on back.			
	a. Sign. D. B. Pattullo and P. Burt. 1.5.1995.	FV	FV	62.50
	b. Sign. Bruce Pattullo and G. Masterton. 25.10.1996.	FV	FV	55.00
	c. Sign. A. Grant and G. Masterton.	Expected New Issue		

		VG	VF	UNC
122	**50 POUNDS**			
	1.5.1995. Dk. green and olive-brown on m/c unpt. Music director and violinists at ctr. on back. Sign. D. B. Pattullo and P. Burt.	FV	FV	125.00

		VG	VF	UNC
123	**100 POUNDS**			
	1995-. Red-violet and red-orange on m/c unpt. Golf outing at ctr. on back.			
	a. Sign. D. B. Pattullo and P. Burt. 17.7.1995.	FV	FV	275.00
	b. Sign. D. B. Pattullo and G. Masterton. 18.8.1997.	FV	FV	235.00

BRITISH LINEN BANK

NOTE: Formerly the British Linen Company. See Vol. I. Merged with the Bank of Scotland in 1970.

1961; 1962 ISSUE

#162-170 sideview of seated Britannia in emblem at l., arms at upper r. Back blue. Printer: TDLR.

		VG	VF	UNC
162	**1 POUND** 30.9.1961. Blue and red.	12.00	25.00	60.00

		VG	VF	UNC
163	**5 POUNDS** 2.1.1961; 3.2.1961. Blue and red.	17.50	65.00	150.00
164	**20 POUNDS** 14.2.1962; 5.3.1962; 4.4.1962. Blue and red.	45.00	100.00	225.00

		VG	VF	UNC
165	**100 POUNDS** 9.5.1962; 1.6.1962. Blue and red.	200.00	300.00	500.00

1962 ISSUE

		VG	VF	UNC
166	**1 POUND** 1962-67. Blue and red. Similar to #162 but reduced size. 150 x 70mm.			
	a. Sign. A. P. Anderson. 31.3.1962.	5.00	15.00	45.00
	b. Test note w/lines for electronic sorting on back. 31.3.1962.	16.00	60.00	200.00
	c. Sign. T. W. Walker. 1.7.1963-13.6.1967.	5.00	12.00	30.00

		VG	VF	UNC
167	**5 POUNDS** 21.9.1962-18.8.1964. Blue and red. Sir Walter Scott at r. 140 x 85mm.			
	a. Sign. A. P. Anderson. 21.9.1962; 20.10.1962; 16.6.1962.	12.50	25.00	60.00
	b. Sign. T. W. Walker. 16.6.1964; 17.7.1964; 18.8.1964.	12.50	25.00	60.00
	c. As b. Test note w/lines for electronic sorting. 17.7.1964.	35.00	100.00	300.00

1967 ISSUE

		VG	VF	UNC
168	**1 POUND** 13.6.1967. Blue on m/c unpt. Similar to #166 but modified design and w/lines for electronic sorting on back.	5.00	15.00	45.00

1968 ISSUE

		VG	VF	UNC
169	**1 POUND** 1968-70. Blue on m/c unpt. Sir W. Scott at r., supported arms at top ctr.			
	a. 29.2.1968; 5.11.1969.	4.00	12.50	25.00
	b. 20.7.1970.	5.00	15.00	40.00

		VG	VF	UNC
170	**5 POUNDS** 22.3.1968; 23.4.1968; 24.5.1968. Blue and red. Similar to #167, but reduced size and many plate changes. 146 x 78 mm.	17.50	35.00	70.00

CLYDESDALE AND NORTH OF SCOTLAND BANK LTD.

Formerly, and later to become the Clydesdale Bank Ltd. again.

1951 ISSUE

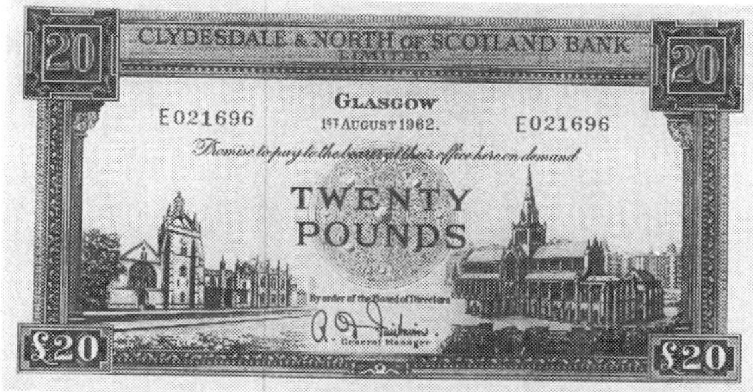

		VG	VF	UNC
193	**20 POUNDS** 2.5.1951-1.8.1962. Green on m/c unpt. 180 x 97mm.			
	a. Sign. J. J. Campbell.	35.00	70.00	110.00
	b. Sign. R. D. Fairbairn.	35.00	70.00	110.00
194	**100 POUNDS** 2.5.1951. Blue. 180 x 97mm. Sign. J. J. Campbell.	175.00	300.00	600.00

1961 ISSUE

#195 and 196 arms at r.

		VG	VF	UNC
195	**1 POUND** 1.3.1961; 2.5.1962; 1.2.1963. Green on m/c unpt. Ship and tug at ctr. on back.	6.00	15.00	40.00

		VG	VF	UNC
196	**5 POUNDS** 20.9.1961; 1.6.1962; 1.2.1963. Dk. blue on m/c unpt. King's College at Aberdeen on back.	12.50	30.00	75.00

CLYDESDALE BANK LIMITED

Formerly the Clydesdale and North of Scotland Bank Ltd. Later became Clydesdale Bank PLC.

1963-64 ISSUE

		VG	VF	UNC
197	**1 POUND** 2.9.1963-3.4.1967. Green on m/c unpt. Like #195.	6.00	15.00	40.00
198	**5 POUNDS** 1963-66. Blue and violet. Like #196.	12.50	30.00	75.00

		VG	VF	UNC
199	**10 POUNDS** 1964-70. Brown on m/c unpt. Arms at r., University of Glasgow on back.	40.00	85.00	200.00

NOTICE

Readers with unlisted dates, signature varieties, etc. are invited to submit photocopies of their notes to: Standard Catalog of World Paper Money, 700 East State St. Iola, WI 54990-0001, fax: 1-715-445-4087, or E-Mail: thernr@krause.com.

		VG	VF	UNC
200	**20 POUNDS** 1964-70. Carmine on m/c unpt. Arms at r. George Square in Glasgow on back.	45.00	100.00	250.00

		VG	VF	UNC
201	**100 POUNDS** 1964-70. Violet on m/c unpt. Multiple arch bridge across river at ctr. on back.	225.00	300.00	575.00

1967 ISSUE

		VG	VF	UNC
202	**1 POUND** 3.4.1967; 1.10.1968; 1.9.1969. Green on m/c unpt. Like #197 but lines for electronic sorting on back.	5.00	12.00	40.00

		VG	VF	UNC
203	**5 POUNDS** 1.5.1967; 1.11.1968; 1.9.1969. Blue and violet on m/c unpt. Like #198 but lines for electronic sorting on back.	12.00	30.00	75.00

1971-81 ISSUE

#204-210 wmk: Old sailing ships.

		VG	VF	UNC
204	**1 POUND** 1971-81. Dk. olive-green on m/c unpt. Robert the Bruce at l. Scene of Battle of Bannockburn, 1314 on back.			
	a. Sign. R. D. Fairbairn, w/title: *GENERAL MANAGER.* 1.3.1971.	6.00	12.50	40.00
	b. Sign. A. R. Macmillan, w/title: *GENERAL MANAGER.* 1.5.1972; 1.8.1973.	6.00	12.50	45.00
	c. Sign. A. R. Macmillan, w/title: *CHIEF GENERAL MANAGER.* 1.3.1974-27.2.1981.	4.00	9.00	20.00

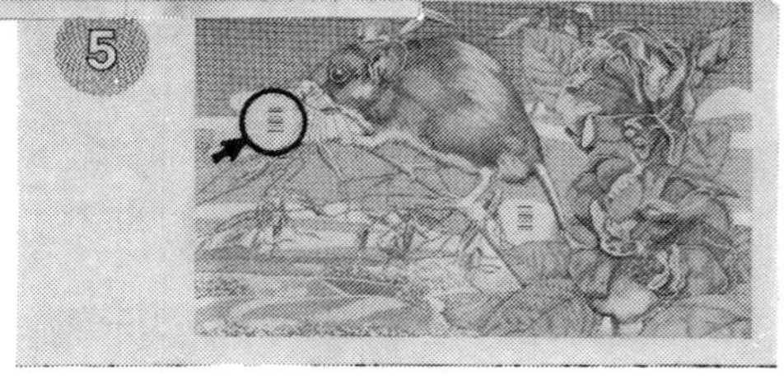

		VG	VF	UNC
205	**5 POUNDS** 1971-80. Grayish lilac on m/c unpt. R. Burns at l. Mouse and rose from Burns' poems on back.			
	a. Sign. R. D. Fairbairn, w/title: *GENERAL MANAGER.* 1.3.1971.	15.00	35.00	100.00
	b. Sign. A. R. Macmillan, w/title: *GENERAL MANAGER.* 1.5.1972; 1.8.1973.	15.00	32.50	85.00
	c. Sign. A. R. Macmillan, w/title: *CHIEF GENERAL MANAGER.* 1.3.1974; 6.1.1975; 2.2.1976; 31.1.1979; 1.2.1980.	15.00	30.00	65.00

#206 *Deleted*. See #205.

		VG	VF	UNC
207	**10 POUNDS** 1972-81. Brown and pale purple. D. Livingstone at l. African scene on back.			
	a. Sign. A. R. MacMillan, w/title: *GENERAL MANAGER.* 1.3.1972; 1.8.1973.	35.00	75.00	175.00
	b. Sign. A. R. MacMillan, w/title: *CHIEF GENERAL MANAGER.* 1.3.1974-27.2.1981.	30.00	60.00	150.00
208	**20 POUNDS** 1972-81. Lilac on m/c unpt. Lord Kelvin at l. Kelvin's lecture room at Glasgow University on back.			
	a. Sign. A. R. MacMillan, w/title: *GENERAL MANAGER.* 1.3.1972.	FV	50.00	175.00
	b. Sign. A. R. MacMillan, w/title: *CHIEF GENERAL MANAGER.* 2.2.1976; 27.2.1981.	FV	45.00	165.00

		VG	VF	UNC
209	**50 POUNDS** 1.9.1981. Olive on m/c unpt. A. Smith at l. Sailing ships, blacksmith implements and farm on back.	90.00	120.00	300.00
210	**100 POUNDS** 1972; 1976. Red on m/c unpt. Lord Kelvin at l. Kelvin's lecture room at Glasgow University on back.			
	a. Sign. A. R. MacMillan, w/title: *GENERAL MANAGER.* 1.3.1972.	FV	225.00	450.00
	b. Sign. A. R. MacMillan, w/title: *CHIEF GENERAL MANAGER.* 2.2.1976.	FV	210.00	425.00

CLYDESDALE BANK PLC

Formerly the Clydesdale Bank Limited.

1982-89 "STERLING" ISSUES

#211-217 wmk: Old sailing ship repeated vertically.

NOTICE

Readers with unlisted dates, signature varieties, etc. are invited to submit photocopies of their notes to: Standard Catalog of World Paper Money, 700 East State St. Iola, WI 54990-0001, fax: 1-715-445-4087, or E-Mail: thernr@krause.com.

		VG	VF	UNC
211	**1 POUND** 1982-88. Dk. olive-green on m/c unpt. Like #204.			
	a. W/sorting marks. Sign. A. R. Macmillan. 29.3.1982.	4.00	9.00	20.00
	b. Like a. Sign. A. R. Cole Hamilton. 5.1.1983.	4.00	9.00	20.00
	c. W/o sorting marks. Sign. A. R. Cole Hamilton. 8.4.1985; 25.11.1985.	FV	6.00	14.00
	d. Sign. title: *CHIEF EXECUTIVE.* 18.9.1987; 9.11.1988.	FV	4.00	10.00

		VG	VF	UNC
212	**5 POUNDS** 1982-89. Blue on m/c unpt. Like #205.			
	a. Sign. A. R. Macmillan. 29.3.1982.	12.50	20.00	50.00
	b. Sign. A. R. Cole Hamilton. 5.1.1983.	10.00	15.00	45.00
	c. W/o sorting marks. Sign. A. R. Cole Hamilton. 18.9.1986.	FV	15.00	45.00
	d. Sign. title: *CHIEF EXECUTIVE.* 18.9.1987; 2.8.1988; 28.6.1989.	FV	13.50	37.50

		VG	VF	UNC
213	**10 POUNDS** 1982-87. Brown and pale purple on m/c unpt. Like #207.			
	a. Sign. A. R. Macmillan. 29.3.1982; 5.1.1983.	25.00	50.00	120.00
	b. Sign. A. R. Cole Hamilton. 8.4.1985; 18.9.1986.	25.00	50.00	110.00
	c. Sign. title: *CHIEF EXECUTIVE.* 18.9.1987.	20.00	45.00	100.00

018601
CLYDESDALE BANK PLC
PROMISE TO PAY TO THE BEARER ON DEMAND AT THEIR OFFICE HERE
TEN POUNDS
STERLING
£10
10
£10
018601

214 10 POUNDS

	VG	VF	UNC
7.5.1988; 3.9.1989; 1.3.1990; 9.11.1990. Dk. brown on m/c unpt. D. Livingstone in front of map at l. Blantyre (Livingstone's birthplace) on back. Wmk: Sailing ships.	FV	27.50	60.00

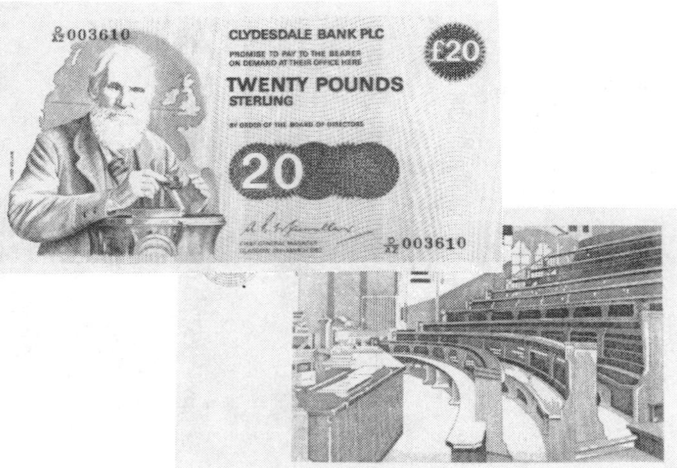

215 20 POUNDS

1982-87. Lilac on m/c unpt. Lord Kelvin at l. Lord Kelvin's lecture room at Glasgow University on back.

	VG	VF	UNC
a. Sign. A. R. Macmillan. 29.3.1982.	FV	55.00	135.00
b. Sign. A. R. Cole Hamilton. 5.1.1983; 8.4.1985.	FV	45.00	110.00
c. Sign. title: *CHIEF EXECUTIVE.* 18.9.1987; 2.8.1990.	FV	42.50	95.00

#216 *Deleted.* See #222.

217 100 POUNDS

1985; 1991. Red on m/c unpt. Like #215. 163 x 90mm.

	VG	VF	UNC
a. Sign. title: *CHIEF GENERAL MANAGER.* 8.4.1985.	225.00	350.00	550.00
b. Sign. title: *CHIEF EXECUTIVE.* 9.11.1991.	200.00	275.00	375.00

1989-96 "STERLING" ISSUE

#218-221 like #212-217 but reduced size notes. Wmk: Old sailing ship repeated vertically.

218 5 POUNDS

1990-97. Black and gray on m/c unpt. Similar to #212, but 135 x 70mm.

	VG	VF	UNC
a. Sign. A. R. Cole Hamilton. 2.4.1990.	FV	FV	20.00
b. Sign. F. Cicutto. 1.9.1994.	FV	FV	18.50
c. Sign. F. Goodwin. 21.7.1996; 1.12.1997.	FV	FV	17.50

219 10 POUNDS

1992-97. Deep brown and green on m/c unpt. Similar to #214 with modified sailing ship outlines at r. 142 x 75mm.

	VG	VF	UNC
a. Sign. A. R. Cole Hamilton. 3.9.1992.	FV	FV	37.50
b. Sign. Charles Love. 5.1.1993.	FV	22.50	45.00
c. Sign. F. Goodwin. 22.3.1996; 27.2.1997.	FV	FV	23.50

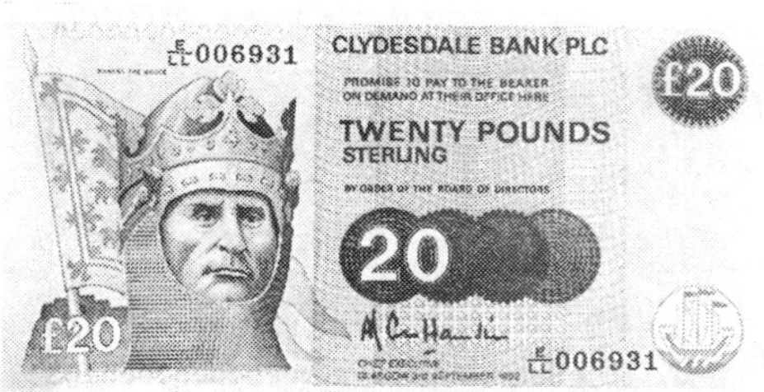

220 20 POUNDS

1990-93. Violet, purple, brown and brown-orange on m/c unpt. Robert the Bruce at l. His equestrian statue, Monymusk reliquary, Stirling Castle and Wallace Monument on back. 148 x 80mm.

	VG	VF	UNC
a. Sign. A. R. Cole Hamilton. 30.11.1990; 2.8.1991; 3.9.1992.	FV	50.00	90.00
b. Sign. Charles Love. 5.1.1993.	FV	55.00	110.00

		VG	VF	UNC
221	**20 POUNDS**			
	1994-96. Purple, dk. brown and deep orange on m/c unpt. Like #220.			
	a. Sign. F. Cicutto. 1.9.1994.	FV	40.00	75.00
	b. Sign. F. Goodwin. 2.12.1996.	FV	40.00	65.00

		VG	VF	UNC
222	**50 POUNDS** 3.9.1989; 20.4.1992. Olive-green on m/c unpt. Similar to #209. Sign. A. R. Cole Hamilton.	FV	125.00	225.00
223	**100 POUNDS** 2.10.1996. Purple, red and violet on m/c unpt. Face similar to #217. Glasgow University on back. Sign. F. Goodwin.	FV	FV	275.00

1996 COMMEMORATIVE ISSUE

#224, Poetry of Robert Burns

		VG	VF	UNC
224	**5 POUNDS**			
	21.7.1996. Black and gray on m/c unpt. Like #218 but w/lines of poetry. Wmk: Sailing ship.			
	a. "A man's a man for a'that - Then let us..."	FV	FV	20.00
	b. "Tam O'Shanter - Now, wha this..."	FV	FV	20.00
	c. "Ae Fond Kiss - But to see..."	FV	FV	20.00
	d. "Scots wha hae - By oppressions woes..."	FV	FV	20.00

NOTE: See Collector's Series #CS1.

1996 REGULAR ISSUE

		VG	VF	UNC
225	**50 POUNDS** 22.3.1996. Olive-green on m/c unpt. Like #222 but reduced size. 157 x 85mm. Sign. F. Goodwin.	FV	FV	120.00

1997 COMMEMORATIVE ISSUES

#226, Work of Mary Slessor

		VG	VF	UNC
226	**10 POUNDS**			
	1997-98. Dk. brown and brown on m/c unpt. M. Slessor at l. and as wmk. Map of Calabar in Nigeria in wreath at ctr., sailing ship at upper l., Slessor seated below and w/children at r.			
	a. Sign. F. Goodwin. 1.5.1997.	FV	FV	25.00
	b. Sign. J. Wright. 5.11.1998.	FV	FV	23.50

NOTE: #226 exists w/serial # prefix *NAB* encapsulated in acrylic plastic w/text: *1987-1997 THE FIRST DECADE.* Market value *$250.*

Non-encapsulated *NAB* market value *$125.*

#227, Commonwealth heads of government meeting in Edinburgh, Oct. 1997

		VG	VF	UNC
227	**20 POUNDS** 30.9.1997. Purple, dk. brown and deep orange on m/c unpt. Face like #221. Edinburgh International Conference Centre at lower r., Clydesdale Bank plaza and Edinburgh Castle in background at ctr. on back. Sign. F. Goodwin.	FV	FV	60.00

NOTE: #227 was issued w/serial # prefix: *CHG* (Special Commemorative prefix). Market value $70.

1997 REGULAR ISSUE

		VG	VF	UNC
228	**20 POUNDS** 1.11.1997. Purple, dk. brown and deep orange on m/c unpt. Like #221 but square design replaces *£20* at lower l., segmented foil over security thread, bank logo added to value panel at lower ctr. r.	FV	FV	60.00

1999 ISSUE

		VG	VF	UNC
229	**20 POUNDS** 1999. M/c. Alex "Greek" Thompson.	FV	FV	60.00

NATIONAL COMMERCIAL BANK OF SCOTLAND LIMITED

Formed by an amalgamation of The Commercial Bank of Scotland Ltd. and The National Bank of Scotland Ltd. in 1959. In 1969 it amalgamated with The Royal Bank of Scotland.

1961 ISSUE

#269 and 270 printer: BWC.

		VG	VF	UNC
269	**1 POUND** 1.11.1961-4.1.1966. Green on m/c unpt. Forth Railway bridge. Reduced size. 151 x 72mm.	3.00	10.00	25.00

		VG	VF	UNC
270	**5 POUNDS** 3.1.1961. Green on m/c unpt. Arms at bottom ctr. r. Forth Railway bridge on back. Reduced size: 159 x 90mm.	17.50	40.00	100.00

1963-67 ISSUE

#271-273 printer: BWC.

		VG	VF	UNC
271	**1 POUND** 4.1.1967. Green on m/c unpt. Like #269, but lines for electronic sorting on back. 152 x 72mm.	6.00	17.50	40.00

		VG	VF	UNC
272	**5 POUNDS** 2.1.1963; 1.8.1963; 1.10.1964; 4.1.1966; 1.8.1966. Blue on m/c unpt. Arms at lower ctr. Landscape w/Edinburgh Castle, National Gallery on back. 142 x 85mm.	15.00	30.00	65.00
273	**10 POUNDS** 18.8.1966. Brown on m/c unpt. Arms at lower ctr. Forth Railway bridge on back. 151 x 94mm.			
	a. Issued note.	175.00	275.00	800.00
	s. Specimen.	—	—	400.00

1967; 1968 ISSUE

#274 and 275 printer: BWC.

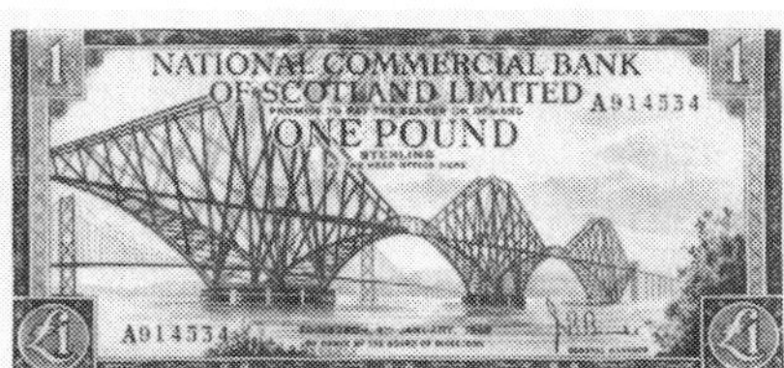

		VG	VF	UNC
274	**1 POUND** 4.1.1968. Green on m/c unpt. Similar to #271, but W/Forth Railway Bridge and road bridge on face. Reduced size. 136 x 67mm.	4.50	15.00	35.00

		VG	VF	UNC
275	**5 POUNDS** 4.1.1968. Blue, red and green on m/c unpt. Like #272 but electronic sorting marks on back.	12.00	25.00	75.00
275A	**20 POUNDS** 1.6.1967. Red on m/c unpt. Arms at lower r. Bridge on back. Printer: TDLR.			
	a. Issued note.	90.00	225.00	750.00
	s. Specimen.	—	—	—
275B	**100 POUNDS** 1.6.1967. Purple on m/c unpt. Arms at lower r. Bridge on back. Printer: TDLR. Specimen.	—	—	—

ROYAL BANK OF SCOTLAND

Later became the Royal Bank of Scotland Limited.

1875; 1887 ISSUE

		GOOD	FINE	XF
318	**10 POUNDS** 1887-1969. Blue and red. Uniface.			
	a. Plate C. 1887-1918.	500.00	950.00	—
	b. Plate D. Yellow unpt. The blue is much darker than plate C. 1918-40.	75.00	200.00	400.00
	c. 1940-69.	35.00	150.00	300.00

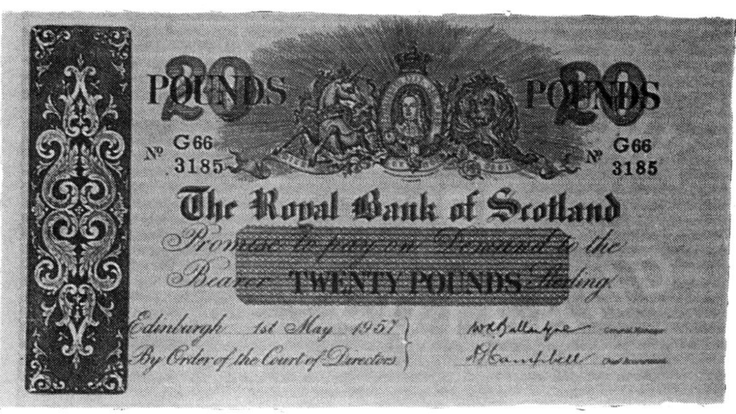

		GOOD	FINE	XF
319	**20 POUNDS** 1877-1969. Blue and red. Uniface.			
	a. Plate C. 1877-1918.	150.00	325.00	500.00
	b. Plate D. Yellow unpt. Imprint: W. & A. K. Johnston 1914-47.	65.00	150.00	225.00
	c. Plates E; F; G; H. Imprint: W. & A. K. Johnston & G. W. Bacon Ltd. Both sign. printed 1947-69.	45.00	70.00	120.00
320	**100 POUNDS** 1877-1969. Blue and red. Uniface.			
	a. Plate C. 1877-1918.	400.00	650.00	—
	b. Plates D; E. Yellow unpt. 1918-60.	185.00	350.00	500.00
	c. Plates F; G. Imprint: W. & A. K. Johnston & G. W. Bacon Ltd. Both sign. printed. 1960-69.	180.00	300.00	425.00

1955 ISSUE

		VG	VF	UNC
324	**1 POUND** 1955-64. Dk. blue on yellow and brown unpt. Sign. W. R. Ballantyne w/title: *General Manager*. 152 x 85mm.			
	a. W/o engraver's name on back. 1.4.1955-1.11.1955.	4.00	12.00	40.00
	b. W/engraver's name W. H. Egan on back. 1.2.1956-1.7.1964.	3.00	9.00	30.00

1964 ISSUE

		VG	VF	UNC
325	**1 POUND** 1964-67. Black and brown on yellow unpt. Like #324, but 150 x 71mm.			
	a. Sign. W. R. Ballantyne. 1.8.1964-1.6.1965.	4.00	12.50	30.00
	b. Sign. G. P. Robertson. 2.8.1965-1.11.1967.	3.00	10.00	25.00
326	**5 POUNDS** 1964-65. Dk. blue, orange-brown and yellow. Uniface. Like #323, but 140 x 85mm.			
	a. 2.11.1964. Sign. W. R. Ballantyne & A. G. Campbell.	25.00	65.00	150.00
	b. 2.8.1965. Sign. G. P. Robertson & A. G. Campbell.	25.00	65.00	150.00

1966; 1967 Issue

#327 and 328 portr. D. Dale at l. and as wmk., bank arms at lower r. Bank head office bldg. at ctr. and upper r. on back.

		VG	VF	UNC
327	**1 Pound** 1.9.1967. Green on m/c unpt.	4.00	10.00	22.50

		VG	VF	UNC
328	**5 Pounds** 1.11.1966; 1.3.1967. Blue on m/c unpt.	15.00	35.00	75.00

Royal Bank of Scotland Limited

Formerly the Royal Bank of Scotland. Later became the Royal Bank of Scotland PLC.

1969 Issue

#329-333 wmk: D. Dale. Sign. G. P. Robertson and J. B. Burke. Printer: BWC.

		VG	VF	UNC
329	**1 Pound** 19.3.1969. Green on m/c unpt. Forth Road Bridge at l. ctr., old Forth Railway bridge in background. Arms at ctr. r. on back.	5.00	10.00	25.00

		VG	VF	UNC
330	**5 Pounds** 19.3.1969. Blue on m/c unpt. Arms at l. Edinburgh Castle on back.	17.50	40.00	80.00

		VG	VF	UNC
331	**10 Pounds** 19.3.1969. Brown on m/c unpt. Arms at ctr. Tay road bridge on back.	40.00	80.00	200.00
332	**20 Pounds** 19.3.1969. Purple on m/c unpt. Forth road bridge on back.	45.00	75.00	250.00

		VG	VF	UNC
333	**100 Pounds** 19.3.1969. Red on m/c unpt. Similar to #332.	180.00	250.00	550.00

1970 Issue

#334 and 335 like #329 and 330 but w/only 1 sign, J. B. Burke.

		VG	VF	UNC
334	**1 Pound** 15.7.1970. Green on m/c unpt.	3.00	10.00	30.00
335	**5 Pounds** 15.7.1970. Blue on m/c unpt.	17.50	35.00	75.00

1972 ISSUE

#336-340 arms at r. Wmk: A. Smith. Printer: BWC.

		VG	VF	UNC
336	**1 POUND** 5.1.1972-1.5.1981. Dk. green on m/c unpt. Edinburgh Castle at l. ctr. on back.	4.00	6.00	15.00

		VG	VF	UNC
337	**5 POUNDS** 5.1.1972-2.4.1973; 1.5.1975; 1.5.1979; 1.5.1981. Blue on m/c unpt. Culzean Castle at l. ctr. on back.	20.00	35.00	80.00

		VG	VF	UNC
338	**10 POUNDS** 5.1.1972; 15.12.1975; 2.5.1978; 10.1.1981. Brown on m/c unpt. Glamis Castle at l. ctr. on back.	27.50	50.00	110.00
339	**20 POUNDS** 5.1.1972; 1.5.1981. Purple on m/c unpt. Brodick Castle on back.	50.00	80.00	175.00

		VG	VF	UNC
340	**100 POUNDS** 5.1.1972; 1.5.1981. Red on m/c unpt. Balmoral Castle on back.	225.00	275.00	550.00

ROYAL BANK OF SCOTLAND PLC

Formerly the Royal Bank of Scotland Limited.

1982-86 ISSUES

#341-345 arms at r. Sign. title varieties.

#341, replacement note: Serial # prefix *Y/1*.

		VG	VF	UNC
341	**1 POUND** 1982-85. Dk. green on m/c unpt. Like #336. Sign. C. Winter. Printer: BWC.			
	a. W/sorting marks. 3.5.1982.	2.50	5.00	25.00
	b. W/o sorting marks. 1.10.1983; 4.1.1984; 3.1.1985.	2.50	5.00	10.00

		VG	VF	UNC
341A	**1 POUND** 1986. Dk. green on m/c unpt. Like #341. Printer: TDLR.			
	a. Sign. C. Winter. 1.5.1986.	2.50	4.00	12.50
	b. Sign. R. M. Maiden. 17.12.1986.	2.50	5.00	15.00

		VG	VF	UNC
342	**5 POUNDS** 1982-86. Blue on m/c unpt. Like #337. Printer: BWC.			
	a. Sign. C. M. Winter. W/sorting marks. 3.5.1982; 5.1.1983.	17.50	25.00	65.00
	b. W/o sorting marks. 4.1.1984.	17.50	25.00	60.00
	c. Sign. C. M. Winter title larger size. 3.1.1985.	17.50	25.00	65.00
	d. Sign. R. M. Maiden. 17.12.1986.	15.00	22.50	55.00

		VG	VF	UNC
343	**10 POUNDS** 1982-86. Brown on m/c unpt. Like #338. Printer: BWC.			
	a. Sign. C. M. Winter. 3.5.1982; 4.1.1984.	27.50	50.00	110.00
	b. Sign. R. M. Maiden. 17.12.1986.	27.50	50.00	100.00

		VG	VF	UNC
344	**20 POUNDS** 3.5.1982; 3.1.1985. Purple on m/c unpt. Like #339. Printer: BWC.	40.00	80.00	200.00
345	**100 POUNDS** 3.5.1982. Red on m/c unpt. Like #340. Printer: BWC.	200.00	250.00	450.00

1987 ISSUE

#346-350 Lord Ilay at r. and as wmk. Printer: TDLR. Replacement notes: Serial # prefix: *Z/1*.

		VG	VF	UNC
346	**1 POUND** 25.3.1987. Dk. green and green on m/c unpt. Edinburgh Castle at l. ctr. on back.	FV	3.00	6.00

NOTICE

Readers with unlisted dates, signature varieties, etc. are invited to submit photocopies of their notes to: Standard Catalog of World Paper Money, 700 East State St. Iola, WI 54990-0001, fax: 1-715-445-4087, or E-Mail: thernr@krause.com.

		VG	VF	UNC
347	**5 POUNDS** 25.3.1987; 22.6.1988. Black and blue-black on m/c unpt. Culzean Castle at l. ctr. on back.	FV	15.00	35.00

		VG	VF	UNC
348	**10 POUNDS** 25.3.1987; 24.2.1988; 22.2.1989; 24.1.1990. Deep brown and brown on m/c unpt. Glamis Castle at l. ctr. on back. Sign. R. M. Maiden.	FV	25.00	50.00

		VG	VF	UNC
349	**20 POUNDS** 25.3.1987; 24.1.1990. Black and purple on m/c unpt. Brodick Castle at l. ctr. on back. Sign. R. M. Maiden.	FV	40.00	85.00

350 **100 POUNDS**
1987-96. Red on m/c unpt. Balmoral Castle at l. ctr. on back.

		VG	VF	UNC
a.	Sign. R. M. Maiden, w/title: *MANAGING DIRECTOR.* 25.3.1987; 24.1.1990.	FV	225.00	400.00
b.	Sign. G. R. Mathewson, w/title: *CHIEF EXECUTIVE.* 28.1.1992; 23.3.1994; 24.1.1996; 26.3.1997.	FV	FV	300.00

1988-92 ISSUE

#351-355 similar to #346-350, but reduced size. Replacement notes: Serial # prefix: *Z/1*.

#351-354 Lord Ilay at r. and as wmk.

351 **1 POUND**
1988-. Dk. green and green on m/c unpt. Similar to #346, but 127 x 65mm. Printer: TDLR.

		VG	VF	UNC
a.	Sign. R. M. Maiden w/title: *MANAGING DIRECTOR.* 13.12.1988; 26.7.1989; 19.12.1990.	FV	3.00	8.00
b.	Sign. C. Winter w/title: *CHIEF EXECUTIVE.* 24.7.1991.	FV	2.50	7.00
c.	Sign. G. R. Mathewson w/title: *CHIEF EXECUTIVE.* 24.3.1992; 24.2.1993; 24.2.1994; 24.1.1996; 1.10.1997.	FV	FV	4.00

352 **5 POUNDS**
1988-. Black and blue-black on m/c unpt. Similar to #347, but 135 x 70mm. Sign. title: *MANAGING DIRECTOR.*

		VG	VF	UNC
a.	Sign. R. M. Maiden. 13.12.1988; 24.1.1990.	FV	FV	17.50
b.	Sign. G. R. Mathewson. 23.3.1994; 24.1.1996; 26.3.1997; 29.4.1998.	FV	FV	13.50

		VG	VF	UNC
353	**10 POUNDS** 28.1.1992; 7.5.1992; 24.2.1993; 23.3.1994. Deep brown and brown on m/c unpt. Similar to #348, but 142 x 75mm. Sign. G. R. Mathewson, w/title: *CHIEF EXECUTIVE.*	FV	FV	32.50

354 **20 POUNDS**
1991-. Black and purple on m/c unpt. Similiar to #349 but 150 x 81mm.

		VG	VF	UNC
a.	Sign. C. Winter w/title: *CHIEF EXECUTIVE.* 27.3.1991.	FV	FV	67.50
b.	Sign. G. R. Mathewson. 28.1.1992; 24.2.1993.	FV	FV	57.50

#355 not assigned.

1992 COMMEMORATIVE ISSUE

#356, European Summit at Edinburgh, Dec. 1992

		VG	VF	UNC
356	**1 POUND** 8.12.1992. Dk. green and green on m/c unpt. Additional blue-violet ovpt. containing commemorative inscription at l. on #351c.	FV	FV	6.00

1994 REGULAR ISSUE

Lord Ilay at r. Replacement note: Serial # prefix *Y/1*.

		VG	VF	UNC
357	**1 POUND** 23.3.1994. Dk. green and green on m/c unpt. Like #351 but w/o wmk. Printer: BABN.	4.00	10.00	50.00

1994 COMMEMORATIVE ISSUE

#358, Centennial - Death of Robert Louis Stevenson

		VG	VF	UNC
358	**1 POUND** 3.12.1994. Dk. green and green on m/c unpt. Commemorative ovpt. in wmk area on #351c. Portr. R. L. Stevenson and images of his life and works on back.	FV	FV	5.00

1997 COMMEMORATIVE ISSUE

#359, 150th Anniversary - Birth of Alexander Graham Bell, 1847-1997

		VG	VF	UNC
359	**1 POUND** 3.3.1997. Dk. green and green on m/c unpt. Ovpt. telephone, text and OVD on wmk. area of face like #351c. Portr. A. G. Bell and images of his life and work on back.	FV	FV	4.50

1999 COMMEMORATIVE ISSUE

#360 Opening of the Scottish Parliament

		VG	VF	UNC
360	**1 POUND** 12.5.1999. Dk. green on m/c unpt. Ovpt. Scottish Parliament text at l. on wmk. area of face like #351c. Scottish Parliament bldg. on back.	FV	FV	4.50

COLLECTOR SERIES

CLYDESDALE BANK PLC

1996 ISSUE

		ISSUE PRICE	MKT. VALUE
CS1	**1996 5 POUNDS** Matched serial # (prefix R/B 0 - R/B 3) set #224a-224d.	60.00	75.00

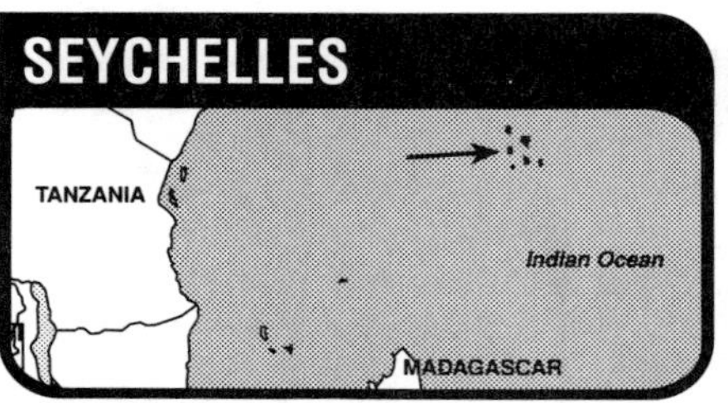

The Republic of Seychelles, an archipelago of 85 granite and coral islands situated in the Indian Ocean 600 miles (965 km.) northeast of Madagascar, has an area of 156 sq. mi. (455 sq. km.) and a population of 76,400. Among these islands are the Aldabra Islands, the Farquhar Group, and Ile Desroches, which the United Kingdom ceded to the Seychelles upon its independence. Capital: Victoria, on Mahe. The economy is based on fishing, a plantation system of agriculture and tourism. Copra, cinnamon and vanilla are exported.

Although the Seychelles are marked on Portuguese charts of the early 16th century, the first recorded visit to the islands, by an English ship, occurred in 1609. The Seychelles were annexed to France by Captain Lazare Picault in 1743 and permanently settled in 1768, with the intention of establishing spice plantations to compete with the Dutch monopoly of the spice trade. British troops seized the islands in 1810, during the Napoleonic Wars; they were formally ceded to Britain by the Treaty of Paris, 1814. The Seychelles were a dependency of Mauritius until Aug. 31, 1903, when they became a separate British Crown Colony. The colony was granted limited internal self-government in 1970, and attained independence on June 28, 1976, becoming Britain's last African possession to do so. Seychelles is a member of the Commonwealth of Nations. The president is the Head of State and of Government.

RULERS:

British to 1976

MONETARY SYSTEM:

1 Rupee = 100 Cents

GOVERNMENT OF SEYCHELLES

1954 ISSUE

#11-13 portr. Qn. Elizabeth II in profile at r. Denominations on back. Various date and sign. varieties. Printer: TDLR.

		VG	VF	UNC
11	**5 RUPEES** 1954; 1960. Lilac and green.			
	a. 1.8.1954.	8.50	35.00	150.00
	b. 1.8.1960.	7.00	20.00	140.00

		VG	VF	UNC
12	**10 RUPEES** 1954-67. Green and red. Like #11.			
	a. 1.8.1954.	12.50	45.00	525.00
	b. 1.8.1960.	10.00	40.00	475.00
	c. 1.5.1963.	10.00	35.00	475.00
	d. 1.1.1967.	10.00	35.00	450.00

NOTICE

Readers with unlisted dates, signature varieties, etc. are invited to submit photocopies of their notes to: Standard Catalog of World Paper Money, 700 East State St. Iola, WI 54990-0001, fax: 1-715-445-4087, or E-Mail: thernr@krause.com.

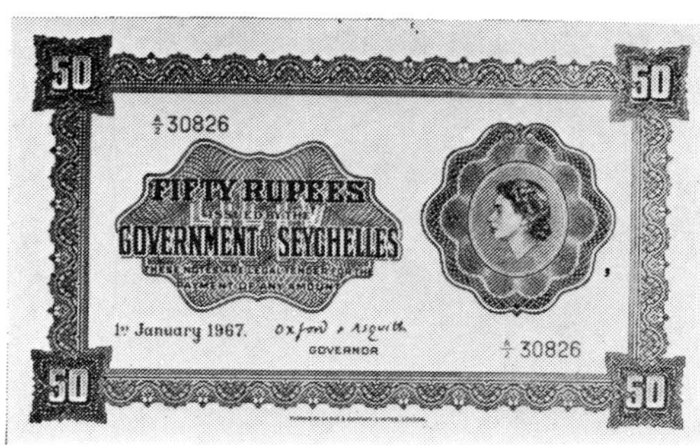

13	50 RUPEES	VG	VF	UNC
	1954-67. Black. Like #11.			
	a. 1.8.1954.	30.00	100.00	800.00
	b. 1.8.1960.	25.00	90.00	750.00
	c. 1.5.1963.	25.00	85.00	750.00
	d. 1.1.1967.	25.00	85.00	750.00

1968 ISSUE

#14-18 Qn. Elizabeth II at r. Wmk: Black parrot's head. Various date and sign. varieties.

14	5 RUPEES	VG	VF	UNC
	1.1.1968. Dk. brown on m/c unpt. Parrot at l.	1.00	5.00	37.50

15	10 RUPEES	VG	VF	UNC
	1968; 1974. Lt. blue on m/c unpt. Sea tortoise at l. ctr.			
	a. 1.1.1968.	3.00	20.00	175.00
	b. 1.1.1974.	2.50	15.00	140.00

16	20 RUPEES	VG	VF	UNC
	1968-74. Purple on m/c unpt. Nesting bird at l. ctr.			
	a. 1.1.1968.	6.00	35.00	350.00
	b. 1.1.1971.	5.00	25.00	250.00
	c. 1.1.1974.	4.00	20.00	185.00

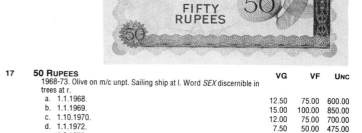

17	50 RUPEES	VG	VF	UNC
	1968-73. Olive on m/c unpt. Sailing ship at l. Word *SEX* discernible in trees at r.			
	a. 1.1.1968.	12.50	75.00	600.00
	b. 1.1.1969.	15.00	100.00	850.00
	c. 1.10.1970.	12.00	75.00	700.00
	d. 1.1.1972.	7.50	50.00	475.00
	e. 1.8.1973.	7.50	50.00	450.00

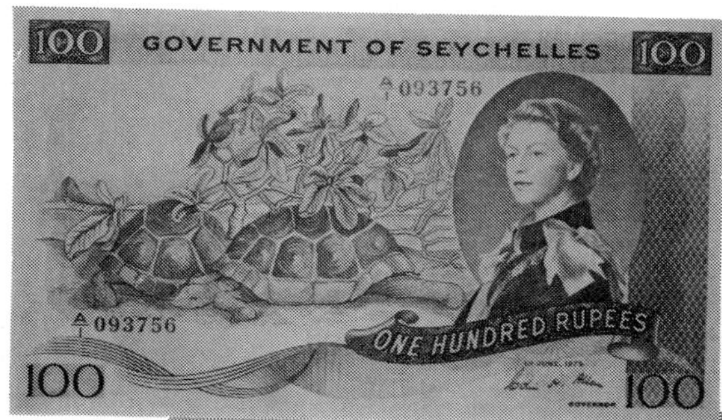

18	100 RUPEES	VG	VF	UNC
	1968-75. Red on m/c unpt. Land turtles at l. ctr.			
	a. 1.1.1968.	37.50	235.00	1500.
	b. 1.1.1969.	75.00	500.00	2500.
	c. 1.1.1972.	50.00	225.00	1250.
	d. 1.8.1973.	45.00	200.00	1200.
	e. 1.6.1975.	45.00	185.00	1000.

REPUBLIC OF SEYCHELLES

1976; 1977 ND ISSUE

#19-22 Pres. J. R. Mancham at r. Wmk: Black parrot's head.

		VG	VF	UNC
19	**10 RUPEES** ND (1976). Dk. blue and blue on m/c unpt. Seashell at lower l. Hut w/boats and cliffs on back.	1.00	2.25	9.00

		VG	VF	UNC
20	**20 RUPEES** ND (1977). Purple on m/c unpt. Sea tortoise at lower l. Sailboat at l. ctr. on back.	2.00	4.50	17.50

		VG	VF	UNC
21	**50 RUPEES** ND (1977). Olive on m/c unpt. Fish at lower l. Fishermen at l. ctr. on back.	5.00	10.00	65.00

		VG	VF	UNC
22	**100 RUPEES** ND (1977). Red and m/c. 2 birds at lower l. Dock area and islands on back.	10.00	20.00	110.00

SEYCHELLES MONETARY AUTHORITY

1979 ND ISSUE

#23-27 vertical format on back. Wmk: Black parrot's head.

		VG	VF	UNC
23	**10 RUPEES** ND (1979). Blue, green and lt. red on m/c unpt. Nesting bird at ctr. Girl picking flowers on back.	FV	1.75	4.00

		VG	VF	UNC
24	**25 RUPEES** ND (1979). Brown, purple and gold on m/c unpt. Coconuts at ctr. Man and basket on back.	FV	4.00	16.50

		VG	VF	UNC
25	**50 RUPEES** ND (1979). Olive-green, brown and lilac on m/c unpt. Turtle at ctr. Bldgs. and palm trees on back.	FV	8.00	40.00

NOTICE

Readers with unlisted dates, signature varieties, etc. are invited to submit photocopies of their notes to: Standard Catalog of World Paper Money, 700 East State St. Iola, WI 54990-0001, fax: 1-715-445-4087, or E-Mail: thernr@krause.com.

26 **100 RUPEES** — VG | VF | UNC
ND (1979). Red and lt. blue on m/c unpt. Tropical fish at ctr. Man w/tools, swordfish on back. — 22.50 | 55.00 | 240.00

NOTE: A shipment of #26 was lost at sea, only serial # A000,001 - A300,000 are valid numbers for exchange.

1980 ND ISSUE

27 **100 RUPEES** — VG | VF | UNC
ND (1980). Brown and lt. blue on m/c unpt. Like #26. — FV | 22.50 | 80.00

CENTRAL BANK OF SEYCHELLES

1983 ND ISSUE

#28-31 like previous issue except for new bank name and sign. title. Wmk: Black parrot's head.

28 **10 RUPEES** — VG | VF | UNC
ND (1983). Blue, green and lt. red on m/c unpt. Like #23. — FV | FV | 5.50

29 **25 RUPEES**
ND (1983). Brown, purple and gold on m/c unpt. Like #24. — FV | FV | 12.50

30 **50 RUPEES** — VG | VF | UNC
ND (1983). Olive-green, brown and lilac on m/c unpt. Like #25. — FV | FV | 30.00

31 **100 RUPEES**
ND (1983). Brown and lt. blue on m/c unpt. Like #27. — FV | FV | 55.00

LABANK SANTRAL SESEL

CENTRAL BANK OF SEYCHELLES

1989 ND ISSUE

#32-35 bank at ctr., flying fish at l. and ctr. r. Wmk: Black parrot's head.

32 **10 RUPEES** — VG | VF | UNC
ND (1989). Blue-black and deep blue-green on m/c unpt. Boy scouts at lower l., image of man w/flags and broken chain at r. Local people dancing to drummer at ctr. on back. — FV | FV | 6.00

33 **25 RUPEES** — VG | VF | UNC
ND (1989). Purple on m/c unpt. 2 men w/coconuts at lower l., boy near palms at upper r. Primitive ox-drawn farm equipment on back. — FV | FV | 13.50

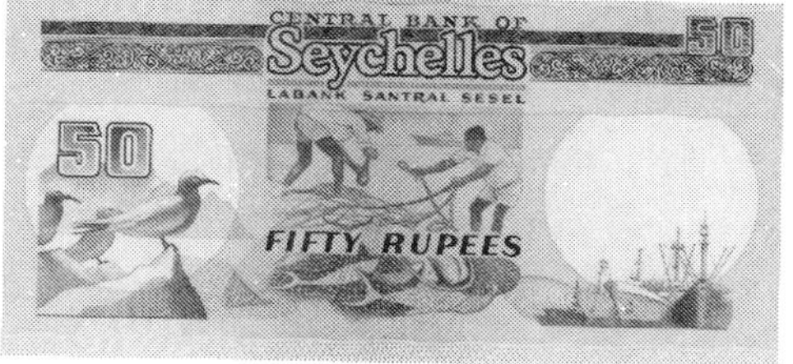

34 **50 RUPEES** — VG | VF | UNC
ND (1989). Dk. green and brown on m/c unpt. 2 men in boat, Seychelles man at lower l., prow of boat in geometric outline at upper r. Seagulls at lower l., fishermen w/nets at ctr., modern cargo ships at r. on back. — FV | FV | 21.50

		VG	VF	UNC
35	**100 RUPEES** ND (1989). Red and brown on m/c unpt. Men in ox-cart at lower l., girl w/shell at upper r. Bldg. at ctr. on back.	FV	FV	42.50

1998 ND ISSUE

#36-39 arms at upper l. Cowry shells at upper l. on back. Wmk: Sea tortoise. Ascending serial #.

		VG	VF	UNC
36	**10 RUPEES** ND (1998). Deep blue, dk. green and green on m/c unpt. Coco-de-Mer palm at ctr., black-spotted trigger fish at lower l. Coco-de-Mer palm fruit at lower l. Fairy Terns at ctr., Hawksbill turtle at lower r. on back.	FV	FV	5.50

		VG	VF	UNC
37	**25 RUPEES** ND (1998). Purple, violet and blue-violet on m/c unpt. "Wrights gardenia" flower at ctr., Lion fish at lower l. Bi-Centennary monument at lower l., coconut crab at ctr., Seychelles blue pigeon at r. on back.	FV	FV	12.50

		VG	VF	UNC
38	**50 RUPEES** ND (1998). Dk. green, deep olive-green and brown on m/c unpt. "Paille en Que" orchids at ctr., Angel fish at lower l. Clock tower, autos at lower l., Yellow fin tuna at ctr., Flightle white throated rail or "Tiomitio" at r. on back.	FV	FV	20.00

		VG	VF	UNC
39	**100 RUPEES** ND (1998). Red, brown-orange and violet on m/c unpt. Pitcher plant at ctr., Vielle Babone Cecile fish at lower l. Shoreline at lower l., Bridled terns at ctr., giant land tortoise at lower r. on back.	FV	FV	40.00

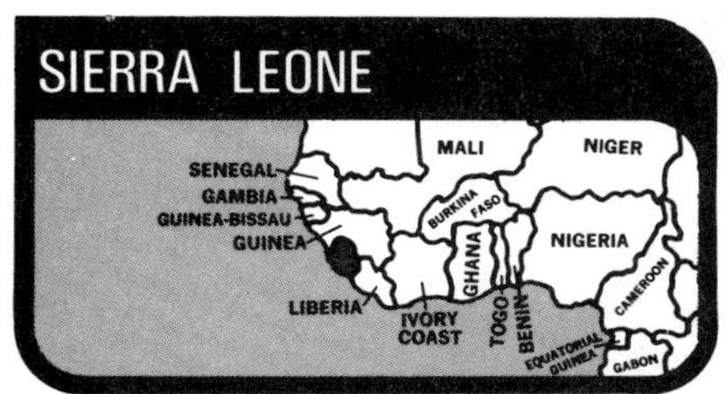

The Republic of Sierra Leone, a British Commonwealth nation located in western Africa between Guinea and Liberia, has an area of 27,699 sq. mi. (71,740 sq. km.) and a population of 4.46 million. Capital: Freetown. The economy is predominantly agricultural but mining contributes significantly to export revenues. Diamonds, iron ore, palm kernels, cocoa and coffee are exported.

The coast of Sierra Leone was first visited by Portuguese and British slavers in the 15th and 16th centuries. The first settlement at Freetown was established in 1787 as a refuge for freed slaves within the British Empire, runaway slaves from the United States and blacks discharged from the British armed forces. The first settlers were virtually wiped out by tribal attacks and disease. The colony was re-established under the auspices of the Sierra Leone Company and transferred to the British Crown in 1907. The interior region was secured and established as a protectorate in 1896. Sierra Leone became independent within the Commonwealth on April 27, 1961, and adopted a republican constitution ten years later. It is a member of the Commonwealth of Nations. The president is Chief of State and Head of Government.

RULERS:

British to 1971

MONETARY SYSTEM:

1 Leone = 100 Cents

REPUBLIC

BANK OF SIERRA LEONE

1964 ND ISSUE

#1-3 w/300-year-old cottonwood tree and court bldg. on face. Sign. varieties. Wmk: Lion's head. Printer: TDLR.

		VG	VF	UNC
1	**1 LEONE** ND (1964-70). Green on m/c unpt. Diamond mining on back.			
	a. ND (1964). Prefix A/1-A/6.	4.50	13.50	65.00
	b. ND (1969). Prefix A/7-A/8.	6.00	18.50	75.00
	c. ND (1970). Prefix A/9-A/12.	2.75	8.00	45.00

#2d replacement notes: Serial # prefix *Z1*.

		VG	VF	UNC
2	**2 LEONES** ND (1964-70). Red on m/c unpt. Village scene on back.			
	a. ND (1964). Prefix B/1-B/21.	5.00	15.00	60.00
	b. ND (1967). Prefix B/22-B/25.	6.00	18.50	75.00
	c. ND (1969). Prefix B/26-B/30.	6.00	18.50	75.00
	d. ND (1970). Prefix B/31-B/41.	5.00	16.00	70.00

		VG	VF	UNC
3	**5 LEONES** ND (1964). Purple on m/c unpt. Dockside at Freetown at ctr. r. w/boats in harbor on back. Prefix C/1.	30.00	90.00	365.00

1974-80 ISSUE

#4-8 Pres. S. Stevens at l. Printer: TDLR. Replacement notes: Serial # prefix *Z/1*.

		VG	VF	UNC
4	**50 CENTS** ND; 1979-84. Dk. brown on m/c unpt. Arms at upper l., flowers in unpt. at r. Central bank bldg. at ctr. on back.			
	a. ND (1972). Prefix D/1-D/2.	.75	2.00	6.00
	b. ND (1974). Prefix D/3-D/5.	.60	1.50	4.00
	c. Prefix D/6-D/8. 1.7.1979.	.50	1.00	3.00
	d. Prefix D/9. 1.7.1981.	.15	.50	1.50
	e. 4.8.1984.	.10	.25	.75

#5-8 arms at upper r. on back. Wmk: Lion's head.

		VG	VF	UNC
5	**1 LEONE** 1974-84. Olive-green and dk. green on m/c unpt. Central bank bldg. at ctr. r. on back.			
	a. Prefix A/1-A/7. 19.4.1974.	.75	2.25	7.50
	b. Prefix A/8-A/12. 1.1.1978.	1.00	4.00	10.00
	c. Prefix A/13-A/17. 1.3.1980.	.25	1.00	4.00
	d. Prefix A/18. 1.7.1981.	.25	.50	2.00
	e. 4.8.1984.	.25	.50	1.00

		VG	VF	UNC
6	**2 LEONES** 1974-85. Red, deep red-orange and dk. brown on m/c unpt. Central bank bldg. at ctr. r. on back.			
	a. Prefix B/1-B/20. 19.4.1974.	1.25	3.50	10.00
	b. Prefix B/21-B/22. 1.1.1978.	6.00	15.00	45.00
	c. Prefix B/23-B/27. 1.7.1978.	1.00	4.00	12.50
	d. Prefix B/28-B/31. 1.7.1979.	.75	2.00	7.50
	e. Prefix B/32. 1.5.1980.	.75	2.00	7.00
	f. 1.7.1983.	.35	.75	3.00
	g. 4.8.1984.	.20	.45	1.25
	h. 4.8.1985.	.20	.45	1.25

		VG	VF	UNC
7	**5 LEONES** 1975-85. Purple and blue-black on m/c unpt. Plant leaves at ctr. Parliament bldg. at ctr. r. on back.			
	a. Prefix C/1. 4.8.1975.	3.00	10.00	32.50
	b. Prefix C/2. 1.7.1978.	2.00	7.00	25.00
	c. Prefix C/3. 1.3.1980.	1.00	4.00	12.50
	d. Prefix C/4-C/6. 1.7.1981.	.75	3.00	7.50
	e. 19.4.1984.	.50	1.00	3.75
	f. 4.8.1984.	.50	1.00	3.50
	g. 4.8.1985.	.50	1.00	3.25

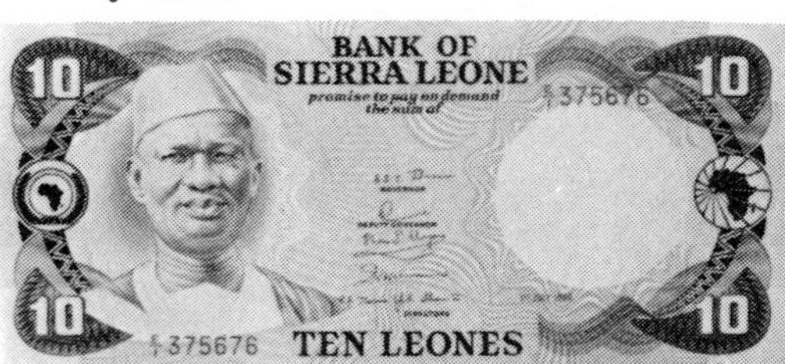

		VG	VF	UNC
8	**10 LEONES** 1980; 1984. Blue-gray, black and blue-green on m/c unpt. Dredging operation at ctr. r. on back.			
	a. Prefix E/1. 1.7.1980.	1.00	4.00	12.50
	b. 19.4.1984.	.40	1.00	3.25
	c. 4.8.1984.	.40	1.00	3.00

1980 COMMEMORATIVE ISSUE

#9-13, Commemorating The Organisation of African Unity Conference in Freetown

NOTE: #9-13 were prepared in special booklets (1800 sets).

		VG	VF	UNC
9	**50 CENTS** 1.7.1980. Dk. brown on m/c unpt. Red ovpt. in 4 lines at upper l. ctr. on #4.	1.00	4.00	15.00

#10-13 red ovpt. in circle around wmk. area at r., date below.

		VG	VF	UNC
10	**1 LEONE** 1.7.1980. Olive-green and dk. green on m/c unpt. Ovpt. on #5.	1.25	5.00	15.00

		VG	VF	UNC
11	**2 LEONES** 1.7.1980. Red, deep red-orange and dk. brown on m/c unpt. Ovpt. on #6.	1.65	6.50	20.00

NOTICE

Readers with unlisted dates, signature varieties, etc. are invited to submit photocopies of their notes to: Standard Catalog of World Paper Money, 700 East State St. Iola, WI 54990-0001, fax: 1-715-445-4087, or E-Mail: thernr@krause.com.

		VG	VF	UNC
12	**5 LEONES** 1.7.1980. Purple and blue-black on m/c unpt. Ovpt. on #7.	2.25	8.50	22.50

		VG	VF	UNC
13	**10 LEONES** 1.7.1980. Blue-gray, black and blue-green on m/c unpt. Ovpt. on #8.	2.50	10.00	30.00

1982 ISSUE

		VG	VF	UNC
14	**20 LEONES** 1982; 1984. Brown and green on m/c unpt. Tree at ctr., Pres. S. Stevens at r. 2 youths pan mining (gold or diamonds) on back. Printer: BWC. Wmk: Lion's head.			
	a. 24.8.1982.	1.00	2.50	10.00
	b. 24.8.1984.	.40	1.10	4.00

1988-93 ISSUE

#15-21 arms at upper ctr. Wmk: Lion's head. Replacement notes: Serial # prefix *Z/1*.

#15-19 Pres. Dr. Joseph Saidu Momoh at r.

		VG	VF	UNC
15	**10 LEONES** 27.4.1988. Dk. green and purple on m/c unpt. Steer at l., farmer harvesting at ctr. on back.	FV	.50	2.00

		VG	VF	UNC
16	**20 LEONES** 27.4.1988. Brown, red and green on m/c unpt. Like #14, but new president at r.	FV	.65	2.50

		VG	VF	UNC
17	**50 LEONES** 1988-89. Purple, blue and black on m/c unpt. Sports stadium at ctr. Dancers at l. ctr. on back.			
	a. W/o imprint. 27.4.1988.	FV	1.50	3.00
	b. Printer: TDLR. 27.4.1989.	FV	.75	2.00

		VG	VF	UNC
18	**100 LEONES** 1988-90. Blue and black on m/c unpt. Bldg. and ship at l. ctr. Local designs at l. and r., Central Bank bldg. at l. ctr. on back.			
	a. W/o imprint. 27.4.1988.	FV	1.00	5.00
	b. Printer: TDLR. 27.4.1989.	FV	.65	2.25
	c. 26.9.1990.	FV	FV	2.00

		VG	VF	UNC
19	**500 LEONES** 27.4.1991. Red-brown and dark green on m/c unpt. Modern bldg. below arms at l. ctr. 2 boats on back.	FV	1.00	3.75

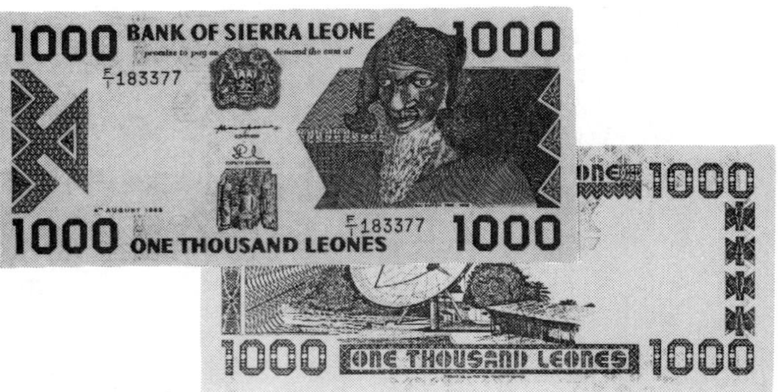

20 **1000 LEONES** | VG | VF | UNC
4.8.1993. Red and yellow on m/c unpt. B. Bureh at r., carving at lower ctr. Dish antenna at l. ctr. on back. Printer: TDLR. | FV | 1.50 | 5.50

21 **5000 LEONES** | VG | VF | UNC
4.8.1993. Blue and violet on m/c unpt. S. Pieh at r., bldg. at lower ctr. Dam at l. ctr. on back. Printer: TDLR. | FV | 6.50 | 22.50

1995 ISSUE

#22 and 23 Not assigned.

24 **500 LEONES** | VG | VF | UNC
27.4.1995 (1996). Blue-green, brown and green on m/c unpt. K. Londo at r., arms at upper ctr., spearhead at l., bldg. at lower ctr. Fishing boats at l. ctr., artistic carp at r. on back. Wmk: Lion's head. Printer: TDLR. | FV | FV | 3.00

COLLECTOR SERIES

BANK OF SIERRA LEONE

1972 ND ISSUE

#CS1, First Anniversary of Republic, 1972

CS1 **ND (19.4.1972) - 50 CENTS** | ISSUE PRICE | MKT. VALUE
#4 laminated in plastic w/2 50 cent coins in special maroon case. | — | 10.00

NOTE: #CS1 note has serial # all zeros but w/o specimen ovpt.

1979 ND ISSUE

CS2 **ND (1979) 50 CENTS - 5 LEONES** | ISSUE PRICE | MKT. VALUE
#4, 5b-7b w/ovpt: *SPECIMEN* and serial # prefix Maltese cross. | 14.00 | 20.00

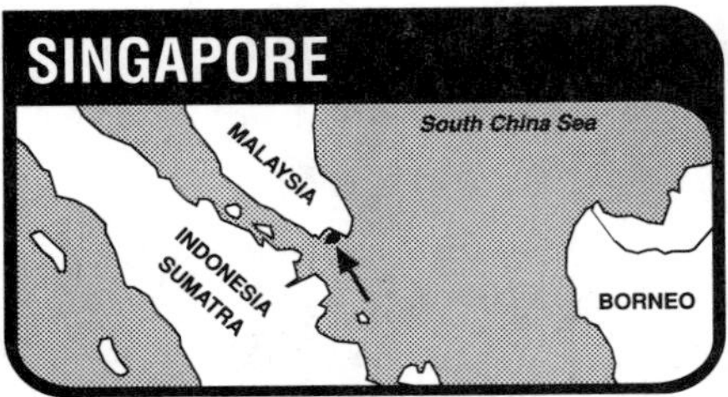

The Republic of Singapore, a British Commonwealth nation situated at the southern tip of the Malay peninsula, has an area of 230 sq. mi. (648 sq. km.) and a population of 3.9 million. Capital: Singapore. The economy is based on manufacturing of computers, disk drives, integrated circuits, sound cards, pharmaceuticals and shipbuilding/repairs. It is a world financial, business services, E-commerce, oil refining and air services center, besides having the busiest port in terms of shipping tonnage and containers handled.

Singapore's modern history - it was an important shipping center in the 14th century before the rise of Malacca and Penang - began in 1819 when Sir Thomas Stamford Raffles, an agent for the British East India Company, founded the town of Singapore. By 1825 its trade exceeded that of Malacca and Penang combined. The opening of the Suez Canal (1869) and the demand for rubber and tin created by the automobile and packaging industries combined to make Singapore one of the major ports of the world. In 1826 Singapore, Penang and Malacca were combined to form the Straits Settlements, which was made a Crown Colony in 1867. Singapore became a separate Crown Colony in 1946 when the Straits Settlements was dissolved. It joined in the formation of Malaysia in 1963, but broke away on Aug. 9, 1965, to become an independent republic. Continued economic prosperity has made Singapore an influential member of the Asian economic community. Singapore is a member of the Commonwealth of Nations. The president is Chief of State. The prime minister is Head of Government.

MONETARY SYSTEM:

1 Dollar = 100 Cents

REPUBLIC

BOARD OF COMMISSIONERS OF CURRENCY

SIGNATURE SEAL VARIETIES

SIGNATURE SEAL VARIETIES	

Type I: Dragon, seal script, lion	Type II: Seal script w/symbol

1967-73 ND ISSUE

#1 and 2 wmk: Lion's head. Sign. varieties. Printer: BWC.

		VG	VF	UNC
1	**1 DOLLAR** ND (1967-72) Blue on m/c unpt. Lt. red flowers at ctr., arms at r. Apartment bldgs. on back.			
	a. W/o red seal. Sign. Lim Kim San (1967).	2.00	3.50	12.50
	b. Red sign. seal Type I at center. Sign. Dr. Goh Keng Swee (1970).	2.50	3.00	20.00
	c. W/o red seal. Sign. Hon Sui Sen (1971).	2.00	4.00	15.00
	d. Red sign. seal Type II at ctr. Sign. Hon Sui Sen (1972).	1.00	2.00	6.00

		VG	VF	UNC
2	**5 DOLLARS** ND (1967-73). Green on m/c unpt. Lt. orange flowers at ctr., arms at upper r. Small boats at moorings on back.			
	a. W/o red seal. Sign. Lim Kim San (1967).	5.00	15.00	60.00
	b. Red sign. seal Type I at ctr. Sign. Dr. Goh Keng Swee (1970).	30.00	120.00	350.00
	c. W/o red seal. Sign. Hon Sui Sen (1972).	8.00	20.00	100.00
	d. Red sign. seal Type II at ctr. Sign. Hon Sui Sen (1973).	4.00	12.50	50.00

#3-5 wmk: Lion's head. Printer: TDLR.

3	**10 DOLLARS**	VG	VF	UNC
	ND (1967-73). Red on m/c unpt. Lilac flowers at ctr., arms at lower r. 4 hands clasping wrists over map at l. ctr. on back.			
	a. W/o red seal. Sign. Lim Kim San (1967).	10.00	15.00	60.00
	b. Red sign. seal Type I at ctr. Sign. Dr. Goh Keng Swee (1970).	12.00	25.00	150.00
	c. W/o red seal. Sign. Hon Sui Sen (1972).	8.00	15.00	75.00
	d. Red sign. seal Type II at ctr. Sign. Hon Sui Sen (1973).	7.50	10.00	50.00

4	**25 DOLLARS**	VG	VF	UNC
	ND (1972). Dk. brown on m/c unpt. Yellow flowers at ctr., arms at upper r. Capitol on back.	22.50	40.00	120.00

5	**50 DOLLARS**	VG	VF	UNC
	ND (1967-73). Blue on m/c unpt. Violet flowers at ctr., arms at lower r. Bldgs. and boats on back.			
	a. W/o red seal. Sign. Lim Kim San (1967).	40.00	70.00	150.00
	b. Red sign. seal Type I at ctr. Sign. Dr. Goh Keng Swee (1970).	40.00	70.00	200.00
	c. W/o red seal. Sign. Hon Sui Se Sen (1972).	37.50	60.00	160.00
	d. Red sign. seal Type II at ctr. Sign. Hon Sui Sen (1973).	35.00	50.00	110.00

6	**100 DOLLARS**	VG	VF	UNC
	ND (1967-73). Blue and violet on m/c unpt. Red flowers at ctr., arms at r. Sailing vessels in harbor on back. Wmk: Lion's head. Printer: BWC.			
	a. W/o red seal. Sign. Lim Kim San (1967).	80.00	100.00	250.00
	b. Red sign. seal Type I at ctr. Sign. Dr. Goh Keng Swee (1970).	90.00	350.00	800.00
	c. W/o red seal. Sign. Hon Sui Sen (1972).	80.00	120.00	250.00
	d. Red sign. seal Type II at ctr. Sign. Hon Sui Sen (1973).	80.00	100.00	225.00

#7-8A wmk: Lion's head. Printer: TDLR.

7	**500 DOLLARS**	VG	VF	UNC
	ND (1972). Dk. green, lilac on m/c unpt. Flowers at ctr. Government bldg. on back.	380.00	520.00	800.00

8	**1000 DOLLARS**	VG	VF	UNC
	ND (1967-75). Purple on m/c unpt. Lilac-brown colored flowers at ctr., arms at r. City scene on back.			
	a. W/o red seal. Sign. Lim Kim San (1967).	FV	800.00	1800.
	b. Red sign. seal Type I at ctr. Sign. Dr. Goh Keng Swee (1970).	FV	900.00	1800.
	c. W/o red seal. Sign. Hon Sui Sen (1973).	FV	80.00	1400.
	d. Red sign. seal Type II at ctr. Sign. Hon Sui Sen (1975).	FV	700.00	1200.

8A	**10,000 DOLLARS**	VG	VF	UNC
	ND (1973). Green on m/c unpt. Orchids at ctr., arms at r. Bldg. at l. ctr. on back. Sign. Hon Sui Sen.	FV	FV	10,000.

1976-80 ND Issue

#9-17 city skyline along bottom, arms at upper r. Wmk: Lion's head.

#9 and 10 printer: BWC.

		VG	VF	UNC
9	**1 Dollar** ND (1976). Blue-black on m/c unpt. Tern at l. Parade passing lg. bldg. at ctr. r. on back.	FV	FV	3.00

		VG	VF	UNC
10	**5 Dollars** ND (1976). Green and brown on m/c unpt. Red-whiskered bulbul at l. Skylift above w/ships docked along river on back.	FV	6.00	8.00

		VG	VF	UNC
11	**10 Dollars** ND (1976). Red and dk. blue on m/c unpt. Kingfisher at l. Modern bldgs. at ctr. r. on back. Printer: TDLR.			
	a. W/security thread (1979).	FV	12.50	50.00
	b. W/segmented foil over security thread (1980).	FV	10.00	17.50

		VG	VF	UNC
12	**20 Dollars** ND (1979). Brown and yellow on m/c unpt. Yellow-breasted sunbird at l. Back brown; dancer at l., Concorde over airport at ctr. r. Printer: BWC.	FV	15.00	30.00

		VG	VF	UNC
13	**50 Dollars** ND (1976). Dk. blue on m/c unpt. Bird of Paradise at l. High school band playing in formation on back. Printer: TDLR.			
	a. W/security thread.	FV	50.00	70.00
	b. W/segmented foil over security thread.	FV	50.00	75.00

		VG	VF	UNC
14	**100 Dollars** ND (1977). Blue on m/c unpt. Blue-throated bee eater at l. Dancers on back. Printer: BWC.	FV	90.00	120.00

		VG	VF	UNC
15	**500 Dollars** ND (1977). Green and m/c. Oriole at l. Back green; view of island and refinery at ctr. Printer: TDLR.	FV	450.00	550.00

		VG	VF	UNC
16	**1000 Dollars** ND (1978). Violet and brown on m/c unpt. Brahminy Kite bird at l. Ship on back. Printer: TDLR.	FV	850.00	1000.

17 **10,000 DOLLARS**
ND (1980). Green on m/c unpt. White-bellied sea eagle at l. 19th century Singapore River scene above, modern view below on back. Printer: TDLR.

	VG	VF	UNC
a. Issued note.	FV	FV	8500.
s. Specimen, punched hole cancelled.	—	—	750.00

1984-89 ND ISSUE

#18-25 arms at upper l. Wmk: Lion's head. Printer: TDLR. Replacement notes: Serial # prefix *Z/1*, *Z/2*, etc.

18 **1 DOLLAR**
ND (1987). Deep blue and green. Sailing ship at l. Flowers and satellite tracking station at ctr. on back.

	VG	VF	UNC
a. Sign. Goh Keng Swee.	FV	1.25	2.00
b. Sign. Hu Tsu Tau.	FV	1.25	2.00

19 **5 DOLLARS**
ND (1989). Green and red-violet on m/c unpt. "Twakow" boats at l. PSA container terminal at r. on back.

VG	VF	UNC
FV	5.00	7.00

20 **10 DOLLARS**
ND (1988). Red-orange and violet on m/c unpt. Trader vessel "Palari" at l. Stylized map at ctr., public housing at r. on back.

VG	VF	UNC
FV	8.00	10.00

#21 Not assigned.

22 **50 DOLLARS**
ND (1987). Blue on m/c unpt. Coaster vessel "Perak" at l. 2 raised areas in circles at lower r. for the blind. Bridge and city view on back.

	VG	VF	UNC
a. W/security thread.	FV	FV	65.00
b. W/segmented foil over security thread.	FV	FV	55.00

23 **100 DOLLARS**
ND (1985; 1995). Dk. brown, violet and orange-brown on m/c unpt. Passenger liner "Chusan" at l. ctr. 3 raised areas in circles at lower r. for the blind. Airplane above w/Changi air terminal at ctr. r. on back.

	VG	VF	UNC
a. W/security thread. Sign. Dr. Goh Keng Swee. (1985).	67.50	85.00	125.00
b. W/segmented foil over "clear text" security thread w/$100 *SINGAPORE* in 4 languages. (1995).	FV	FV	100.00
c. As b. Sign. Hu Tsu Tau.	FV	FV	90.00

24 **500 DOLLARS**
ND (1988). Green on m/c unpt. Cargo vessel "Neptune Sardonys at l. National defense members on back.

VG	VF	UNC
FV	FV	500.00

25 **1000 DOLLARS**
ND (1984). Purple and red on m/c unpt. Container ship "Neptune Garnet" at l. ctr. Repair ship on back.

	VG	VF	UNC
a. Sign. Dr. Goh Keng Swee.	FV	FV	800.00
b. Sign. Dr. Hu Tsu Tau.	FV	FV	775.00

		VG	VF	UNC
26	**10,000 DOLLARS** ND (1987). Red and purple on m/c unpt. General bulk carrier "Neptune Canopus" at l., statuary at ctr. r. 1987 National Day parade on back.	FV	FV	7750.

1990 ND ISSUE

#27 and 28 printer: TDLR. Replacement notes: Serial prefix *ZZ*.

		VG	VF	UNC
27	**2 DOLLARS** ND (ca.1990). Orange and red on yellow-green unpt. Arms at upper l., "Tongkang" boat and 2 smaller boats at ctr. Chingay procession on back. Wmk: Lion's head. Printer: TDLR.	FV	FV	3.25

		VG	VF	UNC
28	**2 DOLLARS** ND (1992). Deep purple and brown-violet on m/c unpt. Like #27, but w/ascending size serial #, one of which is vertical.	FV	FV	3.00

NOTE: #28 also issued in various uncut sheets from 2 to 40 subjects.

1992 COMMEMORATIVE ISSUES

#29, 25th Anniversary - Board of Commissioners of Currency

		VG	VF	UNC
29	**2 DOLLARS** ND(1992). Deep purple and brown-violet on m/c unpt. Ovpt: *25 YEARS OF CURRENCY 1967-1992...* on #28. (5000).			
	a. Issued note.	—	—	160.00
	x. W/ovpt. text: *COMMISSONERS* (error).	—	—	300.00

#30 and 31 25th Anniversary of Independence

		VG	VF	UNC
30	**50 DOLLARS** 9.8.1990. Red and purple on m/c unpt. Silver hologram of Yusof bin Ishak at ctr. Old harbor scene at l., modern bldgs. at r. First parliament at l., group of people below flag and arms at r. on back. Plastic.	FV	FV	60.00

NOTE: #30 issued in a special commemorative folder.

		VG	VF	UNC
31	**50 DOLLARS** ND (1990). Red and purple on m/c unpt. Like #30 but w/o date.	FV	FV	50.00

1994 ND COMMEMORATIVE ISSUE

#31A, 25th Anniversary - Board of Commissioners of Currency

		VG	VF	UNC
31A	**2 DOLLARS** ND (1994). Red ovpt. logo of the Board at l. beneath arms on #28.	—	—	75.00

NOTE: Issued w/book *Prudence at the Helm, 1967-1992.*

1994 REGULAR ISSUE

		VG	VF	UNC
32	**50 DOLLARS** ND (1994). Deep blue and red on m/c unpt. Like #22. W/segmented foil over security thread.	FV	FV	52.50

1996 ND COMMEMORATIVE ISSUE

#33, 25th Anniversary of Monetary Authority, 1971-1996

		VG	VF	UNC
33	**25 DOLLARS** ND (1996). Red-brown and green on m/c unpt. Arms at upper l., Monetary Authority bldg. at ctr. Optical variable device at l. ctr. Financial sector skyline on back. Wmk: Lion's head. Sign. Hu Tsu Tau.	FV	FV	50.00

NOTE: #33 was offered in 2 varieties of special booklets, wide and narrow and uncut sheets of 20 subjects.

1997 ND REGULAR ISSUE

#34 and 35 wmk: Lion's head. Printer: H&S.

		VG	VF	UNC
34	**2 DOLLARS** ND (1997). Deep purple and brown-violet on m/c unpt. Like #28.	FV	FV	2.25

		VG	VF	UNC
35	**5 DOLLARS** ND (1997). Green and red-violet on m/c unpt. Like #19.	FV	FV	4.50
36	**50 DOLLARS** ND (1997). Slate gray and red on m/c unpt. Like #32. W/segmented foil over "Cleartext" security thread. W/$50 *SINGAPORE* in 4 languages. Wmk: Lion's head.	FV	FV	42.50

1998 ND ISSUE

		VG	VF	UNC
37	**2 DOLLARS** ND(1998). Deep purple and brown-violet on m/c unpt. Like #34. Wmk: Lion's head. Printer: BABN.	FV	FV	2.25

1999 ND ISSUE

#38-45 Pres. Encik Yusof bin Ishak at r. Wmk. as portr.

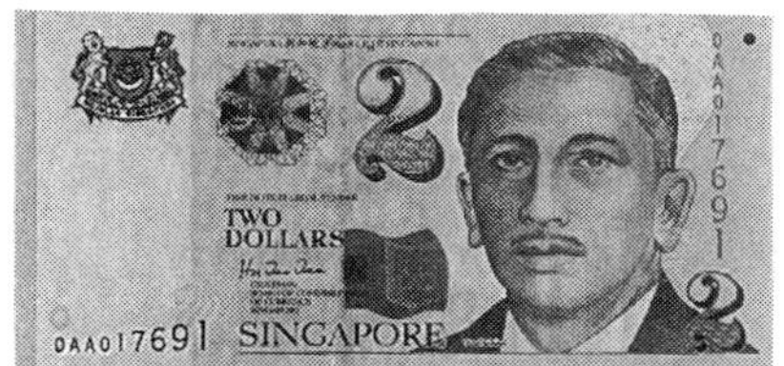

		VG	VF	UNC
38	**2 DOLLARS** ND (1999). Purple, brown and m/c. School and children. Education theme.	FV	FV	2.00

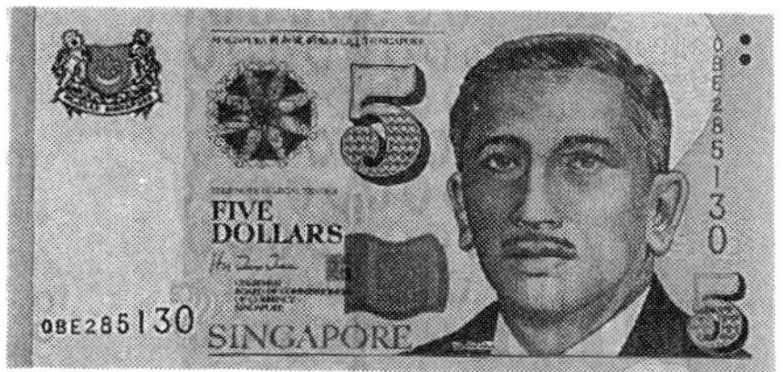

		VG	VF	UNC
39	**5 DOLLARS** ND (1999). Green, red and m/c. Garden City, trees and flowers. Skyline in background.	FV	FV	3.00

		VG	VF	UNC
40	**10 DOLLARS** ND (1999). Red, brown and m/c. Sports - swimming, tennis, soccer, sailing, running.	FV	FV	6.50

		VG	VF	UNC
41	**50 DOLLARS** ND (1999). Slate blue and m/c. Arts - music, graphics.	FV	FV	35.00

		VG	VF	UNC
42	**100 DOLLARS** ND (1999). Orange and m/c. Youth - boy, girl, Sea Scouts, Pioneering Project.	FV	FV	65.00
43	**1000 DOLLARS** ND (1999). M/c. Government bldgs.	FV	FV	450.00
44	**10,000 DOLLARS** ND (1999). M/c. Technology - computer chip research lab.	FV	FV	5500.

COLLECTOR SERIES

SINGAPORE

1989 ND ISSUES

		ISSUE PRICE	MKT. VALUE
CS1	**ND (1989). 1 DOLLAR - 100 DOLLARS** #1a-3a, 5a and 6a ovpt: *SPECIMEN*. (77 sets).	—	1850.
CS2	**ND (1989). 1 DOLLAR - 100 DOLLARS** #1c-3c, 5c and 6c ovpt: *SPECIMEN*. (89 sets).	—	1750.
CS3	**ND (1989). 1 DOLLAR - 100 DOLLARS** #1d-3d, 4, 5d and 6d ovpt: *SPECIMEN*. (82 sets).	—	2400.
CS4	**ND (1989). 1-100 DOLLARS** #9-11, 13 and 14 ovpt: *SPECIMEN*. (311 sets).	—	1250.

SLOVAKIA

Slovakia as a republic has an area of 18,923 sq. mi. (49,011 sq. km.) and a population of almost 5.37 million. Capital: Bratislava. Textiles, steel, and wood products are exported.

Slovakia was settled by Slavic Slovaks in the 6th or 7th century and was incorporated into Greater Moravia in the 9th century. After the Moravian state was destroyed early in the 10th century, Slovakia was conquered by the Magyars and remained a land of the Hungarian crown until 1918, when it joined the Czechs in forming Czechoslovakia. In 1938, the Slovaks declared themselves an autonomous state within a federal Czecho-Slovak state. After the German occupation, Slovakia became nominally independent under the protection of Germany, March 16, 1939. Father Jozef Tiso was appointed President. Slovakia was liberated from German control in Oct. 1944, but in May 1945 ceased to be an independent Slovak state. In 1968 it became a constituent state of Czechoslovakia as Slovak Socialist Republic. In January 1991 the Czech and Slovak Federal Republic was formed, and after June 1992 elections, it was decided to split the federation into the Czech Republic and Slovakia on 1 January, 1993.

MONETARY SYSTEM:

1 Korun = 100 Halierov

REPUBLIC

SLOVENSKA REPUBLIKA

REPUBLIC OF SLOVAKIA

1993 ND PROVISIONAL ISSUE

#15-19 Czechoslovakian issue w/adhesive stamps affixed w/*SLOVENSKA* over arms.

		VG	VF	UNC
15	**20 KORUN** ND (1993- old date 1988). Black and lt. blue adhesive stamp on Czechoslovakia #95.	1.00	2.50	4.00

		VG	VF	UNC
16	**50 KORUN** ND (1993- old date 1987). Black and yellow adhesive stamp on Czechoslovakia #96. Serial # prefixes: *F* and *I*.	2.25	3.50	8.00

		VG	VF	UNC
17	**100 KORUN** ND (1993- old date 1961). Black and orange adhesive stamp on Czechoslovakia #91b. Series G37-.	4.00	5.00	9.00
18	**500 KORUN** ND (1993- old date 1973). Adhesive stamp on Czechoslovakia #93. Serial # prefixes: *Z*, *V* and *W*.	18.50	25.00	50.00
19	**1000 KORUN** ND (1993- old date 1985). Adhesive stamp on Czechoslovakia #98.	35.00	45.00	90.00

NOTICE

Readers with unlisted dates, signature varieties, etc. are invited to submit photocopies of their notes to: Standard Catalog of World Paper Money, 700 East State St. Iola, WI 54990-0001, fax: 1-715-445-4087, or E-Mail: thernr@krause.com.

NÁRODNÁ BANKA SLOVENSKA

SLOVAK NATIONAL BANK

1993 ISSUE

#20-24 shield of arms at lower ctr. r. on back. Sign. varieties.

		VG	VF	UNC
20	**20 KORUN** 1993; 1995. Black and green on m/c unpt. Prince Pribina at r. and as wmk. Nitra Castle at l. on back. Printer: BABN.			
	a. Pale green unpt. 1.9.1993.	FV	FV	3.00
	b. As a. but w/green unpt. at r. Security thread closer at ctr. 1.6.1995.	FV	FV	2.50
	c. As b. 31.10.1997.	FV	FV	2.00
	d. As a. Serial # prefix A. Uncut sheet of 60 (6000 sheets).	—	—	60.00

		VG	VF	UNC
21	**50 KORUN** 1993; 1995. Black, blue and aqua on m/c unpt. St. Cyril and St. Metod at r. and as wmk. Medieval Church at Drazovce and first 7 letters of Slavic alphabet on back. Printer: BABN.			
	a. 1.8.1993.	FV	FV	5.50
	b. Security thread closer to ctr. 1.6.1995.	FV	FV	5.00
	c. As a. Serial # prefix A. Uncut sheet of 45 (4000 sheets).	—	—	100.00

		VG	VF	UNC
22	**100 KORUN** 1.9.1993. Red and black on orange and m/c unpt. Madonna (by master woodcarver Pavel) from the altar of the Birth in St. Jacob's Church in Levoca at r. Levoca town view on back. Printer: TDLR.			
	a. Serial # prefix D.	FV	FV	9.00
	b. Serial # prefix A. Uncut sheet of 35 (4000 sheets).	—	—	165.00

		VG	VF	UNC
23	**500 KORUN** 1.10.1993. Dk. gray and brown on m/c unpt. L. Stúr at r. and as wmk. Bratislava Castle and St. Nicholas' Church at l. on back. Printer: TDLR.			
	a. Serial # prefix E; F.	FV	FV	30.00
	b. Serial # prefix A. Uncut sheet of 28 (2500 sheets).	—	—	525.00

		VG	VF	UNC
24	**1000 KORUN** 1993; 1995. Dk. gray and purple on red-violet and m/c unpt. A. Hlinka at r. and as wmk. Madonna of the church of Liptovké Sliace near Ruzomberok and church of St. Andrew in Ruzomberok at l. ctr. on back. Printer: TDLR.			
	a. 1.10.1993.	FV	FV	55.00
	b. Security thread closer to ctr. 1.6.1995.	FV	FV	52.50
	c. Prefix B. 1.7.1997.	FV	FV	52.50
	d. As a. Serial # prefix A. Uncut sheet of 28 (1500 sheets).	—	—	1050.

1995; 1996 ISSUE

#25-29 shield of arms at lower ctr. r. on back.

		VG	VF	UNC
25	**100 KORUN** 1996-. Like #22 but red-orange replaces dull orange in corners on back.			
	a. Printer as TDLR.	FV	FV	7.00
	b. Serial # prefix: *D, L*. 1.10.1997.	FV	FV	7.00
	c. Printer as DLR. 1.7.1999.	FV	FV	6.00

		VG	VF	UNC
26	**200 Korun** 1.8.1995. Dk. gray and blue-green on m/c unpt. A. Bernolák at r. and as wmk. Trnava town view at l. ctr. on back. Printer: G&D.	FV	FV	13.50

		VG	VF	UNC
27	**500 Korun** 31.10.1996. Like #23 but blue unpt. at l. ctr. and in corners on face and in upper l. ctr. and in corners on back. Dk. brown at ctr. on back.	FV	FV	26.50

		VG	VF	UNC
29	**5000 Korun** 3.4.1995. Brown-violet and pale yellow-brown on m/c unpt. M. R. Štefánik at r., sun and moon at ctr. Štefánik's grave at Bradlo Hill, part of *Ursa Major* constellation, and a pasque flower at l. ctr. on back. Printer: G&D.	FV	FV	200.00

NOTICE

Readers with unlisted dates, signature varieties, etc. are invited to submit photocopies of their notes to: Standard Catalog of World Paper Money, 700 East State St. Iola, WI 54990-0001, fax: 1-715-445-4087, or E-Mail: thernr@krause.com.

1999 Issue

Color shifting design in wmk area: dots in wmk. areas.

		VG	VF	UNC
30	**200 Korun** 31.5.1999. Printer: G&D.	FV	FV	13.50
31	**500 Korun** 1999.			Expected New Issue

		VG	VF	UNC
32	**1000 Korun** 1999.	FV	FV	52.50
33	**5000 Korun**	FV	FV	200.00

2000 Commemorative Issue

Previously issues of Series *A* notes were only available as uncut sheets. These overprints have caused problems with bank counting machines and will not last long in circulation.

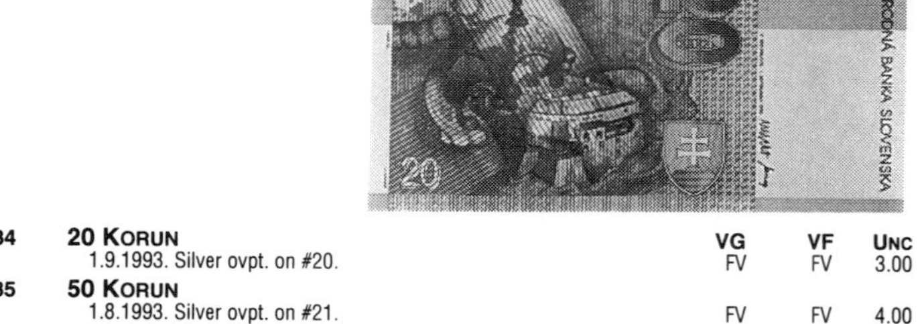

		VG	VF	UNC
34	**20 Korun** 1.9.1993. Silver ovpt. on #20.	FV	FV	3.00
35	**50 Korun** 1.8.1993. Silver ovpt. on #21.	FV	FV	4.00
36	**100 Korun** 1.9.1993. Silver ovpt. on #22.	FV	FV	7.50
37	**200 Korun** 1.8.1995. Silver ovpt. on #26.	FV	FV	15.00
38	**500 Korun** 1.10.1993. Silver ovpt. on #23.	FV	FV	30.00
39	**1000 Korun** 1.10.1993. Silver ovpt. on #24a.	FV	FV	60.00
40	**5000 Korun** 3.4.1995. Gold ovpt. on #29.	FV	FV	225.00

The Republic of Slovenia is bounded in the north by Austria, northeast by Hungary, southeast by Croatia and to the west by Italy. It has an area of 5,246 sq. mi. (20,251 sq. km.) and a population of almost 2.0 million. Capital: Ljubljana. The economy is based on electricity, minerals, forestry, agriculture and fishing. Small industries are being developed during privatization.

The lands originally settled by Slovenes in the 6th century were steadily encroached upon by Germans. Slovenia developed as part of Austro-Hungarian Empire after the defeat of the latter in World War I it became part of the Kingdom of the Serbs, Croats and Slovenes (Yugoslavia) established on December 1, 1918. A legal opposition group, the Slovene League of Social Democrats, was formed in Jan. 1989. In Oct. 1989 the Slovene Assembly voted a constitutional amendment giving it the right to secede from Yugoslavia. On July 2, 1990 the Assembly adopted a 'declaration of sovereignty' and in Sept. proclaimed its control over the territorial defense force on its soil. A referendum on Dec. 23 resulted in a majority vote for independence, which was formally declared on Dec. 26. In Feb. 1991 parliament ruled that henceforth Slovenian law took precedence over federal. On June 25, Slovenia declared independence, but agreed to suspend this for 3 months at peace talks sponsored by the EC. The moratorium having expired, Slovenia (and Croatia) declared their complete independence of the Yugoslav federation on Oct. 8, 1991.

MONETARY SYSTEM:

1 (Tolar) = 1 Yugoslavian Dinar
1 Tolar = 100 Stotinas

REPUBLIC

REPUBLIKA SLOVENIJA

1990-92 ISSUE

#1-10 column pedestal at lower l., denomination numeral in guilloche over a fly in unpt. at ctr. r. Date given as first 2 numerals of serial #. Mountain ridge at l. ctr. on back. Wmk: Symmetrical designs repeated.

NOTE: About 500 sets of Specimens #1s-10s were released to the general collecting public. Specimens exist with normal serial #'s and with 0's as serial #'s. Zero serial #'s are priced to $20.00 each.

		VG	VF	UNC
1	**1 (TOLAR)** (19)90. Dk. olive-green on lt. gray and lt. olive-green unpt.			
	a. Issued note.	.05	.10	.30
	s1. Specimen ovpt: *VZOREC.*	—	—	7.50
	s2. Specimen ovpt. *SPECIMEN.*	—	—	5.00
2	**2 (TOLARJEV)** (19)90. Brown on tan and ochre unpt.			
	a. Issued note.	.05	.10	.40
	s1. Specimen ovpt: *VZOREC.*	—	—	7.50
	s2. Specimen ovpt: *SPECIMEN.*	—	—	5.00
3	**5 (TOLARJEV)** (19)90. Maroon on pale maroon and pink unpt.			
	a. Issued note.	.05	.15	.65
	s1. Specimen ovpt: *VZOREC.*	—	—	7.50
	s2. Specimen ovpt: *SPECIMEN.*	—	—	5.00

		VG	VF	UNC
4	**10 (TOLARJEV)** (19)90. Dk. blue-green and grayish purple on lt. blue-green unpt.			
	a. Issued note.	FV	FV	1.00
	s1. Specimen ovpt: *VZOREC.*	—	—	3.50
	s2. Specimen ovpt: *SPECIMEN.*	—	—	7.50
5	**50 (TOLARJEV)** (19)90. Dk. gray on tan and lt. gray unpt.			
	a. Issued note.	FV	FV	5.00
	s1. Specimen ovpt: *VZOREC.*	—	—	3.50
	s2. Specimen ovpt: *SPECIMEN.*	—	—	7.50

		VG	VF	UNC
6	**100 (TOLARJEV)** (19)90. Reddish brown and violet on orange and lt. violet unpt.			
	a. Issued note.	FV	FV	8.00
	s1. Specimen ovpt: *ZVOREC.*	—	—	3.50
	s2. Specimen ovpt: *SPECIMEN.*	—	—	7.50
7	**200 (TOLARJEV)** (19)90. Greenish black and dk. brown on lt. gray and lt. green unpt.			
	a. Issued note.	FV	FV	25.00
	s1. Specimen ovpt: *VZOREC.*	—	—	3.50
	s2. Specimen ovpt: *SPECIMEN.*	—	—	7.50

		VG	VF	UNC
8	**500 (TOLARJEV)** (19)90; (19)92. Deep lilac and red on pink and pale blue unpt.			
	a. 1990.	FV	FV	25.00
	b. 1992.	FV	FV	40.00
	s1. Specimen ovpt: *VZOREC.*	—	—	3.50
	s2. Specimen ovpt: *SPECIMEN.*	—	—	7.50

		VG	VF	UNC
9	**1000 (TOLARJEV)** (19)91; (19)92. Dk. blue-gray and gray on lt. gray and pale blue unpt.			
	a. 1991.	FV	FV	35.00
	b. 1992.	FV	FV	45.00
	s1. Specimen ovpt: *VZOREC.* Wmk: Column pedestal.	—	—	20.00
	s2. Specimen ovpt: *SPECIMEN.* Wmk: Symmetrical design repeated.	—	—	150.00

(19)92. Purple and lilac on pink unpt.

a. Issued note.	FV	FV	130.00
s1. Specimen ovpt: *VZOREC.*	—	—	25.00
s2. Specimen ovpt: *SPECIMEN.*	—	—	25.00

BANKA SLOVENIJE

1992-93 ISSUE

#11-20 replacement notes: Serial # prefix *ZA*.

11 10 TOLARJEV VG VF UNC

15.1.1992. Black, brown-violet and brown-orange on m/c unpt. P. Trubar at r. and as wmk. Quill pen at l. ctr. Ursuline church in Ljubljana at ctr. on back.

	VG	VF	UNC
a. Issued note.	FV	FV	.50
s. Specimen ovpt: *VZOREC.*	—	—	8.50

12 20 TOLARJEV VG VF UNC

15.1.1992. Brownish black, deep brown and brown-orange on m/c unpt. J. Vajkard Valvasor at r. and as wmk., compass at l. Topographical outlines at l. ctr., cherub arms at r. on back.

	VG	VF	UNC
a. Issued note.	FV	FV	.85
s. Specimen ovpt: *VZOREC.*	—	—	10.00

13 50 TOLARJEV VG VF UNC

15.1.1992. Black, purple and brown-orange on m/c unpt. J. Vega at r. and as wmk., geometric design and calculations at l. ctr. Academy at upper l., planets and geometric design at ctr. on back.

	VG	VF	UNC
a. Issued note.	FV	FV	1.50
s. Specimen ovpt: *VZOREC.*	—	—	12.50

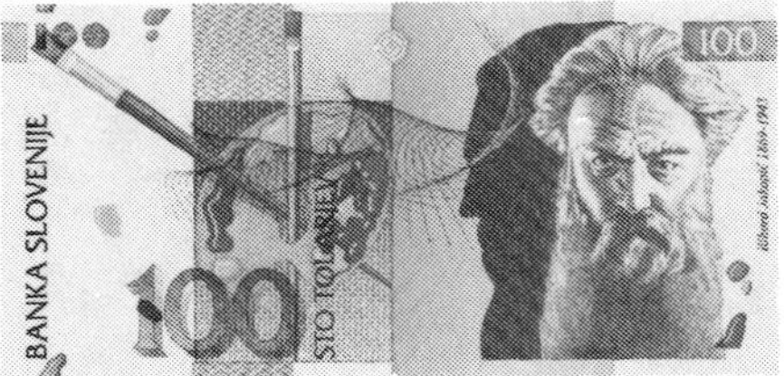

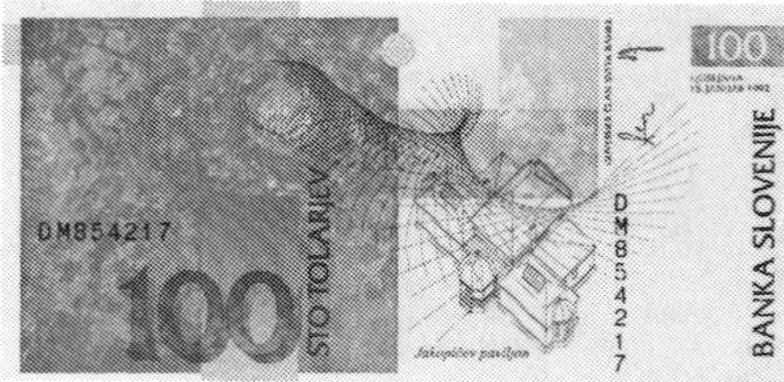

14 100 TOLARJEV VG VF UNC

15.1.1992. Black, blue-black and brown-orange on m/c unpt. R. Jakopic at r. and as wmk. Outline of the Jakopicev Pavilion at ctr. r. on back.

	VG	VF	UNC
a. Issued note.	FV	FV	2.75
s. Specimen ovpt: *VZOREC.*	—	—	15.00

15 200 TOLARJEV VG VF UNC

1992; 1997. Black, violet-brown and brown-orange on m/c unpt. I. Gallus at r. and as wmk., musical facade at l. Drawing of Slovenia's Philharmonic bldg. at upper l., music scores at upper ctr. on back.

	VG	VF	UNC
a. 15.1.1992.	FV	FV	21.00
b. 9.10.1997.	FV	FV	3.25
s. Specimen ovpt: *VZOREC.*	—	—	17.50

16 500 TOLARJEV VG VF UNC

15.1.1992. Black, red and brown-orange on m/c unpt. J. Plecnik at r. and as wmk. Drawing of the National and University Library of Ljubljana at l. ctr. on back.

	VG	VF	UNC
a. Issued note.	FV	FV	9.00
s. Specimen ovpt: *VZOREC.*	—	—	20.00

NOTICE

Readers with unlisted dates, signature varieties, etc. are invited to submit photocopies of their notes to: Standard Catalog of World Paper Money, 700 East State St. Iola, WI 54990-0001, fax: 1-715-445-4087, or E-Mail: thernr@krause.com.

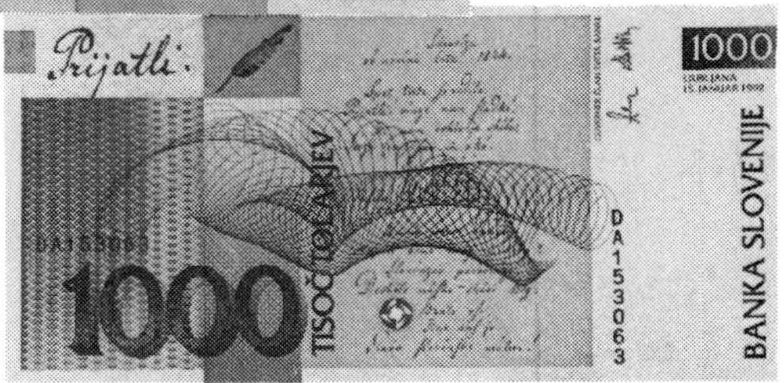

		VG	VF	UNC
17	**1000 TOLARJEV** 15.1.1992. Brownish black, deep green and brown-orange on m/c unpt. F. Preseren at r. and as wmk. The poem "Drinking Toast" at ctr. on back.			
	a. Issued note.	FV	FV	22.50
	s. Specimen ovpt: *VZOREC.*	—	—	25.00

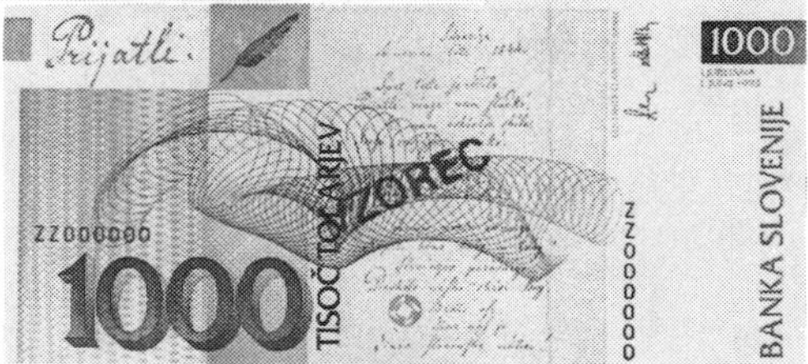

		VG	VF	UNC
18	**1000 TOLARJEV** 1.6.1993. Black, deep blue-green and brown-orange on m/c unpt. Like #17 but modified portrait and other incidental changes including color.			
	a. Issued note.	FV	FV	15.00
	s. Specimen ovpt: *VZOREC.*	—	—	25.00

		VG	VF	UNC
19	**5000 TOLARJEV** 1.6.1993. Brownish black, dk. brown and brown-orange on m/c unpt. I. Kobilika at r. and as wmk. National Gallery in Ljubljana at upper l. on back.			
	a. Issued note.	FV	FV	80.00
	s. Specimen ovpt: *VZOREC.*	—	—	30.00

		VG	VF	UNC
20	**10,000 TOLARJEV** 28.6.1994. Black, purple and brown-orange on m/c unpt. I. Cankar at r. and as wmk. Chrysanthemum blossom at l. on back.			
	a. Issued note.	FV	FV	110.00
	s. Specimen ovpt: *VZOREC.*	—	—	35.00

1997 ISSUE

		VG	VF	UNC
21	**5000 TOLARJEV** 8.10.1997. Brownish black, dk. brown and brown-orange on m/c unpt. Like #19 but w/scalloped kinnegram w/cameo portr.//value.			
	a. Kinnegram 5000 vertical.	FV	FV	50.00
	b. Kinnegram 5000 horizontal.	FV	FV	50.00
	s. Specimen ovpt: *VZOREC.*	—	—	25.00

The Solomon Islands, located in the Southwest Pacific east of Papua New Guinea, has an area of 10,983 sq. mi. (28,450 sq. km.) and an estimated population of 426,855. Capital: Honiara. The most important islands of the Solomon chain are Guadalcanal (scene of some of the fiercest fighting of World War II), Malaitia, New Georgia, Florida, Vella Lavella, Choiseul, Rendova, San Cristobal, the Lord Howe group, the Santa Cruz islands, and the Duff group. Copra is the only important cash crop but it is hoped that timber will become an economic factor.

The Solomon Islands were discovered by Spanish navigator Alvaro de Mendana in 1567, and in 1569 he made an unsuccessful attempt to colonize them. European knowledge of the group would not be completed until the end of the 18th century. Germany declared a protectorate over the northern Solomons in 1885. The British protectorate over the southern Solomons was established in 1893. In 1899 Germany transferred its claim to all Solomon Islands except Buka and Bougainville to Great Britain in exchange for recognition of German claims in western Samoa. Australia occupied the two German held islands in 1914, and administered them after 1920.

The Japanese invaded the Solomons during 1942-43, but were driven out by an American counteroffensive after a series of bloody clashes.

Following World War II the islands returned to the status of a British protectorate. In 1976 the protectorate was abolished and the Solomons became a self-governing dependency. Full independence was achieved on July 7, 1978. Solomon Islands is a member of the Commonwealth of Nations. Elizabeth II is Head of State as Queen of the Solomon Islands.

RULERS:

British

MONETARY SYSTEM:

1 Shilling = 12 Pence
1 Pound = 20 Shillings to 1966
1 Dollar = 100 Cents, 1966-

SIGNATURE/TITLE VARIETIES					
1	Chairman	Member	4	Governor	Director
2			5		
3			6		

SOLOMON ISLANDS MONETARY AUTHORITY

1977; 1981 ND ISSUE

Dollar System

#5-8 Qn. Elizabeth II at r. Wmk: Falcon. Printer: TDLR (w/o imprint). Replacement notes: Serial # prefix: *Z/1*.

		VG	VF	UNC
5	**2 DOLLARS** ND (1977). Dk. green on pink and pale green unpt. Fishermen on back. Sign. 1.	1.00	2.00	10.00

		VG	VF	UNC
6	**5 DOLLARS** ND (1977). Dk. blue on m/c unpt. Long boats and hut on back.			
	a. Sign. 1.	2.25	4.00	20.00
	b. Sign. 2.	2.25	5.00	25.00

		VG	VF	UNC
7	**10 DOLLARS** ND (1977). Purple and violet on m/c unpt. Weaver on back.			
	a. Sign. 1.	4.00	7.50	27.50
	b. Sign. 2.	4.00	8.00	35.00

		VG	VF	UNC
8	**20 DOLLARS** ND (1981). Brown and deep orange on m/c unpt. Line of people on back. Sign. 3.	7.00	15.00	50.00

CENTRAL BANK OF SOLOMON ISLANDS

1984 ND ISSUE

#11 and 12 like #7 and 8 except for new bank name. Wmk: Falcon. Sign. 4. Replacement notes: Serial # prefix *Z/1*.

		VG	VF	UNC
11	**10 DOLLARS** ND (1984). Purple and violet on m/c unpt.	FV	FV	22.50

		VG	VF	UNC
12	**20 DOLLARS** ND (1984). Brown and dk. orange on m/c unpt.	FV	FV	36.50

1986 ND ISSUE

#13-17 arms at r. Wmk: Falcon. Sign. 5. Replacement notes: Replacement notes: Serial # prefix *Y/1*.

#13-16 backs like #5-8.

		VG	VF	UNC
13	**2 DOLLARS** ND (1986). Green on m/c unpt.	FV	FV	2.25

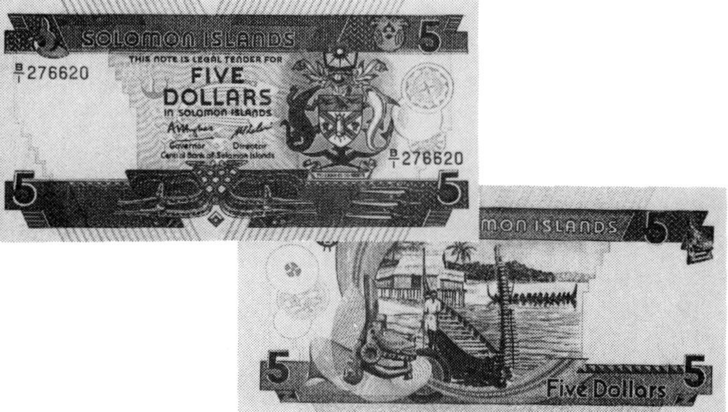

		VG	VF	UNC
14	**5 DOLLARS** ND (1986). Dk. blue, deep purple and violet on m/c unpt.	FV	FV	6.00

		VG	VF	UNC
15	**10 DOLLARS** ND (1986). Purple and violet on m/c unpt.	FV	FV	8.50
16	**20 DOLLARS** ND (1986). Brown and deep orange on m/c unpt.	FV	FV	20.00

		VG	VF	UNC
17	**50 DOLLARS** ND (1986). Blue-green and purple on m/c unpt. Butterflies and reptiles on back.	FV	FV	45.00

1996; 1997 ND ISSUE

#18-22 similar to #13-17 but w/added security devices. Printing in wmk. area on back. Ascending size serial #. W/security thread. Wmk: Falcon. Replacement notes: Serial # prefix *X/1*.

		VG	VF	UNC
18	**2 DOLLARS** ND (1997). Greenish black and olive-green on m/c unpt.	FV	FV	2.50

		VG	VF	UNC
19	**5 DOLLARS** ND (1997). Dk. blue, deep purple and violet on m/c unpt.	FV	FV	4.00

		VG	VF	UNC
20	**10 DOLLARS** ND (1996). Purple and red-violet on m/c unpt.	FV	FV	7.00

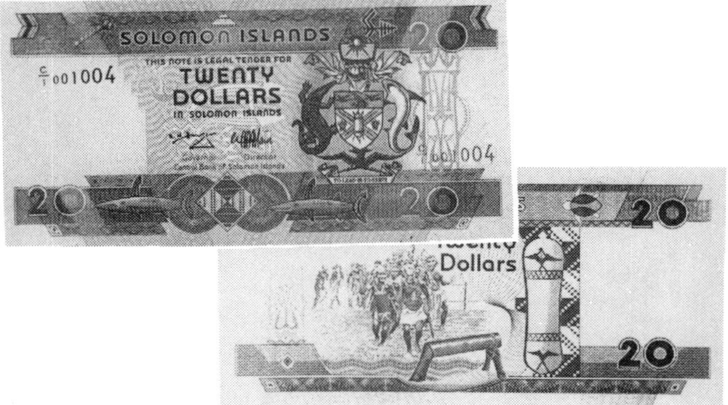

		VG	VF	UNC
21	**20 DOLLARS** ND (1996). Brown and brown-orange on m/c unpt.	FV	FV	13.50

		VG	VF	UNC
22	**50 DOLLARS** ND (1996). Green, Blue-gray and purple on m/c unpt.	FV	FV	30.00

COLLECTOR SERIES

SOLOMON ISLANDS MONETARY AUTHORITY

1979 ND ISSUE

		ISSUE PRICE	MKT. VALUE
CS1	**ND (1979) 2-10 DOLLARS** #5, 6b, 7b w/ovpt: *SPECIMEN* and serial # prefix Maltese cross.	14.00	25.00

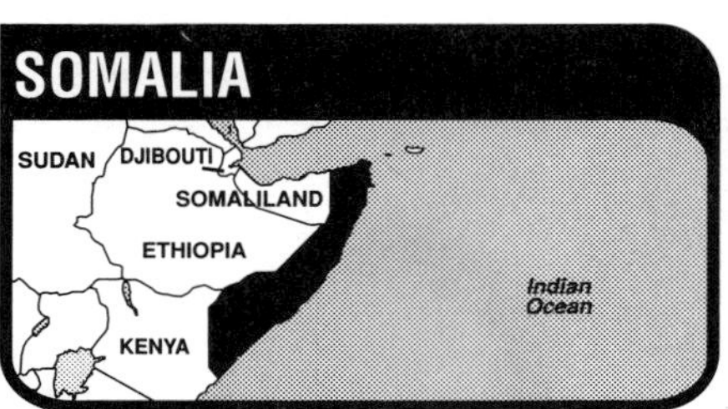

Somalia, the Somali Democratic Republic, comprising the former Italian Somaliland, is located on the coast of the eastern projection of the African continent commonly referred to as the "Horn". It has an area of 178,201 sq. mi. (461,657 sq. km.). Capital: Mogadishu. The economy is pastoral and agricultural. Livestock, bananas and hides are exported. The area of the British Somaliland Protectorate was known to the Egyptians at least 1,500 years B.C., and was occupied by the Arabs and Portuguese before British sea captains obtained trading and anchorage rights in 1827. The land of sandy clay and sporadic rainfall acquired a strategic importance with the opening of the Suez Canal in 1869. After negotiating treaties with the tribes, Britain declared the area a protectorate in 1888. Italy acquired Italian Somaliland in 1895 by purchase from the sultan of Zanzibar. Britain occupied Italian Somaliland in 1941 and administered it until April 1, 1950, when it was returned to Italy as a U.N. trusteeship. The British Somaliland protectorate became independent on June 26, 1960. Five days later it joined with Italian Somaliland to form the Somali Republic. The country was under a revolutionary military regime installed Oct. 21, 1969. After 11 years of civil war rebel forces fought their way into the capital. A. M. Muhammad became president in Aug. 1991 but interfactional fighting continued. A UN-sponsored truce was signed in March 1992 and a peace plan and pact was signed Jan. 15, 1993. The northern Somali National Movements (SNM) declared a secession of the northwestern Somaliland Republic on May 17, 1991 which is not recognized by the Somali Democratic Republic.

MONETARY SYSTEM:

1 Scellino = 1 Shilling = 100 Centesimi
1 Shilin = 1 Shilling = 100 Centi

REPUBLIC

BANCA NAZIONALE SOMALA

1962 ISSUE

#1-4 sign. title: *PRESIDENTE* at l. Wmk: Leopard's head. Printer OCV.

		VG	VF	UNC
1	**5 SCELLINI = 5 SHILLINGS** 1962. Red on green and orange unpt. Antelope at l. Back orange-brown; dhow at ctr.			
	a. Issued note.	15.00	35.00	200.00
	s. Specimen.	—	—	110.00

		VG	VF	UNC
2	**10 SCELLINI = 10 SHILLINGS** 1962. Green on red-brown and green unpt. Flower at l. Back brown and green; river scene at ctr. r.			
	a. Issued note.	20.00	55.00	325.00
	s. Specimen.	—	—	185.00

3	20 SCELLINI = 20 SHILLINGS	VG	VF	UNC
	1962. Brown on blue and gold unpt. Banana plant at l. Back brown and blue; bank bldg. at ctr. r.			
	a. Issued note.	25.00	75.00	475.00
	s. Specimen.	—	—	335.00

4	100 SCELLINI = 100 SHILLINGS	VG	VF	UNC
	1962. Blue on green and orange unpt. Artcraft at l. Back blue and red; bldg.			
	a. Issued note.	35.00	125.00	550.00
	s. Specimen.	—	—	400.00

1966 ISSUE

#5-8 slight changes in colors and design elements (w/o imprint). Wmk: Leopard's head.

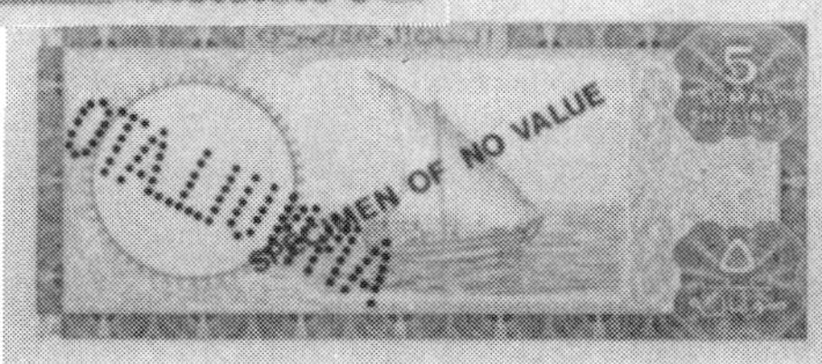

5	5 SCELLINI = 5 SHILLINGS	VG	VF	UNC
	1966. Similar to #1 but different guilloche in unpt. Back w/blue unpt.			
	a. Issued note.	10.00	30.00	175.00
	s. Specimen perforated: *ANNULLATO.*	—	—	100.00

NOTICE

Readers with unlisted dates, signature varieties, etc. are invited to submit photocopies of their notes to: Standard Catalog of World Paper Money, 700 East State St. Iola, WI 54990-0001, fax: 1-715-445-4087, or E-Mail: thernr@krause.com.

6	10 SCELLINI = 10 SHILLINGS	VG	VF	UNC
	1966. Similar to #2 but different guilloche in unpt. Back green w/lt. tan unpt.			
	a. Issued note.	15.00	50.00	325.00
	s. Specimen perforated: *ANNULLATO.*	—	—	225.00

7	20 SCELLINI = 20 SHILLINGS	VG	VF	UNC
	1966. Similar to #3 but unpt. is pink, blue and green. Brown bank bldg. on back.			
	a. Issued note.	25.00	65.00	450.00
	s. Specimen perforated: *ANNULLATO.*	—	—	325.00

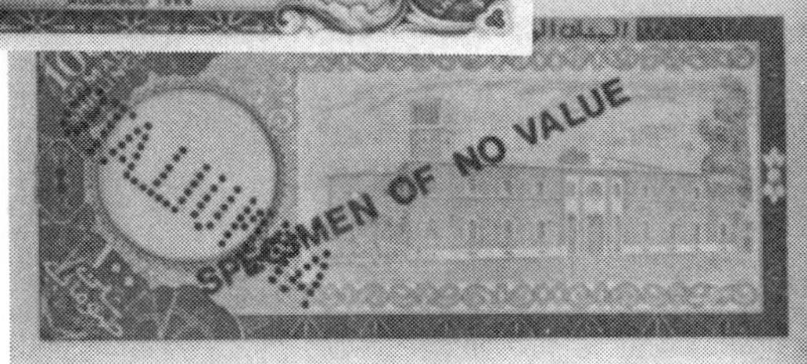

8	100 SCELLINI = 100 SHILLINGS	VG	VF	UNC
	1966. Similar to #4 but unpt. is green, purple and tan.			
	a. Issued note.	35.00	120.00	600.00
	s. Specimen perforated: *ANNULLATO.*	—	—	435.00

1968 ISSUE

#9-12 Wmk: Leopard's head. Sign. title *Governatore* at l.

9	5 SCELLINI = 5 SHILLINGS	VG	VF	UNC
	1968. Red on green and orange unpt. Like #5.	12.50	35.00	200.00
10	10 SCELLINI = 10 SHILLINGS			
	1968. Green on red-brown and green unpt. Like #6.	20.00	55.00	425.00
11	20 SCELLINI = 20 SHILLINGS			
	1968. Brown on blue and gold unpt. Like #7.	27.50	85.00	525.00
12	100 SCELLINI = 100 SHILLINGS			
	1968. Blue on green and orange unpt. Like #8.	37.50	125.00	750.00

DEMOCRATIC REPUBLIC

BANCA NAZIONALE SOMALA

1971 ISSUE

#13-16 like #9-12. Wmk: Leopard's head. Sign. title: *GOVERNATORE* and *CASSIERE* at r.

		VG	VF	UNC
13	**5 SCELLINI = 5 SHILLINGS** 1971. Purple-brown on blue, green and gold unpt. Like #9.			
	a. Issued note.	8.00	22.50	185.00
	s. Specimen.	—	—	110.00

		VG	VF	UNC
14	**10 SCELLINI = 10 SHILLINGS** 1971. Green on red-brown and green unpt. Like #10.			
	a. Issued note.	10.00	27.50	275.00
	s. Specimen.	—	—	175.00

		VG	VF	UNC
15	**20 SCELLINI = 20 SHILLINGS** 1971. Brown on blue and gold unpt. Like #11.			
	a. Issued note.	15.00	40.00	425.00
	s. Specimen.	—	—	275.00

		VG	VF	UNC
16	**100 SCELLINI = 100 SHILLINGS** 1971. Blue on green and orange unpt. Like #12.			
	a. Issued note.	17.50	60.00	525.00
	s. Specimen.	—	—	375.00

BANKIGA QARANKA SOOMAALIYEED

SOMALI NATIONAL BANK

LAW OF 11.12.1974

#17-20 arms at l. Wmk: S. M. A. Hassan.

		VG	VF	UNC
17	**5 SHILIN = 5 SHILLINGS** 1975. Purple on gold and m/c unpt. Gnus and zebras at bottom ctr. Banana harvesting at ctr. r. on back.	1.50	5.00	20.00

		VG	VF	UNC
18	**10 SHILIN = 10 SHILLINGS** 1975. Dk. green on pink and m/c unpt. Lighthouse at l. ctr. Shipbuilders at work at ctr. r. on back.	2.00	6.50	37.50

		VG	VF	UNC
19	**20 SHILIN = 20 SHILLINGS** 1975. Brown on m/c unpt. Bank bldg. at ctr. Cattle on back.	2.25	6.50	100.00

		VG	VF	UNC
20	**100 SHILIN = 100 SHILLINGS** 1975. Blue on gold and m/c unpt. Woman w/baby, rifle and farm tools at l. ctr. Dagathur Monument at ctr. r. Workers in factory on back.	7.00	20.00	125.00

BANKIGA DHEXE EE SOOMAALIYA

CENTRAL BANK OF SOMALIA

LAW OF 6.12.1977

#20A-24 arms at l. Black series and serial #. Wmk: S. M. A. Hassan.

		VG	VF	UNC
20A	**5 SHILIN = 5 SHILLINGS** 1978. Purple on gold and m/c unpt. Like #17.	4.00	10.00	35.00

		VG	VF	UNC
21	**5 SHILIN = 5 SHILLINGS** 1978. Purple on gold and m/c unpt. Similar to #20A but Cape Buffalo herd at bottom l. ctr.	.50	2.00	12.50
22	**10 SHILIN = 10 SHILLINGS** 1978. Dk. green on pink and m/c unpt. Like #18.	1.00	4.00	25.00

		VG	VF	UNC
23	**20 SHILIN = 20 SHILLINGS** 1978. Brown on m/c unpt. Like #19.	1.75	8.00	42.50
24	**100 SHILIN = 100 SHILLINGS** 1978. Blue on gold and m/c unpt. Like #20.	2.25	10.00	70.00

LAW OF 5.4.1980

#26-28 arms at l. Red series and serial #. Different sign. title at l. Wmk: S. M. A. Hassan. Replacement notes: Serial # prefix *Z001*.

#25 *Deleted*.

		VG	VF	UNC
26	**10 SHILIN = 10 SHILLINGS** 1980. Dk. green on pink and m/c unpt. Like #22.	.60	2.50	10.00

		VG	VF	UNC
27	**20 SHILIN = 20 SHILLINGS** 1980. Brown on m/c unpt. Like #23.	1.00	5.00	20.00

		VG	VF	UNC
28	**100 SHILIN = 100 SHILLINGS** 1980. Blue on gold and m/c unpt. Like #24.	2.25	9.00	35.00

LAW OF 9.12.1981

#29-30 wmk: S. M. A. Hassan. Replacement notes: Serial # prefix *ZZ001*.

		VG	VF	UNC
29	**20 SHILIN = 20 SHILLINGS** 1981. Brown on m/c unpt. Like #27.	1.00	5.50	37.50

		VG	VF	UNC
30	**100 SHILIN = 100 SHILLINGS** 1981. Blue on gold and m/c unpt. Like #28.	4.00	12.00	32.50

LAW OF 30.12.1982; 1983 ISSUE

#31-35 arms at top l. ctr., star at or near lower ctr. Reduced size notes. Replacement notes: Serial # prefix *Z001*.

		VG	VF	UNC
31	**5 SHILIN = 5 SHILLINGS** 1983-87. Brown-violet. Cape Buffalo herd at l. ctr. Harvesting bananas on back.			
	a. 1983.	.10	.50	2.50
	b. 1986.	.10	.40	2.00
	c. 1987.	.10	.25	1.00

#32-35 wmk: S. M. A. Hassan.

		VG	VF	UNC
32	**10 SHILIN = 10 SHILLINGS** 1983-87. Green and m/c. Lighthouse at l. Shipbuilders at ctr. r. on back.			
	a. 1983.	.25	.75	3.00
	b. 1986.	.20	.60	2.00
	c. 1987.	.15	.50	1.75

		VG	VF	UNC
33	**20 SHILIN = 20 SHILLINGS** 1983-89. Brown and m/c. Bank at l. Back similar to #19.			
	a. 1983.	.35	1.50	5.00
	b. 1986.	.25	1.00	4.00
	c. 1987.	.20	.75	3.00
	d. 1989.	.15	.50	2.00

		VG	VF	UNC
34	**50 SHILIN = 50 SHILLINGS** 1983-89. Red-brown and m/c unpt. Walled city at l. and ctr. Watering animals at ctr. r. on back.			
	a. 1983.	.50	1.50	6.00
	b. 1986; 1987. 2 sign. varieties for 1987.	.15	.40	4.00
	c. 1988.	.15	.50	2.50
	d. 1989.	.10	.40	2.00

		VG	VF	UNC
35	**100 SHILIN = 100 SHILLINGS** 1983-89. Blue-black, dk. blue and dk. green on m/c unpt. Similar to #20.			
	a. 1983.	.60	2.50	7.50
	b. 1986; 1987. 2 sign. varieties for 1987.	.30	1.00	4.00
	c. 1988.	.15	.50	2.50
	d. 1989.	.15	.40	2.00

LAW OF 1.1.1989

#36 and 37 arms at top l. ctr. Wmk: S. M. A. Hussan.

		VG	VF	UNC
36	**500 SHILIN = 500 SHILLINGS** 1989; 1990. Green and aqua on m/c unpt. Fishermen mending net at l. ctr. Mosque at l. ctr. on back. 2 sign. varieties.	FV	FV	5.00

LAW OF 1.1.1990; 1990 ISSUE

		VG	VF	UNC
37	**1000 SHILIN = 1000 SHILLINGS** 1990; 1996. Violet and orange on m/c unpt. Women seated weaving baskets at l. ctr.; arms above. City view at bottom, Port of Mogadishu at upper ctr. r. on back.			
	a. 1990.	FV	FV	2.50
	b. 1996.	FV	FV	3.50
38	**1000 SHILIN = 1000 SHILLINGS** 1996. Like #37.	FV	FV	3.00

REGIONAL

In Mogadishu-North, forces loyal to warlord Ali Mahdi Mohammed have issued currency valued in "N" Shilin. The notes may have originally been part of a plan to replace older currency.

MOGADISHU NORTH FORCES

1991 ISSUE

#R1 and R2 arms at top l. ctr. Wmk: S. M. A. Hassan.

		VG	VF	UNC
R1	**20 N SHILIN = 20 N SHILLINGS** 1991. Violet, red-brown, brown-orange and olive-green on m/c unpt. Trader leading camel in unpt. at l. ctr. Picking cotton at ctr. r. on back.	.50	1.50	7.00

		VG	VF	UNC
R2	**50 N SHILIN = 50 N SHILLINGS** 1991. Brown, green and black on m/c unpt. Man working loom. Young person leading a donkey w/3 children on back.	1.75	5.00	15.00

NOTICE

Readers with unlisted dates, signature varieties, etc. are invited to submit photocopies of their notes to: Standard Catalog of World Paper Money, 700 East State St. Iola, WI 54990-0001, fax: 1-715-445-4087, or E-Mail: thernr@krause.com.

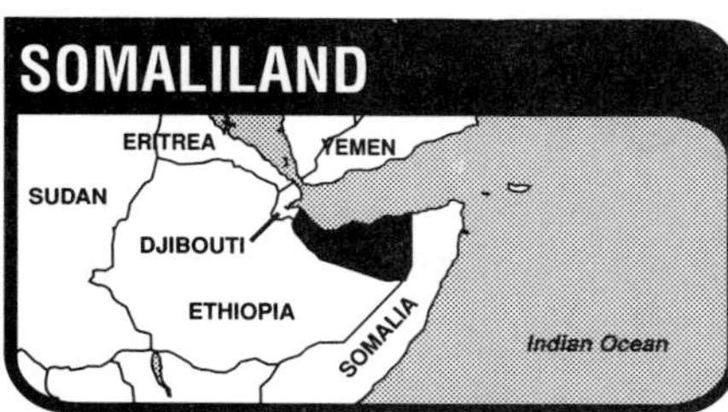

The Somaliland Republic, comprising the former British Somaliland Protectorate, is located on the coast of the northeastern projection of the African continent commonly referred to as the "Horn" on the southwestern end of the Gulf of Aden.

Bordered by Eritrea to the west, Ethiopia to west and south and Somalia to the east, it has an area of 68,000* sq. mi. (176,000* sq. km). Capital: Hargeysa. It is mostly arid and mounainous except for the gulf shoreline.

The Protectorate of British Somaliland was established in 1888 and from 1905 the territory was administered by a commissioner under the British Colonial Office. Italian Somaliland was administered as a colony from 1893 to 1941, when the territory was occupied by British forces. In 1950 the United Nations allowed Italy to resume control of Italian Somaliland under a trusteeship. In 1960 British and Italian Somaliland were united as Somalia, an independent republic outside the Commonwealth.

Civil War erupted in the late 1970's and continued until the capital of Somalia was taken in 1990. The United Nations provided aid and peacekeepers. A UN sponsored truce was signed in March 1992 and a peace plan and pact was signed Jan. 15, 1993. The northern Somali National Movement (SMN) declared a secession of the Somaliland Republic on May 17, 1991 which is not recognized by the Somali Democratic Republic.

The currency issued by the East African Currency Board was used in British Somaliland from 1945 to 1961. Somali currency was then used until 1995.

MONETARY SYSTEM:

1 Somaliland Shilling = 1 Shilin

SIGNATURE VARIETIES					
1	Guddoomiyaha	Lacaghayaha	2	Lacaghayaha	Guddoomiyaha

REPUBLIC

BAANKA SOMALILAND

1994 ISSUE

#1-4 bldg. at ctr. Greater Kudu at r. Traders w/camels on back.

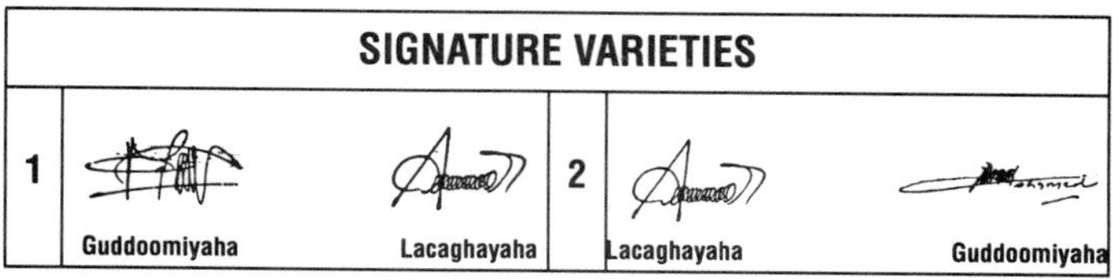

		VG	VF	UNC
1	**5 SHILLINGS = 5 SHILIN** 1994. Bright green, olive-green and red-brown on m/c unpt.	FV	FV	1.00

		VG	VF	UNC
2	**10 SHILLINGS = 10 SHILIN** 1994-. Violet, purple and red-brown on m/c unpt.			
	a. 1994.	FV	FV	1.25
	b. 1996.	FV	FV	1.00

		VG	VF	UNC
3	**20 SHILLINGS = 20 SHILIN** 1994-. Brown and red-brown on m/c unpt.			
	a. 1994.	FV	FV	2.25
	b. 1996.	FV	FV	2.00

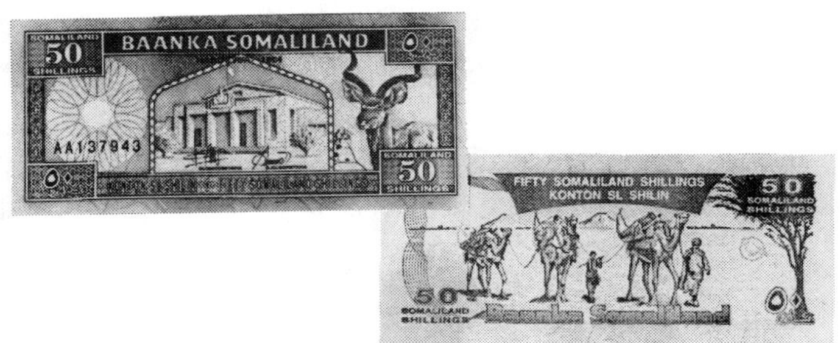

4 **50 SHILLINGS = 50 SHILIN** | VG | VF | UNC
1994-. Blue-violet, blue-gray and red-brown on m/c unpt.

	VG	VF	UNC
a. 1994.	FV	FV	4.00
b. 1996.	FV	FV	3.50

#5 and 6 bldg. at ctr. Ship dockside in background, herdsmen w/sheep at front ctr. on back.

5 **100 SHILLINGS = 100 SHILIN**
1994-. Brownish black and red-violet on m/c unpt.

	VG	VF	UNC
a. 1994.	FV	FV	6.50
b. 1996.	FV	FV	4.75

6 **500 SHILLINGS = 500 SHILIN**
1994-. Purple, blue-black and blue-green on m/c unpt.

	VG	VF	UNC
a. 1994.	FV	FV	15.00
b. 1996.	FV	FV	10.00

1996 ISSUE

7 **50 SHILLINGS = 50 SHILIN**
1996. Blue-violet, blue-gray and violet on m/c unpt. Like #4 but increased size. 130 x 58mm.

	VG	VF	UNC
a. Sign. 1.	FV	FV	2.50
b. Sign. 2.	FV	FV	2.25

1996 "BRONZE" COMMEMORATIVE ISSUE

#8-13, 5th Anniversary of Independence

#8-13 bronze ovpt: *5th Anniversary of Independence 18 May 1996 - Sanad Gurada 5ee Gobanimadda 18 May 1996*

8 **5 SHILLINGS = 5 SHILIN**
18.5.1996 (- old date 1994). Ovpt. on #1.

VG	VF	UNC
FV	FV	1.75

9 **10 SHILLINGS = 10 SHILIN**
18.5.1996 (- old date 1994). Ovpt. on #2a.

VG	VF	UNC
FV	FV	2.00

10 **20 SHILLINGS = 20 SHILIN**
18.5.1996 (- old date 1994). Ovpt. on #3a.

VG	VF	UNC
FV	FV	3.00

11 **50 SHILLINGS = 50 SHILIN**
18.5.1996.

	VG	VF	UNC
a. Ovpt. on #4a. (- old date 1994).	FV	FV	4.25
b. Ovpt. on #4b. 1996.	FV	FV	3.00

11A **50 SHILLINGS = 50 SHILIN**
18.5.1996. Blue-violet, blue-gray and violet on m/c unpt. Bronze ovpt. on #7a.

VG	VF	UNC
FV	FV	3.50

12 **100 SHILLINGS = 100 SHILIN**
18.5.1996 (- old date 1994). Ovpt. on #5a.

VG	VF	UNC
FV	FV	7.50

13 **500 SHILLINGS = 500 SHILIN**
18.5.1996 (- old date 1994). Ovpt. on #6a.

VG	VF	UNC
FV	FV	26.50

1996 "SILVER" COMMEMORATIVE ISSUE

#14-19, 5th Anniversary of Independence

#14-19 silver ovpt: *Sanad Gurada 5ee Gobanimadda 18 May 1996*

		VG	VF	UNC
14	**5 SHILLINGS = 5 SHILIN** 18.5.1996 (- old date 1994). Ovpt. on #1.	FV	FV	1.75

		VG	VF	UNC
15	**10 SHILLINGS = 10 SHILIN** 18.5.1996 (- old date 1994). Ovpt. on #2a.	FV	FV	2.00

		VG	VF	UNC
16	**20 SHILLINGS = 20 SHILIN** 18.5.1996 (- old date 1994). Ovpt. on #3a.	FV	FV	3.00

		VG	VF	UNC
17	**50 SHILLINGS = 50 SHILIN** 18.5.1996.			
	a. Ovpt. on #4a. (- old date 1994).	FV	FV	4.25
	b. Ovpt. on #4b. 1996.	FV	FV	3.00

		VG	VF	UNC
17A	**50 SHILLINGS = 50 SHILIN** 1996. Blue-violet, blue-gray and violet on m/c unpt. Ovpt. on #7b.	FV	FV	3.50

		VG	VF	UNC
18	**100 SHILLINGS = 100 SHILIN** 18.5.1996 (- old date 1994). Ovpt. on #5a.	FV	FV	7.50

		VG	VF	UNC
19	**500 SHILLINGS = 500 SHILIN** 18.5.1996 (- old date 1994). Ovpt. on #6a.	FV	FV	26.50

SOUTH AFRICA

CONGO DEMOCRATIC REPUBLIC · TANZANIA · MALAWI · ANGOLA · ZAMBIA · NAMIBIA · ZIMBABWE · MOZAMBIQUE · BOTSWANA · MADAGASCAR · SWAZILAND · LESOTHO

The Republic of South Africa, located at the southern tip of Africa, has an area, including the enclave of Walvis Bay, of 472,359 sq. mi. (1,221,040 sq. km.) and a population of 41.5 million. Capital: Administrative, Pretoria; Legislative, Cape Town; Judicial, Bloemfontein. Manufacturing, mining and agriculture are the principal industries. Exports include wool, diamonds, gold and metallic ores.

Portuguese navigator Bartholomeu Diaz became the first European to sight the region of South Africa when he rounded the Cape of Good Hope in 1488, but throughout the 16th century the only white men to come ashore were the survivors of ships wrecked while attempting the stormy Cape passage. The first permanent settlement was established by Jan van Riebeeck of the Dutch East India Company in 1652. In subsequent decades additional Dutch, Germans and Huguenot refugees from France settled in the Cape area to form the Afrikaner segment of today's population.

Great Britain captured the Cape colony in 1795, and again in 1806, receiving permanent title in 1814. To escape British political rule and cultural dominance, many Afrikaner farmers (Boers) migrated northward (the Great Trek) beginning in 1836, and established the independent Boer republics of the Transvaal (the South African Republic, Zuid-Afrikaansche Republiek) in 1852, and the Orange Free State in 1854. British political intrigues against the two republics, coupled with the discovery of diamonds and gold in the Boer-settled regions, led to the bitter Boer Wars (1880-1881, 1899-1902) and the incorporation of the Boer republics into the British Empire.

On May 31, 1910, the two former Boer republics (Transvaal and Orange Free State) were joined with the British colonies of Cape of Good Hope and Natal to form the Union of South Africa, a dominion of the British Empire. In 1934 the Union achieved status as a sovereign state within the British Empire. Political integration of the various colonies did not still the conflict between the Afrikaners and the English-speaking groups, which continued to have a significant impact on political developments. A resurgence of Afrikaner nationalism in the 1940s and 1950s led to a referendum in the white community authorizing the relinquishment of dominion status and the establishment of a republic. The decision took effect on May 31, 1961. The Republic of South Africa withdrew from the British Commonwealth in Oct., 1961. The apartheid era ended on April 27, 1994 with the first democratic election for all people of South Africa. Nelson Mandela was inaugurated as president on May 10, 1994. South Africa was readmitted to the Commonwealth of Nations.

South African currency carries inscriptions in both Afrikaans and English.

RULERS:

British to 1961

MONETARY SYSTEM:

1 Rand = 100 Cents (= 10 Shillings), 1961-

SIGNATURE VARIETIES

3	M. H. de Kock, 1.7.1945-30.6.1962	4	G. Rissik, 1.7.1962-30.6.1967
5	T. W. de Jongh, 1.7.1967-31.12.1980	6	G. P. C. de Kock, 1.1.1981-7.8.1989
7	C. L. Stals, 8.8.1989-7.8.1999	8	T.T. Mboweni, 8.8.1999-

REPUBLIC OF SOUTH AFRICA
SOUTH AFRICAN RESERVE BANK

1961 ND ISSUE

#102-108A portr. Jan van Riebeeck at l. and as wmk.

#102-105 replacement notes: Serial # prefix *Z/1; Y/1; X/1; W/1* respectively.

		VG	VF	Unc
102	**1 Rand** ND (1961-62). Rust brown. First line of bank name and value in English. 135 x 77mm.			
	a. Sign. 3. (1961).	3.75	13.50	40.00
	b. Sign. 4. (1962).	2.00	10.00	27.50

		VG	VF	Unc
103	**1 Rand** ND (1961-62). Rust brown. Like #102 but first line of bank name and value in Afrikaans. 137 x 78mm.			
	a. Sign. 3. (1961).	3.75	13.50	40.00
	b. Sign. 4. (1962).	3.00	10.00	27.50

		VG	VF	Unc
104	**2 Rand** ND (1961-62). Blue. First line of bank name and value in English. 150 x 85mm.			
	a. Sign. 3. (1961).	2.50	7.00	25.00
	b. Sign. 4. (1962).	1.50	4.00	15.00

		VG	VF	Unc
105	**2 Rand** ND (1961-62). Like #104 but first line of bank name and value in Afrikaans. 150 x 85mm.			
	a. Sign. 3. (1961).	2.50	7.00	25.00
	b. Sign. 4. (1962).	1.50	4.00	15.00

		VG	VF	Unc
106	**10 Rand** ND (1961-62). Green and brown on m/c unpt. First line of bank name and value in English. Sailing ship on back. 170 x 97mm.			
	a. Sign. 3. (1961).	6.00	17.50	60.00
	b. Sign. 4. (1962).	4.00	12.00	40.00

		VG	VF	Unc
107	**10 Rand** ND (1961-62). Green and brown on m/c unpt. Like #106 but first line of bank name and value in Afrikaans. 170 x 97mm.			
	a. Sign. 3. (1961).	6.00	17.50	60.00
	b. Sign. 4. (1962).	4.00	12.00	40.00
108	**20 Rand** ND (1961-62). Brown-violet. First line of bank name and value in English. Machinery on back. Sign. 3.	11.00	35.00	110.00

		VG	VF	UNC
108A	**20 RAND** ND (1962). Like #108 but first line of bank name in Afrikaans. Sign. 4.	12.00	40.00	135.00

1966 ND ISSUE

#109-114 J. van Riebeeck at l. Replacement notes: Serial # prefix *Z/1; Y/1; X/1; W/1* respectively.

		VG	VF	UNC
109	**1 RAND** ND (1966-72). Dk. reddish brown on m/c unpt. First lines of bank name and value in English. Rams in field on back. 126 x 64mm. Wmk: Springbok.			
	a. Sign. 4. (1966).	1.50	4.00	12.50
	b. Sign. 5. (1967).	1.00	2.50	8.00

		VG	VF	UNC
110	**1 RAND** ND (1966-72). Dk. reddish brown on m/c unpt. Like #109 but first lines of bank name and value in Afrikaans. 126 x 64mm. Wmk: Springbok.			
	a. Sign. 4. (1966).	1.50	4.00	12.50
	b. Sign. 5. (1967).	1.00	2.50	8.00
111	**5 RAND** ND (1966-76). Purple on m/c unpt. Covered wagons on trail at r. corner. First lines of bank name and value in English. Factory w/train on back. 133 x 70mm.			
	a. Sign. 4. Wmk: Springbok (1966).	7.00	20.00	62.50
	b. Sign. 5. Wmk: Springbok (1967-74).	2.50	5.00	20.00
	c. Sign. 5. Wmk: J. van Riebeeck (1975).	2.75	5.25	21.50

		VG	VF	UNC
112	**5 RAND** ND (1966-76). Purple on m/c unpt. Like #111 but first lines of bank name and value in Afrikaans.			
	a. Sign. 4. Wmk: Springbok (1966).	7.00	20.00	62.50
	b. Sign. 5. Wmk: Springbok (1967-74).	2.25	5.00	20.00
	c. Sign. 5. Wmk: J. van Riebeeck (1975).	2.25	5.50	21.50

		VG	VF	UNC
113	**10 RAND** ND (1966-76). Dk. green and brown on m/c unpt. Capital bldg. at ctr. First lines of bank name and value in English. Old sailing ships on back. 140 x 76mm.			
	a. Sign. 4. Wmk: Springbok (1966).	7.00	12.00	35.00
	b. Sign. 5. Wmk: Springbok (1967-74).	5.00	7.50	20.00
	c. Sign. 5. Wmk: J. van Riebeeck (1975).	3.75	5.50	21.50

		VG	VF	UNC
114	**10 RAND** ND (1966-76). Dk. green and brown on m/c unpt. Like #113 but first lines of bank name and value in Afrikaans. 140 x 76mm.			
	a. Sign. 4. Wmk: Springbok (1966).	7.00	12.00	35.00
	b. Sign. 5. Wmk: Springbok (1967-74).	5.00	7.50	20.00
	c. Sign. 5. Wmk: J. van Riebeeck (1975).	3.75	5.50	21.50

1973-84 ISSUE

#115-122 J. van Riebeeck at l.

		VG	VF	UNC
115	**1 RAND** ND (1973-75). Dk. reddish brown on m/c unpt. Like #109 but 120 x 57mm. Sign. 5.			
	a. Wmk: Springbok (1973).	.40	1.25	5.00
	b. Wmk: J. van Riebeeck (1975).	.40	1.25	5.00

NOTICE

Readers with unlisted dates, signature varieties, etc. are invited to submit photocopies of their notes to: Standard Catalog of World Paper Money, 700 East State St. Iola, WI 54990-0001, fax: 1-715-445-4087, or E-Mail: thernr@krause.com.

116 1 Rand

ND (1973-75). Dk. reddish brown on m/c unpt. Like #110 but 120 x 57mm. Sign. 5.

	VG	VF	Unc
a. Wmk: Springbok (1973).	.40	1.25	5.00
b. Wmk: J. van Riebeeck (1975).	.40	1.25	5.00

117 2 Rand

ND (1973-76). Blue on m/c unpt. First lines of bank name and value in Afrikaans. Hydroelectric dam on back. 127 x 62mm. Sign. 5.

	VG	VF	Unc
a. Wmk: Springbok (1974).	.75	4.00	12.00
b. Wmk: J. van Riebeeck (1976).	.75	5.00	16.00

#118-122 wmk: J. van Riebeek.

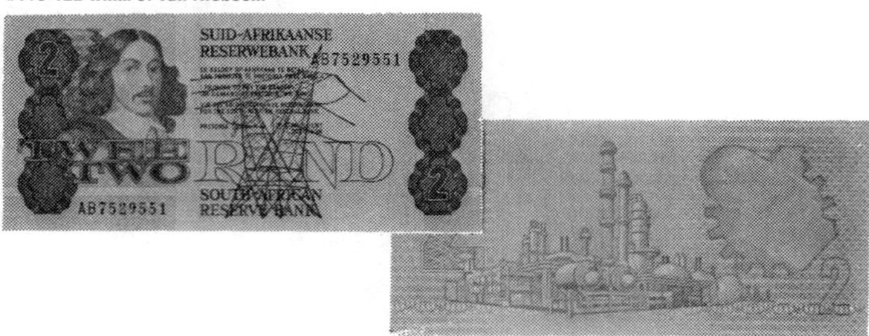

118 2 Rand

ND (1978-90). Blue on m/c unpt. Electrical tower at ctr. Refinery at l. ctr. on back. 120 x 57mm.

	VG	VF	Unc
a. Sign. 5. (1978-81).	.65	2.00	6.50
b. Sign. 6. Fractional numbering system. W/o security thread (1981).	1.00	5.00	18.00
c. As b. but w/security thread. (1981-83).	.50	1.25	4.00
d. As b. Alpha-numeric system. (1983-90).	.50	.75	2.50
e. Sign. 7. (1990).	.75	3.50	10.00

NOTE: #118b exists w/Serial # w/sm. fractional letters and lg. numerals or larger letters w/sm. numerals.

119 5 Rand

ND (1978-94). Purple on m/c unpt. First lines of bank name and value in English. Diamond at ctr. Grain storage at l. ctr. on back. 127 x 63mm.

	VG	VF	Unc
a. Sign. 5. (1978-81).	1.25	3.50	11.00
b. Sign. 6. Fractional numbering system. W/o security thread (1981).	9.00	35.00	125.00
c. As b. W/security thread. (1981-89).	1.00	3.00	9.00
d. As c. Alpha-numeric system. (1989-90).	1.00	3.00	9.50
e. Sign. 7. (1990-94).	1.00	2.00	8.00

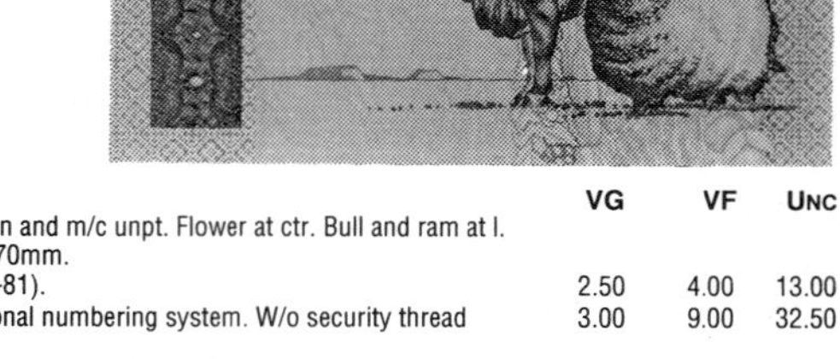

120 10 Rand

ND (1978-93). Green and m/c unpt. Flower at ctr. Bull and ram at l. ctr. on back. 134 x 70mm.

	VG	VF	Unc
a. Sign. 5. (1978-81).	2.50	4.00	13.00
b. Sign. 6. Fractional numbering system. W/o security thread (1981).	3.00	9.00	32.50
c. As b. w/security thread. (1982-85).	2.50	4.50	14.00
d. As c. Alpha-numeric system. (1985-90).	2.50	3.50	13.00
e. Sign. 7. (1990-93).	2.50	3.50	9.00

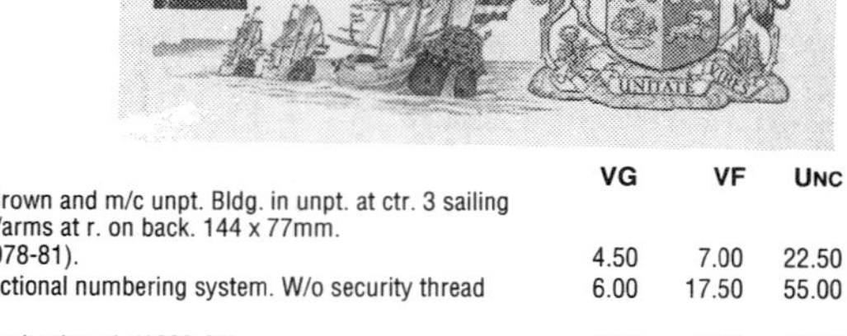

121 20 Rand

ND (1984-93). Brown and m/c unpt. Bldg. in unpt. at ctr. 3 sailing ships at l. ctr. w/arms at r. on back. 144 x 77mm.

	VG	VF	Unc
a. Sign. 5. (1978-81).	4.50	7.00	22.50
b. Sign. 6. Fractional numbering system. W/o security thread (1981).	6.00	17.50	55.00
c. As b. w/security thread. (1982-85).	4.50	6.00	18.00
d. As c. Alpha-numeric system. (1985-90).	4.50	8.00	22.50
e. Sign. 7. (1990-93).	4.50	5.50	23.00

122 50 Rand

ND (1984-90). Red on m/c unpt. Lion in unpt. at ctr. First lines of bank name and value in Afrikaans. Local animals at lower l., mountains at ctr., plants at r. on back. 147 x 83mm.

	VG	VF	Unc
a. Sign. 6. (1984).	13.50	20.00	40.00
b. Sign. 7. (1990).	15.00	25.00	50.00

1992-94 ISSUE

		VG	VF	UNC
123	**10 RAND** ND(1993; 1999). Dk. green and dk. blue on brown and m/c unpt. White rhinoceros at ctr., lg. white rhino at r. and as wmk. Ram's head over sheep at l. on back.			
	a. Sign. 7. (1993).	FV	FV	6.50
	b. Sign. 8. (1999).	FV	FV	4.00

		VG	VF	UNC
124	**20 RAND** ND(1993; 1999). Deep brown and red-brown on m/c unpt. Elephants at ctr., lg. elephant head at r. and as wmk. Open pit mining at l. ctr. on back.			
	a. Sign. 7 (1993).	FV	FV	10.00
	b. Sign. 8 (1999).	FV	FV	7.00

		VG	VF	UNC
125	**50 RAND** ND(1992; 1999). Maroon and deep blue-green on m/c unpt. Lions w/cub drinking water at ctr., male lion head at r. and as wmk. Sasol oil refinery at lower l. ctr. on back.			
	a. Sign. 7 (1992).	FV	FV	22.50
	b. Sign. 8 (1999).	FV	FV	22.50
	x. Like a. Wmk. on wrong side. Serial # prefix: *BP*.	FV	22.50	50.00

		VG	VF	UNC
126	**100 RAND** ND(1994; 1999). Blue-violet and dk. gray on m/c unpt. Water buffalo at ctr. and lg. water buffalo head at r. and as wmk. Zebras along bottom from l. to ctr. on back.			
	a. Sign. 7 (1994).	FV	FV	40.00
	b. Sign. 8 (1999).	FV	FV	32.00

		VG	VF	UNC
127	**200 RAND** ND(1994; 1999). Orange on m/c unpt. Leopard at ctr., lg. leopard's head at r. Dish antenna at upper l., modern bridge at lower l. on back.			
	a. Sign. 7 (1994).	FV	FV	70.00
	b. Sign. 8 (1999).	FV	FV	60.00

The Spanish State, forming the greater part of the Iberian Peninsula of southwest Europe, has an area of 194,884 sq. mi. (504,750 sq. km.) and a population of *40.5 million including the Balearic and the Canary Islands. Capital: Madrid. The economy is based on agriculture, industry and tourism. Machinery, fruit, vegetables and chemicals are exported.

It is not known when man first came to the Iberian Peninsula - the Altamira caves off the Cantabrian coast approximately 50 miles west of Santander were fashioned in Paleolithic times. Spain was a battleground for centuries before it became a united nation, fought for by Phoenicians, Carthaginians, Greeks, Celts, Romans, Vandals, Visigoths and Moors. Ferdinand and Isabella destroyed the last Moorish stronghold in 1492, freeing the national energy and resources for the era of discovery and colonization that would make Spain the most powerful country in Europe during the 16th century. After the destruction of the Spanish Armada, 1588, Spain never again played a major role in European politics. Napoleonic France ruled Spain between 1808 and 1814. The monarchy was restored in 1814 and continued, interrupted by the short-lived republic of 1873-74, until the exile of Alfonso XIII in 1931, when the Second Republic was established. A bloody civil war ensued in 1936, and Francisco Franco established himself as ruler of fascist Spain after his forces, aided by the Italians and especially the Germans, defeated the Republican forces.

The monarchy was reconstituted in 1947 under the regency of General Francisco Franco, the king designate to be crowned after Franco's death. Franco died on Nov. 30, 1975. Two days after his passing, Juan Carlos de Borbón, the grandson of Alfonso XIII, was proclaimed King of Spain.

RULERS:

Francisco Franco, regent, 1937-1975
Juan Carlos I, 1975-

MONETARY SYSTEM:

1 Peseta = 100 Centimos 1874-

REPUBLIC

BANCO DE ESPAÑA

1965 (1970; 1971) ISSUE

#150-151 printer: FNMT.

		VG	VF	UNC
150	**100 PESETAS** 19.11.1965 (1970). Brown on m/c unpt. G.A. Bécquer at ctr. r., couple near fountain at lower l. Woman w/parasol at ctr., Cathedral of Sevilla at l. on back. Wmk: Woman's head.	1.00	3.00	7.00

		VG	VF	UNC
151	**1000 PESETAS** 19.11.1965 (1971). Green on m/c unpt. S. Isidoro at l. Imaginary figure w/basilica behind on back.	8.50	20.00	40.00

1970-71 ISSUE

152 and 153 printer: FNMT.

		VG	VF	UNC
152	**100 PESETAS** 17.11.1970 (1974). Brown on pale orange and m/c unpt. M. de Falla at r. and as wmk. Patio garden scene in Granada, villa in background at l. ctr. on back.	1.00	2.00	4.00

		VG	VF	UNC
153	**500 PESETAS** 23.7.1971 (1973). Blue-gray and black on m/c unpt. J. Verdaguer at r. and as wmk. View of Mt.Canigó w/village of Vignolas d'Oris on back.	4.50	15.00	35.00

NOTICE

Readers with unlisted dates, signature varieties, etc. are invited to submit photocopies of their notes to: Standard Catalog of World Paper Money, 700 East State St. Iola, WI 54990-0001, fax: 1-715-445-4087, or E-Mail: thernr@krause.com.

1974 COMMEMORATIVE ISSUE

#154, Centennial of the Banco de España's becoming the sole issuing bank, 1874-1974

		VG	VF	UNC
154	**1000 PESETAS** 17.9.1971 (1974). Green and black on m/c unpt. J. Echegaray at r. and as wmk. Bank of Spain in Madrid and commemorative legend on back. Printer: FNMT.	8.50	11.50	20.00

1976 ISSUE

		VG	VF	UNC
155	**5000 PESETAS** 6.2.1976 (1978). Purple and brown on m/c unpt. Kg. Carlos III at r. Museum of Prado in Madrid at l. ctr. on back.	FV	45.00	80.00

1982-87 ISSUE

#156-161 printer: FNMT.

		VG	VF	UNC
156	**200 PESETAS** 16.9.1980 (1984). Brown and orange on m/c unpt. L. Alas Clarín at r. and as wmk., cross at lower ctr. Tree at l., cross at ctr. on back.	1.75	6.00	15.00

		VG	VF	UNC
157	**500 PESETAS** 23.10.1979 (1983). Dk. blue and black on m/c unpt. R. de Castro at r. and as wmk. Villa at l. ctr. on back.	4.50	8.00	15.00

		VG	VF	UNC
158	**1000 PESETAS** 23.10.1979 (1982). Gray-blue and green on m/c unpt. Tree at ctr., B. Pérez Galdos at r. and as wmk. Rock formations, mountains and map of Canary Islands on back.	8.50	10.00	12.50

		VG	VF	UNC
159	**2000 PESETAS** 22.7.1980 (1983). Deep red and orange on m/c unpt. Rose at ctr., J. R. Jiménez at r. and as wmk. Villa de la Rosa at l. ctr. on back.	16.50	22.50	35.00

		VG	VF	UNC
160	**5000 PESETAS** 23.10.1979 (1982). Brown and violet on m/c unpt. Fleur-de-lis at ctr., Kg. Juan Carlos I at r. and as wmk. Royal Palace in Madrid at l. ctr. on back.	40.00	45.00	62.50

		VG	VF	UNC
161	**10,000 PESETAS** 24.9.1985 (1987). Gray-black on m/c unpt. Arms at ctr., Kg. Juan Carlos I at r. and as wmk. Back blue-gray on m/c unpt. Prince of Asturias at l., view of the Escorial at ctr.	FV	85.00	110.00

1992 ISSUE

		VG	VF	UNC
162	**2000 PESETAS** 24.4.1992. Red-violet and orange on m/c unpt. J. C. Mutis observing flower at r. and as wmk. Royal Botanical Garden and title page of Mutis' work on vertical format back. 2 serial #.	FV	15.00	30.00

1992 (1996) ISSUE

#163-166 w/blurred *BANCO DE ESPAÑA* at r. margin.

NOTE: Issued for the 5th Centennial of the Discovery of America by Spain.

		VG	VF	UNC
163	**1000 PESETAS** 12.10.1992 (1996). Dk. green, purple and red-brown on m/c unpt. H. Cortes at r. F. Pizarro on vertical format back and as wmk.	FV	FV	13.50

		VG	VF	UNC
164	**2000 PESETAS** 24.4.1992 (1996). Red-violet and orange on m/c unpt. Like #162 but w/modified portr. 1 serial #.	FV	FV	27.50

		VG	VF	UNC
165	**5000 PESETAS** 12.10.1992 (1996). Violet-brown, brown and red-brown on m/c unpt. C. Columbus at r. and as wmk. Astrolabe at lower ctr. on vertical format back.	FV	FV	50.00

166 **10,000 PESETAS**
12.10.1992 (1996). Slate blue on m/c unpt. Kg. Juan Carlos I at r. Casa de América in Madrid at lower ctr. A. de Ulloa y de Jorge Juan and as wmk. above astronomical navigation diagram on vertical format back.

VG	VF	UNC
FV	FV	100.00

SRI (SHRI) LANKA

The Democratic Socialist Republic of Sri (Shri) Lanka (formerly Ceylon), situated in the Indian Ocean 18 miles (29 km.) southeast of India, has an area of 25,332 sq. mi. (65,610 sq. km.) and a population of 18.7 million. Capital: Colombo. The economy is chiefly agricultural. Tea, coconut products and rubber are exported.

The earliest known inhabitants of Ceylon, the Veddahs, were subjugated by the Sinhalese from northern India in the 6th century BC. Sinhalese rule was maintained until 1505 when the costal areas came under Portuguese control which was maintained for 150 years. The Portuguese were supplanted by the Dutch in 1658, who were in turn supplanted by the British who seized the Dutch colonies in 1796, and made them into Crown Colony in 1802. In 1815, the British conquered the independent Kingdom of Kandy in the central part of the island. Constitutional changes in 1931 and 1946 granted the Ceylonese a measure of autonomy and a parliamentary form of government. Ceylon became a self-governing dominion of the British Commonwealth on February 4, 1948. On May 22, 1972, the Ceylonese adopted a new constitution which declared Ceylon to be the Republic of Sri Lanka - 'Resplendent Island'. Sri Lanka is a member of the Commonwealth of Nations. The president is Chief of State. The prime minister is Head of Government.

See also Ceylon for earlier listings.

RULERS:
British, 1796-1972

MONETARY SYSTEM:
1 Rupee = 100 Cents, ca. 1830-

REPUBLIC

CENTRAL BANK OF CEYLON

1977 ISSUE

#81 and 82 Sri Lanka arms at r. Wmk: Chinze. Printer: BWC.

81 **50 RUPEES**
26.8.1977. Purple and green on m/c unpt. Terraced hillside on back.

VG	VF	UNC
2.50	6.00	30.00

82 **100 RUPEES**
26.8.1977. Purple and black on m/c unpt. Shrine at l. ctr. on back.

VG	VF	UNC
4.00	10.00	55.00

1979 ISSUE

#83-88 backs vertical format. Wmk: Chinze. Replacement notes: Serial # prefix *Z/1*.

		VG	VF	UNC
83	**2 RUPEES** 26.3.1979. Red on m/c unpt. Fish at r. Butterfly and lizard on back.	.30	.75	3.50

		VG	VF	UNC
84	**5 RUPEES** 26.3.1979. Gray on m/c unpt. Butterfly and lizard at r. Flying squirrel and bird on back.	.50	1.75	6.50

		VG	VF	UNC
85	**10 RUPEES** 26.3.1979. Green and black on m/c unpt. Bird in tree at ctr. Flowers and animals on back.	.60	2.00	12.50

		VG	VF	UNC
86	**20 RUPEES** 26.3.1979. Brown and green on m/c unpt. Bird at ctr., monkey at r. Bird, tree and animals on back.	1.35	2.75	20.00

		VG	VF	UNC
87	**50 RUPEES** 26.3.1979. Blue and brown on m/c unpt. Butterfly at ctr., bird at r. Lizard and birds on back.	3.50	8.50	60.00

		VG	VF	UNC
88	**100 RUPEES** 26.3.1979. Gold and green on m/c unpt. Snakes and tree at ctr., birds at r. Bird in tree, butterfly below on back.	5.00	12.50	100.00

1981 ISSUE

#89 and 90 backs vertical format. Wmk: Chinze.

		VG	VF	UNC
89	**500 RUPEES** 1.1.1981; 1.1.1985. Brown and purple on m/c unpt. Elephant w/rider at r. Abhayagiri Stupa, Anuradhapura temple on hill on back.	15.00	35.00	110.00

		VG	VF	UNC
90	**1000 RUPEES** 1.1.1981. Green on m/c unpt. Dam at r. Peacock and mountains on back.	40.00	90.00	175.00

1982 ISSUE

#91-95 backs vertical format. Wmk: Chinze. Printer: BWC.

		VG	VF	UNC
91	**5 RUPEES** 1.1.1982. Lt. red on m/c unpt. Ruins at r. Stone carving of deity and child on back.	FV	.35	2.75

		VG	VF	UNC
92	**10 RUPEES** 1.1.1982; 1.1.1985. Olive-green on m/c unpt. Temple of the Tooth at r. Shrine on back.	FV	.50	4.50

		VG	VF	UNC
93	**20 RUPEES** 1.1.1982; 1.1.1985. Violet on m/c unpt. Moonstone Anuradhapura at r. Shrine on back.	FV	.75	6.00

		VG	VF	UNC
94	**50 RUPEES** 1.1.1982. Dk. blue and dk. brown on m/c unpt. Tomb at r. Ruins at ctr. on back.	FV	3.00	11.50

		VG	VF	UNC
95	**100 RUPEES** 1.1.1982. Orange and brown on m/c unpt. Stone carving of lion at lower r. Parliament bldg. on back.	2.00	4.00	18.50

SRÍ LANKÁ MAHA BÄNKUVA

CENTRAL BANK OF SRI LANKA

1987-89 ISSUE

#96-101 wmk: Chinze.

#96-100 similar to #89 and 91-95 but w/bank name changed in English from *CEYLON* to *Sri Lanka*. Printer: BWC.

		VG	VF	UNC
96	**10 RUPEES** 1.1.1987; 21.11.1988; 21.2.1989; 5.4.1990. Green on m/c unpt.	FV	.40	2.50

		VG	VF	UNC
97	**20 RUPEES** 1988-90. Purple on m/c unpt.			
	a. 21.11.1988.	.75	2.50	15.00
	b. 21.2.1989; 5.4.1990.	FV	.75	3.75

		VG	VF	UNC
98	**50 RUPEES** 21.2.1989. Blue and brown on m/c unpt.	FV	1.75	7.00
99	**100 RUPEES** 1.1.1987; 1.2.1988; 21.2.1989; 5.4.1990. Orange and brown on m/c unpt.	FV	2.75	11.00
100	**500 RUPEES** 1.1.1987; 21.11.1988; 21.2.1989; 5.4.1990. Brown and purple on m/c unpt. Similar to #89 but w/clearer wmk. area, vertical silver security markings, bird and borders deeper red brown. Hill and temple in purple on back.	FV	13.50	50.00

		VG	VF	UNC
101	**1000 RUPEES** 1.1.1987; 21.2.1989; 5.4.1990. Deep green and purple on m/c unpt. Victoria Dam at r. Peacock and University of Ruhuna on back. Printer: BWC.	FV	25.00	90.00

1991 ISSUE

#102-107 backs vertical format. Wmk: Chinze. Printer: TDLR. Replacement notes: Serial # prefix *Z/1*.

		VG	VF	UNC
102	**10 RUPEES** 1.1.1991; 1.7.1992, 19.8.1994. Deep brown and green on m/c unpt. Sinhalese Chinze at r. Crane above Presidential Secretariat bldg. in Colombo, flowers in lower foreground on back.	FV	.25	1.25

		VG	VF	UNC
103	**20 RUPEES** 1.1.1991; 1.7.1992; 19.8.1994. Purple and red on m/c unpt. Native bird mask at r. Two youths fishing, sea shells on back.	FV	.30	2.25

		VG	VF	UNC
104	**50 RUPEES** 1.1.1991; 1.7.1992; 19.8.1994. Brown-violet, deep blue and blue-green on m/c unpt. Male dancer w/local headdress at r. Butterflies above temple ruins, w/shield and ornamental sword hilt in lower foreground on back.	FV	.35	4.00

NOTICE

Readers with unlisted dates, signature varieties, etc. are invited to submit photocopies of their notes to: Standard Catalog of World Paper Money, 700 East State St. Iola, WI 54990-0001, fax: 1-715-445-4087, or E-Mail: thernr@krause.com.

		VG	VF	UNC
105	**100 RUPEES** 1991; 1992. Orange and dk. brown on m/c unpt. Decorative urn at r. Tea leaf pickers, 2 parrots at bottom on back.			
	a. W/o dot on value in Tamil at l. 1.1.1991.	FV	FV	10.00
	b. W/dot on value in Tamil at l. 1.1.1991.	FV	FV	6.00
	c. 7.1.1992.	FV	FV	6.00

		VG	VF	UNC
106	**500 RUPEES** 1.1.1991. Dk. brown, purple and brown-orange on m/c unpt. Musicians at r., dancer at l. ctr. Kingfisher above temple and orchids on back.	FV	FV	32.50

		VG	VF	UNC
107	**1000 RUPEES** 1.1.1991; 1.7.1992. Brown, dk. green and purple on m/c unpt. Chinze at lower l., 2-headed bird at bottom ctr., elephant w/trainer at r. Peacocks on palace lawn; lotus flowers above and Octagon of Temple of the Tooth in Kandy on back.	FV	FV	55.00

1995 ISSUE

#108-113 have a vertical format back.

		VG	VF	UNC
108	**10 RUPEES** 15.11.1995. Like #102. Additional security features.	FV	FV	1.00
109	**20 RUPEES** 15.11.1995. Like #103 but w/additional security features.	FV	FV	2.00
110	**50 RUPEES** 15.11.1995. Like #104 but w/additional security features.	FV	FV	4.00

		VG	VF	UNC
111	**100 RUPEES** 15.11.1995. Dk. brown and orange on m/c unpt. Like #105 but back orange on m/c unpt. Printer: TDLR.	FV	FV	5.50
112	**500 RUPEES** 15.11.1995. Like #106 but w/additional security features.	FV	FV	32.50
113	**1000 RUPEES** 15.11.1995. Like #107 but w/additional security features.	FV	FV	50.00

1998 COMMEMORATIVE ISSUE

#114, 50th Anniversary of Independence, 1948-1998

		VG	VF	UNC
114	**200 RUPEES** 4.2.1998. Deep olive-green, black and dull purple on m/c unpt. Temple at upper ctr. r. above a collage of modern scenes across lower l. to r. Palace at upper l. ctr. above collage of medieval scenes of British landing across lower l. to r. on back. Polymer.			
	a. Red serial # in folder.	FV	FV	15.00
	b. Black serial #.	FV	FV	12.50

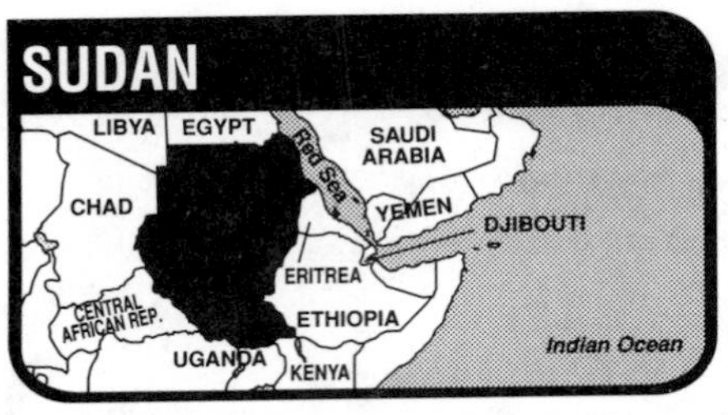

The Democratic Republic of the Sudan, located in northeast Africa on the Red Sea between Egypt and Ethiopia, has an area of 967,500 sq. mi. (2,505,810 sq. km.) and a population of 32.6 million. Capital: Khartoum. Agriculture and livestock raising are the chief occupations. Cotton, gum arabic and peanuts are exported.

The Sudan, site of the powerful Nubian kingdom of Roman times, was a collection of small independent states from the 14th century until 1820-22 when it was conquered and united by Mohammed Ali, Pasha of Egypt. Egyptian forces were driven from the area during the Mahdist revolt, 1881-98, but the Sudan was retaken by Anglo-Egyptian expeditions, 1896-98, and established as an Anglo-Egyptian condominium in 1899. Britain supplied the administrative apparatus and personnel, but the appearance of joint Anglo-Egyptian administration was continued until Jan. 9, 1954, when the first Sudanese self-government parliament was inaugurated.

The Sudan achieved independence on Jan. 1, 1956 with the consent of the British and Egyptian governments. On June 30, 1989 Gen. Omar Hassan Ahmad al-Bashir overthrew the civilian government in a military coup. The rebel guerrilla PLA forces are active in the south. Notes of Egypt were in use before 1956.

RULERS:

British, 1899-1954

MONETARY SYSTEM:

1 Ghirsh (Piastre) = 10 Millim (Milliemes)
1 Sudanese Pound = 100 Piastres to 1992
1 Dinar = 10 Old Sudanese Pounds, 1992

REPUBLIC

BANK OF SUDAN

1961-64 ISSUE

#6-10 various date and sign. varieties. Arms (desert camel rider) on back.

6	**25 PIASTRES**	VG	VF	UNC
	1964-68. Red on m/c unpt. Soldiers in formation at l.			
	a. 6.3.1964.	6.00	16.50	165.00
	b. 25.1.1967.	5.00	15.00	155.00
	c. W/o Arabic text *al-Khartoum*. 7.2.1968.	5.00	13.50	150.00

7	**50 PIASTRES**	VG	VF	UNC
	1964-68. Green on m/c unpt. Elephants at l.			
	a. 6.3.1964.	15.00	55.00	450.00
	b. 25.1.1967.	12.50	52.50	425.00
	c. W/o Arabic text *al-Khartoum*. 7.2.1968.	12.00	50.00	400.00

8	**1 POUND**	VG	VF	UNC
	1961-68. Blue on yellow and m/c unpt. Dam at l.			
	a. 8.4.1961.	8.00	25.00	225.00
	b. 2.3.1965.	7.00	18.50	210.00
	c. 20.1.1966.	6.00	17.50	200.00
	d. 25.1.1967.	5.50	15.00	185.00
	e. W/o Arabic text *al-Khartoum*. 7.2.1968.	5.00	14.00	175.00

NOTICE

Readers with unlisted dates, signature varieties, etc. are invited to submit photocopies of their notes to: Standard Catalog of World Paper Money, 700 East State St. Iola, WI 54990-0001, fax: 1-715-445-4087, or E-Mail: thernr@krause.com.

9	**5 POUNDS**	VG	VF	UNC
	1962-68. Lilac-brown on m/c unpt. Dhow at l.			
	a. 1.7.1962.	12.50	50.00	575.00
	b. 2.3.1965.	11.50	45.00	550.00
	c. 20.1.1966.	10.00	42.50	500.00
	d. 25.1.1967.	9.00	40.00	475.00
	e. W/o Arabic text *al-Khartoum*. 7.2.1968.	8.00	38.50	450.00

10	**10 POUNDS**	VG	VF	UNC
	1964-68. Gray-black on m/c unpt. Bank of Sudan bldg. at l.			
	a. 6.3.1964.	13.50	50.00	575.00
	b. 20.1.1966.	12.50	45.00	550.00
	c. 25.1.1967.	11.50	42.50	525.00
	d. W/o Arabic text *al-Khartoum*. 7.2.1968.	10.00	40.00	500.00

1970 ISSUE

#11-15 Bank of Sudan at l. on face. Various date and sign. varieties. Printer: TDLR.

11	**25 PIASTRES**	VG	VF	UNC
	1970-80. Red on m/c unpt. Textile industry on back.			
	a. Jan. 1970; Jan. 1971; Jan. 1972.	1.00	5.00	40.00
	b. 1.4.1973-28.5.1978.	.75	2.50	10.00
	c. 2.1.1980.	.50	1.00	4.50

12	**50 PIASTRES**	VG	VF	UNC
	1970-80. Green on m/c unpt. University of Khartoum on back.			
	a. Jan. 1970; Jan. 1971; Jan. 1972.	1.50	5.50	50.00
	b. 1.4.1973-28.5.1978.	1.00	2.50	10.00
	c. 2.1.1980.	.75	1.50	9.00

13 1 POUND

	VG	VF	UNC
1970-80. Blue on m/c unpt. Ancient temple on back.			
a. Wmk: Rhinoceros head. Jan. 1970; Jan. 1971.	7.00	30.00	165.00
b. Wmk: Arms (secretary bird). Jan. 1972-28.5.1978.	1.00	3.00	20.00
c. 2.1.1980.	1.00	3.00	22.50

14 5 POUNDS

	VG	VF	UNC
1970-80. Brown and lilac on m/c unpt. Domestic and wild animals on back.			
a. Wmk: Rhinoceros head. Jan. 1970.	17.50	65.00	300.00
b. Wmk: Arms. Jan. 1971-28.5.1978.	5.00	15.00	120.00
c. 2.1.1980.	5.00	15.00	100.00

15 10 POUNDS

	VG	VF	UNC
1970-80. Purple and green on m/c unpt. Transportation elements (ship, plane, etc.) on back.			
a. Wmk: Rhinoceros head. Jan. 1970.	27.50	90.00	450.00
b. Wmk: Arms. Jan. 1971-28.5.1978.	7.50	20.00	70.00
c. 2.1.1980.	5.00	15.00	35.00

1981 ISSUE

#16-21 Pres. J. Nimeiri wearing national headdress at l., arms at ctr.

#18-21 wmk: Arms.

16 25 PIASTRES

	VG	VF	UNC
1.1.1981. Brown on m/c unpt. Kosti bridge on back.	.40	1.00	2.50

17 50 PIASTRES

	VG	VF	UNC
1.1.1981. Purple on brown unpt. Bank of Sudan on back.	.60	1.25	3.75

18 1 POUND

	VG	VF	UNC
1.1.1981. Blue on m/c unpt. People's Assembly on back.	1.00	3.50	13.50

19 5 POUNDS

	VG	VF	UNC
1.1.1981. Green and brown on m/c unpt. Back green; Islamic Centre Mosque in Khartoum at r.	2.00	5.00	20.00

		VG	VF	UNC
20	**10 POUNDS** 1.1.1981. Blue and brown on m/c unpt. Kenana sugar factory on back.	5.00	15.00	75.00
21	**20 POUNDS** 1.1.1981. Green on m/c unpt. Like #22 but w/o commemorative text.	5.50	20.00	85.00

1981 COMMEMORATIVE ISSUE

#22, 25th Anniversary of Independence

		VG	VF	UNC
22	**20 POUNDS** 1.1.1981. Green on m/c unpt. Pres. J. Nimeiri w/native headdress at l., map at ctr., commemorative legend in circle at r. around wmk., monument at r. Unity Monument at l., People's Palace at ctr. r. on back.	7.50	22.50	85.00

1983-84 ISSUE

#23-29 like previous issue but some in different colors.

		VG	VF	UNC
23	**25 PIASTRES** 1.1.1983. Red-orange on pale yellow unpt. Like #16.	.25	.50	1.75
24	**50 PIASTRES** 1.1.1983. Purple on brown unpt. Like #17.	.60	1.25	2.25
25	**1 POUND** 1.1.1983. Blue on m/c unpt. Like #18 but bldg. on back is blue only.	.50	1.25	3.00

		VG	VF	UNC
26	**5 POUNDS** 1.1.1983. Green. Like #19.	1.00	2.50	12.50
27	**10 POUNDS** 1.1.1983. Purple and red-brown on m/c unpt. Like #20.	2.50	7.50	30.00
28	**20 POUNDS** 1.1.1983. Green on m/c unpt. Like #21.	5.00	10.00	45.00

		VG	VF	UNC
29	**50 POUNDS** 25.5.1984. Brown-orange and blue on m/c unpt. Pres. Nimeiri at l. Back blue on m/c unpt.; sailing ship at ctr., modern oil tanker at r. Wmk: Arms.	7.50	22.50	65.00

LAW OF 30.6.1985/AH1405

#30-36 outline map of Sudan at ctr. Bank of Sudan at ctr. on back. Wmk: Arms. Sign. title w/2 lines of Arabic text (Acting Governor).

Replacement notes: Serial # prefix *Z/1; Z11; Z21; Z31/ Z41/ Z51/ Z61; Z71*.

		VG	VF	UNC
30	**25 PIASTRES** *L.1985.* Purple on m/c unpt. Camels at l.	.10	.40	1.50

		VG	VF	UNC
31	**50 PIASTRES** *L.1985.* Red on lilac and peach unpt. Lyre and drum at l., peanut plant at r.	.15	.50	2.50

#32-36 wmk: Arms.

		VG	VF	UNC
32	**1 POUND** *L.1985.* Green and blue on m/c unpt. Cotton boll at l. Back blue on m/c unpt.	.20	.75	3.00

		VG	VF	UNC
33	**5 POUNDS** *L.1985.* Olive and brown on m/c unpt. Cattle at l.	.50	3.00	22.50

		VG	VF	UNC
34	**10 POUNDS** *L.1985.* Brown on m/c unpt. City gateway at l.	2.00	6.00	40.00

		VG	VF	UNC
35	**20 POUNDS** *L.1985.* Green and purple on m/c unpt. Dhow at l.	10.00	25.00	185.00

		VG	VF	UNC
36	**50 POUNDS** *L.1985.* Brown, purple and red-orange on m/c unpt. Columns along pool below National Museum at l., spear at r. Back red.	7.50	22.50	165.00

1987-90 ISSUE

#37-43 sign. title in 1 line of Arabic text (Governor).

		VG	VF	UNC
37	**25 PIASTRES** 1987. Purple on m/c unpt. Like #30.	.05	.15	.35

		VG	VF	UNC
38	**50 PIASTRES** 1987. Red on lilac and peach unpt. Like #31.	.05	.25	1.00

		VG	VF	UNC
39	**1 POUND** 1987. Green and blue on m/c unpt. Like #32.	.10	.50	.75

#40-44 wmk: Arms.

		VG	VF	UNC
40	**5 POUNDS** 1987-90. Olive and brown on m/c unpt. Like #33.			
	a. 1987.	.25	.75	7.50
	b. 1989.	.25	.75	7.00
	c. 1990.	.25	.65	6.50

		VG	VF	UNC
41	**10 POUNDS** 1987-90. Brown on m/c unpt. Like #34.			
	a. 1987.	.50	1.50	17.50
	b. 1989.	.75	3.00	35.00
	c. 1990.	.75	3.00	35.00

		VG	VF	UNC
42	**20 POUNDS** 1987-90. Green and purple on m/c unpt. Like #35.			
	a. 1987.	.50	1.00	7.50
	b. 1989.	.50	1.00	7.50
	c. 1990.	.50	1.25	10.00

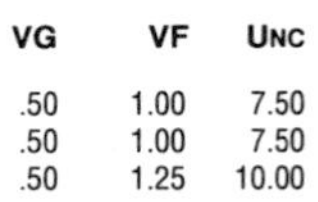

		VG	VF	UNC
43	**50 POUNDS** 1987; 1989. Brown, purple and red-orange on m/c unpt. Like #36.			
	a. 1987.	.75	2.50	5.00
	b. 1989.	1.00	2.75	7.50

		VG	VF	UNC
44	**100 POUNDS** 1988-90. Brown, purple and deep green on m/c unpt. Shield, University of Khartoum bldg. at l., open book at lower r. Bank of Sudan and shiny coin design on back.			
	a. 1988.	1.50	3.00	7.50
	b. 1989; 1990.	.55	1.00	3.00

1991 ISSUE

#45-50 like #40-44. Wmk: Arms.

		VG	VF	UNC
45	**5 POUNDS** 1991/AH1411. Red, orange and violet on m/c unpt. Like #40. Back red-orange on m/c unpt.	.20	.60	2.25

		VG	VF	UNC
46	**10 POUNDS** 1991/AH1411. Black and deep green on m/c unpt. Like #41. Back black on m/c unpt.	.30	.90	2.50

		VG	VF	UNC
47	**20 POUNDS** 1991/AH1411. Purple and violet on m/c unpt. Like #42. Back violet on m/c unpt.	.25	.75	3.25

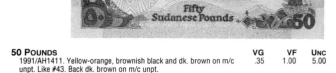

		VG	VF	UNC
48	**50 POUNDS** 1991/AH1411. Yellow-orange, brownish black and dk. brown on m/c unpt. Like #43. Back dk. brown on m/c unpt.	.35	1.00	5.00

		VG	VF	UNC
49	**100 POUNDS** 1991/AH1411. Ultramarine and blue-green on m/c unpt. Like #44. Ultramarine shield at l., lt. blue-green map image at ctr. Shiny lt. green coin design at r. on back (partially engraved).	1.00	2.00	7.50

		VG	VF	UNC
50	**100 POUNDS** 1991/AH1411; 1992/AH1412. Similar to #49 but colors rearranged. Blue-green shield at l., darker details on bldg. and ultramarine map image at ctr. Pink coin design at r. on back. (litho).	.60	1.25	5.00

1992-96 ISSUE

#51-55 People's Palace at ctr. or lower r. Wmk: Domed bldg. w/tower.

NOTE: First issues w/fractional serial # prefix (Type I) replaced w/local printings w/double letter serial # prefix (Type II).

		VG	VF	UNC
51	**5 DINARS** 1993/AH1413. Dk. brown and red-orange on m/c unpt. Plants including sunflowers at l. ctr. on back. Serial # Type II. Replacement note: *GZ*.	FV	FV	2.50

		VG	VF	UNC
52	**10 DINARS** 1993/AH1413. Deep red and dk. brown on m/c unpt. Domed bldg. w/tower at l. ctr. on back. Serial # Type II. Replacement note: *H-Z*.	FV	FV	3.50

		VG	VF	UNC
53	**25 DINARS** 1992/AH1412. Brownish black and green on m/c unpt. Circular design at l. on back.			
	a. W/artist's name *DOSOUGI* at lower r. Serial # Type I.	FV	FV	10.00
	b. W/o artist's name. Serial # Type I. Replacement note: *IZ*.	FV	FV	2.25
	c. As b. Serial # Type II.	FV	FV	2.00
54	**50 DINARS** 1992/AH1412. Dk. blue-green, black and purple on m/c unpt.			
	a. W/artist's name *DOSOUGI* at lower r. below palace. Serial # Type I.	FV	FV	20.00
	b. W/o artist's name. 2 sign. varieties. Serial # Type I.	FV	FV	4.50
	c. As b. Serial # Type II. Replacement note: *JZ*.	FV	FV	3.50
	d. As c. Segmented security thread.	FV	FV	3.50

		VG	VF	UNC
55	**100 DINARS** 1994/AH1414. Black and deep brown-violet on m/c unpt. Double doorway at ctr. Bldg. at l. ctr. on back. Serial # Type I. Replacement note: *KZ*.	FV	FV	7.50
56	**100 DINARS** 1994/AH1414. Black and deep brown-violet on m/c unpt. Like #55 but w/segmented foil over security thread. Serial # Type II. Replacement note: *LZ*.	FV	FV	6.50
57	**1000 DINARS** 1996/AH1416. M/c. Seal at l. ctr., bldg. in background at ctr. Bldg. on back. Serial # Type II. Replacement note: *MZ*.	FV	FV	20.00

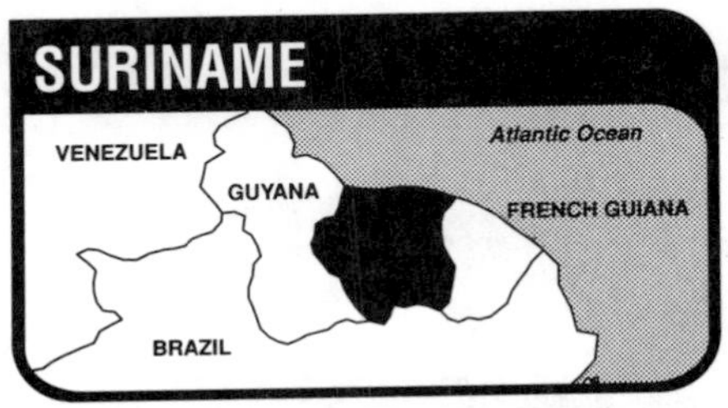

The Republic of Surinam, formerly known as Dutch Guiana, located on the north central coast of South America between Guyana and French Guiana, has an area of 63,037 sq. mi. (163,270 sq. km.) and a population of 417,000. Capital: Paramaribo. The country is rich in minerals and forests, and self-sufficient in rice, the staple food crop. The mining, processing and exporting of bauxite is the principal economic activity.

Lieutenants of Amerigo Vespucci sighted the Guiana coast in 1499. Spanish explorers of the 16th century, disappointed at finding no gold, departed leaving the area to be settled by the British in 1652. The colony prospered and the Netherlands acquired it in 1667 in exchange for the Dutch rights in Nieuw Nederland (state of New York). During the European wars of the 18th and 19th centuries, which were fought in part in the New World, Surinam was occupied by the British from 1799-1814. Surinam became an autonomous part of the Kingdom of the Netherlands on Dec. 15, 1954. Full independence was achieved on Nov. 25, 1975.

RULERS:
Dutch to 1975

MONETARY SYSTEM:
1 Gulden = 1 Florin = 100 Cents

MUNTBILJET

LAW 8.4.1960

#23-24 various date and sign. varieties. Printer: JEZ. Replacement notes: 6-digit serial number beginning with "1".

		VG	VF	UNC
23	**1 GULDEN** 1961-86. Dk. green w/black text on pale olive-green and brown unpt. Bldg. w/tower and flag at l. Back brown and green.			
	a. Sign. title: *De Minister van Financien* w/printed sign. but w/o name. 1.8.1961-1.4.1969.	.75	3.00	9.00
	b. Sign. in facsimile w/printed name below. 1.4.1971.	.50	2.00	7.00
	c. Similar to b., but name of signer at r. 1.11.1974.	.50	2.00	5.50
	d. Similar to a., but shorter text, and sign. title centered. 1.11.1974; 25.6.1979.	.40	1.50	7.00
	e. Similar to d., but sign. title: *De Minister van Financien en Planning*. 1.9.1982.	.15	.50	2.50
	f. 2.1.1984.	.15	.45	2.25
	g. 1.12.1984.	.15	.45	2.25
	h. 1.10.1986.	.15	.40	2.00

		VG	VF	UNC
24	**2 1/2 GULDEN** 1961; 1967. Red-brown. Girl wearing hat at l. Back red-brown and brown.			
	a. 2.1.1961.	.85	2.50	10.00
	b. 2.7.1967.	.75	2.25	7.50

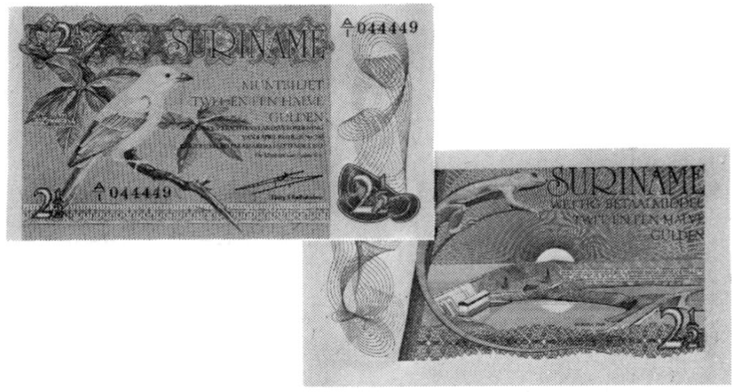

		VG	VF	UNC
24A	**2 1/2 GULDEN** 1973; 1978. Red-brown, lt. blue and m/c. Bird on branch at l. 3 lines of text above sign. title at ctr. Lizard and Afobaka Dam on back. Printer: BWC.			
	a. Sign. title: *De Minister van Financien*. Printed name below sign. 1.9.1973.	.50	2.25	9.00
	b. W/o printed name below sign. 1.8.1978.	.20	.85	4.50

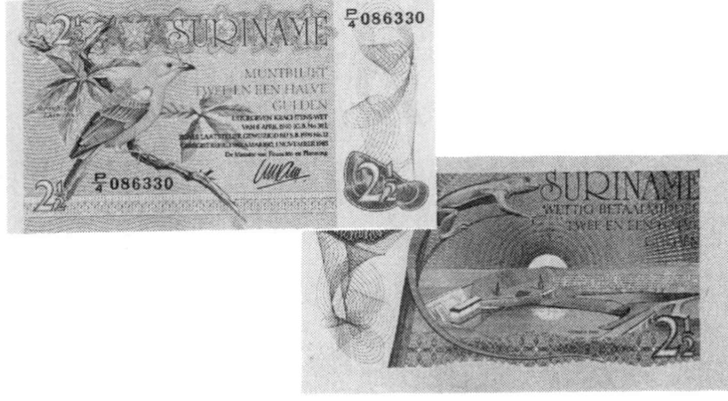

		VG	VF	UNC
24B	**2 1/2 GULDEN** 1.11.1985. Like #24A but 4 lines of text above sign. W/sign. title: *De Minister van Financien en Planning* at ctr.	.20	.75	3.50

CENTRALE BANK VAN SURINAME

1963 ISSUE

#30-34 different arms than 1957 issue on back. Wmk: Toucan's head. Printer: JEZ. Replacement notes: Serial # prefix *ZZ*.

		VG	VF	UNC
30	**5 GULDEN** 1.9.1963. Blue on m/c unpt. 2 serial # varieties.	.10	.25	.75

		VG	VF	UNC
31	**10 GULDEN** 1.9.1963. Orange on m/c unpt.	.10	.25	1.00

		VG	VF	UNC
32	**25 GULDEN** 1.9.1963. Green on m/c unpt.	2.50	7.50	20.00

		VG	VF	UNC
33	**100 GULDEN** 1.9.1963. Purple on m/c unpt.	8.00	20.00	65.00

		VG	VF	UNC
34	**1000 GULDEN** 1.9.1963. Brown on m/c unpt.	7.50	15.00	50.00

NOTE: #34 was recently sold in quantity by the Central Bank to the numismatic community.

NOTICE

Readers with unlisted dates, signature varieties, etc. are invited to submit photocopies of their notes to: Standard Catalog of World Paper Money, 700 East State St. Iola, WI 54990-0001, fax: 1-715-445-4087, or E-Mail: thernr@krause.com.

REPUBLIC

CENTRALE BANK VAN SURINAME

1982 ISSUE

#35-39 soldiers and woman at r. Bldg. w/flag on back. Wmk: Toucan's head. Printer: JEZ.

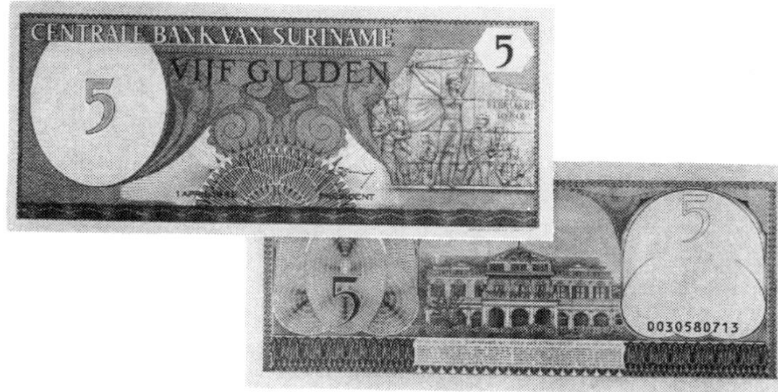

		VG	VF	UNC
35	**5 GULDEN** 1.4.1982. Blue on m/c unpt.	.15	.35	1.00
36	**10 GULDEN** 1.4.1982. Red on m/c unpt.	.15	.40	1.25

		VG	VF	UNC
37	**25 GULDEN** 1982; 1985. Green on m/c unpt.			
	a. 1.4.1982.	1.00	3.00	10.00
	b. 1.11.1985.	.10	.25	.75

		VG	VF	UNC
38	**100 GULDEN** 1982; 1985. Purple on m/c unpt.			
	a. 1.4.1982.	5.00	15.00	45.00
	b. 1.11.1985.	.30	1.25	3.50

		VG	VF	UNC
39	**500 GULDEN** 1.4.1982. Brown on m/c unpt.	.30	2.00	10.00

NOTE: 1000 new notes of #39 were sold by the Central Bank to the numismatic community for USA $2.00 each.

1986-88 ISSUE

#40-44 Anton DeKom at l., militia at r., row of bldgs. across bottom. Toucan at l., speaker w/people at r. on back. Wmk: Toucan. Printer: TDLR.

		VG	VF	UNC
40	**5 GULDEN** 1986; 1988. Blue on m/c unpt.			
	a. 1.7.1986.	FV	.75	3.00
	b. 9.1.1988.	FV	.65	2.75

		VG	VF	UNC
41	**10 GULDEN** 1.7.1986; 9.1.1988. Orange and red on m/c unpt.	FV	1.25	4.00
42	**25 GULDEN** 1.7.1986; 9.1.1988. Green on m/c unpt.	FV	2.00	8.00
43	**100 GULDEN** 1.7.1986; 9.1.1988. Purple on m/c unpt. 2 serial # varieties.	FV	7.50	20.00
44	**250 GULDEN** 9.1.1988. Blue-gray on m/c unpt.	FV	7.50	35.00

		VG	VF	UNC
45	**500 GULDEN** 1.7.1986. Brown on m/c unpt.	FV	15.00	75.00

1991-97 ISSUE

#46-54 Central Bank bldg., Paramaribo at ctr. Toucan at l. ctr. and as wmk., arms at upper r. on back. Printer: TDLR.

		VG	VF	UNC
46	**5 GULDEN** 1991; 1995. Deep blue and green on m/c unpt. Log trucks at upper l. Logging at ctr. r. on back.			
	a. 9.7.1991.	FV	FV	1.50
	b. 1.6.1995.	FV	FV	.25

		VG	VF	UNC
47	**10 GULDEN** 1991; 1995. Red and dk. green on m/c unpt. Bananas at upper l. Banana harvesting at ctr. r. on back.			
	a. 9.7.1991.	FV	FV	2.75
	b. 1.6.1995.	FV	FV	.25

		VG	VF	UNC
48	**25 GULDEN** 1991; 1995. Green and brown-orange on m/c unpt. Track participants at upper l. Competition swimmer (Olympian Anthony Neste) in butterfly stroke at ctr. r. on back.			
	a. 9.7.1991.	FV	FV	4.00
	b. 1.6.1995.	FV	FV	3.50

		VG	VF	UNC
49	**100 GULDEN** 9.7.1991. Violet and purple on m/c unpt. Factory at upper l. Strip mining at ctr. r. on back.	FV	FV	6.50

50 **500 GULDEN**
9.7.1991. Brown and red-orange on m/c unpt. Crude oil pump at upper l. Drilling for crude oil at ctr. r. on back.

	VG	VF	UNC
	FV	FV	10.00

51 **1000 GULDEN**
1993; 1995. Black and red on m/c unpt. Combine at upper l. Combining grain at ctr. r. on back.

	VG	VF	UNC
a. 1.7.1993.	FV	FV	10.00
b. 1.3.1995.	FV	FV	5.50

		VG	VF	UNC
52	**2000 GULDEN** 1.6.1995. Purple and green on m/c unpt. Back like #46.	FV	FV	10.00
53	**5000 GULDEN** 5.10.1997. Purple on m/c unpt. Bird, banana bunches on back.	FV	FV	20.00
54	**10,000 GULDEN** 5.10.1997. M/c. Bird, industrial complex on back.	FV	FV	38.50

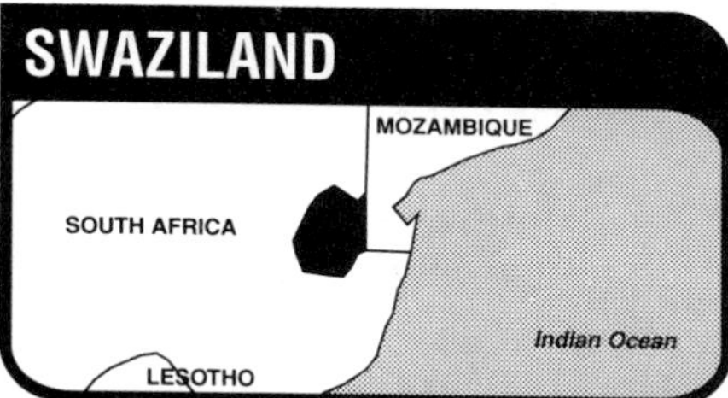

The Kingdom of Swaziland, located in southeastern Africa, has an area of 6,704 sq. mi. (17,360 sq. km.) and a population of 966,000. Capital: Mbabane (administrative); Lobamba (legislative). The diversified economy includes mining, agriculture and light industry. Asbestos, iron ore, wood pulp and sugar are exported.

The people of the present Swazi nation established themselves in an area including what is now Swaziland in the early 1800s. The first Swazi contact with the British came early in the reign of the extremely able Swazi leader King Mswati II when he asked the British for aid against Zulu raids into Swaziland. The British and Transvaal responded by guaranteeing the independence of Swaziland, 1881. South Africa assumed the power of protection and administration in 1894 and Swaziland continued under this administration until the conquest of the Transvaal during the Anglo-Boer War, when administration was transferred to the British government. After World War II, Britain began to prepare Swaziland for independence, which was achieved on Sept. 6, 1968 under the leadership of King Sobhuza II whose reign was of 61 years. His son, Prince Makhosetive was crowned King Mswati III on Apr. 25, 1986 at the age of 18 years. The kingdom is a member of the Commonwealth of Nations. The king of Swaziland is Chief of State. The prime minister is Head of Government.

RULERS:

British to 1968
Sobhuza II, 1968-82
Queen Ntombi, as regent, 1982-86
King Mswati III, 1986-

MONETARY SYSTEM:

1 Lilangeni = 100 Cents
(plural: Emalangeni)

SIGNATURE/TITLE VARIETIES		
	Minister For Finance	Governor
1	R. P. Stephens 1.6.1972-11.1.1979	E. A. Z. Mayisela 1.4.1974-31.10.1976
	J.L.F. Simelane 12.1.1979 - 20.11.1983	Deputy Governor H. B. B. Oliver 1.11.1976-30.6.1978 Acting Governor: A. D. Ockenden 1.6.1978-30.6.1981
2	J. L. F. Simelane 12.1.1979-20.11.1983	H. B. B. Oliver 1.7.1981-30.6.1992
3	Dr. S. S. Nxumalo 21.11.1983-8.6.1984	H. B. B. Oliver 1.7.1981-30.6.1992
4	B. S. Dlamini 27.8.1984-5.11.1993	H. B. B. Oliver 1.7.1981-30.6.1992
5	B. S. Dlamini 27.8.1984-5.11.1993	J. Nxumalo 1.7.1992-30.6.1997
6	I. S. Shabangu 10.11.1993-3.3.1995	J. Nxumalo 1.7.1992-30.6.1997
7a	Dr. D. von Wissell 3.3.1995-12.11.1996	J. Nxumalo 1.7.1992-30.6.1997
7b	Dr. D. von Wissell 3.3.1995-12.11.1996	J. Nxumalo 1.7.1992-30.6.1997

8	T. Masuku 12.11.1996-19.11.1998	J. Nxumalo 1.7.1992-30.6.1997
9a	T. Masuku 12.11.1996-19.11.1998	M. G. Dlamini 1.7.1997-
9b	T. Masuku 12.11.1996-19.11.1998	M. G. Dlamini 1.7.1997-
10	J. Charmichael 20.11.1998-	

KINGDOM

MONETARY AUTHORITY OF SWAZILAND

1974-78 ND ISSUE

#1-5 Kg. Sobhuza II at l., Parliament House at bottom ctr. r. Sign. 1. Wmk: Shield and spears. Printer: TDLR. Replacement notes: Serial # prefix *Z*.

		VG	VF	UNC
1	**1 LILANGENI** ND (1974). Red-brown on m/c unpt. Princesses taking part in the "Newala" (kingship ceremony).			
	a. Issued note.	.50	1.50	6.00
	s. Specimen. Serial # prefix *A; G.*	—	—	100.00

		VG	VF	UNC
2	**2 EMALANGENI** ND (1974). Dk. brown on pink and m/c unpt. Sugar mill on back.			
	a. Issued note.	1.25	2.75	10.00
	s. Specimen. Serial # prefix *A; C.*	—	—	100.00

		VG	VF	UNC
3	**5 EMALANGENI** ND (1974). Dk. green on yellow-green and m/c unpt. Mantenga Falls and landscape on back.			
	a. Issued note.	2.00	7.00	30.00
	s. Specimen. Serial # prefix *A; B.*	—	—	100.00

		VG	VF	UNC
4	**10 EMALANGENI** ND (1974). Blue-black on blue and m/c unpt. Asbestos mine on back.			
	a. Issued note.	7.50	20.00	75.00
	s. Specimen. Serial # prefix *A; B.*	—	—	100.00

		VG	VF	UNC
5	**20 EMALANGENI** ND (1978). Purple and green on m/c unpt. Agricultural products and cows on back.			
	a. Issued note.	15.00	45.00	150.00
	s. Specimen. Serial # prefix *A.*	—	—	100.00

CENTRAL BANK OF SWAZILAND

1981 COMMEMORATIVE ISSUE

#6 and 7, Diamond Jubilee of Kg. Sobhuza II

#6 and 7 printer: TDLR.

		VG	VF	UNC
6	**10 EMALANGENI** 1981. Blue-black on blue and m/c unpt. Black commemorative text on wmk. area. Back like #4. Wmk: Shield and spears. Sign. 2.			
	a. Issued note.	25.00	80.00	250.00
	s. Specimen. Serial # prefix *K.*	—	—	165.00

7 20 EMALANGENI

1981. Purple and green on m/c unpt. Like #8. Back like #5. Wmk: Shield and spears. Sign. 2.

	VG	VF	UNC
a. Issued note.	25.00	80.00	250.00
s. Specimen. Serial # prefix *C*.	—	—	165.00

1982; 1983 ND ISSUE

#8-11 wmk: Shield and spears. Printer: TDLR. Replacement notes: Serial # prefix *Z*.

8 2 EMALANGENI

ND (1983-86). Dk. brown on pink and m/c unpt. Like #2 but new issuer's name at top.

	VG	VF	UNC
a. Sign. 2. (1983).	1.75	3.75	12.50
b. Sign. 4. (1984).	.75	1.50	4.50
s1. As a. Specimen. Serial # prefix *F*.	—	—	90.00
s2. As b. Specimen. Serial # prefix *G, J*.	—	—	90.00

9 5 EMALANGENI

ND (1982-86). Dk. green on yellow-green and m/c unpt. Like #3 but new issuer's name at top.

	VG	VF	UNC
a. Sign. 2. (1982).	2.50	6.00	35.00
b. Sign. 4. (1984).	1.75	2.25	8.00
s1. As a. Specimen. Serial # prefix *D; E*.	—	—	90.00
s2. As b. Specimen. Serial # prefix *F*.	—	—	90.00

10 10 EMALANGENI

ND (1982-86). Blue-black on blue and m/c unpt. Like #6 but w/o commemorative inscription on face.

	VG	VF	UNC
a. Sign. 2. (1982).	10.00	17.50	65.00
b. Sign. 3. (1984).	5.00	15.00	80.00
c. Sign. 4. (1985).	1.50	4.00	20.00
s1. As a. Specimen. Serial # prefix *Q*.	—	—	90.00
s2. As b. Specimen. Serial # prefix *U*.	—	—	90.00
s3. As c. Specimen. Serial # prefix *W*.	—	—	90.00

11 20 EMALANGENI

ND (1984-86). Purple and green on m/c unpt. Like #7 but w/o commemorative inscription on face.

	VG	VF	UNC
a. Sign. 3. (1984).	7.00	25.00	150.00
b. Sign. 4. (1985).	FV	8.50	35.00
s1. As a. Specimen. Serial # prefix *E*.	—	—	90.00
s2. As b. Specimen. Serial # prefix *F*.	—	—	90.00

1986 ND ISSUE

12 20 EMALANGENI

ND (1986). Purple and green on m/c unpt. Kg. Mswati III at l., otherwise like #11. Printer: TDLR. Sign. 4.

	VG	VF	UNC
a. Issued note.	3.50	8.00	25.00
s. Specimen. Serial # prefix *A*.	—	—	90.00

1986; 1987 ND ISSUES

#13-16 Facing portr. of young Kg. Mswati III at l., arms at lower ctr. Wmk: Shield and spears. Sign. 4. Printer: TDLR. Replacement notes: Serial # prefix *Z*.

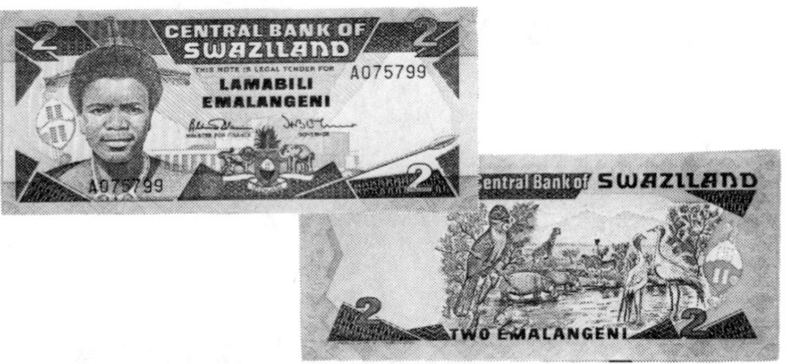

		VG	VF	UNC
13	**2 EMALANGENI** ND (1987). Dk. brown and orange on m/c unpt. Wildlife on back.			
	a. Issued note.	FV	1.00	5.00
	s. Specimen. Serial # prefix *A*.	—	—	90.00

		VG	VF	UNC
14	**5 EMALANGENI** ND (1987). Dk. green, dk. brown and bright green on m/c unpt. Warriors on back.			
	a. Issued note.	FV	2.25	9.00
	s. Specimen. Serial # prefix *A*.	—	—	90.00

		VG	VF	UNC
15	**10 EMALANGENI** ND (1986). Dk. blue and black on m/c unpt. Hydroelectric plant at Luphohlo and bird on back.			
	a. Issued note.	FV	4.00	17.50
	s. Specimen. Serial # prefix *A*; *F*.	—	—	90.00
16	**20 EMALANGENI** ND (1986). Violet, brown and purple on m/c unpt. Cattle and truck on back.			
	a. Issued note.	FV	20.00	80.00
	s. Specimen. Serial # prefix *A*.	—	—	90.00

1989 COMMEMORATIVE ISSUE

#17, 21st Birthday of Kg. Mswati III

		VG	VF	UNC
17	**20 EMALANGENI** 19.4.1989. Like #16, w/silver commemorative text and dates ovpt. on wmk. area. Sign. 4.			
	a. Issued note.	5.50	8.50	30.00
	s. Specimen. Serial # prefix *A*.	—	—	80.00

NOTICE

Readers with unlisted dates, signature varieties, etc. are invited to submit photocopies of their notes to: Standard Catalog of World Paper Money, 700 East State St. Iola, WI 54990-0001, fax: 1-715-445-4087, or E-Mail: thernr@krause.com.

1990; 1992 ND ISSUE

#18-21 similar to #13-16 but w/older portr. of Kg. Mswati III at l. facing half r. Backs like #13-16. Wmk: Shield and spears. Replacement notes: Serial # prefix *Z*.

		VG	VF	UNC
18	**2 EMALANGENI** ND (1992-95). Dk. brown on m/c unpt. Like #13.			
	a. Sign. 4. (1992).	FV	1.50	3.50
	b. Sign. 6. (1994).	FV	.75	9.00
	s1. As a. Specimen. Serial # prefix *M*.	—	—	80.00
	s2. As b. Specimen. Serial # prefix *S*.	—	—	70.00

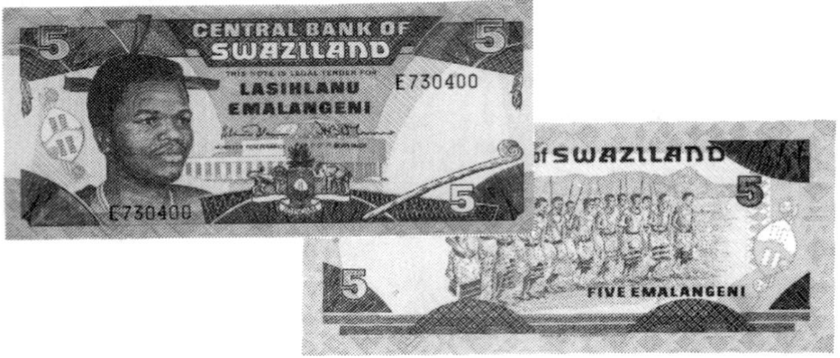

		VG	VF	UNC
19	**5 EMALANGENI** ND (1990-95). Dk. green, dk. brown and bright green on m/c unpt. Like #14.			
	a. Sign. 4. (1990).	FV	2.25	7.00
	b. Sign. 6. (1994).	FV	4.00	20.00
	s1. As a. Specimen. Serial # prefix *D*.	—	—	80.00
	s2. As b. Specimen. Serial # prefix *J*.	—	—	70.00

		VG	VF	UNC
20	**10 EMALANGENI** ND (1990-95). Dk. blue and black on m/c unpt. Like #15.			
	a. Sign. 4. (1990).	FV	4.00	18.00
	b. Sign. 5. (1992).	FV	4.50	18.00
	s1. As a. Specimen. Serial # prefix *J*.	—	—	80.00
	s2. As b. Specimen. Serial # prefix *N*.	—	—	80.00

		VG	VF	UNC
21	**20 EMALANGENI** ND (1990-95). Violet, brown and purple on m/c unpt. Like #16.			
	a. Sign. 4. (1990).	FV	7.00	30.00
	b. Sign. 5. (1992).	FV	7.00	28.00
	s1. As a. Specimen. Serial # prefix *D*.	—	—	80.00
	s2. As b. Specimen. Serial # prefix *G*.	—	—	80.00

22 50 EMALANGENI

ND (1990-95). Dull red-brown, orange and dk. green on m/c unpt. Kg. Mswati at l. Central Bank seal at l. ctr., head office bldg. at r. on back. Wmk: Shield and spears. Printer: TDLR.

	VG	VF	UNC
a. Sign. 4. (1990).	FV	16.50	65.00
b. Sign. 6. (1995).	12.50	40.00	160.00
s1. As a. Specimen. Serial # prefix *A.*	—	—	80.00
s2. As b. Specimen. Serial # prefix *C.*	—	—	70.00

1995 ND; 1995-98 ISSUE

#23-25 w/segmented foil over security thread.

23 5 EMALANGENI

ND (1995). Dk. green, dk. brown and bright green on m/c unpt. Like #19 but warriors on back in dk. brown. Ascending serial #. Sign. 7a. Printer: H&S.

	VG	VF	UNC
a. Issued note.	FV	FV	6.00
s. Specimen. Serial # prefix *AA.*	—	—	70.00

#24 and 25 printer: F-CO.

24 10 EMALANGENI

ND (1995); 1997; 1998. Dk. blue and black on m/c unpt. Like #20.

	VG	VF	UNC
a. Sign. 7a. ND.	FV	FV	12.50
b. Sign. 8. 8.4.1997.	FV	FV	10.00
c. Sign. 9a. 1.4.1998.	FV	FV	5.00
s1. As a. Specimen. Serial # prefix *AA.*	—	—	70.00
s2. As b. Specimen. Serial # prefix *AG.*	—	—	70.00
s3. As c. Specimen. Serial # prefix *AK, AL, AN.*	—	—	70.00

25 20 EMALANGENI

ND (1995); 1997; 1998. Violet, brown and purple on m/c unpt. Like #21.

	VG	VF	UNC
a. Sign. 7a. ND.	FV	FV	20.00
b. Sign. 8. 8.4.1997.	FV	FV	18.50
c. Sign. 9a. 1.4.1998.	FV	FV	9.00
s1. As a. Specimen. Serial # prefix *AA.*	—	—	70.00
s2. As b. Specimen. Serial # prefix *AF; AG.*	—	—	70.00
s3. As c. Specimen. Serial # prefix *AK, AL.*	—	—	70.00

#26 and 27 OVD strip at r. w/C B of S repeated. Printer: G&D.

26 50 EMALANGENI

1995; 1998. Dull red-brown and dk. green on m/c unpt. Like #22.

	VG	VF	UNC
a. Sign. 7b. 1.4.1995.	FV	FV	40.00
b. Sign. 9b. 1.4.1998.	FV	FV	16.50
s1. As a. Specimen. Serial # prefix *AA.*	—	—	70.00
s2. As b. Specimen. Serial # prefix *AA.*	—	—	70.00

27 100 EMALANGENI

6.9.1996. Dk. brown on m/c unpt. Central Bank seal at upper l. ctr., rock formation at ctr. on back. Sign. 7b.

	VG	VF	UNC
a. Issued note.	FV	FV	40.00
s. Specimen. Serial # prefix *AA.*	—	—	70.00

1998 Commemorative Issue

#28, 30th Anniversary of Independence

		VG	VF	Unc
28	**200 Emalangeni** 6.9.1998. Dk. green and green on m/c unpt. Face like #27. Swazi villagers by thatched circular domed and fenced huts at ctr. on back. Printer: G&D. Sign. 9b.			
	a. Issued note.	FV	FV	60.00
	s. Specimen. Serial # prefix *AA*.	—	—	70.00

Collector Series

Monetary Authority of Swaziland

1974 Issue

		Issue Price	Mkt. Value
CS1	**ND (1974). 1-20 Emalangeni** #1-5 w/ovpt: *SPECIMEN* and serial # prefix Maltese cross.	14.00	30.00

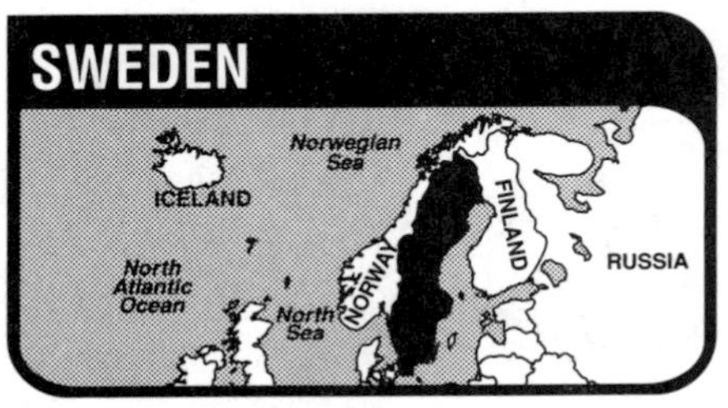

The Kingdom of Sweden, a limited constitutional monarchy located in northern Europe between Norway and Finland, has an area of 173,732 sq. mi. (449,960 sq. km.) and a population of 8.87 million. Capital: Stockholm. Mining, lumbering and a specialized machine industry dominate the economy. Machinery, paper, iron and steel, motor vehicles and wood pulp are exported.

Sweden was founded as a Christian stronghold by Olaf Skotkonung late in the 10th century. After conquering Finland late in the 13th century, Sweden, together with Norway, came under the rule of Denmark, 1397-1523, in an association known as the Union of Kalmar. Modern Sweden had its beginning in 1523 when Gustavus Vasa drove the Danes out of Sweden and was himself chosen king. Under Gustavus Adolphus II and Charles XII, Sweden was one of the great powers of the 17th century Europe - until Charles invaded Russia, 1708, and was defeated at the Battle of Pultowa in June 1709. Early in the 18th century, a coalition of Russia, Poland and Denmark took away Sweden's Baltic empire and in 1809 Sweden was forced to cede Finland to Russia. Norway was ceded to Sweden by the Treaty of Kiel in January 1814. The Norwegians resisted for a time but later signed the Act of Union at the Convention of Moss in August 1814. The Union was dissolved in 1905 and Norway became independent.

A new constitution which took effect on Jan. 1, 1975, restricts the function of the king to a ceremonial role.

RULERS:

Gustaf VI Adolf, 1950-1973
Carl XVI Gustaf, 1973-

MONETARY SYSTEM:

1 Krona = 100 Öre

Kingdom

Sw(v)eriges Riksbank

1952-55 Issue

#42 and 43 replacement notes: Serial # suffix star.

		VG	VF	Unc
42	**5 Kronor** 1954-61. Dk. brown on red and blue unpt. Beige paper. Portr. Kg. Gustaf VI Adolf at r. ctr. and as wmk. Svea standing w/shield on back.			
	a. W/2 safety letters at lower r. just above the digit 5. 1954-56.	1.00	2.00	4.50
	b. W/o safety letters. 1959-61.	1.00	2.00	4.50

		VG	VF	Unc
43	**10 Kronor** 1953-62. Gray-blue. Portr. G. Vasa at l. and as wmk. Blue date and serial #.			
	a. 1953-54.	1.65	2.25	5.00
	b. 1955-56.	1.65	2.25	5.00
	c. 1957-59.	1.65	2.25	5.00
	d. 1960.	2.00	3.50	8.00
	e. 1962.	1.65	2.25	5.50
	f. W/star. 1956-60; 1962.	12.50	35.00	120.00

		VG	VF	UNC
44	**50 KRONOR** 1955-58. Like #35. No safety letter after 6 digit serial #.			
	a. 1947-54. Single lg. letter at lower l. and r. on back.	15.00	30.00	100.00
	b. 1955-58. Two sm. letters at lower l. and r. on back.	10.00	25.00	80.00
	c. w/star. 1956-58.	60.00	150.00	300.00
45	**100 KRONOR** 1955-59. Like #11. 6 digit serial # w/o safety letter.			
	a. 1947-54. Single lg. letter at lower l. and r. on back.	25.00	50.00	100.00
	b. 1955-59. Two sm. letters at lower l. and r. on back.	20.00	40.00	80.00
	c. W/star. 1956-58.	60.00	100.00	200.00
46	**1000 KRONOR** 1952-73. Brown and m/c. Svea standing. Kg. Gustaf V on back and as wmk.			
	a. Blue and red safety fibers. 1952.	165.00	250.00	500.00
	b. 1957.	165.00	250.00	500.00
	c. 1962.	165.00	225.00	450.00
	d. 1965.	165.00	250.00	450.00
	e. One vertical filament. 1971.	165.00	200.00	400.00
	f. 1973.	165.00	200.00	400.00

1958; 1959 ISSUE

#47 and 48 replacement notes: Serial # star suffix.

		VG	VF	UNC
47	**50 KRONOR** 1959-62. Second sign. at l. Sm. date and serial #.			
	a. 1959-62.	10.00	17.50	45.00
	b. W/star. 1959-62.	17.50	40.00	100.00
48	**100 KRONOR** 1959-63. Second sign. at l. Sm. date and serial #.			
	a. 1959-63.	17.50	30.00	60.00
	b. W/star. 1959-63.	20.00	60.00	120.00

		VG	VF	UNC
49	**10,000 KRONOR** 1958. Green and m/c. King Gustav VI Adolf at r. and as wmk. Seva standing w/shield at crt. on back.	1600.	2000.	3000.

1962 ISSUE

		VG	VF	UNC
50	**5 KRONOR** 1962-63. Dk. brown on red and blue unpt. Portr. Kg. Gustaf VI Adolf at ctr. Sven standing w/shield on back. Wmk: E. Tegner. W/security thread.			
	a. 1962.	1.00	3.00	6.00
	b. 1963.	1.00	2.00	4.00

1963-76 ISSUE

#51-55 replacement notes: Serial # suffix star.

		VG	VF	UNC
51	**5 KRONOR** 1965-81. Purple, green and orange. G. Vasa at r. Back blue and reddish brown; abstract design of rooster crowing at l. on back. Beige paper. Wmk: Square w/*5* repeated.			
	a. W/year in dk. red letter press. 1965-69.	FV	1.50	4.00
	b. W/year in deep red offset. 1970.	FV	FV	3.00
	c. As a. 1972-74; 1976-77.	FV	FV	2.50
	d. W/year in pale red offset. 1977-79; 1981.	FV	FV	2.25

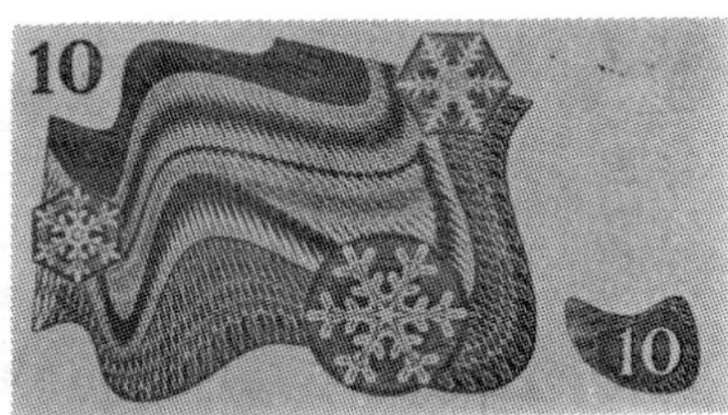

52	10 KRONOR	VG	VF	UNC
	1963-90. Dk. green, w/red and blue guilloche at ctr. Kg. Gustaf Adolf at r., arms at ctr. Northern lights and snowflakes at l. ctr. on back. Pale blue paper. Wmk: A. Strindberg (repeated).			
	a. W/year in dk. red letter press. 1963.	FV	FV	6.00
	b. As a. 1966; 1968.	FV	FV	5.00
	c. As a. 1971; 1972; 1975.	FV	FV	4.50
	d. W/year in pale red offset. Engraved sign. 1976-77; 1979; 1983; 1985.	FV	FV	4.00
	e. As d. but w/offset sign. 1980; 1981; 1983; 1984; 1987-90.	FV	FV	3.50

53	50 KRONOR	VG	VF	UNC
	1965-90. Blue, green and brown. Beige paper. Kg. Gustaf III at r. C. von Linné (Linnaeus) at ctr. on back. Wmk: Anna Maria Lenngren (repeated).			
	a. Sm. wmk. 1965; 1967; 1970.	FV	10.00	22.50
	b. Lg. wmk. w/year in dk. red letter press. 1974; 1976.	FV	FV	20.00
	c. Lg. wmk. as b. w/year in red-brown offset. 1978; 1979; 1981.	FV	FV	18.50
	d. As c. Black serial #. 1982; 1984; 1986; 1989; 1990.	FV	FV	17.50

54	100 KRONOR	VG	VF	UNC
	1965-85. Red-brown, blue and gray on lt. blue paper. King Gustav II Adolf at r. Figure head at l., Admiral ship *Vasa* of 1628 in ctr. on back. Wmk: A. Oxenstierna.			
	a. Sm. wmk. 22mm. 1965; 1968; 1970.	FV	20.00	35.00
	b. Lg. wmk. 27mm. w/year in dk. blue letter press. 1971; 1972; 1974; 1976.	FV	FV	32.50
	c. Lg. wmk. as b. w/year in blue-green offset. 1978; 1980-83; 1985.	FV	FV	30.00

55	1000 KRONOR	VG	VF	UNC
	1976-88. Red-brown on green and violet unpt. Carl XIV Johan at r. Bessemer steel process on back. Wmk: J. Berzelius.			
	a. 1976-78.	FV	FV	275.00
	b. 1980; 1981; 1983-86; 1988.	FV	FV	250.00

1968 COMMEMORATIVE ISSUE

#56, 300th Anniversary Sveriges Riksbank, 1668-1968

56	10 KRONOR	VG	VF	UNC
	1968. Deep blue on m/c unpt. Svea standing w/ornaments at r. Back violet-brown; old Riksbank bldg. at l. ctr. Wmk: Crowned monogram Kg. Charles XI.			
	a. Issued note.	FV	2.00	5.00
	b. In printed banquet program folder w/bank name, date and seal.	—	—	65.00

1985-89 REGULAR ISSUES

#57-63 replacement notes: Serial # suffix star.

NOTE: The last digit of the year is first digit of the serial #.

57	100 KRONOR	VG	VF	UNC
	(198)6-(199)9. Blue-green and brown-violet on m/c unpt. C. von Linné (Linnaeus) at r. and as wmk., bldg. in background. Plants at l. ctr. Bee pollinating flowers at ctr. on back.			
	a. Wmk: Lg. portrait. Sign. B. Dennis. (198)6-(198)8; (199)2.	FV	FV	20.00
	b. Wmk: Sm. portrait repeated vertically. Sign. U. Bäckström. (199)6; (199)8; (199)9.	FV	FV	26.50

58 **500 KRONOR**
(198)5-(198)6. Gray-blue and red-brown. Kg. Carl XI at r. and as wmk. C. Polhem seated at l. ctr. on back.

	VG	VF	UNC
a. (198)5.	FV	100.00	180.00
b. (198)6.	FV	100.00	140.00

59 **500 KRONOR**
(198)9; (199)1; (199)5; (199)7; (199)9. Red and m/c unpt. Similar to #58 but w/o white margin on face, also other slight changes.

	VG	VF	UNC
a. Sign. B. Dennis. (198)9; (199)1; 2.	FV	FV	110.00
b. Sign. U. Bäckström. (199)4; 5; 7; 8; 9.	FV	FV	110.00

60 **1000 KRONOR**
(198)9-(199)2. Brownish black on m/c unpt. Kg G. Vasa at r. and as wmk. Medieval harvest and threshing scene at l. ctr. on back.

	VG	VF	UNC
a. (198)9-(199)0.	FV	FV	200.00
b. (199)0; 1; 2.	FV	FV	200.00

1991; 1996 ISSUE

61 **20 KRONOR**
(199)1-2; (199)4; 5. Dk. blue on m/c unpt. Horse-drawn carriage at lower ctr., Selma Lagerlöf at r. and as wmk. Story scene w/small boy riding a goose in flight at l. ctr. on back. 130 x 72mm.

	VG	VF	UNC
a. Sign. B. Dennis. (199)1; 2.	FV	FV	5.50
b. Sign. U. Bäckström. (199)4; 5.	FV	FV	5.50

		VG	VF	UNC
62	**50 KRONOR** (199)6; 7. Deep olive-brown on m/c unpt. J. Lind at ctr. and as wmk. (repeated), music lines at l., stage at r. Violin, treble clef w/line of notes, abstract musical design on back.	FV	FV	13.50

1997 ISSUE

		VG	VF	UNC
63	**20 KRONOR** (199)7; 8. Violet on m/c unpt. Like #61 but reduced size, 120 x 67mm.	FV	FV	6.00

The Swiss Confederation, located in central Europe north of Italy and south of Germany, has an area of 15,941 sq. mi. (41,290 sq. km.) and a population of 7.06 million. Capital: Bern. The economy centers about a well developed manufacturing industry, however the most important economic factor is services (banks and insurance).

Switzerland, the habitat of lake dwellers in prehistoric times, was peopled by the Celtic Helvetians when Julius Caesar made it a part of the Roman Empire in 58 BC. After the decline of Rome, Switzerland was invaded by Teutonic tribes, who established small temporal holdings which, in the Middle Ages, became a federation of fiefs of the Holy Roman Empire. As a nation, Switzerland originated in 1291 when the districts of Nidwalden, Schwyz and Uri united to defeat Austria and attain independence as the Swiss Confederation. After acquiring new cantons in the 14th century, Switzerland was made independent from the Holy Roman Empire by the 1648 Treaty of Westphalia. The revolutionary armies of Napoleonic France occupied Switzerland and set up the Helvetian Republic, 1798-1803. After the fall of Napoleon, the Congress of Vienna, 1815, recognized the independence of Switzerland and guaranteed its neutrality. The Swiss Constitutions of 1848, 1874, and 1999 established a union modeled upon that of the United States.

MONETARY SYSTEM:

1 Franc (Franken) = 10 Batzen = 100 Centimes (Rappen)
Plural: Francs, Franchi or Franken.

SIGNATURE VARIETIES

	President, Bank Council	Director	Cashier
39	Dr. Brenno Galli 1959-78	Dr.Walter Schweghler	Otto Kunz 1954-66
40	Dr. Brenno Galli	Dr. Riccardo Motta 1955-66	Otto Kunz
41	Dr. Brenno Galli	Dr Max Lkle 1956-68	Otto Kunz
42	Dr. Brenno Galli 1959-78	Dr. Edwin Stopper 1966-74	Rudolf Aebersold 1954-66
43	Dr. Brenno Galli	Alexandre Hay 1966-75	Rudolf Aebersold
44	Dr. Brenno Galli	Dr. Max Lkle	Rudolf Aebersold
45	Dr. Brenno Galli	Dr. Fritz Leutwiler 1968-84	Rudolf Aebersold
46	Dr. Brenno Galli	Dr. Leo Schürmann 1974-80	Rudolf Aebersold
47	Dr. Brenno Galli	Dr. Pierre Languetin 1976-88	Rudolf Aebersold

NOTE: From #180 onward w/o the Chief Cashier's signature.

	President, Bank Council	Director
48	Dr. Brenno Galli	Dr. Leo Schürmann
49	Dr. Brenno Galli	Alexandre Hay

SIGNATURE VARIETIES

	President, Bank Council	Director
50	Dr. Brenno Galli	Dr. Fritz Leutwiler
51	Dr. Brenno Galli	Dr. Pierre Languetin
52	Dr. Edmund Wyss 1978-86	Dr. Leo Schürmann
53	Dr. Edmund Wyss	Dr. Pierre Languetin
54	Dr. Edmund Wyss	Dr. Fritz Leutwiler
55	Dr. Edmund Wyss	Dr. Markus Lusser 1981-96
56	Dr. Edmund Wyss	Dr. Hans Meyer 1985-
57	Dr. François Schaller 1986-89	Dr. Markus Lusser
58	Dr. François Schaller	Dr. Pierre Languetin
59	Dr. François Schaller	Dr. Hans Meyer
60	Dr. François Schaller	Jean Zwahlen (18mm) 1988-96
61	Peter Gerber 1989-93	Dr. Markus Lusser
62	Peter Gerber	Jean Zwahlen (18mm)
63	Peter Gerber	Jean Zwahlen (15mm)
64	Peter Gerber	Dr. Hans Meyer
65	Dr. Jakob Schönenberger 1993-99	Dr. Markus Lusser
66	Dr. Jakob Schönenberger	Dr. Hans Meyer

SIGNATURE VARIETIES

	President, Bank Council	Director
67	Dr. Jakob Schönenberger	Jean Zwahlen (12mm)
68	Dr. Jakob Schönenberger	Dr. Jean-Pierre Roth 1996-
69	Dr. Jakob Schönenberger	Dr. Bruno Gehrig 1986-
70	Eduard Belser 1999	Dr. Hans Meyer
71	Eduard Belser	Dr. Jean-Pierre Roth
72	Eduard Belser	Dr. Bruno Gehrig

CONFEDERATION

SCHWEIZERISCHE NATIONALBANK

SWISS NATIONAL BANK

1954-57 ISSUE

#174-175 printer: OFZ.

NOTE: Sign. varieties listed after date.

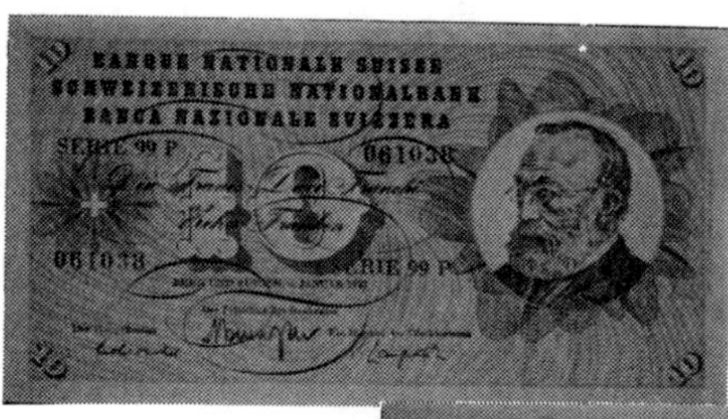

		VG	VF	UNC
174	**10 FRANKEN** 1955-77. Purple on red brown unpt. Gottfried Keller at r. Carnation flower at l. ctr. on back. Printer: OFZ.			
	a. 25.8.1955 (34,36,37); 20.10.1955 (34,36,37).	10.00	10.00	27.50
	b. 29.11.1956 (34,37,38).	FV	FV	25.00
	c. 18.12.1958 (34,37,38).	FV	10.00	35.00
	d. 23.12.1959 (39,40,41); 22.12.1960 (39, 40, 41); 26.10.1961 (39, 40, 41); 28.3.1963 (39, 40, 41); 2.4.1964 (39, 40, 41); 21.1.1965 (39, 40, 41); 23.12.1965 (39, 40, 41).	FV	FV	21.50
	e. 1.1.1967 (42, 43, 44); 30.6.1967 (42, 43, 44); 15.5.1968 (42, 43, 45); 15.1.1969 (42, 43, 45).	FV	FV	17.50
	f. 5.1.1970 (42, 43, 45); 10.2.1971 (42, 43, 45; 24.1.1972 (42, 43, 45); 7.3.1973 (42, 43, 45); 7.2.1974 (42, 43, 45); 6.1.1977 (45, 46, 47).	FV	FV	13.50

		VG	VF	UNC
175	**20 FRANKEN** 1954-76. Blue on m/c. unpt. Gen. G. H. Dufour at r. Silver thistle at l. ctr. on back. Printer: OFZ.			
	a. 1.7.1954 (34, 35, 36).	15.00	17.50	70.00
	b. 7.7.1955 (34, 36, 37); 20.10.1955 (34, 36,37; 5.7.1956 (34, 37, 38); 4.10.1957 (34, 37, 38).	FV	25.00	50.00
	c. 18.12.1958 (34, 37, 38).	FV	17.50	62.50
	d. 23.12.1959 (39, 40, 41); 22.12.1960 (39, 40, 41); 26.10.1961 (39, 40, 41); 28.3.1963 (39, 40, 41); 2.4.1964 (39, 40, 41); 21.1.1965 (39, 40, 41); 23.12.1965 (39, 40, 41).	FV	FV	30.00
	e. 1.1.1967 (42, 43, 44); 30.6.1967 (42, 43, 44); 15.5.1968 (42, 43, 45); 15.1.1969 (42, 43, 45).	FV	FV	27.50
	f. 5.1.1970 (42, 43, 45); 10.2.1971 (42, 43, 45); 24.1.1972 (42, 43, 45); 7.3.1973 (42, 43, 45); 7.2.1974 (42, 43, 45); 9.4.1976 (45, 46, 47).	FV	FV	25.00
176	**50 FRANKEN** 1955-58. Green and red on m/c unpt. Girl at upper r. Apple harvesting scene on back (symbolizing fertility). Printer: W&S.			
	a. 7.7.1955 (34, 36, 37).	FV	50.00	100.00
	b. 4.10.1957 (34, 37, 38).	FV	FV	85.00
	c. 18.12.1958 (34, 37, 38).	FV	45.00	135.00

		VG	VF	UNC
177	**100 FRANKEN** 1956-73. Blue and brown on m/c unpt. Boy's head at upper r w/lamb. St. Martin sharing his cape at ctr. r. on back. Printer: TDLR.			
	a. 25.10.1956 (34, 37, 38).	FV	90.00	175.00
	b. 1.10.1957 (34, 37, 38).	FV	80.00	140.00
	c. 18.12.1958 (34, 37, 38).	FV	FV	210.00
	d. 21.12.1961 (39, 40, 41); 28.3.1963 (39, 40, 41); 2.4.1964 (39, 40, 41); 21.1.1965 (39, 40, 41); 23.12.1965 (39, 40, 41).	FV	FV	135.00
	e. 1.1.1967 (42, 43, 44); 30.6.1967 (42, 43, 44); 15.1.1969 (42, 43, 45).	FV	FV	120.00
	f. 5.1.1970 (42, 43, 45); 10.2.1971 (42, 43, 45); 24.1.1972 (42, 43, 45); 7.3.1973 (42, 43, 45).	FV	FV	100.00

		VG	VF	UNC
178	**500 FRANKEN** 31.1.1957; 4.10.1957; 18.12.1958. Brown-orange and olive on m/c unpt. Woman looking in mirror at r. Elders w/4 girls bathing at ctr. r. on back (Fountain of Youth). Printer: W&S.			
	a. 31.1.1957 (34, 37, 38); 4.10.1957 (34, 37, 38).	FV	375.00	700.00
	b. 18.12.1958 (34, 37, 38).	FV	375.00	750.00

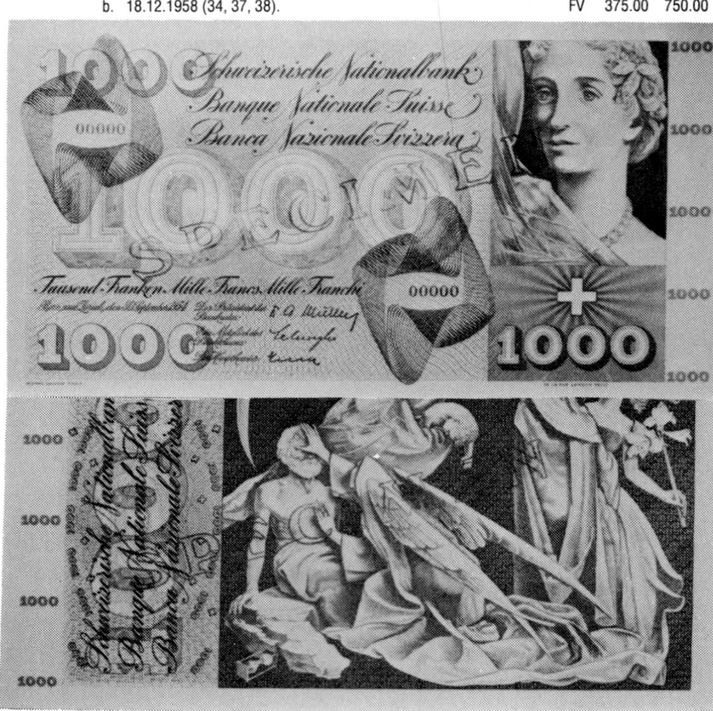

		VG	VF	UNC
179	**1000 FRANKEN** 1954-74. Purple and blue on m/c unpt. Female head at upper r. Allegorical scene "dance macabre" on back. Printer: TDLR.			
	a. 30.9.1954 (34, 35, 36).	FV	900.00	1350.
	b. 4.10.1957 (34, 37, 38).	FV	850.00	1250.
	c. 18.12.1958 (34, 37, 38).	FV	FV	1350.
	d. 22.12.1960 (39, 40, 41); 21.12.1961 (39, 40, 41); 28.3.1963 (39, 40, 41).	FV	FV	1200.
	e. 21.1.1965 (39, 40, 41); 1.1.1967 (42, 43, 44).			
	f. 5.1.1970 (42, 43, 45); 10.2.1971 (42, 43, 45); 24.1.1972 (42, 43, 45); 1.10.1973 (42, 43, 45); 7.2.1974 (42, 43, 45).	FV	FV	1000.

1961 ISSUE

#179A and 179B printer: TDLR.

These notes will cease to be redeemable on 30.4.2000.

NOTE: Sign. varieties follow date listings.

		VG	VF	UNC
179A	**50 FRANKEN** 1961-74. Green and red on m/c unpt. Girl at r. Apple harvesting scene on back (symbolizing fertility).			
	a. 4.5.1961 (39, 40, 41); 21.12.1961 (39, 40, 41); 28.3.1963 (39, 40, 41); 2.4.1964 (39, 40, 41); 21.1.1965 (39, 40, 41); 23.12.1965 (39, 40, 41).	FV	FV	75.00
	b. 30.6.1967 (42, 43, 44); 15.5.1968 (42, 43, 45); 15.1.1969 (42, 43, 45).	FV	FV	70.00
	c. 5.1.1970 (42, 43, 45); 10.2.1971 (42, 43, 45); 24.1.1972 (42, 43, 45); 7.3.1973 (42, 43, 45); 7.2.1974 (42, 43, 45).	FV	FV	65.00

		VG	VF	UNC
179B	**500 FRANKEN** 1961-74. Brown-orange and olive on m/c unpt. Woman looking in mirror at r. Elders w/4 girls bathing at ctr. r. on back (Fountain of Youth).			
	a. 21.12.1961 (39, 40, 41); 28.3.1963 (39, 40, 41); 2.4.1964 (39, 40, 41); 21.1.1965 (39, 40, 41).	FV	FV	625.00
	b. 1.1.1967 (42, 43, 44); 15.5.1968 (42, 43, 45); 15.1.1969 (42, 43, 45).	FV	FV	580.00
	c. 5.1.1970 (42, 43, 45); 10.2.1971 (42, 43, 45); 24.1.1972 (42, 43, 45); 7.3.1973 (42, 43, 45); 7.2.1974 (42, 43, 45).	FV	FV	550.00

1976-79 ISSUE; 6TH SERIES

#180-185 series of notes printed in 4 languages - the traditional German, French and Italian plus Romansch; (Rhaeto - Romanic), the language of the mountainous areas of Graubünden Canton. Wmk. as portr. The first 2 numerals before the serial # prefix letter are date (year) indicators. Printer: OFZ.

NOTE: Sign. varieties listed after date.

		VG	VF	UNC
180	**10 FRANKEN** (19)79-92. Orange-brown and m/c. L. Euler at r. Water turbine, light rays through lenses and Solar System in vertical format on back.			
	a. 1979 (52, 53, 54); 1980 (52, 53, 54).	FV	FV	14.00
	b. 1981 (53, 54, 55); 1982 (53, 54, 55).	FV	FV	13.50
	c. 1983 (53, 54, 55); 1986 (53, 55, 56).	FV	FV	13.00
	d. 1987 (57, 58, 59).	FV	FV	12.00
	e. 1990 (62).	FV	FV	17.50
	f. 1990 (61, 63, 64); 1991 (61, 63, 64); 1992 (61, 63, 64).	FV	FV	10.00

		VG	VF	UNC
181	**20 FRANKEN** (19)78-92. Blue and m/c. H-B. de Saussure at r. Fossil and early mountain expedition team hiking on vertical format back.			
	a. 1978 (52, 53, 54). 2mm distance between end of unpt. and upper edge line on face.	FV	FV	27.50
	b. 1978 (52, 53, 54). No distance.	Reported Not Confirmed		
	c. 1980 (52, 53, 54).	FV	FV	27.50
	d. 1981 (53, 54, 55); 1982 (53, 54, 55); 1983 (53, 54, 55).	FV	FV	25.00
	e. 1986 (57, 58, 59); 1987 (57, 58, 59).	FV	FV	20.00
	f. 1989 (61, 62, 64); 1990 (61, 63, 64); 1992 (61, 63, 64).	FV	FV	17.50
	s. Perforated: *SPECIMEN.*	—	—	250.00

182	50 FRANKEN	VG	VF	UNC
	(19)78-88. Green and m/c. K. Gessner at r. Eagle owl, *Primula auricula* plant and stars on vertical format back.			
	a. 1978 (48, 50, 51).	FV	FV	60.00
	b. 1979 (52, 53, 54); 1980 (52, 53, 54); 1981 (53, 54, 55).	FV	FV	55.00
	c. 1983 (53, 54, 55); 1985 (53, 55, 56).	FV	FV	52.50
	d. 1987 (57, 58, 59); 1988 (57, 59, 60).	FV	FV	42.50
	s. Perforated: *SPECIMEN.*	—	—	350.00

183	100 FRANKEN	VG	VF	UNC
	(19)75-93. Blue and m/c. F. Borromini at r. Baroque architectural drawing and view of S. Ivo alla Sapienza. Vertical format back.			
	a. 1975 (49).	FV	FV	125.00
	b. 1975 (48, 50); 1977 (48, 50, 51).	FV	FV	100.00
	c. 1980 (52, 53, 54).	FV	FV	95.00
	d. 1981 (53, 54, 55); 1982 (53, 54, 55); 1983 (53, 54, 55); 1984 (53, 54, 55).	FV	FV	90.00
	e. 1986 (57, 58, 59); 1988 (57, 59, 60); 1989 (57, 59, 60).	FV	FV	85.00
	f. 1991 (61, 63, 64); 1992 (61, 63, 64); 1993 (61, 63, 64).	FV	FV	80.00
	s. Perforated: *SPECIMEN.*	—	—	400.00

184	500 FRANKEN	VG	VF	UNC
	(19)76-92. Brown and m/c. A. von Haller at r. Anatomical muscles of the back, schematic blood circulation and a purple orchid flower on vertical format back.			
	a. 1976 (48, 50, 51).	FV	FV	500.00
	b. 1986 (57, 58, 59).	FV	FV	450.00
	c. 1992 (61, 63, 64).	FV	FV	425.00
	s. Perforated: *SPECIMEN.*	—	—	500.00

185	1000 FRANKEN	VG	VF	UNC
	(19)77-93. Purple on m/c unpt. A. Forel at r. Ants and ant hill on vertical format back.			
	a. 1977 (48, 50, 51).	FV	FV	1000.
	b. 1980 (52, 53, 54); 1984 (53, 54, 55).	FV	FV	900.00
	c. 1987 (57, 58, 59); 1988 (57, 59, 60).	FV	FV	875.00
	d. 1993 (61, 63, 64).	FV	FV	850.00
	s. Perforated: *SPECIMEN.*	—	—	1000.

1994-98 ISSUE; 8TH SERIES

#186-191 vertical format, reduced size. New standard language "Rumantsch Grischun" (Rhaeto-Romanic) text. Many sophisticated security features added.

NOTE: There is a full series of notes (7th Series) of 10 through 1000 Francs held in storage by the SNB in case of extensive forgery. No other information is available.

NOTE: Sign. varieties listed after date.

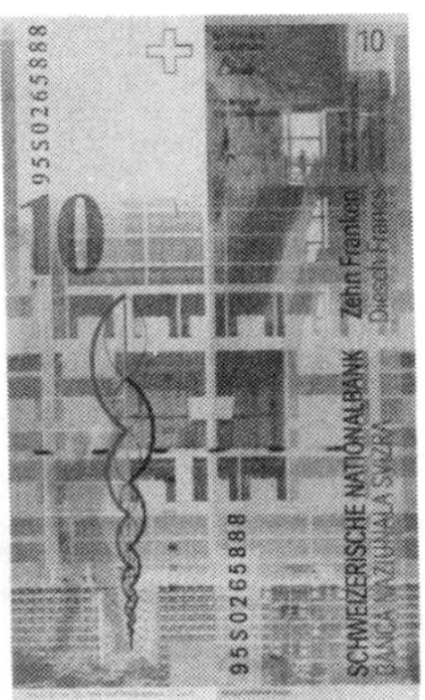

186	10 FRANKEN	VG	VF	UNC
	(19)95 (65, 66, 67). Brown-orange, dk. brown and blue on m/c unpt. Architect Le Corbusier (aka Ch. E. Jeanneret-Gris) at upper l. and bottom ctr. and as wmk. "Modular" measuring system and bldgs. in Chandigarh designed by Le Corbusier on back.	FV	FV	10.00

		VG	VF	UNC
187	**20 FRANKEN** (19)94 (65, 66, 67). Red and green on m/c unpt. Composer A. Honegger at upper l. and bottom ctr. and as wmk. Trumpet valves at top, steam locomotive wheel at ctr., musical score and piano keys at bottom on back.	FV	FV	18.00

		VG	VF	UNC
188	**50 FRANKEN** (19)94 (65, 66, 67). Deep olive-green and purple on m/c unpt. Artist S. Taeuber-Arp at upper l., bottom and as wmk. Examples of her abstract art works on back.	FV	FV	40.00

		VG	VF	UNC
189	**100 FRANKEN** (19)96 (66, 68, 69); (19)97 (66, 68, 69). Dk. blue, purple and brown-orange on m/c unpt. A. Giacometti (artist) at upper l., bottom and as wmk. Bronze bust "Lotar II" at top, sculpture "Homme Qui Marche I" repeated at ctr., time-space relationship scheme at lower ctr. on back.	FV	FV	75.00

		VG	VF	UNC
190	**200 FRANKEN** (19)96 (66, 68, 69). Brown and purple on m/c unpt. Author Ch. F. Ramuz at upper l. and at bottom ctr. and as wmk. Diablerets massif at top, Lavaux area by Lake Geneva repeated at ctr. to bottom w/partial manuscript overlay on back.	FV	FV	160.00
191	**1000 FRANKEN** (19)96 (66, 68, 69). Purple and violet on m/c unpt. J. Burckhardt (art historian) at upper l., bottom and as wmk. Section of the Pergamon Altar at top, the Rotunda of the Pantheon in Rome and a section of the Facade of Palazzo Strozzi in Florence at ctr., overlapped by Burckhardt's view of history scheme on back.	FV	FV	750.00

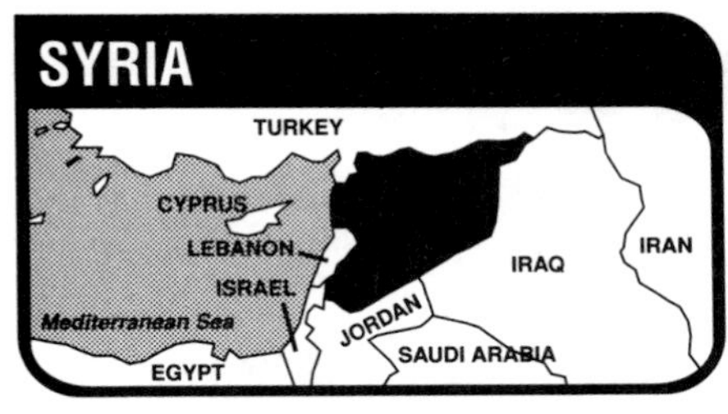

The Syrian Arab Republic, located in the Near East at the eastern end of the Mediterranean Sea, has an area of 71,498 sq. mi. (185,180 sq. km.) and a population of 16.14 million. Capital: Greater Damascus. Agriculture and animal breeding are the chief industries. Cotton, crude oil and livestock are exported.

Ancient Syria, a land bridge connecting Europe, Africa and Asia, has spent much of its history in thrall to the conqueror's whim. Its subjection by Egypt about 1500 BC was followed by successive conquests by the Hebrews, Phoenicians, Babylonians, Assyrians, Persians, Macedonians, Romans, Byzantines and finally, in 636 AD, by the Moslems. The Arabs made Damascus, one of the oldest continuously inhabited cities of the world, the trade center and capital of an empire stretching from India to Spain. In 1517, following the total destruction of Damascus by the Mongols of Tamerlane, Syria fell to the Ottoman Turks and remained a Turkish province until World War I. The League of Nations gave France a mandate to the Levant states of Syria and Lebanon in 1920. In 1930, following a series of uprisings, France recognized Syria as an independent republic, but still subject to the mandate. Lebanon became fully independent on Nov. 22, 1943, and Syria on Jan. 1, 1944.

On Feb. 1, 1958, Egypt and Syria formed the United Arab Republic. Yemen joined on March 8 in an association known as the United Arab States. Syria withdrew from the United Arab Republic on Sept. 29, 1961, and on Dec. 26 Egypt dissolved its ties with Yemen in the United Arab States. Between 1961 and 1970 five coups brought in Lieut. Gen. Hafez el Assad as Prime Minister and in 1973 a new constitution was approved.

MONETARY SYSTEM:

1 Pound (Livre) = 100 Piastres

REPUBLIC

CENTRAL BANK OF SYRIA

1963-66 ISSUE

#93-98 wmk: Arabian horse's head. W/o imprint.

#93-95 worker at r.

93	**1 POUND**	VG	VF	UNC
	1963-82/AH1383-1402. Brown on m/c unpt. Water wheel of Hama on back.			
	a. W/o security thread. 1963/AH1383.	1.00	3.00	10.00
	b. 1967/AH1387.	.60	2.00	6.00
	c. 1973/AH1393.	.25	.75	2.00
	d. Security thread w/*Central Bank of Syria* in sm. letters. 1978/AH1398.	.15	.50	2.00
	e. 1982/AH1402.	.15	.50	2.00
	s. As a. Specimen.	—	—	85.00

94	**5 POUNDS**	VG	VF	UNC
	1963-73/AH1383-93. Green on m/c unpt. Citadel of Aleppo on back.			
	a. 1963/AH1383.	2.50	10.00	40.00
	b. 1967/AH1387.	1.75	6.00	35.00
	c. 1970.	1.00	4.00	25.00
	d. 1973/AH1393.	.50	2.50	20.00

95	**10 POUNDS**	VG	VF	UNC
	1965-73/AH138x-93. Purple on m/c unpt. Courtyard of Omayad Mosque on back.			
	a. 1965.	3.00	8.50	50.00
	b. 1968.	2.00	6.00	40.00
	c. 1973/AH1393.	1.00	3.50	22.50

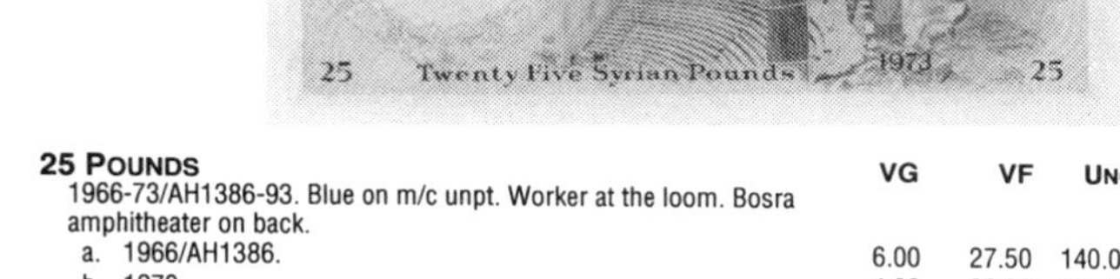

96	**25 POUNDS**	VG	VF	UNC
	1966-73/AH1386-93. Blue on m/c unpt. Worker at the loom. Bosra amphitheater on back.			
	a. 1966/AH1386.	6.00	27.50	140.00
	b. 1970.	4.00	20.00	110.00
	c. 1973/AH1393.	3.00	17.50	85.00

97	**50 POUNDS**	VG	VF	UNC
	1966-73/AH1386-93. Brown and olive-green on m/c unpt. Arab w/agricultural machine at l. Fortress on back.			
	a. 1966/AH1386; 1970.	10.00	30.00	150.00
	b. 1973/AH1393.	5.00	25.00	80.00

98	**100 POUNDS**	VG	VF	UNC
	1966-74/AH1386-139x. Green and blue on m/c unpt. Port installation at l. Back purple; dam at ctr.			
	a. 1966/AH1386.	12.50	40.00	125.00
	b. 1968.	15.00	50.00	150.00
	c. 1971/AH1391.	12.50	40.00	125.00
	d. 1974.	10.00	30.00	90.00

		VG	VF	UNC
99	**1 POUND** 1977/AH1397. Orange and brown on m/c unpt. Omayyad Mosque at ctr., craftsman at r. Back red-brown; cutting wheat at ctr.	1.00	4.00	10.00

		VG	VF	UNC
100	**5 POUNDS** 1977-91/AH1397-1412. Dk. green on m/c unpt. Bosra amphitheater and statue of female warrior at r. Cotton picking and spinning frame on back.			
	a. Security thread. 1977/AH1397.	.75	2.50	7.50
	b. Security thread. W/*Central Bank of Syria* in sm. letters. 1978/AH1398.	FV	FV	4.00
	c. 1982/AH1402.	FV	FV	3.00
	d. 1988/AH1408.	—	—	1.00
	e. 1991/AH1412.	—	—	.45

		VG	VF	UNC
101	**10 POUNDS** 1977-91/AH1397-1412. Purple and violet on m/c unpt. Al-Azem Palace in Damascus at ctr., dancing woman at r. Water treatment plant on back.			
	a. Like #100a. 1977/AH1397.	1.50	4.00	10.00
	b. Like #100b. 1978/AH1398.	FV	FV	3.50
	c. 1982/AH1402.	FV	FV	2.50
	d. 1988/AH1408.	FV	FV	1.00
	e. 1991/AH1412.	FV	FV	.50

		VG	VF	UNC
102	**25 POUNDS** 1977-91/AH1397-1412. Dk. blue and dk. green on m/c unpt. Krak des Chevaliers castle at ctr., Saladdin at r. Central Bank bldg. on back.			
	a. Like #100a. 1977/AH1397.	3.00	8.00	20.00
	b. Like #100b. 1978/AH1398.	FV	1.00	5.00
	c. 1982/AH1402.	FV	FV	4.00
	d. 1988/AH1408.	FV	FV	3.00
	e. 1991/AH1412.	FV	FV	2.00

		VG	VF	UNC
103	**50 POUNDS** 1977-91/AH1397-1412. Brown, black and green on m/c unpt. Dam at ctr., ancient statue at r. Citadel of Aleppo on back.			
	a. Like #100a. 1977/AH1397.	4.50	10.00	25.00
	b. Like #100b. 1978/AH1398.	FV	3.00	12.00
	c. 1982/AH1402.	FV	FV	7.50
	d. 1988/AH1408.	FV	FV	4.50
	e. 1991/AH1412.	FV	FV	2.75

		VG	VF	UNC
104	**100 POUNDS** 1977-90/AH1397-1411. Dk. blue and dk. green on dk. brown on m/c unpt. Ancient Palmyra ruins at ctr., Qn. Zenobia bust at r. Grain silos at Lattakia on back.			
	a. Like #100a. 1977/AH1397.	5.00	15.00	50.00
	b. Like #100b. 1978/AH1398.	FV	6.50	17.50
	c. 1982/AH1402.	FV	FV	9.00
	d. 1990/AH1411.	FV	FV	5.00

		VG	VF	UNC
105	**500 POUNDS** 1976-90/AH1396-1411. Dk. violet-brown and brown on m/c unpt. Like #92.			
	a. 1976/AH1396.	12.50	15.00	60.00
	b. 1979.	15.00	40.00	180.00
	c. 1982/AH1402.	FV	FV	55.00
	d. 1986.	FV	FV	45.00
	e. 1990/AH1411.	FV	FV	32.50
	f. 1992/AH1413.	FV	FV	17.50

1997-98 ISSUE

		VG	VF	UNC
106	**25 POUNDS** 199x/AH141x.	Expected New Issue		
107	**50 POUNDS** 1998/AH1419. Aleppo Citadel at ctr., Al-Assad library and stadium on back.	FV	FV	4.00
108 (106)	**100 POUNDS** 1998/AH1419. Bosra amphitheater at ctr., bust of Philip at r. Hijaz railway locomotive and Damascus station on back.	FV	FV	7.50

		VG	VF	UNC
109	**200 POUNDS** 1997/AH1418. Red and orange on m/c unpt. Omayyad Mosque main entrance, Islamic coin, and clay tablet in ctr, oil industry workers at l. Cotton weaving and energy plant on back.	FV	FV	7.50
110 (108)	**500 POUNDS** 199x/AH141x.	Expected New Issue		

		VG	VF	UNC
111 (109)	**1000 POUNDS** 1997/AH1418. Green, blue and lt. brown on m/c unpt. Hafez Al-Assad at r. Agriculture, industry and services on back.	FV	FV	30.00

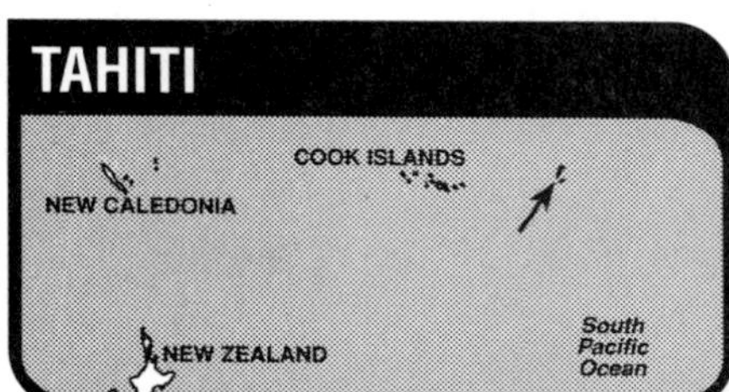

Tahiti, the largest island of the central South Pacific French overseas territory of French Polynesia, has an area of 402 sq. mi. (1,042 sq. km.) and a population of 79,500. Papeete on the northwest coast is the capital and administrative center of French Polynesia. Copra, sugar cane, vanilla and coffee are exported. Tourism is an important industry.

Capt. Samuel Wallis of the British Navy discovered Tahiti in 1768 and named it King George III Island. Louis-Antoine de Bougainville arrived the following year and claimed it for France. Subsequent English visits were by James Cook in 1769 and William Bligh in the HMS "Bounty" in 1788.

Members of the Protestant London Missionary Society established the first European settlement in 1797, and with the aid of the local Pomare family gained control of the entire island and established a "missionary kingdom" with a scriptural code of law. Nevertheless, Tahiti was subsequently declared a French protectorate (1842) and a colony (1880), and since 1958 is part of the overseas territory of French Polynesia.

RULERS:
French

MONETARY SYSTEM:
1 Franc = 100 Centimes

SIGNATURE/TITLE VARIETIES

	DIRECTEUR GÉNÉRAL	PREÉSIDENT DU CONSEIL DE SURVEILLANCE
1	André POSTEL-VINAY 1967-1972	Bernard CLAPPIER 1966-1972
2	Claude PANOUILLOT , 1972-1973	André DE LATTRE 1973
3	Claude PANOUILLOT 1974-1978	Marcel THERON 1974-1979
4	Yves ROLAND-BILLECART 1979-1984	Gabriel LEFORT 1980-1984
5	Yves ROLAND-BILLECART, 1985-	Jacques WAITZENEGGER, 1985-

FRENCH INFLUENCE
BANQUE DE L'INDOCHINE
PAPEETE BRANCH

1939-40 ND ISSUE

		GOOD	FINE	XF
14	**100 FRANCS** ND (1939-65). Brown and m/c. woman wearing wreath and holding sm. figure of Athena at ctr. Angkor statue on back.			
	a. Sign. M. Borduge and P. Baudouin w/titles: *LE PRÉSIDENT* and *LE ADMINISTRATEUR DIRECTEUR GÉNÉRAL.*	6.00	20.00	60.00
	b. Sign. titles: *LE PRÉSIDENT* and *LE ADMINISTRATEUR DIRECTEUR GÉNÉRAL.*	5.00	17.50	50.00
	c. Sign. titles: *LE PRÉSIDENT* and *LE VICE-PRÉSIDENT DIRECTEUR GÉNÉRAL.*	4.00	15.00	35.00
	d. Sign. titles: *LE PRÉSIDENT* and *LE DIRECTEUR GÉNÉRAL.*	3.00	12.50	27.50

1951 ND ISSUE

		VG	VF	UNC
21	**20 FRANCS** ND (1951-63). M/c. Youth at l., flute player at r. Fruit at l., woman at r. on back. Wmk: Man w/hat.			
	a. Sign. titles: *LE PRÉSIDENT* and *LE DIRECTEUR GAL.* (1951).	3.50	9.00	35.00
	b. Sign. titles: *LE PRÉSIDENT* and *LE VICE-PRÉSIDENT DIRECTEUR GÉNÉRAL* (1954-1958).	1.50	6.00	20.00
	c. Sign. titles: *LE PRÉSIDENT* and *LE DIRECTEUR GÉNÉRAL.* (1963).	1.25	5.00	15.00

Institut d'Emission d'Outre-Mer

Papeete Branch

1969-71 ND Issues

#		VG	VF	Unc
23	**100 Francs** ND (1969). Brown and m/c. Girl wearing wreath holding guitar at r., w/o *REPUBLIQUE FRANCAISE* near bottom ctr. Girl at l., town scene at ctr. on back. Sign. 1. Printed from engraved copper plates.	3.00	10.00	65.00

#		VG	VF	Unc
24	**100 Francs** ND. (1971; 1973). M/c. Like #23 but w/ovpt: *REPUBLIQUE FRANCAISE* at bottom ctr. Sign. 1.			
	a. Printed from engraved copper plates. (1971).	1.00	4.50	32.50
	b. Offset printing. (1973).	1.00	4.00	25.00

#		VG	VF	Unc
25	**500 Francs** ND (1970-83). Blue and m/c. Harbor view w/boat in background at ctr., fisherman at lower r. Man at l., objects at r. on back.			
	a. Sign. 1. (1970).	FV	7.50	32.50
	b. Sign. 3. (1977).	FV	7.00	27.50
	c. Sign. 4. (1983).	FV	7.00	22.50
	d. Sign. 5. (1985).	FV	7.00	15.00

#		VG	VF	Unc
26	**1000 Francs** ND (1969). Dk. brown on red and m/c unpt. Hut under palms at l., girl at r. W/o *REPUBLIQUE FRANCAISE* ovpt. at bottom ctr. Birds, animals, bldgs., native carvings on back. Wmk: Marianne. Sign. 1.	12.00	35.00	165.00

#		VG	VF	Unc
27	**1000 Francs** ND (1971; 1983). Dk. brown on m/c unpt. Like #26 but w/ovpt: *REPUBLIQUE FRANCAISE* at lower l.			
	a. Sign. 1. (1971).	FV	12.50	32.50
	b. Sign. 3. (1977).	FV	12.50	27.50
	c. Sign. 4. (1983).	FV	12.50	27.50
	d. Sign. 5. (1985).	FV	FV	20.00

#		VG	VF	Unc
28	**5000 Francs** ND (1971-84). Brown w/black text on olive-green and m/c unpt. Bougainville at l., sailing ships at ctr. Admiral Febvrier-Despointes at r., sailboat at ctr. r. on back.			
	a. Sign. 1. (1971).	FV	65.00	165.00
	b. Sign. 2. (1975).	FV	62.50	135.00
	c. Sign. 4. (1982; 1984).	FV	60.00	120.00
	d. Sign. 5. (1985).	FV	60.00	100.00

The Republic of Tajikistan (Tadjiquistan), was formed from those regions of Bukhara and Turkestan where the population consisted mainly of Tajiks. It is bordered in the north and west by Uzbekistan and Kyrgyzstan, in the east by China and in the south by Afghanistan. It has an area of 55,240 sq. miles (143,100 sq. km.) and a population of 5.95 million. It includes 2 provinces of Khudzand and Khatlon together with the Gorno-Badakhshan Autonomous Region with a population of 5,092,603. Capital: Dushanbe. Tajikistan was admitted as a constituent republic of the Soviet Union on Dec. 5, 1929. In Aug. 1990 the Tajik Supreme Soviet adopted a declaration of republican sovereignty, and in Dec. 1991 the republic became a member of the CIS.

After demonstrations and fighting, the Communist government was replaced by a Revolutionary Coalition Council on May 7, 1992. Following further demonstrations President Nabiev was ousted on Sept. 7, 1992. Civil war broke out, and the government resigned on Nov. 10, 1992. On Nov. 30, 1992 it was announced that a CIS peacekeeping force would be sent to Tajikistan. A state of emergency was imposed in Jan. 1993. A ceasefire was signed in 1996 and a peace agreement signed in June 1997.

MONETARY SYSTEM:

1 Ruble = 100 Tanga

REPUBLIC

БОНКИ МИЛЛИИ ЧУМХУРИИ ТОЧИКИСТОН

NATIONAL BANK OF THE REPUBLIC OF TAJIKISTAN

1994 ISSUE

#1-8 arms at upper l. or l. Bldg. w/flag at ctr. r. on back. Wmk: Multiple stars.

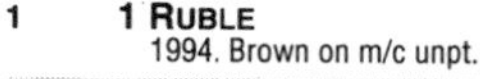

		VG	VF	UNC
1	**1 RUBLE** 1994. Brown on m/c unpt.	FV	FV	.40

		VG	VF	UNC
2	**5 RUBLES** 1994. Deep blue on m/c unpt.	FV	FV	.65

		VG	VF	UNC
3	**10 RUBLES** 1994. Deep red on m/c unpt.	FV	FV	1.00

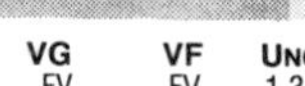

		VG	VF	UNC
4	**20 RUBLES** 1994. Purple on m/c unpt.	FV	FV	1.35

		VG	VF	UNC
5	**50 RUBLES** 1994. Dk. olive-green on m/c unpt.	FV	FV	2.50

		VG	VF	UNC
6	**100 RUBLES** 1994. Blue-black and brown on m/c unpt.	FV	FV	3.75

		VG	VF	UNC
7	**200 RUBLES** 1994. Deep olive-green and pale violet on m/c unpt.	FV	FV	8.00

		VG	VF	UNC
8	**500 RUBLES** 1994. Brown-violet on m/c unpt.	FV	FV	16.50
9	**1000 RUBLES** 1999. M/c.	FV	FV	30.00

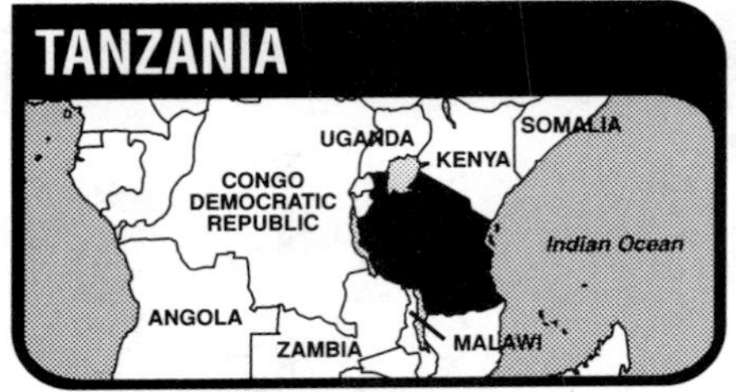

The United Republic of Tanzania, located on the east coast of Africa between Kenya and Mozambique, consists of Tanganyika and the islands of Zanzibar and Pemba. It has an area of 364,900 sq. mi. (945,090 sq. km.) and a population of 29.5 million. Capital: Dar es Salaam (Haven of Peace). The chief exports are cotton, coffee, diamonds, sisal, cloves, petroleum products and cashew nuts.

German East Africa (Tanganyika), located on the coast of east-central Africa between British East Africa (now Kenya) and Portuguese East Africa (now Mozambique), had an area of 362,284 sq. mi. (938,216 sq. km.) and a population of about 6 million. Capital: Dar es Salaam. Chief products prior to German control were ivory and slaves; after German control, sisal, coffee and rubber. Germany acquired control of the area by treaties with coastal chiefs in 1884, established it as a protectorate in 1891, and proclaimed it the Colony of German East Africa in 1897. After World War I, Tanganyika was entrusted to Great Britain as a League of Nations mandate, and after World War II as a United Nations trust territory. Tanganyika became an independent nation within the British Commonwealth on Dec. 9, 1961.

The British Protectorate of Zanzibar and Pemba, and adjacent small islands, located in the Indian Ocean 22 miles (35 km.) off the coast of Tanganyika, comprised a portion of British East Africa. Zanzibar was also the name of a sultanate which included the Zanzibar and Kenya protectorates. Zanzibar has an area of 637 sq. mi. (1,651 sq. km.). Chief city: Zanzibar. Pemba has an area of 380 sq. mi. (984 sq. km.). Chief city: Chake Chake. The islands are noted for their cloves, of which Zanzibar is the world's foremost producer.

Zanzibar and Pemba share a common history. Zanzibar came under Portuguese control in 1503, was conquered by the Omani Arabs in 1698, became independent of Oman in 1860, and (with Pemba) came under British control in 1890. Britain granted the protectorate self-government in 1961, and independence within the British Commonwealth on Dec. 19, 1963. On April 26, 1964, Tanganyika and Zanzibar (with Pemba) united to form the United Republic of Tanganyika and Zanzibar. The name of the country was changed to Tanzania on Oct. 29, 1964. The president is Chief of State.

Also see East Africa and Zanzibar, (Vol. 2).

MONETARY SYSTEM:

1 Shilingi (Shilling) = 100 Senti

REPUBLIC

BANK OF TANZANIA

SIGNATURE VARIETIES

	MINISTER FOR FINANCE	GOVERNOR		MINISTER FOR FINANCE	GOVERNOR
1			2		
3			4		
5			6	WAZIRI WA FEDHA	GAVANA
7	WAZIRI WA FEDHA	GAVANA	8		
9			10		
11			12		

1966 ND ISSUE

NOTE: Sign. 3-5 w/English titles on #2 and 3, changed to Swahili titles for later issues.

#1-5 arms at ctr., Pres. J. Nyerere at r. Wmk: Giraffe's head. Replacement notes: Serial # prefix *ZZ; ZY*.

NOTICE

Readers with unlisted dates, signature varieties, etc. are invited to submit photocopies of their notes to: Standard Catalog of World Paper Money, 700 East State St. Iola, WI 54990-0001, fax: 1-715-445-4087, or E-Mail: thernr@krause.com.

1	**5 SHILLINGS**	VG	VF	UNC
	ND (1966). Brown on m/c unpt. Sign. 1. Mountain view on back.	1.00	3.00	11.50

2	**10 SHILLINGS**	VG	VF	UNC
	ND (1966). Green on m/c unpt. Sisal drying on back.			
	a. Sign. 1.	1.50	3.00	7.50
	b. Sign. 2.	2.00	4.00	10.00
	c. Sign. 3.	7.50	30.00	185.00
	d. Sign. 4.	1.00	2.00	7.50
	e. Sign. 5.	1.00	2.00	6.00

3	**20 SHILLINGS**	VG	VF	UNC
	ND (1966). Blue on m/c unpt. Work bldgs. on back.			
	a. Sign. 1.	2.00	5.00	12.50
	b. Sign. 2.	2.00	5.00	12.50
	c. Sign. 3.	3.00	7.00	17.50
	d. Sign. 4.	2.00	5.00	12.50
	e. Sign. 5.	1.50	3.00	11.00

4	**100 SHILLINGS**	VG	VF	UNC
	ND (1966). Red on m/c unpt. Masai herdsman w/animals on back. Sign. 1.	15.00	50.00	300.00

		VG	VF	UNC
5	**100 SHILLINGS** ND (1966). Red on m/c unpt. Various animals on back.			
	a. Sign. 1.	15.00	50.00	275.00
	b. Sign. 3.	10.00	40.00	225.00

BENKI KUU YA TANZANIA

1977-78 ND ISSUE

#6-8 arms at top ctr., Pres. J. Nyerere at r. Wmk: Giraffe's head. Replacement notes: Serial # prefix *ZZ; ZY*.

NOTE: For #6-8, sign. are shown in chronological order of appearance. It seems sign. 3 was used again following several later combinations.

		VG	VF	UNC
6	**10 SHILINGI** ND (1978). Green on m/c unpt. Monument and mountain at ctr. on back.			
	a. Sign. 5.	.25	1.50	4.00
	b. Sign. 6.	.25	1.00	3.00
	c. Sign. 3.	.25	.75	2.25

		VG	VF	UNC
7	**20 SHILINGI** ND (1978). Blue on m/c unpt. Cotton knitting machine on back.			
	a. Sign. 5.	.50	2.50	6.50
	b. Sign. 6.	.50	2.25	4.50
	c. Sign. 3.	.50	2.25	5.50

		VG	VF	UNC
8	**100 SHILINGI** ND (1977). Purple on m/c unpt. Teacher and students at l., farmers at ctr. on back.			
	a. Sign. 4.	2.50	8.00	25.00
	b. Sign. 5.	2.00	7.00	20.00
	c. Sign. 6.	2.00	6.50	17.50
	d. Sign. 3.	1.50	6.00	15.00

1985 ND ISSUE

#9-11 portr. of an older Pres. J. Nyerere at r., torch at l., arms at ctr. Islands of Mafia, Pemba and Zanzibar are omitted from map on back. Sign. 3. Wmk: Giraffe's head. Replacement notes: Serial # prefix *ZZ; ZY*.

		VG	VF	UNC
9	**20 SHILINGI** ND (1985). Purple, brown on m/c unpt. Tire factory scene on back.	.15	.50	3.00

		VG	VF	UNC
10	**50 SHILINGI** ND (1985). Red-orange, lt. brown on m/c unpt. Brick making on back.	.30	1.50	6.00

		VG	VF	UNC
11	**100 SHILINGI** ND (1985). Blue, purple on m/c unpt. Graduation procession on back.	.50	3.00	10.00

1986 ND ISSUE

#12-14 like #9-11 but w/islands of Mafia, Pemba and Zanzibar now included in map on back. Replacement notes: Serial # prefix *ZZ; ZY*.

		VG	VF	UNC
12	**20 SHILINGI** ND (1986). Like #9 but w/islands in map on back. Sign. 3.	.15	.60	2.25

		VG	VF	UNC
13	**50 SHILINGI** ND (1986). Like #10 but w/islands in map on back. Sign. 3.	.25	1.00	4.50

		VG	VF	UNC
14	**100 SHILINGI** ND (1986). Like #11 but w/islands in map on back.			
	a. Sign. 3 w/titles: *WAZIRI WA FEDHA* and *GAVANA*.	.50	2.00	6.75
	b. Sign. 8.	.25	1.25	6.25

1986-90 ND ISSUE

#15-18 arms at ctr., Pres. Mwinyi at r. Wmk: Giraffe's head. Replacement notes: Serial # prefix *ZZ; ZY*.

		VG	VF	UNC
15	**20 SHILINGI** ND (1987). Purple, red-brown on m/c unpt. Back like #12. Sign. 3 but w/titles: *WAZIRI WA FEDHA* and *GAVANA*.	.10	.40	3.00

		VG	VF	UNC
16	**50 SHILINGI** ND (1986). Red-orange, lt. brown on m/c unpt. Back like #13.			
	a. Sign. 3 but w/titles: *WAZIRI WA FEDHA* and *GAVANA*.	.30	1.00	5.00
	b. Sign. 7.	.20	.75	3.00

		VG	VF	UNC
18	**200 SHILINGI** ND (1986). Black, orange and ochre on m/c unpt. 2 fishermen on back.			
	a. Sign. 3 but w/titles: *WAZIRI WA FEDHA* and *GAVANA*.	.50	2.00	6.50
	b. Sign. 7.	.65	2.25	8.00

1989-92 ND ISSUE

#19-22 similar to #16 and #18 but w/modified portr. Wmk: Giraffe's head. Replacement notes: Serial # prefix *ZZ; ZY*.

		VG	VF	UNC
19	**50 SHILINGI** ND (1992). Red-orange and lt. brown on m/c unpt. Sign. 8.	.10	.50	1.75

		VG	VF	UNC
20	**200 SHILINGI** ND (1992). Black, orange and ochre on m/c unpt. Sign. 8.	.50	1.50	6.00

		VG	VF	UNC
21	**500 SHILINGI** ND (1989). Dk. blue on m/c unpt. Zebra at lower l. Harvesting on back.			
	a. Sign. 3 but w/titles: *WAZIRI WA FEDHA* and *GAVANA*.	2.50	10.00	37.50
	b. Sign. 7.	1.50	5.00	15.00
	c. Sign. 8.	1.25	3.00	12.50

		VG	VF	UNC
22	**1000 SHILINGI** ND (1990). Green, brown on m/c unpt. Elephants at lower l. Kiwira Coal Mine at l. ctr., door to the Peoples Bank of Zanzibar at lower r. on back. Sign. 8.	2.50	6.00	22.50

1993; 1995 ND ISSUE

#23, 25-27 arms at ctr., Pres. Mwinyi at r. Wmk: Giraffe's head. Reduced size. Replacement notes: Serial # prefix *ZZ; ZY*.

		VG	VF	UNC
23	**50 SHILINGI** ND (1993). Red-orange, brown on m/c unpt. Animal grazing at l. Men making bricks on back. Sign. 9.	FV	FV	2.00

		VG	VF	UNC
24	**100 SHILINGI** ND (1993). Blue, aqua on m/c unpt. Kudu at l., arms at ctr., J. Nyerere at r. Graduation procession on back. Sign. 9.	FV	FV	2.75

		VG	VF	UNC
25	**200 SHILINGI** ND (1993). Black and orange on m/c unpt. Leopards at l. Back similar to #18.			
	a. Sign. 9.	FV	FV	3.50
	b. Sign. 11.	FV	FV	3.00

		VG	VF	UNC
26	**500 SHILINGI** ND (1993). Purple, blue-green and violet on m/c unpt. Zebra at lower l. Back similar to #21 w/arms at lower r.			
	a. Sign. 9.	FV	FV	8.00
	b. Sign. 10.	FV	FV	5.00
	c. Sign. 11.	FV	FV	4.50

		VG	VF	UNC
27	**1000 SHILINGI** ND (1993). Dk. green, brown and orange-brown on m/c unpt. Similar to #22.			
	a. Sign. 9.	FV	FV	12.50
	b. Sign. 10.	FV	FV	10.00
	c. Sign. 11.	FV	FV	7.50

		VG	VF	UNC
28	**5000 SHILINGI** ND (1995). Brown on m/c unpt. Giraffes w/Mt. Kilimanjaro in background on back.			
	a. Sign. 10.	FV	FV	27.50
	b. Sign. 11.	Reported Not Confirmed		
29	**10,000 SHILINGI** ND (1995). M/c. Lion at lower l.			
	a. Sign. 10.	FV	FV	48.50
	b. Sign. 11.	Reported Not Confirmed		

1997 ND ISSUE

#30-33 arms at upper ctr., giraffe's head at r. and as wmk. Sign. 12.

		VG	VF	UNC
30	**500 SHILINGI** ND (1997). Blue-black and dk. green on m/c unpt. Zebra at lower l., woman harvesting cloves at l. ctr. on back.	FV	FV	3.00

		VG	VF	UNC
31	**1000 SHILINGI** ND (1997). Deep olive-green, red-orange and dk. brown on m/c unpt. Elephants at lower l. Industrial bldgs. at l. ctr., door to the Peoples Bank of Zanzibar at lower r. on back.	FV	FV	6.00

		VG	VF	UNC
32	**5000 SHILINGI** ND (1997). Dk. brown and purple on m/c unpt. Rhinoceros at lower l. Giraffes w/Mt. Kilimanjaro in background on back. Segmented foil over security thread.	FV	FV	25.00

		VG	VF	UNC
33	**10,000 SHILINGI** ND (1997). Blue-black and dk. gray on m/c unpt. Lion at lower l. Vertical foil strip at r. Bank of Tanzania Head Office bldg. at l. ctr., Zanzibar House of Wonder at lower r. on back.	FV	FV	50.00

Tatarstan, an autonomous republic in the Russian Federation, is situated between the middle of the Volga River and its tributary Kama, extends east to the Ural mountains, covering 26,500 sq. mi. (68,000 sq. km.) and as of the 1970 census has a population of 3,743,600. Captial: Kazan. Tatarstan's economy combines its ancient traditions in the craftsmanship of wood, leather, cloth and ceramics with modern engineering, chemical, and food industries.

Colonized by the Bulgars in the 5th century, the territory of the Volga-Kama Bulgar State was inhabited by Turks. In the 13th century, Ghengis Khan conquered the area and established control until the 15th century when residual Mongol influence left Tatarstan as the Tatar Khanate, seat of the Kazar (Tatar) Khans. In 1552, under Ivan IV (the Terrible), Russia conquered, absorbed and controlled Tatarstan until the dissolution of the U.S.S.R. in the late 20th century.

Constituted as an autonomous republic on May 27, 1990, and as a sovereign state equal with Russia in April, 1992, Tatarstan, with Russia's president, signed a treaty in February, 1994, defining Tatarstan as a state united with Russia (Commonwealth of Independent States), but this has yet to be ratified by Russia's parliament.

MONETARY SYSTEM:

1 Ruble = 100 Kopeks

ТАТАРСКАЯ С.С.Р.

REPUBLIC OF TATARSTAN

TREASURY

1992 ND КУРОН - RUBLE CONTROL COUPON ISSUES

#1-3 red and green stripes w/black ТАТАРСКАЯ repeated on back.

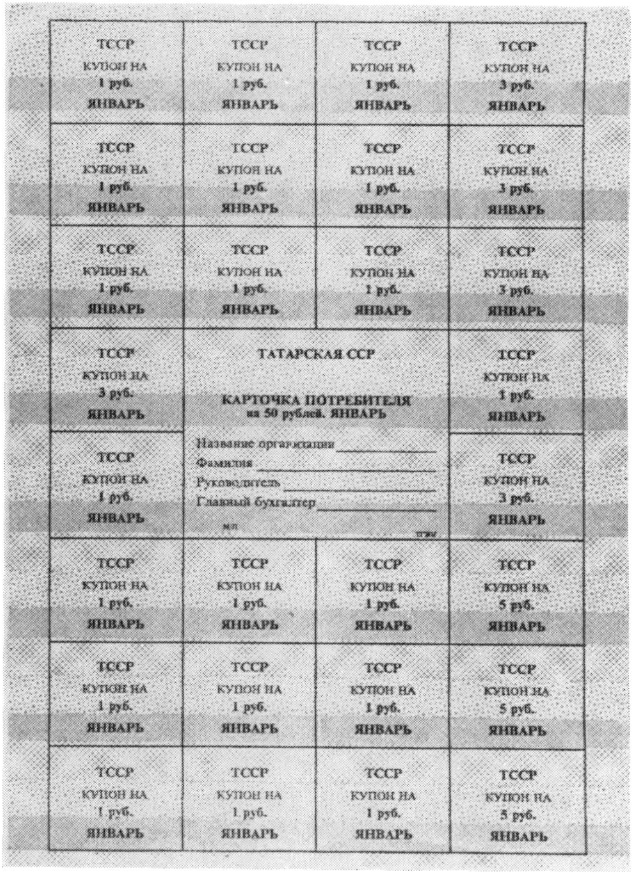

		VG	VF	UNC
1	**50 RUBLES** ND (1992). Black text on green unpt. w/month: ЯНВАРЬ (January).			
	a. Issued full sheet.	4.50	10.00	16.00
	b. Remainder full sheet.	2.50	6.00	10.00
	c. Coupon.	.05	.20	.50
2	**50 RUBLES** ND (1992). Black text on pink unpt. w/month: ФЕВЯАЛЬ (February).			
	a. Issued full sheet.	4.00	8.00	14.00
	b. Remainder full sheet.	2.00	5.00	9.00
	c. Coupon.	.05	.20	.50
3	**50 RUBLES** ND (1992). Black text on blue unpt. w/month: МАРТ (March).			
	a. Issued full sheet.	3.00	8.00	14.00
	b. Remainder full sheet.	1.50	4.50	8.00
	c. Coupon.	.05	.20	.50

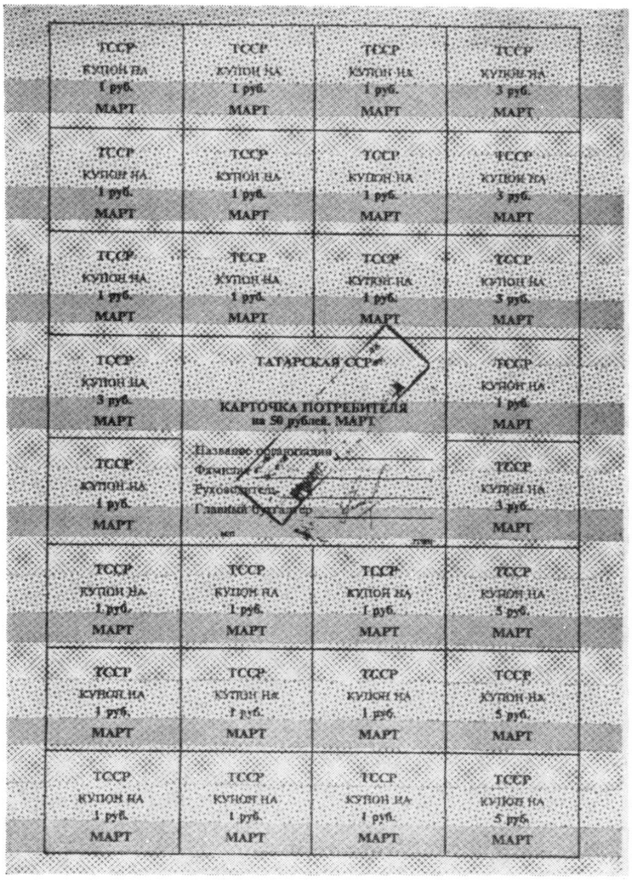

GOVERNMENT

1993 PRIVATIZATION CHECK ISSUE

		VG	VF	UNC
4A	**30,000 RUBLES** 1993. Black text on green unpt. Arms w/number. Back black text on white. Printer: USBN.			
	a. Issued note. W/registration and w/o privatization book.	—	25.00	40.00
	b. Issued note. W/registration and w/privatization book.	—	40.00	80.00
	c. Not issued. All w/coupons and w/o registration.	—	—	50.00
4B	**40,000 RUBLES** 1993. Black text on green. Arms w/number. Back black text on white. Printer: USBN.			
	a. Issued note. W/registration and w/o privatization book.	—	18.50	30.00
	b. Issued note. W/registration and w/privatization book.	—	30.00	50.00
	c. Not issued. All w/coupons and w/o registration.	—	—	50.00

NOTICE

Readers with unlisted dates, signature varieties, etc. are invited to submit photocopies of their notes to: Standard Catalog of World Paper Money, 700 East State St. Iola, WI 54990-0001, fax: 1-715-445-4087, or E-Mail: thernr@krause.com.

4C (4) 60,000 RUBLES
1993. Black text on green unpt. Arms w/number. Back black text on white. Printer: USBN (w/o imprint).

	VG	VF	UNC
a. Issued note. W/registration and w/o privatization book.	—	20.00	35.00
b. Issued note. W/registration and w/privatization book.	—	35.00	60.00
c. Not issued. All w/coupons and w/o registration.	—	—	50.00

4D 80,000 RUBLES
1993. Black text on green. Arms w/number. Back black text on white. Printer: USBN.

	VG	VF	UNC
a. Issued note. W/registration and w/o privatization book.	—	25.00	40.00
b. Issued note. W/registration and w/privatization book.	—	40.00	75.00
c. Not issued. All w/coupons and w/o registration.	—	—	50.00

4E 90,000 RUBLES
1993. Black text on green. Arms w/number. Black text on white. Printer: USBN.

	VG	VF	UNC
a. Issued note. W/registration and w/o privatization book.	—	30.00	50.00
b. Issued note. W/registration and w/privatization book.	—	40.00	80.00
c. Not issued. All w/coupons and w/o registration.	—	—	50.00

4F 100,000 RUBLES
1993. Black text on green. Arms w/number. Black text on white. Printer: USBN.

	VG	VF	UNC
a. Issued note. W/registration and w/o privatization book.	—	35.00	60.00
b. Issued note. W/registration and w/privatization book.	—	45.00	85.00
c. Not issued. All w/coupons and w/o registration.	—	—	—

1991; 1993 ND FIRST CURRENCY CHECK ISSUE

#5 and 6 state flag inside circle at l., stylized image of old castle Suumbeky in Kazan (ca. 16th century) in ornate frame at r. Uniface.

5 (100 RUBLES)
ND (1991-92). Blue-gray. 138 x 66mm. Wmk: Lozenges.

	VG	VF	UNC
a. Gray unpt.	—	10.00	25.00
b. Red unpt.	—	12.50	40.00
c. Yellow unpt.	—	12.50	40.00
d. Orange unpt.	—	12.50	40.00

NOTE: Issued statewide. Checks probably printed in 1991, as coat of arms was accepted later than flag, but issued to circulation in 1992.

6 (100 RUBLES)
ND (1993). Red and green arms at l., stylized image of old castle Suumbeky in ornate frame at r. Wmk: Lozenges. Uniface.

	VG	VF	UNC
a. Gray unpt.	—	10.00	20.00
b. Violet on pink unpt.	—	8.00	15.00
c. Dk. blue on pale blue unpt.	—	10.00	20.00
d. Brown unpt.	—	8.00	15.00
e. Olive-green unpt.	—	10.00	20.00

NOTE: Issued for circulation in Kazan.

1994 ND SECOND CURRENCY CHECK ISSUE

7 (200 RUBLES)
ND (1994). Medical emblem inside oval at r., stylized image of old castle Suumbeky in Kazan (ca. 16th century) at l. 105 x 53mm. Wmk: Lozenges. Uniface.

	VG	VF	UNC
a. Blue-black and pale blue on m/c unpt.	FV	8.00	12.50
b. Deep olive-green and green on tan and pale green unpt.	FV	8.00	12.50

NOTE: Circulated in the republic from 3.10.1994 to 1.7.1995.

1993-95 ND THIRD CURRENCY CHECK ISSUE

#8-12 arms at top ctr., Kazan Kremlin (ca. 16th century) at lower l., Arabic *Tatar* at r.

#8-11 wmk.: Mosaic.

		VG	VF	UNC
8	**(500 RUBLES)** ND (1993). Red on m/c unpt. Women feeding geese on back. 105 x 53mm.	FV	5.00	9.00

		VG	VF	UNC
9	**(500 RUBLES)** ND (1993). Green on m/c unpt. Horses galloping at ctr. on back. 105 x 53mm.	FV	5.00	9.00
10	**(1000 RUBLES)** ND (1994). Pink on m/c unpt. Gulls flying over raging waves on back. 105 x 53mm.	FV	5.00	9.00
11	**(1000 RUBLES)** ND (1995). Blue on m/c unpt. Deer at watering hole on back. 105 x 53mm.	FV	5.00	9.00

NOTE: Checks #8-11 found in circulation before Aug. 1996.

1996 ND FOURTH CURRENCY CHECK ISSUE

12 (50 SHAMIL = 5000 RUBLES)
ND (1996). Kazan Kremlin (ca. 16th century) w/English and Russian text "Tatarstan" in frame below. Women from national epic on back. 135 x 65mm. Wmk: Lt. lines.

	VG	VF	UNC
a. Dk. blue on pale blue-gray unpt.	FV	4.50	8.00
b. Deep green on pale green unpt.	FV	6.00	10.00

NOTE: Check #12 found in circulation from Aug. 1996 to this day.

The Kingdom of Thailand (formerly Siam), a constitutional monarchy located in the center of mainland southeast Asia between Burma and Laos, has an area of 198,457 sq. mi. (514,000 sq. km.) and a population of 59.45 million. Capital: Bangkok. The economy is based on agriculture and mining. Rubber, rice, teakwood, tin and tungsten are exported.

The history of Thailand, the only country in south and southeast Asia that was never colonized by an European power, dates from the 6th century AD when tribes of the Thai stock migrated into the area from the Asiatic continent, a process that accelerated with the Mongol invasion of China in the 13th century. After 400 years of sporadic warfare with the neighboring Burmese, King Taksin won the last battle in 1767. He founded a new capital, Dhonburi, on the west bank of Chao Praya River. King Rama I moved the capital to Bangkok in 1782.

The Thai were introduced to the Western world by the Portuguese, who were followed by the Dutch, British and French. Rama III of the present ruling dynasty negotiated a treaty of friendship and commerce with Britain in 1826, and in 1896 the independence of the kingdom was guaranteed by an Anglo-French accord. The absolute monarchy was changed into a constitutional monarchy in 1932.

In 1909 Siam ceded to Great Britain its suzerain rights over the dependencies of Kedah, Kelantan, Trengganu and Perlis, Malay states situated in southern Siam just north of British Malaya. This eliminated any British jurisdiction in Siam proper.

On Dec. 8, 1941, after five hours of fighting, Thailand agreed to permit Japanese troops passage through the country to invade northern British Malaya. This eventually led to increased Japanese intervention and finally occupation of the country. On Jan. 25, 1942, Thailand declared war on Great Britain and the United States. A free Thai guerrilla movement was soon organized to counteract the Japanese. In July 1943, Japan transferred the four northern Malay States back to Thailand. These were returned to Great Britain after peace treaties were signed in 1946.

RULERS:

Rama IX (Bhumiphol Adulyadej), 1946-

MONETARY SYSTEM:

1 Baht (Tical) = 100 Satang

SIGNATURE VARIETIES

	MINISTER OF FINANCE รัฐมนตรีว่าการกระทรวงการคลัง	GOVERNOR OF THE BANK OF THAILAND ผู้ว่าการธนาคารแห่งประเทศไทย
34		
35		
36		
37		
38		
39	Chote Kvnakasem -no error-	Chote Kvnakasem
40		
41	S. Vinichchaikul	Puey Ungpakorn
42	S. Vinichchaikul	Bisudhi Nimmanhaemin
43	Boonma Wongsesawan**	Bisudhi Nimmanhaemin
44	Sommai Hoontrakul	Bisudhi Nimmanhaemin
45	Sawet Piempongsarn	Bisudhi Nimmanhaemin
46	Boonchu Rojanasathien	Bisudhi Nimmanhaemin
47	Boonchu Rojanasathien	Sanoh Unakul
48	Sawet Piempongsarn	Sanoh Unakul
	MINISTER OF FINANCE รัฐมนตรีว่าการกระทรวงการคลัง	GOVERNOR OF THE BANK OF THAILAND ผู้ว่าการธนาคารแห่งประเทศไทย
49	Suphat Suthatham	Sanoh Unakul
50	Gen. K. Chomanan	Sanoh Unakul
51	Gen. K. Chomanan	Nukul Prachuabmoh
52	Amnuey Virawan	Nukul Prachuabmoh
53	Sommai Hoontrakul	Nukul Prachuabmoh
54	Sommai Hoontrakul	Kamchorn Sathirakul
55	Suthee Singsaneh	Kamchorn Sathirakul
56	Pramual Sabhavasu	Kamchorn Sathirakul
57	Pramual Sabhavasu	Chavalit Thanachanan
57a	Virabongsa Ramangkul	Chavalit Thanachanan
58	Virabongsa Ramangkul	Vigit Supinit
59	Baham Silpa-acha	Vigit Supinit
60	Suthee Singsaneh	Vigit Supinit
61		Vigit Supinit

**signed as Undersecretary/Deputy Finance Minister

62	Panat Sumasathien	Vigit Supinit
63	Tharin Nimanhaemin	Vigit Supinit
64	Sukariart Satirathai	Vigit Supinit
65	Bhodi Joonanord	Vigit Supinit
66	Bhodi Joonanord	Rerngchai Marakanond
67	Amnuey Virawan	Rerngchai Marakanond
68	Thanon Pithaya	Rerngchai Marakanond
69	Thanon Pithaya	Chaiwat Viboon
70	Kasit Pampiern	Chaiwat Viboon
71	Tharin Nimanhaemin	Chaiwat Viboon

KINGDOM

GOVERNMENT OF THAILAND

1953-56 ND ISSUE

#74-78 slightly modified Kg. in Field Marshall's uniform w/collar insignia and 3 decorations. Black serial #. Printer: TDLR.

Small letters in 2-line text on back.

Large letters in 2-line text on back.

		VG	VF	UNC
74	**1 BAHT** ND (1955). Blue on m/c unpt. Like #69.			
	a. Wmk: Constitution. Red and blue security threads. Sign. 34.	.20	1.00	6.00
	b. Wmk: Constitution. Metal security strip. Sign. 34; 35 (lg. size).	.20	1.00	5.00
	c. Wmk: Kg. profile. Sm. letters in 2-line text on back. Sign. 35.	.20	1.00	5.00
	d. Wmk: Kg. profile. Larger letters in 2-line text on back. Sign. 36; 37; 38; 39; 40; 4l.	.10	.75	4.00

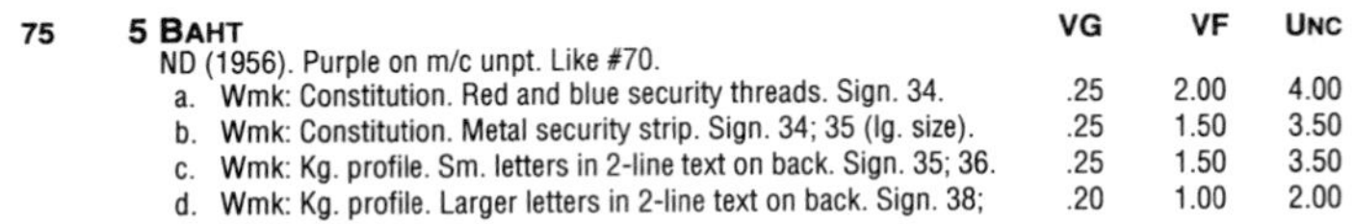

		VG	VF	UNC
75	**5 BAHT** ND (1956). Purple on m/c unpt. Like #70.			
	a. Wmk: Constitution. Red and blue security threads. Sign. 34.	.25	2.00	4.00
	b. Wmk: Constitution. Metal security strip. Sign. 34; 35 (lg. size).	.25	1.50	3.50
	c. Wmk: Kg. profile. Sm. letters in 2-line text on back. Sign. 35; 36.	.25	1.50	3.50
	d. Wmk: Kg. profile. Larger letters in 2-line text on back. Sign. 38; 39; 40; 41.	.20	1.00	2.00

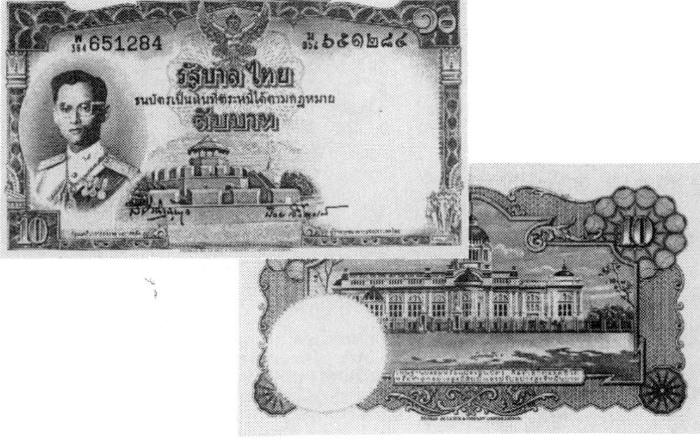

		VG	VF	UNC
76	**10 BAHT** ND (1953). Brown on m/c unpt. Like #71.			
	a. Wmk: Constitution. Red and blue security threads. Sign. 34.	.50	3.50	8.00
	b. Wmk: Constitution. Metal security strip. Sign. 34; 35 (lg. size).	.50	2.00	5.00
	c. Wmk: Kg. profile. Sm. letters in 2-line text on back. Sign. 35; 36; 37; 38.	.30	1.00	3.00
	d. Wmk: Kg. profile. Larger letters in 2-line text on back. Sign. 39; 40; 41; 42; 44.	.30	1.00	3.00

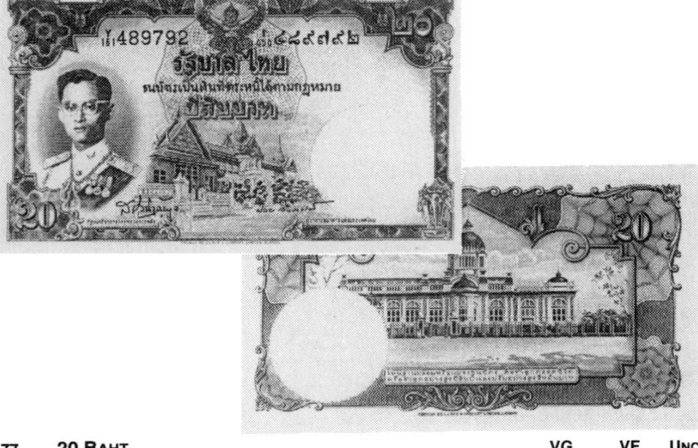

		VG	VF	UNC
77	**20 BAHT** ND (1953). Olive-green on m/c unpt. Like #72.			
	a. Wmk: Constitution. Red and blue security threads. Sign. 34.	1.00	3.50	15.00
	b. Wmk: Constitution. Metal security strip. Sign. 34; 35 (lg. size).	1.00	3.00	10.00
	c. Wmk: Kg. profile. Sm. letters in 2-line text on back. Sign. 35; 37-42; 44.	.60	1.25	5.00
	d. Wmk: Kg. profile. Larger letters in 2-line text on back. Sign. 35; 37-42; 44.	.60	1.25	5.00

NOTE: Sign. for #77c and 77d include 35; 37; 38; 39; 40; 41; 42; 44.

		VG	VF	UNC
78	**100 BAHT** ND (1955). Red on m/c unpt. Like #73.			
	a. Wmk: Constitution. Red and blue security threads. Sign. 34.	4.50	10.00	25.00
	b. Wmk: Constitution. Metal security strip. Sign. 34; 35; 37; 38.	4.25	10.00	25.00
	c. Wmk: Kg. profile. Sm. letters in 2-line text on back. Sign. 38-41.	2.25	6.00	15.00
	d. Wmk: Kg. profile. Larger letters in 2-line text on back. Sign. 38-41.	2.25	6.00	15.00

NOTE: Sign. for #78c and 78d include 38; 39; 40; 41.

BANK OF THAILAND

1968 ISSUE; SERIES 10

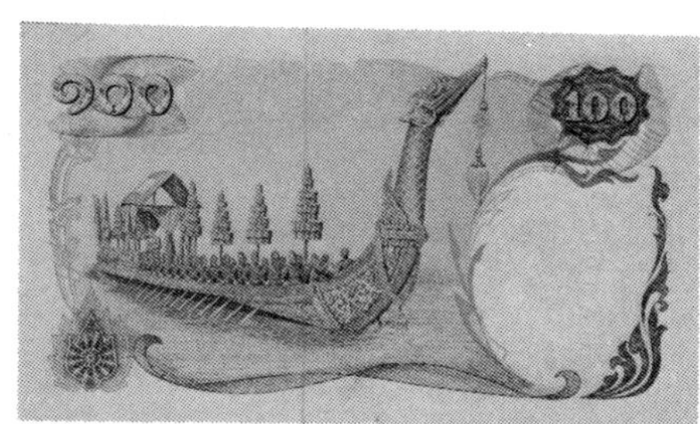

79 **100 BAHT** | VG 4.50 | VF 7.00 | UNC 15.00
ND (1968). Red, blue and m/c. Rama IX in uniform at r. and as wmk. Royal barge on back. Sign. 41; 42. Printer: TDLR.

1969 COMMEMORATIVE ISSUE

SERIES 11

Printed in Thailand by the Thai Banknote Printing Works. Officially described as "Series Eleven". Kg. Rama IX wearing traditional robes at r., sign. of Finance Minister (above) and Governor of the Bank of Thailand (below) at ctr. Wmk: Rama IX. Reportedly 6,000 or 7,000 sets issued.

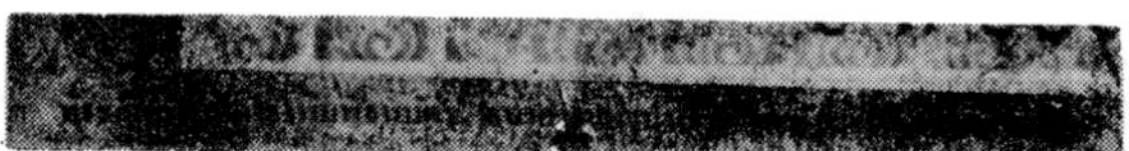

#80 and 81 text at bottom: *opening of the Thai Banknote Printing Works 24 June 2512* (1969).

80 **5 BAHT** | VG 5.00 | VF 25.00 | UNC 250.00
24.6.1969. Purple and m/c. Abhorn Pimoke Throne Hall on back. Serial # prefix 00A. Sign. 41.

81 **10 BAHT** | VG 5.00 | VF 25.00 | UNC 250.00
24.6.1969. Brown on m/c unpt. Wat Benchamabophitr temple on back. Serial # and sign. like #80.

1969-75 ND ISSUE; SERIES 11

#82-86 replacement notes: Serial # prefix *S-(W)*.

82 **5 BAHT** | VG .25 | VF .75 | UNC 3.00
ND (1969). Purple and m/c unpt. Like #80 but w/o commemorative line at bottom. Sign. 41; 42.

83 **10 BAHT** | VG .30 | VF .85 | UNC 3.50
ND (1969-78). Brown and m/c. Like #81 but w/o commemorative line at bottom. Sign. 41; 42; 43; 44; 45; 46; 47; 48; 49; 50; 51; 52; 53.

84 **20 BAHT** | VG .65 | VF 1.00 | UNC 4.00
ND (1971-81). Dk. green, olive-green and m/c. Royal barge at l. ctr. on back. Sign. 41; 42; 43; 44; 45; 46; 47; 48; 49; 50; 51; 52; 53.

NOTICE

Readers with unlisted dates, signature varieties, etc. are invited to submit photocopies of their notes to: Standard Catalog of World Paper Money, 700 East State St. Iola, WI 54990-0001, fax: 1-715-445-4087, or E-Mail: thernr@krause.com.

		VG	VF	UNC
85	**100 BAHT** ND (1969-78). Red-brown and m/c. Emerald Buddha section of Grand Palace on back.			
	a. W/o black Thai ovpt. on face. Sign. 42; 43; 44; 45; 46; 47; 48; 49.	3.00	4.50	12.50
	b. Black Thai ovpt. line just below upper sign. for change of title. Sign. 43.	10.00	17.50	40.00

		VG	VF	UNC
86	**500 BAHT** ND (1975-88). Purple and m/c. Pra Prang Sam Yod Lopburi (3 towers) on back. Sign. 47; 49; 50; 51; 52; 53; 54; 55.	15.00	22.50	50.00

1978-81 ND ISSUE; SERIES 12

#87-89 Kg. Rama IX wearing dk. Field Marshal's uniform at r. and as wmk. Sign. of Finance Minister (upper) and Governor of the Bank of Thailand (lower) at ctr. Replacement notes: Serial # prefix *S-(W)*.

		VG	VF	UNC
87	**10 BAHT** ND (1980). Dk. brown on m/c unpt. Mounted statue of Kg. Chulalongkorn on back. Sign. 52; 53; 54; 55;56; 60; 62; 64. 64.	FV	.50	1.50

		VG	VF	UNC
88	**20 BAHT** ND (1981-84). Dk. green on m/c unpt. Kg. Taksin's statue at Chantaburi w/3 armed men on back. Sign. 53; 54; 55; 56; 59; 61; 62; 64; 65.	FV	.90	2.75

		VG	VF	UNC
89	**100 BAHT** ND (1978). Violet, red and orange on m/c unpt. Kg. Narasuan the Great atop elephant on back. Sign. 49-62.	FV	3.25	10.00

1985-92 ND ISSUE; SERIES 12

#90-92 replacement notes: Serial # prefix *S-(W)*.

		VG	VF	UNC
90	**50 BAHT** ND (1985-). Dk. blue and purple on m/c unpt. Kg. Rama IX facing at r., wearing traditional robe and as wmk. Palace at l., statue of Kg. Rama VII at ctr., his arms and sign. at upper l. on back.			
	a. Kg. w/pointed eartips. Sign. 54.	FV	2.00	6.00
	b. Darker blue color obscuring pointed eartips. Sign. 54-62.	FV	2.00	5.00

		VG	VF	UNC
91	**500 BAHT** ND(1988-). Purple and violet on m/c unpt. Kg. Rama IX at r. in Field Marshal's uniform and as wmk. Statue at ctr. r., palace in background in unpt. at l. ctr. on back. Sign. 54-62.	FV	15.00	35.00

		VG	VF	UNC
92	**1000 BAHT** ND (1992-). Gray, brown, orange and m/c. Kg. at ctr. r. and as wmk. Kg. Rama IX and Qn. Sirikit greeting children at l. ctr. in unpt., viewing map at ctr. r. on back. Sign. 61-70.	FV	28.50	75.00

1987 COMMEMORATIVE ISSUE

#93, King's 60th Birthday

		VG	VF	UNC
93	**60 BAHT** BE2530 (5.12.1987). Dk. brown on m/c unpt. Kg. Rama IX seated on throne at ctr., Victory crown at l., Royal regalia at r. Royal family seated w/subjects on back. Sign. 55.			
	a. Issued note.	—	2.00	6.00
	s. Specimen in blue folder.	—	—	100.00

NOTE: A 40 Baht surcharge was added to issue price of #93, for charity work and the expense of the special envelope which came with each issued note.

1992 COMMEMORATIVE ISSUE

#94 and 95, 90th Birthday of Princess Mother

		VG	VF	UNC
94	**50 BAHT** ND (1992). Blue on m/c unpt. Similar to #90. 2 lines of text added under Princess Mother's wmk. on face. Sign. 57.	FV	2.00	6.00

		VG	VF	UNC
95	**500 BAHT** ND (1992). Purple and m/c. Similar to #91. 2 lines of text added under Princess Mother's wmk. on face. Sign. 57.	FV	FV	37.50

#96, Qn. Sirikit's 60th Birthday

		VG	VF	UNC
96	**1000 BAHT** ND (1992). Black, deep olive-green and yellow-brown on m/c unpt. Like #92 but w/commemorative text in 3 lines under Qn. Sirikit's wmk. on face and back. Sign. 62.	FV	FV	85.00

1994 ND Issue

		VG	VF	Unc
97	**100 Baht** ND (1994). Violet, red and brown-orange on m/c unpt. Kg. Rama IX at r. Statue of Kg. and prince at ctr. r. between children on back. Sign. 63, 64, 65, 67, 68, 69, 70, 71.	FV	FV	10.00

1995 Commemorative Issue

Text at lower margin:

๑๒๐ ปี กระทรวงการคลัง วันที่ ๑๔ เมษายน พุทธศักราช ๒๕๓๘

#98, 120th Anniversary of the Ministry of Finance

		VG	VF	Unc
98	**10 Baht** ND (1995). Dk. brown on m/c unpt. Like #87 but w/Commemorative text in lower margin. Sign. 59; 63.	FV	FV	2.50

1996 Commemorative Issue

#99 and 101, 50th Anniversary of Reign

		VG	VF	Unc
99	**50 Baht** ND (1996). Purple on lt. blue and m/c unpt. Kg. Rama IX wearing Field Marshal's uniform at r. and as a shadow design in clear area at l., royal seal of kingdom at upper r. Back like #94. Polymer plastic. Sign. 66, 67. Printer: NPA (w/o imprint).	FV	FV	6.00

		VG	VF	Unc
100	**500 Baht** ND (1996). Purple and red-violet on m/c unpt. Similar to #103 but w/Crowned Royal seal w/*50* at ctr. r., arms above dancers at r. replacing crowned radiant Chakra at l. ctr. Sign. 64.	FV	FV	37.50

		VG	VF	Unc
101	**500 Baht** ND(1996). M/c. Kg. Rama IX seated in royal attire at ctr. r., hologram of Kg. at upper r. Kg. holding map at ctr., waterfalls at l., farmers in terraced landscape at r. on back. Polymer plastic. Sign. 64; 65. Printer: NPA (w/o imprint).	FV	FV	100.00

1996; 1997 ND Regular Issue

		VG	VF	Unc
102	**50 Baht** ND(1997). Black on lt. blue and m/c unpt. Kg. Rama IX in Field Marshall's uniform at ctr. r., arms at upper l. Kg. Rama VI seated at table at ctr. r., royal arms at upper l. ctr., medieval ship's prow at lower r. on back. Sign. 65; 67. Polymer plastic. Printer: NPA (w/o imprint).	FV	FV	4.00
103	**500 Baht** ND (1996). Purple and red-violet on m/c unpt. Kg. Rama IX at r. and as wmk. Arms at upper l., radiant crowned Chakra seal on platform at l. ctr. Palace at l. ctr., 2 statues at ctr. r. on back. Sign. 63-71.	FV	FV	75.00

1999 COMMEMORATIVE ISSUE

#104, 60th Anniversary of Coronation

		VG	VF	UNC
104	**1000 BAHT** 1999. M/c.	FV	FV	125.00

COLLECTOR SERIES

1991 COMMEMORATIVE ISSUE

#CS1, World Bank Group/IMF Annual Meetings

		ISSUE PRICE	MKT. VALUE
CS1	**1991 10, 20, 50, 100, 500 BAHT** #87-91 w/ovpt: 1991 World Bank Group/IMF Annual Meetings in English and Thai. Specimen. (Issued in blue hanging folder).	—	600.00

MILITARY - VIETNAM WAR

AUXILIARY MILITARY PAYMENT CERTIFICATE COUPONS

Issued to Thai troops in Vietnam to facilitate their use of United States MPC. These coupons could not be used as currency by themselves.

FIRST SERIES

#M1-M8 issued probably from January to April or May, 1970. Larger shield at ctr. on face and back. Words *Coupon* below shield or at r., *Non Negotiable* at r. Small Thai symbol only at upper l. corner; denomination at 3 corners. Black print on check-type security paper.

		GOOD	FINE	XF
M1	**5 CENTS** ND (1970). Yellow paper. Seahorse shield design.	100.00	250.00	—
M2	**10 CENTS** ND (1970). Lt. gray paper. Shield w/leaping panther and *RTAVF. Non Negotiable* under shield; *Coupon* deleted.	100.00	250.00	—
M3	**25 CENTS** ND (1970). Pink paper. Shield w/*Victory Vietnam. Coupon* at r.	160.00	400.00	—
M4	**50 CENTS** ND (1970). Lt. blue paper. Circle w/shaking hands and *Royal Thai Forces Vietnam.*	160.00	400.00	—
M5	**1 DOLLAR** ND (1970). Yellow paper. Inscription *Victory Vietnam. Coupon* at r.	160.00	400.00	—
M6	**5 DOLLARS** ND (1970). Lt. gray paper. Seahorse in shield.	200.00	500.00	—
M7	**10 DOLLARS** ND (1970). Yellow paper. Shield w/leaping panther.	225.00	550.00	—
M8	**20 DOLLARS** ND (1970). Lt. green paper. Circle w/hands shaking.	225.00	550.00	—

SECOND SERIES

#M9-M16 issued April or May, 1970 to possibly Oct. 7, 1970. Shield designs similar to previous issue, but paper colors are different. Larger shield outline around each shield at l. ctr. *Coupon* in margin at lower ctr., denomination at all 4 corners.

		GOOD	FINE	XF
M9	**5 CENTS** ND (1970). Yellow paper. Shield similar to #M1.	40.00	100.00	—

		GOOD	FINE	XF
M10	**10 CENTS** ND (1970). Lt. green paper. Shield similar to #M2.	50.00	125.00	—

		GOOD	FINE	XF
M11	**25 CENTS** ND (1970). Yellow paper. Shield similar to #M3.	60.00	150.00	—
M12	**50 CENTS** ND (1970). Lt. gray paper. Shield similar to #M4.	60.00	150.00	—
M13	**1 DOLLAR** ND (1970). Pink paper. Shield similar to #M5.	60.00	150.00	—
M14	**5 DOLLARS** ND (1970). Lt. green paper. Shield similar to #M6.	160.00	400.00	—
M15	**10 DOLLARS** ND (1970). Pale yellow paper. Shield similar to #M7.	160.00	400.00	—

		GOOD	FINE	XF
M16	**20 DOLLARS** ND (1970). Lt. green paper. Shield similar to #M8.	180.00	450.00	—

THIRD SERIES

#M17-M23 date of issue not known (Oct., 1970?). All notes w/hands shaking in shield at lower r. on face. Different shield designs at upper l. on back. More elaborate design across face and back.

		VG	VF	UNC
M17	**5 CENTS** ND. Lt. gray, maroon and green.	22.50	75.00	300.00

		VG	VF	UNC
M18	**10 CENTS** ND. Lt. yellow and green.	22.50	75.00	300.00

		VG	VF	UNC
M19	**25 CENTS** ND. Green, pink and maroon.	40.00	125.00	350.00

		VG	VF	UNC
M20	**50 CENTS** ND. Yellow, green, blue and red.	40.00	125.00	350.00

		VG	VF	UNC
M21	**1 DOLLAR**			
	ND. Pink, blue and green.			
	a. Issued note.	125.00	225.00	—
	r. Remainder w/o serial #.	—	—	300.00

		VG	VF	UNC
M22	**5 DOLLARS**			
	ND. Yellow, green, blue and red.			
	a. Issued note.	600.00	950.00	—
	r. Remainder w/o serial #.	—	—	375.00

		VG	VF	UNC
M23	**10 DOLLARS**			
	ND. Green, maroon and dk. red.			
	a. Issued note.	125.00	225.00	—
	r. Remainder w/o serial #.	—	—	350.00

TIMOR

Timor, now an island of Indonesia between the Savu and Timor Seas, has an area, including the former colony of Portuguese Timor, of 11,883 sq. mi. (30,775 sq. km.) and a population of 1.5 million. Western Timor is administered as part of Nusa Tenggara Timur (East Nusa Tenggara) province. Capital: Kupang. The eastern half of the island, the former Portuguese colony, forms a single province, Timor Timur (East Timor). Originally the Portuguese colony also included the area around Ocussi-Ambeno and the small island of Atauro (Pulau Kambing) located north of Dili. Capital: Dili. Timor exports sandalwood, coffee, tea, hides, rubber and copra.

Portuguese traders reached Timor about 1520, and moved to the north and east when the Dutch established themselves in Kupang, a sheltered bay at the southwestern tip, in 1613. Treaties effective in 1860 and 1914 established the boundaries between the two colonies. Japan occupied the entire island during World War II. The former Dutch colony in the western part of the island became part of Indonesia in 1950.

At the end of Nov., 1975, the Portuguese Province of Timor attained independence as the People's Democratic Republic of East Timur. In Dec., 1975 or early in 1976 the government of the People's Democratic Republic was seized by a guerilla faction sympathetic to the Indonesian territorial claim to East Timur which ousted the constitutional government and replaced it with the Provisional Government of East Timur. On July 17, 1976, the Provisional Government enacted a law which dissolved the free republic and made East Timur the 24th province of Indonesia.

NOTE: For later issues see Indonesia.

MONETARY SYSTEM:

1 Escudo = 100 Centavos, 1958-1975

SIGNATURE VARIETIES

	O ADMINISTRADOR	O GOVERNADOR
1		
2		
3		
4		
5		
6		
7		
8		

NOTE: The signatures illustrated are presented only for convenience. They may not be necessarily in chronological order for every denomination. Further information is requested.

NOTICE

Readers with unlisted dates, signature varieties, etc. are invited to submit photocopies of their notes to: Standard Catalog of World Paper Money, 700 East State St. Iola, WI 54990-0001, fax: 1-715-445-4087, or E-Mail: thernr@krause.com.

PORTUGUESE INFLUENCE
BANCO NACIONAL ULTRAMARINO

DECRETOS - LEI 39221E 44891; 1963-68 ISSUE

#26-30 portr. R. D. Aleixo at r. Bank ship seal at l., crowned arms at ctr. on back. Printer: BWC.

		VG	VF	UNC
26	**20 ESCUDOS** 24.10.1967. Olive-brown on m/c unpt. Sign. 3-7.	.50	4.00	12.50

		VG	VF	UNC
27	**50 ESCUDOS** 24.10.1967. Blue on m/c unpt. Sign. 2; 5; 6; 8.	2.00	4.00	15.00

		VG	VF	UNC
28	**100 ESCUDOS** 25.4.1963. Brown on m/c unpt. Sign. 1-3; 8.			
	a. Issued note.	2.50	5.00	17.50
	s. Specimen. Punched hole cancelled.	—	—	50.00

		VG	VF	UNC
29	**500 ESCUDOS** 25.4.1963. Dk. brown on m/c unpt. Sign. 1-3; 8; 9.	10.00	20.00	55.00

		VG	VF	UNC
30	**1000 ESCUDOS** 21.3.1968. Green on m/c unpt. Sign. 2-8.	15.00	30.00	90.00

1969 ND PROVISIONAL ISSUE

		VG	VF	UNC
31	**20 ESCUDOS** ND. Green on m/c unpt. Régulo Jose Nunes at l. Bank seal at ctr., local huts on pilings at r. on back. Specimen.	—	—	—
32	**500 ESCUDOS** ND (1969 - old date 22.3.1967). Brown and violet on m/c unpt. Ovpt: *PAGAVEL EM TIMOR* on Mozambique #110, face and back.	125.00	300.00	550.00

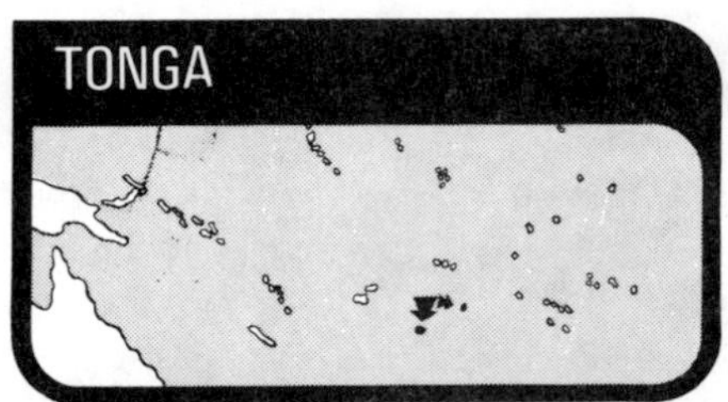

The Kingdom of Tonga (or Friendly Islands), a member of the British Commonwealth, is an archipelago situated in the southern Pacific Ocean south of Western Samoa and east of Fiji comprising 150 islands. Tonga has an area of 270 sq. mi. (748 sq. km.) and a population of 107,300. Capital: Nuku'alofa. Primarily agricultural, the kingdom exports bananas and copra.

Dutch navigators Willem Schouten and Jacob Lemaire were the first Europeans to visit Tonga in 1616. They were followed by the noted Dutch explorer Abel Tasman who visited the Tongatapu group in 1643. No further European contact was made until 1773 when British navigator Capt. James Cook arrived and, impressed by the peaceful deportment of the natives, named the islands the Friendly Islands. Within a few years of Cook's visit, Tonga was embroiled in a civil war that lasted until the great chief Taufa'ahau, who reigned as George Tubou I (1845-93), was converted to Christianity and brought unity and peace to the islands. Tonga became a self-governing protectorate of Great Britain in 1900 and a fully independent state on June 4, 1970. The monarchy is a member of the Commonwealth of Nations. The monarch is Chief of State and Head of Government.

RULERS:

Queen Salote III, 1918-1965
King Taufa'ahau IV, 1967-

MONETARY SYSTEM:

1 Shilling = 12 Pence
1 Pound = 20 Shillings to 1967
1 Pa'anga = 100 Seniti, 1967-

KINGDOM
GOVERNMENT OF TONGA

1939-42 ISSUE

#9-12 w/denomination spelled out on both sides of arms at ctr. Printer: TDLR.

		VG	VF	UNC
9	**4 SHILLINGS** 1941-66. Brown on m/c unpt. *FOUR SHILLINGS* at l. and r.			
	a. 1.12.1941-22.10.1946. 3 sign.	25.00	100.00	—
	b. 7.2.1949; 15.2.1951; 20.7.1951; 6.9.1954.	22.50	100.00	—
	c. 19.9.1955-30.11.1959.	7.50	25.00	75.00
	d. 24.10.1960-27.9.1966.	3.00	10.00	35.00
	e. 3.11.1966. 2 sign.	2.00	5.00	22.50
10	**10 SHILLINGS** 1941-66. Green on m/c unpt. *TEN SHILLINGS* at l. and r.			
	a. 19.5.1939; 17.10.1941-28.11.1944. 3 sign.	35.00	200.00	—
	b. 9.7.1949-1955.	30.00	125.00	—
	c. 2.5.1956; 22.7.1957; 10.12.1958.	7.50	30.00	—
	d. 24.10.1960; 28.11.1962; 29.7.1964; 22.6.1965.	3.00	10.00	65.00
	e. 3.11.1966. 2 sign.	2.00	7.50	30.00

		VG	VF	UNC
11	**1 POUND** 1940-66. Red on m/c unpt. *ONE POUND* at l. and r.			
	a. 3.5.1940-7.11.1944. 3 sign.	35.00	150.00	—
	b. 15.6.1951; 11.9.1951; 19.9.1955.	30.00	120.00	—
	c. 2.5.1956; 10.12.1958; 30.11.1959; 12.12.1961.	10.00	25.00	85.00
	d. 28.11.1962; 30.10.1964; 2.11.1965; 3.11.1966.	5.00	12.00	55.00
	e. 2.12.1966. 2 sign.	3.00	10.00	37.50

		VG	VF	UNC
12	**5 POUNDS** 1942-66. Dk. blue on m/c unpt. *FIVE POUNDS* at l. and r.			
	a. 11.3.1942-1945. 3 sign.	550.00	1000.	—
	b. 15.6.1951; 5.7.1955; 11.9.1956; 26.6.1958.	300.00	650.00	—
	c. 30.11.1959; 2.11.1965.	150.00	400.00	—
	d. 2.12.1966. 2 sign.	10.00	25.00	70.00

PULE' ANGA 'O TONGA
GOVERNMENT OF TONGA

1967 ISSUE

#13-17 arms at lower l., Qn. Salote III at r. Various date and sign. varieties.

		VG	VF	UNC
13	**1/2 PA'ANGA** 1967-73. Dk. brown on pink unpt. Back brown and blue; coconut workers at l.			
	a. 3.4.1967; 10.3.1970; 16.6.1970; 4.2.1971; 24.7.1972. 3 sign.	1.50	7.50	40.00
	b. 13.6.1973. 2 sign.	2.00	10.00	60.00
14	**1 PA'ANGA** 1967; 70-71. Olive-green on m/c unpt. Back olive and blue; river scene, palm trees.			
	a. 3.4.1967; 12.4.1967; 2.10.1967; 8.12.1967.	2.00	7.50	75.00
	b. 10.3.1970.	2.50	8.50	80.00
	c. 19.10.1971.	3.00	10.00	95.00

		VG	VF	UNC
15	**2 PA'ANGA** 1967-73. Red on m/c unpt. Back red and brown; women making Tapa cloth.			
	a. 3.4.1967; 2.10.1967; 8.12.1967.	3.00	12.00	100.00
	b. 19.5.1969; 10.3.1970; 19.10.1971; 2.8.1973.	3.50	15.00	125.00
	c. 12.11.1973. 2 sign.	5.00	30.00	—

16 **5 PA'ANGA**
1967; 1973. Purple on m/c unpt. Back purple and olive-green; Ha'amonga stone gateway.

	VG	VF	UNC
a. 3.4.1967.	7.00	25.00	165.00
b. 13.6.1973.	8.50	30.00	225.00
c. 6.12.1973. 2 sign.	10.00	50.00	—

17 **10 PA'ANGA**

	VG	VF	UNC
3.4.1967; 2.10.1967; 8.12.1967. Dk. blue on m/c unpt. Back blue and purple; Royal Palace.	12.50	65.00	400.00

1974; 1985 ISSUE

#18-22 arms at lower l., Portr. Kg. Taufa'ahau at r. Various date and sign. varieties. Replacement notes: Serial # prefix *Z/1*.

18 **1/2 PA'ANGA**
1974-83. Dk. brown on pink unpt. Back like #13.

	VG	VF	UNC
a. 2 sign. 2.10.1974; 19.6.1975.	1.00	2.50	11.00
b. 3 sign. 12.1.1977; 17.5.1977; 10.9.1979.	.60	1.25	12.50
c. As b. 28.11.1979; 27.8.1980; 31.7.1981; 17.8.1982; 29.7.1983.	.50	1.00	7.50

19 **1 PA'ANGA**
1974-89. Olive-green on m/c unpt. Back like #14.

	VG	VF	UNC
a. 2 sign. 31.7.1974; 19.6.1975; 21.8.1975; 21.1.1981; 18.5.1983.	FV	1.50	6.00
b. 3 sign. 17.5.1977-11.6.1980; 31.7.1981-28.10.1982; 27.7.1983-30.6.1989.	FV	FV	4.50

20 **2 PA'ANGA**
1974-89. Red on m/c unpt. Back like #15.

	VG	VF	UNC
a. 2 sign. 2.10.1974; 19.6.1975; 21.8.1975; 21.1.1981.	FV	2.00	10.00
b. 3 sign. 12.1.1977-27.8.1980; 31.7.1981-30.6.1989.	FV	FV	5.00

21 **5 PA'ANGA**
1974-89. Purple on m/c unpt. Back like #16.

	VG	VF	UNC
a. 2 sign. 2.10.1974; 19.6.1975; 21.1.1981.	FV	4.00	20.00
b. 3 sign. 21.12.1976-28.11.1980; 27.5.1981-30.6.1989.	FV	FV	10.00

22 **10 PA'ANGA**
1974-89. Dk. blue on m/c unpt. Back like #17.

	VG	VF	UNC
a. 2 sign. 31.7.1974; 3.9.1974; 19.6.1975; 21.1.1981.	FV	7.50	40.00
b. 3 sign. 12.12.1976-28.11.1980; 19.1.1982-30.6.1989.	FV	FV	22.50

23 **20 PA'ANGA**
1985-89. Orange on green and m/c unpt. Kg. in new design at ctr. r. and as wmk., arms at r. Tonga Development Bank on back.

	VG	VF	UNC
a. 4.7.1985.	FV	25.00	85.00
b. 18.7.1985; 8.1.1986; 27.2.1987; 28.9.1987.	FV	FV	40.00
c. 20.5.1988; 14.12.1988; 23.1.1989; 30.6.1989.	FV	FV	37.50

NOTE: #23a was made in limited quantities in celebration of the king's birthday.

KINGDOM OF TONGA

1988 ISSUE

24 **50 PA'ANGA**
1988-89. Brown and green on m/c unpt. Kg. in new design at ctr. r. and as wmk., arms at r. Vava'u Harbour on back.

	VG	VF	UNC
a. 4.7.1988.	FV	50.00	150.00
b. 14.12.1988; 30.6.1989.	FV	FV	85.00

NOTE: #24a was made in limited quantities in celebration of the king's birthday. (5,000 pcs.).

NATIONAL RESERVE BANK OF TONGA

1992 ND ISSUE

#25-29 designs like #19-23. 2 sign. w/Tongan titles beneath.

		VG	VF	UNC
25	**1 PA'ANGA** ND (1992-95). Olive-green on m/c unpt.	FV	FV	3.00

		VG	VF	UNC
26	**2 PA'ANGA** ND (1992-95). Red on m/c unpt.	FV	FV	5.00

		VG	VF	UNC
27	**5 PA'ANGA** ND (1992-95). Purple on m/c unpt.	FV	FV	13.50
28	**10 PA'ANGA** ND (1992-95). Dk. blue on m/c unpt.	FV	FV	21.50
29	**20 PA'ANGA** ND (1992-95). Orange and green on m/c unpt.	FV	FV	42.50

1989 COMMEMORATIVE ISSUE

#30, Inauguration of National Reserve Bank of Tonga

		VG	VF	UNC
30	**20 PA'ANGA** 1.7.1989. Orange on green and m/c unpt. w/commemorative text in circle on wmk. area on face and back.	FV	20.00	45.00

1995 ISSUE

#31-34 Kg. Taufa'ahau at upper ctr. r. and as wmk., arms at r. Printer: TDLR.

		VG	VF	UNC
31	**1 PA'ANGA** ND (1995). Olive-green on m/c unpt. River scene, palm trees on back.	FV	FV	2.75

		VG	VF	UNC
32	**2 PA'ANGA** ND (1995). Red on m/c unpt. Woman making Tapa cloth on back.	FV	FV	4.50

		VG	VF	UNC
33	**5 PA'ANGA** ND (1995). Purple on m/c unpt. Ha'amonga stone gateway on back.	FV	FV	12.50
34	**10 PA'ANGA** ND (1995). Dk. blue on m/c unpt. Royal Palace on back.	FV	FV	22.50

COLLECTOR SERIES

GOVERNMENT OF TONGA

1978 ISSUE

		ISSUE PRICE	MKT. VALUE
CS1	**1978 1-10 PA'ANGA** #19b-22b ovpt: *SPECIMEN* and prefix serial # Maltese cross.	14.00	25.00

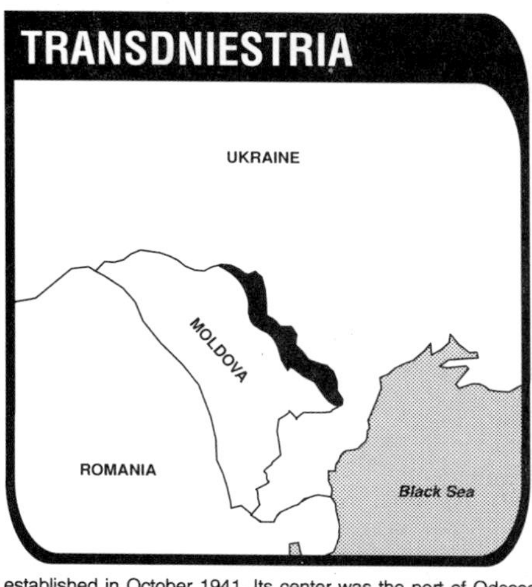

The Transnistria Moldavian Republic was formed in 1990, even before the separation of Moldavia from Russia. It has an area of 11,544 sq. mi. (29,900 sq. km). and a population of 700,000. Capital: Tiraspol.

The area was conquered from the Turks in the last half of the 18th Century, and in 1792 the capital city of Tiraspol was founded. After 1812, the area called Bessarabia (present Moldova and part of the Ukraine) became part of the Russian Empire. During the Russian Revolution, in 1918, the area was taken by Romanian troops, and in 1924 the Moldavian Autonomous SSR was formed on the left bank of the Dniester River. On June 22, 1941, Romania declared war on the U.S.S.R. and Romanian troops fought alongside the Germans up to Stalingrad. A Romanian occupation area between the Dniester and Bug Rivers called *Transnistria* was established in October 1941. Its center was the port of Odessa. A special issue of notes for use in Transnistria was made by the Romanian government. In 1944 the Russians recaptured Transnistria, advancing into Romania itself and occupying Bucharest in August of that year.

Once the Moldavian SSR declared independence in August 1991. Transnistria did not want to be a part of Moldavia. In 1992 Moldova tried to solve the issue militarily with battles in Bendery and Doubossary. The conflict was ended with Russian mediation and Russian peacekeeping forces were stationed there.

Transnistria has a president, parliament, army and police forces, but as yet it is lacking international recognition.

REPUBLIC

GOVERNMENT

1994 ND PROVISIONAL ISSUES

#1-15 issued 24.1.1994, invalidated on 1.12.1994.

The Bank purchased used Russian notes and placed stickers on them. Most collectors feel that "uncirculated" notes currently available were made after 1994, using overstruck notes and stamps.

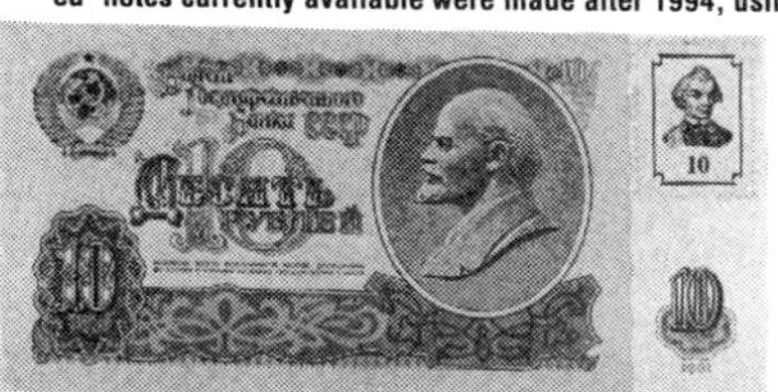

		VG	VF	UNC
1	**10 RUBLEI** ND (1994- old date 1961). Green on pink tint adhesive stamp on Russia #233.	.15	.50	2.00

		VG	VF	UNC
2	**10 RUBLEI** ND (1994- old date 1991). Green on pink tint adhesive stamp on Russia #240.	.10	.50	2.00

		VG	VF	UNC
3	**25 RUBLEI** ND (1994- old date 1961). Red-violet on buff tint adhesive stamp on Russia #234.	.10	.40	2.50
4	**50 RUBLEI** ND (1994- old date 1991). Red on pale green tint adhesive stamp on Russia #241.	.20	1.00	7.00

		VG	VF	UNC
5	**50 RUBLEI** ND (1994- old date 1992). Red on pale green tint adhesive stamp on Russia #247.	.15	.80	4.00
6	**100 RUBLEI** ND (1994- old date 1991). Black on pale blue tint adhesive stamp on Russia #242.	.40	2.00	7.50

		VG	VF	UNC
7	**100 RUBLEI** ND (1994- old date 1991). Black on pale blue tint adhesive stamp on Russia #243.	.15	.85	4.50
8	**200 RUBLEI** ND (1994- old date 1991). Green on yellow tint adhesive stamp on Russia #244.	.50	4.00	18.50
9	**200 RUBLEI** ND (1994- old date 1992). Green on yellow tint adhesive stamp on Russia #248.	.10	.40	3.50
10	**500 RUBLEI** ND (1994- old date 1991). Blue adhesive stamp on Russia #245.	.50	4.00	22.50

		VG	VF	UNC
11	**500 RUBLEI** ND (1994- old date 1992). Blue adhesive stamp on Russia #249.	.05	.20	3.50
12	**1000 RUBLEI** ND (1994- old date 1991). Violet on yellow tint adhesive stamp on Russia #246.	.50	4.00	20.00

		VG	VF	UNC
13	**1000 RUBLEI** ND (1994- old date 1992). Violet on yellow tint adhesive stamp on Russia #250.	.05	.25	3.00

		VG	VF	UNC
14	**5000 RUBLEI** ND (1994- old date 1992). Dk. brown on pale blue-gray tint adhesive stamp on Russia #252.	.15	.75	3.50
14A	**5000 RUBLEI** ND (1994 -old date 1961). Adhesive stamp on Russia 5 Rubles #224.	.10	.50	2.00
14B	**5000 RUBLEI** ND (1994 -old date 1991). Adhesive stamp on Russia 5 Rubles #239.	.10	.50	3.50

		VG	VF	UNC
15	**10,000 RUBLEI** ND (1994- old date 1992). Purple on yellow tint adhesive stamp on Russia #253.	.20	.75	4.00

БАНКА НИСТРЯНЭ
Banka Nistriana

1993; 1994 КУПОН Kupon Issue

#16-18 A. V. Suvorov at r. Parliament bldg. at ctr. on back. Wmk: Block design.

NOTE: Postal adhesive stamps have been seen affixed to #16-18 to imitate revalidated notes.

		VG	VF	Unc
16	**1 Ruble** 1994. Dk. green on m/c unpt.	FV	.10	.30

		VG	VF	Unc
17	**5 Rublei** 1994. Blue on m/c unpt.	FV	.10	.40

		VG	VF	Unc
18	**10 Rublei** 1994. Red-violet on m/c unpt.	FV	.10	.50

#19-24 equestrian statue of A. V. Suvorov at r. Parliament bldg. on back. Wmk: Block design.

		VG	VF	Unc
19	**50 Rublei** 1993 (1994). Green on m/c unpt.	FV	.15	1.00

		VG	VF	Unc
20	**100 Rublei** 1993 (1994). Dk. brown on m/c unpt.	FV	.20	1.00

		VG	VF	Unc
21	**200 Rublei** 1993 (1994). Red-violet on m/c unpt.	FV	.25	2.00

		VG	VF	Unc
22	**500 Rublei** 1993 (1994). Blue on m/c unpt.	FV	.30	2.50

		VG	VF	Unc
23	**1000 Rublei** 1993 (1994). Purple and red-violet on m/c unpt.	FV	.40	2.00

		VG	VF	Unc
24	**5000 Rublei** 1993 (1995). Black on deep olive-green and m/c unpt.	FV	1.00	3.50

#25 Not assigned.

1994 (1995) Issue

Currency Reform

1 Ruble = 1000 "Old" Rublei

		VG	VF	Unc
26	**1000 Rublei = 100,000 Rublei** 1994 (1995). Violet and purple. V. Suvorov at r. Parliament bldg. on back.	FV	1.00	3.50

1995; ND (1996) PROVISIONAL ISSUE

27 **50,000 RUBLEI ON 5 RUBLEI** — VG FV, VF FV, UNC 2.00
ND (1996 - old date 1994). Blue on m/c unpt. Hologram w/*50,000* at upper l. on #17.

28 **50,000 RUBLEI = 500,000 RUBLEI** — VG FV, VF FV, UNC 7.50
1995 (1996). Brown-violet and brown on m/c unpt. B. Khmelnytsky at r. Drama and comedy theatre on back.

1996 ND PROVISIONAL ISSUE

29 **10,000 RUBLEI ON 1 RUBLE** — VG FV, VF FV, UNC .75
ND (1996 - old date 1994). Dk. green on m/c unpt. Ovpt. on #16.

30 **50,000 RUBLEI ON 5 RUBLEI** — VG FV, VF FV, UNC 1.50
ND (1996 - old date 1994). Blue on m/c unpt. Ovpt. on #17.

31 **100,000 RUBLEI ON 10 RUBLEI** — VG FV, VF FV, UNC 2.00
ND (1996 - old date 1994). Red-violet on m/c unpt. Ovpt. on #18.

1997 REGULAR ISSUE

32 **500,000 RUBLEI** — VG FV, VF FV, UNC 3.00
1997. Purple and violet on m/c unpt. Like #24.

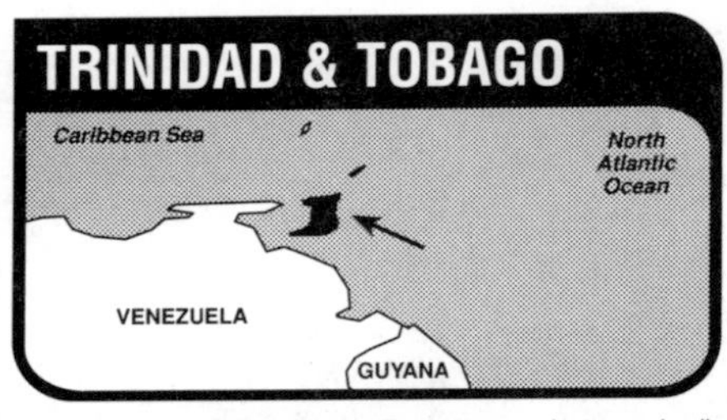

The Republic of Trinidad and Tobago, a member of the British Commonwealth, situated 7 miles (11 km.) off the coast of Venezuela, has an area of 1,981 sq. mi. (5,130 sq. km.) and a population of 1.27 million. Capital: Port-of-Spain. The Island of Trinidad contains the world's largest natural asphalt bog. Birds of Paradise live on little Tobago, the only place outside of their native New Guinea where they can be found in a wild state. Petroleum and petroleum products are the mainstay of the economy. Petroleum products, crude oil and sugar are exported.

Trinidad and Tobago were discovered by Columbus in 1498. Trinidad remained under Spanish rule from the time of its settlement in 1592 until its capture by the British in 1797. It was ceded to the British in 1802. Tobago was occupied at various times by the French, Dutch and British before being ceded to Britain in 1814. Trinidad and Tobago were merged into a single colony in 1888. The colony was part of the Federation of the West Indies until Aug. 31, 1962, when it became an independent member of the Commonwealth of Nations. A new constitution establishing a republican form of government was adopted on Aug. 1, 1976. The president is Chief of State. The prime minister is Head of Government.

Notes of the British Caribbean Territories circulated between 1950-1964.

RULERS:

British to 1976

MONETARY SYSTEM:

1 Dollar = 100 Cents
5 Dollars = 1 Pound 10 Pence

SIGNATURE VARIETIES			
1	J. F. Pierce	2	A. N. McLeod
3	J. E. Bruce	4	Linn OHB
5	W. Demas	6	N. Hareward
7	M. Duberan		

REPUBLIC

CENTRAL BANK OF TRINIDAD AND TOBAGO

1964 CENTRAL BANK ACT

#26-29 arms at l., Portr. Qn. Elizabeth II at ctr. Central Bank bldg. at ctr. r. on back. Wmk: Bird of Paradise.

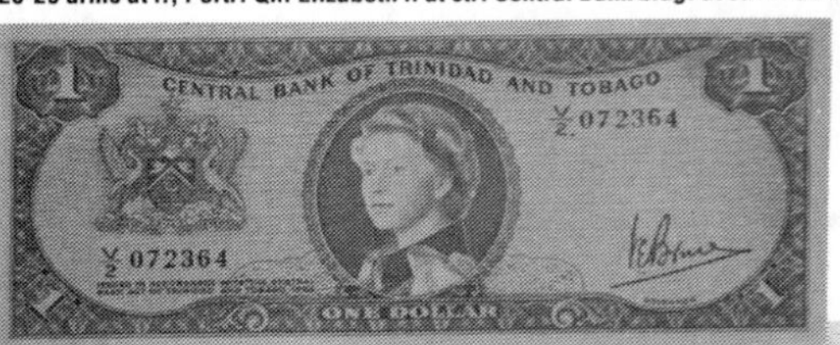

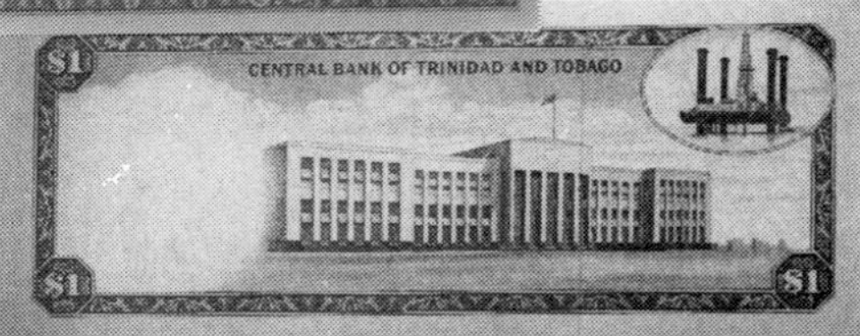

		VG	VF	UNC
26	**1 DOLLAR** *L.1964*. Red on m/c unpt. Oil rig in water at upper r. on back.			
	a. Sign. 1.	1.50	3.50	27.50
	b. Sign. 2. Serial # single letter or fractional letters prefix.	2.00	4.50	40.00
	c. Sign. 3.	1.00	2.50	22.50
	s. As a. Specimen.	—	—	100.00

		VG	VF	UNC
27	**5 DOLLARS** *L.1964*. Green on m/c unpt. Crane loading sugar cane at upper r. on back.			
	a. Sign. 1.	7.50	30.00	250.00
	b. Sign. 2.	5.00	12.50	150.00
	c. Sign. 3.	2.00	7.50	75.00
	s. As a. Specimen.	—	—	150.00

		VG	VF	UNC
28	**10 DOLLARS** *L.1964*. Dk. brown on m/c unpt. Factory at upper r. on back.			
	a. Sign. 1.	10.00	50.00	550.00
	b. Sign. 2.	9.00	40.00	500.00
	c. Sign. 3.	5.00	20.00	200.00
	s. As a. Specimen.	—	—	275.00

		VG	VF	UNC
29	**20 DOLLARS** *L.1964*. Purple on m/c unpt. Cocoa pods at upper r. on back.			
	a. Sign. 1.	15.00	65.00	750.00
	b. Sign. 2.	12.50	50.00	650.00
	c. Sign. 3.	7.50	20.00	265.00
	s. As a. Specimen.	—	—	335.00

1977 ND ISSUE

#30-35 authorization date 1964. Arms at ctr. Back like #26-29. Wmk: Bird of Paradise. Replacement notes: Serial # prefix *XX*.

		VG	VF	UNC
30	**1 DOLLAR** *L.1964* (1977). Red on m/c unpt. 2 flying birds at l.			
	a. Sign. 3.	FV	.50	3.00
	b. Sign. 4.	FV	1.00	4.00

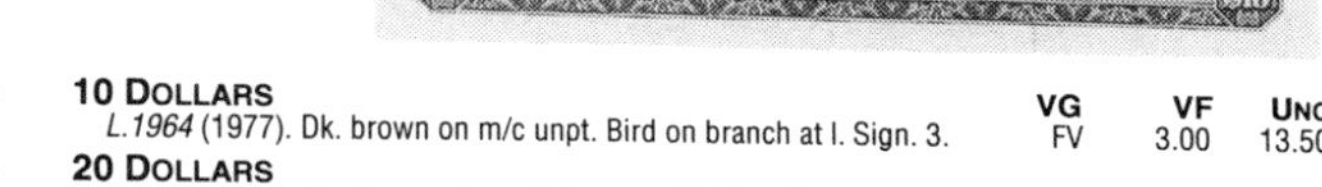

		VG	VF	UNC
31	**5 DOLLARS** *L.1964* (1977). Dk. green on m/c unpt. Branches and leaves at l.			
	a. Sign. 3.	FV	1.00	6.00
	b. Sign. 4.	FV	2.00	12.00

		VG	VF	UNC
32	**10 DOLLARS** *L.1964* (1977). Dk. brown on m/c unpt. Bird on branch at l. Sign. 3.	FV	3.00	13.50
33	**20 DOLLARS** *L.1964* (1977). Purple on m/c unpt. Flowers at l. Sign. 3.	FV	6.00	27.50

		VG	VF	UNC
34	**50 DOLLARS** *L.1964* (1977). Dk. brown on m/c unpt. Hummingbird at l. Net fishing at upper r. on back. Sign. 3.			
	a. 1963 (error date in authorization).	25.00	40.00	200.00
	b. 1964 (corrected authorization date).	30.00	75.00	385.00

		VG	VF	UNC
35	**100 DOLLARS** *L.1964* (1977). Deep blue on m/c unpt. Branch w/leaves and berries at l. Huts and palm trees at upper r. on back.			
	a. Sign. 3.	FV	30.00	125.00
	b. Sign. 4.	FV	35.00	150.00

CENTRAL BANK ACT CHAP. 79.02; 1985 ND ISSUE

#36-41 arms at ctr. Twin towered modern bank bldg. at ctr. on back. Wmk: Bird of Paradise. Replacement notes: Serial # prefix *XX*.

		VG	VF	UNC
36	**1 DOLLAR** ND (1985). Red-orange and purple on m/c unpt. 2 birds at l. Oil refinery at r. on back.			
	a. Sign. 4.	FV	FV	1.50
	b. Sign. 5.	FV	FV	1.50
	c. Sign. 6.	FV	FV	1.25
	d. Sign. 7.	FV	FV	1.00

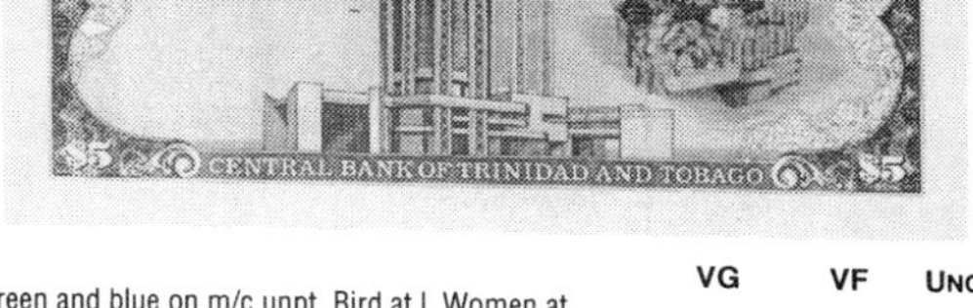

		VG	VF	UNC
37	**5 DOLLARS** ND (1985). Dk. green and blue on m/c unpt. Bird at l. Women at roadside produce stand at r. on back.			
	a. Sign. 4.	FV	FV	5.50
	b. Sign. 5.	FV	FV	3.25
	c. Sign. 6.	FV	FV	2.25

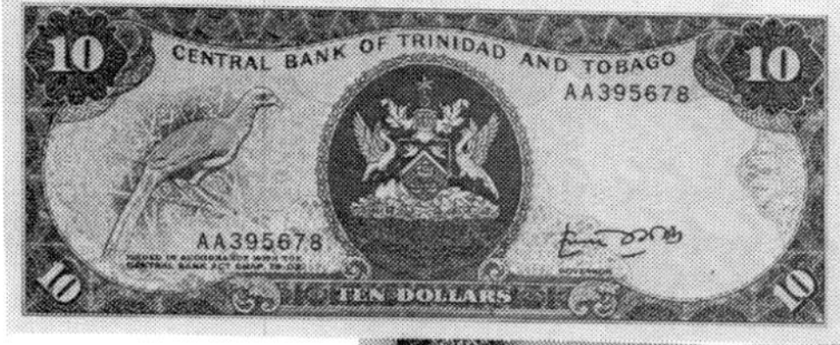

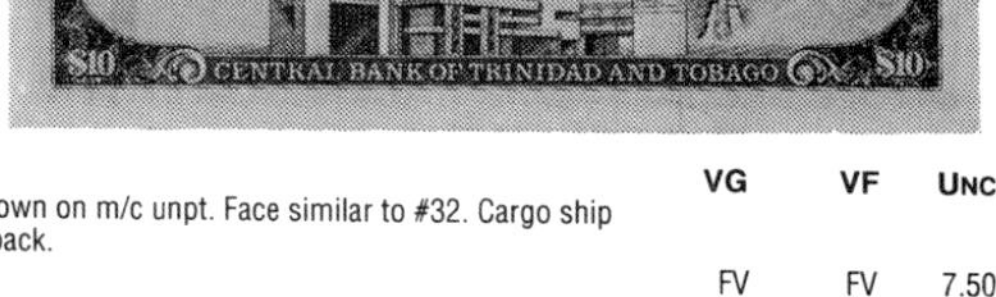

		VG	VF	UNC
38	**10 DOLLARS** ND (1985). Dk. brown on m/c unpt. Face similar to #32. Cargo ship dockside at r. on back.			
	a. Sign. 4.	FV	FV	7.50
	b. Sign. 5.	FV	FV	6.25
	c. Sign. 6.	FV	FV	4.25

NOTICE

Readers with unlisted dates, signature varieties, etc. are invited to submit photocopies of their notes to: Standard Catalog of World Paper Money, 700 East State St. Iola, WI 54990-0001, fax: 1-715-445-4087, or E-Mail: thernr@krause.com.

39	20 DOLLARS	VG	VF	UNC
	ND (1985). Purple on m/c unpt. Hummingbird in flowers at l. Steel drums at r. on back.			
	a. Sign. 4.	FV	FV	12.50
	b. Sign. 5.	FV	FV	7.50
	c. Sign. 6.	FV	FV	6.00

40	100 DOLLARS	VG	VF	UNC
	ND (1985). Deep blue on m/c unpt. Bird at l. Oil rig at r. on back.			
	a. Sign. 4.	FV	FV	50.00
	b. Sign. 5.	FV	FV	37.50
	c. Sign. 6.	FV	FV	30.00

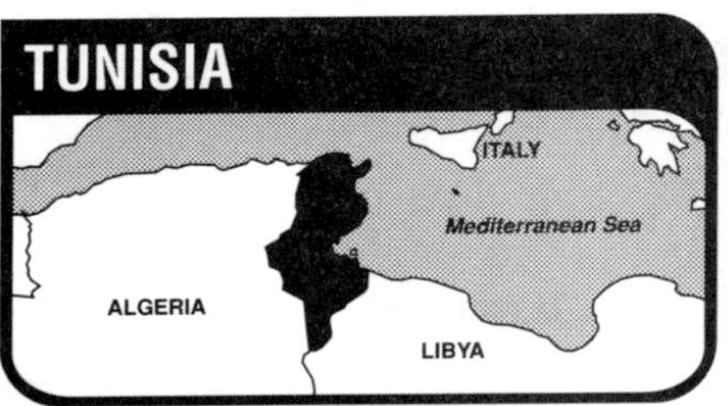

The Republic of Tunisia, located on the northern coast of Africa between Algeria and Libya, has an area of 63,170 sq. mi. (163,610 sq. km.) and a population of 9.1 million. Capital: Tunis. Agriculture is the backbone of the economy. Crude oil, phosphates, olive oil, and wine are exported.

Tunisia, settled by the Phoenicians in the 12th century BC, was the center of the seafaring Carthaginian empire. After the total destruction of Carthage, Tunisia became part of Rome's African province. It remained a part of of the Roman Empire (except for the 439-533 interval Vandal conquest) until taken by the Arabs, 648, who administered it until the Turkish invasion of 1570. Under Turkish control, the public revenue was heavily dependent upon the piracy of Mediterranean shipping, an endeavor that wasn't abandoned until 1819 when a coalition of powers threatened appropriate reprisal. Deprived of its major source of income, Tunisia underwent a financial regression that ended in bankruptcy, enabling France to establish a protectorate over the country in 1881. National agitation and guerrilla fighting forced France to grant Tunisia internal autonomy in 1955 and to recognize Tunisian independence on March 20, 1956. Tunisia abolished the monarchy and established a republic on July 25, 1957.

In 1975 the constitution was changed to make Bourguiba president for life. A two party system was started in 1981, but in the 1986 elections, all but the Front Nationals boycotted. Bourguiba was ousted in 1987. His successor, Zine el Abidine Ben Ali introduced some democratic reforms, but a struggle with Islamic Fundamentalists has lead to sporadic violence.

RULERS:

French, 1881-1956

MONETARY SYSTEM:

1 Franc = 100 Centimes to 1960
1 Dinar = 1000 Millimes, 1960-

REPUBLIC
BANQUE CENTRALE DE TUNISIE

1962 ISSUE

61	5 DINARS	VG	VF	UNC
	20.3.1962. Blue on m/c unpt. H. Bourguiba at r., bridge at l. Archways on back. Wmk: Arms.	7.00	45.00	215.00

1965-69 ISSUE

#63-65 H. Bourguiba at r. and as wmk.

62	1/2 DINAR	VG	VF	UNC
	1.6.1965. Blue on m/c unpt. H. Bourguiba at l. and as wmk., mosque at r. Mosaic from Monastir on back.	5.00	35.00	120.00

63	1 DINAR	VG	VF	UNC
	1.6.1965. Blue on m/c unpt. Factory at l. Mosaic on back.	6.00	30.00	80.00

		VG	VF	UNC
64	**5 DINARS** 1.6.1965. Lilac-brown and green on m/c unpt. Sadiki College at l. Mosaic w/woman in sprays at l., arch at ctr., Sunface at lower r. on back.	10.00	40.00	125.00

		VG	VF	UNC
65	**10 DINARS** 1.6.1969. M/c. Refinery at l. Palm trees in field on back.	12.50	35.00	100.00

1972 ISSUE

#66-68 H. Bourguiba at r. and as wmk. Printer: (T)DLR.

		VG	VF	UNC
66	**1/2 DINAR** 3.8.1972. Brown on m/c unpt. City w/river at l. View of Tunis on back.	1.00	9.00	15.00

		VG	VF	UNC
67	**1 DINAR** 3.8.1972. Purple on m/c unpt. Old fort at l. Minaret at l., girl at ctr. on back.	2.00	15.00	30.00

		VG	VF	UNC
68	**5 DINARS** 3.8.1972. Green on m/c unpt. Modern bldg. at l. Amphitheater at El-Djem on back.	6.00	20.00	70.00

1973 ISSUE

#69-72 H. Bourguiba at l. ctr. and as wmk.

		VG	VF	UNC
69	**1/2 DINAR** 15.10.1973. Green on m/c unpt. Man w/camel and trees at l. Landscape w/sheep and assorted produce on back.	1.50	6.50	10.00

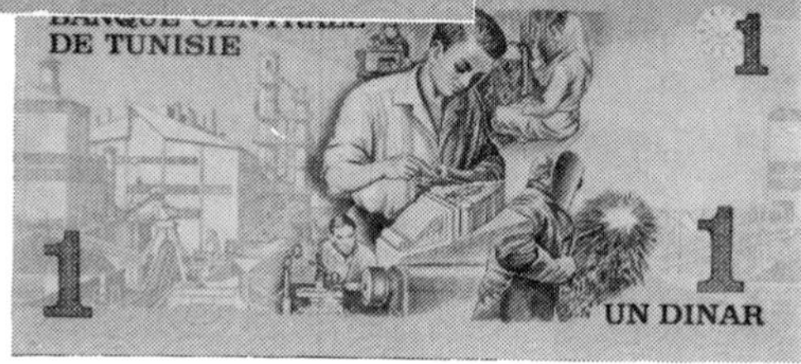

		VG	VF	UNC
70	**1 DINAR** 15.10.1973. Blue and green on m/c unpt. Bldg. at r. Industrial scenes on back.	2.00	6.00	25.00

NOTICE

Readers with unlisted dates, signature varieties, etc. are invited to submit photocopies of their notes to: Standard Catalog of World Paper Money, 700 East State St. Iola, WI 54990-0001, fax: 1-715-445-4087, or E-Mail: thernr@krause.com.

		VG	VF	UNC
71	**5 Dinars** 15.10.1973. Dk. brown on m/c unpt. City view at l. Montage of old and new on back.	FV	10.00	25.00

		VG	VF	UNC
72	**10 Dinars** 15.10.1973. Purple and brown on m/c unpt. Refinery in background at ctr. Montage w/students, column, train and drummers on back.	FV	12.50	45.00

1980 Issue

#74, 75 and 77 H. Bourguiba at r. and as wmk.

		VG	VF	UNC
74	**1 Dinar** 15.10.1980. Red-brown on dk. red and m/c unpt. Amphitheater at ctr. Town w/sea and mountain on back.	1.00	3.00	9.00

		VG	VF	UNC
75	**5 Dinars** 15.10.1980. Brown, red-brown and olive-green on m/c unpt. Bldgs. at ctr. Bridge and hills at l. on back.	FV	7.50	25.00
76	**10 Dinars** 15.10.1980. Blue-green on bistre and m/c unpt. H. Bourguiba at l., bldg. at ctr. Reservoir at ctr. on back.	FV	10.00	40.00

		VG	VF	UNC
77	**20 Dinars** 15.10.1980. Dk. blue-green and brown on m/c unpt. Amphitheater at ctr. Rowboats dockside on back.	FV	30.00	85.00

1983 Issue

#79-81 H. Bourguiba on face and as wmk.

		VG	VF	UNC
79	**5 Dinars** 3.11.1983. Red-brown and purple on lilac unpt. H. Bourguiba at l., desert scene at bottom ctr. Hydroelectric dam at ctr. r. on back.	FV	6.00	12.50

80 **10 DINARS**

3.11.1983. Blue and lilac on m/c unpt. Workers at lower l. ctr., H. Bourguiba at ctr., offshore oil rig at r. Modern bldg. at ctr., old city gateways at r. on back.

VG	VF	UNC
FV	15.00	38.50

81 **20 DINARS**

3.11.1983. Lt. blue and dk. blue on green and m/c unpt. H. Bourguiba at l., bldg. at bottom ctr. Bldg. at lower l., aerial view of harbor at r. on back.

VG	VF	UNC
FV	22.00	50.00

1986 ISSUE

#82 and 83 Held in reserve.

84 **10 DINARS**

20.3.1986. Yellow-brown on green unpt. H. Bourguiba at l. ctr. and as wmk., agricultural scene at bottom ctr. Offshore oil rig at l. ctr. on back.

VG	VF	UNC
FV	12.50	25.00

#85 Held in reserve.

1992-97 ISSUE

#86-89 replacement notes: *R* in denomination of lower r. serial #.

86 **5 DINARS**

7.11.1993. Green, olive-brown and black. Head of Hannibal at l. ctr. and as wmk., harbor fortress at r. "Dec. 7, 1987" collage at l. ctr. on back.

VG	VF	UNC
FV	FV	8.00

87 **10 DINARS**

7.11.1994. Purple, blue-green and red-brown on m/c unpt. ibn Khaldoun at ctr. and as wmk. Open book of "7 Novembre" at l. ctr. on back.

VG	VF	UNC
FV	FV	15.00

88 **20 DINARS**

7.11.1992. Deep purple, blue-black and red-brown on m/c unpt. K. Ettounsi on horseback at l. ctr., his head as wmk., bldgs. in background. Montage of city view; a "7" over flag on stylized dove at ctr. on back.

VG	VF	UNC
FV	FV	35.00

89 **30 DINARS**

7.11.1997. Green and yellow on m/c unpt. Abou El Kacem Chebbi at r. and as wmk. Schoolgirls, sheep and weaver on back.

VG	VF	UNC
FV	FV	50.00

The Republic of Turkey, a parliamentary democracy of the Near East located partially in Europe and partially in Asia between the Black and the Mediterranean seas, has an area of 301,382 sq. mi. (780,580 sq. km.) and a population of 63.53 million. Capital: Ankara. Turkey exports cotton, hazelnuts and tobacco, and enjoys a virtual monopoly in meerschaum.

The Ottoman Turks, a tribe from Central Asia, first appeared in the early 13th century, and by the 17th century had established the Ottoman Empire which stretched from the Persian Gulf to the southern frontier of Poland, and from the Caspian Sea to the Algerian plateau. The defeat of the Turkish navy by the Holy League in 1571, and of the Turkish forces besieging Vienna in 1683, began the steady decline of the Ottoman Empire which, accelerated by the rise of nationalism, contracted its European border, and by the end of World War I deprived it of its Arab lands. The present Turkish boundaries were largely fixed by the Treaty of Lausanne in 1923. The sultanate and caliphate, the political and spiritual ruling institutions of the old empire, were separated and the sultanate abolished in 1922 by Mustafa Kemal Atatürk. On Oct. 29, 1923, Turkey formally became a republic and Atatürk was selected as the first president.

MONETARY SYSTEM:

1 Lira (Livre, Pound) = 100 Piastres

REPUBLIC

TÜRKIYE CÜMHURIYET MERKEZ BANKASI
CENTRAL BANK OF TURKEY

LAW 11 HAZIRAN 1930; 1961-65 ND ISSUE

#173-178 Pres. K. Atatürk at r. and as wmk. Printer: DBM-A (w/o imprint).

		VG	VF	UNC
173	**5 LIRA** *L.1930* (25.10.1961). Blue w/orange, blue and m/c guilloche. Back blue; 3 peasant women w/baskets of hazelnuts at ctr.	3.00	10.00	60.00

		VG	VF	UNC
174	**5 LIRA** *L.1930* (4.1.1965). Blue-green. Back blue-gray, like #173.	2.00	6.00	45.00

		VG	VF	UNC
175	**50 LIRA** *L.1930* (1.6.1964). Brown on m/c unpt. Different sign. Soldier holding rifle at ctr. on back.	5.00	18.50	75.00
176	**100 LIRA** *L.1930* (15.3.1962). Olive on orange and m/c guilloche. Park w/bridge in Ankara on back.	12.50	50.00	125.00

		VG	VF	UNC
177	**100 LIRA** *L.1930* (1.10.1964). Like #176, but guilloche blue, lilac and m/c. Different sign.	8.50	35.00	100.00
178	**500 LIRA** *L.1930* (1.12.1962). Brown on m/c unpt. Square w/mosque on back.	50.00	150.00	400.00

LAW 11 HAZIRAN 1930; 1966-69 ND ISSUE

#179-183 Pres. Atatürk at r. and as wmk. 3 sign. Printer: DBM-A (w/o imprint).

		VG	VF	UNC
179	**5 LIRA** *L.1930* (8.1.1968). Grayish purple on m/c unpt. Waterfalls at l. ctr. on back.	.25	1.00	4.00

		VG	VF	UNC
180	**10 LIRA** *L.1930* (4.7.1966). Green on m/c unpt. Lighthouse at l., town view at ctr. on back.	.50	2.00	7.00

		VG	VF	UNC
181	**20 LIRA** *L.1930* (15.6.1966). Red-brown on m/c unpt. Back dull brown on pale green unpt., monument at l., tomb of Atatürk at ctr. on back.	1.25	2.50	12.50

		VG	VF	UNC
182	**100 LIRA** *L.1930* (17.3.1969). Like #176 but modified guilloche in pinkish red, blue and m/c unpt. Different sign.	10.00	30.00	90.00
183	**500 LIRA** *L.1930* (3.6.1968). Purple, brown and m/c. Like #178.	25.00	75.00	225.00

#184 Held in reserve.

LAW OCAK 14 (JAN. 26), 1970; 1971-82 ND ISSUES

#185-191 Pres. Atatürk at r. and as wmk. 2 sign.

#185, 188, 190 and 191 replacement notes: Serial # prefix *Z91-Z95*.

		VG	VF	UNC
185	**5 LIRA** *L.1970.* Like #179.	.15	.40	2.00

		VG	VF	UNC
186	**10 LIRA** *L.1970.* Like #180.	.30	1.25	4.00

		VG	VF	UNC
187	**20 LIRA** *L.1970.* Like #181.			
	a. Black sign. 2 varieties.	.30	1.50	4.50
	b. Brown sign.	.20	.50	1.00

		VG	VF	UNC
187A	**50 LIRA** *L.1970* (2.8.1971). Brown on m/c unpt. Like #175 except for different inscription at ctr., Pres. Atatürk at r. Soldier w/rifle on back. 2 sign. Series O-Y. Printer: Devlet Banknot Matbassi (w/o imprint).	1.00	2.50	9.00

		VG	VF	UNC
188	**50 LIRA** *L.1970.* Dk. brown on m/c unpt. New portr. at r. Fountain on back. 2 sign. varieties.	.50	.85	1.75

		VG	VF	UNC
189	**100 LIRA** *L.1970* (15.5.1972). Blue-green on m/c unpt. Face similar to #188. Back brown; Mt. Ararat. 2 sign. varieties.	.50	1.00	2.00

		VG	VF	UNC
190	**500 LIRA** *L.1970* (1.9.1971). Blue-black and dk. green on m/c unpt. Gate of the University of Istanbul on back. 2 sign. varieties.	2.00	8.00	15.00

		VG	VF	UNC
191	**1000 LIRA** *L.1970.* Deep purple and brown-violet on m/c unpt. Bosphorus River w/boat and suspension bridge on back. Sign. varieties.	1.00	2.00	5.50

LAW OCAK 14 (JAN. 26), 1970; 1984-97 ND ISSUES

#192-204 Pres. Atatürk at r. and as wmk.

Some sign. varieties.

		VG	VF	UNC
192	**10 LIRA** *L.1970.* Dull gray-green on m/c unpt. Young boy and girl in medallion in unpt. at ctr. Children presenting flowers to Atatürk on back.	.10	.20	.50
193	**10 LIRA** *L.1970.* Black on m/c unpt. Like #192.	.10	.20	.50

		VG	VF	UNC
194	**100 LIRA** *L.1970* (1984). Violet and brown on m/c unpt. Bldg., castle on hill, document and M. A. Ersoy on back.			
	a. Wmk.: Head sm., bust facing r., dotted security thread.	.15	.30	1.25
	b. Wmk.: Head lg., bust facing 3/4 r.	.10	.25	1.00

		VG	VF	UNC
195	**500 LIRA** *L.1970* (1984). Blue on m/c unpt. Tower monument at l. ctr. on back. Wmk. varieties.	.20	.50	1.50

		VG	VF	UNC
196	**1000 LIRA** *L.1970* (1986). Purple and blue on m/c unpt. One dot for blind at lower l. Coastline at l., Fatin Sultan Mehmed at ctr. r. on back.	.25	.65	1.75

		VG	VF	UNC
196A	**5000 LIRA** *L.1970* (1985). Dk. brown and olive-green on m/c unpt. Mevlana Museum at ctr. on back.	1.00	2.50	12.50

		VG	VF	UNC
197	**5000 LIRA** *L.1970* (1985). Dk. brown, red-brown and blue on m/c unpt. Seated Mevlana at l. ctr., Mevlana Museum at ctr. on back.	.75	2.50	7.50

		VG	VF	UNC
198	**5000 LIRA** *L.1970* (ca.1992). Deep brown and deep green on m/c unpt. Afsin-Elbistan thermal power plant at l. ctr. on back.	.30	1.25	4.00

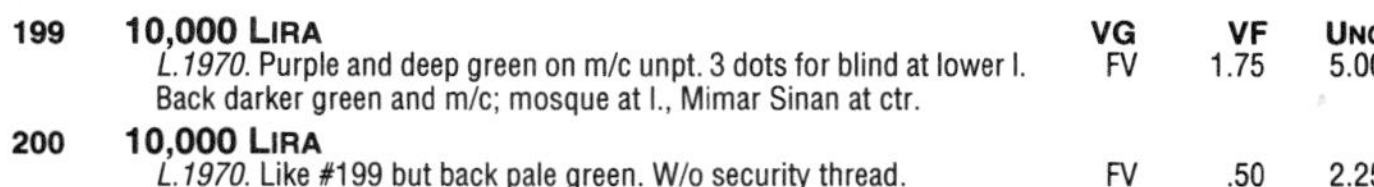

		VG	VF	UNC
199	**10,000 LIRA** *L.1970.* Purple and deep green on m/c unpt. 3 dots for blind at lower l. Back darker green and m/c; mosque at l., Mimar Sinan at ctr.	FV	1.75	5.00
200	**10,000 LIRA** *L.1970.* Like #199 but back pale green. W/o security thread.	FV	.50	2.25

		VG	VF	UNC
201	**20,000 LIRA** *L.1970* (1988). Red-brown and violet on m/c unpt. Central Bank bldg. in Ankara at l. ctr. on back.	FV	FV	7.00
202	**20,000 LIRA** *L.1970* (1995). Like #201 but w/yellow unpt. on litho back. Red sign. Series G-.	FV	FV	2.75

		VG	VF	UNC
203	**50,000 LIRA** *L.1970* (1989). Black and blue-green on m/c unpt. National Parliament House in Ankara at l. ctr. on back.	FV	FV	9.00
204	**50,000 LIRA** *L.1970* (1995). Like #203 but w/value in gray on back. Series K-.	FV	FV	2.50

#205-211 Pres. Atatürk facing at ctr. r. and as wmk.

		VG	VF	UNC
205	**100,000 LIRA** *L.1970* (1991). Reddish brown, dk. brown and black on m/c unpt. Equestrian statue of Atatürk at lower l. ctr. Children presenting flowers to Atatürk at l. ctr. on back.	FV	FV	7.50
206	**100,000 LIRA** *L.1970* (1997). M/c. Like #205 but w/o security device at upper r.	FV	FV	2.25

		VG	VF	UNC
207	**250,000 LIRA** *L.1970* (1992). Blue-gray, dk. green and violet on m/c unpt. Triangular security device at upper r. Kizilkale Fortress at Alunya at ctr. on back.	FV	FV	13.50

		VG	VF	UNC
208	**500,000 LIRA** *L.1970* (1993). Purple blue-black and violet on m/c unpt. Square security device at upper r. Aerial view of Canakkale Martyrs Monument on back.	FV	FV	21.50

		VG	VF	UNC
209	**1,000,000 LIRA** *L.1970* (1995). Claret red and blue-gray on m/c unpt. Atatürk dam in Sanli Urfa on back.	FV	FV	35.00

		VG	VF	UNC
210	**5,000,000 LIRA** *L.1970* (1997). Dk. brown and red-brown on m/c unpt. Gold oval seal w/AH1329 date at r. Anitkabir bldg. complex in Ankara at l. ctr. on back.	FV	FV	40.00

1998-99 ND ISSUE

		VG	VF	UNC
211	**250,000 LIRA** *L.1970* (1998). Blue-gray and violet on m/c unpt. Like #207 but triangular security device at upper r. printed in solid ink. Back blue litho.	FV	FV	3.00
212	**500,000 LIRA** *L.1970* (1998). Purple, blue-black and violet on m/c unpt. Like #208 but w/o square security device at upper r.	FV	FV	5.50
213	**10,000,000 LIRA** *L.1970* (1999). M/c.	FV	FV	12.50

The Turkmenistan Republic covers the territory of the Trans-Caspian Region of Turkestan, the Charjiui Vilayet of Bukhara and the part of Khiva located on the right bank of the Oxus. Bordered on the north by the Autonomous Kara-Kalpak Republic (a constituent of Uzbekistan), by Iran and Afghanistan on the south, by the Uzbek Republic on the east and the Caspian Sea on the west. It has an area of 186,400 sq. mi. (488,100 sq. km.) and a population of 4.2 million. Capital: Ashkhabad (formerly Poltoratsk). Main occupation is agricultural products including cotton and maize. It is rich in minerals, oil, coal, sulphur and salt,and is also famous for it's carpets, Turkoman horses and Karakul sheep.

The Turkomans arrived in Transcaspia as nomadic Seluk Turks in the 11th century. It often became subjected to one of the neighboring states. Late in the 19th century the Czarist Russians invaded with their first victory at Kyzyl Arvat in 1877, arriving in Ashkhabad in 1882 resulting in submission of the Turkmen tribes. By March 18, 1884 the Transcaspian province of Russian Turkestan was formed. During WW I the Czarist government tried to conscript the Turkmen; this led to a revolt in Oct. 1916 under the leadership of Aziz Chapykov. In 1918 the Turks captured Baku from the Red army and the British sent a contingent to Merv to prevent a German-Turkish offensive toward Afghanistan and India. In mid-1919 a Bureau of Turkistan Moslem Communist Organization was formed in Moscow hoping to develop one large republic including all surrounding Turkic areas within a Soviet federation. A Turkistan Autonomous Soviet Socialist Republic was formed and plans to partition Turkistan into five republics according to the principle of nationalities was quickly implemented by Joseph Stalin. On Oct. 27, 1924, Turkmenistan became a Soviet Socialist Republic and was accepted as a member of the U.S.S.R. on Jan. 29, 1925. The Bureau of T.M.C.O. was disbanded in 1934. In Aug. 1990 the Turkmen Supreme Soviet adopted a declaration of sovereignty followed by a declaration of independence in Oct. 1991 joining the Commonwealth of Independent States in Dec. A new constitution was adopted in 1992 providing for an executive presidency.

REPUBLIC

TÜRKMENISTANYÑ MERKEZI DÖWLET BANKY

CENTRAL BANK OF TURKMENISTAN

1993 ND; 1995-98 ISSUE

#1-9 arms at l. on back. Wmk: Rearing Arabian horse. Replacement notes: Serial # prefix *ZZ*.

		VG	VF	UNC
1	**1 MANAT** ND (1993). Brown and tan on m/c unpt. Ylymlar Academy at ctr., native craft at r. Shield at l., Temple at ctr. on back.	FV	FV	.60

		VG	VF	UNC
2	**5 MANAT** ND (1993). Blue and green on m/c unpt. Bldg. at ctr. Bldg. at ctr. on back.	FV	FV	1.00

#3-10 Pres. S. Niazov at r.

> **NOTICE**
>
> Readers with unlisted dates, signature varieties, etc. are invited to submit photocopies of their notes to: Standard Catalog of World Paper Money, 700 East State St. Iola, WI 54990-0001, fax: 1-715-445-4087, or E-Mail: thernr@krause.com.

		VG	VF	UNC
3	**10 MANAT** ND (1993). Brown and pale orange on m/c unpt. Govt. bldg. at ctr. Govt. bldg. on back.	FV	FV	1.40

		VG	VF	UNC
4	**20 MANAT** ND (1993); 1995. Blue-gray and blue on m/c unpt. National library at ctr. Lg. bldg. at ctr. on back.			
	a. ND (1993).	FV	FV	3.25
	b. 1995.	FV	FV	1.50

		VG	VF	UNC
5	**50 MANAT** ND (1993); 1995. Brown and green on m/c unpt. Monument at ctr. Mosque ruins on back.			
	a. ND (1993).	FV	FV	5.00
	b. 1995.	FV	FV	1.75

		VG	VF	UNC
6	**100 MANAT** ND (1993); 1995. Dk. blue and dk. gray on m/c unpt. Presidential Palace at ctr. Sultan Sanjaryn mausoleum on back.			
	a. ND (1993).	FV	FV	6.50
	b. 1995.	FV	FV	1.75

7	**500 MANAT**	VG	VF	UNC
	ND (1993); 1995. Violet, dk. brown and orange on m/c unpt. National theatre at ctr. Hanymyn mausoleum on back.			
	a. ND (1993).	FV	FV	11.50
	b. 1995.	FV	FV	5.00

		VG	VF	UNC
8	**1000 MANAT** 1995. Green on m/c unpt. Bldg. at ctr. Arms at ctr. on back.	FV	FV	7.25
9	**5000 MANAT** 1996. Violet, purple and red on m/c unpt. Bldg. at ctr. Coat of arms on back.	FV	FV	8.50
10	**10,000 MANAT** 1996. Dk. brown on m/c unpt. Presidential palace at ctr. Arms on back.	FV	FV	10.00

		VG	VF	UNC
11	**20,000 MANAT** 1998. Lt. blue, lt. brown, and red on m/c unpt. Palace of Turkmenbashy. Back: lt. blue, violet, and purple on m/c unpt., mosque of Saparmurat.	FV	FV	10.00

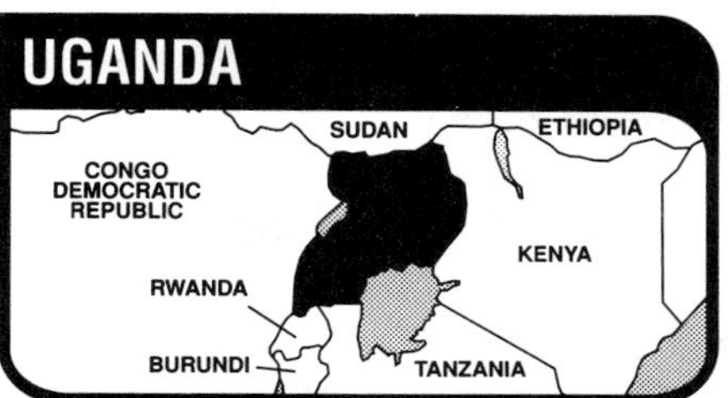

The Republic of Uganda, a former British protectorate located astride the equator in east-central Africa, has an area of 91,134 sq. mi. (236,036 sq. km.) and a population of 15.25 million. Capital: Kampala. Agriculture, including livestock, is the basis of the economy; there is some mining of copper, tin, gold and lead. Coffee, cotton, copper and tea are exported.

Uganda was first visited by Arab slavers in the 1830s. They were followed in the 1860s by British explorers searching for the headwaters of the Nile. The explorers, and the missionaries who followed them into the Lake Victoria region of south-central Africa in 1877-1879, found well developed African kingdoms dating back several centuries. In 1894 the local native Kingdom of Buganda was established as a British protectorate that was extended in 1896 to encompass an area substantially the same as the present Republic of Uganda. The protectorate was given a ministerial form of government in 1955, full internal self-government on March 1, 1962, and complete independence on Oct. 9, 1962. Uganda is a member of the Commonwealth of Nations. The president is Chief of State and Head of Government.

Notes of East African Currency Board circulated before Bank of Uganda notes were available. Also see East Africa.

MONETARY SYSTEM:

1 Shilling = 100 Cents

CAUTION: Several years ago the Bank of Uganda sold quantities of demonetized notes, most of which were made available for only $1.00 per note. Condition of notes thus sold is not reported. A listing of some pieces NOT available from the bank includes #4, 6a, 7a, 8a and b, 9a and b, 13a, 14a, 16b, 23, and 24a and b.

REPUBLIC

BANK OF UGANDA

1966 ND ISSUE

#1-5 sign. titles: *GOVERNOR* and *SECRETARY*. Wmk: Hand. Replacement notes: Serial # prefix *Z/1* (5/ and 10/); *Y/1; X/1; W/1* respectively.

1	**5 SHILLINGS**	VG	VF	UNC
	ND (1966). Dk. blue on m/c unpt. Arms at r. River and waterfall on back.	.65	2.00	5.00

2	**10 SHILLINGS**	VG	VF	UNC
	ND (1966). Brown on m/c unpt. Arms at ctr. Workers picking cotton on back.	1.25	2.50	5.00

		VG	VF	UNC
3	**20 SHILLINGS** ND (1966). Purple on m/c unpt. Arms at l. African animals on back.	1.00	2.00	5.00

		VG	VF	UNC
4	**100 SHILLINGS** ND (1966). Green on m/c unpt. Crested crane at l., w/o *FOR BANK OF UGANDA* just below value at ctr. Bldg. at r. on back.	20.00	85.00	750.00

		VG	VF	UNC
5	**100 SHILLINGS** ND (1966). Green on m/c unpt. Like #4 but w/text: *FOR BANK OF UGANDA* under value.	.75	1.50	6.00

1973-77 ND ISSUE

SIGNATURE VARIETIES					
1	GOVERNOR	SECRETARY	2	GOVERNOR	SECRETARY

#5A-9 Pres. Idi Amin at l., arms at lower r. Wmk: Crested crane. Replacement notes: Serial # prefix *Z/1* (5/ and 10/); *Y/1*; *X/1*; *W/1* respectively.

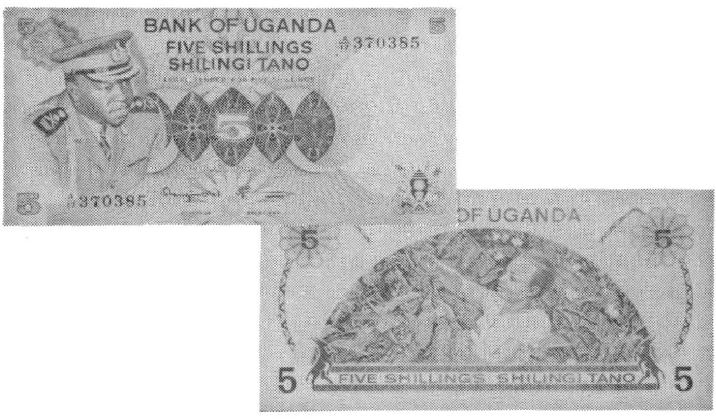

		VG	VF	UNC
5A	**5 SHILLINGS** ND (1977). Blue on m/c unpt. Woman picking coffee beans on back.	.35	.75	2.50

		VG	VF	UNC
6	**10 SHILLINGS** ND (1973). Brown on m/c unpt. Elephants, antelope and hippopotamus on back.			
	a. Sign. titles: *GOVERNOR* and *DIRECTOR.*	5.00	35.00	225.00
	b. Sign. titles: *GOVERNOR* and *SECRETARY.* Sign. 1.	1.00	2.50	12.50
	c. Sign. titles as b. Sign. 2.	.35	1.00	4.00
	s. As a. Specimen.	—	—	80.00

		VG	VF	UNC
7	**20 SHILLINGS** ND (1973). Purple and brown on m/c unpt. Lg. bldg. on back.			
	a. Sign. titles: *GOVERNOR* and *DIRECTOR.*	7.50	40.00	250.00
	b. Sign. titles: *GOVERNOR* and *SECRETARY.* Sign. 1.	1.00	3.00	35.00
	c. Sign. titles as b. Sign. 2.	.75	2.25	7.50
	s. As a. Specimen.	—	—	90.00

		VG	VF	UNC
8	**50 SHILLINGS**			
	ND (1973). Blue (shade) on m/c unpt. Hydroelectric dam on back.			
	a. Sign. titles: *GOVERNOR* and *DIRECTOR*.	8.50	40.00	200.00
	b. Sign. titles: *GOVERNOR* and *SECRETARY*. Sign. 1.	2.00	5.00	50.00
	c. Sign. titles as b. Sign. 2.	.75	2.00	6.00
	s. As a. Specimen.	—	—	135.00

		VG	VF	UNC
9	**100 SHILLINGS**			
	ND (1973). Green (shades) on m/c unpt. Scene of lake and hills on back.			
	a. Sign. titles: *GOVERNOR* and *DIRECTOR*.	8.00	30.00	175.00
	b. Sign. titles: *GOVERNOR* and *SECRETARY*. Sign. 1.	3.00	10.00	75.00
	c. Sign. titles as b. Sign. 2.	.75	2.00	8.50
	s. As a. Specimen.	—	—	110.00

1979 ISSUE

#10-14 Bank of Uganda at l. Sign. titles: *GOVERNOR* and *DIRECTOR*. Wmk: Crested crane's head. Replacement notes: Serial # prefix *Z/1* (5/ and 10/); *Y/1; X/1; W/1* respectively.

		VG	VF	UNC
10	**5 SHILLINGS**			
	ND (1979). Blue on m/c unpt. Back like #5A.	.05	.20	1.00

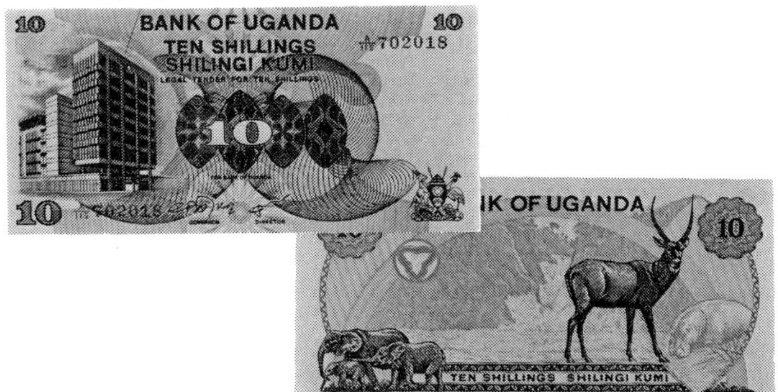

		VG	VF	UNC
11	**10 SHILLINGS**			
	ND (1979). Brown on m/c unpt. Back like #6.			
	a. Lt. printing on bank.	.25	1.50	4.50
	b. Dk. printing on bank.	.30	.90	3.25

		VG	VF	UNC
12	**20 SHILLINGS**			
	ND (1979). Purple and brown on m/c unpt. Back like #7.			
	a. Lt. printing on bank.	.40	2.50	6.50
	b. Dk. printing on bank.	.25	.75	4.00

		VG	VF	UNC
13	**50 SHILLINGS**			
	ND (1979). Dk. blue and purple on m/c unpt. Back like #8.			
	a. Lt. printing on bank.	5.00	17.50	100.00
	b. Dk. printing on bank.	.35	1.00	4.50

		VG	VF	UNC
14	**100 SHILLINGS**			
	ND (1979). Green (shades) on m/c unpt. Back like #9.			
	a. Lt. printing on bank.	1.50	4.00	11.00
	b. Dk. printing on bank.	1.00	3.00	8.50

1982 ISSUE

#15-19 arms at l. Sign. titles: *GOVERNOR* and *SECRETARY*. Wmk: Crested crane's head. Replacement notes: Serial # prefix *Z/1* (5/ and 10/); *Y/1; X/1; W/1* respectively.

		VG	VF	UNC
15	**5 SHILLINGS** ND (1982). Olive-green on m/c unpt. Back like #5A.	.10	.25	1.50

		VG	VF	UNC
16	**10 SHILLINGS** ND (1982). Purple on m/c unpt. Back like #6.	.15	.40	2.75

		VG	VF	UNC
17	**20 SHILLINGS** ND (1982). Green, red and m/c. Back like #7.	.30	1.50	4.50

		VG	VF	UNC
18	**50 SHILLINGS** ND (1982). Brown, orange and m/c. Back like #8.			
	a. Sign. titles: *GOVERNOR* and *SECRETARY.*	.25	.75	2.75
	b. Sign. titles: *GOVERNOR* and *DEPUTY GOVERNOR.*	.25	.85	10.00

		VG	VF	UNC
19	**100 SHILLINGS** ND (1982). Red-violet, orange and m/c. Back like #9.			
	a. Sign. titles: *GOVERNOR* and *SECRETARY.*	.65	1.50	5.00
	b. Sign. titles: *GOVERNOR* and *DEPUTY GOVERNOR.* Sm. or lg. prefix letter and # before serial #.	.25	1.00	3.75

NOTICE

Readers with unlisted dates, signature varieties, etc. are invited to submit photocopies of their notes to: Standard Catalog of World Paper Money, 700 East State St. Iola, WI 54990-0001, fax: 1-715-445-4087, or E-Mail: thernr@krause.com.

1983-85 ISSUE

#20-23 Pres. Milton Obote at l. on face. Sign. titles: *GOVERNOR* and *DEPUTY GOVERNOR.* Wmk: Hand. Replacement notes: Serial # prefix *X/1; W/1; U/1; T/1; S/1* respectively.

		VG	VF	UNC
20	**50 SHILLINGS** ND (1985). Brown and orange on m/c unpt. Back like #8.	.50	1.00	3.00
21	**100 SHILLINGS** ND (1985). Red-violet and orange on m/c unpt. Back like #9.	1.00	2.50	15.00

		VG	VF	UNC
22	**500 SHILLINGS** ND (1983). Blue, purple and m/c. Cattle and harvesting on back. Serial # prefix varieties as #19b.			
	a. Issued note.	.30	1.25	5.50
	s. Specimen.	—	—	10.00

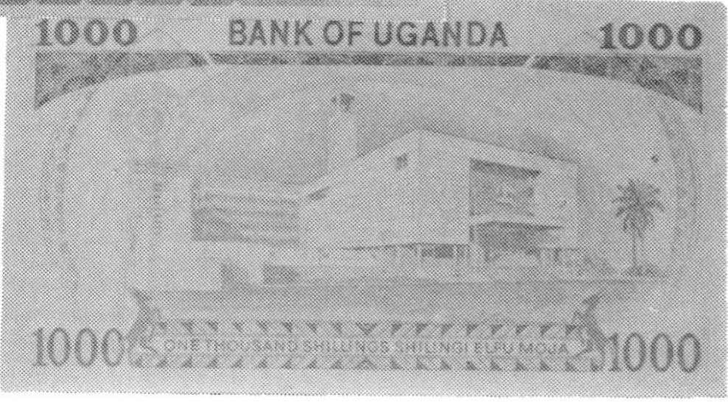

		VG	VF	UNC
23	**1000 SHILLINGS** ND (1983). Red and m/c. Bldg. on back. Serial # prefix varieties as #19b.			
	a. Issued note.	1.50	4.00	20.00
	s. Specimen.	—	—	12.50

24 **5000 SHILLINGS** — VG / VF / UNC

1985-86. Purple and m/c. Arms at l. Bldg. w/clock tower at ctr. r. on back.

	VG	VF	UNC
a. Wmk: Hand. 1985.	2.50	5.50	27.50
b. Wmk: Crested crane. 1986.	.75	2.00	5.00

1985-86 ISSUE

#25 and 26 face similar to #24. Wmk: Crested crane's head. Replacement notes: Serial # prefix *U/1; T/1* respectively.

25	500 SHILLINGS	VG	VF	UNC
	1986. Blue, purple and m/c. Back like #22.	.25	.65	3.00

26	1000 SHILLINGS	VG	VF	UNC
	1986. Red and m/c. Back like #23.	.35	1.00	3.75

1987 ISSUE

#27-34 replacement notes: Serial # prefix *ZZ*.

#27-32 arms at upper l., map at ctr. Printer: TDLR.

27	5 SHILLINGS	VG	VF	UNC
	1987. Brown on m/c unpt. Arms at r. also. African wildlife on back.	.10	.40	1.25

28	10 SHILLINGS	VG	VF	UNC
	1987. Green on m/c unpt. Arms at r. also. 2 antelope grazing, 2 men fishing in canoe at ctr. on back.	.10	.30	1.75

#29-34 wmk: Crested crane's head.

29	20 SHILLINGS	VG	VF	UNC
	1987-88. Purple, blue-black and violet on m/c unpt. Modern bldgs. at ctr. r. on back.			
	a. Imprint on back. 1987.	.15	.40	2.50
	b. W/o imprint. 1988.	.05	.35	2.25

		VG	VF	UNC
30	**50 SHILLINGS** 1987-98. Red, orange and dk. brown on m/c unpt. Parliament bldg. at ctr. r. on back.			
	a. Imprint on back. 1987.	.20	.50	2.25
	b. W/o imprint. 1988; 1989.	.15	.40	2.00
	c. 1994; 1996; 1997; 1998.	.10	.25	1.25

		VG	VF	UNC
31	**100 SHILLINGS** 1987-98. Deep blue-violet, black and aqua on m/c unpt. High Court bldg. w/clock tower at ctr. r. on back.			
	a. Sign. titles: *GOVERNOR* and *SECRETARY, TREASURY.* Imprint on back. 1987.	.25	1.00	5.00
	b. As a. but w/o imprint on back. 1988.	.15	.85	3.00
	c. As b. but w/sign. titles: *GOVERNOR* and *SECRETARY.* 1994; 1996; 1997; 1998.	.10	.20	1.50

		VG	VF	UNC
32	**200 SHILLINGS** 1987-98. Brown, orange and olive-brown on m/c unpt. Worker in textile factory at ctr. r. on back.			
	a. 1987.	.20	.60	3.00
	b. 1991; 1994; 1996; 1998.	.15	.50	2.00

1991 ISSUE

		VG	VF	UNC
33	**500 SHILLINGS** 1991. Dk. brown and deep purple on m/c unpt. Elephant at l., arms at upper ctr. and lower r. Uganda Independence Monument at l., municipal bldg. w/clock tower at ctr. on back.			
	a. Sign. titles: *GOVERNOR* and *SECRETARY, TREASURY.*	.65	.80	3.00
	b. Sign. titles: *GOVERNOR* and *SECRETARY.*	FV	.65	3.50
	s. As a. Specimen.	—	—	25.00

		VG	VF	UNC
34	**1000 SHILLINGS** 1991. Black, deep brown-violet and dk. green on m/c unpt. Farmers at l., arms at upper ctr. and lower r. Grain storage facility at ctr. on back.			
	a. Sign. titles: *GOVERNOR* and *SECRETARY, TREASURY.*	1.25	2.00	6.50
	b. Sign. titles: *GOVERNOR* and *SECRETARY.*	FV	1.25	5.00

1993-95 ISSUE

#35-38 arms at upper ctr. Wmk: Crested crane's head. Replacement notes: Serial # prefix *ZZ*.

		VG	VF	UNC
35	**500 SHILLINGS** 1994; 1996; 1998. Like #33. Segmented foil over security thread. Ascending serial # at l.			
	a. 1994; 1996.	FV	FV	3.00
	b. 1998.	.75	2.50	6.00

NOTICE

Readers with unlisted dates, signature varieties, etc. are invited to submit photocopies of their notes to: Standard Catalog of World Paper Money, 700 East State St. Iola, WI 54990-0001, fax: 1-715-445-4087, or E-Mail: thernr@krause.com.

36 **1000 SHILLINGS**

	VG	VF	UNC
1994; 1996; 1998. Like #34. Segmented foil over security thread. Ascending serial # at l.	FV	1.25	3.50

37 **5000 SHILLINGS**

	VG	VF	UNC
1993. Red-violet, deep purple and dk. green on m/c unpt. Lake Bunyoni, terraces at l. Railroad cars being loaded onto Kaawa Ferry at ctr., plant at lower r. on back.	FV	6.00	13.50

38 **10,000 SHILLINGS**

1995. Green and red on m/c unpt. Musical instruments at l. Owen Falls dam, kudu on back.	FV	11.00	25.00

Ukraine (formerly the Ukrainian Soviet Socialist Republic) is bordered by Russia to the east, Russia and Belarus to the north, Poland, Slovakia and Hungary to the west, Romania and Moldova to the southwest and in the south by the Black Sea and the Sea of Azov. It has an area of 233,088 sq. mi. (603,700 sq. km.) and a population of 50.9 million. Capital: Kyiv (Kiev). Ukraine was the site of the Chernobyl nclear power station disaster in 1986. Coal, grain, vegetables and heavy industrial machinery are major exports.

The territory of Ukraine has been inhabited for over 30,000 years. As the result of its location, Ukraine has served as the gateway to Europe for millennia and its early history has been recorded by Arabic, Greek, Roman, as well as Ukrainian historians.

Ukraine, which was known as Rus' until the sixteenth century (and from which the name Russia was derived in the 17th century), became the major political and cultural center of Eastern Europe in the 9th century. The Rus' Kingdom, under a dynasty of Varangian origin, due to its position on the intersection of the north-south Scandinavia to Byzantium and the east-west Orient to Europe trade routes, became a focal point of world trade. At its apex Rus' stretched from the Baltic to the Black Sea and from the upper Volga River in the east, almost to the Vistula River in the west. It has family ties to many European dynasties. In 988 knyaz (king) Volodymyr adopted Christianity from Byzantium. With it came church books written in the Cyrillic alphabet, which originated in Bulgaria. The Mongol invasion in 1240 brought an end to the might of the Rus' Kingdom.

In the seventeenth century, after almost four hundred years of Mongol, Lithuanian, Polish, and Turkish domination, the Cossack State under Hetman Bohdan Khmelnytsky regained Ukrainian independence. The Hetman State lasted until the mid-eighteenth century and was followed by a period of foreign rule: Eastern Ukraine was controlled by Russia, which enforced russification through introduction of the Russian language and prohibiting the use of the Ukrainian language in schools, books and public life. Western Ukraine came under relatively benign Austro-Hungarian rule.

With the disintegration of the Russian and Austro-Hungarian Empires in 1917 and 1918, Eastern Ukraine declared its full independence on January 22, 1918 and Western Ukraine followed suit on November 1 of that year. On January 22, 1919 both parts united into one state that had to defend itself on three fronts: from the "Red" Bolsheviks and their puppet Ukrainian Soviet Republic formed in Kharkiv, from the "White" czarist Russian forces, and from Poland. Ukraine lost the war. In 1920 Eastern Ukraine was occupied by the Bolsheviks and in 1922 was incorporated into the Soviet Union. There followed a brief resurgence of Ukrainian language and culture until Stalin suppressed it in 1928. The artificial famine-genocide of 1932-33 killed 7-10 million Ukrainians, and Stalinist purges in the mid-1930s took a heavy toll. Western Ukraine was partitioned between Poland, Romania, Hungary and Czechoslovakia.

On August 24, 1991 Ukraine once again declared its independence. On December 1, 1991 over 90% of Ukraine's electorate approved full independence from the Soviet Union. On December 5, 1991 the Ukrainian Parliament abrogated the 1922 treaty which incorporated Ukraine into the Soviet Union. Later, Leonid Kravchuk was elected president by a 65% majority.

During the changeover from the Ruble currency of the Soviet Union to the Karbovanets of Ukraine, as a transition measure and to restrict unlicensed export of scarce goods, coupon cards (202 x 82mm), similar to ration cards, were issued in various denominations They were valid for one month and were given to employees in amounts equal to their pay. Each card contained multiples of 1, 3, 5, 10, 25 and sometimes 50 Karbovanets valued coupons, to be cut apart. They were supposed to be used for purchases together with ruble notes. In January 1992 Ukraine began issuing individual coupons in Karbovanets denominations from 1 krb to 100 krb (printed in France and dated 1991). They were replaced by the Hryvnia.

Ukraine is a charter member of the United Nations and has inherited the third largest nuclear arsenal in the world, which by agreement with the USA will be dismantled within the next decade. Ukrainians in the homeland and the diaspora make up 1% of the world's population.

MONETARY SYSTEM:

1 Karvovanets (Karbovantsiv) КАРБОВАНЕЦЬ, КАРБОВАНЦІВ = 1 Russian Ruble, 1991-96
1 Hryvnia (Hryvni, Hryven) ГРИВНЯ (ГРИВНІ, ГРИВЕНЬ) = 100,000 Karbovantsiv, 1996-

УКРАЇНСЬКА Р.С.Р.

TREASURY

1990 ND КУПОН RUBLE CONTROL COUPON ISSUE

#68 various authorization handstamps in registry. Uniface.

68 **KARBOVANTSIV - VARIOUS AMOUNTS**

	VG	VF	UNC
ND (1990). Sheet of 28 coupons and registry. Жовтень.	—	—	4.00

#69-74 not assigned.

1991 КУПОН RUBLE CONTROL COUPON ISSUE

#75 various authorization handstamps in registry. Uniface.

#		VG	VF	UNC
75	**KARBOVANTSIV - VARIOUS AMOUNTS** 1991. Sheet of 28 coupons and registry.	—	—	4.00

#76-80 not assigned.

НАЦІОНАЛЬНИЙ БАНК УКРАЇНИ
UKRAINIAN NATIONAL BANK

1991 КУПОН CONTROL COUPON ISSUE

Karbovanets System

Originally issued at par and temporarily to be used jointly with Russian rubles in commodity purchases as a means of currency control (similar to Ruble Control Coupons above). They soon became more popular while the ruble slowly depreciated in exchange value. This did not last very long and the karbovanets has since suffered a higher inflation rate than the Russian ruble.

#81-87 Libyd, Viking sister of the founding brothers, at l. Cathedral of St. Sophia in Kiev at l. ctr. on back. All notes w/o serial #. Wmk. paper. All denominations had the value, i.e. *3 KRB*, printed sideways with fluorescent ink at l.

#		VG	VF	UNC
81	**1 KARBOVANETS** 1991. Dull brown and pale orange on yellow unpt.	.05	.10	.25

#		VG	VF	UNC
82	**3 KARBOVANTSI** 1991. Greenish gray and pale orange on yellow unpt.	.05	.10	.25
83	**5 KARBOVANTSIV** 1991. Dull blue-violet and pale orange on yellow unpt.	.05	.20	.40

#		VG	VF	UNC
84	**10 KARBOVANTSIV** 1991. Pink and pale orange on yellow unpt.	.05	.20	.50
85	**25 KARBOVANTSIV** 1991. Red-violet and pale orange on yellow unpt.	.15	.50	1.50

#		VG	VF	UNC
86	**50 KARBOVANTSIV** 1991. Blue-green and pale orange on yellow unpt.	.10	.35	1.50
87	**100 KARBOVANTSIV** 1991. Brown-violet and pale orange on yellow unpt.	.50	1.50	4.50

1992 ISSUE

#88-91 founding Viking brothers Kyi, Shchek and Khoryv w/sister Libyd in bow of boat at l. Backs like #81-87. All notes w/serial #. Wmk. paper. Replacement notes: Serial # prefix *.../99* in denominator. Printer: TDLR.

#		VG	VF	UNC
88	**100 KARBOVANTSIV** 1992. Orange on lilac and ochre unpt.			
	a. Issued note.	.10	.40	1.75
	s. Specimen.	—	—	10.00

#		VG	VF	UNC
89	**200 KARBOVANTSIV** 1992. Dull brown and silver on lilac and ochre unpt.			
	a. Issued note.	.25	1.25	5.00
	s. Specimen.	—	—	10.00

#		VG	VF	UNC
90	**500 KARBOVANTSIV** 1992. Blue-green and silver on lilac and ochre unpt.			
	a. Issued note.	.25	.75	2.00
	s. Specimen.	—	—	10.00

		VG	VF	UNC
91	**1000 KARBOVANTSIV** 1992. Red-violet and lt. green on lilac and ochre unpt.			
	a. Issued note.	.25	.75	2.25
	s. Specimen.	—	—	10.00

GOVERNMENT

TREASURY

1992 СЕРТИФІКАТ - COMPENSATION CERTIFICATE ISSUE

#91A and 91B church at l., small arms at upper r. Text on back. The exact use of these notes has come into question.

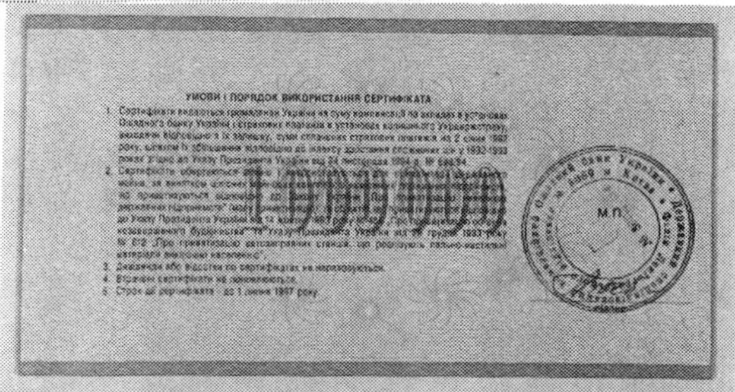

		VG	VF	UNC
91A	**1,000,000 KARBOVANTSIV** 1992. Dull blue-green, orange and gray on pale orange and pale green unpt.	.75	2.00	5.00

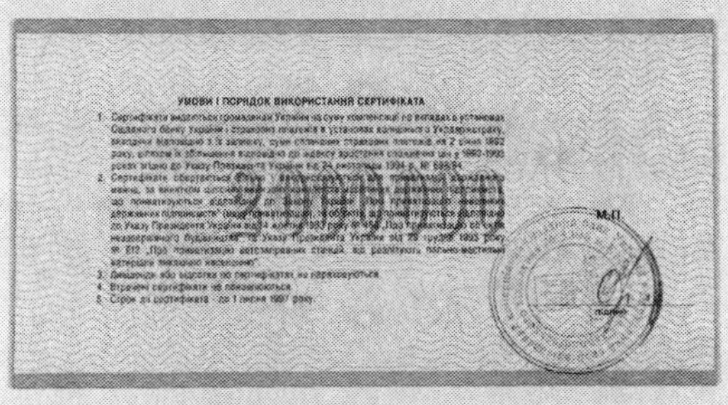

		VG	VF	UNC
91B	**2,000,000 KARBOVANTSIV** 1992. Green, orange and pink w/black text on lt. blue, pink and m/c unpt.	1.00	3.00	8.00

НАЦІОНАЛЬНИЙ БАНК УКРАЇНИ

UKRAINIAN NATIONAL BANK

1993 ISSUE

#92 and 93 similar to #88-91, but trident symbol added at l. on face; at r. on back. Replacement notes: Serial # prefix *001/92-001/99; 001/99* for notes dated 1993. Printer: TDLR.

		VG	VF	UNC
92	**2000 KARBOVANTSIV** 1993. Blue and olive-green on aqua and gold unpt.			
	a. Issued note.	.25	.75	2.50
	s. Specimen.	—	—	10.00

		VG	VF	UNC
93	**5000 KARBOVANTSIV** 1993; 1995. Red-orange and olive-brown on pale blue and ochre unpt.			
	a. 1993.	.10	.25	1.25
	b. 1995.	.05	.10	.50
	s. Specimen. 1993; 1995.	—	—	10.00

#94-97 statue of St. Volodymyr standing w/long cross at l. Bldg. facade at l. on back. Trident at l. on face, at r. on back. Wmk: Ornamental shield repeated vertically. Replacement notes: Serial # prefix *001/92-001/99; 001/99* for notes dated 1993. Printer: TDLR.

		VG	VF	UNC
94	**10,000 KARBOVANTSIV** 1993-96. Apple green and tan pale blue and ochre unpt. Printer: TDLR (w/o imprint).			
	a. 1993.	.10	.25	2.00
	b. 1995.	.05	.20	.65
	c. 1996. Wmk: Zig-zag of 4 bars.	.10	.35	1.50
	s. Specimen. 1993; 1995; 1996.	—	—	10.00

		VG	VF	UNC
95	**20,000 KARBOVANTSIV** 1993-96. Lilac and tan on blue and yellow unpt.			
	a. 1993.	.15	.50	2.00
	b. 1994; 1995.	.10	.25	1.00
	c. Wmk: Zig-zag of 4 bars. 1996.	.15	.50	2.00
	s. Specimen. 1993-96.	—	—	10.00

#		VG	VF	UNC
96	**50,000 KARBOVANTSIV** 1993-95. Dull orange and blue on m/c unpt.			
	a. 1993; 1994.	.15	.50	2.00
	b. 1995.	.40	1.25	8.00
	s. Specimen. 1993-95.	—	—	10.00

#		VG	VF	UNC
97	**100,000 KARBOVANTSIV** 1993; 1994. Gray-green and ochre on m/c unpt.			
	a. Prefix fraction before serial #. Wmk: НБУ. 1993.	.40	1.25	8.00
	b. Prefix letters w/serial #. Wmk: Trident shield repeated. 1994.	.25	.75	3.00
	s. Specimen. 1993; 1994.	—	—	10.00

#98 and 99 statue of St. Volodymyr standing w/long cross at r. Opera house at l. ctr. on back. Replacement notes: Serial # prefix *001/92-001/99; 001-99* for notes dated 1993.

#		VG	VF	UNC
98	**200,000 KARBOVANTSIV** 1993; 1994. Dull red-brown and lt. blue on aqua and gray unpt. Back m/c.			
	a. Prefix fraction before serial #. Wmk: НБУ. 1993; 1994.	.65	2.50	10.00
	b. Prefix letters w/serial #. Wmk: Trident shield repeated. 1994.	.50	1.50	5.00
	s. Specimen. 1993; 1994.	—	—	10.00

#		VG	VF	UNC
99	**500,000 KARBOVANTSIV** 1994. Lt. blue and lilac on yellow and gray unpt. Wmk: Trident shield repeated.			
	a. Issued note.	1.00	3.00	18.00
	s. Specimen.	—	—	15.00

1995 ISSUE

#		VG	VF	UNC
100	**1,000,000 KARBOVANTSIV** 1995. Dk. brown on pale orange, lt. blue and m/c unpt. Statue of T. G. Shevchenko at r., arms at lower l. Kiev State University at l. ctr., arms at lower r. on back.			
	a. Issued note.	1.50	4.50	18.00
	s. Specimen.	—	—	15.00

1995 PRIVATIZATION CERTIFICATE ISSUE

#101. 3 different notes available.

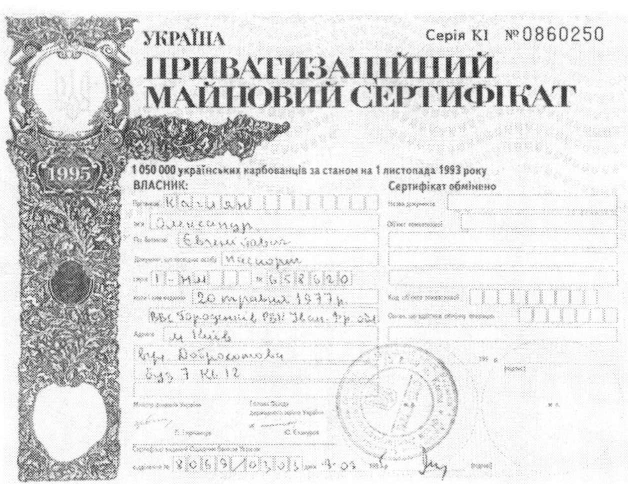
УКРАЇНА Серія КІ №0860250

ПРИВАТИЗАЦІЙНИЙ МАЙНОВИЙ СЕРТИФІКАТ

1995

1 050 000 українських карбованців за станом на 1 листопада 1993 року

ВЛАСНИК:

Сертифікат обмінено

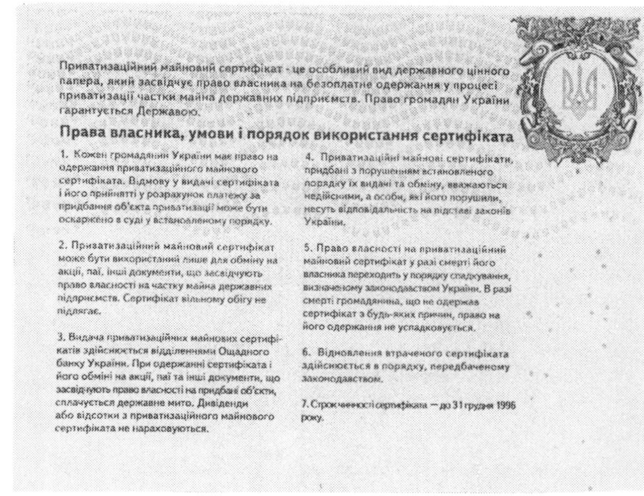
Приватизаційний майновий сертифікат - це особливий вид державного цінного папера, який засвідчує право власника на безоплатне одержання у процесі приватизації частки майна державних підприємств. Право громадян України гарантується Державою.

Права власника, умови і порядок використання сертифіката

1. Кожен громадянин України має право на одержання приватизаційного майнового сертифіката. Відмову у видачі сертифіката і його прийнятті у розрахунок платежу за придбання об'єкта приватизації може бути оскаржено в суді у встановленому порядку.

2. Приватизаційний майновий сертифікат може бути використаний лише для обміну на акції, паї, інші документи, що засвідчують право власності на частку майна державних підприємств. Сертифікат вільному обігу не підлягає.

3. Видача приватизаційних майнових сертифікатів здійснюється відділеннями Ощадного банку України. При одержанні сертифіката і його обміні на акції, паї та інші документи, що засвідчують право власності на придбані об'єкти, сплачується державне мито. Дивіденди або відсотки з приватизаційного майнового сертифіката не нараховуються.

4. Приватизаційні майнові сертифікати, придбані з порушенням встановленого порядку їх видачі та обміну, вважаються недійсними, а особи, які його порушили, несуть відповідальність на підставі законів України.

5. Право власності на приватизаційний майновий сертифікат у разі смерті його власника переходить у порядку спадкування, визначеному законодавством України. В разі смерті громадянина, що не одержав сертифікат з будь-яких причин, право на його одержання не успадковується.

6. Відновлення втраченого сертифіката здійснюється в порядку, передбаченому законодавством.

7. Строк чинності сертифіката — до 31 грудня 1996 року.

#		VG	VF	UNC
101	**1,050,000 KARBOVANTSIV** 1995. Dk. gray on lt. gray and ochre unpt. Arms at upper l. Text on back.	2.00	8.00	25.00

#102 not assigned.

1992 (1996) REGULAR ISSUE

SIGNATURE VARIETIES			
1	В.Гетьмаан	2	В.Матвієнко
3	В.Ющенко		

#103-107 wmk: Trident repeated. Printer: CBNC (w/o imprint). Replacement notes: First digit of serial # is *9*.

		VG	VF	UNC
103	**1 HRYVNIA** 1992 (1996). Olive-brown on m/c unpt. St. Volodymyr at ctr. Ancient city of Khersonnes at ctr. on back.			
	a. Sign. 2.	FV	FV	1.00
	b. Sign. 3.	FV	FV	1.00

		VG	VF	UNC
104	**2 HRYVNI** 1992 (1996). Brown on m/c unpt. Prince Yaroslav "The Wise" at ctr. Cathedral of St. Sophia at ctr. on back.			
	a. Sign. 1.	FV	FV	1.50
	b. Sign. 2.	FV	FV	1.50
	c. Sign. 3.	FV	FV	1.50

		VG	VF	UNC
105	**5 HRYVEN** 1992 (1996). Blue-gray on m/c unpt. B. Khmelnytsky at ctr. Illinska Church in Subotiv at ctr. on back.			
	a. Sign. 1.	FV	FV	2.50
	b. Sign. 2.	FV	FV	2.50
	c. Sign. 3.	FV	FV	2.50
106	**10 HRYVEN** 1992 (1996). Violet on m/c unpt. I. Mazepa at ctr. Kyiv-Pecherska Monastery at ctr. on back.			
	a. Sign. 2.	FV	FV	4.50
	b. Sign. 3.	FV	FV	4.50
107	**20 HRYVEN** 1992 (1996). Brown on m/c unpt. I. Franko at ctr. The Lviv Opera House at ctr. on back.			
	a. Sign. 2.	FV	FV	8.50
	b. Sign. 3.	FV	FV	8.50
107A	**50 HRYVEN** 1992. Man at ctr. (Not issued). Printer: CBNC.	—	—	—
107B	**100 HRYVEN** 1992. Man at ctr. (Not issued). Printer: CBNC.	—	—	—

1994-98 ND AND DATED ISSUE

		VG	VF	UNC
108	**1 HRYVNIA** 1994 (1996); 1995. Grayish brown and green on m/c unpt. St. Volodymyra at ctr. r. and as wmk. City of Khersonnes at ctr. on back. Sign. 3.			
	a. 1994.	FV	FV	1.00
	b. 1995.	FV	FV	1.00
	s. Specimen. 1994.	—	—	35.00

		VG	VF	UNC
109	**2 HRYVNI** 1995 (1997). M/c. Yaroslav the Wise at r. and as wmk. Cathedral of St. Sophia in Kyiv on back.	FV	FV	1.50

		VG	VF	UNC
110	**5 HRYVEN** 1994 (1997). M/c. Bohdan Khmelnytsky at ctr. r. Illinska Church in Subotiv at ctr. Printer: TDLR (w/o imprint).	FV	FV	2.50

		VG	VF	UNC
111	**10 HRYVEN** 1994 (1997). M/c. I. Mazepa at ctr. r. and as wmk. Kyiv-Pecherska Monastery at ctr. on back.	FV	FV	4.50

		VG	VF	UNC
112	**20 HRYVEN** 1995 (1997). M/c. I. Franko at r. and as wmk. Opera House in Lviv on back.			
	a. W/metallic security thread.	FV	FV	8.50
	b. W/o metallic security thread.	FV	FV	8.50

		VG	VF	UNC
113	**50 HRYVEN** ND (1996). Purple and dk. blue-gray on m/c unpt. M. Hrushevsky at r. and as wmk. Parliament bldg. at ctr. on back.			
	a. Sign. 2.	FV	FV	20.00
	b. Sign. 3.	FV	FV	20.00
	s. Specimen.	—	—	60.00
	x. Wmk. T. Shevchenko (error).	—	Rare	—

		VG	VF	UNC
114	**100 HRYVEN** ND (1996). Brown and dk. green on m/c unpt. T. Shevchenko at r. and as wmk. Cathedral of St. Sophia in Kyiv at ctr., statue of St. Volodymyr standing at l. on back.			
	a. Sign. 2.	FV	FV	35.00
	b. Sign. 3.	FV	FV	35.00
	s. Specimen.	—	—	100.00
115	**200 HRYVEN** ND (199x). L. Ukrainka on back.		Expected New Issue	

1997 (1998) ISSUE

		VG	VF	UNC
116	**5 HRYVEN** 1997 (1998). M/c. Like #110.	FV	FV	2.50

COLLECTOR SERIES

НАЦІОНАЛЬНИЙ БАНК УКРАЇНИ

UKRAINIAN NATIONAL BANK

1996 ISSUE

		ISSUE PRICE	MKT. VALUE
CS1	**1 HRYVNIA** #103 and 2 Karbovantsiv 1996 Independence coins in a folder.	—	—

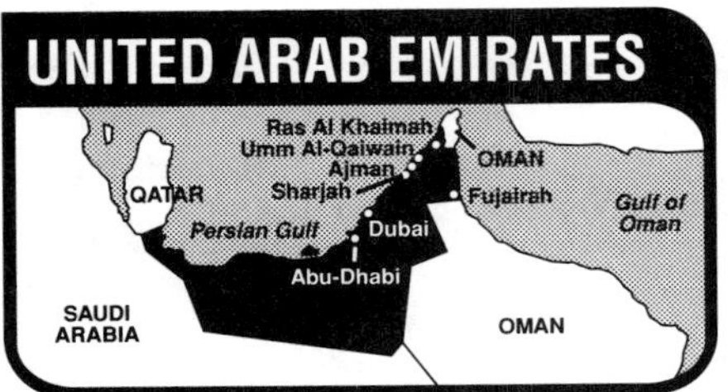

The seven United Arab Emirates (formerly known as the Trucial Sheikhdoms or States), located along the southern shore of the Persian Gulf, are comprised of the Sheikhdoms of Abu Dhabi, Dubai, Sharjah, Ajman, Umm al Qaiwain, Ras al-Khaimah and Fujairah. They have a combined area of about 32,000 sq. mi. (83,600 sq. km.) and a population of 2.3 million. Capital: Abu Zaby (Abu Dhabi). Since the oil strikes of 1958-60, the economy has centered on petroleum.

The Trucial States came under direct British influence in 1892 when the maritime truce treaty, enacted after the suppression of pirate activity along the Trucial Coast, was enlarged to enjoin the states from disposing of any territory, or entering into any foreign agreements, without British consent in return for British protection from external aggression. In March of 1971 Britain reaffirmed its decision to terminate its treaty relationships with the Trucial Sheikhdoms, whereupon the seven states joined with Bahrain and Qatar in an effort to form a union of Arab emirates under British protection. When the prospective members failed to agree on terms of union, Bahrain and Qatar declared their respective independence in Aug. and Sept. 1971. Six of the Sheikhdoms united to form the United Arab Emirates on Dec. 2, 1971. Ras al-Khaimah joined a few weeks later.

MONETARY SYSTEM:

1 Dirham = 1000 Fils

SHEIKHDOMS

UNITED ARAB EMIRATES CURRENCY BOARD

1973; 1976 ND ISSUE

#1-6 dhow, camel caravan, palm tree and oil derrick at l. Wmk: Arabian horse's head. Non-redeemable after 2.2.1989.

		VG	VF	UNC
1	**1 DIRHAM** ND (1973). Green on m/c unpt. Police station at ctr. r. on back.			
	a. Issued note.	1.00	4.00	10.00
	s. Specimen.	—	—	30.00

		VG	VF	UNC
2	**5 DIRHAMS** ND (1973). Purple on m/c unpt. Fortress Fujairah at ctr. r. on back.			
	a. Issued note.	2.00	7.50	25.00
	s. Specimen.	—	—	35.00

		VG	VF	UNC
3	**10 DIRHAMS** ND (1973). Gray-blue on m/c unpt. Aerial view of Umm al-Qaiwan at ctr. r. on back.			
	a. Issued note.	2.00	8.00	27.50
	s. Specimen.	—	—	40.00

		VG	VF	UNC
4	**50 DIRHAMS** ND (1973). Red on m/c unpt. Sheikh's Palace of Ajman at ctr. r. on back.			
	a. Issued note.	7.50	30.00	140.00
	s. Specimen.	—	—	100.00

#5 and 6 printer: (T)DLR.

		VG	VF	UNC
5	**100 DIRHAMS** ND (1973). Olive-green on m/c unpt. Ras al-Khaimah city at ctr. r. on back.			
	a. Issued note.	11.50	55.00	250.00
	s. Specimen.	—	—	225.00

		VG	VF	UNC
6	**1000 DIRHAMS** ND (1976). Blue on m/c unpt. Fortress at ctr. r. on back.			
	a. Issued note.	100.00	500.00	1000.
	s. Specimen.	—	—	675.00

UNITED ARAB EMIRATES CENTRAL BANK

1982; 1983 ND ISSUE

#7-11 arms at upper ctr., sparrowhawk at l. on back. Wmk: Sparrowhawk's head.

		VG	VF	UNC
7	**5 DIRHAMS** ND (1982). Brown on m/c unpt. Arms at ctr., Sharjah Market at r. Seacoast cove w/tower on back.			
	a. Issued note.	FV	2.00	6.00
	s. Specimen.	—	—	25.00

		VG	VF	UNC
8	**10 DIRHAMS** ND (1982). Green on m/c unpt. Arms at ctr., Arab dagger at r. Ideal farm w/trees at l. ctr. on back.			
	a. Issued note.	FV	3.75	11.00
	s. Specimen.	—	—	30.00

		VG	VF	UNC
9	**50 DIRHAMS** ND (1982). Purple, dk. brown and olive on m/c unpt. Oryx at r. Al Jahilie Fort at l. ctr. on back.			
	a. Issued note.	FV	17.50	33.50
	s. Specimen.	—	—	35.00

		VG	VF	UNC
10	**100 DIRHAMS** ND (1982). Red, violet and black on m/c unpt. Al Fahidie Fort at r. Dubai Trade Ctr. at l. ctr. on back.			
	a. Issued note.	FV	33.50	62.50
	s. Specimen.	—	—	45.00

		VG	VF	UNC
11	**500 DIRHAMS** ND (1983). Dk. blue, purple and brown on m/c unpt. Sparrowhawk at r. Mosque in Dubai at l. ctr. on back.			
	a. Issued note.	FV	150.00	240.00
	s. Specimen.	—	—	175.00

1989-96 ISSUES

#12-15 and 17 similar to #7-11 w/condensed Arabic text in titles, modified designs and slight color variations. Wmk: Sparrowhawk's head.

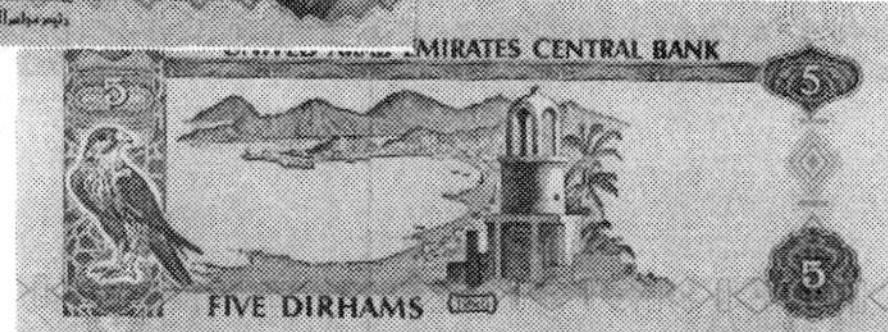

		VG	VF	UNC
12	**5 DIRHAMS** 1993-/AH1414-. Dk. brown, red-orange and violet on m/c unpt. Similar to #7.			
	a. 1993/AH1414.	FV	FV	3.50
	b. 1995/AH1416.	FV	FV	3.00

		VG	VF	UNC
13	**10 DIRHAMS** 1993-/AH1414-. Green and pale olive-green on m/c unpt. Similar to #8.			
	a. 1993/AH1414.	FV	FV	7.50
	b. 1995/AH1416.	FV	FV	6.25

		VG	VF	UNC
14	**50 DIRHAMS** 1995-/AH1415-. Purple, black and violet on m/c unpt. W/segmented foil over security thread. Similar to #9.			
	a. 1995/AH1415.	FV	FV	32.50
	b. 1996/AH1417.	FV	FV	30.00

		VG	VF	UNC
15	**100 DIRHAMS** 1993-/AH1414-. Red, red-violet and black on m/c unpt. Fortress at l. ctr. on back. W/segmented foil over security thread. Similar to #10.			
	a. 1993/AH1414.	FV	FV	50.00
	b. 1995/AH1416.	FV	FV	47.50

16	**200 DIRHAMS** 1989/AH 1410. Brown, green and m/c. Sharia Court bldg. and Zayed Sports City on face. Central bank bldg. at l. ctr. on back. W/segmented foil over security thread.	FV	FV	75.00

		VG	VF	UNC
17	**500 DIRHAMS** 1993/AH1414. Dk. blue, black, purple and silver on m/c unpt. W/segmented foil over security thread. Similar to #11.	FV	FV	215.00

		VG	VF	UNC
18	**500 DIRHAMS** 1996/AH1416. Dk. blue, black, purple and silver on m/c unpt. Like #17 but w/kinegram added at lower l.	FV	FV	180.00

1997-98 ISSUE

		VG	VF	UNC
19	**5 DIRHAMS** 1997-98.	Expected New Issue		
20	**10 DIRHAMS** 1998/AH1419. Similar to #13.	FV	FV	7.25

		VG	VF	UNC
21 (19)	**20 DIRHAMS** 1997/AH1418. Dhow bldg. Dhow on back.	FV	FV	14.50

NOTICE

Readers with unlisted dates, signature varieties, etc. are invited to submit photocopies of their notes to: Standard Catalog of World Paper Money, 700 East State St. Iola, WI 54990-0001, fax: 1-715-445-4087, or E-Mail: thernr@krause.com.

22 **50 DIRHAMS**
1997-98. Expected New Issue

23 **100 DIRHAMS**
1998/AH1419. Similar to #15.

VG	VF	UNC
FV	FV	40.00

24 **1000 DIRHAMS**
(20) 1998/AH1419. Castle at r. City view on back.

VG	VF	UNC
FV	FV	325.00

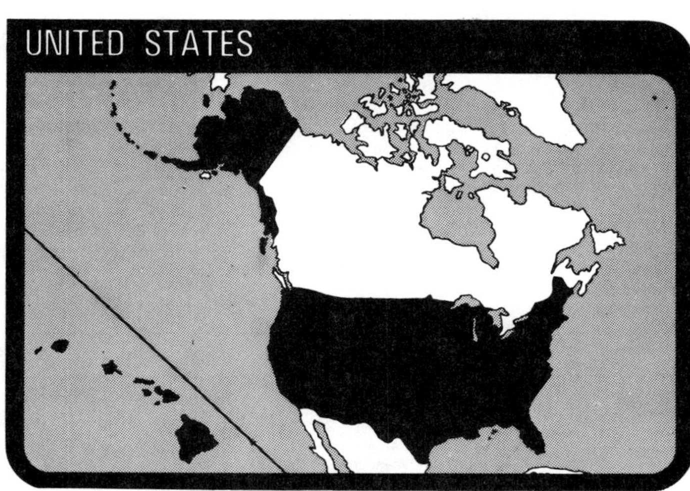

The United States of America as politically organized under the Articles of Confederation consisted of the 13 former British-American colonies - New Hampshire, Massachusetts, Rhode Island, Connecticut, New York, New Jersey, Pennsylvania, Delaware, Maryland, Virginia, North Carolina, South Carolina and Georgia - clustered along the eastern seaboard of North America between the forests of Maine (then part of Massachusetts) and the marshes of Georgia. The United States had no national capital; Philadelphia, where the Contintenal Congress met, was the "seat of the government." The population during this formative phase of America's history (1777-1789) was about 3 million, most of whom lived on self-sufficient family farms. Fishing, lumbering and the production of grains for export were major economic endeavors. Rapid strides were also being made in industry and manufacturing, as well as mining one-seventh of the world's production of raw iron.

On the basis of the voyage of John Cabot to the North American mainland in 1497, England claimed the entire continent. France and Spain also claimed extensive territory in North America. At the end of the French and Indian War (1763), England acquired all of the territory east of the Mississippi River, including East and West Florida. During the colonial and Confederation period, individual states each retained the right to issue money and did so. Independence from Great Britain was declared on July 4, 1776 and ratified in 1783 at the end of the American Revolution. The Constitution which organized and governs the present United States was ratified on Nov. 21, 1788 and became effective in 1789, removing from the states the right to issue money.

1775 Declaration of Independence; 1789 George Washington first president; 1861-1865 Civil War and defeat of the Confederate States by the Union. Originally 13 states, in 1959 Alaska joined the Union as 49th and Hawaii as the 50th state.

MONETARY SYSTEM:

1 Dollar = 100 Cents

SIGNATURE VARIETIES

Series	Treasurer	Secretary
1963	Kathryn O'Hay Granahan	C. Douglas Dillon
1963A	Kathryn O'Hay Granahan	Henry H. Fowler
1963B	Kathryn O'Hay Granahan	Joseph W. Barr
1969	Dorothy Andrews Elston	David M. Kennedy
1969A	Dorothy Andrews Kabis	David M. Kennedy
1969B	Dorothy Andrews Kabis	John B. Connally
1969C	Romana Acosta Banuelos	John B. Connally
1969D	Romana Acosta Banuelos	George P. Schultz
1974	Francine I. Neff	William E. Simon
1977	Azie Taylor Morton	W. Michael Blumenthal
1977A	Azie Taylor Morton	J. William Miller
1981	Angela M. Buchanan	Donald T. Regan
1981A	Katherine Davalos Ortega	Donald T. Regan
1985	Katherine Davalos Ortega	John A. Baker III
1988	Katherine Davalos Ortega	Nicholas F. Brady

Series	Treasurer	Secretary
1988A	Catalina Vasquez Villalpando	Nicholas F. Brady
1993	Mary Ellen Withrow	Lloyd Bentson
1995,1996	Mary Ellen Withrow	Robert E. Rubin
1999	Mary Ellen Withrow	Lawrence Summers

BANKNOTE DESIGNS	
1 DOLLAR	Portr. G. Washington. Great Seal flanking ONE on back.
2 DOLLAR	Portr. T. Jefferson. Monticello on back to 1963, signing of the Declaration of Independence, 1976; 1995 series.
5 DOLLAR	Portr. A. Lincoln. Lincoln Memorial on back.
10 DOLLAR	Portr. A. Hamilton. U.S. Treasury bldg. on back.
20 DOLLAR	Portr. A. Jackson. White House on back.
50 DOLLAR	Portr. U. S. Grant. U.S. Capital bldg. on back.
100 DOLLAR	Portr. B. Franklin. Independence Hall on back.

REPLACEMENT NOTES:

All issues since about 1916 have a star either before or after the serial number, depending on type of note.

MPC's: Any with prefix and w/o suffix letter.

All government notes of the United States, since issue of the Demand Notes in 1861, are still valid as legal tender. The different types of currency are treated in a number of specialized catalogs such as the following:

Friedberg, Robert; *Paper Money of the United States.*

Hickman, John and Oakes, Dean; *Standard Catalog of National Bank Notes.*

Krause, Chester L. and Lemke, Robert F.; *United States Paper Money.*

Detailed information, as given in these catalogs, is not repeated here. The following listing is limited to the individual types and their principal varieties.

REPUBLIC

UNITED STATES NOTES - SMALL SIZE

Red Treasury seal.

SERIES OF 1963

Replacement Notes: Serial # suffix is an *.

		VG	VF	UNC
382	**2 DOLLARS** 1963.			
	a. 1963.	FV	FV	7.50
	b. 1963A.	FV	FV	7.50
383	**5 DOLLARS** 1963.	FV	8.00	12.00

SERIES OF 1966

		VG	VF	UNC
384	**100 DOLLARS** 1966.			
	a. 1966.	FV	130.00	300.00
	b. 1966A.	FV	225.00	750.00

FEDERAL RESERVE NOTES - SMALL SIZE

Green Treasury seal.

Replacement notes: Serial # suffix is an *.

Imprinted #, letter and name (in seal at l.) of 1 of the 12 Federal Reserve Banks:

A-1: Boston	E-5: Richmond	I-9: Minneapolis
B-2: New York	F-6: Atlanta	J-10: Kansas City
C-3: Philadelphia	G-7: Chicago	K-11: Dallas
D-4: Cleveland	H-8: St. Louis	L-12: San Francisco

SERIES OF 1963

		VG	VF	UNC
443	**1 DOLLAR** 1963.			
	a. 1963. (A-L).	FV	FV	3.00
	b. 1963A. (A-L).	FV	FV	3.00
	c. 1963B. (B; E; G; J; L).	FV	FV	3.50

		VG	VF	UNC
444	**5 DOLLARS** 1963.			
	a. 1963. (A-D; F-H: J-L).	FV	FV	14.00
	b. 1963A. (A-L).	FV	FV	12.00

		VG	VF	UNC
445	**10 DOLLARS** 1963.			
	a. 1963. (A-H; J-L).	FV	FV	20.00
	b. 1963A. (A-L).	FV	FV	20.00

	20 DOLLARS	VG	VF	UNC
446	1963.			
	a. 1963. (A-B; D-H; J-L).	FV	FV	35.00
	b. 1963A. (A-L).	FV	FV	30.00

	50 DOLLARS	VG	VF	UNC
447	1963A. (A-L).	FV	FV	100.00

	100 DOLLARS	VG	VF	UNC
448	1963A. (A-L).	FV	FV	200.00

SERIES OF 1969

		VG	VF	UNC
449	**1 DOLLAR**			
	1969.			
	a. 1969. (A-L).	FV	FV	2.50
	b. 1969A. (A-L).	FV	FV	2.50
	c. 1969B. (A-L).	FV	FV	2.50
	d. 1969C. (B; D-L).	FV	FV	2.50
	e. 1969D. (A-L).	FV	FV	2.50
450	**5 DOLLARS**			
	1969.			
	a. 1969. (A-L).	FV	FV	10.00
	b. 1969A. (A-L).	FV	FV	12.00
	c. 1969B. (A-L).	FV	FV	14.00
	d. 1969C. (A-L).	FV	FV	10.00
451	**10 DOLLARS**			
	1969.			
	a. 1969. (A-L).	FV	FV	20.00
	b. 1969A. (A-L).	FV	FV	20.00
	c. 1969B. (A-L).	FV	FV	25.00
	d. 1969C. (A-L).	FV	FV	18.00
452	**20 DOLLARS**			
	1969.			
	a. 1969. (A-L).	FV	FV	30.00
	b. 1969A. (A-L).	FV	FV	30.00
	c. 1969B. (B; D-L).	FV	FV	40.00
	d. 1969C. (A-L).	FV	FV	30.00

		VG	VF	UNC
453	**50 DOLLARS**			
	1969.			
	a. 1969. (A-L).	FV	FV	100.00
	b. 1969A. (A-L).	FV	FV	90.00
	c. 1969B. (A-B; E-G; K).	FV	FV	90.00
	d. 1969C. (A-L).	FV	FV	70.00
454	**100 DOLLARS**			
	1969.			
	a. 1969. (A-L).	FV	FV	175.00
	b. 1969A. (A-L).	FV	FV	175.00
	c. 1969C. (A-L).	FV	FV	150.00

SERIES OF 1974

		VG	VF	UNC
455	**1 DOLLAR**			
	1974. (A-L).	FV	FV	2.00
456	**5 DOLLARS**			
	1974. (A-L).	FV	FV	10.00
457	**10 DOLLARS**			
	1974. (A-L).	FV	FV	17.00
458	**20 DOLLARS**			
	1974. (A-L).	FV	FV	30.00
459	**50 DOLLARS**			
	1974. (A-L).	FV	FV	100.00
460	**100 DOLLARS**			
	1974. (A-L).	FV	FV	150.00

SERIES OF 1976

#461, U.S. Bicentennial - Trumbell's painting *Signing of the Declaration of Independence*

	2 DOLLARS	VG	VF	UNC
461	1976. (A-L).	FV	FV	4.00

NOTE: #461 is also available in uncut sheets of 4, 16 and 32 notes.

SERIES OF 1977

		VG	VF	UNC
462	**1 DOLLAR**			
	1977.			
	a. 1977. (A-L).	FV	FV	2.00
	b. 1977A. (A-L).	FV	FV	2.00
463	**5 DOLLARS**			
	1977.			
	a. 1977. (A-L).	FV	FV	10.00
	b. 1977A. (A-L).	FV	FV	10.00
464	**10 DOLLARS**			
	1977.			
	a. 1977. (A-L).	FV	FV	17.00
	b. 1977A. (A-L).	FV	FV	16.00
465	**20 DOLLARS**			
	1977. (A-L).	FV	FV	30.00
466	**50 DOLLARS**			
	1977. (A-L).	FV	FV	95.00

		VG	VF	UNC
467	**100 DOLLARS** 1977. (A-L).	FV	FV	150.00

SERIES OF 1981

NOTE: Since Oct. 1981 the Bureau of Engraving and Printing has made available to collectors uncut sheets of 4, 16, and 32 notes of the $1.00 and $2.00 denominations.

		VG	VF	UNC
468	**1 DOLLAR** 1981.			
	a. 1981. (A-L).	FV	FV	2.00
	b. 1981A. (A-L).	FV	FV	2.00
469	**5 DOLLARS** 1981.			
	a. 1981. (A-L).	FV	FV	10.00
	b. 1981A. (A-L).	FV	FV	10.00
470	**10 DOLLARS** 1981.			
	a. 1981. (A-L).	FV	FV	15.00
	b. 1981A. (A-L).	FV	FV	15.00
471	**20 DOLLARS** 1981.			
	a. 1981. (A-L).	FV	FV	30.00
	b. 1981A. (A-L).	FV	FV	30.00

		VG	VF	UNC
472	**50 DOLLARS** 1981.			
	a. 1981. (A-L).	FV	FV	85.00
	b. 1981A. (A-L).	FV	FV	80.00

		VG	VF	UNC
473	**100 DOLLARS** 1981.			
	a. 1981. (A-L).	FV	FV	200.00
	b. 1981A. (A-L).	FV	FV	200.00

SERIES OF 1985

		VG	VF	UNC
474	**1 DOLLAR** 1985. (A-L).	FV	FV	2.00
475	**5 DOLLARS** 1985. (A-L).	FV	FV	10.00
476	**10 DOLLARS** 1985. (A-L).	FV	FV	15.00
477	**20 DOLLARS** 1985. (A-L).	FV	FV	30.00
478	**50 DOLLARS** 1985. (A-L).	FV	FV	75.00
479	**100 DOLLARS** 1985. (A-L).	FV	FV	175.00

SERIES OF 1988

		VG	VF	UNC
480	**1 DOLLAR** 1988.			
	a. 1988. (A-L).	FV	FV	2.50
	b. 1988A. (A-L).	FV	FV	2.00
	c. 1988A FW web. (A-C; E-G).	FV	3.00	35.00
481	**5 DOLLARS** 1988.			
	a. 1988. (A-L).	FV	FV	10.00
	b. 1988A. (A-L).	FV	FV	10.00
482	**10 DOLLARS** 1988A (A-L).	FV	FV	15.00
483	**20 DOLLARS** 1988A (A-L).	FV	FV	30.00
484	**50 DOLLARS** 1988 (A-L).	FV	FV	65.00
485	**100 DOLLARS** 1988 (A-L).	FV	FV	150.00

SERIES OF 1990

#486-489 w/additional row of micro-printing: *THE UNITED STATES OF AMERICA* repeated around portr. Filament w/value and *U.S.A.* repeated inversely at l.

		VG	VF	UNC
486	**10 DOLLARS** 1990. (A-L).	FV	FV	15.00
487	**20 DOLLARS** 1990. (A-L).	FV	FV	30.00

		VG	VF	UNC
488	**50 DOLLARS** 1990. (A-L).	FV	FV	65.00
489	**100 DOLLARS** 1990. (A-L).	FV	FV	125.00

SERIES OF 1993

		VG	VF	UNC
490	**1 DOLLAR** 1993.			
	a. 1993. (A-L).	FV	FV	2.00
	b. 1993 Ft. Worth web. (B-C).	FV	3.00	12.50
491	**5 DOLLARS** 1993 (A-C; E-L).	FV	FV	10.00
492	**10 DOLLARS** 1993 (A-D, F-H, J, L).	FV	FV	15.00
493	**20 DOLLARS** 1993. (A-L).	FV	FV	30.00
494	**50 DOLLARS** 1993 (A, B, D, E, G, H, J, K).	FV	FV	75.00
495	**100 DOLLARS** 1993. (A-L).	FV	FV	120.00

SERIES OF 1995

		VG	VF	UNC
496	**1 DOLLAR** 1995.			
	a. (A-L).	FV	FV	2.00
	b. Ft. Worth web. (A; B; D; F).	FV	3.00	12.50
497	**2 DOLLARS** 1995. (F).	FV	FV	3.50
498	**5 DOLLARS** 1995 (A-L).	FV	FV	10.00

		VG	VF	UNC
499	**10 DOLLARS** 1995 (A-L).	FV	FV	15.00

		VG	VF	UNC
500	**20 DOLLARS** 1995 (B-L).	FV	FV	30.00

Federal Reserve Bank codes below serial # at upper l. for notes starting in 1996.

A-1: (Boston)	E-5: (Richmond)	I-9: (Minneapolis)
B-2: (New York)	F-6: (Atlanta)	J-10: (Kansas City)
C-3: (Philadelphia)	G-7: (Chicago)	K-11: (Dallas)
D-4: (Cleveland)	H-8: (St. Louis)	L-12: (San Francisco)

SERIES OF 1996

#501-503 redesigned and enlarged portr. on face at l. ctr. and as wmk. Green value at lower r. Security thread at l. Backs similar to #493-495.

		VG	VF	UNC
501	**20 DOLLARS** 1996. (A1-L12).	FV	FV	30.00

		VG	VF	UNC
502	**50 DOLLARS** 1996 (A1-L12).	FV	FV	60.00

		VG	VF	UNC
503	**100 DOLLARS** 1996 (A1-L12).	—	—	115.00

SERIES OF 1999

		VG	VF	UNC
504	**1 DOLLAR** 1999.	FV	FV	1.50

#505-507 have redesigned and enlarged portr. on face at l. ctr. and as wmk.

		VG	VF	UNC
505	**5 DOLLARS** 1999.	FV	FV	6.50
506	**10 DOLLARS** 1999.	FV	FV	11.50
507	**20 DOLLARS** 1999.	FV	FV	22.50

MILITARY PAYMENT CERTIFICATES

Replacement Notes: Can be identified by serial # which will have a prefix letter but no suffix letter. All replacement notes are much scarcer than regular issues which have prefix and suffix letters. Issued after World War II for use by American military and certain civilian personnel in 21 various occupied areas or military bases.

SERIES 591

26.5.1961 to 6.1.1964.

#M43-M46 Liberty at r.

		VF	XF	UNC
M43	**5 CENTS** ND (1961). Lilac on green and yellow unpt.	6.00	13.00	55.00
M44	**10 CENTS** ND (1961). Blue on lilac unpt.	7.00	15.00	65.00
M45	**25 CENTS** ND (1961). Green on purple unpt.	28.00	50.00	135.00

		VF	XF	UNC
M46	**50 CENTS** ND (1961). Brown on aqua unpt.	40.00	85.00	235.00

		VF	XF	UNC
M47	**1 DOLLAR** ND (1961). Red. Portr. woman facing l. at r.	40.00	85.00	275.00
M48	**5 DOLLARS** ND (1961). Blue. Woman at l.	550.00	1500.	4000.

		VF	XF	UNC
M49	**10 DOLLARS** ND (1961). Green. Portr. woman 3/4 facing l. at r.	200.00	325.00	2000.

SERIES 611

6.1.1964 to 28.4.1969.

#M50-M53 Liberty head facing r. at l.

		VF	XF	UNC
M50	**5 CENTS** ND (1964). Blue.	2.00	3.00	10.00
M51	**10 CENTS** ND (1964). Green.	3.00	6.00	17.00
M52	**25 CENTS** ND (1964). Brown.	5.00	8.00	25.00
M53	**50 CENTS** ND (1964). Lilac	6.00	15.00	55.00

		VF	XF	UNC
M54	**1 DOLLAR** ND (1964). Green. Portr. woman w/tiara facing at l.	6.00	15.00	85.00
M55	**5 DOLLARS** ND (1964). Red. Woman at ctr.	100.00	175.00	600.00

		VF	XF	UNC
M56	**10 DOLLARS** ND (1964). Blue. Portr. woman facing l. at ctr.	130.00	200.00	550.00

SERIES 641

31.8.1965 to 21.10.1968.

#M57-M60 woman at l.

		VF	XF	UNC
M57	**5 CENTS** ND (1965). Violet on blue.	1.00	2.00	5.00
M58	**10 CENTS** ND (1965). Green.	1.00	3.00	6.00
M59	**25 CENTS** ND (1965). Red.	2.00	4.00	12.00
M60	**50 CENTS** ND (1965). Orange.	3.00	6.00	18.00
M61	**1 DOLLAR** ND (1965). Lilac. Woman at r.	3.50	8.00	30.00
M62	**5 DOLLARS** ND (1965). Green. Woman w/wreath of flowers at ctr.	35.00	75.00	250.00

		VF	XF	UNC
M63	**10 DOLLARS** ND (1965). Brown. Portr. woman facing r. at ctr.	30.00	60.00	200.00

SERIES 661

21.10.1968 to 11.8.1969.

#M64-M67 woman wearing scarf at l.

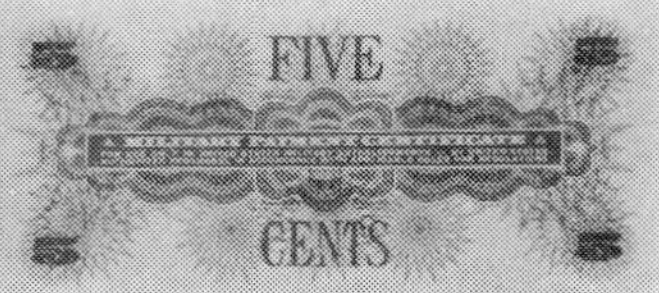

		VF	XF	UNC
M64	**5 CENTS** ND (1968). Green and lilac.	.50	2.00	6.00
M65	**10 CENTS** ND (1968). Blue and violet.	1.00	2.00	7.00
M66	**25 CENTS** ND (1968). Brown and orange.	2.00	4.00	15.00
M67	**50 CENTS** ND (1968). Red and green.	3.00	6.00	18.00

		VF	XF	UNC
M68	**1 DOLLAR** ND (1968). Blue. Portr. woman 3/4 facing l. at r. Mountain scene on back.	3.00	6.00	17.50
M69	**5 DOLLARS** ND (1968). Dk. brown. Woman holding flowers at ctr.	3.00	6.00	16.00

		VF	XF	UNC
M70	**10 DOLLARS** ND (1968). Red. Woman holding fasces at l.	250.00	450.00	1250.
M71	**20 DOLLARS** ND (1968). Black, brown and blue. Woman at ctr.	200.00	300.00	800.00

SERIES 651

28.4.1969 to 19.11.1973.

#M72A-M74 similar to Series 641 except for colors and the addition of a "Minuteman statue" at l.

		VF	XF	UNC
M72A	**5 CENTS** ND (1969).	—	—	2800.
M72B	**10 CENTS** ND (1969).	—	—	2800.
M72C	**25 CENTS** ND (1969).	—	—	2800.
M72D	**50 CENTS** ND (1969).	1250.	1500.	2500.

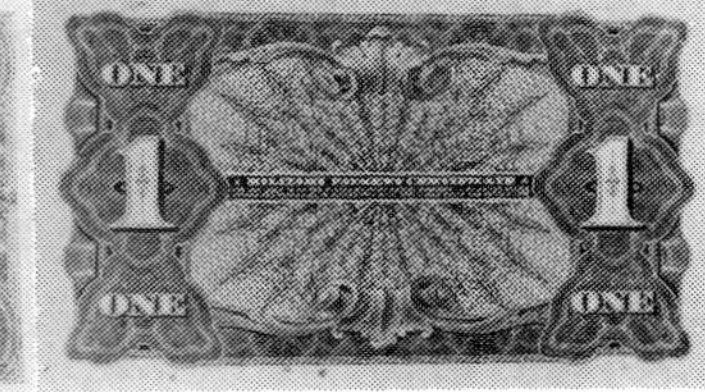

		VF	XF	UNC
M72E	**1 DOLLAR** ND (1969). Green. Portr. woman facing l. at r.	3.00	8.00	32.50

		VF	XF	UNC
M73	**5 DOLLARS** ND (1969). Brown. Portr. woman facing w/wreath of flowers at ctr.	35.00	75.00	150.00
M74	**10 DOLLARS** ND (1969). Violet. Woman at ctr.	35.00	80.00	200.00

SERIES 681

11.8.1969 to 7.10.1970.

#M75-M78 submarine at r.

		VF	XF	UNC
M75	**5 CENTS** ND (1969). Green and blue.	1.00	2.00	6.00

		VF	XF	UNC
M76	**10 CENTS** ND (1969). Violet.	1.00	2.00	8.00
M77	**25 CENTS** ND (1969). Claret and blue.	2.00	5.00	15.00
M78	**50 CENTS** ND (1969). Brown and blue.	3.00	6.00	18.00
M79	**1 DOLLAR** ND (1969). Violet. Air Force pilot at r.	2.00	4.00	12.00

		VF	XF	UNC
M80	**5 DOLLARS** ND (1969). Purple and green. Sailor at ctr.	5.00	12.00	35.00

		VF	XF	UNC
M81	**10 DOLLARS** ND (1969). Blue-green. Infantryman at ctr.	20.00	35.00	160.00

		VF	XF	UNC
M82	**20 DOLLARS** ND (1969). Brown, pink and blue. Portr. soldier facing wearing helmet at ctr.	20.00	45.00	160.00

SERIES 692

7.10.1970 to 15.3.1973.

#M83-M86 seated Roman warrior at l.

		VF	XF	UNC
M83	**5 CENTS** ND (1970). Brown.	1.00	2.00	7.00
M84	**10 CENTS** ND (1970). Green.	1.50	2.50	9.00
M85	**25 CENTS** ND (1970). Blue.	3.00	4.50	15.00
M86	**50 CENTS** ND (1970). Violet.	4.00	6.00	22.00

		VF	XF	UNC
M87	**1 DOLLAR** ND (1970). Blue green. Portr. woman facing r. at l., flowers at bottom ctr. Buffalo at ctr. on back.	8.00	12.00	30.00
M88	**5 DOLLARS** ND (1970). Brown. Girl and flowers at ctr.	75.00	170.00	250.00

		VF	XF	UNC
M89	**10 DOLLARS** ND (1970). Blue. Indian Chief Hollow Horn Bear at ctr.	130.00	250.00	550.00

		VF	XF	UNC
M90	**20 DOLLARS** ND (1970). Violet. Indian Chief Ouray at ctr.	100.00	220.00	450.00

The Oriental Republic of Uruguay (so called because of its location on the east bank of the Uruguay River) is situated on the Atlantic coast of South America between Argentina and Brazil. This most advanced of South American countries has an area of 68,536 sq. mi. (176,220 sq. km.) and a population of 3.27 million. Capital: Montevideo. Uruguay's chief economic asset is its rich, rolling grassy plains. Meat, wool, hides and skins are exported.

Uruguay was discovered in 1516 by Juan Diaz de Solis, a Spaniard, but settled by the Portuguese who founded Colonia in 1680. Spain contested Portuguese possession and, after a long struggle, gained control of the country in 1778. During the general South American struggle for independence, Uruguay's first attempt was led by gaucho soldier José Gervasio Artigas leading the Banda Oriental which was quelled by Spanish and Portuguese forces in 1811. The armistice was soon broken and Argentine forces from Buenos Aires cast off the Spanish bond in the Plata region in 1814, only to be reconquered by the Portuguese from Brazil in the struggle of 1816-20. Revolt flared anew in 1825 and independence was reasserted in 1828 with the help of Argentina. The Uruguayan Republic was established in 1830.

In 1919, a new constitution established a plural executive, but this was abolished in 1933. A presidential government existed from 1933 to 1951 at which time a collective form of leadership was formed through 1966. Strikes and riots in the 1960's brought the military to power until 1985 when Julio Maria Sanguinetti established a government of national unity.

MONETARY SYSTEM:

1 Peso = 100 Centésimos, 1860-1975
1 Doblon = 10 Pesos, 1860-1875
1 Nuevo Peso = 1000 Old Pesos, 1975-1993
1 Peso Uruguayo = 1000 Nuevos Pesos, 1993-

REPUBLIC

BANCO CENTRAL DEL URUGUAY

1967 ND PROVISIONAL ISSUE

#42-45 Banco Central was organized in 1967 and used notes of previous issuing authority w/Banco Central sign. title ovpt. Series D.

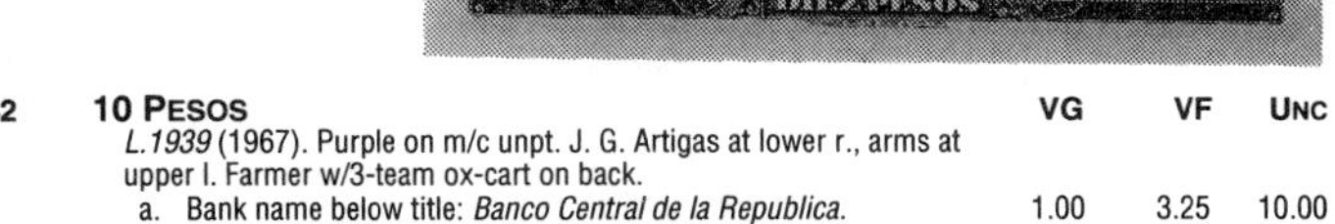

		VG	VF	UNC
42	**10 PESOS** *L.1939* (1967). Purple on m/c unpt. J. G. Artigas at lower r., arms at upper l. Farmer w/3-team ox-cart on back.			
	a. Bank name below title: *Banco Central de la Republica.*	1.00	3.25	10.00
	b. Bank name below title: *Banco Central del Uruguay.*	.75	2.50	7.50

		VG	VF	UNC
42A	**50 PESOS** *L.1939* (1967). Blue and brown. Warrior wearing helmet at r., arms at upper l. Group of people w/flag on back.			
	a. Bank name below all 3 sign.	.75	2.00	6.00
	b. Bank name below 2 sign. at r.	.75	2.50	7.50

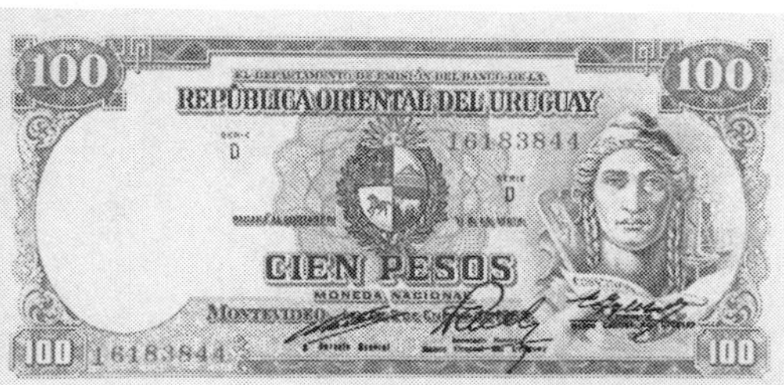

		VG	VF	UNC
43	**100 PESOS** *L.1939* (1967). Red and brown. "Constitution" at r., arms at ctr. People in town square on back.			
	a. Bank name below 3 sign. at r.: *Banco Central del Uruguay*. Sign. title: *PRESIDENTE* at r.	1.00	3.00	10.00
	b. Bank name below 2 sign. at l.: *Banco Central del Uruguay*. Sign. title: *VICE PRESIDENTE* at r.	—	—	—
	c. Bank name below 2 sign. at r.	1.00	3.00	10.00

		VG	VF	UNC
44	**500 PESOS** *L.1939.* Green and blue. "Industry" at r., arms at upper l. People w/symbols of agriculture on back.			
	a. Sign. like #42b.	1.50	5.00	15.00
	b. Sign. like #42a.	1.50	5.00	15.00

		VG	VF	UNC
45	**1000 PESOS** *L.1939.* Purple and black on pale yellow unpt. J. C. Artigas at r., arms at upper l. Man on horseback at ctr. on back. Sign. like #42a.	3.00	7.00	20.00

1967 ND ISSUE

#46-51 J. G. Artigas at ctr. Sign. and sign. title varieties. Printer: TDLR.

		VG	VF	UNC
46	**50 PESOS** ND (1967). Deep blue on lt. green and lilac unpt. Arms at l. Group of 33 men w/flag on back. Series A.	.10	.25	1.75

		VG	VF	UNC
47	**100 PESOS** ND (1967). Red on lilac and lt. gold unpt. Arms at l. Man presiding at independence meeting on back.	.10	.25	1.75

#48-51 wmk: Arms.

		VG	VF	UNC
48	**500 PESOS** ND (1967). Green and blue on orange and lt. green unpt. Dam on back.	.50	1.25	5.00

		VG	VF	UNC
49	**1000 PESOS** ND (1967). Purple and black on blue and yellow unpt. Lg. bldg. on back.	.50	1.25	5.00

		VG	VF	UNC
50	**5000 PESOS** ND (1967). Brown and blue-green on lilac and lt. blue unpt. Bank on back.			
	a. Series A; B.	2.00	5.00	20.00
	b. Series C.	.40	1.00	4.25
51	**10,000 PESOS** ND (1967). Dk. green and black on yellow and lt. orange unpt. Bldg. on back. Series A; B.			
	a. R. sign. title: *PRESIDENTE.*	5.00	12.50	30.00
	b. R. sign. title: *VICE-PRESIDENTE.*	6.00	15.00	35.00

1974 ND ISSUE

#52 and 53 sign. varieties. Wmk: Artigas.

#52 replacement notes: Serial # prefix *R*.

		VG	VF	UNC
52 (51A)	**1000 PESOS** ND (1974). Violet and dk. green on m/c unpt. Arms at upper ctr., Artigas at r. Bldg. on back. Printer: CdeM-A.	.30	1.00	3.00

#53 replacement notes: First digit of 8 digit serial # is *9*.

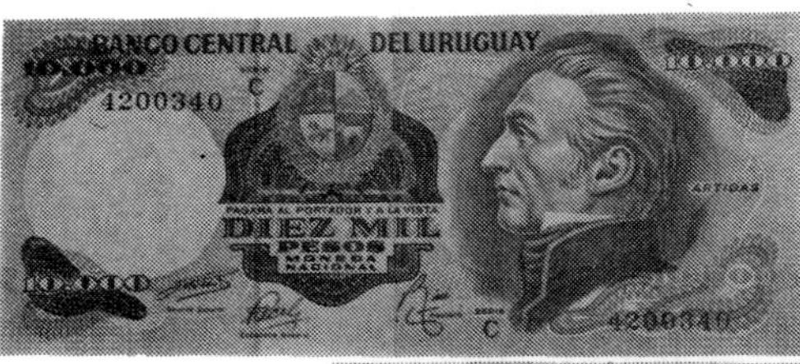

		VG	VF	UNC
53	**10,000 PESOS** ND (1974). Orange on m/c unpt. arms at upper ctr., J. G. Artigas at r. Palace Esteze at l. ctr. on back. Printer: TDLR.			
	a. Series A.	.90	2.50	7.50
	b. Series B.	.75	2.00	6.00
	c. Series C.	.65	1.75	5.50

1975 ND PROVISIONAL ISSUE

#54-58 new value ovpt. on wmk. area.

		VG	VF	UNC
54	**0.50 NUEVO PESO ON 500 PESOS** ND (1975). Ovpt. on #48.	.10	.35	1.50

		VG	VF	UNC
55	**1 NUEVO PESO ON 1000 PESOS** ND (1975). Ovpt. on #49.	.25	.75	3.25

#56 and 57 replacement notes: 8 digit serial # prefix *R*.

		VG	VF	UNC
56	**1 NUEVO PESO ON 1000 PESOS** ND (1975). Ovpt. on #52.	.25	.75	2.75

		VG	VF	UNC
57	**5 NUEVOS PESOS ON 5000 PESOS** ND (1975). Brown on m/c unpt. J. G. Artigas at r., arms at ctr., ovpt. new value at l. Old Banco de la República on back. Printer: CdM-A.	.35	.85	3.50

NOTICE

Readers with unlisted dates, signature varieties, etc. are invited to submit photocopies of their notes to: Standard Catalog of World Paper Money, 700 East State St. Iola, WI 54990-0001, fax: 1-715-445-4087, or E-Mail: thernr@krause.com.

58	10 NUEVOS PESOS ON 10,000 PESOS	VG	VF	UNC
	ND (1975). Ovpt. on #53c.	1.00	3.25	11.50

LEY NO. 14.316; 1975 ND ISSUE

#59-60 arms near ctr., J. G. Artigas at r. and as wmk. Old govt. palace on back. Printer: TDLR.

59	50 NUEVOS PESOS	VG	VF	UNC
	ND (1975). Deep blue on m/c unpt. Series A. 3 sign.	2.00	4.50	7.00

60	100 NUEVOS PESOS	VG	VF	UNC
	ND (1975). Olive-green on m/c unpt. Series A. 3 sign.	4.00	8.00	12.00

LEY NO. 14.316; 1978-88 ND ISSUES

#61-64A similar to previous issue but w/o text: *PAGARA .... A LA VISTA* at ctr. Printer: TDLR.

Replacement notes: 8 digit serial # starting w/*9*.

61	50 NUEVOS PESOS	VG	VF	UNC
	ND (1978-87). Similar to #59.			
	a. 2 sign. Series B (1978).	.40	1.65	5.00
	b. 3 sign. Series C (1980).	.25	1.00	3.00
	c. 2 sign. Series D (1981).	.15	.65	2.00
	d. 3 sign. Series E (1987).	.10	.35	1.00

61A	50 NUEVOS PESOS	VG	VF	UNC
	ND (1988-89). Like #61 but J. G. Artigas portr. printed in wmk. area. Series F (1988); Series G (1989).	.05	.20	.75

62	100 NUEVOS PESOS	VG	VF	UNC
	ND (1978-86). Similar to #60.			
	a. 2 sign. Series B (1978).	.50	2.00	5.00
	b. 3 sign. Series C (1980); Series D (1981).	.15	.65	2.00
	c. Series E (1985); Series F (1986).	.05	.15	.50

62A	100 NUEVOS PESOS	VG	VF	UNC
	ND. Olive-green on m/c unpt. Like #62 but J. G. Artigas portr. printed in wmk. area. Series G (1987).	.05	.30	1.35

63	500 NUEVOS PESOS	VG	VF	UNC
	ND(1978-85). Red on m/c unpt.			
	a. 2 sign. Series A (1978).	.90	3.50	10.00
	b. 3 sign. Series B (1978); Series C (1985).	.20	.80	2.50

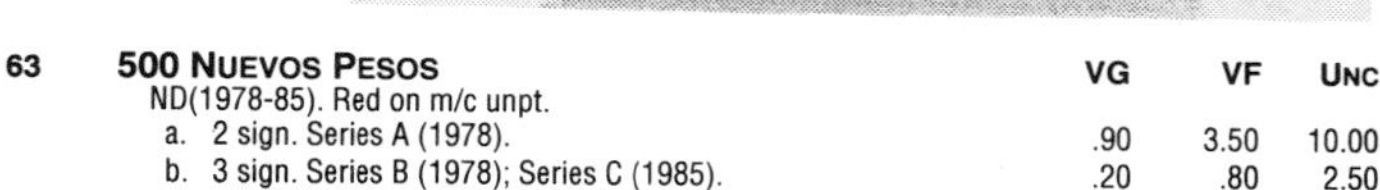

63A	500 NUEVOS PESOS	VG	VF	UNC
	ND. Red on m/c unpt. Like #63 but J. G. Artigas portr. printed in wmk. area. Series D (1991).	.15	.45	1.25

64	1000 NUEVOS PESOS	VG	VF	UNC
	ND(1978-81). Purple on m/c unpt.			
	a. 2 sign. Series A (1978).	2.00	4.50	10.00
	b. 3 sign. Series B (1981).	.40	1.50	4.50

#65-67 wmk: J. G. Artigas.

64A	1000 NUEVOS PESOS	VG	VF	UNC
	ND. Purple on m/c unpt. Like #64 but J. G. Artigas portr. printed in wmk. area.			
	a. Series C (1991).	.35	.75	2.50
	b. Series D (1992).	.10	.35	2.00

65	5000 NUEVOS PESOS	VG	VF	UNC
	ND (1983). Deep brown, red-brown and blue on m/c unpt. Arms at top ctr., Brig. Gen. J. A. Lavalleja at r. Back m/c; 1830 scene of pledging allegiance at ctr. Series A; B; C. Printer: TDLR.	.35	1.00	3.50

LEY NO. 14.316; 1986-88 ND ISSUE

#66 replacement notes: Series A-*R*.

66	200 NUEVOS PESOS	VG	VF	UNC
	1986. Dk. and lt. green on brown and m/c unpt. Quill and scroll at l., arms at ctr., J. E. Rodo at r. Rodo Monument at ctr., statuary at l. and ctr. on back. Series A. Printer: Ciccone S.A.	.10	.35	1.00

67	10,000 NUEVOS PESOS	VG	VF	UNC
	ND (1987). Purple, dk. blue, dk. olive-green and violet on m/c unpt. Plaza of Democracy w/flag at ctr. 19 departmental arms on back. Wmk: J. G. Artigas. Printer: ABNC.			
	a. Ovpt. gold gilt bars on description and law designation. Series A.	7.50	25.00	75.00
	b. No ovpt. bars on new inscription at l., *DECRETO-LEY NO. 14.316* at upper. r. Series B; C.	.75	2.00	8.00
	s. Entire note as printed and w/o ovpt. Series A. Specimen.	—	—	—

NOTE: On #67 the description *Plaza de la Nacionalidad Oriental/Monumento a la bandera and LEY 14.316* ovpt. was being blocked out because of a change of government from military to elected civil administration before the notes were released. The new government took the prepared notes, ovpt. the legend relating to the old government and issued them (Series A). Only Specimen notes are known w/o the ovpt.

1989-92 ISSUE

#68-73 arms at upper l., silver oval latent image at upper r. w/letters B/CU. Wmk: Portr. J. G. Artigas. Printer: TDLR.

68	2000 NUEVOS PESOS	VG	VF	UNC
	1989. Dk. brown and orange on m/c unpt. J. M. Blanes at ctr. r. Altar of the Homeland (allegory of the Republic) on back. Series A.	.25	.50	2.00

69	20,000 NUEVOS PESOS	VG	VF	UNC
	1989; 1991. Dk. green and violet on m/c unpt. Dr. J. Zorrilla de San Martin at ctr. r. Manuscript and allegory of the legend of the homeland (Victory w/wings) on back. Series A.	FV	3.50	7.50

70 **50,000 Nuevos Pesos** — VG FV; VF 7.50; UNC 17.50
1989; 1991. Black and violet on m/c unpt. J. P. Varela at ctr. r. Varela Monument at l. on back. Series A.

71 **100,000 Nuevos Pesos** — VG FV; VF 15.00; UNC 32.50
1991. Purple and dk. brown on m/c unpt. E. Fabini at r. ctr. Musical allegory on back. Series A.

72 **200,000 Nuevos Pesos** — VG FV; VF 27.50; UNC 65.00
1992. Dk. brown and violet and orange on m/c unpt. P. Figari at ctr. r. Old dance at l. on back. Series A.

73 **500,000 Nuevos Pesos** — VG FV; VF 65.00; UNC 125.00
1992. Blue-gray, violet and pale red on m/c unpt. A. Vaquez Acevedo at ctr. r. University of Montevideo at l. on back. Series A.

1994-97 Issue

Currency Reform

1 Peso Uruguayo = 1000 Nuevos Pesos, 1993-

73A **5 Pesos Uruguayos** — VG FV; VF FV; UNC 2.00
ND (1997). Dk. brown, red-brown and blue on m/c unpt. Like 5000 Nuevos Pesos #65. Series A.

73B **10 Pesos Uruguayos**
ND (1995). Purple, dk. blue, dk. olive-green and violet on m/c unpt. Like 10,000 Nuevos Pesos #67. Printer: G&D.

	VG	VF	UNC
a. W/Ley No.14.316 (error). Series A.	FV	FV	4.00
b. W/o Ley. Series B.	FV	FV	2.50

#74-77 like #69-73 but w/new denominations. Arms at upper l. Series A. Wmk: J. G. Artigas. Printer: TDLR.

74 **20 Pesos Uruguayos** — VG FV; VF FV; UNC 4.50
1994. Dk. green and violet on m/c unpt. Like #69.

75 **50 Pesos Uruguayos** — VG FV; VF FV; UNC 10.00
1994. Black, red and violet on m/c unpt. Like #70.

		VG	VF	UNC
76	**100 PESOS URUGUAYOS** 1994. Purple and dk. brown on m/c unpt. Like #71.	FV	FV	18.50

		VG	VF	UNC
77	**200 PESOS URUGUAYOS** 1995. Dk. brown-violet on m/c unpt. Like #72.	FV	FV	36.50

		VG	VF	UNC
78	**500 PESOS URUGUAYOS** 1994. Blue-gray, violet and pale red on m/c unpt. Like #73.	FV	FV	75.00

		VG	VF	UNC
79	**1000 PESOS URUGUAYOS** 1995. Brown and olive-green on m/c unpt. J. de Ibarbourou at r. Palm tree in Ibarbourou Square at l., books on back.	FV	FV	140.00

1998 ISSUE

		VG	VF	UNC
80	**5 PESOS URUGUAYOS** 1998. Joaquín Torres Garcia at r. ctr. Garcia's painting on back.	FV	FV	2.00
81	**10 PESOS URUGUAYOS** 1998.	FV	FV	3.00

The Republic of Uzbekistan (formerly the Uzbek S.S.R.), is bordered on the north by Kazakhstan, to the east by Kirghizia and Tajikistan, on the south by Afghanistan and on the west by Turkmenistan. The republic is comprised of the regions of Andizhan, Bukhara, Dzhizak, Ferghana, Kashkadar, Khorezm (Khiva), Namangan, Navoi, Samarkand, Surkhan-Darya, Syr-Darya, Tashkent and the Karakalpak Autonomous Republic. It has an area of 172,741 sq. mi. (447,400 sq. km.) and a population of 23.5 million. Capital: Tashkent. Crude oil, natural g2as, coal, copper and gold deposits make up the chief resources, while intensive farming, based on artificial irrigation, provides an abundance of cotton.

The original population was believed to be Iranian towards the north while the southern part hosted the satrapies of Sogdiana and Bactria, members of the Persian empire and once part of the empire of Alexander of Macedon. In the 2nd century B.C. they suffered an invasion by easterners referred to by the Chinese as Yue-chi and Hiung-nu. At the end of the 7th century and into the 8th century an Arab army under Emir Kotaiba ibu Muslim conquered Khiva (Khorezm) and Bukhara (Sogdiana). Persian influence developed from the Abbasid caliphs of Baghdad. About 874 the area was conquered by the Persian Saminids of Balkh.

In 999 a Turkic Karakhanid dynasty, the first to embrace Islam, supplanted the Samanids in Samarkand and Bukhara. At the beginning of the 11th century the Seljuk Turks passed through Transoxiana and appointed a hereditary governor at Khorezm. In 1141 another dynasty appeared in Transoxiana, the Kara Kitai from north China. Under the Seljuk shahs Khorezm remained a Moslem outpost.

The Mongol invasion of Jenghiz Khan in 1219-20 brought destruction and great ethnic changes among the population. The conquerors became assimilated and adopted the Turkic language "Chagatai." At the beginning of the 16th century Turkestan was conquered by another wave of Turkic nomads, the Uzbeks (Usbegs). The term Uzbek was used in the 15th century to indicate Moslem. In the 18th century Khokand made itself independent from the emirate of Bukhara, but was soon subject to China, which had conquered eastern Turkestan (now called Sinkiang). The khanate of Khiva, in 1688, became a vassal of Persia, but recovered its independence in 1747. While the Uzbek emirs and khans ruled central Turkestan, in the north were the Kazakhs, in the west lived the nomadic Turkmens, in the east dwelled the Kirghiz, and in the southeast was the homeland of the Persian-speaking Tajiks. In 1714-17 Peter the Great sent a military expedition against Khiva which ended in a disaster. In 1853 Ak-Mechet ("White Mosque," renamed Perovsk, later Kzyl Orda), was conquered by the Russians, and the following year the fortress of Vernoye (later Alma-Ata) was established. On July 29, 1867, Gen. C. P. Kaufmann was appointed governor general of Turkestan with headquarters in Tashkent. On July 5 Mozaffar ed-Din, emir of Bukhara, signed a treaty making his country a Russian vassal state with much-reduced territory. Khiva was conquered by Gen. N. N. Golovachev, and on Aug. 24, 1873, Khan Mohammed Rakhim Kuli had to become a vassal of Russia. Furthermore, all his possessions east of the Amu Darya were annexed to the Turkestan governor-generalship. The khanate of Khokand was suppressed and on March 3, 1876, became the Fergana province. On the eve of WW I Khiva and Bukhara were enclaves within a Russian Turkestan divided into five provinces or *oblasti.* The czarist government did not attempt to Russify the indigenous Turkic or Tajik populations, preferring to keep them backward and illiterate. The revolution of March 1917 created a confused situation in the area. In Tashkent there was a Turkestan committee of the provisional government; a Communist-controlled council of workers', soldiers' and peasants' deputies; also a Moslem Turkic movement, Shuro-i-Islamiya, and a Young-Turkestan or Jaddidi (Renovation) party. The last-named party claimed full political autonomy for Turkestan and the abolition of the emirate of Bukhara and the khanate of Khiva. After the Communist *coup d'état* Petrograd, the council of people's commissars on Nov. 24 (Dec. 7), 1917, published an appeal to "all toiling Moslems in Russia and in the east" proclaiming their right to build their national life "freely and unhindered." In response, the Moslem and Jaddidi organizations in Dec. 1917 convoked a national congress in Khokand which appointed a provisional government headed by Mustafa Chokayev (or Chokaigolu; 1890-1941) and resolved to elect a constituent assembly to decide whether Turkestan should remain within a Russian federal state or proclaim its independence. In the spring of 1919 a Red army group defeated Kolchak and in September its commander, M.V. Frunze, arrived in Tashkent with V.V. Kuibyshev as political commissar. The Communists were still much too weak in Turkestan to proclaim the country part of Soviet Russia. Faizullah Khojayev organized a Young Bukhara movement, which on Sept. 14, 1920, proclaimed the dethronement of Emir Mir Alim. Bukhara was then made a S.S.R. In 1920 the Tashkent Communist government declared war on Junaid, who took to flight, and Khiva became another S.S.R. In Oct. 1921 Enver Pasha, the former leader of the Young Turks, appeared in Bukhara and assumed command of the Basmachi movement. In Aug. 1922 he was forced to retreat into Tajikistan and died on Aug. 4, in a battle near Baljuvan. Khiva concluded a treaty of alliance with the Russian S.F.S.R. in Sept. 1920, and Bukhara followed suit in March 1921. Theoret On June 20, 1990 the Uzbek Supreme Soviet adopted a declaration of sovereignty, and in Aug. 1991, following the unsuccessful coup, it declared itself independent as the 'Republic of Uzbekistan', which was confirmed by referendum in December. That same month Uzbekistan became a member of the CIS.

Monetary System:

1 Sum (Ruble) = 100 Kopeks, 1991
1 Sum = 1,000 Sum Coupon, 1994
1 СЎМ (Sum) = 100 ТИЙИН (Tiyin)

REPUBLIC
GOVERNMENT
КУПОНГА КАРТОЧКА - 1993 RUBLE CONTROL COUPONS

#43-52 and 58 uniface.

		VG	VF	UNC
43	**10 AND 25 COUPONS** ND (1993). Black on pale blue unpt.			
	a. Full sheet of 35 coupons w/2 registries.	—	—	3.00
	b. Top half sheet of 10 coupons w/registry.	—	—	2.00
	c. Bottom half sheet of 25 coupons w/registry.	—	—	2.00
	d. Coupon.	—	—	.10
44	**10 AND 25 COUPONS** ND (1993). Black on orange unpt.			
	a. Full sheet of 35 coupons w/2 registries.	—	—	3.00
	b. Top half sheet of 10 coupons w/registry.	—	—	2.00
	c. Bottom half sheet of 25 coupons w/registry.	—	—	2.00
	d. Coupon.	—	—	.10
45	**10 AND 25 COUPONS** ND (1993). Black on pink unpt.			
	a. Full sheet of 35 coupons w/2 registries.	—	—	5.00
	b. Top half sheet of 10 coupons w/registry.	—	—	2.00
	c. Bottom half sheet of 25 coupons w/registry.	—	—	2.00
	d. Coupon.	—	—	.10
46	**50 COUPONS** ND (1993). Black on pale ochre unpt.			
	a. Full sheet of 28 coupons w/registry.	—	—	3.00
	b. Coupon.	—	—	.10
47	**100 COUPONS** ND (1993). Black on violet unpt.			
	a. Full sheet of 100 coupons w/registry.	—	—	3.00
	b. Coupon.	—	—	.10
48	**100 COUPONS** ND (1993). Black on tan unpt.			
	a. Full sheet of 100 coupons w/registry.	—	—	3.00
	b. Coupon.	—	—	.10
49	**100 COUPONS** ND (1993). Black on lt. blue unpt.			
	a. Full sheet of 100 coupons w/registry.	—	—	3.00
	b. Coupon.	—	—	.10

		VG	VF	UNC
50	**150 COUPONS** ND (1993). Red on pale gray unpt.			
	a. Full sheet of 150 coupons w/registry.	—	—	3.00
	b. Coupon.	—	—	.10
51	**200 COUPONS** ND (1993). Black on pink unpt.			
	a. Full sheet of 200 coupons w/registry.	—	—	3.00
	b. Coupon.	—	—	.10
52	**200 COUPONS** ND (1993). Black on tan unpt.			
	a. Full sheet of 200 coupons w/registry.	—	—	.10
	b. Coupon.	FV	FV	.10

#53-57 not assigned.

		VG	VF	UNC
58	**2000 COUPONS** ND (1993). Blue on pink unpt. Uniface.			
	a. Full sheet of 28 coupons w/registry.	—	—	4.00
	b. Coupon.	—	—	.10

#59 and 60 not assigned.

УЗБЕКИСТОН ДАВПАТ БАНКИ

BANK OF UZBEKISTAN

1992 (1993) ISSUE

#61-72 arms at l. Mosque at ctr. on back. Printer: H&S (w/o imprint).

#61-65 wmk: Flower pattern repeated.

61	1 SUM	VG	VF	UNC
	1992 (1993). Blue-gray on lt. blue and gold unpt.			
	a. Issued note.	.05	.10	.35
	s. Specimen.	—	—	25.00

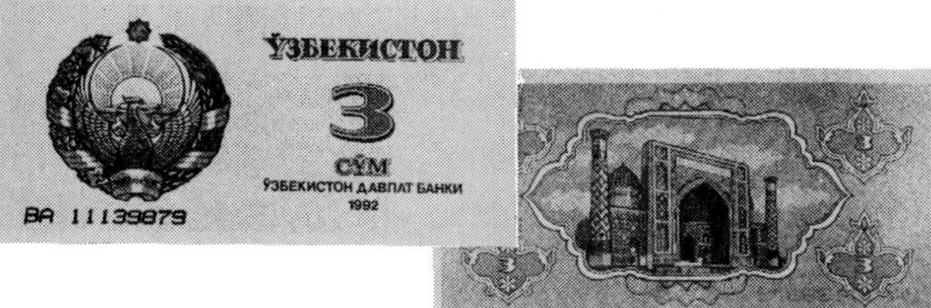

62	3 SUM	VG	VF	UNC
	1992 (1993). Green and blue.			
	a. Issued note.	.05	.10	.50
	s. Specimen.	—	—	25.00

63	5 SUM	VG	VF	UNC
	1992 (1993). Purple on lt. blue and gold unpt.			
	a. Issued note.	.05	.10	.60
	s. Specimen.	—	—	25.00

64	10 SUM	VG	VF	UNC
	1992 (1993). Red on lt. blue and gold unpt.			
	a. Issued note.	.05	.10	.75
	s. Specimen.	—	—	25.00

65	25 SUM	VG	VF	UNC
	1992 (1993). Blue-green on lt. blue and pale orange unpt. Back green.			
	a. Issued note.	—	.20	.85
	s. Specimen.	—	—	25.00

#66-72 wmk: Lg. flower.

66	50 SUM	VG	VF	UNC
	1992 (1993). Rose on blue unpt.			
	a. Issued note.	.10	.35	1.25
	s. Specimen.	—	—	25.00

67	100 SUM	VG	VF	UNC
	1992 (1993). Dk. brown on blue unpt.			
	a. Issued note.	.10	.40	2.00
	s. Specimen.	—	—	25.00

68	200 SUM	VG	VF	UNC
	1992 (1993). Violet on blue unpt.			
	a. Issued note.	.15	.75	4.50
	s. Specimen.	—	—	25.00

69	500 SUM	VG	VF	UNC
	1992 (1993). Orange on lt. blue unpt.			
	a. Larger and italicized serial #.	.10	.60	2.00
	b. Smaller and regular serial #.	.50	1.50	5.00
	s. Specimen.	—	—	25.00

70	1000 SUM	VG	VF	UNC
	1992 (1993). Brown on green unpt.			
	a. Prefix letters same size as the numbers.	.15	.75	3.00
	b. Specimen.	.15	.75	4.00
	s. Serial # prefix letters taller than the numbers.	—	—	30.00

71	5000 SUM	VG	VF	UNC
	1992 (1993). Blue-gray on lilac and pale green unpt.			
	a. Issued note.	.50	2.50	12.50
	s. Specimen.	—	—	25.00

72	10,000 SUM	VG	VF	UNC
	1992 (1993). Red-orange on lilac and pale green unpt.			
	a. Issued note.	.40	2.00	10.00
	s. Specimen.	—	—	30.00

ЎЗБЕКИСТОН РЕСПУБЛИКАСИ МАРКАЗИЙ БАНКИ

CENTRAL BANK OF UZBEKISTAN REPUBLIC

1994; 1997 ISSUE

#73-80 wmk. paper. Replacement notes: serial # prefix *ZZ*.

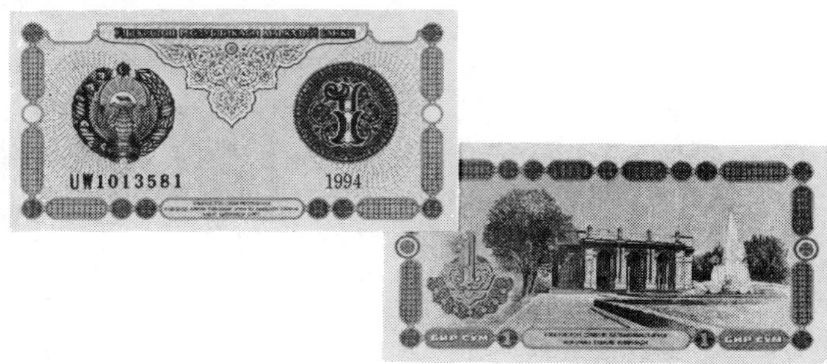

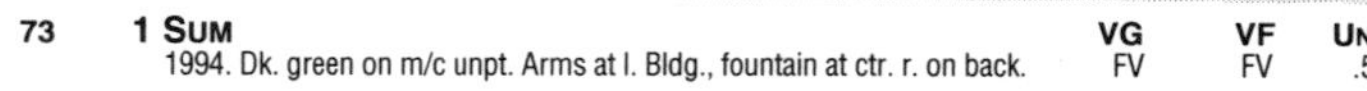

73	1 SUM	VG	VF	UNC
	1994. Dk. green on m/c unpt. Arms at l. Bldg., fountain at ctr. r. on back.	FV	FV	.50

74	3 SUM	VG	VF	UNC
	1994. Violet on m/c unpt. Arms at l. Mosque of Çaçma Ayub Mazar in Bukhara on back.	FV	FV	1.50

#75-79 arms at upper ctr. and as wmk.

75	5 SUM	VG	VF	UNC
	1994. Dk. blue and red-violet on m/c unpt. Ali Shir Nawai Monument in Tashkent at ctr. on back.	FV	FV	2.75

76	10 SUM	VG	VF	UNC
	1994. Violet and blue-gray on m/c unpt. Mosque of Mohammed Amin Khan in Khiva on back.	FV	FV	4.50

77	25 SUM	VG	VF	UNC
	1994. Dk. blue and brown on m/c unpt. Mausoleum Kazi Zadé Rumi in the necropolis Shakhi-Zinda in Samarkand at ctr. r. on back.	FV	FV	3.00

78	50 SUM	VG	VF	UNC
	1994. Dk. brown, olive-brown and dull brown-orange on m/c unpt. Esplanade in Reghistan and the 2 Medersas in Samarkand at ctr. r. on back.	FV	FV	3.50

		VG	VF	UNC
79	**100 SUM** 1994. Purple and blue on m/c unpt. Stylized facing peacocks at l. *Drubja Narodov* palace in Tashkent on back.	FV	FV	5.00

		VG	VF	UNC
80	**200 SUM** 1997. Dk. blue, black, deep purple on m/c unpt. Arms at l. and as wmk. Sunface over tiger at ctr. on back.	FV	FV	5.50

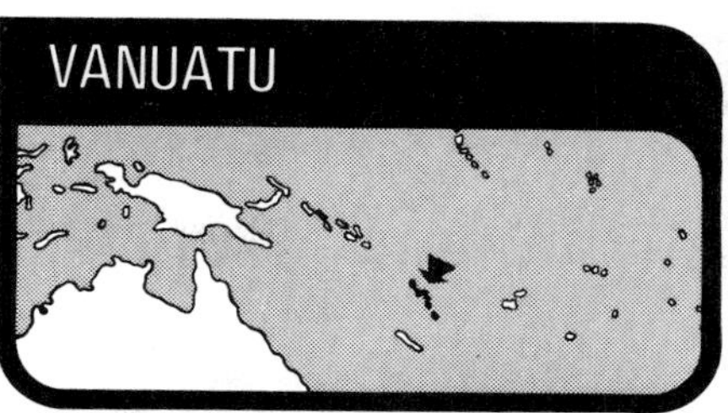

Vanuatu (formerly the New Hebrides Condominium), a group of islands located in the South Pacific 500 miles (800 km.) west of Fiji, were under the joint sovereignty of Great Britain and France. The islands have an area of 5,700 sq. mi. (14,763 sq. km.) and a population of *181,350, mainly Melanesians of mixed blood. Capital: Vila. The volcanic and coral islands, while malarial and subject to frequent earthquakes, are extremely fertile, and produce copra, coffee, tropical fruits and timber for export.

The New Hebrides were discovered by Portuguese navigator Pedro de Quiros in 1606, visited by French explorer Bougainville in 1768, and named by British navigator Capt. James Cook in 1774. Ships of all nations converged on the islands to trade for sandalwood prompting France and Britain to relinquish their individual claims and declare the islands a neutral zone in 1878. The New Hebrides were placed under the control of a mixed Anglo-French commission of naval officers during the native uprisings of 1887, and established as a condominium under the joint sovereignty of France and Great Britain in 1906. Independence for the area was attained in 1982 under the new name of Vanuatu.

RULERS:

British and French to 1982

MONETARY SYSTEM:

100 Vatu = 100 Francs

SIGNATURE VARIETIES					
1	PRESIDENT	GENERAL MANAGER	2	GOVERNOR	MINISTER OF FINANCE
3	PRESIDENT	GENERAL MANAGER	4	GOVERNOR	MINISTER OF FINANCE

BANQUE CENTRALE DE VANUATU
CENTRAL BANK OF VANUATU/CENTRAL BANK BLONG VANUATU

1982; 1989 ND ISSUE

#1-4 arms w/Melanesian chief standing w/spear at ctr. r. Wmk: Melanesian male head. Printer: BWC.

		VG	VF	UNC
1	**100 VATU** ND (1982). Dk. green on m/c unpt. Cattle among palm trees at l. ctr. on back. Sign. 1.	1.25	2.50	15.00

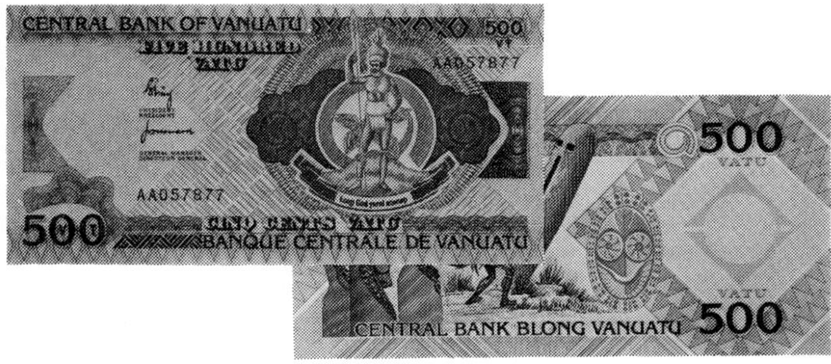

		VG	VF	UNC
2	**500 VATU** ND (1982). Red on m/c unpt. 3 carved statues at l., 2 men beating upright hollow log drums at l. ctr. on back. Sign. 1.	FV	6.50	20.00

		VG	VF	UNC
3	**1000 VATU** ND (1982). Black, lt. orange and green on m/c unpt. 3 carvings at lower l., 3 men in outrigger sailboat at ctr. on back. Sign. 1.	FV	12.50	35.00

		VG	VF	UNC
4	**5000 VATU** ND(1989). Brown and lilac on m/c unpt. Man watching another *Gol* diving from log tower at ctr. on back. Sign. 2.	FV	50.00	95.00

BANQUE DE RESERVE DE VANUATU

RESERVE BANK OF VANUATU/RESERVE BANK BLONG VANUATU

1993 ND ISSUE

#5-7 like #2-4 but w/new bank name. Sign. 3. Wmk: Melanesian male head.

		VG	VF	UNC
5	**500 VATU** ND (1993). Dk. green on m/c unpt. Like #2.	FV	FV	11.50

NOTICE

Readers with unlisted dates, signature varieties, etc. are invited to submit photocopies of their notes to: Standard Catalog of World Paper Money, 700 East State St. Iola, WI 54990-0001, fax: 1-715-445-4087, or E-Mail: thernr@krause.com.

		VG	VF	UNC
6	**1000 VATU** ND (1993). Red on m/c unpt. Like #3.	FV	FV	22.50
7	**5000 VATU** ND.	Expected New Issue		

1995 ND ISSUE

		VG	VF	UNC
8	**200 VATU** ND (1995). Purple and violet on m/c unpt. Arms w/Melanesian chief standing w/spear at ctr. Statue of family life, "Traditional parliament in session" and flag on back. Wmk: Melanesian male head. Printer: TDLR.	FV	FV	6.50

1995 COMMEMORATIVE ISSUE

#9, 15th Anniversary of Independence

		VG	VF	UNC
9	**200 VATU** ND (1995). Purple on m/c unpt. Ovpt. at upper l. on #8.	FV	FV	35.00

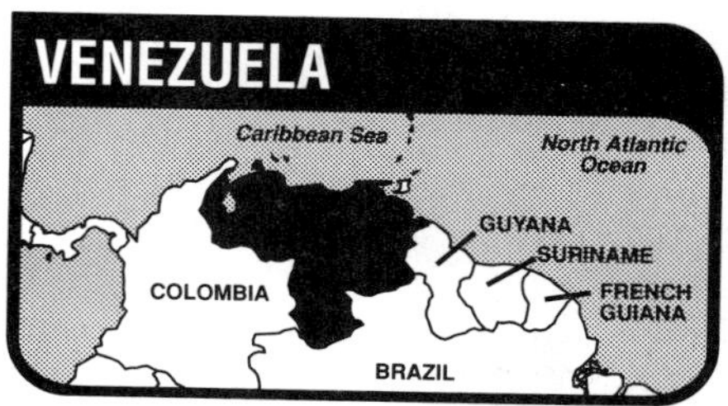

The Republic of Venezuela ("Little Venice"), located on the northern coast of South America between Colombia and Guyana, has an area of 352,145 sq. mi. (912,050 sq. km.) and a population of 21.8 million. Capital: Caracas. Petroleum and mining provide 90 percent of Venezuela's exports although they employ less than 2 percent of the work force. Coffee, grown on 60,000 plantations, is the chief crop.

Columbus discovered Venezuela on his third voyage in 1498. Initial exploration did not reveal Venezuela to be a land of great wealth. An active pearl trade operated on the off-shore islands and slavers raided the interior in search of Indians to be sold into slavery, but, no significant mainland settlements were made before 1567 when Caracas was founded. Venezuela, the home of Bolívar, was among the first South American colonies to revolt against Spain in 1810. Independence was attained in 1821 but not recognized by Spain until 1845. Together with Ecuador, Panama and Colombia, Venezuela was part of "Gran Colombia" until 1830 when it became a sovereign and independent state.

MONETARY SYSTEM:

1 Bolívar = 100 Centimos, 1879-

REPUBLIC

BANCO CENTRAL DE VENEZUELA

Established in 1940. Sign. and date varieties.

NOTE: Many specimen notes were "liberated" about 1982. Up to 200 of each are known for many of the more common types which are being incorporated in these listings.

1940-47 ISSUES

#31-37 arms on back. Printer: ABNC.

		VG	VF	UNC
34	**100 BOLÍVARES** 11.12.1940-3.7.1962. Brown on m/c unpt. Portr. S. Bolívar at ctr. Arms at ctr. on back.			
	a. 1940-52.	20.00	60.00	200.00
	b. 1953-58.	15.00	45.00	150.00
	c. 1959-62.	10.00	30.00	100.00
	s. As a. Specimen. W/o sign. Punched hole cancelled.	—	—	175.00

1947 ISSUE

		VG	VF	UNC
37	**500 BOLÍVARES** 1947-71. Orange on m/c unpt.			
	a. 14.8.1947-21.8.1952.	60.00	150.00	—
	b. 23.7.1953-29.5.1958.	25.00	55.00	165.00
	c. 11.3.1960-17.8.1971.	20.00	50.00	135.00
	s. Punched hole cancelled. As b. Specimen. W/o sign.	—	—	135.00

1960; 1961 ISSUE

#42-44 printer: TDLR.

		VG	VF	UNC
42	**10 BOLÍVARES** 6.6.1961. Purple on m/c unpt. Portr. S. Bolívar at l., A. J. de Sucre at r. Arms at l., monument to Battle of Caraboba at ctr. on back.			
	a. Issued note.	2.50	9.00	25.00
	s. Specimen w/black ovpt: *SPECIMEN*. Serial # prefix *E*.	—	—	11.50

		VG	VF	UNC
43	**20 BOLÍVARES** 11.3.1960-10.5.1966. Dk. green on m/c unpt. Portr. S. Bolívar at r., bank name in 1 line. Monument at ctr. on back.			
	a. Issued note.	4.00	12.00	30.00
	s1. Specimen w/red ovpt: *SPECIMEN*. Paper w/colored planchettes. Serial # prefix *X*.	—	—	12.50
	s2. Specimen w/red ovpt: *ESPECIMEN SIN VALOR*. Paper w/security thread. Punched hole cancelled.	—	—	12.50
	s3. Specimen w/black ovpt: *SPECIMEN*. Serial # prefix *U*.	—	—	12.50

		VG	VF	UNC
44	**50 BOLÍVARES** 6.6.1961; 7.5.1963. Black. Modified effigy of S. Bolívar at l. Back orange; monument at ctr. on back.			
	a. Issued note.	8.00	25.00	75.00
	s. Specimen w/red ovpt: *SPECIMEN SIN VALOR*. Punched hole cancelled.	—	—	15.00

1963-67 ISSUE

#45-48 monument to Battle of Carabobo on back similar to #42-44. Printer: TDLR.

		VG	VF	UNC
45	**10 BOLÍVARES** 7.5.1963-27.1.1970. Purple on m/c unpt. Similar to #42 but much different portr. of A. J. de Sucre at r.			
	a. Issued note.	1.00	2.50	7.50
	s. Specimen w/red ovpt: *ESPECIMEN SIN VALOR*. ND. Punched hole cancelled.	—	—	30.00

		VG	VF	UNC
46	**20 BOLÍVARES** 8.8.1967-29.1.1974. Green on orange and blue unpt. Portr. S. Bolívar at r., and as wmk., bank name in 3 lines. Arms w/o circle at l. on back.			
	a. 8.8.1967.	1.35	4.00	16.50
	b. 5.3.1968.	1.25	3.75	15.00
	c. 30.9.1969.	1.10	3.50	14.00
	d. 21.1.1970.	1.00	3.25	13.00
	e. 29.1.1974. Serial # prefix *Y-Z* (7 digits); *A-C* (7 or 8 digits).	1.00	3.00	12.50
	s1. Specimen w/red ovpt: *ESPECIMEN SIN VALOR*. ND. Punched hole cancelled.	—	—	11.50
	s2. Specimen w/red ovpt. as a. 27.1.1970.	—	—	11.50
47	**50 BOLÍVARES** 2.6.1964-22.2.1972. Black on orange and green unpt. Portr. S. Bolívar at l. *CINCUENTA BOLÍVARES* above *50* at ctr. Back orange.			
	a. Issued note.	2.00	6.00	30.00
	s. Specimen w/red ovpt: *ESPECIMEN SIN VALOR*. ND.	—	—	35.00

48	100 BOLÍVARES	VG	VF	UNC
	7.5.1963-6.2.1973. Brown. Portr. S. Bolívar at r.			
	a. Issued note.	2.00	5.00	30.00
	s1. Specimen w/red ovpt: *ESPECIMEN SIN VALOR.* ND.	—	—	17.50
	s2. Specimen w/red ovpt: *SPECIMEN* and TDLR oval stampings. ND. Punched hole cancelled.	—	—	95.00

1966 COMMEMORATIVE ISSUE

#49, 400th Anniversary - Founding of Caracas 1567-1967

49	5 BOLÍVARES	VG	VF	UNC
	10.5.1966. Blue on green and yellow unpt. Scene of the founding and commemorative text at ctr. and l., portr. S. Bolívar at r. Back blue; city arms at l., early map (1578) of the city at ctr., national arms at r. Printer: ABNC. Serial # prefix *A-D.*	FV	3.00	15.00

1968-71 ISSUE

#51-52 printer: ABNC.

50	5 BOLÍVARES	VG	VF	UNC
	1968-74. Red on m/c unpt. S. Bolívar at l., F. de Miranda at r. Arms at l., National Pantheon at ctr. on back. Printer: TDLR.			
	a. 24.9.1968. Serial # prefix *E; F.*	.75	2.25	10.00
	b. 29.4.1969. Serial # prefix *H-J.*	.65	2.00	9.00
	c. 30.9.1969. Serial # prefix *G; H.*	.60	1.75	7.50
	d. 27.1.1970. Serial # prefix *J-M.*	.50	1.50	6.50
	e. 22.6.1971. Serial # prefix *M-P.*	.45	1.40	5.50
	f. 11.4.1972. Serial # prefix *P; R.*	.40	1.25	4.50
	g. 13.3.1973. Serial # prefix *S; T.*	.35	1.10	4.00
	h. 29.1.1974. Serial # prefix *U-Z* (7 digits); *A-E* (7 or 8 digits).	.30	1.00	4.00
	r. Remainder w/o date, sign. or serial #.	—	—	7.50
	s. Specimen.	—	—	8.50

51	10 BOLÍVARES	VG	VF	UNC
	1971-79. Purple on green and lilac unpt. Similar to #45.			
	a. 22.6.1971. Dk. blue serial # w/prefix *U-A.*	.75	2.25	10.00
	b. 11.4.1972. Serial # prefix *A-H.*	.65	2.00	9.00
	c. 13.3.1973. Serial # prefix *H-R.*	.60	1.85	8.50
	d. 29.1.1974. Serial # prefix *R-Z; A-H.*	.60	1.80	8.00
	e. 27.1.1976. Serial # prefix *J-Y.*	.60	1.75	7.50
	f. 7.7.1977. Serial # prefix *Y-C.*	.55	1.65	7.00
	g. 18.9.1979. Black serial # w/prefix *C; D.*	.50	1.50	6.50
	s1. Specimen w/red ovpt: *MUESTRA.* Punched hole cancelled. 11.4.1972.	—	—	10.00
	s2. Specimen w/red ovpt: *MUESTRA.* Punched hole cancelled. 27.1.1976.	—	—	10.00
	s3. Specimen w/red ovpt: *MUESTRA.* Punched hole cancelled. 7.6.1977.	—	—	10.00
	s4. Specimen w/red ovpt: *MUESTRA.* Punched hole cancelled. 18.9.1979.	—	—	10.00

52	20 BOLÍVARES	VG	VF	UNC
	1971; 1972. Dk. green on m/c unpt. Similar to #46.			
	a. 22.6.1971.	.75	2.25	10.00
	b. 11.4.1972.			
	s. Specimen w/red ovpt: *MUESTRA.* Punched hole cancelled. 11.4.1972.	—	—	10.00

1971-74 ISSUE

53	20 BOLÍVARES	VG	VF	UNC
	1974-79. Dk. green on m/c unpt. J. Antonio Paez at r. and as wmk. Arms at l., monument to Battle of Carabobo at ctr. on back. Printer: ABNC.			
	a. 23.4.1974.	.60	1.75	7.50
	b. 7.6.1977.	.50	1.50	6.50
	c. 18.9.1979.	.45	1.40	6.00
	s1. Specimen w/red ovpt: *ESPECIMEN SIN VALOR.* 23.4.1974.	—	—	7.50
	s2. Specimen w/red ovpt: *MUESTRA.* Punched hole cancelled. 7.6.1977.	—	—	7.50
	s3. Specimen w/red ovpt: *MUESTRA.* Punched hole cancelled. 18.9.1979.	—	—	7.50

		VG	VF	UNC
54	**50 BOLÍVARES** 1972-77. Purple, orange and m/c. Academic bldg. at ctr., A. Bello at r. and as wmk. Back orange; arms at l., bank at ctr. Printer: TDLR.			
	a. 21.11.1972.	1.00	3.25	12.50
	b. 29.1.1974.	1.00	3.00	12.00
	c. 27.1.1976.	.85	2.85	11.50
	d. 7.6.1977.	.75	2.75	11.00
	s. Specimen w/red ovpt: *ESPECIMEN SIN VALOR.* 21.11.1972.	—	—	12.50

		VG	VF	UNC
55	**100 BOLÍVARES** 1972-81. Dk. brown and brown-violet on m/c unpt. S. Bolívar at r. and as wmk. National Capitol at l., arms at r. on back. Printer: BDDK.			
	a. Red serial #. 21.11.1972.	3.75	11.50	55.00
	b. Wmk: Bolívar. 5.3.1974.	3.00	10.00	40.00
	c. Blue serial #. *B-C* added to wmk. 27.1.1976.	1.75	5.50	22.50
	d. 23.11.1976.	1.85	5.50	22.50
	e. 12.12.1978.	1.65	5.00	20.00
	f. 18.9.1979.	1.50	4.75	18.50
	g. 1.9.1981.	1.35	4.50	17.50
	s1. Specimen w/red ovpt: *ESPECIMEN SIN VALOR.* 21.11.1972.	—	—	12.50
	s2. Specimen. 27.1.1976.	—	—	12.50

		VG	VF	UNC
56	**500 BOLÍVARES** 9.11.1971; 11.1.1972. Brown and blue on m/c unpt. S. Bolívar at l. and as wmk., horsemen w/rifles riding at ctr. Back brown; dam at ctr., arms at r. Printer: TDLR.			
	a. 9.11.1971.	2.50	5.00	25.00
	b. 11.1.1972.	1.25	2.50	20.00
	s. Specimen w/red ovpt: *ESPECIMEN SIN VALOR.* ND.	—	—	20.00

1980 ISSUE

		VG	VF	UNC
57	**10 BOLÍVARES** 29.1.1980. Purple on m/c unpt. A. J. de Sucre at r. Arms at l., officers on horseback at ctr. r. on back. Printer: ABNC.			
	a. Issued note.	.50	1.00	2.50
	s. Specimen w/red ovpt: *MUESTRA.* Punched hole cancelled.	—	—	8.50

1980-81 COMMEMORATIVE ISSUES

#58, Bicentennial - Birth of Andres Bello, 1781-1981

		VG	VF	UNC
58	**50 BOLÍVARES** 27.1.1981. Dk. brown and green on m/c unpt. A. Bello at r. and as wmk. Arms at l., scene showing Bello teaching young Bolívar on back. Printer: TDLR.	1.00	2.50	8.00

#59, 150th Anniversary - Death of Simon Bolívar, 1830-1980

		VG	VF	UNC
59	**100 BOLÍVARES** 29.1.1980. Red and purple on m/c unpt. S. Bolívar at r. and as wmk., his tomb at ctr. r. Arms at l., scene of hand to hand combat on back. Printer: TDLR.			
	a. Issued note.	2.00	5.00	22.50
	s. Specimen w/red ovpt: *ESPECIMEN SIN VALOR.*	—	—	12.50

1981-87 ISSUES

#60-67 w/o imprint.

		VG	VF	UNC
60	**10 BOLÍVARES** 6.10.1981. Purple on lt. blue unpt. Similar to #57 but unpt. is different, and there are many significant plate changes. Printer: CdM-B (w/o imprint).			
	a. Issued note. 7 or 8 digits serial #.	FV	.75	2.75
	s. Specimen w/red ovpt: *MUESTRA*.	—	—	10.00

		VG	VF	UNC
61	**10 BOLÍVARES** 1986-95. Purple on lt. green and lilac unpt. Like #51, but *CARACAS* removed from upper ctr. beneath bank title. Printer: ABNC (w/o imprint).			
	a. 18.3.1986.	FV	FV	1.75
	b. 31.5.1990.	FV	FV	1.00
	c. 8.12.1992.	FV	FV	.75
	d. 5.6.1995.	FV	FV	1.00

		VG	VF	UNC
62	**10 BOLÍVARES** 3.11.1988. Purple on ochre unpt. Like #45, but *CARACAS* removed from upper ctr. beneath bank title. Printer: TDLR (w/o imprint).	FV	FV	1.00

		VG	VF	UNC
63	**20 BOLÍVARES** 1981-92. Dk. green on m/c unpt. Similar to #53 but *CARACAS* deleted under bank title. Title 82mm, horizontal central design in l. ctr. guilloche. Printer: TDLR (w/o imprint).			
	a. 6.10.1981.	FV	FV	2.75
	b. 7.9.1989.	FV	FV	2.00
	c. 31.5.1990.	FV	FV	1.75
	d. 8.12.1992.	FV	FV	1.50
	e. 5.6.1995.	FV	FV	.75
	s. Specimen.	—	—	8.00

NOTE: Central design in l.h. guilloche: … or …

		VG	VF	UNC
64	**20 BOLÍVARES** 25.9.1984. Dk. green on m/c unpt. Like #63, but title 84mm and w/o central design in l. ctr. guilloche, also other minor plate differences. Latent image *BCV* in guilloches easily seen. Printer: CdM-B (w/o imprint).	FV	FV	2.25

		VG	VF	UNC
64A	**20 BOLÍVARES** 7.7.1987. Dk. green on m/c unpt. Like #63 but printer: ABNC (w/o imprint).	FV	FV	2.00

		VG	VF	UNC
65	**50 BOLÍVARES** 1985-98. Purple, black and orange on m/c unpt. Like #54, but *CARACAS* removed under bank name. Printer: BDDK (w/o imprint).			
	a. Issued note. 10.12.1985-5.6.1995.	FV	FV	3.00
	b. 2.5.1998.	FV	FV	1.50
	s. Specimen. 10.12.1985. Serial # prefix *N*.	—	—	20.00

66	100 BOLÍVARES	VG	VF	UNC
	1987-92. Dk. brown and brown-violet on m/c unpt. Like #55 but w/o imprint. Printer: BDDK (w/o imprint).			
	a. 3.2.1987.	FV	FV	4.00
	b. 16.3.1989.	FV	FV	3.50
	c. 31.5.1990.	FV	FV	3.50
	d. 12.5.1992.	FV	FV	2.75
	e. 8.12.1992.	FV	FV	2.75
	f. 2.5.1998.	FV	FV	2.75

67	500 BOLÍVARES	VG	VF	UNC
	1981-90. Purple and black on m/c unpt. S. Bolívar at r. and as wmk. Back green and m/c; arms at l., orchids at ctr. Printer: BDDK (w/o imprint).			
	a. 25.9.1981.	FV	5.00	20.00
	b. 3.2.1987.	FV	FV	15.00
	c. 16.3.1989.	FV	FV	15.00
	d. 31.5.1990.	FV	FV	4.00
	e. 5.6.1995.	FV	FV	4.00

1989 ISSUE

#68-70 w/o imprint.

#68 and 69 replacement notes: Serial # prefix *X* and *XX*.

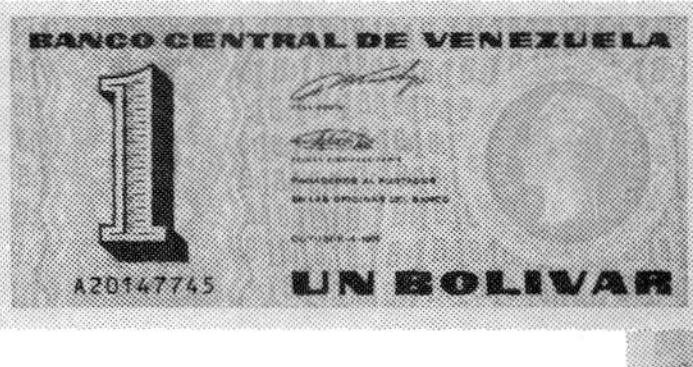

68	1 BOLÍVAR	VG	VF	UNC
	5.10.1989. Purple on blue and green unpt. Lg. *1* at l., coin w/S. Bolívar at r. Arms at l., rosette at r. on back. Wmk. paper. Printer: BDDK.	FV	FV	.35

69	2 BOLÍVARES	VG	VF	UNC
	5.10.1989. Blue and black on lt. blue unpt. Coin head of S. Bolívar at r. Lg. *2* at l., arms at r. on back. Printer: USBNC.	FV	FV	.50

70	5 BOLÍVARES	VG	VF	UNC
	21.9.1989. Red on m/c unpt. Like #50, but *CARACAS* removed from upper ctr. beneath bank title on face and back. Lithographed. Printer: TDLR.			
	a. 7 digit serial #.	FV	FV	.75
	b. 8 digit serial #.	FV	FV	.60

1989 COMMEMORATIVE ISSUE

#71, Bicentennial - Birth of Rafael Urdaneta, 1789-1989

71	20 BOLÍVARES	VG	VF	UNC
	20.10.1987 (1989). Deep green and black on m/c unpt. Gen. R. Urdaneta at r. and as wmk. Battle of Lake Maracaibo on back.	FV	FV	1.50

1990-94 ISSUE

#72 and 73 w/o imprint.

72	50 BOLÍVARES	VG	VF	UNC
	31.5.1990. Purple, black and orange on m/c unpt. Similar to #65 but modified plate design, ornaments in "50's". Back deeper orange.	FV	FV	2.25

#73-75 arms at upper r. on back.

73	1000 BOLÍVARES	VG	VF	UNC
	1991-94. Red-violet on m/c unpt. Part of independence text at far l., S. Bolívar at l. and as wmk. Signing of the Declaration of Independence at ctr. r., arms at upper r. on back.			
	a. Dot instead of accent above *i* (error) in *Bolivares* on face and back. 8.8.1991.	3.25	10.00	40.00
	b. Accent above *í* in *Bolívares* on face and back. 30.7.1992.	FV	FV	20.00
	c. As b. 30.7.1992; 8.12.1992.	FV	FV	4.00
	d. As b. 17.3.1994.	FV	FV	3.00
	e. As b. 5.2.1998.	—	—	—
	s1. As a. Specimen.	—	—	40.00
	s2. As b. Specimen.	—	—	40.00

		VG	VF	UNC
74	**2000 Bolívares** 1994; 1995. Dk. green and black on m/c unpt. A. J. de Sucre at r. and as wmk. Scene of Battle of Ayacucho at l. ctr. on back.			
	a. 12.5.1994.	FV	FV	7.50
	b. 21.12.1995. Large serial #.	FV	FV	5.00

		VG	VF	UNC
75	**5000 Bolívares** 1994; 1996. Dk. brown and brown-violet on m/c unpt. S. Bolívar at r. and as wmk. Gathering at palace for Declaration of Independence at ctr. on back.			
	a. 12.5.1994.	FV	FV	15.00
	b. 14.3.1996.	FV	FV	12.50

1995-98 Issue

		VG	VF	UNC
76	**1000 Bolívares** 5.6.1995. Red-violet on m/c unpt. Like #73 but w/green OVD *1000* at lower r.	FV	FV	3.00
77	**2000 Bolívares** 1997. Dk. green, brown and black on m/c unpt. Like #74 but w/*2000* at lower l. in brown.			
	a. 1997.	FV	FV	9.00
	b. 8.6.1998.	FV	FV	8.50

		VG	VF	UNC
78	**10,000 Bolívares** 10.2.1998. Black, red and olive-brown on m/c unpt. S. Bolívar at r. and as wmk. Teresa Carreno Theatre at l. ctr., arms at top ctr. r. on back.	FV	FV	27.50
79	**20,000 Bolívares** 199x. M/c.		Expected New Issue	
80	**50,000 Bolívares** 199x. M/c.		Expected New Issue	

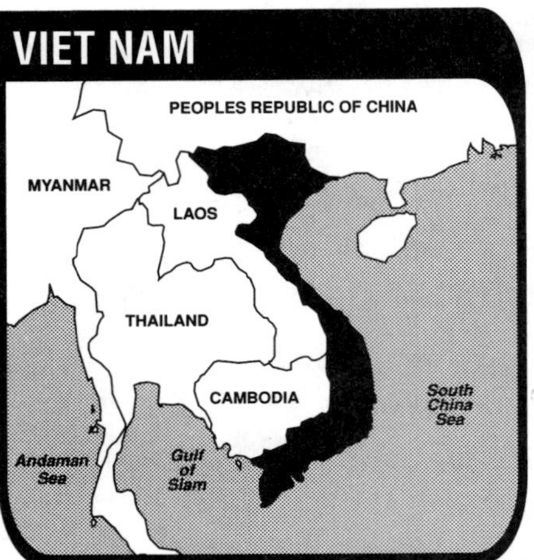

The Socialist Republic of Viet Nam, located in Southeast Asia west of the South China Sea, has an area of 127,300 sq. mi. (329,560 sq. km.) and a population of 76 million. Capital: Hanoi. Agricultural products, coal and mineral ores are exported.

The Viet Namese originated in North China, from where they were driven southward by the Han Chinese. They settled in the Red River Delta in northern Viet Nam; by 208 BC, much of present-day southern China and northern Viet Nam was incorporated into the independent kingdom of Nam Viet. China annexed Nam Viet in 111 BC and ruled it until 939, when independence was reestablished. The new state then expanded until it included much of Cambodia and southern Viet Nam. Viet Nam was reconquered by the Chinese in 1407; they were finally driven out, but the country was divided into two, not to be reunited until 1802.

During the latter half of the 19th century, the French gradually overran Viet Nam. Cochin-China, an alluvial plain of the Mekong Delta, fell to the French in 1862-67. In 1884, France established protectorates over Annam, an historic kingdom on the east coast of Indochina, and Tonkin in the north. Cambodia, Cochin-China, Annam and Tonkin were incorporated into the Indo-Chinese Union in 1887.

Viet Namese nationalists never really acquiesced to French domination, but continued to resist through a number of clandestine extra-legal organizations. At the start of World War II, many nationalists, communist and non-communist alike, fled to China where Ho Chi Minh organized the League for the Independence of Viet Nam ("Viet Minh") to free Viet Nam from French rule. The Japanese occupied Viet Nam during World War II. As the end of the war drew near, they the Vichy French administration and granted Viet Nam independence under a puppet government headed by Bao Dai, emperor of Annam. The Bao Dai government collapsed at the end of the war, and on Sept. 2, 1945, Ho Chi Minh proclaimed the existence of an independent Viet Nam consisting of Cochin-China, Annam and Tonkin, and set up a provisional Communist government of the Democratic Republic of Viet Nam. France recognized the new government as a free state, but later reneged and in 1949 reinstalled Bao Dai as ruler of Viet Nam and extended the regime independence within the French Union. Ho Chi Minh led a guerrilla war, in the first Indochina War, against the French puppet state that raged on to the disastrous defeat of the French by the Viet Minh at Dien Bien Phu on May 7, 1954.

An agreement signed at Geneva on July 21, 1954, provided for a temporary division of Viet Nam at the 17th parallel of latitude, with the Communist dominated Democratic Republic of Viet Nam (North Viet Nam) to the north, and the US/French-supported Republic of Viet Nam (South Viet Nam) to the south. In October 1955, South Viet Nam deposed Bao Dai by referendum and authorized the establishment of a new republic with Ngo Dinh Diem as president. This Republic of Viet Nam was proclaimed on October 26, 1955, and was recognized immediately by the Western powers.

The Democratic Republic of Viet Nam, working through Viet Cong guerrillas, instigated subversion in South Viet Nam which led to US armed intervention and the second Indochina War. This war, from the viewpoint of the North merely a continuation of the first (anti-French) war, was a bitter, protracted military conflict which came to a brief halt in 1973 (when a cease-fire was arranged and US and its other allied forces withdrew), but did not end until April 30, 1975 when South Viet Nam surrendered unconditionally. The National Liberation Front for South Viet Nam, the political arm of the Viet Cong, assumed governmental power when on July 2, 1976, North and South Vietnam were united as the Socialist Republic of Viet Nam with Hanoi as the capital.

MONETARY SYSTEM:

1 Hao = 10 Xu
1 Dông = 100 Xu to 1985
1 Dông = 10 "Old" Dông, 1985-95

NOTE: HCM - Ho Chi Minh

Democratic Republic

Ngân-Hàng Nhà-Nu'ó'c Viêt-Nam

State Bank of Viet Nam

1964 ND; 1972; 1975 Issue

		VG	VF	UNC
75	**2 Xu** ND (1964). Purple on green unpt. Arms at ctr.			
	a. Issued note.	2.00	8.00	37.50
	s. Specimen.	—	—	20.00

		VG	VF	UNC
76	**5 Xu** 1975 (date in lt. brown above *VIET* at lower l. ctr.). Violet on brown unpt. Arms at upper r.			
	a. Wmk: 15mm stars.	.25	1.25	6.50
	b. Wmk: 30mm radiant star.	.25	1.25	6.50
	s. Specimen w/o wmk.	—	—	45.00

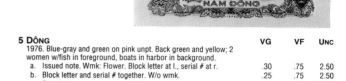

		VG	VF	UNC
77	**1 HAO** 1972. Violet on m/c unpt. Arms at ctr. Woman feeding pigs on back. 103 x 57mm.			
	a. Wmk: 15mm stars. Series KG-?.	.25	1.25	6.50
	b. Wmk: 32mm encircled stars. Series MK-?.	.25	1.25	6.50
	c. W/o wmk. Series ML.	.25	1.25	5.00
	s. Specimen w/o wmk.	—	—	50.00
77A	**1 HAO** 1972. Violet on m/c unpt. Like #77 but reduced size, 96 x 48mm. Specimen.	—	—	20.00

		VG	VF	UNC
78	**2 HAO** 1975. Brownish purple on green and peach unpt. Arms at ctr. 2 men spraying rice field on back.			
	a. Issued note.	.25	1.25	6.50
	s. Specimen.	—	—	50.00

SOCIALIST REPUBLIC

Working through Viet Cong guerrillas with material help from China and Russia, and finally with years of armed conflict, the Democratic Republic of Viet Nam (North Viet Nam) toppled the U.S.A. supported Democratic government of the South. Reunion of North and South Viet Nam took place on July 2, 1976, and the Socialist Republic of Viet Nam was established.

NGÂN-HÀNG NHÀ-NU'Ó'C VIÊT-NAM

STATE BANK OF VIET NAM

1976 DATED ISSUE

Issued in 1978, these notes unified the monetary systems of the South with that of the DRVN. Exchanged at par with the old DRVN notes, these replaced South Viet Nam (Ngan Hang Viet Nam) transitional series (see South Viet Nam #37-44) at 1 "new" = 0.8 "old South".

#79-82 arms at ctr. Wmk. paper.

		VG	VF	UNC
79	**5 HAO** 1976. Purple on m/c unpt. Coconut palms amd river scene on back.			
	a. Issued note.	.25	.75	2.50
	s. Specimen.	—	—	20.00

		VG	VF	UNC
80	**1 DÔNG** 1976. Brown on m/c unpt. Arms at ctr. Factory on back.			
	a. Issued note.	.25	.65	2.00
	s. Specimen.	—	—	20.00

NOTICE

Readers with unlisted dates, signature varieties, etc. are invited to submit photocopies of their notes to: Standard Catalog of World Paper Money, 700 East State St. Iola, WI 54990-0001, fax: 1-715-445-4087, or E-Mail: thernr@krause.com.

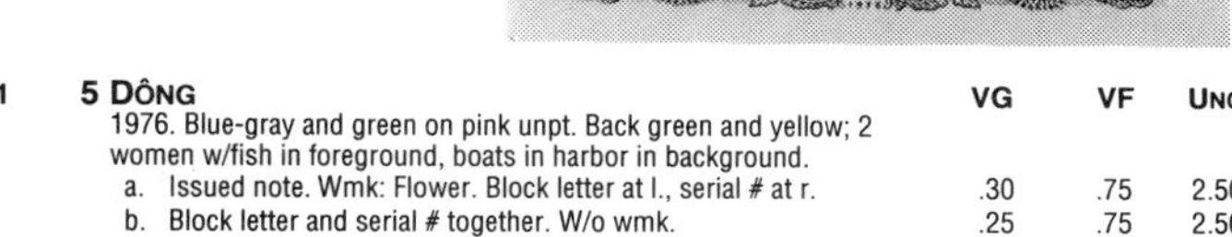

		VG	VF	UNC
81	**5 DÔNG** 1976. Blue-gray and green on pink unpt. Back green and yellow; 2 women w/fish in foreground, boats in harbor in background.			
	a. Issued note. Wmk: Flower. Block letter at l., serial # at r.	.30	.75	2.50
	b. Block letter and serial # together. W/o wmk.	.25	.75	2.50
	s. Specimen.	—	—	25.00

		VG	VF	UNC
82	**10 DÔNG** 1976. Purple and brown on m/c unpt. Elephants logging at ctr. on back.			
	a. Issued note.	.35	1.00	4.50
	s. Specimen.	—	—	30.00

		VG	VF	UNC
83	**20 DÔNG** 1976. Blue on pink and green unpt. HCM at r., arms at l. Tractors and dam on back.			
	a. Issued note.	.30	1.25	5.00
	s. Specimen.	—	—	30.00

		VG	VF	UNC
84	**50 DÔNG** 1976. Reddish purple on pink and green unpt. HCM at r., arms at l. Open pit mining scene in Hongay on back. 2 serial # varieties.			
	a. Issued note.	.30	1.25	5.00
	s. Specimen.	—	—	40.00

SOCIALIST REPUBLIC OF VIET NAM

NGÂN-HÀNG NHÀ-NƯ'Ó'C VIÊT-NAM

STATE BANK OF VIET NAM

1980; 1981 ISSUE

		VG	VF	UNC
85	**2 DÔNG** 1980 (1981). Brown on m/c unpt. Arms at ctr. River scene on back.			
	a. Issued note.	.20	.75	1.75
	s. Specimen.	—	—	40.00

		VG	VF	UNC
86	**10 DÔNG** 1980 (1981). Brown on m/c unpt. Arms at r. House and trees on back.			
	a. Issued note.	.25	.75	2.00
	s. Specimen.	—	—	30.00

		VG	VF	UNC
87	**30 DÔNG** 1981 (1982). Purple, brown and m/c. Arms at l. ctr., HCM at r. Harbor scene on back.			
	a. Issued note.	.25	1.00	5.00
	s1. Specimen ovpt: *SPECIMEN.*	—	—	25.00
	s2. Specimen ovpt: *GIAY MÂU.*	—	—	35.00

		VG	VF	UNC
88	**100 DÔNG** 1980 (1981). Brown, dk. blue and m/c. Portr. HCM at r. and as wmk., arms at ctr. Back blue, purple and brown; boats and rock formations in sea cove. Lg. 6-digit or sm. 7-digit serial #.			
	a. Issued note.	.25	1.00	5.00
	s. Specimen.	—	—	35.00

1985 ISSUE

#89-93 tower at l. ctr. on face.

		VG	VF	UNC
89	**5 HAO** 1985. Red-violet on lt. blue unpt.			
	a. Issued note.	.25	2.00	5.00
	s. Specimen.	—	—	25.00

		VG	VF	UNC
90	**1 DÔNG** 1985. Blue-green on m/c unpt. Sampans along rocky coastline on back.			
	a. Issued note.	.15	.40	1.25
	s. Specimen.	—	—	25.00

		VG	VF	UNC
91	**2 DÔNG** 1985. Purple on m/c unpt. Sampans anchored along coastline on back.			
	a. Issued note.	.20	.60	1.75
	s. Specimen.	—	—	25.00

		VG	VF	UNC
92	**5 DÔNG** 1985. Green on m/c unpt. Sampans anchored in river on back.			
	a. Issued note.	.15	.40	1.00
	s. Specimen.	—	—	25.00

		VG	VF	UNC
93	**10 DÔNG**			
	1985. Brown-violet on m/c unpt. Village along stream at ctr. on back.			
	a. Issued note.	.25	.75	2.00
	s. Specimen.	—	—	35.00

#94-99 HCM at r.

		VG	VF	UNC
94	**20 DÔNG**			
	1985 (1986). Brown, dk. purple and m/c. One pillar pagoda in Hanoi on back.			
	a. Issued note.	.25	.75	2.00
	s. Specimen.	—	—	30.00

		VG	VF	UNC
95	**30 DÔNG**			
	1985 (1986). Blue and m/c. Lg. bldg. w/clock tower at ctr. on back.			
	a. Issued note.	.50	1.25	5.00
	s. Specimen.	—	—	30.00

		VG	VF	UNC
96	**50 DÔNG**			
	1985. Green, brown and m/c. Reservoir and electric power station on back.			
	a. Issued note.	.50	1.50	6.00
	s. Specimen.	—	—	30.00

		VG	VF	UNC
97	**50 DÔNG**			
	1985 (1987). Blue-gray on orange and m/c unpt. Bridge at ctr. on back.			
	a. Issued note.	.25	.75	2.50
	s. Specimen.	—	—	35.00

		VG	VF	UNC
98	**100 DÔNG**			
	1985. Brown, yellow and m/c. Planting rice on back. Wmk: HCM.			
	a. Issued note.	1.00	3.00	12.50
	s. Specimen.	—	—	35.00

		VG	VF	UNC
99	**500 DÔNG**			
	1985. Red on blue and m/c unpt. Factory at l. ctr. on back. Wmk: HCM.			
	a. Issued note.	1.25	3.25	10.00
	s. Specimen.	—	—	40.00

1987; 1988 ISSUE

#100-104 HCM at r.

		VG	VF	UNC
100	**200 DÔNG**			
	1987. Red-brown and tan on m/c unpt. Field workers at l. and tractor at ctr. r. on back.			
	a. Issued note.	.10	.35	1.00
	s. Specimen.	—	—	35.00

101 500 DÔNG

1988 (1989). Red-brown and red on m/c unpt. Dockside view on back.

	VG	VF	UNC
a. Issued note.	.25	.50	2.00
s. Specimen.	—	—	35.00

#102-104 wmk: HCM.

102 1000 DÔNG

1987 (1988). Purple, dk. brown and deep olive-green on m/c unpt. Open pit mining equipment at l. ctr. on back.

	VG	VF	UNC
a. Issued note.	1.00	3.50	10.00
s. Specimen.	—	—	35.00

103 2000 DÔNG

1987 (1988). Brown, purple and olive-green on m/c unpt. Industrial plant at l. ctr. on back.

	VG	VF	UNC
a. Issued note.	.85	3.00	8.50
s. Specimen.	—	—	35.00

104 5000 DÔNG

1987 (1989). Deep blue, purple and green on m/c unpt. Offshore oil rigs at l. ctr. on back.

	VG	VF	UNC
a. Issued note.	.30	1.00	4.00
s. Specimen.	—	—	35.00

1988-91 ISSUE

#106-111 HCM at r.

105 100 DÔNG

1991 (1992). Brown on m/c unpt. Arms at l. Temple and pagoda at l. ctr. on back.

	VG	VF	UNC
a. Issued note.	.05	.15	.75
s1. Specimen w/ovpt: *TIEN MÂU.*	—	—	45.00
s2. Specimen w/ovpt: *SPECIMEN.*	—	—	40.00

106 1000 DÔNG

1988 (1989). Purple on gold and m/c unpt. Arms at l. ctr. Elephant logging on back.

	VG	VF	UNC
a. Issued note.	.10	.30	1.50
s. Specimen.	—	—	40.00

107 2000 DÔNG

1988 (1989). Brownish purple on lilac and m/c unpt. Arms at l. Women workers in textile factory on back.

	VG	VF	UNC
a. Issued note.	.15	.50	2.00
s. Specimen.	—	—	35.00

108 5000 DÔNG

1991 (1993). Dk. blue on m/c unpt. Arms at l. Electric lines on back.

	VG	VF	UNC
a. Issued note.	.25	.75	3.00
s. Specimen.	—	—	35.00

#109-111 wmk: HCM.

		VG	VF	UNC
109	**10,000 DÔNG** 1990 (1992). Red and red-violet on m/c unpt. Arms at ctr. Junks along coastline on back.			
	a. Issued note.	FV	FV	5.50
	s. Specimen.	—	—	65.00

		VG	VF	UNC
110	**20,000 DÔNG** 1991 (1993). Blue-green on m/c unpt. Arms at ctr. Packing factory on back.			
	a. Issued note.	FV	FV	12.50
	s. Specimen.	—	—	75.00
111	**50,000 DÔNG** 1990 (1993). Dk. olive-green and black on m/c unpt. Arms at upper l. ctr. Date at lower r. Dockside view on back.			
	a. Issued note.	FV	FV	25.00
	s. Specimen.	—	—	75.00

1992 BANK CHEQUE ISSUE

#112-114A Negotiable Bank Cheques/Certificates with expiration dates used between banks, businesses.

		VG	VF	UNC
112	**100,000 DÔNG** 1992-99.	20.00	50.00	100.00
113	**500,000 DÔNG** 1992-99.	25.00	75.00	150.00
114	**1,000,000 DÔNG** 1992-99.	50.00	100.00	250.00
114A	**5,000,000 DÔNG** 1992-99.	100.00	300.00	600.00

1993; 1994 REGULAR ISSUE

		VG	VF	UNC
115	**10,000 DÔNG** 1993. Red and red-violet on m/c unpt. Like #109 but w/optical registry device at lower l., modified unpt. color around arms. Back brown-violet on m/c unpt.			
	a. Issued note.	FV	FV	3.00
	s. Specimen.	—	—	60.00

		VG	VF	UNC
116	**50,000 DÔNG** 1994. Dk. olive-green and black on m/c unpt. Like #111 but w/date under HCM.			
	a. Issued note.	FV	FV	13.00
	s. Specimen.	—	—	65.00

FOREIGN EXCHANGE CERTIFICATES
NGÂN HANG N GOAI THU'O'NG
BANK FOR FOREIGN T RADE

1987 ND DÔNG B ISSUE

#FX1-FX5 green on pale blue and yellow unpt. Back pale blue.

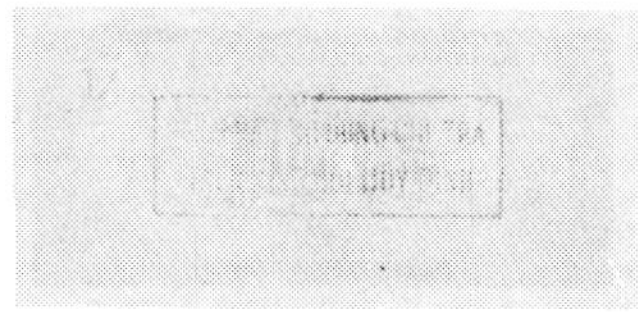

		VG	VF	UNC
FX1	**10 DÔNG B** ND (1987). Back pale blue.			
	a. Series AA; AB (not issued).	—	—	2.50
	s. Specimen. Series EE.	—	—	10.00
FX2	**50 DÔNG B** ND (1987). Back pale blue.			
	a. Series AD (not issued).	—	—	2.50
	s. Specimen. Series EE.	—	—	10.00
FX3	**100 DÔNG B** ND (1987). Back pale blue.			
	a. Series AC (not issued).	—	—	2.50
	s. Specimen. Series EE.	—	—	10.00
FX4	**200 DÔNG B** ND (1987). Back pale blue.			
	a. Series AD (not issued).	—	—	2.50
	s. Specimen. Series EE.	—	—	10.00
FX5	**500 DÔNG B** ND (1987). Back pale blue.			
	a. Series AC (not issued).	—	—	2.50
	s. Specimen. Series EE.	—	—	10.00

		VG	VF	UNC
FX6	**1000 DÔNG B** ND (1987). Red-violet on pink and pale orange unpt. Back pink.			
	a. Issued note. Series AE.	—	—	2.50
	s. Specimen. Series EE.	—	—	10.00
FX7	**5000 DÔNG B** ND (1987). Brown on ochre unpt. Back ochre.			
	a. Issued note. Series AA; AB.	—	—	2.50
	s. Specimen. Series EE.	—	—	10.00

PHIÊU' THAY NGOAI TÊ

1981 US DOLLAR A ISSUE

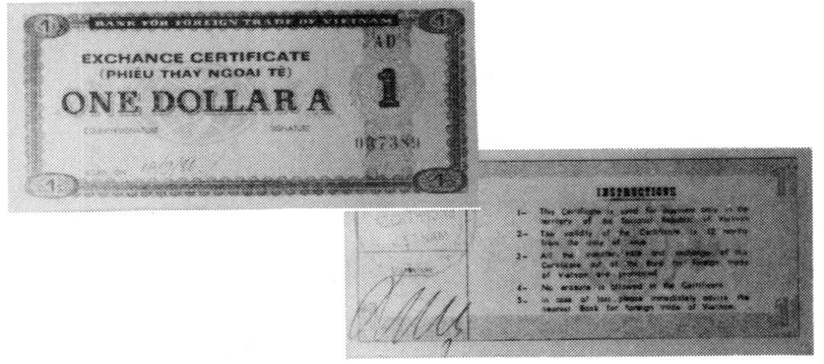

		GOOD	FINE	XF
FX8	**1 DOLLAR** 1981-84. Green on peach and lt. blue unpt. Series AD.	150.00	400.00	—

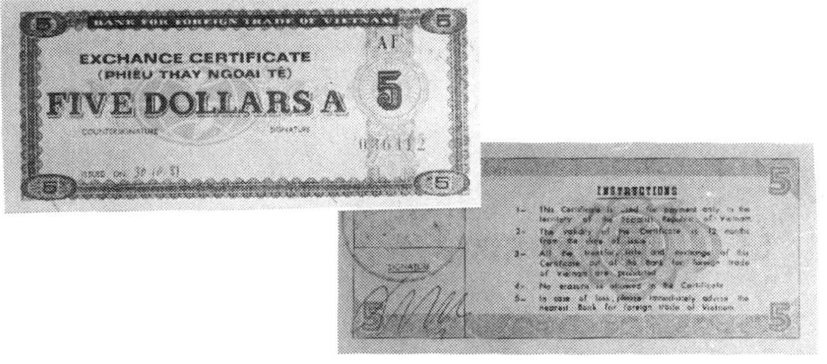

		GOOD	FINE	XF
FX9	**5 DOLLARS** 1981-84. Purple on peach and lt. blue unpt. Series AF.	300.00	900.00	—

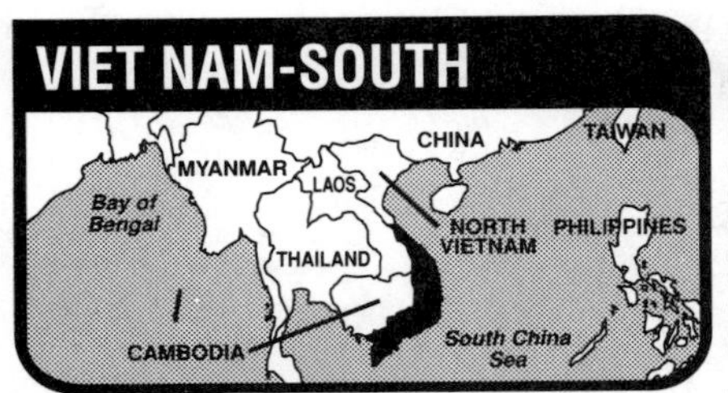

South Viet Nam (the former Republic of Viet Nam), located in Southeast Asia, bounded by North Viet Nam on the north, Laos and Cambodia on the west, and the South China Sea on the east and south, had an area of 66,280 sq. mi. (171,665 sq. km.) and a population of 20 million. Capital: Saigon (now Ho Chi Minh City). The economy of the are is predominantly agricultural.

South Viet Nam, the direct successor to the French-dominated Emperor Bao Dai regime (also known as the State of Viet Nam), was created after the first Indochina War (between the French and the Viet-Minh) by the Geneva agreement of 1954 which divided Viet Nam at the 17th parallel of latitude. The National Bank of Viet Nam, with headquarters in the old Bank of Indochina building in Saigon, came into being on December 31, 1954. Elections which would have reunified North and South Viet Nam in 1956 never took place, and the North continued the war for unification of Viet Nam under the communist government of the Democratic Republic of Viet Nam begun at the close of World War II. South Viet Nam surrendered unconditionally on April 30, 1975. There followed a short period of coexistence of the two Viet Namese states, but the South was governed by the North through the Peoples Revolutionary Government (PRG). On July 2, 1976, South and North Viet Nam joined to form the Socialist Republic of Viet Nam.

Also see Viet Nam.

MONETARY SYSTEM

1 Dông = 100 Xu

VIET NAM - SOUTH

NGÂN-HÀNG QUÔ'C-GIA VIÊT-NAM

NATIONAL BANK OF VIET NAM

1962 ND ISSUE

		VG	VF	UNC
5	**10 DÔNG** ND (1962). Red. Young farm couple at l. Ornate arch on back. Shade varieties.			
	a. Issued note.	.50	1.75	5.50
	s. Specimen.	—	—	200.00

		VG	VF	UNC
6	**20 DÔNG** ND (1962). Brown. Ox cart at l. Woman digging on back.			
	a. Issued note.	.75	3.00	12.00
	s. Specimen.	—	—	200.00

		VG	VF	UNC
6A	**500 DÔNG** ND (1962). Green-blue on gold and pinkish unpt. Dragon at l., palace-like bldg. at l. ctr. Farmer w/2 water buffalos at r. on back. Wmk: Ngo Dinh Diem.			
	a. Issued note.	50.00	150.00	500.00
	s. Specimen.	—	—	400.00

1964; 1966 ND ISSUES

		VG	VF	UNC
15	**1 DÔNG** ND (1964). Lt. and dk. brown on orange and lt. blue unpt. Back red-brown; farm tractor at r. Wmk: Plant.			
	a. Issued note.	.20	.60	2.50
	s. Specimen.	—	—	225.00

		VG	VF	UNC
16	**20 DÔNG** ND (1964). Green on m/c unpt. Stylized fish at ctr. on back. Wmk: Dragon's head.			
	a. Issued note.	.25	.75	5.00
	s. Specimen.	—	—	225.00

		VG	VF	UNC
17	**50 DÔNG** ND (1966). Purple on m/c unpt. Leaf tendrils at r.			
	a. Issued note.	1.00	5.00	25.00
	s. Specimen.	—	—	225.00

18	100 DÔNG	VG	VF	UNC
	ND (1966). Lt. and dk. brown on lt. blue unpt. Bldg. w/domed roof at r. Quarry and hills on back. Wmk: Plant.			
	a. Issued note.	1.00	5.00	25.00
	s1. Specimen. Red ovpt.	—	—	250.00
	s2. Specimen. Black ovpt.	—	—	250.00

19	100 DÔNG	VG	VF	UNC
	ND (1966). Red on m/c unpt. Le Van Duyet in national costume at l. Bldg. and ornate gateway at ctr. r. on back.			
	a. Wmk: Demon's head.	.50	2.50	10.00
	b. Wmk: Le Van Duyet.	1.00	7.50	20.00
	s1. As a. Specimen.	—	—	250.00
	s2. As b. Specimen.	—	—	250.00

20	200 DÔNG	VG	VF	UNC
	ND (1966). Dk. brown on m/c unpt. Nguyen-Hue, warrior at l. Warrior on horseback leading soldiers on back.			
	a. Wmk: Demon's head.	2.50	10.00	25.00
	b. Wmk: Nguyen Hue's head.	.25	4.00	10.00
	s1. As a. Specimen.	—	—	250.00
	s2. As b. Specimen.	—	—	250.00

#21 *Deleted.* See #6A.

22	500 DÔNG	VG	VF	UNC
	ND (1964). Brown on m/c unpt. Museum in Saigon at ctr. Stylized creatures at ctr. on back. Wmk: Demon's head.			
	a. Issued note.	4.00	12.50	35.00
	s. Specimen.	—	—	275.00

23	500 DÔNG	VG	VF	UNC
	ND (1966). Blue on m/c unpt. Trâ'n-Hu'ng-Dao, warrior at l. and as wmk. Sailboat and rocks in water on back.			
	a. Issued note.	2.50	10.00	25.00
	s. Specimen.	—	—	225.00
	x. Counterfeit. Series S; U; X.	—	—	5.00

1969-71 ND ISSUE

#24-29 bank bldg. at r. Lathework on all backs. Wmk. as #23.

24	20 DÔNG	VG	VF	UNC
	ND (1969). Red on m/c unpt.			
	a. Issued note.	.25	.50	2.50
	s. Specimen.	—	—	175.00

25	50 DÔNG	VG	VF	UNC
	ND (1969). Blue-green on m/c unpt.			
	a. Issued note.	.25	.50	2.50
	s. Specimen.	—	—	175.00

26	100 DÔNG	VG	VF	UNC
	ND (1970). Dk. green on m/c unpt.			
	a. Issued note.	.25	.75	5.00
	s. Specimen.	—	—	185.00

	200 DÔNG	VG	VF	UNC
27	ND (1970). Purple on m/c unpt.			
	a. Issued note.	.50	1.25	7.50
	s. Specimen.	—	—	200.00

	500 DÔNG	VG	VF	UNC
28	ND (1970). Orange and dk. brown on m/c unpt. Back orange and pale olive-green on m/c unpt.			
	a. Issued note.	.25	.75	5.00
	s. Specimen.	—	—	200.00

#28A *Deleted*. See #28.

NOTE: Authorities currently agree that the brown and black variety previously listed as #28A is believed to be the result of oxidation.

	1000 DÔNG	VG	VF	UNC
29	ND (1971). Turquoise on m/c unpt.			
	a. Issued note.	1.00	7.50	20.00
	s. Specimen.	—	—	225.00

1972; 1975 ND Issue

#30-36 Palace of Independence at r. Wmk: Young woman's head in profile.

	50 DÔNG	VG	VF	UNC
30	ND (1972). Blue-gray on m/c unpt. 3 horses at l. ctr. on back.			
	a. Issued note.	.25	.75	5.00
	s. Specimen.	—	—	175.00

	100 DÔNG	VG	VF	UNC
31	ND (1972). Green on m/c unpt. Farmer w/2 water buffalos at l. ctr. on back.			
	a. Issued note.	.25	.75	5.00
	s. Specimen.	—	—	185.00

	200 DÔNG	VG	VF	UNC
32	ND (1972). Wine red on m/c unpt. 3 deer at l. ctr. on back.			
	a. Issued note.	1.00	2.50	11.00
	s. Specimen.	—	—	200.00

	500 DÔNG	VG	VF	UNC
33	ND (1972). Orange and olive-green on m/c unpt. Tiger at l. ctr. on back.			
	a. Issued note.	.50	1.25	7.50
	s. Specimen.	—	—	225.00

NOTE: The brown and olive-brown variety previously listed as #33A is believed to be the result of oxidation by leading authorities.

#33A *Deleted*. See #33.

		VG	VF	UNC
34	**1000 DÔNG** ND (1972). Blue on m/c unpt. 3 elephants carrying loads at l. ctr. on back.			
	a. Issued note.	.50	1.25	7.50
	s. Specimen.	—	—	225.00

		VG	VF	UNC
34A	**1000 DÔNG** ND(1975). Green and m/c. Stylized fish at l., Truong Cong Dinh at r. Dinh's tomb at upper l., stylized fish at r. on back. Specimen. (Not issued).	—	—	1200.

#35 and 36 printer: TDLR.

		VG	VF	UNC
35	**5000 DÔNG** ND (1975). Brown, blue and m/c. Leopard at l. ctr. on back. (Not issued).			
	a. Normal serial #.	—	80.00	250.00
	s. Specimen.	—	—	250.00

		VG	VF	UNC
36	**10,000 DÔNG** ND (1975). Violet and m/c. Water buffalo at l. ctr. on back. (Not issued).			
	a. Normal serial #.	—	80.00	250.00
	s. Specimen.	—	—	250.00

NGÂN-HÀNG VIÊT-NAM

1966 DATED (1975) TRANSITIONAL ISSUE

#37-44 constitute a transitional issue of the communist National Liberation Front (Viet Cong) government which took over on April 30, 1975. Dated 1966 but not issued until 1975, they were used until the South's economic system was merged with that of the DRVN (North Viet Nam) into a unified Socialist Republic of Viet Nam.

		VG	VF	UNC
37	**10 XU** 1966 (1975). Brown on m/c unpt. Drying salt at ctr. Unloading boats on back.			
	a. Issued note.	.50	1.25	4.00
	s. Specimen.	—	—	50.00

		VG	VF	UNC
38	**20 XU** 1966 (1975). Blue on m/c unpt. Workers on rubber plantation at ctr. Soldiers greeting farmers w/oxen on back.			
	a. Issued note.	.75	2.50	7.50
	s. Specimen.	—	—	50.00

		VG	VF	UNC
39	**50 XU** 1966 (1975). Brownish purple on m/c unpt. Harvesting cane at ctr. Women weaving rugs on back.			
	a. Issued note.	1.00	3.75	12.50
	s. Specimen.	—	—	70.00

		VG	VF	UNC
40	**1 DÔNG** 1966 (1975). Red-orange on m/c unpt. Boats on canal at ctr. Workers in field on back.			
	a. Issued note.	1.00	3.00	12.50
	s. Specimen.	—	—	75.00
41	**2 DÔNG** 1966 (1975). Blue and green on m/c. Houseboats under a bridge at ctr. Soldiers and workers on back.			
	a. Issued note.	2.50	7.50	30.00
	s. Specimen.	—	—	80.00

		VG	VF	UNC
42	**5 DÔNG** 1966 (1975). Purple on m/c unpt. 4 women in textile factory at ctr. Armed soldiers w/downed helicopters on back.			
	a. Issued note.	3.50	10.00	30.00
	s. Specimen.	—	—	80.00

43 **10 DÔNG**
1966 (1975). Red on m/c unpt. 3 women and train at ctr. Soldiers and people w/flag on back.

	VG	VF	UNC
a. Issued note.	5.00	30.00	60.00
s. Specimen.	—	—	125.00

44 **50 DÔNG**
1966 (1975). Green and blue on m/c unpt. Workers in factory at ctr. Combine harvester on back.

	VG	VF	UNC
a. Issued note.	15.00	75.00	200.00
s. Specimen.	—	—	150.00

REGIONAL

ÚY BAN TRUNG U'O'NG

CENTRAL COMMITTEE OF THE NATIONAL FRONT FOR THE LIBERATION OF SOUTH VIETNAM

1963 ND ISSUE

#R1-R8 were printed in China for use in territories under control of the National Liberation Front. They were never issued, but many were captured during a joint US/South Viet Nam military operation into Cambodia. Except for #R2, relatively few survived in uncirculated condition.

		VG	VF	UNC
R1	**10 XU** ND (1963). Purple and m/c. Star at ctr.	.25	.75	3.00

		VG	VF	UNC
R2	**20 XU** ND (1963). Red-brown on aqua and m/c unpt. Star at ctr.	.25	.75	3.00

		VG	VF	UNC
R3	**50 XU** ND (1963). Green and m/c. Star at ctr.	.30	1.50	5.00

		VG	VF	UNC
R4	**1 DÔNG** ND (1963). Lt. brown on m/c unpt. Harvesting at ctr. Schoolroom on back.	1.00	4.00	15.00

		VG	VF	UNC
R5	**2 DÔNG** ND (1963). Blue on m/c unpt. Women in convoy at ctr. Fishermen w/boats on back.	2.00	7.00	35.00

		VG	VF	UNC
R6	**5 DÔNG** ND (1963). Lilac on m/c unpt. Women harvesting at ctr. Women militia patrol on back.	1.50	6.50	25.00

		VG	VF	UNC
R7	**10 DÔNG** ND (1963). Green on m/c unpt. Harvesting scene at ctr. War scene on back.	4.50	18.50	75.00

		VG	VF	UNC
R8	**50 DÔNG** ND (1963). Orange on m/c unpt. Truck convoy at ctr. Soldiers shooting down helicopters on back.	6.00	25.00	100.00

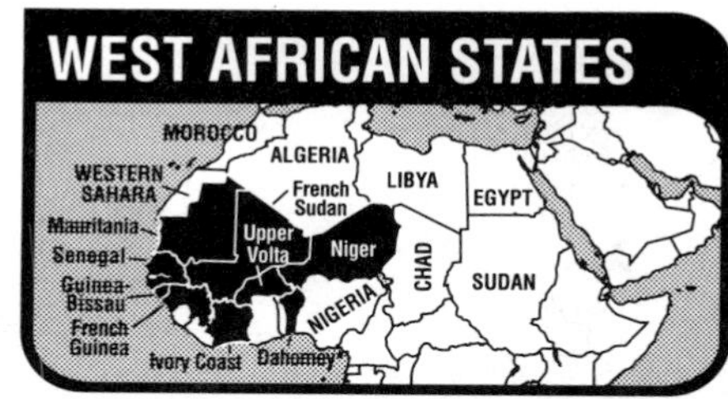

The West African States, a former federation of eight French colonial territories on the northwest coast of Africa, had an area of 1,813,079 sq. mi. (4,742,495 sq. km.) and a population of about 60 million. Capital: Dakar. The constituent territories were Mauritania, Senegal, Dahomey, French Sudan, Ivory Coast, Upper Volta, Niger and French Guinea.

The members of the federation were overseas territories within the French Union until Sept. of 1958 when all but French Guinea approved the constitution of the Fifth French Republic, thereby electing to become autonomous members of the new French Community. French Guinea voted to become the fully independent Republic of Guinea. The other seven attained independence in 1960. The French West Africa territories were provided with a common currency, a practice which was continued as the monetary union of the West African States which provides a common currency to the autonomous republics of Dahomey (now Benin), Mali, Senegal, Upper Volta, Ivory Coast, Togo, Niger, and Guinea-Bissau.

MONETARY SYSTEM:

1 Franc = 100 Centimes

DATING:

The year of issue on the current 500, 1000 and 2500 Francs appears in the first 2 digits of the serial number, i.e. (19)91, (19)92, etc.

SIGNATURE VARIETIES

	LE PRÉSIDENT	LE DIRECTEUR GÉNÉRAL	Date
1			Various dates – 1959 20.3.1961
2			20.3.1961
3			2.12.1964
4			2.3.1965; ND
5			ND
6			ND
7			ND
8			ND
9			ND
	LE PRÉSIDENT DU CONSEIL DES MINISTRES	LE GOUVERNEUR	Date
10			ND
11			ND (1977); 1977
12			ND (1978); 1978; 1979
13			ND (1980); 1980
14			ND (1977); 1977; 1988; 1989
	LE PRÉSIDENT DU CONSEIL DES MINISTRES	LE GOUVERNEUR	Date
15			ND (1981); 1981; 1982
16			ND (1983); 1983
17			1981; 1983; 1984
18			ND (1984); 1984
19			1984; 1985
20			1986; 1987
21			1989
22			1991
23			1992
24			1992
25			1993
26			1994
27			1994; 1995
28			1996; 1997

WEST AFRICAN STATES

NOTE: Beginning with signatures #21 the position has been reversed on the 500 Francs.

BANQUE CENTRALE DES ETATS DE L'AFRIQUE DE L'OUEST

Notes of this bank were issued both w/and w/o code letters in the upper r. and lower l. corners. The code letter follows the control number and indicates which member country the note was issued for. Those w/o code letters are general issues. The code letters are as follows:

A for Cote d' Ivoire	D for Mali	K for Senegal
B for Benin (Dahomey)	E for Mauritania	S for Guinea-Bissau
C for Burkina Faso (Upper Volta)	H for Niger	T for Togo

A for Cote d'Ivoire (Ivory Coast)

1959-65; ND Issue

101A 100 Francs
1961-65; ND. Dk. brown, orange and m/c. Design like #2.

	VG	VF	Unc
a. Engraved. Sign. 1. 20.3.1961.	8.00	20.00	65.00
b. Sign. 2. 20.3.1961.	8.00	20.00	65.00
c. Litho. Sign. 2. 20.3.1961.	10.00	25.00	70.00
d. Sign. 3. 2.12.1964.	10.00	25.00	70.00
e. Sign. 4. 2.3.1965.	8.00	20.00	65.00
f. Sign. 4. ND.	5.00	15.00	45.00
g. Sign. 5. ND.	5.00	15.00	45.00

102A 500 Francs
1959-64; ND. Brown, green and m/c. Field workers at l., mask carving at r. Woman at l., farmer on tractor at r. on back. Wmk: Woman's head.

	VG	VF	Unc
a. Engraved. Sign. 1. 15.4.1959.	25.00	55.00	150.00
b. Sign. 1. 20.3.1961.	12.00	35.00	90.00
c. Sign. 2. 20.3.1961.	12.00	35.00	90.00
d. Sign. 3. 2.12.1964.	25.00	55.00	150.00
e. Sign. 5. ND.	12.00	35.00	90.00
f. Sign. 6. ND.	10.00	30.00	75.00
g. Litho. Sign. 6. ND.	13.00	40.00	100.00
h. Sign. 7. ND.	12.00	35.00	90.00
i. Sign. 8. ND.	20.00	50.00	120.00
j. Sign. 9. ND.	8.00	25.00	60.00
k. Sign. 10. ND.	5.00	15.00	45.00
l. Sign. 11. ND.	5.00	15.00	40.00
m. Sign. 12. ND.	13.00	40.00	100.00

103A 1000 Francs
1959-65; ND. Brown, blue and m/c. Man and woman at ctr. Man w/rope suspension bridge in background and pineapples on back. Wmk: Man's head.

	VG	VF	Unc
a. Engraved. Sign. 1. 17.9.1959.	—	—	—
b. Sign. 1. 20.3.1961.	15.00	45.00	110.00
c. Sign. 2. 20.3.1961.	15.00	45.00	110.00
d. Sign. 4. 2.3.1965.	30.00	80.00	—
e. Sign. 5. ND.	8.00	25.00	60.00
f. Sign. 6. ND.	8.00	25.00	60.00
g. Litho. Sign. 6. ND.	8.00	25.00	60.00
h. Sign. 7. ND.	10.00	30.00	70.00
i. Sign. 8. ND.	12.00	40.00	90.00
j. Sign. 9. ND.	8.00	25.00	60.00
k. Sign. 10. ND.	5.00	15.00	40.00
l. Sign. 11. ND.	5.00	15.00	35.00
m. Sign. 12. ND.	5.00	15.00	35.00
n. Sign. 13. ND.	5.00	15.00	35.00

104A 5000 Francs
1961-65; ND. Blue, brown and m/c. Bearded man at l., bldg. at ctr. Woman, corn grinders and huts on back.

	VG	VF	Unc
a. Sign. 1. 20.3.1961.	35.00	100.00	300.00
b. Sign. 2. 20.3.1961.	25.00	75.00	200.00
c. Sign. 3. 2.12.1964.	25.00	75.00	200.00
d. Sign. 4. 2.3.1965.	35.00	100.00	—
e. Sign. 6. ND.	25.00	50.00	175.00
f. Sign. 7. ND.	25.00	50.00	175.00
g. Sign. 8. ND.	35.00	100.00	—
h. Sign. 9. ND.	20.00	45.00	160.00
i. Sign. 10. ND.	20.00	40.00	140.00
j. Sign. 11. ND.	20.00	40.00	140.00

1977-81; ND Issue

#105A-109A smaller size notes.

105A 500 Francs
1979-80. Lilac, lt. olive-green and m/c. Artwork at l., long horn animals at ctr., man wearing hat at r. Cultivated palm at l., aerial view at ctr., mask at r. on back. Wmk: Woman in profile.

	VG	VF	Unc
a. Sign. 12. 1979.	3.00	8.00	20.00
b. Sign. 13. 1980.	3.00	7.00	18.00

106A 500 Francs
1981-90. Pale olive-green and m/c. Design like #105A.

	VG	VF	Unc
a. Sign. 14. 1988.	FV	FV	6.00
b. Sign. 15. 1981. (BF).	5.00	15.00	35.00
c. Sign. 15. 1981. (F-CO).	FV	3.00	7.00
d. Sign. 15. 1982. (BF).	6.00	20.00	50.00
e. Sign. 17. 1981. (F-CO).	6.00	20.00	50.00
f. Sign. 17. 1983.	FV	3.00	7.00
g. Sign. 18. 1984.	FV	3.00	7.00
h. Sign. 19. 1984.	FV	3.00	7.00
i. Sign. 19. 1985.	FV	3.00	7.00
j. Sign. 20. 1986.	FV	FV	6.00
k. Sign. 20. 1987.	FV	3.00	10.00
l. Sign. 21 (reversed order). 1989.	FV	FV	5.00
m. Sign. 22. 1990.	FV	FV	5.00

NOTE: #106A w/10-digit small serial # were printed by Banque de France (BF) while those w/9-digit large serial # were printed by F-CO.

107A 1000 Francs
1981-90. Brown on m/c unpt. Artwork at l., open pit mine at ctr., woman at r. and as wmk. Wood carver w/finished works on back.

	VG	VF	Unc
a. Sign. 14. 1988.	FV	FV	10.00
b. Sign. 15. 1981.	FV	4.00	12.00
c. Sign. 17. 1981.	FV	4.00	12.00
d. Sign. 18. 1984.	FV	4.00	12.00
e. Sign. 19. 1984.	5.00	11.00	30.00
f. Sign. 19. 1985.	FV	4.00	12.00
g. Sign. 20. 1986.	FV	FV	10.00
h. Sign. 20. 1987.	FV	FV	10.00
i. Sign. 21. 1989.	FV	FV	9.00
j. Sign. 22. 1990.	FV	FV	9.00

108A 5000 Francs
1977-91. Black and red on m/c unpt. Woman at l., fish and boats on shore at ctr., carving at r. Carvings, fishing boats and mask on back.

	VG	VF	Unc
a. Sign. 11. 1977.	15.00	25.00	60.00
b. Sign. 12. 1978.	15.00	25.00	60.00
c. Sign. 12. 1979.	25.00	45.00	100.00
d. Sign. 13. 1980.	25.00	50.00	110.00
e. Sign. 14. 1977.	20.00	35.00	80.00
f. Sign. 14. 1988.	FV	FV	35.00
g. Sign. 14. 1989.	FV	FV	35.00
h. Sign. 15. 1981.	FV	20.00	50.00

	VG	VF	UNC
i. Sign. 15. 1982.	FV	20.00	50.00
j. Sign. 16. 1983.	35.00	60.00	—
k. Sign. 17. 1983.	20.00	35.00	80.00
l. Sign. 18. 1984.	15.00	25.00	60.00
m. Sign. 19. 1984.	FV	20.00	50.00
n. Sign. 19. 1985.	FV	20.00	50.00
o. Sign. 20. 1986.	20.00	35.00	80.00
p. Sign. 20. 1987.	FV	FV	35.00
q. Sign. 21. 1990.	FV	FV	35.00
r. Sign. 22. 1991.	FV	FV	40.00

109A 10,000 FRANCS
ND (1977-92). Red-brown on m/c unpt. 2 men seated operating primitive spinning apparatus, woman w/headwear at r. and as wmk. Figurine and girl at l., modern textile spinning machine at ctr. on back.

	VG	VF	UNC
a. Sign. 11. ND.	20.00	35.00	85.00
b. Sign. 12. ND.	20.00	35.00	95.00
c. Sign. 13. ND.	20.00	35.00	95.00
d. Sign. 14. ND.	FV	FV	60.00
e. Sign. 15. ND.	FV	FV	65.00
f. Sign. 18. ND.	20.00	35.00	85.00
g. Sign. 19. ND.	20.00	35.00	95.00
h. Sign. 20. ND.	FV	FV	60.00
i. Sign. 21. ND.	FV	FV	55.00
j. Sign. 22. ND.	FV	FV	55.00
k. Sign. 23. ND.	FV	FV	55.00

1991-92 ISSUE

#113A and 114A were first issued on 19.9.1994.

110A 500 FRANCS
(19)91-. Dk. brown and dk. green on m/c unpt. Male at r. and as wmk., flood control dam at ctr. Farmer riding spray rig behind garden tractor at ctr., native art at l. on back.

	VG	VF	UNC
a. Sign. 22. (19)91.	FV	FV	4.00
b. Sign. 23. (19)92.	FV	4.00	10.00
c. Sign. 25. (19)93.	FV	FV	4.00
d. Sign. 26. (19)94.	FV	FV	4.00
e. Sign. 27. (19)95.	FV	FV	3.00
f. Sign. 28. (19)96.	FV	FV	3.00
g. Sign. 28. (19)97.	FV	FV	3.00
h. Sign. 28. (19)98.	FV	FV	3.00

111A 1000 FRANCS
(19)91-. Dk. brown-violet on tan, yellow and m/c unpt. Workmen hauling peanuts to storage at ctr., woman's head at r. and as wmk. Twin statues and mask at l., 2 women w/baskets, elevated riverside storage bins in background at ctr. on back.

	VG	VF	UNC
a. Sign. 22. (19)91.	FV	FV	7.00
b. Sign. 23. (19)92.	FV	FV	7.00
c. Sign. 25. (19)93.	FV	FV	7.00
d. Sign. 26. (19)94.	FV	FV	7.00
e. Sign. 27. (19)95.	FV	FV	6.00
f. Sign. 28. (19)96.	FV	FV	6.00
g. Sign. 28. (19)97.	FV	FV	6.00
h. Sign. 28. (19)98.	FV	FV	6.00

112A 2500 FRANCS
(19)92-. Deep purple and dk. brown on lilac and m/c unpt. Dam at ctr., young woman's head at r. and as wmk. Statue at l., harvesting and spraying of fruit at l. ctr. on back.

	VG	VF	UNC
a. Sign. 23. (19)92.	FV	FV	20.00
b. Sign. 25. (19)93.	FV	FV	20.00
c. Sign. 27. (19)94.	FV	FV	20.00

113A 5000 FRANCS
(19)92-. Dk. brown and deep blue on m/c unpt. Woman wearing headdress adorned w/cowrie shells at r. and as wmk., smelting plant at ctr. Women w/children and various pottery at l. ctr. on back.

	VG	VF	UNC
a. Sign. 23. (19)92.	FV	FV	27.00
b. Sign. 25. (19)93.	FV	FV	27.00
c. Sign. 27. (19)94.	FV	FV	27.00
d. Sign. 27. (19)95.	FV	FV	26.00
e. Sign. 28. (19)96.	FV	FV	26.00
f. Sign. 28. (19)97.	FV	FV	26.00
g. Sign. 28. (19)98.	FV	FV	26.00
h. Sign. 29. (19)98.	FV	FV	26.00

114A 10,000 FRANCS
(19)92-. Dk. brown on m/c unpt. Headman w/scepter at r. and as wmk., skyscraper at ctr. Native art at l., woman crossing vine bridge over river at ctr. on back.

	VG	VF	UNC
a. Sign. 25. (19)92.	FV	FV	50.00
b. Sign. 27. (19)94.	FV	FV	50.00
c. Sign. 27. (19)95.	FV	FV	45.00
d. Sign. 28. (19)96.	FV	FV	45.00
e. Sign. 28. (19)97.	FV	FV	45.00
f. Sign. 20. (19)98.	FV	FV	45.00
g. Sign. 29. (19)98.	FV	FV	45.00

B FOR BENIN (DAHOMEY)

1959-65; ND ISSUE

201B 100 FRANCS
1961-65; ND. Like #101A.

	VG	VF	UNC
a. Engraved. Sign. 1. 20.3.1961.	12.00	40.00	120.00
b. Sign. 2. 20.3.1961.	10.00	35.00	100.00
c. Litho. Sign. 2. 20.3.1961.	10.00	35.00	100.00
d. Sign. 3. 2.12.1964.	12.00	40.00	120.00
e. Sign. 4. 2.3.1965.	8.00	20.00	65.00
f. Sign. 4. ND.	5.00	15.00	45.00

202B 500 FRANCS
1961-65; ND. Like #102A.

	VG	VF	UNC
a. Sign. 1. 20.3.1961.	50.00	—	—
b. Engraved Sign. 2. 20.3.1961.	25.00	65.00	150.00
d. Sign. 3. 2.12.1964.	—	—	—
e. Sign. 4. 2.3.1965.	50.00	—	—
f. Sign. 5. ND.	20.00	55.00	130.00
g. Sign. 6. ND.	10.00	30.00	80.00
h. Litho. Sign. 7. ND.	12.00	35.00	90.00
i. Sign. 9. ND.	8.00	25.00	75.00
k. Sign. 10. ND.	5.00	20.00	60.00
l. Sign. 11. ND.	4.00	15.00	45.00

203B 1000 FRANCS
1961-65; ND. Like #103A.

	VG	VF	UNC
a. Engraved. Sign. 1. 17.9.1959.	35.00	90.00	—
b. Sign. 1. 20.3.1961.	35.00	90.00	—
c. Sign. 2. 20.3.1961.	35.00	90.00	—
d. Sign. 4. 2.3.1965.	25.00	60.00	140.00
g. Sign. 6. ND.	8.00	30.00	70.00
h. Litho. Sign. 6. ND.	7.00	25.00	60.00
i. Sign. 7. ND.	25.00	60.00	150.00
j. Sign. 8. ND.	10.00	35.00	100.00
k. Sign. 9. ND.	10.00	35.00	100.00
l. Sign. 10. ND.	5.00	15.00	50.00
m. Sign. 11. ND.	5.00	15.00	45.00
n. Sign. 12. ND.	5.00	15.00	50.00

204B 5000 FRANCS
1961; ND. Like #104A.

	VG	VF	UNC
a. Sign. 1. 20.3.1961.	50.00	150.00	—
b. Sign. 2. 20.3.1961.	50.00	150.00	—
h. Sign. 6. ND.	25.00	75.00	200.00
j. Sign. 7. ND.	25.00	75.00	200.00
k. Sign. 9. ND.	20.00	50.00	175.00
l. Sign. 10. ND.	20.00	50.00	175.00

1977-81; ND ISSUE

#205B-209B smaller size notes.

205B 500 FRANCS
1979-80. Like #105A.

	VG	VF	UNC
a. Sign. 12. 1979.	6.00	20.00	50.00
b. Sign. 13. 1980.	3.00	8.00	20.00

206B 500 FRANCS
1981-90. Like #106A.

	VG	VF	UNC
a. Sign. 14. 1988.	4.00	12.00	—
b. Sign. 15. 1981. (BF).	FV	3.00	10.00
c. Sign. 15. 1981. (F-CO).	FV	3.00	10.00
d. Sign. 15. 1982. (BF).	6.00	25.00	—
e. Sign. 17. 1981. (F-CO).	6.00	25.00	—
f. Sign. 17. 1983. (BF).	6.00	25.00	—
g. Sign. 18. 1984.	FV	3.00	10.00
h. Sign. 19. 1984.	FV	3.00	10.00
i. Sign. 19. 1985.	FV	8.00	20.00
j. Sign. 20. 1986.	FV	FV	6.00
k. Sign. 20. 1987.	FV	8.00	20.00
l. Sign. 21. 1989.	FV	8.00	20.00
m. Sign. 22. 1990.	FV	FV	6.00

NOTE: #206B w/10-digit small serial # were printed by Banque de France (BF) while those w/9-digit large serial # were printed by F-CO.

207B 1000 FRANCS
1981-90. Like #107A.

	VG	VF	UNC
a. Sign. 14. 1988.	FV	FV	12.00
b. Sign. 15. 1981.	FV	5.00	20.00
c. Sign. 18. 1984.	FV	4.00	14.00
d. Sign. 19. 1984.	10.00	40.00	—
e. Sign. 19. 1985.	FV	4.00	14.00
f. Sign. 20. 1986.	FV	FV	12.00
g. Sign. 20. 1987.	FV	FV	12.00
h. Sign. 21. 1989.	5.00	25.00	—
i. Sign. 22. 1990.	FV	FV	10.00

208B 5000 FRANCS
1977-92. Like #108A.

	VG	VF	UNC
a. Sign. 12. 1979.	20.00	35.00	75.00
b. Sign. 14. 1977.	20.00	35.00	80.00
c. Sign. 14. 1988.	35.00	75.00	—
d. Sign. 14. 1989.	FV	FV	35.00
e. Sign. 15. 1981.	FV	25.00	65.00
f. Sign. 15. 1982.	FV	20.00	55.00
g. Sign. 17. 1983.	35.00	75.00	—
h. Sign. 18. 1984.	35.00	75.00	—
i. Sign. 19. 1985.	35.00	75.00	—
j. Sign. 20. 1986.	35.00	75.00	—
k. Sign. 20. 1987.	FV	20.00	55.00
l. Sign. 21. 1990.	FV	FV	35.00
m. Sign. 22. 1991.	FV	FV	55.00
n. Sign. 22. 1992.	FV	FV	30.00
o. Sign. 23. 1992.	FV	FV	30.00
p. Sign. 24. 1992.	20.00	40.00	—

209B 10,000 FRANCS
ND (1977-92). Like #109A.

	VG	VF	UNC
a. Sign. 11. ND.	40.00	75.00	175.00
b. Sign. 12. ND.	40.00	75.00	—
c. Sign. 14. ND.	FV	40.00	100.00
d. Sign. 15. ND.	FV	35.00	90.00
e. Sign. 16. ND.	40.00	75.00	—
f. Sign. 18. ND.	40.00	75.00	—
g. Sign. 19. ND.	FV	35.00	90.00
h. Sign. 20. ND.	35.00	60.00	—
i. Sign. 21. ND.	FV	FV	60.00
j. Sign. 22. ND.	FV	FV	60.00
k. Sign. 23. ND.	FV	FV	60.00

1991-92 ISSUE

210B 500 FRANCS
(19)91-. Like #110A.

	VG	VF	UNC
a. Sign. 22. (19)91.	FV	FV	5.00
b. Sign. 22. (19)92.	FV	5.00	15.00
c. Sign. 23. (19)92.	FV	5.00	15.00
d. Sign. 25. (19)93.	FV	FV	5.00
e. Sign. 26. (19)94.	FV	FV	5.00
f. Sign. 27. (19)95.	FV	FV	4.00
g. Sign. 28. (19)96.	FV	FV	4.00
h. Sign. 28. (19)97.	FV	FV	4.00

211B 1000 FRANCS
(19)91-. Like #111A.

	VG	VF	UNC
a. Sign. 22. (19)91.	FV	FV	8.00
b. Sign. 22. (19)92.	FV	5.00	15.00
c. Sign. 23. (19)92.	FV	5.00	15.00
d. Sign. 25. (19)93.	FV	5.00	15.00
e. Sign. 26. (19)94.	FV	FV	8.00
f. Sign. 27. (19)95.	FV	FV	7.00
g. Sign. 28. (19)96.	FV	FV	7.00
h. Sign. 28. (19)97.	FV	FV	6.00
i. Sign. 28. (19)98.	FV	FV	6.00

212B 2500 Francs	VG	VF	Unc
(19)92-. Like #112A.			
a. Sign. 23. (19)92.	FV	FV	20.00
b. Sign. 25. (19)93.	FV	FV	20.00
c. Sign. 27. (19)94.	FV	FV	20.00

213B 5000 Francs	VG	VF	Unc
(19)92-. Like #113A.			
a. Sign. 23. (19)92.	FV	FV	28.00
b. Sign. 25. (19)93.	FV	FV	28.00
c. Sign. 27. (19)94.	FV	FV	28.00
d. Sign. 27. (19)95.	FV	FV	28.00
e. Sign. 28. (19)98.	FV	FV	27.00

214B 10,000 Francs	VG	VF	Unc
(19)92-. Like #114A.			
a. Sign. 25. (19)92.	FV	FV	50.00
b. Sign. 27. (19)94.	FV	FV	50.00
c. Sign. 27. (19)95.	FV	FV	45.00
d. Sign. 28. (19)96.	FV	FV	45.00

C for Burkina Faso (Upper Volta)

1961; ND Issue

301C 100 Francs	VG	VF	Unc
1961-65; ND. Like #101A.			
a. Engraved. Sign. 1. 20.3.1961.	15.00	45.00	140.00
b. Sign. 2. 20.3.1961.	12.00	40.00	120.00
c. Litho. Sign. 2. 20.3.1961.	30.00	60.00	—
d. Sign. 3. 2.12.1964.	—	—	—
e. Sign. 4. 2.3.1965.	8.00	25.00	75.00
f. Sign. 4. ND.	7.00	18.00	55.00

302C 500 Francs	VG	VF	Unc
1961-65; ND. Like #102A.			
c. Engraved. Sign. 2. 20.3.1961.	25.00	75.00	160.00
d. Sign. 4. 20.3.1961.	25.00	65.00	—
e. Sign. 4. 2.3.1965.	25.00	75.00	—
f. Sign. 5. ND.	50.00	—	—
g. Sign. 6. ND.	15.00	40.00	110.00
h. Litho. Sign. 6. ND.	10.00	30.00	100.00
i. Sign. 7. ND.	20.00	60.00	140.00
k. Sign. 8. ND.	15.00	40.00	90.00
k. Sign. 9. ND.	8.00	25.00	75.00
m. Sign. 11. ND.	5.00	15.00	45.00
n. Sign. 12. ND.	5.00	15.00	50.00

303C 1000 Francs	VG	VF	Unc
1961; ND. Like #103A.			
b. Sign. 1. 20.3.1961.	75.00	—	—
d. Sign. 2. 20.3.1961.	30.00	90.00	—
e. Sign. 5. ND.	—	—	—
f. Sign. 6. ND.	25.00	60.00	140.00
i. Sign. 7. ND.	20.00	45.00	120.00
j. Sign. 8. ND.	25.00	60.00	150.00
k. Sign. 9. ND.	10.00	30.00	80.00
l. Sign. 10. ND.	5.00	15.00	50.00
m. Sign. 11. ND	5.00	15.00	45.00
n. Sign. 12. ND.	5.00	15.00	50.00
o. Sign. 13. ND.	8.00	20.00	55.00

304C 5000 Francs	VG	VF	Unc
1961; ND. Like #104A.			
a. Sign. 1. 20.3.1961.	35.00	90.00	300.00
d. Sign. 4. 2.3.1965.	100.00	—	—
h. Sign. 6. ND.	25.00	75.00	—
i. Sign. 7. ND.	25.00	75.00	—
k. Sign. 9. ND.	20.00	60.00	190.00
l. Sign. 11. ND.	20.00	50.00	175.00

1977-81; ND Issues

#305C-309C smaller size notes.

305C 500 Francs	VG	VF	Unc
1979-80. Like #105A.			
a. Sign. 12. 1979.	3.00	8.00	20.00
b. Sign. 13. 1980.	2.75	7.00	18.00

306C 500 Francs	VG	VF	Unc
1981-90. Like #106A.			
a. Sign. 14. 1988.	FV	FV	7.00
b. Sign. 15. 1981. (BF).	FV	3.00	10.00
c. Sign. 15. 1981. (F-CO).	FV	3.00	8.00
d. Sign. 15. 1982. (BF).	6.00	15.00	40.00
e. Sign. 17. 1981. (F-CO).	6.00	15.00	—
f. Sign. 17. 1983. (BF).	6.00	15.00	—
g. Sign. 18. 1984.	FV	3.00	8.00
h. Sign. 19. 1984.	FV	3.00	8.00
i. Sign. 19. 1985.	FV	3.00	8.00
j. Sign. 20. 1986.	FV	3.00	8.00
k. Sign. 20. 1987.	3.00	10.00	—
l. Sign. 21. 1989.	3.00	10.00	—
m. Sign. 22. 1990.	FV	FV	7.00

NOTE: #306C w/10-digit small serial # were printed by Banque de France (BF) while those w/9-digit large serial # were printed by F-CO.

307C 1000 Francs	VG	VF	Unc
1981-90. Like #107A.			
a. Sign. 14. 1988.	FV	FV	11.00
b. Sign. 15. 1981.	FV	4.00	14.00
c. Sign. 17. 1981.	5.00	30.00	—
d. Sign. 18. 1984.	5.00	30.00	—
e. Sign. 19. 1984.	5.00	30.00	—
f. Sign. 19. 1985.	5.00	30.00	—
g. Sign. 20. 1986.	FV	4.00	15.00
h. Sign. 20. 1987.	FV	FV	11.00
i. Sign. 21. 1989.	FV	4.00	15.00
j. Sign. 22. 1990.	FV	FV	10.00

308C 5000 Francs	VG	VF	Unc
1977-92. Like #108A.			
a. Sign. 12. 1978.	20.00	35.00	80.00
b. Sign. 12. 1979.	20.00	35.00	80.00
c. Sign. 14. 1977.	20.00	35.00	80.00
d. Sign. 14. 1988.	FV	FV	35.00
e. Sign. 14. 1989.	FV	FV	40.00
f. Sign. 15. 1981.	FV	20.00	60.00
g. Sign. 15. 1982.	FV	20.00	55.00
h. Sign. 17. 1983.	FV	20.00	55.00
i. Sign. 18. 1984.	20.00	35.00	80.00
k. Sign. 19. 1985.	FV	20.00	60.00
l. Sign. 20. 1986.	FV	25.00	75.00
m. Sign. 20. 1987.	FV	25.00	70.00
n. Sign. 21. 1990.	FV	FV	35.00
o. Sign. 22. 1991.	FV	FV	35.00
p. Sign. 22. 1992.	FV	FV	35.00
q. Sign. 23. 1992.	FV	FV	35.00
r. Sign. 24. 1992.	20.00	40.00	—

		VG	VF	UNC
309C	**10,000 FRANCS** ND (1977-92). Like #109A.			
	a. Sign. 11. ND.	40.00	75.00	175.00
	b. Sign. 12. ND.	25.00	50.00	100.00
	c. Sign. 13. ND.	25.00	50.00	100.00
	d. Sign. 14. ND.	30.00	65.00	150.00
	e. Sign. 15. ND.	25.00	55.00	120.00
	f. Sign. 20. ND.	FV	30.00	80.00
	g. Sign. 21. ND.	FV	FV	55.00
	h. Sign. 22. ND.	FV	FV	55.00
	i. Sign. 23. ND.	FV	FV	55.00

1991 ISSUE

		VG	VF	UNC
310C	**500 FRANCS** (19)91-. Like #110A.			
	a. Sign. 22. (19)91.	FV	FV	5.00
	b. Sign. 23. (19)92.	FV	5.00	15.00
	c. Sign. 25. (19)93.	FV	FV	7.00
	d. Sign. 26. (19)94.	FV	FV	5.00
	e. Sign. 27. (19)95.	FV	FV	4.00
	f. Sign. 28. (19)96.	FV	FV	3.00
	g. Sign. 28. (19)97.	FV	FV	3.00
	h. Sign. 28. (19)98.	FV	FV	3.00
311C	**1000 FRANCS** (19)91-. Like #111A.			
	a. Sign. 22. (19)91.	FV	FV	8.00
	b. Sign. 22. (19)92.	3.00	6.00	15.00
	c. Sign. 23. (19)92.	3.00	6.00	15.00
	d. Sign. 25. (19)93.	FV	FV	8.00
	e. Sign. 26. (19)94.	FV	FV	7.00
	f. Sign. 27. (19)95.	FV	FV	6.00
	g. Sign. 28. (19)96.	FV	FV	6.00
	h. Sign. 28. (19)97.	FV	FV	6.00
	i. Sign. 28. (19)98.	FV	FV	6.00

		VG	VF	UNC
312C	**2500 FRANCS** (19)92-. Like #112A.			
	a. Sign. 23. (19)92.	FV	FV	20.00
	b. Sign. 25. (19)93.	FV	FV	25.00
	c. Sign. 27. (19)94.	FV	FV	20.00
313C	**5000 FRANCS** (19)92-. Like #113A.			
	a. Sign. 23. (19)92.	FV	FV	28.00
	b. Sign. 25. (19)93.	FV	FV	28.00
	c. Sign. 27. (19)94.	FV	FV	28.00
	d. Sign. 27. (19)95.	FV	FV	26.00
	e. Sign. 28. (19)96.	FV	FV	26.00
	f. Sign. 28. (19)97.	FV	FV	26.00
	g. Sign. 28. (19)98.	FV	FV	26.00
314C	**10,000 FRANCS** (19)92-. Like #114A.			
	a. Sign. 25. (19)92.	FV	FV	50.00
	b. Sign. 27. (19)94.	FV	FV	50.00
	c. Sign. 27. (19)95.	FV	FV	45.00
	d. Sign. 28. (19)96.	FV	FV	45.00
	e. Sign. 28. (19)97.	FV	FV	45.00
	f. Sign. 28. (19)98.	FV	FV	45.00

D FOR MALI

1959-61; ND ISSUE

		GOOD	FINE	XF
401D	**100 FRANCS** 20.3.1961. Like #101A. Sign. I.	65.00	175.00	—
402D	**500 FRANCS** 1959; 1961. Like #102A.			
	a. Sign. I. 15.4.1959.	90.00	250.00	—
	b. Sign. I. 20.3.1961.	—	—	—
403D	**1000 FRANCS** 1959; 1961. Like #103A.			
	a. Sign. I. 17.9.1959.	75.00	200.00	400.00
	b. Sign. I. 20.3.1961.	75.00	200.00	450.00
404D	**5000 FRANCS** 20.3.1961. Like #104A. Sign. I.	125.00	300.00	600.00

1981; ND ISSUE

#405D-408D smaller size notes.

		VG	VF	UNC
405D	**500 FRANCS** 1981-90. Like #106A.			
	a. Sign. 14. 1988.	FV	FV	7.00
	b. Sign. 15. 1981. (BF).	FV	3.00	9.00
	c. Sign. 17. 1981. (F-CO).	FV	3.00	9.00
	e. Sign. 19. 1985.	FV	FV	8.00
	f. Sign. 20. 1986.	FV	8.00	20.00
	g. Sign. 20. 1987.	FV	4.00	12.00
	h. Sign. 21. 1989.	FV	8.00	20.00
	i. Sign. 22. 1990.	FV	FV	5.00

NOTE: #405D w/10-digit small serial # were printed by Banque de France (BF) while those w/9-digit large serial # were printed by F-CO.

		VG	VF	UNC
406D	**1000 FRANCS** 1981-90. Like #107A.			
	a. Sign. 14. 1988.	FV	FV	10.00
	b. Sign. 15. 1981.	FV	4.00	12.00
	c. Sign. 17. 1981.	4.00	9.00	25.00
	f. Sign. 19. 1985.	4.00	9.00	25.00
	g. Sign. 20. 1986	4.00	9.00	25.00
	h. Sign. 20. 1987.	4.00	11.00	30.00
	i. Sign. 21. 1989.	FV	FV	9.00
	j. Sign. 22. 1990.	FV	FV	10.00
407D	**5000 FRANCS** 1981-92. Like #108A.			
	a. Sign. 14. 1988.	FV	FV	50.00
	b. Sign. 14. 1989.	20.00	35.00	75.00
	c. Sign. 15. 1981.	FV	20.00	50.00
	d. Sign. 17. 1984.	FV	20.00	50.00
	e. Sign. 18. 1984.	25.00	45.00	80.00
	f. Sign. 19. 1985.	FV	20.00	50.00
	g. Sign. 20. 1986.	FV	20.00	50.00
	h. Sign. 20. 1987.	FV	20.00	50.00
	i. Sign. 21. 1990.	FV	FV	40.00
	j. Sign. 22. 1991.	FV	FV	35.00
	k. Sign. 23. 1992.	FV	FV	40.00
	l. Sign. 24. 1992.	FV	20.00	50.00
408D	**10,000 FRANCS** ND (1981-92). Like #109A.			
	a. Sign. 14. ND.	FV	25.00	80.00
	b. Sign. 15. ND.	FV	25.00	80.00
	c. Sign. 18. ND.	25.00	55.00	120.00
	d. Sign. 19. ND.	25.00	55.00	120.00
	e. Sign. 20. ND.	FV	FV	70.00
	f. Sign. 21. ND.	FV	FV	55.00
	g. Sign. 22. ND.	FV	FV	55.00

1991-92 ISSUE

		VG	VF	UNC
410D	**500 FRANCS** (19)91-. Like #110A.			
	a. Sign. 22. (19)91.	FV	FV	4.00
	b. Sign. 23. (19)92.	3.00	6.00	15.00
	c. Sign. 25. (19)93.	FV	FV	4.00
	d. Sign. 26. (19)94.	FV	FV	4.00
	e. Sign. 27. (19)95.	FV	FV	3.00
	f. Sign. 28. (19)96.	FV	FV	3.00
	g. Sign. 28. (19)97.	FV	FV	3.00

		VG	VF	UNC
411D	**1000 FRANCS** (19)91-. Like #111A.			
	a. Sign. 22. (19)91.	FV	FV	7.00
	b. Sign. 23. (19)92.	FV	5.00	15.00
	c. Sign. 25. (19)93.	FV	FV	7.00
	d. Sign. 26. (19)94.	FV	FV	7.00
	e. Sign. 27. (19)95.	FV	FV	6.00
	f. Sign. 28. (19)96.	FV	FV	6.00
	g. Sign. 28. (19)97.	FV	FV	6.00
412D	**2500 FRANCS** (19)92-. Like #112A.			
	a. Sign. 23. (19)92.	FV	FV	20.00
	b. Sign. 25. (19)93.	FV	FV	30.00
	c. Sign. 27. (19)94.	FV	FV	20.00

413D **5000 FRANCS** (19)92-. Like #113A.			
a. Sign. 23. (19)92.	FV	FV	28.00
b. Sign. 27. (19)94.	FV	FV	28.00
c. Sign. 27. (19)95.	FV	FV	28.00
d. Sign. 28. (19)96.	FV	FV	26.00
e. Sign. 28. (19)97.	FV	FV	26.00
f. Sign. 28. (19)98.	FV	FV	26.00
414D **10,000 FRANCS** (19)92-. Like #114A.			
a. Sign. 25. (19)92.	FV	FV	50.00
b. Sign. 27. (19)94.	FV	FV	50.00
c. Sign. 27. (19)95.	FV	FV	45.00
d. Sign. 28. (19)96.	FV	FV	45.00
e. Sign. 28. (19)97.	FV	FV	45.00
f. Sign. 28. (19)98.	FV	FV	45.00

E FOR MAURITANIA

1959-64; ND ISSUE

	GOOD	FINE	XF
501E **100 FRANCS** 1961-65; ND. Like #101A.			
b. Sign. 1. 20.3.1961.	30.00	90.00	250.00
c. Sign. 3. 2.12.1964.	30.00	90.00	250.00
e. Sign. 4. 2.3.1965.	25.00	85.00	225.00
f. Sign. 4. ND.	25.00	85.00	225.00
502E **500 FRANCS** 1959-64; ND. Like #102A.			
a. Engraved. Sign. 1. 15.4.1959.	55.00	120.00	400.00
b. Sign. 1. 20.3.1961.	45.00	100.00	350.00
c. Sign. 2. 20.3.1961.	45.00	100.00	350.00
e. Sign. 4. 2.3.1965.	45.00	100.00	350.00
f. Sign. 5. ND.	45.00	100.00	350.00
g. Sign. 6. ND.	45.00	100.00	350.00
h. Litho. Sign. 6. ND.	45.00	100.00	350.00
i. Sign. 7. ND.	45.00	100.00	350.00
503E **1000 FRANCS** 1961-65; ND. Like #103A.			
b. Engraved. Sign. 1. 20.3.1961.	55.00	130.00	400.00
e. Sign. 4. 2.3.1965.	45.00	130.00	350.00
g. Sign. 6. ND.	45.00	120.00	350.00
h. Litho. Sign. 6. ND.	45.00	120.00	350.00
504E **5000 FRANCS** 1961-65; ND. Like #104A.			
a. Sign. 1. 20.3.1961.	65.00	150.00	450.00
b. Sign. 2. 20.3.1961.	65.00	150.00	450.00
c. Sign. 4. 2.3.1965.	65.00	150.00	450.00
d. Sign. 6. ND.	60.00	130.00	400.00
e. Sign. 7. ND.	60.00	130.00	400.00

H FOR NIGER

1959-65; ND ISSUE

	VG	VF	UNC
601H **100 FRANCS** 1961-65; ND. Like #101A.			
a. Engraved. Sign. 1. 20.3.1961.	15.00	45.00	140.00
b. Sign. 2. 20.3.1961.	12.00	40.00	120.00
c. Litho. Sign. 2. 20.3.1961.	12.00	40.00	120.00
d. Sign. 3. 2.12.1964.	20.00	55.00	160.00
e. Sign. 4. 2.3.1965.	8.00	25.00	75.00
f. Sign. 4. ND.	7.00	18.00	55.00
602H **500 FRANCS** 1959-65; ND. Like #102A.			
a. Engraved. Sign. 1. 15.4.1959.	50.00	125.00	—
d. Sign. 3. 2.12.1964.	25.00	75.00	175.00
e. Sign. 4. 2.3.1965.	25.00	75.00	175.00
f. Sign. 5. ND.	50.00	—	—
g. Sign. 6. ND.	10.00	30.00	100.00
h. Litho. Sign. 6. ND.	10.00	30.00	100.00
i. Sign. 7. ND.	20.00	65.00	150.00
j. Sign. 8. ND.	10.00	30.00	100.00
k. Sign. 9. ND.	8.00	25.00	80.00
l. Sign. 10. ND.	75.00	—	—
m. Sign. 11. ND.	5.00	15.00	55.00
603H **1000 FRANCS** 1959-65; ND. Like #103A.			
a. Sign. 1. 17.9.1959.	—	—	—
b. Sign. 1. 20.3.1961.	30.00	65.00	175.00
c. Sign. 2. 20.3.1961.	75.00	—	—
e. Sign. 4. 2.3.1965.	30.00	65.00	175.00
f. Sign. 5. ND.	30.00	65.00	175.00
g. Sign. 6. ND.	10.00	35.00	90.00
h. Litho. Sign. 6. ND.	20.00	45.00	125.00
i. Sign. 7. ND.	10.00	35.00	100.00
j. Sign. 8. ND.	30.00	65.00	—
k. Sign. 9. ND	8.00	30.00	70.00
l. Sign. 10. ND.	5.00	15.00	50.00
m. Sign. 11. ND.	5.00	15.00	45.00
n. Sign. 12. ND.	5.00	15.00	50.00
o. Sign. 13. ND.	5.00	20.00	60.00
604H **5000 FRANCS** 1961; 1965; ND. Like #104A.			
a. Sign. 1. 20.3.1961.	100.00	—	—
b. Sign. 2. 20.3.1961.	40.00	150.00	—
d. Sign. 4. 2.3.1965.	40.00	150.00	—
e. Sign. 6. ND.	40.00	150.00	—
i. Sign. 7. ND.	40.00	150.00	—
k. Sign. 9. ND.	20.00	60.00	190.00
l. Sign. 10. ND.	20.00	60.00	190.00
m. Sign. 11. ND.	20.00	50.00	175.00

1977-81; ND ISSUE

#605H-608H smaller size notes.

	VG	VF	UNC
605H **500 FRANCS** 1979-80. Like #105A.			
a. Sign. 12. 1979.	6.00	18.00	40.00
b. Sign. 13. 1980.	3.00	8.00	20.00
606H **500 FRANCS** 1981-90. Like #106A.			
a. Sign. 14. 1988.	FV	FV	7.00
b. Sign. 15. 1981. (BF).	6.00	15.00	35.00
c. Sign. 15. 1981. (F-CO).	FV	3.00	8.00
d. Sign. 15. 1982. (BF).	10.00	—	—
e. Sign. 17. 1981. (F-CO).	FV	3.00	8.00
f. Sign. 18. 1984.	10.00	—	—
g. Sign. 19. 1984.	10.00	—	—
h. Sign. 19. 1985.	8.00	—	—
i. Sign. 20. 1986.	FV	FV	7.00
j. Sign. 20. 1987.	FV	3.00	8.00
k. Sign. 21. 1989.	FV	FV	6.00
l. Sign. 22. 1990.	FV	FV	6.00
607H **1000 FRANCS** 1981-90. Like #107A.			
a. Sign. 14. 1988.	FV	FV	11.00
b. Sign. 15. 1981.	FV	4.00	14.00
c. Sign. 17. 1981.	10.00	—	—
d. Sign. 18. 1984.	5.00	11.00	30.00
e. Sign. 19. 1984.	5.00	11.00	30.00
f. Sign. 19. 1985.	FV	4.00	14.00
g. Sign. 20. 1986.	FV	FV	11.00
h. Sign. 20. 1987.	FV	FV	11.00
i. Sign. 21. 1989.	FV	FV	10.00
j. Sign. 22. 1990.	FV	FV	10.00

		VG	VF	Unc
608H	**5000 Francs** 1977-90. Like #108A.			
	a. Sign. 12. 1978.	20.00	35.00	80.00
	b. Sign. 12. 1979.	20.00	35.00	80.00
	c. Sign. 13. 1980.	30.00	50.00	110.00
	d. Sign. 14. 1977.	20.00	35.00	80.00
	e. Sign. 14. 1989.	FV	FV	35.00
	f. Sign. 15. 1981.	FV	20.00	60.00
	g. Sign. 15. 1982.	FV	20.00	55.00
	h. Sign. 17. 1983.	FV	20.00	55.00
	i. Sign. 18. 1984.	20.00	35.00	80.00
	j. Sign. 19. 1985.	FV	20.00	55.00
	k. Sign. 20. 1986.	FV	20.00	55.00
	l. Sign. 20. 1987.	FV	FV	35.00
	m. Sign. 21. 1990.	FV	FV	35.00
	n. Sign. 27. 1995.	FV	FV	35.00
609H	**10,000 Francs** ND (1977). Like #109A.			
	a. Sign. 11. ND.	30.00	55.00	130.00
	b. Sign. 12. ND.	50.00	—	—
	c. Sign. 13. ND.	50.00	—	—
	d. Sign. 14. ND.	FV	FV	65.00
	e. Sign. 15. ND.	FV	35.00	90.00
	f. Sign. 18. ND.	30.00	55.00	130.00
	g. Sign. 19. ND.	30.00	55.00	130.00
	h. Sign. 20. ND.	FV	FV	65.00
	i. Sign. 21. ND.	FV	FV	60.00
	j. Sign. 22. ND.	FV	FV	50.00

1991-92 Issue

		VG	VF	Unc
610H	**500 Francs** (19)91-. Like #110A.			
	a. Sign. 22. (19)91.	FV	FV	5.00
	b. Sign. 23. (19)92.	FV	5.00	15.00
	c. Sign. 25. (19)93.	FV	FV	5.00
	d. Sign. 26. (19)94.	FV	FV	4.00
	e. Sign. 27. (19)95.	FV	FV	3.00
	f. Sign. 28. (19)96.	FV	FV	3.00
	g. Sign. 28. (19)97.	FV	FV	3.00
611H	**1000 Francs** (19)91-. Like #111A.			
	a. Sign. 22. (19)91.	FV	FV	8.00
	b. Sign. 23. (19)92.	FV	FV	8.00
	c. Sign. 25. (19)93.	FV	FV	8.00
	d. Sign. 26. (19)94.	FV	FV	7.00
	e. Sign. 27. (19)95.	FV	FV	6.00
	f. Sign. 28. (19)96.	FV	FV	6.00
	g. Sign. 28. (19)97.	FV	FV	6.00
612H	**2500 Francs** (19)92-. Like #112A.			
	a. Sign. 23. (19)92.	FV	FV	20.00
	b. Sign. 25. (19)93.	FV	FV	20.00
	c. Sign. 27. (19)94.	FV	FV	20.00
613H	**5000 Francs** (19)92-. Like #113A.			
	a. Sign. 23. (19)92.	FV	FV	28.00
	b. Sign. 27. (19)94.	FV	FV	28.00
	c. Sign. 27. (19)95.	FV	FV	27.00
	d. Sign. 28. (19)96.	FV	FV	27.00
	e. Sign. 28. (19)97.	FV	FV	28.00
614H	**10,000 Francs** (19)92-. Like #114A.			
	a. Sign. 25. (19)92.	FV	FV	50.00
	b. Sign. 27. (19)94.	FV	FV	50.00
	c. Sign. 27. (19)95.	FV	FV	45.00
	d. Sign. 28. (19)96.	FV	FV	45.00
	e. Sign. 28. (19)96.	FV	FV	45.00

K for Senegal

1959-65; ND Issue

		VG	VF	Unc
701K	**100 Francs** 1961-65; ND. Like #101A.			
	a. Engraved. Sign. 1. 20.3.1961.	15.00	35.00	100.00
	b. Sign. 2. 20.3.1961.	10.00	25.00	70.00
	c. Litho. Sign. 2. 20.3.1961.	10.00	25.00	70.00
	d. Sign. 3. 2.12.1964.	11.00	28.00	80.00
	e. Sign. 4. 2.3.1965.	8.00	20.00	65.00
	f. Sign. 4. ND.	5.00	15.00	45.00
	g. Sign. 5. ND.	15.00	35.00	100.00
702K	**500 Francs** 1959-65; ND. Like #102A.			
	a. Engraved. Sign. 1. 15.4.1959.	25.00	55.00	150.00
	b. Sign. 1. 20.3.1961.	15.00	45.00	120.00
	c. Sign. 2. 20.3.1961.	15.00	45.00	120.00
	d. Sign. 3. 2.12.1964.	15.00	45.00	120.00
	e. Sign. 4. 2.3.1965.	12.00	40.00	100.00
	f. Sign. 5. ND.	18.00	50.00	130.00
	g. Sign. 6. ND.	8.00	25.00	75.00
	h. Litho. Sign. 6. ND.	8.00	25.00	75.00
	i. Sign. 7. ND.	12.00	40.00	100.00
	j. Sign. 8. ND.	12.00	40.00	100.00
	k. Sign. 9. ND.	5.00	20.00	60.00
	l. Sign. 10. ND.	4.00	15.00	50.00
	m. Sign. 11. ND.	4.00	12.00	40.00
	n. Sign. 12. ND.	4.00	15.00	45.00

		VG	VF	Unc
703K	**1000 Francs** 1959-65; ND. Like #103A.			
	a. Engraved. Sign. 1. 17.9.1959.	20.00	60.00	150.00
	b. Sign. 1. 20.3.1961.	20.00	60.00	150.00
	c. Sign. 2. 20.3.1961.	12.00	45.00	110.00
	e. Sign. 4. 2.3.1965.	12.00	45.00	110.00
	f. Sign. 5. ND.	35.00	90.00	—
	g. Sign. 6. ND.	35.00	90.00	—
	h. Litho. Sign. 6. ND.	5.00	15.00	50.00
	i. Sign. 7. ND.	8.00	20.00	60.00
	j. Sign. 8. ND.	8.00	20.00	60.00
	k. Sign. 9. ND.	5.00	15.00	50.00
	l. Sign. 10. ND.	4.00	12.00	40.00
	m. Sign. 11. ND.	4.00	10.00	35.00
	n. Sign. 12. ND.	4.00	12.00	40.00
	o. Sign. 13. ND.	4.00	12.00	40.00
704K	**5000 Francs** 1961-65; ND. Like #104A.			
	b. Sign. 1. 20.3.1961.	30.00	80.00	225.00
	c. Sign. 2. 20.3.1961.	30.00	80.00	225.00
	d. Sign. 3. 2.12.1964.	30.00	80.00	225.00
	e. Sign. 4. 2.3.1965.	25.00	65.00	180.00
	h. Sign. 6. ND.	20.00	45.00	150.00
	i. Sign. 7. ND.	25.00	65.00	180.00
	j. Sign. 9. ND.	20.00	45.00	160.00
	k. Sign. 10. ND.	20.00	45.00	160.00
	m. Sign. 11. ND.	20.00	40.00	140.00

1977-81; ND Issue

#705K-709K smaller size notes.

		VG	VF	Unc
705K	**500 Francs** 1979-80. Like #105A.			
	a. Sign. 12. 1979.	3.00	8.00	20.00
	b. Sign. 13. 1980.	3.00	7.00	18.00

706K 500 FRANCS
1981-90. Like #106A.

	VG	VF	UNC
a. Sign. 14. 1988.	FV	FV	6.00
b. Sign. 15. 1981 (BF).	5.00	15.00	35.00
c. Sign. 15. 1981. (F-CO).	FV	3.00	7.00
d. Sign. 15. 1982. (BF).	FV	4.00	9.00
e. Sign. 17. 1981. (F-CO).	FV	3.00	7.00
f. Sign. 17. 1983. (BF).	FV	4.00	9.00
g. Sign. 18. 1984.	FV	3.00	7.00
h. Sign. 19. 1985.	FV	3.00	7.00
i. Sign. 20. 1986.	FV	FV	6.00
j. Sign. 20. 1987.	FV	FV	6.00
k. Sign. 21. (reversed order). 1989.	FV	FV	5.00
l. Sign. 22. 1990.	FV	FV	5.00

NOTE: #706K w/10-digit small serial # were printed by Banque de France (BF) while those w/9-digit large serial # were printed by F-CO.

707K 1000 FRANCS
1981-90. Like #107A.

	VG	VF	UNC
a. Sign. 14. 1988.	FV	FV	10.00
b. Sign. 15. 1981.	FV	4.00	12.00
c. Sign. 17. 1981.	FV	4.00	12.00
d. Sign. 18. 1984.	FV	4.00	12.00
e. Sign. 19. 1984.	5.00	20.00	—
f. Sign. 19. 1985.	FV	4.00	12.00
g. Sign. 20. 1986.	FV	FV	10.00
h. Sign. 20. 1987.	FV	FV	10.00
i. Sign. 21. 1989.	FV	FV	9.00
j. Sign. 22. 1990.	FV	FV	9.00

708K 5000 FRANCS
1977-92. Like #108A.

	VG	VF	UNC
a. Sign. 12. 1978.	15.00	25.00	60.00
b. Sign. 12. 1979.	20.00	35.00	90.00
c. Sign. 13. 1980.	25.00	45.00	110.00
d. Sign. 14. 1977.	15.00	25.00	60.00
e. Sign. 14. 1989.	FV	15.00	50.00
f. Sign. 15. 1982.	25.00	45.00	110.00
g. Sign. 16. 1983.	30.00	50.00	130.00
h. Sign. 17. 1983.	15.00	25.00	60.00
i. Sign. 18. 1984.	18.00	25.00	60.00
j. Sign. 19. 1985.	20.00	50.00	—
k. Sign. 20. 1986.	20.00	50.00	—
l. Sign. 20. 1987.	FV	FV	35.00
m. Sign. 21. 1990.	FV	FV	35.00
n. Sign. 22. 1991.	FV	FV	35.00
o. Sign. 22. 1992.	FV	FV	35.00
p. Sign. 23. 1992.	FV	FV	35.00
q. Sign. 24. 1992.	FV	FV	35.00

709K 10,000 FRANCS
ND. (1977-92). Like #109A.

	VG	VF	UNC
a. Sign. 11. ND.	20.00	35.00	95.00
b. Sign. 12. ND.	20.00	35.00	95.00
c. Sign. 13. ND.	20.00	40.00	100.00
d. Sign. 14. ND.	FV	FV	60.00
e. Sign. 15. ND.	FV	FV	65.00
f. Sign. 16. ND.	20.00	45.00	110.00
h. Sign. 18. ND.	FV	25.00	75.00
i. Sign. 19. ND.	20.00	35.00	100.00
j. Sign. 20. ND.	FV	FV	60.00
k. Sign. 21. ND.	FV	FV	55.00
l. Sign. 22. ND.	FV	FV	55.00
m. Sign. 23. ND.	FV	FV	55.00

1991-92 ISSUE

710K 500 FRANCS
(19)91-. Like #110A.

	VG	VF	UNC
a. Sign. 22. (19)91.	FV	FV	4.00
b. Sign. 23. (19)92.	FV	FV	4.00
c. Sign. 25. (19)93.	FV	FV	4.00
d. Sign. 26. (19)94.	FV	FV	4.00
e. Sign. 27. (19)95.	FV	FV	3.00
f. Sign. 28. (19)96.	FV	FV	3.00
g. Sign. 28. (19)97.	FV	FV	3.00

711K 1000 FRANCS
(19)91-. Like #111A.

	VG	VF	UNC
a. Sign. 22. (19)91.	FV	FV	7.00
b. Sign. 23. (19)92.	FV	FV	7.00
c. Sign. 25. (19)93.	FV	FV	7.00
d. Sign. 26. (19)94.	FV	FV	10.00
e. Sign. 27. (19)95.	FV	FV	6.00
f. Sign. 28. (19)96.	FV	FV	6.00
g. Sign. 28. (19)97.	FV	FV	6.00

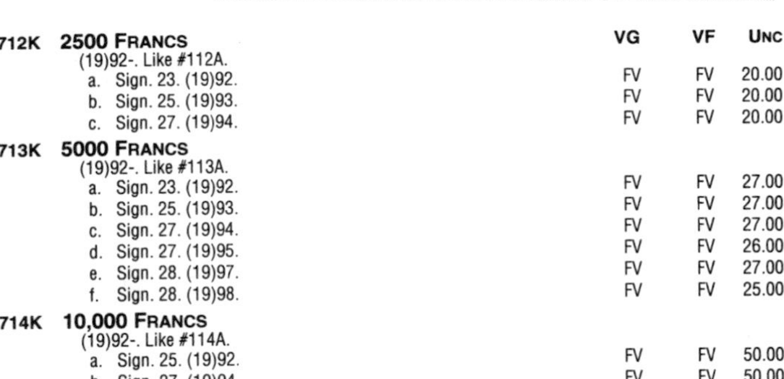

712K 2500 FRANCS
(19)92-. Like #112A.

	VG	VF	UNC
a. Sign. 23. (19)92.	FV	FV	20.00
b. Sign. 25. (19)93.	FV	FV	20.00
c. Sign. 27. (19)94.	FV	FV	20.00

713K 5000 FRANCS
(19)92-. Like #113A.

	VG	VF	UNC
a. Sign. 23. (19)92.	FV	FV	27.00
b. Sign. 25. (19)93.	FV	FV	27.00
c. Sign. 27. (19)94.	FV	FV	27.00
d. Sign. 27. (19)95.	FV	FV	26.00
e. Sign. 28. (19)97.	FV	FV	27.00
f. Sign. 28. (19)98.	FV	FV	25.00

714K 10,000 FRANCS
(19)92-. Like #114A.

	VG	VF	UNC
a. Sign. 25. (19)92.	FV	FV	50.00
b. Sign. 27. (19)94.	FV	FV	50.00
c. Sign. 27. (19)95.	FV	FV	45.00
d. Sign. 28. (19)96.	FV	FV	45.00
e. Sign. 28. (19)97.	FV	FV	45.00
f. Sign. 28. (19)95.	FV	FV	45.00

T FOR TOGO

1959-65; ND ISSUE

801T 100 FRANCS
1961-65; ND. Like #101A.

	VG	VF	UNC
a. Engraved. Sign. 1. 20.3.1961.	15.00	35.00	100.00
b. Sign. 2. 20.3.1961.	10.00	25.00	70.00
c. Litho. Sign. 2. 20.3.1961.	10.00	25.00	70.00
d. Sign. 3. 2.12.1964.	11.00	28.00	80.00
e. Sign. 4. 2.3.1965.	8.00	20.00	60.00
f. Sign. 4. ND.	5.00	15.00	45.00
g. Sign. 5. ND.	11.00	28.00	80.00

802T 500 FRANCS
1959-61; ND. Like #102A.

	VG	VF	UNC
a. Engraved. Sign. 1. 15.4.1959.	25.00	55.00	150.00
b. Sign. 1. 20.3.1961.	35.00	100.00	—
c. Sign. 2. 20.3.1961.	35.00	100.00	—
f. Sign. 5. ND.	25.00	55.00	150.00
g. Sign. 6. ND.	8.00	25.00	75.00
i. Litho. Sign. 7. ND.	20.00	50.00	130.00
j. Sign. 8. ND.	20.00	50.00	130.00
k. Sign. 9. ND.	5.00	20.00	60.00
l. Sign. 10. ND.	10.00	30.00	90.00
m. Sign. 11. ND.	FV	5.00	30.00

803T 1000 FRANCS
1959-65; ND. Like #103A.

	VG	VF	UNC
a. Engraved. Sign. 1. 17.9.1959.	75.00	—	—
b. Sign. 1. 20.3.1961.	20.00	60.00	150.00
c. Sign. 2. 20.3.1961.	35.00	90.00	—
e. Sign. 4. 2.3.1965.	20.00	60.00	140.00
f. Sign. 5. ND.	20.00	60.00	150.00
g. Sign. 6. ND.	10.00	30.00	70.00
h. Litho. Sign. 6. ND.	25.00	70.00	—
i. Sign. 7. ND.	10.00	30.00	70.00
j. Sign. 8. ND.	35.00	90.00	—
k. Sign. 9. ND.	5.00	20.00	50.00
l. Sign. 10. ND.	5.00	15.00	40.00
m. Sign. 11. ND.	4.00	10.00	35.00
n. Sign. 12. ND.	5.00	15.00	40.00
o. Sign. 13. ND.	5.00	15.00	40.00

804T 5000 FRANCS
1961; ND. Like #104A.

	VG	VF	UNC
b. Sign. 1. 20.3.1961.	35.00	90.00	250.00
h. Sign. 6. ND.	25.00	75.00	200.00
i. Sign. 7. ND.	50.00	150.00	—
j. Sign. 8. ND.	50.00	150.00	—
k. Sign. 9. ND.	25.00	65.00	175.00
m. Sign. 11. ND.	20.00	40.00	140.00

1977-81; ND ISSUE

#805T-809T smaller size notes.

805T 500 FRANCS

	VG	VF	UNC
1979. Like #105A. Sign. 12.	3.00	8.00	20.00

806T 500 FRANCS
1981-90. Like #106A.

	VG	VF	UNC
a. Sign. 14. 1988.	6.00	15.00	—
b. Sign. 15. 1981. (BF).	FV	3.00	7.00
c. Sign. 15. 1981. (F-CO).	FV	3.00	7.00
d. Sign. 15. 1982. (BF).	FV	5.00	20.00
e. Sign. 17. 1981. (F-CO).	FV	5.00	20.00
f. Sign. 18. 1984.	6.00	15.00	—
g. Sign. 19. 1984.	FV	5.00	11.00
h. Sign. 19. 1985.	FV	3.00	7.00
i. Sign. 20. 1986.	FV	FV	6.00
j. Sign. 20. 1987.	FV	FV	6.00
k. Sign. 21. 1989.	FV	FV	5.00
l. Sign. 22. 1990.	FV	FV	5.00

NOTE: #806T w/10-digit small serial # were printed by Banque de France (BF) while those w/9-digit large serial # were printed by F-CO.

807T 1000 FRANCS
1981-90. Like #107A.

	VG	VF	UNC
a. Sign. 14. 1988.	FV	FV	10.00
b. Sign. 15. 1981.	FV	4.00	12.00
c. Sign. 17. 1981.	FV	6.00	25.00
d. Sign. 18. 1984.	FV	6.00	25.00
e. Sign. 19. 1984.	5.00	11.00	—
f. Sign. 19. 1985.	FV	4.00	12.00
g. Sign. 20. 1986.	5.00	11.00	—
h. Sign. 20. 1987.	FV	FV	10.00
i. Sign. 21. 1989.	FV	FV	9.00
j. Sign. 22. 1990.	FV	FV	9.00

808T 5000 FRANCS
1977-92. Like #108A.

	VG	VF	UNC
a. Sign. 12. 1978.	20.00	35.00	90.00
b. Sign. 12. 1979.	20.00	35.00	90.00
c. Sign. 14. 1977.	15.00	25.00	60.00
d. Sign. 14. 1989.	FV	FV	35.00
e. Sign. 15. 1981.	25.00	45.00	—
f. Sign. 15. 1982.	25.00	45.00	—
g. Sign. 17. 1983.	40.00	—	—
h. Sign. 18. 1984.	15.00	25.00	60.00
i. Sign. 20. 1987.	FV	FV	35.00
j. Sign. 21. 1990.	FV	FV	35.00
k. Sign. 22. 1991.	25.00	—	35.00
l. Sign. 22. 1992.	FV	FV	35.00
m. Sign. 23. 1992.	FV	FV	35.00
n. Sign. 24. 1992.	FV	FV	35.00

NOTICE

Readers with unlisted dates, signature varieties, etc. are invited to submit photocopies of their notes to: Standard Catalog of World Paper Money, 700 East State St. Iola, WI 54990-0001, fax: 1-715-445-4087, or E-Mail: thernr@krause.com.

		VG	VF	UNC
809T	**10,000 FRANCS** ND. (1977-92). Like #109A.			
	a. Sign. 11. ND.	20.00	40.00	95.00
	b. Sign. 12. ND.	35.00	90.00	—
	c. Sign. 13. ND.	35.00	90.00	—
	d. Sign. 14. ND.	35.00	90.00	
	e. Sign. 15. ND.	FV	FV	65.00
	f. Sign. 16. ND.	20.00	45.00	110.00
	h. Sign. 18. ND.	FV	FV	65.00
	k. Sign. 22. ND.	FV	FV	55.00
	l. Sign. 23. ND.	FV	FV	55.00

1991-92 ISSUE

		VG	VF	UNC
810T	**500 FRANCS** (19)91-. Like #110A.			
	a. Sign. 22. (19)91.	FV	FV	4.00
	b. Sign. 23. (19)92.	FV	5.00	15.00
	c. Sign. 25. (19)93.	FV	FV	4.00
	d. Sign. 26. (19)94.	FV	FV	4.00
	e. Sign. 27. (19)95.	FV	FV	3.00
	f. Sign. 28. (19)96.	FV	FV	3.00
	g. Sign. 28. (19)97.	FV	FV	3.00
	h. Sign. 28. (19)98.	FV	FV	3.00

		VG	VF	UNC
811T	**1000 FRANCS** (19)91-. Like #111A.			
	a. Sign. 22. (19)91.	FV	FV	7.00
	b. Sign. 23. (19)92.	FV	FV	7.00
	c. Sign. 25. (19)93.	FV	FV	7.00

		VG	VF	UNC
	d. Sign. 26. (19)94.	FV	FV	7.00
	e. Sign. 27. (19)95.	FV	FV	6.00
	f. Sign. 28. (19)96.	FV	FV	6.00
	g. Sign. 28. (19)97.	FV	FV	6.00
	h. Sign. 28. (19)98.	FV	FV	6.00

		VG	VF	UNC
812T	**2500 FRANCS** (19)92-. Like #112A.			
	a. Sign. 23. (19)92.	FV	FV	20.00
	b. Sign. 25. (19)93.	FV	FV	20.00
	c. Sign. 27. (19)94.	FV	FV	20.00
813T	**5000 FRANCS** (19)92-. Like #113A.			
	a. Sign. 23. (19)92.	FV	FV	27.00
	b. Sign. 25. (19)93.	FV	FV	27.00
	c. Sign. 27. (19)94.	FV	FV	27.00
	d. Sign. 27. (19)95.	FV	FV	26.00
	e. Sign. 28. (19)96.	FV	FV	26.00
814T	**10,000 FRANCS** (19)92-. Like #114A.			
	a. Sign. 25. (19)92.	FV	FV	50.00
	b. Sign. 27. (19)94.	FV	FV	50.00
	c. Sign. 27. (19)95.	FV	FV	45.00
	d. Sign. 28. (19)96.	FV	FV	45.00

S FOR GUINEA-BISSAU

1997 ISSUE

		VG	VF	UNC
910S	**500 FRANCS** (19)97. Like #110A. Sign. 28.	FV	FV	5.00

		VG	VF	UNC
911S	**1000 FRANCS** (19)97. Like #111A. Sign. 28.	FV	FV	8.00

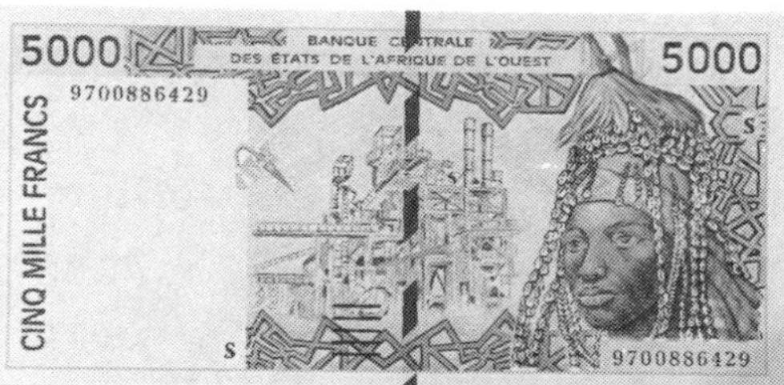

		VG	VF	UNC
913S	**5000 FRANCS** (19)97. Like #113A. Sign. 28.	FV	FV	35.00

		VG	VF	UNC
914S	**10,000 FRANCS** (19)97. Like #114A. Sign. 28.	FV	FV	55.00

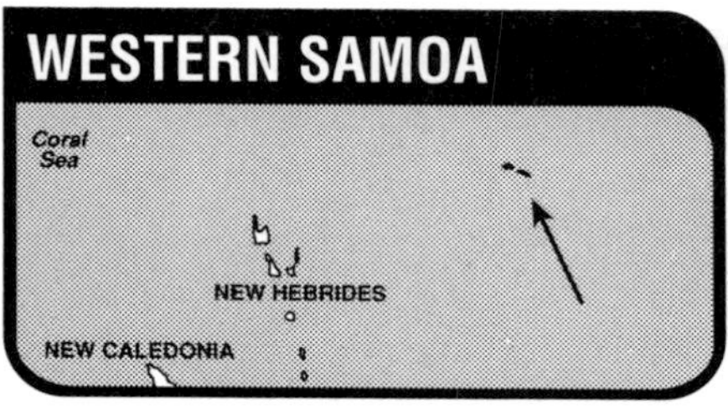

The Independent State of Western Samoa (formerly German Samoa), located in the Pacific Ocean 1,600 miles (2,574 km.) northeast of New Zealand, has an area of 1,097 sq. mi. (2,860 sq. km.) and a population of 157,000. Capital: Apia. The economy is based on agriculture, fishing and tourism. Copra, cocoa and bananas are exported.

The Samoan group of islands was discovered by Dutch navigator Jacob Roggeveen in 1772. Great Britain, the United States and Germany established consular representation at Apia in 1847, 1853 and 1861 respectively. The conflicting interests of the three powers produced the Berlin agreement of 1889 which declared Samoa neutral and had the effect of establishing a tripartite protectorate over the islands. A further agreement, 1899, recognized the rights of the United States in those islands east of 171 deg. west longitude (American Samoa) and of Germany in the other islands (Western Samoa). New Zealand occupied Western Samoa at the start of World War I and administered it as a League of Nations mandate and U.N. trusteeship until Jan. 1, 1962, when it became an independent state.

Western Samoa is a member of the Commonwealth of Nations. The Chief Executive is Chief of State. The prime minister is the Head of Government. The present Head of State, Malietoa Tanumafili II, holds his position for life. Future Heads of State will be elected by the Legislature Assembly for five-year terms.

RULERS:

British, 1914-1962
Malietoa Tanumafili II, 1962-

MONETARY SYSTEM:

1 Shilling = 12 Pence
1 Pound = 20 Shillings to 1967
1 Tala = 100 Sene, 1967-

NEW ZEALAND ADMINISTRATION

TERRITORY OF WESTERN SAMOA

1920-22 TREASURY NOTE ISSUE

By Authority of New Zealand Government

#7-9 various date and sign. varieties. Printer: BWC.

#8 and 9 *STERLING* appears close beneath spelled out denominations at ctr. until about 1953.

NOTE: Some of these notes may appear to be ND, probably through error or washed out, faded or worn off hand-stamped dates.

		GOOD	FINE	XF
7	**10 SHILLINGS** 1922-59. Black on brown and green unpt. Palm trees along beach at ctr.			
	a. 3.3.1922.	—	Rare	—
	b. Sign. title: *MINISTER OF EXTERNAL AFFAIRS FOR NEW ZEALAND* at l. 24.4.1939-21.11.1949.	50.00	175.00	425.00
	c. Sign. title: *MINISTER OF ISLAND TERRITORIES FOR NEW ZEALAND* at l. 25.9.1953-27.5.1958.	75.00	300.00	650.00
	d. Sign. title: *HIGH COMMISSIONER* at l. 20.3.1957-22.12.1959.	35.00	150.00	325.00

#8-9 STERLING appears close beneath spelled out denomination at ctr. until about 1953.

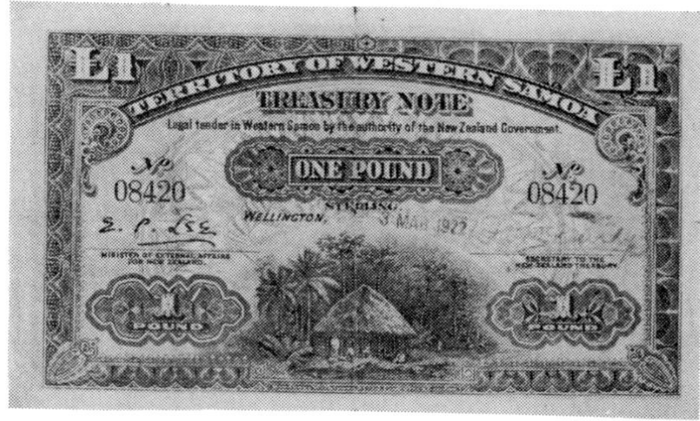

		Good	Fine	XF
8	**1 Pound** 1922-61. Purple on m/c unpt. Hut, palm trees at ctr.			
	a. 3.3.1922.	—	Rare	—
	b. Sign. title: *MINISTER OF EXTERNAL AFFAIRS FOR NEW ZEALAND* at l. 16.1.1939-12.1.1947.	65.00	200.00	500.00
	c. Sign. title: *MINISTER OF ISLAND TERRITORIES FOR NEW ZEALAND* at l. 21.6.1951-1.4.1958. 7.8. 1958.	85.00	300.00	700.00
	d. Sign. title: *HIGH COMMISSIONER* at l. 20.4.1959; 10.12.1959; 1.5.1961.	50.00	175.00	400.00
9	**5 Pounds** 1920-59. Purple on m/c unpt. Boat at lower ctr.			
	a. (1920's).	—	Rare	—
	b. Sign. title: *MINISTER OF EXTERNAL AFFAIRS FOR NEW ZEALAND* at l. 1.11.1944.	700.00	1800.	—
	c. Sign. title: *MINISTER OF ISLAND TERRITORIES FOR NEW ZEALAND* at l. 11.4.1956.	500.00	1300.	—
	d. Sign. title: *HIGH COMMISSIONER* at l. 13.10.1958; 10.12.1959.	350.00	1000.00	2250.

Bank of Western Samoa

1960-61 Provisional Issue

#10-12 red ovpt: *Bank of Western Samoa, Legal Tender in Western Samoa by virtue of the Bank of Western Samoa Ordinance 1959* on older notes. Various date and sign. varieties.

		Good	Fine	XF
10	**10 Shillings** ND; 1960-61. Ovpt. on #7.			
	a. Sign. title: *HIGH COMMISSIONER* blocked out at lower l., w/*MINISTER OF FINANCE* below. 8.12.1960; 1.5.1961.	25.00	75.00	250.00
		25.00	75.00	225.00

b. ND. Sign. title: *MINISTER OF FINANCE* in plate w/o ovpt., at lower l. 1.5.1961.

		Good	Fine	XF
11	**1 Pound** 1960-61. Ovpt. on #8.			
	a. Sign. title: *HIGH COMMISSIONER* blocked out at lower l., w/*MINISTER OF FINANCE* below. 8.11.1960; 1.5.1961.	35.00	125.00	400.00
	b. Sign. title: *MINISTER OF FINANCE* in plate w/o ovpt., at lower l. 1.5.1961.	35.00	100.00	350.00
12	**5 Pounds** 1.5.1961. Ovpt. on #9.	300.00	1000.	2500.

State

Fale Tupe o Samoa I Sisifo

Bank of Western Samoa

1963 ND Issue

		VG	VF	Unc
13	**10 Shillings** ND (1963). Dk. green on m/c unpt. Arms at l., boat at r. Hut and 2 palms at ctr. on back.	2.50	10.00	65.00

		VG	VF	Unc
14	**1 Pound** ND (1963). Blue on m/c unpt. Palms and rising sun at l. and r., arms at ctr. Sm. bldg. and lagoon at ctr. on back. 159 x 83mm.	5.00	20.00	100.00

		VG	VF	UNC
15	**5 POUNDS** ND (1963). Brown on m/c unpt. Rava bowl at l., flag over arms at r. Shoreline, sea and islands on back. 166 x 89mm.	20.00	50.00	175.00

1967 ND ISSUE

Tala System

SIGNATURE VARIETIES			
1	MANAGER	2	MANAGER
3	MANAGER	4	SENIOR MANAGER

#16-18 sign. varieties. Wmk: BWS repeated.

		VG	VF	UNC
16	**1 TALA** ND (1967). Dk. green on m/c unpt. Like #13.			
	a. Sign. 1.	1.50	8.00	35.00
	b. Sign. 2.	1.25	7.00	30.00
	c. Sign. 3.	1.00	7.00	20.00
	d. Sign. 4.	1.50	8.00	30.00
	s. Sign. as b. Specimen.	—	—	40.00

		VG	VF	UNC
17	**2 TALA** ND (1967). Blue on m/c unpt. Like #14, but 144 x 77mm.			
	a. Sign. 1.	3.00	7.50	45.00
	b. Sign. 3.	2.50	5.00	40.00
	c. Sign. 4.	4.00	8.00	50.00
	s. Sign. as b. Specimen.	—	—	50.00

		VG	VF	UNC
18	**10 TALA** ND (1967). Brown on m/c unpt. Like #15, but 150 x 76mm.			
	a. Sign. 3.	11.50	25.00	135.00
	b. Sign. 4.	12.50	30.00	150.00
	s. Sign. as b. Specimen.	—	—	60.00

KOMITI FAATINO O TUPE A SAMOA I SISIFO

MONETARY BOARD OF WESTERN SAMOA

1980-84 ND ISSUE

#19-23 national flag at l. ctr. on face and ctr. r. on back. Arms at lower ctr. r. on back. Wmk: M. Tanumafili II.

		VG	VF	UNC
19	**1 TALA** ND (1980). Dk. green on m/c unpt. 2 weavers at r. 2 fishermen in canoe at l. ctr. on back.	.75	2.00	9.00

		VG	VF	UNC
20	**2 TALA** ND (1980). Deep blue-violet on m/c unpt. Woodcarver at r. Hut w/palms on sm. island at l. ctr. on back.	1.50	3.00	13.50

		VG	VF	UNC
21	**5 TALA** ND (1980). Red on m/c unpt. Child writing at r. Sm. port city at l. ctr. on back.	3.50	7.00	27.50

		VG	VF	UNC
22	**10 TALA** ND (1980). Dk. brown and purple on m/c unpt. Man picking bananas at r. Shoreline landscape on back.	7.00	22.50	110.00
23	**20 TALA** ND (1984). Brown and orange-brown on m/c unpt. Fisherman w/net at r. Round bldg. at l. on back.	30.00	100.00	300.00

#24 not assigned.

FALETUPE TUTOTONU O SAMOA

CENTRAL BANK OF SAMOA

1985 ND ISSUE

#25-30 like #20-23 but w/new issuer's name. Wmk: M. Tanumafili II.

		VG	VF	UNC
25	**2 TALA** ND (1985). Deep blue-violet on m/c unpt. Like #20.	FV	FV	4.00

		VG	VF	UNC
26	**5 TALA** ND (1985). Red on m/c unpt. Like #21.	FV	FV	6.50

		VG	VF	UNC
27	**10 TALA** ND (1985). Dk. brown and purple on m/c unpt. Like #22.	FV	FV	10.00

		VG	VF	UNC
28	**20 TALA** ND (1985). Brown and orange-brown on m/c unpt. Like #23.	FV	FV	22.50

#29-30 M. Tanumafili II at r.

		VG	VF	UNC
29	**50 TALA** ND (ca.1990). Green on m/c unpt. Former home of R. L. Stevenson, current residence of Head of State at ctr. Man performing traditional knife dance on back.	FV	FV	45.00

		VG	VF	UNC
30	**100 TALA** ND (ca.1990). Violet and lt. brown on m/c unpt. Flag and Parliament bldg. at ctr. Harvest scene on back.	FV	FV	75.00

1990 COMMEMORATIVE ISSUE

#31, Golden Jubilee of Service of the Head of State, Susuga Malietoa Tanumafili II, 1990

		VG	VF	UNC
31	**2 TALA** ND (1990). Brown, blue and purple on m/c unpt. Samoan village at ctr., M. Tanumafili II at r. Clear area at lower r. containing a Rava bowl visible from both sides. Family scene at ctr., arms at upper r. on back. Polymer. Printer: NPA (w/o imprint).			
	a. Text on face partly engraved. Serial # prefix *AAA*.	FV	FV	6.50
	b. Printing as a. Uncut sheet of 4 subjects. Serial # prefix *AAB*.	—	—	25.00
	c. Face completely lithographed, deeper blue, purple and dull brown. Serial # prefix *AAC*.	FV	FV	3.50
	d. Serial # prefix: *AAD*.	FV	FV	3.50
	e. Serial # prefix: *AAE*.	FV	FV	3.25

NOTE: #31a was also issued in a special folder.

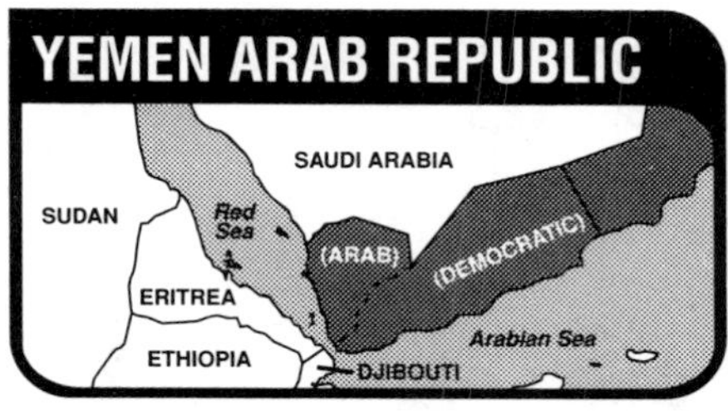

The Yemen Arab Republic, located in the southwestern corner of the Arabian Peninsula, has an area of 75,290 sq. mi. (195,000 sq. km.) and a population of 15.8 million. Capital: San'a. The industries of Yemen, one of the world's poorest countries, are agriculture and local handicrafts. Qat (a mildly narcotic leaf), coffee, cotton and rock salt are exported.

One of the oldest centers of civilization in the Near East, Yemen was once part of the Minaean Kingdom and of the ancient Kingdom of Sheba, after which it was captured successively by Egyptians, Ethiopians and Romans. It was converted to the Moslem religion in 628 AD and administered as a caliphate until 1538, when it came under Turkish occupation which was maintained until 1918 when autonomy was achieved through revolution.

On Feb. 1, 1958, Egypt and Syria formed the United Arab Republic. Yemen joined on March 8 in an association known as the United Arab States. Syria withdrew from the United Arab Republic on Sept. 29, 1961, and on Dec. 26 Egypt dissolved its ties with Yemen in the United Arab States.

Provoked by the harsh rule of Imam Mohammed al-Badr, last ruler of the Kingdom of Mutawwakkilite, the National Liberation Front seized control of the government on Sept. 27, 1962. Badr fled to Saudi Arabia.

An agreement for a constitution for a unified state was reached in Dec. 1989 uniting the Yemen Arab Republic with the People's Democratic Republic of Yemen into the Republic of Yemen on May 22, 1990. Both currencies circulated for a number of years, but the PDR dinar lost legal tender status on June 11, 1996.

RULERS:

Imam Ahmad, AH1367-1382/1948-1962AD
Imam al-Badr, AH1382-1388/1962-1968AD

MONETARY SYSTEM:

1 Rial = 40 Buqshas
1 Rial = 100 Fils (from April 1, 1995).

SIGNATURE VARIETIES

No.	Signature	No.	Signature
1	Minister of the Treasury Abdul Ghani Ali, 1964	2	Minister of the Treasury and Economy Abdul Ghani Ali, 1967
3	Minister of the Treasury Ahmad al-Ruhumi, 1966 (actually inverted)	4	Minister of the Treasury Ahmad Abdu Said, 1968
5	Governor & Chairman, CBY Abdul Aziz Abdul Ghani, 1971-75	6	Governor & Chairman, CBY Abdulla Mohamed al-Sanabani, 1978-85
7	Governor & Chairman, CBY Abdulla Mohamed al-Sanabani, 1978-85	8	Governor, CBY Muhammad Ahmad Gunaid, 1985-94
9	Governor, CBY Aluwi Salih al-Salami, 1994	10	Governor, CBY Ahmed Abdul Rahman al-Samani, 1997-

ARAB REPUBLIC

YEMEN CURRENCY BOARD

1964 ND ISSUE

#1-3 wmk: Arms.

		VG	VF	UNC
1	**1 RIAL** ND (1964; 1967). Green on m/c unpt. Arms at l. Houses in Sana'a w/minaret at ctr. on back.			
	a. Sign. 1. (1964).	3.00	20.00	100.00
	b. Sign. 2. (1967).	4.00	25.00	125.00

		VG	VF	UNC
2	**5 RIALS** ND (1964; 1967). Red on m/c unpt. Arms at l. Lion of Timna sculpture at r. on back.			
	a. Sign. 1. (1964).	7.00	70.00	275.00
	b. Sign. 2. (1967).	8.00	75.00	300.00

		VG	VF	UNC
3	**10 RIALS** ND (1964; 1967). Blue-green on m/c unpt. Arms at l. Dam at r. on back.			
	a. Sign. 1. (1964).	15.00	80.00	325.00
	b. Sign. 2. (1967).	15.00	80.00	325.00

1966-71 ND ISSUE

#4-10 wmk: Arms.

		VG	VF	UNC
4	**10 BUQSHAS** ND (1966). Brown on m/c unpt. Lion of Timna sculpture at l. Ancient dedication stone from a temple at Ma'rib at r. on back. Sign. 3.	1.25	4.00	17.50

		VG	VF	UNC
5	**20 BUQSHAS** ND (1966). Green on m/c unpt. Tall alabaster head at l. Back olive-green; ruins of the Bara'an temple at r. Sign. 3.	1.00	5.00	17.50

		VG	VF	UNC
6	**1 RIAL** ND (1969). Green on m/c unpt. Alabaster head at l. House in Sana'a w/minaret on back. Sign. 4.	3.50	15.00	60.00

		VG	VF	UNC
7	**5 RIALS** ND (1969). Red on m/c unpt. Bronze lion's head sculpture at l. Lion of Timna sculpture at r. on back. Sign. 4.	5.00	35.00	150.00

		VG	VF	UNC
8	**10 RIALS** ND (1969). Blue-green on m/c unpt. Shadhili Mosque at l. Dam at r. on back. Sign. 4.	8.00	35.00	150.00

		VG	VF	UNC
9	**20 RIALS** ND (1971). Violet and blue-green on m/c unpt. Palace on the rock at Wadi Dahr. Back violet and gold; city view of Sana'a. Sign. 4.	12.50	40.00	175.00

		VG	VF	UNC
10	**50 RIALS** ND (1971). Dk. olive-green on m/c unpt. Crossed *jambiyas* (daggers) at l. Coffee branch and tree, mountains in background at ctr. r. on back. Sign. 4.	7.50	35.00	175.00

CENTRAL BANK OF YEMEN

1973-77 ND ISSUES

#11-16 wmk: Arms.

		VG	VF	UNC
11	**1 RIAL** ND (1973). Green on m/c unpt. al Baqiliyah Mosque at l. Coffee plants w/mountains in background at ctr. on back.			
	a. Sign. 5.	.10	.40	2.50
	b. Sign. 7.	.10	.40	2.50

		VG	VF	UNC
12	**5 RIALS** ND (1973). Red on m/c unpt. Bldgs. in Wadi Du'an at l. Beit al Midie on high rock hill at ctr. on back. Sign. 5.	.60	2.50	10.00

		VG	VF	UNC
13	**10 RIALS** ND (1973). Blue-green on m/c unpt. Bronze head of Kg. Dhamer Ali at l. Republican Palace in Sana'a at ctr. on back.			
	a. Sign. 5.	1.00	4.00	20.00
	b. Sign. 7.	.75	3.00	15.00

		VG	VF	UNC
14	**20 RIALS** ND (1973). Purple on m/c unpt. Marble sculpture of seated figure w/grapes at l. Back purple and brown; terraced slopes along mountain at ctr. r. Sign. 5.	1.00	4.00	20.00

		VG	VF	UNC
15	**50 RIALS** ND (1973). Dk. olive-green on m/c unpt. Bronze statue of Ma'adkarib at l. Bab al Yemen (main gate of Sana'a) on back.			
	a. Sign. 5.	1.00	3.50	15.00
	b. Sign. 7.	.65	2.00	10.00

		VG	VF	UNC
16	**100 RIALS** ND (1976). Red-violet on m/c unpt. Marble sculpture of cherub and griffin at l. View of Ta'izz on back. Sign. 5.	4.50	13.50	65.00

1979-85 ND ISSUES

#16B-21 wmk: Arms.

		VG	VF	UNC
16B	**1 RIAL** ND (1983). Like #11, but darker green and smaller serial #. Clearer unpt. design over wmk. area at r. Sign. 7.	.10	.25	1.00

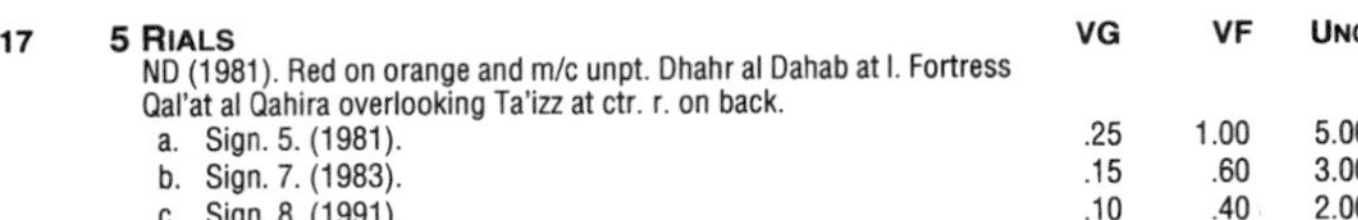

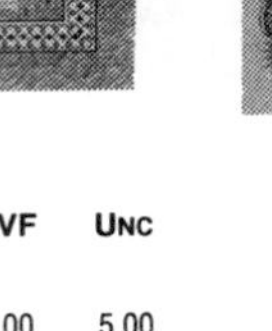

#		VG	VF	UNC
17	**5 RIALS** ND (1981). Red on orange and m/c unpt. Dhahr al Dahab at l. Fortress Qal'at al Qahira overlooking Ta'izz at ctr. r. on back.			
	a. Sign. 5. (1981).	.25	1.00	5.00
	b. Sign. 7. (1983).	.15	.60	3.00
	c. Sign. 8. (1991).	.10	.40	2.00

#		VG	VF	UNC
18	ND (1981). Blue-green on m/c unpt. Village of Thulla at l. al Baqiliyah Mosque on back.			
	a. Sign. 5. (1981).	.50	2.00	10.00
	b. Sign. 7. (1983).	.30	1.25	6.00

#		VG	VF	UNC
19	**20 RIALS** ND (1985). Purple on m/c unpt. Face like #14. View of Sana'a on back.			
	a. Bank title on tan unpt. on back. Sign. 7. (1983). 4mm serial #.	1.00	3.00	15.00
	b. As a. Sign. 8. 3mm serial #.	.60	2.00	10.00
	c. Bank title on lt. brown unpt. of vertical lines on back. Sign. 8.	.50	1.50	7.50

#20 *Deleted*. See #26.

#		VG	VF	UNC
21	**100 RIALS** ND (1979). Red-violet on m/c unpt. al Ashrafiya Mosque and Ta'izz city view. View of Sana'a w/mountains on back. Sign. 6.	1.25	3.50	17.50

#		VG	VF	UNC
21A	**100 RIALS** ND (1984). Red-violet on m/c unpt. Face like #16 but different sign. Central Bank of Yemen bldg. at ctr. r. on back. Sign. 7.	1.00	2.50	6.50

1990-98 ND ISSUES

#23-31 wmk: Arms.

#		VG	VF	UNC
23	**10 RIALS** ND (1990-). Blue and black on m/c unpt. al Baqilyah Mosque at l. Ma'rib Dam at ctr. r., *10* at upper corners on back. 2 wmk. varieties. Sign. 8.	FV	FV	3.00

#		VG	VF	UNC
24	**10 RIALS** ND (ca.1992). Face like #23. Back like #23, but w/*10* at upper l. and lower r. *10* w/Arabic text: *Sadd Marib* near lower r. Sign. 8.	FV	FV	2.50

NOTICE

Readers with unlisted dates, signature varieties, etc. are invited to submit photocopies of their notes to: Standard Catalog of World Paper Money, 700 East State St. Iola, WI 54990-0001, fax: 1-715-445-4087, or E-Mail: thernr@krause.com.

		VG	VF	UNC
25	**20 RIALS** ND (1995). Dk. brown on m/c unpt. Arch ends straight border across upper ctr. Marble sculpture of cupid w/grapes at l. Coastal view of Aden, dhow on back. Sign. 8.	FV	FV	4.00

		VG	VF	UNC
26	**20 RIALS** ND (1990). Dk. brown on m/c unpt. Face like #25. Different city view w/o minarets or dhow at ctr. r. on back of Sana'a on back. Sign. 8.			
	a. W/o shading around title of the bank.	FV	FV	4.00
	b. W/shading around title of the bank.	FV	FV	3.00

		VG	VF	UNC
27	**50 RIALS** ND (1993). Black and deep olive-brown on m/c unpt. Face like #15. Shibam city view at ctr. r. w/o Arabic title at lower l. on back. Sign. 8.	FV	FV	4.50

		VG	VF	UNC
27A	**50 RIALS** ND (199?). Black and deep olive-brown on m/c unpt. Like #27 but w/Arabic title *Shibam Hadramaut* at lower l. on back. Sign. 8.	FV	FV	2.50

		VG	VF	UNC
28	**100 RIALS** ND (1993). Violet, purple and black on m/c unpt. Ancient culvert in Aden at l. City view of Sana'a on back. Sign. 8.	FV	FV	2.50

		VG	VF	UNC
29	**200 RIALS** ND (1996). Deep blue-green on m/c unpt. Alabaster sculpture of a man at l. Harbor view of Mukalla at ctr. r. on back. Sign. 9.	FV	FV	5.50

		VG	VF	UNC
30	**500 RIALS** ND (1997). Red-brown, blue-violet and deep purple on m/c unpt. Central Bank of Yemen bldg. at l. Bara'an temple ruins at r. on back. Sign. 9.	FV	FV	12.50

		VG	VF	UNC
31	**1000 RIALS** ND (1998). Dk. brown and dk. green on m/c unpt. Sultan's palace in Seiyun, Hadramaut at ctr. Bab al-Yemen and old city of Sana'a on back. Sign. 10.	FV	FV	19.00

The People's Democratic Republic of Yemen, (formerly the Peoples Republic of Southern Yemen) was located on the southern coast of the Arabian Peninsula. It had an area of 128,560 sq. mi. (332,968 sq. km.). Capital: Aden. It consisted of the port city of Aden, 17 states of the former South Arabian Federation, 3 small sheikhdoms, 3 large sultanates, Quaiti, Kathiri and Mahri, which made up the Eastern Aden Protectorate, and Socotra, the largest island in the Arabian Sea. The port of Aden is the area's most valuable natural resource. Cotton, fish, coffee and hides are exported.

Between 1200 BC and the 6th century AD, what is now the People's Democratic Republic of Yemen was part of the Minaean kingdom. In subsequent years it was controlled by Persians, Egyptians and Turks. Aden, one of the cities mentioned in the Bible, had been a port for trade between the East and West for 2,000 years. British rule began in 1839 when the British East India Co. seized control to put an end to the piracy threatening trade with India. To protect their foothold in Aden, the British found it necessary to extend their control into the area known historically as the Hadramaut, and to sign protection treaties with the sheikhs of the hinterland. Eventually, 15 of the 16 Western Protectorate states, the Wahidi state of the Eastern Protectorate, and Aden Colony joined to form the Federation of South Arabia. In 1959, Britain agreed to prepare South Arabia for full independence, which was achieved on Nov. 30, 1967, at which time South Arabia, including Aden, changed its name to the People's Republic of Southern Yemen. On Dec. 1, 1970, following the overthrowing of the new government by the National Liberation Front, Southern Yemen changed its name to the People's Democratic Republic of Yemen. On May 22, 1990 the People's Democratic Republic merged with the Yemen Arab Republic into a unified Republic of Yemen. The YDR currency ceased to circulate on June 11, 1996.

MONETARY SYSTEM:

1 Dinar = 1000 Fils

FEDERATED STATE

SIGNATURE VARIETIES

SIGNATURE VARIETIES			
1		2	
3		4	

SOUTH ARABIAN CURRENCY AUTHORITY

1965 ND ISSUE

#1-5 Aden harbor, dhow at ctr. Wmk: Camel's head. Printer: TDLR.

		VG	VF	UNC
1	**250 FILS** ND (1965). Brown on m/c unpt. Date palm at ctr. on back.			
	a. Sign. 1.	2.50	7.50	35.00
	b. Sign. 2.	.50	2.00	13.50

		VG	VF	UNC
2	**500 FILS** ND (1965). Green on m/c unpt. Date palm at ctr., heads of wheat at lower l. on back.			
	a. Sign. 1.	3.00	9.00	65.00
	b. Sign. 2.	2.00	6.00	35.00

		VG	VF	UNC
3	**1 DINAR** ND (1965). Blue-black on m/c unpt. Date palm at ctr., branch of a cotton plant on back.			
	a. Sign. 1.	6.50	20.00	125.00
	b. Sign. 2.	3.75	15.00	55.00

		VG	VF	UNC
4	**5 DINARS** ND (1965). Red on m/c unpt. Date palm at ctr., cotton plant branch and millet flanking on back.			
	a. Sign. 1.	17.50	45.00	250.00
	b. Sign. 2.	12.50	35.00	175.00
5	**10 DINARS** ND (1967). Deep olive-green on m/c unpt. Date palm at ctr;, cotton branch, corn cobs and heads of wheat around on back. Sign. 2.	22.50	90.00	365.00

PEOPLES DEMOCRATIC REPUBLIC

BANK OF YEMEN

1984 ND ISSUE

#6-9 similar to #1-5 but w/o English on face and w/new bank name on back. Capital: *ADEN* added to bottom r. on back. Wmk: Camel's head.

		VG	VF	UNC
6	**500 FILS** ND (1984). Green on m/c unpt. Similar to #2.	.65	2.00	12.50

		VG	VF	UNC
7	**1 DINAR** ND (1984). Blue-black on m/c unpt. Similar to #3.	1.00	2.50	17.50

		VG	VF	UNC
8	**5 DINARS** ND (1984). Red on m/c unpt. Similar to #4.			
	a. Sign. 3.	5.00	15.00	100.00
	b. Sign. 4.	3.25	10.00	45.00

		VG	VF	UNC
9	**10 DINARS** ND (1984). Deep olive-green on m/c unpt. Similar to #5.			
	a. Sign. 3.	10.00	30.00	140.00
	b. Sign. 4.	6.50	20.00	75.00

The Federal Republic of Yugoslavia is a Balkan country located on the east shore of the Adriatic Sea bordering Bosnia-Herzegovina and Croatia to the west, Hungary and Romania to the north, Bulgaria to the east, and Albania and Macedonia to the south. It has an area of 39,449 sq. mi. (102,173 sq. km.) and a population of *10.4 million. Capital: Belgrade. The chief industries are agriculture, mining, manufacturing and tourism. Machinery, nonferrous metals, meat and fabrics are exported.

The first South-Slavian State - Yugoslavia was proclaimed on Dec. 1, 1918, after the union of the Kingdom of Serbia, Montenegro and the South Slav territories of Austria-Hungary; and changed its official name from the Kingdom of the Serbs, Croats, and Slovenes to the Kingdom of Yugoslavia on Oct. 3, 1929. The Royal government of Yugoslavia attempted to remain neutral in World War II but, yielding to German pressure, aligned itself with the Axis powers in March of 1941; a few days later it was overthrown by a military led coup and its neutrality reasserted. The Nazis occupied the country on April 17, and throughout the remaining years were resisted by a number of guerrilla armies, notably that of Marshal Josip Broz known as Tito. After the defeat of the Axis powers, a leftist coalition headed by Tito abolished the monarchy and, on Jan. 31, 1946, established a "People's Republic". Tito's rival General Draza Mihajlovic, who led the Chetniks against the Germans and Tito's forces, was arrested on March 13, 1946 and executed the following day being convicted by a partisan court.

The Federal Republic of Yugoslavia was composed of six autonomous republics: Serbia, Croatia, Slovenia, Bosnia-Herzegovina, Macedonia and Montenegro with two autonomous provinces within Serbia: Kosovo-Metohija and Vojvodina. The collapse of the Socialist Federal Republic of Yugoslavia during 1991-92 has resulted in the autonomous republics of Croatia, Slovenia, Bosnia-Herzegovina and Macedonia declaring their respective independence.

The Federal Republic of Yugoslavia was proclaimed in 1992 and it consists of the former Republics of Serbia and Montenegro.

RULERS:

Peter I, 1918-1921
Alexander I, 1921-1934

MONETARY SYSTEM:

1 Dinar = 100 Para
1 Dinar = 100 *Old* Dinara, 1965
1 Dinar = 10,000 *Old* Dinara, 1990-91
1 Dinar = 10 *Old* Dinara, 1992
1 Dinar = 1 Million *Old* Dinara, 1993
1 Dinara = 1 Milliard *Old* Dinara, 1.1.1994

SIGNATURE CHART

Vice Governor	Governor
Isak Sion	Nikola Maljanich
Borivoje Jelich	Nikola Maljanich
Branislav Colanovich	Nikola Maljanich
Branislav Colanovich	Ivo Perishin
Joshko Shtrukelj	Branislav Colanovich
Ilija Marjanovich	Ksente Bogoev
Miodrag Veljkovich	Radovan Makich
Dr. Slobodan Stanojevich	Radovan Makich

SIGNATURE CHART	
Vice Governor	Governor
Dr. Slobodan Stanojevich	Dushan Vlatkovich
Mitja Gaspari	Dushan Vlatkovich
	Dushan Vlatkovich
	Vuk Ognjanovich
	Borivoje Atanockovich
Bozidar Gazivoda	
Bozidar Gazivoda	Dragoslav Avramovich

SOCIALIST FEDERAL REPUBLIC

НАРОДНА БАНКА ЈУГОСЛАВИЈЕ

NARODNA BANKA JUGOSLAVIJE

NATIONAL BANK OF YUGOSLAVIA

1963 ISSUE

#73-76 sign. 5. Replacement notes: Serial # prefix *ZA*.

		VG	VF	UNC
73	**100 DINARA** 1.5.1963. Red on m/c unpt. Woman wearing national costume at l. View of Dubrovnik at ctr. on back.			
	a. Issued note.	.10	.30	1.75
	s. Specimen.	—	—	40.00

		VG	VF	UNC
74	**500 DINARA** 1.5.1963. Dk. green on m/c unpt. Farm woman w/sickle at l. 2 combine harvesters at ctr. on back.			
	a. Issued note.	.25	.50	3.00
	s. Specimen.	—	—	50.00

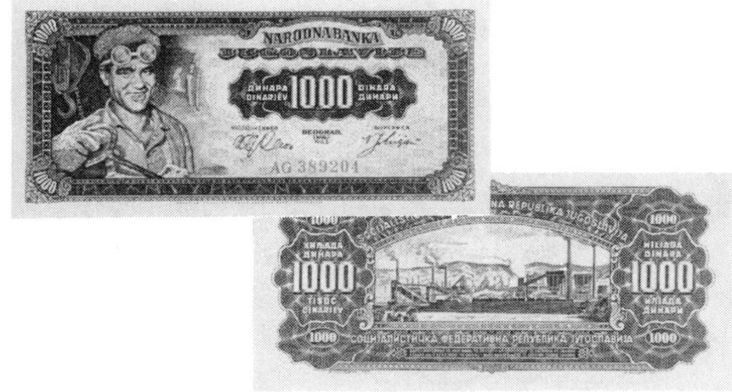

		VG	VF	UNC
75	**1000 DINARA** 1.5.1963. Dk. brown on m/c unpt. Male steelworker at l. Factory complex at ctr. on back.			
	a. Issued note.	.30	.60	4.00
	s. Specimen.	—	—	30.00
76	**5000 DINARA** 1.5.1963. Blue-black on m/c unpt. Relief of Mestrovic at l. Parliament bldg. (National Assembly) in Belgrade at ctr. on back.			
	a. Issued note.	4.00	25.00	75.00
	s. Specimen.	—	—	30.00

1965 ISSUE

#77-80 sign. 6. Replacement notes: Serial # prefix *ZA*.

		VG	VF	UNC
77	**5 DINARA** 1.8.1965. Dk. green on m/c unpt. Like #74. 134 x 64mm.			
	a. Sm. numerals in serial #.	.20	.50	7.50
	b. Lg. numerals in serial #.	.20	.50	10.00
	s. Specimen.	—	—	40.00
78	**10 DINARA** 1.8.1965. Dk. brown on m/c unpt. Like #75. 143 x 66mm.			
	a. Serial # like #77a.	.20	.50	10.00
	b. Serial # like #77b.	.20	.50	15.00
	s. Specimen.	—	—	40.00
79	**50 DINARA** 1.8.1965. Dk. blue on m/c unpt. Like #76. 151 x 72mm.			
	a. Serial # like #77a.	.50	2.75	28.50
	b. Serial # like #77b.	.30	3.50	35.00
	s. Specimen.	—	—	40.00

		VG	VF	UNC
80	**100 DINARA** 1.8.1965. Red on m/c unpt. Equestrian statue "Peace of Augustincic" in garden of United Nations, New York at l.			
	a. Serial # like #77a.	1.00	6.00	20.00
	b. Serial # like #77b, but w/o security thread.	.50	3.00	10.00
	c. Serial # like #77b, but w/security thread. 7 digit serial #.	.25	1.00	5.00
	s. Specimen.	—	—	40.00

1968-70 Issue

#81-84 lg. numerals of value at l. ctr. on back. Sign. 7 or 8. Replacement notes: Serial # prefix *ZA*.

		VG	VF	Unc
81	**5 Dinara** 1.5.1968. Dk. green on m/c unpt. Face like #77. 123 x 59mm.			
	a. Serial # like #77a.	.05	.20	.50
	b. Serial # like #77b.	.05	.20	.50
	s. Specimen.	—	—	30.00

		VG	VF	Unc
82	**10 Dinara** 1.5.1968. Dk. brown on m/c unpt. Face like #78. 131 x 63mm.			
	a. Serial # like #77a.	.50	2.00	15.00
	b. Serial # like #80b.	.20	.50	1.00
	c. Serial # like #80c.	.05	.15	.35
	s. Specimen.	—	—	30.00

		VG	VF	Unc
83	**50 Dinara** 1.5.1968. Blue-black on m/c unpt. Face like #79. 139 x 66mm.			
	a. Serial # like #77a.	.75	3.00	12.50
	b. Serial # like #80b.	.20	.65	4.00
	c. Serial # like #80c.	.10	.35	1.00
	s. Specimen.	—	—	45.00

		VG	VF	Unc
84	**500 Dinara** 1.8.1970. Dk. olive-green on m/c unpt. Statue of N. Tesla seated w/open book at l.			
	a. W/o security thread. Sign. 8.	.15	.50	4.00
	b. W/security thread.	.50	2.00	6.00

1974 Issue

#85 and 86 sign. 9. Replacement notes: Serial # prefix *ZA*.

		VG	VF	Unc
85	**20 Dinara** 19.12.1974. Purple on m/c unpt. Ship dockside at l. 6 or 7-digit serial #.	.15	.40	1.50
86	**1000 Dinara** 19.12.1974. Blue-black on m/c unpt. Woman w/fruit at l.	.30	1.50	4.50

1978 Issue

#87-92 long, 2-line sign. title at l. and different sign. Replacement notes: Serial # prefix *ZA; ZB; ZC*.

		VG	VF	Unc
87	**10 Dinara** 1978; 1981. Dk. brown on m/c unpt. Like #82.			
	a. Sign. 10. 12.8.1978.	.10	.20	.75
	b. Sign. 11. 4.11.1981.	.10	.20	.75
88	**20 Dinara** 1978; 1981. Purple on m/c unpt. Like #85.			
	a. Sign. 10. 12.8.1978.	.05	.15	.75
	b. Sign. 11. 4.11.1981.	.15	.50	3.00
89	**50 Dinara** 1978; 1981. Blue-black on m/c unpt. Like #83.			
	a. Sign. 10. 12.8.1978.	.05	.20	1.00
	b. Sign. 11. 4.11.1981.	.05	.20	1.00

		VG	VF	Unc
90	**100 Dinara** 1978. Red on m/c unpt. Like #80.			
	a. Sign. 10. 12.8.1978.	.10	.30	1.25
	b. Sign. 11. 4.11.1981.	.10	.30	1.25
	c. Sign. 13. 16.5.1986.	.05	.20	1.00

		VG	VF	Unc
91	**500 Dinara** 1978; 1981; 1986. Dk. olive-green on m/c unpt. Like #84.			
	a. Sign. 10. 12.8.1978.	.15	.50	2.00
	b. Sign. 11. 4.11.1981.	.10	.40	1.25
	c. Sign. 13. 16.5.1986.	.20	.75	3.00

		VG	VF	UNC
92	**1000 DINARA**			
	1978; 1981. Blue-black on m/c unpt. Like #86.			
	a. Sign. 10 w/title: *Governor* in Latin w/o letter *R* (engraving error). Series AF. 12.8.1978.	.25	1.00	8.00
	b. As a. Series AR.	1.25	5.00	20.00
	c. Corrected sign. title.	.15	.50	4.00
	d. Sign. 11. 4.11.1981.	.05	.25	1.25

1985-89 ISSUE

		VG	VF	UNC
93	**5000 DINARA**			
	1.5.1985. Deep blue on m/c unpt. Tito at l. and as wmk., arms at ctr. Jajce in Bosnia at ctr. on back. Sign. 12.			
	a. Error. Date *1930.*	.10	.50	3.50
	b. Corrected. Date 1980.			
	x. Error. Date *1930* instead of *1980* (Tito's death year).	1.75	7.50	30.00

#94 Held in reserve.

		VG	VF	UNC
95	**20,000 DINARA** 1.5.1987. Brown on m/c unpt. Miner at l. and as wmk., arms at ctr. Mining equipment at ctr. on back. Sign. 13.	.05	.30	1.00

		VG	VF	UNC
96	**50,000 DINARA** 1.5.1988. Green and blue on m/c unpt. Girl at l. and as wmk. City of Dubrovnik at ctr. on back. Sign. 13.	.10	.50	3.00

#97-100 sign. 14.

		VG	VF	UNC
97	**100,000 DINARA** 1.5.1989. Violet and red on m/c unpt. Young girl at l. and as wmk. Abstract design w/letters and numbers at ctr. r. on back.	.25	1.00	4.50

		VG	VF	UNC
98	**500,000 DINARA**			
	Aug. 1989. Deep purple and blue on lilac unpt. Arms at l., Partisan monument "Kozara" at r. Partisan monument "Sutjeska" at ctr. on back.			
	a. Issued note.	.35	1.25	8.50
	s. Specimen.	—	—	50.00

		VG	VF	UNC
99	**1,000,000 DINARA** 1.11.1989. Lt. olive-green on orange and gold unpt. Young woman at l. and as wmk. Stylized stalk of wheat on back.	.40	1.75	11.00

		VG	VF	UNC
100	**2,000,000 DINARA** Aug. 1989. Pale olive-green and brown on lt. orange unpt. Face like #98. Partisan "V3" monument at Kragujevac at ctr. on back.			
	a. Issued note.	2.75	12.50	50.00
	s. Specimen.	—	—	50.00

1990 FIRST ISSUE

#101 and 102 sign. 14. Replacement notes: Serial # prefix *ZA*.

		VG	VF	UNC
101	**50 DINARA** 1.1.1990. Purple on lilac unpt. Similar to #98.			
	a. Issued note.	.50	2.50	12.50
	s. Specimen.	—	—	50.00

		VG	VF	UNC
101A	**100 DINARA** ND (1990). Black and dk. olive-green on pink and yellow-green unpt. Marshal Tito at r., flags in unpt. at ctr., arms at upper l. Partisan monument "Sutjeska" at ctr. on back. (Not issued).	—	—	*1250.*
102	**200 DINARA** 1.1.1990. Pale olive-green and brown on lt. orange unpt. Similar to #100.			
	a. Issued note.	1.00	4.50	22.50
	s. Specimen.	—	—	50.00

1990 SECOND ISSUE

#103-107 arms at ctr. Sign. 14. Replacement notes: Serial # prefix *ZA*.

		VG	VF	UNC
103	**10 DINARA** 1.9.1990. Violet and red on m/c unpt. Similar to #97.	.05	.20	1.50

		VG	VF	UNC
104	**50 DINARA** 1.6.1990. Purple. Young boy at l. and as wmk. Roses at ctr. r. on back.	.05	.25	1.50
105	**100 DINARA** 1.3.1990. Lt. olive-green on orange and gold unpt. Similar to #99.	.20	1.00	7.00
106	**500 DINARA** 1.3.1990. Blue and purple. Young man at l. and as wmk. Mountain scene on back.	.20	1.00	7.00
106A	**500 DINARA** Brown and orange. Like #106. (Not issued).	—	—	225.00

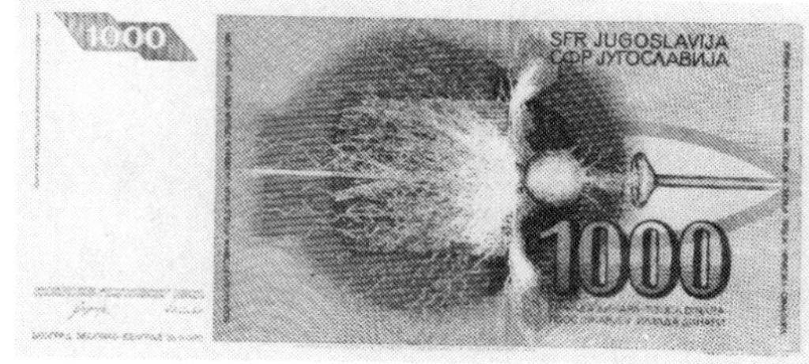

		VG	VF	UNC
107	**1000 DINARA** 26.11.1990. Brown and orange. N. Tesla at l. and as wmk. High frequency transformer on back.	.40	2.00	12.50

1991 ISSUE

#107A-111 year date only. Sign. 15. Replacement notes: Serial # prefix *ZA*.

		VG	VF	UNC
107A	**10 DINARA** 1991. Purple, black and lilac. Like #103. (Not issued).	—	—	175.00
107B	**50 DINARA** 1991. Orange and red. Like #104. (Not issued).	—	—	175.00

		VG	VF	UNC
108	**100 DINARA** 1991. Black and olive-brown on yellow unpt. Similar to #105.	.10	.50	2.50

		VG	VF	UNC
109	**500 DINARA** 1991. Brown, dk. brown and orange on tan unpt. Similar to #106.	.25	.75	4.00

		VG	VF	UNC
110	**1000 DINARA** 1991. Blue and purple. Similar to #107.	.20	1.00	7.00

		VG	VF	UNC
111	**5000 DINARA** 1991. Purple, red-orange and violet on gray unpt. I. Andric at l. and as wmk. Multiple arch stone bridge on the Drina River at Visegrad at ctr. on back.	.75	4.00	20.00

1992 ISSUE

#112-117 National Bank monogram arms at ctr. Similar to previous issues. Replacement notes: Serial # prefix *ZA*.

#112-115 sign. 15.

		VG	VF	UNC
112	**100 DINARA** 1992. Pale blue and purple. Similar to #105.	.25	.50	1.50

		VG	VF	UNC
113	**500 DINARA** 1992. Pale purple and lilac. Similar to #106.	.15	.75	4.00

		VG	VF	UNC
114	**1000 DINARA** 1992. Red, orange and purple on lilac unpt. Similar to #107.	.25	1.50	8.00

		VG	VF	UNC
115	**5000 DINARA** 1992. Deep blue-green, purple and deep olive-brown on gray unpt. Similar to #111.	.40	1.50	6.50

		VG	VF	UNC
116	**10,000 DINARA** 1992. Varied shades of brown and salmon on tan unpt. Similar to #103. Sign. 16.			
	a. W/dot after date.	.15	.20	2.00
	b. W/o dot after date.	.10	.30	2.00

		VG	VF	UNC
117	**50,000 DINARA** 1992. Purple, olive-green and deep blue-green. Similar to #104. Sign. 16.	.50	1.50	4.50

1993 ISSUE

#118-127 replacement notes: Serial # prefix *ZA*.

#118-123 sign. 16.

		VG	VF	UNC
118	**100,000 DINARA** 1993. Olive-green on orange and gold unpt. Face like #112. Sunflowers at ctr. r. on back.	.15	1.00	5.00

		VG	VF	UNC
119	**500,000 DINARA** 1993. Blue-violet and orange on m/c unpt. Young man at l. and as wmk. Koponik Sky Center on back.	.60	3.00	17.50

		VG	VF	UNC
120	**1,000,000 DINARA** 1993. Purple on blue, orange and m/c unpt. Face like #117. Iris flowers at ctr. r. on back.	.60	3.00	13.00

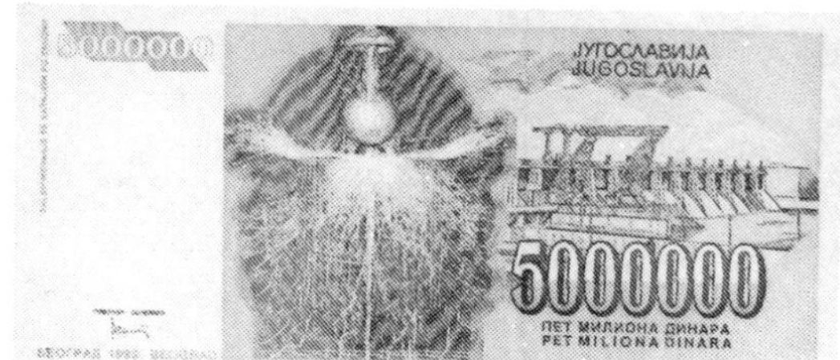

		VG	VF	UNC
121	**5,000,000 DINARA** 1993. Violet, lilac, turquoise and m/c. Face like #114. Vertical rendition of high frequency transformer at ctr., hydroelectric dam at r. on back.	.15	.50	2.50

		VG	VF	UNC
122	**10,000,000 DINARA** 1993. Slate blue, lt. and dk. brown. Face like #115. National library at ctr. r. on back.	.20	.60	3.00
123	**50,000,000 DINARA** 1993. Black and orange. Face like #116. Belgrade University on back.	.25	.75	5.00

#124-127 sign. 17.

		VG	VF	UNC
124	**100,000,000 DINARA** 1993. Grayish purple and blue. Face like #113. Academy of Science at ctr. r. on back.	.20	.60	3.00

		VG	VF	UNC
125	**500,000,000 DINARA** 1993. Black and lilac. Face like #118. Dept. of Agriculture bldg. on back.	.45	1.35	6.00

		VG	VF	UNC
126	**1,000,000,000 DINARA** 1993. Red and purple on orange and blue-gray unpt. Face like #123. Parliament bldg. (National Assembly) at ctr. on back.	.30	2.00	9.00

127	10,000,000,000 DINARA	VG	VF	UNC
	1993. Black, purple and red. Face like #121. Back like #114.	.60	3.00	15.00

1993 REFORM ISSUE

#128-137 replacement notes: Serial # prefix *ZA*.

#128-130 sign. 17.

128	5000 DINARA	VF	VF	UNC
	1993. Pale reddish brown, pale olive-green and orange. Face like #114. Tesla Museum at ctr. r. on back.	.20	1.00	6.00

129	10,000 DINARA	VG	VF	UNC
	1993. Orange, gray and olive-green. S. Karadzic at l. Orthodox church, house on back.	.25	.75	5.00

130	50,000 DINARA	VG	VF	UNC
	1993. Blue and pink. Petar II, Prince-Bishop of Montenegro at l. Monastery in Cetinje at r. on back.	.10	.50	3.25

#131-137 sign. 18.

131	500,000 DINARA	VG	VF	UNC
	1993. Dk. green on blue-green and yellow-orange unpt. D. Obradovic at l. Monastery Hopovo at ctr. r. on back.	.25	.75	5.00

132	5,000,000 DINARA	VG	VF	UNC
	1993. Dk. brown on orange, blue-green and pale olive-brown unpt. K. Petrovich, Prince of Serbia at l. Orthodox church at ctr. r. on back.	.25	.75	5.00

133	50,000,000 DINARA	VG	VF	UNC
	1993. Red and purple on orange and lilac unpt. M. Pupin at l. Telephone Exchange bldg. at ctr. r. on back.	.25	1.00	6.00

134	500,000,000 DINARA	VG	VF	UNC
	1993. Purple on aqua, brown-orange and dull pink unpt. J. Cvijich at l. University at ctr. r. on back.	.25	1.00	5.00

135 5,000,000,000 DINARA
1993. Olive-brown on lt. green, ochre and orange unpt. D. Jaksich at l. Monastery in Vrazcevsnitza at ctr. r. on back.

	VG	VF	UNC
a. Issued note.	.25	.60	5.00
s. Specimen w/red ovpt.	—	—	60.00

136 50,000,000,000 DINARA
1993. Dk. brown on blue-violet, orange, red-violet and gray unpt. Serbian Prince M. Obrenovich at l. Villa of Obrenovich at ctr. r. on back.

VG	VF	UNC
.30	1.00	6.00

137 500,000,000,000 DINARA
1993. Red-violet on orange, pale blue-gray and olive-brown unpt. Poet J. J. Zmaj at l. National Library at ctr. r. on back.

	VG	VF	UNC
a. Issued note.	.35	1.25	10.00
s. Specimen w/red ovpt.	—	—	70.00

1994 ISSUE

#138-143 wmk. paper. Sign. 18.

138 10 DINARA
1994. Chocolate brown on brown and gray-green unpt. J. Panchic at l. Back aqua; mountain view, pine trees at ctr. r. on back. W/o serial #.

	VG	VF	UNC
a. Issued note w/o serial #.	.10	.50	1.50
b. W/serial #, serial # prefix *AR*.	—	—	—
s. Specimen w/red ovpt.	—	—	40.00

NOTE: Violet or orange specimen ovpts. are forgeries.

139 100 DINARA
1994. Grayish purple on pink and aqua unpt. Similar to #128.

	VG	VF	UNC
a. Issued note w/o serial #.	.10	.25	1.50
s. Specimen w/red ovpt.	—	—	40.00

140 1000 DINARA
1994. Dk. olive-gray on red-orange, olive-brown and lilac unpt. Similar to #130.

	VG	VF	UNC
a. Issued note.	1.25	.50	2.50
s. Specimen w/red ovpt.	—	—	40.00

141 5000 DINARA
1994. Dk. blue on lilac, orange and aqua unpt. Similar to #131.

	VG	VF	UNC
a. Issued note.	.25	1.00	4.50
s. Specimen w/red ovpt.	—	—	40.00

142 50,000 DINARA
1994. Dull red and lilac on orange unpt. Similar to #132.

	VG	VF	UNC
a. Issued note.	.45	1.25	4.00
s. Specimen w/red ovpt.	—	—	40.00

142A 100,000 DINARA
1994. Red-brown on ochre and pale olive-green unpt. Like #133. M. Pupin at l. Telephone Exchange bldg. on back. W/o serial #. (Not issued).

VG	VF	UNC
—	—	350.00

143 500,000 DINARA
1994. Dull olive-green and orange on yellow unpt. Similar to #134.

	VG	VF	UNC
a. Issued note.	.15	.75	3.00
s. Specimen w/red ovpt.	—	—	40.00

1994 PROVISIONAL ISSUE

144 10,000,000 DINARA
1994 (-old date 1993). Red ovpt: *1994* on face and back w/new silver ovpt. sign. 18 and sign. title on back on #122.

	VG	VF	UNC
a. Issued note.	.20	1.00	4.00
s. Specimen w/red ovpt.	—	—	50.00

1994 REFORM ISSUES

#145-147 wmk: Diamond grid. Sign. 19.

NOTE: #145-147 withdrawn from circulation on 1.1.1995.

145 1 NOVI DINAR
1.1.1994. Blue-gray and brown on pale olive-green and tan unpt. Similar to #138.

VG	VF	UNC
.25	1.00	3.50

146 5 NOVIH DINARA
1.1.1994. Red-brown and pink on ochre and pale orange unpt. Similar to #139.

VG	VF	UNC
.35	1.75	7.50

147 10 NOVIH DINARA
1.1.1994. Purple and pink on aqua and olive-green unpt. Similar to #140.

VG	VF	UNC
.60	3.00	13.50

1994; 1996 ISSUE

#148-152 arms w/double-headed eagle at upper ctr. Wmk: Symmetrical design repeated.

#148-150 sign. 20. Replacement notes: Serial # prefix *3A*.

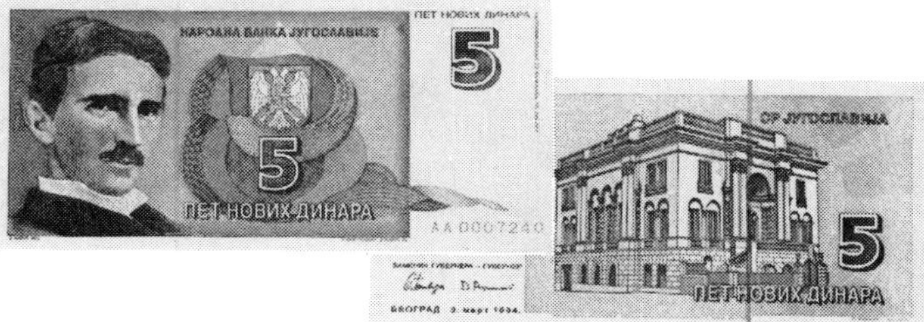

148 5 NOVIH DINARA
3.3.1994. Deep purple and violet. N. Tesla at l. Back like #146.

VG	VF	UNC
FV	FV	3.50

149 10 NOVIH DINARA
3.3.1994. Purple, violet and brown. Like #147.

VG	VF	UNC
FV	FV	6.00

150 20 NOVIH DINARA
3.3.1994. Greenish black, brown-orange and brown. Similar to #135.

VG	VF	UNC
FV	FV	9.50

#151 and 152 sign. 19. Replacement notes: Serial # prefix *ZA*.

151 50 NOVIH DINARA
June 1996. Black and blue. Similar to #136.

VG	VF	UNC
FV	FV	17.50

152 100 NOVIH DINARA
Oct. 1996. Black on olive-brown and grayish green unpt. Similar to #141.

VG	VF	UNC
FV	FV	45.00

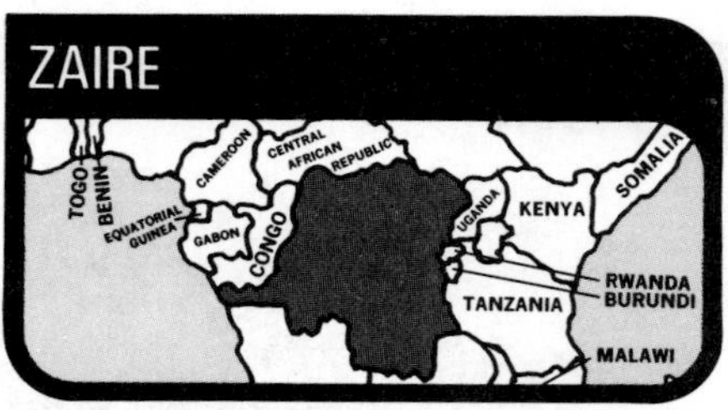

The Republic of Zaïre (formerly the Congo Democratic Republic) located in the south-central part of Africa, has an area of 905,568 sq. mi. (2,345,409 sq. km.) and a population of 43.81 million. Capital: Kinshasa. The mineral-rich country produces copper, tin, diamonds, gold, zinc, cobalt and uranium.

In ancient times the territory comprising Zaïre was occupied by Negrito peoples (Pygmies) pushed into the mountains by Bantu and Nilotic invaders. The interior was first explored by the American correspondent Henry Stanley, who was subsequently commissioned by King Leopold II of Belgium to conclude development treaties with the local chiefs. The Berlin conference of 1885 awarded the area to Leopold, who administered and exploited it as his private property until it was annexed to Belgium in 1908. Following the eruption of bloody independence riots in 1959, Belgium granted the Belgian Congo independence as the Republic of the Congo on June 30, 1960. The Belgian Congo attained independence with the distinction of being the most ill-prepared country to ever undertake self-government. Without a single doctor, lawyer or engineer, with no organized unit capable of maintaining law and order, independence disintegrated into an orgy of anarchy. Provinces seceded. Intertribal warfare erupted. Belgian troops intervened to protect Belgian citizens from retributive massacre. By 1961, four groups were fighting for political dominance. The most serious threat to the viability of the country was posed by the secession of mineral-rich Katanga province on July 11, 1960.

After two and one-half years of sporadic warfare with a U.N. military force, Katanga's leaders capitulated, Jan. 14, 1963 and the rebellious province was partioned into three provinces. The nation officially changed its name to Zaïre on Oct. 27, 1971. In May 1997, the dictator was overthrown after a three-year rebellion. The country changed its name to the Democratic Republic of the Congo.

See also Rwanda, Rwanda-Burundi and Congo Democratic Republic.

MONETARY SYSTEM:

1 Franc = 100 Centimes to 1967
1 Zaïre = 100 Makuta, 1967-1993
1 Nouveaux Zaïre = 100 N Makuta = 3 million "old" Zaïres, 1993-1998

Banque du Zaïre			
	Governor		Governor
3	J. Sambwa Mbagui	4	Bofossa W. Amba
5	EmonyJ	6	Sambwa Mbagui
7	Pay Pay wa Syakassighe	8	Nyembo Shabanga
9	B. Mushaba	10	Ndiang Kabul
11	L. O. Djamboleka	12	

Republic

Banque du Zaïre

1971-80 Issues

#16-25 Mobutu at l. and as wmk., leopard at lower r. facing r. Various date and sign. varieties. Printer: G&D. Replacement notes: Serial # suffix *Z*.

		VG	VF	Unc
16	**50 Makuta** 1973-78. Red, brown and m/c. Man and structure in water on back. Intaglio.			
	a. Red guilloche at l. on back. Sign. 3. 30.6.1973; 4.10.1974; 4.10.1975; 24.6.1976.	.60	2.50	10.00
	b. Red and purple guilloche at ctr. on back. Sign. 3. 24.6.1977; Sign. 4. 20.5.1978.	.30	1.50	7.00

		VG	VF	Unc
17	**50 Makuta** 1979; 1980. Like #16 but slight color differences and lithographed.			
	a. Sign. 5. 24.11.1979.	.35	1.00	3.50
	b. Sign. 3. 14.10.1980.	.35	1.00	3.00

		VG	VF	Unc
18	**1 Zaïre** 1972-77. Brown and m/c. Factory, pyramid, flora and elephant tusks at ctr. r. on back. Intaglio.			
	a. Sign. 3 w/title: *LE GOUVERNEUR* placed below line. 15.3.1972; 27.10.1974; 20.5.1975; 27.10.1975; 27.10.1976.	.60	2.00	8.50
	b. Sign. 4 w/title: *LE GOUVERNEUR* placed above line. 27.10.1977.	.30	1.20	4.00

		VG	VF	Unc
19	**1 Zaïre** 1979-81. Like #18 but slight color differences and lithographed.			
	a. Sign. 5. 22.10.1979.	.15	.50	3.50
	b. Sign. 3. 27.10.1980; 20.5.1981.	.15	.50	2.75

20	5 ZAÏRES	VG	VF	UNC
	24.11.1972. Green, black and m/c. Like #14 except for bank name. Sign. 3.	15.00	35.00	110.00

21	5 ZAÏRES	VG	VF	UNC
	1974-77. Green, black and m/c. Similar to #20 but Mobutu w/cap.			
	a. Sign. 3. 30.11.1974; 30.6.1975; 24.11.1975; 24.11.1976.	2.75	8.50	25.00
	b. Sign. 4. 24.11.1977.	.60	1.50	10.00
	s. As a. Specimen.	—	—	75.00

22	5 ZAÏRES	VG	VF	UNC
	1979; 1980. Blue, brown and m/c. Like #21.			
	a. Sign. 5. 20.5.1979.	.60	2.00	8.50
	b. Sign. 3. 27.10.1980.	.60	2.00	8.00
	s. Specimen. 20.5.1979.	—	—	65.00

23	10 ZAÏRES	VG	VF	UNC
	1972-77. Dk. brown and blue on m/c unpt. Similar to #15 but arms w/hand holding torch at l. ctr. on back.			
	a. Sign. 3. 30.6.1972; 22.6.1974; 30.6.1975; 30.6.1976; 27.10.1976.	3.00	9.00	40.00
	b. Sign. 4. 27.10.1977.	1.00	3.00	12.50
	s. As a. Specimen w/o serial #.	—	—	85.00

24	10 ZAÏRES	VG	VF	UNC
	1979; 1981. Green and m/c. Like #23.			
	a. Sign. 5. 24.6.1979.	1.00	3.00	11.00
	b. Sign. 3. 4.1.1981.	1.00	3.00	10.00
	s. Specimen. 24.6.1979.	—	—	85.00

25	50 ZAÏRES	VG	VF	UNC
	1980. Red, violet, brown and m/c. Face similar to #21. Arms at l. ctr. on back.			
	a. Sign. 5. 4.2.1980.	5.00	17.50	45.00
	b. Sign. 3. 24.11.1980.	5.00	17.50	40.00
	s. Specimen. 4.2.1980.	—	—	100.00

1982-85 ISSUES

#26-31 replacement notes: Serial # suffix *Z*. #26-29 leopard at lower l. facing l. Mobutu in civilian dress at ctr. r. and as wmk. Sign. varieties.

26	5 ZAÏRES	VG	VF	UNC
	17.11.1982. Blue, black and m/c. Hydroelectric dam at ctr. r. on back. Printer: G&D. Sign. 6.			
	a. Issued note.	.30	.75	3.50
	s. Specimen.	—	—	85.00

		VG	VF	UNC
26A	**5 ZAÏRES**			
	24.11.1985. Like #26, but printer: HdMZ. Sign. 7.	.20	.40	2.00
27	**10 ZAÏRES**	**VG**	**VF**	**UNC**
	27.10.1982. Green, black and m/c. Arms w/hand holding torch on back. Printer: G&D. Sign. 6.			
	a. Issued note.	.50	1.20	4.00
	s. Specimen.	—	—	50.00
27A	**10 ZAÏRES**			
	27.10.1985. Like #27, but printer: HdMZ. Sign. 7.	.20	.40	2.00

#28 and 29 printer: G&D.

		VG	VF	UNC
28	**50 ZAÏRES**			
	1982; 1985. Purple, blue and m/c. Back blue and m/c; men fishing w/stick nets at ctr.			
	a. Sign. 6. 24.11.1982.	.75	2.50	9.00
	b. Sign. 7. 24.6.1985.	.50	1.75	7.50
	s. Specimen.	—	—	50.00

		VG	VF	UNC
29	**100 ZAÏRES**			
	1983; 1985. Brown, orange and m/c. Bank of Zaïre at ctr. r. on back.			
	a. Sign. 6. 30.6.1983.	.60	1.75	10.00
	b. Sign. 7. 30.6.1985.	.25	.75	4.00
	s. Specimen.	—	—	50.00

#30 and 31 leopard at lower l. facing l., Mobutu in military dress at ctr. r. and as wmk., arms at lower r. Printer: G&D.

		VG	VF	UNC
30	**500 ZAÏRES**			
	1984; 1985. Brown, purple and m/c. Suspension bridge over river at ctr. r. on back.			
	a. Sign. 6. 14.10.1984.	1.50	8.00	40.00
	b. Sign. 7. 14.10.1985.	1.25	6.00	25.00
	s. Specimen.	—	75.00	100.00

		VG	VF	UNC
31	**1000 ZAÏRES**			
	24.11.1985. Blue-black and green on m/c unpt. Civic bldg., water fountain at ctr. r. on back. Sign. 7.			
	a. Issued note.	1.50	6.50	25.00
	s. Specimen.	—	85.00	125.00

1988-92 ISSUES

#32-46 Mobutu in military dress at r. and as wmk., leopard at lower l. ctr. facing l., arms at lower r. Reduced size notes.

#32-36 printer: HdMZ.

		VG	VF	UNC
32	**50 ZAÏRES**			
	30.6.1988. Green and m/c. Men fishing w/stick nets on back. Similar to #28. Sign. 7.			
	a. Issued note.	.10	.25	1.25
	s. Specimen.	—	45.00	55.00

33 **100 ZAÏRES**
14.10.1988. Blue and m/c. Bank of Zaïre at l. ctr. on back. Similar to #29. Sign. 7.

	VG	VF	UNC
a. Issued note.	.15	.40	2.00
s. Specimen.	—	45.00	55.00

34 **500 ZAÏRES**
24.6.1989. Brown, orange and m/c. Suspension bridge over river at l. ctr. on back. Similar to #30. Sign. 7.

	VG	VF	UNC
a. Issued note.	.20	.75	5.50
s. Specimen.	—	50.00	65.00

35 **1000 ZAÏRES**
24.11.1989. Purple, brown and m/c. Back similar to #31. Sign. 7.

	VG	VF	UNC
a. Issued note.	.50	2.00	12.50
s. Specimen.	—	60.00	75.00

36 **2000 ZAÏRES**
1.10.1991. Purple and peach on m/c unpt. Men fishing w/stick nets at l., carved figure at ctr. r. on back. (Smaller size than #35.) Sign. 8.

	VG	VF	UNC
a. Issued note.	.25	.75	2.00
s. Specimen.	—	55.00	65.00

#37 and 38 printer: G&D. Replacement notes: Serial # suffix *Z*.

37 **5000 ZAÏRES**
20.5.1988. Blue, green and m/c. Factory at l., elephant tusks and plants at ctr. on back. Sign. 7.

	VG	VF	UNC
a. Brown triangle at lower r.	2.00	6.50	25.00
b. Green triangle at lower r.	.30	1.00	4.00

38 **10,000 ZAÏRES**
24.11.1989. Purple, brown-orange and red on m/c unpt. Govt. bldg. complex at l. ctr. on back. Sign. 7.

	VG	VF	UNC
a. Issued note.	.30	1.00	4.50
s. Specimen.	—	50.00	65.00

39 **20,000 ZAÏRES**
1.7.1991. Black on m/c unpt. Bank of Zaïre at l., other bldgs. across ctr. on back. Printer: HdMZ. Sign. 8.

	VG	VF	UNC
a. Issued note.	.25	.50	3.00
s. Specimen.	—	60.00	70.00

NOTICE

Readers with unlisted dates, signature varieties, etc. are invited to submit photocopies of their notes to: Standard Catalog of World Paper Money, 700 East State St. Iola, WI 54990-0001, fax: 1-715-445-4087, or E-Mail: thernr@krause.com.

#40 and 41 printer: G&D. Replacement notes: Serial # suffix *Z*.

		VG	VF	UNC
40	**50,000 ZAÏRES** 24.4.1991. Wine and blue-black on m/c unpt. Family of gorillas on back. Sign. 7.			
	a. Issued note.	.75	2.00	6.00
	s. Specimen.	—	60.00	70.00

		VG	VF	UNC
41	**100,000 ZAÏRES** 4.1.1992. Black and deep olive-green on m/c unpt. Domed bldg. at l. ctr. on back. Sign. 8.			
	a. Issued note.	.50	1.50	5.50
	s. Specimen.	—	50.00	65.00

		VG	VF	UNC
42	**200,000 ZAÏRES** 1.3.1992. Deep purple and deep blue on m/c unpt. Civic bldg., water fountain at l. ctr. Printer HdMZ. Sign. 8.			
	a. Issued note.	.50	1.50	6.00
	s. Specimen.	—	50.00	65.00

#43 and 44 printer: G&D.

		VG	VF	UNC
43	**500,000 ZAÏRES** 15.3.1992. Brown and orange on m/c unpt. Hydroelectric dam at l. ctr. on back. Sign. 8.			
	a. Issued note.	.50	1.50	7.50
	s. Specimen.	—	50.00	65.00

		VG	VF	UNC
44	**1,000,000 ZAÏRES** 31.7.1992. Red-violet and deep red on m/c unpt. Suspension bridge at l. ctr. on back. Sign. 8.	.50	1.25	5.50

1992-93

		VG	VF	UNC
45	**1,000,000 ZAÏRES** 1993. Like #44. Printer: HdMZ.			
	a. Sign. 8. 15.3.1993.	.60	2.00	12.50
	b. Sign. 9. 17.5.1993; 30.6.1993.	.50	1.25	7.00
	s. Specimen.	—	60.00	85.00

		VG	VF	UNC
46	**5,000,000 ZAÏRES** 1.10.1992. Deep brown and brown on m/c unpt. Factory, pyramids at ctr., flora and elephant tusks at l. on back. Printer: H&S. Sign. 8.			
	a. Issued note.	.50	1.50	5.00
	s. Specimen.	—	60.00	75.00

1993 ISSUE

#47-58 leopard at lower l., Mobutu in military dress at r., arms at lower r.

#47 and 48 Independence Monument at l. on back. W/o wmk. Printer: G&D.

		VG	VF	UNC
47	**1 NOUVEAU LIKUTA** 24.6.1993. Lt. brown on pink and m/c unpt. Sign. 9.	.05	.20	.60

		VG	VF	UNC
48	**5 NOUVEAUX MAKUTA** 24.6.1993. Black on pale violet and blue-green unpt. Sign. 9.	.05	.20	.75

#49 and 51 printer: HdMZ (CdM-A).

#49-58 wmk: Mobutu.

		VG	VF	UNC
49	**10 NOUVEAUX MAKUTA** 24.6.1993. Green on m/c unpt. Factory, pyramids at ctr., flora and elephant tusks at l. on back. Sign. 9.	.10	.30	1.00

#50 *Deleted.*

		VG	VF	UNC
51	**50 NOUVEAUX MAKUTA** 24.6.1993. orange on lt. green and m/c unpt. Chieftain at l., men fishing w/stick nets at ctr. on back. Sign. 9.	.10	.30	1.25

#52-54 printer: G&D.

		VG	VF	UNC
52	**1 NOUVEAU ZAÏRE** 24.6.1993. Violet and purple on m/c unpt. Banque du Zaïre at l. ctr. on back. Sign. 9.	.10	.30	1.25

		VG	VF	UNC
53	**5 NOUVEAUX ZAÏRES** 24.6.1993. Brown on m/c unpt. Back like #41.			
	a. Sign. 9.	.20	.50	1.50
	b. Sign. 10.	.20	.50	1.50

		VG	VF	Unc
54	**10 Nouveaux Zaïres** 24.6.1993. Dk. gray and dk. blue-green on m/c unpt. Back like #42. Sign. 9.	.50	1.00	3.00
55	**10 Nouveaux Zaïres** 24.6.1993. Dk. gray and dk. blue-green on m/c unpt. Back like #42. Printer: HdMZ (CdM-A). Sign. 9.	.15	.40	1.50

#56 and 57 printer: HdMZ (CdM-A).

		VG	VF	Unc
56	**20 Nouveaux Zaïres** 24.6.1993. Brown and blue on pale green and lilac unpt. Back similar to #42. Sign. 9.	.25	.75	2.25

		VG	VF	Unc
57	**50 Nouveaux Zaïres** 24.6.1993. Brown and deep red on m/c unpt. Back like #43. Sign. 9.	.25	1.00	6.50

		VG	VF	Unc
58	**100 Nouveaux Zaïres** 1993-94. Grayish purple and blue-violet on aqua and ochre unpt. Back like #44. Printer: G&D.			
	a. Sign. 9. 24.6.1993.	.75	2.50	4.00
	b. Sign. 10. 15.2.1994.	.40	2.00	4.50
58A	**100 Nouveaux Zaïres** 1993. As 58a but printer: HdMZ.	.75	2.50	4.00

1994-96 Issues

#59-77 a leopard at lower l. ctr., Mobutu in military dress at r. and as wmk., arms at lower r.

#59-61 printer: HdMZ.

		VG	VF	Unc
59	**50 Nouveaux Zaïres** 15.2.1994. Dull red-violet and red on m/c unpt. Like #57. Sign. 10.	.40	1.25	6.00

		VG	VF	Unc
60	**100 Nouveaux Zaïres** 15.2.1994. Grayish purple and blue-violet on aqua and ochre unpt. Like #58. Sign. 10.	.25	1.00	6.50
61	**200 Nouveaux Zaïres** 15.2.1994. Deep olive-brown on orange and m/c unpt. Men fishing w/stick nets at l. ctr. on back. Sign. 10.	.05	.25	2.50

		VG	VF	Unc
62	**200 Nouveaux Zaïres** 15.2.1994. Deep olive-brown on orange and m/c unpt. Like #61. Printer: G&D.	.10	.50	2.75

		VG	VF	Unc
63	**500 Nouveaux Zaïres** 15.2.1994. Gray and deep olive-green on m/c unpt. Banque du Zaïre at l. ctr. on back. Printer: HdMZ.	.05	.25	1.40

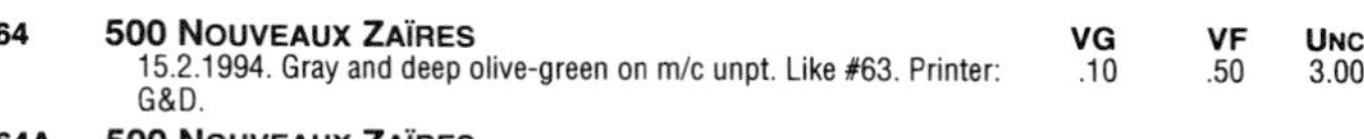

		VG	VF	UNC
64	**500 NOUVEAUX ZAÏRES** 15.2.1994. Gray and deep olive-green on m/c unpt. Like #63. Printer: G&D.	.10	.50	3.00
64A	**500 NOUVEAUX ZAÏRES** 15.2.1994. As #63. Serial # prefix *X*. Printed in Argentina.	—	1.50	5.00

		VG	VF	UNC
65	**500 NOUVEAUX ZAÏRES** 30.1.1995. Blue on m/c unpt. Lg. value on back. Sign. 11.	.05	.30	1.50

		VG	VF	UNC
66	**1000 NOUVEAUX ZAÏRES** 30.1.1995. Olive-gray and olive-green on m/c unpt. Printer: G&D. Sign. 11.	.15	.80	5.00
67	**1000 NOUVEAUX ZAÏRES** 30.1.1995. Like #66. Printer: HdMZ. Sign. 11.	.10	.60	3.50

		VG	VF	UNC
68	**5000 NOUVEAUX ZAÏRES** 30.1.1995. Brown-violet and red-violet on m/c unpt. Printer: G&D. Sign. 11.	.25	1.35	8.00

		VG	VF	UNC
69	**5000 NOUVEAUX ZAÏRES** 30.1.1995. Like #68. Printer: HdMZ. Sign. 11.	.20	1.00	5.50

#70-77 w/OVD vertical band at l.

		VG	VF	UNC
70	**10,000 NOUVEAUX ZAÏRES** 30.1.1995. Blue-violet and deep purple on m/c unpt. Printer: G&D. Sign. 11.	.20	1.00	6.50

		VG	VF	UNC
71	**10,000 NOUVEAUX ZAÏRES** 30.1.1995. Blue-violet and deep purple on m/c unpt. Printer: HdMZ. Sign. 11.	.20	1.00	5.00

		VG	VF	UNC
72	**20,000 Nouveaux Zaïres** 30.1.1996. Brown on m/c unpt. Printer: G&D. Sign. 11.	.20	1.00	6.00
73	**20,000 Nouveaux Zaïres** 30.1.1996. Brown on m/c unpt. Like #72. Printer: HdMZ. Sign. 11.	.20	1.00	5.50

		VG	VF	UNC
74	**50,000 Nouveaux Zaïres** 30.1.1996. Violet and pale blue on m/c unpt. Printer: G&D. Sign. 11.	.40	2.50	12.50
75	**50,000 Nouveaux Zaïres** 30.1.1996. Violet and pale blue on m/c unpt. Like #74. Printer: HdMZ. Sign. 11.	.50	2.00	10.00

		VG	VF	UNC
76	**100,000 Nouveaux Zaïres** 30.6.1996. Dull orange on m/c unpt. Printer: G&D. Sign. 11.	.30	1.50	8.00
77	**100,000 Nouveaux Zaïres** 30.6.1996. Green and blue on m/c unpt. Sign. 11. Printer: HdMZ.	.30	1.50	7.50
77A	**100,000 Nouveaux Zaïres** 30.6.1996. Gray and blue-green on m/c unpt. Like #76 and 77. Printer: HdMZ.	.65	3.00	15.00

#78 and 79 Mobutu at r. and as wmk. Printer: G&D. Sign. 11.

		VG	VF	UNC
78	**500,000 Nouveaux Zaïres** 25.10.1996. Green and yellow-green on m/c unpt. Map of Zaïre, family in canoe on back.			
	a. Issued note.	3.00	12.50	50.00
	s. Specimen.	—	—	50.00

		VG	VF	UNC
79	**1,000,000 Nouveaux Zaïres** 25.10.1996. Lt. violet and red on m/c unpt. Diamonds at lower l. ctr. Map of Zaïre, mining facility on back.			
	a. Issued note.	2.00	10.00	25.00
	s. Specimen.	—	—	100.00

Regional

Validation Ovpt:

Type I: Circular handstamp: *REPUBLIQUE DU ZAÏRE-REGION DU BAS-ZAÏRE; GARAGE - STA/BANANA* around arms.

Banque du Zaïre Branches

NOTE: #R3 and R4 are just 2 examples of handstamps applied to notes being turned in for exchange for a new issue. It appears that in some locations (i.e. Bas Fleuve, Bas Zaïre and Shaba Sons) there were not enough of the new notes to trade for the older ones. In such cases, an ovpt. was applied to the older piece indicating its validity and acceptability for future redemption into new currency. A number of different ovpt. are known, and more information is needed.

1980's ND Provisional Issue

		Good	Fine	XF
R3	**5 Zaïres** 1980's ND (- old date 24.11.1972; 30.11.1974; 24.11.1975; 24.11.1976; or 24.11.1977). Handstamp on #21b.	5.00	15.00	50.00

		Good	Fine	XF
R4	**10 Zaïres** 1980's ND (-old date 30.6.1976). Handstamp on #23b.	5.00	15.00	50.00

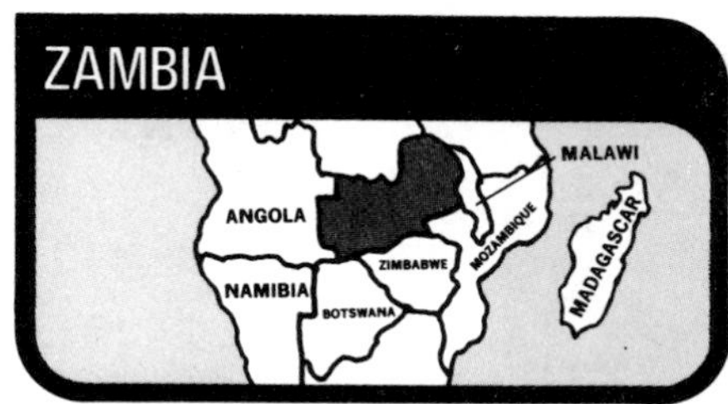

The Republic of Zambia (formerly Northern Rhodesia), a landlocked country in south-central Africa, has an area of 290,586 sq. mi. (752,614 sq. km.) and a population of nearly 9.35 million. Capital: Lusaka. The economy is based principally on copper, of which Zambia is the world's third largest producer. Copper, zinc, lead, cobalt and tobacco are exported.

The area that is now Zambia was brought within the British sphere of influence in 1888 by empire builder Cecil Rhodes, who obtained mining concessions in south-central Africa from indigenous chiefs. The territory was ruled by the British South Africa Company, which Rhodes established, until 1924 when its administration was transferred to the British government as a protectorate. In 1953, Northern Rhodesia was joined with Nyasaland and the colony of Southern Rhodesia to form the Federation of Rhodesia and Nyasaland. Northern Rhodesia seceded from the Federation on Oct. 24, 1964, and became the independent Republic of Zambia. It is a member of the Commonwealth of Nations. The president is Chief of State.

Zambia adopted a decimal currency system on Jan. 16, 1969.

Also see Rhodesia and Malawi.

RULERS:

British to 1964

MONETARY SYSTEM:

1 Shilling = 12 Pence
1 Pound = 20 Shillings to 1968
1 Kwacha = 100 Ngwee, 1968-

SIGNATURE VARIETIES			
1	R. C. Hallet, 1964-67	2	Dr. J. B. Zulu, 1967-70
3	V. S. Musakanya, 1970-72	4	B. R. Kuwani, 1972-76, 1982-84
5	L. J. Mwananshiku, 1976-81	6	D. A. R. Phiri, 1984-86
7	Dr. L. S. Chivuno, 1986-88	8	F. Nkhoma, 1988-91
9	J. A. Bussiere, 1991- (ca.1993)	10	D. Mulaisho, 1993-95
11	Dr. J. Mwanza, 1995-		

REPUBLIC

BANK OF ZAMBIA

1963 ND ISSUE

		VG	VF	UNC
A1	**1 POUND** 1963. Blue on lilac unpt. Fisherman w/net and boat at ctr., portr. Qn. Elizabeth II at r. Back purple; bird at l. ctr. Imprint: H&S. (Not issued).	—	—	2750.

1964 ND ISSUE

#1-3 sign. R. C. Hallet. Arms at upper ctr. Wmk: Wildebeest's head. Printer: TDLR .

		VG	VF	UNC
1	**10 SHILLINGS** ND (1964). Brown on m/c unpt. Chaplins Barbet bird at r. Farmers plowing w/tractor and oxen on back.	15.00	55.00	300.00

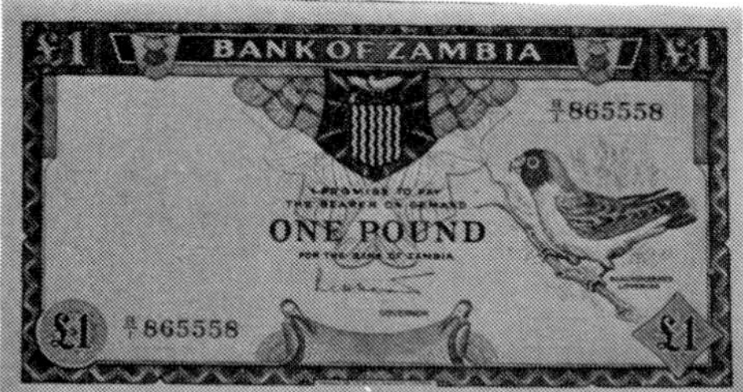

		VG	VF	UNC
2	**1 POUND** ND (1964). Green on m/c unpt. Lovebird at r. Mining tower and conveyors at l. ctr. on back.	15.00	110.00	650.00

		VG	VF	UNC
3	**5 POUNDS** ND (1964). Blue on m/c unpt. Wildebeest at r. Waterfalls at l. ctr. on back.	25.00	125.00	1200.

1968 ND ISSUE

#4-8 Pres. K. Kaunda at r. Dot between letter and value. Sign. 2. Printer: TDLR. Replacement notes: Serial # prefix *1/Z; 1/Y; 1/X; 1/W; 1/V* respectively.

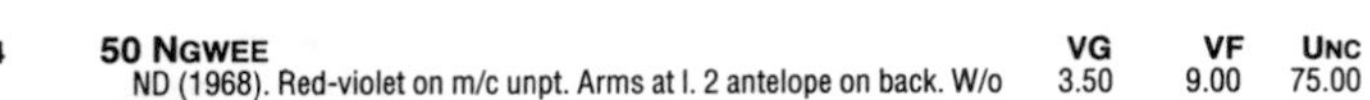

		VG	VF	UNC
4	**50 NGWEE** ND (1968). Red-violet on m/c unpt. Arms at l. 2 antelope on back. W/o wmk.	3.50	9.00	75.00

#5-8 arms at upper ctr. Wmk: Kaunda.

		VG	VF	UNC
5	**1 KWACHA** ND (1968). Dk. brown on m/c unpt. Farmers plowing w/tractor and oxen on back.	4.00	15.00	75.00

		VG	VF	UNC
6	**2 KWACHA** ND (1968). Green on m/c unpt. Mining tower and conveyors at l. ctr. on back.	4.00	17.50	125.00
7	**10 KWACHA** ND (1968). Blue on m/c unpt. Waterfalls on back.	15.00	55.00	450.00
8	**20 KWACHA** ND (1968). Purple on m/c unpt. National Assembly on back.	25.00	85.00	550.00

1969 ND ISSUE

#9-13 Pres. K. Kaunda at r., w/o dot between letter and value. Backs and wmks. like #4-8. Replacement notes: Serial # prefix *1/Z; 1/Y; 1/X; 1/W; 1/V* respectively.

		VG	VF	UNC
9	**50 NGWEE** ND (1969). Red-violet on m/c unpt. Like #4.			
	a. Sign. 2.	Reported Not Confirmed		
	b. Sign. 3.	2.00	7.50	50.00
	c. Sign. 4.	1.00	3.50	27.50
	s. As c. Specimen.	—	—	40.00

		VG	VF	UNC
10	**1 KWACHA** ND (1969). Dk. brown on m/c unpt.			
	a. Sign. 2.	4.00	9.00	85.00
	b. Sign. 3.	3.00	7.00	55.00
11	**2 KWACHA** ND (1969). Green on m/c unpt.			
	a. Sign. 2.	3.00	11.50	150.00
	b. Sign. 3.	2.50	10.00	120.00
	c. Sign. 4.	2.00	7.00	120.00
	s. As s. Specimen.	—	—	40.00

		VG	VF	UNC
12	**10 KWACHA** ND (1969). Blue on m/c unpt.			
	a. Sign. 2.	7.50	22.50	225.00
	b. Sign. 3.	12.50	37.50	375.00
	c. Sign. 4.	8.00	25.00	250.00

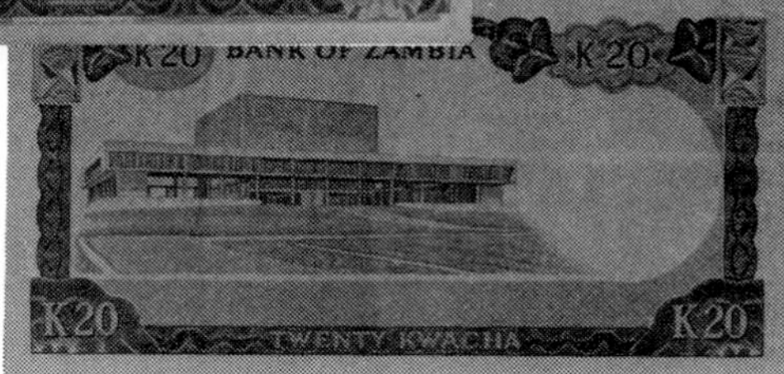

		VG	VF	UNC
13	**20 KWACHA** ND (1969). Purple on m/c unpt.			
	a. Sign. 2.	12.00	50.00	375.00
	b. Sign. 3.	25.00	75.00	500.00
	c. Sign. 4.	6.00	22.50	250.00

NOTICE

Readers with unlisted dates, signature varieties, etc. are invited to submit photocopies of their notes to: Standard Catalog of World Paper Money, 700 East State St. Iola, WI 54990-0001, fax: 1-715-445-4087, or E-Mail: thernr@krause.com.

1973 ND Issue

#14 and 15 Pres. K. Kaunda at r. and as wmk., arms at upper ctr. Replacement notes: Serial # prefix *1/Z; 1/U* respectively.

		VG	VF	UNC
14	**50 Ngwee** ND (1973). Black on purple and m/c unpt. Miners on back. W/o wmk. Printer: TDLR. Sign. 4.			
	a. Issued note.	.50	1.50	8.00
	s. Specimen.	—	—	30.00
15	**5 Kwacha** ND (1973). Red-violet. Children by school on back. Sign. 4.			
	a. Issued note.	15.00	100.00	350.00
	s. Specimen.	—	—	150.00

1973 ND Commemorative Issue

#16, Birth of the Second Republic, December 13, 1972

		VG	VF	UNC
16	**1 Kwacha** ND (1973). Red-orange and brown on m/c unpt. Pres. K. Kaunda at r. and as wmk. Document signing, commemorative text and crowd on back. Printer: TDLR. Sign. 4.			
	a. Issued note.	2.50	10.00	40.00
	s. Specimen.	—	—	30.00

1974 ND Issue

#17 and 18 Pres. K. Kaunda at r. and as wmk., arms at upper ctr. Sign. 4. Printer: BWC. Replacement notes: Serial # prefix *1/W; 1/V* respectively.

		VG	VF	UNC
17	**10 Kwacha** ND (1974). Blue on m/c unpt. Waterfalls at l. ctr. on back.	10.00	55.00	275.00

		VG	VF	UNC
18	**20 Kwacha** ND (1974). Purple and red on m/c unpt. National Assembly on back.	10.00	50.00	270.00

1974-76 ND Issue

#19-22A earlier frame design, arms at upper ctr. Older Pres. K. Kaunda at r. but same wmk. as previous issues. Printer: TDLR. Replacement notes: Serial # prefix *1/Y; 1/X; 1/U; 1/W* respectively.

		VG	VF	UNC
19	**1 Kwacha** ND (1976). Brown on m/c unpt. Back like #5. Sign. 5.	.50	2.00	10.00
20	**2 Kwacha** ND (1974). Green on m/c unpt. Back like #6. Sign. 4.	1.00	3.00	17.50

		VG	VF	UNC
21	**5 Kwacha** ND (1976). Brown and violet on m/c unpt. Back like #16. Sign. 5.	3.00	10.00	42.50

		VG	VF	UNC
22	**10 Kwacha** ND (1976). Blue on m/c unpt. Back like #17. Sign. 5.			
	a. Issued note.	5.00	20.00	125.00
	s. Specimen.	—	—	60.00

		VG	VF	Unc
22A	**20 Kwacha** ND. Purple, red and m/c. Back like #13 (not issued).	—	—	—

1980; 1986 ND Issue

#23-28 Pres. K. Kaunda at r. and as wmk., fish eagle at ctr. Printer: TDLR. Replacement notes: Serial # prefix *Z/1*.

		VG	VF	Unc
23	**1 Kwacha** ND (1980-88). Brown on m/c unpt. Workers picking cotton at l. ctr. on back.			
	a. Sign. 5.	.20	.50	3.00
	b. Sign. 7.	.15	.40	2.00
	s. Specimen.	—	—	20.00

		VG	VF	Unc
24	**2 Kwacha** ND (1980-88). Olive-green on m/c unpt. Teacher w/student at l., school bldg. at ctr. on back.			
	a. Sign. 5.	.50	1.00	7.50
	b. Sign. 6.	.25	.75	3.00
	c. Sign. 7.	.10	.50	1.25
	s. Specimen.	—	—	25.00

		VG	VF	Unc
25	**5 Kwacha** ND (1980-88). Brown on m/c unpt. Hydroelectric dam at l. ctr. on back.			
	a. Sign. 5.	.40	1.00	8.00
	b. Sign. 4.	.50	3.00	15.00
	c. Sign. 6.	.10	.35	1.50
	d. Sign. 7.	.10	.25	1.25
	s. Specimen.	—	—	25.00

		VG	VF	Unc
26	**10 Kwacha** ND (1980-88). Blue and green on m/c unpt. Bank at l. ctr. on back.			
	a. Sign. 5.	1.50	6.00	37.50
	b. Sign. 4 in black.	1.25	4.50	35.00
	c. Sign. 4 in blue.	1.25	3.25	28.50
	d. Sign. 6.	.50	1.00	5.00
	e. Sign. 7.	.40	1.00	4.00
	s. Specimen.	—	—	30.00

		VG	VF	Unc
27	**20 Kwacha** ND (1980-88). Green on m/c unpt. Woman w/basket on head at ctr. r. on back.			
	a. Sign. 5.	2.25	6.50	45.00
	b. Sign. 4 in black.	2.25	6.50	42.50
	c. Sign. 4 in dk. green.	2.00	5.00	35.00
	d. Sign. 6.	.50	1.50	6.00
	e. Sign. 7.	.50	1.25	4.00
	s. Specimen.	—	—	40.00

		VG	VF	Unc
28	**50 Kwacha** ND (1986-88). Purple, violet and m/c. "Chainbreaker" statue at l., modern bldg. at l. ctr. on back. Sign. 7.			
	a. Issued note.	.50	1.00	7.50
	s. Specimen.	—	—	50.00

NOTICE

Readers with unlisted dates, signature varieties, etc. are invited to submit photocopies of their notes to: Standard Catalog of World Paper Money, 700 East State St. Iola, WI 54990-0001, fax: 1-715-445-4087, or E-Mail: thernr@krause.com.

1989 ND ISSUE

#29-33 Pres. K. Kaunda at r. and as wmk., fish eagle at lower l., butterfly over arms at ctr. "Chainbreaker" statue at l. on back.

		VG	VF	UNC
29	**2 KWACHA** ND (1989). Olive-brown on m/c unpt. Rhinoceros head at lower l. facing l., cornfield at ctr., tool at r. on back. Sign. 8.			
	a. Issued note.	.10	.30	1.50
	s. Specimen.	—	—	25.00
30	**5 KWACHA** ND (1989). Brown and red-orange on m/c unpt. Back brown; lion cub head facing at lower l., bldg. at ctr., jar at r. Sign. 8.			
	a. Issued note.	.10	.30	1.50
	s. Specimen.	—	—	25.00

		VG	VF	UNC
31	**10 KWACHA** ND (1989-91). Black, dk. blue and red-violet on m/c unpt. Back dk. blue; giraffe head at lower l. facing l., bldg. at ctr., carving of man's head at r.			
	a. Sign. 8.	.15	.40	4.00
	b. Sign. 9.	.10	.30	1.75
	s. Specimen.	—	—	25.00

		VG	VF	UNC
32	**20 KWACHA** ND (1989-91). Dk. olive-green and brown on m/c unpt. Back dk. green; Dama gazelle head at lower l. facing 3/4 l., bldg. at ctr., carving of man's head at r.			
	a. Sign. 8.	.15	.50	9.00
	b. Sign. 9.	.10	.35	2.50
	s. Specimen.	—	—	40.00

		VG	VF	UNC
33	**50 KWACHA** ND (1989-91). Red-violet and purple on m/c unpt. Zebra head at lower l. facing l., manufacturing at ctr., carving of woman's bust at r. on back.			
	a. Sign. 8.	.50	4.00	25.00
	b. Sign. 9.	.45	2.25	12.50
	s. Specimen.	—	—	50.00

1991 ND ISSUE

#34-35 older Pres. K. Kaunda at r. and as wmk., fish eagle at l., tree over arms at ctr. "Chainbreaker" statue at l. on back. Sign. 9.

		VG	VF	UNC
34	**100 KWACHA** ND (1991). Purple on m/c unpt. Water buffalo head at l. facing, Victoria Falls of Zambezi w/rainbow through ctr. on back.			
	a. Issued note.	.25	1.00	7.50
	s. Specimen.	—	—	30.00
35	**500 KWACHA** ND (1991). Brown on m/c unpt. Elephant at l., workers picking cotton at ctr. on back.			
	a. Issued note.	.50	1.25	8.50
	s. Specimen.	—	—	50.00

1992; 1996 ND ISSUE

#36-42 seal of arms w/date at lower l., fish eagle at r. Wmk: Fish eagle's head. "Chainbreaker" statue at lower ctr. r. on back. Printer: TDLR. Replacement notes: Serial # prefix *1/X*.

		VG	VF	UNC
36	**20 KWACHA** 1992. Green on m/c unpt. Kudu at l. 3/4 facing l., govt. bldg. at ctr. on back.			
	a. Sign. 10.	FV	.20	1.25
	b. Sign. 11.	FV	.20	1.00
	s. Specimen.	—	—	25.00

		VG	VF	UNC
37	**50 KWACHA** 1992. Red on m/c unpt. Zebra at l. facing, foundry worker at ctr. on back.			
	a. Sign. 10.	FV	.30	1.75
	b. Sign. 11.	FV	.25	1.25
	s. Specimen.	—	—	25.00

		VG	VF	UNC
38	**100 KWACHA** 1992. Deep purple on m/c unpt. Water buffalo head facing at l., waterfalls at ctr. on back.			
	a. Sign. 10.	FV	.35	2.00
	b. Sign. 11.	FV	.20	1.50
	s. Specimen.	—	—	40.00

		VG	VF	UNC
39	**500 KWACHA** 1992. Brown on m/c unpt. Elephant head at l., workers picking cotton at ctr. on back.			
	a. Sign. 10.	FV	.75	5.00
	b. Sign. 11.	FV	.75	3.00
	s. Specimen.	—	—	40.00

		VG	VF	UNC
40	**1000 KWACHA** 1992 (1996). Red-violet, deep orange and dk. olive-green on m/c unpt. Aardvark at l., farmer on tractor at ctr. on back. Sign. 11.			
	a. Issued note.	FV	FV	4.00
	s. Specimen.	—	—	40.00

		VG	VF	UNC
41	**5000 KWACHA** 1992 (1996). Purple, dk. brown and deep red on m/c unpt. Lion facing at l., plant at ctr. Sign. 11.			
	a. Issued note.	FV	FV	10.00
	s. Specimen.	—	—	40.00

		VG	VF	UNC
42	**10,000 KWACHA** 1992 (1996). Aqua, brown-violet and yellow-brown on m/c unpt. Porcupine at l., harvesting at ctr. on back. Sign. 11.			
	a. Issued note.	.50	1.50	18.50
	s. Specimen.	—	—	50.00

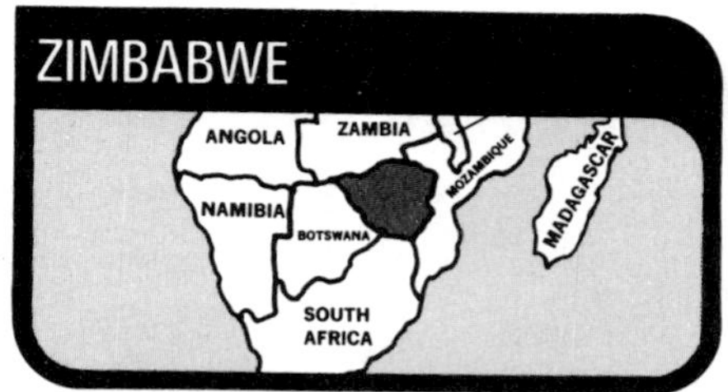

The Republic of Zimbabwe (formerly Rhodesia or Southern Rhodesia), located in the east-central part of southern Africa, has an area of 150,820 sq. mi. (390,580 sq. km.) and a population of 11.54 million. Capital: Harare (formerly Salisbury). The economy is based on agriculture and mining. Tobacco, sugar, asbestos, copper and chrome ore and coal are exported.

The Rhodesian area, the habitat of paleolithic man, contains extensive evidence of earlier civilizations, notably the world-famous ruins of Zimbabwe, a gold-trading center that flourished about the 14th or 15th century AD. The Portuguese of the 16th century were the first Europeans to attempt to develop south-central Africa, but it remained for Cecil Rhodes and the British South Africa Co. to open the hinterlands. Rhodes obtained a concession for mineral rights from local chiefs in 1888 and administered his African empire (named Southern Rhodesia in 1895) through the British South Africa Co. until 1923, when the British government annexed the area after the white settlers voted for existence as a separate entity, rather than for incorporation into the Union of South Africa. From Sept. of 1953 through 1963 Southern Rhodesia was joined with the British protectorates of Northern Rhodesia and Nyasaland into a multiracial federation. When the federation was dissolved at the end of 1963, Northern Rhodesia and Nyasaland became the independent states of Zambia and Malawi.

Britain was prepared to grant independence to Southern Rhodesia but declined to do so when the politically dominant white Rhodesians refused to give assurances of representative government. In November 1965, the white minority government of Southern Rhodesia unilaterally declared Southern Rhodesia an independent dominion. The United Nations and the British Parliament both proclaimed this unilateral declaration of independence null and void. In 1970, the government proclaimed a republic, but this too received no recognition. In 1979, the government purported to change the name of the colony to Zimbabwe Rhodesia, but again this was never recognized. Following a conference in London in December 1979, the opposition government conceded and it was agreed that the British government should resume control. A British governor soon returned to Southern Rhodesia. One of his first acts was to affirm the nullification of the purported declaration of independence. On April 18, 1980, pursuant to an act of the British Parliament, the Colony of Southern Rhodesia became independent within the Commonwealth as the Republic of Zimbabwe.

For earlier issues see Rhodesia.

MONETARY SYSTEM:

1 Dollar = 100 Cents

SIGNATURE VARIETIES			
GOVERNOR		GOVERNOR	
1	D. Crough	2	K. Movana
3	L. Tshumba		

ZIMBABWEAN BIRD WATERMARK VARIETIES		
Type A Profile short neck	Type B 3/4 view medium neck	Type C 3/4 view long neck

REPUBLIC

RESERVE BANK OF ZIMBABWE

1980 ISSUE

#1-4 Re Matapos Rocks at ctr. r. Sign. varieties. Wmk: Zimbabwe bird. Replacement notes: Serial # prefix: *AW; BW; CW; DW* respectively.

		VG	VF	UNC
1	**2 DOLLARS** 1980 (1981); 1983; 1994. Blue and m/c. Water buffalo at l. Tigerfish at ctr., Kariba Dam and reservoir at r. on back.			
	a. Sign. 1. Salisbury. 1980.	FV	1.50	6.50
	b. Sign. 2. Harare. 1983.	FV	.75	3.00
	c. Sign. 3. Wmk: Type A. 1994.	FV	.50	2.50
	d. Sign. 3. Wmk: Type B.	1.00	5.50	38.50

		VG	VF	UNC
2	**5 DOLLARS** 1980 (1981); 1982-83; 1994. Green and m/c. Zebra at l. Village scene w/2 workers on back.			
	a. Sign. 1. Salisbury. 1980.	1.50	4.50	17.50
	b. Sign. 1. Harare. 1982.	1.00	4.00	15.00
	c. Sign. 2. 1983.	FV	.75	5.00
	d. Sign. 3. 1994. Wmk: Type A.	FV	2.00	7.50
	e. Sign. 3. 1994. Wmk: Type B.	FV	1.00	4.00

		VG	VF	UNC
3	**10 DOLLARS** 1980 (1981); 1982-83; 1994. Red and m/c. Sable antelope at l. View of Harare and Freedom Flame monument on back.			
	a. Sign. 1. Salisbury. 1980.	2.50	10.00	30.00
	b. Sign. 1. Salisbury. 1982 (error).	4.00	16.50	65.00
	c. Sign. 1. Harare. 1982.	3.75	15.00	55.00
	d. Sign. 2. 1983.	.65	1.50	8.00
	e. Sign. 3. 1994.	FV	1.50	5.50

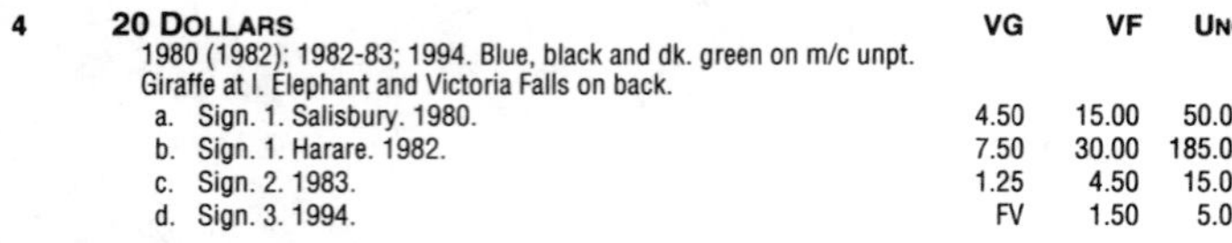

4	20 Dollars	VG	VF	Unc
	1980 (1982); 1982-83; 1994. Blue, black and dk. green on m/c unpt. Giraffe at l. Elephant and Victoria Falls on back.			
	a. Sign. 1. Salisbury. 1980.	4.50	15.00	50.00
	b. Sign. 1. Harare. 1982.	7.50	30.00	185.00
	c. Sign. 2. 1983.	1.25	4.50	15.00
	d. Sign. 3. 1994.	FV	1.50	5.00

1994; 1997 Issue

#5-6 Re Matapos Rocks at l. ctr. Wmk: Zimbabwe bird, Type C. Sign. 3. Replacement notes: Serial # prefix *AA; AB; AC; AD; AE;* and *AF* respectively.

5	5 Dollars	VG	VF	Unc
	1997. Brown, red-orange and purple on m/c unpt. Terraced hills at ctr. r. on back.	FV	FV	1.25

6	10 Dollars	VG	VF	Unc
	1997. Red-brown, deep green and blue-black on m/c unpt. Chilolo Cliffs at ctr. r. on back.	FV	FV	2.50

7	20 Dollars	VG	VF	Unc
	1997. Deep blue, purple and gray-green on m/c unpt. Victoria Falls at ctr. r.	FV	FV	2.50

8	50 Dollars	VG	VF	Unc
	1994. Dk. brown, olive-brown and red-orange on m/c unpt. Great Zimbabwe ruins on back.	FV	FV	5.00

9	100 Dollars	VG	VF	Unc
	1995. Brownish black and purple on m/c unpt. Aerial view of Kariba Dam and reservoir at ctr. r. on back.	FV	FV	8.00

GLOSSARY

ALTERATION — A note with a major feature or denomination fraudulently changed to raise its value or make it passable.

BACK — The reverse side of a note.

BANKNOTE or BANK NOTE — In its most literal sense, a promissory note issued by a bank. In practice, the common name for any note issued by authority of a nation and fulfilling whatever specifications are laid down by that nation for the production of paper money.

BEARER CHECK — An item resembling a check but payable for its specified amount to anyone possessing it, and without endorsement. Bearer checks have served as a form of emergency currency in a number of countries.

BLOCK NUMBERS — Numbers designating printing sequence or run of an issue of notes.

BONS — "Good fors," taken from the wording of early 19th century private note issues of Canadian merchants, manufacturers, railways, etc.

CANCELLED — Notes rendered worthless as money by official cancellation with punched holes, pin perforations, cutting, overprinting, or handwriting. Such notes with their legal tender status removed are worth much less to collectors today than uncancelled notes.

CHECK — A written order directing a bank to pay a certain amount as indicated. Usually payable only as written and only with endorsement. Old checks are often collected by paper money and sometimes autograph collectors.

COMMEMORATIVE ISSUE — A note made in remembrance of some person or event, usually containing special dates, appropriate text or special serial numbers.

CONTROL COUPONS — Government issued ration coupons to be exchanged in combination with currency to control or localize commodity exchanges during transitional periods.

COUNTERFEIT—Unauthorized, illegal reproduction of a banknote.

COUNTERIFOIL — The part of a note cut with or without perforations and retained by the issuer as a record at release.

CUT NOTES — Paper money officially halved, quartered or otherwise divided, with each division given its own value, often indicated by overprinting. Usually an emergency measure to provide small change during a coin shortage.

DEMONETIZED NOTES — Paper money officially withdrawn from circulation and no longer redeemable. Not to be confused with notes no longer legal tender but still redeemable by the issuing authority or its designates.

DEVIL'S HEAD NOTES — Bank of Canada 1954 notes with a "devil's head design" in the curls of Queen Elizabeth's hairdo. Because the public objected to their use, the notes were withdrawn and new plates engraved to remove this hidden design.

EMERGENCY ISSUES — Note issues made under emergency conditions. Often printed or overprinted on earlier notes.

ESSAY NOTE — A trial print made to test a new design, to try a manufacturing or printing concept, or to otherwise preview certain features before a note is officially authorized. Essays are rarely available to collectors, but since demand is low, they may or may not bring high prices.

FACE — The front side of a note, similar to the term "obverse" used for coins.

FANTASY NOTE — A totally invented or concocted design or denomination of paper money, whether or not in imitation of an actual note. Political parties have issued numerous varieties in pre-elections.

FEDERAL RESERVE NOTES — U.S. paper money issued since 1914 backed the Federal Government, rather than the individual bank through which it is issued.

FIAT MONEY — Money not convertible into precious metal or specie of equivalent face value. Current U.S. Federal Reserve Notes are an excellent example.

FIDUCIARY ISSUES — Bank notes without the backing of gold or other securities.

FOIL NOTE—A process by which 2 thin layers of metal (gold, silver, etc.) are bonded to a paper center, then a design impression is made.

FOXING — Yellowish-brown aging stains sometimes found on older paper money, generally detracting from its value.

GREENBACKS — Commonly used term for U.S. governmental paper money issues. The name derives from the deep green ink used on the backs of virtually all such issues since 1861.

GUILLOCHE — The geometric design frequently surrounding the denomination of a note.

HALVED NOTE — Paper money issues cut into two equal portions as a precaution against loss during transportation from branches to the main offices of a bank. These are to be differentiated from "cut notes" (q.v.).

HELL MONEY — Name given to varieties of specially printed fantasy paper money burned at Oriental funeral rites.

INFLATION MONEY — Very high denomination notes issued in periods of hyperinflation, often caused by war. In this century such issues were common in China, Germany, Hungary, Greece, Romania, Russia, Yugoslavia, Zaire, and others. The issues were demonetized at the end of the inflationary period and the currency system completely reformed.

INTAGLIO — Process of printing postage stamps, paper money, souvenir cards, etc. After etching a mirror image design onto a plate, the plate is inked and applied to paper, creating a normal image that often feels "raised" to the fingertip.

LITHOGRAPHY — A technique developed in 1798 by a German map inspector, based on the principle that water and grease repel each other. The image is transferred to a plate, combining the use of ink-absorbent and ink-repellent materials, then applied to paper. The final product lacks the detail and definition of intaglio as the ink is thoroughly absorbed into the paper (often used for emergency purposes or counterfeiting).

LOW NUMBERED NOTES — Notes bearing very low serial numbers, indicating they were among the first printed of a specific issue. Such notes usually command a premium, especially the #1 serial number.

MILITARY CURRENCY — Official paper money issues of military authorities for use by troops. Military currency includes invasion, occupation, liberation and partisan issues (q.v.).

MILITARY PAYMENT CERTIFICATES (MPC) — U.S. military notes for use only by military personnel at U.S. military establishments to combat black market activities.

MODEL — A paste-up design for a proposed note issue. May or may not be identical to notes as issued.

MULE — A note made from two plates not originally intended to be used together.

MULTILINGUAL NOTES — Paper money issued with legends in more than one language, as in India, Belgium, Cyprus, the USSR, etc.

MULTIPLE DENOMINATIONS — A note bearing denominations in more than one monetary system to facilitate exchange.

NEGOTIABLE NOTES — Notes that are still redeemable.

OVERPRINT — Official printing added to a paper money issue for purposes of reissue, revaluation, cancellation, etc.

PAPER MONEY — The general term for all forms of money inscribed on paper.

PAYABLE CLAUSE — Usually refers "to bearer" and sometimes to office of redemption.

PILGRIM RECEIPTS — Overprinted currency indicating usage only by pilgrims in another country. Pakistan, for example, overprinted some notes for use in Saudi Arabia by pilgrims only.

PLATE LETTERS — Letters such as A, B, C, D indicating sheet position of the note at printing.

PLATE NUMBERS — Figures often appearing in very small type on notes to indicate the number of the plate from which they were printed. Do not confuse with Block Numbers (q.v.).

POLYMER (PLASTIC) NOTES — Material patented and used exclusively by Note Printing Australia for production of modern notes for Australia, Brunei, etc.

PORTRAIT — The image of a person as seen on a note.

PROMISSORY NOTES — Negotiable fiscal paper promising to pay on demand, usually after a fixed period of time, a specific amount of money to the person named, or the bearer. All bank notes are promissory notes.

PROOF — A whole or partial note design without such authorizing marks as signatures, serial numbers, etc., as it is not intended for circulation, May be a color trial of a note's face or back design, a progressive color trial of two or more colors, or an imprint on large paper or paper that is otherwise different from that used for circulation notes. Proofs of notes and/or vignettes prepared by bank note printers for quality control, counterfeit detectors or salesman's samples are sometimes encountered among collectors. See also Essay.

PROPAGANDA NOTES — Counterfeit notes or facsimiles of notes imprinted with a propaganda message, usually by a nation at war. Such notes were often air-dropped behind enemy lines. The similitude to genuine money of the nation caused military personnel and civilians to pick them up and read the message which could be derogatory and might also include surrender terms. Such notes have been used in both world wars and frequently since.

PSYWAR NOTES — Similar to propaganda notes (q.v.), except that they are not made in representation of specific enemy notes. Usually intended to demoralize enemy forces.

REISSUES — Withdrawn issues placed back in circulation after a lapse of time, often with an overprint, such as a new issuer's name.

REPLACEMENT NOTES — Notes issued to replace damaged notes during production. They do not run in normal serial number sequence and usually bear a star, asterisk, special prefix letter or similar device in the serial number to indicate their status. Naturally scarcer than other notes, they sometimes command a significant premium.

REPRINT — Notes printed from the original plate(s), but subsequent to the original issue, usually many years later, and often after the plates have fallen into hands other than the original issuing authority. Some notes are known only in reprint form, the originals being unavailable.

REVALIDATED NOTES — Paper money bearing an official overprint, stamp or other marking to indicate renewed status as legal tender, despite previous invalidating of the note.

REVALUE — An overprint to change the value of a note. Frequently this is caused by monetary reform, though sometimes inflation or occupation is the cause.

SERIAL NUMBERS/LETTERS — The system of numbering notes to check the quantity put into circulation and guard against counterfeiting. Often important to collectors of certain types of paper money.

SHORT SNORTER — Term was first applied to a single piece of paper money signed by individuals who had made transoceanic flights. In World War II, the term came to be applied to notes attached end to end, autographed by service buddies, etc. If a serviceman entered a tavern without his "short snorter" notes he was obliged "to buy" a round of drinks.

SILVER CERTIFICATES — The series of U.S. paper money first authorized in 1878, and redeemable in silver by the U.S. Treasury. This redemption privilege was revoked in 1968, although the notes are still currently legal tender for their face value.

SMALL SIZE NOTES — Collectors' terminology for the reduced size U.S. paper money that first appeared July 10, 1929 and which is still in use.

SPECIMENS — Sample notes, usually bearing special or all zero serial numbers and overprinted or perforated with the word "Specimen" in the language of the country of origin. Usually distributed on a restricted basis between national banks, treasuries and law enforcement agencies to familiarize them with newly issued currency.

STAGE MONEY — Fantasy notes (q.v.) or imitations of genuine notes, made for use instead of real money in movies, plays, television and the like. A number of paper money collectors seek such notes.

STAMPED NOTES — Paper money issued with revenue or other adhesive stamps attached to add to the face value or to validate the notes.

STAR NOTES — Replacement notes (q.v.) issued in the U.S., so called for the star preceding the serial number on earlier issues and following it currently.

SUBJECT — The name given to an individual note that is part of a sheet containing multiple impressions. Thus, a 32-subject sheet of $2 notes contains 32 single impressions of this issue.

TYPOGRAPHY — Basic form of printing involving setting type - used very little today for paper money with the exception of adding type in margins of dates, bank branches, etc.

UNCUT SHEETS — Paper money basically as it was printed in sheet form before separation into individual notes for circulation. Special formats such as 8, 16 and 32 subjects of U.S. currency have been released to the collector market.

VALIDATING STAMPS — A handstamp added to notes either upon issue or on older notes for authorization in an area other than originally intended.

VIGNETTE — A pictorial design on a note, as distinguished from frame, lettering, etc. Vignettes may be scenes, objects, buildings, allegorical figures, portraits, and the like.

ESSENTIAL BUYING AND SELLING POWER

STANDARD CATALOG OF WORLD COINS SERIES

For thousands of coin prices from around the world, experienced and beginning collectors turn to the Standard Catalog of World Coins series from Krause Publications. Each volume, authored by Chester Krause & Clifford Mishler - edited by Colin R. Bruce III, contains crisp clear photographs and pricing in up to four grades of condition listed by country and denomination.

Standard Catalog of World Coins 1901-present
Softcover • 8-1/2 x 11 • 2,016 pages
47,700 b&w photos
SC28 • $49.95

Standard Catalog of World Coins, 1801-1900
Softcover • 8-1/2 x 11 • 1,032 pages
24,000+ b&w photos
SCN02 • $45.00

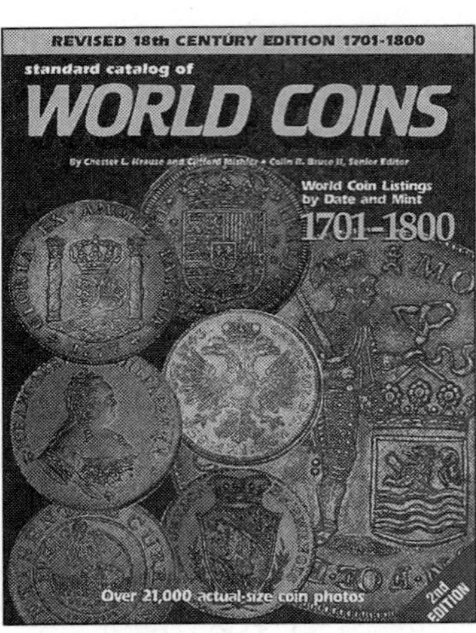

Standard Catalog of World Coins, 1701-1800
Softcover • 8-1/2 x 11 • 1248 pages
20,000 b&w photos
SE02 • $65.00

Standard Catalog of World Coins, 1601-1700
Softcover • 8-1/2 x 11 • 1,272 pages
18,500 b&w photos
C402 • $65.00

Chinese Cash
Identification and Price Guide
by David Jen

This is the first collector's guide providing a comprehensive overview of the complex, but fascinating world of Chinese cash coins. Covering more than 3,000 years of numismatic history, this long-awaited volume lists, illustrates and values in multiple condition grades, a variety of monetary forms issued in Imperial China. You'll find historical and production details for thousands of issues, including many newly discovered varieties not listed in any other reference source.

Softcover • 8-1/2 x 11 • 352 pages
1,500 illustrations
CHINA • $42.95

Standard Catalog of German Coins
1601-Present, 2nd Edition
by N. Douglas Nicol, edited by Fred J. Borgmann, Colin R. Bruce II, Senior Editor

Amass a fortune of essential buying and selling power with tens of thousands of fully detailed coins - priced in up to four grades of preservation - from every dynasty, kingdom, and republic, within the German possessions since 1601. Crisp photos, historic maps and instant identifiers bring you the riches of the Empire.

Softcover • 8-1/2 x 11 • 1,064 pages
18,000 b&w photos
GE02 • $59.00

For a FREE catalog or to place a credit card order

Call 800-258-0929

Dept. NUBR

M-F, 7 am - 8 pm • Sat, 8 am - 2 pm, CST
Krause Publications, 700 E State St, Iola, WI 54990
www.krausebooks.com

Numismatic News
WORLD COINS
BANK NOTE REPORTER
Coins
COIN PRICES

Retailers: Call toll-free 888-457-2873 ext 880, M-F, 8 am - 5 pm
Shipping and Handling: $3.25 1st book; $2 ea. add'l. Call for UPS rates. Foreign orders $15 per shipment plus $5.95 per book.
Sales tax: CA 7.25%, IA 6%, IL 6.25%, PA 6%, TN 8.25%, VA 4.5%, WA 8.2%, WI 5.5%
Satisfaction Guarantee: If for any reason you are not completely satisfied with your purchase, simply return it within 14 days and receive a full refund, less shipping.

NOTES

NOTES